CONSTITUTIONAL LAW

Carolina Academic Press
Context and Practice Series
Michael Hunter Schwartz
Series Editor

Administrative Law
Richard Henry Seamon

Civil Procedure for All States
Benjamin V. Madison, III

Constitutional Law
David S. Schwartz and Lori A. Ringhand

Contracts
Michael Hunter Schwartz and Denise Riebe

Current Issues in Constitutional Litigation
Sarah E. Ricks, with contributions by Evelyn M. Tenenbaum

Employment Discrimination
Susan Grover, Sandra F. Sperino, and Jarod S. Gonzalez

Evidence
Pavel Wonsowicz

International Women's Rights, Equality, and Justice
Christine M. Venter

The Lawyer's Practice
Kris Franklin

Professional Responsibility
Barbara Glesner Fines

Sales
Edith R. Warkentine

Torts Law
Paula J. Manning

Workers' Compensation Law
Michael C. Duff

CONSTITUTIONAL LAW
A Context and Practice Casebook

Revised Printing

David S. Schwartz
UNIVERSITY OF WISCONSIN LAW SCHOOL

Lori A. Ringhand
UNIVERSITY OF GEORGIA SCHOOL OF LAW

CAROLINA ACADEMIC PRESS
Durham, North Carolina

Revised Printing

ISBN 978-1-61163-527-0
LCCN 2013946821

Carolina Academic Press
700 Kent Street
Durham, North Carolina 27701
Telephone (919) 489-7486
Fax (919) 493-5668
www.cap-press.com

Printed in the United States of America

We dedicate this book to John Kidwell.

John was our teacher, mentor, colleague and friend.
He inspired us in so many ways,
and was taken from us much too soon.

Summary of Contents

Contents

List of Diagrams and Figures

Table of Cases

Note: Boldface page numbers indicate principal cases.

Series Editor's Preface

Welcome to a new type of casebook. Designed by leading experts in law school teaching and learning, Context and Practice casebooks assist law professors and their students to work together to learn, minimize stress, and prepare for the rigors and joys of practicing law. Student learning and preparation for law practice are the guiding ethics of these books.

Why would we depart from the tried and true? Why have we abandoned the legal education model by which we were trained? Because legal education can and must improve.

In Spring 2007, the Carnegie Foundation published *Educating Lawyers: Preparation for the Practice of Law* and the Clinical Legal Education Association published *Best Practices for Legal Education*. Both works reflect in-depth efforts to assess the effectiveness of modern legal education, and both conclude that legal education, as presently practiced, falls quite short of what it can and should be. Both works criticize law professors' rigid adherence to a single teaching technique, the inadequacies of law school assessment mechanisms, and the dearth of law school instruction aimed at teaching law practice skills and inculcating professional values. Finally, the authors of both books express concern that legal education may be harming law students. Recent studies show that law students, in comparison to all other graduate students, have the highest levels of depression, anxiety and substance abuse.

The problems with traditional law school instruction begin with the textbooks law teachers use. Law professors cannot implement *Educating Lawyers* and *Best Practices* using texts designed for the traditional model of legal education. Moreover, even though our understanding of how people learn has grown exponentially in the past 100 years, no law school text to date even purports to have been designed with educational research in mind.

The Context and Practice Series is an effort to offer a genuine alternative. Grounded in learning theory and instructional design and written with *Educating Lawyers* and *Best Practices* in mind, Context and Practice casebooks make it easy for law professors to change.

I welcome reactions, criticisms, and suggestions; my e-mail address is michael.schwartz@ washburn.edu. Knowing the author(s) of these books, I know they, too, would appreciate your input; we share a common commitment to student learning. In fact, students, if your professor cares enough about your learning to have adopted this book, I bet s/he would welcome your input, too!

Professor Michael Hunter Schwartz, Series Designer and Editor
Co-Director, Institute for Law Teaching and Learning
Associate Dean for Faculty and Academic Development

Acknowledgments

Writing a Constitutional Law casebook is a daunting task. The field is vast, and there are many wonderful books by renowned authors already available. But the Context and Practice Series is special. Michael Schwartz and his team of editors at Carolina Academic Press have a powerful vision of what legal education should and can be. That vision is one that we share, and we are honored to be a part of this unique series.

Any undertaking of this nature could not be successful without a great deal of help. We offer our sincere thanks to the numerous friends and colleagues who read various chapters of the book. We particularly acknowledge the help of Andrew Coan, Dan Coenen, Anuj Desai, Hillel Levin, Dan Lorentz, Timothy Meyer, Elizabeth Sanger, Brad Snyder, Sonja West and BethAnne Yeager. We also thank Michael for his optimism and good advice, and Linda Lacy and Karen Clayton at CAP for their tireless help in preparing the manuscript. Stacy Harvey played a special role in keeping us on track and organized throughout the project, for which we are much indebted. We also thank our institutions for supporting this project.

CONSTITUTIONAL LAW

Introduction: Constitutional Litigation and Analysis

A. Overview

In this chapter, we explain a number of substantive and procedural matters that will give context to the materials in this book—most of which consist of edited Supreme Court decisions. We'll start by setting out some very broad structures that shape how constitutional questions arise and how to begin going about resolving them. We'll then talk about constitutional actors and how "constitutional law" disputes arise. Then we will zero in on the process of constitutional litigation itself. Constitutional cases do not simply appear fully formed in the U.S. Supreme Court and end with the Supreme Court's decision. Rather, they arise out of real-world disputes that find their way into court because they have taken a form suitable for judicial resolution (or because the very question of that suitability for judicial resolution has been called into question—see "Justiciability," explained in Chapter 6).

Opinions differ on when the material in this chapter will be the most helpful to you. Many law professors believe in providing a "big picture" or "road map" before zeroing in on specific points to enable you, the student, to understand where the specific point belongs and how it fits into the broader scheme of things. On the other hand, a road map is not necessarily helpful to someone who has never read a map before. If you were teaching someone to read a map, you might start with an example of a specific road trip. In other words, starting out with concrete examples or specific cases might provide a better basis on which to ground big picture principles.

There is probably some validity to both approaches. For that reason, we suggest that you at least skim this chapter early in the semester, but that you also return to the chapter later on, once you are well-immersed in your study of constitutional law. As questions arise in your later reading, you may find the explanations in this chapter particularly helpful.

The study of constitutional law necessarily compresses a broad range of doctrine, "black letter rules," and complex concepts into one or two semester-long courses. This makes it necessary for casebook authors to take some short-cuts that, unfortunately, can hide some of the practical aspects of constitutional litigation that might help put the doctrines in context. Opinions that appear in Constitutional Law casebooks are edited down, often drastically, from their original length, and this book is no exception. What virtually all other constitutional law texts also do—and here, we do try to be an exception—is edit out the most or all of the facts and procedural history from the cases. There's little question that reading assignments for law students have to be kept within manageable limits, and that requires heavy editing. But what often gets lost in the shuffle are key facts telling us who the parties are, what happened in the world that brought the parties into conflict and eventually into court, what remedies they were seeking in court, what rulings were made in the lower courts, and what remedies the parties ended up with. That information is of great interest to the parties and the lawyers, of course, but it also provides insights and perspectives on the meaning of the Supreme Court's decision in the case. These insights and perspectives can also shed light on the practice of law, whether constitutional law or other fields, by showing how practical concerns can shape judicial decisions and how certain kinds of arguments or procedures can be used to achieve one's clients' goals. In this book, we provide some of that background information. This chapter complements these efforts by explaining in general terms the kinds of case information that is out there if you take the time to look for it.

B. What Is Constitutional Law?

The United States Constitution is fundamentally a set of arrangements, memorialized in a written document, defining the extent of governmental powers. These arrangements are set out expressly or impliedly in the written Constitution. The Constitution consists primarily of grants of power, limitations on power, or procedural rules for governmental institutions. For the most part, the Constitution does not create rights or duties between private parties, as you would find in tort, contract or property law, for example.[1]

In the subsections that follow, we introduce you to the Constitution itself, and then to five categories of what we call "constitutional actors." Constitutional law can be understood as a series of rules and principles for allocating social and political decisionmaking power between and among those actors. Finally, we consider which of these constitutional actors have the power to interpret the Constitution.

1. The Constitution

U.S. Supreme Court opinions take up the great bulk of the pages in this, or any, Constitutional Law casebook. That makes it all too easy to lose sight of a simple truth: it is *the Constitution* we are studying here.

With every constitutional issue you study, you should always begin with the text of the Constitution itself. You should read the Constitution early (at the very start of the course) and often (going back to the text and re-reading it throughout the course). All constitutional arguments start—or should start—with the text of the most pertinent constitutional provisions. To be sure, constitutional arguments rarely start *and end* with the Constitution's text: there are likely to be at least a few, and possibly dozens of Supreme Court precedents creating a doctrinal overlay interpreting the relevant provision. But, in our view, skipping over the applicable constitutional section or clause and going straight to the case law is a kind of malpractice. It is a neglect of the right and duty of each citizen to try to determine what the Constitution means and says. It may even be legal malpractice, if it were to cause you to miss viable constitutional arguments on behalf of your client.

---

1. There are arguable exceptions to this statement. The now-defunct "fugitive slave clause" (Art. IV, §2, cl. 3), and the Thirteenth Amendment, which abolished slavery, govern what had been deemed a private property relationship. In addition, some disagreement exists as to whether the Fourteenth Amendment can be read to prohibit discrimination by private parties, an argument rejected by the Supreme Court. (See Chapters 1, 8.)

To promote our view, we quote the text of the relevant constitutional provision at the start of each section where that provision is introduced.

The Constitution was drafted by a national convention in Philadelphia in 1787. The constitutional convention was called for the express purpose of strengthening the union of states that had declared independence from Great Britain in 1776. The relatively loose "confederation" formed by the states and maintained during and after the Revolutionary War had proven unsatisfactory: the Convention was called "to form a more perfect Union," in the words of the Constitution's preamble. The Convention adopted the proposed Constitution on September 17, 1787 for submission to state ratifying conventions. Article VII of the Constitution provides: "The ratification of the conventions of nine states, shall be sufficient for the establishment of this Constitution between the states so ratifying the same." New Hampshire became the ninth state to ratify, on June 21, 1788; resolutions of the existing Continental Congress called for elections for the new national Congress and President, and set March 4, 1789, as the date by which proceedings under the new Constitution would commence. Three more states ratified the Constitution in 1789, and Rhode Island became the last of the original 13 states to ratify, in May 1790.

On September 25, 1789, the new, first Congress of the United States adopted a proposed set of amendments, the "Bill of Rights," and submitted those for ratification by at least three fourths of the state legislatures; this occurred effective December 15, 1791. The Bill of Rights thereby became the first ten amendments to the Constitution.

The Constitution's first three articles establish, respectively, the Legislative, Executive and Judicial branches of the national government, and assign their functions. The continued existence of the states as sovereign entities that retained "powers not delegated to the United States by the Constitution, nor prohibited by it to the states" (U.S. Const., Tenth Amendment), was implicitly recognized in numerous provisions. Several additional provisions limit governmental power by recognizing rights of individuals — primarily, but not exclusively found in the Bill of Rights, the Thirteenth through Fifteenth Amendments, and a handful of other provisions.

As you will see, most (though not all) constitutional law cases involve judicial review of "laws." Figure 1, which we call the "ladder of law," shows the hierarchical relationship of lawmaking institutions and the laws they create under the constitutional scheme.

In a nutshell: federal law trumps state law, federal statutes trump administrative agency "regulations," and the U.S. Constitution trumps all.

2. Constitutional Actors

Constitutional law allocates social and political decisionmaking power among five categories of "constitutional actors." These are people or institutions who have powers, duties, or rights under the Constitution and who may therefore be in a position to interpret the Constitution by basing their conduct (at least in part) on some constitutional provision. The five categories are: (1) legislative bodies; (2) executive officials and agencies; (3) courts; (4) individuals; and (5) non-governmental institutions.

Legislative bodies are those institutions, at all levels of government (federal, state, local), that consist of members elected to create laws. *Executive officials and agencies* consist of an elected "chief executive" of the political unit (the President, state governor, county executive, mayor, etc.) and the (frequently un-elected) officials working under the authority of that chief executive. These include cabinet secretaries, but also bureaucratic appointees

Figure 1. Ladder of Law

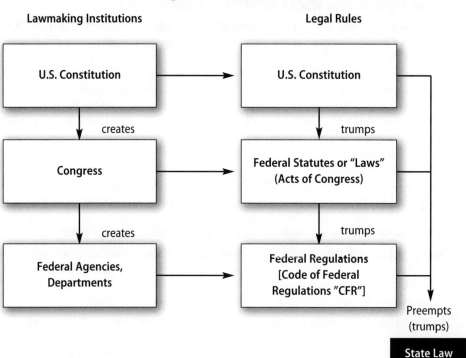

and hirees, police officers, and others. *Courts* are the federal and state judicial branch tribunals and their judges (exclusive of administrative or executive branch tribunals). *Individuals* are people who are not acting in any official governmental capacity. *Non-governmental institutions* are business and non-profit corporations, unincorporated private associations and, perhaps most significantly, the "free market"—that is, the system of private, consensual interactions among these non-governmental institutions and private individuals.

Different labels are used to describe these power allocations depending on which of the five above categories are involved, as shown in Figure 2.

Figure 2. Constitutional Law Categories

Allocation of power between or among			Constitutional label
Legislative, executive or judicial branch	and	Legislative, executive or judicial branch	*Separation of powers*
Federal governmental branch	and	State governmental branch	*Federalism*
Federal or state government	and	Individual and/or non-governmental institution	*Individual rights* (e.g., due process, equal protection, First Amendment)

3. The Power to Interpret the Constitution

It is a commonplace to assume that constitutional interpretation is the job of the courts, and the Supreme Court above all. The first year of law school tends to reinforce this idea by presenting "law" as a series of judicial rulings interpreting constitutional provisions or statutes, or creating rules from courts' own prior decisions. A more sophisticated version of this idea, from an eminent commentator, suggests that "law" is a prediction of how judges will rule in the next case.[2] The Supreme Court has itself claimed to be the final arbiter of what the Constitution means.

There is much truth to this, in Constitutional Law and other subjects, given the courts' role in interpreting and applying the law to specific cases. But the Constitution itself nowhere says that the Judicial Branch is superior to its co-equal branches when it comes to interpreting the Constitution. The Constitution creates the Congress and the President, as well as the Judicial Branch, and members of all three branches are sworn to uphold the Constitution. Assuming that these government officials act in good faith toward their constitutional obligations, it is fair to say that members of the legislative and executive branches must, and do, interpret the Constitution in carrying out many of their functions. Unless it intentionally exceeds, or is heedless toward, the limits on its constitutional power in enacting legislation, Congress implicitly (and sometimes expressly) interprets the Constitution by passing bills. The President interprets the Constitution by signing a bill into law, or vetoing the bill on constitutional grounds. When acting in ways that push the limits of their power, members of the Executive branch may be basing their actions on constitutional interpretations and arguments. The extent to which each branch of government has the authority to interpret the Constitution independently when writing on a clean slate, and to follow its own constitutional views when the Supreme Court has ruled on a question, remains subject to debate.

It is, therefore, a mistake to confuse the opinions of the Supreme Court with the Constitution itself. Compared to the text of the Constitution, which remains relatively constant subject only to an arduous amendment process, the opinions of the Supreme Court on constitutional meaning change over time. Whether this is good or bad is a matter of much debate; the opaque nature of much of the Constitution's text, and the changing nature of the social, political, and legal ideas that underlie judicial decisions, probably make such change inevitable. Despite stare decisis (the principle of following its precedents), the Court has overruled itself on numerous doctrines in its two-and-a-quarter century history, sometimes in a span of just a decade. Far more often than formally overruling its precedents, the Court will distinguish earlier cases in ways that alter the direction of legal doctrine, sometimes subtly, sometimes dramatically. It is fair to say that some precedents and principles are more stable than others. Getting a feel for which is which is an art, not a science, and an art that we hope you will begin to master in your Constitutional Law course.

Of course, the bulk of what you will study in Constitutional Law consists of Supreme Court decisions. But you should always have two important facts in the back of your mind. The first is that many acts of constitutional interpretation—and even disputes over how the Constitution should be interpreted—never reach the courts. The second is that, even when constitutional disputes reach the courts in the form of cases, the Con-

---

2. "[A] legal duty so called is nothing but a prediction that if a man does or omits certain things he will be made to suffer in this or that way by judgment of the court; and so of a legal right." Oliver Wendell Holmes, Jr., *The Path of the Law*, 10 Harv. L. Rev. 457 (1897).

stitution will have already been interpreted in the events leading up to that dispute by some constitutional actor other than the reviewing court.

Exercise: Constitutional Law

Try to create a list of five examples of constitutional actors—other than judges or litigators filing a case in court—taking some action based on their own constitutional interpretation. Example: a police officer making a judgment call about how much force can properly be used in arresting a suspect, pursuant to the Fourth Amendment's requirement that seizures be "reasonable."

C. Constitutional Cases

1. The Requirement of Governmental Action

As noted above, the Constitution is a set of arrangements granting, allocating and limiting governmental power. It follows that every constitutional law dispute necessarily involves an underlying governmental action, and, in particular, a claim that some governmental actor or institution has exceeded or abused its power. No government action, no constitutional dispute.

Constitutional disputes that wind up in the courts necessarily involve a claim that one or more officials or institutions of government have caused an injury to the claimant by exceeding their constitutional powers. In most cases, the government action is not difficult to discern. Any legislative enactment, by Congress or a state or local legislative body, will suffice. Any regulation, decision or action by a federal, state or local administrative body will do, too, as will any enforcement action by any executive officer, from a local police officer all the way up to the President of the United States. Note here that we're not saying there will be a valid claim, or even a claim that the courts will agree to decide; we're simply saying that a key threshold requirement—government action—is met in these examples.

In the context of Fourteenth Amendment cases, which are primarily individual rights challenges to state and local governmental action, this concept goes under the heading of "state action." (See Chapter 8.) But the "state action requirement" of Fourteenth Amendment claims is simply a subcategory of this broader requirement of government action in any constitutional claim.

"State" or "government" action may be less apparent in cases where the primary disputants seem to be private parties. But there may be government action lurking in the background that can suffice to meet the requirement. In *Shelley v. Kraemer*, 334 U.S. 1 (1948), the Supreme Court found "state action" for Fourteenth Amendment purposes in a case where the plaintiffs sought to enforce a "racially restrictive covenant" (a private agreement affecting real estate) against a black family that bought a home in their neighborhood. The actions of the state court to enforce these covenants, the Supreme Court held, qualified as state action.

Exercise: State Action

Christy Brzonkala sued Antonio Morrison for money damages arising out of an alleged sexual assault, under a provision of the Violence Against Women Act that created a federal cause of action for a sexual assault victim against the person who assaulted her. This lawsuit resulted in a major constitutional ruling by the Supreme Court. (See *United States v. Morrison*, Chapter 1.) What do you think the government action was in that case? Which party do you think asserted the constitutional right?

---

2. Eight Patterns of Constitutional Cases

It would be tidy if every constitutional claimant — the challenger to the alleged excess of government power — were the plaintiff and the challenged government actor or institution were the defendant in every case. But constitutional law is not so tidy, and that particular array of parties only occurs in some constitutional cases. The constitutional "challenger" may be the plaintiff or the defendant, the parties may be government officials or institutions or non-governmental institutions or individuals. The cases may be civil or criminal.

Most of the cases in this book are civil cases, for two reasons. First, as mentioned above, constitutional cases all involve a challenge to some type of governmental act, and the majority of governmental acts do not directly involve the creation or enforcement of criminal laws. Second, the Constitutional Law courses to which this book is directed omit coverage of so-called "constitutional criminal law" — the interplay between criminal prosecution and the Fourth, Fifth, Sixth and Eight Amendments, which deal respectively with search and seizure, self-incrimination, right to counsel and confrontation, and cruel or unusual punishment. (The due process clause of the Fifth Amendment, as opposed to the self-incrimination clause, forms a significant part of this book, however.) Those issues are traditionally broken out and covered in a Criminal Procedure course.

But several cases in this book do arise out of criminal law. Enactment and enforcement of criminal statutes represent a significant assertion of governmental power. Although these activities represent a minority of governmental activities in general, they are a significant minority. Challenges to criminal legislation and enforcement can be based on constitutional principles that are central to this book, such as federalism, separation of powers, due process, or free speech. Some of the cases you study will therefore be criminal cases.

The following is a list of eight patterns of constitutional cases that you will find in this book. We think this list is both detailed and exhaustive, though some cases may be difficult to categorize (or may fall into more than one category); and it certainly is possible to categorize types of constitutional cases in a different way. To help organize the information presented, we've broken the eight patterns into two groups:

a. Patterns 1 through 4: Constitutional Right Asserted as Litigation Defense

Pattern 1: Private party defends against government civil enforcement action. Numerous federal or state laws authorize the federal or state governments to take non-criminal enforcement measures against private parties. Under some statutes, the government is authorized to file suit; under other statutes, the government may act administratively, and the affected party will have the right to some sort of administrative hearing process and judicial review. In this pattern, the private party defendant asserts that the non-criminal law or regulation that the government is trying to enforce is unconstitutional.

Illustrative examples: *NLRB v. Jones & Laughlin Steel Corp.*; *United States v. Butler* (Chapter 1); *Immigration and Naturalization Service v. Chadha* (Chapter 4); *FCC v. Pacifica Foundation* (Chapter 9).

Pattern 2: Private party defends against federal or state criminal prosecution. The federal or state governments initiate a standard criminal prosecution. The defendant challenges the constitutionality of the particular criminal statute, typically, by making a motion to dismiss the indictment (or the charging document in state court); or by challenging the sentence.

Illustrative examples: *United States v. Darby, United States v. Lopez* (Chapter 1); *Mistretta v. United States* (Chapter 4); *Lochner v. New York, Roe v. Wade* (Chapter 7); *Brandenburg v. Ohio* (Chapter 9).

Pattern 3: State or state official defends against private party suit. This pattern of case involves a private party claim authorized by federal law against a state or state official. The claim is directly based on the statute, not the Constitution. The constitutional issue arises as a defense: the state defendant asserts that the federal statute is unconstitutional.

Illustrative examples: *Garcia v. SAMTA, Nevada Department of Human Resources v. Hibbs* (Chapter 1).

Pattern 4: Private party sues private party. Some constitutional challenges arise entirely between private litigants. Many federal and state laws—either legislative enactments or judicially created rights—structure relations among individuals and non-governmental institutions by recognizing rights that can be asserted as a claim or defense in private litigation. If such a right is challenged as violating the Constitution, then a constitutional issue arises in the private party lawsuit.

The party asserting the federal right is not necessarily relied on to defend its constitutionality; typically, the government will be allowed to intervene to do so. This procedure brought the federal government into the case to defend the Violence Against Women Act in *United States v. Morrison*.

Illustrative examples: *Gibbons v. Ogden, Carter v. Carter Coal Co.* (Chapter 1); *Geier v. American Honda Co.* (Chapter 2); *Stern v. Marshall* (Chapter 4); *Dred Scott v. Sanford* (Chapter 5); *New York Times v. Sullivan* (Chapter 9).

b. Patterns 5 through 8: Constitutional Right as Basis for Claim

Pattern 5: One federal branch, institution, or official sues another. Federal government officials or institutions may sue one another to resolve difficult disputed issues regarding separation of powers or the structure of government. These cases are often civil in nature, but they may also arise as collateral ("side") issues in criminal cases—for example, as a motion to quash a subpoena. As a percentage of cases on federal court dockets, these cases are probably overrepresented in our book, but they offer some of the courts' prime opportunities to address these questions.

Illustrative examples: *United States v. Nixon, Campbell v. Clinton, Morrison v. Olson* (Chapter 3); *Powell v. McCormack, Raines v. Byrd, Nixon v. United States* (Chapter 6).

Pattern 6: State sues federal government in opposition to non-judicial federal enforcement action. The federal government directly asserts some regulatory authority over state or local governments or officials, and the states or officials challenge the action on constitutional grounds. If the federal government files suit, the state's argument is an affirmative defense; if the federal government acts through executive enforcement, the state might file suit to challenge the action.

Illustrative examples: *South Dakota v. Dole, Katzenbach v. Morgan* (Chapter 1); *Clinton v. City of New York* (Chapter 4).

Pattern 7: Private party or state proactively sues to block enforcement of federal or state law. In this pattern of case, challengers who anticipate being harmed by a federal or state law do not wait for the law to be enforced against them; instead, they get out in front of any potential enforcement action by seeking to block enforcement proactively. Challengers may be individuals, non-governmental organizations, even state governments or officials, or a combination of all of the above. Typically, such challenges are brought very soon after the law is enacted. Many "public interest law" constitutional suits are brought in this manner. Because such claims are brought prior to enforcement, they can raise justiciability problems such as "ripeness" or "standing." (See Chapter 6.) Also, because the harm has not yet occurred, it is unusual for such cases to involve requests for monetary damages; instead, such suits typically seek injunctive or declaratory relief.

Illustrative examples: *New York v. United States, Printz v. United States* (Chapter 1); *Raines v. Byrd* (Chapter 6); *Romer v. Evans* (Chapter 8); *Reno v. ACLU* (Chapter 9).

Pattern 8: Private party sues based on direct constitutional claim against federal or state agency or official. Here, the constitutional challenger is a plaintiff who claims injury directly resulting from unconstitutional government action. The challenger sues for damages, or declaratory or injunctive relief.

Several habeas corpus cases are contained in this book. Habeas corpus is a challenge to allegedly illegal imprisonment (or other detention). It is structured, technically, as a civil suit against the executive officials in charge of the detention facility. (This is so despite the fact that many habeas cases are post-conviction challenges to procedures in an underlying criminal prosecution leading to a sentence of imprisonment.) While habeas cases could be a ninth category unto themselves, we think they also fall into this eighth pattern.

Illustrative examples: *Youngstown Sheet & Tube Co. v. Sawyer, Dames & Moore v. Regan, Nixon v. Fitzgerald, Myers v. United States, Humphreys' Executor v. United States* (Chapter 3); *Marbury v. Madison* (Chapter 5); *Lujan v. Defenders of Wildlife* (Chapter 6); *Brown v. Board of Education* (Chapter 8); *Clark v. Community for Creative Nonviolence, Garcetti v. Ceballos* (Chapter 9).

In addition, any of the habeas corpus cases, such as: *Ex parte Milligan, Hamdi v. Rumsfeld* (Chapter 3); *Ex parte McCardle* (Chapter 5).

Exercises: Patterns of Constitutional Cases

1. Based on what you know about *NFIB v. Sebelius* (the Affordable Care Act case) — either from having studied it in Chapter 1 or read about it in the news — see if you can categorize the case as fitting one of the eight patterns.

2. As you read the various cases in this book, try to place them in one of the eight patterns.

D. Litigation Procedure in Constitutional Cases

1. In General

Generally speaking, constitutional claims are handled procedurally in the same manner as any other claim of substantive or procedural rights. What makes a claim "constitutional" is the source of the legal argument asserted: Constitutional claims are based on arguments from the Constitution. To be sure, constitutional cases can raise some issues that fall outside familiar patterns. For example, certain special rules arise when federal or state governmental actors are parties to litigation — such as rules relating to "sovereign immunity." (*See, e.g.,* Chapter 1 (Eleventh Amendment); Chapter 3 (Executive Privilege or Immunity).) In addition, some constitutional claims raise special problems of "justiciability." (See Chapter 6.) But for the most part, the familiar rules of civil or criminal procedure that you study in those procedural courses also govern constitutional cases.

In many of the constitutional law cases that you read in this book, it is worth giving some thought to the underlying procedural steps that would have occurred before the case got to the Supreme Court. For example, if a case was dismissed on a Rule 12(b)(6) motion in the district court before working its way up to the Supreme Court, the facts of the case recited in the Supreme Court opinion should be derived from the allegations of the complaint — following basic civil procedure, at that stage of the litigation, the facts alleged in the complaint must be assumed true for purposes of making legal rulings on them. Similarly, where a case is dismissed at the summary judgment stage and reaches the Supreme Court on appeal, the source of facts for the Court's opinion should be those presented at the summary judgment hearing: the affidavits of witnesses (not their live testimony), with any attached discovery materials, such as deposition transcripts and responses to discovery requests.

It is also useful to be aware of appellate procedure, since virtually all the cases in this book are appellate opinions. Certain appellate procedures are generic and may be familiar to you from Civil Procedure, while others are particular to the Supreme Court of the United States. Some of these are described in subsections 4 through 7, below.

2. The Court System

The federal court system, and most state court systems, consist of a three-level hierarchy with trial courts at the bottom, intermediate appellate courts in the middle, and a supreme court at the top.[3] The chart in Figure 3 shows this system.

Figure 3. Hierarchy of Court Systems of the United States

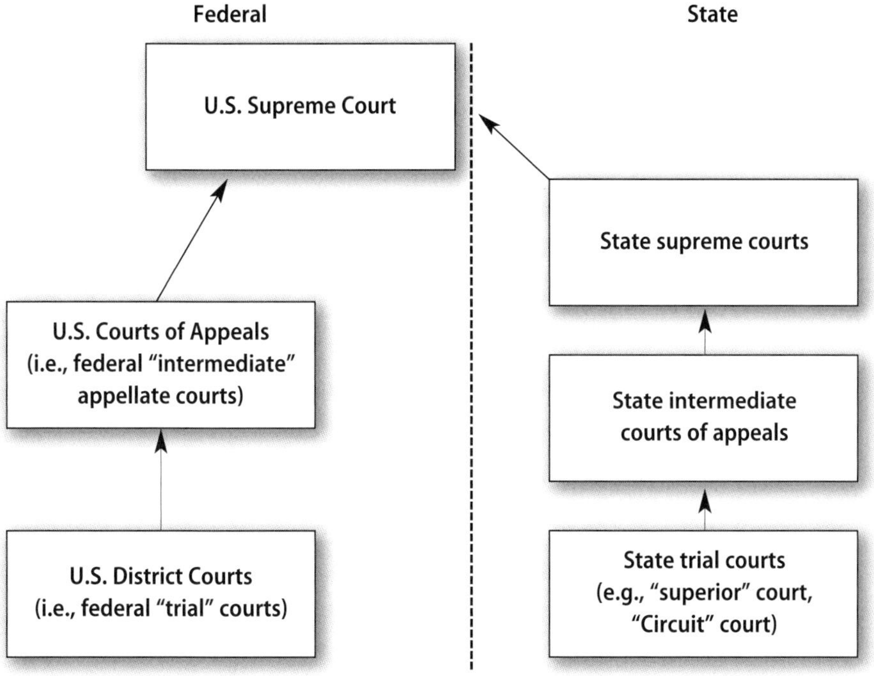

Federal

State

U.S. Supreme Court

State supreme courts

U.S. Courts of Appeals
(i.e., federal "intermediate" appellate courts)

State intermediate courts of appeals

U.S. District Courts
(i.e., federal "trial" courts)

State trial courts
(e.g., "superior" court, "Circuit" court)

The federal court system, as depicted in Figure 3, is established in part by the U.S. Constitution, and in part by federal statutes. (State courts are set up by state constitutions and statutes.) Five provisions of the Constitution speak to the structure of the courts. Here are the first two:

> [The Congress shall have power ...] To constitute tribunals inferior to the Supreme Court [Art. I, §8, cl. 9]

> The judicial power of the United States, shall be vested in one Supreme Court, and in such inferior courts as the Congress may from time to time ordain and establish. The judges, both of the supreme and inferior courts, shall hold their offices during good behaviour, and shall, at stated times, receive for their services, a compensation, which shall not be diminished during their continuance in office. [Art. III, §1]

These two provisions tell us, among other things, that the Constitution itself establishes only a (the) Supreme Court. Lower federal courts "may" be established by Congress. The

---

3. The court systems of several smaller states (as well as the District of Columbia, a federal enclave governed ultimately by Congress) have only trial courts and an ultimate appellate (i.e., supreme) court.

third provision (Art. III, § 2, cl. 1) sets out the jurisdiction of the federal courts (i.e., their power to hear and decide cases):

> The judicial power shall extend to all cases, in law and equity, arising under this Constitution, the laws of the United States, and treaties made, or which shall be made, under their authority;—to all cases affecting ambassadors, other public ministers and consuls;—to all cases of admiralty and maritime jurisdiction;—to controversies to which the United States shall be a party;—to controversies between two or more states;—between a state and citizens of another state;—between citizens of different states;—between citizens of the same state claiming lands under grants of different states, and between a state, or the citizens thereof, and foreign states, citizens or subjects.

The fourth provision (Art. III, § 2, cl. 2) sets out the Supreme Court's jurisdiction in particular:

> In all cases affecting ambassadors, other public ministers and consuls, and those in which a state shall be party, the Supreme Court shall have original jurisdiction. In all the other cases before mentioned, the Supreme Court shall have appellate jurisdiction, both as to law and fact, with such exceptions, and under such regulations as the Congress shall make.

Note that the Constitution gives Congress power over the jurisdiction of the lower courts (it can create them from scratch and so presumably can limit their jurisdiction), and over the Supreme Court's appellate jurisdiction (the "exceptions and regulations" clause, discussed in Chapter 5). The remaining provision relating at all to court structure is the "appointments clause," Art. II, which provides that federal judges and justices are to be appointed by the president "with the advice and consent of the Senate." The Constitution says nothing about the number of justices to be appointed to the Supreme Court, which by implication, and as confirmed by historical precedent, is left to the control of Congress. (The First Congress enacted the Judiciary Act of 1789, which established six seats on the Supreme Court.[4])

Although there have always been lower federal courts,[5] it appears to have been the framers' assumption that state courts would handle a substantial amount of federal judicial business.[6] This assumption is implicit in the above-quoted constitutional provisions. The Supreme Court has very limited "original jurisdiction"—extending only to "cases affecting ambassadors and other public ministers and consuls" (i.e., emissaries of foreign governments), and cases "in which a state shall be a party." Original

---

4. Judiciary Act of 1789, § 1,1 Stat. 73 (Sep. 24, 1789).

5. The Judiciary Act of 1789 created a system of lower federal courts. Each of the 11 states that had ratified the constitution as of September 1789 was formed into a federal district with one federal district judge (except for Virginia and Massachusetts, which had two districts each). The 13 districts were grouped into three circuits. The Circuit Courts were comprised of the district judge plus two Supreme Court justices riding circuit—traveling to the Circuit court locations to hear cases. Circuit court jurisdiction included both appeals from the district courts as well as original jurisdiction (i.e., trial) in major felony cases and civil cases involving larger dollar amounts. Judiciary Act of 1789, §§ 2-5, 1 Stat. 73 (Sep. 24, 1789).

6. See The Federalist, No. 82 (Hamilton) (Rossiter ed. 1961), at 493("[I]n every case in which they were not expressly excluded by the future acts of the national legislature, they will of course take cognizance of the [cases] to which those acts gave birth."). The 1789 Judiciary Act gave federal courts exclusive jurisdiction only in admiralty and federal criminal cases, and implied that state courts would be deciding federal questions: hence, the need to establish U. S. Supreme Court review of such cases in section 25.

jurisdiction is the power of a court to act as the initial judicial forum, in which the case originates; this typically includes the basic fact-finding and trial-supervision functions that we associate with "trial courts." In contrast, "appellate" courts review cases initiated in lower courts of original jurisdiction, and essentially supervise their legal rulings. If the Supreme Court was and is to be primarily an "appellate" court, and if the Constitution merely allows, but does not require, Congress to create lower federal courts, then by implication, state trial courts could be expected to act as courts of original jurisdiction for many federal cases. Indeed, even today, state courts have "concurrent jurisdiction" (concurrent with the federal courts) over many, perhaps most, federal law claims and defenses.

Congress expressly provided for the U.S. Supreme Court having ultimate appellate authority over all judicial decisions on questions of federal law. Under Section 25 of the 1789 Judiciary Act, the Supreme Court was empowered to review cases whose resolution required an interpretation of a federal statute or treaty, or of the U.S. Constitution. (The text of this provision, and the leading case interpreting it, *Martin v. Hunters' Lessee*, are presented in Chapter 5.) A slightly revised version of this provision is now found at 28 U.S.C. § 1257.

3. Initiating the Constitutional Case

Constitutional law cases virtually always begin in a "trial court" of a state or the federal court system.[7] The function of trial courts is to make the first-line resolution of the case, while compiling whatever evidence the parties choose to present and resolving disputes in the evidence. Trial courts are usually presided over by a single trial judge — the federal district judge, in federal courts. On rare occasions, a few of which can be found in this book, the federal district court will sit as a "three judge court."[8]

If the case is a criminal prosecution or a civil enforcement action by the government (patterns 1 and 2, above), the government initiates the case and the constitutional argument, if any, is raised as a defense. If the case is initiated by a private party, against another private party or a state or state official (patterns 3 and 4), the constitutional issue most likely arises as a defense: that the claim is based on an unconstitutional statute (or is preempted by federal law — see Chapter 2).

In all the other constitutional cases (patterns 5 through 8) the party making the constitutional claim initiates a civil suit as the plaintiff (or "petitioner," in a habeas corpus case). The constitutional right becomes the basis, in essence, for a "cause of action" in the complaint.

---

7. One noteworthy exception is *Marbury v. Madison*, in which Marbury, invoking the Supreme Court's original jurisdiction, initiated his case in the Supreme Court. Less noteworthy, but more common, are categories of cases that are heard by administrative tribunals that can be appealed directly to intermediate appellate courts.

8. While three-judge district courts are unusual, they crop up a bit more frequently in constitutional cases. From 1948 to 1976, for example, a three-judge district court had to be convened whenever a party sought to enjoin a state statute on grounds of unconstitutionality. See 28 U.S.C. § 2281 (repealed). Under current law, a three-judge court is required to hear a constitutional challenge to a legislative reapportionment of congressional voting districts. See 28 U.S.C. § 2284. A handful of substantive federal laws include a provision that a constitutional challenge to the law must be heard by a three judge district court; such was the case, for example, in *Reno v. ACLU* (Chapter 9), a challenge to the Communications Decency Act of 1996. *See* 104-104, Title V, Subtitle C, § 561, 110 Stat. 142 (1996).

Who are the defendants in this latter group of constitutional cases (patterns 5 through 8)? That depends on a number of factors. The basic principle of any civil suit, which applies to constitutional cases as well, is that a plaintiff wants to sue defendants who (a) have at least some responsibility for causing the harm to the plaintiff; and (b) have the means to supply the remedy sought by the plaintiff. "Means" could be money if the desired remedy is monetary damages. But in many constitutional cases, the desired remedy is declaratory or injunctive relief: a declaration that a law is unconstitutional, or an order to an executive official to act or refrain from acting. A defendant with "means" to supply the latter remedies is an official or agency with legal authority to order the doing of (or refraining from) the act.[9]

The ins and outs of naming defendants in constitutional litigation can get complex, and take up a significant chunk of an advanced course that might be called "Constitutional [or Civil Rights] Litigation." We will make just two points here.

First, to the extent that there is any "law" about who should be named as defendants in constitutional cases, it consists of a narrow set of rules about who *cannot* be sued — not necessarily who *should be* sued. These rules are called "immunity" rules, and include the doctrine of "sovereign immunity" as well as individual "official immunity." Generally speaking, a sovereign government — federal or state — cannot be sued without its consent. This greatly limits the ability of a plaintiff in patterns 5 through 8 cases to name "the United States" or "the State of Alabama" as defendants. On the other hand, agencies of a government do not necessarily have this sovereign immunity, and many government officials can be sued for their official acts (though there are some exceptions). In sum, the rules of "appropriate defendants" in constitutional cases might be understood as "whoever is responsible and does not have immunity."

Second, the choices by attorneys in naming one or more defendants from this category may be driven largely by intuition. Legal rules about what government officials to sue — who is responsible for an alleged constitutional violation — are frequently unclear. This tends to prompt lawyers who draft complaints in patterns 5 through 8 cases to "throw the names up against the wall and see who sticks." Thus, it is common in patterns 5 through 8 litigation to see many officials and agencies named as defendants in a single case.

Constitutional cases are generally litigated in trial courts under the rules of procedure and evidence that govern ordinary litigation. Where the specific factual narrative of the parties' dispute may bear heavily on the constitutional issues, a constitutional case will look the same as any other civil or criminal case. But many constitutional cases are focused far more on the legal issue than on the disputed narrative facts that might dominate in ordinary litigation. If the constitutional claim is that Congress lacks the authority to prohibit the possession of a gun in a school zone, the argument will revolve around the meaning of the commerce clause and perhaps on some questions of statutory interpretation or legislative history of the law; the story of Alfonso Lopez, and what he was doing with a gun near a school, becomes somewhat tangential background. (See *United States v. Lopez*, Chapter 1.) In a case dominated by the legal issues, the case facts will have, at most, a persuasive impact as an exemplar of what is at stake in a particular constitutional controversy.

When the facts underlying a constitutional case are sociological in nature, how are those facts introduced into the case? For example, in the Affordable Care Act litigation (*NFIB v. Sebelius*), the court recited extensive background facts about the health care system; in

---

9. For reasons explained below, subsection D. 8 ("Remedies"), legislators are rarely if ever appropriate defendants in cases challenging the constitutionality of the laws they have enacted.

United States v. Morrison, there were extensive background facts about violence against women; and in *ACLU v. Reno*, there was an extensive factual record about internet use and what sort of parental controls on web browsing was technologically feasible. Ambiguities in the rules of procedure and evidence lead to an ambiguous answer to the question of how these facts enter the lawsuit. In some cases, the parties present them as evidence to the trial court, through documents and "expert witness" testimony. In other cases, the courts seem willing to consider background information supplied in the legislative findings that led up to enactment of a law, or even in briefs submitted by parties to the appellate courts.

4. Appeals

A "final judgment" by a federal district court—a ruling that disposes of all of the issues in the case such that there is nothing left to decide on the "merits"(the core substantive claims of the case)—is appealable to the United States Court of Appeals. See 28 U.S.C. § 1291.[10]

The federal system has one level of "intermediate" appellate court, known as the United States Court of Appeals and divided into thirteen Circuits: the First through Eleventh and District of Columbia Circuits have geographically defined authority over the District Courts in their respective circuits; the Federal Circuit has authority over appeals from the U.S. Court of Claims and other specialized federal courts. An appeal from a U.S. district court to one of these Circuit Courts of Appeals is "an appeal as of right"—that is to say, the losing litigant has a right to take this appeal, and the Court of Appeals must hear it (assuming it has jurisdiction). In contrast, as will be seen, there is generally no right to have one's appeal heard by the U.S. Supreme Court. Most state court systems have an analogous court structure.[11]

Appellate courts typically do not consider new evidence, but instead confine their consideration of case facts to those developed by the trial court—they consider only evidence that is "in the record" created by the trial court. If for some reason there are grounds to allow the introduction of new evidence, the case must be sent back ("remanded") to the trial court to hear the new evidence. In short, trial courts are evidence-taking courts, appellate courts are not.

Appellate courts follow a few broad principles to determine whether or not to give deference to the decisions of lower courts. Deferential review means that the trial court's decision will be upheld if it is debatably correct, meaning that if the decision is reasonable it will be upheld, even if the appellate judges would have decided differently had they sat as the trial judge. Findings of fact are reviewed deferentially: a trial court's determination of a disputed factual issue will be reversed on appeal only if it is "clearly erroneous." Discretionary rulings by trial courts (these include decisions about whether to admit or exclude evidence and decisions about case management) are also reviewed deferentially

---

10. In very limited circumstances, an appeal can be taken from something other than a final judgment—called an "interlocutory" decision. See 28 U.S.C. § 1292.

11. In the modern "administrative state" (our present governmental structure which comprises numerous administrative agencies at both the federal and state levels), many adjudications begin in administrative agency hearings rather than in a trial court. The administrative hearing may function in many ways like a court—with a neutral hearing officer or "administrative law judge" taking evidence and resolving factual disputes. Such administrative hearings are created by statutes. While there is probably a constitutional right to have many of these kinds of cases heard by a court, judicial review of an agency hearing decision might go first to a district court or directly to an appellate court— depending on the procedure specified in the applicable statute.

and will be reversed on appeal only if they constitute an "abuse of discretion"—a standard that means something like an "unreasonable" decision.

Non-deferential review means that there is no presumption of correctness afforded to the lower court decision, and no need to give any particular weight to the lower court ruling. The reviewing court in such situations allows itself free rein to substitute its judgment for that of the lower court. Rulings on legal principles are reviewed non-deferentially. This standard is typically called "de novo" review, meaning "from the start." Appellate courts, thus, take a fresh look at a question of law on appeal. Most constitutional issues decided by the Supreme Court are questions of law, on which the Court gives non-deferential review to the lower court decisions, though there may be certain underlying factual issues that the Supreme Court supposedly reviews deferentially.

5. Reaching the Supreme Court

When it comes to getting one's case reviewed by the Supreme Court, the plain fact is that "many have tried, but few are chosen." The Supreme Court has discretionary review authority—it can pick and choose cases from among those in which litigants seek Supreme Court review. The Supreme Court exercises its discretion to grant review very sparingly. Each year, the Court grants review in 90 or so cases out of several thousand appeals and petitions.[12] It hears around 75 to 80 oral arguments, and issues a slightly lesser number of decisions based on full opinions.

Under current procedures, cases most commonly reach the Supreme Court on a "writ of certiorari," after they have been decided by one of the federal courts of appeals, 28 U.S.C. §1254(1), or a state appellate court. 28 U.S.C. §1257(a). Certiorari (known as "cert" to its friends)is a process historically derived from the common law for *discretionary* appellate review of a case. As Supreme Court Rule 10 states, "Review on a writ of certiorari is not a matter of right, but of judicial discretion." Writs of certiorari are technically issued by the Supreme Court to the court that issued the most recent judgment in the case. Hence, in a full opinion (not, typically, an edited casebook version), you will see a sentence like this, following the case caption:

On Writ of Certiorari to the United States Court of Appeals for the Fourth Circuit

This means that the Supreme Court has ordered the Fourth Circuit to transfer the authority to issue judgments in the case, together with the physical court records, to the Supreme Court. Where the case has worked its way up through the state system, the Supreme Court issues the writ of certiorari to the "the highest court of a state in which a decision could

---

12. About 9,000 cases are filed seeking review in the Supreme Court annually. About 7,000 of these are "in forma pauperis," that is, by parties whose lack of financial means meets the requirement for a waiver of the filing fee. Although the Court does not break down the data in this way, it is probably the case that most of these 7,000 cases consist of routine federal criminal appeals and perhaps some "pro se" cases (parties unrepresented by lawyers). The Court grants review in only about 10 to 15, or about 0.18%, of these 7,000 in forma pauperis cases.

An additional 2000 or so cases are filed by parties who pay filing fees. These "fee paying" cases are more likely than the in forma pauperis group to be winnowed down by lawyers advising their clients about the unlikelihood of a grant of review. A lawyer who would charge a fee to prepare a cert petition should advise his client if, in her opinion, the case is not "cert worthy" and highly likely to result in a denial of review. As a result, a higher proportion of these fees-paid cases are likely to meet the Court's criteria for granting review. The Court grants review in around 70 to 80, or about 3%, of the 2,000 "fee paying" cases filed. *See* www.uscourts.gov/Statistics/JudicialBusiness.aspx.

be had." 28 U.S.C. § 1257(a). Typically, this means the Supreme Court reviews a decision of the state supreme court. But states with three-tiered court systems typically afford their state supreme courts discretionary review power much like the U.S. Supreme Court, so there may be cases in which the U.S. Supreme Court grants certiorari in a case where a decision was rendered by the state's intermediate appellate court, but the state's supreme court denied review. The above-quoted language from § 1257(a) has been construed to cover this situation.

In unusual circumstances, a "direct appeal" may be taken to the Supreme Court (skipping the intermediate appellate courts) from the judgment of a district court. Direct appeals to the Supreme Court are provided in cases where a three-judge district court has been convened, 28 U.S.C. § 1253, and, until 1988, in cases where the district court had struck down an Act of Congress as unconstitutional. 28 U.S.C. § 1252 (repealed 1988).[13] ("Direct appeals" from certain state court decisions also used to be allowed.) Cases also can reach the Supreme Court via the Court's original jurisdiction, in which the Court acts as a factfinding or trial court rather than an appellate court, but these are quite rare.[14]

The key points to remember about the Supreme Court's docket, then, are that: (1) review of a case in the Supreme Court is fundamentally a matter of the Court's discretion; (2) most requests for Supreme Court review are sought by filing a petition for writ of certiorari; and (3) most requests for Supreme Court review are turned down. A litigant must, therefore, take on quite a challenge to persuade the Supreme Court to grant review. Supreme Court Rule 10 lays out the criteria for the persuasive case a litigant must make if review is to be granted:

> Review on a writ of certiorari is not a matter of right, but of judicial discretion. A petition for a writ of certiorari will be granted only for compelling reasons. The following, although neither controlling nor fully measuring the Court's discretion, indicate the character of the reasons the Court considers:
>
>> (a) a United States court of appeals has entered a decision in conflict with the decision of another United States court of appeals on the same important matter; has decided an important federal question in a way that conflicts with a decision by a state court of last resort; or has so far departed from the accepted and usual course of judicial proceedings, or sanctioned such a departure by a lower court, as to call for an exercise of this Court's supervisory power;

---

13. Technically speaking, a direct appeal (in contrast to a writ of certiorari) is not a discretionary procedure; by traditional understanding, appeals are mandatory on the reviewing court — provided they have jurisdiction. Under long-standing practice, the Supreme Court has finessed the mandatory nature of appeals by making them depend on a finding of "probable jurisdiction" (a decision that is discretionary in practice). For this reason, in the handful of direct appeal cases where the Court decides to grant review (some of which are found in this book), it does so by "noting" that it has "probable jurisdiction."

14. Article III, § 2, cl. 2, quoted above, provides that the Supreme Court has original jurisdiction only in cases involving foreign emissaries or in which a state is a party. Congress has further specified that the Court must take original jurisdiction only where the suit is "between two or more states." 28 U.S.C. § 1251(a). Otherwise, the Court has "original but not exclusive jurisdiction" of cases by or against (but not between) one or more states and cases involving foreign emissaries. 28 U.S.C. § 1251(b). This means that the Court may decline original jurisdiction in § 1251(b) cases. See Supreme Court Rule 17(3) (requiring motion for leave to file original case in Supreme Court).

A fourth route to the Supreme Court, exceedingly unusual, occurs when the Court grants a Court of Appeals' request to decide a case or issue by "certification" — which essentially means that the appellate court passes the case along to the Supreme Court without deciding it. 28 U.S.C. § 1254(2).

(b) a state court of last resort has decided an important federal question in a way that conflicts with the decision of another state court of last resort or of a United States court of appeals;

(c) a state court or a United States court of appeals has decided an important question of federal law that has not been, but should be, settled by this Court, or has decided an important federal question in a way that conflicts with relevant decisions of this Court.

A petition for a writ of certiorari is rarely granted when the asserted error consists of erroneous factual findings or the misapplication of a properly stated rule of law.

A petition for a writ of certiorari does not focus on why the petitioner should win the case, but rather why the case is important enough—and meets the criteria for—discretionary Supreme Court review. The same criteria apply when the review mechanism is direct appeal, rather than certiorari.[15] The affirmative vote of four justices is required to grant review.

If certiorari (or appellate jurisdiction) is denied, the judgment or order of the lower court stands. If certiorari is granted, the fun begins. The Court sets a briefing schedule. Lawyers and groups from around the country with an interest in the case and the issues it raises are likely to join the act by filing amicus curiae ("friend of the court") briefs, arguing aspects of the case on behalf of one side or the other, or perhaps advocating some neutral or middle ground. Often, the litigants themselves will recruit amicus support by soliciting helpful amicus briefs from allied organizations, or experts on one or more issues raised in the case. The Court tends to be fairly liberal about granting permission to "amici" to file briefs. In particularly momentous cases, dozens of amicus briefs may be filed. (In the recent health care litigation, there were over 100 amicus briefs.)

One extremely important document in addition to the briefs is the "joint appendix," a summary of key documents from the lower court record, compiled specially for the Supreme Court by the litigants. The Court receives the "full record" on appeal. In a conceptual sense, "the record" comprises the universe of facts and procedural history that the Supreme Court (like the intermediate appellate courts before it) will consider: as we have said, appellate courts do not conduct independent fact-finding. In a physical sense, "the record" includes all of the written and recorded matter that comprises the case file, from its very beginning in the trial court, including all pleadings, motions and briefs filed with the lower courts; all evidence submitted; and all transcripts of hearings and proceedings in the lower courts. The full (physical) record is typically so voluminous that important items can be easy to overlook. The Court thus requires the "joint appendix" to include certain "relevant" matter, such as the lower court docket and the decision under review, plus "any other parts of the record that the parties particularly wish to bring to the court's attention." Supreme Court Rule 26(1). As the name implies, this is supposed to be a "joint" document. ("The parties are encouraged to agree on the contents of the joint appendix." Id., Rule 26(2).) When Supreme Court opinions recite case facts and procedural history, they will often cite to the "JA" or "joint appendix."

The Court hears oral arguments over the course of a nine-month term beginning in October and ending in June the following year. At the end of each week of oral argument, the justices meet in conference to decide the cases argued that week. A preliminary vote is taken to determine whether there is a majority judgment and which justices are in the majority. The senior justice voting in the majority—the Chief Justice or, if the Chief is

---

15. On direct appeal, the appellant files a "jurisdictional statement" that must "follow, insofar as practicable, the form for a petition for writ of certiorari[.]" Supreme Court Rule 18(3).

in the dissent, the longest-serving associate justice—will assign the writing of the majority opinion to one of the majority justices (including herself). Over the next several weeks or months, the justices draft opinions in the case and circulate them internally. Because the initial vote is not binding, justices can (and not infrequently, do) change their minds during this time. The justices' deliberative process continues via informal conversations between justices and discussions about draft opinions circulated before the final decision is solidified.

A judgment of the Supreme Court requires an agreement of five justices. The "judgment" is the outcome with respect to the decision below, but is not in itself a statement of legal principles or reasons for the judgment. The different types of appellate court judgment indicators (affirmed, reversed, vacated) are described below, in section D.7.

An "opinion" is a statement of legal principles and reasons in support of a judgment (or would-be judgment, in the case of dissenting opinions). An opinion becomes the "opinion of the court" or "majority opinion" only if it gains the assent of a majority of justices (five, assuming the Court's current nine positions are all occupied).[16] In some instances, five or more justices agree on a judgment without any five agreeing on the supporting legal principles and reasoning; the judgment will issue, but the lead opinion— the one with the largest number of votes among those in voting for the majority judgment (four or perhaps three)—is in this situation called a "plurality" opinion and not deemed a precedent accorded full precedential effect.

Even in the usual case, where five or more justices agree to a single majority opinion, additional opinions may be issued by individual or groups of justices:

- A "**concurring opinion**" or "**concurrence**" is a separate opinion issued by a justice who signs onto the reasoning of the majority opinion but feels the need to add some further explanation or qualification.

- An opinion "**concurring in the judgment**" is the opinion of a justice who agrees with the majority (or plurality) result only—i.e., the judgment—but not the key legal principles and reasons. A justice "concurring in the judgment" does *not* sign onto the majority (or plurality) opinion.

- A "**dissenting opinion**" or "**dissent**" is one that disagrees with *both* the *opinion* of the majority (or plurality) *and* the *judgment* of the court.

- Where a decision has multiple aspects, individual judges might mix and match these possibilities: e.g., "**concurring in part, dissenting in part**," or "**concurring in the judgment in part, dissenting in part**."

Frequently, one or more justices will join the separate opinions (concurrence, concurrence in the judgment, or dissent) written by other justices. All this information is conveyed in summary form in tag lines at the outset of the opinions; but in order to find the detailed bases for agreements and disagreements among the justices, some of which can be quite subtle, you have to read the opinions.

Majority opinions sometimes suffer from their need to attract support from multiple justices. Since they must bring together the views of at least five typically strong-minded and independent individuals, majority opinions must at times reflect compromises that

---

16. The Constitution says nothing about the number of justices to constitute the Supreme Court. That number has been set by Congress, at various points through U.S. history, at 5, 6, 9 and 10. It has stood at nine for well over a century. In theory, if there were two unfilled vacancies, the Court could decide a case with a majority of four.

affect writing style and even clarity. Separate opinions sometimes come across as clearer and stronger, given that the author is freed from the constraints of coalition-building and editing-by-committee.

6. A Note on Party Designations and Case Captions

Party designations vary from court to court. In civil cases, as you know, the party initiating the suit is the plaintiff, and the party being sued is the defendant.[17] Case captions often use the same terms in criminal cases—with the prosecution being referred to formally as the "plaintiff."

Habeas corpus cases are different. Habeas is a "petition," for a "writ." The complaining party, the one who initiates the habeas case, is thus the "petitioner," and the opposing party is the "respondent."

Appellate courts also use different terminology, reflecting the parties' roles with respect to the appellate procedures. In the federal system, the party who loses in the district court and takes the appeal to the intermediate court of appeals is the "appellant," and the party opposing the appeal (the winner below) is the "appellee" (or, in some state court systems, the "respondent").

In the U.S. Supreme Court, party designations depend on the procedure used. In the minority of cases that reach the Supreme Court on direct appeal, the party initiating the appeal is, again, the "appellant" and the opposing party the "respondent." But in the more frequently employed certiorari procedure, the party seeking review of the lower court decision is the "petitioner," and the opposing party the "respondent." It is customary for the Court to refer to the parties with those labels in its opinions.[18]

Case captions also follow a set pattern. In the district court, captions are structured as Plaintiff v. Defendant. Where there are multiple parties, it is typical for most purposes to shorten case names to include only the first named plaintiff and the first named defendant. (Electronic case databases are inconsistent in their practice on this; and brief-writers in the Supreme Court are given the option whether or not to list the names of all parties.)

In the U.S. Court of Appeals, the case caption from the district court is retained, with the addition of the appeal designations. In other words, the plaintiff is named first, whether he is the appellant or the appellee. The caption will look something like this:

(1) *Ann Smith, Plaintiff-Appellant v. John Jones, Defendant-Appellee*

(2) *Jane Doe, Plaintiff-Appellee v. Richard Roe, Defendant-Appellant*

In the first example, the plaintiff lost in the trial court; in the second example, the plaintiff won.

Captioning practice changes in the U.S. Supreme Court. There, the petitioner is always named first, even if he was the defendant in the trial court. If Ann Smith wins

---

17. Specialty courts may use different terminology, like "libellant" in admiralty court.

18. In sections 22 and 29 of the 1789 Judiciary Act, a "writ of error" was expressly identified as the mechanism for seeking Supreme Court review of lower federal and state court decisions. The writ of error was displaced by the writ of certiorari in 1891. The party seeking the writ of error was referred to as "the plaintiff in error" in many older cases. That phrase is meant to convey not that the plaintiff was mistaken, but that he was bringing an action for a writ of error.

in the Court of Appeals, in example (1) above, and Jones petitions for cert, the caption will be:

John Jones, Petitioner v. Ann Smith, Respondent

In this way, *Smith v. Jones* in the lower courts becomes *Jones v. Smith* in the Supreme Court — but it's same case.

Exercise: Party Designations and Case Captions

United States v. Lopez, 514 U.S. 549 (1995), was a federal criminal prosecution in which the defendant challenged the constitutionality of the criminal statute in question, the Gun Free School Zones Act. Can you make an educated guess, based on the case caption, what the ruling was in the Court of Appeals?

---

7. Proceedings on Remand

Cases don't end in the Supreme Court.[19] Technically speaking, authority to issue final binding judgments over litigants lies with the trial court — the court exercising "original" jurisdiction. Appellate courts therefore act on the parties only indirectly, by issuing instructions to trial courts. Appellate opinions, therefore, typically conclude with some sort of instructional phrase or sentence directed to a lower court. There are three basic forms of judgment issued by appellate courts, including the U.S. Supreme Court:

- **"Affirmed"**: the judgment of the lower court is approved and adopted (again, its judgment only, and not its principles or reasoning).
- **"Reversed"**: the judgment of the lower court is rejected and the opposite judgment adopted.
- **"Vacated"**: the judgment of the lower court is erased, and the lower court is directed to re-decide the case with the guidance of the new Supreme Court decision.

Usually, one of these three judgment indicators will come at the end of the majority opinion. Where a judgment has multiple aspects to it, the Supreme Court judgment might be different for the different parts: e.g., "Reversed in part, affirmed in part." Where the instructions to the lower court are particularly complex, the wrap-up might be phrased as an instruction to undertake "further proceedings consistent with this opinion" or similar language.

Sometimes the judgment tag will be "reversed and remanded" or "vacated and remanded" (though never, apparently, "affirmed and remanded"). The word "remanded" probably goes without saying, but it does have a technical meaning that is worth understanding. The power to issue a judgment in a case, called the "mandate," is passed up the appellate ladder as the parties appeal the case to successively higher levels of court. An appellate court's judgment power is limited to issuing orders to the immediately lower court. If a case reaches the Supreme Court, it will, in issuing its judgment, pass the mandate back down one level to the Court of Appeals or state appellate court from whence it came,

---

19. The only exception to this is when the Supreme Court exercises original jurisdiction.

with instructions as to what that lower court is to do. Ultimately, the mandate returns to the court of original jurisdiction—the trial court—which alone has the power to issue a judgment that acts directly on the parties. The word used to describe an appellate court passing the mandate back down the appellate ladder is "remand."

Because the final judgment in any case is always issued by the court in which the case was originally filed, that means a Supreme Court decision is not technically the very end of the case. That is so even where the Supreme Court decision resolves all merits issues: the case will still be returned back through the intermediate appellate court to the original trial court for final disposition, even if no substantive rulings remain to be made. Where the Supreme Court decides all the merits issues in a way that leaves no further substantive rulings, the proceedings on remand will be terse and purely formal.

But in many cases, the Supreme Court's decision does *not* resolve all merits issues. In some cases, the Court will expressly decide that one or more claims should go forward. In other cases, the Court will have granted review on only of some substantive issues but not others; even a ruling resulting in the claims being dismissed by the Supreme Court might not, in such a case, end all of the claims on the merits. Thus a party who loses in the Supreme Court might still go on and win her case on the merits in the lower courts. Or, the parties might settle the remaining claims following a Supreme Court decision. From the parties' vantage point, then, a Supreme Court decision may not be the final act of the drama.

8. Remedies and the Impact of Unconstitutionality Rulings

Many Supreme Court decisions conclude with a decision that a government action or statute is "unconstitutional." But few, if any, say exactly what that means in practice. What happens to the government officials who have acted unconstitutionally? What happens to a law that is "declared" unconstitutional? The phrase "strike down" is used in the popular press, in academic commentary, and even in some judicial opinions to describe a ruling that a law is unconstitutional, but what exactly does that mean?

Somewhat surprisingly, the answers to these questions are not as clear as you might think they should be. A critical starting point is to consider the pattern of the constitutional case. Let's first consider patterns 1 through 4 (listed above). In these patterns, the constitutional right is asserted as a defense to legal action (a civil suit or criminal prosecution). The defendant's argument is that the law under which the plaintiff or prosecutor has initiated the suit (or criminal prosecution) is unconstitutional. A favorable ruling requires that the court dismiss the case, or at least the unconstitutional part of it.

In patterns 5 through 8, where the constitutional right is the basis for the plaintiff's claim, the result of an "unconstitutionality" ruling depends on the remedy sought by the constitutional claimant. While the specific details can be more complicated in particular cases, as a general matter the parties in pattern 5 through 8 cases will be seeking one or more of three types of "relief" or remedy: money damages, injunction (or "coercive" court order), or declaratory judgment.

In a money damages case (pattern 8), the plaintiff has suffered physical or pecuniary losses due to conduct allegedly violating the Constitution. The constitutional issue is whether the Constitution in fact recognizes the right in question. "Constitutional tort" claims—the most common form of this case—are typically covered in an upper level Constitutional or Civil Rights Litigation course.[20] This casebook contains only a handful of money damages cases, all of them involving allegedly wrongful employment discharges.[21] The key point is that the recognition of the constitutional right allows the damage claim to go forward.

Most pattern 5 through 8 cases seek injunction-type remedies or declaratory relief. An injunction is a court order requiring the defendant to do something or refrain from doing something. Given that these cases challenge unconstitutional acts or the enforcement of unconstitutional laws, an injunction is an apt remedy. The Court might order an executive official to cease and desist from its unconstitutional seizure of private steel mills, for example; or to refrain from investigating or prosecuting violators of a law found to be unconstitutional.[22]

The problem with injunctions is that they are strong medicine—arguably, they are the most aggressive and far-reaching judicial remedy. In the constitutional setting, an injunction represents a direct judicial command to an official of a state or of a coordinate branch of the federal government. Aside from the appearance of disrespect to other governmental units or agents that such orders entail, injunctions can be problematic to enforce. Violation of an injunction is typically treated as a contempt of court, and is punishable by fines or imprisonment. Think about the potential embarrassment of a district judge ordering the arrest of a cabinet official for contempt. The potential for government officials to disregard injunctions and face judicial enforcement efforts is the stuff of constitutional crises. At a minimum, it is fair to say that injunctive relief directed at a state government raises federalism concerns, and when issued to a co-equal branch of the federal government raises separation of powers concerns.

One response to the above concerns might be to say that government officials can be counted on to respect the judgments of the courts and comply with them voluntarily. But if that's true, then perhaps the strong medicine of injunctive relief isn't needed to begin with. Hence the declaratory judgment. Declaratory relief is "non-coercive"—it declares the rights of the parties without ordering anyone to do (or not do) anything. The hope is that the losing parties will comply voluntarily. If a law is declared unconstitutional by means of a declaratory judgment, the assumption is that the relevant state or federal officials will not thereafter attempt to enforce that law. If they do, the case will wind up back in court, and the party who won the declaratory judgment will be able to assert that declaratory judgment as a defense to the government enforcement action. Declaratory judgments thus put off the potential constitutional showdown between the court and the possibly recalcitrant official to some later day.

Finally, it's important to consider just whose rights are affected by a decision, and how. Clearly, a constitutional remedy decides the rights of the parties to the specific case—that, after all, is the fundamental nature and purpose of adjudication. In some cases, the parties can represent a broad swathe of society, at least in theory. If the defendant is a cabinet

---

20. See, e.g., SARAH E. RICKS & EVELYN M. TENENBAUM, CURRENT ISSUES IN CONSTITUTIONAL LITIGATION (Carolina Academic Press, 2011).

21. *See Nixon v. Fitzgerald, Myers v. United States, Humphreys' Executor v. United States* (Chapter 3); *Garcetti v. Ceballos* (Chapter 11).

22. In a habeas corpus case, the traditional remedy is a court order directed to the executive official to release the prisoner from custody (or transfer him from one custodial authority to another, or to order a new trial).

secretary in charge of nationwide enforcement of a statute, and the plaintiffs represent a nationwide class in a pattern 7 case, the judgment would be nationwide in its impact. But relatively few constitutional cases are class actions, and many involve only a small number of named parties. In the more typical case, an unconstitutionality ruling will affect the rights of parties not before the court indirectly, through the mechanism of precedent. If it is unconstitutional to prosecute Alfonso Lopez for possession of a gun in a school zone on the ground that the Gun Free School Zones Act exceeds Congress's power under the commerce clause (*United States v. Lopez*, Chapter 1), then it is likewise unconstitutional to prosecute Jane Smith, John Jones, etc., under that statute. If such a subsequent prosecution were brought, the trial court would be obligated to dismiss the case on the ground that the Supreme Court's *Lopez* decision is a binding precedent. One would hope, therefore, that the prosecutor would not file such a case, but would instead respect the Supreme Court's decision.

But what if the unconstitutionality ruling was made by a lower court in a case that never reached the Supreme Court—perhaps because it was settled by the parties before the Supreme Court could decide, or because the Supreme Court denied review? The situation arises less frequently than you might suppose, because the Supreme Court is likely to grant review of cases where a federal law has been struck down on federal constitutional grounds by a lower court.[23] Still, there will be windows of time before the Supreme Court decides to hear such a case. What are the government's obligations to treat a lower court's unconstitutionality ruling as a binding precedent?[24] One would think that the obligation of government officials outside the judicial branch should be no greater than that of a court: if the Fourth Circuit has struck down the Gun Free School Zones Act, federal prosecutors in the Fifth, Sixth, and other circuits could still prosecute these cases—perhaps the other circuits would uphold the law. Until the Supreme Court has decided a case, the obligation of government officials to obey a lower court ruling as to others than the parties to the judgment may boil down to a policy decision whether or not to enforce the supposedly unconstitutional law prior to a Supreme Court determination.

What about the obligation of governmental actors to obey decisions of the Supreme Court? Even that question does not generate clear-cut answers. We discuss that question further in Chapters 3 and 5.

What manifestly has *not* occurred when a court—even the Supreme Court—"strikes down" a law as unconstitutional is the formal repeal of that law. Repeal is a legislative act that removes a law from the books. The repealed law ceases to exist as a law. But a law declared unconstitutional by the Supreme Court is not removed from the books. As the above discussion suggests, non-judicial constitutional actors may in practice treat the unconstitutional law as a nullity. They may, in other words, treat it as though it were repealed. If they tried to enforce it, a subsequent court would be obligated to treat the Supreme Court's unconstitutionality ruling as binding precedent, and render judgment accordingly.

---

23. Because federal laws apply throughout the nation, the need for uniformity of judicial application of that law is more pressing: having a single federal law that is enforceable in some districts or circuits and unconstitutional (and thus unenforceable) in others, creates an unstable situation that the Supreme Court will not tolerate for long. State laws can present a different situation. If a state law is one found in many states around the country, the need for uniformity—and thus, a definitive Supreme Court ruling—will be comparable to the need for national uniformity in application of a single federal law. (It would be doctrinally unstable to have similar abortion laws, for example, deemed enforceable in some federal circuits but not others.) In contrast, when a state law is somewhat unique, the U.S. Supreme Court justices may feel less urgency in addressing a particular circuit court's constitutional ruling.

24. Similarly, what are the obligations of the officials of one state to adhere to a lower federal court ruling striking down a very similar law in another state?

But the unconstitutional law continues to exist. This can be significant *if the Supreme Court later overrules its earlier decision.* Assuming the Gun Free School Zones Act has not been repealed by Congress, if the Supreme Court were to overrule its own *Lopez* decision, the formerly unconstitutional law would be valid and enforceable once again, without further legislative action.

This last point follows from the relationship of remedies to defendants. As discussed above, the appropriate defendant in any pattern 5 through 8 constitutional cases is an individual or entity who has both caused the wrong and has the means to make it right. If an executive official's conduct is unconstitutional, a remedy aimed at that official to prevent, deter, or punish that conduct normally suffices. If the problem is that an underlying statute is unconstitutional, a remedy preventing enforcement of that law—again, aimed at the executive official who enforces the law—normally suffices. Since executive officials don't enact laws, they cannot be ordered to repeal them (or enact a new, constitutional substitute for the unconstitutional law); hence, the normal constitutional remedy is not the repeal of an unconstitutional law. In theory, perhaps, Congress or a state legislature could be named as a defendant in a case challenging an unconstitutional law enacted by that body; but the remedy—ordering the repeal of the law, say—is almost inconceivable coming from a court.[25] In any event, the Supreme Court has held that federal and state legislators are absolutely immune from suit for their legislative activities.[26]

Exercise: Remedies

What would the state of the law on abortion be if the Supreme Court overruled its decision in *Roe v. Wade*?

E. Reading Supreme Court Opinions: Form and Format

Supreme Court opinions can present some technical challenges to readers unfamiliar with their form and format, while also providing some useful information, if you know

---

25. Consider the difficulties. First, in the federal system, where the President's signature is required for legislation, the order would have to direct both the Congress and the President to legislate. Second, what would the order to the legislature look like? Would all members have to vote in conformity with the Court order, or just a majority? If the latter, which legislators would be allowed to vote against the Court order? Third, if there were multiple ways to fix the unconstitutional legislation, how would the law be drafted? Would the Court direct the drafting? The separation of powers and federalism problems in such a scenario are so challenging that a court will always opt for the less problematic approach of blocking enforcement of the unconstitutional law and leaving the legislature free to try again if it wishes.

26. The "speech or debate" clause, Art. I, §6, provides that "for any speech or debate in either House, [the Senators and Representatives] shall not be questioned in any other place." This provision has been interpreted to afford absolute immunity from suit for legislative activities; and a similar principle has been found for state and local legislators. *See* Kilbourn v. Thompson, 103 U.S. 168, 202–04 (1881) (members of Congress); Bogan v. Scott-Harris, 523 U.S. 44, 49 (1997) (state and local legislators).

where to look for it. In this section we'll discuss these issues, starting with how Supreme Court opinions appear in their original "print" versions (both paper and electronic) and then explaining how we present the cases in this book.

1. Un-Edited or Original Print Supreme Court Opinions

Let's start by looking at the very first and last lines framing the opinion of the Court. A short statement identifying the opinion writers and joiners immediately precedes the opinion of the Court. The last line of the opinion indicates the judgment of the Court. The more detailed, case specific aspects of the judgment—who wins on what issues, and what are the implications for the case and the parties—are sometimes summarized by the Court in a concluding paragraph, but often they are not: in most cases, you have to read the opinion, and in particular the procedural background of the case, in order to figure this out.

But recall that the judgment in itself is the result of the case without the underlying reasoning. The reasoning leading to the judgment—which creates the doctrinal rules— is found in the body of the majority opinion.

The majority opinion of a modern Supreme Court case typically adheres to the following format. A short introduction states the overall legal issue and perhaps (not always) indicates the judgment and even briefly summarizes the fundamental reasoning. Then follows a series of numbered sections, using traditional outline numbering: roman I, II, III etc. for major sections; A, B and C, for subsections, and 1, 2 and 3 for sub-subsections. Obviously, these vary depending on complexity of the case. Typically, section I states the facts giving rise to the case, followed by the procedural history of the suit leading up to the Supreme Court's decision to hear the case. In cases involving complex statutory frameworks or legislative proceedings, these may also be covered in a background section. Where these background materials are lengthy or complex, they may take up a couple of sections. The main body of the opinion follows: this is the legal analysis. There is no fixed rule for organizing this part of the opinion. In some cases, each issue in a case gets a separate roman numeral; in others, the roman numerals are steps in the analysis. The key point is that, for stylistic reasons that appear to be lost to history, the Court does not typically provide helpful descriptive headings for any of its sections. The tradition is simply to number its sections, outline-style.

Dissenting opinions are often presented as full blown alternatives to the majority opinion, perhaps including a recitation of the case facts and even procedural history. This is particularly noteworthy when the dissent places a markedly different spin on the case background, illustrating how seemingly objective facts can look very different depending on one's view of the case. Concurrences may also give this full treatment, though that is less common.

Some opinions of the Court are identified as "per curiam" (Latin for "by the court") rather than by name of the authoring justice. This practice of declining to name the opinion's author is sometimes used in important and controversial cases to suggest that the court wishes to speak as a whole, or perhaps to shield the author behind a cloak of anonymity. "Per curiam" might also be used for the opposite reason: because the decision is rendered in such a short, summary fashion that no one justice takes pride of authorship.

2. Case Citations and Case Envelopes

Supreme Court opinions are published in a variety of places. These outlets (we assume and hope) print the main text verbatim, but they vary in the "envelope" material they add. So the appearance of the case can be different depending on where you find it. There are two official prints of Supreme Court opinions issued by the government. "Slip opinions" are small booklets (or electronic reproductions on PDF files) that are made available when the decision is issued. Eventually these are compiled into official bound volumes called the United States Reports.

Here, we have to pause to acknowledge the transitional period of legal publication we find ourselves in. Those of us who went to law school before the mid-1990s relied heavily on paper books to read judicial opinions. An entire traditional system of legal citation is based on printed books. Thus, the official citation for Supreme Court cases refers to the United States Reports by page and volume number: "301 U.S. 1 (1937)" tells you to find the first page of the case (*NLRB v. Jones & Laughlin Steel Corp.*, as it happens) at page 1 of volume 301 of the U.S. Reports, and also tells you that the decision was issued in 1937. This citation system is sensible and meaningful in a world of books, but somewhat arbitrary in a world of on-line databases, where any unique code number would be enough. But because the page-and-volume system does generate a unique code for each case, it works well enough with electronic databases, and is unlikely to be deserted soon.

Until 1875, the official Supreme Court reports volumes were indexed by an abbreviation of the last name of the Reporter of Decisions, an official charged with overseeing the publication of Supreme Court decisions. These older cases were subsequently renumbered as volumes of the "U.S." reports going all the way back to one. Current "Bluebook" form (i.e., the generally accepted citation form) gives the U.S. report volume followed by the abbreviated-name-of-the-reporter volume when citing pre-1875 cases. Example: *McCulloch v. Maryland*, 17 U.S. (4 Wheat.) 316 (1819). Volume 17 of the U.S. Reports is the same as volume 4 of the reports during Henry Wheaton's tenure as Reporter of Decisions.

Various unofficial, commercial case reporters, such as S. Ct. (West Publishing Company's Supreme Court Reports), and L. Ed. 2d (Lawyers' Edition, Second Series, now owned by LEXIS/NEXIS), also publish Supreme Court opinions. Because they are faster to press than the U.S. Reports, their page cites are established earlier. U.S. Reports bound volumes, with their official "U.S." pagination, can lag a year or two behind the issuance of the decision. During that time, it is customary to cite the case "___ U.S. ___" followed by a citation to S. Ct. or L. Ed. 2d.

The "envelope" information that precedes the actual opinions varies depending on the publisher. The official U.S. Reports, both in their slip opinions and bound volumes, begin with something called the "syllabus," which is an abstract or summary of the issues presented to, and conclusions reached by the Court. The syllabus is compiled by the Reporter of Decisions of the Supreme Court, and is intended as a convenience; but it is not authored by the justices and not formally part of the opinion of the Court. Older volumes of the U.S. Reports also provided summaries of arguments of counsel presented at oral argument, compiled by the Reporter of Decisions from his notes of the oral argument. These are not presented as Q and A transcripts, but look a lot like briefs or opinions, with embedded legal citations. These can be quite lengthy, and when reading older cases in their original forms, it is important to be aware whether you are reading the summary of arguments or the justices' opinions. The U.S. Reports, in addition to the case caption giving the parties' names, also sct out the Supreme Court's docket number assigned to the case, the dates of oral argument and decision, and an indication of the review-granting mechanism (e.g., "On Writ of Certiorari to the Eleventh Circuit").

The unofficial commercial publishers provide additional envelope information. First, they provide a short case abstract of their own (shorter than, and presented before, the syllabus). They next provide a series of "headnotes," in which they extract what they deem to be key legal points from the opinion and index them to the topical headings of their legal research products. They also identify the lawyers and organizations who filed briefs on behalf of the parties or amici, and those who presented the oral arguments in the Court.

3. Edited Supreme Court Opinions in This Book

To streamline your study of Constitutional Law, we follow the practice of all law casebook authors by heavily editing the opinions we reproduce in these pages. As a general matter, we have cut out at least 50–60% of the material in any given case.

In doing this editing, our goal is to make sure that the key elements of the majority reasoning, and the key points of disagreement among the justices (if any) are presented with reasonable clarity and completeness. But it is good for you to know in general the kinds of things we have removed. Our editorial cuts can be grouped into five broad categories:

1. *Citations.* Supreme Court opinions are filled with citations, often long strings of them. We have cut most citations from the opinions, retaining only those to cases included in our textbook and other cases that are important to the particular area of doctrine.

2. *Prolixity.* We're just going to come out and say this: Supreme Court opinions are rarely concise. Casebook editors save a lot of space simply by deleting wordiness and redundancy from the opinions, without sacrificing meaning.

3. *Low-priority precedents.* A lot of space in Supreme Court decisions is devoted to lengthy discussions of precedents whose importance has receded over time. These are not particularly meaningful to students who will not be asked to read those cited precedents in a general Constitutional Law course.

4. *Tangential matter.* A lot of detail that may be pertinent to an in-depth study of a particular case is tangential in a course devoted to the broad themes and doctrines of constitutional law. This includes highly technical details of facts, underlying statutes or narrow doctrines, as well as side- or threshold issues that do not go to the core doctrinal holding of a case.

5. *Separate opinions.* Concurrences and dissents are retained to the extent that they expose flaws in or important counter-arguments to the majority opinion. We also include those that illustrate doctrinal controversies of historical or contemporary importance, or prefigure shifts in the prevailing judicial outlook. These points can often come across clearly even in significantly abridged separate opinions, since the majority opinion can be relied on to lay out the facts and set up the basic issues. Separate opinions that do not serve one of the foregoing functions are cut entirely.

Why are we telling you all this? It's not simply that we want you to be informed consumers, though that is certainly part of our motivation. It's also that you should know that these edited cases are not exactly what the real cases look like, and are not necessarily the best exemplars on which to model your own legal writing. At a minimum, in writing briefs and legal memoranda, you will want to include citations in places we've often cut them out—whenever you quote something and whenever you make an assertion about what the law is. You may also need to spend more time explaining the facts and holdings of controlling precedents than you will see done in these pages.

Where the factual and procedural background is particularly lengthy relative to the rest of the edited version of the case, we supply an abridgment in brackets. Where we have cut material from the opinion, we indicate that with ellipses. Outline headers from the original opinions (roman numerals, letters, Arabic numbers) are retained where that seems to be helpful, to indicate a change of topic, to distinguish points agreed or disagreed on by the justices, or to break up a long edited version of an opinion. Otherwise, we cut them.

A unique feature of our book is that we provide the voting breakdown of each case at the beginning of the opinion. We identify the writers of the majority and separate opinions in bold italics, and indicate opinion "joiners" in ordinary roman type. We do this to help you develop a sense of the jurisprudence of many of the justices and to help put you in a position to assess the consistency of individual justices' views from case to case. Because the Supreme Court is often described in terms of time periods defined by the tenure of the successive Chief Justices (e.g., "the Warren Court," "the Rehnquist Court"), we identify the Chief Justice in each case with the parenthetical "(CJ)." We list opinion writers first, and the joining justices in order of seniority.

F. Reading Supreme Court Opinions: Substance

Up to this point, we have been giving you a lot of background and context. Now we're ready to address the foreground: What is going on substantively in the constitutional law cases you will read in this course? In this section, we will identify and summarize some of the major themes and concepts that underlie constitutional arguments and the legal analysis of constitutional problems. These ideas recur throughout the book and will be useful to you in understanding the cases.

So, what should you look for when you read the cases? The mastery of any skill or area of knowledge requires recognizing that there are multiple, increasingly deep levels at which the skill or knowledge can be understood—and then trying to understand and eventually master those levels. We think it's useful to identify four levels of depth at which you can understand constitutional law in general, and Supreme Court decisions in particular. Your ability to make sophisticated constitutional law arguments will be greatly enhanced the better you perceive and can function at each of the four levels. Of possibly more immediate concern (we get it!), functioning competently at levels 1 and 2 will get you into the B range gradewise; getting an A is likely to require some comfort on your part in articulating your understandings at levels 3 and 4.

We'll explain each of these levels in a moment, but first let's agree on what it means to "understand" or "function competently" at each of these levels. It is all too common for students to read a case in a casebook, think silently about it, decide "I get this" and then move on to the next piece of the assignment. That's not what we mean by understanding or functioning competently. At a minimum, you have to be able to restate the key concept of the case in your own words in a way that another person (someone with at least your level of legal training) can understand. To test your understanding of a concept, you should try to explain it to a classmate. Better yet, explain it in writing in a sentence or a paragraph. Even better, do both. This "say it/write it" test is a great first step in understanding new ideas. To *master* the concept, however, you need to take a further step and *apply* it: use the concept to solve a hypothetical problem or to make an argument in a new case. We give you opportunities and suggestions for testing yourself in this way throughout the book.

1. Level 1: Holdings

Level 1 requires that you read a case and articulate its holding. Identifying the "holding" of a case can be challenging. Many law students (and lawyers) mistakenly believe that a holding is simply an abstract legal rule derived from a case. This understanding is not accurate. A holding is a rule-statement that incorporates three elements: the abstract legal rule, the key case fact(s), and the case result. Here's an example:

Figure 4. Holding of United States v. Lopez

Abstract rule:	Holding:
• "Lopez stands for the proposition that commerce power does not extend to regulation of non-economic activities that are not an essential part of a larger economic regulation."	– Facts/rule/result • "Lopez held that mere possession of a gun in a school zone fell outside the commerce power because it was non-economic activity that was not an essential part of a larger economic regulation. Therefore, the GFSZA was unconstitutional."

The version on the left is not wrong—as far as it goes. But it's not a holding, because it is missing the factual and result elements. The version on the right has the case facts (boiled down to their essence, "mere possession of a gun in a school zone"); the legal rule ("non-economic activity that is not an essential part of a larger economic regulation falls outside the commerce power"); and the result (GFSZA is unconstitutional).

Note that you cannot understand or articulate the holding unless you understand the key facts of the case! Indeed, the holding of a case can be varied, spun, or distinguished by adding or omitting case facts.

2. Level 2: Reasoning/Argument

The Court's explanation of, and justification for, its holding takes up most of the space in the cases and most of our time when reading the cases. This is where the Court lays out and applies the nitty-gritty details of the "black letter" law: the background legal principles, and the legal tests and frameworks used to decide the case. One of the big challenges in studying judicial opinions of any sort is to sift through this part of the case for indications of the arguments that the court found persuasive or determinative, and those the court rejected.

While far from a fail-safe guide to all judicial opinions, the IRAC ("issue-rule-analysis/application-conclusion") structure that characterizes much legal writing can help you decode many opinions. Often, opinions will identify the legal issue under consideration, and then proceed to the "rule" framework—the broad background principles and settled black-letter doctrine, sometimes is laid out at great length—before getting down to the "analysis" or application of the legal rule framework to the facts of the case at hand. Sometimes the analysis will be framed as a response to the losing side's arguments; in other cases, rebuttals to rejected arguments will follow the analysis as further justification for the result.

There's no substitute for getting immersed in this part of the case as you read, but there is a pitfall associated with doing so. It's tiring. Even professors and practicing lawyers can get worn down by lengthy opinions, and the details of arguments can lead you to lose sight of the big picture. But whatever you do, don't lose sight of the holding.

3. Level 3: Broad Themes

This third level of understanding demands that you go beyond the "black letter" rules and holdings of the cases and try to grapple with the way judicial opinions reveal the judges' mentality, their approach to judging, and their techniques of argument. This level might include what is sometimes referred to as "judicial philosophy," although the term "philosophy" implies a more systematic, consistent and developed set of ideas than what most judges actually rely on to guide their thinking.

You could probably come up with other lists than ours, but we want to suggest five broad themes that come up again and again in the judicial opinions in these cases, from *Marbury v. Madison* (1803), the oldest case in this book to *NFIB v. Sebelius* (2012), the most recent. These five themes are sometimes deployed as principles that guide how one or more justices believe the case should be decided. Sometimes, however, they are used more opportunistically as rhetorical ploys. Other times they surface as mere intuitions that underlie a more developed argument. Despite these different usages, identifying and watching for these themes will help you be a better analyzer of opinions.

The five themes are: (1) deference; (2) democracy; (3) neutral principles; (4) the nature of rules (bright lines, balancing tests, and slippery slopes); and (5) modes of constitutional interpretation. Each of these themes requires some further explanation: We will go into the details in section G, below. For now, the key point is that these themes are generic and repeated forms of argument that recur explicitly in numerous opinions.

4. Level 4: Between the Lines Decision Factors

It is simply not possible to gain a thorough understanding of a Supreme Court decision without trying to discern the deepest level of analysis, the subtle and sometimes hidden or between-the-lines factors that ultimately drive many decisions. At the same time, we caution you against addressing this level of analysis by glibly asserting that judges are only "result-oriented" and simply decide cases based on their personal values or political affiliations. Those concerns are not irrelevant, but reality is more complicated.

A more nuanced way to think about these issues is to start with the realization that judges are part of the government. They are appointed to use the processes of adjudication to help govern the state or the nation. That task imposes practical responsibilities on them. We want them to recognize that their decisions have practical impact; indeed, it would be a poor judge who viewed every case as some sort of theoretical abstraction with no regard to practical consequences.

With this realization in mind, we can identify a few broad categories of factors that might influence judges' decisions in any particular case. As a model of judicial decisionmaking, we suggest that all of these factors are present in every case; but that their relative weights in the mind of a given judge will vary from case to case. Consequently, your ability to predict how a given judge will decide a case will not be well served by assuming an unrealistic degree of consistency: e.g., that this judge *always* follows precedent, or *always* decides in favor of the Democratic party's position.

A final challenge to analyzing cases at this fourth level is that the judges are not always explicit about these factors. Particularly where revealing a motivation would make the judge seem inconsistent, intellectually dishonest, result-oriented, or political, the "level 4" motivation is likely to be buried beneath or couched in "level 3" language.

The "Between the Lines" decision factors worth watching for are these:

Precedent/stare decisis. The policy of faithfulness to precedents (see Section H, below) is clearly an important decisional factor in many, if not most cases. Stare decisis provides a universally accepted "neutral principle" for deciding cases, and it engages the reasoning process at the very heart of our legal system (both in practice and in legal education). It is how judges are "supposed to" decide cases. For these reasons, it is all too easy to overestimate its influence in any given Supreme Court constitutional case.

Obviously, if the Court overrules its precedent in deciding a case, other factors predominated in that decision. But let's set that circumstance aside, and examine cases where the Court says it is following precedent.

Was precedent a decisive factor? Assuming so is problematic, for several reasons. (1) Distinguishing or otherwise getting around precedents is not all that hard. (2) No reviewing Court sits over the Supreme Court's shoulder to make the justices adhere faithfully to precedents. (3) In many fields of constitutional law, the precedents are thin on the ground—the issue in question just hasn't arisen all that much, if at all. (4) Other decisional factors are often more compelling.

It is, however, fair to say that when judges don't really care much about the practical or political issues raised in a case, precedent is more likely to be a predominant factor, particularly when there are not compelling lines of precedent pointing to a different outcome.

Institutional factors. The prestige of the Court is important to its authority. The judicial branch is famously the "least dangerous" (i.e., practically weakest) of the three branches of the federal government, lacking "sword" or "purse" (armed force or budgetary authority), in the words of the Federalist Papers. The judicial branch often depends on voluntary cooperation of other branches of government for the enforcement of its judgments. An important part of its prestige is to appear to be above the fray of partisan politics. Making (or appearing to make) decisions based on non-partisan legal principles may be crucial to maintaining this prestige, and can be a constraining and, at times, determining factor in a decision. (In this sense, stare decisis is a particularly notable type of institutional factor.) The Court may need to shape decisions in ways that avoid entering political controversies or partisan confrontations with other government actors or with public opinion.

Workable rules. The Supreme Court should be, and usually is, highly conscious of its role of setting legal policy for the courts of the nation. Its members therefore are attentive to the need to create workable legal rules. For example, to hold that a person's speech may never under any circumstances be restricted under the First Amendment ("Congress shall make no law ... abridging the freedom of speech") is to create a frankly unworkable rule. Social order could not be maintained under such a rule, and the Court's interest in creating workable rules forecloses any such interpretation of the First Amendment.

Other practical concerns. Your professor is likely to stress the importance of the historical context of any given case. That's because pragmatic factors stemming from social reality or the unfolding of historical events can be heavily influential on the justices' decisionmaking. It would be naïve to think that the hard-pressed military position of the U.S. and its allies in 1942 was irrelevant to the Court's decisions to sustain the military authorities in cases like *Korematsu* and *Quirin* (Chapter 3). Awareness that a return to a pre-1937 understanding of the Commerce Clause would mean dismantling hundreds of billions of dollars of federal programs is likely to make today's justices reluctant to attempt to impose such a thing by judicial fiat.

Individual factors. Factors about the justices as individuals also may influence their decisionmaking. Like all of us, justices are likely to be influenced by their own "judicial philosophy" or set of values and approaches to constitutional adjudication. And although we cautioned against undue cynicism in assuming that partisan politics is always a dominant factor, it would be equally mistaken to go the other way and assume a justice's partisan political affiliations never affect their decisions. These political affiliations might result from political activities prior to assuming the bench, loyalty to the appointing President, bitterness against a party opposing the justice's nomination in the Senate, or other things. Even more personal factors can deeply influence judges, as human beings: their personal experiences or history, their sex or race, or their interpersonal relationships on the Court. Finally, a justice's own sense of her place in the Court's and nation's history might influence her decisionmaking. A justice might not want to go down in history as the deciding vote for X or against Y.

These "level 4 factors" may or may not predominate in any given case, and their influence is likely to vary from case to case, justice to justice, and even within the jurisprudence of a particular justice. The factors also vary a great deal in how plainly they emerge in the written opinion, or how much instead they are hidden behind more "judicial" language.

G. Level 3 Broad Themes

In this section, we return to the five "broad themes" identified at what we have called the third level of depth in reading Supreme Court cases.

1. Deference

Constitutional cases all involve judicial review of a government action that is claimed to have exceeded the limits of government power. Embedded within every government action is a decision of some kind. So judicial review always entails second-guessing another government actor's decision.

Whenever one decisionmaker reviews the decision of another, the question logically arises, how much deference should be given to the earlier decisionmaker? We see this in all areas of life, and of law. Decisions that are non-deferential allow the reviewing court to completely second-guess the original decisionmaker: the question might be framed as "what would I do if I were in this person's shoes faced with this decision?" Non-deferential review is about identifying mistaken decisions and correcting them.

Deferential review, in contrast, poses the question differently. Rather than ask "how do I think the decision should have been made," a deferential reviewer asks "could a reasonable person make that decision, even if I personally might have decided differently?" Deferential review affords a range of discretion and judgment to the decisionmaker, and is more tolerant of mistaken decisions. In close calls, the decision will stand; only clear mistakes will be corrected.

In constitutional law, the degree of deference to be given other governmental decisionmakers is continually debated. The question of whether minimal (deferential) or strict (non-deferential) scrutiny should be applied in reviewing legislative acts challenged under the doctrines of equal protection, due process, or the First Amendment are questions about degrees of deference. The Justices repeatedly recite their duty to defer to legislative judgments about policy, but these bland statements rarely decide the question presented (and are frequently followed by words like "but in this case …").

2. Democracy

Courts in constitutional cases are typically asked to override the decisions, and thus by extension, the policy judgments, of the so-called "political" branches of government: those run by elected officials. Congress consists entirely of members who must stand for election and re-election at regular intervals. The executive branch is filled with people who may not have been elected to their posts, but are ultimately answerable to the President, who is elected and whose own re-election chances could suffer if his or her policies are distasteful to the people.

Federal judges are not elected. They have life tenure and salary security. Their positions have been intentionally insulated from direct democratic accountability. Judges are acutely aware of this, and we see them again and again forswearing any power to make policy judgments or implement their personal values the way that elected officials would be entitled to. Judges express this in several ways. When they argue against finding a constitutional right, they frequently tell the losing claimant that his remedy lies in getting the laws changed through the democratic process. When they argue against their colleagues' "judicial activism," they make sure to point out that the democratic process can and should be allowed to resolve the question without judicial interference.

Yet, we all know, or quickly discern in our law school careers, that judges make policy judgments all the time. We know, too, that when they accuse one another of usurping the legislative role of policymaking, they are sometimes being disingenuous. But it is a mistake to jump from that perception to the view that there is nothing real about judges' anxiety about the "undemocratic" quality of their decisions. In some cases, or some doctrinal areas, judges feel very confident and empowered by constitutional law to impose their views; in other cases and doctrinal areas, they feel themselves to be on thin ice. One of your tasks in this course is to begin to develop your own intuitions about which is which.

3. Neutral Principles

The term "neutral principles" captures an idea embedded in the very logic of adjudication in our legal culture.[27] It is closely related to the democracy theme. Since judges are not supposed to be free to implement their personal values or policy choices, their decisions to override the actions of the political branches must be based on a "neutral" constitutional principle; that is, one that is justified without reference to disputed political values. Some would say that a neutral principle must be one that has bi-partisan or non-partisan consensus. (E.g., the First Amendment prohibits the government from jailing a person for criticizing the President.) Others would say that a neutral principle is one that we would find acceptable even when applied by a judge whose political values differ from ours. According to this definition of neutral principles, if "liberty" in the due process includes what a liberal judge deems to be fundamental rights (e.g., the right of a woman to terminate a pregnancy), then it should also include what a conservative judge deems to be fundamental rights (e.g., the right of an employer to terminate an employee for trying to unionize).

The appeal of neutral principles is that they, in theory, generate a consistent and predictable set of constitutional decisions without regard to whether the judges are "liberal" or "conservative." They are, in other words, the opposite of "result-oriented" judging. Much of constitutional theorizing involves a quest for sufficiently neutral principles to support controversial decisions.

4. The Nature of Rules: Balancing Tests, Bright Lines, Slippery Slopes

Ultimately, Supreme Court decisions struggle to formulate rules that can be applied in future cases. By their nature, rules present certain logical or structural difficulties, and Supreme Court justices often argue with one another through their opinions about the *structure* of the rule to be established by the case.

Three issues that commonly come up in rule-structure debates are ideas about "balancing tests," "bright lines," and "slippery slopes." A "balancing test" is a concept employed when the Court acknowledges, and tries to accommodate, valid interests on both sides of the issue. For instance, in *Frisby v. Schultz* (Chapter 9), where anti-abortion protesters picketed in front of a doctor's house, the interest in free speech was balanced against the interest in the privacy of the home. Balancing tests try to accommodate both interests. The levels of scrutiny in Equal Protection and Due Process cases embody balancing tests, because they weigh the government's interest underlying the law against the intrusion on a fundamental right or the invasiveness of certain class-based distinctions.

---

27. The phrase is attributed to Professor Herbert Wechsler, who wrote a highly controversial law review article *Toward Neutral Principles of Constitutional Law*, 73 Harv. L. Rev. 1 (1959), arguing that the decision in *Brown v. Board of Education* was not supported by a neutral principle. While that argument has not stood up well against the test of time, the phrase "neutral principles" expresses an idea of lasting theoretical importance.

"Bright line" rules are the foil of balancing tests. Debates frequently occur because one bloc of justices prefers a bright line rule, and the other prefers a balancing test. A bright line rule creates a categorical distinction and generates a yes-or-no result depending on how the facts fit the category. For example, Commerce Clause analysis (superficially) follows a "bright line" approach: If a subject of regulation meets the definition of "interstate commerce," Congress has the power to enact the law; if it is not interstate commerce, Congress does not have that power (at least not under the Commerce Clause). In the *Frisby* example, then, a bright line approach (not adopted by the Court) might have been to hold "no picketing in front of a person's home, ever."

Both approaches have pros and cons. Bright line rules are easy to articulate, and *seem* to generate clear yes-or-no answers. On the other hand, bright line rules are inflexible, and when the need is great enough, the rule is likely to be bent or abandoned. Also, bright lines are illusory: they seem "bright" in the abstract but can become very dim, gray, and debatable in specific cases. Look, for example, at the disagreements over whether something is "interstate commerce."

Balancing tests, on the other hand, are flexible and pragmatic. They don't pretend to be crystal clear, and they are highly adaptable to individual cases. However, they can be mushy and indeterminate. Critics claim, with some justification, that balancing tests can be used to reach any result, thus giving too much discretion to judges. Balancing tests also are challenged on semantic grounds: if a "test" is something that generates a clear answer, balancing tests, to critics, are not really "tests" at all but merely ways to structure an analysis or argument.

Few justices consistently prefer one type of rule over another. Justice Hugo Black is probably the most salient "bright line rule" jurist (he and Justice William O. Douglas tended to prefer bright lines in free speech cases). For the most part, though, justices tend to pick and choose, sometimes based on the logic of the problem presented (e.g., bright lines seem to make sense in determining the scope of Congress's enumerated powers), but sometimes more opportunistically, based on which tools are more likely to generate the outcome the justice prefers.

A "slippery slope" is an argument that a rule, which might be relatively unobjectionable when applied to the facts of the case at hand, will inevitably lead to unacceptable results in future cases. Slippery slope arguments sometimes go by other names, such as "parade of horribles," "Pandora's box," "can of worms," or "we don't want to go there." This problem of an unacceptable potential consequences is endemic to judging, because judges (particularly appellate judges) have to balance two competing sets of concerns in every case: the demand to do justice in the case immediately at hand and the need to think about the implications of setting a precedent. The precedent-setting factor is particularly strong at the Supreme Court level, since that court sets legal policy for the entire nation.

Slippery slope arguments can easily be exaggerated, by overstating both the horror of the future case and the ease of sliding into it. Balancing tests have an inherently self-limiting quality, because the countervailing interest can be given greater weight in the next case to stop a "slide" down the slippery slope. Even in cases using bright line rules, it may be possible to create principled "stopping points" without abandoning the rule. As Justice Ginsburg said in *NFIB v. Sebelius*, just because you see a slippery slope doesn't mean you have to ski all the way to the bottom.

It is not always clear what rule structure is at stake in a particular case, and sometimes, the structure can be manipulated by changing how one frames the rule. The key point is to be able to recognize these arguments when you see them in judicial opinions.

Exercise: Rule Structures

Choose a constitutional case or principle and try to state it as a bright line rule and recast it is a balancing test. Then try to create a slippery slope argument for or against the rule.

---

5. Modes of Constitutional Argument

There are several modes of constitutional argument that you will see used in the cases presented in this book.[28] Some jurists and legal commentators associate some of these modes of interpretation with normative (i.e., moral, philosophical, or values-based) theories about judicial review. However, few — if any — judges have been thoroughly consistent in adopting and adhering to a particular interpretive method in constitutional cases. Far more common is the tendency of judges to "mix and match" — relying on one mode in one case, and switching in another. Not infrequently, more than one mode of interpretation will be used in a single opinion — perhaps because the author finds that an eclectic approach will cover the bases more thoroughly. At times, this switching of interpretive modes reflects opportunism. Perhaps more frequently one mode is (or seems) better suited to addressing a particular type of constitutional problem. When reading Supreme Court cases, it can be useful to be aware of the different modes of constitutional interpretation to see how they are deployed in argument. You should also consider whether, in a given case, a justice is using a particular interpretive method as a tool, or if he or she is going further and arguing that his or her preferred mode of interpretation is normatively superior.

1. Textual. Some constitutional arguments assert that there is a clearly correct understanding of an applicable provision of the Constitution's text that determines the answer to a particular constitutional question. There are times when this seems plainly true. Consider Article II, § 1, cl. 5 ("No person ... shall be eligible to the office of President ... who shall not have attained the age of 35 years"). This provision rather clearly tells us that a 29-year-old candidate for President is disqualified. At the other end of this spectrum of determinacy, however, is something like Article II, § 2, cl. 1 ("The President shall be commander in chief of the Army and Navy"). This text may be a starting point, but hardly in itself answers the question whether President Bush had the inherent constitutional authority to order the trial of suspected terrorists by military tribunal. In the middle is language that is somewhat determinate: for example, the inference that state judges have the power and duty to apply federal law. (See provisions quoted and discussed in Sections D. 2 and D. 3, above.) Constitutional arguments often are arguments over whether the text (sometimes supplemented by other interpretive methods) is or is not sufficient to answer the question presented.

2. Historical. Historical arguments look at the actions of non-judicial constitutional actors (see section B. 2, above) as precedents that shed light on constitutional meaning. If Congress has always acted on the assumption that it may determine the number of Supreme

---

28. The classic exposition of the various "modalities" of constitutional interpretation and argument is found in Philip Bobbitt, Constitutional Interpretation 12–13 (1991). The typology here departs from Bobbitt's significantly, though there is necessarily some overlap.

Court justices, and no other branch of government has challenged that view, then the Constitution's silence on the proper number of justices can be taken to mean that Congress indeed has that power. In this way, historical practice provides a "gloss" or interpretive explanation on the meaning of the Constitution. *See Youngstown Sheet & Tube Co. v. Sawyer*, 343 U.S. 579, 610 (1952) (Frankfurter, J., concurring). In such arguments, the actions of constitutional actors closer in time to the drafting of the Constitution are often treated as more significant historical precedents on the theory that they were closer to the "original understanding," which is, in this view, presumed to be binding when knowable.

3. Structural. Some constitutional arguments draw inferences from the "structure" of the Constitution—its overall gist, or logical inferences derived from key elements. The "anti-commandeering rule" of *Printz v. United States* (Chapter 1) that Congress cannot order state executive officials to enforce federal law, is a "structural postulate" that is said to flow from the retention of the states as sovereign entities within the federal system. There is no specific textual indication of this particular rule, and the historical precedents were debatable.

4. Policy. Policy-based arguments use the policy objectives as the guiding principle to decide a case and interpret constitutional text accordingly, typically by assigning policy objectives to open-textured language in the constitution. (By "open-textured," we mean language broad enough to accommodate a relatively wide array of substantive interpretations.) For example, a policy of promoting national security may be associated with the Article II "commander in chief" clause and used to justify the trial of suspected terrorists by military tribunals created by the President. The First Amendment may be said to support a policy of unrestrained political debate, which in turn is used to justify striking down limits on corporate spending in election campaigns. Such policy-based arguments may overlap with "structural" arguments or use structural arguments as a starting point.

5. Fundamental rights. Fundamental rights arguments are like policy arguments and overlap with them to a degree. Fundamental rights arguments assign broad principles to "open-textured" constitutional language, but the principles tend to revolve around broader normative concepts such as equality, justice, freedom from racial discrimination, and privacy. These kinds of arguments typically arise in individual rights cases.

6. Originalism versus non-originalism. An "originalist" argument asserts that the Constitution must be interpreted according to some version of original understanding of the Constitution. The precise arguments embraced by originalism have shifted significantly over time. We identify three important variants here. An "original intent" approach looks at the intent of the framers or ratifiers of the Constitution. For example, such an argument might assert that, if integrated public schools or same sex marriage were not specifically intended by the framers or ratifiers of the Fourteenth Amendment to be included in the concepts of due process or equal protection, we should not interpret the Fourteenth Amendment to embrace those practices today. A "textualist" variant focuses on "original public meaning" rather than original intent. In this view, the relevant understanding is not that of the framers, but that of the people who ratified the relevant text. Since it is the ratifier's understandings that matter, the best way to understand the original meaning is not to look to the subjective intent of the framers, but to the objective meaning the words had at the time of the ratification of the Constitution (or amendment), because these are the meanings that would have been ascertainable to the ratifiers.

Yet another group of originalists use what they call a "text and principles" approach. These originalists agree that the original meaning of the constitution is binding, but resist the efforts of other originalists to read the Constitution as embodying only rules. The Constitution, these originalists argue, also embraces standards. Fidelity to original meaning thus requires ascertaining the level of abstraction at which a particular provision was intended to be applied. For example, if the original purpose of the Equal Protection clause was to embrace a broad principle of equal citizenship, than what is protected under the clause must change over time as necessary to ensure that that promise continues to be fulfilled.

"Non-originalists" differ from originalists in that they do not source their arguments in fidelity to original meaning, however defined. Instead, advocates of this position argue for a "living Constitution" whose interpretation evolves to incorporate changes in contemporary fundamental values. A non-originalist might argue that racially segregated schools violate contemporary norms of equality and therefore are unconstitutional, whatever mid-19th century politicians may have believed. Note that non-originalists and text and principle originalists will often reach the same result in particular cases, but will just do so for different reasons. Note also that it is *not* always the case that non-originalist arguments are more protective of individual rights. (See Justice Scalia's dissent in *Hamdi v. Rumsfeld* (Chapter 3) for an arguable example of originalism being more rights-protective.)

7. Formalism versus "functionalism." Formalistic constitutional arguments are premised on the view that the Constitution presents a set of well-defined concepts, procedures, and structures that generate clear answers to constitutional problems. Formalistic arguments tend to eschew subtle distinctions and favor bright line rules over balancing tests. They tend to extol the virtues of rigidity over flexibility. A classic example of a formalistic argument is Justice Black's opinion for the Court in *Youngstown Sheet & Tube Co. v. Sawyer* (Chapter 3), in which he argued that "the President's power to see that the laws are faithfully executed refutes the idea that he is to be a lawmaker." The underlying premise is that the distinction between executive and legislative functions is clear and well-defined; that seizing a steel mill is clearly a legislative act; and that the President is flatly prohibited from exercising legislative powers. The virtue of a formalistic argument is its simplicity and clarity, and the predictability of results generated by its application. But the drawback of such arguments is their tendency to break down at the margins, in close cases. Their simplicity, clarity, and predictability, therefore, often are illusory. How clear are any of the three underlying premises in the *Youngstown* example, after all?

A classic functionalist approach was that taken by Justice Jackson in his *Youngstown* concurrence: "The actual art of governing under our Constitution does not, and cannot," Jackson wrote, "conform to judicial definitions of the power of any of its branches based on isolated clauses, or even single Articles torn from context." Functionalist arguments embrace ambiguity and seek to craft flexible solutions to constitutional problems. They tend to favor answering difficult constitutional questions on a case-by-case basis, often by employing balancing tests. They try to accommodate competing interests and make room for innovative structures and processes where not expressly prohibited by the Constitution. The virtue of a functionalist approach is realism, but its drawback is a lack of consistency or predictability. Functionalist "rules" are excessively malleable. Note that formalist and functionalist approaches are not necessarily always in opposition, and at times can reach the same conclusion. For example, Black and Jackson agreed that the President's seizure of the steel mills was unconstitutional.

8. A note on "judicial activism." The term "judicial activism" is frequently bandied about by commentators and even some judges. We consider this term to be too imprecise and politically loaded to constitute a meaningful category of constitutional argument. The underlying idea seems to be that judges who substitute their own value choices for what the Constitution "requires" are judicial activists and therefore bad judges. The label initially was strongly associated with judges or decisions using open-textured constitutional text (such as that of the Equal Protection clause) to reach "liberal" results on social issues. As such, it frequently was contrasted with ideas about "strict construction" or judicial deference, both of which hold that when the Constitution is unclear, the Court should not intervene. The terminology arose in an era where constraining judicial power in constitutional cases usually tilted in a politically conservative direction. But, the liberal/conservative connotations make little sense in historical contexts where political conservatives advocate using broad interpretations of open-textured constitutional text to strike down laws supported by political liberals. (Some observers characterize the *Lochner* era, as well as the Rehnquist and Roberts Courts, in this way.) To the extent that the terms have any useful meaning, that meaning is better captured by the idea of deference (or lack thereof) to democratic institutions. (See sections G. 1 and G. 2, above.)

Exercise: Modes of Constitutional Argument

Separation of powers arguments frequently pit "formalistic" against "functionalistic" arguments. As you read Chapter 3, try to answer following questions (or go back if you've already read Chapter 3):

1. Can you categorize the Douglas and Frankfurter opinions in *Youngstown* as formalistic or functionalistic?

2. Identify the opinions you read (or have read) in Chapters 3 and 4 as formalistic or functionalistic.

H. Precedent and Stare Decisis

The court systems of the United States have a small number of well-defined rules regarding precedent. The primary distinction drawn in these rules is whether a precedent is "binding" or merely "persuasive." A court is free to disregard merely persuasive authority if it finds the reasoning of the precedent to be unpersuasive. But a court must follow binding authority, unless the precedent can be "distinguished," which means showing that it is factually different in a way that matters to the legal rule and result.

Trial court decisions bind only the parties to that particular case, and are never binding precedents in later cases. In the federal system, intermediate appellate decisions are binding within the circuit that issued the decision. For example, a decision by the U.S. Court of Appeals for the Seventh Circuit is binding on future Seventh Circuit panels and binding on all the district courts within the Seventh Circuit (the various federal judicial districts in the states of Wisconsin, Illinois, and Indiana). But the Seventh Circuit's decisions are merely persuasive authority for district courts and appellate courts outside the Seventh Circuit.

Decisions by the U.S. Supreme Court are binding authority on all federal and state courts in the United States. However—and this is a key point—the Supreme Court's decisions are not binding in subsequent Supreme Court cases: that Court is always at liberty to overrule itself, meaning that its prior decisions are merely "persuasive" authority in subsequent Supreme Court cases.

How persuasive is persuasive? The answer to that question is encapsulated in the doctrine of "stare decisis," a Latin phrase meaning "to stand by what has been decided." Stare decisis is a prudential doctrine rather than a legal requirement. It is justified on a few key, related grounds. Adhering to precedent promotes the institutional stability of the Supreme Court, promotes stability and predictability of the law, and reduces the disruptions that might be created by changes to the law among the people and institutions who conform their behavior to the law as interpreted by the Supreme Court. As Chief Justice Roberts recently summarized the doctrine:

> Fidelity to precedent — the policy of stare decisis — is vital to the proper exercise of the judicial function. "Stare decisis is the preferred course because it promotes the evenhanded, predictable, and consistent development of legal principles, fosters reliance on judicial decisions, and contributes to the actual and perceived integrity of the judicial process." For these reasons, we have long recognized that departures from precedent are inappropriate in the absence of a "special justification."

> At the same time, stare decisis is neither an "inexorable command," nor "a mechanical formula of adherence to the latest decision," especially in constitutional cases. If it were, segregation would be legal, minimum wage laws would be unconstitutional, and the Government could wiretap ordinary criminal suspects without first obtaining warrants.

> Stare decisis is instead a "principle of policy." When considering whether to reexamine a prior erroneous holding, we must balance the importance of having constitutional questions *decided* against the importance of having them decided *right*....

> [S]tare decisis is not an end in itself. It is instead "the means by which we ensure that the law will not merely change erratically, but will develop in a principled and intelligible fashion." Its greatest purpose is to serve a constitutional ideal — the rule of law. It follows that in the unusual circumstance when fidelity to any particular precedent does more to damage this constitutional ideal than to advance it, we must be more willing to depart from that precedent.[29]

In sum, stare decisis means that there is a very strong presumption in favor of following precedents, but the presumption is not absolute. Stare decisis is one factor that guides Supreme Court decisionmaking; it is an important factor that is sometimes, but not always determinative. A crucial aspect of legal argument is developing a feel for when a precedent will be followed and when, instead, there is an opening to challenge it.

The Roberts quotation also suggests that stare decisis not as strong in constitutional cases. This is an allusion to the Court's policy, stated expressly elsewhere, that stare decisis "has special force" in statutory interpretation, as opposed to constitutional, cases. This is because Congress can (in theory) overrule the Supreme Court's interpretation of a statute simply by amending the statute. Consequently, if a statutory interpretation decision needs correcting, the Court can rely in part on Congress to make the correction. When Congress fails to do so, letting a statutory interpretation decision by the Supreme Court stand undisturbed for many years, the Court often construes that inaction as a tacit en-

---

29. *Citizens United v. Federal Election Commission*, ___ U.S. ___, 130 S. Ct. 876, 920 (2010) (Roberts, C.J., concurring).

dorsement of the decision's correctness, thus providing further reason not to overrule it judicially.

It is extremely important to understand that stare decisis does not simply present the stark decision either to overrule or follow a precedent. Things are more complicated. As you will learn (or have learned already), a core element of your legal training is to develop an ability to *distinguish* precedents from the case at hand. Courts can thus work around precedents without overruling them. Precedents can be narrowly interpreted, misinterpreted, "limited to their facts," "eroded" (their scope and legal force weakened), or even practically (though not formally) overruled.

I. The Role of Statutes in Constitutional Cases

Although constitutional cases can involve judicial review of any governmental action, the paradigm example of judicial review is a constitutional challenge to a statute. Most of the cases in this book follow that pattern. This requires you to gain some comfort and familiarity in reading statutes and understanding how courts interpret them.

When law schools emerged in the late nineteenth century, the prevailing ideology in most law schools was that courts held a privileged position in the making and interpretation of law. Modern law schools have never fully overcome those origins: the dominant teaching texts remain casebooks dominated by edited cases, as though "law" comes primarily from judges. This is wrong as a matter of sociological fact, and it is dubious in terms of democratic theory. Most law comes from elected legislatures, in the form of statutes.

1. Reading Statutes

Statutes can be tedious to read. They lack the narratives of litigated cases, are typically written in awkward language, and are formatted in ways that discourage casual browsing. They break lengthy grammatical sentences into sections and subsections on separate lines. They contain often cumbersome definitions, and are filled with cross-references that prevent them from being read and understood sequentially.

Despite these issues, and the fact that your study of law tends to shunt statutes to the background, it is essential for you as a lawyer to recognize that statutes are the main source of law in our system, and to learn to love them — or at least not dislike them to the point where you can't bring yourself to read them.

When reading a statute, a good practice is to assume that you'll have to read it through at least twice. In the first read-through, you should skim to identify the key elements: (1) who is the regulated party; (2) what is the act required or prohibited of the regulated party; (3) what is the consequence of doing the prohibited thing or failing to do the required thing.

When you have identified these three elements, go back and read the statute again more thoroughly to pick up the details and nuances. Here, you will be trying to distinguish more important from less important language. It's a good idea to assume all of the language in a statute has a reason for being there. But some of the words are more important than others, particularly in the context of the case at hand. Suppose you are reading a statute that adds the phrase "in interstate commerce" as a "jurisdictional element" to invoke the commerce power as the basis for enacting the statute (see *Lopez* and *Morrison* in Chapter 1); if the case does not involve a Commerce Clause challenge, that language probably does not bear on the relevant analysis.

Another technique for reading statutes is to try to "chunk" or "group" statutory terms. A long list of related or synonymous terms is probably intended to create a single broad category, and might be reducible to its gist. In *Reno v. ACLU* (Chapter 9), for instance, the statute prohibited a "comment, request, suggestion, proposal, image, or other communication" of an "indecent" nature to a minor. The listed synonyms were all types of "communication" or "message," with the list consisting of illustrative examples. In other instances, however, word lists might be intended to be exhaustive.

2. Facial versus As-Applied Challenges

There are two basic types of constitutional challenges to statutes: "facial" challenges and "as-applied" challenges. It is important to understand the distinction, because courts approach the two types of challenges differently.

A "facial challenge" is a claim that the law is unconstitutional "on its face." As the Court has defined this term, a facial challenge argues that the statute is unconstitutional in all its applications, i.e., in the case at hand and all potential cases.

On the other hand, if the Court can conceive of some constitutional applications of the statute, it will not strike down the law as unconstitutional on its face. In this situation, the challenger might succeed with an "as-applied" challenge. This is an argument that the statute is unconstitutional as applied to the particular facts and circumstances of the case.

In *NFIB v. Sebelius* (the Affordable Care Act case discussed in Chapter 1), the Court considered a facial challenge to the "individual mandate." The argument was that the requirement that individuals either purchase health insurance or pay a tax was unconstitutional with respect to everyone covered by that provision of the statute. An "as-applied" challenge, in contrast, might have argued that the statute was unconstitutional only as applied to healthy people who have signed a sworn document that they will never seek emergency room treatment without paying for it.

A significant modification of this doctrine is used in free speech cases. Where a statute is "substantially overbroad"—that is, where it is unconstitutional in many though not all of its applications—it can be subject to a facial challenge. *Reno v. ACLU* (Chapter 9) is an example. There, provisions of an internet censorship law were struck down as substantially overbroad based on a facial challenge, even though it could have been constitutionally applied to prohibit the communication of certain obscene matter.

3. The Doctrine of Constitutional Avoidance

The doctrine of "constitutional avoidance" is a principle of statutory interpretation according to which courts will try to interpret a statute to avoid constitutional problems with it. Under this doctrine, if a statute challenged on constitutional grounds can "reasonably" be interpreted in a way that would maintain its constitutionality, the Court should adopt that interpretation.

However, the interpretation that preserves constitutionality must be both plausible in light of the language of the statute, and also consistent with the intent of the statute's drafters.

Exercises

1. This exercise is called the "Interpretive Treasure Hunt through the United States Constitution." Read the entire Constitution of the United States, and then identify the provision or provisions that do the following:

   a) empower the Senate to confirm judicial nominees.

   b) empower Congress to override a presidential veto of legislation.

   c) authorize Congress to abolish the slave trade.

   d) give federal judges life tenure.

   e) provide that a federal law can supersede a state law.

   f) grant former slaves the right to vote.

   g) authorize states to raise the legal drinking age to 21.

   h) prohibit states from raising the voting age above 18.

   i) give rise to the argument that a same-sex couple legally married in a state recognizing same-sex marriages can move to another state and have their marriage legally recognized.

2. Not all provisions of the Constitution are enforceable in court; put another way, not all constitutional provisions create a legal rule of decision on which legal cases are decided by courts. Try to identify at least two such provisions.

3. For each of the problems below, identify all the provisions of the Constitution that seem applicable and construct an argument to resolve the constitutional question. Do not refer to any legal authorities outside the Constitution itself. You may, however, include arguments based on your knowledge of history, the "intent of the framers" and similar matters which you believe shed light on your interpretation of the constitutional text.

   a) In 2001, then-president George W. Bush issued an order to establish "military tribunals" to try suspected terrorists outside of Article III federal courts. Was that order constitutional?

   b) Senate Rule 22 in effect authorizes the "filibuster," a procedure in which a bill can be effectively denied a vote of the full Senate unless 3/5 of the members of the Senate vote for "cloture" (to end debate). This procedure has been employed numerous times in the Senate's history to block bills and presidential nominees when 2/5 or more members of the Senate band together to oppose cloture. Is the filibuster constitutional?

   c) The Minimal Essential Coverage Provision of the 2010 Patient Protection and Affordable Care Act requires every U.S. citizen to maintain a minimum level of health insurance by 2014 or else pay a tax penalty. Is the provision constitutional?

PART ONE

LEGISLATIVE POWER AND FEDERALISM

A. Overview

This part consists of two chapters, which focus on the legislative powers of Congress and federalism. The Constitution, as you know, divides power between the federal government and the states. The federal government has only those powers given to it by the Constitution, while the states retain all powers except those the Constitution takes away. The cases you will read in this part all support this basic proposition. Where they differ is in their understanding of what it means to say that the Constitution gives the federal government a power or takes a power away from the states. Should grants of congressional power be read strictly or broadly? What should be done with express grants of power that are themselves worded in broad terms? Are there congressional powers that are necessarily implied by the very creation of a federal government? Likewise, are there things states simply cannot do once a federal government exists? Did the founding generation mean to enshrine a specific division of power, or a broad blueprint for a generally federalist regime? Should the founders' intentions even matter in a world so utterly unimaginable to them? These are the questions the Supreme Court struggles with in the cases in Chapters 1 and 2. As we will see, the Court's answers have varied over time.

Chapter 1 deals with the affirmative grants of power to Congress as well as express and implied limitations on that power. Chapter 2 examines the ways in which state power is limited by the Constitution. There is some overlap between the two chapters: in some situations, the powers granted to Congress and those taken away from the states are two sides of the same coin. In others, the powers overlap and the dispute is which entity—state or federal—should trump in cases of conflict.

To help you get started, we suggest you (re)read certain parts of the Constitution. We recommend that you read Art. I, §§ 8–10; Arts. IV–VII, and the Tenth, Eleventh, Thirteenth, Fourteenth and Fifteenth Amendments. Note the affirmative grants of power to Congress, as well as powers reserved to or removed from the states.

B. The Concept of Enumerated Powers

The framers of the Constitution were determined to create a national government that was considerably stronger and more unified than the loose confederation of sovereign states that had formed the United States before 1787 under the Articles of Confederation. The Articles, approved by Congress in 1777 and effective as of 1781 when nine of the 13 states had ratified it, was more like a mutual defense league than a unified nation. Its second and third articles provide:

> Each state retains its sovereignty, freedom, and independence, and every power, jurisdiction, and right, which is not by this Confederation expressly delegated to the United States, in Congress assembled.... The said States hereby severally enter into a firm league of friendship with each other, for their common defense, the security of their liberties, and their mutual and general welfare, binding themselves to assist each other, against all force offered to, or attacks made upon them, or any of them....

The Constitution of the United States, drafted by the Constitutional Convention in Philadelphia in 1787, was written "to form a more perfect Union" than that formed under the Articles. (U.S. Const., Preamble.) The question of how strong that Union should be, and how much the states delegated their sovereign powers to the national government (see Tenth Amendment) has been debated ever since.

While the extent of national governmental powers can be debated, it is axiomatic that the government of the United States is one of limited powers: the states did not grant all of their power to the new union. Instead, only those powers "enumerated"—or listed—are given. The idea is that federal powers are restricted to those that are enumerated and—as we will see in *McCulloch v. Maryland* in Chapter 1—those that can be implied from the enumerated powers.

Chief Justice John Roberts, in a recent major case that we will present in Chapter 1, began the opinion with the following explanation of enumerated powers. His words are worth quoting at length.

CASE NOTE: *National Federation of Independent Business v. Sebelius*, 567 U.S. ___, 132 S. Ct. 2566 (2012).

CHIEF JUSTICE ROBERTS:

.... The Federal Government "is acknowledged by all to be one of enumerated powers." McCulloch v. Maryland, 4 Wheat. (17 U.S.) 316 (1819). That is, rather than granting general authority to perform all the conceivable functions of government, the Constitution lists, or enumerates, the Federal Government's powers. Congress may, for example, "coin Money," "establish Post Offices," and "raise and support Armies." Art. I, § 8, cls. 5, 7, 12. The enumeration of powers is also a limitation of powers, because "[t]he enumeration presupposes something not enumerated." Gibbons v. Ogden, 9 Wheat. (22 U.S.) 1 (1824). The Constitution's express conferral of some powers makes clear that it does not grant others. And the Federal Government "can exercise only the powers granted to it." McCulloch, supra, at 405.

Today, the restrictions on government power foremost in many Americans' minds are likely to be affirmative prohibitions, such as contained in the Bill of Rights. These affirmative prohibitions come into play, however, only where the Government possesses authority to act in the first place. If no enumerated power authorizes Congress to pass a certain law, that law may not be enacted, even if it would not violate any of the express prohibitions in the Bill of Rights or elsewhere in the Constitution.

Indeed, the Constitution did not initially include a Bill of Rights at least partly because the Framers felt the enumeration of powers sufficed to restrain the Government. As Alexander Hamilton put it, "the Constitution is itself, in every rational sense, and to every useful purpose, A BILL OF RIGHTS." The Federalist No. 84, p. 515 (C. Rossiter ed. 1961). And when the Bill of Rights was ratified, it made express what the enumeration of powers necessarily implied: "The powers not delegated to the United States by the Constitution ... are reserved to the States respectively, or to the people." U.S. Const., Amdt. 10. The Federal Government has expanded dramatically over the past two centuries, but it still must show that a constitutional grant of power authorizes each of its actions.

The same does not apply to the States, because the Constitution is not the source of their power. The Constitution may restrict state governments — as it does, for example, by forbidding them to deny any person the equal protection of the laws. But where such prohibitions do not apply, state governments do not need constitutional authorization to act. The States thus can and do perform many of the vital functions of modern government — punishing street crime, running public schools, and zoning property for development, to name but a few — even though the Constitution's text does not authorize any government to do so. Our cases refer to this general power of governing, possessed by the States but not by the Federal Government, as the "police power."

"State sovereignty is not just an end in itself: Rather, federalism secures to citizens the liberties that derive from the diffusion of sovereign power." New York v. United States, 505 U.S. 144, 181 (1992). Because the police power is controlled by 50 different States instead of one national sovereign, the facets of governing that touch on citizens' daily lives are normally administered by smaller governments closer to the governed. The Framers thus ensured that powers which "in the ordinary course of affairs, concern the lives, liberties, and properties of the people" were held by governments more local and more accountable than a distant federal bureaucracy. The Federalist No. 45, at 293 (J. Madison). The independent power of the States also serves as a check on the power of the Federal Government: "By denying any one government complete jurisdiction over all the concerns of public life, federalism protects the liberty of the individual from arbitrary power." Bond v. United States, 564 U.S. ___, ___, 131 S. Ct. 2355, 2364 (2011).

Figure I.1 illustrates the most significant of Congress's enumerated powers.

As you can see from Figure I.1, some powers are more specific than others. Not surprisingly, those powers expressed in more general, open-ended terms have tended to lead to more legislative activity by Congress. For example, far more laws have been enacted under the power to regulate interstate commerce than under the power to establish a post office. In addition, the meaning of interstate commerce — as you will see — is far more open to interpretation and debate than the meaning of the postal power or the bankruptcy clause. For these and other related reasons, constitutional controversies relating to the powers of Congress have tended to cluster around a few particular powers: the Necessary and Proper clause, the Commerce Clause, the taxing and spending power, and the Fourteenth Amendment enforcement power.

Figure I.1. Enumerated Powers: Article I, §8 (selections)

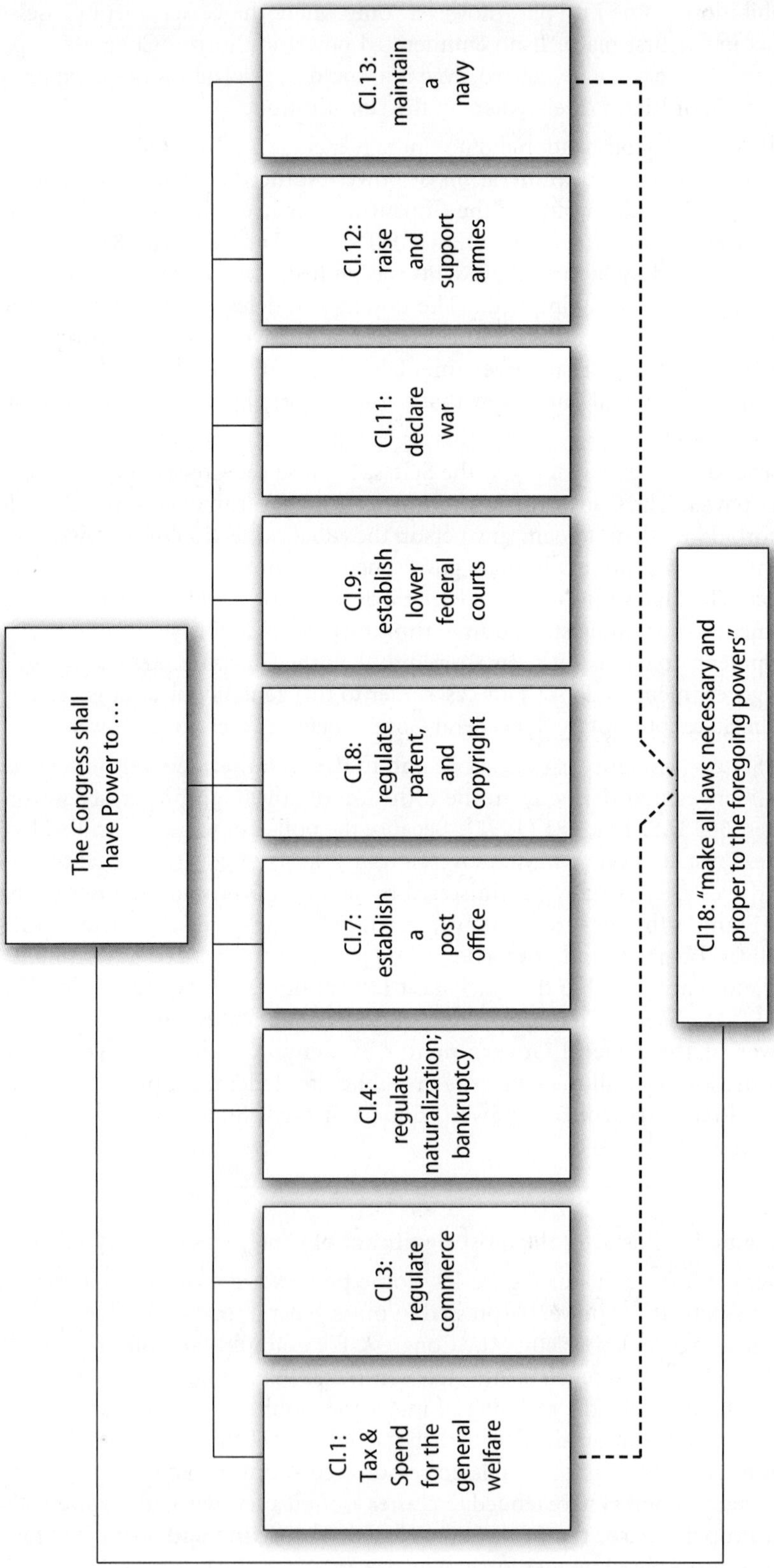

The Congress shall have Power to . . .

Cl.1: Tax & Spend for the general welfare

Cl.3: regulate commerce

Cl.4: regulate naturalization; bankruptcy

Cl.7: establish a post office

Cl.8: regulate patent, and copyright

Cl.9: establish lower federal courts

Cl.11: declare war

Cl.12: raise and support armies

Cl.13: maintain a navy

Cl18: "make all laws necessary and proper to the foregoing powers"

Chapter 1

Legislative Power

A. Overview: The Affordable Care Act Case

In late June 2012, the Supreme Court decided various constitutional challenges to the Patient Protection and Affordable Care Act of 2010. The decision consolidated several lower court cases under the caption *National Federation of Independent Business v. Sebelius*. This case captured more public and media attention than any Supreme Court case in recent years, because it involved a major law that was the centerpiece of the Obama administration's legislative agenda.

The case provides an unusually comprehensive vehicle to study constitutional law and litigation. It involves challenges based on three key enumerated powers of Congress, all of which raise significant federalism questions. It therefore presents a unique opportunity to use an important, highly contested, and recent case as an organizing principle to study the question of federal legislative power.

The opinions issued in the case are exceedingly lengthy. (When finally published in the U.S. Reports, they are likely to take up 150 pages or more.) For this reason, and because the opinion spans three major doctrinal areas, we divide the decision up throughout this chapter. For ease of reference we will refer to the case as the "Affordable Care Act" or the "ACA" case, or by a short form of its caption, *NFIB v. Sebelius*.

Here, we introduce the case and the constitutional issues it raises, by presenting excerpts from Chief Justice Roberts' opinion for the Court. This excerpt summarizes the main issues and lays out the factual and procedural background of the case.

National Federation of Independent Business v. Sebelius
567 U.S. ___, 132 S. Ct. 2566 (2012)

CHIEF JUSTICE ROBERTS announced the judgment of the Court....

Today we resolve constitutional challenges to two provisions of the Patient Protection and Affordable Care Act of 2010: the individual mandate, which requires individuals to purchase a health insurance policy providing a minimum level of coverage; and the Medicaid expansion, which gives funds to the States on the condition that they provide specified health care to all citizens whose income falls below a certain threshold. We do not consider whether the Act embodies sound policies. That judgment is entrusted to the Nation's elected leaders. We ask only whether Congress has the power under the Constitution to enact the challenged provisions.

In our federal system, the National Government possesses only limited powers; the States and the people retain the remainder. Nearly two centuries ago, Chief Justice Marshall observed that "the question respecting the extent of the powers actually granted" to the

Federal Government "is perpetually arising, and will probably continue to arise, as long as our system shall exist." McCulloch v. Maryland, 4 Wheat. (17 U.S.) 316 (1819). In this case we must again determine whether the Constitution grants Congress powers it now asserts, but which many States and individuals believe it does not possess. Resolving this controversy requires us to examine both the limits of the Government's power, and our own limited role in policing those boundaries....

In 2010, Congress enacted the Patient Protection and Affordable Care Act, 124 Stat. 119. The Act aims to increase the number of Americans covered by health insurance and decrease the cost of health care. The Act's 10 titles stretch over 900 pages and contain hundreds of provisions. This case concerns constitutional challenges to two key provisions, commonly referred to as the individual mandate and the Medicaid expansion.

The individual mandate requires most Americans to maintain "minimum essential" health insurance coverage. 26 U.S.C. § 5000A.... Many individuals will receive the required coverage through their employer, or from a government program such as Medicaid or Medicare. See § 5000A(f). But for individuals who are not exempt and do not receive health insurance through a third party, the means of satisfying the requirement is to purchase insurance from a private company.

Beginning in 2014, those who do not comply with the mandate must make a "[s]hared responsibility payment" to the Federal Government. § 5000A(b)(1). That payment, which the Act describes as a "penalty," is calculated as a percentage of household income, subject to a floor based on a specified dollar amount and a ceiling based on the average annual premium the individual would have to pay for qualifying private health insurance. § 5000A(c). In 2016, for example, the penalty will be 2.5 percent of an individual's household income, but no less than $695 and no more than the average yearly premium for insurance that covers 60 percent of the cost of 10 specified services (e.g., prescription drugs and hospitalization). 42 U.S.C. § 18022. The Act provides that the penalty will be paid to the Internal Revenue Service with an individual's taxes, and "shall be assessed and collected in the same manner" as tax penalties, such as the penalty for claiming too large an income tax refund. 26 U.S.C. § 5000A(g)(1). The Act, however, bars the IRS from using several of its normal enforcement tools, such as criminal prosecutions and levies. § 5000A(g)(2). And some individuals who are subject to the mandate are nonetheless exempt from the penalty—for example, those with income below a certain threshold and members of Indian tribes. § 5000A(e).

On the day the President signed the Act into law, Florida and 12 other States filed a complaint in the Federal District Court for the Northern District of Florida. Those plaintiffs—who are both respondents and petitioners here, depending on the issue—were subsequently joined by 13 more States, several individuals, and the National Federation of Independent Business. The plaintiffs alleged, among other things, that the individual mandate provisions of the Act exceeded Congress's powers under Article I of the Constitution. The District Court agreed, holding that Congress lacked constitutional power to enact the individual mandate. 780 F. Supp. 2d 1256 (N.D. Fla. 2011). The District Court determined that the individual mandate could not be severed from the remainder of the Act, and therefore struck down the Act in its entirety.

The Court of Appeals for the Eleventh Circuit affirmed in part and reversed in part. The court affirmed the District Court's holding that the individual mandate exceeds Congress's power. 648 F.3d 1235 (2011). The panel unanimously agreed that the individual mandate did not impose a tax, and thus could not be authorized by Congress's power to "lay and collect Taxes." U.S. Const., Art. I, § 8, cl. 1. A majority also held that the individual mandate was not supported by Congress's power to "regulate Commerce … among the several States." Id., cl. 3. According to the majority, the Commerce Clause does not empower the Federal Government to order individuals to engage in commerce, and the Government's efforts to cast the individual mandate in a different light were unpersuasive.…

Having held the individual mandate to be unconstitutional, the majority examined whether that provision could be severed from the remainder of the Act. The majority determined that, contrary to the District Court's view, it could. The court thus struck down only the individual mandate, leaving the Act's other provisions intact. 648 F. 3d, at 1328.

Other Courts of Appeals have also heard challenges to the individual mandate. The Sixth Circuit and the D. C. Circuit upheld the mandate as a valid exercise of Congress's commerce power. See Thomas More Law Center v. Obama, 651 F.3d 529 (6th Cir. 2011); Seven-Sky v. Holder, 661 F.3d 1 (D.C. Cir. 2011).…

The second provision of the Affordable Care Act directly challenged here is the Medicaid expansion. Enacted in 1965, Medicaid offers federal funding to States to assist pregnant women, children, needy families, the blind, the elderly, and the disabled in obtaining medical care. See 42 U.S.C. § 1396a(a)(10). In order to receive that funding, States must comply with federal criteria governing matters such as who receives care and what services are provided at what cost. By 1982 every State had chosen to participate in Medicaid. Federal funds received through the Medicaid program have become a substantial part of state budgets, now constituting over 10 percent of most States' total revenue.

The Affordable Care Act expands the scope of the Medicaid program and increases the number of individuals the States must cover. For example, the Act requires state programs to provide Medicaid coverage to adults with incomes up to 133 percent of the federal poverty level, whereas many States now cover adults with children only if their income is considerably lower, and do not cover childless adults at all. See § 1396a(a)(10)(A)(i)(VIII). The Act increases federal funding to cover the States' costs in expanding Medicaid coverage, although States will bear a portion of the costs on their own. § 1396d(y)(1). If a State does not comply with the Act's new coverage requirements, it may lose not only the federal funding for those requirements, but all of its federal Medicaid funds. See § 1396c.

Along with their challenge to the individual mandate, the state plaintiffs in the Eleventh Circuit argued that the Medicaid expansion exceeds Congress's constitutional powers. The Court of Appeals unanimously held that the Medicaid expansion is a valid exercise of Congress's power under the Spending Clause. U.S. Const., Art. I, § 8, cl. 1. And the court rejected the States' claim that the threatened loss of all federal Medicaid funding violates the Tenth Amendment by coercing them into complying with the Medicaid expansion. 648 F. 3d, at 1264, 1268.

We granted certiorari to review the judgment of the Court of Appeals for the Eleventh Circuit with respect to both the individual mandate and the Medicaid expansion. Because no party supports the Eleventh Circuit's holding that the individual mandate can be completely severed from the remainder of the Affordable Care Act, we appointed an amicus curiae to defend that aspect of the judgment below.…

We will return to the ACA case in a series of exercises at various points through the course of this chapter, either as questions at the end of cases, or else as major case excerpts in the Commerce Clause, taxing power and spending power sections. When reading the cases presented below, therefore, you should consider their implications for the questions presented in the ACA case.

B. Foundational Doctrine

McCulloch v. Maryland is one of the first, and many argue one of the most important, Supreme Court decisions addressing the question of how power should be divided between the federal and state governments under the Constitution. The case centered around the constitutionality of the Second Bank of the United States.

The question of a national bank was one of the first major political and constitutional controversies facing the new nation.[1] The United States in 1789 faced various financial difficulties, including massive debts from the Revolutionary War, the lack of a uniform national currency, and an absence of a rationalized system for raising and spending revenue. Alexander Hamilton, appointed by President Washington as the first Secretary of the newly created Treasury Department, strongly advocated the creation of a national bank as a key element of his comprehensive plan to overhaul the nation's finances. The national bank would be a federally chartered private corporation that would act as the depository for all federal funds, centralize revenue collection activities, pay federal debts, and issue banknotes that would be legal tender for all sums owed to the United States. While a variety of political and financial interests opposed creation of a national bank, the debate in Congress eventually coalesced around the constitutional question of whether Congress had the authority to create a bank. Since chartering corporations in general, and banks in particular, was not among the specifically enumerated powers of Congress, the arguments gravitated toward whether the power could be implied by virtue of the Necessary and Proper clause. Madison, among others, argued that the bank bill under consideration in Congress was unconstitutional.

After extensive debates, the bill establishing the first Bank of the United States with a 20-year charter passed the Senate and then the House. It was presented to President Washington for signature on February 14, 1791. The Constitution gave the President until February 25 (10 days excluding Sundays, Art. I, § cl. 2) either to sign the bill or return it with his objections (veto it). Over the next 10 days the constitutional debate therefore shifted to the executive branch. Washington asked his top three advisors — Attorney General Edmund Randolph, Secretary of State Thomas Jefferson, and Treasury Secretary Alexander Hamilton — for their opinions on the constitutionality of the bill (the only ground on which Washington believed he could properly veto it). In arguments echoing those that would be made to the Supreme Court 28 years later, Randolph and Jefferson gave Washington written opinions arguing that the bank was unconstitutional. Jefferson argued that Congress's "necessary and proper" powers were restricted to those implied powers "without which the grant of the [enumerated] power would be nugatory." Equating "necessary and proper" with "convenient," he argued, "would swallow up all of the delegated powers[.]" (Washington also consulted informally with Madison, who made similar arguments against the bank's constitutionality). With a few days to go, Washington turned to Hamilton for his opinion. Hamilton rapidly drafted point-by-point responses to the Randolph and Jefferson memoranda, arguing that the bank was constitutional: "If the

---

1. This summary of the historical background of McCulloch is largely derived from Professor Killenbeck's excellent study. Mark R. Killenbeck, M'Culloch v. Maryland: Securing a Nation (2006).

end be clearly comprehended within any of the specific powers, & if the measure have an obvious relation to that end, and is not forbidden by any particular provision of the constitution — it may safely be deemed to come within the compass of the national government." Washington followed Hamilton's advice and signed the bank bill into law on February 25, 1791.

Over the next 20 years, the first Bank of the United States fulfilled its intended purposes, and opposition to it died down, at least for a while. As presidents, both Jefferson and Madison came around to at least grudging support of the Bank. Their Secretary of the Treasury, Albert Gallatin, became a strong proponent of the Bank, and Jefferson signed a bill in 1804 authorizing the Bank to establish branch offices in the states. When the issue of renewing the Bank's charter arose in Congress in 1809 (the charter was due to expire in 1811), President Madison took the position that the constitutionality of the bank had been "settled" by the factual and historical precedent of its operating without major objections for 18 years. However, serious political opposition began to materialize in 1810, due to a combination of concern over foreign ownership of the bank's stock, personal enmities raised by some impolitic moves by the bank, and renewed constitutional objections. The bill to renew the bank's charter was rejected when a tie vote was broken by Vice President George Clinton. Vice President Clinton voted against the bill, perhaps as a finger in the eye of his political enemies, Gallatin and Madison. The Bank of the United States closed its doors forever when its charter expired in February 1811.

But the need for a national bank quickly reasserted itself. The War of 1812 drained the federal treasury, and the government's credit rating was in a shambles. There was still no uniform currency. Specie (gold and silver coin) was in short supply, creating a gap in a circulating medium of exchange that was filled by the more than 200 private banks in existence. These banks, many of which emerged after the demise of the national bank, often issued more paper money than they could redeem with specie. The need for a new national bank was, consequently, widely acknowledged, and supported by President Madison. Bills to recreate the bank were introduced and debated throughout 1814 and 1815; and while there was considerable disagreement over particulars, there was little if any objection on constitutional grounds.

On April 10, 1816, Madison signed legislation creating the Second Bank of the United States. The Second Bank, like the First, was fundamentally a private corporation, with some government participation. Of its 25 directors (all of whom were required to be U.S. citizens), five were to be appointed by the President, and 20% of the Bank's stock would be owned by the federal government. The Second Bank began operations in January 1817. Unlike the First Bank, it promptly established branch offices in sixteen states, which enabled it to fulfill one of its functions of moving federal funds around the country. Unfortunately, the Second Bank was ineptly managed in some key respects. Most importantly for our purposes, it undertook a policy of aggressive competition with state-chartered private banks. This tended to stimulate reactions from state legislatures, many of which sought to impose taxes on the Bank, motivated either by a distrust of banks generally or to curtail the Second Bank's competitive position. The Second Bank also found itself overextended due to its aggressive lending policy, and in late 1818 it abruptly and aggressively began calling in many of its loans. The rapid contraction of credit exacerbated (if it did not cause) a depression that became known as the Panic of 1819. The public perception of the Bank turned increasingly negative.

This was the context in which *McCulloch v. Maryland* arose. James McCulloch was the "cashier" — the manager — of the Baltimore branch of the Second Bank of the United

States.[2] In February 1818, Maryland enacted a law "to impose a Tax on all Banks or Branches thereof in the State of Maryland not chartered by the [Maryland] Legislature." The tax was imposed on notes issued by the bank (negotiable commercial paper that the bank was obligated to redeem for cash, and that functioned, like cash, as a medium of exchange), ranging from 10 cents to $20, depending on the amount of the note. Failure to pay the tax was punishable by fines of $100 for each offense. A bank could obtain a waiver of the tax by paying $15,000. When the law went into effect in May 1818, McCulloch issued notes without paying the tax, and a Maryland treasury official brought an action for debt against McCulloch, as Bank cashier, to collect $2,500 in penalties on five notes. The parties agreed on a statement of facts and a Baltimore county court ruled that the Bank owed the tax. The Maryland Court of Appeals (then the state's highest court) affirmed. The case was argued before the U.S. Supreme Court beginning on February 22, 1819. Some of the leading lawyers in the nation argued the case, including Daniel Webster for the Bank. The argument lasted several days, wrapping up on March 3. Three days later, the Court issued its decision.

Guided Reading Questions: *McCulloch v. Maryland*

1. The opinion has two main parts. In the first, the Court considers whether Congress has the power to create a national bank. In the second part, the Court considers whether a state can tax an entity created by the national government. Is an answer to the first question necessary to decide the second? If so, why?

2. Under the state's theory of national power, what would give the Congress the right to charter a national bank?

3. Under Marshall's opinion, what gives Congress the right to charter a national bank?

4. How does Maryland argue the Necessary and Proper clause should be interpreted? How does Marshall interpret it?

5. Why is the tax imposed by Maryland unconstitutional? (Be careful here!)

McCulloch v. Maryland

17 U.S. (4 Wheat.) 316 (1819)

Unanimous decision: *Marshall* (CJ), Washington, Johnson, Livingston, Todd, Duvall, Story

MARSHALL, Ch. J., delivered the opinion of the court.

In the case now to be determined, the defendant, a sovereign state, denies the obligation of a law enacted by the legislature of the Union, and the plaintiff, on his part, contests the validity of an act which has been passed by the legislature of that state. The constitution

---

2. Apparently, the correct spelling of his name was actually "McCulloh" (without the final "c"). The official reports spelled his name "M'Culloch," using an upside-down and backwards apostrophe, because that was how 19th century printers rendered a lower-case superscript "c," which was itself an abbreviation for "Mac." Michael G. Collins, *M'Culloch and the Turned Comma*, 12 Green Bag 2d 265, 266 (2009). The second "c" at the end of his name was a misspelling in the court records. *See* KILLENBECK, *supra* note 1, at 90. Although not an issue in the case, McCulloch was engaged in extensive financial manipulations and some fraud in connection with the Bank.

of our country, in its most interesting and vital parts, is to be considered; the conflicting powers of the government of the Union and of its members, as marked in that constitution, are to be discussed; and an opinion given, which may essentially influence the great operations of the government. No tribunal can approach such a question without a deep sense of its importance, and of the awful responsibility involved in its decision. But it must be decided peacefully, or remain a source of hostile legislation, perhaps, of hostility of a still more serious nature; and if it is to be so decided, by this tribunal alone can the decision be made. On the supreme court of the United States has the constitution of our country devolved this important duty.

The first question made in the cause is—has congress power to incorporate a bank? It has been truly said, that this can scarcely be considered as an open question, entirely unprejudiced by the former proceedings of the nation respecting it. The principle now contested was introduced at a very early period of our history, has been recognised by many successive legislatures, and has been acted upon by the judicial department, in cases of peculiar delicacy, as a law of undoubted obligation.…

The power now contested was exercised by the first congress elected under the present constitution. The bill for incorporating the Bank of the United States did not steal upon an unsuspecting legislature, and pass unobserved. Its principle was completely understood, and was opposed with equal zeal and ability. After being resisted, first, in the fair and open field of debate, and afterwards, in the executive cabinet, with as much persevering talent as any measure has ever experienced, and being supported by arguments which convinced minds as pure and as intelligent as this country can boast, it became a law. The original act was permitted to expire; but a short experience of the embarrassments to which the refusal to revive it exposed the government, convinced those who were most prejudiced against the measure of its necessity, and induced the passage of the present law. It would require no ordinary share of intrepidity, to assert that a measure adopted under these circumstances, was a bold and plain usurpation, to which the constitution gave no countenance. These observations belong to the cause; but they are not made under the impression, that, were the question entirely new, the law would be found irreconcilable with the constitution.

In discussing this question, the counsel for the state of Maryland have deemed it of some importance, in the construction of the constitution, to consider that instrument, not as emanating from the people, but as the act of sovereign and independent states. The powers of the general government, it has been said, are delegated by the states, who alone are truly sovereign; and must be exercised in subordination to the states, who alone possess supreme dominion. It would be difficult to sustain this proposition. The convention which framed the constitution was indeed elected by the state legislatures. But the instrument, when it came from their hands, was a mere proposal, without obligation, or pretensions to it. It was reported to the then existing congress of the United States, with a request that it might "be submitted to a convention of delegates, chosen in each state by the people thereof, under the recommendation of its legislature, for their assent and ratification." This mode of proceeding was adopted; and by the convention, by congress, and by the state legislatures, the instrument was submitted to the people. They acted upon it in the only manner in which they can act safely, effectively and wisely, on such a subject, by assembling in convention. It is true, they assembled in their several states—and where else should they have assembled? No political dreamer was ever wild enough to think of breaking down the lines which separate the states, and of compounding the American people into one common mass. Of consequence, when they act, they act in their states. But the measures they adopt do not, on that account, cease to be the measures of the people themselves, or become the measures of the state governments.

From these conventions, the constitution derives its whole authority. The government proceeds directly from the people; is "ordained and established," in the name of the people; and is declared to be ordained, "in order to form a more perfect union, establish justice, insure domestic tranquillity, and secure the blessings of liberty to themselves and to their posterity." The assent of the states, in their sovereign capacity, is implied, in calling a convention, and thus submitting that instrument to the people. But the people were at perfect liberty to accept or reject it; and their act was final. It required not the affirmance, and could not be negatived, by the state governments. The constitution, when thus adopted, was of complete obligation, and bound the state sovereignties.

It has been said, that the people had already surrendered all their powers to the state sovereignties, and had nothing more to give. But, surely, the question whether they may resume and modify the powers granted to government, does not remain to be settled in this country. Much more might the legitimacy of the general government be doubted, had it been created by the states. The powers delegated to the state sovereignties were to be exercised by themselves, not by a distinct and independent sovereignty, created by themselves. To the formation of a league, such as was the confederation, the state sovereignties were certainly competent. But when, "in order to form a more perfect union," it was deemed necessary to change this alliance into an effective government, possessing great and sovereign powers, and acting directly on the people, the necessity of referring it to the people, and of deriving its powers directly from them, was felt and acknowledged by all. The government of the Union, then (whatever may be the influence of this fact on the case), is, emphatically and truly, a government of the people. In form, and in substance, it emanates from them. Its powers are granted by them, and are to be exercised directly on them, and for their benefit.

This government is acknowledged by all, to be one of enumerated powers. The principle, that it can exercise only the powers granted to it, would seem too apparent, to have required to be enforced by all those arguments, which its enlightened friends, while it was depending before the people, found it necessary to urge; that principle is now universally admitted. But the question respecting the extent of the powers actually granted, is perpetually arising, and will probably continue to arise, so long as our system shall exist. In discussing these questions, the conflicting powers of the general and state governments must be brought into view, and the supremacy of their respective laws, when they are in opposition, must be settled.

If any one proposition could command the universal assent of mankind, we might expect it would be this—that the government of the Union, though limited in its powers, is supreme within its sphere of action. This would seem to result, necessarily, from its nature. It is the government of all; its powers are delegated by all; it represents all, and acts for all. Though any one state may be willing to control its operations, no state is willing to allow others to control them. The nation, on those subjects on which it can act, must necessarily bind its component parts. But this question is not left to mere reason: the people have, in express terms, decided it, by saying, "this constitution, and the laws of the United States, which shall be made in pursuance thereof," "shall be the supreme law of the land," and by requiring that the members of the state legislatures, and the officers of the executive and judicial departments of the states, shall take the oath of fidelity to it. The government of the United States, then, though limited in its powers, is supreme; and its laws, when made in pursuance of the constitution, form the supreme law of the land, "anything in the constitution or laws of any state to the contrary notwithstanding."

Among the enumerated powers, we do not find that of establishing a bank or creating a corporation. But there is no phrase in the instrument which, like the articles of confederation, excludes incidental or implied powers; and which requires that everything granted shall be expressly and minutely described. Even the 10th amendment, which was framed for the purpose of quieting the excessive jealousies which had been excited, omits the word "expressly," and declares only, that the powers "not delegated to the United States, nor prohibited to the states, are reserved to the states or to the people"; thus leaving the question, whether the particular power which may become the subject of contest, has been delegated to the one government, or prohibited to the other, to depend on a fair construction of the whole instrument. The men who drew and adopted this amendment had experienced the embarrassments resulting from the insertion of this word in the articles of confederation, and probably omitted it, to avoid those embarrassments. A constitution, to contain an accurate detail of all the subdivisions of which its great powers will admit, and of all the means by which they may be carried into execution, would partake of the prolixity of a legal code, and could scarcely be embraced by the human mind. It would, probably, never be understood by the public. Its nature, therefore, requires, that only its great outlines should be marked, its important objects designated, and the minor ingredients which compose those objects, be deduced from the nature of the objects themselves. That this idea was entertained by the framers of the American constitution, is not only to be inferred from the nature of the instrument, but from the language. Why else were some of the limitations, found in the 9th section of the 1st article, introduced? It is also, in some degree, warranted, by their having omitted to use any restrictive term which might prevent its receiving a fair and just interpretation. In considering this question, then, we must never forget that it is a constitution we are expounding.

Although, among the enumerated powers of government, we do not find the word "bank" or "incorporation," we find the great powers, to lay and collect taxes; to borrow money; to regulate commerce; to declare and conduct a war; and to raise and support armies and navies. The sword and the purse, all the external relations, and no inconsiderable portion of the industry of the nation, are intrusted to its government. It can never be pretended that these vast powers draw after them others of inferior importance, merely because they are inferior. Such an idea can never be advanced. But it may with great reason be contended, that a government, intrusted with such ample powers, on the due execution of which the happiness and prosperity of the nation so vitally depends, must also be intrusted with ample means for their execution. The power being given, it is the interest of the nation to facilitate its execution. It can never be their interest, and cannot be presumed to have been their intention, to clog and embarrass its execution, by withholding the most appropriate means. Throughout this vast republic, from the St. Croix to the Gulf of Mexico, from the Atlantic to the Pacific, revenue is to be collected and expended, armies are to be marched and supported. The exigencies of the nation may require, that the treasure raised in the north should be transported to the south, that raised in the east, conveyed to the west, or that this order should be reversed. Is that construction of the constitution to be preferred, which would render these operations difficult, hazardous and expensive? Can we adopt that construction (unless the words imperiously require it), which would impute to the framers of that instrument, when granting these powers for the public good, the intention of impeding their exercise, by withholding a choice of means? If, indeed, such be the mandate of the constitution, we have only to obey; but that instrument does not profess to enumerate the means by which the powers it confers may be executed; nor does it prohibit the creation of a corporation, if the existence of such a being be essential, to the beneficial exercise of those powers. It is, then, the subject of fair inquiry, how far such means may be employed.

It is not denied, that the powers given to the government imply the ordinary means of execution. That, for example, of raising revenue, and applying it to national purposes, is admitted to imply the power of conveying money from place to place, as the exigencies of the nation may require, and of employing the usual means of conveyance. But it is denied, that the government has its choice of means; or, that it may employ the most convenient means, if, to employ them, it be necessary to erect a corporation. On what foundation does this argument rest? On this alone: the power of creating a corporation, is one appertaining to sovereignty, and is not expressly conferred on congress. This is true. But all legislative powers appertain to sovereignty. The original power of giving the law on any subject whatever, is a sovereign power; and if the government of the Union is restrained from creating a corporation, as a means for performing its functions, on the single reason that the creation of a corporation is an act of sovereignty; if the sufficiency of this reason be acknowledged, there would be some difficulty in sustaining the authority of congress to pass other laws for the accomplishment of the same objects. The government which has a right to do an act, and has imposed on it, the duty of performing that act, must, according to the dictates of reason, be allowed to select the means; and those who contend that it may not select any appropriate means, that one particular mode of effecting the object is excepted, take upon themselves the burden of establishing that exception.

The creation of a corporation, it is said, appertains to sovereignty. This is admitted. But to what portion of sovereignty does it appertain? Does it belong to one more than to another? In America, the powers of sovereignty are divided between the government of the Union, and those of the states. They are each sovereign, with respect to the objects committed to it, and neither sovereign, with respect to the objects committed to the other....

But the constitution of the United States has not left the right of congress to employ the necessary means, for the execution of the powers conferred on the government, to general reasoning. To its enumeration of powers is added, that of making "all laws which shall be necessary and proper, for carrying into execution the foregoing powers, and all other powers vested by this constitution, in the government of the United States, or in any department thereof." The counsel for the state of Maryland have urged various arguments, to prove that this clause, though, in terms, a grant of power, is not so, in effect; but is really restrictive of the general right, which might otherwise be implied, of selecting means for executing the enumerated powers. In support of this proposition, they have found it necessary to contend, that this clause was inserted for the purpose of conferring on congress the power of making laws. That, without it, doubts might be entertained, whether congress could exercise its powers in the form of legislation.

But could this be the object for which it was inserted? A government is created by the people, having legislative, executive and judicial powers. Its legislative powers are vested in a congress, which is to consist of a senate and house of representatives. Each house may determine the rule of its proceedings; and it is declared, that every bill which shall have passed both houses, shall, before it becomes a law, be presented to the president of the United States. The 7th section describes the course of proceedings, by which a bill shall become a law; and, then, the 8th section enumerates the powers of congress. Could it be necessary to say, that a legislature should exercise legislative powers, in the shape of legislation? After allowing each house to prescribe its own course of proceeding, after describing the manner in which a bill should become a law, would it have entered into the mind of a single member of the convention, that an express power to make laws was necessary, to enable the legislature to make them? That a legislature, endowed with legislative powers, can legislate, is a proposition too self-evident to have been questioned.

But the argument on which most reliance is placed, is drawn from that peculiar language of this clause. Congress is not empowered by it to make all laws, which may have relation to the powers conferred on the government, but such only as may be "necessary and proper" for carrying them into execution. The word "necessary" is considered as controlling the whole sentence, and as limiting the right to pass laws for the execution of the granted powers, to such as are indispensable, and without which the power would be nugatory. That it excludes the choice of means, and leaves to congress, in each case, that only which is most direct and simple.

Is it true, that this is the sense in which the word "necessary" is always used? Does it always import an absolute physical necessity, so strong, that one thing to which another may be termed necessary, cannot exist without that other? We think it does not. If reference be had to its use, in the common affairs of the world, or in approved authors, we find that it frequently imports no more than that one thing is convenient, or useful, or essential to another. To employ the means necessary to an end, is generally understood as employing any means calculated to produce the end, and not as being confined to those single means, without which the end would be entirely unattainable. Such is the character of human language, that no word conveys to the mind, in all situations, one single definite idea; and nothing is more common than to use words in a figurative sense. Almost all compositions contain words, which, taken in their rigorous sense, would convey a meaning different from that which is obviously intended. It is essential to just construction, that many words which import something excessive, should be understood in a more mitigated sense—in that sense which common usage justifies.

The word "necessary" is of this description. It has not a fixed character, peculiar to itself. It admits of all degrees of comparison; and is often connected with other words, which increase or diminish the impression the mind receives of the urgency it imports. A thing may be necessary, very necessary, absolutely or indispensably necessary. To no mind would the same idea be conveyed by these several phrases. The comment on the word is well illustrated by the passage cited at the bar, from the 10th section of the 1st article of the constitution. It is, we think, impossible to compare the sentence which prohibits a state from laying "imposts, or duties on imports or exports, except what may be absolutely necessary for executing its inspection laws," with that which authorizes congress "to make all laws which shall be necessary and proper for carrying into execution" the powers of the general government, without feeling a conviction, that the convention understood itself to change materially the meaning of the word "necessary," by prefixing the word "absolutely." This word, then, like others, is used in various senses; and, in its construction, the subject, the context, the intention of the person using them, are all to be taken into view.

Let this be done in the case under consideration. The subject is the execution of those great powers on which the welfare of a nation essentially depends. It must have been the intention of those who gave these powers, to insure, so far as human prudence could insure, their beneficial execution. This could not be done, by confiding the choice of means to such narrow limits as not to leave it in the power of congress to adopt any which might be appropriate, and which were conducive to the end. This provision is made in a constitution, intended to endure for ages to come, and consequently, to be adapted to the various crises of human affairs. To have prescribed the means by which government should, in all future time, execute its powers, would have been to change, entirely, the character of the instrument, and give it the properties of a legal code. It would have been an unwise attempt to provide, by immutable rules, for exigencies which, if foreseen at all, must have been seen dimly, and which can be best provided for as they occur. To have declared, that the best means shall not be used, but those alone, without which the power given would be nugatory, would have been to deprive the legislature of the capacity to avail itself of experience, to exercise its reason, and to accommodate its legislation to circumstances. If we apply this principle of construction to any of the powers of the government, we shall find it so pernicious in its operation that we shall be compelled to discard it....

Take, for example, the power "to establish post-offices and post-roads." This power is executed, by the single act of making the establishment. But, from this has been inferred the power and duty of carrying the mail along the post-road, from one post-office to another. And from this implied power, has again been inferred the right to punish those who steal letters from the post-office, or rob the mail. It may be said, with some plausibility, that the right to carry the mail, and to punish those who rob it, is not indispensably necessary to the establishment of a post-office and post-road. This right is indeed essential to the beneficial exercise of the power, but not indispensably necessary to its existence. So, of the punishment of the crimes of stealing or falsifying a record or process of a court of the United States, or of perjury in such court. To punish these offences, is certainly conducive to the due administration of justice. But courts may exist, and may decide the causes brought before them, though such crimes escape punishment.

The baneful influence of this narrow construction on all the operations of the government, and the absolute impracticability of maintaining it, without rendering the government incompetent to its great objects, might be illustrated by numerous examples drawn from the constitution, and from our laws. The good sense of the public has pronounced, without hesitation, that the power of punishment appertains to sovereignty, and may be exercised, whenever the sovereign has a right to act, as incidental to his constitutional powers. It is a means for carrying into execution all sovereign powers, and may be used, although not indispensably necessary. It is a right incidental to the power, and conducive to its beneficial exercise.

If this limited construction of the word "necessary" must be abandoned, in order to punish, whence is derived the rule which would reinstate it, when the government would carry its powers into execution, by means not vindictive in their nature? If the word "necessary" means "needful," "requisite," "essential," "conducive to," in order to let in the power of punishment for the infraction of law; why is it not equally comprehensive, when required to authorize the use of means which facilitate the execution of the powers of government, without the infliction of punishment?

In ascertaining the sense in which the word "necessary" is used in this clause of the constitution, we may derive some aid from that with which it is associated. Congress shall have power "to make all laws which shall be necessary and proper to carry into execution" the powers of the government. If the word "necessary" was used in that strict and rigorous sense for which the counsel for the state of Maryland contend, it would be an extraordinary departure from the usual course of the human mind, as exhibited in composition, to add a word, the only possible effect of which is, to qualify that strict and rigorous meaning; to present to the mind the idea of some choice of means of legislation, not strained and compressed within the narrow limits for which gentlemen contend.

But the argument which most conclusively demonstrates the error of the construction contended for by the counsel for the state of Maryland, is founded on the intention of the convention, as manifested in the whole clause. To waste time and argument in proving that, without it, congress might carry its powers into execution, would be not much less idle, than to hold a lighted taper to the sun. As little can it be required to prove, that in the absence of this clause, congress would have some choice of means. That it might employ those which, in its judgment, would most advantageously effect the object to be accomplished. That any means adapted to the end, any means which tended directly to the execution of the constitutional powers of the government, were in themselves constitutional. This clause, as construed by the state of Maryland, would abridge, and almost annihilate, this useful and necessary right of the legislature to select its means. That this could not be intended, is, we should think, had it not been already controverted, too apparent for controversy.

We think so for the following reasons: 1st. The clause is placed among the powers of congress, not among the limitations on those powers. 2d. Its terms purport to enlarge, not to diminish the powers vested in the government. It purports to be an additional power, not a restriction on those already granted. No reason has been, or can be assigned, for thus concealing an intention to narrow the discretion of the national legislature, under words which purport to enlarge it. The framers of the constitution wished its adoption, and well knew that it would be endangered by its strength, not by its weakness. Had they been capable of using language which would convey to the eye one idea, and, after deep reflection, impress on the mind, another, they would rather have disguised the grant of power, than its limitation. If, then, their intention had been, by this clause, to restrain the free use of means which might otherwise have been implied, that intention would have been inserted in another place, and would have been expressed in terms resembling these. "In carrying into execution the foregoing powers, and all others," &c., "no laws shall be passed but such as are necessary and proper." Had the intention been to make this clause restrictive, it would unquestionably have been so in form as well as in effect.

The result of the most careful and attentive consideration bestowed upon this clause is, that if it does not enlarge, it cannot be construed to restrain the powers of congress, or to impair the right of the legislature to exercise its best judgment in the selection of measures to carry into execution the constitutional powers of the government. If no other motive for its insertion can be suggested, a sufficient one is found in the desire to remove all doubts respecting the right to legislate on that vast mass of incidental powers which must be involved in the constitution, if that instrument be not a splendid bauble.

We admit, as all must admit, that the powers of the government are limited, and that its limits are not to be transcended. But we think the sound construction of the constitution must allow to the national legislature that discretion, with respect to the means by which the powers it confers are to be carried into execution, which will enable that body to perform the high duties assigned to it, in the manner most beneficial to the people. Let the end be legitimate, let it be within the scope of the constitution, and all means which are appropriate, which are plainly adapted to that end, which are not prohibited, but consist with the letter and spirit of the constitution, are constitutional.

…. Should congress, in the execution of its powers, adopt measures which are prohibited by the constitution; or should congress, under the pretext of executing its powers, pass laws for the accomplishment of objects not entrusted to the government; it would become the painful duty of this tribunal, should a case requiring such a decision come before it, to say, that such an act was not the law of the land. But where the law is not prohibited, and is really calculated to effect any of the objects entrusted to the government, to undertake here to inquire into the degree of its necessity, would be to pass the line which circumscribes the judicial department, and to tread on legislative ground. This court disclaims all pretensions to such a power. After this declaration, it can scarcely be necessary to say, that the existence of state banks can have no possible influence on the question. No trace is to be found in the constitution, of an intention to create a dependence of the government of the Union on those of the states, for the execution of the great powers assigned to it.

Its means are adequate to its ends; and on those means alone was it expected to rely for the accomplishment of its ends. To impose on it the necessity of resorting to means which it cannot control, which another government may furnish or withhold, would render its course precarious, the result of its measures uncertain, and create a dependence on other governments, which might disappoint its most important designs, and is incompatible with the language of the constitution. But were it otherwise, the choice of means implies a right to choose a national bank in preference to state banks, and congress alone can make the election.

After the most deliberate consideration, it is the unanimous and decided opinion of this court, that the act to incorporate the Bank of the United States is a law made in pursuance of the constitution, and is a part of the supreme law of the land....

It being the opinion of the court, that the act incorporating the bank is constitutional; and that the power of establishing a branch in the state of Maryland might be properly exercised by the bank itself, we proceed to inquire—Whether the state of Maryland may, without violating the constitution, tax that branch? That the power of taxation is one of vital importance; that it is retained by the states; that it is not abridged by the grant of a similar power to the government of the Union; that it is to be concurrently exercised by the two governments—are truths which have never been denied. But such is the paramount character of the constitution, that its capacity to withdraw any subject from the action of even this power, is admitted. The states are expressly forbidden to lay any duties on imports or exports, except what may be absolutely necessary for executing their inspection laws. If the obligation of this prohibition must be conceded—if it may restrain a state from the exercise of its taxing power on imports and exports—the same paramount character would seem to restrain, as it certainly may restrain, a state from such other exercise of this power, as is in its nature incompatible with, and repugnant to, the constitutional laws of the Union. A law, absolutely repugnant to another, as entirely repeals that other as if express terms of repeal were used.

On this ground, the counsel for the bank place its claim to be exempted from the power of a state to tax its operations. There is no express provision for the case, but the claim has been sustained on a principle which so entirely pervades the constitution, is so intermixed with the materials which compose it, so interwoven with its web, so blended with its texture, as to be incapable of being separated from it, without rending it into shreds. This great principle is, that the constitution and the laws made in pursuance thereof are supreme; that they control the constitution and laws of the respective states, and cannot be controlled by them. From this, which may be almost termed an axiom, other propositions are deduced as corollaries, on the truth or error of which, and on their application to this case, the cause has been supposed to depend. These are, 1st. That a power to create implies a power to preserve: 2d. That a power to destroy, if wielded by a different hand, is hostile to, and incompatible with these powers to create and to preserve: 3d. That where this repugnancy exists, that authority which is supreme must control, not yield to that over which it is supreme.

These propositions, as abstract truths, would, perhaps, never be controverted. Their application to this case, however, has been denied; and both in maintaining the affirmative and the negative, a splendour of eloquence, and strength of argument, seldom, if ever, surpassed, have been displayed. The power of congress to create, and of course, to continue, the bank, was the subject of the preceding part of this opinion; and is no longer to be considered as questionable. That the power of taxing it by the states may be exercised so as to destroy it, is too obvious to be denied.... It is admitted, that the power of taxing the people and their property, is essential to the very existence of government, and may be legitimately exercised on the objects to which it is applicable, to the utmost extent to which the government may choose to carry it. The only security against the abuse of this power, is found in the structure of the government itself. In imposing a tax, the legislature acts upon its constituents. This is, in general, a sufficient security against erroneous and oppressive taxation.

The people of a state, therefore, give to their government a right of taxing themselves and their property, and as the exigencies of government cannot be limited, they prescribe no limits to the exercise of this right, resting confidently on the interest of the legislator, and on the influence of the constituent over their representative, to guard them against its abuse. But the means employed by the government of the Union have no such security, nor is the right of a state to tax them sustained by the same theory. Those means are not given by the people of a particular state, not given by the constituents of the legislature, which claim the right to tax them, but by the people of all the states. They are given by all, for the benefit of all — and upon theory, should be subjected to that government only which belongs to all.

.... That the power to tax involves the power to destroy; that the power to destroy may defeat and render useless the power to create; that there is a plain repugnance in conferring on one government a power to control the constitutional measures of another, which other, with respect to those very measures, is declared to be supreme over that which exerts the control, are propositions not to be denied.... Would the people of any one state trust those of another with a power to control the most insignificant operations of their state government? We know they would not. Why, then, should we suppose, that the people of any one state should be willing to trust those of another with a power to control the operations of a government to which they have confided their most important and most valuable interests? In the legislature of the Union alone, are all represented. The legislature of the Union alone, therefore, can be trusted by the people with the power of controlling measures which concern all, in the confidence that it will not be abused. This, then, is not a case of confidence, and we must consider it is as it really is. If we apply the principle for which the state of Maryland contends, to the constitution, generally, we shall find it capable of changing totally the character of that instrument. We shall find it capable of arresting all the measures of the government, and of prostrating it at the foot of the states. The American people have declared their constitution and the laws made in pursuance thereof, to be supreme; but this principle would transfer the supremacy, in fact, to the states.... This was not intended by the American people. They did not design to make their government dependent on the states....

The court has bestowed on this subject its most deliberate consideration. The result is a conviction that the states have no power, by taxation or otherwise, to retard, impede, burden, or in any manner control, the operations of the constitutional laws enacted by congress to carry into execution the powers vested in the general government. This is, we think, the unavoidable consequence of that supremacy which the constitution has declared. We are unanimously of opinion, that the law passed by the legislature of Maryland, imposing a tax on the Bank of the United States, is unconstitutional and void.

Review Questions and Explanations: *McCulloch*

1. What ideas about state and national sovereignty are raised as arguments in the case? How do these theories relate to the question at hand (whether the national government can charter a national bank)?

2. What visions of national and state sovereignty does Marshall's opinion accept?

3. If the state's theory of national power were accepted, what consequences would that have for national legislative power more generally?

4. Marshall's opinion in this case includes one of the most famous statements in constitutional law: "We must never forget that it is a Constitution we are expounding." What does this mean? What do you think it meant to Marshall?

Figure 1.1. Second Bank of the United States Building, Philadelphia. (One of casebook authors, foreground, for scale.)

5. The *McCulloch* opinion did not, in fact, "settle" the controversy over the Second Bank of the United States. The Bank remained an object of controversy, with opponents continuing to raise constitutional, as well as practical and political objections to it. Andrew Jackson was a vociferous opponent of the Bank, both before and during his presidency. In 1832, with the expiration of the Second Bank's charter still four years away, Jackson's political opponents gambled that the Bank was sufficiently popular that Jackson's re-election chances would be undermined if he were forced to veto a bank charter renewal bill on the eve of the 1832 presidential election. The recharter bill narrowly passed Congress, Jackson vetoed it, a veto override failed, and Jackson was re-elected. (Jackson's constitutional objections to the bank were set out in a lengthy veto message, which we present in Chapter 3.)

The second Bank of the United States shut down at the end of Jackson's second term, in 1836; no national Bank was ever again chartered, though the issue (including the Bank's constitutionality) continued to be debated by politicians

(Whigs favoring the national bank, Democrats opposing it), until slavery eclipsed the bank as a political issue at the end of the 1840s.

Exercise: Necessary and Proper Clause

For years, Congress has been under pressure to respond to public concerns about "sexual predators"—individuals convicted of sex-related crimes who either have been repeat violators or are seen as likely to repeat their crimes. Congress eventually responded to this pressure by passing a law authorizing court-ordered civil commitment by the federal government of: (1) "sexually dangerous" persons who are already in the custody of the Bureau of Prisons, but who are coming to the end of their federal prison sentences, and (2) "sexually dangerous" persons who are in the custody of the Attorney General because they have been found mentally incompetent to stand trial. Assume that the law only applies to federal prisoners charged with otherwise valid federal laws (such as laws involving kidnapping across state boarders, or crimes that occurred on federal property). Use Justice Marshall's understanding of the Necessary and Proper Clause to argue that this statute is constitutional. Be as precise in your argument as you can. Now use Maryland's understanding of the Clause to argue that the law is unconstitutional. Remember to focus your arguments on the question of Congressional power (i.e., do not make arguments based on the individual rights of criminal defendants).

C. The Commerce Clause

The power to regulate commerce among the states, found in the Commerce Clause, is one of the most important of Congress's enumerated powers. It is useful to think about the Court's Commerce Clause jurisprudence as composed of four distinct time periods: 1) the early period, in which the Court interpreted congressional power broadly (as seen in *McCulloch*); 2) the late 1800s to 1937, when the Court aggressively constrained congressional power; 3) 1937 to 1995, when the Court more or less abstained from imposing any restraint on Congress; and 4) the current era, in which the Court is struggling to find workable restrictions on congressional authority.

This "four era" story is oversimplified. Careful historical research has shown that the Court's jurisprudence in the second era (called the *Lochner* era after a famous case in which the Court struck down working-hours legislation intended to protect bakers) was more mixed than common wisdom allows. Likewise, the Court in the third era, while not actively using its power to restrict the reach of the Commerce Clause, never conceded that it could not or would not do so in an appropriate case. The four-era story, nonetheless, is helpful in organizing our thinking about the Court's Commerce Clause cases, and we will reference the framework throughout this section.

You have already read one case—*McCulloch*—from the first era. Think about Justice Marshall's understanding of the Commerce Clause while you read the following materials. Also remember that most of the cases in the second era have, as noted above, been directly or indirectly overturned. As you read those cases, think about what problem the Court was trying to solve and why the Court's solution was eventually deserted. In reading cases from the current era, ask yourself if the Court has successfully addressed concerns you had about decisions from the earlier time periods.

The materials covered in this part differ from most of the materials in the book in that we have included several cases that have been overturned. We do this because these cases are a critical element to the historical development of the Court's jurisprudence in this area. As you will see, that history continues to shape arguments about congressional power. Understanding the debates about current doctrine thus requires some understanding of these earlier cases. These cases also warn against looking for easy answers to the issues presented: the Court has tried many approaches over the years, none of which have turned out to be completely satisfactory.

1. Doctrinal Origins

The first major Supreme Court decision interpreting the reach of the Commerce Clause was Chief Justice John Marshall's opinion in *Gibbons v. Ogden* (1824). Whatever influence the *Gibbons* decision may have had in its own day in establishing a consensus understanding of Congress's commerce power, it has long been viewed as the authoritative starting point for Commerce Clause analysis — or at least Commerce Clause rhetoric — since the late 19th century. While over time the Supreme Court has given both narrower and broader scope to Congress's commerce power, *Gibbons* is cited and quoted in nearly every important Commerce Clause opinion, by both the majority and the dissent. *Gibbons* has thus taken on an almost scriptural quality, both for its revered place in doctrinal arguments and for its amenability to being quoted in support of opposing viewpoints. For this reason, *Gibbons* can rarely if ever function as a controlling precedent that dictates the outcome in a contemporary case. However, when it was decided, *Gibbons* settled a crucial controversy over which government (state or federal) had ultimate authority to regulate a major emerging industry.

Guided Reading Questions: *Gibbons v. Ogden*

1. What are claimed legal rights underlying the dispute, and where do the claimed rights come from?

2. Why does the Court spend so much time on the question of whether "navigation" is "commerce"?

3. How does Ogden define "commerce among the states"?

Gibbons v. Ogden

22 U.S. (9 Wheat.) 1 (1824)

Majority: *Marshall* (CJ), Washington, Todd, Duvall, Story

Concurrence: *Johnson* (Thompson took no part in the case).

MR. CHIEF JUSTICE MARSHALL delivered the opinion of the Court.

[Ogden had a license, issued by the State of **New York**, giving him the exclusive right to "navigation of all the waters within the jurisdiction of that State, with boats moved by fire or steam, for a term of years." Gibbons, acting under a license issued pursuant to a Congressional statute, operated two steamboats that ran in and between New York and New Jersey. Ogden sued to stop Gibbons from operating in the waterways in which he held — under New York law — an exclusive monopoly. Ogden defended the validity of his state-issued monopoly by arguing that Congress did not have power under the Commerce Clause to regulate navigation.]

As preliminary to the very able discussions of the constitution, which we have heard from the bar, and as having some influence on its construction, reference has been made to the political situation of these States, anterior to its formation. It has been said, that they were sovereign, were completely independent, and were connected with each other only by a league. This is true. But, when these allied sovereigns converted their league into a government, when they converted their Congress of Ambassadors, deputed to deliberate on their common concerns, and to recommend measures of general utility, into a Legislature, empowered to enact laws on the most interesting subjects, the whole character in which the States appear, underwent a change, the extent of which must be determined by a fair consideration of the instrument by which that change was effected.

This instrument contains an enumeration of powers expressly granted by the people to their government. It has been said, that these powers ought to be construed strictly. But why ought they to be so construed? Is there one sentence in the constitution which gives countenance to this rule? In the last of the enumerated powers, that which grants, expressly, the means for carrying all others into execution, Congress is authorized "to make all laws which shall be necessary and proper" for the purpose. But this limitation on the means which may be used, is not extended to the powers which are conferred; nor is there one sentence in the constitution, which has been pointed out by the gentlemen of the bar, or which we have been able to discern, that prescribes this rule. We do not, therefore, think ourselves justified in adopting it. What do gentlemen mean, by a strict construction? If they contend only against that enlarged construction, which would extend words beyond their natural and obvious import, we might question the application of the term, but should not controvert the principle. If they contend for that narrow construction which, in support of some theory not to be found in the constitution, would deny to the government those powers which the words of the grant, as usually understood, import, and which are consistent with the general views and objects of the instrument; for that narrow construction, which would cripple the government, and render it unequal to the object for which it is declared to be instituted, and to which the powers given, as fairly understood, render it competent; then we cannot perceive the propriety of this strict construction, nor adopt it as the rule by which the constitution is to be expounded. As men, whose intentions require no concealment, generally employ the words which most directly and aptly express the ideas they intend to convey, the enlightened patriots who framed our constitution, and the people who adopted it, must be understood to have employed words in their natural sense, and to have intended what they have said. If, from the imperfection of human language, there should be serious doubts respecting the extent of any given power, it is a well settled rule, that the objects for which it was given, especially when those objects are expressed in the instrument itself, should have great influence in the construction. We know of no reason for excluding this rule from the present case. The grant does not convey power which might be beneficial to the grantor, if retained by himself, or which can ensure solely to the benefit of the grantee; but is an investment of power for the general advantage, in the hands of agents selected for that purpose; which power can never be exercised by the people themselves, but must be placed in the hands of agents, or lie dormant. We know of no rule for construing the extent of such powers, other than is given by the language of the instrument which confers them, taken in connection with the purposes for which they were conferred.

The words are, "Congress shall have power to regulate commerce with foreign nations, and among the several States, and with the Indian tribes."

The subject to be regulated is commerce; and our constitution being, as was aptly said at the bar, one of enumeration, and not of definition, to ascertain the extent of the power, it becomes necessary to settle the meaning of the word. The counsel for the appellee would limit it to traffic, to buying and selling, or the interchange of commodities, and do not admit that it comprehends navigation. This would restrict a general term, applicable to many objects, to one of its significations. Commerce, undoubtedly, is traffic, but it is something more: it is intercourse. It describes the commercial intercourse between nations, and parts of nations, in all its branches, and is regulated by prescribing rules for carrying on that intercourse. The mind can scarcely conceive a system for regulating commerce between nations, which shall exclude all laws concerning navigation, which shall be silent on the admission of the vessels of the one nation into the ports of the other, and be confined to prescribing rules for the conduct of individuals, in the actual employment of buying and selling, or of barter.

If commerce does not include navigation, the government of the Union has no direct power over that subject, and can make no law prescribing what shall constitute American vessels, or requiring that they shall be navigated by American seamen. Yet this power has been exercised from the commencement of the government, has been exercised with the consent of all, and has been understood by all to be a commercial regulation. All America understands, and has uniformly understood, the word "commerce," to comprehend navigation. It was so understood, and must have been so understood, when the constitution was framed. The power over commerce, including navigation, was one of the primary objects for which the people of America adopted their government, and must have been contemplated in forming it. The convention must have used the word in that sense, because all have understood it in that sense; and the attempt to restrict it comes too late....

To what commerce does this power extend? The constitution informs us, to commerce "with foreign nations, and among the several States, and with the Indian tribes."

It has, we believe, been universally admitted, that these words comprehend every species of commercial intercourse between the United States and foreign nations. No sort of trade can be carried on between this country and any other, to which this power does not extend. It has been truly said, that commerce, as the word is used in the constitution, is a unit, every part of which is indicated by the term.

If this be the admitted meaning of the word, in its application to foreign nations, it must carry the same meaning throughout the sentence, and remain a unit, unless there be some plain intelligible cause which alters it.

The subject to which the power is next applied, is to commerce "among the several States." The word "among" means intermingled with. A thing which is among others, is intermingled with them. Commerce among the States, cannot stop at the external boundary line of each State, but may be introduced into the interior.

It is not intended to say that these words comprehend that commerce, which is completely internal, which is carried on between man and man in a State, or between different parts of the same State, and which does not extend to or affect other States. Such a power would be inconvenient, and is certainly unnecessary.

Comprehensive as the word "among" is, it may very properly be restricted to that commerce which concerns more States than one. The phrase is not one which would probably have been selected to indicate the completely interior traffic of a State, because it is not an apt phrase for that purpose; and the enumeration of the particular classes of commerce, to which the power was to be extended, would not have been made, had the intention been to extend the power to every description. The enumeration presupposes something not enumerated; and that something, if we regard the language or the subject of the sentence, must be the exclusively internal commerce of a State. The genius and character of the whole government seem to be, that its action is to be applied to all the external concerns of the nation, and to those internal concerns which affect the States generally; but not to those which are completely within a particular State, which do not affect other States, and with which it is not necessary to interfere, for the purpose of executing some of the general powers of the government. The completely internal commerce of a State, then, may be considered as reserved for the State itself....

We are now arrived at the inquiry—What is this power?

It is the power to regulate; that is, to prescribe the rule by which commerce is to be governed. This power, like all others vested in Congress, is complete in itself, may be exercised to its utmost extent, and acknowledges no limitations, other than are prescribed in the constitution. These are expressed in plain terms, and do not affect the questions which arise in this case, or which have been discussed at the bar. If, as has always been understood, the sovereignty of Congress, though limited to specified objects, is plenary as to those objects, the power over commerce with foreign nations, and among the several States, is vested in Congress as absolutely as it would be in a single government, having in its constitution the same restrictions on the exercise of the power as are found in the constitution of the United States. The wisdom and the discretion of Congress, their identity with the people, and the influence which their constituents possess at elections, are, in this, as in many other instances, as that, for example, of declaring war, the sole restraints on which they have relied, to secure them from its abuse. They are the restraints on which the people must often rely solely, in all representative governments.

The power of Congress, then, comprehends navigation, within the limits of every State in the Union; so far as that navigation may be, in any manner, connected with "commerce with foreign nations, or among the several States, or with the Indian tribes." It may, of consequence, pass the jurisdictional line of New York, and act upon the very waters to which the prohibition now under consideration applies....

This opinion has been frequently expressed in this Court, and is founded, as well on the nature of the government as on the words of the constitution. In argument, however, it has been contended, that if a law passed by a State, in the exercise of its acknowledged sovereignty, comes into conflict with a law passed by Congress in pursuance of the con-stitution, they affect the subject, and each other, like equal opposing powers.

But the framers of our constitution foresaw this state of things, and provided for it, by declaring the supremacy not only of itself, but of the laws made in pursuance of it. The nullity of any act, inconsistent with the constitution, is produced by the declaration, that the constitution is the supreme law. The appropriate application of that part of the clause which confers the same supremacy on laws and treaties, is to such acts of the State Legislatures as do not transcend their powers, but, though enacted in the execution of acknowledged State powers, interfere with, or are contrary to the laws of Congress, made in pursuance of the constitution, or some treaty made under the authority of the United States. In every such case, the act of Congress, or the treaty, is supreme; and the law of the State, though enacted in the exercise of powers not controverted, must yield to it....

Powerful and ingenious minds, taking, as postulates, that the powers expressly granted to the government of the Union, are to be contracted by construction, into the narrowest possible compass, and that the original powers of the States are retained, if any possible construction will retain them, may, by a course of well digested, but refined and metaphysical reasoning, founded on these premises, explain away the constitution of our country, and leave it, a magnificent structure, indeed, to look at, but totally unfit for use. They may so entangle and perplex the understanding, as to obscure principles, which were before thought quite plain, and induce doubts where, if the mind were to pursue its own course, none would be perceived. In such a case, it is peculiarly necessary to recur to safe and fundamental principles to sustain those principles, and when sustained, to make them the tests of the arguments to be examined.

[The congressional law is found to be within Congress's Commerce Clause power, and the conflicting New York licensing scheme is therefore invalidated under the Supremacy Clause.]

MR. JUSTICE JOHNSON.

.... The "power to regulate commerce," here meant to be granted, was that power to regulate commerce which previously existed in the States. But what was that power? The States were, unquestionably, supreme.... The power of a sovereign state over commerce, therefore, amounts to nothing more than a power to limit and restrain it at pleasure. And since the power to prescribe the limits to its freedom, necessarily implies the power to determine what shall remain unrestrained, it follows, that the power must be exclusive; it can reside but in one potentate; and hence, the grant of this power [to Congress] carries with it the whole subject, leaving nothing for the State to act upon.

Review Questions and Explanations: *Gibbons*

1. What were the stakes in this case for national commercial policy? What would happen to interstate businesses if each state had the power to grant a monopoly to a home-state business?

2. Identify three types of things that Congress could regulate under Ogden's definition.

3. Identify three types of things that Congress could *not* regulate under Chief Justice Marshall's definition.

4. Justice Johnson's concurrence implies that states' power to regulate interstate commerce is entirely displaced by the grant of that power to Congress. What

does Marshall say on this point? Johnson's view has been given a narrow application in the so-called "dormant Commerce Clause" doctrine, discussed in the next chapter.

NOTE: Daniel Webster's Argument for *Gibbons*. The following is an excerpt of the oral argument presented to the Court by Gibbons' attorney, Daniel Webster. Webster was a member of Congress from 1813 until his death in 1852, mostly in the Senate (and with a hiatus to serve as Secretary of State). He was also a practicing lawyer (it was not uncommon then for members of Congress to maintain active law practices) and was viewed as one the greatest orators and litigators of his time. He argued numerous cases to the U.S. Supreme Court, including arguing *McCulloch* on behalf of the Bank. Read Webster's argument. How much have arguments about the scope of Commerce Clause power changed since John Marshall's time? (Note: this is a summary of Webster's argument written by the Supreme Court's "Reporter of Decisions," which explains why Webster is referred to in the third person.)

..... [T]he power of Congress to regulate commerce, was complete and entire, and, to a certain extent, necessarily exclusive; that the acts in question were regulations of commerce, in a most important particular; and affecting it in those respects, in which it was under the exclusive authority of Congress. He stated this first proposition guardedly. He did not mean to say that *all* regulations which might, in their operation, affect commerce, were exclusively in the power of Congress; but that *such power* as had been exercised in this case, did not remain with the States. Nothing was more complex than commerce; and in such an age as this, no words embraced a wider field than *commercial regulation*. Almost all the business and intercourse of life may be connected, incidentally, more or less, with *commercial regulations*....

It was in vain to look for a precise and exact *definition* of the powers of Congress, on several subjects. The constitution did not undertake the task of making such exact definitions. In conferring powers, it proceeded in the way of *enumeration*, stating the powers conferred, one after another, in few words; and, where the power was general, or complex in its nature, the extent of the grant must necessarily be judged of, and limited, by its object, and by the nature of the power.

Few things were better known, than the immediate causes which led to the adoption of the present constitution; and he thought nothing clearer, than that the prevailing motive was *to regulate commerce;* to rescue it from the embarrassing and destructive consequences, resulting from the legislation of so many different States, and to place it under the protection of a uniform law. The great objects were commerce and revenue; and they were objects indissolubly connected. By the confederation, diverse restrictions had been imposed on the States; but these had not been found sufficient. No State, it was true, could send or receive an embassy; nor make any treaty; nor enter into any compact with another State, or with a foreign power; nor lay duties, interfering with treaties which had been entered into by Congress. But all these were found to be far short of what the actual condition of the country. The States could still, each for itself, regulate commerce, and the consequence was, a perpetual jarring and hostility of commercial regulation.

2. The *Lochner* Era: 1880s to 1937

The following cases were decided in the Court's so-called "*Lochner* era." This era, which begin in the late 1800s and extended through 1937, has become one of the most controversial in the Court's history. The Court throughout this time period used its power to invalidate numerous laws seeking to regulate business and the economy. The Court was seen by many as improperly obstructing governmental efforts to protect workers from the negative consequences of the early industrial age and to correct market dysfunctions. Although not all such protective legislation reviewed by the Court in this era was struck down, laws setting minimum wages, maximum working hours, and imposing other worker safety requirements frequently were invalidated.

Lochner v. New York, the case for which this era is named, was a U.S. Supreme Court decision invalidating a *state* law. The mechanism often used to strike state legislation was the so-called "liberty of contract" doctrine, developed by the Court under the Due Process clause (covered in Chapter 7).[3]

In this chapter, our concern is with the Court's response to *federal* law. At the federal level, the Court used different tools to strike down regulations similar to that struck down in *Lochner*. Because Congress, unlike the states, only has those powers given to it by the Constitution, these tools involved various ways of arguing that the federal law being challenged was beyond the scope of the enumerated power under which it was enacted. In practice, this meant that the Court would frequently hold that the federal law at issue was beyond the scope of Congress's Commerce Clause power, or was otherwise prohibited by the Tenth Amendment.

Each of the cases shows a slightly different way in which "commerce among the states" was defined by the Court in this era. As a group, the cases also illustrate how a good lawyer can adapt her arguments to exploit "loopholes" — doctrinal kinks that have not yet been ironed out — in evolving areas of law. Reading these cases therefore gives you a good opportunity to develop this important lawyering skill. As you read the cases, think about how the government's argument in each case shifts slightly to take advantage of opportunities left open in the preceding case. Specifically, pay attention to the different tests the Court uses to define the scope of the Commerce Clause, and the arguments the United States makes to try to fit its defense of the statute at issue into the those tests.

Hammer also introduces the relationship between the Commerce Clause and the Tenth Amendment. Note this in your reading, but do not concern yourself too much with it just yet.

---

3. The basic idea was that the substantive component of the Due Process clause prohibited governments from interfering with the ability of people to enter into a contract on whatever terms they wanted. The *Lochner* Court used this doctrine to strike down a state law limiting to ten the number of hours per day bakers could work. The state argued that the regulation was necessary because working longer hours endangered the health of bakers by forcing them to repeatedly inhale flour and fumes common in the industrial bakeshops of the day. The Court disagreed, holding that the law unconstitutionally prevented bakers (and their employers) from entering into whatever type of contracts they saw fit.

Guided Reading Questions: *Hammer, Schechter* **and** *Carter Coal*

1. What is the test in these cases for whether an act of Congress falls within the commerce power? Why are the laws unconstitutional or constitutional in each case?

2. In *Hammer*, Congress had tried to regulate goods being shipped to markets across state lines. Why wasn't that sufficient to come within Congress's power to regulate interstate commerce?

3. In *Schechter* and *Carter Coal*, unlike in *Hammer*, the challenged laws do not purport to regulate the interstate *movement* of any goods or services. Instead, they try to regulate goods or services that may have traveled across state lines, or that affect the economy of more than one state. Why aren't those qualities of the regulated activity sufficient, to the Court, to qualify as "interstate commerce" regulation?

Hammer v. Dagenhart

247 U.S. 251 (1918)

Majority: *Day*, White (CJ), Pitney, Van Devanter, McReynolds

Dissent: *Holmes*, McKenna, Brandeis, Clarke

MR. JUSTICE DAY delivered the opinion of the Court.

A bill was filed in the United States District Court for the Western District of North Carolina by a father in his own behalf and as next friend of his two minor sons, one under the age of fourteen years and the other between the ages of fourteen and sixteen years, employees in a cotton mill at Charlotte, North Carolina, to enjoin the enforcement of the act of Congress intended to prevent interstate commerce in the products of child labor.

The District Court held the act unconstitutional and entered a decree enjoining its enforcement. This appeal brings the case here. [The Act reads as follows]:

> That no producer, manufacturer, or dealer shall ship or deliver for shipment in interstate or foreign commerce any article or commodity the product of any mine or quarry, situated in the United States, in which within thirty days prior to the time of the removal of such product therefrom children under the age of sixteen years have been employed or permitted to work, or any article or commodity the product of any mill, cannery, workshop, factory, or manufacturing establishment, situated in the United States, in which within thirty days prior to the removal of such product therefrom children under the age of fourteen years have been employed or permitted to work, or children between the ages of fourteen years and sixteen years have been employed or permitted to work more than eight hours in any day, or more than six days in any week, or after the hour of seven o'clock postmeridian, or before the hour of six o'clock antemeridian.

The controlling question for decision is: Is it within the authority of Congress in regulating commerce among the states to prohibit the transportation in interstate commerce of manufactured goods, the product of a factory in which, within thirty days prior to their removal therefrom children under the age of fourteen have been employed or permitted to work, or children between the ages of fourteen and sixteen years have been employed or permitted to work more than eight hours in any day, or more than six days in any week, or after the hour of 7 o'clock p.m., or before the hour of 6 o'clock a.m.?

The power essential to the passage of this act, the government contends, is found in the commerce clause of the Constitution which authorizes Congress to regulate commerce with foreign nations and among the states.

In Gibbons v Ogden, Chief Justice Marshall, speaking for this court, and defining the extent and nature of the commerce power, said, 'It is the power to regulate; that is, to prescribe the rule by which commerce is to be governed.' In other words, the power is one to control the means by which commerce is carried on, which is directly the contrary of the assumed right to forbid commerce from moving and thus destroying it as to particular commodities. But it is insisted that adjudged cases in this court establish the doctrine that the power to regulate given to Congress incidentally includes the authority to prohibit the movement of ordinary commodities and therefore that the subject is not open for discussion. The cases demonstrate the contrary. They rest upon the character of the particular subjects dealt with and the fact that the scope of governmental authority, state or national, possessed over them is such that the authority to prohibit is as to them but the exertion of the power to regulate.

The first of these cases is Champion v. Ames, the so-called Lottery Case, in which it was held that Congress might pass a law having the effect to keep the channels of commerce free from use in the transportation of tickets used in the promotion of lottery schemes. In Hipolite Egg Co. v. United States, this court sustained the power of Congress to pass the Pure Food and Drug Act, which prohibited the introduction into the states by means of interstate commerce of impure foods and drugs. In Hoke v. United States, this court sustained the constitutionality of the so-called 'White Slave Traffic Act' (Act June 25, 1910, c. 395, 36 Stat. 825 [Comp. St. 1916, §§ 8812–8819]), whereby the transportation of a woman in interstate commerce for the purpose of prostitution was forbidden. In that case we said, having reference to the authority of Congress, under the regulatory power, to protect the channels of interstate commerce:

> If the facility of interstate transportation can be taken away from the demoralization of lotteries, the debasement of obscene literature, the contagion of diseased cattle or persons, the impurity of food and drugs, the like facility can be taken away from the systematic enticement to, and the enslavement in prostitution and debauchery of women, and, more insistently, of girls.

In Caminetti v. United States, we held that Congress might prohibit the transportation of women in interstate commerce for the purposes of debauchery and kindred purposes. In Clark Distilling Co. v. Western Maryland Railway, Co., the power of Congress over the transportation of intoxicating liquors was sustained. In the course of the opinion it was said:

> The power conferred is to regulate, and the very terms of the grant would seem to repel the contention that only prohibition of movement in interstate commerce was embraced. And the cogency of this is manifest, since if the doctrine were applied to those manifold and important subjects of interstate commerce as to which Congress from the beginning has regulated, not prohibited, the existence of government under the Constitution would be no longer possible.

And concluding the discussion which sustained the authority of the Government to prohibit the transportation of liquor in interstate commerce, the court said: "The exceptional nature of the subject here regulated is the basis upon which the exceptional power exerted must rest and affords no ground for any fear that such power may be constitutionally extended to things which it may not, consistently with the guaranties of the Constitution embrace."

In each of these instances the use of interstate transportation was necessary to the accomplishment of harmful results. In other words, although the power over interstate transportation was to regulate, that could only be accomplished by prohibiting the use of the facilities of interstate commerce to effect the evil intended.

This element is wanting in the present case. The thing intended to be accomplished by this statute is the denial of the facilities of interstate commerce to those manufacturers in the states who employ children within the prohibited ages. The act in its effect does not regulate transportation among the states, but aims to standardize the ages at which children may be employed in mining and manufacturing within the states. The goods shipped are of themselves harmless. The act permits them to be freely shipped after thirty days from the time of their removal from the factory. When offered for shipment, and before transportation begins, the labor of their production is over, and the mere fact that they were intended for interstate commerce transportation does not make their production subject to federal control under the commerce power.

Commerce "consists of intercourse and traffic ... and includes the transportation of persons and property, as well as the purchase, sale and exchange of commodities." The making of goods and the mining of coal are not commerce, nor does the fact that these things are to be afterwards shipped, or used in interstate commerce, make their production a part thereof.

Over interstate transportation, or its incidents, the regulatory power of Congress is ample, but the production of articles, intended for interstate commerce, is a matter of local regulation.... If it were otherwise, all manufacture intended for interstate shipment would be brought under federal control to the practical exclusion of the authority of the states, a result certainly not contemplated by the framers of the Constitution when they vested in Congress the authority to regulate commerce among the States.

It is further contended that the authority of Congress may be exerted to control interstate commerce in the shipment of child made goods because of the effect of the circulation of such goods in other states where the evil of this class of labor has been recognized by local legislation, and the right to thus employ child labor has been more rigorously restrained than in the state of production. In other words, that the unfair competition, thus engendered, may be controlled by closing the channels of interstate commerce to manufacturers in those states where the local laws do not meet what Congress deems to be the more just standard of other states.

There is no power vested in Congress to require the states to exercise their police power so as to prevent possible unfair competition. Many causes may co-operate to give one state, by reason of local laws or conditions, an economic advantage over others. The commerce clause was not intended to give to Congress a general authority to equalize such conditions. In some of the states laws have been passed fixing minimum wages for women, in others the local law regulates the hours of labor of women in various employments. Business done in such states may be at an economic disadvantage when compared with states which have no such regulations; surely, this fact does not give Congress the power to deny transportation in interstate commerce to those who carry on business where the hours of labor and the rate of compensation for women have not been fixed by a standard in use in other states and approved by Congress.

The grant of power of Congress over the subject of interstate commerce was to enable it to regulate such commerce, and not to give it authority to control the states in their exercise of the police power over local trade and manufacture.

The grant of authority over a purely federal matter was not intended to destroy the local power always existing and carefully reserved to the states in the Tenth Amendment to the Constitution....

In interpreting the Constitution it must never be forgotten that the nation is made up of states to which are entrusted the powers of local government. And to them and to the people the powers not expressly delegated to the national government are reserved. The power of the states to regulate their purely internal affairs by such laws as seem wise to the local authority is inherent and has never been surrendered to the general government. To sustain this statute would not be in our judgment a recognition of the lawful exertion of congressional authority over interstate commerce, but would sanction an invasion by the federal power of the control of a matter purely local in its character, and over which no authority has been delegated to Congress in conferring the power to regulate commerce among the states.

We have neither authority nor disposition to question the motives of Congress in enacting this legislation. The purposes intended must be attained consistently with con-stitutional limitations and not by an invasion of the powers of the states. This court has no more important function than that which devolves upon it the obligation to preserve inviolate the constitutional limitations upon the exercise of authority federal and state to the end that each may continue to discharge, harmoniously with the other, the duties entrusted to it by the Constitution.

In our view the necessary effect of this act is, by means of a prohibition against the movement in interstate commerce of ordinary commercial commodities to regulate the hours of labor of children in factories and mines within the states, a purely state authority. Thus the act in a two-fold sense is repugnant to the Constitution. It not only transcends the authority delegated to Congress over commerce but also exerts a power as to a purely local matter to which the federal authority does not extend. The far reaching result of upholding the act cannot be more plainly indicated than by pointing out that if Congress can thus regulate matters entrusted to local authority by prohibition of the movement of commodities in interstate commerce, all freedom of commerce will be at an end, and the power of the states over local matters may be eliminated, and thus our system of government be practically destroyed.

For these reasons we hold that this law exceeds the constitutional authority of Congress. It follows that the decree of the District Court must be affirmed.

MR. JUSTICE HOLMES, dissenting.

The single question in this case is whether Congress has power to prohibit the shipment in interstate or foreign commerce of any product of a cotton mill situated in the United States, in which within thirty days before the removal of the product children under fourteen have been employed, or children between fourteen and sixteen have been employed more than eight hours in a day, or more than six days in any week, or between seven in the evening and six in the morning. The objection urged against the power is that the States have exclusive control over their methods of production and that Congress cannot meddle with them, and taking the proposition in the sense of direct intermeddling I agree to it and suppose that no one denies it. But if an act is within the powers specifically conferred upon Congress, it seems to me that it is not made any less constitutional because of the indirect effects that it may have, however obvious it may be that it will have those effects, and that we are not at liberty upon such grounds to hold it void.

The first step in my argument is to make plain what no one is likely to dispute — that the statute in question is within the power expressly given to Congress if considered only as to its immediate effects and that if invalid it is so only upon some collateral ground.

The statute confines itself to prohibiting the carriage of certain goods in interstate or foreign commerce. Congress is given power to regulate such commerce in unqualified terms. It would not be argued today that the power to regulate does not include the power to prohibit. Regulation means the prohibition of something, and when interstate commerce is the matter to be regulated I cannot doubt that the regulation may prohibit any part of such commerce that Congress sees fit to forbid....

But I had thought that the propriety of the exercise of a power admitted to exist in some cases was for the consideration of Congress alone and that this Court always had disavowed the right to intrude its judgment upon questions of policy or morals. It is not for this Court to pronounce when prohibition is necessary to regulation if it ever may be necessary—to say that it is permissible as against strong drink but not as against the product of ruined lives.

Figure 1.2. Commerce Power v. "General Police Power"

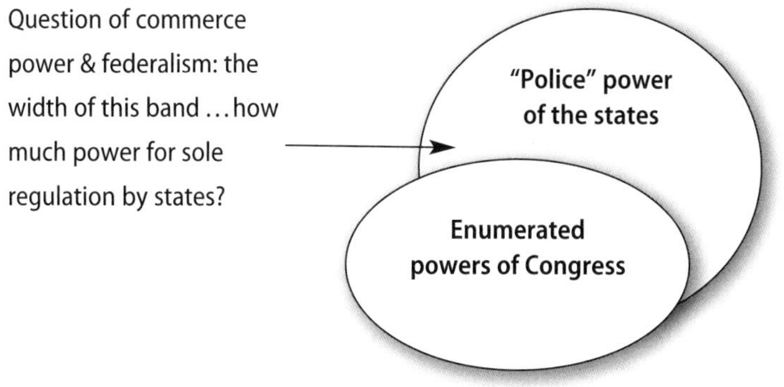

Question of commerce power & federalism: the width of this band ... how much power for sole regulation by states?

"Police" power of the states

Enumerated powers of Congress

A.L.A. Schechter Poultry Corp. v. United States
295 U.S. 495 (1935)

Unanimous decision: *Hughes* (CJ), Van Devanter, McReynolds, Brandeis, Sutherland, Butler, Roberts

Concurrence: *Cardozo*, Stone (omitted)

MR. CHIEF JUSTICE HUGHES delivered the opinion of the court.

New York City is the largest live poultry market in the United States. Ninety-six per cent of the live poultry there marketed comes from other states. Three-fourths of this amount arrives by rail and is consigned to commission men or receivers. Most of these freight shipments (about 75 per cent.) come in at the Manhattan Terminal of the New York Central Railroad, and the remainder at one of the four terminals in New Jersey serving New York City. The commission men transact by far the greater part of the business on a commission basis, representing the shippers as agents, and remitting to them the proceeds of sale, less commissions, freight, and handling charges. Otherwise, they buy for their own account. They sell to slaughterhouse operators who are also called marketmen.

The defendants are slaughterhouse operators of the latter class. A.L.A. Schechter Poultry Corporation and Schechter Live Poultry Market are corporations conducting wholesale poultry slaughterhouse markets in Brooklyn, New York City. Joseph Schechter operated the latter corporation and also guaranteed the credits of the former corporation, which was operated by Martin, Alex, and Aaron Schechter. Defendants ordinarily purchase their live poultry from commission men at the West Washington Market in New York City or at the railroad terminals serving the city, but occasionally they purchase from commission men in Philadelphia. They buy the poultry for slaughter and resale. After the poultry is trucked to their slaughterhouse markets in Brooklyn, it is there sold, usually within twenty-four hours, to retail poultry dealers and butchers who sell directly to consumers. The poultry purchased from defendants is immediately slaughtered, prior to delivery, by shochtim in defendants' employ. Defendants do not sell poultry in interstate commerce.

The "Live Poultry Code" was promulgated under section 3 of the National Industrial Recovery Act.... The code fixes the number of hours for workdays. It provides that no employee, with certain exceptions, shall be permitted to work in excess of forty hours in any one week, and that no employees, save as stated, "shall be paid in any pay period less than at the rate of fifty (50) cents per hour." The article containing "general labor provisions" prohibits the employment of any person under 16 years of age, and declares that employees shall have the right of "collective bargaining" and freedom of choice with respect to labor organizations.... These provisions relate to the hours and wages of those employed by defendants in their slaughterhouses in Brooklyn and to the sales there made to retail dealers and butchers.

Were these transactions "in" interstate commerce? Much is made of the fact that almost all the poultry coming to New York is sent there from other states. But the code provisions, as here applied, do not concern the transportation of the poultry from other states to New York, or the transactions of the commission men or others to whom it is consigned, or the sales made by such consignees to defendants. When defendants had made their purchases, whether at the West Washington Market in New York City or at the railroad terminals serving the city, or elsewhere, the poultry was trucked to their slaughterhouses in Brooklyn for local disposition. The interstate transactions in relation to that poultry then ended. Defendants held the poultry at their slaughterhouse markets for slaughter and local sale to retail dealers and butchers who in turn sold directly to consumers. Neither the slaughtering nor the sales by defendants were transactions in interstate commerce.

The undisputed facts thus afford no warrant for the argument that the poultry handled by defendants at their slaughterhouse markets was in a "current" or "flow" of interstate commerce, and was thus subject to congressional regulation. The mere fact that there may be a constant flow of commodities into a state does not mean that the flow continues after the property has arrived and has become commingled with the mass of property within the state and is there held solely for local disposition and use. So far as the poultry here in question is concerned, the flow in interstate commerce had ceased. The poultry had come to a permanent rest within the state. It was not held, used, or sold by defendants in relation to any further transactions in interstate commerce and was not destined for transportation to other states. Hence decisions which deal with a stream of interstate commerce—where goods come to rest within a state temporarily and are later to go forward in interstate commerce—and with the regulations of transactions involved in that practical continuity of movement, are not applicable here....

In determining how far the federal government may go in controlling intrastate transactions upon the ground that they "affect" interstate commerce, there is a necessary and well-established distinction between direct and indirect effects. The precise line can be drawn only as individual cases arise, but the distinction is clear in principle. Direct effects are illustrated by the railroad cases we have cited, as, e.g., the effect of failure to use prescribed safety appliances on railroads which are the highways of both interstate and intrastate commerce, injury to an employee engaged in interstate transportation by the negligence of an employee engaged in an intrastate movement, the fixing of rates for intrastate transportation which unjustly discriminate against interstate commerce. But where the effect of intrastate transactions upon interstate commerce is merely indirect, such transactions remain within the domain of state power. If the commerce clause were construed to reach all enterprises and transactions which could be said to have an indirect effect upon interstate commerce, the federal authority would embrace practically all the activities of the people, and the authority of the state over its domestic concerns would exist only by sufferance of the federal government.

Carter v. Carter Coal Co.

298 U.S. 238 (1936)

Majority: *Sutherland*, Butler, McReynolds, Roberts, Van Devanter

Concurrence in part, dissent in part: *Hughes* (CJ) (omitted)

Dissent: *Cardozo*, Brandeis, Stone

MR. JUSTICE SUTHERLAND delivered the opinion of the Court.

The purposes of the "Bituminous Coal Conservation Act of 1935," involved in these suits, as declared by the title, are to stabilize the bituminous coal-mining industry and promote its interstate commerce; to provide for co-operative marketing of bituminous coal; to levy a tax on such coal and provide for a drawback under certain conditions; to declare the production, distribution, and use of such coal to be affected with a national public interest; to conserve the national resources of such coal; to provide for the general welfare, and for other purposes. The constitutional validity of the act is challenged in each of the suits....

Section 1 [of the Act] is a detailed assertion of circumstances thought to justify the act. It declares that the mining and distribution of bituminous coal throughout the United States by the producer are affected with a national public interest; and that the service of such coal in relation to industrial activities, transportation facilities, health and comfort of the people, conservation by controlled production and economical mining and marketing, maintenance of just and rational relations between the public, owners, producers, and employees, the right of the public to constant and adequate supplies of coal at reasonable prices, and the general welfare of the Nation, require that the bituminous coal industry should be regulated as the act provides.

Section 1, among other things, further declares that the production and distribution by producers of such coal bear upon and directly affect interstate commerce, and render regulation of production and distribution imperative for the protection of such commerce; that certain features connected with the production, distribution, and marketing have led to waste of the national coal resources, disorganization of interstate commerce in such coal, and burdening and obstructing interstate commerce therein; that practices prevailing in the production of such coal directly affect interstate commerce and require regulation for the protection of that commerce; and that the right of mine workers to organize and collectively bargain for wages, hours of labor, and conditions of employment should be guaranteed in order to prevent constant wage cutting and disparate labor costs detrimental to fair interstate competition, and in order to avoid obstructions to interstate commerce that recur in industrial disputes over labor relations at the mines....

Without repeating the long and involved provisions with regard to the fixing of minimum prices, it is enough to say that the act confers the power to fix the minimum price of coal at each and every coal mine in the United States, with such price variations as the board may deem necessary and proper. There is also a provision authorizing the commission, when deemed necessary in the public interest, to establish maximum prices in order to protect the consumer against unreasonably high prices....

The ruling and firmly established principle is that the powers which the general government may exercise are only those specifically enumerated in the Constitution, and such implied powers as are necessary and proper to carry into effect the enumerated powers. Whether the end sought to be attained by an act of Congress is legitimate is wholly a matter of constitutional power and not at all of legislative discretion. Legislative congressional discretion begins with the choice of means and ends with the adoption of methods and details to carry the delegated powers into effect. The distinction between these two things — power and discretion — is not only very plain but very important. For while the powers are rigidly limited to the enumerations of the Constitution, the means which may be employed to carry the powers into effect are not restricted, save that they must be appropriate, plainly adapted to the end, and not prohibited by, but consistent with, the letter and spirit of the Constitution. McCulloch v. Maryland. Thus, it may be said that to a constitutional end many ways are open; but to an end not within the terms of the Constitution, all ways are closed.

The proposition, often advanced and as often discredited, that the power of the federal government inherently extends to purposes affecting the Nation as a whole with which the states severally cannot deal or cannot adequately deal, and the related notion that Congress, entirely apart from those powers delegated by the Constitution, may enact laws to promote the general welfare, have never been accepted but always definitely rejected by this court. Mr. Justice Story, as early as 1816, laid down the cardinal rule, which has ever since been followed — that the general government "can claim no powers which are not granted to it by the constitution, and the powers actually granted, must be such as are expressly given, or given by necessary implication." Martin v. Hunter's Lessee. In the Framers Convention, the proposal to confer a general power akin to that just discussed was included in Mr. Randolph's resolutions, the sixth of which, among other things, declared that the National Legislature ought to enjoy the legislative rights vested in Congress by the Confederation, and "moreover to legislate in all cases to which the separate States are incompetent, or in which the harmony of the United States may be interrupted by the exercise of individual Legislation." The convention, however, declined to confer upon Congress power in such general terms; instead of which it carefully limited the powers which it thought wise to intrust to Congress by specifying them, thereby denying all others not granted expressly or by necessary implication....

The general rule with regard to the respective powers of the national and the state governments under the Constitution is not in doubt. The states were before the Constitution; and, consequently, their legislative powers antedated the Constitution. Those who framed and those who adopted that instrument meant to carve from the general mass of legislative powers, then possessed by the states, only such portions as it was thought wise to confer upon the federal government; and in order that there should be no uncertainty in respect of what was taken and what was left, the national powers of legislation were not aggregated but enumerated — with the result that what was not embraced by the enumeration remained vested in the states without change or impairment.... And since every addition to the national legislative power to some extent detracts from or invades the power of the states, it is of vital moment that, in order to preserve the fixed balance intended by the Constitution, the powers of the general government be not so extended as to embrace any not within the express terms of the several grants or the implications necessarily to be drawn therefrom....

The determination of the Framers Convention and the ratifying conventions to preserve complete and unimpaired state self-government in all matters not committed to the general government is one of the plainest facts which emerges from the history of their deliberations. And adherence to that determination is incumbent equally upon the federal government and the states. State powers can neither be appropriated on the one hand nor abdicated on the other. As this court said in Texas v. White, "The preservation of the States, and the maintenance of their governments, are as much within the design and care of the Constitution as the preservation of the Union and the maintenance of the National government. The Constitution, in all its provisions, looks to an indestructible Union, composed of indestructible States." Every journey to a forbidden end begins with the first step; and the danger of such a step by the federal government in the direction of taking over the powers of the states is that the end of the journey may find the states so despoiled of their powers, or—what may amount to the same thing—so relieved of the responsibilities which possession of the powers necessarily enjoins, as to reduce them to little more than geographical subdivisions of the national domain. It is safe to say that if, when the Constitution was under consideration, it had been thought that any such danger lurked behind its plain words, it would never have been ratified....

We have set forth, perhaps at unnecessary length, the foregoing principles, because it seemed necessary to do so in order to demonstrate that the general purposes which the act recites, and which, therefore, unless the recitals be disregarded, Congress undertook to achieve, are beyond the power of Congress except so far, and only so far, as they may be realized by an exercise of some specific power granted by the Constitution. Proceeding by a process of elimination, which it is not necessary to follow in detail, we shall find no grant of power which authorizes Congress to legislate in respect of these general purposes unless it be found in the commerce clause—and this we now consider....

Since the validity of the act depends upon whether it is a regulation of interstate commerce, the nature and extent of the power conferred upon Congress by the commerce clause becomes the determinative question in this branch of the case.... The function to be exercised is that of regulation. The thing to be regulated is the commerce described. In exercising the authority conferred by this clause of the Constitution, Congress is powerless to regulate anything which is not commerce, as it is powerless to do anything about commerce which is not regulation....

But [the Act] now under review declares that all production and distribution of bituminous coal "bear upon and directly affect its interstate commerce"; and that regulation thereof is imperative for the protection of such commerce. The contention of the government is that the labor provisions of the act may be sustained in that view.

That the production of every commodity intended for interstate sale and transportation has some effect upon interstate commerce may be, if it has not already been, freely granted; and we are brought to the final and decisive inquiry, whether here that effect is direct, as [the preamble to the Act] recites, or indirect. The distinction is not formal, but substantial in the highest degree, as we pointed out in Schechter: "If the commerce clause were construed," we there said, "to reach all enterprises and transactions which could be said to have an indirect effect upon interstate commerce, the federal authority would embrace practically all the activities of the people, and the authority of the state over its domestic concerns would exist only by sufferance of the federal government. Indeed, on such a theory, even the development of the state's commercial facilities would be subject to federal control." It was also pointed out that "the distinction between direct and indirect effects of intrastate transactions upon interstate commerce must be recognized as a fundamental one, essential to the maintenance of our constitutional system."

Whether the effect of a given activity or condition is direct or indirect is not always easy to determine. The word "direct" implies that the activity or condition invoked or blamed shall operate proximately—not mediately, remotely, or collaterally—to produce the effect. It connotes the absence of an efficient intervening agency or condition. And the extent of the effect bears no logical relation to its character. The distinction between a direct and an indirect effect turns, not upon the magnitude of either the cause or the effect, but entirely upon the manner in which the effect has been brought about. If the production by one man of a single ton of coal intended for interstate sale and shipment, and actually so sold and shipped, affects interstate commerce indirectly, the effect does not become direct by multiplying the tonnage, or increasing the number of men employed, or adding to the expense or complexities of the business, or by all combined. It is quite true that rules of law are sometimes qualified by considerations of degree, as the government argues. But the matter of degree has no bearing upon the question here, since that question is not—What is the extent of the local activity or condition, or the extent of the effect produced upon interstate commerce? But—What is the relation between the activity or condition and the effect?

Much stress is put upon the evils which come from the struggle between employers and employees over the matter of wages, working conditions, the right of collective bargaining, etc., and the resulting strikes, curtailment, and irregularity of production and effect on prices; and it is insisted that interstate commerce is greatly affected thereby. But, in addition to what has just been said, the conclusive answer is that the evils are all local evils over which the federal government has no legislative control. The relation of employer and employee is a local relation. At common law, it is one of the domestic relations. The wages are paid for the doing of local work. Working conditions are obviously local conditions. The employees are not engaged in or about commerce, but exclusively in producing a commodity. And the controversies and evils, which it is the object of the act to regulate and minimize, are local controversies and evils affecting local work undertaken to accomplish that local result. Such effect as they may have upon commerce, however extensive it may be, is secondary and indirect. An increase in the greatness of the effect adds to its importance. It does not alter its character.

MR. JUSTICE CARDOZO (dissenting):

.... Mining and agriculture and manufacture are not interstate commerce considered by themselves, yet their relation to that commerce may be such that for the protection of the one there is need to regulate the other. Sometimes it is said that the relation must be "direct" to bring that power into play. In many circumstances such a description will be sufficiently precise to meet the needs of the occasion. But a great principle of constitutional law is not susceptible of comprehensive statement in an adjective.... At times, as in [*Schechter*], the waves of causation will have radiated so far that their undulatory motion, if discernible at all, will be too faint or obscure, too broken by crosscurrents, to be heeded by the law. In such circumstances the holding is not directed at prices or wages considered in the abstract, but at prices or wages in particular conditions. The relation may be tenuous or the opposite according to the facts. Always the setting of the facts is to be viewed if one would know the closeness of the tie. Perhaps, if one group of adjectives is to be chosen in preference to another, "intimate" and "remote" will be found to be as good as any. At all events, "direct" and "indirect," even if accepted as sufficient, must not be read too narrowly.... [The] words have been interpreted with suppleness of adaptation and flexibility of meaning. The power is as broad as the need that evokes it....

All this may be said, and with equal, if not greater force, of the conditions and practices in the bituminous coal industry, not only at the enactment of this statute in August, 1935, but for many years before. Overproduction was at a point where free competition had been degraded into anarchy. Prices had been cut so low that profit had become impossible for all except the lucky handful. Wages came down along with prices and with profits. There were strikes, at times nation-wide in extent, at other times spreading over broad areas and many mines, with the accompaniment of violence and bloodshed and misery and bitter feeling. The sordid tale is unfolded in many a document and treatise. During the twenty-three years between 1913 and 1935, there were nineteen investigations or hearings by Congress or by specially created commissions with reference to conditions in the coal mines. The hope of betterment was faint unless the industry could be subjected to the compulsion of a code. In the weeks immediately preceding the passage of this Act the country was threatened once more with a strike of ominous proportions. The plight of the industry was not merely a menace to owners and to mine workers: it was and had long been a menace to the public, deeply concerned in a steady and uniform supply of a fuel so vital to the national economy.

Congress was not condemned to inaction in the face of price wars and wage wars so pregnant with disaster. Commerce had been choked and burdened; its normal flow had been diverted from one state to another; there had been bankruptcy and waste and ruin alike for capital and for labor.... After making every allowance for difference of opinion as to the most efficient cure, the student of the subject is confronted with the indisputable truth that there were ills to be corrected, and ills that had a direct relation to the maintenance of commerce among the states without friction or diversion. An evil existing, and also the power to correct it, the lawmakers were at liberty to use their own discretion in the selection of the means.

Review Questions and Explanations: *Hammer, Schechter* and *Carter Coal*

1. Are there some subjects of regulation that the *Lochner*-era Court views as off-limits to regulation by Congress — even if they might qualify as "interstate commerce"? If so, what is the constitutional basis for such a limitation?

2. Each of these cases seems to be based on two possibly overlapping arguments: one about whether the subject of regulation is interstate commerce and the other about whether the Tenth Amendment bars the regulation even if it might otherwise fall within the commerce power. Try to identify these separate arguments.

3. Are you persuaded that industries like "manufacturing" and "mining" are "local" activities that do not qualify as interstate commerce, notwithstanding their impact on the interstate economy?

4. How might low-cost child labor in a state with no restrictions on child labor affect the economies of neighboring states that prohibited child labor?

Exercises: The *Lochner* Era

1. With one or more classmates, brainstorm to come up with a list of at least five federal laws that regulate economic activities in ways that you think are important (e.g., federal minimum wage law — you can put that on your list if you like). Once you have your list, consider each law separately and analyze whether it would withstand a Commerce Clause challenge under *Hammer, Schechter,* and *Carter Coal.*

2. Apply Chief Justice Marshall's Necessary and Proper clause reasoning to *Carter Coal.* Then consider the pros and cons of each approach examined so far. Which do you prefer? Be prepared to defend your preference in class.

3. The New Deal Turnaround and the Reaction to the *Lochner* Era: 1937 to 1995

The Court's proactive use of judicial review to restrain the government's efforts to mediate the effect of the industrial revolution ended with a bang during the Great Depression. President Franklin D. Roosevelt, frustrated by the Court's repeated invalidation of New Deal legislation, began aggressively attacking the Court in his speeches and public statements. In February of 1937 he sent his famous "Court-packing" plan (the Judicial Reorganization Bill) to Congress. The plan would have increased the size of the Supreme Court by creating one vacancy for every sitting justice over the age of 70. The plan received decidedly mixed reviews in Congress, but it did put the issue of judicial interference with economic regulation squarely on the political table. The justices seemed to respond: later that year, the Court issued a series of decisions signaling that its active resistance to the New Deal was over.

Historians dispute the impact of the Court-packing plan on the Court's decision to stop engaging in vigorous oversight of economic regulation. Whether attributable to the Court-packing plan or not, however, the battle over congressional power seemed to be over. The cases you are about to read demonstrate this more relaxed judicial attitude to economic regulation. *Darby* and *Wickard* present traditional economic regulation of the type routinely upheld since 1937. When reading these cases, try to ascertain what restrictions — if any — the Court is imposing on Congress's Commerce Clause power.

The second set of cases, *Heart of Atlanta Motel* and *Katzenbach,* introduce a different type of problem: congressional power to enact civil rights legislation. For reasons that will be examined more fully below, federal civil rights legislation has frequently been enacted under Congress's Commerce Clause authority rather than under the authority granted by the Civil Rights Amendments (the Thirteenth, Fourteenth and Fifteenth Amendments). *Heart of Atlanta Motel* and *Katzenbach* explore this issue. When reading these cases, consider how the Civil Rights Movement may have influenced the Court in these cases. Should the Court be sensitive to social movements like the Civil Rights Movement, or should it ignore the social and political consequences of its decisions? Is there an appropriate middle ground in between these two options?

While reading these cases, also pay particular attention to the way the Court is treating Congress's factual findings. Congressional findings are the way Congress articulates the facts it relied on when developing a particular piece of legislation. One of the important questions in this area of law is the extent to which the Court should defer to Congress in regard to such findings. These cases merely introduce you to this idea; the question of deference to factual findings becomes more important in sub-section 4 ("Current Doctrine").

Although we have placed the following cases in the third of four "eras" of the Court's Commerce Clause jurisprudence, and prior to the section called "Current doctrine," it is important to note that the cases in this period all remain good law. The current Court has taken pains to make its current Commerce Clause decisions consistent with these cases, or at least to harmonize them. As you will see, however, the justices sometimes disagree over the precise meaning of these precedents—especially *Wickard v. Filburn*.

Guided Reading Questions: *Jones & Laughlin, Darby, Wickard*

1. In what way does the Court in *Jones & Laughlin* depart from the *Lochner*-era cases?

2. Do *Darby* and *Wickard* suggest a broader, more lenient view, toward congressional assertions of commerce power than that implicit in *Jones & Laughlin*?

3. What is the new test applied by the Court for determining whether legislation is within the commerce power of Congress?

4. What if anything do these cases tell us about whether there are subjects of legislation—such as employment or manufacturing—that are reserved exclusively for state regulation under the Tenth Amendment?

National Labor Relations Board v. Jones & Laughlin Steel Corp.

301 U.S. 1 (1937)

Majority: *Hughes* (CJ), Brandeis, Stone, Roberts, Cardozo

Dissent: *McReynolds*, Van Devanter, Sutherland, Butler (omitted)

MR. CHIEF JUSTICE HUGHES delivered the opinion of the Court.

.... The scheme of the National Labor Relations Act—which is too long to be quoted in full—may be briefly stated. The first section sets forth findings with respect to the injury to commerce resulting from the denial by employers of the right of employees to organize and from the refusal of employers to accept the procedure of collective bargaining. There follows a declaration that it is the policy of the United States to eliminate these causes of obstruction to the free flow of commerce. The act then defines the terms it uses, including the terms "commerce" and "affecting commerce." ...

The respondent argues that the act is in reality a regulation of labor relations and not of interstate commerce [and] that the act can have no application to the respondent's relations with its production employees because they are not subject to regulation by the federal government....

The facts as to the nature and scope of the business of the Jones & Laughlin Steel Corporation have been found by the Labor Board, and, so far as they are essential to the determination of this controversy, they are not in dispute.... It manufactures and distributes a widely diversified line of steel and pig iron, being the fourth largest producer of steel in the United States. With its subsidiaries—nineteen in number—it is a completely integrated enterprise, owning and operating ore, coal and limestone properties, lake and river transportation facilities and terminal railroads located at its manufacturing plants. It owns or controls mines in Michigan and Minnesota. It operates four ore steamships on the Great

Lakes, used in the transportation of ore to its factories. It owns coal mines in Pennsylvania. It operates towboats and steam barges used in carrying coal to its factories. It owns limestone properties in various places in Pennsylvania and West Virginia. It owns the Monongahela connecting railroad which connects the plants of the Pittsburgh works and forms an interconnection with the Pennsylvania, New York Central and Baltimore & Ohio Railroad systems. It owns the Aliquippa & Southern Railroad Company, which connects the Aliquippa works with the Pittsburgh & Lake Erie, part of the New York Central system.

Much of its product is shipped to its warehouses in Chicago, Detroit, Cincinnati and Memphis—to the last two places by means of its own barges and transportation equipment. In Long Island City, New York, and in New Orleans it operates structural steel fabricating shops in connection with the warehousing of semifinished materials sent from its works. Through one of its wholly-owned subsidiaries it owns, leases, and operates stores, warehouses, and yards for the distribution of equipment and supplies for drilling and operating oil and gas wells and for pipe lines, refineries and pumping stations. It has sales offices in twenty cities in the United States and a wholly-owned subsidiary which is devoted exclusively to distributing its product in Canada. Approximately 75 per cent. of its product is shipped out of Pennsylvania....

To carry on the activities of the entire steel industry, 33,000 men mine ore, 44,000 men mine coal, 4,000 men quarry limestone, 16,000 men manufacture coke, 343,000 men manufacture steel, and 83,000 men transport its product. Respondent has about 10,000 employees in its Aliquippa plant, which is located in a community of about 30,000 persons....

The act is challenged in its entirety as an attempt to regulate all industry, thus invading the reserved powers of the States over their local concerns. It is asserted that the references in the act to interstate and foreign commerce are colorable at best; that the act is not a true regulation of such commerce or of matters which directly affect it, but on the contrary has the fundamental object of placing under the compulsory supervision of the federal government all industrial labor relations within the nation....

The critical words of this provision, prescribing the limits of the Board's authority in dealing with the labor practices, are "affecting commerce." The act specifically defines the "commerce" ... "The term 'commerce' means trade, traffic, commerce, transportation, or communication among the several States, or between the District of Columbia or any Territory of the United States and any State or other Territory, or between any foreign country and any State, Territory, or the District of Columbia, or within the District of Columbia or any Territory, or between points in the same State but through any other State or any Territory or the District of Columbia or any foreign country."

There can be no question that the commerce thus contemplated by the act (aside from that within a Territory or the District of Columbia) is interstate and foreign commerce in the constitutional sense. The act also defines the term "affecting commerce" ... "The term 'affecting commerce' means in commerce, or burdening or obstructing commerce or the free flow of commerce, or having led or tending to lead to a labor dispute burdening or obstructing commerce or the free flow of commerce."

This definition is one of exclusion as well as inclusion. The grant of authority to the Board does not purport to extend to the relationship between all industrial employees and employers. Its terms do not impose collective bargaining upon all industry regardless of effects upon interstate or foreign commerce. It purports to reach only what may be deemed to burden or obstruct that commerce and, thus qualified, it must be construed as contemplating the exercise of control within constitutional bounds. It is a familiar principle that acts which directly burden or obstruct interstate or foreign commerce, or its free flow, are within the reach of the congressional power. Acts having that effect are not rendered immune because they grow out of labor disputes....

Respondent says that, whatever may be said of employees engaged in interstate commerce, the industrial relations and activities in the manufacturing department of respondent's enterprise are not subject to federal regulation. The argument rests upon the proposition that manufacturing in itself is not commerce....

We do not find it necessary to determine whether these features of defendant's business dispose of the asserted analogy to the "stream of commerce" cases. The instances in which that metaphor has been used are but particular, and not exclusive, illustrations of the protective power which the government invokes in support of the present act. The congressional authority to protect interstate commerce from burdens and obstructions is not limited to transactions which can be deemed to be an essential part of a "flow" of interstate or foreign commerce. Burdens and obstructions may be due to injurious action springing from other sources. The fundamental principle is that the power to regulate commerce is the power to enact "all appropriate legislation" for its "protection or advancement"; to adopt measures "to promote its growth and insure its safety"; "to foster, protect, control, and restrain." That power is plenary and may be exerted to protect interstate commerce "no matter what the source of the dangers which threaten it." ... Although activities may be intrastate in character when separately considered, if they have such a close and substantial relation to interstate commerce that their control is essential or appropriate to protect that commerce from burdens and obstructions, Congress cannot be denied the power to exercise that control. Schechter Corporation v. United States.

Undoubtedly the scope of this power must be considered in the light of our dual system of government and may not be extended so as to embrace effects upon interstate commerce so indirect and remote that to embrace them, in view of our complex society, would effectually obliterate the distinction between what is national and what is local and create a completely centralized government. The question is necessarily one of degree. As the Court said in Board of Trade v. City of Chicago, repeating what had been said in Stafford v. Wallace, supra: "Whatever amounts to more or less constant practice, and threatens to obstruct or unduly to burden the freedom of interstate commerce is within the regulatory power of Congress under the commerce clause, and it is primarily for Congress to consider and decide the fact of the danger and to meet it." ... [In] the first Coronado Case the Court also said that "if Congress deems certain recurring practices though not really part of interstate commerce, likely to obstruct, restrain or burden it, it has the power to subject them to national supervision and restraint." ...

In the Schechter Case, we found that the effect there was so remote as to be beyond the federal power. To find "immediacy or directness" there was to find it "almost everywhere," a result inconsistent with the maintenance of our federal system. In the Carter Case, supra, the Court was of the opinion that the provisions of the statute relating to production were invalid upon several grounds,—that there was improper delegation of legislative power, and that the requirements not only went beyond any sustainable measure of protection of interstate commerce but were also inconsistent with due process. These cases are not controlling here.

Giving full weight to respondent's contention with respect to a break in the complete continuity of the "stream of commerce" by reason of respondent's manufacturing operations, the fact remains that the stoppage of those operations by industrial strife would have a most serious effect upon interstate commerce. In view of respondent's far-flung activities, it is idle to say that the effect would be indirect or remote. It is obvious that it would be immediate and might be catastrophic. We are asked to shut our eyes to the plainest facts of our national life and to deal with the question of direct and indirect effects in an intellectual vacuum. Because there may be but indirect and remote effects upon interstate commerce in connection with a host of local enterprises throughout the country, it does not follow that other industrial activities do not have such a close and intimate relation to interstate commerce as to make the presence of industrial strife a matter of the most urgent national concern. When industries organize themselves on a national scale, making their relation to interstate commerce the dominant factor in their activities, how can it be maintained that their industrial labor relations constitute a forbidden field into which Congress may not enter when it is necessary to protect interstate commerce from the paralyzing consequences of industrial war? We have often said that interstate commerce itself is a practical conception. It is equally true that interferences with that commerce must be appraised by a judgment that does not ignore actual experience....

The steel industry is one of the great basic industries of the United States, with ramifying activities affecting interstate commerce at every point.... It is not necessary again to detail the facts as to respondent's enterprise. Instead of being beyond the pale, we think that it presents in a most striking way the close and intimate relation which a manufacturing industry may have to interstate commerce and we have no doubt that Congress had constitutional authority to safeguard the right of respondent's employees to self-organization and freedom in the choice of representatives for collective bargaining.

By the time of the next two decisions, the Court was dominated by pro-New Deal justices, most of whom had been appointed by President Franklin Roosevelt. By 1941, Justice McReynolds was the only remaining member of the "four horsemen," who had dissented in *Jones & Laughlin*. He joined in the unanimous *Darby* decision, having either changed his views or given up the fight in his last days on the Court. He retired at the end of the 1940–41 term, and was replaced by James Byrnes. Thus, when *Wickard* was decided, seven of the nine Justices were Roosevelt appointees, and an eighth, Stone, was elevated from an associate justice position to the chief justiceship by Roosevelt. (All eight of those Roosevelt appointments were made after the Court-packing plan had been made public.)

United States v. Darby Lumber Co.

312 U.S. 100 (1941)

Unanimous decision: *Stone*, Hughes (CJ), McReynolds, Roberts, Black, Reed, Frankfurter, Douglas, Murphy

MR. JUSTICE STONE delivered the opinion of the Court.

[One of the principal questions in this case was whether Congress has constitutional power to prohibit the shipment in interstate commerce of lumber manufactured by employees whose wages are less than a prescribed minimum or whose weekly hours of labor at that wage are greater than a prescribed maximum.]

The Fair Labor Standards Act set up a comprehensive legislative scheme for preventing the shipment in interstate commerce of certain products and commodities produced in the United States under labor conditions as respects wages and hours which fail to conform to standards set up by the Act. Its purpose, as we judicially know from the declaration of policy in § 2(a) of the Act ... is to exclude from interstate commerce goods produced for the commerce and to prevent their production for interstate commerce, under conditions detrimental to the maintenance of the minimum standards of living necessary for health and general well-being; and to prevent the use of interstate commerce as the means of competition in the distribution of goods so produced, and as the means of spreading and perpetuating such substandard labor conditions among the workers of the several states.

The indictment charges that appellee is engaged, in the state of Georgia, in the business of acquiring raw materials, which he manufactures into finished lumber with the intent, when manufactured, to ship it in interstate commerce to customers outside the state, and that he does in fact so ship a large part of the lumber so produced....

The district court quashed the indictment in its entirety upon the broad grounds that the Act, which it interpreted as a regulation of manufacture within the states, is unconstitutional. It declared that manufacture is not interstate commerce and that the regulation by the Fair Labor Standards Act of wages and hours of employment of those engaged in the manufacture of goods which it is intended at the time of production 'may or will be' after production 'sold in interstate commerce in part or in whole' is not within the congressional power to regulate interstate commerce. The effect of the court's decision and judgment are thus to deny the power of Congress to prohibit shipment in interstate commerce of lumber produced for interstate commerce under the proscribed substandard labor conditions of wages and hours ...

Since this section is not violated unless the commodity shipped has been produced under labor conditions prohibited by § 6 and § 7, the only question arising under the commerce clause with respect to such shipments is whether Congress has the constitutional power to prohibit them.

While manufacture is not of itself interstate commerce the shipment of manufactured goods interstate is such commerce and the prohibition of such shipment by Congress is indubitably a regulation of the commerce. The power to regulate commerce is the power 'to prescribe the rule by which commerce is to be governed.' Gibbons v. Ogden. It extends not only to those regulations which aid, foster and protect the commerce, but embraces those which prohibit it.

But it is said that the present prohibition falls within the scope of none of these categories; that while the prohibition is nominally a regulation of the commerce its motive or purpose is regulation of wages and hours of persons engaged in manufacture, the control of which has been reserved to the states ...

The power of Congress over interstate commerce 'is complete in itself, may be exercised to its utmost extent, and acknowledges no limitations, other than are prescribed by the constitution.' Gibbons v. Ogden.... Congress, following its own conception of public policy concerning the restrictions which may appropriately be imposed on interstate commerce, is free to exclude from the commerce articles whose use in the states for which they are destined it may conceive to be injurious to the public health, morals or welfare, even though the state has not sought to regulate their use.... Such regulation is not a forbidden invasion of state power merely because either its motive or its consequence is to restrict the use of articles of commerce within the states of destination and is not prohibited unless by other Constitutional provisions. It is no objection to the assertion of the power to regulate interstate commerce that its exercise is attended by the same incidents which attend the exercise of the police power of the states.... The motive and purpose of a regulation of interstate commerce are matters for the legislative judgment upon the exercise of which the Constitution places no restriction and over which the courts are given no control....

In the more than a century which has elapsed since the decision of Gibbons v. Ogden, these principles of constitutional interpretation have been so long and repeatedly recognized by this Court as applicable to the Commerce Clause, that there would be little occasion for repeating them now were it not for the decision of this Court twenty-two years ago in Hammer v. Dagenhart. In that case it was held by a bare majority of the Court over the powerful and now classic dissent of Mr. Justice Holmes setting forth the fundamental issues involved, that Congress was without power to exclude the products of child labor from interstate commerce. The reasoning and conclusion of the Court's opinion there cannot be reconciled with the conclusion which we have reached, that the power of Congress under the Commerce Clause is plenary to exclude any article from interstate commerce subject only to the specific prohibitions of the Constitution.

Hammer v. Dagenhart has not been followed. The distinction on which the decision was rested that Congressional power to prohibit interstate commerce is limited to articles which in themselves have some harmful or deleterious property—a distinction which was novel when made and unsupported by any provision of the Constitution—has long since been abandoned.... It should be and now is overruled.

There remains the question whether such restriction on the production of goods for commerce is a permissible exercise of the commerce power. The power of Congress over interstate commerce is not confined to the regulation of commerce among the states. It extends to those activities intrastate which so affect interstate commerce or the exercise of the power of Congress over it as to make regulation of them appropriate means to the attainment of a legitimate end, the exercise of the granted power of Congress to regulate interstate commerce. McCulloch v. Maryland.

Congress, having by the present Act adopted the policy of excluding from interstate commerce all goods produced for the commerce which do not conform to the specified labor standards, it may choose the means reasonably adapted to the attainment of the permitted end, even though they involve control of intrastate activities. Such legislation has often been sustained with respect to powers, other than the commerce power granted to the national government, when the means chosen, although not themselves within the granted power, were nevertheless deemed appropriate aids to the accomplishment of some purpose within an admitted power of the national government.

The means adopted by [the statute] for the protection of interstate commerce by the suppression of the production of the condemned goods for interstate commerce is so related to the commerce and so affects it as to be within the reach of the commerce power.... Congress, to attain its objective in the suppression of nationwide competition in interstate commerce by goods produced under substandard labor conditions, has made no distinction as to the volume or amount of shipments in the commerce or of production for commerce by any particular shipper or producer. It recognized that in present day industry, competition by a small part may affect the whole and that the total effect of the competition of many small producers may be great.... So far as Carter v. Carter Coal Co is inconsistent with this conclusion, its doctrine is limited in principle by the decisions under the Sherman Act and the National Labor Relations Act, which we have cited and which we follow....

Our conclusion is unaffected by the Tenth Amendment which provides: 'The powers not delegated to the United States by the Constitution, nor prohibited by it to the States, are reserved to the States respectively, or to the people.' The amendment states but a truism that all is retained which has not been surrendered. There is nothing in the history of its adoption to suggest that it was more than declaratory of the relationship between the national and state governments as it had been established by the Constitution before the amendment or that its purpose was other than to allay fears that the new national government might seek to exercise powers not granted, and that the states might not be able to exercise fully their reserved powers.

From the beginning and for many years the amendment has been construed as not depriving the national government of authority to resort to all means for the exercise of a granted power which are appropriate and plainly adapted to the permitted end. Martin v. Hunter's Lessee. Whatever doubts may have arisen of the soundness of that conclusion they have been put at rest by the decisions under the Sherman Act and the National Labor Relations Act which we have cited.

Wickard v. Filburn
317 U.S. 111 (1942)

Unanimous decision: *Jackson*, Stone (CJ), Roberts, Black, Reed, Frankfurter, Douglas, Murphy, Byrnes

MR. JUSTICE JACKSON delivered the opinion of the Court.

The appellee filed his complaint against the Secretary of Agriculture of the United States, three members of the County Agricultural Conservation Committee for Montgomery County, Ohio, and a member of the State Agricultural Conservation Committee for Ohio. He sought to enjoin enforcement against himself of the marketing penalty imposed by the amendment of May 26, 1941, to the Agricultural Adjustment Act of 1938, upon that part of his 1941 wheat crop which was available for marketing in excess of the marketing quota established for his farm. He also sought a declaratory judgment that the wheat marketing quota provisions of the Act as amended and applicable to him were unconstitutional because not sustainable under the Commerce Clause. [The appellee also made several other claims not discussed here.]

The appellee for many years past has owned and operated a small farm in Montgomery County, Ohio, maintaining a herd of dairy cattle, selling milk, raising poultry, and selling poultry and eggs. It has been his practice to raise a small acreage of winter wheat, sown in the Fall and harvested in the following July; to sell a portion of the crop; to feed part to poultry and livestock on the farm, some of which is sold; to use some in making flour for home consumption; and to keep the rest for the following seeding. The intended disposition of the crop here involved has not been expressly stated.

In July of 1940, pursuant to the Agricultural Adjustment Act of 1938, as then amended, there were established for the appellee's 1941 crop a wheat acreage allotment of 11.1 acres and a normal yield of 20.1 bushels of wheat an acre. He was given notice of such allotment in July of 1940 before the Fall planting of his 1941 crop of wheat, and again in July of 1941, before it was harvested. He sowed, however, 23 acres, and harvested from his 11.9 acres of excess acreage 239 bushels, which under the terms of the Act as amended on May 26, 1941, constituted farm marketing excess, subject to a penalty of 49 cents a bushel, or $117.11 in all.

The general scheme of the Agricultural Adjustment Act of 1938 as related to wheat is to control the volume moving in interstate and foreign commerce in order to avoid surpluses and shortages and the consequent abnormally low or high wheat prices and obstructions to commerce. Within prescribed limits and by prescribed standards the Secretary of Agriculture is directed to ascertain and proclaim each year a national acreage allotment for the next crop of wheat, which is then apportioned to the states and their counties, and is eventually broken up into allotments for individual farms. Loans and payments to wheat farmers are authorized in stated circumstances....

Appellee says that this is a regulation of production and consumption of wheat. Such activities are, he urges, beyond the reach of Congressional power under the Commerce Clause, since they are local in character, and their effects upon interstate commerce are at most 'indirect.' In answer the Government argues that the statute regulates neither production nor consumption, but only marketing; and, in the alternative, that if the Act does go beyond the regulation of marketing it is sustainable as a 'necessary and proper' implementation of the power of Congress over interstate commerce....

At the beginning Chief Justice Marshall described the Federal commerce power with a breadth never yet exceeded. Gibbons v. Ogden. He made emphatic the embracing and penetrating nature of this power by warning that effective restraints on its exercise must proceed from political rather than from judicial processes.

For nearly a century, however, decisions of this Court under the Commerce Clause dealt rarely with questions of what Congress might do in the exercise of its granted power under the Clause and almost entirely with the permissibility of state activity which it was claimed discriminated against or burdened interstate commerce. During this period there was perhaps little occasion for the affirmative exercise of the commerce power, and the influence of the Clause on American life and law was a negative one, resulting almost wholly from its operation as a restraint upon the powers of the states. In discussion and decision the point of reference instead of being what was 'necessary and proper' to the exercise by Congress of its granted power, was often some concept of sovereignty thought to be implicit in the status of statehood. Certain activities such as 'production,' 'manufacturing,' and 'mining' were occasionally said to be within the province of state governments and beyond the power of Congress under the Commerce Clause....

It was not until 1887 with the enactment of the Interstate Commerce Act that the interstate commerce power began to exert positive influence in American law and life. This first important federal resort to the commerce power was followed in 1890 by the Sherman Anti-Trust Act and, thereafter, mainly after 1903, by many others. These statutes ushered in new phases of adjudication, which required the Court to approach the interpretation of the Commerce Clause in the light of an actual exercise by Congress of its power thereunder....

Not long after the decision of United States v. E. C. Knight Co., supra, Mr. Justice Holmes, in sustaining the exercise of national power over intrastate activity, stated for the Court that 'commerce among the states is not a technical legal conception, but a practical one, drawn from the course of business.'

In the Shreveport Rate Cases, the Court held that railroad rates of an admittedly intrastate character and fixed by authority of the state might, nevertheless, be revised by the Federal Government because of the economic effects which they had upon interstate commerce. The opinion of Mr. Justice Hughes found federal intervention constitutionally authorized because of 'matters having such a close and substantial relation to interstate traffic that the control is essential or appropriate to the security of that traffic, to the efficiency of the interstate service, and to the maintenance of the conditions under which interstate commerce may be conducted upon fair terms and without molestation or hindrance.'

The Court's recognition of the relevance of the economic effects in the application of the Commerce Clause exemplified by this statement has made the mechanical application of legal formulas no longer feasible. Once an economic measure of the reach of the power granted to Congress in the Commerce Clause is accepted, questions of federal power cannot be decided simply by finding the activity in question to be 'production' nor can consideration of its economic effects be foreclosed by calling them 'indirect.' The present Chief Justice has said in summary of the present state of the law: 'The commerce power is not confined in its exercise to the regulation of commerce among the states. It extends to those activities intrastate which so affect interstate commerce, or the exertion of the power of Congress over it, as to make regulation of them appropriate means to the attainment of a legitimate end, the effective execution of the granted power to regulate interstate commerce. The power of Congress over interstate commerce is plenary and complete in itself, may be exercised to its utmost extent, and acknowledges no limitations other than are prescribed in the Constitution[.]' ... But even if appellee's activity be local and though it may not be regarded as commerce, it may still, whatever its nature, be reached by Congress if it exerts a substantial economic effect on interstate commerce and this irrespective of whether such effect is what might at some earlier time have been defined as 'direct' or 'indirect.' ...

The effect of consumption of homegrown wheat on interstate commerce is due to the fact that it constitutes the most variable factor in the disappearance of the wheat crop. Consumption on the farm where grown appears to vary in an amount greater than 20 per cent of average production. The total amount of wheat consumed as food varies but relatively little, and use as seed is relatively constant.

The maintenance by government regulation of a price for wheat undoubtedly can be accomplished as effectively by sustaining or increasing the demand as by limiting the supply. The effect of the statute before us is to restrict the amount which may be produced for market and the extent as well to which one may forestall resort to the market by producing to meet his own needs. That appellee's own contribution to the demand for wheat may be trivial by itself is not enough to remove him from the scope of federal regulation where, as here, his contribution, taken together with that of many others similarly situated, is far from trivial....

This record leaves us in no doubt that Congress may properly have considered that wheat consumed on the farm where grown if wholly outside the scheme of regulation would have a substantial effect in defeating and obstructing its purpose to stimulate trade therein at increased prices....

It is said, however, that this Act, forcing some farmers into the market to buy what they could provide for themselves, is an unfair promotion of the markets and prices of specializing wheat growers. It is of the essence of regulation that it lays a restraining hand on the self interest of the regulated and that advantages from the regulation commonly fall to others. The conflicts of economic interest between the regulated and those who advantage by it are wisely left under our system to resolution by the Congress under its more flexible and responsible legislative process. Such conflicts rarely lend themselves to judicial determination. And with the wisdom, workability, or fairness, of the plan of regulation we have nothing to do.

Review Questions and Explanations: *Jones & Laughlin, Darby, Wickard*

1. *Jones & Laughlin* is viewed as one of the two cases in which the "switch in time saved nine." The "switch" was the vote of Justice Roberts to support the idea that Congress could regulate otherwise "intrastate" activities that have a "substantial effect" on interstate commerce. Does the "substantial effects test" evolve at all in

the five year span from *Jones & Laughlin* to *Wickard*? Note that there was no change in personnel on the Court between *Carter Coal* and *Jones & Laughlin*. There was considerable turnover between *Jones & Laughlin* and *Wickard*. See Figure 1.3.

Figure 1.3. The Transformation of the Supreme Court under FDR

1936	1937	1941	1942
Carter Coal	*West Coast Hotel*	*Darby*	*Wickard*
298 US 238	300 US 379	312 US 100	317 US 111
	Jones & Laughlin		
Majority:	301 US 1	**Unanimous:**	**Unanimous:**
Van Devanter		Hughes (CJ)	**Stone** (CJ)
McReynolds	**Majority:**	McReynolds	Roberts
Butler	Hughes (CJ)	Stone	**Black**
Sutherland	Cardozo	Roberts	**Reed**
Roberts	Brandeis	**Black**	**Frankfurter**
	Stone	**Reed**	**Douglas**
Partial dissent:	Roberts	**Frankfurter**	**Murphy**
Hughes (CJ)		**Douglas**	**Byrnes**
	Dissent:	**Murphy**	**Jackson**
Dissent:	Van Devanter		
Cardozo	McReynolds		
Brandeis	Butler		
Stone	Sutherland		

Note: F.D. Roosevelt's nominees in **bold italics**. Stone was originally nominated by Coolidge; elevated to Chief Justiceship by Roosevelt.

2. *Jones & Laughlin* was probably a strong test case for the adoption of the substantial effects test, given the massive size and interstate scope of the steel industry, as detailed in the opinion. Agriculture was also a major interstate industry, even looking at the sub-field of wheat production. The problem in *Wickard*, of course, is that the regulation is being applied to a private wheat field of a single farmer. How does the *Wickard* Court use the substantial effects test to cover that situation?

3. *Jones & Laughlin, Darby* and *Wickard* each dismantle part of the Court's pre-1937 jurisprudence in this area. In doing so, these cases also provide the foundation for the Court's current Commerce Clause jurisprudence. Identify both the old and the new doctrine in each of these cases. Do this by articulating the specific piece of the old doctrine rejected in each case and also the new doctrine the Court replaced it with. It will help to consider which of the pre-1937 cases each of these cases most closely resembles.

Exercises: The New Deal Turnaround

1. At this point, you have all the building blocks of contemporary Commerce Clause jurisprudence. Try your hand at writing out what you think the current doctrinal "test" is, based on your reading of these cases. (It took the Court decades to doctrinalize these cases, so this is not an easy task. But give it a try.)

2. Return to the list you made of important federal statutes that regulate economic activity. Are these laws constitutional under the doctrinal test of *Jones, Darby,* and *Wickard*?

From the "New Deal Turnaround" until 1995, the Court did not strike down a single act of Congress as exceeding the commerce power. It would be a mistake, however, to read this period as one in which the Court viewed the Commerce Clause as an unlimited grant of national legislative power. The Court continued to acknowledge theoretical or implicit limits in its decisions during this period. However, it is fair to say that the Court adopted a deferential view toward congressional determinations that a particular law regulated conduct that had a "substantial effect" on interstate commerce.

Arguably the most significant assertion of the federal commerce power in this period came in connection with the Civil Rights Act of 1964. Undoubtedly the most important civil rights legislation in our nation's history, the Act prohibited discrimination on the basis of "race, color, religion, sex or national origin" in employment, education, federally funded programs and places of public accommodation. The case took on added significance, in that the Civil Rights Act of 1964 was strikingly similar to legislation passed by Congress nearly 100 years earlier. In that legislation, the Civil Rights Act of 1875, Congress had sought to prohibit race discrimination by private business owners. Congress had based the earlier act on its power to enforce the Equal Protection clause of the Fourteenth amendment. The Court struck down the law in the *Civil Rights Cases* (1886), holding that the Fourteenth Amendment only prohibited discrimination by state and local officials, and not by private persons. The Civil Rights Act of 1875 and the Court's decision in the *Civil Rights Cases* are discussed in Chapter 8. In order to reach private conduct, Congress based the 1964 Civil Rights Act on the commerce power, in addition to the Fourteenth Amendment's enforcement power.

Guided Reading Questions: *Heart of Atlanta Motel*

1. Can you explain in your own words why Congress relied on both the Commerce Clause and section 5 of the Fourteenth Amendment as bases for the 1964 Civil Rights Act?

2. What exactly is being regulated by the Civil Rights Act of 1964? Is there more than one way to answer that question, and, if so, does the answer make a difference to whether the regulation is "interstate commerce"?

Heart of Atlanta Motel v. United States

379 U.S. 241 (1964)

Unanimous decision: *Clark,* Warren (CJ), Black, Douglas, Clark, Harlan, Brennan, Stewart, White, Goldberg

Concurrences: *Black, Douglas, Goldberg*

MR. JUSTICE CLARK delivered the opinion of the Court.

.... Appellant owns and operates the Heart of Atlanta Motel which has 216 rooms available to transient guests. The motel.... is readily accessible to interstate highways 75 and 85 and state highways 23 and 41. Appellant solicits patronage from outside the State of Georgia through various national advertising media, including magazines of national circulation; it maintains over 50 billboards and highway signs within the State, soliciting patronage for the motel; it accepts convention trade from outside Georgia and approximately 75% of its registered guests are from out of State. Prior to passage of the Act the motel had followed a practice of refusing to rent rooms to Negroes, and it alleged that it intended to continue to do so. In an effort to perpetuate that policy this suit was filed. [The motel sued to strike down the Civil Rights Act, and the government counterclaimed to enforce the Act against the motel. The government won in the court below, and the motel appealed.]

The appellant contends that Congress in passing this Act exceeded its power to regulate commerce....

.... In 1883 this Court struck down the public accommodations sections of the 1875 [Civil Rights] Act in the Civil Rights Cases, 109 U.S. 3. No major legislation in this field had been enacted by Congress for [more than 80 years].

The [Civil Rights] Act as finally adopted was most comprehensive, undertaking to prevent through peaceful and voluntary settlement discrimination in voting, as well as in places of accommodation and public facilities, federally secured programs and in employment. [Title II, dealing with places of accommodation] is the only portion under attack here.... [Section 201(a)] provides that:

> All persons shall be entitled to the full and equal enjoyment of the goods, services, facilities, privileges, advantages, and accommodations of any place of public accommodation, as defined in this section, without discrimination or segregation on the ground of race, color, religion, or national origin.

There are listed in § 201 (b) four classes of business establishments, each of which "serves the public" and "is a place of public accommodation" within the meaning of § 201 (a) "if its operations affect commerce, or if discrimination or segregation by it is supported by State action." The covered establishments are [inns, hotels, restaurants, movie houses, and "any establishment ... which is physically located within the premises of any establishment otherwise covered by this subsection"].... A person aggrieved may bring suit, in which the Attorney General may be permitted to intervene....

It is admitted that the operation of the motel brings it within the provisions of § 201 (a) of the Act and that appellant refused to provide lodging for transient Negroes because of their race or color and that it intends to continue that policy unless restrained.

The sole question posed is, therefore, the constitutionality of the Civil Rights Act of 1964 as applied to these facts. The legislative history of the Act indicates that Congress based the Act on § 5 and the Equal Protection Clause of the Fourteenth Amendment as well as its power to regulate interstate commerce under Art. I, § 8, cl. 3, of the Constitution.

.... [We] think [the Civil Rights Cases] inapposite, and without precedential value in determining the constitutionality of the present Act. Unlike Title II of the present legislation, the 1875 Act broadly proscribed discrimination in "inns, public conveyances on land or water, theaters, and other places of public amusement," without limiting the categories of affected businesses to those impinging upon interstate commerce. In contrast, the applicability of Title II is carefully limited to enterprises having a direct and substantial relation to the interstate flow of goods and people, except where state action is involved. Further, the fact that certain kinds of businesses may not in 1875 have been sufficiently involved in interstate commerce to warrant bringing them within the ambit of the commerce power is not necessarily dispositive of the same question today. Our populace had not reached its present mobility, nor were facilities, goods and services circulating as readily in interstate commerce as they are today. Although the principles which we apply today are those first formulated by Chief Justice Marshall in Gibbons v. Ogden, 9 Wheat. 1 (1824), the conditions of transportation and commerce have changed dramatically, and we must apply those principles to the present state of commerce. The sheer increase in volume of interstate traffic alone would give discriminatory practices which inhibit travel a far larger impact upon the Nation's commerce than such practices had on the economy of another day. Finally, there is language in the Civil Rights Cases which indicates that the Court did not fully consider whether the 1875 Act could be sustained as an exercise of the commerce power....

While the Act as adopted carried no congressional findings[,] the record of its passage through each house is replete with evidence of the burdens that discrimination by race or color places upon interstate commerce. [Hearing] testimony included the fact that our people have become increasingly mobile with millions of people of all races traveling from State to State; that Negroes in particular have been the subject of discrimination in transient accommodations, having to travel great distances to secure the same; that often they have been unable to obtain accommodations and have had to call upon friends to put them up overnight, S. Rep. No. 872, supra, at 14–22; and that these conditions had become so acute as to require the listing of available lodging for Negroes in a special guidebook which was itself "dramatic testimony to the difficulties" Negroes encounter in travel. These exclusionary practices were found to be nationwide, the Under Secretary of Commerce testifying that there is "no question that this discrimination in the North still exists to a large degree" and in the West and Midwest as well. Id., at 735, 744. This testimony indicated a qualitative as well as quantitative effect on interstate travel by Negroes.... We shall not burden this opinion with further details since the voluminous testimony presents overwhelming evidence that discrimination by hotels and motels impedes interstate travel.

.... In framing Title II of this Act Congress was ... dealing with what it considered a moral problem. But that fact does not detract from the overwhelming evidence of the disruptive effect that racial discrimination has had on commercial intercourse. It was this burden which empowered Congress to enact appropriate legislation, and, given this basis for the exercise of its power, Congress was not restricted by the fact that the particular obstruction to interstate commerce with which it was dealing was also deemed a moral and social wrong.

It is said that the operation of the motel here is of a purely local character. But, assuming this to be true, "if it is interstate commerce that feels the pinch, it does not matter how local the operation which applies the squeeze." As Chief Justice Stone put it in United States v. Darby, supra:

> The power of Congress over interstate commerce is not confined to the regulation of commerce among the states. It extends to those activities intrastate which so affect interstate commerce or the exercise of the power of Congress over it as to make regulation of them appropriate means to the attainment of a legitimate end, the exercise of the granted power of Congress to regulate interstate commerce. See McCulloch v. Maryland.

Thus the power of Congress to promote interstate commerce also includes the power to regulate the local incidents thereof, including local activities in both the States of origin and destination, which might have a substantial and harmful effect upon that commerce.

One need only examine the evidence which we have discussed above to see that Congress may—as it has—prohibit racial discrimination by motels serving travelers, however "local" their operations may appear.

.... It may be argued that Congress could have pursued other methods to eliminate the obstructions it found in interstate commerce caused by racial discrimination. But this is a matter of policy that rests entirely with the Congress not with the courts. How obstructions in commerce may be removed—what means are to be employed—is within the sound and exclusive discretion of the Congress. It is subject only to one caveat—that the means chosen by it must be reasonably adapted to the end permitted by the Constitution. We cannot say that its choice here was not so adapted. The Constitution requires no more. Affirmed.

MR. JUSTICE BLACK, concurring.

.... It requires no novel or strained interpretation of the Commerce Clause to sustain Title II.... At least since Gibbons v. Ogden, 9 Wheat. 1, decided in 1824 in an opinion by Chief Justice John Marshall, it has been uniformly accepted that the power of Congress to regulate commerce among the States is plenary, "complete in itself, may be exercised to its utmost extent, and acknowledges no limitations, other than are prescribed in the constitution." 9 Wheat., at 196. Nor is "Commerce" as used in the Commerce Clause to be limited to a narrow, technical concept. It includes not only, as Congress has enumerated in the Act, "travel, trade, traffic, commerce, transportation, or communication," but also all other unitary transactions and activities that take place in more States than one. That some parts or segments of such unitary transactions may take place only in one State cannot, of course, take from Congress its plenary power to regulate them in the national interest....

MR. JUSTICE DOUGLAS, concurring.

Though I join the Court's opinions, I am somewhat reluctant here, as I was in Edwards v. California, 314 U.S. 160, 177, to rest solely on the Commerce Clause. My reluctance is not due to any conviction that Congress lacks power to regulate commerce in the interests of human rights. It is rather my belief that the right of people to be free of state action that discriminates against them because of race, like the "right of persons to move freely from State to State" (Edwards v. California, supra, at 177), "occupies a more protected position in our constitutional system than does the movement of cattle, fruit, steel and coal across state lines." Ibid. Moreover, ... the result reached by the Court is for me much more obvious as a protective measure under the Fourteenth Amendment than under the Commerce Clause. For the former deals with the constitutional status of the individual not with the impact on commerce of local activities or vice versa.

Hence I would prefer to rest on the assertion of legislative power contained in § 5 of the Fourteenth Amendment....

MR. JUSTICE GOLDBERG, concurring.

I join in the opinions and judgments of the Court.... The primary purpose of the Civil Rights Act of 1964, however, as the Court recognizes, and as I would underscore, is the vindication of human dignity and not mere economics.... [In] my view, Congress clearly had authority under both § 5 of the Fourteenth Amendment and the Commerce Clause to enact the Civil Rights Act of 1964.

CASE NOTE: *Katzenbach v. McClung,* 379 U.S. 294 (1964). On the same day it decided *Heart of Atlanta,* the Court rejected a second Commerce Clause challenge to the 1964 Civil Rights Act in another unanimous opinion authored by Justice Clark. *Katzenbach v. McClung,* 379 U.S. 294 (1964). The plaintiff McClung was the owner of a restaurant called

Ollie's Barbecue that refused to seat black customers. He argued that his restaurant was too small and local to be regulated as "interstate commerce." The Court disagreed. Noting that Ollie's purchased close to half its food supplies from out of state, the Court held that the restaurant could be subject to Title II of the 1964 Civil Rights Act under the commerce clause. The court also relied on *Wickard v. Filburn*'s statement that "even if appellee's activity be local and though it may not be regarded as commerce, it may still, whatever its nature, be reached by Congress if it exerts a substantial economic effect on interstate commerce."

Review Questions and Explanations: *Heart of Atlanta Motel*

1. Is there language in *Wickard* that could have been relied on to make *Heart of Atlanta* an easy case? What language? Did the *Heart of Atlanta* Court rely on that simple approach? If not, why not?

2. Is *Heart of Atlanta* more expansive in its application of the "substantial effects" test than *Wickard*?

3. As you read the next set of cases, consider whether the constitutionality of federal law prohibiting discrimination in employment and in places of public accommodation (established in the Civil Rights Act of 1964) is cast in doubt by them.

---

4. The Modern Era: The Commerce Clause Since 1995

The Modern Era of the Supreme Court's Commerce Clause jurisprudence began in 1995, when the Court for the first time since 1937 invalidated a federal law as beyond the reach of Congress's Commerce Clause power. The Court has decided only a handful of Commerce Clause cases since then. These cases do not appear to overrule any post-1937 cases and therefore are—probably—not truly revolutionary in a doctrinal sense. Rather, they evidence an increased effort on the part of the Court to impose some restrictions on Congress while operating within the existing doctrinal paradigm. Legal scholars disagree on whether the Court's efforts have been effective, as well as whether they are constitutionally warranted.

The three cases in this section—*Lopez, Morrison* and *Raich*—work together to show the doctrine developed by the Court in this era. *Lopez* reviews prior case law and provides three categories of congressional action in which Commerce Clause power can be properly exercised. When reading *Lopez*, think about how those categories tie back to the earlier cases you have read. *Morrison* and *Raich* work within and provide more detail to the framework set forth in *Lopez*. When reading these cases, also consider whether the individual justices are applying their preferred doctrines consistently.

Guided Reading Questions: *United States v. Lopez*

1. Identify the three categories of congressional actions that the Court says are within Congress's Commerce Clause authority. Where do they come from?

2. Which category does the majority say the law being challenged falls into?

3. The majority opinion in Lopez gives three distinct reasons why the law being challenged is constitutionally problematic. Identify each of these reasons. Can you tell from the majority opinion which is/are fatal to the law?

4. What role does the distinction between "economic" and "non-economic" activity play in the *Lopez* decision? Why is the dissent uncomfortable with that distinction as the basis for determining the extent of Congress's interstate commerce power? What importance, if any, is the term "activity" playing in the case?

United States v. Lopez

514 U.S. 549 (1995)

Majority: *Rehnquist* (CJ), O'Connor, Scalia, Kennedy, Thomas,

Concurrences: *Kennedy*, O'Connor; *Thomas*

Dissents: *Stevens* (omitted), *Souter, Breyer*, Ginsburg

CHIEF JUSTICE REHNQUIST delivered the opinion of the Court.

In the Gun-Free School Zones Act of 1990, Congress made it a federal offense "for any individual knowingly to possess a firearm at a place that the individual knows, or has reasonable cause to believe, is a school zone." 18 U.S.C. § 922(q)(1)(A) (1988 ed., Supp. V). The Act neither regulates a commercial activity nor contains a requirement that the possession be connected in any way to interstate commerce. We hold that the Act exceeds the authority of Congress "[t]o regulate Commerce ... among the several States...." U.S. Const., Art. I, § 8, cl. 3.

On March 10, 1992, respondent, who was then a 12th-grade student, arrived at Edison High School in San Antonio, Texas, carrying a concealed .38 caliber handgun and five bullets. Acting upon an anonymous tip, school authorities confronted respondent, who admitted that he was carrying the weapon. He was arrested and charged under Texas law with firearm possession on school premises. See Tex. Penal Code Ann. § 46.03(a)(1) (Supp. 1994). The next day, the state charges were dismissed after federal agents charged respondent ... with violating the Gun-Free School Zones Act of 1990....

We start with first principles. The Constitution creates a Federal Government of enumerated powers.... This constitutionally mandated division of authority "was adopted by the Framers to ensure protection of our fundamental liberties".... The Court, through Chief Justice Marshall, first defined the nature of Congress' commerce power in Gibbons v. Ogden, 9 Wheat. 1, 189–190 (1824): "Commerce, undoubtedly, is traffic, but it is something more: it is intercourse. It describes the commercial intercourse between nations, and parts of nations, in all its branches, and is regulated by prescribing rules for carrying on that intercourse."

The commerce power "is the power to regulate; that is, to prescribe the rule by which commerce is to be governed. This power, like all others vested in Congress, is complete in itself, may be exercised to its utmost extent, and acknowledges no limitations, other than are prescribed in the constitution." Id., at 196. The Gibbons Court, however, acknowledged that limitations on the commerce power are inherent in the very language of the Commerce Clause....

For nearly a century thereafter, the Court's Commerce Clause decisions dealt but rarely with the extent of Congress' power, and almost entirely with the Commerce Clause as a limit on state legislation that discriminated against interstate commerce. Under this line of precedent, the Court held that certain categories of activity such as "production," "manufacturing," and "mining" were within the province of state governments, and thus were beyond the power of Congress under the Commerce Clause. See Wickard v. Filburn, 317 U.S. 111, 121 (1942) (describing development of Commerce Clause jurisprudence).

In 1887, Congress enacted the Interstate Commerce Act, 24 Stat. 379, and in 1890, Congress enacted the Sherman Antitrust Act, 26 Stat. 209, as amended, 15 U.S.C. § 1 et seq. These laws ushered in a new era of federal regulation under the commerce power. When cases involving these laws first reached this Court, we imported from our negative Commerce Clause cases the approach that Congress could not regulate activities such as "production," "manufacturing," and "mining." See, e.g., United States v. E. C. Knight Co., 156 U.S. 1, 12 (1895) ("Commerce succeeds to manufacture, and is not part of it"); Carter v. Carter Coal Co., 298 U.S. 238, 304 (1936) ("Mining brings the subject matter of commerce into existence. Commerce disposes of it"). Simultaneously, however, the Court held that, where the interstate and intrastate aspects of commerce were so mingled together that full regulation of interstate commerce required incidental regulation of intrastate commerce, the Commerce Clause authorized such regulation. See, e.g., Houston, E. & W. T. R. Co. v. United States, 234 U.S. 342 (1914) (Shreveport Rate Cases).

In A. L. A. Schechter Poultry Corp. v. United States, 295 U.S. 495, 550 (1935), the Court struck down regulations that fixed the hours and wages of individuals employed by an intrastate business because the activity being regulated related to interstate commerce only indirectly. In doing so, the Court characterized the distinction between direct and indirect effects of intrastate transactions upon interstate commerce as "a fundamental one, essential to the maintenance of our constitutional system." Id., at 548. Activities that affected interstate commerce directly were within Congress' power; activities that affected interstate commerce indirectly were beyond Congress' reach. Id., at 546. The justification for this formal distinction was rooted in the fear that otherwise "there would be virtually no limit to the federal power and for all practical purposes we should have a completely centralized government." Id., at 548.

Two years later, in the watershed case of NLRB v. Jones & Laughlin Steel Corp., 301 U.S. 1 (1937), the Court upheld the National Labor Relations Act against a Commerce Clause challenge, and in the process, departed from the distinction between "direct" and "indirect" effects on interstate commerce. Id., at 36–38 ("The question [of the scope of Congress' power] is necessarily one of degree"). The Court held that intrastate activities that "have such a close and substantial relation to interstate commerce that their control is essential or appropriate to protect that commerce from burdens and obstructions" are within Congress' power to regulate. Id., at 37.

In United States v. Darby, 312 U.S. 100 (1941), the Court upheld the Fair Labor Standards Act, stating:

> The power of Congress over interstate commerce is not confined to the regulation of commerce among the states. It extends to those activities intrastate which so affect interstate commerce or the exercise of the power of Congress over it as to make regulation of them appropriate means to the attainment of a legitimate end, the exercise of the granted power of Congress to regulate interstate commerce.

In Wickard v. Filburn, the Court upheld the application of amendments to the Agricultural Adjustment Act of 1938 to the production and consumption of home-grown wheat. The Court explicitly rejected earlier distinctions between direct and indirect effects on interstate commerce, stating:

> Even if appellee's activity be local and though it may not be regarded as commerce, it may still, whatever its nature, be reached by Congress if it exerts a substantial economic effect on interstate commerce, and this irrespective of whether such effect is what might at some earlier time have been defined as "direct" or "indirect."

The Wickard Court emphasized that although Filburn's own contribution to the demand for wheat may have been trivial by itself, that was not "enough to remove him from the scope of federal regulation where, as here, his contribution, taken together with that of many others similarly situated, is far from trivial."

Jones & Laughlin Steel, Darby, and Wickard ushered in an era of Commerce Clause jurisprudence that greatly expanded the previously defined authority of Congress under that Clause. In part, this was a recognition of the great changes that had occurred in the way business was carried on in this country. Enterprises that had once been local or at most regional in nature had become national in scope. But the doctrinal change also reflected a view that earlier Commerce Clause cases artificially had constrained the authority of Congress to regulate interstate commerce.

But even these modern-era precedents which have expanded congressional power under the Commerce Clause confirm that this power is subject to outer limits. In Jones & Laughlin Steel, the Court warned that the scope of the interstate commerce power "must be considered in the light of our dual system of government and may not be extended so as to embrace effects upon interstate commerce so indirect and remote that to embrace them, in view of our complex society, would effectually obliterate the distinction between what is national and what is local and create a completely centralized government." ... Since that time, the Court has heeded that warning and undertaken to decide whether a rational basis existed for concluding that a regulated activity sufficiently affected interstate commerce.

Consistent with this structure, we have identified three broad categories of activity that Congress may regulate under its commerce power.... First, Congress may regulate the use of the channels of interstate commerce. See, e.g., Darby, Heart of Atlanta Motel, supra, at 256 ("[T]he authority of Congress to keep the channels of interstate commerce free from immoral and injurious uses has been frequently sustained, and is no longer open to question."). Second, Congress is empowered to regulate and protect the instrumentalities of interstate commerce, or persons or things in interstate commerce, even though the threat may come only from intrastate activities. See, e.g., Shreveport Rate Cases, 234 U.S. 342 (1914); Southern R. Co. v. United States, 222 U.S. 20 (1911).... Finally, Congress' commerce authority includes the power to regulate those activities having a substantial relation to interstate commerce, Jones & Laughlin Steel, i.e., those activities that substantially affect interstate commerce....

Within this final category, admittedly, our case law has not been clear whether an activity must "affect" or "substantially affect" interstate commerce in order to be within Congress' power to regulate it under the Commerce Clause.... We conclude, consistent with the great weight of our case law, that the proper test requires an analysis of whether the regulated activity "substantially affects" interstate commerce.

We now turn to consider the power of Congress, in the light of this framework, to enact § 922(q). The first two categories of authority may be quickly disposed of: § 922(q) is not a regulation of the use of the channels of interstate commerce, nor is it an attempt to prohibit the interstate transportation of a commodity through the channels of commerce; nor can § 922(q) be justified as a regulation by which Congress has sought to protect an instrumentality of interstate commerce or a thing in interstate commerce. Thus, if § 922(q) is to be sustained, it must be under the third category as a regulation of an activity that substantially affects interstate commerce.

First, we have upheld a wide variety of congressional Acts regulating intrastate economic activity where we have concluded that the activity substantially affected interstate commerce. Examples include the regulation of intrastate coal mining; Hodel, supra, intrastate extortionate credit transactions, Perez, supra, restaurants utilizing substantial interstate supplies, McClung, supra, inns and hotels catering to interstate guests, Heart of Atlanta Motel, supra, and production and consumption of home-grown wheat, Wickard v. Filburn. These examples are by no means exhaustive, but the pattern is clear. Where economic activity substantially affects interstate commerce, legislation regulating that activity will be sustained.

Even Wickard, which is perhaps the most far reaching example of Commerce Clause authority over intrastate activity, involved economic activity in a way that the possession of a gun in a school zone does not.... Section 922(q) is a criminal statute that by its terms has nothing to do with "commerce" or any sort of economic enterprise, however broadly one might define those terms. Section 922(q) is not an essential part of a larger regulation of economic activity, in which the regulatory scheme could be undercut unless the intrastate activity were regulated. It cannot, therefore, be sustained under our cases upholding regulations of activities that arise out of or are connected with a commercial transaction, which viewed in the aggregate, substantially affects interstate commerce.

Second, § 922(q) contains no jurisdictional element which would ensure, through case-by-case inquiry, that the firearm possession in question affects interstate commerce. For example, in United States v. Bass (1971), the Court interpreted former 18 U.S.C. § 1202(a), which made it a crime for a felon to "receiv[e], posses[s], or transpor[t] in commerce or affecting commerce ... any firearm." The Court interpreted the possession component of § 1202(a) to require an additional nexus to interstate commerce both because the statute was ambiguous and because "unless Congress conveys its purpose clearly, it will not be deemed to have significantly changed the federal-state balance." Id., at 349. The Bass Court set aside the conviction because although the Government had demonstrated that Bass had possessed a firearm, it had failed "to show the requisite nexus with interstate commerce." Id., at 347. The Court thus interpreted the statute to reserve the constitutional question whether Congress could regulate, without more, the "mere possession" of firearms....

Although as part of our independent evaluation of constitutionality under the Commerce Clause we of course consider legislative findings, and indeed even congressional committee findings, regarding effect on interstate commerce, the Government concedes that "[n]either the statute nor its legislative history contain[s] express congressional findings regarding the effects upon interstate commerce of gun possession in a school zone." Brief for United States 5–6. We agree with the Government that Congress normally is not required to make formal findings as to the substantial burdens that an activity has on interstate commerce.... But to the extent that congressional findings would enable us to evaluate the legislative judgment that the activity in question substantially affected interstate commerce, even though no such substantial effect was visible to the naked eye, they are lacking here....

The Government's essential contention, in fine, is that we may determine here that § 922(q) is valid because possession of a firearm in a local school zone does indeed substantially affect interstate commerce. The Government argues that possession of a firearm in a school zone may result in violent crime and that violent crime can be expected to affect the functioning of the national economy in two ways. First, the costs of violent crime are substantial, and, through the mechanism of insurance, those costs are spread throughout the population. Second, violent crime reduces the willingness of individuals to travel to areas within the country that are perceived to be unsafe. The Government also argues that the presence of guns in schools poses a substantial threat to the educational process by threatening the learning environment. A handicapped educational process, in turn, will result in a less productive citizenry. That, in turn, would have an adverse effect on the Nation's economic well-being. As a result, the Government argues that Congress could rationally have concluded that §922(q) substantially affects interstate commerce.

We pause to consider the implications of the Government's arguments. The Government admits, under its "costs of crime" reasoning, that Congress could regulate not only all violent crime, but all activities that might lead to violent crime, regardless of how tenuously they relate to interstate commerce. Similarly, under the Government's "national productivity" reasoning, Congress could regulate any activity that it found was related to the economic productivity of individual citizens: family law (including marriage, divorce, and child custody), for example. Under the theories that the Government presents in support of §922(q), it is difficult to perceive any limitation on federal power, even in areas such as criminal law enforcement or education where States historically have been sovereign. Thus, if we were to accept the Government's arguments, we are hard-pressed to posit any activity by an individual that Congress is without power to regulate....

Admittedly, a determination whether an intrastate activity is commercial or noncommercial may in some cases result in legal uncertainty. But, so long as Congress' authority is limited to those powers enumerated in the Constitution, and so long as those enumerated powers are interpreted as having judicially enforceable outer limits, congressional legislation under the Commerce Clause always will engender "legal uncertainty." As Chief Justice Marshall stated in McCulloch v. Maryland, 4 Wheat. 316 (1819):

> The [federal] government is acknowledged by all to be one of enumerated powers. The principle, that it can exercise only the powers granted to it ... is now universally admitted. But the question respecting the extent of the powers actually granted, is perpetually arising, and will probably continue to arise, as long as our system shall exist.

The Constitution mandates this uncertainty by withholding from Congress a plenary police power that would authorize enactment of every type of legislation. Congress has operated within this framework of legal uncertainty ever since this Court determined that it was the judiciary's duty "to say what the law is." Any possible benefit from eliminating this "legal uncertainty" would be at the expense of the Constitution's system of enumerated powers.

.... The possession of a gun in a local school zone is in no sense an economic activity that might, through repetition elsewhere, substantially affect any sort of interstate commerce. Respondent was a local student at a local school; there is no indication that he had recently moved in interstate commerce, and there is no requirement that his possession of the firearm have any concrete tie to interstate commerce....

To uphold the Government's contentions here, we would have to pile inference upon inference in a manner that would bid fair to convert congressional authority under the Commerce Clause to a general police power of the sort retained by the States. Admittedly, some of our prior cases have taken long steps down that road, giving great deference to congressional action. The broad language in these opinions has suggested the possibility of additional expansion, but we decline here to proceed any further. To do so would require us to conclude that the Constitution's enumeration of powers does not presuppose something not enumerated, and that there never will be a distinction between what is truly national and what is truly local. This we are unwilling to do. For the foregoing reasons the judgment of the Court of Appeals is affirmed.

JUSTICE KENNEDY, with whom JUSTICE O'CONNOR joins, concurring.

The history of the judicial struggle to interpret the Commerce Clause during the transition from the economic system the Founders knew to the single, national market still emergent in our own era counsels great restraint before the Court determines that the Clause is insufficient to support an exercise of the national power. That history gives me some pause about today's decision, but I join the Court's opinion with these observations on what I conceive to be its necessary though limited holding....

The case that seems to mark the Court's definitive commitment to the practical conception of the commerce power is NLRB v. Jones & Laughlin Steel Corp, where the Court sustained labor laws that applied to manufacturing facilities, making no real attempt to distinguish Carter, supra, and Schechter, supra. The deference given to Congress has since been confirmed. United States v. Darby (1941), overruled Hammer v. Dagenhart, supra. And in Wickard v. Filburn, (1942), the Court disapproved E. C. Knight and the entire line of direct-indirect and manufacture-production cases, explaining that "broader interpretations of the Commerce Clause [were] destined to supersede the earlier ones," id., at 122, and "whatever terminology is used, the criterion is necessarily one of degree and must be so defined. This does not satisfy those who seek mathematical or rigid formulas. But such formulas are not provided by the great concepts of the Constitution" ...

The history of our Commerce Clause decisions contains at least two lessons of relevance to this case. The first, as stated at the outset, is the imprecision of content-based boundaries used without more to define the limits of the Commerce Clause. The second, related to the first but of even greater consequence, is that the Court as an institution and the legal system as a whole have an immense stake in the stability of our Commerce Clause jurisprudence as it has evolved to this point. Stare decisis operates with great force in counselling us not to call in question the essential principles now in place respecting the congressional power to regulate transactions of a commercial nature. That fundamental restraint on our power forecloses us from reverting to an understanding of commerce that would serve only an 18th-century economy, dependent then upon production and trading practices that had changed but little over the preceding centuries; it also mandates against returning to the time when congressional authority to regulate undoubted commercial activities was limited by a judicial determination that those matters had an insufficient connection to an interstate system. Congress can regulate in the commercial sphere on the assumption that we have a single market and a unified purpose to build a stable national economy....

While it is doubtful that any State, or indeed any reasonable person, would argue that it is wise policy to allow students to carry guns on school premises, considerable disagreement exists about how best to accomplish that goal. In this circumstance, the theory and utility of our federalism are revealed, for the States may perform their role as laboratories for experimentation to devise various solutions where the best solution is far from clear. See San Antonio Independent School Dist. v. Rodriguez, 411 U.S. 1, 49–50 (1973); New State Ice Co. v. Liebmann, 285 U.S. 262, 311 (1932) (Brandeis, J., dissenting).

If a State or municipality determines that harsh criminal sanctions are necessary and wise to deter students from carrying guns on school premises, the reserved powers of the

States are sufficient to enact those measures. Indeed, over 40 States already have criminal laws outlawing the possession of firearms on or near school grounds.

Other, more practicable means to rid the schools of guns may be thought by the citizens of some States to be preferable for the safety and welfare of the schools those States are charged with maintaining. See Brief for National Conference of State Legislatures et al. as Amici Curiae 26–30 (injection of federal officials into local problems causes friction and diminishes political accountability of state and local governments). These might include inducements to inform on violators where the information leads to arrests or confiscation of the guns; programs to encourage the voluntary surrender of guns with some provision for amnesty; penalties imposed on parents or guardians for failure to supervise the child, or programs for expulsion with assignment to special facilities.

The statute now before us forecloses the States from experimenting and exercising their own judgment in an area to which States lay claim by right of history and expertise.... Absent a stronger connection or identification with commercial concerns that are central to the Commerce Clause, that interference contradicts the federal balance the Framers designed and that this Court is obliged to enforce.

JUSTICE THOMAS, concurring.

.... Although I join the majority, I write separately to observe that our case law has drifted far from the original understanding of the Commerce Clause.... We have said that Congress may regulate not only "Commerce ... among the several States," but also anything that has a "substantial effect" on such commerce. This test, if taken to its logical extreme, would give Congress a "police power" over all aspects of American life....

.... [T]he sweeping nature of our current test enables the dissent to argue that Congress can regulate gun possession. But it seems to me that the power to regulate "commerce" can by no means encompass authority over mere gun possession, any more than it empowers the Federal Government to regulate marriage, littering, or cruelty to animals, throughout the 50 States. Our Constitution quite properly leaves such matters to the individual States, notwithstanding these activities' effects on interstate commerce. Any interpretation of the Commerce Clause that even suggests that Congress could regulate such matters is in need of reexamination....

JUSTICE SOUTER, dissenting.

.... [T]he notion that the commerce power diminishes the closer it gets to customary state concerns ... has been flatly rejected, and not long ago. The commerce power, we have often observed, is plenary [and] ".... may override countervailing state interests[.]"

.... The practice of deferring to rationally based legislative judgments "is a paradigm of judicial restraint." ... In judicial review under the Commerce Clause, it reflects our respect for the institutional competence of the Congress on a subject expressly assigned to it by the Constitution and our appreciation of the legitimacy that comes from Congress's political accountability in dealing with matters open to a wide range of possible choices.

JUSTICE BREYER, with whom JUSTICE STEVENS, JUSTICE SOUTER, and JUSTICE GINSBURG join, dissenting.

.... [T]he Constitution requires us to judge the connection between a regulated activity and interstate commerce, not directly, but at one remove. Courts must give Congress a degree of leeway in determining the existence of a significant factual connection between the regulated activity and interstate commerce—both because the Constitution delegates the commerce power directly to Congress and because the determination requires an empirical judgment of a kind that a legislature is more likely than a court to make with accuracy. The traditional words "rational basis" capture this leeway. Thus, the specific question before us, as the Court recognizes, is not whether the "regulated activity sufficiently affected interstate commerce," but, rather, whether Congress could have had "a rational basis" for so concluding....

[Why cannot Congress conclude] that a widespread, serious, and substantial physical threat to teaching and learning also substantially threatens the commerce to which that teaching and learning is inextricably tied? That is to say, guns in the hands of six percent of inner-city high school students and gun-related violence throughout a city's schools must threaten the trade and commerce that those schools support....

In sum, a holding that the particular statute before us falls within the commerce power would not expand the scope of that Clause. Rather, it simply would apply pre-existing law to changing economic circumstances. See Heart of Atlanta Motel, Inc. v. United States (1964). It would recognize that, in today's economic world, gun-related violence near the classroom makes a significant difference to our economic, as well as our social, well-being. In accordance with well-accepted precedent, such a holding would permit Congress "to act in terms of economic ... realities," would interpret the commerce power as "an affirmative power commensurate with the national needs," and would acknowledge that the "commerce clause does not operate so as to render the nation powerless to defend itself against economic forces that Congress decrees inimical or destructive of the national economy."

Review Questions and Explanations: *Lopez*

1. The majority, concurrences and dissents all go into great detail about the doctrinal history of the Commerce Clause. Why do you think they do that?

2. What is Justice Kennedy's point in his concurrence?

3. What is Justice Thomas getting at? What would be the implications for society and government if his suggestion were taken up?

4. What role does federalism play in the Court's decisions? Note that here, the legislative jurisdiction prior to the Court's ruling was concurrent — the federal government and the states both regulated the area. How, if at all, did the federal law intrude on state autonomy, and how, if at all, did the majority protect state autonomy?

5. Does *Lopez* call the constitutionality of the 1964 Civil Rights Act into question? How can you tell?

Exercises: *Lopez*

1. Good lawyers working in evolving areas of law know how to exploit avenues of argument left open by the Court in its earlier cases. Suppose you are legal counsel to a Senator who wants to pass a new version of the Gun Free School Zones Act that could withstand a Commerce Clause challenge under the test developed in *Lopez*. How would you write the statute to increase the chances that the Court would uphold it?

2. A great deal of economic, social, and civil rights legislation has been enacted by Congress since the New Deal. Much of this legislation has become an assumed part of the background of American life. For example, in *Jones & Laughlin, Darby* and *Heart of Atlanta*, the court upheld the constitutionality of, respectively,

federal labor law, wage and hour laws and anti-discrimination laws. With this in mind, write 1–2 paragraphs addressing the following three questions:

a) Try to identify three other aspects of federal regulation of commerce, different from those just listed above, that people rely on and take for granted. If you did the earlier exercise generating the list of five statutes to consider under the pre-New Deal cases, you can rely on those.

b) What would happen to these laws if the Court reconsidered the "substantial effects" test, as suggested by Justice Thomas in his *Lopez* concurrence? Is this question relevant to the question of how the Court should interpret the Constitution? Why or why not?

c) In what way might the existence of, and society's reliance on, these federal laws constrain or shape contemporary Commerce Clause doctrine?

Guided Reading Questions: *United States v. Morrison*

1. Unlike its enactment of the Gun Free School Zones Act (at issue in *Lopez*), Congress made extensive findings of fact before enacting the Violence Against Women Act (VAWA). What were these findings, and how did the government argue that they related to "commerce among the states"?

2. What role does the distinction between "economic" and "non-economic" play in the *Morrison* decision? What role, if any, does the term "activity" play?

3. The majority opinion in *Morrison* cites *Wickard v. Filburn* approvingly. Under the Court's reasoning, what is the legally significant fact distinguishing *Wickard* from *Morrison*?

4. Justice Souter argues in his *Morrison* dissent that the Court must defer to congressional judgments about what does and does not substantially affect commerce. What reasons does he give for this position? How does the majority respond to his point?

5. Justice Breyer argues that the majority's "economic/non-economic" distinction will not protect the federalism values purportedly at stake in the case. What reasons does he give for this position? How does the majority respond to his point?

United States v. Morrison
529 U.S. 598 (2000)

Majority: *Rehnquist* (CJ), O'Connor, Scalia, Kennedy, Thomas,

Concurrence: *Thomas* (omitted)

Dissents: *Souter; Breyer;* Stevens, Ginsburg

CHIEF JUSTICE REHNQUIST delivered the opinion of the Court.

In these cases we consider the constitutionality of 42 U.S.C. § 13981, which provides a federal civil remedy for the victims of gender-motivated violence.

[Petitioner Christy Brzonkala, an undergraduate at Virginia Polytechnic Institute (Virginia Tech), alleged that she was raped on the Virginia Tech campus by respondents

Antonio Morrison and James Crawford, who were both students at Virginia Tech and members of its varsity football team. Brzonkala pursued remedies under University policies, but the university ultimately declined to punish the respondents. Brzonkala then sued Morrison, Crawford, and Virginia Tech in federal court, alleging that Morrison's attack violated VAWA § 13981. The court dismissed Brzonkala's § 13981 claim, on the ground that Congress lacked authority to enact the section. The Court of Appeals reversed, reinstating Brzonkala's § 13981 claim; but that decision was reversed by the Court of Appeals in a rehearing en banc: the en banc court affirmed the District Court's conclusion that § 13981 was unconstitutional. The Supreme Court granted certiorari.]

.... [Section] 13981 was part of the Violence Against Women Act of 1994. It states that "[a]ll persons within the United States shall have the right to be free from crimes of violence motivated by gender." 42 U.S.C. § 13981(b). To enforce that right, subsection (c) declares:

> A person (including a person who acts under color of any statute, ordinance, regulation, custom, or usage of any State) who commits a crime of violence motivated by gender and thus deprives another of the right declared in subsection (b) of this section shall be liable to the party injured, in an action for the recovery of compensatory and punitive damages, injunctive and declaratory relief, and such other relief as a court may deem appropriate.

.... Congress explicitly.... said that a "federal civil rights cause of action" is established "[p]ursuant to the affirmative power of Congress ... under section 8 of Article I of the Constitution." 42 U.S.C. § 13981(a)....

Petitioners.... seek to sustain § 13981 as a regulation of activity that substantially affects interstate commerce.... Lopez's review of Commerce Clause case law demonstrates that in those cases where we have sustained federal regulation of intrastate activity based upon the activity's substantial effects on interstate commerce, the activity in question has been some sort of economic endeavor.... Gender-motivated crimes of violence are not, in any sense of the phrase, economic activity. While we need not adopt a categorical rule against aggregating the effects of any noneconomic activity in order to decide these cases, thus far in our Nation's history our cases have upheld Commerce Clause regulation of intrastate activity only where that activity is economic in nature. See, e.g., id., at 559–560, and the cases cited therein.

Like the Gun-Free School Zones Act at issue in Lopez, § 13981 contains no jurisdictional element establishing that the federal cause of action is in pursuance of Congress' power to regulate interstate commerce.... In contrast with the lack of congressional findings that we faced in Lopez, § 13981 is supported by numerous findings regarding the serious impact that gender-motivated violence has on victims and their families. But the existence of congressional findings is not sufficient, by itself, to sustain the constitutionality of Commerce Clause legislation. As we stated in Lopez, "[S]imply because Congress may conclude that a particular activity substantially affects interstate commerce does not necessarily make it so." ...

In these cases, Congress' findings are substantially weakened by the fact that they rely so heavily on a method of reasoning that we have already rejected as unworkable if we are to maintain the Constitution's enumeration of powers.... The reasoning that petitioners advance seeks to follow the but-for causal chain from the initial occurrence of violent crime (the suppression of which has always been the prime object of the States' police power) to every attenuated effect upon interstate commerce. If accepted, petitioners' reasoning would allow Congress to regulate any crime as long as the nationwide, aggregated impact of that crime has substantial effects on employment, production, transit, or consumption. Indeed, if Congress may regulate gender-motivated violence, it would be able to regulate murder or any other type of violence since gender-motivated violence, as a subset of all violent crime, is certain to have lesser economic impacts than the larger class of which it is a part....

Petitioners' reasoning, moreover, will not limit Congress to regulating violence but may, as we suggested in Lopez, be applied equally as well to family law and other areas of traditional state regulation since the aggregate effect of marriage, divorce, and childrearing on the national economy is undoubtedly significant. Congress may have recognized this specter when it expressly precluded § 13981 from being used in the family law context. See 42 U.S.C. § 13981(e)(4) ...

We accordingly reject the argument that Congress may regulate noneconomic, violent criminal conduct based solely on that conduct's aggregate effect on interstate commerce. The Constitution requires a distinction between what is truly national and what is truly local.... [W]e can think of no better example of the police power, which the Founders denied the National Government and reposed in the States, than the suppression of violent crime and vindication of its victims....

[Petitioner] Brzonkala's complaint alleges that she was the victim of a brutal assault.... If the allegations here are true, no civilized system of justice could fail to provide her a remedy for the conduct of respondent Morrison. But under our federal system that remedy must be provided by the Commonwealth of Virginia, and not by the United States. The judgment of the Court of Appeals is affirmed.[4]

JUSTICE SOUTER, with whom JUSTICE STEVENS, JUSTICE GINSBURG, and JUSTICE BREYER join, dissenting.

.... Congress has the power to legislate with regard to activity that, in the aggregate, has a substantial effect on interstate commerce. See Wickard v. Filburn, (1942); Hodel v. Virginia Surface Mining & Reclamation Assn., (1981). The fact of such a substantial effect is not an issue for the courts in the first instance, but for the Congress, whose institutional capacity for gathering evidence and taking testimony far exceeds ours. By passing legislation, Congress indicates its conclusion, whether explicitly or not, that facts support its exercise of the commerce power. The business of the courts is to review the congressional assessment, not for soundness but simply for the rationality of concluding that a jurisdictional basis exists in fact. See ibid. Any explicit findings that Congress chooses to make, though not dispositive of the question of rationality, may advance judicial review by identifying factual authority on which Congress relied. Applying those propositions in these cases can lead to only one conclusion.

One obvious difference from United States v. Lopez, is the mountain of data assembled by Congress, here showing the effects of violence against women on interstate commerce. Passage of the Act in 1994 was preceded by four years of hearings, which included testimony from physicians and law professors; from survivors of rape and domestic violence; and from representatives of state law enforcement and private business.... Indeed, the legislative record here is far more voluminous than the record compiled by Congress and found sufficient in two prior cases upholding Title II of the Civil Rights Act of 1964 against

---

4. Editors' note: Congress expressly based the Violence Against Women Act on both its commerce power and its power to enforce the equal protection guarantee of the Fourteenth Amendment. But the Court also rejected that ground for sustaining VAWA. That portion of the opinion is excerpted below, in section F of this chapter.

Commerce Clause challenges. [See Heart of Atlanta Motel, Inc. v. United States, and Katzenbach v. McClung.]

While Congress did not, to my knowledge, calculate aggregate dollar values for the nationwide effects of racial discrimination in 1964, in 1994 it did rely on evidence of the harms caused by domestic violence and sexual assault, citing annual costs of $3 billion in 1990. Equally important, though, gender-based violence in the 1990s was shown to operate in a manner similar to racial discrimination in the 1960s in reducing the mobility of employees and their production and consumption of goods shipped in interstate commerce. Like racial discrimination, "[g]ender-based violence bars its most likely targets—women—from full partic[ipation] in the national economy."

.... Supply and demand for goods in interstate commerce will also be affected by the deaths of 2,000 to 4,000 women annually at the hands of domestic abusers, see S. Rep. No. 101-545, at 36, and by the reduction in the work force by the 100,000 or more rape victims who lose their jobs each year or are forced to quit, see id., at 56, H. R. Rep. No. 103-395, at 25–26. Violence against women may be found to affect interstate commerce and affect it substantially....

Thus the elusive heart of the majority's analysis in these cases is its statement that Congress's findings of fact are "weakened" by the presence of a disfavored "method of reasoning." This seems to suggest that the "substantial effects" analysis is not a factual enquiry, for Congress in the first instance with subsequent judicial review looking only to the rationality of the congressional conclusion, but one of a rather different sort, dependent upon a uniquely judicial competence.

This new characterization of substantial effects has no support in our cases....

The premise that the enumeration of powers implies that other powers are withheld is sound; the conclusion that some particular categories of subject matter are therefore presumptively beyond the reach of the commerce power is, however, a non sequitur. From the fact that Art. I, §8, cl. 3 grants an authority limited to regulating commerce, it follows only that Congress may claim no authority under that section to address any subject that does not affect commerce. It does not at all follow that an activity affecting commerce nonetheless falls outside the commerce power, depending on the specific character of the activity, or the authority of a State to regulate it along with Congress. My disagreement with the majority is not, however, confined to logic, for history has shown that categorical exclusions have proven as unworkable in practice as they are unsupportable in theory....

Why is the majority tempted to reject the lesson so painfully learned in 1937? An answer emerges from contrasting Wickard with one of the predecessor cases it superseded. It was obvious in Wickard that growing wheat for consumption right on the farm was not "commerce" in the common vocabulary, but that did not matter constitutionally so long as the aggregated activity of domestic wheat growing affected commerce substantially. Just a few years before Wickard, however, it had certainly been no less obvious that "mining" practices could substantially affect commerce, even though Carter Coal Co., supra, had held mining regulation beyond the national commerce power. When we try to fathom the difference between the two cases, it is clear that they did not go in different directions because the Carter Coal Court could not understand a causal connection that the Wickard Court could grasp; the difference, rather, turned on the fact that the Court in Carter Coal had a reason for trying to maintain its categorical, formalistic distinction, while that reason had been abandoned by the time Wickard was decided. The reason was laissez-faire economics, the point of which was to keep government interference to a minimum. The Court in Carter Coal was still trying to create a laissez-faire world out of the 20th-century economy, and formalistic commercial distinctions were thought to be useful instruments in achieving that object. The Court in Wickard knew it could not do any such thing and in the aftermath of the New Deal had long since stopped attempting the impossible. Without the animating economic theory, there was no point in contriving formalisms in a war with Chief Justice Marshall's conception of the commerce power.

.... [I]n the minds of the majority there is a new animating theory that makes categorical formalism seem useful again.... It is the instrument by which assertions of national power are to be limited in favor of preserving a supposedly discernible, proper sphere of state autonomy to legislate or refrain from legislating as the individual States see fit. The legitimacy of the Court's current emphasis on the noncommercial nature of regulated activity, then, does not turn on any logic serving the text of the Commerce Clause or on the realism of the majority's view of the national economy....

The objection to reviving traditional state spheres of action as a consideration in commerce analysis, however, not only rests on the portent of incoherence, but is compounded by a further defect just as fundamental. The defect, in essence, is the majority's rejection of the Founders' considered judgment that politics, not judicial review, should mediate between state and national interests as the strength and legislative jurisdiction of the National Government inevitably increased through the expected growth of the national economy. Whereas today's majority takes a leaf from the book of the old judicial economists in saying that the Court should somehow draw the line to keep the federal relationship in a proper balance, Madison, [James] Wilson, and Marshall understood the Constitution very differently....

JUSTICE BREYER, with whom JUSTICE STEVENS joins, and with whom JUSTICE SOUTER and JUSTICE GINSBURG join as to Part I-A, dissenting.

.... The "economic/noneconomic" distinction is not easy to apply. Does the local street corner mugger engage in "economic" activity or "noneconomic" activity when he mugs for money? Would evidence that desire for economic domination underlies many brutal crimes against women save the present statute?

The line becomes yet harder to draw given the need for exceptions. The Court itself would permit Congress to aggregate, hence regulate, "noneconomic" activity taking place at economic establishments. See Heart of Atlanta Motel, Inc. v. United States, 379 U.S. 241 (1964) (upholding civil rights laws forbidding discrimination at local motels); Katzenbach v. McClung, 379 U.S. 294 (1964) (same for restaurants); Lopez, supra, at 559 (recognizing congressional power to aggregate, hence forbid, noneconomically motivated discrimination at public accommodations); ante, at 9–10 (same). And it would permit Congress to regulate where that regulation is "an essential part of a larger regulation of economic activity, in which the regulatory scheme could be undercut unless the intrastate activity were regulated." Lopez, supra, at 561; cf. Controlled Substances Act, 21 U.S.C. § 801 et seq. (regulating drugs produced for home consumption). Given the former exception, can Congress simply rewrite the present law and limit its application to restaurants, hotels, perhaps universities, and other places of public accommodation? Given the latter exception, can Congress save the present law by including it, or much of it, in a broader "Safe Transport" or "Workplace Safety" act?

More important, why should we give critical constitutional importance to the economic, or noneconomic, nature of an interstate-commerce-affecting cause? If chemical emanations through indirect environmental change cause identical, severe commercial harm outside a State, why should it matter whether local factories or home fireplaces release them? The Constitution itself refers only to Congress' power to "regulate Commerce ... among the several States," and to make laws "necessary and proper" to implement that power. Art. I, § 8, cls. 3, 18. The language says nothing about either the local nature, or the economic nature, of an interstate-commerce-affecting cause.

This Court has long held that only the interstate commercial effects, not the local nature of the cause, are constitutionally relevant. Nothing in the Constitution's language, or that of earlier cases prior to Lopez, explains why the Court should ignore one highly relevant characteristic of an interstate-commerce-affecting cause (how "local" it is), while placing critical constitutional weight upon a different, less obviously relevant, feature (how "economic" it is).

Most important, the Court's complex rules seem unlikely to help secure the very object that they seek, namely, the protection of "areas of traditional state regulation" from federal intrusion. The Court's rules, even if broadly interpreted, are underinclusive. The local pickpocket is no less a traditional subject of state regulation than is the local gender-motivated assault. Regardless, the Court reaffirms, as it should, Congress' well-established and frequently exercised power to enact laws that satisfy a commerce-related jurisdictional prerequisite — for example, that some item relevant to the federally regulated activity has at some time crossed a state line....

And in a world where most everyday products or their component parts cross interstate boundaries, Congress will frequently find it possible to redraft a statute using language that ties the regulation to the interstate movement of some relevant object, thereby regulating local criminal activity or, for that matter, family affairs. See, e.g., Child Support Recovery Act of 1992, 18 U.S.C. § 228. Although this possibility does not give the Federal Government the power to regulate everything, it means that any substantive limitation will apply randomly in terms of the interests the majority seeks to protect. How much would be gained, for example, were Congress to reenact the present law in the form of "An Act Forbidding Violence Against Women Perpetrated at Public Accommodations or by Those Who Have Moved in, or through the Use of Items that Have Moved in, Interstate Commerce"? Complex Commerce Clause rules creating fine distinctions that achieve only random results do little to further the important federalist interests that called them into being. That is why modern (pre-Lopez) case law rejected them.

The majority, aware of these difficulties, is nonetheless concerned with what it sees as an important contrary consideration. To determine the lawfulness of statutes simply by asking whether Congress could reasonably have found that aggregated local instances significantly affect interstate commerce will allow Congress to regulate almost anything. Virtually all local activity, when instances are aggregated, can have "substantial effects on employment, production, transit, or consumption." Hence Congress could "regulate any crime," and perhaps "marriage, divorce, and childrearing" as well, obliterating the "Constitution's distinction between national and local authority."

This consideration, however, while serious, does not reflect a jurisprudential defect, so much as it reflects a practical reality. We live in a Nation knit together by two centuries of scientific, technological, commercial, and environmental change. Those changes, taken together, mean that virtually every kind of activity, no matter how local, genuinely can affect commerce, or its conditions, outside the State — at least when considered in the aggregate. Heart of Atlanta Motel, 379 U.S. at 251. And that fact makes it close to impossible for courts to develop meaningful subject-matter categories that would exclude some kinds of local activities from ordinary Commerce Clause "aggregation" rules without, at the same time, depriving Congress of the power to regulate activities that have a genuine and important effect upon interstate commerce.

Since judges cannot change the world, the "defect" means that, within the bounds of the rational, Congress, not the courts, must remain primarily responsible for striking the appropriate state/federal balance. Congress is institutionally motivated to do so. Its Members represent state and local district interests. They consider the views of state and local officials when they legislate, and they have even developed formal procedures to ensure that such consideration takes place. Moreover, Congress often can better reflect state concerns for autonomy in the details of sophisticated statutory schemes than can the judiciary, which cannot easily gather the relevant facts and which must apply more general legal rules and categories. Not surprisingly, the bulk of American law is still state law, and overwhelmingly so....

Review Questions and Explanations: *Morrison*

1. What role does federalism play in the Court's decisions? Does the majority in *Morrison* succeed in grounding its discussion of federalism in the Constitution?

2. Once again, the majority seems concerned with an application of the substantial effects test that would authorize Congress to regulate "family law and other areas of traditional state regulation since the aggregate effect of marriage, divorce, and childrearing on the national economy is undoubtedly significant." Is the concern here federalism pure and simple — or does the Court have other concerns as well?

3. Is this case distinguishable from *Heart of Atlanta*? If so, how? If not, is the Civil Rights Act of 1964 in danger of being held unconstitutional?

4. Do congressional findings matter in these cases, or not?

Exercises: *Lopez* and *Morrison*

1. Suppose Congress enacts a law making "car-jacking" (stealing a car at gunpoint while the driver is in the vehicle) a federal crime. Under *Lopez* and *Morrison*, is this law a constitutional exercise of Congress's Commerce Clause power? What type of facts, findings or additional statutory provisions can you think of that would increase the chances that the statute would be found constitutional? What would hurt its chances?

2. Under *Lopez* and *Morrison*, can Congress enact a law making it a crime to grow small amounts of marijuana for purely personal consumption, without requiring proof that the marijuana plants or seeds were bought or sold, or that they were transported across state lines?

Exercise: The ACA Case

The ACA sought to address the fact that millions of Americans had no health insurance, yet actively participated in the health care market, consuming health care services for which they did not pay. The provision addressing this issue is the Affordable Care Act's "minimum coverage provision," also known as the "individual mandate."

The following excerpt from one of the lower court decisions addressing the ACA, *Thomas Moore Law Center v. Obama*, 651 F.3d 529 (6th Cir. 2011), provides some relevant background:

> Congress found that the minimum coverage provision is an essential cog in the Affordable Care Act's comprehensive scheme to reform the national markets in health care delivery and health insurance.... [T]he Act bars certain practices in the insurance industry that have prevented individuals from obtaining and maintaining health insurance. The guaranteed issue requirement bars insurance companies from denying coverage to individuals with pre-existing conditions, and the community rating requirement prohibits insurance companies from charging higher rates to individuals based on their medical history.... Congress determined that "the Federal Government has a significant role in regulating health insurance," and "[t]he requirement is an essential part of this larger regulation of economic activity." 42 U.S.C. § 18091(a)(2)(H). Congress found that without the minimum coverage provision, other provisions in the Act, in particular the guaranteed issue and community rating requirements, would increase the incentives for individuals to "wait to purchase health insurance until they needed care." *Id.* § 18091(a)(2)(I). This would exacerbate the current problems in the markets for health care delivery and health insurance. *See id.* Conversely, Congress found that "[b]y significantly reducing the number of the uninsured, the [minimum coverage] requirement, together with the other provisions of this Act, will lower health insurance premiums." *Id.* § 18091(a)(2)(F). Congress concluded that the minimum coverage provision "is essential to creating effective health insurance markets in which improved health insurance products that are guaranteed issue and do not exclude coverage of pre-existing conditions can be sold." *Id.* § 18091(a)(2)(I).

The ACA was challenged by various private individuals, groups and states. The challenge was based in part on the ground that the individual mandate exceeds Congress's power under the Commerce Clause. In a nutshell, the challengers' argument is this: under the substantial effects test, as construed by *Lopez* and *Morrison*, Congress can regulate only "economic activity" that has a substantial effect on interstate commerce. But the individual mandate, by requiring the purchase of health insurance (to avoid becoming liable for a tax "penalty"), regulates *inactivity*.

With one or more fellow students, develop the arguments for and against this position, and argue them to one of your fellow students playing the role of judge.

When reading the next case, *Gonzales v. Raich*, you will notice that the five-to-four alignment of justices present in *Lopez* and *Morrison* breaks down. It will be helpful in understanding the case, therefore, to think through why the deviating justices did not vote as you might have anticipated. What legally significant differences did they see between this case and *Lopez* and *Morrison*? Also ask yourself whether *Raich* applied or *changed* the test developed in *Lopez* and *Morrison*.

Guided Reading Questions: *Gonzales v. Raich*

1. *Lopez* and *Morrison* tell us that the Commerce Clause allows Congress to regulate things moving in interstate commerce, the channels and instrumentalities of interstate commerce, and things that substantially effect interstate commerce. To avoid congressional reach, the challengers in *Raich* tried to keep their conduct out of the first two categories. What efforts did they make to do so?

2. Why did the Court find that the challengers' marijuana use "substantially affected" interstate commerce? What assumptions (or facts) did the Court rely on in reaching this decision?

3. Is *Wickard* an on-point precedent, or can you distinguish it from *Raich* in a legally meaningful way?

4. *Lopez* and *Morrison* distinguished "economic" from "non-economic" activity. What, if anything, does *Raich* add to our understanding of those terms?

5. Read Justice Scalia's concurring opinion carefully. What is his constitutional argument?

6. The majority and dissent seem to disagree about whether the plaintiffs/respondents (Raich and Monson) are or are not within a distinct, separable group from illegal drug traffickers. What is the factual basis for this disagreement? What is the legal implication of deciding whether they are distinct and separable?

Gonzales v. Raich

545 U.S. 1 (2005)

Majority: *Stevens*, Kennedy, Souter, Ginsburg, Breyer

Concurrence in the judgment: *Scalia*

Dissents: *O'Connor*, Rehnquist (CJ), *Thomas*

JUSTICE STEVENS delivered the opinion of the Court.

California is one of at least nine States that authorize the use of marijuana for medicinal purposes.... In 1996, California voters passed Proposition 215, now codified as the Compassionate Use Act of 1996. The proposition was designed to ensure that "seriously ill" residents of the State have access to marijuana for medical purposes, and to encourage Federal and State Governments to take steps towards ensuring the safe and affordable distribution of the drug to patients in need. The Act creates an exemption from criminal prosecution for physicians, as well as for patients and primary caregivers who possess or cultivate marijuana for medicinal purposes with the recommendation or approval of a physician. A "primary caregiver" is a person who has consistently assumed responsibility for the housing, health, or safety of the patient.

Respondents Angel Raich and Diane Monson are California residents who suffer from a variety of serious medical conditions and have sought to avail themselves of medical marijuana pursuant to the terms of the Compassionate Use Act. They are being treated by licensed, board-certified family practitioners, who have concluded, after prescribing a host of conventional medicines to treat respondents' conditions and to alleviate their associated symptoms, that marijuana is the only drug available that provides effective treatment. Both women have been using marijuana as a medication for several years pursuant to their doctors' recommendation, and both rely heavily on cannabis to function on a daily basis. Indeed, Raich's physician believes that forgoing cannabis treatments would certainly cause Raich excruciating pain and could very well prove fatal.

Respondent Monson cultivates her own marijuana, and ingests the drug in a variety of ways including smoking and using a vaporizer. Respondent Raich, by contrast, is unable to cultivate her own, and thus relies on two caregivers, litigating as "John Does," to provide her with locally grown marijuana at no charge. These caregivers also process the cannabis into hashish or keif, and Raich herself processes some of the marijuana into oils, balms, and foods for consumption.

On August 15, 2002, county deputy sheriffs and agents from the federal Drug Enforcement Administration (DEA) came to Monson's home. After a thorough investigation, the county officials concluded that her use of marijuana was entirely lawful as a matter of California law. Nevertheless, after a 3-hour standoff, the federal agents seized and destroyed all six of her cannabis plants.

Respondents thereafter brought this action against the Attorney General of the United States and the head of the DEA seeking injunctive and declaratory relief prohibiting the enforcement of the federal Controlled Substances Act (CSA), 84 Stat. 1242, 21 U.S.C. § 801 et seq., to the extent it prevents them from possessing, obtaining, or manufacturing cannabis for their personal medical use....

The District Court denied respondents' motion for a preliminary injunction.... A divided panel of the Court of Appeals for the Ninth Circuit reversed and ordered the District Court to enter a preliminary injunction. Raich v. Ashcroft, 352 F.3d 1222 (2003). The court found that respondents had "demonstrated a strong likelihood of success on their claim that, as applied to them, the CSA is an unconstitutional exercise of Congress' Commerce Clause authority." ...

The obvious importance of the case prompted our grant of certiorari. The case is made difficult by respondents' strong arguments that they will suffer irreparable harm because, despite a congressional finding to the contrary, marijuana does have valid therapeutic purposes. The question before us, however, is not whether it is wise to enforce the statute in these circumstances; rather, it is whether Congress' power to regulate interstate markets for medicinal substances encompasses the portions of those markets that are supplied with drugs produced and consumed locally. Well-settled law controls our answer. The CSA is a valid exercise of federal power, even as applied to the troubling facts of this case. We accordingly vacate the judgment of the Court of Appeals.

II

.... [I]n 1970, after declaration of the national "war on drugs," federal drug policy underwent a significant transformation.... [Title II of the Controlled Substances Act of 1970] repealed most of the earlier antidrug laws in favor of a comprehensive regime to combat the international and interstate traffic in illicit drugs. The main objectives of the CSA were to conquer drug abuse and to control the legitimate and illegitimate traffic in controlled substances.

> FN20.... [Congress found, among other things, that] "(4) Local distribution and possession of controlled substances contribute to swelling the interstate traffic in such substances." "(5) Controlled substances manufactured and distributed intrastate cannot be differentiated from controlled substances manufactured and distributed interstate. Thus, it is not feasible to

distinguish, in terms of controls, between controlled substances manufactured and distributed interstate and controlled substances manufactured and distributed intrastate." "(6) Federal control of the intrastate incidents of the traffic in controlled substances is essential to the effective control of the interstate incidents of such traffic." 21 U.S.C. § 801(1)–(6).

Congress was particularly concerned with the need to prevent the diversion of drugs from legitimate to illicit channels.

To effectuate these goals, Congress devised a closed regulatory system making it unlawful to manufacture, distribute, dispense, or possess any controlled substance except in a manner authorized by the CSA. 21 U.S.C. §§ 841(a)(1), 844(a). The CSA categorizes all controlled substances into five schedules. § 812. The drugs are grouped together based on their accepted medical uses, the potential for abuse, and their psychological and physical effects on the body. §§ 811, 812. Each schedule is associated with a distinct set of controls regarding the manufacture, distribution, and use of the substances listed therein. §§ 821–830....

In enacting the CSA, Congress classified marijuana as a Schedule I drug. 21 U.S.C. § 812(c). This preliminary classification was based, in part, on the recommendation of the Assistant Secretary of HEW "that marihuana be retained within schedule I at least until the completion of certain studies now underway." Schedule I drugs are categorized as such because of their high potential for abuse, lack of any accepted medical use, and absence of any accepted safety for use in medically supervised treatment. § 812(b)(1). These three factors, in varying gradations, are also used to categorize drugs in the other four schedules. For example, Schedule II substances also have a high potential for abuse which may lead to severe psychological or physical dependence, but unlike Schedule I drugs, they have a currently accepted medical use. § 812(b)(2). By classifying marijuana as a Schedule I drug, as opposed to listing it on a lesser schedule, the manufacture, distribution, or possession of marijuana became a criminal offense, with the sole exception being use of the drug as part of a Food and Drug Administration pre-approved research study. §§ 823(f), 841(a)(1), 844(a).

The CSA provides for the periodic updating of schedules and delegates authority to the Attorney General, after consultation with the Secretary of Health and Human Services, to add, remove, or transfer substances to, from, or between schedules. § 811. Despite considerable efforts to reschedule marijuana, it remains a Schedule I drug.

III

Respondents in this case do not ... contend that any provision or section of the CSA amounts to an unconstitutional exercise of congressional authority. Rather, respondents' challenge is actually quite limited; they argue that the CSA's categorical prohibition of the manufacture and possession of marijuana as applied to the intrastate manufacture and possession of marijuana for medical purposes pursuant to California law exceeds Congress' authority under the Commerce Clause.

In assessing the validity of congressional regulation, none of our Commerce Clause cases can be viewed in isolation. As charted in considerable detail in United States v. Lopez, our understanding of the reach of the Commerce Clause, as well as Congress' assertion of authority thereunder, has evolved over time. The Commerce Clause emerged as the Framers' response to the central problem giving rise to the Constitution itself: the absence of any federal commerce power under the Articles of Confederation. For the first century of our history, the primary use of the Clause was to preclude the kind of discriminatory state legislation that had once been permissible. Then, in response to rapid industrial development and an increasingly interdependent national economy, Congress "ushered in a new era of federal regulation under the commerce power," beginning with the enactment of the Interstate Commerce Act in 1887, and the Sherman Antitrust Act in 1890.

Our case law firmly establishes Congress' power to regulate purely local activities that are part of an economic "class of activities" that have a substantial effect on interstate commerce. See, e.g., Perez, 402 U.S., at 151; Wickard v. Filburn, 317 U.S. 111, 128–129 (1942). As we stated in Wickard, "even if appellee's activity be local and though it may not be regarded as commerce, it may still, whatever its nature, be reached by Congress if it exerts a substantial economic effect on interstate commerce." Id., at 125. We have never required Congress to legislate with scientific exactitude. When Congress decides that the "total incidence" of a practice poses a threat to a national market, it may regulate the entire class. In this vein, we have reiterated that when "a general regulatory statute bears a substantial relation to commerce, the de minimis character of individual instances arising under that statute is of no consequence." E.g., Lopez, 514 U.S., at 558.

Our decision in Wickard is of particular relevance. In Wickard, we upheld the application of regulations promulgated under the Agricultural Adjustment Act of 1938, which were designed to control the volume of wheat moving in interstate and foreign commerce in order to avoid surpluses and consequent abnormally low prices. The regulations established an allotment of 11.1 acres for Filburn's 1941 wheat crop, but he sowed 23 acres, intending to use the excess by consuming it on his own farm. Filburn argued that even though we had sustained Congress' power to regulate the production of goods for commerce, that power did not authorize "federal regulation [of] production not intended in any part for commerce but wholly for consumption on the farm." Wickard, 317 U.S., at 118. Justice Jackson's opinion for a unanimous Court rejected this submission. He wrote:

> The effect of the statute before us is to restrict the amount which may be produced for market and the extent as well to which one may forestall resort to the market by producing to meet his own needs. That appellee's own contribution to the demand for wheat may be trivial by itself is not enough to remove him from the scope of federal regulation where, as here, his contribution, taken together with that of many others similarly situated, is far from trivial.

Wickard thus establishes that Congress can regulate purely intrastate activity that is not itself "commercial," in that it is not produced for sale, if it concludes that failure to regulate that class of activity would undercut the regulation of the interstate market in that commodity.

The similarities between this case and Wickard are striking. Like the farmer in Wickard, respondents are cultivating, for home consumption, a fungible commodity for which there is an established, albeit illegal, interstate market. Just as the Agricultural Adjustment Act was designed "to control the volume [of wheat] moving in interstate and foreign commerce in order to avoid surpluses ..." and consequently control the market price a primary purpose of the CSA is to control the supply and demand of controlled substances in both lawful and unlawful drug markets. In Wickard, we had no difficulty concluding that Congress had a rational basis for believing that, when viewed in the aggregate, leaving home-consumed wheat outside the regulatory scheme would have a substantial influence on price and market conditions. Here too, Congress had a rational basis for concluding that leaving home-consumed marijuana outside federal control would similarly affect price and market conditions.

More concretely, one concern prompting inclusion of wheat grown for home consumption in the 1938 Act was that rising market prices could draw such wheat into the interstate market, resulting in lower market prices. The parallel concern making it appropriate to include marijuana grown for home consumption in the CSA is the likelihood that the high demand in the interstate market will draw such marijuana into that market. While the diversion of homegrown wheat tended to frustrate the federal interest in stabilizing prices by regulating the volume of commercial transactions in the interstate market, the diversion of homegrown marijuana tends to frustrate the federal interest in eliminating commercial transactions in the interstate market in their entirety. In both cases, the regulation is squarely within Congress' commerce power because production of the commodity meant for home consumption, be it wheat or marijuana, has a substantial effect on supply and demand in the national market for that commodity.

> FN29. To be sure, the wheat market is a lawful market that Congress sought to protect and stabilize, whereas the marijuana market is an unlawful market that Congress sought to eradicate. This difference, however, is of no constitutional import. It has long been settled that Congress' power to regulate commerce includes the power to prohibit commerce in a particular commodity.

The fact that Wickard's own impact on the market was "trivial by itself" was not a sufficient reason for removing him from the scope of federal regulation. That the Secretary of Agriculture elected to exempt even smaller farms from regulation does not speak to his power to regulate all those whose aggregated production was significant, nor did that fact play any role in the Court's analysis. Moreover, even though Wickard was indeed a commercial farmer, the activity he was engaged in — the cultivation of wheat for home consumption — was not treated by the Court as part of his commercial farming operation. See Wickard, 317 U.S., at 125 (recognizing that Wickard's activity "may not be regarded as commerce"). And while it is true that the record in the Wickard case itself established the causal connection between the production for local use and the national market, we have before us findings by Congress to the same effect....

In assessing the scope of Congress' authority under the Commerce Clause, we stress that the task before us is a modest one. We need not determine whether respondents' activities, taken in the aggregate, substantially affect interstate commerce in fact, but only whether a "rational basis" exists for so concluding. Given the enforcement difficulties that attend distinguishing between marijuana cultivated locally and marijuana grown elsewhere, and concerns about diversion into illicit channels, we have no difficulty concluding that Congress had a rational basis for believing that failure to regulate the intrastate manufacture and possession of marijuana would leave a gaping hole in the CSA. Thus, as in Wickard, when it enacted comprehensive legislation to regulate the interstate market in a fungible commodity, Congress was acting well within its authority to "make all Laws which shall be necessary and proper" to "regulate Commerce ... among the several States." U.S. Const., Art. I, § 8. That the regulation ensnares some purely intrastate activity is of no moment. As we have done many times before, we refuse to excise individual components of that larger scheme.

IV

.... [Respondents rely heavily on] Lopez and Morrison.... At issue in Lopez was the validity of the Gun-Free School Zones Act of 1990, which was a brief, single-subject statute making it a crime for an individual to possess a gun in a school zone.... Distinguishing our earlier cases holding that comprehensive regulatory statutes may be validly applied to local conduct that does not, when viewed in isolation, have a significant impact on interstate commerce, we held the statute invalid. We explained:

> .... Section 922(q) is not an essential part of a larger regulation of economic activity, in which the regulatory scheme could be undercut unless the intrastate

activity were regulated. It cannot, therefore, be sustained under our cases upholding regulations of activities that arise out of or are connected with a commercial transaction, which viewed in the aggregate, substantially affects interstate commerce. 514 U.S., at 56.

The statutory scheme that the Government is defending in this litigation is at the opposite end of the regulatory spectrum. As explained above, the CSA, enacted in 1970 as part of the Comprehensive Drug Abuse Prevention and Control Act, was a lengthy and detailed statute creating a comprehensive framework for regulating the production, distribution, and possession of five classes of "controlled substances." ... [Listing marijuana on Schedule I] was merely one of many "essential part[s] of a larger regulation of economic activity, in which the regulatory scheme could be undercut unless the intrastate activity were regulated." Lopez, 514 U.S., at 561. Our opinion in Lopez casts no doubt on the validity of such a program.

Unlike those at issue in Lopez and Morrison, the activities regulated by the CSA are quintessentially economic. "Economics" refers to "the production, distribution, and consumption of commodities." Webster's Third New International Dictionary 720 (1966). The CSA is a statute that regulates the production, distribution, and consumption of commodities for which there is an established, and lucrative, interstate market. Prohibiting the intrastate possession or manufacture of an article of commerce is a rational (and commonly utilized) means of regulating commerce in that product. Such prohibitions include specific decisions requiring that a drug be withdrawn from the market as a result of the failure to comply with regulatory requirements as well as decisions excluding Schedule I drugs entirely from the market. Because the CSA is a statute that directly regulates economic, commercial activity, our opinion in Morrison casts no doubt on its constitutionality.

The Court of Appeals was able to conclude otherwise only by isolating a "separate and distinct" class of activities that it held to be beyond the reach of federal power, defined as "the intrastate, noncommercial cultivation, possession and use of marijuana for personal medical purposes on the advice of a physician and in accordance with state law." The court characterized this class as "different in kind from drug trafficking." The differences between the members of a class so defined and the principal traffickers in Schedule I substances might be sufficient to justify a policy decision exempting the narrower class from the coverage of the CSA. The question, however, is whether Congress' contrary policy judgment, i.e., its decision to include this narrower "class of activities" within the larger regulatory scheme, was constitutionally deficient. We have no difficulty concluding that Congress acted rationally in determining that none of the characteristics making up the purported class, whether viewed individually or in the aggregate, compelled an exemption from the CSA; rather, the subdivided class of activities defined by the Court of Appeals was an essential part of the larger regulatory scheme.

First,.... the mere fact that marijuana—like virtually every other controlled substance regulated by the CSA—is used for medicinal purposes cannot possibly serve to distinguish it from the core activities regulated by the CSA.

Nor can it serve as an "objective marker" or "objective factor" to arbitrarily narrow the relevant class as the dissenters suggest. More fundamentally, if ... the personal cultivation, possession, and use of marijuana for medicinal purposes is beyond the "outer limits of Congress' Commerce Clause authority," it must also be true that such personal use of marijuana (or any other homegrown drug) for recreational purposes is also beyond those "outer limits," whether or not a State elects to authorize or even regulate such use.... One need not have a degree in economics to understand why a nationwide exemption for the vast quantity of marijuana (or other drugs) locally cultivated for personal use (which presumably would include use by friends, neighbors, and family members) may have a substantial impact on the interstate market for this extraordinarily popular substance. The congressional judgment that an exemption for such a significant segment of the total market would undermine the orderly enforcement of the entire regulatory scheme is entitled to a strong presumption of validity. Indeed, that judgment is not only rational, but "visible to the naked eye," Lopez, 514 U.S., at 563, under any commonsense appraisal of the probable consequences of such an open-ended exemption.

Second, limiting the activity to marijuana possession and cultivation "in accordance with state law" cannot serve to place respondents' activities beyond congressional reach. The Supremacy Clause unambiguously provides that if there is any conflict between federal and state law, federal law shall prevail. It is beyond peradventure that federal power over commerce is "superior to that of the States to provide for the welfare or necessities of their inhabitants," however legitimate or dire those necessities may be.... [S]tate action cannot circumscribe Congress' plenary commerce power.

> FN38. That is so even if California's current controls (enacted eight years after the Compassionate Use Act was passed) are "[e]ffective," as the dissenters would have us blindly presume. California's decision (made 34 years after the CSA was enacted) to impose "stric[t] controls" on the "cultivation and possession of marijuana for medical purposes," (Thomas, J., dissenting), cannot retroactively divest Congress of its authority under the Commerce Clause. Indeed, Justice Thomas' urgings to the contrary would turn the Supremacy Clause on its head, and would resurrect limits on congressional power that have long since been rejected....

Respondents acknowledge this proposition, but nonetheless contend that their activities were not "an essential part of a larger regulatory scheme" because they had been "isolated by the State of California, and [are] policed by the State of California," and thus remain "entirely separated from the market." Tr. of Oral Arg. 27. The dissenters fall prey to similar reasoning. The notion that California law has surgically excised a discrete activity that is hermetically sealed off from the larger interstate marijuana market is a dubious proposition, and, more importantly, one that Congress could have rationally rejected.

Indeed, that the California exemptions will have a significant impact on both the supply and demand sides of the market for marijuana is not just "plausible" as the principal dissent concedes, it is readily apparent. The exemption for physicians provides them with an economic incentive to grant their patients permission to use the drug. In contrast to most prescriptions for legal drugs, which limit the dosage and duration of the usage, under California law the doctor's permission to recommend marijuana use is open-ended. The authority to grant permission whenever the doctor determines that a patient is afflicted with "any other illness for which marijuana provides relief," Cal. Health & Safety Code Ann. § 11362.5(b)(1)(A) (West Supp. 2005), is broad enough to allow even the most scrupulous doctor to conclude that some recreational uses would be therapeutic. And our cases have taught us that there are some unscrupulous physicians who overprescribe when it is sufficiently profitable to do so.

The exemption for cultivation by patients and caregivers can only increase the supply of marijuana in the California market.

> FN41. The state policy allows patients to possess up to eight ounces of dried marijuana, and to cultivate up to 6 mature or 12 immature plants. Cal. Health & Safety Code Ann. § 11362.77(a) (West Supp. 2005). However, the quantity limitations serve only as a floor. Based on a doctor's recommendation, a patient can possess whatever quantity is

necessary to satisfy his medical needs, and cities and counties are given carte blanche to establish more generous limits. Indeed, several cities and counties have done just that....

The likelihood that all such production will promptly terminate when patients recover or will precisely match the patients' medical needs during their convalescence seems remote; whereas the danger that excesses will satisfy some of the admittedly enormous demand for recreational use seems obvious.

> FN42. For example, respondent Raich attests that she uses 2.5 ounces of cannabis a week. App. 82. Yet as a resident of Oakland, she is entitled to possess up to 3 pounds of processed marijuana at any given time, nearly 20 times more than she uses on a weekly basis.

Moreover, that the national and international narcotics trade has thrived in the face of vigorous criminal enforcement efforts suggests that no small number of unscrupulous people will make use of the California exemptions to serve their commercial ends whenever it is feasible to do so. Taking into account the fact that California is only one of at least nine States to have authorized the medical use of marijuana, a fact Justice O'Connor's dissent conveniently disregards in arguing that the demonstrated effect on commerce while admittedly "plausible" is ultimately "unsubstantiated," Congress could have rationally concluded that the aggregate impact on the national market of all the transactions exempted from federal supervision is unquestionably substantial....

V

.... As the Solicitor General confirmed during oral argument, the statute authorizes procedures for the reclassification of Schedule I drugs. But perhaps even more important than these legal avenues is the democratic process, in which the voices of voters allied with these respondents may one day be heard in the halls of Congress. Under the present state of the law, however, the judgment of the Court of Appeals must be vacated. The case is remanded for further proceedings consistent with this opinion.

JUSTICE SCALIA, concurring in the judgment.

I agree with the Court's holding that the Controlled Substances Act (CSA) may validly be applied to respondents' cultivation, distribution, and possession of marijuana for personal, medicinal use. I write separately because my understanding of the doctrinal foundation on which that holding rests is, if not inconsistent with that of the Court, at least more nuanced.

.... [U]nlike the channels, instrumentalities, and agents of interstate commerce, activities that substantially affect interstate commerce are not themselves part of interstate commerce, and thus the power to regulate them cannot come from the Commerce Clause alone.... Congress's regulatory authority over intrastate activities that are not themselves part of interstate commerce (including activities that have a substantial effect on interstate commerce) derives from the Necessary and Proper Clause. And the category of "activities that substantially affect interstate commerce," Lopez, supra, at 559, is *incomplete* because the authority to enact laws necessary and proper for the regulation of interstate commerce is not limited to laws governing intrastate activities that substantially affect interstate commerce. Where necessary to make a regulation of interstate commerce effective, Congress may regulate even those intrastate activities that do not themselves substantially affect interstate commerce.

.... In Lopez and Morrison, the Court—conscious of the potential of the "substantially affects" test to "obliterate the distinction between what is national and what is local," Lopez, supra, at 566–567 (quoting A. L. A. Schechter Poultry Corp. v. United States,

295 U.S. 495, 554 (1935)—rejected the argument that Congress may regulate noneconomic activity based solely on the effect that it may have on interstate commerce through a remote chain of inferences....

As we implicitly acknowledged in Lopez, however, Congress's authority to enact laws necessary and proper for the regulation of interstate commerce is not limited to laws directed against economic activities that have a substantial effect on interstate commerce. Though the conduct in Lopez was not economic, the Court nevertheless recognized that it could be regulated as "an essential part of a larger regulation of economic activity, in which the regulatory scheme could be undercut unless the intrastate activity were regulated." 514 U.S., at 561. This statement referred to those cases permitting the regulation of intrastate activities "which in a substantial way interfere with or obstruct the exercise of the granted power." Wrightwood Dairy Co., 315 U.S., at 119.... [W]here Congress has the authority to enact a regulation of interstate commerce, "it possesses every power needed to make that regulation effective." Id.

.... The regulation of an intrastate activity may be essential to a comprehensive regulation of interstate commerce even though the intrastate activity does not itself "substantially affect" interstate commerce. Moreover, as the passage from Lopez quoted above suggests, Congress may regulate even noneconomic local activity if that regulation is a necessary part of a more general regulation of interstate commerce. The relevant question is simply whether the means chosen are "reasonably adapted" to the attainment of a legitimate end under the commerce power ....

.... As Lopez itself states, and the Court affirms today, Congress may regulate noneconomic intrastate activities only where the failure to do so "could ... undercut" its regulation of interstate commerce. This is not a power that threatens to obliterate the line between "what is truly national and what is truly local."

Lopez and Morrison.... do not declare noneconomic intrastate activities to be categorically beyond the reach of the Federal Government. Neither case involved the power of Congress to exert control over intrastate activities in connection with a more comprehensive scheme of regulation; Lopez expressly disclaimed that it was such a case, and Morrison did not even discuss the possibility that it was. To dismiss this distinction as "superficial and formalistic," (O'Connor, J., dissenting) is to misunderstand the nature of the Necessary and Proper Clause, which empowers Congress to enact laws in effectuation of its enumerated powers that are not within its authority to enact in isolation. See McCulloch v. Maryland, 17 U.S. 316, 4 Wheat. 316, 421–422 (1819).

And there are other restraints upon the Necessary and Proper Clause authority. As Chief Justice Marshall wrote in McCulloch v. Maryland, even when the end is constitutional and legitimate, the means must be "appropriate" and "plainly adapted" to that end....

The application of these principles to the case before us is straightforward. In the CSA, Congress has undertaken to extinguish the interstate market in Schedule I controlled substances, including marijuana. The Commerce Clause unquestionably permits this.... That simple possession is a noneconomic activity is immaterial to whether it can be prohibited as a necessary part of a larger regulation. Rather, Congress's authority to enact all of these prohibitions of intrastate controlled-substance activities depends only upon whether they are appropriate means of achieving the legitimate end of eradicating Schedule I substances from interstate commerce.

By this measure, I think the regulation must be sustained. Not only is it impossible to distinguish "controlled substances manufactured and distributed intrastate" from "controlled substances manufactured and distributed interstate," but it hardly makes sense to speak in such terms. Drugs like marijuana are fungible commodities. As the Court explains, marijuana that is grown at home and possessed for personal use is never more than an instant from the interstate market — and this is so whether or not the possession is for medicinal use or lawful use under the laws of a particular State. Congress need not accept on faith that state law will be effective in maintaining a strict division between a lawful market for "medical" marijuana and the more general marijuana market. "To impose on [Congress] the necessity of resorting to means which it cannot control, which another government may furnish or withhold, would render its course precarious, the result of its measures uncertain, and create a dependence on other governments, which might disappoint its most important designs, and is incompatible with the language of the constitution." McCulloch, supra, at 424.

Finally, neither respondents nor the dissenters suggest any violation of state sovereignty of the sort that would render this regulation "inappropriate," — except to argue that the CSA regulates an area typically left to state regulation. That is not enough to render federal regulation an inappropriate means. The Court has repeatedly recognized that, if authorized by the commerce power, Congress may regulate private endeavors "even when [that regulation] may pre-empt express state-law determinations contrary to the result which has commended itself to the collective wisdom of Congress[.]" . . .

JUSTICE O'CONNOR, with whom the CHIEF JUSTICE and JUSTICE THOMAS join as to all but Part III, dissenting.

We enforce the "outer limits" of Congress' Commerce Clause authority not for their own sake, but to protect historic spheres of state sovereignty from excessive federal encroachment and thereby to maintain the distribution of power fundamental to our federalist system of government. United States v. Lopez, 514 U.S. 549 (1995); NLRB v. Jones & Laughlin Steel Corp., 301 U.S. 1, 37 (1937). One of federalism's chief virtues, of course, is that it promotes innovation by allowing for the possibility that "a single courageous State may, if its citizens choose, serve as a laboratory; and try novel social and economic experiments without risk to the rest of the country." New State Ice Co. v. Liebmann, 285 U.S. 262, 311 (1932) (Brandeis, J., dissenting).

This case exemplifies the role of States as laboratories. The States' core police powers have always included authority to define criminal law and to protect the health, safety, and welfare of their citizens. Exercising those powers, California (by ballot initiative and then by legislative codification) has come to its own conclusion about the difficult and sensitive question of whether marijuana should be available to relieve severe pain and suffering. Today the Court sanctions an application of the federal Controlled Substances Act that extinguishes that experiment, without any proof that the personal cultivation, possession, and use of marijuana for medicinal purposes, if economic activity in the first place, has a substantial effect on interstate commerce and is therefore an appropriate subject of federal regulation. In so doing, the Court announces a rule that gives Congress a perverse incentive to legislate broadly pursuant to the Commerce Clause — nestling questionable assertions of its authority into comprehensive regulatory schemes — rather than with precision. That rule and the result it produces in this case are irreconcilable with our decisions in Lopez, and United States v. Morrison. Accordingly I dissent. . . .

. . . . Today's decision suggests that the federal regulation of local activity is immune to Commerce Clause challenge because Congress chose to act with an ambitious, all-encompassing statute, rather than piecemeal. In my view, allowing Congress to set the terms of the constitutional debate in this way, i.e., by packaging regulation of local activity in broader schemes, is tantamount to removing meaningful limits on the Commerce Clause. . . .

A number of objective markers are available to confine the scope of constitutional review here. Both federal and state legislation—including the CSA itself, the California Compassionate Use Act, and other state medical marijuana legislation—recognize that medical and nonmedical (i.e., recreational) uses of drugs are realistically distinct and can be segregated, and regulate them differently. Respondents challenge only the application of the CSA to medicinal use of marijuana. Moreover, because fundamental structural concerns about dual sovereignty animate our Commerce Clause cases, it is relevant that this case involves the interplay of federal and state regulation in areas of criminal law and social policy, where "States lay claim by right of history and expertise." Lopez, supra, at 583 (Kennedy, J., concurring). California, like other States, has drawn on its reserved powers to distinguish the regulation of medicinal marijuana. To ascertain whether Congress' encroachment is constitutionally justified in this case, then, I would focus here on the personal cultivation, possession, and use of marijuana for medicinal purposes.

Having thus defined the relevant conduct, we must determine whether, under our precedents, the conduct is economic and, in the aggregate, substantially affects interstate commerce. Even if intrastate cultivation and possession of marijuana for one's own medicinal use can properly be characterized as economic, and I question whether it can, it has not been shown that such activity substantially affects interstate commerce. Similarly, it is neither self-evident nor demonstrated that regulating such activity is necessary to the interstate drug control scheme.

The Court's definition of economic activity is breathtaking. It defines as economic any activity involving the production, distribution, and consumption of commodities. And it appears to reason that when an interstate market for a commodity exists, regulating the intrastate manufacture or possession of that commodity is constitutional either because that intrastate activity is itself economic, or because regulating it is a rational part of regulating its market.... [T]he Court's definition of economic activity for purposes of Commerce Clause jurisprudence threatens to sweep all of productive human activity into federal regulatory reach.

The Court uses a dictionary definition of economics to skirt the real problem of drawing a meaningful line between "what is national and what is local," Jones & Laughlin Steel, 301 U.S. at 37. It will not do to say that Congress may regulate noncommercial activity simply because it may have an effect on the demand for commercial goods, or because the noncommercial endeavor can, in some sense, substitute for commercial activity. Most commercial goods or services have some sort of privately producible analogue. Home care substitutes for daycare. Charades games substitute for movie tickets. Backyard or windowsill gardening substitutes for going to the supermarket. To draw the line wherever private activity affects the demand for market goods is to draw no line at all, and to declare everything economic. We have already rejected the result that would follow—a federal police power. Lopez, supra.

In Lopez and Morrison, we suggested that economic activity usually relates directly to commercial activity. The homegrown cultivation and personal possession and use of marijuana for medicinal purposes has no apparent commercial character. Everyone agrees that the marijuana at issue in this case was never in the stream of commerce, and neither were the supplies for growing it. (Marijuana is highly unusual among the substances subject to the CSA in that it can be cultivated without any materials that have traveled in interstate commerce.) Lopez makes clear that possession is not itself commercial activity. Ibid. And respondents have not come into possession by means of any commercial transaction; they have simply grown, in their own homes, marijuana for their own use, without acquiring, buying, selling, or bartering a thing of value....

Even assuming that economic activity is at issue in this case, the Government has made no showing in fact that the possession and use of homegrown marijuana for medical purposes, in California or elsewhere, has a substantial effect on interstate commerce. Similarly, the Government has not shown that regulating such activity is necessary to an interstate regulatory scheme....

There is simply no evidence that homegrown medicinal marijuana users constitute, in the aggregate, a sizable enough class to have a discernable, let alone substantial, impact on the national illicit drug market—or otherwise to threaten the CSA regime. Explicit evidence is helpful when substantial effect is not "visible to the naked eye." See Lopez, 514 U.S., at 563. And here, in part because common sense suggests that medical marijuana users may be limited in number and that California's Compassionate Use Act and similar state legislation may well isolate activities relating to medicinal marijuana from the illicit market, the effect of those activities on interstate drug traffic is not self-evidently substantial....

Relying on Congress' abstract assertions, the Court has endorsed making it a federal crime to grow small amounts of marijuana in one's own home for one's own medicinal use. This overreaching stifles an express choice by some States, concerned for the lives and liberties of their people, to regulate medical marijuana differently. If I were a California citizen, I would not have voted for the medical marijuana ballot initiative; if I were a California legislator I would not have supported the Compassionate Use Act. But whatever the wisdom of California's experiment with medical marijuana, the federalism principles that have driven our Commerce Clause cases require that room for experiment be protected in this case. For these reasons I dissent.

JUSTICE THOMAS, dissenting.

Respondents Diane Monson and Angel Raich use marijuana that has never been bought or sold, that has never crossed state lines, and that has had no demonstrable effect on the national market for marijuana. If Congress can regulate this under the Commerce Clause, then it can regulate virtually anything—and the Federal Government is no longer one of limited and enumerated powers....

.... Throughout founding-era dictionaries, Madison's notes from the Constitutional Convention, The Federalist Papers, and the ratification debates, the term "commerce" is consistently used to mean trade or exchange—not all economic or gainful activity that has some attenuated connection to trade or exchange.... Certainly no evidence from the founding suggests that "commerce" included the mere possession of a good or some purely personal activity that did not involve trade or exchange for value. In the early days of the Republic, it would have been unthinkable that Congress could prohibit the local cultivation, possession, and consumption of marijuana....

Respondents are not regulable simply because they belong to a large class (local growers and users of marijuana) that Congress might need to reach, if they also belong to a distinct and separable subclass (local growers and users of state-authorized, medical marijuana) that does not undermine the CSA's interstate ban....

California's Compassionate Use Act sets respondents' conduct apart from other intrastate producers and users of marijuana. The Act channels marijuana use to "seriously ill Californians," Cal. Health & Safety Code Ann. § 11362.5(b)(1)(A), and prohibits "the diversion of marijuana for nonmedical purposes," § 11362.5(b)(2).... We normally presume that States enforce their own laws, and there is no reason to depart from that presumption here: Nothing suggests that California's controls are ineffective. The scant evidence that exists suggests that few people—the vast majority of whom are aged 40 or older—register to use medical marijuana. In part because of the low incidence of medical marijuana use, many law enforcement officials report that the introduction of medical marijuana laws has not affected their law enforcement efforts.

… [The] Government [has not] offered any obvious reason why banning medical marijuana use is necessary to stem the tide of interstate drug trafficking. Congress' goal of curtailing the interstate drug trade would not plainly be thwarted if it could not apply the CSA to patients like Monson and Raich.…

The majority's rewriting of the Commerce Clause seems to be rooted in the belief that, unless the Commerce Clause covers the entire web of human activity, Congress will be left powerless to regulate the national economy effectively. The interconnectedness of economic activity is not a modern phenomenon unfamiliar to the Framers. Moreover, the Framers understood what the majority does not appear to fully appreciate: There is a danger to concentrating too much, as well as too little, power in the Federal Government. This Court has carefully avoided stripping Congress of its ability to regulate interstate commerce, but it has casually allowed the Federal Government to strip States of their ability to regulate intrastate commerce — not to mention a host of local activities, like mere drug possession, that are not commercial.

One searches the Court's opinion in vain for any hint of what aspect of American life is reserved to the States. Yet this Court knows that "[t]he Constitution created a Federal Government of limited powers." New York v. United States, 505 U.S. 144, 155 (1992). That is why today's decision will add no measure of stability to our Commerce Clause jurisprudence: This Court is willing neither to enforce limits on federal power, nor to declare the Tenth Amendment a dead letter. If stability is possible, it is only by discarding the stand-alone substantial effects test and revisiting our definition of "Commerce among the several States." Congress may regulate interstate commerce — not things that affect it, even when summed together, unless truly "necessary and proper" to regulating interstate commerce.…

Review Questions and Explanations: *Raich*

1. Are *Lopez* and *Morrison* consistent or inconsistent with *Gonzales v. Raich*?

2. The majority and dissent disagree about whether *Wickard v. Filburn* is distinguishable. Who has the more convincing argument about that? Is the growing of wheat for purely home consumption, when marketing that wheat would violate federal law, more like "commercial/econonomic activity" than the growing of marijuana for personal medical consumption?

3. The majority opinion includes language seen in the *Lopez/Morrison* dissents about the modest task facing the Court in Commerce Clause challenges: not whether the activity substantially affects interstate commerce, but only whether there is a *rational basis* for believing so. Has that idea been "restored" to the law after *Lopez* and *Morrison*? At the same time, note that *Raich* does not overrule *Lopez* and *Morrison*, but seems to accept the economic/non-economic activity distinction that the dissenters objected to. Do you think the *Lopez/Morrison* dissenters needed to do this to win Justice Kennedy's vote in *Raich*? (Notwithstanding Justice Scalia's concurrence in the judgment, Kennedy's vote was needed to make the Stevens opinion a clear majority rather than a plurality opinion.)

4. Do the dissenters say that the Controlled Substances Act cannot constitutionally apply to any aspects of medical marijuana distribution or use that is permitted by California's Compassionate Use Act?

5. The six-Justice majority in *Raich* consisted of the four dissenters from *Lopez* and *Morrison* plus Justices Kennedy and Scalia (concurring in the judgment). The *Lopez-Morrison* dissenters would have upheld Congress's commerce power in all three cases, but Scalia and Kennedy seemed to have switched sides. Are Justices Scalia and Kennedy doctrinally consistent across the three cases?

Exercise: The ACA Case (continued)

Gonzales v. Raich is the last major commerce decision prior to the ACA cases reaching the Supreme Court. Now that you've read it, you are well positioned to make the arguments for and against the ACA's "individual mandate" on commerce clause grounds. Try repeating the exercise set out after *United States v. Morrison*, with the following additions:

    a)   Try to incorporate any helpful arguments and ideas contained in the *Raich* opinions.

    b)   Be sure to address the arguments in Justice Scalia's concurrence. This line of analysis is largely independent of the activity/inactivity distinction that was the focal point of much public debate, as well as the lower court litigation, over the constitutionality of the "individual mandate." Which side, if either, of the ACA case does the Scalia concurrence help?

To assist you in going deeper into these arguments, we provide an excerpt from one of the main briefs filed in the Supreme Court on behalf of the challengers to the individual mandate. The brief was filed in *Department of Health and Human Services v. Florida*, one of three companion cases challenging the Affordable Care Act, that was ultimately consolidated under the name *NFIB v. Sebelius*.

Department of Health and Human Services, et al. v. State of Florida, et al.

No. 11-398
Supreme Court Of The United States
February 6, 2012
On Writ of Certiorari to the
United States Court of Appeals for the Eleventh Circuit
Initial Brief: Appellee-Respondent

Counsel: Karen R. Harned, NFIB Small Business Legal Center, Washington, DC,

Prof. Randy E. Barnett, Georgetown Univ. Law Center, Washington, DC,

Michael A. Carvin, Counsel of Record,

Gregory G. Katsas, C. Kevin Marshall, Hashim M. Mooppan, Yaakov M. Roth,

Jones Day, Washington, DC,

Counsel For Private Respondents

    .... The mandate imposes an extraordinary and unprecedented duty on Americans to enter into costly private contracts. By commanding citizens to subsidize voluntary participants in the insurance industry through disadvantageous contracts, it exemplifies the threat to individual liberty that occurs when Congress exceeds its limited and enumerated powers.

Under the Commerce Clause, Congress has the power to regulate interstate commerce by prescribing the rules that govern interstate commercial intercourse. But forcing people into commerce does not regulate commerce. Otherwise, Congress could compel the purchase of *any* product....

The "substantial effects" cases have turned on whether the regulation is "necessary" — *i.e.*, whether the means selected are plainly adapted or otherwise rationally related to *implementing* the legitimate end of regulating interstate commerce. The Government erroneously reads those cases to allow Congress to choose *any* rational means that *advances or promotes* interstate commerce. But this Court's precedents instead demonstrate that the requisite connection exists only where the regulated conduct *itself* (1) substantially interferes with interstate commerce or its regulation, (2) is either economic in nature or an impediment to the effective execution of a commercial regulatory scheme, and (3) could be regulated without effectively authorizing plenary federal power. None of the mandate's asserted justifications satisfies these requirements.

Congress emphasized that the mandate will lower premiums by forcing healthy individuals into the insurance risk pool. The relevant question, however, is not whether Congress' *regulation* will beneficially affect commerce, but whether the *regulated conduct* negatively affects commerce in a cognizable way. And uninsured status neither interferes with commerce or its regulation nor constitutes economic activity. Instead, the uninsured's *defining* characteristic is their *non-participation* in commerce. If that nonparticipation can be overridden simply to benefit voluntary market participants, then Congress could conscript Americans to purchase *any* product.

.... Congress lacks the power to regulate a practice that is *outside* the commerce power simply because *some* of those who engage in it are also statistically likely to engage in regulable conduct *in the future*....

We now present the Commerce Clause portions of the opinions issued in the ACA Case.

National Federation of Independent Business v. Sebelius

567 U.S. ___, 132 S. Ct. 2566 (2012)

[Editors' note: With Chief Justice Roberts plus the "joint dissent" of Justices Scalia, Kennedy, Thomas, and Alito, five justices voted to hold that the individual mandate exceeded Congress's commerce power. However, the Chief Justice joined Justices Ginsburg, Breyer, Sotomayor, Kagan to uphold the mandate under the taxing power. (Oops — spoiler alert!)]

Judgment of the Court (Commerce Clause): *Roberts* (CJ)

[Concurrence in the judgment*]: Scalia, Kennedy, Thomas, Alito

Partial Dissent (Commerce Clause): *Ginsburg*, Breyer, Sotomayor, Kagan

[* The "joint dissent" is not styled a partial concurrence in the judgment, but it has that effect. See "Review Questions and Explanations," after the case excerpt.]

CHIEF JUSTICE ROBERTS ... [delivered] an opinion with respect to Parts III-A, III-B ...

.... The Constitution authorizes Congress to "regulate Commerce with foreign Nations, and among the several States, and with the Indian Tribes." Art. I, § 8, cl. 3. Our precedents read that to mean that Congress may regulate "the channels of interstate commerce," "persons or things in interstate commerce," and "those activities that substantially affect interstate commerce." Morrison, supra, at 609. The power over activities that substantially affect interstate commerce can be expansive. That power has been held to authorize federal regulation of such seemingly local matters as a farmer's decision to grow wheat for himself and his livestock, and a loan shark's extortionate collections from a neighborhood butcher shop. See Wickard v. Filburn, 317 U.S. 111 (1942); Perez v. United States, 402 U.S. 146 (1971)....

Our permissive reading of these powers is explained in part by a general reticence to invalidate the acts of the Nation's elected leaders. "Proper respect for a coordinate branch of the government" requires that we strike down an Act of Congress only if "the lack of constitutional authority to pass [the] act in question is clearly demonstrated." Members of this Court are vested with the authority to interpret the law; we possess neither the expertise nor the prerogative to make policy judgments. Those decisions are entrusted to our Nation's elected leaders, who can be thrown out of office if the people disagree with them. It is not our job to protect the people from the consequences of their political choices.

Our deference in matters of policy cannot, however, become abdication in matters of law. "The powers of the legislature are defined and limited; and that those limits may not be mistaken, or forgotten, the constitution is written." Marbury v. Madison, 1 Cranch (5 U.S.) 137 (1803). Our respect for Congress's policy judgments thus can never extend so far as to disavow restraints on federal power that the Constitution carefully constructed. "The peculiar circumstances of the moment may render a measure more or less wise, but cannot render it more or less constitutional." Chief Justice John Marshall, Alexandria Gazette, July 5, 1819. And there can be no question that it is the responsibility of this Court to enforce the limits on federal power by striking down acts of Congress that transgress those limits....

III

The Government advances two theories for the proposition that Congress had constitutional authority to enact the individual mandate. First, the Government argues that Congress had the power to enact the mandate under the Commerce Clause. Under that theory, Congress may order individuals to buy health insurance because the failure to do so affects interstate commerce, and could undercut the Affordable Care Act's other reforms. Second, the Government argues that if the commerce power does not support the mandate, we should nonetheless uphold it as an exercise of Congress's power to tax....

A

The Government's first argument is that the individual mandate is a valid exercise of Congress's power under the Commerce Clause and the Necessary and Proper Clause. According to the Government, the health care market is characterized by a significant cost-shifting problem. Everyone will eventually need health care at a time and to an extent they cannot predict, but if they do not have insurance, they often will not be able to pay for it. Because state and federal laws nonetheless require hospitals to provide a certain degree of care to individuals without regard to their ability to pay, see, e.g., 42 U.S.C. § 1395dd; Fla. Stat. Ann. § 395.1041, hospitals end up receiving compensation for only a portion of the services they provide. To recoup the losses, hospitals pass on the cost to insurers through higher rates, and insurers, in turn, pass on the cost to policy holders in the form of higher premiums. Congress estimated that the cost of uncompensated care raises family health insurance premiums, on average, by over $1,000 per year. 42 U.S.C. § 18091(2)(F).

In the Affordable Care Act, Congress addressed the problem of those who cannot obtain insurance coverage because of preexisting conditions or other health issues. It did so through the Act's "guaranteed-issue" and "community-rating" provisions. These provisions together prohibit insurance companies from denying coverage to those with such conditions or charging unhealthy individuals higher premiums than healthy individuals.

The guaranteed-issue and community-rating reforms do not, however, address the issue of healthy individuals who choose not to purchase insurance to cover potential health care needs. In fact, the reforms sharply exacerbate that problem, by providing an incentive for individuals to delay purchasing health insurance until they become sick, relying on the promise of guaranteed and affordable coverage. The reforms also threaten to impose massive new costs on insurers, who are required to accept unhealthy individuals but prohibited from charging them rates necessary to pay for their coverage. This will lead insurers to significantly increase premiums on everyone. See Brief for America's Health Insurance Plans et al. as Amici Curiae in No. 11-393 etc. 8–9.

The individual mandate was Congress's solution to these problems. By requiring that individuals purchase health insurance, the mandate prevents cost-shifting by those who would otherwise go without it. In addition, the mandate forces into the insurance risk pool more healthy individuals, whose premiums on average will be higher than their health care expenses. This allows insurers to subsidize the costs of covering the unhealthy individuals the reforms require them to accept. The Government claims that Congress has power under the Commerce and Necessary and Proper Clauses to enact this solution.

1

The Government contends that the individual mandate is within Congress's power because the failure to purchase insurance "has a substantial and deleterious effect on interstate commerce" by creating the cost-shifting problem. The path of our Commerce Clause decisions has not always run smooth, see United States v. Lopez, 514 U.S. 549, 552–559 (1995), but it is now well established that Congress has broad authority under the Clause....

.... But Congress has never attempted to rely on that power to compel individuals not engaged in commerce to purchase an unwanted product. Legislative novelty is not necessarily fatal; there is a first time for everything. But sometimes "the most telling indication of [a] severe constitutional problem ... is the lack of historical precedent" for Congress's action....

The Constitution grants Congress the power to "regulate Commerce" Art. I, § 8, cl. 3. The power to regulate commerce presupposes the existence of commercial activity to be regulated....

Our precedent also reflects this understanding. As expansive as our cases construing the scope of the commerce power have been, they all have one thing in common: They uniformly describe the power as reaching "activity." It is nearly impossible to avoid the word when quoting them....

The individual mandate, however, does not regulate existing commercial activity. It instead compels individuals to become active in commerce by purchasing a product, on the ground that their failure to do so affects interstate commerce. Construing the Commerce Clause to permit Congress to regulate individuals precisely because they are doing nothing would open a new and potentially vast domain to congressional authority. Every day individuals do not do an infinite number of things. In some cases they decide not to do something; in others they simply fail to do it. Allowing Congress to justify federal regulation by pointing to the effect of inaction on commerce would bring countless decisions an individual could potentially make within the scope of federal regulation, and—under the Government's theory—empower Congress to make those decisions for him....

Wickard has long been regarded as "perhaps the most far reaching example of Commerce Clause authority over intrastate activity," Lopez, 514 U.S., at 560, but the Government's theory in this case would go much further.... The farmer in Wickard was at least actively engaged in the production of wheat, and the Government could regulate that activity because of its effect on commerce. The Government's theory here would effectively override that limitation, by establishing that individuals may be regulated under the Commerce Clause whenever enough of them are not doing something the Government would have them do.

Indeed, the Government's logic would justify a mandatory purchase to solve almost any problem. To consider a different example in the health care market, many Americans do not eat a balanced diet.... The failure of that group to have a healthy diet increases health care costs, to a greater extent than the failure of the uninsured to purchase insurance.... Under the Government's theory, Congress could address the diet problem by ordering everyone to buy vegetables.

People, for reasons of their own, often fail to do things that would be good for them or good for society. Those failures—joined with the similar failures of others—can readily have a substantial effect on interstate commerce. Under the Government's logic, that authorizes Congress to use its commerce power to compel citizens to act as the Government would have them act.

That is not the country the Framers of our Constitution envisioned.... Congress already enjoys vast power to regulate much of what we do. Accepting the Government's theory would give Congress the same license to regulate what we do not do, fundamentally changing the relation between the citizen and the Federal Government.

To an economist, perhaps, there is no difference between activity and inactivity; both have measurable economic effects on commerce. But the distinction between doing something and doing nothing would not have been lost on the Framers, who were "practical statesmen," not metaphysical philosophers.... The Framers gave Congress the power to regulate commerce, not to compel it, and for over 200 years both our decisions and Congress's actions have reflected this understanding. There is no reason to depart from that understanding now.

The Government.... argues that because sickness and injury are unpredictable but unavoidable, "the uninsured as a class are active in the market for health care, which they regularly seek and obtain." Brief for United States 50. The individual mandate "merely regulates how individuals finance and pay for that active participation—requiring that they do so through insurance, rather than through attempted self-insurance with the back-stop of shifting costs to others."

The Government repeats the phrase "active in the market for health care" throughout its brief, but that concept has no constitutional significance. An individual who bought a car two years ago and may buy another in the future is not "active in the car market" in any pertinent sense. The phrase "active in the market" cannot obscure the fact that most of those regulated by the individual mandate are not currently engaged in any commercial activity involving health care, and that fact is fatal to the Government's effort to "regulate the uninsured as a class." Our precedents recognize Congress's power to regulate "class[es] of *activities*," Gonzales v. Raich, 545 U.S. 1, 17 (2005) (emphasis added), not classes of individuals, apart from any activity in which they are engaged.

The individual mandate's regulation of the uninsured as a class is, in fact, particularly divorced from any link to existing commercial activity. The mandate primarily affects healthy, often young adults who are less likely to need significant health care and have other priorities for spending their money. It is precisely because these individuals, as an actuarial class, incur relatively low health care costs that the mandate helps counter the effect of forcing insurance companies to cover others who impose greater costs than their premiums are allowed to reflect. If the individual mandate is targeted at a class, it is a class whose commercial inactivity rather than activity is its defining feature....

The proposition that Congress may dictate the conduct of an individual today because of prophesied future activity finds no support in our precedent.... Everyone will likely participate in the markets for food, clothing, transportation, shelter, or energy; that does not authorize Congress to direct them to purchase particular products in those or other markets today. The Commerce Clause is not a general license to regulate an individual from cradle to grave, simply because he will predictably engage in particular transactions. Any police power to regulate individuals as such, as opposed to their activities, remains vested in the States.

The Government argues that the individual mandate can be sustained as a sort of exception to this rule, because health insurance is a unique product. According to the Government, upholding the individual mandate would not justify mandatory purchases of items such as cars or broccoli because, as the Government puts it, "[h]ealth insurance is not purchased for its own sake like a car or broccoli; it is a means of financing health-care consumption and covering universal risks." Reply Brief for United States 19. But cars and broccoli are no more purchased for their "own sake" than health insurance. They are purchased to cover the need for transportation and food.

The Government says that health insurance and health care financing are "inherently integrated." Brief for United States 41. But that does not mean the compelled purchase of the first is properly regarded as a regulation of the second. No matter how "inherently integrated" health insurance and health care consumption may be, they are not the same thing: They involve different transactions, entered into at different times, with different providers. And for most of those targeted by the mandate, significant health care needs will be years, or even decades, away. The proximity and degree of connection between the mandate and the subsequent commercial activity is too lacking to justify an exception of the sort urged by the Government. The individual mandate forces individuals into commerce precisely because they elected to refrain from commercial activity. Such a law cannot be sustained under a clause authorizing Congress to "regulate Commerce."

2

The Government next contends that Congress has the power under the Necessary and Proper Clause to enact the individual mandate because the mandate is an "integral part of a comprehensive scheme of economic regulation"—the guaranteed-issue and community-rating insurance reforms. Brief for United States 24. Under this argument, it is not necessary to consider the effect that an individual's inactivity may have on interstate commerce; it is enough that Congress regulate commercial activity in a way that requires regulation of inactivity to be effective.

The power to "make all Laws which shall be necessary and proper for carrying into Execution" the powers enumerated in the Constitution, Art. I, § 8, cl. 18, vests Congress with authority to enact provisions "incidental to the [enumerated] power, and conducive to its beneficial exercise," McCulloch, 4 Wheat., at 418. Although the Clause gives Congress authority to "legislate on that vast mass of incidental powers which must be involved in the constitution," it does not license the exercise of any "great substantive and independent power[s]" beyond those specifically enumerated. Id....

.... [T]he individual mandate cannot be sustained under the Necessary and Proper Clause as an essential component of the insurance reforms. Each of our prior cases upholding laws under that Clause involved exercises of authority derivative of, and in service to, a granted power.... The individual mandate, by contrast, vests Congress with the extraordinary ability to create the necessary predicate to the exercise of an enumerated power.

This is in no way an authority that is "narrow in scope," United States v. Comstock, 130 S. Ct. 1949, 1964 (2010), or "incidental" to the exercise of the commerce power, McCulloch, supra, 4 Wheat., at 418. Rather, such a conception of the Necessary and Proper Clause would work a substantial expansion of federal authority. No longer would Congress be limited to regulating under the Commerce Clause those who by some preexisting activity bring themselves within the sphere of federal regulation. Instead, Congress could reach beyond the natural limit of its authority and draw within its regulatory scope those who otherwise would be outside of it. Even if the individual mandate is "necessary" to the Act's insurance reforms, such an expansion of federal power is not a "proper" means for making those reforms effective.

The Government relies primarily on our decision in Gonzales v. Raich. In Raich, we considered "comprehensive legislation to regulate the interstate market" in marijuana. 545 U.S., at 22. Certain individuals sought an exemption from that regulation on the ground that they engaged in only intrastate possession and consumption. We denied any exemption, on the ground that marijuana is a fungible commodity, so that any marijuana could be readily diverted into the interstate market. Congress's attempt to regulate the interstate market for marijuana would therefore have been substantially undercut if it could not also regulate intrastate possession and consumption. Accordingly, we recognized that "Congress was acting well within its authority" under the Necessary and Proper Clause even though its "regulation ensnare[d] some purely intrastate activity." Raich thus did not involve the exercise of any "great substantive and independent power," McCulloch, supra, at 411, of the sort at issue here. Instead, it concerned only the constitutionality of "individual applications of a concededly valid statutory scheme." Raich, supra, at 23.

Just as the individual mandate cannot be sustained as a law regulating the substantial effects of the failure to purchase health insurance, neither can it be upheld as a "necessary and proper" component of the insurance reforms. The commerce power thus does not authorize the mandate. Accord (joint opinion of SCALIA, KENNEDY, THOMAS, and ALITO, JJ., dissenting)....

The Framers created a Federal Government of limited powers, and assigned to this Court the duty of enforcing those limits. The Court does so today. But the Court does not express any opinion on the wisdom of the Affordable Care Act. Under the Constitution, that judgment is reserved to the people.

The judgment of the Court of Appeals for the Eleventh Circuit is affirmed in part and reversed in part.

JUSTICE GINSBURG, with whom JUSTICE SOTOMAYOR joins, and with whom JUSTICE BREYER and JUSTICE KAGAN join as to Parts I, II, III, and IV, concurring in part, concurring in the judgment in part, and dissenting in part.

.... The provision of health care is today a concern of national dimension, just as the provision of old-age and survivors' benefits was in the 1930s. In the Social Security Act,

Congress installed a federal system to provide monthly benefits to retired wage earners and, eventually, to their survivors. Beyond question, Congress could have adopted a similar scheme for health care. Congress chose, instead, to preserve a central role for private insurers and state governments. According to THE CHIEF JUSTICE, the Commerce Clause does not permit that preservation. This rigid reading of the Clause makes scant sense and is stunningly retrogressive.

Since 1937, our precedent has recognized Congress' large authority to set the Nation's course in the economic and social welfare realm. THE CHIEF JUSTICE's crabbed reading of the Commerce Clause harks back to the era in which the Court routinely thwarted Congress' efforts to regulate the national economy in the interest of those who labor to sustain it. It is a reading that should not have staying power.

In enacting the Patient Protection and Affordable Care Act (ACA), Congress comprehensively reformed the national market for healthcare products and services. By any measure, that market is immense. Collectively, Americans spent $2.5 trillion on health care in 2009, accounting for 17.6% of our Nation's economy. 42 U.S.C. § 18091(2)(B) Within the next decade, it is anticipated, spending on health care will nearly double. Ibid.

The healthcare market's size is not its only distinctive feature. Unlike the market for almost any other product or service, the market for medical care is one in which all individuals inevitably participate. Virtually every person residing in the United States, sooner or later, will visit a doctor or other health-care professional....

When individuals make those visits, they face another reality of the current market for medical care: its high cost. In 2010, on average, an individual in the United States incurred over $7,000 in health-care expenses. Over a lifetime, costs mount to hundreds of thousands of dollars. When a person requires nonroutine care, the cost will generally exceed what he or she can afford to pay. A single hospital stay, for instance, typically costs upwards of $10,000. Treatments for many serious, though not uncommon, conditions similarly cost a substantial sum. Brief for Economic Scholars as Amici Curiae in No. 11-398, p. 10 (citing a study indicating that, in 1998, the cost of treating a heart attack for the first 90 days exceeded $20,000, while the annual cost of treating certain cancers was more than $50,000).

Although every U.S. domiciliary will incur significant medical expenses during his or her lifetime, the time when care will be needed is often unpredictable.... To manage the risks associated with medical care—its high cost, its unpredictability, and its inevitability—most people in the United States obtain health insurance. Many (approximately 170 million in 2009) are insured by private insurance companies. Others, including those over 65 and certain poor and disabled persons, rely on government-funded insurance programs, notably Medicare and Medicaid. Combined, private health insurers and State and Federal Governments finance almost 85% of the medical care administered to U.S. residents.

Not all U.S. residents, however, have health insurance. In 2009, approximately 50 million people were uninsured, either by choice or, more likely, because they could not afford private insurance and did not qualify for government aid....

The large number of individuals without health insurance, Congress found, heavily burdens the national health-care market. As just noted, the cost of emergency care or treatment for a serious illness generally exceeds what an individual can afford to pay on her own. Unlike markets for most products, however, the inability to pay for care does not mean that an uninsured individual will receive no care. Federal and state law, as well as professional obligations and embedded social norms, require hospitals and physicians to provide care when it is most needed, regardless of the patient's ability to pay.

As a consequence, medical-care providers deliver significant amounts of care to the uninsured for which the providers receive no payment. In 2008, for example, hospitals, physicians, and other health-care professionals received no compensation for $43 billion worth of the $116 billion in care they administered to those without insurance.

Health-care providers do not absorb these bad debts. Instead, they raise their prices, passing along the cost of uncompensated care to those who do pay reliably: the government and private insurance companies. In response, private insurers increase their premiums, shifting the cost of the elevated bills from providers onto those who carry insurance. The net result: Those with health insurance subsidize the medical care of those without it. As economists would describe what happens, the uninsured "free ride" on those who pay for health insurance.

The size of this subsidy is considerable. Congress found that the cost-shifting just described "increases family [insurance] premiums by on average over $1,000 a year." Higher premiums, in turn, render health insurance less affordable, forcing more people to go without insurance and leading to further cost-shifting.

And it is hardly just the currently sick or injured among the uninsured who prompt elevation of the price of health care and health insurance. Insurance companies and health-care providers know that some percentage of healthy, uninsured people will suffer sickness or injury each year and will receive medical care despite their inability to pay. In anticipation of this uncompensated care, health-care companies raise their prices, and insurers their premiums. In other words, because any uninsured person may need medical care at any moment and because health-care companies must account for that risk, every uninsured person impacts the market price of medical care and medical insurance.

The failure of individuals to acquire insurance has other deleterious effects on the health-care market. Because those without insurance generally lack access to preventative care, they do not receive treatment for conditions—like hypertension and diabetes—that can be successfully and affordably treated if diagnosed early on. When sickness finally drives the uninsured to seek care, once treatable conditions have escalated into grave health problems, requiring more costly and extensive intervention. The extra time and resources providers spend serving the uninsured lessens the providers' ability to care for those who do have insurance.

States cannot resolve the problem of the uninsured on their own. Like Social Security benefits, a universal health-care system, if adopted by an individual State, would be "bait to the needy and dependent elsewhere, encouraging them to migrate and seek a haven of repose." Helvering v.Davis, 301 U.S. 619, 644 (1937). See also Brief for Commonwealth of Massachusetts as Amicus Curiae in No. 11-398, p. 15 (noting that, in 2009, Massachusetts' emergency rooms served thousands of uninsured, out-of-state residents). An influx of unhealthy individuals into a State with universal health care would result in increased spending on medical services. To cover the increased costs, a State would have to raise taxes, and private health-insurance companies would have to increase premiums. Higher taxes and increased insurance costs would, in turn, encourage businesses and healthy in-dividuals to leave the State.

States that undertake health-care reforms on their own thus risk "placing themselves in a position of economic disadvantage as compared with neighbors or competitors." Davis, 301 U.S., at 644. Facing that risk, individual States are unlikely to take the initiative in addressing the problem of the uninsured, even though solving that problem is in all States' best interests. Congress' intervention was needed to overcome this collective-action impasse....

A central aim of the ACA is to reduce the number of uninsured U.S. residents. The minimum coverage provision advances this objective by giving potential recipients of health care a financial incentive to acquire insurance. Per the minimum coverage provision, an individual must either obtain insurance or pay a toll constructed as a tax penalty. See 26 U.S.C. § 5000A....

Before the ACA's enactment, private insurance companies took an applicant's medical history into account when setting insurance rates or deciding whether to insure an individual. Because individuals with preexisting medical conditions cost insurance companies significantly more than those without such conditions, insurers routinely refused to insure these individuals, charged them substantially higher premiums, or offered only limited coverage that did not include the preexisting illness.

To ensure that individuals with medical histories have access to affordable insurance, Congress devised a three-part solution. First, Congress imposed a "guaranteed issue" requirement, which bars insurers from denying coverage to any person on account of that person's medical condition or history. Second, Congress required insurers to use "community rating" to price their insurance policies. Community rating, in effect, bars insurance companies from charging higher premiums to those with preexisting conditions.

But these two provisions, Congress comprehended, could not work effectively unless individuals were given a powerful incentive to obtain insurance.

In the 1990s, several States—including New York, New Jersey, Washington, Kentucky, Maine, New Hampshire, and Vermont—enacted guaranteed-issue and community-rating laws without requiring universal acquisition of insurance coverage. The results were disastrous. "All seven states suffered from skyrocketing insurance premium costs, reductions in individuals with coverage, and reductions in insurance products and providers." ...

Massachusetts, Congress was told, cracked the ... problem. By requiring most residents to obtain insurance, the Commonwealth ensured that insurers would not be left with only the sick as customers. As a result, federal lawmakers observed, Massachusetts succeeded where other States had failed. In coupling the minimum coverage provision with guaranteed-issue and community-rating prescriptions, Congress followed Massachusetts' lead.

In sum, Congress passed the minimum coverage provision as a key component of the ACA to address an economic and social problem that has plagued the Nation for decades: the large number of U.S. residents who are unable or unwilling to obtain health insurance. Whatever one thinks of the policy decision Congress made, it was Congress' prerogative to make it.... under the Commerce and Necessary and Proper Clauses.

II

.... The Framers understood that the "general Interests of the Union" would change over time, in ways they could not anticipate. Accordingly, they recognized that the Constitution was of necessity a "great outlin[e]," not a detailed blueprint, see McCulloch v. Maryland, 4 Wheat. 316, (1819)....

Consistent with the Framers' intent, we have repeatedly emphasized that Congress' authority under the Commerce Clause is dependent upon "practical" considerations, including "actual experience." Jones & Laughlin Steel Corp., 301 U.S., at 41–42; see Wickard v. Filburn, 317 U.S. 111 (1942); United States v. Lopez, 514 U.S. 549, 573 (1995) (KENNEDY, J., concurring).

Until today, this Court's pragmatic approach to judging whether Congress validly exercised its commerce power was guided by two familiar principles. First, Congress has the power to regulate economic activities "that substantially affect interstate commerce." Gonzales v. Raich, 545 U.S. 1, 17 (2005). This capacious power extends even to local activities that, viewed in the aggregate, have a substantial impact on interstate commerce.

Second, we owe a large measure of respect to Congress when it frames and enacts economic and social legislation. See Raich, 545 U.S., at 17. When appraising such legislation, we ask only (1) whether Congress had a "rational basis" for concluding that the regulated activity substantially affects interstate commerce, and (2) whether there is a "reasonable connection between the regulatory means selected and the asserted ends." Id., at 323–324. In answering these questions, we presume the statute under review is constitutional and may strike it down only on a "plain showing" that Congress acted irrationally. United States v. Morrison, 529 U.S. 598, 607 (2000).

Straightforward application of these principles would require the Court to hold that the minimum coverage provision is proper Commerce Clause legislation. Beyond dispute, Congress had a rational basis for concluding that the uninsured, as a class, substantially affect interstate commerce. Those without insurance consume billions of dollars of health-care products and services each year. Those goods are produced, sold, and delivered largely by national and regional companies who routinely transact business across state lines. The uninsured also cross state lines to receive care. Some have medical emergencies while away from home. Others, when sick, go to a neighboring State that provides better care for those who have not prepaid for care.

Not only do those without insurance consume a large amount of health care each year; critically, as earlier explained, their inability to pay for a significant portion of that consumption drives up market prices, foists costs on other consumers, and reduces market efficiency and stability. Given these far-reaching effects on interstate commerce, the decision to forgo insurance is hardly inconsequential or equivalent to "doing nothing"; it is, instead, an economic decision Congress has the authority to address under the Commerce Clause.

The minimum coverage provision, furthermore, bears a "reasonable connection" to Congress' goal of protecting the health-care market from the disruption caused by individuals who fail to obtain insurance. By requiring those who do not carry insurance to pay a toll, the minimum coverage provision gives individuals a strong incentive to insure. This incentive, Congress had good reason to believe, would reduce the number of uninsured and, correspondingly, mitigate the adverse impact the uninsured have on the national health-care market....

THE CHIEF JUSTICE.... insists, the uninsured cannot be considered active in the market for health care, because "[t]he proximity and degree of connection between the [uninsured today] and [their] subsequent commercial activity is too lacking."

This argument has multiple flaws. First, more than 60% of those without insurance visit a hospital or doctor's office each year. Nearly 90% will within five years. An uninsured's consumption of health care is thus quite proximate: It is virtually certain to occur in the next five years and more likely than not to occur this year.

Equally evident, Congress has no way of separating those uninsured individuals who will need emergency medial care today (surely their consumption of medical care is sufficiently imminent) from those who will not need medical services for years to come. No one knows when an emergency will occur, yet emergencies involving the uninsured arise daily. To capture individuals who unexpectedly will obtain medical care in the very near future, then, Congress needed to include individuals who will not go to a doctor anytime soon....

Second, it is Congress' role, not the Court's, to delineate the boundaries of the market the Legislature seeks to regulate. THE CHIEF JUSTICE defines the health-care market as including only those transactions that will occur either in the next instant or within some (unspecified) proximity to the next instant. But Congress could reasonably have viewed the market from a long-term perspective, encompassing all transactions virtually certain to occur over the next decade, not just those occurring here and now.

Third, contrary to THE CHIEF JUSTICE's contention, our precedent does indeed.... acknowledge Congress' authority, under the Commerce Clause, to direct the conduct of an individual today (the farmer in Wickard, stopped from growing excess wheat; the plaintiff in Raich, ordered to cease cultivating marijuana) because of a prophesied future transaction (the eventual sale of that wheat or marijuana in the interstate market). Congress' actions are even more rational in this case, where the future activity (the consumption of medical care) is certain to occur, the sole uncertainty being the time the activity will take place.

.... The inevitable yet unpredictable need for medical care and the guarantee that emergency care will be provided when required are conditions nonexistent in other markets. That is so of the market for cars, and of the market for broccoli as well.... Virtually everyone, I reiterate, consumes health care at some point in his or her life. Health insurance is a means of paying for this care, nothing more. In requiring individuals to obtain insurance, Congress is therefore not mandating the purchase of a discrete, unwanted product. Rather, Congress is merely defining the terms on which individuals pay for an interstate good they consume: Persons subject to the mandate must now pay for medical care in advance (instead of at the point of service) and through insurance (instead of out of pocket). Establishing payment terms for goods in or affecting interstate commerce is quintessential economic regulation well within Congress' domain.

THE CHIEF JUSTICE also calls the minimum coverage provision an illegitimate effort to make young, healthy individuals subsidize insurance premiums paid by the less hale and hardy. This complaint, too, is spurious. Under the current health-care system, healthy persons who lack insurance receive a benefit for which they do not pay: They are assured that, if they need it, emergency medical care will be available, although they cannot afford it. Those who have insurance bear the cost of this guarantee. By requiring the healthy uninsured to obtain insurance or pay a penalty structured as a tax, the minimum coverage provision ends the free ride these individuals currently enjoy.

In the fullness of time, moreover, today's young and healthy will become society's old and infirm. Viewed over a lifespan, the costs and benefits even out: The young who pay more than their fair share currently will pay less than their fair share when they become senior citizens. And even if, as undoubtedly will be the case, some individuals, over their lifespans, will pay more for health insurance than they receive in health services, they have little to complain about, for that is how insurance works. Every insured person receives protection against a catastrophic loss, even though only a subset of the covered class will ultimately need that protection.

.... Nothing in [the Constitution's] language implies that Congress' commerce power is limited to regulating those actively engaged in commercial transactions. Indeed, as the D. C. Circuit observed, "[a]t the time the Constitution was [framed], to 'regulate' meant," among other things, "to require action."

.... THE CHIEF JUSTICE asserts, "[t]he language of the Constitution reflects the natural understanding that the power to regulate assumes there is already something to be regulated." ... This argument is difficult to fathom. Requiring individuals to obtain insurance unquestionably regulates the interstate health-insurance and health-care markets, both of them in existence well before the enactment of the ACA. Thus, the "something to be regulated" was surely there when Congress created the minimum coverage provision.

Nor does our case law toe the activity versus inactivity line. In Wickard, for example, we upheld the penalty imposed on a farmer who grew too much wheat, even though the regulation had the effect of compelling farmers to purchase wheat in the open market. "[F]orcing some farmers into the market to buy what they could provide for themselves" was, the Court held, a valid means of regulating commerce. Id., at 128–129....

.... This Court's former endeavors to impose categorical limits on the commerce power have not fared well. In several pre-New Deal cases, the Court attempted to cabin Congress' Commerce Clause authority by distinguishing "commerce" from activity once conceived to be noncommercial, notably, "production," "mining," and "manufacturing." The Court also sought to distinguish activities having a "direct" effect on interstate commerce, and for that reason, subject to federal regulation, from those having only an "indirect" effect, and therefore not amenable to federal control.

These line-drawing exercises were untenable, and the Court long ago abandoned them. "[Q]uestions of the power of Congress [under the Commerce Clause]," we held in Wickard, "are not to be decided by reference to any formula which would give controlling force to nomenclature such as 'production' and 'indirect' and foreclose consideration of the actual effects of the activity in question upon interstate commerce." 317 U.S., at 120. Failing to learn from this history, THE CHIEF JUSTICE plows ahead with his formalistic distinction between those who are "active in commerce," and those who are not.

It is not hard to show the difficulty courts (and Congress) would encounter in distinguishing statutes that regulate "activity" from those that regulate "inactivity." As Judge Easterbrook noted, "it is possible to restate most actions as corresponding inactions with the same effect." Take this case as an example. An individual who opts not to purchase insurance from a private insurer can be seen as actively selecting another form of insurance: self-insurance.... Wickard is another example. Did the statute there at issue target activity (the growing of too much wheat) or inactivity (the farmer's failure to purchase wheat in the marketplace)? If anything, the Court's analysis suggested the latter. See 317 U.S., at 127–129.

At bottom, THE CHIEF JUSTICE's and the joint dissenters "view that an individual cannot be subject to Commerce Clause regulation absent voluntary, affirmative acts that enter him or her into, or affect, the interstate market expresses a concern for individual liberty that [is] more redolent of Due Process Clause arguments." Plaintiffs have abandoned any argument pinned to substantive due process, however, and now concede that the provisions here at issue do not offend the Due Process Clause.

.... [T]he commerce power [would not] be unbridled, absent THE CHIEF JUSTICE's "activity" limitation. Congress would remain unable to regulate noneconomic conduct that has only an attenuated effect on interstate commerce and is traditionally left to state law....

Other provisions of the Constitution also check congressional overreaching. A mandate to purchase a particular product would be unconstitutional if, for example, the edict impermissibly abridged the freedom of speech, interfered with the free exercise of religion, or infringed on a liberty interest protected by the Due Process Clause.

Supplementing these legal restraints is a formidable check on congressional power: the democratic process. As the controversy surrounding the passage of the Affordable Care Act attests, purchase mandates are likely to engender political resistance. This prospect is borne out by the behavior of state legislators. Despite their possession of unquestioned authority to impose mandates, state governments have rarely done so.

When contemplated in its extreme, almost any power looks dangerous. The commerce power, hypothetically, would enable Congress to prohibit the purchase and home production of all meat, fish, and dairy goods, effectively compelling Americans to eat only vegetables. Yet no one would offer the "hypothetical and unreal possibilit[y]," of a vegetarian state as a credible reason to deny Congress the authority ever to ban the possession and sale of goods. THE CHIEF JUSTICE accepts just such specious logic when he cites the broccoli horrible as a reason to deny Congress the power to pass the individual mandate. Cf. R. Bork, The Tempting of America 169 (1990) ("Judges and lawyers live on the slippery slope of analogies; they are not supposed to ski it to the bottom."). But see, e.g., (joint opinion of SCALIA, KENNEDY, THOMAS, and ALITO, JJ.) (asserting, outlandishly, that if the minimum coverage provision is sustained, then Congress could make "breathing in and out the basis for federal prescription")....

III

The Necessary and Proper Clause "empowers Congress to enact laws in effectuation of its [commerce] powe[r] that are not within its authority to enact in isolation." Raich, 545 U.S., at 39, (SCALIA, J., concurring in judgment). Hence, "[a] complex regulatory program ... can survive a Commerce Clause challenge without a showing that every single facet of the program is independently and directly related to a valid congressional goal." "It is enough that the challenged provisions are an integral part of the regulatory program and that the regulatory scheme when considered as a whole satisfies this test." Ibid. See also Raich, 545 U.S., at 37, (SCALIA, J., concurring in judgment) ("Congress may regulate even noneconomic local activity if that regulation is a necessary part of a more general regulation of interstate commerce. The relevant question is simply whether the means chosen are 'reasonably adapted' to the attainment of a legitimate end under the commerce power.")

Recall that one of Congress' goals in enacting the Affordable Care Act was to eliminate the insurance industry's practice of charging higher prices or denying coverage to individuals with preexisting medical conditions. The commerce power allows Congress to ban this practice, a point no one disputes.... [T]he minimum coverage provision, together with the guaranteed-issue and community-rating requirements, is "'reasonably adapted' to the attainment of a legitimate end under the commerce power": the elimination of pricing and sales practices that take an applicant's medical history into account.

.... How is a judge to decide, when ruling on the constitutionality of a federal statute, whether Congress employed an "independent power," or merely a "derivative" one? Whether the power used is "substantive," or just "incidental"? The instruction THE CHIEF JUSTICE, in effect, provides lower courts: You will know it when you see it....

... [P]erhaps most important, the minimum coverage provision, along with other provisions of the ACA, addresses the very sort of interstate problem that made the commerce power essential in our federal system. The crisis created by the large number of U.S. residents who lack health insurance is one of national dimension that States are "separately incompetent" to handle. Far from trampling on States' sovereignty, the ACA attempts a federal solution for the very reason that the States, acting separately, cannot meet the need. Notably, the ACA serves the general welfare of the people of the United States while retaining a prominent role for the States....

JUSTICE SCALIA, JUSTICE KENNEDY, JUSTICE THOMAS, and JUSTICE ALITO, dissenting.

Congress has set out to remedy the problem that the best health care is beyond the reach of many Americans who cannot afford it. It can assuredly do that, by exercising the powers accorded to it under the Constitution. The question in this case, however, is whether the complex structures and provisions of the Patient Protection and Affordable Care Act (Affordable Care Act or ACA) go beyond those powers. We conclude that they do.

.... The striking case of Wickard v. Filburn, 317 U.S. 111 (1942), which held that the economic activity of growing wheat, even for one's own consumption, affected commerce sufficiently that it could be regulated, always has been regarded as the ne plus ultra of expansive Commerce Clause jurisprudence. To go beyond that, and to say the failure to grow wheat (which is not an economic activity, or any activity at all) nonetheless affects commerce and therefore can be federally regulated, is to make mere breathing in and out the basis for federal prescription and to extend federal power to virtually all human activity....

In Gibbons v. Ogden, 22 U.S. 1, 9 Wheat. 1, 196 (1824), Chief Justice Marshall wrote that the power to regulate commerce is the power "to prescribe the rule by which commerce is to be governed." That understanding is consistent with the original meaning of "regulate" at the time of the Constitution's ratification, when "to regulate" meant "[t]o adjust by rule, method or established mode," 2 N. Webster, An American Dictionary of the English Language (1828); "[t]o adjust by rule or method," 2 S. Johnson, A Dictionary of the English Language (7th ed. 1785); "[t]o adjust, to direct according to rule," 2 J. Ash, New and Complete Dictionary of the English Language (1775) ...

We do not doubt that the buying and selling of health insurance contracts is commerce generally subject to federal regulation. But when Congress provides that (nearly) all citizens must buy an insurance contract, it goes beyond "adjust[ing] by rule or method," Johnson, supra, or "direct[ing] according to rule," Ash, supra; it directs the creation of commerce.

In response, the Government offers two theories as to why the Individual Mandate is nevertheless constitutional. Neither theory suffices to sustain its validity.

.... [T]he Government submits that § 5000A is "integral to the Affordable Care Act's insurance reforms" and "necessary to make effective the Act's core reforms." Congress included a "finding" to similar effect in the Act itself. See 42 U.S.C. § 18091(2)(H).

.... [But] there are many ways other than this unprecedented Individual Mandate by which the regulatory scheme's goals of reducing insurance premiums and ensuring the profitability of insurers could be achieved. For instance, those who did not purchase insurance could be subjected to a surcharge when they do enter the health insurance system. Or they could be denied a full income tax credit given to those who do purchase the insurance....

The Government's second theory in support of the Individual Mandate is that.... the provision directs the manner in which individuals purchase health care services and related goods (directing that they be purchased through insurance) and is therefore a straightforward exercise of the commerce power.

The primary problem with this argument is that § 5000A does not apply only to persons who purchase all, or most, or even any, of the health care services or goods that the mandated insurance covers. Indeed, the main objection many have to the Mandate is that they have no intention of purchasing most or even any of such goods or services and thus no need to buy insurance for those purchases. The Government responds that the health-care market involves "essentially universal participation," The principal difficulty with this response is that it is, in the only relevant sense, not true. It is true enough that everyone consumes "health care," if the term is taken to include the purchase of a bottle of aspirin. But the health care "market" that is the object of the Individual Mandate not only includes but principally consists of goods and services that the young people primarily affected by the Mandate do not purchase. They are quite simply not participants in that market, and cannot be made so (and thereby subjected to regulation) by the simple device of defining participants to include all those who will, later in their lifetime, probably purchase the goods or services covered by the mandated insurance. Such a definition of market participants is unprecedented, and were it to be a premise for the exercise of national power, it would have no principled limits.

In a variation on this attempted exercise of federal power, the Government points out that Congress in this Act has purported to regulate "economic and financial decision[s] to forego [sic] health insurance coverage and [to] attempt to self-insure," 42 U.S.C. § 18091(2)(A), since those decisions have "a substantial and deleterious effect on interstate commerce." But as the discussion above makes clear, the decision to forgo participation in an interstate market is not itself commercial activity (or indeed any activity at all) within Congress' power to regulate. It is true that, at the end of the day, it is inevitable that each American will affect commerce and become a part of it, even if not by choice. But if every person comes within the Commerce Clause power of Congress to regulate by the simple reason that he will one day engage in commerce, the idea of a limited Government power is at an end....

The dissent dismisses the conclusion that the power to compel entry into the health-insurance market would include the power to compel entry into the new-car or broccoli markets. The latter purchasers, it says, "will be obliged to pay at the counter before receiving the vehicle or nourishment," whereas those refusing to purchase health-insurance will ultimately get treated anyway, at others' expense. "[T]he unique attributes of the health-care market ... give rise to a significant free-riding problem that does not occur in other markets." And "a vegetable-purchase mandate" (or a car-purchase mandate) is not "likely to have a substantial effect on the health-care costs" borne by other Americans. Those differences make a very good argument by the dissent's own lights, since they show that the failure to purchase health insurance, unlike the failure to purchase cars or broccoli, creates a national, social-welfare problem that is (in the dissent's view) included among the unenumerated "problems" that the Constitution authorizes the Federal Government to solve. But those differences do not show that the failure to enter the health-insurance market, unlike the failure to buy cars and broccoli, is an activity that Congress can "regulate." (Of course one day the failure of some of the public to purchase American cars may endanger the existence of domestic automobile manufacturers; or the failure of some to eat broccoli may be found to deprive them of a newly discovered cancer-fighting chemical which only that food contains, producing health-care costs that are a burden on the rest of us—in which case, under the theory of JUSTICE GINSBURG's dissent, moving against those inactivities will also come within the Federal Government's unenumerated problem-solving powers.) ...

Review Questions and Explanations: The Affordable Care Act Case
(commerce power excerpt)

1. The voting breakdown in this case was somewhat unusual. The "joint dissent" (called "joint" to indicate shared authorship of the four dissenters)

seems to agree with the analysis and conclusion of Chief Justice Roberts on both the Commerce Clause issue and the "Medicaid expansion" spending power issue (presented below). It dissents from the conclusion that the individual mandate can be upheld under the taxing power; and it argues that the entire 900-page law should have been struck down. The "joint dissent" thus might have more accurately been styled as "concurring in part, dissenting in part." Some commentators have speculated that Chief Justice Roberts had initially agreed with the four "joint dissenters" to a single majority opinion striking down the entire law, but then changed his mind and agreed with the other four justices to use the taxing authority to uphold the "mandate." If so, perhaps there is a bit of spite in the dissenters' refusal to join those portions of the Roberts opinion they agreed with.

2. Chief Justice Roberts' opinion acknowledges "To an economist, perhaps, there is no difference between activity and inactivity; both have measurable economic effects[.]" Arguably, what the "healthy young people" who stay out of the insurance market are doing is "market timing" or "free riding." Why isn't that properly construed as an activity? Roberts' answer seems to be simply to say that the framers were "practical statesmen," not "metaphysical philosophers." What does that mean? Is economics "metaphysical" while a distinction between activity and inactivity is "practical"?

3. Is the activity/inactivity distinction supported by the Court's precedents? Is it supported by the constitutional text? Why can't you "regulate" something by either prohibiting *or* requiring it?

4. If there is an actual or potential major market-failure of an interstate market due to a pervasive free-riding problem, should the Commerce Clause be understood to authorize Congress to try to solve the problem by requiring the free riders to participate?

5. Can Justice Scalia's participation in the "joint dissent" be harmonized with his concurrence in the judgment in *Raich*? There he said, "Congress may regulate even noneconomic local activity if that regulation is a necessary part of a more general regulation of interstate commerce." Professor Randy Barnett, who represented NFIB in the ACA case (and the plaintiffs-respondents in *Raich*) reportedly said that Justice Scalia would be able to distinguish his *Raich* opinion "without breaking a sweat." Sweat or no, do you see a principled distinction?

6. This is a Commerce Clause decision, and therefore asks whether Congress has the power to require the purchase of health insurance. But does some of the language in the Roberts and dissenting opinions, and their use (at least in certain passages) of the term "government" without the qualification "federal," suggest that an insurance mandate violates individual autonomy in a way that is beyond the power of *any* government, federal or state? What about state laws requiring the purchase of car insurance even by safe drivers who will never have an accident?

7. Consider again the individual rights language by Roberts and the dissenters, noted just above. Much of the public discussion (and outrage) about the ACA sounded in ideas of individual liberty, not commerce. The general gist of this objection was that making people buy insurance simply went "too far" and interfered with their "freedoms." To what extent do the opinions of these justices rest on the idea that the Court should actively protect individual liberties, even

when they are not enumerated in the Constitution—the idea, in other words, that even if the Constitution gives Congress the power to regulate the national economy, certain regulations nonetheless go "too far" and must be struck down? As you will see later in your studies, this type of judicially protected, unenumerated liberty interest, operationalized through the Due Process clause, underlies cases like *Roe v. Wade*. It also, as Justice Ginsburg points out, is similar to the Court's efforts to restrain Congress during the *Lochner* era. Can you draw principled distinctions between the role of the Court in protecting these different types of "liberty"?

8. Does the individual mandate project commerce power into a "new" and "limitless" field, as the joint dissent suggests? Why isn't health insurance regulation an old and limited field? *See, e.g.*, Employee Retirement Income Security Act of 1974.

D. The Tenth Amendment

The Tenth Amendment provides:

> The powers not delegated to the United States by the Constitution, nor prohibited by it to the states, are reserved to the states respectively, or to the people.

The Tenth Amendment has been discussed in the Commerce Clause cases you have read so far, but we have not examined it in detail. Pre-1937 cases such *as Hammer v. Dagenhart* and *Carter v. Carter Coal Co.*, tended to interpret the Tenth Amendment as an independent limitation on the power of Congress. Under this view, an array of subjects deemed to be of "purely local" regulatory concern—for example, the employer-employee relationship—were "reserved" to the states and immune from federal legislation. In other words, even a law that might theoretically be a regulation of interstate commerce could be struck down as violative of the Tenth Amendment. This view was forcefully repudiated in *Darby*, where the Court held that the Tenth Amendment did not act as an independent limit on Congressional power: "The amendment states but a truism that all is retained which has not been surrendered." In other words, the Tenth Amendment is a reassurance that states retain their pre-constitutional sovereignty over legislative subjects not given to Congress, but doesn't in itself tell us what specific limits there may be on the powers of Congress.

1. The Unsteady Path: Tenth Amendment Doctrine from the New Deal to 1992

After *Darby* in 1941, the notion of the Tenth Amendment as an independent limitation was banished from the Court's jurisprudence for the next 35 years. However, since 1976, the Court has engaged in limited forays into making an exception to the "mere truism" understanding of the Tenth Amendment. Without questioning *Darby*'s holding as it applies to congressional regulation of *private* conduct, the Court has attempted to carve out limits on the power of federal legislation to regulate conduct by state government actors.

When reading these cases, identify the test developed by the Court in *National League of Cities* and consider why it failed. Specifically, consider the different positions taken by the majority, the dissent, and the concurrence. Why did Justice Blackmun write separately—can you identify what makes his opinion different from that of the majority? Justice Blackmun's opinion matters because he is the justice who changed his vote in *Garcia*.

Guided Reading Questions: *National League of Cities* and *Garcia*

1. *National League of Cities* and *Garcia* both decide the same question. What is it?

2. What principle does the Court announce in *National League of Cities*? Does it revive the Tenth Amendment doctrine from *Hammer* and *Carter Coal*?

3. Try to articulate the principle the Court adopts in *Garcia*.

4. Would *National League of Cities* (assuming for the moment it had not been overturned) limit Congress's ability to impose minimum wage restrictions on private employers? Why or why not?

5. What reasons does Justice Blackmun give for changing his position in *Garcia*?

National League of Cities v. Usery
426 U.S. 833 (1976)

Majority: *Rehnquist*, Burger (CJ), Stewart, Blackmun, Powell

Concurrence: *Blackmun*

Dissent: *Brennan*, White, Marhsall; *Stevens* (omitted)

Mr. Justice REHNQUIST delivered the opinion of the Court.

Nearly 40 years ago Congress enacted the Fair Labor Standards Act, and required employers covered by the Act to pay their employees a minimum hourly wage and to pay them at one and one-half times their regular rate of pay for hours worked in excess of 40 during a work week. The Act required covered employers to keep certain records to aid in the enforcement of the Act, and to comply with specified child labor standards. This Court unanimously upheld the Act as a valid exercise of congressional authority under the commerce power in U.S. v. Darby....

The original Fair Labor Standards Act passed in 1938 specifically excluded the States and their political subdivisions from its coverage. In 1974, however, Congress enacted the most recent of a series of broadening amendments to the Act. By these amendments Congress has extended the minimum wage and maximum hour provisions to almost all public employees employed by the States and by their various political subdivisions. Appellants in these cases include individual cities and States, the National League of Cities, and the National Governors' Conference; they brought an action in the District Court for the District of Columbia which challenged the validity of the 1974 amendments. They asserted in effect that when Congress sought to apply the Fair Labor Standards Act provisions virtually across the board to employees of state and municipal governments it "infringed a constitutional prohibition" running in favor of the States as States....

Appellants in no way challenge these decisions establishing the breadth of authority granted Congress under the commerce power. Their contention, on the contrary, is that when Congress seeks to regulate directly the activities of States as public employers, it transgresses an affirmative limitation on the exercise of its power akin to other commerce power affirmative limitations contained in the Constitution. Congressional enactments which may be fully within the grant of legislative authority contained in the Commerce Clause may nonetheless be invalid because found to offend against the right to trial by jury contained in the Sixth Amendment or the Due Process Clause of the Fifth Amendment. Appellants' essential contention is that the 1974 amendments to the Act, while undoubtedly within the scope of the Commerce Clause, encounter a similar constitutional barrier because they are to be applied directly to the States and subdivisions of States as employers....

This Court has never doubted that there are limits upon the power of Congress to override state sovereignty, even when exercising its otherwise plenary powers to tax or to regulate commerce which are conferred by Article I of the Constitution. In Wirtz, for example, the Court took care to assure the appellants that it had "ample power to prevent ... 'the utter destruction of the State as a sovereign political entity,'" which they feared....

While the Tenth Amendment has been characterized as a "truism," stating merely that "all is retained which has not been surrendered," United States v. Darby, it is not without significance. The Amendment expressly declares the constitutional policy that Congress may not exercise power in a fashion that impairs the States' integrity or their ability to function effectively in a federal system." ...

One undoubted attribute of state sovereignty is the States' power to determine the wages which shall be paid to those whom they employ in order to carry out their governmental functions, what hours those persons will work, and what compensation will be provided where these employees may be called upon to work overtime. The question we must resolve here, then, is whether these determinations are "functions essential to separate and independent existence," so that Congress may not abrogate the States' otherwise plenary authority to make them.

In their complaint appellants advanced estimates of substantial costs which will be imposed upon them by the 1974 amendments.... Judged solely in terms of increased costs in dollars, these allegations show a significant impact on the functioning of the governmental bodies involved. The Metropolitan Government of Nashville and Davidson County, Tenn., for example, asserted that the Act will increase its costs of providing essential police and fire protection, without any increase in service or in current salary levels, by $938,000 per year. Cape Girardeau, Mo., estimated that its annual budget for fire protection may have to be increased by anywhere from $250,000 to $400,000 over the current figure of $350,000. The State of Arizona alleged that the annual additional expenditures which will be required if it is to continue to provide essential state services may total $2.5 million. The State of California, which must devote significant portions of its budget to fire-suppression endeavors, estimated that application of the Act to its employment practices will necessitate an increase in its budget of between $8 million and $16 million.

Increased costs are not, of course, the only adverse effects which compliance with the Act will visit upon state and local governments, and in turn upon the citizens who depend upon those governments. In its complaint in intervention, for example, California asserted that it could not comply with the overtime costs (approximately $750,000 per year) which the Act required to be paid to California Highway Patrol cadets during their academy training program. California reported that it had thus been forced to reduce its academy training program from 2,080 hours to only 960 hours, a compromise undoubtedly of substantial importance to those whose safety and welfare may depend upon the preparedness of the California Highway Patrol.

This type of forced relinquishment of important governmental activities is further reflected in the complaint's allegation that the city of Inglewood, Cal., has been forced to curtail its affirmative action program for providing employment opportunities for men and women interested in a career in law enforcement. The Inglewood police department has abolished a program for police trainees who split their week between on-the-job training and the classroom. The city could not abrogate its contractual obligations to these trainees, and it concluded that compliance with the Act in these circumstances was too financially burdensome to permit continuance of the classroom program. The city of Clovis, Cal., has been put to a similar choice regarding an internship program it was running in cooperation with a California state university. According to the complaint, because the interns' compensation brings them within the purview of the Act the city must decide whether to eliminate the program entirely or to substantially reduce its beneficial aspects by doing away with any pay for the interns.

Quite apart from the substantial costs imposed upon the States and their political sub-divisions, the Act displaces state policies regarding the manner in which they will structure delivery of those governmental services which their citizens require. The Act, speaking directly to the States Qua States, requires that they shall pay all but an extremely limited minority of their employees the minimum wage rates currently chosen by Congress. It may well be that as a matter of economic policy it would be desirable that States, just as private employers, comply with these minimum wage requirements. But it cannot be gainsaid that the federal requirement directly supplants the considered policy choices of the States' elected officials and administrators as to how they wish to structure pay scales in state employment. The State might wish to employ persons with little or no training, or those who wish to work on a casual basis, or those who for some other reason do not possess minimum employment requirements, and pay them less than the federally prescribed minimum wage. It may wish to offer part-time or summer employment to teenagers at a figure less than the minimum wage, and if unable to do so may decline to offer such employment at all. But the Act would forbid such choices by the States. The only "discretion" left to them under the Act is either to attempt to increase their revenue to meet the additional financial burden imposed upon them by paying congressionally prescribed wages to their existing complement of employees, or to reduce that complement to a number which can be paid the federal minimum wage without increasing revenue....

... States as States stand on a quite different footing from an individual or a corporation when challenging the exercise of Congress' power to regulate commerce.... Congress may not exercise that power so as to force directly upon the States its choices as to how essential decisions regarding the conduct of integral governmental functions are to be made. We agree that such assertions of power if unchecked, would indeed, as Mr. Justice Douglas cautioned in his dissent in Wirtz, allow "the National Government [to] devour the essentials of state sovereignty," and would therefore transgress the bounds of the authority granted Congress under the Commerce Clause....

MR. JUSTICE BLACKMUN, concurring.

The Court's opinion and the dissents indicate the importance and significance of this litigation as it bears upon the relationship between the Federal Government and our

States. Although I am not untroubled by certain possible implications of the Court's opinion some of them suggested by the dissents I do not read the opinion so despairingly as does my Brother BRENNAN. In my view, the result with respect to the statute under challenge here is necessarily correct. I may misinterpret the Court's opinion, but it seems to me that it adopts a balancing approach, and does not outlaw federal power in areas such as environmental protection, where the federal interest is demonstrably greater and where state facility compliance with imposed federal standards would be essential. With this understanding on my part of the Court's opinion, I join it.

Mr. Justice BRENNAN, with whom Mr. Justice WHITE and Mr. Justice MARSHALL join, dissenting.

The Court concedes, as of course it must, that Congress enacted the 1974 amendments pursuant to its exclusive power under [Article I] of the Constitution "[t]o regulate Commerce … among the several States." It must therefore be surprising that my Brethren should choose this bicentennial year of our independence to repudiate principles governing judicial interpretation of our Constitution settled since the time of Mr. Chief Justice John Marshall, discarding his postulate that the Constitution contemplates that restraints upon exercise by Congress of its plenary commerce power lie in the political process and not in the judicial process….

My Brethren thus have today manufactured an abstraction without substance, founded neither in the words of the Constitution nor on precedent. An abstraction having such profoundly pernicious consequences is not made less so by characterizing the 1974 amendments as legislation directed against the "States Qua States." … Of course, regulations that this Court can say are not regulations of "commerce" cannot stand … But my Brethren make no claim that the 1974 amendments are not regulations of "commerce"; rather they overrule Wirtz in disagreement with historic principles that United States v. California, supra, reaffirmed: "[W]hile the commerce power has limits, valid general regulations of commerce do not cease to be regulations of commerce because a State is involved. If a State is engaging in economic activities that are validly regulated by the Federal Government when engaged in by private persons, the State too may be forced to conform its activities to federal regulation."

Therefore, my Brethren are also repudiating the long line of our precedents holding that a judicial finding that Congress has not unreasonably regulated a subject matter of "commerce" brings to an end the judicial role. "Let the end be legitimate, let it be within the scope of the constitution, and all means which are appropriate, which are plainly adapted to that end, which are not prohibited, but consist with the letter and spirit of the constitution, are constitutional." McCulloch v. Maryland.

Garcia v. San Antonio Metropolitan Transit Authority
469 U.S. 528 (1985)

Majority: *Blackmun*, Brennan, White, Marshall, Stevens

Dissents: *Powell* (omitted), Burger (CJ), *Rehnquist, O'Connor* (omitted)

JUSTICE BLACKMUN delivered the opinion of the Court.

We revisit in these cases an issue raised in National League of Cities v. Usery. In that litigation, this Court, by a sharply divided vote, ruled that the Commerce Clause does not empower Congress to enforce the minimum-wage and overtime provisions of the Fair Labor Standards Act (FLSA) against the States "in areas of traditional governmental functions." Although National League of Cities supplied some examples of "traditional governmental functions," it did not offer a general explanation of how a "traditional" function is to be distinguished from a "nontraditional" one. Since then, federal and state courts have struggled with the task, thus imposed, of identifying a traditional function for purposes of state immunity under the Commerce Clause.

In the present cases, a Federal District Court concluded that municipal ownership and operation of a mass-transit system is a traditional governmental function and thus, under National League of Cities, is exempt from the obligations imposed by the FLSA. Faced with the identical question, three Federal Courts of Appeals and one state appellate court have reached the opposite conclusion. Our examination of this "function" standard applied in these and other cases over the last eight years now persuades us that the attempt to draw the boundaries of state regulatory immunity in terms of "traditional governmental function" is not only unworkable but is also inconsistent with established principles of federalism and, indeed, with those very federalism principles on which National League of Cities purported to rest. That case, accordingly, is overruled....

The present controversy concerns the extent to which SAMTA [the San Antonio Metropolitan Transit Authority] may be subjected to the minimum-wage and overtime requirements of the FLSA.... The FLSA obligations of public mass-transit systems ... were expanded in 1974 when Congress provided for the progressive repeal of the surviving overtime exemption for mass-transit employees.... Congress simultaneously brought the States and their subdivisions further within the ambit of the FLSA by extending FLSA coverage to virtually all state and local-government employees.... [San Antonio] complied with the FLSA's overtime requirements until 1976, when this Court, in National League of Cities, overruled Maryland v. Wirtz, and held that the FLSA could not be applied constitutionally to the "traditional governmental functions" of state and local governments. Four months after National League of Cities was handed down, [San Antonio] informed its employees that the decision relieved [it] of its overtime obligations under the FLSA....

Appellees have not argued that SAMTA is immune from regulation under the FLSA on the ground that it is a local transit system engaged in intrastate commercial activity. In a practical sense, SAMTA's operations might well be characterized as "local." Nonetheless, it long has been settled that Congress' authority under the Commerce Clause extends to intrastate economic activities that affect interstate commerce. Were SAMTA a privately owned and operated enterprise, it could not credibly argue that Congress exceeded the bounds of its Commerce Clause powers in prescribing minimum wages and overtime rates for SAMTA's employees. Any constitutional exemption from the requirements of the FLSA therefore must rest on SAMTA's status as a governmental entity rather than on the "local" nature of its operations.

The prerequisites for governmental immunity under National League of Cities were summarized by this Court in Hodel, supra. Under that summary, four conditions must be satisfied before a state activity may be deemed immune from a particular federal regulation under the Commerce Clause. First, it is said that the federal statute at issue must regulate "the States as States." Second, the statute must "address matters that are indisputably 'attribute[s] of state sovereignty.'" Third, state compliance with the federal obligation must "directly impair [the States'] ability 'to structure integral operations in areas of traditional governmental functions.'" Finally, the relation of state and federal interests must not be such that "the nature of the federal interest ... justifies state submission." ...

The controversy in the present cases has focused on the third Hodel requirement— that the challenged federal statute trench on "traditional governmental functions." The

District Court voiced a common concern: "Despite the abundance of adjectives, identifying which particular state functions are immune remains difficult." Just how troublesome the task has been is revealed by the results reached in other federal cases. Thus, courts have held that regulating ambulance services, licensing automobile drivers, operating a municipal airport; performing solid waste disposal; and operating a highway authority; are functions protected under National League of Cities. At the same time, courts have held that issuance of industrial development bonds; regulation of intrastate natural gas sales; regulation of traffic on public roads; regulation of air transportation; operation of a telephone system; leasing and sale of natural gas; operation of a mental health facility; and provision of in-house domestic services for the aged and handicapped; are not entitled to immunity. We find it difficult, if not impossible, to identify an organizing principle that places each of the cases in the first group on one side of a line and each of the cases in the second group on the other side. The constitutional distinction between licensing drivers and regulating traffic, for example, or between operating a highway authority and operating a mental health facility, is elusive at best.

Thus far, this Court itself has made little headway in defining the scope of the governmental functions deemed protected under National League of Cities. In that case the Court set forth examples of protected and unprotected functions but provided no explanation of how those examples were identified....

Neither do any of the alternative standards that might be employed to distinguish between protected and unprotected governmental functions appear manageable. We rejected the possibility of making immunity turn on a purely historical standard of "tradition" in Long Island, and properly so. The most obvious defect of a historical approach to state immunity is that it prevents a court from accommodating changes in the historical functions of States, changes that have resulted in a number of once-private functions like education being assumed by the States and their subdivisions. At the same time, the only apparent virtue of a rigorous historical standard, namely, its promise of a reasonably objective measure for state immunity, is illusory. Reliance on history as an organizing principle results in line-drawing of the most arbitrary sort; the genesis of state governmental functions stretches over a historical continuum from before the Revolution to the present, and courts would have to decide by fiat precisely how longstanding a pattern of state involvement had to be for federal regulatory authority to be defeated....

A nonhistorical standard for selecting immune governmental functions is likely to be just as unworkable as is a historical standard. The goal of identifying "uniquely" governmental functions, for example, has been rejected by the Court in the field of governmental tort liability in part because the notion of a "uniquely" governmental function is unmanageable.... another possibility would be to confine immunity to "necessary" governmental services, that is, services that would be provided inadequately or not at all unless the government provided them. The set of services that fits into this category, however, may well be negligible. The fact that an unregulated market produces less of some service than a State deems desirable does not mean that the State itself must provide the service; in most if not all cases, the State can "contract out" by hiring private firms to provide the service or simply by providing subsidies to existing suppliers. It also is open to question how well equipped courts are to make this kind of determination about the workings of economic markets.

We believe, however, that there is a more fundamental problem at work here, a problem that explains why the Court was never able to provide a basis for the governmental/proprietary distinction in the intergovernmental tax-immunity cases and why an attempt to draw similar distinctions with respect to federal regulatory authority under National League of Cities is unlikely to succeed regardless of how the distinctions are phrased. The problem is that neither the governmental/proprietary distinction nor any other that purports to separate out important governmental functions can be faithful to the role of federalism in a democratic society. The essence of our federal system is that within the realm of authority left open to them under the Constitution, the States must be equally free to engage in any activity that their citizens choose for the common weal, no matter how unorthodox or unnecessary anyone else—including the judiciary—deems state involvement to be. Any rule of state immunity that looks to the "traditional," "integral," or "necessary" nature of governmental functions inevitably invites an unelected federal judiciary to make decisions about which state policies it favors and which ones it dislikes. "The science of government ... is the science of experiment."

We therefore now reject, as unsound in principle and unworkable in practice, a rule of state immunity from federal regulation that turns on a judicial appraisal of whether a particular governmental function is "integral" or "traditional." Any such rule leads to inconsistent results at the same time that it disserves principles of democratic self-governance, and it breeds inconsistency precisely because it is divorced from those principles. If there are to be limits on the Federal Government's power to interfere with state functions—as undoubtedly there are—we must look elsewhere to find them. We accordingly return to the underlying issue that confronted this Court in National League of Cities—the manner in which the Constitution insulates States from the reach of Congress' power under the Commerce Clause.

The central theme of National League of Cities was that the States occupy a special position in our constitutional system and that the scope of Congress' authority under the Commerce Clause must reflect that position. Of course, the Commerce Clause by its specific language does not provide any special limitation on Congress' actions with respect to the States. It is equally true, however, that the text of the Constitution provides the beginning rather than the final answer to every inquiry into questions of federalism, for "[b]ehind the words of the constitutional provisions are postulates which limit and control." National League of Cities reflected the general conviction that the Constitution precludes "the National Government [from] devour[ing] the essentials of state sovereignty." ...

What has proved problematic is not the perception that the Constitution's federal structure imposes limitations on the Commerce Clause, but rather the nature and content of those limitations.... We doubt that courts ultimately can identify principled constitutional limitations on the scope of Congress' Commerce Clause powers over the States merely by relying on a priori definitions of state sovereignty. In part, this is because of the elusiveness of objective criteria for "fundamental" elements of state sovereignty, a problem we have witnessed in the search for "traditional governmental functions."

There is, however, a more fundamental reason: the sovereignty of the States is limited by the Constitution itself. A variety of sovereign powers, for example, are withdrawn from the States by Article I, §10. Section 8 of the same Article works an equally sharp contraction of state sovereignty by authorizing Congress to exercise a wide range of legislative powers and (in conjunction with the Supremacy Clause of Article VI) to displace contrary state legislation. By providing for final review of questions of federal law in this Court, Article III curtails the sovereign power of the States' judiciaries to make authoritative determinations of law. See Martin v Hunter's Lessee. Finally, the developed application, through the Fourteenth Amendment, of the greater part of the Bill of Rights to the States limits the sovereign authority that States otherwise would possess to legislate with respect to their citizens and to conduct their own affairs.... As a result, to say that the Constitution assumes the continued role of the States is to say little about the nature of that role....

When we look for the States' "residuary and inviolable sovereignty," The Federalist No. 39, p. 285 (B. Wright ed. 1961) (J. Madison), in the shape of the constitutional scheme rather than in predetermined notions of sovereign power, a different measure of state sovereignty emerges. Apart from the limitation on federal authority inherent in the delegated nature of Congress' Article I powers, the principal means chosen by the Framers to ensure the role of the States in the federal system lies in the structure of the Federal Government itself. It is no novelty to observe that the composition of the Federal Government was designed in large part to protect the States from overreaching by Congress. The Framers thus gave the States a role in the selection both of the Executive and the Legislative Branches of the Federal Government. The States were vested with indirect influence over the House of Representatives and the Presidency by their control of electoral qualifications and their role in Presidential elections. They were given more direct influence in the Senate, where each State received equal representation and each Senator was to be selected by the legislature of his State. The significance attached to the States' equal representation in the Senate is underscored by the prohibition of any constitutional amendment divesting a State of equal representation without the State's consent....

In short, the Framers chose to rely on a federal system in which special restraints on federal power over the States inhered principally in the workings of the National Government itself, rather than in discrete limitations on the objects of federal authority. State sovereign interests, then, are more properly protected by procedural safeguards inherent in the structure of the federal system than by judicially created limitations on federal power.... Of course, we continue to recognize that the States occupy a special and specific position in our constitutional system and that the scope of Congress' authority under the Commerce Clause must reflect that position. But the principal and basic limit on the federal commerce power is that inherent in all congressional action — the built-in restraints that our system provides through state participation in federal governmental action. The political process ensures that laws that unduly burden the States will not be promulgated. In the factual setting of these cases the internal safeguards of the political process have performed as intended.

JUSTICE REHNQUIST, dissenting.

I join both Justice POWELL's and Justice O'CONNOR's thoughtful dissents. Justice POWELL's reference to the "balancing test" approved in National League of Cities is not identical with the language in that case, which recognized that Congress could not act under its commerce power to infringe on certain fundamental aspects of state sovereignty that are essential to "the States' separate and independent existence." Nor is either test, or Justice O'CONNOR's suggested approach, precisely congruent with Justice BLACKMUN's views in 1976, when he spoke of a balancing approach which did not outlaw federal power in areas "where the federal interest is demonstrably greater." But under any one of these approaches the judgment in these cases should be affirmed, and I do not think it incumbent on those of us in dissent to spell out further the fine points of a principle that will, I am confident, in time again command the support of a majority of this Court.

Review Questions and Explanations: *National League of Cities* and *Garcia*

1. The majority in *Garcia* rejects the idea that the Court should actively use the Tenth Amendment to protect general federalism values. Is this an appropriate exercise of judicial deference in light of unhelpful constitutional text, or is it an

abdication of the Court's obligation to impose constitutional restraints on elected officials? Make the best argument you can in support of each position.

2. Do you think the "traditional governmental functions" test rejected in *Garcia* is more or less difficult to apply than other doctrinal tests you have seen so far, in constitutional law or elsewhere?

3. What is the point of Justice Rehnquist's separate dissent in *Garcia*? What are the advantages and disadvantages of a justice signaling his or her future intentions this way?

4. Might there be some "traditional governmental functions" or some way to view "states as states" that should be immune from congressional control?

2. The Tenth Amendment Anti-Commandeering Doctrine, 1992–Present

Garcia was not the Court's last word on the meaning of the Tenth Amendment. In the next two cases, *New York v. United States* and *Printz v. United States*, the Court resurrects the idea of the Tenth Amendment as an affirmative limit on the power of Congress, though on more limited grounds than those stated in *National League of Cities*. The third case, *Reno v. Condon*, seeks to reconcile *New York* and *Printz* with *Garcia*, and show us where Tenth Amendment doctrine currently stands.

The facts of *New York* are complicated. Make sure you understand them before you attempt to work your way through the Court's legal analysis. Also, be aware that the dormant Commerce Clause, a doctrine you will study in Chapter 2, prohibits a state, acting without congressional approval, from simply refusing to accept waste from waste generators located outside of the state, while continuing to accept in-state waste. That is one of the reasons why the states (and Congress) developed the complicated regime set out in the case.

Guided Reading Questions: *New York v. United States*

1. Justice O'Connor's opinion identifies three different techniques by which Congress might try to bring about state legislation in support of a federal legislative objective. Two of these are constitutional, and one isn't. Try to identify each of these three techniques and the reason why it is or is not constitutionally permissible.

2. According to the majority opinion, what precisely is the problem with the scheme adopted by Congress?

3. Does *New York* overrule *Garcia* and return to the *National League of Cities* principle, that Congress cannot regulate traditional state functions?

4. What is the doctrinal principle derived from the Court's holding that the "take title" provision is unconstitutional?

New York v. United States

505 U.S. 144 (1992)

Majority: *O'Connor*, Rehnquist (CJ), Scalia, Kennedy, Souter, Thomas

Dissents: *White*, Blackmun, *Stevens* (omitted)

JUSTICE O'CONNOR delivered the opinion of the Court.

These cases implicate one of our Nation's newest problems of public policy and perhaps our oldest question of constitutional law. The public policy issue involves the disposal of radioactive waste: In these cases, we address the constitutionality of three provisions of the Low-Level Radioactive Waste Policy Amendments Act of 1985. The constitutional question is as old as the Constitution: It consists of discerning the proper division of authority between the Federal Government and the States. We conclude that while Congress has substantial power under the Constitution to encourage the States to provide for the disposal of the radioactive waste generated within their borders, the Constitution does not confer upon Congress the ability simply to compel the States to do so. We therefore find that only two of the Act's three provisions at issue are consistent with the Constitution's allocation of power to the Federal Government.

We live in a world full of low level radioactive waste. Radioactive material is present in luminous watch dials, smoke alarms, measurement devices, medical fluids, research materials, and the protective gear and construction materials used by workers at nuclear power plants. Low level radioactive waste is generated by the Government, by hospitals, by research institutions, and by various industries. The waste must be isolated from humans for long periods of time, often for hundreds of years. Millions of cubic feet of low level radioactive waste must be disposed of each year.

Our Nation's first site for the land disposal of commercial low level radioactive waste opened in 1962 in Beatty, Nevada. Five more sites opened in the following decade: Maxey Flats, Kentucky (1963), West Valley, New York (1963), Hanford, Washington (1965), Sheffield, Illinois (1967), and Barnwell, South Carolina (1971). Between 1975 and 1978, the Illinois site closed because it was full, and water management problems caused the closure of the sites in Kentucky and New York. As a result, since 1979 only three disposal sites—those in Nevada, Washington, and South Carolina—have been in operation. Waste generated in the rest of the country must be shipped to one of these three sites for disposal.

In 1979, both the Washington and Nevada sites were forced to shut down temporarily, leaving South Carolina to shoulder the responsibility of storing low level radioactive waste produced in every part of the country. The Governor of South Carolina, understandably perturbed, ordered a 50% reduction in the quantity of waste accepted at the Barnwell site. The Governors of Washington and Nevada announced plans to shut their sites permanently.

Faced with the possibility that the Nation would be left with no disposal sites for low level radioactive waste, Congress responded by enacting the Low-Level Radioactive Waste Policy Act. Relying largely on a report submitted by the National Governors' Association, Congress declared a federal policy of holding each State "responsible for providing for the availability of capacity either within or outside the State for the disposal of low-level radioactive waste generated within its borders," and found that such waste could be disposed of "most safely and efficiently ... on a regional basis." The 1980 Act authorized States to enter into regional compacts that, once ratified by Congress, would have the authority beginning in 1986 to restrict the use of their disposal facilities to waste generated within member States. The 1980 Act included no penalties for States that failed to participate in this plan.

By 1985, only three approved regional compacts had operational disposal facilities; not surprisingly, these were the compacts formed around South Carolina, Nevada, and Washington, the three sited States. The following year, the 1980 Act would have given these three compacts the ability to exclude waste from nonmembers, and the remaining 31 States would have had no assured outlet for their low level radioactive waste. With this prospect looming, Congress once again took up the issue of waste disposal. The result was the legislation challenged here, the Low-Level Radioactive Waste Policy Amendments Act of 1985.

The 1985 Act was again based largely on a proposal submitted by the National Governors' Association. In broad outline, the Act embodies a compromise among the sited and unsited States. The sited States agreed to extend for seven years the period in which they would accept low level radioactive waste from other States. In exchange, the unsited States agreed to end their reliance on the sited States by 1992.

The mechanics of this compromise are intricate. The Act directs: "Each State shall be responsible for providing, either by itself or in cooperation with other States, for the disposal of ... low-level radioactive waste generated within the State," with the exception of certain waste generated by the Federal Government.... [T]he three States in which the disposal sites are located are permitted to exact a graduated surcharge for waste arriving from outside the regional compact ... After the 7-year transition expires, approved regional compacts may exclude radioactive waste generated outside the region.

The Act provides three types of incentives to encourage the States to comply with their statutory obligation to provide for the disposal of waste generated within their borders.

1. *Monetary incentives....* [This provision creates a federal fund by requiring sited states to pass along one quarter of the surcharges they collect for disposing of waste from unsited states. Moneys in the fund are paid to those states that reach disposal agreements.]

2. *Access incentives....* [This provision authorizes sited states to charge waste producers located in unsited states escalating rates for access to disposal sites, and, eventually to deny that access entirely.]

3. *The take title provision.* The third type of incentive is the most severe. The Act provides:

> If a State (or, where applicable, a compact region) in which low-level radioactive waste is generated is unable to provide for the disposal of all such waste generated within such State or compact region by January 1, 1996, each State in which such waste is generated, upon the request of the generator or owner of the waste, shall take title to the waste, be obligated to take possession of the waste, and shall be liable for all damages directly or indirectly incurred by such generator or owner as a consequence of the failure of the State to take possession of the waste as soon after January 1, 1996, as the generator or owner notifies the State that the waste is available for shipment.

These three incentives are the focus of petitioners' constitutional challenge. The State of New York and the two counties.... [seek] a declaratory judgment that the Act is inconsistent with the Tenth and Eleventh Amendments to the Constitution ...

While no one disputes the proposition that "[t]he Constitution created a Federal Government of limited powers," and while the Tenth Amendment makes explicit that "[t]he powers not delegated to the United States by the Constitution, nor prohibited by it to the States, are reserved to the States respectively, or to the people"; the task of ascertaining the constitutional line between federal and state power has given rise to many of the Court's most difficult and celebrated cases. At least as far back as Martin v. Hunter's Lessee, the Court has resolved questions "of great importance and delicacy" in determining whether particular sovereign powers have been granted by the Constitution to the Federal Government or have been retained by the States.

These questions can be viewed in either of two ways. In some cases the Court has inquired whether an Act of Congress is authorized by one of the powers delegated to Congress in Article I of the Constitution. In other cases the Court has sought to determine whether an Act of Congress invades the province of state sovereignty reserved by the Tenth Amendment. See, e.g., Garcia v. San Antonio Metropolitan Transit Authority. In a case like these, involving the division of authority between federal and state governments, the two inquiries are mirror images of each other. If a power is delegated to Congress in the Constitution, the Tenth Amendment expressly disclaims any reservation of that power to the States; if a power is an attribute of state sovereignty reserved by the Tenth Amendment, it is necessarily a power the Constitution has not conferred on Congress.

It is in this sense that the Tenth Amendment "states but a truism that all is retained which has not been surrendered." United States v. Darby. As Justice Story put it, "[t]his amendment is a mere affirmation of what, upon any just reasoning, is a necessary rule of interpreting the constitution. Being an instrument of limited and enumerated powers, it follows irresistibly, that what is not conferred, is withheld, and belongs to the state authorities." This has been the Court's consistent understanding: "The States unquestionably do retai[n] a significant measure of sovereign authority ... to the extent that the Constitution has not divested them of their original powers and transferred those powers to the Federal Government." Garcia.

Congress exercises its conferred powers subject to the limitations contained in the Constitution. Thus, for example, under the Commerce Clause Congress may regulate publishers engaged in interstate commerce, but Congress is constrained in the exercise of that power by the First Amendment. The Tenth Amendment likewise restrains the power of Congress, but this limit is not derived from the text of the Tenth Amendment itself, which, as we have discussed, is essentially a tautology. Instead, the Tenth Amendment confirms that the power of the Federal Government is subject to limits that may, in a given instance, reserve power to the States. The Tenth Amendment thus directs us to determine, as in this case, whether an incident of state sovereignty is protected by a limitation on an Article I power.

This framework has been sufficiently flexible over the past two centuries to allow for enormous changes in the nature of government. The Federal Government undertakes activities today that would have been unimaginable to the Framers in two senses; first, because the Framers would not have conceived that any government would conduct such activities; and second, because the Framers would not have believed that the Federal Government, rather than the States, would assume such responsibilities. Yet the powers conferred upon the Federal Government by the Constitution were phrased in language broad enough to allow for the expansion of the Federal Government's role. Among the provisions of the Constitution that have been particularly important in this regard, three concern us here.

First, the Constitution allocates to Congress the power "[t]o regulate Commerce ... among the several States." ...

Second, the Constitution authorizes Congress "to pay the Debts and provide for the ... general Welfare of the United States." ...

Finally, the Constitution provides that "the Laws of the United States ... shall be the supreme Law of the Land ... any Thing in the Constitution or Laws of any State to the

Contrary notwithstanding." ... We have observed that the Supremacy Clause gives the Federal Government "a decided advantage in th[e] delicate balance" the Constitution strikes between state and federal power.

The actual scope of the Federal Government's authority with respect to the States has changed over the years, therefore, but the constitutional structure underlying and limiting that authority has not. In the end, just as a cup may be half empty or half full, it makes no difference whether one views the question at issue in these cases as one of ascertaining the limits of the power delegated to the Federal Government under the affirmative provisions of the Constitution or one of discerning the core of sovereignty retained by the States under the Tenth Amendment. Either way, we must determine whether any of the three challenged provisions of the Low-Level Radioactive Waste Policy Amendments Act of 1985 oversteps the boundary between federal and state authority.

Petitioners do not contend that Congress lacks the power to regulate the disposal of low level radioactive waste. Space in radioactive waste disposal sites is frequently sold by residents of one State to residents of another. Regulation of the resulting interstate market in waste disposal is therefore well within Congress' authority under the Commerce Clause. Petitioners likewise do not dispute that under the Supremacy Clause Congress could, if it wished, pre-empt state radioactive waste regulation. Petitioners contend only that the Tenth Amendment limits the power of Congress to regulate in the way it has chosen. Rather than addressing the problem of waste disposal by directly regulating the generators and disposers of waste, petitioners argue, Congress has impermissibly directed the States to regulate in this field.

Most of our recent cases interpreting the Tenth Amendment have concerned the authority of Congress to subject state governments to generally applicable law. The Court's jurisprudence in this area has traveled an unsteady path. [The opinion then presents a lengthy string citation, including the Wirtz-National League of Cities-Garcia line of cases and several others.] This litigation presents no occasion to apply or revisit the holdings of any of these cases, as this is not a case in which Congress has subjected a State to the same legislation applicable to private parties.

This litigation instead concerns the circumstances under which Congress may use the States as implements of regulation; that is, whether Congress may direct or otherwise motivate the States to regulate in a particular field or a particular way. Our cases have established a few principles that guide our resolution of the issue.

As an initial matter, Congress may not simply "commandee[r] the legislative processes of the States by directly compelling them to enact and enforce a federal regulatory program." Hodel v. Virginia Surface Mining & Reclamation Assn., Inc. In Hodel, the Court upheld the Surface Mining Control and Reclamation Act of 1977 precisely because it did *not* "commandeer" the States into regulating mining. The Court found that "the States are not compelled to enforce the steep-slope standards, to expend any state funds, or to participate in the federal regulatory program in any manner whatsoever. If a State does not wish to submit a proposed permanent program that complies with the Act and implementing regulations, the full regulatory burden will be borne by the Federal Government."

While Congress has substantial powers to govern the Nation directly, including in areas of intimate concern to the States, the Constitution has never been understood to confer upon Congress the ability to require the States to govern according to Congress' instructions.... The Court has been explicit about this distinction. "Both the States and the United States existed before the Constitution. The people, through that instrument, established a more perfect union by substituting a national government, acting, with ample power, *directly upon the citizens,* instead of the Confederate government, which acted with powers, greatly restricted, only upon the States."

In providing for a stronger central government, therefore, the Framers explicitly chose a Constitution that confers upon Congress the power to regulate individuals, not States. As we have seen, the Court has consistently respected this choice. We have always understood that even where Congress has the authority under the Constitution to pass laws requiring or prohibiting certain acts, it lacks the power directly to compel the States to require or prohibit those acts. The allocation of power contained in the Commerce Clause, for example, authorizes Congress to regulate interstate commerce directly; it does not authorize Congress to regulate state governments' regulation of interstate commerce.

This is not to say that Congress lacks the ability to encourage a State to regulate in a particular way, or that Congress may not hold out incentives to the States as a method of influencing a State's policy choices. Our cases have identified a variety of methods, short of outright coercion, by which Congress may urge a State to adopt a legislative program consistent with federal interests. Two of these methods are of particular relevance here.

First, under Congress' spending power, "Congress may attach conditions on the receipt of federal funds." ... Second, where Congress has the authority to regulate private activity under the Commerce Clause, we have recognized Congress' power to offer States the choice of regulating that activity according to federal standards or having state law pre-empted by federal regulation....

By either of these methods, as by any other permissible method of encouraging a State to conform to federal policy choices, the residents of the State retain the ultimate decision as to whether or not the State will comply. If a State's citizens view federal policy as sufficiently contrary to local interests, they may elect to decline a federal grant. If state residents would prefer their government to devote its attention and resources to problems other than those deemed important by Congress, they may choose to have the Federal Government rather than the State bear the expense of a federally mandated regulatory program, and they may continue to supplement that program to the extent state law is not pre-empted. Where Congress encourages state regulation rather than compelling it, state governments remain responsive to the local electorate's preferences; state officials remain accountable to the people.

By contrast, where the Federal Government compels States to regulate, the accountability of both state and federal officials is diminished. If the citizens of New York, for example, do not consider that making provision for the disposal of radioactive waste is in their best interest, they may elect state officials who share their view. That view can always be pre-empted under the Supremacy Clause if it is contrary to the national view, but in such a case it is the Federal Government that makes the decision in full view of the public, and it will be federal officials that suffer the consequences if the decision turns out to be detrimental or unpopular. But where the Federal Government directs the States to regulate, it may be state officials who will bear the brunt of public disapproval, while the federal officials who devised the regulatory program may remain insulated from the electoral ramifications of their decision. Accountability is thus diminished when, due to federal coercion, elected state officials cannot regulate in accordance with the views of the local electorate in matters not pre-empted by federal regulation....

The first set of incentives ... authorize[s] States with disposal sites to impose a surcharge on radioactive waste received from other States. [T]he Secretary of Energy collects a portion of this surcharge and places the money in an escrow account. [S]tates achieving a series of milestones receive portions of this fund. [The surcharge] is an unexceptionable exercise of

Congress' power to authorize the States to burden interstate commerce.... The [Secretary's] collection of a percentage of the surcharge, is no more than a federal tax on interstate commerce.... [Finally, the disbursement to complying states] is a conditional exercise of Congress' authority under the Spending Clause: Congress has placed conditions—the achievement of the milestones—on the receipt of federal funds.... [Although] the money collected and redisbursed to the States is kept in an account separate from the general treasury, [and] the Secretary holds the funds only as a trustee [for the states],.... [the] Constitution's grant to Congress of the authority to "pay the Debts and provide for the ... general Welfare" has never, however, been thought to mandate a particular form of accounting.... [or] to deprive Congress of the power to structure federal spending in this manner.

In the second set of incentives, Congress has authorized States and regional compacts with disposal sites gradually to increase the cost of access to the sites, and then to deny access altogether, to radioactive waste generated in States that do not meet federal deadlines.... Where federal regulation of private activity is within the scope of the Commerce Clause, we have recognized the ability of Congress to offer States the choice of regulating that activity according to federal standards or having state law pre-empted by federal regulation.... [The] affected States are not compelled by Congress to regulate, because any burden caused by a State's refusal to regulate will fall on those who generate waste and find no outlet for its disposal, rather than on the State as a sovereign.... [The] Act's second set of incentives thus represents a conditional exercise of Congress' commerce power, along the lines of those we have held to be within Congress' authority. As a result, the second set of incentives does not intrude on the sovereignty reserved to the States by the Tenth Amendment.

The take title provision is of a different character. This third so-called "incentive" offers States, as an alternative to regulating pursuant to Congress' direction, the option of taking title to and possession of the low level radioactive waste generated within their borders and becoming liable for all damages waste generators suffer as a result of the States' failure to do so promptly. In this provision, Congress has crossed the line distinguishing encouragement from coercion.

The take title provision offers state governments a "choice" of either accepting ownership of waste or regulating according to the instructions of Congress. Respondents do not claim that the Constitution would authorize Congress to impose either option as a freestanding requirement. On one hand, the Constitution would not permit Congress simply to transfer radioactive waste from generators to state governments. Such a forced transfer, standing alone, would in principle be no different than a congressionally compelled subsidy from state governments to radioactive waste producers. The same is true of the provision requiring the States to become liable for the generators' damages. Standing alone, this provision would be indistinguishable from an Act of Congress directing the States to assume the liabilities of certain state residents. Either type of federal action would "commandeer" state governments into the service of federal regulatory purposes, and would for this reason be inconsistent with the Constitution's division of authority between federal and state governments. On the other hand, the second alternative held out to state governments—regulating pursuant to Congress' direction—would, standing alone, present a simple command to state governments to implement legislation enacted by Congress. As we have seen, the Constitution does not empower Congress to subject state governments to this type of instruction.

Because an instruction to state governments to take title to waste, standing alone, would be beyond the authority of Congress, and because a direct order to regulate, standing alone, would also be beyond the authority of Congress, it follows that Congress lacks the power to offer the States a choice between the two. Unlike the first two sets of incentives, the take title incentive does not represent the conditional exercise of any congressional power enumerated in the Constitution. In this provision, Congress has not held out the threat of exercising its spending power or its commerce power; it has instead held out the threat, should the States not regulate according to one federal instruction, of simply forcing the States to submit to another federal instruction. A choice between two unconstitutionally coercive regulatory techniques is no choice at all. Either way, "the Act commandeers the legislative processes of the States by directly compelling them to enact and enforce a federal regulatory program," Hodel, an outcome that has never been understood to lie within the authority conferred upon Congress by the Constitution.

JUSTICE WHITE, dissenting.

.... Curiously absent from the Court's analysis is any effort to place the take title provision within the overall context of the legislation. As the discussion in Part I of this opinion suggests, the 1980 and 1985 statutes were enacted against a backdrop of national concern over the availability of additional low-level radioactive waste disposal facilities. Congress could have pre-empted the field by directly regulating the disposal of this waste pursuant to its powers under the Commerce and Spending Clauses, but instead it *unanimously* assented to the States' request for congressional ratification of agreements to which they had acceded. As the floor statements of Members of Congress reveal ... the States wished to take the lead in achieving a solution to this problem and agreed among themselves to the various incentives and penalties implemented by Congress to ensure adherence to the various deadlines and goals. The chief executives of the States proposed this approach, and I am unmoved by the Court's vehemence in taking away Congress' authority to sanction a recalcitrant unsited State now that New York has reaped the benefits of the sited States' concessions....

.... [T]he majority's historical analysis has a distinctly wooden quality. One would not know from reading the majority's account, for instance, that the nature of federal-state relations changed fundamentally after the Civil War. That conflict produced in its wake a tremendous expansion in the scope of the Federal Government's law-making authority, so much so that the persons who helped to found the Republic would scarcely have recognized the many added roles the National Government assumed for itself. Moreover, the majority fails to mention the New Deal era, in which the Court recognized the enormous growth in Congress' power under the Commerce Clause....

Given the scanty textual support for the majority's position, it would be far more sensible to defer to a coordinate branch of government in its decision to devise a solution to a national problem of this kind....

Review Questions and Explanations: *New York*

1. The Court's opinion does not make as clear as it might have why the "take title" provision requires legislative action by the states—a crucial aspect of its constitutional analysis. In essence, the "take title" provision tells the states, "if you don't deal with the radioactive waste by a certain deadline, you own it." Privately "owned" radioactive waste thus becomes owned by the states. But, technically, in order for a state to change property relations, such as ownership—even ownership of negative property, such as waste—the state would have to pass legislation. Hence, the "take title" provision requires states to legislate.

2. Is the principle of *New York*, that Congress cannot "commandeer" state legislatures, different from the *National League of Cities* rule that Congress cannot regulate the "states as states" or dictate their "essential government functions"? If so, how?

3. Justice White argues that it is constitutionally significant that the states agreed to the take title provision. Is that relevant to the question of whether it infringes their sovereign rights? How does the majority respond?

Guided Reading Questions: *Printz v. United States*

1. What does *Printz* add to the rule developed in *New York*?

2. Justice Scalia's majority opinion in *Printz* sets forth two distinct ways in which Congressional "commandeering" harms federalism values. Can you identify both?

3. How does the *Printz* majority say state courts differ from state legislatures and executive officials when it comes to federal "commandeering"? Why the difference?

4. The *Printz* majority also argues that the "commandeering" in this case intrudes on separation of powers. Explain that argument.

Printz v. United States
521 U.S. 898 (1997)

Majority: *Scalia*, Rehnquist (CJ), O'Connor, Kennedy, Thomas

Concurrences: *O'Connor* (omitted), *Thomas* (omitted)

Dissents: *Stevens*, *Souter* (omitted), Ginsburg, *Breyer* (omitted)

JUSTICE SCALIA delivered the opinion of the Court.

The question presented in these cases is whether certain interim provisions of the Brady Handgun Violence Prevention Act, commanding state and local law enforcement officers to conduct background checks on prospective handgun purchasers and to perform certain related tasks, violate the Constitution.

The Gun Control Act of 1968 establishes a detailed federal scheme governing the distribution of firearms. It prohibits firearms dealers from transferring handguns to any person under 21, not resident in the dealer's State, or prohibited by state or local law from purchasing or possessing firearms. It also forbids possession of a firearm by, and transfer of a firearm to, convicted felons, fugitives from justice, unlawful users of controlled substances, persons adjudicated as mentally defective or committed to mental institutions, aliens unlawfully present in the United States, persons dishonorably discharged from the Armed Forces, persons who have renounced their citizenship, and persons who have been subjected to certain restraining orders or been convicted of a misdemeanor offense involving domestic violence.

In 1993, Congress amended the GCA by enacting the Brady Act. The Act requires the Attorney General to establish a national instant background-check system by November 30, 1998 ... and immediately puts in place certain interim provisions until that system becomes operative. Under the interim provisions, a firearms dealer who proposes to transfer a handgun must first: (1) receive from the transferee a statement (the Brady Form) containing the name, address, and date of birth of the proposed transferee along with a sworn statement that the transferee is not among any of the classes of prohibited purchasers; (2) verify the identity of the transferee by examining an identification document; and (3) provide the "chief law enforcement officer" (CLEO) of the transferee's residence with notice of the contents (and a copy) of the Brady Form. With some exceptions, the dealer must then wait five business days before consummating the sale, unless the CLEO earlier notifies the dealer that he has no reason to believe the transfer would be illegal.

The Brady Act creates two significant alternatives to the foregoing scheme. A dealer may sell a handgun immediately if the purchaser possesses a state handgun permit issued after a background check, if state law provides for an instant background check. In States that have not rendered one of these alternatives applicable to all gun purchasers, CLEOs are required to perform certain duties. When a CLEO receives the required notice of a proposed transfer from the firearms dealer, the CLEO must "make a reasonable effort to ascertain within 5 business days whether receipt or possession would be in violation of the law, including research in whatever State and local recordkeeping systems are available and in a national system designated by the Attorney General." The Act does not require the CLEO to take any particular action if he determines that a pending transaction would be unlawful; he may notify the firearms dealer to that effect, but is not required to do so. If, however, the CLEO notifies a gun dealer that a prospective purchaser is ineligible to receive a handgun, he must, upon request, provide the would-be purchaser with a written statement of the reasons for that determination. Moreover, if the CLEO does not discover any basis for objecting to the sale, he must destroy any records in his possession relating to the transfer, including his copy of the Brady Form. Under a separate provision of the GCA, any person who "knowingly violates [the section of the GCA amended by the Brady Act] shall be fined under this title, imprisoned for not more than 1 year, or both."

From the description set forth above, it is apparent that the Brady Act purports to direct state law enforcement officers to participate, albeit only temporarily, in the administration of a federally enacted regulatory scheme.... Petitioners here object to being pressed into federal service, and contend that congressional action compelling state officers to execute federal laws is unconstitutional. Because there is no constitutional text speaking to this precise question, the answer to the CLEOs' challenge must be sought in historical understanding and practice, in the structure of the Constitution, and in the jurisprudence of this Court.

[The Court here surveys laws passed in the early days of the Republic and concludes that there were no such statutes "commandeering" the services of state executive officers. The Court then examines the claim that support for executive commandeering could be found in laws requiring state courts to perform certain federal functions.]

These early laws establish, at most, that the Constitution was originally understood to permit imposition of an obligation on state judges to enforce federal prescriptions, insofar as those prescriptions related to matters appropriate for the judicial power. That assumption was perhaps implicit in one of the provisions of the Constitution, and was explicit in another. In accord with the so-called Madisonian Compromise, Article III, § 1, established only a Supreme Court, and made the creation of lower federal courts optional with the Congress — even though it was obvious that the Supreme Court alone could not hear all federal cases throughout the United States. And the Supremacy Clause, Art. VI, cl. 2, announced that "the Laws of the United States ... shall be the supreme Law of the Land; and the Judges in every State shall be bound thereby." It is understandable why courts should have been viewed distinctively in this regard; unlike legislatures and executives, they applied the law of other sovereigns all the time.... [L]aws which operated elsewhere created obligations in justice that courts of the forum state would enforce. The Constitution itself, in the Full Faith and Credit Clause, Art. IV, § 1, generally required such enforcement with respect to obligations arising in other States.

For these reasons, we do not think the early statutes imposing obligations on state courts imply a power of Congress to impress the state executive into its service.

The constitutional practice we have examined above tends to negate the existence of the congressional power asserted here, but is not conclusive. We turn next to consideration of the structure of the Constitution, to see if we can discern among its "essential postulate[s]," a principle that controls the present cases.

The Framers' experience under the Articles of Confederation had persuaded them that using the States as the instruments of federal governance was both ineffectual and provocative of federal-state conflict. Preservation of the States as independent political entities being the price of union, and "the practicality of making laws, with coercive sanctions, for the States as political bodies" having been, in Madison's words, "exploded on all hands," 2 Records of the Federal Convention of 1787, p. 9 (M. Farrand ed. 1911), the Framers rejected the concept of a central government that would act upon and through the States, and instead designed a system in which the state and federal governments would exercise concurrent authority over the people—who were, in Hamilton's words, "the only proper objects of government," The Federalist No. 15.... "The Framers explicitly chose a Constitution that confers upon Congress the power to regulate individuals, not States." [New York v. United States], at 166. The great innovation of this design was that "our citizens would have two political capacities, one state and one federal, each protected from incursion by the other"— "a legal system unprecedented in form and design, establishing two orders of government, each with its own direct relationship, its own privity, its own set of mutual rights and obligations to the people who sustain it and are governed by it." The Constitution thus con-templates that a State's government will represent and remain accountable to its own citizens. As Madison expressed it: "The local or municipal authorities form distinct and independent portions of the supremacy, no more subject, within their respective spheres, to the general authority than the general authority is subject to them, within its own sphere." The Federalist No. 39.

This separation of the two spheres is one of the Constitution's structural protections of liberty. "Just as the separation and independence of the coordinate branches of the Federal Government serve to prevent the accumulation of excessive power in any one branch, a healthy balance of power between the States and the Federal Government will reduce the risk of tyranny and abuse from either front." Gregory v. Ashcroft, at 458....

.... Federal control of state officers would.... also have an effect upon ... the separation and equilibration of powers between the three branches of the Federal Government itself. The Constitution does not leave to speculation who is to administer the laws enacted by Congress; the President, it says, "shall take Care that the Laws be faithfully executed," Art. II, § 3, personally and through officers whom he appoints (save for such inferior officers as Congress may authorize to be appointed by the "Courts of Law" or by "the Heads of Departments" who are themselves presidential appointees), Art. II, § 2. The Brady Act effectively transfers this responsibility to thousands of CLEOs in the 50 States, who are left to implement the program without meaningful Presidential control (if indeed meaningful Presidential control is possible without the power to appoint and remove). The insistence of the Framers upon unity in the Federal Executive—to insure both vigor and accountability—is well known. That unity would be shattered, and the power of the President would be subject to reduction, if Congress could act as effectively without the President as with him, by simply requiring state officers to execute its laws.

> FN12. There is not, as the dissent believes, "tension" between the proposition that impressing state police officers into federal service will massively augment *federal* power, and the proposition that it will also sap the power of the Federal *Presidency*. It is quite possible to have a more powerful Federal Government that is, by reason of the destruction of its Executive unity, a less efficient one. The dissent is correct, that control by the unitary Federal Executive is also sacrificed when States voluntarily administer federal programs, but the condition of voluntary state participation significantly reduces the ability of Congress to use this device as a means of reducing the power of the Presidency.

The dissent of course resorts to the last, best hope of those who defend ultra vires congressional action, the Necessary and Proper Clause. It reasons, that the power to regulate the sale of handguns under the Commerce Clause, coupled with the power to "make all Laws which shall be necessary and proper for carrying into Execution the foregoing Powers," Art. I, § 8, conclusively establishes the Brady Act's constitutional validity, because the Tenth Amendment imposes no limitations on the exercise of delegated powers but merely prohibits the exercise of powers "not delegated to the United States." What destroys the dissent's Necessary and Proper Clause argument, however, is not the Tenth Amendment but the Necessary and Proper Clause itself.

> FN13. This argument also falsely presumes that the Tenth Amendment is the exclusive textual source of protection for principles of federalism. Our system of dual sovereignty is reflected in numerous constitutional provisions, and not only those, like the Tenth Amendment, that speak to the point explicitly.

When a "Law ... for carrying into Execution" the Commerce Clause violates the principle of state sovereignty reflected in the various constitutional provisions we mentioned earlier, supra, at 19–20, it is not a "Law ... proper for carrying into Execution the Commerce Clause[.]" ...

The Government also maintains that requiring state officers to perform discrete, ministerial tasks specified by Congress does not violate the principle of New York because it does not diminish the accountability of state or federal officials. This argument fails even on its own terms. By forcing state governments to absorb the financial burden of implementing a federal regulatory program, Members of Congress can take credit for "solving" problems without having to ask their constituents to pay for the solutions with higher federal taxes. And even when the States are not forced to absorb the costs of implementing a federal program, they are still put in the position of taking the blame for its burdensomeness and for its defects.... Under the present law, for example, it will be the CLEO and not some federal official who stands between the gun purchaser and immediate possession of his gun. And it will likely be the CLEO, not some federal official, who will be blamed for any error (even one in the designated federal database) that causes a purchaser to be mistakenly rejected....

Finally, the Government puts forward a cluster of arguments that can be grouped under the heading: "The Brady Act serves very important purposes, is most efficiently administered by CLEOs during the interim period, and places a minimal and only temporary burden upon state officers." There is considerable disagreement over the extent of the burden, but we need not pause over that detail. Assuming *all* the mentioned factors were true, they might be relevant if we were evaluating whether the incidental application to the States of a federal law of general applicability excessively interfered with the functioning of state governments. But where, as here, it is the whole *object* of the law to direct the functioning of the state executive, and hence to compromise the structural framework of dual sovereignty, such a "balancing" analysis is inappropriate. It is the very *principle* of separate state sovereignty that such a law offends, and no comparative assessment of the various interests can overcome that fundamental defect....

We held in New York that Congress cannot compel the States to enact or enforce a federal regulatory program. Today we hold that Congress cannot circumvent that prohibition by conscripting the State's officers directly. The Federal Government may neither issue directives requiring the States to address particular problems, nor command the States' officers, or those of their political subdivisions, to administer or enforce a federal regulatory program. It matters not whether policymaking is involved, and no case-by-case weighing of the burdens or benefits is necessary; such commands are fundamentally incompatible with our constitutional system of dual sovereignty. Accordingly, the judgment of the Court of Appeals for the Ninth Circuit is reversed.

JUSTICE STEVENS, with whom JUSTICES SOUTER, GINSBURG and BREYER join, dissenting.

When Congress exercises the powers delegated to it by the Constitution, it may impose affirmative obligations on executive and judicial officers of state and local governments as well as ordinary citizens. This conclusion is firmly supported by the text of the Constitution, the early history of the Nation, decisions of this Court, and a correct understanding of the basic structure of the Federal Government....

These cases do not implicate the more difficult questions associated with congressional coercion of state legislatures addressed in New York. Nor need we consider the wisdom of relying on local officials rather than federal agents to carry out aspects of a federal program, or even the question whether such officials may be required to perform a federal function on a permanent basis. The question is whether Congress, acting on behalf of the people of the entire Nation, may require local law enforcement officers to perform certain duties during the interim needed for the development of a federal gun control program. It is remarkably similar to the question, heavily debated by the Framers of the Constitution, whether Congress could require state agents to collect federal taxes. Or the question whether Congress could impress state judges into federal service to entertain and decide cases that they would prefer to ignore.

Indeed, since the ultimate issue is one of power, we must consider its implications in times of national emergency. Matters such as the enlistment of air raid wardens, the administration of a military draft, the mass inoculation of children to forestall an epidemic, or perhaps the threat of an international terrorist, may require a national response before federal personnel can be made available to respond. If the Constitution empowers Congress and the President to make an appropriate response, is there anything in the Tenth Amendment, "in historical understanding and practice, in the structure of the Constitution, [or] in the jurisprudence of this Court," that forbids the enlistment of state officers to make that response effective? More narrowly, what basis is there in any of those sources for concluding that it is the Members of this Court, rather than the elected representatives of the people, who should determine whether the Constitution contains the unwritten rule that the Court announces today?

Perhaps today's majority would suggest that no such emergency is presented by the facts of these cases. But such a suggestion is itself an expression of a policy judgment. And Congress' view of the matter is quite different from that implied by the Court today....

The text of the Constitution provides a sufficient basis for a correct disposition of these cases.

Article I, §8, grants Congress the power to regulate commerce among the States. Putting to one side the revisionist views expressed by JUSTICE THOMAS in his concurring opinion in *Lopez,* there can be no question that that provision adequately supports the regulation of commerce in handguns effected by the Brady Act. Moreover, the additional grant of authority in that section of the Constitution "[t]o make all Laws which shall be necessary and proper for carrying into Execution the foregoing Powers" is surely adequate to support the temporary enlistment of local police officers in the process of identifying persons who should not be entrusted with the possession of handguns. In short, the affirmative delegation of power in Article I provides ample authority for the congressional enactment.

Unlike the First Amendment, which prohibits the enactment of a category of laws that would otherwise be authorized by Article I, the Tenth Amendment imposes no restriction on the exercise of delegated powers. [It uses] language that plainly refers only to powers that are "*not*" delegated to Congress....

The Amendment confirms the principle that the powers of the Federal Government are limited to those affirmatively granted by the Constitution, but it does not purport to limit the scope or the effectiveness of the exercise of powers that are delegated to Congress. Thus, the Amendment provides no support for a rule that immunizes local officials from obligations that might be imposed on ordinary citizens. Indeed, it would be more reasonable to infer that federal law may impose greater duties on state officials than on private citizens because another provision of the Constitution requires that "all executive and judicial Officers, both of the United States and of the several States, shall be bound by Oath or Affirmation, to support this Constitution."

> FN1. Indeed, the Framers repeatedly rejected proposed changes to the Tenth Amendment that would have altered the text to refer to "powers not *expressly* delegated to the United States." ... This was done, as Madison explained, because "it was impossible to confine a Government to the exercise of express powers; there must necessarily be admitted powers by implication, unless the constitution descended to recount every minutia."

Recognizing the force of the argument, the Court suggests that this reasoning is in error because—even if it is responsive to the submission that the Tenth Amendment roots the principle set forth by the majority today—it does not answer the possibility that the Court's holding can be rooted in a "principle of state sovereignty" mentioned nowhere in the constitutional text. As a ground for invalidating important federal legislation, this argument is remarkably weak. The majority's further claim that, while the Brady Act may be legislation "necessary" to Congress' execution of its undisputed Commerce Clause authority to regulate firearms sales, it is nevertheless not "proper" because it violates state sovereignty, see *ibid.,* is wholly circular, and provides no traction for its argument. Moreover, this reading of the term "proper" gives it a meaning directly contradicted by Chief Justice Marshall in *McCulloch.* As the Chief Justice explained, the Necessary and Proper Clause by "[i]ts terms purport[s] to enlarge, not to diminish the powers vested in the government. It purports to be an additional power, not a restriction on those already granted." ...

Our ruling in New York that the Commerce Clause does not provide Congress the authority to require States to enact legislation—a power that affects States far closer to the core of their sovereign authority—does nothing to support the majority's unwarranted extension of that reasoning today.... There is not a clause, sentence, or paragraph in the entire text of the Constitution of the United States that supports the proposition that a local police officer can ignore a command contained in a statute enacted by Congress pursuant to an express delegation of power enumerated in Article I....

.... Absent even a modicum of textual foundation for its judicially crafted constitutional rule, there should be a presumption that if the Framers had actually intended such a rule, at least one of them would have mentioned it.

The Court's "structural" arguments are not sufficient to rebut that presumption. The fact that the Framers intended to preserve the sovereignty of the several States simply does not speak to the question whether individual state employees may be required to perform federal obligations, such as registering young adults for the draft, 40 Stat. 80–81, creating state emergency response commissions designed to manage the release of hazardous substances, 42 U.S.C. §§ 11001, 11003, collecting and reporting data on underground storage tanks that may pose an environmental hazard, § 6991a, and reporting traffic fatalities, 23 U.S.C. § 402(a), and missing children, 42 U.S.C. § 5779(a), to a federal agency.

As we explained in Garcia v. San Antonio Metropolitan Transit Authority, 469 U.S. 528 (1985): "The principal means chosen by the Framers to ensure the role of the States in the federal system lies in the structure of the Federal Government itself. It is no novelty to observe that the composition of the Federal Government was designed in large part to protect the States from overreaching by Congress." Id., at 550–551. Given the fact that the Members of Congress are elected by the people of the several States, with each State receiving an equivalent number of Senators in order to ensure that even the smallest States have a powerful voice in the legislature, it is quite unrealistic to assume that they will ignore the sovereignty concerns of their constituents. It is far more reasonable to presume that their decisions to impose modest burdens on state officials from time to time reflect a considered judgment that the people in each of the States will benefit therefrom.

Indeed, the presumption of validity that supports all congressional enactments has added force with respect to policy judgments concerning the impact of a federal statute upon the respective States. The majority points to nothing suggesting that the political safeguards of federalism identified in Garcia need be supplemented by a rule, grounded in neither constitutional history nor text, flatly prohibiting the National Government from enlisting state and local officials in the implementation of federal law.

Recent developments demonstrate that the political safeguards protecting Our Federalism are effective. The majority expresses special concern that were its rule not adopted the Federal Government would be able to avail itself of the services of state government officials "at no cost to itself." But this specific problem of federal actions that have the effect of imposing so-called "unfunded mandates" on the States has been identified and meaningfully addressed by Congress in recent legislation.

FN18. The majority also makes the more general claim that requiring state officials to carry out federal policy causes states to "take the blame" for failed programs. The Court cites no empirical authority to support the proposition, relying entirely on the speculations of a law review article. This concern is vastly overstated.

Unlike state legislators, local government executive officials routinely take action in response to a variety of sources of authority: local ordinance, state law, and federal law. It doubtless may therefore require some sophistication to discern under which authority an executive official is acting, just as it may not always be immediately obvious what legal source of authority underlies a judicial decision. In both cases, affected citizens must look past the official before them to find the true cause of their grievance. But the majority's rule neither creates nor alters this basic truth.

The problem is of little real consequence in any event, because to the extent that a particular action proves politically unpopular, we may be confident that elected officials charged with implementing it will be quite clear to their constituents where the source of the misfortune lies. These cases demonstrate the point. Sheriffs Printz and Mack have made public statements, including their decisions to serve as plaintiffs in these actions, denouncing the Brady Act. Indeed, Sheriff Mack has written a book discussing his views on the issue. See R. Mack & T. Walters, From My Cold Dead Fingers: Why America Needs Guns (1994). Moreover, we can be sure that CLEOs will inform disgruntled constituents who have been denied permission to purchase a handgun about the origins of the Brady Act requirements. The Court's suggestion that voters will be confused over who is to "blame" for the statute reflects a gross lack of confidence in the electorate that is at war with the basic assumptions underlying any democratic government.

.... Perversely, the majority's rule seems more likely to damage than to preserve the safeguards against tyranny provided by the existence of vital state governments. By limiting the ability of the Federal Government to enlist state officials in the implementation of its programs, the Court creates incentives for the National Government to aggrandize itself. In the name of State's rights, the majority would have the Federal Government create vast national bureaucracies to implement its policies. This is exactly the sort of thing that the early Federalists promised would not occur, in part as a result of the National Government's ability to rely on the magistracy of the states....

Review Questions and Explanations: *Printz*

1. The federal laws at issue in *National League of Cities* and *Garcia* differ from those at issue in *New York* and *Printz* in a way that the Court sees as legally significant. What is the key difference between them?

2. Does *Printz* seem like a natural extension of the "anti-commandeering rule" in *New York*?

3. Make sure you understand why state judges may be "commandeered"—i.e., must apply federal law in making decisions—while state legislatures and executives cannot be. The relevant passage is the paragraph in the majority opinion starting "Those early state laws establish ..." See also the Supremacy Clause, Art. VI, cl. 2. What does that have to say on the matter?

4. Are *New York* and *Printz* consistent with the "political process" reasoning adopted in *Garcia*—i.e., that the Constitution builds political safeguards into the federal system that protect state interests, such as state representation in Congress?

5. Do *New York* and *Printz* represent yet another reversal of Tenth Amendment doctrine (for the third time in 21 years—the other two being *National League of Cities* (1976) (overruling *Wirtz*); *Garcia* (1985) (overruling *National League of Cities*)? In other words do *New York* and *Printz* overrule *Garcia*? This question is addressed, at least implicitly, in *Reno v. Condon*, presented below.

Exercise: *Printz v. United States*

You are a legislative drafter working for Congress. Can you write a statute that accomplishes the same goals as the schemes struck down either in *New York* or *Printz*, but that passes the test developed in those cases? Be prepared to defend your statute in class.

Guided Reading Questions: *Reno v. Condon*

1. Unlike the other Tenth Amendment cases, many of which were 5–4 decisions, *Reno* is a unanimous opinion. What distinguishes this case from the cases preceding it? In other words, why does the Court find it so clear that the actions required of the state under the federal law at issue in *Reno* do not constitute unconstitutional "commandeering"?

2. How does the court distinguish this case from *Printz*? Is the distinction convincing?

3. Is the Drivers Privacy Protection Act a "generally applicable law"? If so, what makes it so?

Reno v. Condon

528 U.S. 141 (2000)

Unanimous decision: *Rehnquist* (CJ), Stevens, O'Connor, Scalia, Kennedy, Souter, Thomas, Ginsburg, Breyer

CHIEF JUSTICE REHNQUIST delivered the opinion of the Court.

The Driver's Privacy Protection Act of 1994 (DPPA or Act) regulates the disclosure of personal information contained in the records of state motor vehicle departments (DMVs). We hold that in enacting this statute Congress did not run afoul of the federalism principles enunciated in [New York and Printz].

The DPPA regulates the disclosure and resale of personal information contained in the records of state DMVs. State DMVs require drivers and automobile owners to provide personal information, which may include a person's name, address, telephone number, vehicle description, Social Security number, medical information, and photograph, as a condition of obtaining a driver's license or registering an automobile. Congress found that many States, in turn, sell this personal information to individuals and businesses. These sales generate significant revenues for the States.

The DPPA establishes a regulatory scheme that restricts the States' ability to disclose a driver's personal information without the driver's consent.... The DPPA's prohibition of nonconsensual disclosures is also subject to a number of statutory exceptions. For example, the DPPA requires disclosure of personal information "for use in connection with matters of motor vehicle or driver safety and theft, motor vehicle emissions, motor vehicle product alterations, recalls, or advisories, performance monitoring of motor vehicles and dealers by motor vehicle manufacturers, and removal of non-owner records from the original owner records of motor vehicle manufacturers to carry out the purposes of titles I and IV of the Anti-Car Theft Act of 1992, the Automobile Information Disclosure Act, the Clean Air Act....

The DPPA's provisions do not apply solely to States. The Act also regulates the resale and redisclosure of drivers' personal information by private persons who have obtained that information from a state DMV....

South Carolina law conflicts with the DPPA's provisions. Under that law, the information contained in the State's DMV records is available to any person or entity that fills out a form listing the requester's name and address and stating that the information will not be used for telephone solicitation....

Following the DPPA's enactment, South Carolina and its Attorney General, respondent Condon, filed suit in the United States District Court for the District of South Carolina, alleging that the DPPA violates the Tenth ... Amendment[].... The court ... granted summary judgment for the State and permanently enjoined the Act's enforcement against the State and its officers. The Court of Appeals for the Fourth Circuit affirmed.... We granted certiorari and now reverse....

The United States asserts that the DPPA is a proper exercise of Congress' authority to regulate interstate commerce under the Commerce Clause. The United States bases its Commerce Clause argument on the fact that the personal, identifying information that the DPPA regulates is a "thin[g] in interstate commerce," and that the sale or release of that information in interstate commerce is therefore a proper subject of congressional regulation. Lopez. We agree with the United States' contention....

But the fact that drivers' personal information is, in the context of this case, an article in interstate commerce does not conclusively resolve the constitutionality of the DPPA. In New York and Printz, we held federal statutes invalid, not because Congress lacked legislative authority over the subject matter, but because those statutes violated the principles of federalism contained in the Tenth Amendment....

South Carolina contends that the DPPA violates the Tenth Amendment because it "thrusts upon the States all of the day-to-day responsibility for administering its complex provisions," Brief for Respondents 10, and thereby makes "state officials the unwilling implementors of federal policy," id., at 11. South Carolina emphasizes that the DPPA requires the State's employees to learn and apply the Act's substantive restrictions, which are summarized above, and notes that these activities will consume the employees' time and thus the State's resources....

We agree with South Carolina's assertion that the DPPA's provisions will require time and effort on the part of state employees, but reject the State's argument that the DPPA violates the principles laid down in either New York or Printz....

In [South Carolina v Baker] we upheld a statute that prohibited States from issuing unregistered bonds because the law "regulate[d] state activities," rather than "seek[ing] to control or influence the manner in which States regulate private parties."

Like the statute at issue in Baker, the DPPA does not require the States in their sovereign capacity to regulate their own citizens. The DPPA regulates the States as the owners of data bases. It does not require the South Carolina Legislature to enact any laws or regulations, and it does not require state officials to assist in the enforcement of federal statutes regulating private individuals. We accordingly conclude that the DPPA is consistent with the constitutional principles enunciated in New York and Printz....

As a final matter, we turn to South Carolina's argument that the DPPA is unconstitutional because it regulates the States exclusively. The essence of South Carolina's argument is that Congress may only regulate the States by means of "generally applicable" laws, or laws that apply to individuals as well as States. But we need not address the question whether general applicability is a constitutional requirement for federal regulation of the States, because the DPPA is generally applicable. The DPPA regulates the universe of entities that participate as suppliers to the market for motor vehicle information—the States as initial suppliers of the information in interstate commerce and private resellers or redisclosers of that information in commerce. The judgment of the Court of Appeals is therefore reversed.

Review Questions and Explanations: *Reno v. Condon*

1. Does *Reno* tell us whether *New York* and *Printz* overrule *Garcia*?

2. Is "general applicability" a requirement of federal regulation of states? What is general applicability?

3. Explain the distinction between laws that "regulate state activities" and laws that "seek to control or influence the manner in which States regulate private parties." Which type, if either, is constitutional? Which better characterizes the law in *Reno*? *Printz*? *New York*?

NOTE: **"Cooperative federalism."** The doctrines you are learning do more than show lawyers how to structure constitutional challenges to federal laws. They also provide guidance to members of Congress and their legal staffers about how to draft laws to *avoid* constitutional problems.

The last few cases have given you a glimpse at a federal legislative approach known as "cooperative federalism." You can probably think of several federal programs in which states participate through their legislatures, executive officials, or both. Social Security, unemployment insurance, Temporary Assistance to Needy Families (commonly referred to as "welfare") are all examples of such programs. In each of these schemes, the states play key roles in implementing, and in some cases defining, the parameters of a federal legislative program. Also consider the federal requirement in *Dole* (below) that states raise the drinking age to 21. How does Congress get away with creating these types of programs—don't they violate the anti-commandeering rule set out in the cases above?

The answer, implicit in *New York*, is explained by the concept of *cooperative* federalism. In each of these situations, Congress has created inducements for states to opt into federal programs but does not (because it cannot) *require* states to do so. Consider the following regulatory techniques, each of which could be used to design a federal program:

1) **Direct regulation.** Where the subject matter of the law falls within one of Congress's enumerated powers, Congress may regulate people within the states directly. Federal law acts directly on the people. This is probably the most common form of legislation.

2) **"Conditional commerce [or other enumerated power]" regulation.** Where an enumerated power allows Congress to regulate a subject directly, Congress may nevertheless choose to get states involved by offering a "conditional" regulation. The "condition" is as follows: "if you [the state] enact laws that meet our federal standards, your laws will be controlling in your state. If you decline to enact such laws, the federal regulation will take effect by default." This type of law is constitutional because Congress has the power, under its enumerated powers, to impose the regulation directly. But rather than doing so, Congress offers states an opportunity to regulate the area themselves, as long as they do so in compliance with broad federal standards. *Examples:* Occupational Safety and Health Act; "access incentives" in *New York*.

3) **"Conditional spending."** Rather than offer the states the option of directly regulating an area in compliance with federal standards, here the federal government offers monetary subsidies to the states on the condition that they pass laws implementing the federal program. Several major federal programs are implemented this way. States in these cases

may, as in the above situation, have some latitude to vary some aspects of the program so long as they meet minimum federal standards, but the key point is that states failing to implement the law will forfeit otherwise available federal funds. In other words, if states opt out of the program, the federal program does not apply in that state and the state simply does not get the money provided under the program. Several governors made a political point of opting out of the Affordable Care Act on this basis, thereby rejecting the federal funding available to implement the Act. *Examples*: Social Security, unemployment insurance, certain provisions of the Affordable Care Act.

In *New York, Printz,* and *Reno,* the Tenth Amendment challenge to the federal law was made by a state or state government official. Since the mid-1970s, the Court has defined and narrowed the concept of "standing"—a doctrine that examines whether a particular party has the right to litigate in federal court. One aspect of that doctrine, as you will see in Chapter 6, is that parties with only a generalized interest in having government follow the Constitution—who haven't themselves been uniquely affected by a constitutional violation—cannot raise the constitutional claim. That idea of standing raises the question whether the Tenth Amendment is a right of states that can only be raised by states, rather than individuals. This question is addressed in the following case.

Bond v. United States

131 S. Ct. 2355 (2011)

Unanimous decision: *Kennedy*, Roberts (CJ), Scalia, Thomas, Ginsburg, Breyer, Alito, Sotomayor, Kagan

Concurrence: *Ginsburg*, Breyer (omitted)

JUSTICE KENNEDY delivered the opinion of the Court.

.... Petitioner Carol Anne Bond..., discovering that her close friend was pregnant and that the father was Bond's husband, ... sought revenge. Bond subjected the woman to a campaign of harassing telephone calls and letters, acts that resulted in a criminal conviction on a minor state charge. Bond persisted in her hostile acts, placing caustic substances on objects the woman was likely to touch, including her mailbox, car door handle, and front doorknob. Bond's victim suffered a minor burn on her hand and contacted federal investigators, who identified Bond as the perpetrator.

Bond was indicted in the United States District Court for the Eastern District of Pennsylvania for, among other offenses, two counts of violating § 229. Section 229 forbids knowing possession or use of any chemical that "can cause death, temporary incapacitation or permanent harm to humans or animals" where not intended for a "peaceful purpose." The statute was enacted as part of the Chemical Weapons Convention Implementation Act of 1998. The Act implements provisions of the Convention on the Prohibition of the Development, Production, Stockpiling and Use of Chemical Weapons and on their Destruction, a treaty the United States ratified in 1997.

In the District Court, Bond moved to dismiss the § 229 charges, contending the statute was beyond Congress' constitutional authority to enact. The District Court denied the motion. Bond entered a conditional plea of guilty, reserving the right to appeal the ruling on the validity of the statute. She was sentenced to six years in prison.

In the Court of Appeals for the Third Circuit, Bond renewed her challenge to the statute, citing, among other authorities, the Tenth Amendment to the Constitution. The

Court of Appeals [ruled that Bond lacked] standing to raise the Tenth Amendment as a ground for invalidating a federal statute in the absence of a State's participation in the proceedings.

In … the Court of Appeals, the Government took the position that Bond did not have standing.…

When Bond sought certiorari, the Government advised this Court that it had changed its position and that, in its view, Bond does have standing to challenge the constitutionality of §229 on Tenth Amendment grounds. See Brief for United States (filed July 9, 2010). The Court granted certiorari, and appointed an amicus curiae to defend the judgment of the Court of Appeals. Stephen McAllister, a member of the bar of this Court, filed an amicus brief and presented an oral argument that have been of considerable assistance to the Court.…

Amicus contends that federal courts should not adjudicate a claim like Bond's because of the prudential rule that a party "generally must assert his own legal rights and interests, and cannot rest his claim to relief on the legal rights or interests of third parties." Warth v. Seldin, 422 U.S. 490, 499, 500 (1975). In amicus' view, to argue that the National Government has interfered with state sovereignty in violation of the Tenth Amendment is to assert the legal rights and interests of States and States alone. That, however, is not so. As explained below, Bond seeks to vindicate her own constitutional interests. The individual, in a proper case, can assert injury from governmental action taken in excess of the authority that federalism defines. Her rights in this regard do not belong to a State.

The federal system rests on what might at first seem a counterintuitive insight, that "freedom is enhanced by the creation of two governments, not one." Alden v. Maine, 527 U.S. 706 (1999). The Framers concluded that allocation of powers between the National Government and the States enhances freedom, first by protecting the integrity of the governments themselves, and second by protecting the people, from whom all governmental powers are derived.

Federalism has more than one dynamic. It is true that the federal structure serves to grant and delimit the prerogatives and responsibilities of the States and the National Government vis-à-vis one another. The allocation of powers in our federal system preserves the integrity, dignity, and residual sovereignty of the States. The federal balance is, in part, an end in itself, to ensure that States function as political entities in their own right.

But that is not its exclusive sphere of operation. Federalism is more than an exercise in setting the boundary between different institutions of government for their own integrity. "State sovereignty is not just an end in itself: Rather, federalism secures to citizens the liberties that derive from the diffusion of sovereign power." New York v. United States, 505 U.S. 144 (1992).

Some of these liberties are of a political character. The federal structure allows local policies "more sensitive to the diverse needs of a heterogeneous society," permits "innovation and experimentation," enables greater citizen "involvement in democratic processes," and makes government "more responsive by putting the States in competition for a mobile citizenry." Gregory v. Ashcroft, 501 U.S. 452, 458 (1991). Federalism secures the freedom of the individual. It allows States to respond, through the enactment of positive law, to the initiative of those who seek a voice in shaping the destiny of their own times without having to rely solely upon the political processes that control a remote central power. True, of course, these objects cannot be vindicated by the Judiciary in the absence of a proper case or controversy; but the individual liberty secured by federalism is not simply derivative of the rights of the States.

Federalism also protects the liberty of all persons within a State by ensuring that laws enacted in excess of delegated governmental power cannot direct or control their actions. By denying any one government complete jurisdiction over all the concerns of public life, federalism protects the liberty of the individual from arbitrary power. When government acts in excess of its lawful powers, that liberty is at stake.

.... States are not the sole intended beneficiaries of federalism. An individual has a direct interest in objecting to laws that upset the constitutional balance between the National Government and the States when the enforcement of those laws causes injury that is concrete, particular, and redressable. Fidelity to principles of federalism is not for the States alone to vindicate.

The recognition of an injured person's standing to object to a violation of a constitutional principle that allocates power within government is illustrated, in an analogous context, by cases in which individuals sustain discrete, justiciable injury from actions that transgress separation-of-powers limitations. Separation-of-powers principles are intended, in part, to protect each branch of government from incursion by the others. Yet the dynamic between and among the branches is not the only object of the Constitution's concern....

.... [I]ndividuals, too, are protected by the operations of separation of powers and checks and balances; and they are not disabled from relying on those principles in otherwise justiciable cases and controversies. In INS v. Chadha, 462 U.S. 919 (1983), it was an individual who successfully challenged the so-called legislative veto — a procedure that Congress used in an attempt to invalidate an executive determination without presenting the measure to the President. The procedure diminished the role of the Executive, but the challenger sought to protect not the prerogatives of the Presidency as such but rather his own right to avoid deportation under an invalid order. Chadha's challenge was sustained. A cardinal principle of separation of powers was vindicated at the insistence of an individual, indeed one who was not a citizen of the United States but who still was a person whose liberty was at risk.

Chadha is not unique in this respect.... If the constitutional structure of our Government that protects individual liberty is compromised, individuals who suffer otherwise justiciable injury may object.

Just as it is appropriate for an individual, in a proper case, to invoke separation-of-powers or checks-and-balances constraints, so too may a litigant, in a proper case, challenge a law as enacted in contravention of constitutional principles of federalism. That claim need not depend on the vicarious assertion of a State's constitutional interests, even if a State's constitutional interests are also implicated.

In this regard it is necessary to address a misconception in the position the Government now urges this Court to adopt.... The Government contends petitioner asserts only that Congress could not enact the challenged statute under its enumerated powers. Were she to argue, the Government insists, that the statute "interferes with a specific aspect of state sovereignty," either instead of or in addition to her enumerated powers contention, the Court should deny her standing. Brief for United States 18 (filed Dec. 3, 2010)....

There is no basis to support the Government's proposed distinction between different federalism arguments for purposes of prudential standing rules. The principles of limited national powers and state sovereignty are intertwined. While neither originates in the Tenth Amendment, both are expressed by it. Impermissible interference with state sovereignty is not within the enumerated powers of the National Government, see New York, 505 U.S., at 155–159, and action that exceeds the National Government's enumerated powers undermines the sovereign interests of States. See United States v. Lopez, 514 U.S. 549, (1995). The unconstitutional action can cause concomitant injury to persons in individual cases.

An individual who challenges federal action on these grounds is, of course, subject to [standing] requirements.... to show actual or imminent harm that is concrete and particular, fairly traceable to the conduct complained of, and likely to be redressed by a favorable decision....

In this case, however, where the litigant is a party to an otherwise justiciable case or controversy, she is not forbidden to object that her injury results from disregard of the federal structure of our Government. Whether the Tenth Amendment is regarded as simply a 'truism,' New York, supra, at 156, (quoting United States v. Darby, 312 U.S. 100, 124, (1941)), or whether it has independent force of its own, the result here is the same.

There is no basis in precedent or principle to deny petitioner's standing to raise her claims. The ultimate issue of the statute's validity turns in part on whether the law can be deemed "necessary and proper for carrying into Execution" the President's Article II, §2 Treaty Power, see U.S. Const., Art. I, §8, cl. 18. This Court expresses no view on the merits of that argument. It can be addressed by the Court of Appeals on remand. The judgment of the Court of Appeals is reversed....

Review Questions and Explanations: *Bond*

1. Are you surprised by the outcome in *Bond* or the fact that it is unanimous? Why or why not?

2. The government's change of position, and the need to appoint an amicus curiae (friend of the court) to make the abandoned argument is unusual, but not unheard of. *Bond* illustrates the situation in which a case is commenced under one presidential administration and carries over into the next. The changeover could become an issue in cases with significant policy implications. It can take a new administration several months to review pending cases to determine whether arguments made in the case conform to the new administration's policies. Here, the case spanned the transition from the Bush to the Obama administrations.

3. Separation-of-powers questions, like federalism questions, go to the structure of government, and are often framed in terms of a conflict between the powers of one branch versus another. What implications, if any, does *Bond* have for the right of a private individual to challenge a federal law on separation-of-powers grounds?

Recap: *Tenth Amendment*

At this point in the course, you should be able to explain the following Tenth Amendment doctrines and concepts. Try to sit down with a classmate and take turns explaining the following:

1. How the Court conceived of the Tenth Amendment before 1937.

2. The meaning of the claim in *Darby* (quoted in *New York*) that "the tenth amendment states but a truism ..."

3. How Tenth Amendment doctrine shifted from *National League of Cities* to *Garcia*, whether *Garcia* is still good law, and the best arguments that it is and is not.

4. The anticommandeering rules of *New York* and *Printz*.

5. How that principle is or is not applied in *Reno*.

6. Why the anticommandeering rule does not relieve state judges of the duty to apply federal law.

7. The implications of the foregoing for legislative drafting choices.

8. Who can raise Tenth Amendment challenges.

Exercise: *Commandeering*

Consider the ongoing controversy over medical marijuana. Suppose an attorney in your law firm provides counseling to the owner of a medical marijuana dispensary. She assists the owner in negotiating a commercial lease for the dispensary storefront and in understanding and complying with the fairly complex set of state regulations. Your firm and the dispensary both operate in a state that has legalized medical marijuana. The applicable state code of professional responsibility says that an attorney shall be subject to discipline if she counsels a client in the commission of a crime. The issue is brought to the attention of the office of the State Bar prosecutor, who issues a statement saying that no disciplinary proceedings will be brought against any attorney in the state who acts in compliance with state law and counsels clients in good faith on how to comply with state law permitting medical marijuana.

    a) Suppose the United States attorney seeks an injunction in federal court ordering the state bar to pursue disciplinary proceedings against attorneys who counsel medical marijuana dispensaries. Does the Constitution permit such an injunction?

    b) Which, if any of the following acts of Congress would be constitutional?

        i) a law requiring state bar prosecutors to pursue disciplinary proceedings against attorneys who counsel medical marijuana dispensaries;

        ii) a law requiring states to pass laws repealing their permissive medical marijuana laws;

        iii) a law providing that attorneys who have been proven to have counseled medical marijuana dispensaries are barred from practicing in federal court.

E. The Taxing and Spending Powers

Article I, section 8, clause 1, provides:

The Congress shall have power to lay and collect taxes, duties, imposts and excises, to pay the debts and provide for the common defense and general welfare of the United States; but all duties, imposts and excises shall be uniform throughout the United States[.]

This clause encompasses two distinct, albeit related, powers of Congress: the taxing power, and the spending power. We will examine these two powers in turn, beginning with the taxing power.

1. The Taxing Power

The taxing power is an independent grant of power in Art. I, §8. As such, it has long been understood as a basis for legislation, and not simply a means of implementing laws enacted under another enumerated power, such as the commerce power. This, of course, raises a constitutional tension with federalism and the doctrine of limited powers. Since taxation can be used to discourage or encourage activities, a taxing power untethered to any other enumerated power arguably allows Congress to regulate matters that would otherwise fall outside the enumerated powers. For this reason, the Supreme Court has made some efforts to distinguish between "bona fide" taxation to raise revenue and what the Court has taken to be efforts by Congress to regulate outside its enumerated powers under the "guise" of taxation. These judicial efforts to distinguish taxes from regulation have been intermittent and not wholly coherent, as will be seen. This distinction raises the constitutional issue we will consider in this section.[5]

Since 1937, the Court has not invalidated any federal tax on the grounds that it is attempted "regulation" and therefore beyond the enumerated powers of Congress. This may be due in part to the expansive interpretation of the commerce power in that time period. Most conceivable taxes would fall within the broad interpretation of the commerce power, rendering the "tax" versus "regulation" distinction unimportant. If a regulation is within one of its other enumerated powers, Congress may employ taxes as a regulatory tool. The distinction only arises where none of the other enumerated powers authorizes the tax. As Professor Tribe summarized it, if the Court's decisions in *Lopez* and *Morrison* "mark[] the beginning of a new era in which the Court cabins Congress' commerce power, it may also render salient, for the first time in more than half a century, the distinction between 'regulatory' and 'revenue' taxes for purposes of Congress' powers."[6] In light of the ACA case, this comment seems prescient.

---

5. The Constitution places certain express limitations on the taxing power of Congress that we will not consider. The last part of Art. I, §8, cl. 1, states that the various forms of taxation imposed by Congress "shall be uniform throughout the United States." This clause has been interpreted to require geographical uniformity only: so long as a tax does not discriminate between states, it need not be "uniform" with respect to individuals. *See Knowlton v Moore*, 178 U.S. 41 (1900). Greater difficulties were created by Art. I, §9, cl. 4: "No capitation, or other direct, tax shall be laid, unless in proportion to the census or enumeration herein before directed to be taken." The apportionment requirement created a virtually insurmountable practical barrier to income taxation—deemed a form of "direct" tax—until the ratification of the Sixteenth Amendment in 1913, which provided that "The Congress shall have power to lay and collect taxes on incomes, from whatever source derived, without apportionment among the several states, and without regard to any census or enumeration." Another limit on Congress's taxing power is found in Art. I, §9, cl. 5: "No tax or duty shall be laid on articles exported from any state."

6. Laurence H. Tribe, American Constitutional Law 846 (3d ed. 2000).

Guided Reading Questions: *United States v. Doremus, Bailey v. Drexel Furniture*

1. The two categories the Court sets up are a "tax," which raises revenue, and a "penalty," which regulates conduct. When reading the cases, pay attention to the precedents they cite or distinguish. Is there a discernable pattern that helps distinguish "tax" from "penalty"?

2. *Doremus* and *Bailey* reach different results. Can you tell why?

United States v. Doremus
249 U.S. 86 (1919)

Majority: *Day*, Holmes, Pitney, Brandeis, Clarke

Dissent: *White* (CJ), McKenna, Van Devanter, McReynolds

Doremus was indicted for violating § 2 of the so-called Harrison Narcotic Drug Act. 38 Stat. 785; 6 U.S. Comp. Stats. 1916, § 6287g. Upon demurrer to the indictment the District Court held the section unconstitutional for the reason that it was not a revenue measure, and was an invasion of the police power reserved to the States.

.... [T]he indictment ... charges that: Doremus, a physician, duly registered, and who had paid the tax required by the first section of the act, did unlawfully, fraudulently, and knowingly sell and give away and distribute to one Ameris a certain quantity of heroin, to wit, five hundred one-sixth grain tablets of heroin, a derivative of opium, the sale not being in pursuance of a written order on a form issued on the blank furnished for that purpose by the Commissioner of Internal Revenue.

The second count charges in substance that: Doremus did unlawfully and knowingly sell, dispense and distribute to one Ameris five hundred one-sixth grain tablets of heroin not in the course of the regular professional practice of Doremus, and not for the treatment of any disease from which Ameris was suffering, but as was well known by Doremus, Ameris was addicted to the use of the drug as a habit, being a person popularly known as a "dope fiend," and that Doremus did sell, dispense, and distribute the drug, heroin, to Ameris for the purpose of gratifying his appetite for the drug as an habitual user thereof.

Section 1 of the act requires persons who produce, import, manufacture, compound, deal in, dispense, sell, distribute, or give away opium or coca leaves or any compound, manufacture, salt, derivative or preparation thereof, to register with the collector of internal revenue of the district his name or style, place of business, and place or places where such business is to be carried on. At the time of such registry every person who produces, imports, manufactures, compounds, deals in, dispenses, sells, distributes, or gives away any of the said drugs, is required to pay to the collector a special tax of $1.00 per annum. It is made unlawful for any person required to register under the terms of the act to produce, import, manufacture, compound, deal in, dispense, sell, distribute, or give away any of the said drugs without having registered and paid the special tax provided in the act.

Section 2.... makes sales of these drugs unlawful except to persons who have [special] order forms issued by the Commissioner of Internal Revenue, and the order is required to be preserved for two years in such way as to be readily accessible to official inspection....

Section 9 inflicts a fine or imprisonment, or both for violations of the act.

This statute purports to be passed under the authority of the Constitution, Article I, § 8, which gives the Congress power "To lay and collect taxes, duties, imposts and excises, to pay the debts and provide for the common defence and general welfare of the United States; but all duties, imposts and excises shall be uniform throughout the United States."

The only limitation upon the power of Congress to levy excise taxes of the character now under consideration is geographical uniformity throughout the United States. This court has often declared it cannot add others. Subject to such limitation Congress may select the subjects of taxation, and may exercise the power conferred at its discretion. License Tax Cases, 5 Wall. 462, 471. Of course Congress may not in the exercise of federal power exert authority wholly reserved to the States. Many decisions of this court have so declared. And from an early day the court has held that the fact that other motives may impel the exercise of federal taxing power does not authorize the courts to inquire into that subject. If the legislation enacted has some reasonable relation to the exercise of the taxing authority conferred by the Constitution, it cannot be invalidated because of the supposed motives which induced it. Veazie Bank v. Fenno, 8 Wall. 533, 541, in which case this court sustained a tax on a state bank issue of circulating notes. McCray v. United States, 195 U.S. 27, where the power was thoroughly considered, and an act levying a special tax upon oleomargarine artificially colored was sustained....

Nor is it sufficient to invalidate the taxing authority given to the Congress by the Constitution that the same business may be regulated by the police power of the State.

The act may not be declared unconstitutional because its effect may be to accomplish another purpose as well as the raising of revenue. If the legislation is within the taxing authority of Congress—that is sufficient to sustain it.

The legislation under consideration was before us in a case concerning § 8 of the act, and in the course of the decision we said: "It may be assumed that the statute has a moral end as well as revenue in view, but we are of opinion that the District Court, in treating those ends as to be reached only through a revenue measure and within the limits of a revenue measure, was right." Considering the full power of Congress over excise taxation the decisive question here is: Have the provisions in question any relation to the raising of revenue? ... Congress, with full power over the subject, short of arbitrary and unreasonable action which is not to be assumed, inserted these provisions in an act specifically providing for the raising of revenue. Considered of themselves, we think they tend to keep the traffic above-board and subject to inspection by those authorized to collect the revenue. They tend to diminish the opportunity of unauthorized persons to obtain the drugs and sell them clandestinely without paying the tax imposed by the federal law. This case well illustrates the possibility which may have induced Congress to insert the provisions limiting sales to registered dealers and requiring patients to obtain these drugs as a medicine from physicians or upon regular prescriptions. Ameris, being as the indictment charges an addict, may not have used this great number of doses for himself. He might sell some to others without paying the tax, at least Congress may have deemed it wise to prevent such possible dealings because of their effect upon the collection of the revenue.

We cannot agree with the contention that the provisions of § 2, controlling the disposition of these drugs in the ways described, can have nothing to do with facilitating the collection of the revenue, as we should be obliged to do if we were to declare this act beyond the power of Congress acting under its constitutional authority to impose excise taxes. It follows that the judgment of the District Court must be reversed.

THE CHIEF JUSTICE [White] dissents because he is of opinion that the court below correctly held the act of Congress, in so far as it embraced the matters complained of, to be beyond the constitutional power of Congress to enact because to such extent the statute was a mere attempt by Congress to exert a power not delegated, that is, the reserved police power of the States.

Bailey v. Drexel Furniture Co.

(a/k/a "The Child Labor Tax Case")
259 U.S. 20 (1922)

Majority: *Taft* (CJ), McKenna, Holmes, Day, Van Devanter, Pitney, McReynolds, Brandeis

Dissent: *Clarke* (omitted)

[In response to the Court's ruling in Hammer v. Dagenhart, supra, in which the Court struck down the Keating-Owen Act of 1916, prohibiting interstate shipment of child-made manufactured goods, Congress enacted the Child Labor Tax Act, which imposed heavy taxes on child-made goods.]

MR. CHIEF JUSTICE TAFT delivered the opinion of the court.

This case presents the question of the constitutional validity of the Child Labor Tax Law. The plaintiff below, the Drexel Furniture Company, is engaged in the manufacture of furniture in the Western District of North Carolina. On September 20, 1921, it received a notice from Bailey, United States Collector of Internal Revenue for the District, that it had been assessed $6,312.79 for having during the taxable year 1919 employed and permitted to work in its factory a boy under fourteen years of age, thus incurring the tax of ten per cent. on its net profits for that year. The Company paid the tax under protest, and after rejection of its claim for a refund, brought this suit....

The Child Labor Tax Law is Title XII of an act entitled "An Act To provide revenue, and for other purposes", approved February 24, 1919, c. 18, 40 Stat. 1057, 1138. The heading of the title is "Tax on Employment of Child Labor"....

The law is attacked on the ground that it is a regulation of the employment of child labor in the States—an exclusively state function under the Federal Constitution and within the reservations of the Tenth Amendment. It is defended on the ground that it is a mere excise tax levied by the Congress of the United States under its broad power of taxation conferred by § 8, Article I, of the Federal Constitution. We must construe the law and interpret the intent and meaning of Congress from the language of the act. The words are to be given their ordinary meaning unless the context shows that they are differently used. Does this law impose a tax with only that incidental restraint and regulation which a tax must inevitably involve? Or does it regulate by the use of the so-called tax as a penalty? If a tax, it is clearly an excise. If it were an excise on a commodity or other thing of value we might not be permitted under previous decisions of this court to infer solely from its heavy burden that the act intends a prohibition instead of a tax. But this act is more. It provides a heavy exaction for a departure from a detailed and specified course of conduct in business. That course of business is that employers shall employ in mines and quarries, children of an age greater than sixteen years; in mills and factories, children of an age greater than fourteen years, and shall prevent children of less than sixteen years in mills and factories from working more than eight hours a day or six days in the week. If an employer departs from this prescribed course of business, he is to pay to the Government one-tenth of his entire net income in the business for a full year. The amount is not to be proportioned in any degree to the extent or frequency of the departures, but is to be paid by the employer in full measure whether he employs five hundred children for a year, or employs only one for a day. Moreover, if he does not know the child is within the named age limit, he is not to pay; that is to say, it is only where he knowingly departs from the prescribed course that payment is to be exacted. Scienter is associated with penalties not with taxes. The employer's factory is to be subject to inspection at any time not only by the taxing officers of the Treasury, the Department normally charged with the collection of taxes, but also by the Secretary of Labor and his subordinates whose normal function is the advancement and protection of the welfare of the workers. In the light of these features of the act, a court must be blind not to see that the so-called tax is imposed to stop the employment of children within the age limits prescribed. Its prohibitory and regulatory effect and purpose are palpable. All others can see and understand this. How can we properly shut our minds to it? ...

Out of a proper respect for the acts of a coordinate branch of the Government, this court has gone far to sustain taxing acts as such, even though there has been ground for suspecting from the weight of the tax it was intended to destroy its subject. But, in the act before us, the presumption of validity cannot prevail, because the proof of the contrary is found on the very face of its provisions. Grant the validity of this law, and all that Congress would need to do, hereafter, in seeking to take over to its control and one of the great number of subjects of public interest, jurisdiction of which the States have never parted with, and which are reserved to them by the Tenth Amendment, would be to enact a detailed measure of complete regulation of the subject and enforce it by a so-called tax upon departures from it. To give such magic to the word "tax" would be to break down all constitutional limitation of the powers of Congress and completely wipe out the sovereignty of the States.

The difference between a tax and a penalty is sometimes difficult to define and yet the consequences of the distinction in the required method of their collection often are important. Where the sovereign enacting the law has power to impose both tax and penalty the difference between revenue production and mere regulation may be immaterial, but not so when one sovereign can impose a tax only, and the power of regulation rests in another. Taxes are occasionally imposed in the discretion of the legislature on proper subjects with the primary motive of obtaining revenue from them and with the incidental motive of discouraging them by making their continuance onerous. They do not lose their character as taxes because of the incidental motive. But there comes a time in the extension of the penalizing features of the so-called tax when it loses its character as such and becomes a mere penalty with the characteristics of regulation and punishment. Such is the case in the law before us. Although Congress does not invalidate the contract of employment or expressly declare that the employment within the mentioned ages is illegal, it does exhibit its intent practically to achieve the latter result by adopting the criteria of wrongdoing and imposing its principal consequence on those who transgress its standard.

The case before us can not be distinguished from that of Hammer v. Dagenhart, 247 U.S. 251. Congress there enacted a law to prohibit transportation in interstate commerce of goods made at a factory in which there was employment of children within the same ages and for the same number of hours a day and days in a week as are penalized by the act in this case. This court held the law in that case to be void. It said:

> In our view the necessary effect of this act is, by means of a prohibition against the movement in interstate commerce of ordinary commercial commodities, to regulate the hours of labor of children in factories and mines within the States, a purely state authority.

In the case at the bar, Congress in the name of a tax which on the face of the act is a penalty seeks to do the same thing, and the effort must be equally futile.

The analogy of the Dagenhart Case is clear. The congressional power over interstate commerce is, within its proper scope, just as complete and unlimited as the congressional power to tax, and the legislative motive in its exercise is just as free from judicial suspicion and inquiry. Yet when Congress threatened to stop interstate commerce in ordinary and necessary commodities, unobjectionable as subjects of transportation, and to deny the same to the people of a State in order to coerce them into compliance with Congress's regulation of state concerns, the court said this was not in fact regulation of interstate commerce, but rather that of State concerns and was invalid. So here the so-called tax is a penalty to coerce people of a State to act as Congress wishes them to act in respect of a matter completely the business of the state government under the Federal Constitution....

But it is pressed upon us that this court has gone so far in sustaining taxing measures the effect or tendency of which was to accomplish purposes not directly within congressional power that we are bound by authority to maintain this law.

[McCray v. United States, 195 U.S. 27, involved].... a tax on oleomargarine, a substitute for butter. The tax on the white oleomargarine was one-quarter of a cent a pound, and on the yellow oleomargarine was first two cents and was then by the act in question increased to ten cents per pound. This court held that the discretion of Congress in the exercise of its constitutional powers to levy excise taxes could not be controlled or limited by the courts because the latter might deem the incidence of the tax oppressive or even destructive.... Congress in selecting its subjects for taxation might impose the burden where and as it would and that a motive disclosed in its selection to discourage sale or manufacture of an article by a higher tax than on some other did not invalidate the tax.... [T]he law objected to [did not] show on its face as does the law before us the detailed specifications of a regulation of a state concern and business with a heavy exaction to promote the efficacy of such regulation.

[United States v. Doremus, 249 U.S 86,] ... involved the validity of the Narcotic Drug Act, 38 Stat. 785, which imposed a special tax on the manufacture, importation and sale or gift of opium or coca leaves or their compounds or derivatives.... The validity of a special tax in the nature of an excise tax on the manufacture, importation and sale of such drugs was, of course, unquestioned. The provisions for subjecting the sale and distribution of the drugs to official supervision and inspection were held to have a reasonable relation to the enforcement of the tax and were therefore held valid.

The court said that the act could not be declared invalid just because another motive than taxation, not shown on the face of the act, might have contributed to its passage. This case does not militate against the conclusion we have reached in respect of the law now before us. The court, there, made manifest its view that the provisions of the so-called taxing act must be naturally and reasonably adapted to the collection of the tax and not solely to the achievement of some other purpose plainly within state power.

For the reasons given, we must hold the Child Labor Tax Law invalid and the judgment of the District Court is affirmed.

Review Questions and Explanations: *Doremus* and *Bailey*

1. Can you discern any principled distinction between the law struck down in *Bailey* and those upheld in *Doremus* and the cases cited in *Doremus* and *Bailey* (e.g., the tax on oleomargarine)?

2. It is no doubt significant that the taxes upheld in these cases were paralleled by commerce regulations that were also upheld under the Commerce Clause: the Court in the *Lochner* era had upheld federal laws regulating morals (lottery tickets, prostitution) and pure food and drugs under the Commerce Clause; whereas, child labor regulation was struck down as exceeding the commerce power. Significant, but why? The taxing power is grant of legislative authority independent of commerce power.

3. Justice Holmes, the dissenter in *Hammer*, joined the majority in *Bailey*. Why do you think he did that?

Guided Reading Questions: *United States v. Kahriger*

1. What is the nature of the tax in *Kahriger*: the activity and the manner of collection? If no one breaks any gambling laws, would the government collect any tax? Shouldn't that suggest that we're looking at a penalty?

2. What test, if any, does the Court offer to determine whether the tax is valid under the taxing power?

3. Is there any contention that this tax could be upheld as regulation under the commerce power?

United States v. Kahriger

345 U.S. 22 (1953)

Majority: *Reed*, Vinson (CJ), Burton, Clark, Minton

Concurrence: *Jackson*

Dissents: *Black, Frankfurter*, Douglas

MR. JUSTICE REED delivered the opinion of the Court.

The issue raised by this appeal is the constitutionality of the occupational tax provisions of the Revenue Act of 1951, which levy a tax on persons engaged in the business of accepting wagers, and require such persons to register with the Collector of Internal Revenue. The unconstitutionality of the tax is asserted on two grounds. First, it is said that Congress, under the pretense of exercising its power to tax has attempted to penalize illegal intrastate gambling through the regulatory features of the Act (26 U.S.C. (Supp. V) § 3291) and has thus infringed the police power which is reserved to the states. Secondly, it is urged that the registration provisions of the tax violate the privilege against self-incrimination and are arbitrary and vague, contrary to the guarantees of the Fifth Amendment.

... [A]n information was filed against appellee alleging that he was in the business of accepting wagers and that he willfully failed to register for and pay the occupational tax in question. Appellee moved to dismiss on the ground that the sections upon which the information was based were unconstitutional. The District Court sustained the motion on the authority of our opinion in United States v. Constantine, 296 U.S. 287. The court reasoned that ... the legislation was an infringement by the Federal Government on the police power reserved to the states by the Tenth Amendment.

The result below..., in our opinion, is erroneous.

In the term following the Constantine opinion, this Court pointed out in Sonzinsky v. United States, 300 U.S. 506, at 513 (a case involving a tax on a "limited class" of objectionable firearms alleged to be prohibitory in effect and "to disclose unmistakably the legislative purpose to regulate rather than to tax"), that the subject of the tax in Constantine was "described or treated as criminal by the taxing statute." The tax in the Constantine case was a special additional excise tax of $1,000, placed only on persons who carried on a liquor business in violation of state law. The wagering tax with which we are here concerned applies to all persons engaged in the business of receiving wagers, regardless of whether such activity violates state law.

The substance of respondent's position with respect to the Tenth Amendment is that Congress has chosen to tax a specified business which is not within its power to regulate. The precedents are many upholding taxes similar to this wagering tax as a proper exercise of the federal taxing power. In the License Tax Cases, 5 Wall. [72 U.S.] 462 [(1866)], the controversy arose out of indictments for selling lottery tickets and retailing liquor in various states without having first obtained and paid for a license under the Internal Revenue Act of Congress. The objecting taxpayers urged that Congress could not constitutionally tax or regulate activities carried on within a state. P. 470. The Court pointed out that Congress had "no power of regulation nor any direct control" (5 Wall., at 470, 471) over the business there involved. The Court said that, if the licenses were to be regarded as by themselves giving authority to carry on the licensed business, it might be impossible to reconcile the granting of them with the Constitution. P. 471.

> But it is not necessary to regard these laws as giving such authority. So far as they relate to trade within State limits, they give none, and can give none. They simply express the purpose of the government not to interfere by penal proceedings with the trade nominally licensed, if the required taxes are paid. The power to tax is not questioned, nor the power to impose penalties for non-payment of taxes. The granting of a license, therefore, must be regarded as nothing more than a mere form of imposing a tax, and of implying nothing except that the licensee shall be subject to no penalties under national law, if he pays it.

Appellee would have us say that, because there is legislative history indicating a congressional motive to suppress wagering, this tax is not a proper exercise of such taxing power. In the License Tax Cases, supra, it was admitted that the federal license "discouraged" the activities. The intent to curtail and hinder, as well as tax, was also manifest in the following cases, and in each of them the tax was upheld: Veazie Bank v. Fenno, 8 Wall. 533 (tax on paper money issued by state banks); McCray v. United States, 195 U.S. 27, 59 (tax on colored oleomargarine); United States v. Doremus, 249 U.S. 86, and Nigro v. United States, 276 U.S. 332 (tax on narcotics); Sonzinsky v. United States, 300 U.S. 506 (tax on firearms); United States v. Sanchez, 340 U.S. 42 (tax on marihuana).

It is conceded that a federal excise tax does not cease to be valid merely because it discourages or deters the activities taxed. Nor is the tax invalid because the revenue obtained is negligible. Appellee, however, argues that the sole purpose of the statute is to penalize only illegal gambling in the states through the guise of a tax measure. As with the above excise taxes which we have held to be valid, the instant tax has a regulatory effect. But regardless of its regulatory effect, the wagering tax produces revenue. As such it surpasses both the narcotics and firearms taxes which we have found valid.

It is axiomatic that the power of Congress to tax is extensive and sometimes falls with crushing effect on businesses deemed unessential or inimical to the public welfare, or where, as in dealings with narcotics, the collection of the tax also is difficult. As is well known, the constitutional restraints on taxing are few. "Congress cannot tax exports, and it must impose direct taxes by the rule of apportionment, and indirect taxes by the rule of uniformity." License Tax Cases, supra, at 471. The remedy for excessive taxation is in the hands of Congress, not the courts. . . .

The difficulty of saying when the power to lay uniform taxes is curtailed, because its use brings a result beyond the direct legislative power of Congress, has given rise to diverse decisions. In that area of abstract ideas, a final definition of the line between state and federal power has baffled judges and legislators.

. . . . Where federal legislation has rested on other congressional powers, such as the Necessary and Proper Clause or the Commerce Clause, this Court has generally sustained the statutes, despite their effect on matters ordinarily considered state concern. When federal power to regulate is found, its exercise is a matter for Congress. Where Congress has employed the taxing clause a greater variation in the decisions has resulted. The division in this Court has been more acute. Without any specific differentiation between the power to tax and other federal powers, the indirect results from the exercise of the power to tax have raised more doubts. . . . It is hard to understand why the power to tax should raise more doubts because of indirect effects than other federal powers.

Penalty provisions in tax statutes added for breach of a regulation concerning activities in themselves subject only to state regulation have caused this Court to declare the enactments invalid. Unless there are provisions extraneous to any tax need, courts are without authority to limit the exercise of the taxing power. All the provisions of this excise are adapted to the collection of a valid tax.

[The Court went on to reject the respondent's argument that the registration requirement violated the Fifth Amendment privilege against self incrimination. That aspect of the Court's holding was overruled in Marchetti v. United States, 390 U.S. 39 (1968).]

MR. JUSTICE JACKSON, concurring.

. . . Of course, all taxation has a tendency, proportioned to its burdensomeness, to discourage the activity taxed. One cannot formulate a revenue-raising plan that would not have economic and social consequences. Congress may and should place the burden of taxes where it will least handicap desirable activities and bear most heavily on useless or harmful ones. . . .

But here is a purported tax law which requires no reports and lays no tax except on specified gamblers whose calling in most states is illegal. It requires this group to step forward and identify themselves, not because they, like others, have income, but because of its source. This is difficult to regard as a rational or good-faith revenue measure, despite the deference that is due Congress. On the contrary, it seems to be a plan to tax out of existence the professional gambler whom it has been found impossible to prosecute out of existence. Few pursuits are entitled to less consideration at our hands than professional gambling, but the plain unwelcome fact is that it continues to survive because a large and influential part of our population patronizes and protects it.

The United States has a system of taxation by confession. That a people so numerous, scattered and individualistic annually assesses itself with a tax liability, often in highly burdensome amounts, is a reassuring sign of the stability and vitality of our system of self-government. What surprised me in once trying to help administer these laws was not to discover examples of recalcitrance, fraud or self-serving mistakes in reporting, but to discover that such derelictions were so few. It will be a sad day for the revenues if the good will of the people toward their taxing system is frittered away in efforts to accomplish by taxation moral reforms that cannot be accomplished by direct legislation. But the evil that can come from this statute will probably soon make itself manifest to Congress. The evil of a judicial decision impairing the legitimate taxing power by extreme constitutional interpretations might not be transient. Even though this statute approaches the fair limits of constitutionality, I join the decision of the Court.

MR. JUSTICE BLACK, with whom MR. JUSTICE DOUGLAS concurs, dissenting.

The Fifth Amendment declares that no person "shall be compelled in any criminal case to be a witness against himself." The Court nevertheless here sustains an Act which requires a man to register and confess that he is engaged in the business of gambling. I think this confession can provide a basis to convict him of a federal crime for having gambled before registration without paying a federal tax. 26 U.S.C. (Supp. V) §§ 3285, 3290, 3291, 3294. Whether or not the Act has this effect, I am sure that it creates a squeezing device contrived to put a man in federal prison if he refuses to confess himself into a state prison as a violator of state gambling laws. The coercion of confessions is a common but justly criticized practice of many countries that do not have or live up to a Bill of Rights. But we have a Bill of Rights that condemns coerced confessions, however refined or legalistic may be the technique of extortion. I would hold that this Act violates the Fifth Amendment....

MR. JUSTICE FRANKFURTER, dissenting.

The Court's opinion manifests a natural difficulty in reaching its conclusion. Constitutional issues are likely to arise whenever Congress draws on the taxing power not to raise revenue but to regulate conduct. This is so, of course, because of the distribution of legislative power as between the Congress and the State Legislatures in the regulation of conduct.

To review in detail the decisions of this Court, beginning with Veazie Bank v. Fenno, 8 Wall. 533, dealing with this ambivalent type of revenue enactment, would be to rehash the familiar. Two generalizations may, however, safely be drawn from this series of cases. Congress may make an oblique use of the taxing power in relation to activities with which Congress may deal directly, as for instance, commerce between the States. Thus, if the dissenting views of Mr. Justice Holmes in Hammer v. Dagenhart, 247 U.S. 251, 277, had been the decision of the Court, as they became in United States v. Darby, 312 U.S. 100, the effort to deal with the problem of child labor through an assertion of the taxing power in the statute considered in Child Labor Tax Case, 259 U.S. 20, would by the latter case have been sustained. However, when oblique use is made of the taxing power as to matters which substantively are not within the powers delegated to Congress, the Court cannot shut its eyes to what is obviously, because designedly, an attempt to control conduct which the Constitution left to the responsibility of the States, merely because Congress wrapped the legislation in the verbal cellophane of a revenue measure.

Concededly the constitutional questions presented by such legislation are difficult. On the one hand, courts should scrupulously abstain from hobbling congressional choice of policies, particularly when the vast reach of the taxing power is concerned. On the other hand, to allow what otherwise is excluded from congressional authority to be brought within it by casting legislation in the form of a revenue measure could, as so significantly expounded in the Child Labor Tax Case, supra, offer an easy way for the legislative imagination to control "any one of the great number of subjects of public interest, jurisdiction of which the States have never parted with...." Child Labor Tax Case, at 38. I say "significantly" because Mr. Justice Holmes and two of the Justices who had joined his dissent in Hammer v. Dagenhart, McKenna and Brandeis, JJ., agreed with the opinion in the Child Labor Tax Case. Issues of such gravity affecting the balance of powers within our federal system are not susceptible of comprehensive statement by smooth formulas such as that a tax is nonetheless a tax although it discourages the activities taxed, or that a tax may be imposed although it may effect ulterior ends. No such phrase, however fine and well-worn, enables one to decide the concrete case.

What is relevant to judgment here is that, even if the history of this legislation as it went through Congress did not give one the libretto to the song, the context of the circumstances which brought forth this enactment — sensationally exploited disclosures regarding gambling in big cities and small, the relation of this gambling to corrupt politics, the impatient public response to these disclosures, the feeling of ineptitude or paralysis on the part of local law-enforcing agencies — emphatically supports what was revealed on the floor of Congress, namely, that what was formally a means of raising revenue for the Federal Government was essentially an effort to check if not to stamp out professional gambling.

A nominal taxing measure must be found an inadmissible intrusion into a domain of legislation reserved for the States not merely when Congress requires that such a measure is to be enforced through a detailed scheme of administration beyond the obvious fiscal needs, as in the Child Labor Tax Case, supra. That is one ground for holding that Congress was constitutionally disrespectful of what is reserved to the States. Another basis for deeming such a formal revenue measure inadmissible is presented by this case. In addition to the fact that Congress was concerned with activity beyond the authority of the Federal Government, the enforcing provision of this enactment is designed for the systematic confession of crimes with a view to prosecution for such crimes under State law.

It is one thing to hold that the exception, which the Fifth Amendment makes to the duty of a witness to give his testimony when relevant to a proceeding in a federal court, does not include the potential danger to that witness of possible prosecution in a State court, Brown v. Walker, 161 U.S. 591, 606, and, conversely, that the Fifth Amendment does not enable States to give immunity from use in federal courts of testimony given in a State court. Feldman v. United States, 322 U.S. 487. It is a wholly different thing to hold that Congress, which cannot constitutionally grapple directly with gambling in the States, may compel self-incriminating disclosures for the enforcement of State gambling laws, merely because it does so under the guise of a revenue measure obviously passed not for revenue purposes. The motive of congressional legislation is not for our scrutiny, provided only that the ulterior purpose is not expressed in ways which negative what the revenue words on their face express and which do not seek enforcement of the formal revenue purpose through means that offend those standards of decency in our civilization against which due process is a barrier. I would affirm this judgment.

MR. JUSTICE DOUGLAS, while not joining in the entire opinion, agrees with the views expressed herein that this tax is an attempt by the Congress to control conduct which the Constitution has left to the responsibility of the States.

Review Questions and Explanations: *Kahriger*

1. The three taxing power cases, *Doremus, Bailey,* and *Kahriger,* parallel the development of the Commerce Clause (at least up to 1995). *Doremus* upholds an arguably regulatory tax clearly designed to regulate narcotic drug use, a legislative matter that fell outside the commerce power as then understood. *Bailey* then strikes down the Child Labor Tax Act which, in the wake of *Hammer,* tried to use the taxing power to regulate child labor. *Kahriger,* a post-New Deal case, upholds a tax aimed at prohibiting gambling, and it does so by deferring to Congress on the question of whether a tax is a legitimate revenue-raising measure. It is no coincidence how these cases track the Commerce Clause progression from cases like *Champion v. Ames* (upholding federal health/safety/morals regulation under the guise of protecting the "channels" of commerce) to *Hammer* (striking down a comparable law when the subject was labor) to *Darby/Wickard* (upholding laws by deferring to Congress's legislative choices).

2. *Bailey* looks an awful lot like a *Lochner*-era Commerce Clause case, but it has never been overruled—and is therefore, technically, still good law. Can you discern a doctrinal test for when a tax can be upheld under the taxing power? Recall Professor Tribe's comment, at the beginning of this section, that when the Commerce Clause is construed very broadly, most taxes would be valid as regulatory "penalties" as an exercise of the commerce power. The taxing power issue becomes academic. Given the difficulty in drawing a clear line between a tax and a penalty, it is not hard to see why the Court has not chosen to be active in developing doctrine in this area since 1937.

3. Should the Court maintain the deferential approach of *Kahriger* or enter into the difficult terrain of trying to distinguish taxes for revenue-raising from taxes for regulatory purposes?

Exercises: The Taxing Power

1. Can you come up with a coherent and workable distinction between taxes for raising revenue and penalties that are intended to regulate conduct? With one or more classmates, try writing one up a rule that can be employed by the Supreme Court. Don't feel constrained by prior cases: you can write on a clean slate, if you like. Exchange your "rules" with your classmates to see if they stand up to scrutiny.

2. Review the exercise concerning the constitutional challenge to the "minimum coverage" provision of the Affordable Care Act, set out at the beginning of this chapter. Under the provision, individuals who fail to obtain health coverage by 2014 will be required to pay a "penalty" on their income tax returns, scaled to ability to pay as reflected in their tax return. The challengers to the provision argued that this provision exceeded Congress's taxing power. Having read the cases on the taxing power, try to outline your answers to the following questions:

   a) If the minimum coverage provision had been upheld as within Congress's commerce power, should the Court then have gone on to decide whether the so-called penalty provision is a "penalty" or a "tax"?

b) If the minimum coverage provision had been held to fall outside Congress's commerce power, could the provision nevertheless have been upheld if it were deemed to be a revenue-raising tax?

c) What are the arguments for finding the provision to be a "penalty" and those for finding it to be a "tax"?

National Federation of Independent Business v. Sebelius

567 U.S. ___, 132 S. Ct. 2566 (2012)

Majority (Part III-C only): *Roberts* (CJ), Ginsburg, Breyer, Sotomayor, Kagan

Concurrence: *Ginsburg*, Breyer, Sotomayor, Kagan

Dissent (jointly authored): Scalia, Kennedy, Thomas, Alito

CHIEF JUSTICE ROBERTS ... delivered the opinion of the Court with respect to Parts I, II, and III-C....

III

The Government advances two theories for the proposition that Congress had constitutional authority to enact the individual mandate. First, the Government argues that Congress had the power to enact the mandate under the Commerce Clause. Under that theory, Congress may order individuals to buy health insurance because the failure to do so affects interstate commerce, and could undercut the Affordable Care Act's other reforms. Second, the Government argues that if the commerce power does not support the mandate, we should nonetheless uphold it as an exercise of Congress's power to tax. According to the Government, even if Congress lacks the power to direct individuals to buy insurance, the only effect of the individual mandate is to raise taxes on those who do not do so, and thus the law may be upheld as a tax....

C

The exaction the Affordable Care Act imposes on those without health insurance looks like a tax in many respects. The "[s]hared responsibility payment," as the statute entitles it, is paid into the Treasury by "taxpayer[s]" when they file their tax returns. 26 U.S.C. § 5000A(b). It does not apply to individuals who do not pay federal income taxes because their household income is less than the filing threshold in the Internal Revenue Code. § 5000A(e)(2). For taxpayers who do owe the payment, its amount is determined by such familiar factors as taxable income, number of dependents, and joint filing status. §§ 5000A(b)(3), (c)(2), (c)(4). The requirement to pay is found in the Internal Revenue Code and enforced by the IRS, which—as we previously explained—must assess and collect it "in the same manner as taxes." This process yields the essential feature of any tax: it produces at least some revenue for the Government. United States v. Kahriger, 345 U.S. 22, 28, n. 4, (1953). Indeed, the payment is expected to raise about $4 billion per year by 2017. Congressional Budget Office, Payments of Penalties for Being Uninsured Under the Patient Protection and Affordable Care Act (Apr. 30, 2010).

It is of course true that the Act describes the payment as a "penalty," not a "tax." But while that label is fatal to the application of the Anti-Injunction Act, it does not determine whether the payment may be viewed as an exercise of Congress's taxing power. It is up to Congress whether to apply the Anti-Injunction Act to any particular statute, so it makes sense to be guided by Congress's choice of label on that question. That choice does not, however, control whether an exaction is within Congress's constitutional power to tax.

.... We have ... held that exactions not labeled taxes nonetheless were authorized by Congress's power to tax.... We thus ask whether the shared responsibility payment falls within Congress's taxing power, "[d]isregarding the designation of the exaction, and viewing its substance and application."

Our cases confirm this functional approach. For example, in Drexel Furniture, we focused on three practical characteristics of the so-called tax on employing child laborers that convinced us the "tax" was actually a penalty. First, the tax imposed an exceedingly heavy burden—10 percent of a company's net income—on those who employed children, no matter how small their infraction. Second, it imposed that exaction only on those who knowingly employed underage laborers. Such scienter requirements are typical of punitive statutes, because Congress often wishes to punish only those who intentionally break the law. Third, this "tax" was enforced in part by the Department of Labor, an agency responsible for punishing violations of labor laws, not collecting revenue. The same analysis here suggests that the shared responsibility payment may for constitutional purposes be considered a tax, not a penalty: First, for most Americans the amount due will be far less than the price of insurance, and, by statute, it can never be more. It may often be a reasonable financial decision to make the payment rather than purchase insurance, unlike the "prohibitory" financial punishment in Drexel Furniture. Second, the individual mandate contains no scienter requirement. Third, the payment is collected solely by the IRS through the normal means of taxation—except that the Service is not allowed to use those means most suggestive of a punitive sanction, such as criminal prosecution. The reasons the Court in Drexel Furniture held that what was called a "tax" there was a penalty support the conclusion that what is called a "penalty" here may be viewed as a tax.

None of this is to say that the payment is not intended to affect individual conduct. Although the payment will raise considerable revenue, it is plainly designed to expand health insurance coverage. But taxes that seek to influence conduct are nothing new. Some of our earliest federal taxes sought to deter the purchase of imported manufactured goods in order to foster the growth of domestic industry. Today, federal and state taxes can compose more than half the retail price of cigarettes, not just to raise more money, but to encourage people to quit smoking. And we have upheld such obviously regulatory measures as taxes on selling marijuana and sawed-off shotguns. Indeed, "[e]very tax is in some measure regulatory. To some extent it interposes an economic impediment to the activity taxed as compared with others not taxed." Sonzinsky, supra, at 513. That § 5000A seeks to shape decisions about whether to buy health insurance does not mean that it cannot be a valid exercise of the taxing power.

In distinguishing penalties from taxes, this Court has explained that "if the concept of penalty means anything, it means punishment for an unlawful act or omission." While the individual mandate clearly aims to induce the purchase of health insurance, it need not be read to declare that failing to do so is unlawful. Neither the Act nor any other law attaches negative legal consequences to not buying health insurance, beyond requiring a payment to the IRS. The Government agrees with that reading, confirming that if someone chooses to pay rather than obtain health insurance, they have fully complied with the law. Brief for United States 60–61; Tr. of Oral Arg. 49–50 (Mar. 26, 2012).

Indeed, it is estimated that four million people each year will choose to pay the IRS rather than buy insurance. See Congressional Budget Office, supra, at 71. We would expect Congress to be troubled by that prospect if such conduct were unlawful. That Congress apparently regards such extensive failure to comply with the mandate as tolerable suggests that Congress did not think it was creating four million outlaws. It suggests instead that the shared responsibility payment merely imposes a tax citizens may lawfully choose to pay in lieu of buying health insurance....

The joint dissenters argue that we cannot uphold § 5000A as a tax because Congress did not "frame" it as such. In effect, they contend that even if the Constitution permits Congress to do exactly what we interpret this statute to do, the law must be struck down because Congress used the wrong labels.... Interpreting such a law to be a tax would hardly "[i]mpos[e] a tax through judicial legislation." Rather, it would give practical effect to the Legislature's enactment.

Our precedent demonstrates that Congress had the power to impose the exaction in § 5000A under the taxing power, and that § 5000A need not be read to do more than impose a tax. That is sufficient to sustain it. The "question of the constitutionality of action taken by Congress does not depend on recitals of the power which it undertakes to exercise."

Even if the taxing power enables Congress to impose a tax on not obtaining health insurance, any tax must still comply with other requirements in the Constitution. Plaintiffs argue that the shared responsibility payment does not do so, citing Article I, § 9, clause 4. That clause provides: "No Capitation, or other direct, Tax shall be laid, unless in Proportion to the Census or Enumeration herein before directed to be taken." This requirement means that any "direct Tax" must be apportioned so that each State pays in proportion to its population. According to the plaintiffs, if the individual mandate imposes a tax, it is a direct tax, and it is unconstitutional because Congress made no effort to apportion it among the States.

Even when the Direct Tax Clause was written it was unclear what else, other than a capitation (also known as a "head tax" or a "poll tax"), might be a direct tax. Soon after the framing, Congress passed a tax on ownership of carriages, over James Madison's objection that it was an unapportioned direct tax. This Court upheld the tax, in part reasoning that apportioning such a tax would make little sense, because it would have required taxing carriage owners at dramatically different rates depending on how many carriages were in their home State. See Hylton v. United States, 3 Dall. (3 U.S.) 171, 174 (1796) (opinion of Chase, J.). The Court was unanimous, and those Justices who wrote opinions either directly asserted or strongly suggested that only two forms of taxation were direct: capitations and land taxes.

That narrow view of what a direct tax might be persisted for a century.... In 1895, we expanded our interpretation to include taxes on personal property and income from personal property, in the course of striking down aspects of the federal income tax. Pollock v. Farmers' Loan & Trust Co., 158 U.S. 601 (1895). That result was overturned by the Sixteenth Amendment, although we continued to consider taxes on personal property to be direct taxes. See Eisner v. Macomber, 252 U.S. 189 (1920).

A tax on going without health insurance does not fall within any recognized category of direct tax. It is not a capitation. Capitations are taxes paid by every person, "without regard to property, profession, or any other circumstance." Hylton, supra, at 175, 1 L. Ed. 556 (opinion of Chase, J.). The whole point of the shared responsibility payment is that it is triggered by specific circumstances—earning a certain amount of income but not obtaining health insurance. The payment is also plainly not a tax on the ownership of land or personal property. The shared responsibility payment is thus not a direct tax that must be apportioned among the several States.

There may, however, be a more fundamental objection to a tax on those who lack health insurance. Even if only a tax, the payment under § 5000A(b) remains a burden that the Federal Government imposes for an omission, not an act. If it is troubling to interpret the Commerce Clause as authorizing Congress to regulate those who abstain from commerce, perhaps it should be similarly troubling to permit Congress to impose a tax for not doing something.

Three considerations allay this concern. First, and most importantly, it is abundantly clear the Constitution does not guarantee that individuals may avoid taxation through inactivity. A capitation, after all, is a tax that everyone must pay simply for existing, and capitations are expressly contemplated by the Constitution. The Court today holds that our Constitution protects us from federal regulation under the Commerce Clause so long as we abstain from the regulated activity. But from its creation, the Constitution has made no such promise with respect to taxes. See Letter from Benjamin Franklin to M. Le Roy (Nov. 13, 1789) ("Our new Constitution is now established ... but in this world nothing can be said to be certain, except death and taxes").

Whether the mandate can be upheld under the Commerce Clause is a question about the scope of federal authority. Its answer depends on whether Congress can exercise what all acknowledge to be the novel course of directing individuals to purchase insurance. Congress's use of the Taxing Clause to encourage buying something is, by contrast, not new. Tax incentives already promote, for example, purchasing homes and professional educations. See 26 U.S.C. §§ 163(h), 25A. Sustaining the mandate as a tax depends only on whether Congress has properly exercised its taxing power to encourage purchasing health insurance, not whether it can. Upholding the individual mandate under the Taxing Clause thus does not recognize any new federal power. It determines that Congress has used an existing one.

Second, Congress's ability to use its taxing power to influence conduct is not without limits.... More often and more recently we have declined to closely examine the regulatory motive or effect of revenue-raising measures. See Kahriger. We have nonetheless maintained that "there comes a time in the extension of the penalizing features of the so-called tax when it loses its character as such and becomes a mere penalty with the characteristics of regulation and punishment."

We have already explained that the shared responsibility payment's practical characteristics pass muster as a tax under our narrowest interpretations of the taxing power. Because the tax at hand is within even those strict limits, we need not here decide the precise point at which an exaction becomes so punitive that the taxing power does not authorize it. It remains true, however, that the "power to tax is not the power to destroy while this Court sits." Panhandle Oil Co. v. Mississippi ex rel. Knox, 277 U.S. 218, 223 (1928) (Holmes, J., dissenting).

Third, although the breadth of Congress's power to tax is greater than its power to regulate commerce, the taxing power does not give Congress the same degree of control over individual behavior.... Congress's authority under the taxing power is limited to requiring an individual to pay money into the Federal Treasury, no more. If a tax is properly paid, the Government has no power to compel or punish individuals subject to it. We do not make light of the severe burden that taxation-especially taxation motivated by a regulatory purpose—can impose. But imposition of a tax nonetheless leaves an individual with a lawful choice to do or not do a certain act, so long as he is willing to pay a tax levied on that choice.

The Affordable Care Act's requirement that certain individuals pay a financial penalty for not obtaining health insurance may reasonably be characterized as a tax. Because the

Constitution permits such a tax, it is not our role to forbid it, or to pass upon its wisdom or fairness.

D

JUSTICE GINSBURG questions the necessity of rejecting the Government's commerce power argument, given that § 5000A can be upheld under the taxing power. But the statute reads more naturally as a command to buy insurance than as a tax, and I would uphold it as a command if the Constitution allowed it. It is only because the Commerce Clause does not authorize such a command that it is necessary to reach the taxing power question. And it is only because we have a duty to construe a statute to save it, if fairly possible, that § 5000A can be interpreted as a tax. Without deciding the Commerce Clause question, I would find no basis to adopt such a saving construction.

The Federal Government does not have the power to order people to buy health insurance. Section 5000A would therefore be unconstitutional if read as a command. The Federal Government does have the power to impose a tax on those without health insurance. Section 5000A is therefore constitutional, because it can reasonably be read as a tax.

JUSTICE GINSBURG, with whom JUSTICE SOTOMAYOR joins, and with whom JUSTICE BREYER and JUSTICE KAGAN join…, concurring in part….

I agree with THE CHIEF JUSTICE that the Anti-Injunction Act does not bar the Court's consideration of this case, and that the minimum coverage provision is a proper exercise of Congress' taxing power. I therefore join Parts I, II, and III-C of THE CHIEF JUSTICE's opinion….

JUSTICE SCALIA, JUSTICE KENNEDY, JUSTICE THOMAS, and JUSTICE ALITO, dissenting.

…. Congress has attempted to regulate beyond the scope of its Commerce Clause authority, and § 5000A is therefore invalid. The Government contends, however, as expressed in the caption to Part II of its brief, that "THE MINIMUM COVERAGE PROVISION IS INDEPENDENTLY AUTHORIZED BY CONGRESS'S TAXING POWER." Petitioners' Minimum Coverage Brief 52. The phrase "independently authorized" suggests the existence of a creature never hitherto seen in the United States Reports: A penalty for constitutional purposes that is also a tax for constitutional purposes. In all our cases the two are mutually exclusive. The provision challenged under the Constitution is either a penalty or else a tax. Of course in many cases what was a regulatory mandate enforced by a penalty could have been imposed as a tax upon permissible action; or what was imposed as a tax upon permissible action could have been a regulatory mandate enforced by a penalty. But we know of no case, and the Government cites none, in which the imposition was, for constitutional purposes, both…. The issue is not whether Congress had the power to frame the minimum-coverage provision as a tax, but whether it did so….

Our cases establish a clear line between a tax and a penalty: "[A] tax is an enforced contribution to provide for the support of government; a penalty … is an exaction imposed by statute as punishment for an unlawful act." In a few cases, this Court has held that a "tax" imposed upon private conduct was so onerous as to be in effect a penalty. But we have never held—never—that a penalty imposed for violation of the law was so trivial as to be in effect a tax…. When an act "adopt[s] the criteria of wrongdoing" and then imposes a monetary penalty as the "principal consequence on those who transgress its standard," it creates a regulatory penalty, not a tax. Child Labor Tax Case, 259 U.S. 20 (1922).

So the question is, quite simply, whether the exaction here is imposed for violation of the law. It unquestionably is. The minimum-coverage provision is found in 26 U.S.C. § 5000A, entitled *"Requirement* to maintain minimum essential coverage" (emphasis added). It commands that every "applicable individual shall ... ensure that the individual ... is covered under minimum essential coverage." Ibid. And the immediately following provision states that, "[i]f ... an applicable individual ... fails to meet the requirement of subsection (a) ... there is hereby imposed ... a penalty." § 5000A(b). And several of Congress' legislative "findings" with regard to § 5000A confirm that it sets forth a legal requirement and constitutes the assertion of regulatory power, not mere taxing power....

Quite separately, the fact that Congress (in its own words) "imposed ... a penalty," 26 U.S.C. § 5000A(b)(1), for failure to buy insurance is alone sufficient to render that failure unlawful. It is one of the canons of interpretation that a statute that penalizes an act makes it unlawful: .... "If a statute inflicts a penalty for doing an act, the penalty implies a prohibition, and the thing is unlawful, though there be no prohibitory words in the statute." 1 J. Kent, Commentaries on American Law 436 (1826)....

.... [T]he nail in the coffin is that the mandate and penalty are located in Title I of the Act, its operative core, rather than where a tax would be found-in Title IX, containing the Act's "Revenue Provisions."

For all these reasons, to say that the Individual Mandate merely imposes a tax is not to interpret the statute but to rewrite it. Judicial tax-writing is particularly troubling. Taxes have never been popular, Stamp Act of 1765, and in part for that reason, the Constitution requires tax increases to originate in the House of Representatives. See Art. I, § 7, cl. 1. That is to say, they must originate in the legislative body most accountable to the people, where legislators must weigh the need for the tax against the terrible price they might pay at their next election, which is never more than two years off.... We have no doubt that Congress knew precisely what it was doing when it rejected an earlier version of this legislation that imposed a tax instead of a requirement-with-penalty. See Affordable Health Care for America Act, H. R. 3962, 111th Cong., 1st Sess., § 501 (2009); America's Healthy Future Act of 2009, S. 1796, 111th Cong., 1st Sess., § 1301. Imposing a tax through judicial legislation inverts the constitutional scheme, and places the power to tax in the branch of government least accountable to the citizenry.

Finally, we must observe that rewriting § 5000A as a tax in order to sustain its constitutionality would force us to confront a difficult constitutional question: whether this is a direct tax that must be apportioned among the States according to their population. Art. I, §§ 9, cl. 4. Perhaps it is not (we have no need to address the point); but the meaning of the Direct Tax Clause is famously unclear.... [The issue was barely briefed or argued.] One would expect this Court to demand more than fly-by-night briefing and argument before deciding a difficult constitutional question of first impression.

Review Questions and Explanations: ACA Case *(taxing power excerpt)*

1. Does the majority apply the taxing power cases correctly? Or does the dissent? Or does neither? The dissenters argue emphatically that purported taxes intended to "punish for an unlawful act" are clearly penalties, and have never been upheld as taxes. Significantly, the dissenters cherry-pick their citations, never citing *Doremus*, the case upholding the punitive Harrison Narcotic Drug Act, or *Kahriger*, which upheld the tax on illegal bookmaking.

2. Does the majority opinion create a new doctrinal test for the tax/penalty distinction, or is its test reasonably distilled from precedent? Note that Chief Justice Roberts writes: "the shared responsibility payment's practical characteristics pass muster as a tax under our narrowest interpretations of the taxing power." Does the majority overrule any broader prior interpretation?

3. The Anti-Injunction Act provides that "no suit for the purpose of restraining the assessment or collection of any tax shall be maintained in any court by any person, whether or not such person is the person against whom such tax was assessed." 26 U.S.C. §7421(a). This law requires a taxpayer to pay the tax before litigating it, and its application to the ACA Case would have meant dismissing the case for lack of jurisdiction until at least 2014, when the "shared responsibility" payments would fall due. One lower court ruled in just that way. None of the litigants wanted that, nor, apparently, did the Supreme Court. But by holding that the Anti-Injunction Act did not bar a decision, the Court had to deem the payment *not* to be a tax—seemingly the reverse of the taxing power ruling.

The Court resolved this conundrum as follows: "The Anti-Injunction Act and the Affordable Care Act, however, are creatures of Congress's own creation. How they relate to each other is up to Congress ... Congress can, of course, describe something as a penalty but direct that it nonetheless be treated as a tax for purposes of the Anti-Injunction Act." Here, the Court found that Congress meant the law to be a "penalty" for Anti-Injunction Act purposes. What about for taxing power purposes? As you saw in Chief Justice Roberts' opinion, the Court reasoned that Congress' preferences and labels may be determinative under the Anti-Injunction Act, but are not determinative for constitutional analysis of the taxing power.

4. Suppose it is true that the "personal responsibility payment" is intended to deter going without insurance, or to incentivize buying insurance. What would be the practical consequences of a constitutional rule that taxes intended to incentivize behavior are "penalties"? Note that the Internal Revenue Code is filled with incentives of one kind or another.

Recap: The Taxing Power

1. The taxing power is understood as an enumerated power in its own right. That is, Congress has the power to tax even where it cannot rely on one of its other enumerated powers, e.g., commerce. This raises the possibility that, since taxes can easily be used to regulate, the taxing power could be used as an end run around the limits of Congress's legislative power. On the other hand, is there any principled way to distinguish taxes for the (purportedly legitimate) purpose of raising revenue from taxes for the purpose of regulating? Arguably, every tax inevitably does both. Moreover, if a broad power is given in the text of the Constitution itself, why should it be considered a "problem," rather than simply a part of the constitutional scheme, regardless of its potentially expansive consequences?

2. If Congress has the power to regulate a subject under another enumerated power (e.g., commerce), it can use taxes for that regulatory purpose. The taxing power issue arises *only* where there is no other enumerated power that can be invoked. If Congress has the power to regulate (e.g., because the subject is

interstate commerce), the question of whether a tax is for revenue or regulation becomes moot.

2. The Spending Power

The spending power derives from Article I, § 8, cl. 1, authorizing Congress "to lay and collect taxes, duties, imposts and excises, to pay the debts and provide for the common defense and general welfare of the United States[.]" If "provide" were construed to mean "legislate," and the phrase "provide for the common defense and general welfare" were viewed as a grant of power independent of the power to tax, then the clause could be understood as a broad power to pass any laws that "promoted the general welfare." Such a broad grant of power would be all-encompassing, and make the enumerated powers that follow in § 8 superfluous, while undermining the doctrine that Congress has limited powers. In fact, the framers appear to have understood the term "provide" to mean "spend," which makes sense in light of the coupling of that clause with the power to tax.

Even within this narrower understanding of the "spending" clause, however, a difference of opinion emerged. Madison argued that Congress could spend only to carry out the other specifically enumerated powers. Hamilton, in contrast, argued that Congress could spend on any matter that promoted the general welfare. This debate lasted at least until the Civil War. In the twentieth century, Hamilton's reading, which seems to make more sense as a textual matter,[7] was ultimately adopted. The first Supreme Court decision to make this explicit is the next one, *United States v. Butler*. At the same time, the *Butler* decision places limits on the spending power in line with the Court's crabbed pre-1937 views of Congress's commerce power.

Guided Reading Questions: *United States v. Butler*

1. Where does the Court discuss whether the "spending power" is an independent grant of power to Congress (the Hamiltonian view) rather than simply a means of accomplishing other enumerated powers (the Madisonian view)?

2. What does *Butler* say about using spending as a "back door" form of regulation?

3. How can we tell the difference between spending that is "regulatory" and spending that is permissible?

4. What does the Court say about the Tenth Amendment in this case? Based on your reading to this point, can you say whether that aspect of the holding is still good law?

---

7. Madison's argument seems to read the "general welfare clause" as a phrase whose sole function is to modify the taxing power — i.e., that Congress may tax *in order to* "pay the debts and provide for the common defence and general welfare." As such, the clause is not an independent spending authorization, but a description of the taxing power. This reading is strained: it would have made no sense for the drafters of the Constitution to use the phrase "general welfare" to refer to specifically enumerated powers, which were intended to be narrower than the "general welfare." Nor does it make sense to allow Congress to raise revenue "to provide for" matters on which it cannot spend.

United States v. Butler

297 U.S. 1 (1936)

Majority: *Roberts*, Hughes (CJ), Van Devanter, McReynolds, Sutherland, Butler

Dissent: *Stone*, Brandeis, Cardozo

[The Agricultural Adjustment act of 1933, arguably the legislative centerpiece of the first 100 days of the Roosevelt Administration, was a key relief measure aimed at alleviating the severe economic distress in the farming sector by maintaining prices at levels sufficient to support agricultural livelihoods. The statute levied a tax on processors of agricultural products "at such rate as equals the difference between the current average farm price for the commodity and the fair exchange value." In other words, any windfall to agricultural middlemen resulting from depressed farm prices would go to the federal treasury as a tax. This tax, in turn, was to be used to buy up farm surpluses or else pay subsidies to farmers to compensate them for adhering to production limits designed to prevent overproduction that would further depress prices.]

MR. JUSTICE ROBERTS delivered the opinion of the Court.

In this case we must determine whether certain provisions of the Agricultural Adjustment Act, 1933, conflict with the Federal Constitution....

The Government asserts that ... Article I, § 8 of the Constitution authorizes the contemplated expenditure of the funds raised by the tax. This contention presents the great and the controlling question in the case. We approach its decision with a sense of our grave responsibility to render judgment in accordance with the principles established for the governance of all three branches of the Government.

There should be no misunderstanding as to the function of this court in such a case. It is sometimes said that the court assumes a power to overrule or control the action of the people's representatives. This is a misconception. The Constitution is the supreme law of the land ordained and established by the people. All legislation must conform to the principles it lays down. When an act of Congress is appropriately challenged in the courts as not conforming to the constitutional mandate the judicial branch of the Government has only one duty,—to lay the article of the Constitution which is invoked beside the statute which is challenged and to decide whether the latter squares with the former. All the court does, or can do, is to announce its considered judgment upon the question. The only power it has, if such it may be called, is the power of judgment. This court neither approves nor condemns any legislative policy. Its delicate and difficult office is to ascertain and declare whether the legislation is in accordance with, or in contravention of, the provisions of the Constitution; and, having done that, its duty ends.

The question is not what power the Federal Government ought to have but what powers in fact have been given by the people. It hardly seems necessary to reiterate that ours is a dual form of government; that in every state there are two governments,—the state and the United States. Each State has all governmental powers save such as the people, by their Constitution, have conferred upon the United States, denied to the States, or reserved to themselves. The federal union is a government of delegated powers. It has only such as are expressly conferred upon it and such as are reasonably to be implied from those granted. In this respect we differ radically from nations where all legislative power, without restriction or limitation, is vested in a parliament or other legislative body subject to no restrictions except the discretion of its members.... [The Act's] stated purpose is the control of agricultural production, a purely local activity, in an effort to raise the prices paid the farmer. Indeed, the Government does not attempt to uphold the validity of the act on the basis of the commerce clause, which, for the purpose of the present case, may be put aside as irrelevant.

The clause thought to authorize the legislation,—the first,—confers upon the Congress power "to lay and collect Taxes, Duties, Imposts and Excises, to pay the Debts and provide for the common Defence and general Welfare of the United States...." It is not contended that this provision grants power to regulate agricultural production upon the theory that such legislation would promote the general welfare. The Government concedes that the phrase "to provide for the general welfare" qualifies the power "to lay and collect taxes." The view that the clause grants power to provide for the general welfare, independently of the taxing power, has never been authoritatively accepted. Mr. Justice Story points out that if it were adopted "it is obvious that under color of the generality of the words, to 'provide for the common defence and general welfare,' the government of the United States is, in reality, a government of general and unlimited powers, notwithstanding the subsequent enumeration of specific powers." The true construction undoubtedly is that the only thing granteed is the power to tax for the purpose of providing funds for payment of the nation's debts and making provision for the general welfare.

Nevertheless the Government asserts that warrant is found in this clause for the adoption of the Agricultural Adjustment Act. The argument is that Congress may appropriate and authorize the spending of moneys for the "general welfare"; that the phrase should be liberally construed to cover anything conducive to national welfare; that decision as to what will promote such welfare rests with Congress alone, and the courts may not review its determination; and finally that the appropriation under attack was in fact for the general welfare of the United States.

The Congress is expressly empowered to lay taxes to provide for the general welfare. Funds in the Treasury as a result of taxation may be expended only through appropriation. (Art. I, §9, cl. 7.) They can never accomplish the objects for which they were collected unless the power to appropriate is as broad as the power to tax. The necessary implication from the terms of the grant is that the public funds may be appropriated "to provide for the general welfare of the United States." These words cannot be meaningless, else they would not have been used. The conclusion must be that they were intended to limit and define the granted power to raise and to expend money. How shall they be construed to effectuate the intent of the instrument? Since the foundation of the Nation sharp differences of opinion have persisted as to the true interpretation of the phrase. Madison asserted it amounted to no more than a reference to the other powers enumerated in the subsequent clauses of the same section; that, as the United States is a government of limited and enumerated powers, the grant of power to tax and spend for the general national welfare must be confined to the enumerated legislative fields committed to the Congress. In this view the phrase is mere tautology, for taxation and appropriation are or may be necessary incidents of the exercise of any of the enumerated legislative powers. Hamilton, on the other hand, maintained the clause confers a power separate and distinct from those later enumerated, is not restricted in meaning by the grant of them, and Congress consequently has a substantive power to tax and to appropriate, limited only by the requirement that it shall be exercised to provide for the general welfare of the United States. Each contention has had the support of those whose views are entitled to weight. This court has noticed the question, but has never found it necessary to decide which is the true construction. Mr. Justice Story, in his Commentaries, espouses the Hamiltonian position. We shall not review the writings of public men and commentators or discuss the legislative practice. Study of all these leads us to conclude that the reading advocated by Mr. Justice Story is the correct one. While, therefore, the power to tax is not unlimited, its confines are set in the clause which confers it, and not in those of § 8 which bestow and define the legislative powers of the Congress. It results that the power of Congress to authorize expenditure of public moneys for public purposes is not limited by the direct grants of legislative power found in the Constitution.

But the adoption of the broader construction leaves the power to spend subject to limitations.... That the qualifying phrase must be given effect all advocates of broad construction admit. Hamilton, in his well known Report on Manufactures, states that the purpose must be "general, and not local." Monroe, an advocate of Hamilton's doctrine, wrote: "Have Congress a right to raise and appropriate the money to any and to every purpose according to their will and pleasure? They certainly have not." Story says that if the tax be not proposed for the common defence or general welfare, but for other objects wholly extraneous, it would be wholly indefensible upon constitutional principles. And he makes it clear that the powers of taxation and appropriation extend only to matters of national, as distinguished from local welfare....

We are not now required to ascertain the scope of the phrase "general welfare of the United States" or to determine whether an appropriation in aid of agriculture falls within it. Wholly apart from that question, another principle embedded in our Constitution prohibits the enforcement of the Agricultural Adjustment Act. The act invades the reserved rights of the states. It is a statutory plan to regulate and control agricultural production, a matter beyond the powers delegated to the federal government. The tax, the appropriation of the funds raised, and the direction for their disbursement, are but parts of the plan. They are but means to an unconstitutional end.

From the accepted doctrine that the United States is a government of delegated powers, it follows that those not expressly granted, or reasonably to be implied from such as are conferred, are reserved to the states or to the people. To forestall any suggestion to the contrary, the Tenth Amendment was adopted. The same proposition, otherwise stated, is that powers not granted are prohibited. None to regulate agricultural production is given, and therefore legislation by Congress for that purpose is forbidden.

It is an established principle that the attainment of a prohibited end may not be accomplished under the pretext of the exertion of powers which are granted.

[The Court held that the taxing power, by itself, could not sustain the Act, because the tax was regulatory and on a subject outside the other enumerated powers of Congress.]

If the taxing power may not be used as the instrument to enforce a regulation of matters of state concern with respect to which the Congress has no authority to interfere, may it, as in the present case, be employed to raise the money necessary to purchase a compliance which the Congress is powerless to command? The Government asserts that whatever might be said against the validity of the plan if compulsory, it is constitutionally sound because the end is accomplished by voluntary co-operation. There are two sufficient answers to the contention. The regulation is not in fact voluntary. The farmer, of course, may refuse to comply, but the price of such refusal is the loss of benefits. The amount offered is intended to be sufficient to exert pressure on him to agree to the proposed regulation. The power to confer or withhold unlimited benefits is the power to coerce or destroy. If the cotton grower elects not to accept the benefits, he will receive less for his crops; those who receive payments will be able to undersell him. The result may well be financial ruin. The coercive purpose and intent of the statute is not obscured by the fact that it has not been perfectly successful. It is pointed out that, because there still remained a minority whom the rental and benefit payments were insufficient to induce to surrender their independence of action, the Congress has gone further and, in the Bankhead Cotton Act, used the taxing power in a more directly minatory fashion to compel submission. This progression only serves more fully to expose the coercive purpose of the so-called tax imposed by the present act. It is clear that the Department of Agriculture has properly described the plan as one to keep a non-cooperating minority in line. This is coercion by economic pressure. The asserted power of choice is illusory....

We are not here concerned with a conditional appropriation of money, nor with a provision that if certain conditions are not complied with the appropriation shall no longer be available. By the Agricultural Adjustment Act the amount of the tax is appropriated to be expended only in payment under contracts whereby the parties bind themselves to regulation by the Federal Government. There is an obvious difference between a statute stating the conditions upon which moneys shall be expended and one effective only upon assumption of a contractual obligation to submit to a regulation which otherwise could not be enforced. Many examples pointing the distinction might be cited. We are referred to appropriations in aid of education, and it is said that no one has doubted the power of Congress to stipulate the sort of education for which money shall be expended. But an appropriation to an educational institution which by its terms is to become available only if the beneficiary enters into a contract to teach doctrines subversive of the Constitution is clearly bad. An affirmance of the authority of Congress so to condition the expenditure of an appropriation would tend to nullify all constitutional limitations upon legislative power....

Congress has no power to enforce its commands on the farmer to the ends sought by the Agricultural Adjustment Act. It must follow that it may not indirectly accomplish those ends by taxing and spending to purchase compliance. The Constitution and the entire plan of our government negative any such use of the power to tax and to spend as the act undertakes to authorize. It does not help to declare that local conditions throughout the nation have created a situation of national concern; for this is but to say that whenever there is a widespread similarity of local conditions, Congress may ignore constitutional limitations upon its own powers and usurp those reserved to the states....

If the act before us is a proper exercise of the federal taxing power, evidently the regulation of all industry throughout the United States may be accomplished by similar exercises of the same power. It would be possible to exact money from one branch of an industry and pay it to another branch in every field of activity which lies within the province of the states. The mere threat of such a procedure might well induce the surrender of rights and the compliance with federal regulation as the price of continuance in business....

Until recently no suggestion of the existence of any such power in the Federal Government has been advanced. The expressions of the framers of the Constitution, the decisions of this court interpreting that instrument, and the writings of great commentators will be searched in vain for any suggestion that there exists in the clause under discussion or elsewhere in the Constitution, the authority whereby every provision and every fair implication from that instrument may be subverted, the independence of the individual states obliterated, and the United States converted into a central government exercising uncontrolled police power in every state of the Union, superseding all local control or regulation of the affairs or concerns of the states....

Since, as we have pointed out, there was no power in the Congress to impose the contested exaction, it could not lawfully ratify or confirm what an executive officer had done in that regard. Consequently the Act of 1935 does not affect the rights of the parties. The judgment is Affirmed.

MR. JUSTICE STONE, dissenting.... [The majority holds] that a levy unquestionably within the taxing power of Congress may be treated as invalid because it is a step in a plan to regulate agricultural production and is thus a forbidden infringement of state power. The levy is not any the less an exercise of taxing power because it is intended to defray an expenditure for the general welfare rather than for some other support of government. Nor is the levy and collection of the tax pointed to as effecting the regulation. While all federal taxes inevitably have some influence on the internal economy of the states, it is not contended that the levy of a processing tax upon manufacturers using agricultural products as raw material has any perceptible regulatory effect upon either their production or manufacture. The tax is unlike the penalties which were held invalid in the Child Labor Tax Case, 259 U.S. 20, in Hill v. Wallace, 259 U.S. 44, in Linder v. United States, 268 U.S. 5, 17, and in United States v. Constantine, 296 U.S. 287, because they were themselves the instruments of regulation by virtue of their coercive effect on matters left to the control of the states. Here regulation, if any there be, is accomplished not by the tax but by the method by which its proceeds are expended, and would equally be accomplished by any like use of public funds, regardless of their source.

The method may be simply stated. Out of the available fund payments are made to such farmers as are willing to curtail their productive acreage, who in fact do so and who in advance have filed their written undertaking to do so with the Secretary of Agriculture. In saying that this method of spending public moneys is an invasion of the reserved powers of the states, the Court does not assert that the expenditure of public funds to promote the general welfare is not a substantive power specifically delegated to the national government, as Hamilton and Story pronounced it to be. It does not deny that the expenditure of funds for the benefit of farmers and in aid of a program of curtailment of production of agricultural products, and thus of a supposedly better ordered national economy, is within the specifically granted power. But it is declared that state power is nevertheless infringed by the expenditure of the proceeds of the tax to compensate farmers for the curtailment of their cotton acreage. Although the farmer is placed under no legal compulsion to reduce acreage, it is said that the mere offer of compensation for so doing is a species of economic coercion which operates with the same legal force and effect as though the curtailment were made mandatory by Act of Congress. In any event it is insisted that even though not coercive the expenditure of public funds to induce the recipients to curtail production is itself an infringement of state power, since the federal government cannot invade the domain of the states by the "purchase" of performance of acts which it has no power to compel.

Of the assertion that the payments to farmers are coercive, it is enough to say that no such contention is pressed by the taxpayer, and no such consequences were to be anticipated or appear to have resulted from the administration of the Act. The suggestion of coercion finds no support in the record or in any data showing the actual operation of the Act. Threat of loss, not hope of gain, is the essence of economic coercion. Members of a long depressed industry have undoubtedly been tempted to curtail acreage by the hope of resulting better prices and by the proffered opportunity to obtain needed ready money. But there is nothing to indicate that those who accepted benefits were impelled by fear of lower prices if they did not accept, or that at any stage in the operation of the plan a farmer could say whether, apart from the certainty of cash payments at specified times, the advantage would lie with curtailment of production plus compensation, rather than with the same or increased acreage plus the expected rise in prices which actually occurred....

The Constitution requires that public funds shall be spent for a defined purpose, the promotion of the general welfare. Their expenditure usually involves payment on terms which will insure use by the selected recipients within the limits of the constitutional purpose. Expenditures would fail of their purpose and thus lose their constitutional sanction if the terms of payment were not such that by their influence on the action of the recipients the permitted end would be attained. The power of Congress to spend is inseparable from persuasion to action over which Congress has no legislative control. Congress may not command that the science of agriculture be taught in state universities. But if it would aid the teaching of that science by grants to state institutions, it is appropriate, if not necessary, that the grant be on the condition, incorporated in the Morrill Act, 12 Stat. 503, 26 Stat. 417, that it be used for the intended purpose. Similarly it would seem to be compliance with the Constitution, not violation of it, for the government to take and the university to give a contract that the grant would be so used. It makes no difference that there is a promise to do an act which the condition is calculated to induce. Condition and promise are alike valid since both are in furtherance of the national purpose for which the money is appropriated.... The spending power of Congress is in addition to the legislative power and not subordinate to it. This independent grant of the power of the purse, and its very nature, involving in its exercise the duty to insure expenditure within the granted power, presuppose freedom of selection among divers ends and aims, and the capacity to impose such conditions as will render the choice effective. It is a contradiction in terms to say that there is power to spend for the national welfare, while rejecting any power to impose conditions reasonably adapted to the attainment of the end which alone would justify the expenditure.

Review Questions and Explanations: *Butler*

1. The *Butler* decision, one of the last before the "New Deal turnaround," is a problematic decision, although aspects of it remain good law. The *Butler* majority, though adopting the broader "Hamiltonian" version of the spending power, was nevertheless unwilling to embrace spending on matters that it viewed as within the regulatory power of the states.

2. The "spending power"—the power of Congress to spend for the general welfare—has also been construed as an independent grant of Congressional power. Even the pre-1937 Court recognized this in *Butler*. This means that Congress can spend money to promote any policy objective, whether within its enumerated powers or not: e.g., it can give grants of money to local schools.

3. The constitutional issue, again, is whether spending can somehow be used to evade the limits on Congress's legislative power. This question can be posed as whether the spending becomes regulatory. If Congress spent money to hire federal regulators to run local schools, this would most likely be seen as crossing the line from spending to regulation.

4. What about monetary incentives to encourage certain kinds of behaviors, such as cash subsidies to energy companies to develop "clean" energy technology? *Butler* took a narrow view of this spending/regulation distinction, and seemed to hold that positive monetary incentives were inherently coercive—and therefore regulatory. Part of the Agricultural Adjustment Act involved providing cash subsidies to farmers to grow smaller crop yields (to prevent overproduction that would drive prices below subsistence levels). The *Butler* Court held that these subsidies coerced compliance with the growing limits—presumably, it was the proverbial "offer that is too good to refuse"—and was therefore a regulation; since it fell outside the commerce power, according to the *Butler* Court, it was unconstitutional.

Butler's holding that subsidies can be coercive was overruled a year later in two cases upholding welfare programs: *Steward Machine Co. v. Davis* and *Helvering v. Davis* were both "New Deal turnaround cases" decided in 1937, and both upheld the system of federal subsidies to states that provided social safety net programs—unemployment insurance and Social Security, respectively. Those cases continued to recognize the idea that coercive use of the spending power could, at least in theory, be regulatory—and impermissible if not within another enumerated power—but rejected the idea that subsidies (the offer too good to refuse) are coercive.

Since the New Deal, the spending power has been relied on as the legislative basis for many important and far-reaching federal programs. The spending power is frequently used under the "cooperative federalism" approach to legislation discussed above. As you will recall, Congress in some situations induces states to opt into nationwide legislative programs as a condition of receiving federal funds. These programs can extend to matters outside Congress's enumerated powers since the "general welfare" is understood as extending beyond the limits of the enumerated powers. Examples include Social Security and various educational initiatives.

The issue raised in the next case, *South Dakota v. Dole*, is related, but different. Once the federal government is regularly paying subsidies under the spending power (in that case, highway money given to state governments), is it coercive to threaten to withdraw them, in order to incentivize behavior (there, to induce states to raise the drinking age to 21)? In *Dole* the Court said no, so long as the behavioral incentive was reasonably related to the purpose of the spending program (and the other elements of *Dole*'s four-part test were met). *Dole* implies that withdrawal of a large enough percentage of expected funds could be coercive, however.

Guided Reading Questions: *South Dakota v. Dole*

1. What is the federal law that is being challenged? What is its goal, and how does it accomplish that goal?

2. Identify the Court's test for permissible exercises of the spending power.

3. At what point does withholding federal funding become coercive?

4. What is the main point of disagreement between the majority and Justice O'Connor's dissent?

South Dakota v. Dole

483 U.S. 203 (1987)

Majority: *Rehnquist* (CJ), White, Marshall, Blackmun, Powell, Stevens, Scalia

Dissents: *Brennan*, *O'Connor*

CHIEF JUSTICE REHNQUIST delivered the opinion of the Court.

Petitioner South Dakota permits persons 19 years of age or older to purchase beer containing up to 3.2% alcohol. S. D. Codified Laws § 35-6-27 (1986). In 1984 Congress enacted 23 U.S.C. § 158, which directs the Secretary of Transportation to withhold a percentage of federal highway funds otherwise allocable from States "in which the purchase or public possession ... of any alcoholic beverage by a person who is less than twenty-one years of age is lawful." The State sued in United States District Court seeking a declaratory judgment that § 158 violates the constitutional limitations on congressional exercise of the spending power and violates the Twenty-first Amendment to the United States Constitution. The District Court rejected the State's claims, and the Court of Appeals for the Eighth Circuit affirmed. 791 F.2d 628 (1986).

.... Despite the extended treatment of the question by the parties, ... we need not decide in this case whether that Amendment would prohibit an attempt by Congress to legislate directly a national minimum drinking age. Here, Congress has acted indirectly under its spending power to encourage uniformity in the States' drinking ages. As we explain below, we find this legislative effort within constitutional bounds even if Congress may not regulate drinking ages directly.

The Constitution empowers Congress to "lay and collect Taxes, Duties, Imposts, and Excises, to pay the Debts and provide for the common Defence and general Welfare of the United States." Art. I, § 8, cl. 1. Incident to this power, Congress may attach conditions on the receipt of federal funds, and has repeatedly employed the power "to further broad policy objectives by conditioning receipt of federal moneys upon compliance by the recipient with federal statutory and administrative directives." Fullilove v. Klutznick, 448 U.S. 448, 474 (1980) (opinion of Burger, C. J.). The breadth of this power was made clear in United States v. Butler, 297 U.S. 1, 66 (1936), where the Court, resolving a longstanding debate over the scope of the Spending Clause, determined that "the power of Congress to authorize expenditure of public moneys for public purposes is not limited by the direct grants of legislative power found in the Constitution." Thus, objectives not thought to be within Article I's "enumerated legislative fields," id., at 65, may nevertheless be attained through the use of the spending power and the conditional grant of federal funds.

The spending power is of course not unlimited, Pennhurst State School and Hospital v. Halderman, 451 U.S. 1, 17, and n. 13 (1981), but is instead subject to several general restrictions articulated in our cases. The first of these limitations is derived from the language of the Constitution itself: the exercise of the spending power must be in pursuit of "the general welfare." See Helvering v. Davis, 301 U.S. 619, 640–641 (1937); United States v. Butler, supra, at 65. In considering whether a particular expenditure is intended to serve general public purposes, courts should defer substantially to the judgment of Congress. Helvering v. Davis, supra, at 640, 645. Second, we have required that if Congress desires to condition the States' receipt of federal funds, it "must do so unambiguously..., enabl[ing] the States to exercise their choice knowingly, cognizant of the consequences of their participation." Third, our cases have suggested (without significant elaboration) that conditions on federal grants might be illegitimate if they are unrelated "to the federal interest in particular national projects or programs." Finally, we have noted that other constitutional provisions may provide an independent bar to the conditional grant of federal funds.

South Dakota does not seriously claim that § 158 is inconsistent with any of the first three restrictions mentioned above. We can readily conclude that the provision is designed to serve the general welfare, especially in light of the fact that "the concept of welfare or the opposite is shaped by Congress...." Helvering v. Davis, supra, at 645. Congress found that the differing drinking ages in the States created particular incentives for young persons to combine their desire to drink with their ability to drive, and that this interstate problem required a national solution. The means it chose to address this dangerous situation were reasonably calculated to advance the general welfare. The conditions upon which States receive the funds, moreover, could not be more clearly stated by Congress. See 23 U.S.C.

§ 158 (1982 ed., Supp. III). And the State itself, rather than challenging the germaneness of the condition to federal purposes, admits that it "has never contended that the congressional action was … unrelated to a national concern in the absence of the Twenty-first Amendment." Brief for Petitioner 52. Indeed, the condition imposed by Congress is directly related to one of the main purposes for which highway funds are expended — safe interstate travel. See 23 U.S.C. § 101(b). This goal of the interstate highway system had been frustrated by varying drinking ages among the States. A Presidential commission appointed to study alcohol-related accidents and fatalities on the Nation's highways concluded that the lack of uniformity in the States' drinking ages created "an incentive to drink and drive" because "young persons commut[e] to border States where the drinking age is lower." Presidential Commission on Drunk Driving, Final Report 11 (1983). By enacting § 158, Congress conditioned the receipt of federal funds in a way reasonably calculated to address this particular impediment to a purpose for which the funds are expended.

The remaining question about the validity of § 158 — and the basic point of disagreement between the parties — is whether the Twenty-first Amendment constitutes an "independent constitutional bar" to the conditional grant of federal funds.… [The] cases establish that the "independent constitutional bar" limitation on the spending power is not, as petitioner suggests, a prohibition on the indirect achievement of objectives which Congress is not empowered to achieve directly. Instead, we think that the language in our earlier opinions stands for the unexceptionable proposition that the power may not be used to induce the States to engage in activities that would themselves be unconstitutional. Thus, for example, a grant of federal funds conditioned on invidiously discriminatory state action or the infliction of cruel and unusual punishment would be an illegitimate exercise of the Congress' broad spending power. But no such claim can be or is made here. Were South Dakota to succumb to the blandishments offered by Congress and raise its drinking age to 21, the State's action in so doing would not violate the constitutional rights of anyone.

Our decisions have recognized that in some circumstances the financial inducement offered by Congress might be so coercive as to pass the point at which "pressure turns into compulsion." Steward Machine Co. v. Davis, supra, at 590. Here, however, Congress has directed only that a State desiring to establish a minimum drinking age lower than 21 lose a relatively small percentage of certain federal highway funds. Petitioner contends that the coercive nature of this program is evident from the degree of success it has achieved. We cannot conclude, however, that a conditional grant of federal money of this sort is unconstitutional simply by reason of its success in achieving the congressional objective.

When we consider, for a moment, that all South Dakota would lose if she adheres to her chosen course as to a suitable minimum drinking age is 5% of the funds otherwise obtainable under specified highway grant programs, the argument as to coercion is shown to be more rhetoric than fact. As we said a half century ago in Steward Machine Co. v. Davis:

> Every rebate from a tax when conditioned upon conduct is in some measure a temptation. But to hold that motive or temptation is equivalent to coercion is to plunge the law in endless difficulties. The outcome of such a doctrine is the acceptance of a philosophical determinism by which choice becomes impossible. Till now the law has been guided by a robust common sense which assumes the freedom of the will as a working hypothesis in the solution of its problems. 301 U.S., at 589–590.

Here Congress has offered relatively mild encouragement to the States to enact higher minimum drinking ages than they would otherwise choose. But the enactment of such laws remains the prerogative of the States not merely in theory but in fact. Even if Congress might lack the power to impose a national minimum drinking age directly, we conclude that encouragement to state action found in § 158 is a valid use of the spending power. Accordingly, the judgment of the Court of Appeals is affirmed.

JUSTICE BRENNAN, dissenting.

I agree with JUSTICE O'CONNOR that regulation of the minimum age of purchasers of liquor falls squarely within the ambit of those powers reserved to the States by the Twenty-first Amendment.... The Amendment, itself, strikes the proper balance between federal and state authority. I therefore dissent.

JUSTICE O'CONNOR, dissenting.

The Court today upholds the National Minimum Drinking Age Amendment, 23 U.S.C. § 158, as a valid exercise of the spending power conferred by Article I, § 8. But § 158 is not a condition on spending reasonably related to the expenditure of federal funds and cannot be justified on that ground. Rather, it is an attempt to regulate the sale of liquor, an attempt that lies outside Congress' power to regulate commerce because it falls within the ambit of § 2 of the Twenty-first Amendment.

.... I agree with the Court that Congress may attach conditions on the receipt of federal funds to further "the federal interest in particular national projects or programs." I also subscribe to the established proposition that the reach of the spending power "is not limited by the direct grants of legislative power found in the Constitution." Finally, I agree that there are four separate types of limitations on the spending power.... But the Court's application of the requirement that the condition imposed be reasonably related to the purpose for which the funds are expended is cursory and unconvincing.... In my view, establishment of a minimum drinking age of 21 is not sufficiently related to interstate highway construction to justify so conditioning funds appropriated for that purpose.... [I]f the purpose of § 158 is to deter drunken driving, it is far too over- and under-inclusive. It is over-inclusive because it stops teenagers from drinking even when they are not about to drive on interstate highways. It is under-inclusive because teenagers pose only a small part of the drunken driving problem in this Nation.

When Congress appropriates money to build a highway, it is entitled to insist that the highway be a safe one. But it is not entitled to insist as a condition of the use of highway funds that the State impose or change regulations in other areas of the State's social and economic life because of an attenuated or tangential relationship to highway use or safety....

There is a clear place at which the Court can draw the line between permissible and impermissible conditions on federal grants. It is the line identified in the Brief for the National Conference of State Legislatures et al. as Amici Curiae:

> [Congress] has no power under the Spending Clause to impose requirements on a grant that go beyond specifying how the money should be spent. A requirement that is not such a specification is not a condition, but a regulation, which is valid only if it falls within one of Congress' delegated regulatory powers.

This approach harks back to United States v. Butler, 297 U.S. 1 (1936), the last case in which this Court struck down an Act of Congress as beyond the authority granted by the Spending Clause. There the Court wrote that "there is an obvious difference between a statute stating the conditions upon which moneys shall be expended and one effective only upon assumption of a contractual obligation to submit to a regulation which otherwise could not be enforced." Id., at 73. The Butler Court saw the Agricultural Adjustment Act for what it was—an exercise of regulatory, not spending, power. The error in Butler was not the Court's conclusion that the Act was essentially regulatory, but rather its crabbed view of the extent of Congress' regulatory power under the Commerce Clause. The Agricultural Adjustment Act was regulatory but it was regulation that today would likely be considered within Congress' commerce power. See, e.g., Katzenbach v. McClung, 379 U.S. 294 (1964); Wickard v. Filburn, 317 U.S. 111 (1942).

While Butler's authority is questionable insofar as it assumes that Congress has no regulatory power over farm production, its discussion of the spending power and its description of both the power's breadth and its limitations remain sound. The Court's decision in Butler also properly recognizes the gravity of the task of appropriately limiting the spending power. If the spending power is to be limited only by Congress' notion of the general welfare, the reality, given the vast financial resources of the Federal Government, is that the Spending Clause gives "power to the Congress to tear down the barriers, to invade the states' jurisdiction, and to become a parliament of the whole people, subject to no restrictions save such as are self-imposed." United States v. Butler, supra, at 78....

Review Questions and Explanations: *Dole*

1. Why couldn't Congress itself simply pass a law prohibiting alcohol consumption by persons under 21? Aside from any Commerce Clause issues, the answer is found in the Twenty-First Amendment, which famously repeals "prohibition" (specifically, the prohibition of importation, sale or manufacture of alcohol). Section 2 of this amendment is understood to make regulation of alcohol a matter of state law.

2. In a key passage, the Court says: "our cases have suggested (without significant elaboration) that conditions on federal grants might be illegitimate if they are unrelated to the federal interest in particular national projects or programs."

   (a) What does this mean? That spending conditions must be related to the particular project the money is being spent on, or any "particular national projects"?

   (b) Is this a new rule, or does it have something to do with coercion? I.e., is it more coercive to condition funding on unrelated requirements than related ones?

   (c) Might the emphasis be on the "*federal*-ness" of the interest rather than the "relatedness" of the spending condition to the subject matter of the program?

   (d) If this point is about ensuring that spending conditions are closely related to the purposes for which the money is being offered to the states, how close must the relationship be? What do the majority and dissent say about that in this case? Who is more persuasive?

3. Consider whether the doctrine of coercion makes sense as a way to protect federalism: how does it enhance the sovereignty of the states to protect their "right" to be so dependent on federal funds that they find themselves unable, politically, to do without them? Consider also whether the coercion test increases or decreases the type of accountability the Court, particularly Justice O'Connor, was concerned about when developing federalism doctrines in other contexts.

Exercise: The ACA Case and the Spending Power

1. Based on your knowledge of the commerce power, the taxing power and the spending power, as well as current Tenth Amendment doctrine, consider how you might re-write the "minimum coverage" provision to avoid the constitutional problems it eventually encountered.

Note that the minimum coverage provision was the result of a compromise that many observers felt watered down the original proposal. A number of health care advocates supported a "public option" under which uninsured individuals would be automatically covered by an expanded version of Medicaid or Medicare. Would the public option be constitutionally problematic? Is there a constitutional bar to the federal government offering health insurance to anyone who wanted it?

Jot down your ideas in broad outline for a revision to the health care law, with an eye toward avoiding the constitutional arguments the actual law provoked.

2. Return to the ACA exercise, in section A, and review the factual description of the "Medicaid Expansion" provision of the ACA. These are found in the third and fourth paragraphs from the end, starting "The second provision of the Affordable Care Act …"). Here is another excerpt from Chief Justice Roberts' opinion that sets out the Medicaid Expansion provision in greater detail.

> The States also contend that the Medicaid expansion exceeds Congress's authority under the Spending Clause. They claim that Congress is coercing the States to adopt the changes it wants by threatening to withhold all of a State's Medicaid grants, unless the State accepts the new expanded funding and complies with the conditions that come with it. This, they argue, violates the basic principle that the "Federal Government may not compel the States to enact or administer a federal regulatory program." New York, 505 U.S., at 188.
>
> There is no doubt that the Act dramatically increases state obligations under Medicaid. The current Medicaid program requires States to cover only certain discrete categories of needy individuals — pregnant women, children, needy families, the blind, the elderly, and the disabled. 42 U.S.C. § 1396a(a)(10). There is no mandatory coverage for most childless adults, and the States typically do not offer any such coverage. The States also enjoy considerable flexibility with respect to the coverage levels for parents of needy families. § 1396a(a)(10)(A)(ii). On average States cover only those unemployed parents who make less than 37 percent of the federal poverty level, and only those employed parents who make less than 63 percent of the poverty line.
>
> The Medicaid provisions of the Affordable Care Act, in contrast, require States to expand their Medicaid programs by 2014 to cover all individuals under the age of 65 with incomes below 133 percent of the federal poverty line. § 1396a(a)(10)(A)(i)(VIII). The Act also establishes a new "[e]ssential health benefits" package, which States must provide to all new Medicaid recipients — a level sufficient to satisfy a recipient's obligations under the individual mandate. §§ 1396a(k)(1), 1396u-7(b)(5), 18022(b). The Affordable Care Act provides that the Federal Government

will pay 100 percent of the costs of covering these newly eligible individuals through 2016. § 1396d(y)(1). In the following years, the federal payment level gradually decreases, to a minimum of 90 percent. Ibid. In light of the expansion in coverage mandated by the Act, the Federal Government estimates that its Medicaid spending will increase by approximately $100 billion per year, nearly 40 percent above current levels.

Based on *Butler* and *Dole*, outline the arguments for and against the constitutionality of this provision under the spending power. Don't overlook the recent Tenth Amendment cases as potential bases of argument.

National Federation of Independent Business v. Sebelius

567 U.S. ___, 132 S. Ct. 2566 (2012)

Plurality (Medicare expansion): *Roberts* (CJ), Breyer, Kagan

[Partial concurrence in the judgment*]: Scalia, Kennedy, Thomas, Alito

Dissent: *Ginsburg*, Sotomayor

[* The "joint dissent" is not styled a partial concurrence in the judgment, but it has that effect. See "Review Questions and Explanations," after the case excerpt.]

CHIEF JUSTICE ROBERTS announced the judgment of the Court and delivered ... an opinion with respect to Part IV, in which JUSTICE BREYER and JUSTICE KAGAN join ...

IV

.... The Spending Clause grants Congress the power "to pay the Debts and provide for the ... general Welfare of the United States." U.S. Const., Art. I, § 8, cl. 1. We have long recognized that Congress may use this power to grant federal funds to the States, and may condition such a grant upon the States' "taking certain actions that Congress could not require them to take." Such measures "encourage a State to regulate in a particular way, [and] influenc[e] a State's policy choices." New York v. United States, supra, at 166. The conditions imposed by Congress ensure that the funds are used by the States to "provide for the ... general Welfare" in the manner Congress intended.

At the same time, our cases have recognized limits on Congress's power under the Spending Clause to secure state compliance with federal objectives. "We have repeatedly characterized ... Spending Clause legislation as 'much in the nature of a contract.'" The legitimacy of Congress's exercise of the spending power "thus rests on whether the State voluntarily and knowingly accepts the terms of the 'contract.'" Pennhurst State School and Hospital v. Halderman, 451 U.S. 1, 17 (1981). Respecting this limitation is critical to ensuring that Spending Clause legislation does not undermine the status of the States as independent sovereigns in our federal system. That system "rests on what might at first seem a counterintuitive insight, that 'freedom is enhanced by the creation of two governments, not one.'" Bond, 131 S. Ct. 2355....

That insight has led this Court to strike down federal legislation that commandeers a State's legislative or administrative apparatus for federal purposes. See, e.g., Printz, 521 U.S., at 933 (striking down federal legislation compelling state law enforcement officers to perform federally mandated background checks on handgun purchasers); New York, supra, at 174–175. It has also led us to scrutinize Spending Clause legislation to ensure that Congress is not using financial inducements to exert a "power akin to undue influence." Steward Machine Co. v. Davis, 301 U.S. 548, 590 (1937). Congress may use its spending power to create incentives for States to act in accordance with federal policies. But when "pressure turns into compulsion," ibid., the legislation runs contrary to our system of federalism. "[T]he Constitution simply does not give Congress the authority to require the States to regulate." New York, 505 U.S., at 178. That is true whether Congress directly commands a State to regulate or indirectly coerces a State to adopt a federal regulatory system as its own.

Permitting the Federal Government to force the States to implement a federal program would threaten the political accountability key to our federal system. "[W]here the Federal Government directs the States to regulate, it may be state officials who will bear the brunt of public disapproval, while the federal officials who devised the regulatory program may remain insulated from the electoral ramifications of their decision." Id., at 169. Spending Clause programs do not pose this danger when a State has a legitimate choice whether to accept the federal conditions in exchange for federal funds. In such a situation, state officials can fairly be held politically accountable for choosing to accept or refuse the federal offer. But when the State has no choice, the Federal Government can achieve its objectives without accountability, just as in New York and Printz. Indeed, this danger is heightened when Congress acts under the Spending Clause, because Congress can use that power to implement federal policy it could not impose directly under its enumerated powers.

We addressed such concerns in Steward Machine. That case involved a federal tax on employers that was abated if the businesses paid into a state unemployment plan that met certain federally specified conditions. An employer sued, alleging that the tax was impermissibly "driv[ing] the state legislatures under the whip of economic pressure into the enactment of unemployment compensation laws at the bidding of the central government." 301 U.S., at 587. We acknowledged the danger that the Federal Government might employ its taxing [and spending] power to exert a "power akin to undue influence" upon the States. But we observed that Congress adopted the challenged tax and abatement program to channel money to the States that would otherwise have gone into the Federal Treasury for use in providing national unemployment services. Congress was willing to direct businesses to instead pay the money into state programs only on the condition that the money be used for the same purposes. Predicating tax abatement on a State's adoption of a particular type of unemployment legislation was therefore a means to "safeguard [the Federal Government's] own treasury." We held that "[i]n such circumstances, if in no others, inducement or persuasion does not go beyond the bounds of power." ...

As our decision in Steward Machine confirms, Congress may attach appropriate conditions to federal taxing and spending programs to preserve its control over the use of federal funds. In the typical case we look to the States to defend their prerogatives by adopting "the simple expedient of not yielding" to federal blandishments when they do not want to embrace the federal policies as their own. The States are separate and independent sovereigns. Sometimes they have to act like it.

The States, however, argue that the Medicaid expansion.... has "crossed the line distinguishing encouragement from coercion," in the way it has structured the funding: Instead of simply refusing to grant the new funds to States that will not accept the new conditions, Congress has also threatened to withhold those States' existing Medicaid funds. The States claim that this threat serves no purpose other than to force unwilling States to sign up for the dramatic expansion in health care coverage effected by the Act.

Given the nature of the threat and the programs at issue here, we must agree....

In South Dakota v. Dole, we considered a challenge to a federal law that threatened to withhold five percent of a State's federal highway funds if the State did not raise its drinking age to 21. The Court found that the condition was "directly related to one of the main purposes for which highway funds are expended-safe interstate travel." ... We found that the [condition] was not impermissibly coercive, because Congress was offering only "relatively mild encouragement to the States." Dole, 483 U.S., at 211. We observed that "all South Dakota would lose if she adheres to her chosen course as to a suitable minimum drinking age is 5%" of her highway funds. In fact, the federal funds at stake constituted less than half of one percent of South Dakota's budget at the time. See Nat. Assn. of State Budget Officers, The State Expenditure Report 59 (1987); South Dakota v. Dole, 791 F.2d 628, 630 (CA8 1986)....

In this case, the financial "inducement" Congress has chosen is much more than "relatively mild encouragement" — it is a gun to the head. Section 1396c of the Medicaid Act provides that if a State's Medicaid plan does not comply with the Act's requirements, the Secretary of Health and Human Services may declare that "further payments will not be made to the State." 42 U.S.C. § 1396c. A State that opts out of the Affordable Care Act's expansion in health care coverage thus stands to lose not merely "a relatively small percentage" of its existing Medicaid funding, but all of it. Medicaid spending accounts for over 20 percent of the average State's total budget, with federal funds covering 50 to 83 percent of those costs. See Nat. Assn. of State Budget Officers, Fiscal Year 2010 State Expenditure Report, p. 11, Table 5 (2011); 42 U.S.C. § 1396d(b). The Federal Government estimates that it will pay out approximately $3.3 trillion between 2010 and 2019 in order to cover the costs of pre-expansion Medicaid. Brief for United States 10, n. 6. In addition, the States have developed intricate statutory and administrative regimes over the course of many decades to implement their objectives under existing Medicaid. It is easy to see how the Dole Court could conclude that the threatened loss of less than half of one percent of South Dakota's budget left that State with a "prerogative" to reject Congress's desired policy, "not merely in theory but in fact." The threatened loss of over 10 percent of a State's overall budget, in contrast, is economic dragooning that leaves the States with no real option but to acquiesce in the Medicaid expansion....

Here, the Government claims that the Medicaid expansion is properly viewed merely as a modification of the existing program because the States agreed that Congress could change the terms of Medicaid when they signed on in the first place. The Government observes that the Social Security Act, which includes the original Medicaid provisions, contains a clause expressly reserving "[t]he right to alter, amend, or repeal any provision" of that statute. 42 U.S.C. § 1304. So it does. But "if Congress intends to impose a condition on the grant of federal moneys, it must do so unambiguously." Pennhurst, 451 U.S., at 17. A State confronted with statutory language reserving the right to "alter" or "amend" the pertinent provisions of the Social Security Act might reasonably assume that Congress was entitled to make adjustments to the Medicaid program as it developed. Congress has in fact done so, sometimes conditioning only the new funding, other times both old and new.

The Medicaid expansion, however, accomplishes a shift in kind, not merely degree. The original program was designed to cover medical services for four particular categories of the needy: the disabled, the blind, the elderly, and needy families with dependent children. See 42 U.S.C. § 1396a(a)(10). Previous amendments to Medicaid eligibility merely altered and expanded the boundaries of these categories. Under the Affordable Care Act, Medicaid is transformed into a program to meet the health care needs of the entire nonelderly population with income below 133 percent of the poverty level. It is no longer a program to care for the neediest among us, but rather an element of a comprehensive national plan to provide universal health insurance coverage.

Indeed, the manner in which the expansion is structured indicates that while Congress may have styled the expansion a mere alteration of existing Medicaid, it recognized it was enlisting the States in a new health care program. Congress created a separate funding provision to cover the costs of providing services to any person made newly eligible by the expansion. While Congress pays 50 to 83 percent of the costs of covering individuals currently enrolled in Medicaid, § 1396d(b), once the expansion is fully implemented Congress will pay 90 percent of the costs for newly eligible persons, § 1396d(y)(1). The conditions on use of the different funds are also distinct. Congress mandated that newly eligible persons receive a level of coverage that is less comprehensive than the traditional Medicaid benefit package. § 1396a(k)(1); see Brief for United States 9.

As we have explained, "[t]hough Congress' power to legislate under the spending power is broad, it does not include surprising participating States with postacceptance or 'retroactive' conditions." Pennhurst, supra, at 25. A State could hardly anticipate that Congress's reservation of the right to "alter" or "amend" the Medicaid program included the power to transform it so dramatically....

Nothing in our opinion precludes Congress from offering funds under the Affordable Care Act to expand the availability of health care, and requiring that States accepting such funds comply with the conditions on their use. What Congress is not free to do is to penalize States that choose not to participate in that new program by taking away their existing Medicaid funding. Section 1396c gives the Secretary of Health and Human Services the authority to do just that. It allows her to withhold all "further [Medicaid] payments ... to the State" if she determines that the State is out of compliance with any Medicaid requirement, including those contained in the expansion. 42 U.S.C. § 1396c. In light of the Court's holding, the Secretary cannot apply § 1396c to withdraw existing Medicaid funds for failure to comply with the requirements set out in the expansion.

That fully remedies the constitutional violation we have identified. The chapter of the United States Code that contains § 1396c includes a severability clause confirming that we need go no further. That clause specifies that "[i]f any provision of this chapter, or the application thereof to any person or circumstance, is held invalid, the remainder of the chapter, and the application of such provision to other persons or circumstances shall not be affected thereby." § 1303. Today's holding does not affect the continued application of § 1396c to the existing Medicaid program. Nor does it affect the Secretary's ability to withdraw funds provided under the Affordable Care Act if a State that has chosen to participate in the expansion fails to comply with the requirements of that Act.

This is not to say, as the joint dissent suggests, that we are "rewriting the Medicaid Expansion." Instead, we determine, first, that § 1396c is unconstitutional when applied to withdraw existing Medicaid funds from States that decline to comply with the expansion. We then follow Congress's explicit textual instruction to leave unaffected "the remainder of the chapter, and the application of [the challenged] provision to other persons or circumstances." § 1303. When we invalidate an application of a statute because that application is unconstitutional, we are not "rewriting" the statute; we are merely enforcing the Constitution.

The question remains whether today's holding affects other provisions of the Affordable Care Act. In considering that question, "[w]e seek to determine what Congress would have intended in light of the Court's constitutional holding." United States v. Booker, 543 U.S. 220, 246 (2005).... The question here is whether Congress would have wanted the rest of the Act to stand, had it known that States would have a genuine choice whether to participate in the new Medicaid expansion. Unless it is "evident" that the answer is no, we must leave the rest of the Act intact.

We are confident that Congress would have wanted to preserve the rest of the Act. It is fair to say that Congress assumed that every State would participate in the Medicaid expansion, given that States had no real choice but to do so. The States contend that Congress enacted the rest of the Act with such full participation in mind; they point out that Congress made Medicaid a means for satisfying the mandate, 26 U.S.C. § 5000A(f)(1)(A)(ii), and enacted no other plan for providing coverage to many low-income individuals. According to the States, this means that the entire Act must fall.

We disagree. The Court today limits the financial pressure the Secretary may apply to induce States to accept the terms of the Medicaid expansion. As a practical matter, that means States may now choose to reject the expansion; that is the whole point. But that does not mean all or even any will. Some States may indeed decline to participate, either because they are unsure they will be able to afford their share of the new funding obligations, or because they are unwilling to commit the administrative resources necessary to support the expansion. Other States, however, may voluntarily sign up, finding the idea of expanding Medicaid coverage attractive, particularly given the level of federal funding the Act offers at the outset.

We have no way of knowing how many States will accept the terms of the expansion, but we do not believe Congress would have wanted the whole Act to fall, simply because some may choose not to participate. The other reforms Congress enacted, after all, will remain "fully operative as a law," and will still function in a way "consistent with Congress' basic objectives in enacting the statute." Confident that Congress would not have intended anything different, we conclude that the rest of the Act need not fall in light of our constitutional holding....

The judgment of the Court of Appeals for the Eleventh Circuit is affirmed in part and reversed in part.

JUSTICE GINSBURG, with whom JUSTICE SOTOMAYOR joins, ... dissenting in part.

.... I would ... hold that the Spending Clause permits the Medicaid expansion exactly as Congress enacted it....

... The spending power conferred by the Constitution, the Court has never doubted, permits Congress to define the contours of programs financed with federal funds. And to expand coverage, Congress could have recalled the existing legislation, and replaced it with a new law making Medicaid as embracive of the poor as Congress chose.

The question posed by the 2010 Medicaid expansion, then, is essentially this: To cover a notably larger population, must Congress take the repeal/reenact route, or may it achieve the same result by amending existing law? The answer should be that Congress may expand by amendment the classes of needy persons entitled to Medicaid benefits. A ritualistic requirement that Congress repeal and reenact spending legislation in order to enlarge the population served by a federally funded program would advance no constitutional principle and would scarcely serve the interests of federalism. To the contrary, such a requirement would rigidify Congress' efforts to empower States by partnering with them in the implementation of federal programs....

THE CHIEF JUSTICE ... concludes that the 2010 expansion is unduly coercive. His conclusion rests on three premises, each of them essential to his theory. First, the Medicaid expansion is, in THE CHIEF JUSTICE's view, a new grant program,.... [and] Congress,

THE CHIEF JUSTICE maintains, has threatened States with the loss of funds from an old program in an effort to get them to adopt a new one. Second, the expansion was unforeseeable by the States when they first signed on to Medicaid. Third, the threatened loss of funding is so large that the States have no real choice but to participate in the Medicaid expansion....

Medicaid, as amended by the ACA, however, is not two spending programs; it is a single program with a constant aim — to enable poor persons to receive basic health care when they need it. Given past expansions, plus express statutory warning that Congress may change the requirements participating States must meet, there can be no tenable claim that the ACA fails for lack of notice. Moreover, States have no entitlement to receive any Medicaid funds; they enjoy only the opportunity to accept funds on Congress' terms. Future Congresses are not bound by their predecessors' dispositions; they have authority to spend federal revenue as they see fit. The Federal Government, therefore, is not, as THE CHIEF JUSTICE charges, threatening States with the loss of "existing" funds from one spending program in order to induce them to opt into another program. Congress is simply requiring States to do what States have long been required to do to receive Medicaid funding: comply with the conditions Congress prescribes for participation.

A majority of the Court, however, buys the argument that prospective withholding of funds formerly available exceeds Congress' spending power. Given that holding, I entirely agree with THE CHIEF JUSTICE as to the appropriate remedy. It is to bar the withholding found impermissible — not, as the joint dissenters would have it, to scrap the expansion altogether, see post, at 46–48. The dissenters' view that the ACA must fall in its entirety is a radical departure from the Court's normal course. When a constitutional infirmity mars a statute, the Court ordinarily removes the infirmity. It undertakes a salvage operation; it does not demolish the legislation.

.... Since 1965, Congress has amended the Medicaid program on more than 50 occasions, sometimes quite sizably. Most relevant here, between 1988 and 1990, Congress required participating States to include among their beneficiaries pregnant women with family incomes up to 133% of the federal poverty level, children up to age 6 at the same income levels, and children ages 6 to 18 with family incomes up to 100% of the poverty level. These amendments added millions to the Medicaid-eligible population....

Compared to past alterations, the ACA is notable for the extent to which the Federal Government will pick up the tab. Medicaid's 2010 expansion is financed largely by federal outlays. In 2014, federal funds will cover 100% of the costs for newly eligible beneficiaries; that rate will gradually decrease before settling at 90% in 2020.

Nor will the expansion exorbitantly increase state Medicaid spending. The Congressional Budget Office (CBO) projects that States will spend 0.8% more than they would have, absent the ACA.

Finally, any fair appraisal of Medicaid would require acknowledgment of the considerable autonomy States enjoy under the Act.... Subject to its basic requirements, the Medicaid Act empowers States to "select dramatically different levels of funding and coverage, alter and experiment with different financing and delivery modes, and opt to cover (or not to cover) a range of particular procedures and therapies. States have leveraged this policy discretion to generate a myriad of dramatically different Medicaid programs over the past several decades." The ACA does not jettison this approach. States, as first-line administrators, will continue to guide the distribution of substantial resources among their needy populations.

The alternative to conditional federal spending, it bears emphasis, is not state autonomy but state marginalization. In 1965, Congress elected to nationalize health coverage for seniors through Medicare. It could similarly have established Medicaid as an exclusively federal program. Instead, Congress gave the States the opportunity to partner in the program's administration and development. Absent from the nationalized model, of course, is the state-level policy discretion and experimentation that is Medicaid's hallmark; undoubtedly the interests of federalism are better served when States retain a meaningful role in the implementation of a program of such importance....

Congress' authority to condition the use of federal funds is not confined to spending programs as first launched. The legislature may, and often does, amend the law, imposing new conditions grant recipients henceforth must meet in order to continue receiving funds.

Yes, there are federalism-based limits on the use of Congress' conditional spending power.... The Court in Dole mentioned, but did not adopt, a ... limitation, one hypothetically raised a half-century earlier: In "some circumstances," Congress might be prohibited from offering a "financial inducement ... so coercive as to pass the point at which 'pressure turns into compulsion.'" Prior to today's decision, however, the Court has never ruled that the terms of any grant crossed the indistinct line between temptation and coercion....

This case does not present the concerns that led the Court in Dole even to consider the prospect of coercion. In Dole, the condition—set 21 as the minimum drinking age—did not tell the States how to use funds Congress provided for highway construction. Further, in view of the Twenty-First Amendment, it was an open question whether Congress could directly impose a national minimum drinking age.

The ACA, in contrast, relates solely to the federally funded Medicaid program; if States choose not to comply, Congress has not threatened to withhold funds earmarked for any other program. Nor does the ACA use Medicaid funding to induce States to take action Congress itself could not undertake. The Federal Government undoubtedly could operate its own health-care program for poor persons, just as it operates Medicare for seniors' health care.

That is what makes this such a simple case, and the Court's decision so unsettling. Congress, aiming to assist the needy, has appropriated federal money to subsidize state health-insurance programs that meet federal standards. The principal standard the ACA sets is that the state program cover adults earning no more than 133% of the federal poverty line. Enforcing that prescription ensures that federal funds will be spent on health care for the poor in furtherance of Congress' present perception of the general welfare....

The starting premise on which THE CHIEF JUSTICE's coercion analysis rests is that the ACA did not really "extend" Medicaid; instead, Congress created an entirely new program to co-exist with the old. THE CHIEF JUSTICE calls the ACA new, but in truth, it simply reaches more of America's poor than Congress originally covered....

Congress has broad authority to construct or adjust spending programs to meet its contemporary understanding of "the general Welfare." Helvering v. Davis, 301 U.S. 619, 640–641 (1937). Courts owe a large measure of respect to Congress' characterization of the grant programs it establishes. See Steward Machine, 301 U.S., at 594. Even if courts were inclined to second-guess Congress' conception of the character of its legislation, how would reviewing judges divine whether an Act of Congress, purporting to amend a law, is in reality not an amendment, but a new creation? At what point does an extension become so large that it "transforms" the basic law?

Endeavoring to show that Congress created a new program, THE CHIEF JUSTICE cites three aspects of the expansion. First, he asserts that, in covering those earning no more than 133% of the federal poverty line, the Medicaid expansion, unlike pre-ACA Medicaid, does not "care for the neediest among us." What makes that so? Single adults earning no more than $14,856 per year—133% of the current federal poverty level—surely rank among the Nation's poor. Second, according to THE CHIEF JUSTICE, "Congress mandated that newly eligible persons receive a level of coverage that is less comprehensive than the traditional Medicaid benefit package." Ibid. That less comprehensive benefit package, however, is not an innovation introduced by the ACA; since 2006, States have been free to use it for many of their Medicaid beneficiaries. The level of benefits offered therefore does not set apart post-ACA Medicaid recipients from all those entitled to benefits pre-ACA.

Third, THE CHIEF JUSTICE correctly notes that the reimbursement rate for participating States is different regarding individuals who became Medicaid-eligible through the ACA. Ibid. But the rate differs only in its generosity to participating States. Under pre-ACA Medicaid, the Federal Government pays up to 83% of the costs of coverage for current enrollees, § 1396d(b) (2006 ed. and Supp. IV); under the ACA, the federal contribution starts at 100% and will eventually settle at 90%, § 1396d(y). Even if one agreed that a change of as little as 7 percentage points carries constitutional significance, is it not passing strange to suggest that the purported incursion on state sovereignty might have been averted, or at least mitigated, had Congress offered States less money to carry out the same obligations?

Consider also that Congress could have repealed Medicaid. Thereafter, Congress could have enacted Medicaid II, a new program combining the pre-2010 coverage with the expanded coverage required by the ACA. By what right does a court stop Congress from building up without first tearing down? ...

Pennhurst thus instructs that "if Congress intends to impose a condition on the grant of federal moneys, it must do so unambiguously." That requirement is met in this case. Section 2001 does not take effect until 2014. The ACA makes perfectly clear what will be required of States that accept Medicaid funding after that date: They must extend eligibility to adults with incomes no more than 133% of the federal poverty line.

THE CHIEF JUSTICE appears to find in Pennhurst a requirement that, when spending legislation is first passed, or when States first enlist in the federal program, Congress must provide clear notice of conditions it might later impose. If I understand his point correctly, it was incumbent on Congress, in 1965, to warn the States clearly of the size and shape potential changes to Medicaid might take. And absent such notice, sizable changes could not be made mandatory. Our decisions do not support such a requirement....

When future Spending Clause challenges arrive, as they likely will in the wake of today's decision, how will litigants and judges assess whether "a State has a legitimate choice whether to accept the federal conditions in exchange for federal funds"? Are courts to measure the number of dollars the Federal Government might withhold for noncompliance? The portion of the State's budget at stake? And which State's—or States'—budget is de-terminative: the lead plaintiff, all challenging States (26 in this case, many with quite different fiscal situations), or some national median? Does it matter that Florida, unlike most States, imposes no state income tax, and therefore might be able to replace foregone federal funds with new state revenue? Or that the coercion state officials in fact fear is punishment at the ballot box for turning down a politically popular federal grant?

The coercion inquiry, therefore, appears to involve political judgments that defy judicial calculation....

At bottom, my colleagues' position is that the States' reliance on federal funds limits Congress' authority to alter its spending programs. This gets things backwards: Congress, not the States, is tasked with spending federal money in service of the general welfare. And each successive Congress is empowered to appropriate funds as it sees fit. When the 110th Congress reached a conclusion about Medicaid funds that differed from its predecessors' view, it abridged no State's right to "existing," or "pre-existing," funds. For, in fact, there are no such funds. There is only money States anticipate receiving from future Congresses.

… [I]n view of THE CHIEF JUSTICE's disposition, I agree with him that the Medicaid Act's severability clause determines the appropriate remedy.… The Court does not strike down any provision of the ACA. It prohibits only the "application" of the Secretary's authority to withhold Medicaid funds from States that decline to conform their Medicaid plans to the ACA's requirements. Thus the ACA's authorization of funds to finance the expansion remains intact, and the Secretary's authority to withhold funds for reasons other than noncompliance with the expansion remains unaffected.

JUSTICE SCALIA, JUSTICE KENNEDY, JUSTICE THOMAS, and JUSTICE ALITO, dissenting.

…. When Congress makes grants to the States, it customarily attaches conditions, and this Court has long held that the Constitution generally permits Congress to do this.… This practice of attaching conditions to federal funds greatly increases federal power. "[O]bjectives not thought to be within Article I's enumerated legislative fields, may nevertheless be attained through the use of the spending power and the conditional grant of federal funds." Dole, supra, at 207.

This formidable power, if not checked in any way, would present a grave threat to the system of federalism created by our Constitution. If Congress' "Spending Clause power to pursue objectives outside of Article I's enumerated legislative fields," is "limited only by Congress' notion of the general welfare, the reality, given the vast financial resources of the Federal Government, is that the Spending Clause gives 'power to the Congress to tear down the barriers, to invade the states' jurisdiction, and to become a parliament of the whole people, subject to no restrictions save such as are self-imposed,'" Dole, supra, at 217 (O'Connor, J., dissenting).…

…. When a heavy federal tax is levied to support a federal program that offers large grants to the States, States may, as a practical matter, be unable to refuse to participate in the federal program and to substitute a state alternative. Even if a State believes that the federal program is ineffective and inefficient, withdrawal would likely force the State to impose a huge tax increase on its residents, and this new state tax would come on top of the federal taxes already paid by residents to support subsidies to participating States.…

Whether federal spending legislation crosses the line from enticement to coercion is often difficult to determine, and courts should not conclude that legislation is unconstitutional on this ground unless the coercive nature of an offer is unmistakably clear. In this case, however, there can be no doubt.…

… In crafting the ACA, Congress clearly expressed its informed view that no State could possibly refuse the offer that the ACA extends.…

If Congress had thought that States might actually refuse to go along with the expansion of Medicaid, Congress would surely have devised a backup scheme so that the most vulnerable groups in our society, those previously eligible for Medicaid, would not be left out in the cold. But nowhere in the over 900-page Act is such a scheme to be found.

By contrast, because Congress thought that some States might decline federal funding for the operation of a "health benefit exchange," Congress provided a backup scheme; if a State declines to participate in the operation of an exchange, the Federal Government will step in and operate an exchange in that State....

The Federal Government does not dispute the inference that Congress anticipated 100% state participation, but it argues that this assumption was based on the fact that ACA's offer was an "exceedingly generous" gift.... If that offer is "exceedingly generous," as the Federal Government maintains, why have more than half the States brought this lawsuit, contending that the offer is coercive? And why did Congress find it necessary to threaten that any State refusing to accept this "exceedingly generous" gift would risk losing all Medicaid funds? ...

Seven Members of the Court agree that the Medicaid Expansion, as enacted by Congress, is unconstitutional. See (opinion of ROBERTS, C. J., joined by BREYER and KAGAN, JJ.). Because the Medicaid Expansion is unconstitutional, the question of remedy arises....

The Court has applied a two-part guide as the frame-work for severability analysis.... First, if the Court holds a statutory provision unconstitutional, it then determines whether the now truncated statute will operate in the manner Congress intended. If not, the remaining provisions must be invalidated....

Second, even if the remaining provisions can operate as Congress designed them to operate, the Court must determine if Congress would have enacted them standing alone and without the unconstitutional portion. If Congress would not, those provisions, too, must be invalidated....

Major provisions of the Affordable Care Act—i.e., the insurance regulations and taxes, the reductions in federal reimbursements to hospitals and other Medicare spending reductions, the exchanges and their federal subsidies, and the employer responsibility assessment—cannot remain once the Individual Mandate and Medicaid Expansion are invalid. That result follows from the undoubted inability of the other major provisions to operate as Congress intended without the Individual Mandate and Medicaid Expansion. Absent the invalid portions, the other major provisions could impose enormous risks of unexpected burdens on patients, the health-care community, and the federal budget. That consequence would be in absolute conflict with the ACA's design of "shared responsibility," and would pose a threat to the Nation that Congress did not intend....

This Court must not impose risks unintended by Congress or produce legislation Congress may have lacked the support to enact. For those reasons, the unconstitutionality of both the Individual Mandate and the Medicaid Expansion requires the invalidation of the Affordable Care Act's other provisions....

The Court today decides to save a statute Congress did not write. It rules that what the statute declares to be a requirement with a penalty is instead an option subject to a tax. And it changes the intentionally coercive sanction of a total cut-off of Medicaid funds to a supposedly noncoercive cut-off of only the incremental funds that the Act makes available.

The Court regards its strained statutory interpretation as judicial modesty. It is not. It amounts instead to a vast judicial overreaching. It creates a debilitated, inoperable version of health-care regulation that Congress did not enact and the public does not expect. It makes enactment of sensible health-care regulation more difficult, since Congress cannot start afresh but must take as its point of departure a jumble of now senseless provisions, provisions that certain interests favored under the Court's new design will struggle to retain. And it leaves the public and the States to expend vast sums of money on requirements that may or may not survive the necessary congressional revision.…

For the reasons here stated, we would find the Act invalid in its entirety. We respectfully dissent.

Review Questions and Explanations: The Affordable Care Act Case *(spending power excerpt)*

1. The "joint dissent" fundamentally agreed with the analysis in the plurality opinion that the spending power was violated. See note 1 in "Review Questions and Explanations" following the Commerce Clause excerpt of *NFIB v. Sebelius*.

2. Recall the debate between the *Dole* majority and dissent over how close the goal of the funding restriction had to be to the goal of the original funding. Isn't raising the economic cutoff for eligibility for Medicaid even more closely related to the existing program than what was allowed in *Dole*—regulating the drinking age of drivers and non-drivers alike to promote (supposedly) highway safety? Does this suggest that the plurality in the ACA case is siding with Justice O'Connor's *Dole* dissent on this issue?

3. Consider this statement from the plurality opinion: "[Medicaid expansions will cover] the entire nonelderly population with income below 133 percent of the poverty level. It is no longer a program to care for the neediest among us, but rather an element of a comprehensive national plan to provide universal health insurance coverage." Do you agree with the claim that the ACA changes the nature of Medicaid? Note that in 2012, 133% of the poverty level translates into about $30,000 annual income for a family of four. Also, wouldn't Medicaid be part of any "comprehensive universal health coverage plan" even in its current form, so long as it wasn't superseded?

4. The Court ruled that the provision permitting withdrawal of all Medicaid funds from states refusing to participate in Medicaid expansion was unduly coercive under *Dole* and the Tenth Amendment cases. This, in effect, holds the provision invalid "on its face," i.e., in all its potential applications. But the Secretary had discretion to apply far less draconian penalties. Moreover, how likely is it that the Secretary would withdraw all state Medicaid funds—thereby risking leaving that state's Medicaid recipients totally destitute? Could the Court have treated the issue as an "as applied challenge," and waited to see just how far the Secretary would try to go with specific non-complying states, and then see if the level was coercive? Recall that *Dole* upheld a 5% holdback of highway funds as non-coercive; the line where coercion occurs has still yet to be drawn. All we know now is that it lies somewhere between 5% and 100%.

5. Justice Ginsburg argues that Congress could have achieved Medicaid expansion by repealing existing Medicaid and reenacting the new expanded version—making all funding fully conditional on the new version of the program. If so, isn't it unduly formalistic to require that step, as she argues? On the other hand, does the plurality suggest that such a step would be unconstitutional? If that's correct, is the plurality implying that Congress cannot repeal federal funding programs where the states have built up a heavy reliance on the funds?

F. The Civil War Amendments

So far in this chapter, we have examined congressional powers based on Article I, § 8. The following materials introduce an additional source of congressional power: the three amendments enacted within the five years immediately after the Civil War. These Amendments—the Thirteenth, Fourteenth and Fifteenth—vary in their substantive coverage, but each includes an identical "enforcement provision," which states that "Congress shall have the power to enforce this article by appropriate legislation." The enforcement provisions, like the Commerce Clause, are thus an affirmative grant of power to Congress to enact legislation in a given issue area. The dispute in the following cases involves just what is and is not included in that grant of legislative power.

Although each of the Civil War Amendments includes an enforcement provision, our discussion will focus on the application of the clause within the Fourteenth Amendment, which is arguably the broadest in scope of the Civil War Amendments. There are four substantive provisions of the Fourteenth Amendment. The most important one for our purposes is Section 1, which reads in pertinent part as follows:

> No State shall make or enforce any law which shall abridge the privileges or immunities of citizens of the United States; nor shall any State deprive any person of life, liberty, or property, without due process of law; nor deny to any person within its jurisdiction the equal protection of the laws.

The meaning of these words, particularly the final clause (the Equal Protection Clause) is hotly contested and forms the foundation of many of the constitutional disputes about individual rights covered later in this casebook. One of the keys to understanding the materials that follow here is to remember that our focus in this section is not about those disputes. Rather, it is about the nature of the authority granted to Congress, through the enforcement provisions, to legislate to enforce those rights *whatever* they are. Our purpose, in other words, is to understand how the Court evaluates the *relationship* between the underlying right and Congress's power to regulate regarding it, *not* to understand the scope of the right itself.

That said, some understanding about the underlying substantive right being protected is necessary to understand the cases in this section. This section is structured to give to you enough background information about the substantive rights at issue to enable you to understand the enforcement provision cases. But you should not be troubled if you do not fully grasp at this point the reasoning behind the Court's decisions about the substantive content of the underlying right itself.

There are two distinct questions presented by the enforcement provisions. The first is the question just raised: *what* may Congress regulate under these clauses? The second is *whom* Congress can regulate under these clauses.

In regard to the first question—what may Congress regulate—the Court has taken two different approaches. The first approach, set forth in the first case you read below, gives Congress broad authority to regulate most things related to civil rights. The second approach, which is developed in the more recent cases, restricts congressional power to things that either remedy or prevent violations of *judicially* recognized rights—rights the Court (and only the Court) has identified as protected by the substantive provisions of the Fourteenth Amendment. The dispute in cases taking the second approach then becomes the extent to which the Court should defer to congressional judgment about whether a particular piece of legislation is necessary to remedy or prevent such violations.

The second question (*whom* may Congress regulate) is more straightforward, although it does, as we will see, pose some doctrinal challenges.

Several of the cases you will read in this section arise in the context of disputes about the Eleventh Amendment. The Eleventh Amendment, as you will see, prevents states from being subjected to certain types of lawsuits in federal courts. The reason so many enforcement clause cases come up in the context of the Eleventh Amendment is because the Court has held that Congress can authorize otherwise prohibited suits against states when it is acting under its enforcement clause powers, but not when it is acting under its Article I powers. In other words, if Congress wants to abrogate a state's Eleventh Amendment immunity, it can do so *only* when acting under the power granted by the Civil War Amendments. (The reason for this is explained in two of cases examined below, *Fitzpatrick* and *Seminole Tribe*.) Consequently, a key question in Eleventh Amendment cases often is whether the law passed by Congress is in fact a valid exercise of its enforcement provision powers. But keep in mind when reading these cases that your goal at this point is not to learn all the intricacies of Eleventh Amendment doctrine, but rather to know just enough about the Eleventh Amendment to enable you to focus on the enforcement provision doctrine developed and applied in these cases.

Your progress through these materials will be smoother if you remember to keep your eye on the ball of congressional power: what, and whom, do the enforcement provisions allow Congress to regulate? These are the key questions presented in this section; the other materials are just the tools you need to help you answer them.

1. Foundational Doctrine

As noted, the Court has taken two distinct approaches to the question of what Congress can regulate under its Fourteenth Amendment enforcement power. The first case, *Katzenbach v. Morgan,* suggests that Congress has broad authority to promote civil rights. A more restrictive approach, developed in the more recent cases, *City of Boerne v. Flores* and *United States v. Morrison*, limits congressional power to things that either remedy or prevent violations of judicially recognized rights—rights the Court itself has identified as protected by the substantive provisions of the Fourteenth Amendment. The dispute in cases taking the second approach then becomes the extent to which the Court should defer to congressional judgment about whether a particular piece of legislation is necessary to remedy or prevent such violations.

Your goal in reading these cases is to understand the basic structure of how the enforcement provisions work, and to start thinking about the arguments supporting each of the competing interpretations.

Guided Reading Questions: *Katzenbach v. Morgan*

1. How does the majority in *Katzenbach* define Congress's enforcement provision powers? What, in other words, does the majority see as the scope of congressional powers under this clause?

2. Justice Brennan uses textual, structural and historical arguments to support his opinion. Can you separately identify each of these arguments?

Katzenbach v. Morgan
384 U.S. 641 (1966)

Majority: *Brennan*, Warren (CJ), Black, Clark, White, Fortas

Concurrence: *Douglas*

Dissents: *Harlan*, Stewart

MR. JUSTICE BRENNAN delivered the opinion of the Court.

These cases concern the constitutionality of § 4(e) of the Voting Rights Act of 1965. That law, in the respects pertinent in these cases, provides that no person who has successfully completed the sixth primary grade in a public school in, or a private school accredited by, the Commonwealth of Puerto Rico in which the language of instruction was other than English shall be denied the right to vote in any election because of his inability to read or write English. Appellees, registered voters in New York City, brought this suit to challenge the constitutionality of § 4(e) insofar as it *pro tanto* prohibits the enforcement of the election laws of New York requiring an ability to read and write English as a condition of voting. Under these laws many of the several hundred thousand New York City residents who have migrated there from the Commonwealth of Puerto Rico had previously been denied the right to vote, and appellees attack § 4(e) insofar as it would enable many of these citizens to vote. Pursuant to § 14(b) of the Voting Rights Act of 1965, appellees commenced this proceeding in the District Court for the District of Columbia seeking a declaration that § 4(e) is invalid and an injunction prohibiting appellants, the Attorney General of the United States and the New York City Board of Elections, from either enforcing or complying with § 4(e).... We hold that, in the application challenged in these cases, § 4(e) is a proper exercise of the powers granted to Congress by § 5 of the Fourteenth Amendment and that by force of the Supremacy Clause, Article VI, the New York English literacy requirement cannot be enforced to the extent that it is inconsistent with § 4(e)....

The Attorney General of the State of New York argues that an exercise of congressional power under § 5 of the Fourteenth Amendment that prohibits the enforcement of a state law can only be sustained if the judicial branch determines that the state law is prohibited by the provisions of the Amendment that Congress sought to enforce. More specifically, he urges that § 4(e) cannot be sustained as appropriate legislation to enforce the Equal Protection Clause unless the judiciary decides — even with the guidance of a congressional judgment — that the application of the English literacy requirement prohibited by § 4(e) is forbidden by the Equal Protection Clause itself. We disagree. Neither the language nor history of § 5 supports such a construction. As was said with regard to § 5 in Ex parte Com. of Virginia: 'It is the power of Congress which has been enlarged. Congress is authorized to enforce the prohibitions by appropriate legislation. Some legislation is contemplated to make the amendments fully effective.' A construction of § 5 that would require a judicial determination that the enforcement of the state law precluded by Congress violated the Amendment, as a condition of sustaining the congressional enactment, would depreciate both congressional resourcefulness and congressional responsibility for implementing the Amendment. It would confine the legislative power in this context to the insignificant role of abrogating only those state laws that the judicial branch was prepared to adjudge unconstitutional, or of merely informing the judgment of the judiciary by particularizing the 'majestic generalities' of § 1 of the Amendment....

Thus our task in this case is not to determine whether the New York English literacy requirement as applied to deny the right to vote to a person who successfully completed the sixth grade in a Puerto Rican school violates the Equal Protection Clause. Accordingly, our decision in Lassiter v. Northampton County Bd. of Election, sustaining the North Carolina English literacy requirement as not in all circumstances prohibited by the first sections of the Fourteenth and Fifteenth Amendments, is inapposite.... Lassiter did not present the question before us here: Without regard to whether the judiciary would find that the Equal Protection Clause itself nullifies New York's English literacy requirement as so applied, could Congress prohibit the enforcement of the state law by legislating under §5 of the Fourteenth Amendment? In answering this question, our task is limited to determining whether such legislation is, as required by §5, appropriate legislation to enforce the Equal Protection Clause.

By including §5 the draftsmen sought to grant to Congress, by a specific provision applicable to the Fourteenth Amendment, the same broad powers expressed in the Necessary and Proper Clause, Art. I, §8, cl. 18. The classic formulation of the reach of those powers was established by Chief Justice Marshall in McCulloch v. Maryland 'Let the end be legitimate, let it be within the scope of the constitution, and all means which are appropriate, which are plainly adapted to that end, which are not prohibited, but consist with the letter and spirit of the constitution, are constitutional.' Ex parte Com. of Virginia, decided 12 years after the adoption of the Fourteenth Amendment, held that congressional power under §5 had this same broad scope: 'Whatever legislation is appropriate, that is, adapted to carry out the objects the amendments have in view, whatever tends to enforce submission to the prohibitions they contain, and to secure to all persons the enjoyment of perfect equality of civil rights and the equal protection of the laws against State denial or invasion, if not prohibited, is brought within the domain of congressional power.'...

There can be no doubt that §4(e) may be regarded as an enactment to enforce the Equal Protection Clause. Congress explicitly declared that it enacted §4(e) 'to secure the rights under the Fourteenth Amendment of persons educated in American-flag schools in which the predominant classroom language was other than English.' The persons referred to include those who have migrated from the Commonwealth of Puerto Rico to New York and who have been denied the right to vote because of their inability to read and write English, and the Fourteenth Amendment rights referred to include those emanating from the Equal Protection Clause. More specifically, §4(e) may be viewed as a measure to secure for the Puerto Rican community residing in New York nondiscriminatory treatment by government—both in the imposition of voting qualifications and the provision or administration of governmental services, such as public schools, public housing and law enforcement.

Section 4(e) may be readily seen as 'plainly adapted' to furthering these aims of the Equal Protection Clause. The practical effect of §4(e) is to prohibit New York from denying the right to vote to large segments of its Puerto Rican community. Congress has thus prohibited the State from denying to that community the right that is 'preservative of all rights.' Yick Wo v. Hopkins. This enhanced political power will be helpful in gaining nondiscriminatory treatment in public services for the entire Puerto Rican community. Section 4(e) thereby enables the Puerto Rican minority better to obtain 'perfect equality of civil rights and the equal protection of the laws.' It was well within congressional authority to say that this need of the Puerto Rican minority for the vote warranted federal intrusion upon any state interests served by the English literacy requirement. It was for Congress, as the branch that made this judgment, to assess and weigh the various conflicting considerations—the risk or pervasiveness of the discrimination in governmental services, the effectiveness of eliminating the state restriction on the right to vote as a means of dealing with the evil, the adequacy or availability of alternative remedies, and the nature and significance of the state interests that would be affected by the nullification of the

English literacy requirement as applied to residents who have successfully completed the sixth grade in a Puerto Rican school. It is not for us to review the congressional resolution of these factors. It is enough that we be able to perceive a basis upon which the Congress might resolve the conflict as it did. There plainly was such a basis to support § 4(e) in the application in question in this case. Any contrary conclusion would require us to be blind to the realities familiar to the legislators.

The result is no different if we confine our inquiry to the question whether § 4(e) was merely legislation aimed at the elimination of an invidious discrimination in establishing voter qualifications. We are told that New York's English literacy requirement originated in the desire to provide an incentive for non-English speaking immigrants to learn the English language and in order to assure the intelligent exercise of the franchise. Yet Congress might well have questioned, in light of the many exemptions provided, and some evidence suggesting that prejudice played a prominent role in the enactment of the requirement whether these were actually the interests being served. Congress might have also questioned whether denial of a right deemed so precious and fundamental in our society was a necessary or appropriate means of encouraging persons to learn English, or of furthering the goal of an intelligent exercise of the franchise. Finally, Congress might well have concluded that as a means of furthering the intelligent exercise of the franchise, an ability to read or understand Spanish is as effective as ability to read English for those to whom Spanish-language newspapers and Spanish-language radio and television programs are available to inform them of election issues and governmental affairs. Since Congress undertook to legislate so as to preclude the enforcement of the state law, and did so in the context of a general appraisal of literacy requirements for voting, see State of South Carolina v. Katzenbach, supra, to which it brought a specially informed legislative competence, it was Congress' prerogative to weigh these competing considerations. Reversed.

MR. JUSTICE HARLAN, with whom MR. JUSTICE STEWART agrees, dissenting.

When recognized state violations of federal constitutional standards have occurred, Congress is of course empowered by § 5 to take appropriate remedial measures to redress and prevent the wrongs.... But it is a judicial question whether the condition with which Congress has thus sought to deal is in truth an infringement of the Constitution, something that is the necessary prerequisite to bringing the § 5 power into play at all. Thus, in Ex parte Virginia, supra, involving a federal statute making it a federal crime to disqualify anyone from jury service because of race, the Court first held as a matter of constitutional law that 'the Fourteenth Amendment secures, among other civil rights, to colored men, when charged with criminal offences against a State, an impartial jury trial, by jurors in-differently selected or chosen without discrimination against such jurors because of their color.' ... Only then did the Court hold that to enforce this prohibition upon state dis-crimination, Congress could enact a criminal statute of the type under consideration....

A more recent Fifteenth Amendment case also serves to illustrate this distinction. In State of South Carolina v. Katzenbach, decided earlier this Term, we held certain remedial sections of this Voting Rights Act of 1965 constitutional under the Fifteenth Amendment, which is directed against deprivations of the right to vote on account of race. In enacting those sections of the Voting Rights Act the Congress made a detailed investigation of various state practices that had been used to deprive Negroes of the franchise.... In passing upon the remedial provisions, we reviewed first the 'voluminous legislative history' as well as judicial precedents supporting the basic congressional finding that the clear commands of the Fifteenth Amendment had been infringed by various state subterfuges.... Given the existence of the evil, we held the remedial steps taken by the legislature under the Enforcement Clause of the Fifteenth Amendment to be a justifiable exercise of congressional initiative.

Section 4(e), however, presents a significantly different type of congressional enactment. The question here is not whether the statute is appropriate remedial legislation to cure an established violation of a constitutional command, but whether there has in fact been an infringement of that constitutional command, that is, whether a particular state practice or, as here, a statute is so arbitrary or irrational as to offend the command of the Equal Protection Clause of the Fourteenth Amendment. That question is one for the judicial branch ultimately to determine. Were the rule otherwise, Congress would be able to qualify this Court's constitutional decisions under the Fourteenth and Fifteenth Amendments let alone those under other provisions of the Constitution, by resorting to congressional power under the Necessary and Proper Clause. In view of this Court's holding in Lassiter, supra, that an English literacy test is a permissible exercise of state supervision over its franchise, I do not think it is open to Congress to limit the effect of that decision as it has undertaken to do by § 4(e). In effect the Court reads § 5 of the Fourteenth Amendment as giving Congress the power to define the substantive scope of the Amendment. If that indeed be the true reach of § 5, then I do not see why Congress should not be able as well to exercise its § 5 'discretion' by enacting statutes so as in effect to dilute equal protection and due process decisions of this Court. In all such cases there is room for reasonable men to differ as to whether or not a denial of equal protection or due process has occurred, and the final decision is one of judgment. Until today this judgment has always been one for the judiciary to resolve.

I do not mean to suggest in what has been said that a legislative judgment of the type incorporated in § 4(e) is without any force whatsoever. Decisions on questions of equal protection and due process are based not on abstract logic, but on empirical foundations. To the extent 'legislative facts' are relevant to a judicial determination, Congress is well equipped to investigate them, and such determinations are of course entitled to due respect. In State of South Carolina v. Katzenbach, supra, such legislative findings were made to show that racial discrimination in voting was actually occurring. Similarly, in Heart of Atlanta Motel, Inc. v. United States and Katzenback v. McClung, this Court upheld Title II of the Civil Rights Act of 1964 under the Commerce Clause. There again the congressional determination that racial discrimination in a clearly defined group of public accommodations did effectively impede interstate commerce was based on 'voluminous testimony,' ... which had been put before the Congress and in the context of which it passed remedial legislation....

Review Questions and Explanations: *Katzenbach*

1. Both the majority and dissenting opinion discuss *Lassiter v. Northampton County*. *Lassiter* holds that English literacy requirements do not themselves violate the Fourteenth Amendment. Congress nonetheless legislated to prohibit the states (and their subdivisions) from imposing them. This itself is not extraordinary — Congress enacts all kinds of legislation not *required* by the Constitution. The question in such cases is whether Congress has the *power* to enact the legislation. In *Katzenbach*, Congress argued that it had such power under § 5 of the Fourteenth Amendment (the enforcement provision). The question then, is not one of what the Constitution requires, but what it allows. Make sure you understand this point before moving forward.

2. Read carefully the two paragraphs right before the final paragraph of the majority opinion. These paragraphs arguably offer a more limited understanding

of enforcement provision powers than does the rest of the opinion. Can you explain how the argument presented in these paragraphs differs from (and is more limited than) the rest of the majority opinion?

The next case you will read is *City of Boerne v. Flores*. Much of the substantive law at issue in *Boerne* involves assertions of individual rights that do not directly concern us here. However, there are two bits of background information you must know in order to understand the enforcement provision part of the case. The first involves the substantive law of the Free Exercise Clause of the First Amendment. The second is why the Free Exercise Clause has anything at all do to with congressional powers under the Fourteenth Amendment. Each of these issues is discussed in turn below.

a. The Free Exercise Clause of the First Amendment

The Free Exercise Clause of the First Amendment protects people's right to practice their chosen religion. The question presented in free exercise cases is the extent to which government can interfere with this right. Prior to *Boerne*, the Court had decided a Free Exercise clause case called *Employment Division v. Smith*. (You will read *Smith* later in Chapter 10.) *Smith* involves an individual who was denied unemployment benefits after being fired from his job for ingesting peyote, a hallucinogenic drug. Peyote was classified by Oregon as an illegal substance. Mr. Smith argued that he had used peyote as part of a traditional Native American religious ceremony, and that penalizing him for such usage violated his free exercise rights.

Prior to *Smith*, the doctrinal rule governing free exercise cases was that the government could not burden a religious practice unless it had a compelling reason for doing so. (This type of test is often referred to as a *strict scrutiny* test, meaning that the government's reasons for the law must be compelling and that the law must be narrowly tailored to meet those reasons. Strict scrutiny frequently is used in individual rights cases.) The *Smith* Court, in an opinion written by Justice Scalia, rejected Mr. Smith's constitutional claim, holding that strict scrutiny would not apply to laws burdening religious exercise *unless* the law was specifically targeted at suppressing the religious practice or implicated some additional constitutional concern. Generally applicable laws not targeted at religious practices would only have to be supported by rational—not compelling—reasons, and would not have to be narrowly tailored.

Congress was not pleased with the *Smith* decision, and soon passed the Religious Freedom Restoration Act (RFRA). This Act is the law being challenged in *Boerne*. The question presented in *Boerne* is whether Congress had authority under the enforcement provision of the Fourteenth Amendment to enact RFRA.

b. The Incorporation Doctrine

The second bit of background information you need to know before reading *Boerne* is how the interpretation of the Free Exercise clause becomes relevant in a Fourteenth Amendment case. The answer is a complex doctrine called "incorporation" that you will learn about later in this casebook. The nutshell version is this. The original Bill of Rights only imposed limitations on the federal government, not the states—states could not be held to have violated the rights set forth in the Bill of Rights because those rights simply did not restrict the actions of state governments. The Civil War Amendments changed that. The Court held that the Due Process clause of the Fourteenth Amendment "incorporates" against the states most of the individual rights protected in the first eight Amendments, meaning that now neither state governments nor the federal government can do things that violate those rights. This is why many of the individual rights cases you have read so far in law school—such as most of those read in your criminal procedure classes—begin with a statement asserting that one of the parties is arguing that her Fourth (or Fifth or Sixth or Eighth) Amendment *and* her Fourteenth Amendment rights have been violated.

The consequence of incorporation of the First Amendment, for current purposes, is that when a state violates the Free Exercise clause (as asserted in *Smith* and also in *Boerne*) the state is necessarily *also* violating the Fourteenth Amendment. Therefore, whatever power Congress has to remedy or prevent violations of the Fourteenth Amendment also allows it to remedy or prevent violations of these other amendments because they are "incorporated" into—are part of—the Fourteenth Amendment.

Guided Reading Questions: *City of Boerne v. Flores*

1. With these background points in mind, read *Boerne*. When reading the case, pay close attention to the argument the government is making. Why did Congress think RFRA was within its enforcement clause powers, and why does the Court disagree?

2. Under Justice Kennedy's test, can Congress use its enforcement clause powers to prohibit things that are not themselves a violation of a judicially recognized constitutional right?

3. What is the "congruence and proportionality" test and how does Justice Kennedy use it in *Boerne*?

City of Boerne v. Flores

521 U.S. 507 (1997)

Majority: *Kennedy,* Rehnquist (CJ), Stevens, Scalia, Thomas, Ginsburg

Concurrences: *Stevens, Scalia* (both omitted)

Dissents: *O'Connor, Breyer, Souter* (all omitted)

JUSTICE KENNEDY delivered the opinion of the Court.

The parties disagree over whether RFRA is a proper exercise of Congress' § 5 power "to enforce" by "appropriate legislation" the constitutional guarantee that no State shall deprive any person of "life, liberty, or property, without due process of law" nor deny any person "equal protection of the laws."

In defense of the Act, respondent the Archbishop contends, with support from the United States, that RFRA is permissible enforcement legislation. Congress, it is said, is only protecting by legislation one of the liberties guaranteed by the Fourteenth Amendment's

Due Process Clause, the free exercise of religion, beyond what is necessary under *Smith*. It is said the congressional decision to dispense with proof of deliberate or overt discrimination and instead concentrate on a law's effects accords with the settled understanding that § 5 includes the power to enact legislation designed to prevent, as well as remedy, constitutional violations. It is further contended that Congress' § 5 power is not limited to remedial or preventive legislation....

Legislation which deters or remedies constitutional violations can fall within the sweep of Congress' enforcement power even if in the process it prohibits conduct which is not itself unconstitutional and intrudes into "legislative spheres of autonomy previously reserved to the States." For example, the Court upheld a suspension of literacy tests and similar voting requirements under Congress' parallel power to enforce the provisions of the Fifteenth Amendment as a measure to combat racial discrimination in voting, South Carolina v. Katzenbach, despite the facial constitutionality of the tests under Lassiter v. Northampton County Bd. of Elections. We have also concluded that other measures protecting voting rights are within Congress' power to enforce the Fourteenth and Fifteenth Amendments, despite the burdens those measures placed on the States....

It is also true, however, that "[a]s broad as the congressional enforcement power is, it is not unlimited." Oregon v. Mitchell. In assessing the breadth of § 5's enforcement power, we begin with its text. Congress has been given the power "to enforce" the "provisions of this article." We agree with respondent, of course, that Congress can enact legislation under § 5 enforcing the constitutional right to the free exercise of religion. The "provisions of this article," to which § 5 refers, include the Due Process Clause of the Fourteenth Amendment. Congress' power to enforce the Free Exercise Clause follows from our holding in ... that the "fundamental concept of liberty embodied in [the Fourteenth Amendment's Due Process Clause] embraces the liberties guaranteed by the First Amendment." ...

Congress' power under § 5, however, extends only to "enforc[ing]" the provisions of the Fourteenth Amendment. The Court has described this power as "remedial," ... The design of the Amendment and the text of § 5 are inconsistent with the suggestion that Congress has the power to decree the substance of the Fourteenth Amendment's restrictions on the States. Legislation which alters the meaning of the Free Exercise Clause cannot be said to be enforcing the Clause. Congress does not enforce a constitutional right by changing what the right is. It has been given the power "to enforce," not the power to determine what constitutes a constitutional violation. Were it not so, what Congress would be enforcing would no longer be, in any meaningful sense, the "provisions of [the Fourteenth Amendment]."

While the line between measures that remedy or prevent unconstitutional actions and measures that make a substantive change in the governing law is not easy to discern, and Congress must have wide latitude in determining where it lies, the distinction exists and must be observed. There must be a congruence and proportionality between the injury to be prevented or remedied and the means adopted to that end. Lacking such a connection, legislation may become substantive in operation and effect. History and our case law support drawing the distinction, one apparent from the text of the Amendment.

The Fourteenth Amendment's history confirms the remedial, rather than substantive, nature of the Enforcement Clause. The Joint Committee on Reconstruction of the 39th Congress began drafting what would become the Fourteenth Amendment in January 1866. The objections to the Committee's first draft of the Amendment, and the rejection of the draft, have a direct bearing on the central issue of defining Congress' enforcement power. In February, Republican Representative John Bingham of Ohio reported the following draft Amendment to the House of Representatives on behalf of the Joint Committee:

> The Congress shall have power to make all laws which shall be necessary and proper to secure to the citizens of each State all privileges and immunities of citizens in the several States, and to all persons in the several States equal protection in the rights of life, liberty, and property. Cong. Globe, 39th Cong., 1st Sess., 1034 (1866).

The proposal encountered immediate opposition, which continued through three days of debate.... As a result of these objections having been expressed from so many different quarters, the House voted to table the proposal until April.... The congressional action was seen as marking the defeat of the proposal. See The Nation, Mar. 8, 1866, p. 291 ("The postponement of the amendment ... is conclusive against the passage of [it]"); New York Times, Mar. 1, 1866, p. 4 ("It is doubtful if this ever comes before the House again ..."); see also Cong. Globe, 42d Cong., 1st Sess., App., at 115 (statement of Rep. Farnsworth) (The Amendment was "given its quietus by a postponement for two months, where it slept the sleep that knows no waking").... The Amendment in its early form was not again considered. Instead, the Joint Committee began drafting a new article of Amendment, which it reported to Congress on April 30, 1866.

Section 1 of the new draft Amendment imposed self-executing limits on the States. Section 5 prescribed that "[t]he Congress shall have power to enforce, by appropriate legislation, the provisions of this article." ... Under the revised Amendment, Congress' power was no longer plenary but remedial. Congress was granted the power to make the substantive constitutional prohibitions against the States effective. Representative Bingham said the new draft would give Congress "the power ... to protect by national law the privileges and immunities of all the citizens of the Republic ... whenever the same shall be abridged or denied by the unconstitutional acts of any State." Id., at 2542. Representative Stevens described the new draft Amendment as "allow[ing] Congress to correct the unjust legislation of the States." Id., at 2459. See also id., at 2768 (statement of Sen. Howard) (§5 "enables Congress, in case the States shall enact laws in conflict with the principles of the amendment, to correct that legislation by a formal congressional enactment").... The revised Amendment proposal did not raise the concerns expressed earlier regarding broad congressional power to prescribe uniform national laws with respect to life, liberty, and property. See, e.g., Cong. Globe, 42d Cong., 1st Sess., at App. 151 (statement of Rep. Garfield) ("The [Fourteenth Amendment] limited but did not oust the jurisdiction of the State[s]"). After revisions not relevant here, the new measure passed both Houses and was ratified in July 1868 as the Fourteenth Amendment....

The design of the Fourteenth Amendment has proved significant also in maintaining the traditional separation of powers between Congress and the Judiciary. The first eight Amendments to the Constitution set forth self-executing prohibitions on governmental action, and this Court has had primary authority to interpret those prohibitions. The Bingham draft, some thought, departed from that tradition by vesting in Congress primary power to interpret and elaborate on the meaning of the new Amendment through legislation. Under it, "Congress, and not the courts, was to judge whether or not any of the privileges or immunities were not secured to citizens in the several States." Flack, supra, at 64. While this separation-of-powers aspect did not occasion the widespread resistance which was caused by the proposal's threat to the federal balance, it nonetheless attracted the attention of various Members. See Cong. Globe, 39th Cong., 1st Sess., at

1064 (statement of Rep. Hale) (noting that Bill of Rights, unlike the Bingham proposal, "provide[s] safeguards to be enforced by the courts, and not to be exercised by the Legislature"); id., at App. 133 (statement of Rep. Rogers) (prior to Bingham proposal it "was left entirely for the courts ... to enforce the privileges and immunities of the citizens"). As enacted, the Fourteenth Amendment confers substantive rights against the States which, like the provisions of the Bill of Rights, are self-executing.... The power to interpret the Constitution in a case or controversy remains in the Judiciary.

The remedial and preventive nature of Congress' enforcement power, and the limitation inherent in the power, were confirmed in our earliest cases on the Fourteenth Amendment. In the Civil Rights Cases (1883), the Court invalidated sections of the Civil Rights Act of 1875 which prescribed criminal penalties for denying to any person "the full enjoyment of" public accommodations and conveyances, on the grounds that it exceeded Congress' power by seeking to regulate private conduct. The Enforcement Clause, the Court said, did not authorize Congress to pass "general legislation upon the rights of the citizen, but corrective legislation, that is, such as may be necessary and proper for counteracting such laws as the States may adopt or enforce, and which, by the amendment, they are prohibited from making or enforcing...." ... Although the specific holdings of these early cases might have been superseded or modified, see, e.g., Heart of Atlanta Motel, Inc. v. United States, their treatment of Congress' § 5 power as corrective or preventive, not definitional, has not been questioned....

There is language in our opinion in Katzenbach v. Morgan which could be interpreted as acknowledging a power in Congress to enact legislation that expands the rights contained in § 1 of the Fourteenth Amendment. This is not a necessary interpretation, however, or even the best one. In Morgan, the Court considered the constitutionality of § 4(e) of the Voting Rights Act of 1965, which provided that no person who had successfully completed the sixth primary grade in a public school in, or a private school accredited by, the Commonwealth of Puerto Rico in which the language of instruction was other than English could be denied the right to vote because of an inability to read or write English. New York's Constitution, on the other hand, required voters to be able to read and write English. The Court provided two related rationales for its conclusion that § 4(e) could "be viewed as a measure to secure for the Puerto Rican community residing in New York nondiscriminatory treatment by government." ... Under the first rationale, Congress could prohibit New York from denying the right to vote to large segments of its Puerto Rican community, in order to give Puerto Ricans "enhanced political power" that would be "helpful in gaining nondiscriminatory treatment in public services for the entire Puerto Rican community." ... Section 4(e) thus could be justified as a remedial measure to deal with "discrimination in governmental services." ... The second rationale, an alternative holding, did not address discrimination in the provision of public services but "discrimination in establishing voter qualifications." ... The Court perceived a factual basis on which Congress could have concluded that New York's literacy requirement "constituted an invidious discrimination in violation of the Equal Protection Clause." ... Both rationales for upholding § 4(e) rested on unconstitutional discrimination by New York and Congress' reasonable attempt to combat it....

If Congress could define its own powers by altering the Fourteenth Amendment's meaning, no longer would the Constitution be "superior paramount law, unchangeable by ordinary means." It would be "on a level with ordinary legislative acts, and, like other acts, ... alterable when the legislature shall please to alter it." Marbury v. Madison. Under this approach, it is difficult to conceive of a principle that would limit congressional power.... Shifting legislative majorities could change the Constitution and effectively circumvent the difficult and detailed amendment process contained in Article V.

We now turn to consider whether RFRA can be considered enforcement legislation under § 5 of the Fourteenth Amendment.... The Act, it is said, is a reasonable means of protecting the free exercise of religion as defined by Smith. It prevents and remedies laws which are enacted with the unconstitutional object of targeting religious beliefs and practices.... ("[A] law targeting religious beliefs as such is never permissible"). To avoid the difficulty of proving such violations, it is said, Congress can simply invalidate any law which imposes a substantial burden on a religious practice unless it is justified by a compelling interest and is the least restrictive means of accomplishing that interest. If Congress can prohibit laws with discriminatory effects in order to prevent racial discrimination in violation of the Equal Protection Clause ... then it can do the same, respondent argues, to promote religious liberty.

While preventive rules are sometimes appropriate remedial measures, there must be a congruence between the means used and the ends to be achieved. The appropriateness of remedial measures must be considered in light of the evil presented.... Strong measures appropriate to address one harm may be an unwarranted response to another, lesser one.... A comparison between RFRA and the Voting Rights Act is instructive. In contrast to the record which confronted Congress and the Judiciary in the voting rights cases, RFRA's legislative record lacks examples of modern instances of generally applicable laws passed because of religious bigotry. The history of persecution in this country detailed in the hearings mentions no episodes occurring in the past 40 years.... The absence of more recent episodes stems from the fact that, as one witness testified, "deliberate persecution is not the usual problem in this country." ... Rather, the emphasis of the hearings was on laws of general applicability which place incidental burdens on religion. Much of the discussion centered upon anecdotal evidence of autopsies performed on Jewish individuals and Hmong immigrants in violation of their religious beliefs ... and on zoning regulations and historic preservation laws (like the one at issue here), which, as an incident of their normal operation, have adverse effects on churches and synagogues....

It is difficult to maintain that they are examples of legislation enacted or enforced due to animus or hostility to the burdened religious practices or that they indicate some widespread pattern of religious discrimination in this country. Congress' concern was with the incidental burdens imposed, not the object or purpose of the legislation.... This lack of support in the legislative record, however, is not RFRA's most serious shortcoming.... Regardless of the state of the legislative record, RFRA cannot be considered remedial, preventive legislation, if those terms are to have any meaning. RFRA is so out of proportion to a supposed remedial or preventive object that it cannot be understood as responsive to, or designed to prevent, unconstitutional behavior. It appears, instead, to attempt a substantive change in constitutional protections. Preventive measures prohibiting certain types of laws may be appropriate when there is reason to believe that many of the laws affected by the congressional enactment have a significant likelihood of being unconstitutional.... Remedial legislation under § 5 "should be adapted to the mischief and wrong which the [Fourteenth] [A]mendment was intended to provide against." Civil Rights Cases.

RFRA is not so confined. Sweeping coverage ensures its intrusion at every level of government, displacing laws and prohibiting official actions of almost every description and regardless of subject matter. RFRA's restrictions apply to every agency and official of the Federal, State, and local Governments.... RFRA applies to all federal and state law, statutory or otherwise, whether adopted before or after its enactment.... RFRA has no termination date or termination mechanism. Any law is subject to challenge at any time by any individual who alleges a substantial burden on his or her free exercise of religion.... The stringent test RFRA demands of state laws reflects a lack of proportionality or congruence between the means adopted and the legitimate end to be achieved. Judgment of the Court of Appeals reversed.

Review Questions and Explanations: *City of Boerne*

1. Justice Kennedy is not impressed with the factual evidence Congress compiled regarding what it saw as impositions on religious freedom because, in his view, it was not the right type of evidence. What type of evidence was Justice Kennedy looking for? The evidence provided by Congress in these cases, and the extent to which the Court will defer to Congress's judgment about such evidence, becomes important in subsequent cases in this area, so be sure to understand the point raised in this question before moving forward.

2. To what extent does the majority's argument in *Boerne* depend on accepting the view that Congress has no authority to determine the meaning of Fourteenth Amendment rights independently of the Court? Is there an argument for a more robust congressional role? Note that (1) the plain text of section 5 expressly authorizes enforcement of the Fourteenth Amendment by Congress, but nowhere does the Constitution expressly give the Court that power; and (2) the Fourteenth Amendment was intended, at least in part, to overrule the Supreme Court's decision in *Dred Scott*.

The following case, *U.S. v. Morrison*, is a further excerpt from the same case you read when studying the Commerce Clause. In *Morrison*, the government argued that it had authority to enact the Violence Against Women Act *either* under the Commerce Clause *or* under § 5 of the Fourteenth Amendment. The Commerce Clause argument, as discussed above, was rejected by the Court. The portion of the case reprinted below examines the enforcement provision argument.

Guided Reading Questions: *United States v. Morrison*

1. Pay attention to exactly what the Violence Against Women Act does. Be precise in describing the statute.

2. How does Congress argue that the Violence Against Women Act is within its Fourteenth Amendment powers? You should be able to explain its position after reading the case.

3. *Morrison* introduces the question of *who* Congress can regulate under its enforcement clause powers. What is the Court's answer to this question? In what way does Justice Breyer, writing in dissent, disagree with that answer?

United States v. Morrison

529 U.S. 598 (2000)

Majority: *Rehnquist* (CJ), O'Connor, Scalia, Kennedy, Thomas

Concurrence: *Thomas* (omitted)

Dissents: *Souter* (omitted), Stevens, Ginsburg, *Breyer*

CHIEF JUSTICE REHNQUIST delivered the opinion of the Court.

[The facts of the case are presented above in the materials discussing the Commerce Clause. Please review them.]

The District Court dismissed Brzonkala's Title IX claims against Virginia Tech for failure to state a claim upon which relief can be granted.... It then held that Brzonkala's complaint stated a claim against Morrison and Crawford under § 13981 but dismissed the complaint because it concluded that Congress lacked authority to enact the section under either the Commerce Clause or § 5 of the Fourteenth Amendment....

Because we conclude that the Commerce Clause does not provide Congress with authority to enact § 13981, we address petitioners' alternative argument that the section's civil remedy should be upheld as an exercise of Congress' remedial power under § 5 of the Fourteenth Amendment. As noted above, Congress expressly invoked the Fourteenth Amendment as a source of authority to enact § 13981.

The principles governing an analysis of congressional legislation under § 5 are well settled. Section 5 states that Congress may "'enforce' by 'appropriate legislation' the constitutional guarantee that no State shall deprive any person of 'life, liberty, or property, without due process of law,' nor deny any person 'equal protection of the laws.'" City of Boerne v. Flores. Section 5 is "a positive grant of legislative power," Katzenbach v. Morgan, that includes authority to "prohibit conduct which is not itself unconstitutional and [to] intrud[e] into 'legislative spheres of autonomy previously reserved to the States.'" However, "[a]s broad as the congressional enforcement power is, it is not unlimited." In fact, as we discuss in detail below, several limitations inherent in § 5's text and constitutional context have been recognized since the Fourteenth Amendment was adopted.

Petitioners' § 5 argument is founded on an assertion that there is pervasive bias in various state justice systems against victims of gender-motivated violence. This assertion is supported by a voluminous congressional record. Specifically, Congress received evidence that many participants in state justice systems are perpetuating an array of erroneous stereotypes and assumptions. Congress concluded that these discriminatory stereotypes often result in insufficient investigation and prosecution of gender-motivated crime, inappropriate focus on the behavior and credibility of the victims of that crime, and unacceptably lenient punishments for those who are actually convicted of gender-motivated violence.... Petitioners contend that this bias denies victims of gender-motivated violence the equal protection of the laws and that Congress therefore acted appropriately in enacting a private civil remedy against the perpetrators of gender-motivated violence to both remedy the States' bias and deter future instances of discrimination in the state courts.

As our cases have established, state-sponsored gender discrimination violates equal protection unless it "serves 'important governmental objectives and ... the discriminatory means employed' are 'substantially related to the achievement of those objectives.'" However, the language and purpose of the Fourteenth Amendment place certain limitations on the manner in which Congress may attack discriminatory conduct. These limitations are necessary to prevent the Fourteenth Amendment from obliterating the Framers' carefully crafted balance of power between the States and the National Government.... Foremost among these limitations is the time-honored principle that the Fourteenth Amendment, by its very terms, prohibits only state action. "[T]he principle has become firmly embedded in our constitutional law that the action inhibited by the first section of the Fourteenth Amendment is only such action as may fairly be said to be that of the States. That Amendment erects no shield against merely private conduct, however discriminatory or wrongful." Shelly v. Kraemer.

Shortly after the Fourteenth Amendment was adopted, we decided two cases interpreting the Amendment's provisions, United States v. Harris, and the Civil Rights Cases. In Harris, the Court considered a challenge to § 2 of the Civil Rights Act of 1871. That section sought to punish "private persons" for "conspiring to deprive any one of the equal protection of the laws enacted by the State." We concluded that this law exceeded Congress' § 5 power because the law was "directed exclusively against the action of private persons, without reference to the laws of the State, or their administration by her officers." ...

We reached a similar conclusion in the Civil Rights Cases. In those consolidated cases, we held that the public accommodation provisions of the Civil Rights Act of 1875, which applied to purely private conduct, were beyond the scope of the § 5 enforcement power.... The force of the doctrine of *stare decisis* behind these decisions stems not only from the length of time they have been on the books, but also from the insight attributable to the Members of the Court at that time. Every Member had been appointed by President Lincoln, Grant, Hayes, Garfield, or Arthur—and each of their judicial appointees obviously had intimate knowledge and familiarity with the events surrounding the adoption of the Fourteenth Amendment....

Petitioners alternatively argue that, unlike the situation in the Civil Rights Cases, here there has been gender-based disparate treatment by state authorities, whereas in those cases there was no indication of such state action. There is abundant evidence, however, to show that the Congresses that enacted the Civil Rights Acts of 1871 and 1875 had a purpose similar to that of Congress in enacting § 13981: There were state laws on the books bespeaking equality of treatment, but in the administration of these laws there was discrimination against newly freed slaves. The statement of Representative Garfield in the House and that of Senator Sumner in the Senate are representative:

> [T]he chief complaint is not that the laws of the State are unequal, but that even where the laws are just and equal on their face, yet, by a systematic maladministration of them, or a neglect or refusal to enforce their provisions, a portion of the people are denied equal protection under them. Cong. Globe, 42d Cong., 1st Sess., App. 153 (1871) (statement of Rep. Garfield).

> The Legislature of South Carolina has passed a law giving precisely the rights contained in your 'supplementary civil rights bill.' But such a law remains a dead letter on her statute-books, because the State courts, comprised largely of those whom the Senator wishes to obtain amnesty for, refuse to enforce it. Cong. Globe, 42d Cong., 2d Sess., 430 (1872) (statement of Sen. Sumner).

But even if that distinction were valid, we do not believe it would save § 13981's civil remedy. For the remedy is simply not "corrective in its character, adapted to counteract and redress the operation of such prohibited [s]tate laws or proceedings of [s]tate officers." Civil Rights Cases. Or, as we have phrased it in more recent cases, prophylactic legislation under § 5 must have a "congruence and proportionality between the injury to be prevented or remedied and the means adopted to that end." ... Section 13981 is not aimed at proscribing discrimination by officials which the Fourteenth Amendment might not itself proscribe; it is directed not at any State or state actor, but at individuals who have committed criminal acts motivated by gender bias.... Affirmed.

JUSTICE BREYER, with whom JUSTICE STEVENS, JUSTICE SOUTER, and JUSTICE GINSBURG agree, dissenting.

.... Given my conclusion on the Commerce Clause question, I need not consider Congress' authority under § 5 of the Fourteenth Amendment. Nonetheless, I doubt the Court's reasoning rejecting that source of authority. The Court points out that in United States v. Harris, and the Civil Rights Cases, the Court held that § 5 does not authorize Congress to use the Fourteenth Amendment as a source of power to remedy the conduct of *private persons*. That is certainly so. The Federal Government's argument, however, is that Congress used § 5 to remedy the actions of *state actors*, namely, those States which, through discriminatory design or the discriminatory conduct of their officials, failed to provide adequate (or any) state remedies for women injured by gender-motivated violence—a failure that the States, and Congress, documented in depth....

Neither Harris nor the Civil Rights Cases considered this kind of claim. The Court in Harris specifically said that it treated the federal laws in question as "directed exclusively against the action of private persons, without reference to the laws of the State or their administration by her officers." See also Civil Rights Cases (observing that the statute did "not profess to be corrective of any constitutional wrong committed by the States" and that it established "rules for the conduct of individuals in society towards each other, ... without referring in any manner to any supposed action of the State or its authorities").

The Court responds directly to the relevant "state actor" claim by finding that the present law lacks "congruence and proportionality" to the state discrimination that it purports to remedy.... That is because the law, unlike federal laws prohibiting literacy tests for voting, imposing voting rights requirements, or punishing state officials who intentionally discriminated in jury selection ... is not "directed ... at any State or state actor."

But why can Congress not provide a remedy against private actors? Those private actors, of course, did not themselves violate the Constitution. But this Court has held that Congress at least sometimes can enact remedial "[l]egislation ... [that] prohibits conduct which is not itself unconstitutional." City of Boerne. The statutory remedy does not in any sense purport to "determine what constitutes a constitutional violation." Id. It intrudes little upon either States or private parties. It may lead state actors to improve their own remedial systems, primarily through example. It restricts private actors only by imposing liability for private conduct that is, in the main, already forbidden by state law. Why is the remedy "disproportionate"? And given the relation between remedy and violation—the creation of a federal remedy to substitute for constitutionally inadequate state remedies—where is the lack of "congruence"?

The majority adds that Congress found that the problem of inadequacy of state remedies "does not exist in all States, or even most States." ... But Congress had before it the task force reports of at least 21 States documenting constitutional violations. And it made its own findings about pervasive gender-based stereotypes hampering many state legal systems, sometimes unconstitutionally so.... The record nowhere reveals a congressional finding that the problem "does not exist" elsewhere. Why can Congress not take the evidence before it as evidence of a national problem? This Court has not previously held that Congress must document the existence of a problem in every State prior to proposing a national solution. And the deference this Court gives to Congress' chosen remedy under § 5 ... suggests that any such requirement would be inappropriate.

Despite my doubts about the majority's § 5 reasoning, I need not, and do not, answer the § 5 question, which I would leave for more thorough analysis if necessary on another occasion. Rather, in my view, the commerce clause provides an adequate basis for the statute before us. And I would uphold its constitutionality as the "necessary and proper" exercise of legislative power granted to Congress by that Clause.

Review Questions and Explanations: *Morrison*

1. The majority holds that the enactment of the Violence Against Women Act is beyond the scope of Congress' enforcement clause power. Why? Does the Court disagree with Congress' factual findings about the prevalence and cost of violence against women? Does it disagree with Congress' judgment that states are not doing enough to prohibit or prosecute such violence? What exactly is the problem with the statute?

2. Justice Breyer's dissent picks up the argument made at the end of the majority opinion in *Katzenbach*. In doing so, he argues that the Violence Against Women Act is a valid congressional response to what Congress saw as the under-prosecution of such violence by the states. What is Justice Breyer's doctrinal argument on this point?

3. In what way (if at all) does Justice Breyer disagree with the majority's doctrinal statement of who Congress can regulate under its enforcement powers?

Recap

The cases we have read so far illustrate three different approaches to the enforcement clauses. The first, shown by Justice Brennan's majority opinion in *Katzenbach*, gives Congress quite broad power to legislate in areas Congress views as involving civil rights. The second, hinted at in Justice Brennan's *Katzenbach* opinion and taken up by Justice Breyer in *Morrison*, says that Congress must limit itself to remedying or enforcing judicially recognized substantive rights, but gives Congress broad discretion in determining how to do so. The third, shown by the majority opinion in *Morrison*, is more restrictive of congressional power. Does Justice Kennedy's majority opinion in *Boerne* adopt one of these approaches, or does it develop a fourth alternative?

---

2. The Enforcement Clauses and the Eleventh Amendment

The next two cases, *Fitzpatrick* and *Seminole Tribe*, explain the relationship between the enforcement provisions of the Civil War Amendments and the Eleventh Amendment. The Eleventh Amendment reads as follows:

> The Judicial power of the United States shall not be construed to extend to any suit in law or equity, commenced or prosecuted against one of the United States by Citizens of another State, or by Citizens of Subjects of any Foreign State.

The Eleventh Amendment is at its heart an immunity provision — it protects states from certain types of lawsuits brought by certain types of people in certain types of courts. More specifically, the text of the Amendment appears to protect states from being sued "in law or equity" in federal court (the repository of the "judicial power of the United States") by citizens from other states or foreign countries. In fact, however, the Court has interpreted the Eleventh Amendment to give states protection from being sued in federal *or* state courts by citizens, either those of other states *or* of the state itself.

This interpretation *could* have dramatic consequences. It could, for example, forestall any private litigation attempting to force states to stop violating citizens' rights. This has not happened. Instead, this broad interpretation has been tempered by doctrines allowing officers of the state acting in their official capacity to be sued, and by limiting the states' immunity from suit to claims asking for money damages. The result of this is that while states as states do enjoy broad immunity from suit in state and federal courts, suits against state officers, or suits for injunctive or other non-monetary relief, are not barred.

The following cases, *Fitzpatrick* and *Seminole Tribe*, address these issues. They also explain the connection between the Eleventh Amendment and the Civil War Amendments. It is this later issue that you should pay close attention to when reading the cases.

Guided Reading Questions: *Fitzpatrick* and *Seminole Tribe*

1. The Court in *Fitzpatrick* holds that Congress can authorize by statute a suit against a state in federal court. In *Seminole Tribe*, the Court holds Congress cannot authorize the suit against a state. What explains the difference?

2. Which of its enumerated powers did Congress act under when passing the federal statutes at issue in *Seminole Tribe* and *Fitzpatrick?* Were the statutes themselves — excluding for the moment the clauses authorizing suits against the states in federal court — constitutionally valid exercises of congressional power? In other words, where they within the scope of the enumerated power they were enacted under?

3. The Court in *Seminole Tribes* overturned an earlier case, *Pennsylvania v. Union Gas.* How had the Court in *Union Gas* interpreted the Eleventh Amendment? Why does the Court reject that view in *Seminole Tribes*?

Fitzpatrick v. Bitzer

427 U.S. 445 (1976)

Majority: *Rehnquist*, Burger (CJ), Stewart, White, Marshall, Blackmun, Powell

Concurrence: *Brennan; Stevens* (both omitted)

MR. JUSTICE REHNQUIST delivered the opinion of the Court.

In the 1972 Amendments to Title VII of the Civil Rights Act of 1964, Congress, acting under § 5 of the Fourteenth Amendment, authorized federal courts to award money damages in favor of a private individual against a state government found to have subjected that person to employment discrimination on the basis of "race, color, religion, sex, or national origin." The principal question presented by these cases is whether, as against the shield of sovereign immunity afforded the State by the Eleventh Amendment, ... Congress has the power to authorize Federal courts to enter such an award against the State as a means of enforcing the substantive guarantees of the Fourteenth Amendment....

The substantive provisions [of the Fourteenth Amendment] are by express terms directed at the States. Impressed upon them by those provisions are duties with respect to their treatment of private individuals. Standing behind the imperatives is Congress' power to "enforce" them "by appropriate legislation."

The impact of the Fourteenth Amendment upon the relationship between the Federal Government and the States, and the reach of congressional power under § 5, were examined at length by this Court in Ex parte State of Virginia (1880). A state judge had been arrested and indicted under a federal criminal statute prohibiting the exclusion on the basis of race of any citizen from service as a juror in a state court. The judge claimed that the statute was beyond Congress' power to enact under either the Thirteenth or the Fourteenth Amendment.

> FN10. Section 1. Neither slavery nor involuntary servitude, except as a punishment for crime whereof the party shall have been duly convicted, shall exist within the United States, or any place subject to their jurisdiction. Section 2. Congress shall have power to enforce this article by appropriate legislation.

The Court first observed that these Amendments "were intended to be, what they really are, limitations of the power of the States and enlargements of the power of Congress." It then addressed the relationship between the language of § 5 and the substantive provisions of the Fourteenth Amendment:

> The prohibitions of the Fourteenth Amendment are directed to the States, and they are to a degree restrictions of State power. It is these which Congress is empowered to enforce, and to enforce against State action, however put forth, whether that action be executive, legislative, or judicial. Such enforcement is no invasion of State sovereignty. No law can be, which the people of the States have, by the Constitution of the United States, empowered Congress to enact.... It is said the selection of jurors for her courts and the administration of her laws belong to each State; that they are her rights. This is true in the general. But in exercising her rights, a State cannot disregard the limitations which the Federal Constitution has applied to her power. Her rights do not reach to that extent. Nor can she deny to the general government the right to exercise all its granted powers, though they may interfere with the full enjoyment of rights she would have if those powers had not been thus granted. Indeed, every addition of power to the general government involves a corresponding diminution of the governmental powers of the States. It is carved out of them.

> The argument in support of the petition for a Habeas corpus ignores entirely the power conferred upon Congress by the Fourteenth Amendment. Were it not for the fifth section of that amendment, there might be room for argument that the first section is only declaratory of the moral duty of the State.... But the Constitution now expressly gives authority for congressional interference and compulsion in the cases embraced within the Fourteenth Amendment. It is but a limited authority, true, extending only to a single class of cases; but within its limits it is complete. Id. at 346–348.

Ex parte State of Virginia's early recognition of this shift in the federal-state balance has been carried forward by more recent decisions of this Court.... There can be no doubt that this line of cases has sanctioned intrusions by Congress, acting under the Civil War Amendments, into the judicial, executive, and legislative spheres of autonomy previously reserved to the States. The legislation considered in each case was grounded on the expansion of Congress' powers with the corresponding diminution of state sovereignty found to be intended by the Framers and made part of the Constitution upon the States' ratification of those Amendments, a phenomenon aptly described as a "carv(ing) out." ...

It is true that none of these previous cases presented the question of the relationship between the Eleventh Amendment and the enforcement power granted to Congress under § 5 of the Fourteenth Amendment. But we think that the Eleventh Amendment, and the principle of state sovereignty which it embodies, see Hans v. Louisiana (1890), are necessarily limited by the enforcement provisions of § 5 of the Fourteenth Amendment. In that section Congress is expressly granted authority to enforce "by appropriate legislation" the substantive provisions of the Fourteenth Amendment, which themselves embody significant limitations on state authority. When Congress acts pursuant to § 5, not only is it exercising legislative authority that is plenary within the terms of the constitutional grant, it is exercising that authority under one section of a constitutional Amendment whose other sections by their own terms embody limitations on state authority. We think that Congress may, in determining what is "appropriate legislation" for the purpose of enforcing the provisions of the Fourteenth Amendment, provide for private suits against States or state officials which are constitutionally impermissible in other contexts.

> FN11. Apart from their claim that the Eleventh Amendment bars enforcement of the remedy established by Title VII in this case, respondent state officials do not contend that the substantive provisions of Title VII as applied here are not a proper exercise of congressional authority under § 5 of the Fourteenth Amendment.

Reversed in part and affirmed in part.

Seminole Tribe of Florida v. Florida

517 U.S. 44 (1996)

Majority: *Rehnquist* (CJ), O'Connor, Scalia, Kennedy, Thomas

Dissents: *Stevens* (omitted); *Souter*, Ginsburg, Breyer

CHIEF JUSTICE REHNQUIST delivered the opinion of the Court.

The Indian Gaming Regulatory Act provides that an Indian tribe may conduct certain gaming activities only in conformance with a valid compact between the tribe and the State in which the gaming activities are located.... The Act, passed by Congress under the Indian Commerce Clause, ... imposes upon the States a duty to negotiate in good faith with an Indian tribe toward the formation of a compact ... and authorizes a tribe to bring suit in federal court against a State in order to compel performance of that duty.... We hold that notwithstanding Congress' clear intent to abrogate the States' sovereign immunity, the Indian Commerce Clause does not grant Congress that power, and therefore § 2710(d)(7) cannot grant jurisdiction over a State that does not consent to be sued. We further hold that the doctrine of Ex parte Young (1908), may not be used to enforce § 2710(d)(3) against a state official....

[W]e granted certiorari, ... in order to consider two questions: (1) Does the Eleventh Amendment prevent Congress from authorizing suits by Indian tribes against States for prospective injunctive relief to enforce legislation enacted pursuant to the Indian Commerce Clause?; and (2) Does the doctrine of Ex parte Young permit suits against a State's Governor for prospective injunctive relief to enforce the good-faith bargaining requirement of the Act? We answer the first question in the affirmative, the second in the negative, and we therefore affirm the Eleventh Circuit's dismissal of petitioner's suit.

The Eleventh Amendment provides:

> The Judicial power of the United States shall not be construed to extend to any suit in law or equity, commenced or prosecuted against one of the United States by Citizens of another State, or by Citizens or Subjects of any Foreign State.

Although the text of the Amendment would appear to restrict only the Article III diversity jurisdiction of the federal courts, "we have understood the Eleventh Amendment to stand not so much for what it says, but for the presupposition ... which it confirms." ... That presupposition, first observed over a century ago in Hans v. Louisiana, 134 U.S. 1, 10 S.Ct. 504, 33 L.Ed. 842 (1890), has two parts: first, that each State is a sovereign entity in our federal system; and second, that "[i]t is inherent in the nature of sovereignty not to be amenable to the suit of an individual without its consent," ... For over a century we have reaffirmed that federal jurisdiction over suits against unconsenting States "was not contemplated by the Constitution when establishing the judicial power of the United States." ...

Petitioner argues that Congress through the Act abrogated the States' immunity from suit. In order to determine whether Congress has abrogated the States' sovereign immunity, we ask two questions: first, whether Congress has "unequivocally expresse[d] its intent to abrogate the immunity," ... and second, whether Congress has acted "pursuant to a valid exercise of power." ... Here, we agree with the parties, with the Eleventh Circuit in the decision below ... that Congress has ... provided an "unmistakably clear" statement of its intent to abrogate.... we turn now to consider whether the Act was passed "pursuant to a valid exercise of power." ...

Thus our inquiry into whether Congress has the power to abrogate unilaterally the States' immunity from suit is narrowly focused on one question: Was the Act in question passed pursuant to a constitutional provision granting Congress the power to abrogate? See, *e.g.*, Fitzpatrick v. Bitzer, (1976). Previously, in conducting that inquiry, we have found authority to abrogate under only two provisions of the Constitution. In Fitzpatrick, we recognized that the Fourteenth Amendment, by expanding federal power at the expense of state autonomy, had fundamentally altered the balance of state and federal power struck by the Constitution.... We noted that § 1 of the Fourteenth Amendment contained prohibitions expressly directed at the States and that § 5 of the Amendment expressly provided that "The Congress shall have power to enforce, by appropriate legislation, the provisions of this article." ... We held that through the Fourteenth Amendment, federal power extended to intrude upon the province of the Eleventh Amendment and therefore that § 5 of the Fourteenth Amendment allowed Congress to abrogate the immunity from suit guaranteed by that Amendment.

In only one other case has congressional abrogation of the States' Eleventh Amendment immunity been upheld. In Pennsylvania v. Union Gas Co., 491 U.S. 1, 109 (1989), a plurality of the Court found that the Interstate Commerce Clause, Art. I, § 8, cl. 3, granted Congress the power to abrogate state sovereign immunity, stating that the power to regulate interstate commerce would be "incomplete without the authority to render States liable in damages." Id. Justice White added the fifth vote necessary to the result in that case, but wrote separately in order to express that he "[did] not agree with much of [the plurality's] reasoning." Id. (opinion concurring in judgment in part and dissenting in part)....

Both parties make their arguments from the plurality decision in Union Gas, and we, too, begin there.... The Court in Union Gas reached a result without an expressed rationale agreed upon by a majority of the Court. We have already seen that Justice Brennan's opinion received the support of only three other Justices.... (Marshall, Blackmun, and Stevens, JJ., joined Justice Brennan). Of the other five, Justice White, who provided the fifth vote for the result, wrote separately in order to indicate his disagreement with the plurality's rationale ... (opinion concurring in judgment and dissenting in part), and four Justices joined together in a dissent that rejected the plurality's rationale ... (Scalia, J., dissenting, joined by кehnquist, C. J., and O'Connor and кennedy, JJ.). Since it was issued, Union Gas has created confusion among the lower courts that have sought to understand and apply the deeply fractured decision....

Never before the decision in Union Gas had we suggested that the bounds of Article III could be expanded by Congress operating pursuant to any constitutional provision other than the Fourteenth Amendment. Indeed, it had seemed fundamental that Congress could not expand the jurisdiction of the federal courts beyond the bounds of Article III. Marbury v. Madison (1803). The plurality's citation of prior decisions for support was based upon what we believe to be a misreading of precedent.... The plurality's extended reliance upon our decision in Fitzpatrick v. Bitzer (1976), that Congress could under the Fourteenth Amendment abrogate the States' sovereign immunity was also, we believe, misplaced. Fitzpatrick was based upon a rationale wholly inapplicable to the Interstate Commerce Clause, viz., that the Fourteenth Amendment, adopted well after the adoption of the Eleventh Amendment and the ratification of the Constitution, operated to alter the pre-existing balance between state and federal power achieved by Article III and the Eleventh Amendment.... Fitzpatrick cannot be read to justify "limitation of the principle embodied in the Eleventh Amendment through appeal to antecedent provisions of the Constitution."...

In overruling Union Gas today, we reconfirm that the background principle of state sovereign immunity embodied in the Eleventh Amendment is not so ephemeral as to dissipate when the subject of the suit is an area, like the regulation of Indian commerce, that is under the exclusive control of the Federal Government. Even when the Constitution vests in Congress complete law-making authority over a particular area, the Eleventh Amendment prevents congressional authorization of suits by private parties against unconsenting States. The Eleventh Amendment restricts the judicial power under Article III, and Article I cannot be used to circumvent the constitutional limitations placed upon federal jurisdiction. Petitioner's suit against the State of Florida must be dismissed for a lack of jurisdiction.

Petitioner argues that we may exercise jurisdiction over its suit to enforce § 2710(d)(3) against the Governor notwithstanding the jurisdictional bar of the Eleventh Amendment. Petitioner notes that since our decision in Ex parte Young, (1908) we often have found federal jurisdiction over a suit against a state official when that suit seeks only prospective injunctive relief in order to "end a continuing violation of federal law." ... The situation presented here, however, is sufficiently different from that giving rise to the traditional Ex parte Young action so as to preclude the availability of that doctrine.

Here, the "continuing violation of federal law" alleged by petitioner is the Governor's failure to bring the State into compliance with § 2710(d)(3). But the duty to negotiate imposed upon the State by that statutory provision does not stand alone. Rather, as we have seen, supra, at 1120, Congress passed § 2710(d)(3) in conjunction with the carefully crafted and intricate remedial scheme set forth in § 2710(d)(7).

Where Congress has created a remedial scheme for the enforcement of a particular federal right, we have, in suits against federal officers, refused to supplement that scheme with one created by the judiciary.... Here, of course, the question is not whether a remedy should be created, but instead is whether the Eleventh Amendment bar should be lifted, as it was in Ex parte Young, in order to allow a suit against a state officer. Nevertheless, we think that the same general principle applies: Therefore, where Congress has prescribed a detailed remedial scheme for the enforcement against a State of a statutorily created right, a court should hesitate before casting aside those limitations and permitting an action against a state officer based upon Ex parte Young....

The Eleventh Amendment prohibits Congress from making the State of Florida capable of being sued in federal court. The narrow exception to the Eleventh Amendment provided by the Ex parte Young doctrine cannot be used to enforce § 2710(d)(3) because Congress enacted a remedial scheme, § 2710(d)(7), specifically designed for the enforcement of that right. The Eleventh Circuit's dismissal of petitioner's suit is hereby affirmed.

JUSTICE SOUTER, with whom JUSTICE GINSBURG and JUSTICE BREYER agree, dissenting.

In holding the State of Florida immune to suit under the Indian Gaming Regulatory Act, the Court today holds for the first time since the founding of the Republic that Congress has no authority to subject a State to the jurisdiction of a federal court at the behest of an individual asserting a federal right. Although the Court invokes the Eleventh Amendment as authority for this proposition, the only sense in which that amendment might be claimed as pertinent here was tolerantly phrased by Justice STEVENS in his concurring opinion in Pennsylvania v. Union Gas Co. (1989). There, he explained how it has come about that we have two Eleventh Amendments, the one ratified in 1795, the other (so-called) invented by the Court nearly a century later in Hans v. Louisiana (1890)....

It is useful to separate three questions: (1) whether the States enjoyed sovereign immunity if sued in their own courts in the period prior to ratification of the National Constitution; (2) if so, whether after ratification the States were entitled to claim some such immunity when sued in a federal court exercising jurisdiction either because the suit was between a State and a nonstate litigant who was not its citizen, or because the issue in the case raised a federal question; and (3) whether any state sovereign immunity recognized in federal court may be abrogated by Congress.

The answer to the first question is not clear, although some of the Framers assumed that States did enjoy immunity in their own courts. The second question was not debated at the time of ratification, except as to citizen-state diversity jurisdiction; there was no unanimity, but in due course the Court in Chisholm v. Georgia (1793), answered that a state defendant enjoyed no such immunity. As to federal-question jurisdiction, state sovereign immunity seems not to have been debated prior to ratification, the silence probably showing a general understanding at the time that the States would have no immunity in such cases.

The adoption of the Eleventh Amendment soon changed the result in Chisholm, not by mentioning sovereign immunity, but by eliminating citizen-state diversity jurisdiction over cases with state defendants. I will explain why the Eleventh Amendment did not affect federal-question jurisdiction, a notion that needs to be understood for the light it casts on the soundness of Hans' holding that States did enjoy sovereign immunity in federal-question suits. The Hans Court erroneously assumed that a State could plead sovereign immunity against a noncitizen suing under federal-question jurisdiction, and for that reason held that a State must enjoy the same protection in a suit by one of its citizens. The error of Hans' reasoning is underscored by its clear inconsistency with the

Founders' hostility to the implicit reception of common-law doctrine as federal law, and with the Founders' conception of sovereign power as divided between the States and the National Government for the sake of very practical objectives.

The Court's answer today to the third question is likewise at odds with the Founders' view that common law, when it was received into the new American legal system, was always subject to legislative amendment. In ignoring the reasons for this pervasive understanding at the time of the ratification, and in holding that a nontextual common-law rule limits a clear grant of congressional power under Article I, the Court follows a course that has brought it to grief before in our history, and promises to do so again....

The Eleventh Amendment, of course, repudiated Chisholm and clearly divested federal courts of some jurisdiction as to cases against state parties:

> The Judicial power of the United States shall not be construed to extend to any suit in law or equity, commenced or prosecuted against one of the United States by Citizens of another State, or by Citizens or Subjects of any Foreign State.

There are two plausible readings of this provision's text. Under the first, it simply repeals the Citizen-State Diversity Clauses of Article III for all cases in which the State appears as a defendant. Under the second, it strips the federal courts of jurisdiction in any case in which a state defendant is sued by a citizen not its own, even if jurisdiction might otherwise rest on the existence of a federal question in the suit. Neither reading of the Amendment, of course, furnishes authority for the Court's view in today's case, but we need to choose between the competing readings for the light that will be shed on the Hans doctrine and the legitimacy of inflating that doctrine to the point of constitutional immutability as the Court has chosen to do.

The history and structure of the Eleventh Amendment convincingly show that it reaches only to suits subject to federal jurisdiction exclusively under the Citizen-State Diversity Clauses. In precisely tracking the language in Article III providing for citizen-state diversity jurisdiction, the text of the Amendment does, after all, suggest to common sense that only the Diversity Clauses are being addressed. If the Framers had meant the Amendment to bar federal-question suits as well, they could not only have made their intentions clearer very easily, but could simply have adopted the first post-Chisholm proposal, introduced in the House of Representatives by Theodore Sedgwick of Massachusetts on instructions from the Legislature of that Commonwealth.... With its references to suits by citizens as well as non-citizens, the Sedgwick amendment would necessarily have been applied beyond the Diversity Clauses, and for a reason that would have been wholly obvious to the people of the time. Sedgwick sought such a broad amendment because many of the States, including his own, owed debts subject to collection under the Treaty of Paris. Suits to collect such debts would "arise under" that Treaty and thus be subject to federal-question jurisdiction under Article III. Such a suit, indeed, was then already pending against Massachusetts, having been brought in this Court by Christopher Vassall, an erstwhile Bostonian whose move to England on the eve of revolutionary hostilities had presented his former neighbors with the irresistible temptation to confiscate his vacant mansion....

Congress took no action on Sedgwick's proposal, however, and the Amendment as ultimately adopted two years later could hardly have been meant to limit federal-question jurisdiction, or it would never have left the States open to federal-question suits by their own citizens. To be sure, the majority of state creditors were not citizens, but nothing in the Treaty would have prevented foreign creditors from selling their debt instruments (thereby assigning their claims) to citizens of the debtor State. If the Framers of the Eleventh

Amendment had meant it to immunize States from federal-question suits like those that might be brought to enforce the Treaty of Paris, they would surely have drafted the Amendment differently.

Review Questions and Explanations: *Fitzpatrick* and *Seminole Tribe*

1. Justice Souter's dissent takes a much narrower view of the immunity provided by the Eleventh Amendment than does the majority opinion. Who do you think has the better of this argument, the majority or the dissent? Why?

2. If the Civil War Amendments fundamentally restructured the relationship between the federal government and the states, why doesn't that restructuring extend to Congress's Article I powers? Should the guarantees of due process and equal protection, which are enforceable against the states, include all laws enacted by Congress to protect individuals or groups from unfair treatment by states?

3. The question of sovereign immunity is exceedingly complex in judicial doctrine, and gets a considerable amount of course time and attention in at least two upper level courses: Federal Courts/Federal Jurisdiction; and Civil Rights Litigation. Over the years, the Court has developed several doctrinal "work-arounds" to allow plaintiffs to sue for civil rights violations by state actors. For example, a 1907 Supreme Court decision, *Ex Parte Young*, held that state officials can be sued individually in certain circumstances, even though they may have acted in their official capacity in violating the plaintiff's rights. The Court has also held that political subdivisions of states—counties, cities and other municipalities—are not protected by the state's sovereign immunity.

Exercise: The Enforcement Provisions and the Eleventh Amendment

At this point you should understand why questions about the scope of the enforcement provisions found in the Civil War Amendments often arise in the context of Eleventh Amendment disputes about the validity of statutory provisions authorizing suits against the states. Do you? Try explaining it out loud to a non-law student friend or family member.

Since *Seminole Tribe*, the Court has decided several cases involving federal laws giving individuals the right to sue states for violations of civil rights and related matters. In *Alden v. Maine*, 527 U.S. 706 (1999), the Court held in a 5–4 majority opinion written by Justice Kennedy, that the Eleventh Amendment barred suit by a state employee against the state for violation of the federal Fair Labor Standards Act, regardless of whether the suit was brought in federal or (as in this case) state court. It was undisputed that the FLSA—the federal minimum wage and overtime law—was enacted under Congress's Article I powers, not its Fourteenth Amendment enforcement provision powers. In *College Savings Bank v. Florida Prepaid Postsecondary Education Expense Board*, 527 U.S. 666 (1999), decided the same day as *Alden*, the same 5–4 majority ruled that federal copyright laws could not be sustained under section 5 of the Fourteenth Amendment. Congress could pass the laws as Article I legislation (under the copyright clause), but in doing so could not, for the reasons discussed in *Seminole Tribe,* abrogate the states' sovereign immunity.

The following cases—*Kimel v. Florida Board of Regents* and *Nevada Department of Human Resources v. Hibbs*—illustrate how the Court has applied the congruence and proportionality test set forth in *Boerne.* As we mentioned at the beginning of our discussion of the Eleventh Amendment, understanding these cases occasionally requires you to understand some background information about the underlying rights protected by the substantive provisions of the Fourteenth Amendment. This is such an occasion.

Kimel involves an age discrimination suit brought by a state employee under the federal Age Discrimination in Employment Act, while *Hibbs* involves gender discrimination under the Family and Medical Leave Act. The key to understanding these cases is to understand that the substantive provisions of the Fourteenth Amendment, specifically the Equal Protection clause, treat these different types of discrimination differently. Discrimination based on sex or gender is subjected to a form of heightened scrutiny. Generally speaking, heightened scrutiny review means that the government has to have an important (or sometimes compelling) interest in engaging in the discriminatory conduct, and that the law authorizing the discrimination must be substantially or narrowly tailored to advance that interest.[8] In practice, this means that gender discrimination frequently violates the Constitution.

Discriminatory treatment based on age is subjected to less rigorous scrutiny. Laws that differentiate between people on these grounds are subject only to rationality review. This means that the government's reason for the differential treatment need only be reasonable, and that the law authorizing the discrimination need only be rationally related to the government's interest. In practice, this means that most laws authorizing differential treatment on the basis of age or disability will *not* violate the Constitution.

The question presented in these cases is whether Congress has power under the enforcement provisions to prohibit employers from engaging in these different types of discriminatory treatment. Remember: as long as Congress is acting within an enumerated power, it can pass laws doing *more* than is constitutionally required. The question in such cases is not whether the Constitution itself prohibits the discriminatory treatment, but whether Congress has power, under something like the Commerce Clause or the enforcement provisions, to prohibit such treatment by statute if it so chooses.

For the reasons discussed in *Seminole Tribe* and *Fitzpatrick,* these cases arise in the context of the Eleventh Amendment. This is because in each of these statutes Congress wanted not just to prohibit the underlying discriminatory conduct, but also to authorize victims of discriminatory treatment to sue for damages in federal court. As you know, the Eleventh Amendment restricts the power of Congress to authorize such suits.

Guided Reading Questions: *Kimel* and *Hibbs*

1. The Court's application of the congruence and proportionately test is closely tied to the different "tiers" or levels of scrutiny discussed above. Pay attention

---

8. The standard of review used by courts in Equal Protection claims is more complex than the basic outline presented here indicates. You will learn about this later in this book; for now, it is enough to know that laws discriminating on the basis of gender (and race, although that is not at issue in the cases below) are subject to a more rigorous scrutiny than are laws drawing distinctions on things like age.

when reading *Kimel* and *Hibbs* to how these things are connected, and try to explain the connection in your own words before moving on to the next case.

2. Pay attention to how the Court uses congressional findings of fact in both cases. Is the Court giving Congress the same level of deference in both cases?

Kimel v. Florida Board of Regents

528 U.S. 62 (2000)

Majority: *O'Connor*, Rehnquist (CJ), Scalia, Kennedy, Thomas

Dissent: *Stevens*, Souter, Ginsburg, Breyer (omitted)[9]

JUSTICE O'CONNOR delivered the opinion of the Court.

The Age Discrimination in Employment Act of 1967 ... makes it unlawful for an employer, including a State, "to fail or refuse to hire or to discharge any individual or otherwise discriminate against any individual ... because of such individual's age." ... In these cases, three sets of plaintiffs filed suit under the Act, seeking money damages for their state employers' alleged discrimination on the basis of age. In each case, the state employer moved to dismiss the suit on the basis of its Eleventh Amendment immunity. The District Court in one case granted the motion to dismiss, while in each of the remaining cases the District Court denied the motion. Appeals in the three cases were consolidated before the Court of Appeals for the Eleventh Circuit, which held that the ADEA does not validly abrogate the States' Eleventh Amendment immunity. In these cases, we are asked to consider whether the ADEA contains a clear statement of Congress' intent to abrogate the States' Eleventh Amendment immunity and, if so, whether the ADEA is a proper exercise of Congress' constitutional authority. We conclude that the ADEA does contain a clear statement of Congress' intent to abrogate the States' immunity, but that the abrogation exceeded Congress' authority under §5 of the Fourteenth Amendment.... We granted certiorari, ... to resolve a conflict among the Federal Courts of Appeals on the question whether the ADEA validly abrogates the States' Eleventh Amendment immunity....

The Eleventh Amendment states:

> The Judicial power of the United States shall not be construed to extend to any suit in law or equity, commenced or prosecuted against one of the United States by Citizens of another State, or by Citizens or Subjects of any Foreign State.

Although today's cases concern suits brought by citizens against their own States, this Court has long "understood the Eleventh Amendment to stand not so much for what it says, but for the presupposition ... which it confirms." Seminole Tribe of Fla. v. Florida. Accordingly, for over a century now, we have made clear that the Constitution does not provide for federal jurisdiction over suits against nonconsenting States. Hans v. Louisiana (1890). Petitioners nevertheless contend that the States of Alabama and Florida must defend the present suits

---

9. The voting breakdown in the full case was slightly more complicated. The 5–4 breakdown stated above went to the ultimate conclusion that the ADEA was not a valid exercise of section 5 enforcement power. On the threshold question of whether Congress *intended* to abrogate state sovereign immunity in enacting the ADEA, omitted from this excerpt, seven justices (*O'Connor*, Rehnquist (CJ), Scalia, Stevens, Souter, Ginsburg, Breyer) agreed that the ADEA was so intended. (Kennedy and Thomas dissented on this point.)

on the merits because Congress abrogated their Eleventh Amendment immunity in the ADEA. To determine whether petitioners are correct, we must resolve two predicate questions: first, whether Congress unequivocally expressed its intent to abrogate that immunity; and second, if it did, whether Congress acted pursuant to a valid grant of constitutional authority....

To determine whether a federal statute properly subjects States to suits by individuals, we apply a "simple but stringent test: 'Congress may abrogate the States' constitutionally secured immunity from suit in federal court only by making its intention unmistakably clear in the language of the statute.'" ... We agree with petitioners that the ADEA satisfies that test....

This is not the first time we have considered the constitutional validity of the 1974 extension of the ADEA to state and local governments. In EEOC v. Wyoming, we held that the ADEA constitutes a valid exercise of Congress' power "[t]o regulate Commerce ... among the several States," ... and that the Act did not transgress any external restraints imposed on the commerce power by the Tenth Amendment. Because we found the ADEA valid under Congress' Commerce Clause power, we concluded that it was unnecessary to determine whether the Act also could be supported by Congress' power under § 5 of the Fourteenth Amendment.... Resolution of today's cases requires us to decide that question....

Today we adhere to our holding in Seminole Tribe: Congress' powers under Article I of the Constitution do not include the power to subject States to suit at the hands of private individuals.... Section 5 of the Fourteenth Amendment, however, does grant Congress the authority to abrogate the States' sovereign immunity. In Fitzpatrick v. Bitzer, we recognized that "the Eleventh Amendment, and the principle of state sovereignty which it embodies, are necessarily limited by the enforcement provisions of § 5 of the Fourteenth Amendment." ... Since our decision in Fitzpatrick, we have reaffirmed the validity of that congressional power on numerous occasions.... Accordingly, the private petitioners in these cases may maintain their ADEA suits against the States of Alabama and Florida if, and only if, the ADEA is appropriate legislation under § 5....

As we recognized most recently in City of Boerne v. Flores, § 5 is an affirmative grant of power to Congress. "It is for Congress in the first instance to 'determin[e] whether and what legislation is needed to secure the guarantees of the Fourteenth Amendment,' and its conclusions are entitled to much deference." ... Congress' § 5 power is not confined to the enactment of legislation that merely parrots the precise wording of the Fourteenth Amendment. Rather, Congress' power "to enforce" the Amendment includes the authority both to remedy and to deter violation of rights guaranteed thereunder by prohibiting a somewhat broader swath of conduct, including that which is not itself forbidden by the Amendment's text....

Nevertheless, we have also recognized that the same language that serves as the basis for the affirmative grant of congressional power also serves to limit that power. For example, Congress cannot "decree the *substance* of the Fourteenth Amendment's restrictions on the States. It has been given the power 'to enforce,' not the power to determine *what constitutes* a constitutional violation." The ultimate interpretation and determination of the Fourteenth Amendment's substantive meaning remains the province of the Judicial Branch.... In City of Boerne, we noted that the determination whether purportedly prophylactic legislation constitutes appropriate remedial legislation, or instead effects a substantive redefinition of the Fourteenth Amendment right at issue, is often difficult. The line between the two is a fine one. Accordingly, recognizing that "Congress must have wide latitude in determining where [that line] lies," we held that "[t]here must be a congruence and proportionality between the injury to be prevented or remedied and the means adopted to that end." ...

In City of Boerne, we applied that "congruence and proportionality" test and held that the Religious Freedom Restoration Act of 1993 (RFRA) was not appropriate legislation under §5. We first noted that the legislative record contained very little evidence of the unconstitutional conduct purportedly targeted by RFRA's substantive provisions. Rather, Congress had uncovered only "anecdotal evidence" that, standing alone, did not reveal a "widespread pattern of religious discrimination in this country." ... Second, we found that RFRA is "so out of proportion to a supposed remedial or preventive object that it cannot be understood as responsive to, or designed to prevent, unconstitutional behavior."

Applying the same "congruence and proportionality" test in these cases, we conclude that the ADEA is not "appropriate legislation" under §5 of the Fourteenth Amendment. Initially, the substantive requirements the ADEA imposes on state and local governments are disproportionate to any unconstitutional conduct that conceivably could be targeted by the Act. We have considered claims of unconstitutional age discrimination under the Equal Protection Clause three times. In all three cases, we held that the age classifications at issue did not violate the Equal Protection Clause. Age classifications, unlike governmental conduct based on race or gender, cannot be characterized as "so seldom relevant to the achievement of any legitimate state interest that laws grounded in such considerations are deemed to reflect prejudice and antipathy." ... Older persons, again, unlike those who suffer discrimination on the basis of race or gender, have not been subjected to a "history of purposeful unequal treatment." ... Old age also does not define a discrete and insular minority because all persons, if they live out their normal life spans, will experience it.... Accordingly, as we recognized in Murgia, Bradley, and Gregory, age is not a suspect classification under the Equal Protection Clause....

States may discriminate on the basis of age without offending the Fourteenth Amendment if the age classification in question is rationally related to a legitimate state interest. The rationality commanded by the Equal Protection Clause does not require States to match age distinctions and the legitimate interests they serve with razorlike precision. As we have explained, when conducting rational basis review "we will not overturn such [government action] unless the varying treatment of different groups or persons is so unrelated to the achievement of any combination of legitimate purposes that we can only conclude that the [government's] actions were irrational." In contrast, when a State discriminates on the basis of race or gender, we require a tighter fit between the discriminatory means and the legitimate ends they serve. Under the Fourteenth Amendment, a State may rely on age as a proxy for other qualities, abilities, or characteristics that are relevant to the State's legitimate interests. The Constitution does not preclude reliance on such generalizations. That age proves to be an inaccurate proxy in any individual case is irrelevant. "[W]here rationality is the test, a State 'does not violate the Equal Protection Clause merely because the classifications made by its laws are imperfect.' Finally, because an age classification is presumptively rational, the individual challenging its constitutionality bears the burden of proving that the "facts on which the classification is apparently based could not reasonably be conceived to be true by the governmental decision maker." ...

Judged against the backdrop of our equal protection jurisprudence, it is clear that the ADEA is "so out of proportion to a supposed remedial or preventive object that it cannot be understood as responsive to, or designed to prevent, unconstitutional behavior." City of Boerne. The Act, through its broad restriction on the use of age as a discriminating factor, prohibits substantially more state employment decisions and practices than would likely be held unconstitutional under the applicable equal protection, rational basis standard.... The ADEA makes unlawful, in the employment context, all "discriminat[ion] against any individual ... because of such individual's age." ...

That the ADEA prohibits very little conduct likely to be held unconstitutional, while significant, does not alone provide the answer to our §5 inquiry. Difficult and intractable problems often require powerful remedies, and we have never held that § 5 precludes Congress from enacting reasonably prophylactic legislation. Our task is to determine whether the ADEA is in fact just such an appropriate remedy or, instead, merely an attempt to substantively redefine the States' legal obligations with respect to age discrimination. One means by which we have made such a determination in the past is by examining the legislative record containing the reasons for Congress' action.... "The appropriateness of remedial measures must be considered in light of the evil presented. Strong measures appropriate to address one harm may be an unwarranted response to another, lesser one."...

Our examination of the ADEA's legislative record confirms that Congress' 1974 extension of the Act to the States was an unwarranted response to a perhaps inconsequential problem. Congress never identified any pattern of age discrimination by the States, much less any discrimination whatsoever that rose to the level of constitutional violation. The evidence compiled by petitioners to demonstrate such attention by Congress to age discrimination by the States falls well short of the mark. That evidence consists almost entirely of isolated sentences clipped from floor debates and legislative reports.... The statements of Senator Bentsen on the floor of the Senate are indicative of the strength of the evidence relied on by petitioners. See, *e.g.,* 118 Cong. Rec. 24397 (1972) (stating that "there is ample evidence that age discrimination is broadly practiced in government employment," but relying on newspaper articles about federal employees); id., at 7745 ("Letters from my own State have revealed that State and local governments have also been guilty of discrimination toward older employees"); ibid. ("[T]here are strong indications that the hiring and firing practices of governmental units discriminate against the elderly")....

A review of the ADEA's legislative record as a whole, then, reveals that Congress had virtually no reason to believe that state and local governments were unconstitutionally discriminating against their employees on the basis of age. Although that lack of support is not determinative of the § 5 inquiry, ... Congress' failure to uncover any significant pattern of unconstitutional discrimination here confirms that Congress had no reason to believe that broad prophylactic legislation was necessary in this field. In light of the indiscriminate scope of the Act's substantive requirements, and the lack of evidence of widespread and unconstitutional age discrimination by the States, we hold that the ADEA is not a valid exercise of Congress' power under § 5 of the Fourteenth Amendment. The ADEA's purported abrogation of the States' sovereign immunity is accordingly invalid.

Our decision today does not signal the end of the line for employees who find themselves subject to age discrimination at the hands of their state employers. We hold only that, in the ADEA, Congress did not validly abrogate the States' sovereign immunity to suits by private individuals. State employees are protected by state age discrimination statutes, and may recover money damages from their state employers, in almost every State of the Union. Those avenues of relief remain available today, just as they were before this decision. Affirmed.

Nevada Department of Human Resources v. Hibbs

538 U.S. 721 (2003)

Majority opinion: *Rehnquist* (CJ), O'Connor, Souter, Ginsburg, Breyer

Concurrence: *Souter*, Ginsburg, Breyer; *Stevens* (both omitted)

Dissent: *Scalia; Kennedy*, Scalia, Thomas (both omitted)

CHIEF JUSTICE REHNQUIST delivered the opinion of the Court.

The Family and Medical Leave Act of 1993 (FMLA or Act) entitles eligible employees to take up to 12 work weeks of unpaid leave annually for any of several reasons, including the onset of a "serious health condition" in an employee's spouse, child, or parent. The Act creates a private right of action to seek both equitable relief and money damages "against any employer (including a public agency) in any Federal or State court of competent jurisdiction," should that employer "interfere with, restrain, or deny the exercise of" FMLA rights. We hold that employees of the State of Nevada may recover money damages in the event of the State's failure to comply with the family-care provision of the Act.

[Respondent William Hibbs, an employee of the Welfare Division of the Nevada Department of Human Resources, sought leave from work under the FMLA to care for his ailing wife, who was recovering from a car accident and neck surgery. Although the Department granted him some leave, it eventually fired Hibbs for failing to return to work. Hibbs filed suit for money damages under the FMLA, claiming that the FMLA entitled him to more leave than was granted by the Department. The district court granted summary judgment for Nevada on the grounds that the FMLA claim was barred by the Eleventh Amendment; the Ninth Circuit reversed.]

For over a century now, we have made clear that the Constitution does not provide for federal jurisdiction over suits against nonconsenting States. Congress may, however, abrogate such immunity in federal court if it makes its intention to abrogate unmistakably clear in the language of the statute and acts pursuant to a valid exercise of its power under § 5 of the Fourteenth Amendment. In enacting the FMLA, Congress relied on two of the powers vested in it by the Constitution: its Article I commerce power and its power under § 5 of the Fourteenth Amendment to enforce that Amendment's guarantees. Congress may not abrogate the States' sovereign immunity pursuant to its Article I power over commerce. Seminole Tribe. Congress may, however, abrogate States' sovereign immunity through a valid exercise of its § 5 power, for "the Eleventh Amendment, and the principle of state sovereignty which it embodies, are necessarily limited by the enforcement provisions of § 5 of the Fourteenth Amendment." Fitzpatrick....

The FMLA aims to protect the right to be free from gender-based discrimination in the workplace. We have held that statutory classifications that distinguish between males and females are subject to heightened scrutiny. For a gender-based classification to withstand such scrutiny, it must "serv[e] important governmental objectives," and "the discriminatory means employed [must be] substantially related to the achievement of those objectives. The State's justification for such a classification "must not rely on overbroad generalizations about the different talents, capacities, or preferences of males and females." We now inquire whether Congress had evidence of a pattern of constitutional violations on the part of the States in this area....

Congress responded to [the nation's early history of gender discrimination] by abrogating States' sovereign immunity in Title VII of the Civil Rights Act of 1964 and we sustained this abrogation in Fitzpatrick. But state gender discrimination did not cease. "[I]t can hardly be doubted that ... women still face pervasive, although at times more subtle, discrimination ... in the job market." According to evidence that was before Congress when it enacted the FMLA, States continue to rely on invalid gender stereotypes in the employment context, specifically in the administration of leave benefits. Reliance on such stereotypes cannot justify the States' gender discrimination in this area. The long and extensive history of sex discrimination prompted us to hold that measures that differentiate on the basis of gender warrant heightened scrutiny; here, as in Fitzpatrick, the persistence of such unconstitutional discrimination by the States justifies Congress' passage of prophylactic § 5 legislation.

As the FMLA's legislative record reflects, a 1990 Bureau of Labor Statistics (BLS) survey stated that 37 percent of surveyed private-sector employees were covered by maternity leave policies, while only 18 percent were covered by paternity leave policies.... While these data show an increase in the percentage of employees eligible for such leave, they also show a widening of the gender gap during the same period. Thus, stereotype-based beliefs about the allocation of family duties remained firmly rooted, and employers' reliance on them in establishing discriminatory leave policies remained widespread.

Congress also heard testimony that "[p]arental leave for fathers ... is rare. Even ... [w]here child-care leave policies do exist, men, *both in the public and private sectors,* receive notoriously discriminatory treatment in their requests for such leave." Joint Hearing 147 (Washington Council of Lawyers). Many States offered women extended "maternity" leave that far exceeded the typical 4- to 8-week period of physical disability due to pregnancy and childbirth, but very few States granted men a parallel benefit: Fifteen States provided women up to one year of extended maternity leave, while only four provided men with the same.... This and other differential leave policies were not attributable to any differential physical needs of men and women, but rather to the pervasive sex-role stereotype that caring for family members is women's work.... Finally, Congress had evidence that, even where state laws and policies were not facially discriminatory, they were applied in discriminatory ways. It was aware of the "serious problems with the discretionary nature of family leave," because when "the authority to grant leave and to arrange the length of that leave rests with individual supervisors," it leaves "employees open to discretionary and possibly unequal treatment." Testimony supported that conclusion, explaining that "[t]he lack of uniform parental and medical leave policies in the work place has created an environment where [sex] discrimination is rampant." ...

In sum, the States' record of unconstitutional participation in, and fostering of, gender-based discrimination in the administration of leave benefits is weighty enough to justify the enactment of prophylactic § 5 legislation ... We reached the opposite conclusion in Garrett and Kimel. In those cases, the § 5 legislation under review responded to a purported tendency of state officials to make age- or disability-based distinctions. Under our equal protection case law, discrimination on the basis of such characteristics is not judged under a heightened review standard, and passes muster if there is "a rational basis for doing so at a class-based level, even if it 'is probably not true' that those reasons are valid in the majority of cases." Kimel. Thus, in order to impugn the constitutionality of state discrimination against the disabled or the elderly, Congress must identify, not just the existence of age- or disability-based state decisions, but a "widespread pattern" of irrational reliance on such criteria. We found no such showing with respect to the ADEA and Title I of the Americans with Disabilities Act of 1990(ADA)....

Here, however, Congress directed its attention to state gender discrimination, which triggers a heightened level of scrutiny.... Because the standard for demonstrating the constitutionality of a gender-based classification is more difficult to meet than our rational-basis test—it must "serv[e] important governmental objectives" and be "substantially related to the achievement of those objectives," ... it was easier for Congress to show a pattern of state constitutional violations....

The judgment of the Court of Appeals is therefore affirmed.

Review Questions and Explanations: *Kimel* and *Hibbs*

1. The Age Discrimination in Employment Act at issue in *Kimel* prohibits employers, including state governments, from discriminating against their

employees on the basis of age. The ADEA also authorizes employees who believe they have been subject to such discrimination to sue their employers (including employers who are state governments) in federal court for damages. Excluding for the moment the authorization of suit part of the statute, is the ADEA a valid exercise of Congress's Commerce Clause power? Explain why or why not.

2. Does the ADEA violate the Tenth Amendment, as interpreted in *New York* and *Printz*?

3. If Congress had developed a long record showing that non-governmental employers had repeatedly discriminated against people on the basis of age, would that have been sufficient to show that the remedy chosen by Congress (the authorization of suit) was congruent and proportional to an underlying constitutional violation?

4. What evidence of unconstitutional discrimination did Congress rely on in enacting the FMLA? Why was this evidence sufficient when the evidence compiled by Congress in relation to the ADEA was not?

It may be helpful in evaluating these cases to envision the congruence and proportionality test as a dartboard. In the center of the board is the bullseye. Sitting within the bullseye is the underlying constitutional violation, as defined by the Court's individual rights jurisprudence. There has to be *something* in that bullseye that Congress is aiming at—there must be, in other words, an underlying constitutional violation that Congress is attempting to remedy or prevent. So the first question presented in these cases is whether Congress's factual findings adequately evidence an actual underlying constitutional violation, under the applicable doctrinal test (for example, heightened scrutiny or rational basis review).

Figure 1.4. Hitting the Bullseye

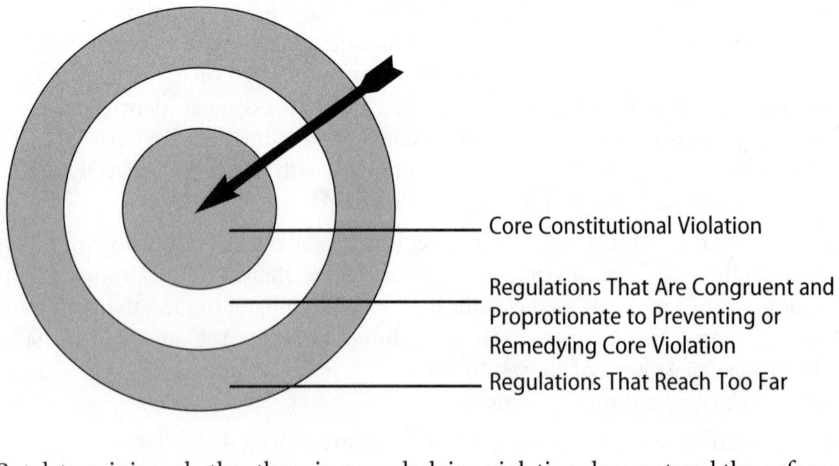

Core Constitutional Violation

Regulations That Are Congruent and Proprotionate to Preventing or Remedying Core Violation

Regulations That Reach Too Far

But determining whether there is an underlying violation does not end the enforcement provision inquiry. We also must consider whether Congress' effort to remedy or prevent constitutional violations is congruent and proportional to that underlying violation. This is where the rest of the dartboard comes in. In trying to remedy or prevent the violation—in trying to hit the bullseye—Congress gets some margin of error. As long as it is *aiming* for a constitutionally recognized violation, it will get points for coming close, just like a dart player gets points for hitting the board near, but not quite in, the bullseye. Hitting the bartender in the eye with a dart, however, is a different story. That is not within the margin of error—it is not "coming close" to your target. So a regulatory effort that is the functional equivalent of hitting the bartender—a congressional effort to regulate something that is just too far removed from the core constitutional violation—is invalid.

Trying to hit the bullseye with an axe is likewise invalid, because the tool being used is disproportionate to the size of the target. We can illustrate this point by using the facts presented in *Kimel.* Because congressional record compiled in *Kimel* failed to show a likelihood of any underlying constitutional violation (it hadn't shown that states themselves were unconstitutionally—as opposed to unwisely or unkindly—discriminating on the basis of age) there was nothing in the bullseye for Congress to be aiming at. So any effort was like throwing an axe at the board—it was disproportionate to the underlying (in this case nonexistent) constitutional violation.

G. The Modern Necessary and Proper Clause

The "necessary and proper" clause continues to receive attention from the Court as a possible basis for assertions of congressional power. As seen above, the majority in *Printz v. United States* brushed aside the dissent's argument that commandeering of local law enforcement officials was "necessary and proper" to federal Commerce Clause regulation of gun purchases, calling the Necessary and Proper clause "the last, best hope of those who defend ultra vires congressional action." Perhaps ironically, the author of *Printz,* Justice Scalia, based his concurrence in the judgment in *Raich* on the Necessary and Proper clause. In the Affordable Care Act case, the Court rejected an argument that the "individual mandate" was "necessary and proper" to regulation of the interstate health care market.

CASE NOTE: *United States v. Comstock,* 560 U.S. ___, 130 S. Ct. 1949 (2010). Comstock involved a challenge to the a federal statute providing for ongoing detention, via "civil commitment" to a mental institution, of mentally ill individuals about to be released from federal prison who have been found to be "sexually dangerous to others." See 18 U.S.C. §§ 4247–4248. Under the statute, if found to be "sexually dangerous" by a federal judge following a hearing, such individuals must be committed by the Attorney General to an appropriate mental institution unless state authorities agree to do so. Comstock and several others challenged the statute on the ground that it exceeded the powers granted to Congress by Art. I, § 8. The Court upheld the statute by a 7–2 vote. A five justice majority opinion concluded that the statute was a valid exercise of authority "necessary and proper" to Congress's acknowledged power to imprison violators of federal criminal laws, since the law dealt with terms and conditions of release from federal criminal detention. The majority adopted a five-factor test for analyzing "necessary and proper" clause arguments: (1) the breadth of the Necessary and Proper Clause, (2) the history of federal involvement in the legislative arena, (3) the federal interests underlying the statute, (4) the statute's accommodation of state interests, and (5) the narrowness of the statute's scope. Justices Kennedy and Alito concurred in the judgment. Justice Thomas, in a dissent joined by Justice Scalia, argued "[t]he Necessary and Proper Clause does not provide Congress with authority to enact any law simply because it furthers other laws Congress has enacted in the exercise of its incidental authority; the Clause plainly requires a showing that every federal statute 'carr[ies] into Execution' one or more of the Federal Government's enumerated powers." Here, the power to detain federal prisoners was already one step removed from any enumerated power. *Comstock*, by the way, is the Court's answer to the exercise on the Necessary and Proper clause immediately following *McCulloch*, in section B of this chapter.

H. The Treaty Power

The "treaty power" belongs to the President and the Senate: the President "shall have power, by and with the advice and consent of the Senate, to make treaties, provided two thirds of the Senators present concur." Art. II, § 2, cl. 2. Although they do not stem from the legislative power of Congress, treaties are "laws" in an important sense, as stated in the Supremacy Clause, Art. VI, cl. 2:

> This Constitution, and the laws of the United States which shall be made in pursuance thereof; *and all treaties made*, or which shall be made, under the authority of the United States, shall be the supreme law of the land; and the judges in every state shall be bound thereby. (Emphasis added.)

Some treaties might, at least in theory, have the force of domestic federal law in and of themselves. Other treaties might require some sort of follow-up implementation, by an act of Congress or perhaps orders or regulations emanating from the Executive Branch. Treaties, therefore, implicate congressional powers even though they are not technically among Congress's enumerated powers. The next case considers whether the treaty power is subject to the kinds of limits imposed on ordinary congressional legislation by the enumeration of powers in Article I, § 8.

Guided Reading Questions: *Missouri v. Holland*

1. What is the relationship between the December 8, 1916 treaty between the U.S. and Great Britain and the "Migratory Bird Treaty Act of July 3, 1918"?

2. Under what constitutional power is the treaty enacted? Under what power is the statute enacted?

Missouri v. Holland
252 U.S. 416 (1920)

Majority: *Holmes*, White (CJ), McKenna, Day, McReynolds, Brandeis, Clarke

Dissents (without opinion): Van Devanter, Pitney

MR. JUSTICE HOLMES delivered the opinion of the court.

This is a bill in equity brought by the State of Missouri to prevent a game warden of the United States from attempting to enforce the Migratory Bird Treaty Act of July 3,

1918, and the regulations made by the Secretary of Agriculture in pursuance of the same.... A motion to dismiss was sustained by the District Court on the ground that the act of Congress is constitutional. The State appeals.

On December 8, 1916, a treaty between the United States and Great Britain was proclaimed by the President. It recited that many species of birds in their annual migrations traversed certain parts of the United States and of Canada, that they were of great value as a source of food and in destroying insects injurious to vegetation, but were in danger of extermination through lack of adequate protection. It therefore provided for specified close seasons and protection in other forms, and agreed that the two powers would take or propose to their law-making bodies the necessary measures for carrying the treaty out. The above mentioned Act of July 3, 1918, entitled an act to give effect to the convention, prohibited the killing, capturing or selling any of the migratory birds included in the terms of the treaty except as permitted by regulations compatible with those terms, to be made by the Secretary of Agriculture. Regulations were proclaimed on July 31, and October 25, 1918. It is unnecessary to go into any details, because ... the question raised is the general one whether the treaty and statute are void as an interference with the rights reserved to the States.

To answer this question it is not enough to refer to the Tenth Amendment, reserving the powers not delegated to the United States, because by Article II, ß 2, the power to make treaties is delegated expressly, and by Article VI treaties made under the authority of the United States, along with the Constitution and laws of the United States made in pursuance thereof, are declared the supreme law of the land. If the treaty is valid there can be no dispute about the validity of the statute under Article I, ß 8, as a necessary and proper means to execute the powers of the Government....

It is said that a treaty cannot be valid if it infringes the Constitution, that there are limits, therefore, to the treaty-making power, and that one such limit is that what an act of Congress could not do unaided, in derogation of the powers reserved to the States, a treaty cannot do....

[It] is obvious that there may be matters of the sharpest exigency for the national well being that an act of Congress could not deal with but that a treaty followed by such an act could, and it is not lightly to be assumed that, in matters requiring national action, "a power which must belong to and somewhere reside in every civilized government" is not to be found. Andrews v. Andrews, 188 U.S. 14, 33. What was said in that case with regard to the powers of the States applies with equal force to the powers of the nation in cases where the States individually are incompetent to act. We are not yet discussing the particular case before us but only are considering the validity of the test proposed. With regard to that we may add that when we are dealing with words that also are a constituent act, like the Constitution of the United States, we must realize that they have called into life a being the development of which could not have been foreseen completely by the most gifted of its begetters. It was enough for them to realize or to hope that they had created an organism; it has taken a century and has cost their successors much sweat and blood to prove that they created a nation. The case before us must be considered in the light of our whole experience and not merely in that of what was said a hundred years ago. The treaty in question does not contravene any prohibitory words to be found in the Constitution. The only question is whether it is forbidden by some invisible radiation from the general terms of the Tenth Amendment. We must consider what this country has become in deciding what that Amendment has reserved.

The State as we have intimated founds its claim of exclusive authority upon an assertion of title to migratory birds, an assertion that is embodied in statute. No doubt it is true that as between a State and its inhabitants the State may regulate the killing and sale of such birds, but it does not follow that its authority is exclusive of paramount powers. To put the claim of the State upon title is to lean upon a slender reed. Wild birds are not in the possession of anyone; and possession is the beginning of ownership. The whole foundation of the State's rights is the presence within their jurisdiction of birds that yesterday had not arrived, tomorrow may be in another State and in a week a thousand miles away. If we are to be accurate we cannot put the case of the State upon higher ground than that the treaty deals with creatures that for the moment are within the state borders, that it must be carried out by officers of the United States within the same territory, and that but for the treaty the State would be free to regulate this subject itself.

As most of the laws of the United States are carried out within the States and as many of them deal with matters which in the silence of such laws the State might regulate, such general grounds are not enough to support Missouri's claim. Valid treaties of course "are as binding within the territorial limits of the States as they are elsewhere throughout the dominion of the United States." Baldwin v. Franks, 120 U.S. 678, 683. No doubt the great body of private relations usually fall within the control of the State, but a treaty may override its power....

Here a national interest of very nearly the first magnitude is involved. It can be protected only by national action in concert with that of another power. The subject-matter is only transitorily within the State and has no permanent habitat therein. But for the treaty and the statute there soon might be no birds for any powers to deal with. We see nothing in the Constitution that compels the Government to sit by while a food supply is cut off and the protectors of our forests and our crops are destroyed. It is not sufficient to rely upon the States. The reliance is vain, and were it otherwise, the question is whether the United States is forbidden to act. We are of opinion that the treaty and statute must be upheld. Decree affirmed.

Review Questions and Explanations: *Missouri v. Holland*

1. Recall what you have learned about the limited scope of the Commerce Clause, and the broad scope of the Tenth Amendment prior to 1937. Would the Court in 1920 have upheld a federal statute regulating hunting seasons for migratory birds as within the commerce power or other enumerated power of Congress, in the absence of a treaty?

2. If the answer to question 1 is "no," what difference does the treaty make?

Professional Development Reflection Questions

1. What do you think motivates Supreme Court justices to decide a particular constitutional decision in a particular way? Consider the following possibilities:

(1) stare decisis; (2) consistency with case precedent more generally (in the absence of a controlling decision); (3) the Court's proper role in the scheme of separation of powers (e.g., deference to legislative choices); (4) the justice's personal view of how best to interpret the Constitution; (5) respect for the justified, settled expectations of individuals and institutional actors who would be affected by the decision; (6) the

justice's moral or ideological beliefs; (7) the justice's social policy preferences; (8) the justice's political party affiliation.

Do you think one or more of these factors enter into the individual justices decisions? Which ones? Do the relative weights of the factors vary from case to case? What factors should enter into their decisions? Note that judges' decisions are often called "result-oriented" if they are dominated by factors 5, 6 or 7. Does factor 4 belong with that group, or with the grouping preceding it? What do you think forms the basis of judicial beliefs about the best interpretive methods? What forms the basis of your beliefs? How would you decide cases if you were a Supreme Court justice? You might find it easier to think about these questions in the context of a specific case rather than in the abstract.

2. Suppose you are a lawyer representing a health insurance company that is vehemently opposed to the minimum coverage provision of the Affordable Care Act. The in-house "general counsel" for your client tells you that the client wants you to argue in a brief to the Supreme Court that *Heart of Atlanta Motel*, the case upholding the constitutionality of the Civil Rights Act of 1964 (federal anti-discrimination law), represented an unwarranted extension of the Commerce Clause and should be overruled (and therefore, a fortiori, the minimum coverage provision is unconstitutional). You believe overruling *Heart of Atlanta Motel* would be bad for the nation and that the Court could easily strike down the minimum coverage provision without overruling *Heart of Atlanta Motel*.

Consider how you would handle the following two variations of this scenario. What would you say to the client in each situation?

1) You are convinced that the argument will be rejected by most or all of the justices.

2) You are concerned that you might succeed in persuading at least some, and perhaps five, justices at least to consider overruling *Heart of Atlanta Motel*.

With a classmate, assume the roles of the lawyer and the general counsel, and have this conversation.

3. Suppose you are an Assistant United States Attorney handling criminal prosecutions for the federal government. You have been assigned the cases of Angel Raich and Diane Monson, and your DEA case agent has provided you a file with evidence showing that you could charge them with possession of marijuana in violation of the Controlled Substances Act. What will you do with these cases? What should the policy of your office be in such cases? With whom should you discuss that policy?

4. Suppose you are a state bar prosecutor responsible for bringing disciplinary actions against errant attorneys in your state, which happens to be a state that has legalized medical marijuana. It has come to your attention that several attorneys in your state have been counseling clients about running medical marijuana dispensaries or otherwise providing legal assistance to distributers of medical marijuana. The activities are all legal under state law, but appear to constitute counseling the commission of a crime under federal law. The attorney ethics code in your state says that it is attorney misconduct to counsel a person in the commission of a crime. Should you initiate disciplinary proceedings against these attorneys?

5. Suppose you are an associate at a large law firm that has a vague pro bono policy that states only "the firm encourages its members and associates to engage in pro bono work." You have an opportunity to write an amicus curiae brief in a constitutional law case pending in the U.S. Supreme Court on behalf of a client who cannot afford to pay you. You have determined that there is no conflict of interest with any of the firm's clients for you to take on this project, but the partner whom you work with says he thinks you are too busy. What will you do?

Chapter 2

Limitations on State Powers

A. Overview

This chapter examines the ways in which the Constitution limits the power of states. As you know from your earlier readings, the states, unlike the federal government, retain all powers not taken away by the Constitution. These retained state powers frequently are referred to as "police powers," and generally include the power to regulate broadly for the health, safety and welfare of the residents of the state.

The Constitution does, however, impose some limitations on state power. Not all powers, in other words, *are* retained. Many of these limitations prohibit states from infringing the individual civil and political rights of people within their jurisdiction. The Amendments enacted after the Civil War (the Thirteenth, Fourteenth, and Fifteenth Amendments) and the "incorporation" of the original Bill of Rights against the states (a process mentioned in Chapter 1 and described later in this book) are examples of this type of limitation.

But the Constitution also imposes important restrictions on state power that are not directly associated with individual rights, particularly in Article I. It is these structural restrictions that we will examine here. Specifically, we will look at the "dormant" Commerce Clause, the Supremacy Clause, the Privileges and Immunities clause, and the Full Faith and Credit clause. The dormant Commerce Clause, which we examine first, is a judicially crafted doctrine derived from the Commerce Clause. Generally speaking, the doctrine prohibits states from doing things that interfere with the congressional prerogative to regulate commerce among the states. The Supremacy Clause limits the power of states by making state laws subordinate to the Constitution, treaties, and federal law. The Privileges and Immunities clause limits the ability of states to treat outsiders differently than it treats its own residents, while the Full Faith and Credit clause requires states to respect certain types of actions taken by other states.

B. The Dormant Commerce Clause

Dormant Commerce Clause doctrine is complex. In teaching these materials, we have found it useful to provide students with a basic outline before studying the cases. While this may tempt some students to believe we have done the hard work for them, rest assured we have not. As you will see, the most analytically difficult part of these materials is not identifying the black letter law, but applying it.

The dormant Commerce Clause applies to situations in which states, broadly speaking, act in ways that interfere with the national market. State laws can do this blatantly, by doing things like prohibiting within the state the sale of a product made by an out of state manufacturer. They also can do so indirectly, by passing laws, like consumer protection laws requiring certain disclosures on food labels, that impose unique costs on nationwide businesses. In analyzing dormant Commerce Clause cases, courts make a preliminary distinction between these two different types of state laws. Laws that discriminate against out of state people, business or interests (like in the first example) are subject to a different test than those (like the second example) that do not discriminate but that nonetheless "burden" interstate commerce.

If a law is discriminatory, it must serve a legitimate state interest and the state must show it is unable to advance that interest through less discriminatory means. A law can under this analysis be discriminatory either facially *or* in purpose or effect. Discriminatory laws rarely pass this test and thus are rarely constitutional.

A law that is burdensome but non-discriminatory is subjected to a balancing test, sometimes called the *Pike* balancing test after the case in which it was first introduced. Under this test, a state law is unconstitutional only if the burdens imposed on interstate commerce by the law are not outweighed by the benefits provided to the state by the law. Note that a desire to protect a state's economic interest at the expensive of outsiders is *not* an acceptable benefit. Since a major goal of the dormant Commerce Clause is to prevent exactly that type of protectionist behavior, a protectionist motive or effect would make the law less, not more, likely to survive constitutional scrutiny.

Some illustrations may be helpful at this point. An example of a facially discriminatory law would be a Kentucky law that prohibits tobacco grown in Virginia from being sold in Kentucky. Such a law discriminates on its face against an out of state product. Laws of this kind are considered protectionist and are subject to a virtually *per se* rule of invalidity. An example of a facially neutral but nonetheless discriminatory law would be a Kentucky law that does not specify on its face that Virginia tobacco cannot be sold in Kentucky, but rather says that all tobacco sold in Kentucky must be of the Cavendish variety, a variety that the enacting legislature knows can be grown only in Kentucky's Bluegrass region.

An example of a law that is non-discriminatory but that burdens interstate commerce would be a law that requires all tobacco sold in Kentucky to be mixed with a particular percentage of non-nicotine fillers. Such laws—when not passed with protectionist motives—are usually enacted by states to promote or protect the health and safety of their citizens. Although these laws are non-discriminatory (in-state goods, businesses, and industries are treated no differently than their out-of-state counterparts), they nonetheless burden the free flow of interstate commerce because they require manufacturers to either forgo the Kentucky market or change their ordinary business practices to do business in one particular state. Because these laws are not protectionist in purpose or effect, they are subject to the less restrictive *Pike* balancing test. Laws subject to this test are often—although certainly not always—upheld.

As we will see when we examine the cases, laws enacted in the real world rarely fall as neatly as do the above examples into one or the other of these categories. A large part of the challenge in these cases is figuring out whether a law *is* discriminatory or not. These examples nonetheless should help you understand the categories and tests used by the Court, and the things the Court is looking for when deciding which test to apply.

One final doctrinal point. The Court has crafted several exceptions to these general rules. The exceptions will be discussed later in this chapter. But to complete our doctrinal overview, we briefly sketch them out here. First, and most importantly, state laws that would otherwise violate the dormant Commerce Clause are constitutional if passed with congressional permission. Recall that the entire purpose of the doctrine is to protect

Congress' prerogative to regulate interstate commerce. Consequently, if Congress *chooses* to empower states to enact discriminatory or burdensome laws, those laws are not subject to judicial invalidation under the dormant Commerce Clause. Second, states acting as "market participants" can do things that would be prohibited by the dormant Commerce Clause if the state was acting in its more traditional regulatory role. States act as market participants when they do things unrelated to their regulatory powers, such as when they buy goods or services. The reasons for this exception will be discussed after we examine the core cases. Finally, the Court has developed distinct criteria governing a few specific issue areas in which states treat outsiders differently than insiders. These include the sale of liquor, the regulation of ground water, and use of differential taxation and subsidy schemes to favor insiders at the expensive of outsiders. These issues are better handled in specialized courses and are not discussed here.

1. Foundational Doctrine

The following case, *H.P. Hood & Sons v. Du Mond,* introduces you to the doctrine outlined above. It also explores the policy considerations underlying the dormant Commerce Clause, and illustrates the difficulty of applying the black letter law in actual case.

Guided Reading Questions: *H.P. Hood & Sons, Inc. v. Du Mond*

1. How does the Court decide whether the law at issue discriminates against out-of-staters or not? When thinking about this question, focus on the consequences of the state's action: what happens to milk prices within the state when milk cannot readily be shipped out of state?

2. What test does the Court apply, and how does it apply the test to the facts?

3. How does the challenged law operate in practice? A useful way to do this is to think through who is advantaged and who is disadvantaged under the challenged legislation.

H.P. Hood & Sons, Inc. v. Du Mond
336 U.S. 525 (1949)

Majority: *Jackson*, Reed, Douglas, Burton, Vinson (CJ)

Dissents: *Frankfurter*, Rutledge; *Black*, Murphy (omitted)

MR. JUSTICE JACKSON delivered the opinion of the Court.

This case concerns the power of the State of New York to deny additional facilities to acquire and ship milk in interstate commerce where the grounds of denial are that such limitation upon interstate business will protect and advance local economic interests.

H. P. Hood & Sons, Inc., a Massachusetts corporation, has long distributed milk and its products to inhabitants of Boston. That city obtains about 90% of its fluid milk from states other than Massachusetts. Dairies located in New York State since about

1900 have been among the sources of Boston's supply, their contribution having varied but during the last ten years approximately 8%. The area in which Hood has been denied an additional license to make interstate purchases has been developed as a part of the Boston milkshed from which both the Hood Company and a competitor have shipped to Boston.

The state courts have held and it is conceded here that Hood's entire business in New York, present and proposed, is interstate commerce. This Hood has conducted for some time by means of three receiving depots, where it takes raw milk from farmers. The milk is not processed in New York but is weighed, tested and, if necessary, cooled and on the same day shipped as fluid milk to Boston. These existing plants have been operated under license from the State and are not in question here as the State has licensed Hood to continue them. The controversy concerns a proposed additional plant for the same kind of operation at Greenwich, New York....

The Commissioner found that Hood, if licensed at Greenwich, would permit its present suppliers, at their option, to deliver at the new plant rather than the old ones and for a substantial number this would mean shorter hauls and savings in delivery costs. The new plant also would attract twenty to thirty producers, some of whose milk Hood anticipates will or may be diverted from other buyers. Other large milk distributors have plants within the general area and dealers serving Troy obtain milk in the locality. He found that Troy was inadequately supplied during the preceding short season....

Our decision in a milk litigation most relevant to the present controversy deals with the converse of the present situation. Baldwin v. G.A.F. Seelig, Inc. In that case, New York placed conditions and limitations on the local sale of milk imported from Vermont designed in practical effect to exclude it, while here its order proposes to limit the local facilities for purchase of additional milk so as to withhold milk from export. The State agreed then, as now, that the Commerce Clause prohibits it from directly curtailing movement of milk into or out of the State. But in the earlier case, it contended that the same result could be accomplished by controlling delivery, bottling and sale after arrival, while here it says it can do so by curtailing facilities for its purchase and receipt before it is shipped out. In neither case is the measure supported by health or safety considerations but solely by protection of local economic interests, such as supply for local consumption and limitation of competition. This Court unanimously rejected the State's contention in the Seelig case and held that the Commerce Clause, even in the absence of congressional action, prohibits such regulations for such ends.... It recognized, as do we, broad power in the State to protect its inhabitants against perils to health or safety, fraudulent traders and highway hazards even by use of measures which bear adversely upon interstate commerce. But it laid repeated emphasis upon the principle that the State may not promote its own economic advantages by curtailment or burdening of interstate commerce.

The Constitution, said Mr. Justice Cardozo for the unanimous Court [in Baldwin] 'was framed upon the theory that the peoples of the several states must sink or swim together, and that in the long run prosperity and salvation are in union and not division.' He reiterated that the economic objective, as distinguished from any health, safety and fair-dealing purpose of the regulation, was the root of its invalidity. The action of the State would 'neutralize the economic consequences of free trade among the states.' Such a power, if exerted, will set a barrier to traffic between one state and another as effective as if customs duties, equal to the price differential, and been laid upon the thing transported. 'If New York, in order to promote the economic welfare of her farmers, may guard them against competition, with the cheaper prices of Vermont, the door has been opened to rivalries and reprisals that were meant to be averted by subjecting commerce between the states to the power of the nation.' And again, 'Neither the power to tax nor the police power may be used by the state of destination with the aim and effect of establishing an economic barrier against competition with the products of another state or the labor of its residents. Restrictions so contrived are an unreasonable clog upon the mobility of commerce. They set up what is equivalent to a rampart of customs duties designed to neutralize advantages belonging to the place of origin. They are thus hostile in conception as well as burdensome in result.

This distinction between the power of the State to shelter its people from menaces to their health or safety and from fraud, even when those dangers emanate from interstate commerce, and its lack of power to retard, burden or constrict the flow of such commerce for their economic advantage, is one deeply rooted in both our history and our law.

When victory relieved the Colonies from the pressure for solidarity that war had exerted, a drift toward anarchy and commercial warfare between states began. '[E]ach state would legislate according to its estimate of its own interests, the importance of its own products, and the local advantages or disadvantages of its position in a political or commercial view.' This came 'to threaten at once the peace and safety of the Union.'...

The Commerce Clause is one of the most prolific sources of national power and an equally prolific source of conflict with legislation of the state. While the Constitution vests in Congress the power to regulate commerce among the states, it does not say what the states may or may not do in the absence of congressional action, nor how to draw the line between what is and what is not commerce among the states. Perhaps even more than by interpretation of its written word, this Court has advanced the solidarity and prosperity of this Nation by the meaning it has given to these great silences of the Constitution.

Baldwin ... is an explicit, impressive, recent and unanimous condemnation by this Court of economic restraints on interstate commerce for local economic advantage, but it does not stand along. This Court consistently has rebuffed attempts of states to advance their own commercial interests by curtailing the movement of articles of commerce, either into or out of the state, while generally supporting their right to impose even burdensome regulations in the interest of local health and safety....

The State, however, insists that denial of the license for a new plant does not restrict or obstruct interstate commerce, because petitioner has been licensed at its other plants without condition or limitation as to the quantities it may purchase. Hence, it is said, all that has been denied petitioner is a local convenience—that of being able to buy and receive at Greenwich, quantities of milk it is free to buy at Eagle Bridge and Salem. It suggests that, by increased efficiency or enlarged capacity at its other plants, petitioner might sufficiently increase its supply through those facilities.

The weakness of this contention is that a buyer has to buy where there is a willing seller, and the peculiarities of the milk business necessitate location of a receiving and cooling station for nearby producers. The Commissioner has not made and there is nothing to persuade us that he could have made findings that petitioner can obtain such additional supplies through its existing facilities; indeed he found that 'applicant has experienced some difficulty during the flush season because of the inability of the plant facilities to handle the milk by 9 a.m.,' the time its receipt is required by Boston health authorities unless it is cooled by the farmer before delivery, and a substantial part of it is not....

The judgment is reversed and the cause remanded for proceedings not inconsistent with this opinion.

MR. JUSTICE FRANKFURTER, with whom MR. JUSTICE RUTLEDGE joins, dissenting.

If the Court's opinion has meaning beyond deciding this case in isolation, its effect is to hold that no matter how important to the internal economy of a State may be the prevention of destructive competition, and no matter how unimportant the interstate commerce affected, a State cannot as a means of preventing such competition deny an applicant access to a market within the State if that applicant happens to intend the out-of-state shipment of the product that he buys. I feel constrained to dissent because I cannot agree in treating what is essentially a problem of striking a balance between competing interests as an exercise in absolutes.... Broadly stated, the question is whether a State can withhold from interstate commerce a product derived from local raw materials upon a determination by an administrative agency that there is a local need for it....

Review Questions and Explanations: *H.P. Hood*

1. Justice Jackson's opinion is one of the Court's strongest endorsements of the dormant Commerce Clause doctrine. He makes several related but distinct arguments in support of a robust doctrine. Identify and evaluate each of his arguments.

2. What is the point of disagreement between the majority and the dissent? Do they disagree about the facts, the law, or something else?

3. What type of test are the dissenters advocating? What would be the advantages and disadvantages of this type of test?

4. Many of the early dormant Commerce Clause cases involved agriculture. Why do you think that was?

2. Facially Discriminatory Laws

Guided Reading Questions: *City of Philadelphia v. New Jersey* and *C&A Carbone v. Clarkstown*

1. The dispute in *City of Philadelphia v. New Jersey* is not about whether the law at issue is discriminatory: both the majority and the dissent agree that it is. When you read the case, focus on figuring out what the actual point of disagreement is and why it is legally relevant.

2. In *C&A Carbone v. Clarkstown*, the parties *do* disagree about whether the challenged law is discriminatory. The town of Clarkstown argues that the challenged law is not discriminatory, while Carbone argues that it is. Can you put the arguments made by both sides into your own words? Taking the time before class to write out your best understanding of the competing positions presented in a case is a good way to improve your case reading skills by forcing you to focus on the issues the Court is grappling with.

City of Philadelphia v. New Jersey
437 U.S. 617 (1978)

Majority: *Stewart*, Brennan, White, Marshall, Blackmun, Powell, Stevens

Dissent: *Rehnquist*, Burger (CJ)

MR. JUSTICE STEWART delivered the opinion of the Court.

A New Jersey law prohibits the importation of most "solid or liquid waste which originated or was collected outside the territorial limits of the State...." In this case we are required to decide whether this statutory prohibition violates the Commerce Clause of the United States Constitution....

Apart from a few narrow exceptions [N]ew Jersey closed its borders to all waste from other States.... Immediately affected by these developments were the operators of private landfills in New Jersey, and several cities in other States that had agreements with these operators for waste disposal. They brought suit against New Jersey and its Department of Environmental Protection in state court, attacking the statute and regulations on a number of state and federal grounds. In an oral opinion granting the plaintiffs' motion for summary judgment, the trial court declared the law unconstitutional because it discriminated against interstate commerce....

Although the Constitution gives Congress the power to regulate commerce among the States, many subjects of potential federal regulation under that power inevitably escape congressional attention "because of their local character and their number and diversity." ... In the absence of federal legislation, these subjects are open to control by the States so long as they act within the restraints imposed by the Commerce Clause itself.... The bounds of these restraints appear nowhere in the words of the Commerce Clause, but have emerged gradually in the decisions of this Court giving effect to its basic purpose....

The state court additionally found that New Jersey's existing landfill sites will be exhausted within a few years; that to go on using these sites or to develop new ones will take a heavy environmental toll, both from pollution and from loss of scarce open lands; that new techniques to divert waste from landfills to other methods of disposal and resource recovery processes are under development, but that these changes will require time; and finally, that "the extension of the lifespan of existing landfills, resulting from the exclusion of out-of-state waste, may be of crucial importance in preventing further virgin wetlands or other undeveloped lands from being devoted to landfill purposes." Based on these findings, the court concluded that ch. 363 was designed to protect, not the State's economy, but its environment, and that its substantial benefits outweigh its "slight" burden on interstate commerce....

This dispute about ultimate legislative purpose need not be resolved, because its resolution would not be relevant to the constitutional issue to be decided in this case. Contrary to the evident assumption of the state court and the parties, the evil of protectionism can reside in legislative means as well as legislative ends. Thus, it does not matter whether the ultimate aim of ch. 363 is to reduce the waste disposal costs of New Jersey residents or to save remaining open lands from pollution, for we assume New Jersey has every right to protect its residents' pocketbooks as well as their environment. And it may be assumed as well that New Jersey may pursue those ends by slowing the flow of *all* waste into the State's remaining landfills, even though interstate commerce may incidentally be affected. But whatever New Jersey's ultimate purpose, it may not be accomplished by discriminating against articles of commerce coming from outside the

State unless there is some reason, apart from their origin, to treat them differently. Both on its face and in its plain effect, ch. 363 violates this principle of nondiscrimination.... The Court has consistently found parochial legislation of this kind to be constitutionally invalid....

The New Jersey law at issue in this case falls squarely within the area that the Commerce Clause puts off limits to state regulation. On its face, it imposes on out-of-state commercial interests the full burden of conserving the State's remaining landfill space. It is true that in our previous cases the scarce natural resource was itself the article of commerce, whereas here the scarce resource and the article of commerce are distinct. But that difference is without consequence. In both instances, the State has overtly moved to slow or freeze the flow of commerce for protectionist reasons. It does not matter that the State has shut the article of commerce inside the State in one case and outside the State in the other. What is crucial is the attempt by one State to isolate itself from a problem common to many by erecting a barrier against the movement of interstate trade.

The judgment is reversed.

MR. JUSTICE REHNQUIST, with whom MR. CHIEF JUSTICE BURGER joins, dissenting.

.... The health and safety hazards associated with landfills present appellees with a currently unsolvable dilemma. Other, hopefully safer, methods of disposing of solid wastes are still in the development stage and cannot presently be used. But appellees obviously cannot completely stop the tide of solid waste that its citizens will produce in the interim. For the moment, therefore, appellees must continue to use sanitary landfills to dispose of New Jersey's own solid waste despite the critical environmental problems thereby created.

The question presented in this case is whether New Jersey must also continue to receive and dispose of solid waste from neighboring States, even though these will inexorably increase the health problems discussed above. The Court answers this question in the affirmative. New Jersey must either prohibit *all* landfill operations, leaving itself to cast about for a presently nonexistent solution to the serious problem of disposing of the waste generated within its own borders, or it must accept waste from every portion of the United States, thereby multiplying the health and safety problems which would result if it dealt only with such wastes generated within the State. Because past precedents establish that the Commerce Clause does not present appellees with such a Hobson's choice, I dissent....

C&A Carbone v. Town of Clarkstown
511 U.S. 383 (1994)

Majority: *Kennedy*, Stevens, Scalia, Thomas, Ginsburg

Concurrence in the judgment: *O'Connor* (omitted)

Dissent: *Souter*, Rehnquist (CJ), Blackmun

JUSTICE KENNEDY delivered the opinion of the Court.

We consider a so-called flow control ordinance, which requires all solid waste to be processed at a designated transfer station before leaving the municipality. The avowed purpose of the ordinance is to retain the processing fees charged at the transfer station to amortize the cost of the facility. Because it attains this goal by depriving competitors, including out-of-state firms, of access to a local market, we hold that the flow control ordinance violates the Commerce Clause.

The town of Clarkstown, New York, lies in the lower Hudson River Valley, just upstream from the Tappan Zee Bridge and by highway minutes from New Jersey. Within the town limits are the village of Nyack and the hamlet of West Nyack. In August 1989, Clarkstown entered into a consent decree with the New York State Department of Environmental Conservation. The town agreed to close its landfill located on Route 303 in West Nyack and build a new solid waste transfer station on the same site. The station would receive bulk solid waste and separate recyclable from nonrecyclable items. Recyclable waste would be baled for shipment to a recycling facility; nonrecyclable waste, to a suitable landfill or incinerator.

The cost of building the transfer station was estimated at $1.4 million. A local private contractor agreed to construct the facility and operate it for five years, after which the town would buy it for $1. During those five years, the town guaranteed a minimum waste flow of 120,000 tons per year, for which the contractor could charge the hauler a so-called tipping fee of $81 per ton. If the station received less than 120,000 tons in a year, the town promised to make up the tipping fee deficit. The object of this arrangement was to amortize the cost of the transfer station: The town would finance its new facility with the income generated by the tipping fees.

The problem, of course, was how to meet the yearly guarantee. This difficulty was compounded by the fact that the tipping fee of $81 per ton exceeded the disposal cost of unsorted solid waste on the private market. The solution the town adopted was the flow control ordinance here in question, Local Laws 1990, No. 9 of the Town of Clarkstown (full text in Appendix). The ordinance requires all nonhazardous solid waste within the town to be deposited at the Route 303 transfer station. Id., § 3.C (waste generated within the town), § 5.A (waste generated outside and brought in). Noncompliance is punishable by as much as a $1,000 fine and up to 15 days in jail.

The petitioners in this case are C & A Carbone, Inc., a company engaged in the processing of solid waste, and various related companies or persons, all of whom we designate Carbone. Carbone operates a recycling center in Clarkstown, where it receives bulk solid waste, sorts and bales it, and then ships it to other processing facilities—much as occurs at the town's new transfer station. While the flow control ordinance permits recyclers like Carbone to continue receiving solid waste, § 3.C, it requires them to bring the nonrecyclable residue from that waste to the Route 303 station. It thus forbids Carbone to ship the nonrecyclable waste itself, and it requires Carbone to pay a tipping fee on trash that Carbone has already sorted....

While the immediate effect of the ordinance is to direct local transport of solid waste to a designated site within the local jurisdiction, its economic effects are interstate in reach. The Carbone facility in Clarkstown receives and processes waste from places other than Clarkstown, including from out of State. By requiring Carbone to send the nonrecyclable portion of this waste to the Route 303 transfer station at an additional cost, the flow control ordinance drives up the cost for out-of-state interests to dispose of their solid waste. Furthermore, even as to waste originating in Clarkstown, the ordinance prevents everyone except the favored local operator from performing the initial processing step. The ordinance thus deprives out-of-state businesses of access to a local market. These economic effects are more than enough to bring the Clarkstown ordinance within the purview of the Commerce Clause. It is well settled that actions are within the domain of the Commerce Clause if they burden interstate commerce or impede its free flow....

The real question is whether the flow control ordinance is valid despite its undoubted effect on interstate commerce. For this inquiry, our case law yields two lines of analysis:

first, whether the ordinance discriminates against interstate commerce ... and second, whether the ordinance imposes a burden on interstate commerce that is "clearly excessive in relation to the putative local benefits," Pike v. Bruce Church, Inc. As we find that the ordinance discriminates against interstate commerce, we need not resort to the Pike test....

Clarkstown protests that its ordinance does not discriminate because it does not differentiate solid waste on the basis of its geographic origin. All solid waste, regardless of origin, must be processed at the designated transfer station before it leaves the town. Unlike the statute in Philadelphia, says the town, the ordinance erects no barrier to the import or export of any solid waste but requires only that the waste be channeled through the designated facility.

Our initial discussion of the effects of the ordinance on interstate commerce goes far toward refuting the town's contention that there is no discrimination in its regulatory scheme. The town's own arguments go the rest of the way. As the town itself points out, what makes garbage a profitable business is not its own worth but the fact that its possessor must pay to get rid of it. In other words, the article of commerce is not so much the solid waste itself, but rather the service of processing and disposing of it.... In this light, the flow control ordinance is just one more instance of local processing requirements that we long have held invalid.... The flow control ordinance has the same design and effect. It hoards solid waste, and the demand to get rid of it, for the benefit of the preferred processing facility.... State and local governments may not use their regulatory power to favor local enterprise by prohibiting patronage of out-of-state competitors or their facilities. We reverse the judgment and remand the case for proceedings not inconsistent with this decision.

JUSTICE SOUTER, with whom CHIEF JUSTICE REHNQUIST and JUSTICE BLACK-MUN join, dissenting.

The majority may invoke "well-settled principles of our Commerce Clause jurisprudence," but it does so to strike down an ordinance unlike anything this Court has ever invalidated. Previous cases have held that the "negative" or "dormant" aspect of the Commerce Clause renders state or local legislation unconstitutional when it discriminates against out-of-state or out-of-town businesses such as those that pasteurize milk, hull shrimp, or mill lumber, and the majority relies on these cases because of what they have in common with this one: out-of-state processors are excluded from the local market (here, from the market for trash processing services). What the majority ignores, however, are the differences between our local processing cases and this one: the exclusion worked by Clarkstown's Local Law 9 bestows no benefit on a class of local private actors, but instead directly aids the government in satisfying a traditional governmental responsibility. The law does not differentiate between all local and all out-of-town providers of a service, but instead between the one entity responsible for ensuring that the job gets done and all other enterprises, regardless of their location. The ordinance thus falls outside that class of tariff or protectionist measures that the Commerce Clause has traditionally been thought to bar States from enacting against each other, and when the majority subsumes the ordinance within the class of laws this Court has struck down as facially discriminatory (and so avails itself of our "virtually *per se* rule" against such statutes ...) the majority is in fact greatly extending the Clause's dormant reach.

There are, however, good and sufficient reasons against expanding the Commerce Clause's inherent capacity to trump exercises of state authority such as the ordinance at issue here. There is no indication in the record that any out-of-state trash processor has been harmed, or that the interstate movement or disposition of trash will be affected one whit. To the degree Local Law 9 affects the market for trash processing services, it does so only by subjecting Clarkstown residents and businesses to burdens far different from the burdens of local favoritism that dormant Commerce Clause jurisprudence seeks to root out. The town has found a way to finance a public improvement, not by transferring its cost to out-of-state economic interests, but by spreading it among the local generators of trash, an equitable result with tendencies that should not disturb the Commerce Clause and should not be disturbed by us....

Review Questions and Explanations: *City of Philadelphia* and *C&A Carbone*

1. The dissent in *City of Philadelphia* implies that the majority has left New Jersey helpless to deal with its landfill problems. Is this correct? What could New Jersey do to address these problems while also complying with the Court's decision?

2. Is the law challenged in *City of Philadelphia* discriminatory on its face, discriminatory in purpose, or discriminatory in effect?

3. Does the Court find that the law challenged in *Carbone* is discriminatory on its face, discriminatory in purpose, or discriminatory in effect?

4. Why does the Court strike down the law at issue in *Carbone*? Be precise — what test did the Court apply, and what prong or element of the test did the law fail?

3. Facially Neutral Laws

Guided Reading Questions: *Hunt v. Washington Apple Advertising* and *Minnesota v. Clover Leaf Creamery*

1. Remember that a facially neutral law can still be discriminatory in purpose or effect. When reading these cases, pay attention to the parties' arguments on this point, and note how the Court resolves them. Does the Court find the laws in either of these cases to be discriminatory in purpose or effect? Why or why not?

2. When reading the cases, think about how the challenged state actions differ from the laws at issue in *City of Philadelphia* and *Carbone*.

Hunt v. Washington State Apple Advertising Commission
432 U.S. 333 (1977)

Unanimous decision: *Burger* (CJ), Brennan, Stewart, White, Marshall, Blackmun, Powell, Rehnquist, Stevens

MR. CHIEF JUSTICE BURGER delivered the opinion of the Court.

In 1973, North Carolina enacted a statute which required, inter alia, all closed containers of apples sold, offered for sale, or shipped into the State to bear "no grade other than the applicable U.S. grade or standard." ...

Washington State is the Nation's largest producer of apples, its crops accounting for approximately 30% of all apples grown domestically and nearly half of all apples shipped in closed containers in interstate commerce. As might be expected, the production and sale of apples on this scale is a multimillion dollar enterprise which plays a significant role in Washington's economy. Because of the importance of the apple industry to the State, its legislature has undertaken to protect and enhance the reputation of Washington apples by establishing a stringent, mandatory inspection program, administered by the State's Department of Agriculture, which requires all apples shipped in interstate commerce to be tested under strict quality standards and graded accordingly. In all cases, the Washington State grades, which have gained substantial acceptance in the trade, are the equivalent of, or superior to, the comparable grades and standards adopted by the United States Department of Agriculture (USDA). Compliance with the Washington inspection scheme costs the State's growers approximately $1 million each year....

In 1972, the North Carolina Board of Agriculture adopted an administrative regulation, unique in the 50 States, which in effect required all closed containers of apples shipped into or sold in the State to display either the applicable USDA grade or none at all. State grades were expressly prohibited. In addition to its obvious consequence prohibiting the display of Washington State apple grades on containers of apples shipped into North Carolina, the regulation presented the Washington apply industry with a marketing problem of potentially nationwide significance. Washington apple growers annually ship in commerce approximately 40 million closed containers of apples, nearly 500,000 of which eventually find their way into North Carolina, stamped with the applicable Washington State variety and grade. It is the industry's practice to purchase these containers preprinted with the various apple varieties and grades, prior to harvest. After these containers are filled with apples of the appropriate type and grade, a substantial portion of them are placed in cold-storage warehouses where the grade labels identify the product and facilitate its handling. These apples are then shipped as needed throughout the year....

Since the ultimate destination of these apples is unknown at the time they are placed in storage, compliance with North Carolina's unique regulation would have required Washington growers to obliterate the printed labels on containers shipped to North Carolina, thus giving their product a damaged appearance. Alternatively, they could have changed their marketing practices to accommodate the needs of the North Carolina market, i.e., repack apples to be shipped to North Carolina in containers bearing only the USDA grade, and/or store the estimated portion of the harvest destined for that market in such special containers. As a last resort, they could discontinue the use of the preprinted containers entirely. None of these costly and less efficient options was very attractive to the industry. Moreover, in the event a number of other States followed North Carolina's lead, the resultant inability to display the Washington grades could force the Washington growers to abandon the State's expensive inspection and grading system which their customers had come to know and rely on over the 60-odd years of its existence....

We turn finally to the appellants' claim that the District Court erred in holding that the North Carolina statute violated the Commerce Clause insofar as it prohibited the display of Washington State grades on closed containers of apples shipped into the State. Appellants do not really contest the District Court's determination that the challenged statute burdened the Washington apple industry by increasing its costs of doing business in the North Carolina market and causing it to lose accounts there. Rather, they maintain that any such burdens on the interstate sale of Washington apples were far outweighed by the local benefits flowing from what they contend was a valid exercise of North Carolina's inherent police powers designed to protect its citizenry from fraud and deception in the marketing of apples....

As the District Court correctly found, the challenged statute has the practical effect of not only burdening interstate sales of Washington apples, but also discriminating against them. This discrimination takes various forms. The first, and most obvious, is the statute's consequence of raising the costs of doing business in the North Carolina market for Washington apple growers and dealers, while leaving those of their North Carolina counterparts unaffected. As previously noted, this disparate effect results from the fact that North Carolina apple producers, unlike their Washington competitors, were not forced to alter their marketing practices in order to comply with the statute. They were still free to market their wares under the USDA grade or none at all as they had done prior to the statute's enactment. Obviously, the increased costs imposed by the statute would tend to shield the local apple industry from the competition of Washington apple growers and dealers who are already at a competitive disadvantage because of their great distance from the North Carolina market.

Second, the statute has the effect of stripping away from the Washington apple industry the competitive and economic advantages it has earned for itself through its expensive inspection and grading system....

Third, by prohibiting Washington growers and dealers from marketing apples under their State's grades, the statute has a leveling effect which insidiously operates to the advantage of local apple producers. As noted earlier, the Washington State grades are equal or superior to the USDA grades in all corresponding categories. Hence, with free market forces at work, Washington sellers would normally enjoy a distinct market advantage vis-a-vis local producers in those categories where the Washington grade is superior....

Despite the statute's facial neutrality, the Commission suggests that its discriminatory impact on interstate commerce was not an unintended byproduct and there are some indications in the record to that effect. The most glaring is the response of the North Carolina Agriculture Commissioner to the Commission's request for an exemption following the statue's passage in which he indicated that before he could support such an exemption, he would "want to have the sentiment from our apple producers since they were mainly responsible for this legislation being passed...."... Moreover, we find it somewhat suspect that North Carolina singled out only closed containers of apples, the very means by which apples are transported in commerce, to effectuate the statute's ostensible consumer protection purpose when apples are not generally sold at retail in their shipping containers. However, we need not ascribe an economic protection motive to the North Carolina Legislature to resolve this case; we conclude that the challenged statute cannot stand insofar as it prohibits the display of Washington State grades even if enacted for the declared purpose of protecting consumers from deception and fraud in the marketplace.

When discrimination against commerce of the type we have found is demonstrated, the burden falls on the State to justify it both in terms of the local benefits flowing from the statute and the unavailability of nondiscriminatory alternatives adequate to preserve the local interests at stake....

[I]t appears that nondiscriminatory alternatives to the outright ban of Washington State grades are readily available. For example, North Carolina could effectuate its goal by permitting out-of-state growers to utilize state grades only if they also marked their shipments with the applicable USDA label. In that case, the USDA grand would serve as a benchmark against which the consumer could evaluate the quality of the various state grades. If this alternative was for some reason inadequate to eradicate problems caused by state grades inferior to those adopted by the USDA, North Carolina might consider banning those state grades which, unlike Washington's could not be demonstrated to be equal or superior to the corresponding USDA categories. Concededly, even in this latter instance, some potential for "confusion" might persist. However, it is the type of "confusion" that the national interest in the free flow of goods between the States demands be tolerated.... Affirmed.

Figure 2.1. Minnesota

Minnesota v. Clover Leaf Creamery
449 U.S. 456 (1981)

Majority: *Brennan*, Burger (CJ), Stewart, White, Marshall, Blackmun

Concurrence/dissent: *Powell* (omitted)

Dissent: *Stevens* (omitted) (Justice Rehnquist took no part.)

JUSTICE BRENNAN delivered the opinion of the Court:

In 1977, the Minnesota Legislature enacted a statute banning the retail sale of milk in plastic nonreturnable, nonrefillable containers, but permitting such sale in other nonreturnable, nonrefillable containers, such as paperboard milk cartons.... Respondents contend that the statute violates the ... Commerce Clauses of the Constitution.

The purpose of the Minnesota statute is set out as § 1:

> The legislature finds that the use of nonreturnable, nonrefillable containers for the packaging of milk and other milk products presents a solid waste management problem for the state, promotes energy waste, and depletes natural resources. The legislature therefore, in furtherance of the policies stated in (citation omitted) determines that the use of nonreturnable, nonrefillable containers for packaging milk and other milk products should be discouraged and that the use of returnable and reusable packaging for these products is preferred and should be encouraged.

Section 2 of the Act forbids the retail sale of milk and fluid milk products, other than sour cream, cottage cheese, and yogurt, in nonreturnable, nonrefillable rigid or semi-rigid containers composed at least 50% of plastic....

When legislating in areas of legitimate local concern, such as environmental protection and resource conservation, States are nonetheless limited by the Commerce Clause.... If a state law purporting to promote environmental purposes is in reality "simple economic protectionism," we have applied a "virtually *per se* rule of invalidity." ... Even if a statute regulates "evenhandedly," and imposes only "incidental" burdens on interstate commerce, the courts must nevertheless strike it down if "the burden imposed on such commerce is clearly excessive in relation to the putative local benefits." (citing Pike). Moreover, "the extent of the burden that will be tolerated will of course depend on the nature of the local interest involved, and on whether it could be promoted as well with a lesser impact on interstate activities." ...

Minnesota's statute does not affect "simple protectionism," but "regulates evenhandedly" by prohibiting all milk retailers from selling their products in plastic, nonreturnable milk containers, without regard to whether the milk, the containers, or the sellers are from outside the State. This statute is therefore unlike statutes discriminating against interstate commerce, which we have consistently struck down.... Since the statute does not discriminate between interstate and intrastate commerce, the controlling question is whether the incidental burden imposed on interstate commerce by the Minnesota Act is "clearly excessive in relation to the putative local benefits." Pike v. Bruce Church. We conclude that it is not.

The burden imposed on interstate commerce by the statute is relatively minor. Milk products may continue to move freely across the Minnesota border, and since most dairies package their products in more than one type of containers, the inconvenience of having to conform to different packaging requirements in Minnesota and the surrounding States should be slight.... Within Minnesota, business will presumably shift from manufacturers of plastic nonreturnable containers to producers of paperboard cartons, refillable bottles, and plastic pouches, but there is no reason to suspect that the gainers will be Minnesota firms, or the losers out-of-state firms. Indeed, two of the three dairies, the sole milk retailer, and the sole milk container producer challenging the statute in this litigation are Minnesota firms.

Pulpwood producers are the only Minnesota industry likely to benefit significantly from the Act at the expense of out-of-state firms. Respondents point out that plastic resin, the raw material used for making plastic nonreturnable milk jugs, is produced entirely by non-Minnesota firms, while pulpwood, used for making paperboard, is a major Minnesota product. Nevertheless, it is clear that respondents exaggerate the degree of burden on out-of-state interests, both because plastics will continue to be used in the production of plastic pouches, plastic returnable bottles, and paperboard itself, and because out-of-state pulpwood producers will presumably absorb some of the business generated by the Act.

Even granting that the out-of-state plastics industry is burdened relatively more heavily than the Minnesota pulpwood industry, we find that this burden is not "clearly excessive" in light of the substantial state interest in promoting conservation of energy and other natural resources and easing solid waste disposal problems, which we have already reviewed in the context of equal protection analysis.... We find these local benefits ample to support Minnesota's decision under the Commerce Clause.... Judgment of the Minnesota Supreme Court reversed.

Review Questions and Explanations: *Hunt* and *Clover Leaf Creamery*

1. Why is the statute at issue in *Hunt* not facially discriminatory?

2. The Washington Apple Advertisers argue that the North Carolina labeling law discriminates against Washington apples. In what way? Do you agree with the Court that this constitutes a discriminatory effect—meaning it effectively treats out-of-state growers differently than in-state growers—rather than a burden on interstate commerce? You will recall from the beginning of this chapter that this is a key distinction in dormant Commerce Clause cases. Consider how the Court applied the distinction here.

3. The challengers in *Cloverleaf Creamery* argued that the law prohibiting milk from being sold in plastic containers was protectionist (a form of discrimination) in purpose or effect. What was their argument? (Hint: Take another look at Figure 2.1).

4. What does the Court see as the legally relevant difference between the regulations challenged in *Hunt* and *Cloverleaf Creamery*?

---

4. Analysis if Discriminatory

Guided Reading Questions: *Dean Milk v. City of Madison* and *Maine v. Taylor*

1. In each of the following cases, the Court found the statute at issue discriminatory and asked whether the state had a sufficient interest in enacting the law and whether the challenged law was the least discriminatory way of advancing that interest. When reading these cases, consider what types of interests the Court accepts as sufficient. When a law fails the test, consider whether it failed the state interest prong or the least restrictive alternative prong.

2. Note that in *Dean Milk* the restriction being challenged was a county ordinance rather than a state law. Does this fact matter to the Court?

3. In reading *Dean Milk*, consider how the state action being challenged is like and unlike the regulation challenged in *Hunt*.

4. What is the key fact distinguishing *Maine v. Taylor* from *Dean Milk*?

Dean Milk v. City of Madison
340 U.S. 349 (1951)

Majority: *Clark*, Vinson (CJ), Reed, Frankfurter, Jackson, Burton

Dissent: *Black*, Douglas, Minton (omitted)

MR. JUSTICE CLARK delivered the opinion of the Court.

This appeal challenges the constitutional validity of two sections of an ordinance of the City of Madison, Wisconsin, regulating the sale of milk and milk products within the municipality's jurisdiction. One section in issue makes it unlawful to sell any milk as pasteurized unless it has been processed and bottled at an approved pasteurization plant within a radius of five miles from the central square of Madison. Another section, which prohibits the sale of milk, or the importation, receipt or storage of milk for sale, in Madison unless from a source of supply possessing a permit issued after inspection by Madison officials, is attacked insofar as it expressly relieves municipal authorities from any duty to inspect farms located beyond twenty-five miles from the center of the city.

Appellant is an Illinois corporation engaged in distributing milk and milk products in Illinois and Wisconsin. It contended below, as it does here, that both the five-mile limit on pasteurization plants and the twenty-five-mile limit on sources of milk violate the Commerce Clause and the Fourteenth Amendment to the Federal Constitution....

The City of Madison is the county seat of Dane County. Within the county are some 5,600 dairy farms with total raw milk production in excess of 600,000,000 pounds annually and more than ten times the requirements of Madison. Aside from the milk supplied to Madison, fluid milk produced in the county moves in large quantities to Chicago and more distant consuming areas, and the remainder is used in making cheese, butter and other products. At the time of trial the Madison milkshed was not of 'Grade A' quality by the standards recommended by the United States Public Health Service, and no milk labeled 'Grade A' was distributed in Madison.

The area defined by the ordinance with respect to milk sources encompasses practically all of Dane County and includes some 500 farms which supply milk for Madison. Within the five-mile area for pasteurization are plants of five processors, only three of which are engaged in the general wholesale and retail trade in Madison. Inspection of these farms and plants is scheduled once every thirty days and is performed by two municipal inspectors, one of whom is full-time. The courts below found that the ordinance in question promotes convenient, economical and efficient plant inspection.

Appellant purchases and gathers milk from approximately 950 farms in northern Illinois and southern Wisconsin, none being within twenty-five miles of Madison. Its pasteurization plants are located at Chemung and Huntley, Illinois, about 65 and 85 miles respectively from Madison. Appellant was denied a license to sell its products within Madison solely because its pasteurization plants were more than five miles away.

It is conceded that the milk which appellant seeks to sell in Madison is supplied from farms and processed in plants licensed and inspected by public health authorities of Chicago, and is labeled 'Grade A' under the Chicago ordinance which adopts the rating standards recommended by the United States Public Health Service. Both the Chicago and Madison ordinances, though not the sections of the latter here in issue, are largely patterned after the Model Milk Ordinance of the Public Health Service. However, Madison contends and we assume that in some particulars its ordinance is more rigorous than that of Chicago.... [W]e agree with appellant that the ordinance imposes an undue burden on interstate commerce.

This is not an instance in which an enactment falls because of federal legislation which, as a proper exercise of paramount national power over commerce, excludes measures which might otherwise be within the police power of the states.... Nor can there be objection to the avowed purpose of this enactment. We assume that difficulties in sanitary regulation of milk and milk products originating in remote areas may present a situation in which 'upon a consideration of all the relevant facts and circumstances it appears that the matter is one which may appropriately be regulated in the interest of the safety, health and well-being of local communities.'... We also assume that since Congress has not spoken to the contrary, the subject matter of the ordinance lies within the sphere of state regulation even though interstate commerce may be affected....

But this regulation, like the provision invalidated in Baldwin v. G.A.F. Seelig, Inc., supra, in practical effect excludes from distribution in Madison wholesome milk produced and pasteurized in Illinois.... In thus erecting an economic barrier protecting a major local industry against competition from without the State, Madison plainly discriminates against interstate commerce. This it cannot do, even in the exercise of its unquestioned power to protect the health and safety of its people, if reasonable nondiscriminatory alternatives, adequate to conserve legitimate local interests, are available.... A different view, that the ordinance is valid simply because it professes to be a health measure, would mean that the Commerce Clause of itself imposes no limitations on state action other than those laid down by the Due Process Clause, save for the rare instance where a state artlessly discloses an avowed purpose to discriminate against interstate goods. Cf. H. P. Hood & Sons v. Du Mond, supra. Our issue then is whether the discrimination inherent in the Madison ordinance can be justified in view of the character of the local interests and the available methods of protecting them.

FN4. It is immaterial that Wisconsin milk from outside the Madison area is subjected to the same proscription as that moving in interstate commerce.

It appears that reasonable and adequate alternatives are available. If the City of Madison prefers to rely upon its own officials for inspection of distant milk sources, such inspection is readily open to it without hardship for it could charge the actual and reasonable cost of such inspection to the importing producers and processors.... Moreover, appellee Health Commissioner of Madison testified that as proponent of the local milk ordinance he had submitted the provisions here in controversy and an alternative proposal based on s 11 of the Model Milk Ordinance recommended by the United States Public Health Service. The model provision imposes no geographical limitation on location of milk sources and processing plants but excludes from the municipality milk not produced and pasteurized conformably to standards as high as those enforced by the receiving city. In implementing such an ordinance, the importing city obtains milk ratings based on uniform standards and established by health authorities in the jurisdiction where production and processing occur. The receiving city may determine the extent of enforcement of sanitary standards in the exporting area by verifying the accuracy of safety ratings of specific plants or of the milkshed in the distant jurisdiction through the United States Public Health Service, which routinely and on request spot checks the local ratings. The Commissioner testified that Madison consumers 'would be safeguarded adequately' under either proposal and that he had expressed no preference. The milk sanitarian of the Wisconsin State Board of Health testified that the State Health Department recommends the adoption of a provision based on the Model Ordinance. Both officials agreed that a local health officer would be justified in relying upon the evaluation by the Public Health Service of enforcement conditions in remote producing areas.

To permit Madison to adopt a regulation not essential for the protection of local health interests and placing a discriminatory burden on interstate commerce would invite a multiplication of preferential trade areas destructive of the very purpose of the Commerce Clause. Under the circumstances here presented, the regulation must yield to the principle that 'one state in its dealings with another may not place itself in a position of economic isolation.'... Judgment vacated and cause remanded for further proceedings.

Maine v. Taylor

477 U.S. 131 (1986)

Majority: *Blackmun*, Burger (CJ), Brennan, White, Marshall, Powell, Rehnquist, O'Connor

Dissent: *Stevens*

JUSTICE BLACKMUN delivered the opinion of the Court.

Once again, a little fish has caused a commotion.... The fish in this case is the golden shiner, a species of minnow commonly used as live bait in sport fishing.

Appellee Robert J. Taylor (hereafter Taylor or appellee) operates a bait business in Maine. Despite a Maine statute prohibiting the importation of live baitfish, he arranged to have 158,000 live golden shiners delivered to him from outside the State. The shipment was intercepted, and a federal grand jury in the District of Maine indicted Taylor for violating and conspiring to violate the Lacey Act Amendments of 1981, ... makes it a federal crime "to import, export, transport, sell, receive, acquire, or purchase in interstate or foreign commerce ... any fish or wildlife taken, possessed, transported, or sold in violation of any law or regulation of any State or in violation of any foreign law."... Taylor moved to dismiss the indictment on the ground that Maine's import ban unconstitutionally burdens interstate commerce....

The Commerce Clause of the Constitution grants Congress the power "[t]o regulate Commerce with foreign Nations, and among the several States, and with the Indian Tribes."... "Although the Clause thus speaks in terms of powers bestowed upon Congress, the Court long has recognized that it also limits the power of the States to erect barriers against interstate trade."... Maine's statute restricts interstate trade in the most direct manner possible, blocking all inward shipments of live baitfish at the State's border. Still, as both the District Court and the Court of Appeals recognized, this fact alone does not render the law unconstitutional. The limitation imposed by the Commerce Clause on state regulatory power "is by no means absolute," and "the States retain authority under their general police powers to regulate matters of 'legitimate local concern,' even though interstate commerce may be affected."...

In determining whether a State has overstepped its role in regulating interstate commerce, this Court has distinguished between state statutes that burden interstate transactions only incidentally, and those that affirmatively discriminate against such transactions. While statutes in the first group violate the Commerce Clause only if the burdens they impose on interstate trade are "clearly excessive in relation to the putative local benefits," Pike v. Bruce Church, Inc., statutes in the second group are subject to more demanding scrutiny. The Court explained in Hughes v. Oklahoma that once a state law is shown to discriminate against interstate commerce "either on its face or in practical effect," the burden falls on the State to demonstrate both that the statute "serves a legitimate local purpose," and that this purpose could not be served as well by available nondiscriminatory means....

Three scientific experts testified for the prosecution and one for the defense. The prosecution experts testified that live baitfish imported into the State posed two significant threats to Maine's unique and fragile fisheries. First, Maine's population of wild fish—including its own indigenous golden shiners—would be placed at risk by three types of parasites prevalent in out-of-state baitfish, but not common to wild fish in Maine.... Second, nonnative species inadvertently included in shipments of live baitfish could disturb Maine's aquatic ecology to an unpredictable extent by competing with native fish for food or habitat, by preying on native species, or by disrupting the environment in more subtle ways.... The prosecution experts further testified that there was no satisfactory way to inspect shipments of live baitfish for parasites or commingled species. According to their testimony, the small size of baitfish and the large quantities in which they are shipped made inspection for commingled species "a physical impossibility." ... Parasite inspection posed a separate set of difficulties because the examination procedure required destruction of the fish.... Although statistical sampling and inspection techniques had been developed for salmonids (*i.e.*, salmon and trout), so that a shipment could be certified parasite-free based on a standardized examination of only some of the fish, no scientifically accepted procedures of this sort were available for baitfish....

No matter how one describes the abstract issue whether "alternative means could promote this local purpose as well without discriminating against interstate commerce," ... the more specific question whether scientifically accepted techniques exist for the sampling and inspection of live baitfish is one of fact, and the District Court's finding that such techniques have not been devised cannot be characterized as clearly erroneous. Indeed, the record probably could not support a contrary finding. Two prosecution witnesses testified to the lack of such procedures, and appellee's expert conceded the point, although he disagreed about the need for such tests.... That Maine has allowed the importation of other freshwater fish after inspection hardly demonstrates that the District Court clearly erred in crediting the corroborated and uncontradicted expert testimony that standardized inspection techniques had not yet been developed for baitfish. This is particularly so because the text of the permit statute suggests that it was designed specifically to regulate importation of salmonids, for which, the experts testified, testing procedures *had* been developed.

Before this Court, appellee does not argue that sampling and inspection procedures already exist for baitfish; he contends only that such procedures "could be easily developed." ... Unlike the proposition that the techniques already exist, the contention that they could readily be devised enjoys some support in the record. Appellee's expert testified that developing the techniques "would just require that those experts in the field ... get together and do it." ... He gave no estimate of the time and expense that would be involved, however, and one of the prosecution experts testified that development of the testing procedures for salmonids had required years of heavily financed research.... In light of this testimony, we cannot say that the District Court clearly erred in concluding ... that the development of sampling and inspection techniques for baitfish could be expected to take a significant amount of time.

More importantly, we agree with the District Court that the "abstract possibility" ... of developing acceptable testing procedures, particularly when there is no assurance as to their effectiveness, does not make those procedures an "[a]vailabl[e] ... nondiscriminatory alternativ[e]," ... for purposes of the Commerce Clause. A State must make reasonable efforts to avoid restraining the free flow of commerce across its borders, but it is not required to develop new and unproven means of protection at an uncertain cost. Appellee, of course, is free to work on his own or in conjunction with other bait dealers to develop scientifically acceptable sampling and inspection procedures for golden shiners; if and when such procedures are developed, Maine no longer may be able to justify its import ban. The State need not join in those efforts, however, and it need not pretend they already have succeeded....

The evidence in this case amply supports the District Court's findings that Maine's ban on the importation of live baitfish serves legitimate local purposes that could not adequately be served by available nondiscriminatory alternatives. This is not a case of arbitrary discrimination against interstate commerce; the record suggests that Maine has legitimate reasons, "apart from their origin, to treat [out-of-state baitfish] differently," Philadelphia v. New Jersey. The judgment of the Court of Appeals setting aside appellee's conviction is therefore reversed.

JUSTICE STEVENS dissenting.

There is something fishy about this case. Maine is the only State in the Union that blatantly discriminates against out-of-state baitfish by flatly prohibiting their importation. Although golden shiners are already present and thriving in Maine (and, perhaps not coincidentally, the subject of a flourishing domestic industry), Maine excludes golden shiners grown and harvested (and, perhaps not coincidentally sold) in other States. This kind of stark discrimination against out-of-state articles of commerce requires rigorous justification by the discriminating State. "When discrimination against commerce of the type we have found is demonstrated, the burden falls on the State to justify it both in terms of the local benefits flowing from the statute and the unavailability of nondiscriminatory alternatives adequate to preserve the local interests at stake." Hunt v. Washington State Apple Advertising.

.... Since the State engages in obvious discrimination against out-of-state commerce, it should be put to its proof. Ambiguity about dangers and alternatives should actually defeat, rather than sustain, the discriminatory measure.

This is not to derogate the State's interest in ecological purity. But the invocation of environmental protection or public health has never been thought to confer some kind of special dispensation from the general principle of nondiscrimination in interstate commerce. "A different view, that the ordinance is valid simply because it professes to be a health measure, would mean that the Commerce Clause of itself imposes no restraints on state action other than those laid down by the Due Process Clause, save for the rare instance where a state artlessly discloses an avowed purpose to discriminate against interstate goods." (citing Dean Milk). If Maine wishes to rely on its interest in ecological preservation, it must show that interest, and the infeasibility of other alternatives, with far greater specificity. Otherwise, it must further that asserted interest in a manner far less offensive to the notions of comity and cooperation that underlie the Commerce Clause....

Review Questions and Explanations: *Dean Milk* and *Taylor*

1. The Court in *Dean Milk* was willing to impose fairly significant burdens on Wisconsin milk inspectors rather than allow the discriminatory regime to stand. Are there similar burdens that could have been (but were not) undertaken to protect the state interest asserted in *Maine v. Taylor*?

2. The law at issue in *Maine v. Taylor* is one of the very few discriminatory laws to be upheld by the courts. That makes it an important case for lawyers arguing by analogy that other discriminatory statutes should likewise be upheld.

To successfully analogize a new set of facts to those presented in *Taylor*, however, you must understand what convinced the Court to uphold the Maine law. What do *you* think made these minnows so special?

3. Can you think of one fact you could change in *Maine* that would make the Court come out the other way?

5. Analysis if Not Discriminatory

Guided Reading Questions: *Bibb v. Navajo Freight Lines*

1. The following case shows how the Court applies the balancing test to non-discriminatory state laws that nonetheless impose burdens on interstate commerce. You should use this case to review what you've learned about the difference between discriminatory and nondiscriminatory statues. Why was this statute, unlike those discussed above, treated as merely burdensome rather than discriminatory?

Bibb v. Navajo Freight Lines
359 U.S. 520 (1959)

Majority: *Douglas*, Warren (CJ), Black, Frankfurter, Clark, Brennan, Whittaker
Concurrence: *Harlan*, Stewart (omitted)

Mr. Justice DOUGLAS delivered the opinion of the Court.

We are asked in this case to hold that an Illinois statute requiring the use of a certain type of rear fender mudguard on trucks and trailers operated on the highways of that State conflicts with the Commerce Clause of the Constitution....

Appellees, interstate motor carriers holding certificates from the Interstate Commerce Commission, challenged the constitutionality of the Illinois Act. A specially constituted three-judge District Court concluded that it unduly and unreasonably burdened and obstructed interstate commerce, because it made the conventional or straight mudflap, which is legal in at least 45 States, illegal in Illinois, and because the statute, taken together with a Rule of the Arkansas Commerce Commission requiring straight mudflaps, rendered the use of the same motor vehicle equipment in both States impossible. The statute was declared to be violative of the Commerce Clause and appellants were enjoined from enforcing it....

The power of the State to regulate the use of its highways is broad and pervasive. We have recognized the peculiarly local nature of this subject of safety, and have upheld state statutes applicable alike to interstate and intrastate commerce, despite the fact that they may have an impact on interstate commerce.... These safety measures carry a strong presumption of validity when challenged in court....

The District Court found that 'since it is impossible for a carrier operating in interstate commerce to determine which of its equipment will be used in a particular area, or on a particular day, or days, carriers operating into or through Illinois...will be required to equip all their trailers in accordance with the requirements of the Illinois Splash Guard statute.' With two possible exceptions the mudflaps required in those States which have mudguard regulations would not meet the standards required by the Illinois statute. The cost of installing the contour mudguards is $30 or more per vehicle. The District Court found that the initial cost of installing those mudguards on all the trucks owned by the appellees ranged from $4,500 to $45,840. There was also evidence in the record to indicate that the cost of maintenance and replacement of these guards is substantial.

Illinois introduced evidence seeking to establish that contour mudguards had a decided safety factor in that they prevented the throwing of debris into the faces of drivers of passing cars and into the windshields of a following vehicle. But the District Court in its opinion stated that it was 'conclusively shown that the contour mud flap possesses no advantages over the conventional or straight mud flap previously required in Illinois and presently required in most of the states,' ... and that 'there is rather convincing testimony that use of the contour flap creates hazards previously unknown to those using the highways.' ... These hazards were found to be occasioned by the fact that this new type of mudguard tended to cause an accumulation of heat in the brake drum, thus decreasing the effectiveness of brakes, and by the fact that they were susceptible of being hit and bumped when the trucks were backed up and of falling off on the highway....

It was also found that the Illinois statute seriously interferes with the 'interline' operations of motor carriers — that is to say, with the interchanging of trailers between an originating carrier and another carrier when the latter serves an area not served by the former. These 'interline' operations provide a speedy through-service for the shipper. Interlining contemplates the physical transfer of the entire trailer; there is no unloading and reloading of the cargo. The interlining process is particularly vital in connection with shipment of perishables, which would spoil if unloaded before reaching their destination, or with the movement of explosives carried under seal. Of course, if the originating carrier never operated in Illinois, it would not be expected to equip its trailers with contour mudguards. Yet if an interchanged trailer of that carrier were hauled to or through Illinois, the statute would require that it contain contour guards. Since carriers which operate in and through Illinois cannot compel the originating carriers to equip their trailers with contour guards, they may be forced to cease interlining with those who do not meet the Illinois requirements.... This is summary is the rather massive showing of burden on interstate commerce which appellees made at the hearing....

This is one of those cases — few in number — where local safety measures that are nondiscriminatory place an unconstitutional burden on interstate commerce. This conclusion is especially underlined by the deleterious effect which the Illinois law will have on the 'interline' operation of interstate motor carriers. The conflict between the Arkansas regulation and the Illinois regulation also suggests that this regulation of mudguards is not one of those matters 'admitting of diversity of treatment, according to the special requirements of local conditions,' to use the words of Chief Justice Hughes.... A State which insists on a design out of line with the requirements of almost all the other States may sometimes place a great burden of delay and inconvenience on those interstate motor carriers entering or crossing its territory. Such a new safety device — out of line with the requirements of the other States — may be so compelling that the innovating State need not be the one to give way. But the present showing — balanced against the clear burden on commerce — is far too inconclusive to make this mudguard meet that test.

We deal not with absolutes but with questions of degree. The state legislatures plainly have great leeway in providing safety regulations for all vehicles — interstate as well as local. Our decisions so hold. Yet the heavy burden which the Illinois mudguard law places on the interstate movement of trucks and trailers seems to us to pass the permissible limits even for safety regulations.... Affirmed.

Exercises: Applying the Dormant Commerce Clause

1. A Louisiana statute prohibits the transportation or shipment of minnows for sale outside of the state if the minnows were procured from within the state. Louisiana argues that the statute is necessary because it protects the state's minnow population from the dangers of over-fishing. What test would the Court apply when deciding if the Louisiana law violated the dormant Commerce Clause? Under the applicable test, is the Louisiana law likely to be upheld or struck down?

2. Illinois recently passed a law requiring that any fruit transported in or through Illinois be certified as organically grown. Illinois claims that the law is necessary to protect the state's organic farms from the "super bugs" many scientists believe evolve in response to repeated application of pesticides to agricultural products. If the shipper cannot provide this certification, the fruit cannot pass through the state. The statute has been challenged by a shipper who routinely carries Florida oranges to the sun-deprived upper Midwest. Does the law violate the dormant Commerce Clause? Why or why not?

6. Exceptions

Guided Reading Questions: *Reeves v. Stake* and *South Central Timber v. Wunnicke*

1. The following two cases explore the "market participant" exception to the Court's dormant Commerce Clause jurisprudence. When reading *Reeves*, pay close attention to the arguments made for and against this exception.

2. *South Central Timber* also identifies three possible exceptions to the market participant exception itself. When reading the case, identify these exceptions and consider why the Court believes they should be exceptions to the exception.

3. *South Central Timber* introduces the congressional approval exception. What is the black letter law regarding this exception?

Reeves v. Stake

447 U.S. 429 (1980)

Majority: *Blackmun*, Stewart, Marshall, Burger (CJ), Rehnquist

Dissent: *Powell*, Brennan, White, Stevens

MR. JUSTICE BLACKMUN delivered the opinion of the Court.

The issue in this case is whether, consistent with the Commerce Clause, U. S. Const., Art. I, §8, cl. 3, the State of South Dakota, in a time of shortage, may confine the sale of the cement it produces solely to its residents.

In 1919, South Dakota undertook plans to build a cement plant. The project, a product of the State's then prevailing Progressive political movement, was initiated in response to recent regional cement shortages that "interfered with and delayed both public and private enterprises," and that were "threatening the people of this state." Eakin v. South Dakota State Cement Comm'n. In 1920, the South Dakota Cement Commission anticipated "[t]hat there would be a ready market for the entire output of the plant within the state."... The plant, however, located at Rapid City, soon produced more cement than South Dakotans could use. Over the years, buyers in no less than nine nearby States purchased cement from the State's plant.... Between 1970 and 1977, some 40% of the plant's output went outside the State.

> FN1. ... The backdrop against which the South Dakota cement project was initiated is described in H. Schell, History of South Dakota 268–269 (3d ed. 1975):
>
> Although a majority of the voters [in 1918] had seemingly subscribed to a state-ownership philosophy, it was a question how far the Republican administration at Pierre would go in fulfilling campaign promises. As [Governor] Norbeck entered upon his second term, he again urged a state hail insurance law and advocated steps toward a state-owned coal mine, cement plant, and state-owned stockyards. He also recommended an appropriation for surveying dam sites for hydroelectric development. The lawmakers readily enacted these recommendations into law, except for the stockyards proposal.... In retrospect, [Norbeck's] program must be viewed as a part of the Progressives' campaign against monopolistic prices. There was, moreover, the fervent desire to make the services of the state government available to agriculture.... These were basic tenets of the Progressive philosophy of government.

The plant's list of out-of-state cement buyers included petitioner Reeves, Inc. Reeves is a ready-mix concrete distributor organized under Wyoming law and with facilities in Buffalo, Gillette, and Sheridan, Wyo. From the beginning of its operations in 1958, and until 1978, Reeves purchased about 95% of its cement from the South Dakota plant.... In 1977, its purchases were $1,172,000.... In turn, Reeves has supplied three northwestern Wyoming counties with more than half their ready-mix concrete needs.... For 20 years the relationship between Reeves and the South Dakota cement plant was amicable, uninterrupted, and mutually profitable....

Reeves, which had no pre-existing long-term supply contract, was hit hard and quickly by this development. On June 30, 1978, the plant informed Reeves that it could not continue to fill Reeves' orders, and on July 5, it turned away a Reeves truck.... Unable to find another supplier, ... Reeves was forced to cut production by 76% in mid-July....

On July 19, Reeves brought this suit against the Commission, challenging the plant's policy of preferring South Dakota buyers, and seeking injunctive relief.... After conducting a hearing and receiving briefs and affidavits, the District Court found no substantial issue of material fact and permanently enjoined the Commission's practice. The court reasoned that South Dakota's "hoarding" was inimical to the national free market envisioned by the Commerce Clause....

[Our earlier case, Alexandria Scrap], concerned a Maryland program designed to remove abandoned automobiles from the State's roadways and junkyards. To encourage recycling, a "bounty" was offered for every Maryland-titled junk car converted into scrap. Processors located both in and outside Maryland were eligible to collect these subsidies. The legislation, as initially enacted in 1969, required a processor seeking a bounty to present documentation evidencing ownership of the wrecked car. This requirement however, did not apply to "hulks," inoperable automobiles over eight years old. In 1974, the statute was amended to extend documentation requirements to hulks, which comprised a large majority of the junk cars being processed. Departing from prior practice, the new law imposed more exacting documentation requirements on out-of-state than in-state processors. By making it less remunerative for suppliers to transfer vehicles outside Maryland, the reform triggered a "precipitate decline in the number of bounty-eligible hulks supplied to appellee's [Virginia] plant from Maryland sources." ... Indeed, "[t]he practical effect was substantially the same as if Maryland had withdrawn altogether the availability of bounties on hulks delivered by unlicensed suppliers to licensed non-Maryland processors." ...

Invoking the Commerce Clause, a three-judge District Court struck down the legislation.... It observed that the amendment imposed "substantial burdens upon the free flow of interstate commerce," ... and reasoned that the discriminatory program was not the least disruptive means of achieving the State's articulated objective. See generally Pike v. Bruce Church, Inc.

> **FN6.** Maryland sought to justify its reform as an effort to reduce bounties paid to out-of-state processors on Maryland-titled cars abandoned outside Maryland. The District Court concluded that Maryland could achieve this goal more satisfactorily by simply restricting the payment of bounties to only those cars abandoned in Maryland.

This Court reversed. It recognized the persuasiveness of the lower court's analysis if the inherent restrictions of the Commerce Clause were deemed applicable. In the Court's view, however, Alexandria Scrap did not involve "the kind of action with which the Commerce Clause is concerned." ... Unlike prior cases voiding state laws inhibiting interstate trade, "Maryland has not sought to prohibit the flow of hulks, or to regulate the conditions under which it may occur. Instead, it has entered into the market itself to bid up their price, ... as a purchaser, in effect, of a potential article of interstate commerce," and has restricted "its trade to its own citizens or businesses within the State." ...

Having characterized Maryland as a market participant, rather than as a market regulator, the Court found no reason to "believe the Commerce Clause was intended to require independent justification for [the State's] action." ... The Court couched its holding in unmistakably broad terms. "Nothing in the purposes animating the Commerce Clause prohibits a State, in the absence of congressional action, from participating in the market and exercising the right to favor its own citizens over others."

> **FN8.** The dissent's central criticisms of the result reached here seem to be that the South Dakota policy does not emanate from "the power of governments to supply their own needs," and that it threatens "the natural functioning of the interstate market." The same observations, however, apply with equal force to the subsidy program challenged in Alexandria Scrap.

The basic distinction drawn in Alexandria Scrap between States as market participants and States as market regulators makes good sense and sound law. As that case explains, the Commerce Clause responds principally to state taxes and regulatory measures impeding free private trade in the national marketplace. Id., citing H. P. Hood & Sons v. Du Mond (1949) (referring to "home embargoes," "customs duties," and "regulations" excluding imports). There is no indication of a constitutional plan to limit the ability of the States themselves to operate freely in the free market. See L. Tribe, American Constitutional Law 336 (1978) ("the commerce clause was directed, as an historical matter, only at regulatory and taxing actions taken by states in their sovereign capacity"). The precedents comport with this distinction.

Restraint in this area is also counseled by considerations of state sovereignty, the role of each State "as guardian and trustee for its people," ... and "the long recognized right of trader or manufacturer, engaged in an entirely private business, freely to exercise his own independent discretion as to parties with whom he will deal." United States v. Colgate & Co. (1919). Moreover, state proprietary activities may be, and often are, burdened with the same restrictions imposed on private market participants. Evenhandedness suggests that, when acting as proprietors, States should similarly share existing freedoms from federal constraints, including the inherent limits of the Commerce Clause.... Finally, as this case illustrates, the competing considerations in cases involving state proprietary action often will be subtle, complex, politically charged, and difficult to assess under traditional Commerce Clause analysis. Given these factors, Alexandria Scrap wisely recognizes that, as a rule, the adjustment of interests in this context is a task better suited for Congress than this Court.

South Dakota, as a seller of cement, unquestionably fits the "market participant" label more comfortably than a State acting to subsidize local scrap processors. Thus, the general rule of Alexandria Scrap plainly applies here. Petitioner argues, however, that the exemption for marketplace participation necessarily admits of exceptions. While conceding that possibility, we perceive in this case no sufficient reason to depart from the general rule.

... [I]t is suggested that the South Dakota program is infirm because it places South Dakota suppliers of ready-mix concrete at a competitive advantage in the out-of-state market; Wyoming suppliers, such as petitioner, have little chance against South Dakota suppliers who can purchase cement from the State's plant and freely sell beyond South Dakota's borders.

The force of this argument is seriously diminished, if not eliminated by several considerations. The argument necessarily implies that the South Dakota scheme would be unobjectionable if sales in other States were totally barred. It therefore proves too much, for it would tolerate even a greater measure of protectionism and stifling of interstate commerce than the challenge system allows.... Nor is it to be forgotten that Alexandria Scrap approved a state program that "not only ... effectively protect[ed] scrap processors with existing plants in Maryland from the pressures of competitors with nearby out-of-state plants, but [that] implicitly offer[ed] to extend similar protection to any competitor ... willing to erect a scrap processing facility within Maryland's boundaries." ... Finally, the competitive plight of out-of-state ready-mix suppliers cannot be laid solely at the feet of South Dakota. It is attributable as well to their own States' not providing or attracting alternative sources of supply and to the suppliers' own failure to guard against shortages by executing long-term supply contracts with the South Dakota plant....

We conclude, then, that the arguments for invalidating South Dakota's resident-preference program are weak at best. Whatever residual force inheres in them is more than offset by countervailing considerations of policy and fairness. Reversal would discourage similar state projects, even though this project demonstrably has served the needs of state residents and has helped the entire region for more than a half century. Reversal also would rob South Dakota of the intended benefit of its foresight, risk, and industry. Under these circumstances, there is no reason to depart from the general rule of Alexandria Scrap.

FN 19. The risk borne by South Dakota in establishing the cement plant is not to be underestimated. As explained in n. 1, *supra*, the cement plant was one of several projects through which the Progressive state government sought to deal with local problems. The fate of other similar projects illustrates the risk borne by South Dakota taxpayers in setting up the cement plant at a cost of some $2 million. Thus, "[t]he coal mine was sold in early 1934 for $5,500 with an estimated loss of nearly $175,000 for its fourteen years of operation. The 1933 Legislature also liquidated the state bonding department and the state hail insurance project. The total loss to the taxpayers from the latter venture was approximately $265,000." H. Schell, History of South Dakota, 286 (3d ed. 1975).

The judgment of the United States Court of Appeals is affirmed.

MR. JUSTICE POWELL, with whom MR. JUSTICE BRENNAN, MR. JUSTICE WHITE, and MR. JUSTICE STEVENS join, dissenting.

The South Dakota Cement Commission has ordered that in times of shortage the state cement plant must turn away out-of-state customers until all orders from South Dakotans are filled. This policy represents precisely the kind of economic protectionism that the Commerce Clause was intended to prevent. The Court, however, finds no violation of the Commerce Clause, solely because the State produces the cement. I agree with the Court that the State of South Dakota may provide cement for its public needs without violating the Commerce Clause. But I cannot agree that South Dakota may withhold its cement from interstate commerce in order to benefit private citizens and businesses within the State.

> FN1. By "protectionism," I refer to state policies designed to protect private economic interests within the State from the forces of the interstate market. I would exclude from this term policies relating to traditional governmental functions, such as education, and subsidy programs like the one at issue in Hughes v. Alexandria Scrap Corp. (1976).

The need to ensure unrestricted trade among the States created a major impetus for the drafting of the Constitution. "The power over commerce ... was one of the primary objects for which the people of America adopted their government...." Gibbons v. Ogden (1824). Indeed, the Constitutional Convention was called after an earlier convention on trade and commercial problems proved inconclusive. C. Beard, An Economic Interpretation of the Constitution 61–63 (1935)....

The Commerce Clause has proved an effective weapon against protectionism. The Court has used it to strike down limitations on access to local goods, be they animal, Hughes v. Oklahoma (1979) (minnows); vegetable, Pike v. Bruce Church, Inc. (1970) (cantalopes); or mineral, Pennsylvania v. West Virginia (1923) (natural gas). Only this Term, the Court held ... [that] "this Nation is a common market in which state lines cannot be made barriers to the free flow of both raw materials and finished goods in response to the economic laws of supply and demand."

This case presents a novel constitutional question. The Commerce Clause would bar legislation imposing on private parties the type of restraint on commerce adopted by South Dakota. See Pennsylvania v. West Virginia, supra. Conversely, a private business constitutionally could adopt a marketing policy that excluded customers who come from another State. This case falls between those polar situations. The State, through its Commission, engages in a commercial enterprise and restricts its own interstate distribution. The question is whether the Commission's policy should be treated like state regulation of private parties or like the marketing policy of a private business.

The application of the Commerce Clause to this case should turn on the nature of the governmental activity involved. If a public enterprise undertakes an "integral operatio[n] in areas of traditional governmental functions," National League of Cities v. Usery (1976), the Commerce Clause is not directly relevant. If, however, the State enters the private market and operates a commercial enterprise for the advantage of its private citizens, it may not evade the constitutional policy against economic Balkanization.

This distinction derives from the power of governments to supply their own needs, see Atkin v. Kansas (1903), and from the purpose of the Commerce Clause itself, which is designed to protect "the natural functioning of the interstate market," Hughes v. Alexandria Scrap Corp. In procuring goods and services for the operation of government, a State may act without regard to the private marketplace and remove itself from the reach of the Commerce Clause.... But when a State itself becomes a participant in the private market for other purposes, the Constitution forbids actions that would impede the flow of interstate commerce. These categories recognize no more than the "constitutional line between the State as government and the State as trader." New York v. United States (1946).

The Court holds that South Dakota, like a private business, should not be governed by the Commerce Clause when it enters the private market. But precisely because South Dakota is a State, it cannot be presumed to behave like an enterprise "engaged in an entirely private business."... A State frequently will respond to market conditions on the basis of political rather than economic concerns. To use the Court's terms, a State may attempt to act as a "market regulator" rather than a "market participant." ... In that situation, it is a pretense to equate the State with a private economic actor. State action burdening interstate trade is no less state action because it is accomplished by a public agency authorized to participate in the private market....

South-Central Timber Development v. Wunnicke
467 U.S. 82 (1984)

Majority: *White*, Brennan, Blackmun, Stevens

Concurrences: *Brennan; Powell*, Burger (CJ) (omitted)

Dissent: *Rehnquist*, O'Connor (omitted)

JUSTICE WHITE delivered the opinion of the Court.

We granted certiorari in this case to review a decision of the Court of Appeals for the Ninth Circuit that held that Alaska's requirement that timber taken from state lands be processed within the State prior to export was "implicitly authorized" by Congress and therefore does not violate the Commerce Clause.... We hold that it was not authorized and reverse the judgment of the Court of Appeals.

In September 1980, the Alaska Department of Natural Resources published a notice that it would sell approximately 49 million board-feet of timber in the area of Icy Cape, Alaska, on October 23, 1980. The notice of sale, the prospectus, and the proposed contract for the sale all provided, pursuant to 11 Alaska Admin.Code § 76.130 (1974), that "[p]rimary manufacture within the State of Alaska will be required as a special provision of the contract." ... Under the primary-manufacture requirement, the successful bidder must partially process the timber prior to shipping it outside of the State. The requirement is imposed by contract and does not limit the export of unprocessed timber not owned by the State. The stated purpose of the requirement is to "protect existing industries, provide for the establishment of new industries, derive revenue from all timber resources, and manage the State's forests on a sustained yield basis." ... When it imposes the requirement, the State charges a significantly lower price for the timber than it otherwise would.

> FN1. The proposed contract, which the successful bidder on the timber sale would have been required to sign, provided: "Section 68. Primary Manufacture. Timber cut under this contract shall not be transported for primary manufacture outside the State of Alaska without written approval of the State. "Primary Manufacture is defined under 11 AAC 76.130 and the Governor's policy statement of May 1974."

FN2. 11 Alaska Admin. Code §76.130 (1974) (repealed 1982), which authorized the contractual provision in question, provided: "PRIMARY MANUFACTURE" (a) The director may require that primary manufacture of logs, cordwood, bolts or other similar products be accomplished within the State of Alaska. "(b) The term primary manufacture means manufacture which is first in order of time or development. When used in relation to sawmilling, it means "(1) the breakdown process wherein logs have been reduced in size by a head saw or gang saw to the extent that the residual cants, slabs, or planks can be processed by resaw equipment of the type customarily used in log processing plants; or "(2) manufacture of a product for use without further processing, such as structural timbers (subject to a firm showing of an order or orders for this form of product). "(c) Primary manufacture, when used in reference to pulp ventures, means the breakdown process to a point where the wood fibers have been separated. Chips made from timber processing wastes shall be considered to have received primary manufacture. With respect to veneer or plywood production, it means the production of green veneer. Poles and piling, whether treated or untreated, when manufactured to American National Institute Standards specifications are considered to have received primary manufacture." The local-processing requirement is now authorized by Alaska Admin.Code (1982).

The major method of complying with the primary-manufacture requirement is to convert the logs into cants, which are logs slabbed on at least one side. In order to satisfy the Alaska requirement, cants must be either sawed to a maximum thickness of 12 inches or squared on four sides along their entire length.

Petitioner, South-Central Timber Development, Inc, is an Alaska corporation engaged in the business of purchasing standing timber, logging the timber, and shipping the logs into foreign commerce, almost exclusively to Japan. It does not operate a mill in Alaska and customarily sells unprocessed logs. When it learned that the primary-manufacture requirement was to be imposed on the Icy Cape sale, it brought an action in Federal District Court seeking an injunction, arguing that the requirement violated the negative implications of the Commerce Clause. The District Court agreed and issued an injunction.... The Court of Appeals for the Ninth Circuit reversed, finding it unnecessary to reach the question whether, standing alone, the requirement would violate the Commerce Clause, because it found implicit congressional authorization in the federal policy of imposing a primary-manufacture requirement on timber taken from federal land in Alaska.

FN5. Although it would appear at first blush that it would be economically more efficient to have the primary processing take place within Alaska, that is apparently not the case. Material appearing in the record suggests that the slabs removed from the log in the process of making cants are often quite valuable, but apparently cannot be used and are burned. It appears that because of the wasted wood, cants are actually worth less than the unprocessed logs. An affidavit of a vice president of South-Central states in part: "5. It is also my observation that within Alaska there is absolutely no market for domestic resawing of 'cant' or 'square' manufactured to State of Alaska specifications. In other words, a cant or square manufactured in Alaska would be virtually unsaleable within local Alaska sawmill markets."

Although the Commerce Clause is by its text an affirmative grant of power to Congress to regulate interstate and foreign commerce, the Clause has long been recognized as a self-executing limitation on the power of the States to enact laws imposing substantial burdens on such commerce.... The Court of Appeals held that Congress had done just that by consistently endorsing primary-manufacture requirements on timber taken from federal land.... Although the court recognized that cases of this Court have spoken in terms of express approval by Congress, it stated:

But such express authorization is not always necessary. There will be instances, like the case before us, where federal policy is so clearly delineated that a state may enact a parallel policy without explicit congressional approval, even if the purpose and effect of the state law is to favor local interests.

We agree that federal policy with respect to federal land is "clearly delineated," but the Court of Appeals was incorrect in concluding either that there is a clearly delineated federal policy approving Alaska's local-processing requirement or that Alaska's policy with respect to its timber lands is authorized by the existence of a "parallel" federal policy with respect to federal lands.

Since 1928, the Secretary of Agriculture has restricted the export of unprocessed timber cut from National Forest lands in Alaska. The current regulation, upon which the State places heavy reliance, provides:

> Unprocessed timber from National Forest System lands in Alaska may not be exported from the United States or shipped to other States without prior approval of the Regional Forester. This requirement is necessary to ensure the development and continued existence of adequate wood processing capacity in that State for the sustained utilization of timber from the National Forests which are geographically isolated from other processing facilities.

From 1969 to 1973, Congress imposed a maximum export limitation of 350 million board-feet of unprocessed timber from federal lands lying west of the 100th meridian (a line running from central North Dakota through central Texas).... Beginning in 1973, Congress imposed, by way of a series of annual riders to appropriation Acts, a complete ban on foreign exports of unprocessed logs from western lands except those within Alaska.... These riders limit only foreign exports and do not require in-state processing before the timber may be sold in domestic interstate commerce. The export limitation with respect to federal land in Alaska, rather than being imposed by statute, was imposed by the above-quoted regulation, and applies to exports to other States, as well as to foreign exports.

Alaska argues that federal statutes and regulations demonstrate an affirmative expression of approval of its primary-manufacture requirement for three reasons: (1) federal timber export policy has, since 1928, treated federal timber land in Alaska differently from that in other States; (2) the Federal Government has specifically tailored its policies to ensure development of wood-processing capacity for utilization of timber from the National Forests; and (3) the regulation forbidding without prior approval the export from Alaska of unprocessed timber or its shipment to other States demonstrates that it is the Alaska wood-processing industry in particular, not the domestic wood-processing industry generally, that has been the object of federal concern.

Acceptance of Alaska's three factual propositions does not mandate acceptance of its conclusion. Neither South-Central nor the United States challenges the existence of a federal policy to restrict the out-of-state shipment of unprocessed Alaska timber from federal lands. They challenge only the derivation from that policy of an affirmative expression of federal approval of a parallel policy with respect to state timber. They argue that our cases dealing with congressional authorization of otherwise impermissible state interference with interstate commerce have required an "express" statement of such authorization, and that no such authorization may be implied.

FN6. The United States appears as amicus curiae in support of the position of South-Central.

It is true that most of our cases have looked for an express statement of congressional policy prior to finding that state regulation is permissible. For example, in Sporhase v.

Nebraska ex rel. Douglas, supra, the Court declined to find congressional authorization for state-imposed burdens on interstate commerce in ground water despite 37 federal statutes and a number of interstate compacts that demonstrated Congress' deference to state water law. We noted that on those occasions in which consent has been found, congressional intent and policy to insulate state legislation from Commerce Clause attack have been "expressly stated." ... Similarly, in New England Power Co. v. New Hampshire, we rejected a claim by the State of New Hampshire that its restriction on the interstate flow of privately owned and produced electricity was authorized by § 201(b) of the Federal Power Act. That section provides that the Act "shall not ... deprive a State or State commission of its lawful authority now exercised over the exportation of hydroelectric energy which is transmitted across a State line." ... We found nothing in the statute or legislative history "evinc[ing] a congressional intent 'to alter the limits of state power otherwise imposed by the Commerce Clause.'" ...

Alaska relies in large part on this Court's recent opinion in White v. Massachusetts Council of Construction Employers, Inc. (1983), for its "implicit approval" theory. At issue in White was an executive order issued by the Mayor of Boston requiring all construction projects funded by the city or by funds that the city had authority to administer, to be performed by a work force consisting of at least 50% residents of the city. A number of the projects were funded in part with federal Urban Development Action Grants. The Court held that insofar as the city expended its own funds on the projects, it was a market participant unconstrained by the dormant Commerce Clause; insofar as the city expended federal funds, "the order was affirmatively sanctioned by the pertinent regulations of those programs." ... Alaska relies on the Court's statements in White that the federal regulations "affirmatively permit" and "affirmatively sanctio[n]" the executive order and that the order "sounds a harmonious note" with the federal regulations, and it finds significance in the fact that the Court did not use the words "expressly stated."

Rather than supporting the position of the State, we believe that White undermines it. If approval of state burdens on commerce could be implied from parallel federal policy, the Court would have had no reason to rely upon the market-participant doctrine to uphold the executive order. Instead, the order could have been upheld as being in harmony with federal policy as expressed in regulations governing the expenditure of federal funds.

There is no talismanic significance to the phrase "expressly stated," however; it merely states one way of meeting the requirement that for a state regulation to be removed from the reach of the dormant Commerce Clause, congressional intent must be unmistakably clear. The requirement that Congress affirmatively contemplate otherwise invalid state legislation is mandated by the policies underlying dormant Commerce Clause doctrine. It is not, as Alaska asserts, merely a wooden formalism. The Commerce Clause was designed "to avoid the tendencies toward economic Balkanization that had plagued relations among the Colonies and later among the States under the Articles of Confederation." Hughes v. Oklahoma (1979). Unrepresented interests will often bear the brunt of regulations imposed by one State having a significant effect on persons or operations in other States. Thus, "when the regulation is of such a character that its burden falls principally upon those without the state, legislative action is not likely to be subjected to those political restraints which are normally exerted on legislation where it affects adversely some interests within the state." South Carolina State Highway Dept. v. Barnwell Brothers, Inc. On the other hand, when Congress acts, all segments of the country are represented, and there is significantly less danger that one State will be in a position to exploit others. Furthermore, if a State is in such a position, the decision to allow it is a collective one. A rule requiring a clear expression of approval by Congress ensures that there is, in fact, such a collective decision and reduces significantly the risk that unrepresented interests will be adversely affected by restraints on commerce.

The fact that the state policy in this case appears to be consistent with federal policy — or even that state policy furthers the goals we might believe that Congress had in mind — is an insufficient indicium of congressional intent. Congress acted only with respect to federal lands; we cannot infer from that fact that it intended to authorize a similar policy with respect to state lands. Accordingly, we reverse the contrary judgment of the Court of Appeals.

We now turn to the issues left unresolved by the Court of Appeals. The first of these issues is whether Alaska's restrictions on export of unprocessed timber from state-owned lands are exempt from Commerce Clause scrutiny under the "market-participant doctrine."

Our cases make clear that if a State is acting as a market participant, rather than as a market regulator, the dormant Commerce Clause places no limitation on its activities.... The precise contours of the market-participant doctrine have yet to be established, however, the doctrine having been applied in only three cases of this Court to date.

The first of the cases, Hughes v. Alexandria Scrap Corp., supra, involved a Maryland program designed to reduce the number of junked automobiles in the State. A "bounty" was established on Maryland-licensed junk cars, and the State imposed more stringent documentation requirements on out-of-state scrap processors than on in-state ones. The Court rejected a Commerce Clause attack on the program, although it noted that under traditional Commerce Clause analysis the program might well be invalid because it had the effect of reducing the flow of goods in interstate commerce.... The Court concluded that Maryland's action was not "the kind of action with which the Commerce Clause is concerned," ibid., because "[n]othing in the purposes animating the Commerce Clause prohibits a State, in the absence of congressional action, from participating in the market and exercising the right to favor its own citizens over others." ...

In Reeves, Inc. v. Stake, supra, the Court upheld a South Dakota policy of restricting the sale of cement from a state-owned plant to state residents, declaring that "[t]he basic distinction drawn in Alexandria Scrap between States as market participants and States as market regulators makes good sense and sound law." ... The Court relied upon "the long recognized right of trader or manufacturer, engaged in an entirely private business, freely to exercise his own independent discretion as to parties with whom he will deal." ... In essence, the Court recognized the principle that the Commerce Clause places no limitations on a State's refusal to deal with particular parties when it is participating in the interstate market in goods....

The State of Alaska contends that its primary-manufacture requirement fits squarely within the market-participant doctrine, arguing that "Alaska's entry into the market may be viewed as precisely the same type of subsidy to local interests that the Court found unobjectionable in Alexandria Scrap." ... However, when Maryland became involved in the scrap market it was as a purchaser of scrap; Alaska, on the other hand, participates in the timber market, but imposes conditions downstream in the timber-processing market. Alaska is not merely subsidizing local timber processing in an amount "roughly equal to the difference between the price the timber would fetch in the absence of such a requirement and the amount the state actually receives." ... If the State directly subsidized the timber-processing industry by such an amount, the purchaser would retain the option of taking advantage of the subsidy by processing timber in the State or forgoing the benefits of the subsidy and exporting unprocessed timber. Under the Alaska requirement, however, the choice is made for him: if he buys timber from the State he is not free to take the timber out of state prior to processing.

The State also would have us find Reeves controlling. It states that "Reeves made it clear that the Commerce Clause imposes no limitation on Alaska's power to choose the terms on which it will sell its timber." Such an unrestrained reading of Reeves is unwarranted. Although the Court in Reeves did strongly endorse the right of a State to deal with whomever it chooses when it participates in the market, it did not—and did not purport to—sanction the imposition of any terms that the State might desire. For example, the Court expressly noted in Reeves that "Commerce Clause scrutiny may well be more rigorous when a restraint on foreign commerce is alleged," ... that a natural resource "like coal, timber, wild game, or minerals," was not involved, but instead the cement was "the end product of a complex process whereby a costly physical plant and human labor act on raw materials," ... and that South Dakota did not bar resale of South Dakota cement to out-of-state purchasers.... In this case, all three of the elements that were not present in Reeves—foreign commerce, a natural resource, and restrictions on resale—are present....

The limit of the market-participant doctrine must be that it allows a State to impose burdens on commerce within the market in which it is a participant, but allows it to go no further. The State may not impose conditions, whether by statute, regulation, or contract, that have a substantial regulatory effect outside of that particular market Unless the "market" is relatively narrowly defined, the doctrine has the potential of swallowing up the rule that States may not impose substantial burdens on interstate commerce even if they act with the permissible state purpose of fostering local industry....

There are sound reasons for distinguishing between a State's preferring its own residents in the initial disposition of goods when it is a market participant and a State's attachment of restrictions on dispositions subsequent to the goods coming to rest in private hands. First, simply as a matter of intuition a state market participant has a greater interest as a "private trader" in the immediate transaction than it has in what its purchaser does with the goods after the State no longer has an interest in them.... Second, downstream restrictions have a greater regulatory effect than do limitations on the immediate transaction. Instead of merely choosing its own trading partners, the State is attempting to govern the private, separate economic relationships of its trading partners; that is, it restricts the post-purchase activity of the purchaser, rather than merely the purchasing activity. [T]his restriction on private economic activity takes place after the completion of the parties' direct commercial obligations, rather than during the course of an ongoing commercial relationship in which the city retained a continuing proprietary interest in the subject of the contract. In sum, the State may not avail itself of the market-participant doctrine to immunize its downstream regulation of the timber-processing market in which it is not a participant....

We are buttressed in our conclusion that the restriction is invalid by the fact that foreign commerce is burdened by the restriction. It is a well-accepted rule that state restrictions burdening foreign commerce are subjected to a more rigorous and searching scrutiny. It is crucial to the efficient execution of the Nation's foreign policy that "the Federal Government ... speak with one voice when regulating commercial relations with foreign governments." ... In light of the substantial attention given by Congress to the subject of export restrictions on unprocessed timber, it would be peculiarly inappropriate to permit state regulation of the subject. The judgment of the Court of Appeals is reversed, and the case is remanded for proceedings consistent with the opinion of this Court.

Review Questions and Explanations: *Reeves* and *South Central Timber*

1. You can use *Reeves* to review your understanding of dormant Commerce Clause doctrine. Why was the law discriminatory, what test did the Court apply in deciding the case, and what key facts guided the Court's decision?

2. Can you explain in your own words what it means to say that the state is acting as a "market participant" rather than a "market regulator"?

3. Identify the policy reasons behind the market participant exception. Do you agree that they justify the exception?

4. What test does the Court use in *South Central Timber* to determine if the state action qualified for the congressional permission exception?

C. The Privileges and Immunities Clause

The materials covered so far in this chapter have explored the limitations imposed on states by the dormant Commerce Clause. As noted in the introductory materials, however, the dormant Commerce Clause is just one of several constitutional doctrines and clauses restricting state actions. We now turn to a second such restriction: the Privileges and Immunities clause.

Actually, there are *two* Privileges and (or) Immunities clauses in the Constitution. The first, found in section 2 of Article IV, is called the Privileges *and* Immunities clause, and says that "The Citizens of each State shall be entitled to all Privileges and Immunities of Citizens in the several States." The second, called the Privileges *or* Immunities clause, was enacted after the Civil War as part of the Fourteenth Amendment. It states that "No State shall make or enforce any law which shall abridge the Privileges or Immunities of citizens of the United States" The Article IV clause originated in the Articles of Confederation and limits the ability of states to treat their own citizens differently than they treat citizens of other states. The Fourteenth Amendment clause focuses on what states can and cannot do to their own residents. Like all of the Civil War Amendments, this clause was driven in large part by concerns about how state governments in the former Confederacy would treat the newly freed slaves living in their jurisdictions. It restructured the relationship between the states and the federal government by putting a layer of federal protection between states and the people they governed. As discussed in Part IV of this casebook, the Fourteenth Amendment's Privileges *or* Immunities clause was stripped of most meaning by the Supreme Court shortly after it was enacted. The materials presented here focus on the Privileges **and** Immunities clause of the original Constitution.

The first step in analyzing a Privileges and Immunities clause claim is to determine whether the privilege or immunity being claimed is one protected by the clause. The second step is to decide whether the state's interest in treating residents and non-residents differently is sufficiently important to warrant the differential treatment. This part of the analysis should sound familiar: it is similar to what the Court does in dormant Commerce Clause cases. The tests are not, however, exactly the same. The clauses are doing different things, were developed for different reasons, and apply under different circumstances.

Generally speaking, the dormant Commerce Clause is concerned with the burdens states try to impose on commercial activity, while the Privileges and Immunities clause is concerned with burdens states try to impose on individuals. The Privileges and Immunities clause, in other words, sounds in individual rights, rather than economic regulation. Pay attention to the consequences of this while reading the cases below.

Hicklin v. Orbeck
437 U.S. 518 (1978)

Unanimous decision: *Brennan*, Burger (CJ), Stewart, White, Marshall, Blackmun, Powell, Rehnquist, Stevens

MR. JUSTICE BRENNAN delivered the opinion of the Court.

In 1972, professedly for the purpose of reducing unemployment in the State, the Alaska Legislature passed an Act entitled "Local Hire Under State Leases." The key provision of "Alaska Hire," as the Act has come to be known, is the requirement that "all oil and gas leases, easements or right-of-way permits for oil or gas pipeline purposes, unitization agreements, or any renegotiation of any of the preceding to which the state is a party" contain a provision "requiring the employment of qualified Alaska residents" in preference to nonresidents.... Appellants, individuals desirous of securing jobs covered by the Act but unable to qualify for the necessary resident cards, challenge Alaska Hire as violative of ... the Privileges and Immunities Clause of Art. IV, § 2.

... [T]he appellants, all but one of whom had previously worked on the pipeline, were prevented from obtaining pipeline-related work.... By a vote of 3 to 2, however, the [Alaskan Supreme Court] held that the Act's general preference for Alaska residents was constitutionally permissible. Appellants appealed the State Supreme Court's judgment insofar as it embodied the latter holding, and we noted probable jurisdiction. We reverse....

Appellants' principal challenge to Alaska Hire is made under the Privileges and Immunities Clause of Art. IV, § 2: "The Citizens of each State shall be entitled to all Privileges and Immunities of Citizens in the several States." That provision, which "appears in the so-called States' Relations Article, the same Article that embraces the Full Faith and Credit Clause, the Extradition Clause..., the provisions for the admission of new States, the Territory and Property Clause, and the Guarantee Clause," Baldwin v. Montana Fish and Game (1978), "establishes a norm of comity," that is to prevail among the States with respect to their treatment of each other's residents. The purpose of the Clause, as described in Paul v. Virginia (1869), is "to place the citizens of each State upon the same footing with citizens of other States, so far as the advantages resulting from citizenship in those States are concerned. It relieves them from the disabilities of alienage in other States; it inhibits discriminating legislation against them by other States; it gives them the right of free ingress into other States, and egress from them; it insures to them in other States the same freedom possessed by the citizens of those States in the acquisition and enjoyment of property and in the pursuit of happiness; and it secures to them in other States the equal protection of their laws. It has been justly said that no provision in the Constitution has tended so strongly to constitute the citizens of the United States one people as this."

Appellants' appeal to the protection of the Clause is strongly supported by this Court's decisions holding violative of the Clause state discrimination against nonresidents seeking to ply their trade, practice their occupation, or pursue a common calling within the State. For example, in Ward v. Maryland (1871), a Maryland statute regulating the sale of most goods in the city of Baltimore fell to the privileges and immunities challenge of a New Jersey resident against whom the law discriminated. The statute discriminated against nonresidents of Maryland in several ways: It required nonresident merchants to obtain licenses in order to practice their trade without requiring the same of certain similarly situated Maryland merchants; it charged nonresidents a higher license fee than those Maryland residents who were required to secure licenses; and it prohibited both resident and nonresident merchants from using nonresident salesmen, other than their regular employees, to sell their goods in the city. In holding that the statute violated the Privileges and Immunities Clause, the Court observed that "the clause plainly and unmistakably secures and protects the right of a citizen of one State to pass into any other State of the Union for the purpose of engaging in lawful commerce, trade, or business without molestation." Ward thus recognized that a resident of one State is constitutionally entitled to travel to another State for purposes of employment free from discriminatory restrictions in favor of state residents imposed by the other State.

Again, Toomer v. Witsell (1948), the leading modern exposition of the limitations the Clause places on a State's power to bias employment opportunities in favor of its own residents, invalidated a South Carolina statute that required nonresidents to pay a fee 100 times greater than that paid by residents for a license to shrimp commercially in the three-mile maritime belt off the coast of that State. The Court reasoned that although the Privileges and Immunities Clause "does not preclude disparity of treatment in the many situations where there are perfectly valid independent reasons for it does bar discrimination against citizens of other States where there is no substantial reason for the discrimination beyond the mere fact that they are citizens of other States."

A "substantial reason for the discrimination" would not exist, the Court explained, "unless there is something to indicate that non-citizens constitute a peculiar source of the evil at which the [discriminatory] statute is aimed." Moreover, even where the presence or activity of nonresidents causes or exacerbates the problem the State seeks to remedy, there must be a "reasonable relationship between the danger represented by non-citizens, as a class, and the … discrimination practiced upon them." …

Even assuming that a State may validly attempt to alleviate its unemployment problem by requiring private employers within the State to discriminate against nonresidents—an assumption made at least dubious by Ward—it is clear that under the Toomer analysis … Alaska Hire's discrimination against nonresidents cannot withstand scrutiny under the Privileges and Immunities Clause. For although the statute may not violate the Clause if the State shows "something to indicate that noncitizens constitute a peculiar source of the evil at which the statute is aimed." [B]eyond this, the State "has no burden to prove that its laws are not violative of the … Clause," Baldwin v. Montana Fish and Game (Brennan, J., dissenting), certainly no showing was made on this record that nonresidents were "a peculiar source of the evil" Alaska Hire was enacted to remedy, namely, Alaska's "uniquely high unemployment." What evidence the record does contain indicates that the major cause of Alaska's high unemployment was not the influx of nonresidents seeking employment, but rather the fact that a substantial number of Alaska's jobless residents—especially the unemployed Eskimo and Indian residents—were unable to secure employment either because of their lack of education and job training or because of their geographical remoteness from job opportunities; and that the employment of nonresidents threatened to deny jobs to Alaska residents only to the extent that jobs for which untrained residents were being prepared might be filled by nonresidents before the residents' training was completed.

Moreover, even if the State's showing is accepted as sufficient to indicate that nonresidents were "a peculiar source of evil," Toomer compel[s] the conclusion that Alaska Hire nevertheless fails to pass constitutional muster. For the discrimination the Act works against nonresidents does not bear a substantial relationship to the particular "evil" they are said to present. Alaska Hire simply grants all Alaskans, regardless of their employment status, education, or training, a flat employment preference for all jobs covered by the Act. A highly skilled and educated resident who has never been unemployed is entitled to precisely the same preferential treatment as the unskilled, habitually unemployed Arctic Eskimo enrolled in a job-training program. If Alaska is to attempt to ease its unemployment problem by forcing employers within the State to discriminate against nonresidents—again, a policy which may present serious constitutional questions—the means by which it does so must be more closely tailored to aid the unemployed the Act is intended to benefit. Even if a statute granting an employment preference to unemployed residents or to residents enrolled in job-training programs might be permissible, Alaska Hire's across-the-board grant of a job preference to all Alaskan residents clearly is not.

... Alaska contends that because the oil and gas that are the subject of Alaska Hire are *owned* by the State, this ownership, of itself, is sufficient justification for the Act's discrimination against nonresidents, and takes the Act totally without the scope of the Privileges and Immunities Clause. As the State sees it "the privileges and immunities clause [does] not apply, and was never meant to apply, to decisions by the states as to how they would permit, if at all, the use and distribution of the natural resources which they own...." Brief for Appellees 20 n. 14. We do not agree that the fact that a State owns a resource, of itself, completely removes a law concerning that resource from the prohibitions of the Clause. Although some courts, including the court below, have read [prior case law] as creating an "exception" to the Privileges and Immunities Clause, we have just recently confirmed that "[i]n more recent years ... the Court has recognized that the States' interest in regulating and controlling those things they claim to 'own' ... is by no means absolute." Baldwin. Rather than placing a statute completely beyond the Clause, a State's ownership of the property with which the statute is concerned is a factor—although often the crucial factor—to be considered in evaluating whether the statute's discrimination against noncitizens violates the Clause. Dispositive though this factor may be in many cases in which a State discriminates against nonresidents, it is not dispositive here.

The reason is that Alaska has little or no proprietary interest in much of the activity swept within the ambit of Alaska Hire; and the connection of the State's oil and gas with much of the covered activity is sufficiently attenuated so that it cannot justifiably be the basis for requiring private employers to discriminate against nonresidents....

Although appellants raise no Commerce Clause challenge to the Act, the mutually reinforcing relationship between the Privileges and Immunities Clause of Art. IV, §2, and the Commerce Clause—a relationship that stems from their common origin in the Fourth Article of the Articles of Confederation and their shared vision of federalism, renders several Commerce Clause decisions appropriate support for our conclusion. West v. Kansas Natural Gas (1911), struck down an Oklahoma statutory scheme that completely prohibited the out-of-state shipment of natural gas found within the State. The Court reasoned that if a State could so prefer its own economic well-being to that of the Nation as a whole, "Pennsylvania might keep its coal, the Northwest its timber, [and] the mining States their minerals," so that "embargo may be retaliated by embargo" with the result that "commerce [would] be halted at state lines." was held to be controlling in Pennsylvania v. West Virginia (1923), where a West Virginia statute that effectively required natural gas companies within the State to satisfy all fuel needs of West Virginia residents before transporting any natural gas out of the State was held to violate the Commerce Clause. West and Pennsylvania v. West Virginia thus established that the location in a given State of a resource bound for interstate commerce is an insufficient basis for preserving the benefits of the resource exclusively or even principally for that State's residents.

West [and] Pennsylvania v. West Virginia thus establish that the Commerce Clause circumscribes a State's ability to prefer its own citizens in the utilization of natural resources found within its borders, but destined for interstate commerce.... Alaska's oil and gas here are bound for out-of-state consumption. Indeed, the construction of the Trans-Alaska Pipeline, on which project appellants' nonresidency has prevented them from working, was undertaken expressly to accomplish this end. Although the fact that a state-owned resource is destined for interstate commerce does not, of itself, disable the State from preferring its own citizens in the utilization of that resource, it does inform analysis under the Privileges and Immunities Clause as to the permissibility of the discrimination the State visits upon nonresidents based on its ownership of the resource. Here, the oil and gas upon which Alaska hinges its discrimination against nonresidents are of profound national importance. On the other hand, the breadth of the discrimination mandated by Alaska Hire goes far beyond the degree of resident bias Alaska's ownership of the oil and gas can justifiably support. The confluence of these realities points to but one conclusion: Alaska Hire cannot withstand constitutional scrutiny. As Mr. Justice Cardozo observed in Baldwin v. Seelig, the Constitution "was framed upon the theory that the peoples of the several states must sink or swim together, and that in the long run prosperity and salvation are in union and not division." Reversed.

Review Questions and Explanations: *Hicklin*

1. What privileges and immunities are protected by the Privileges and Immunities clause?

2. What test does the Court use to determine whether the Privileges and Immunities clause has been violated?

3. Can you think of a law that would violate the Privileges and Immunities clause but would not violate the dormant Commerce Clause? [Hint: read the next case.]

United Building and Construction Trades Council v. City of Camden
465 U.S. 208 (1984)

Majority: *Rehnquist*, Burger (CJ), Brennan, White, Marshall, Powell, Stevens, O'Connor

Dissent: *Blackmun* (omitted)

Justice REHNQUIST delivered the opinion of the Court.

A municipal ordinance of the city of Camden, New Jersey requires that at least 40% of the employees of contractors and subcontractors working on city construction projects be Camden residents. Appellant, the United Building and Construction Trades Council of Camden and Vicinity (the Council), challenges that ordinance as a violation of the Privileges and Immunities Clause, Article IV, § 2, of the United States Constitution. The Supreme Court of New Jersey rejected appellant's privileges and immunities attack on the ground that the ordinance discriminates on the basis of *municipal,* not state, residency. The court "decline[d] to apply the Privileges and Immunities Clause in the context of a municipal ordinance that has identical effects upon out-of-state citizens and New Jersey citizens not residing in the locality." We conclude that the challenged ordinance is properly subject to the strictures of the Clause. We therefore reverse the judgment of the Supreme Court of New Jersey and remand the case for a determination of the validity of the ordinance under the appropriate constitutional standard.

The New Jersey court sustained the Treasurer's action as consistent both with state law and the federal constitution. Citing Reeves v. Stake and Hughes v. Alexandria Scrap, the [state] court held that the resident quota was not subject to challenge under the Commerce Clause because the State was acting as a market participant rather than as a market regulator. The [state] court also held that the quota did not violate the Privileges and Immunities Clause because it was not aimed primarily at out-of-state residents. "It almost certainly affects more New Jersey residents not living in Camden than it does out-of-state residents. Because the Camden ordinance does not affect 'the States' ... treatment of each other's residents,' ... it does not violate any privilege of state citizenship." Finally, the New Jersey Supreme Court held that the one-year residency requirement did not violate the right to travel protected by the Equal Protection Clause, concluding that only a rational basis is required to uphold a residency requirement for city employment.

The first argument can be quickly rejected. The fact that the ordinance in question is a municipal, rather than a state, law does not somehow place it outside the scope of the Privileges and Immunities Clause. First of all, one cannot easily distinguish municipal from state action in this case: the municipal ordinance would not have gone into effect without express approval by the State Treasurer.

More fundamentally, a municipality is merely a political subdivision of the State from which its authority derives. It is as true of the Privileges and Immunities Clause as of the Equal Protection Clause that what would be unconstitutional if done directly by the State can no more readily be accomplished by a city deriving its authority from the State. Thus, even if the ordinance had been adopted solely by Camden, and not pursuant to a state program or with state approval, the hiring preference would still have to comport with the Privileges and Immunities Clause.

The second argument merits more consideration. The New Jersey Supreme Court concluded that the Privileges and Immunities Clause does not apply to an ordinance that discriminates solely on the basis of *municipal* residency. The Clause is phrased in terms of *state* citizenship and was designed "to place the citizens of each State upon the same footing with citizens of other States, so far as the advantages resulting from citizenship in those States are concerned." Hicklin v. Orbeck (1978).... Municipal residency classifications, it is argued, simply do not give rise to the same concerns.

We cannot accept this argument. We have never read the Clause so literally as to apply it only to distinctions based on state citizenship.... A person who is not residing in a given State is *ipso facto* not residing in a city within that State. Thus, whether the exercise of a privilege is conditioned on state residency or on municipal residency he will just as surely be excluded.

Given the Camden ordinance, an out-of-state citizen who ventures into New Jersey will not enjoy the same privileges as the New Jersey citizen residing in Camden. It is true that New Jersey citizens not residing in Camden will be affected by the ordinance as well as out-of-state citizens. And it is true that the disadvantaged New Jersey residents have no claim under the Privileges and Immunities Clause. The Slaughterhouse Cases (1872). But New Jersey residents at least have a chance to remedy at the polls any discrimination against them. Out-of-state citizens have no similar opportunity, and they must "not be restricted to the uncertain remedies afforded by diplomatic processes and official retaliation." Toomer v. Witsell (1948). We conclude that Camden's ordinance is not immune from constitutional review at the behest of out-of-state residents merely because some in-state residents are similarly disadvantaged.

Application of the Privileges and Immunities Clause to a particular instance of discrimination against out-of-state residents entails a two-step inquiry. As an initial matter, the court must decide whether the ordinance burdens one of those privileges and immunities protected by the Clause. Not all forms of discrimination against citizens of other States are constitutionally suspect.

> Some distinctions between residents and nonresidents merely reflect the fact that this is a Nation composed of individual States, and are permitted; other distinctions are prohibited because they hinder the formation, the purpose, or the development of a single Union of those States. Only with respect to those 'privileges' and 'immunities' bearing upon the vitality of the Nation as a single entity must the State treat all citizens, resident and nonresident, equally. Baldwin v. Montana Fish and Game.

As a threshold matter, then, we must determine whether an out-of-state resident's interest in employment on public works contracts in another State is sufficiently "fundamental" to the promotion of interstate harmony so as to "fall within the purview of the Privileges and Immunities Clause." ... Certainly, the pursuit of a common calling is one of the most fundamental of those privileges protected by the Clause. Many, if not most, of our cases expounding the Privileges and Immunities Clause have dealt with this basic and essential activity. See, *e.g.*, Hicklin v. Orbeck (1978). Public employment, however, is qualitatively different from employment in the private sector; it is a subspecies of the broader opportunity to pursue a common calling. We have held that there is no fundamental right to government employment for purposes of the Equal Protection Clause. And in White we held that for purposes of the Commerce Clause everyone employed on a city public works project is, "in a substantial if informal sense, 'working for the city.'"

It can certainly be argued that for purposes of the Privileges and Immunities Clause everyone affected by the Camden ordinance is also "working for the city" and, therefore, has no grounds for complaint when the city favors its own residents. But we decline to transfer mechanically into this context an analysis fashioned to fit the Commerce Clause. Our decision in White turned on a distinction between the city acting as a market participant and the city acting as a market regulator. The question whether employees of contractors and subcontractors on public works projects were or were not, in some sense, working for the city was crucial to that analysis. The question had to be answered in order to chart the boundaries of the distinction. But the distinction between market participant and market regulator relied upon in White to dispose of the Commerce Clause challenge is not dispositive in this context. The two Clauses have different aims and set different standards for state conduct.

The Commerce Clause acts as an implied restraint upon state regulatory powers. Such powers must give way before the superior authority of Congress to legislate on (or leave unregulated) matters involving interstate commerce. When the State acts solely as a market participant, no conflict between state *regulation* and federal regulatory authority can arise. The Privileges and Immunities Clause, on the other hand, imposes a direct restraint on state action in the interests of interstate harmony. Hicklin v. Orbeck. This concern with comity cuts across the market regulator—market participant distinction that is crucial under the Commerce Clause. It is discrimination against out-of-state residents on matters of fundamental concern which triggers the Clause, not regulation affecting interstate commerce. Thus, the fact that Camden is merely setting conditions on its expenditures for goods and services in the marketplace does not preclude the possibility that those conditions violate the Privileges and Immunities Clause.

In *Hicklin,* we struck down as a violation of the Privileges and Immunities Clause an "Alaska Hire" statute containing a resident hiring preference for all employment related to the development of the State's oil and gas resources. Alaska argued in that case "that because the oil and gas that are the subject of Alaska Hire are *owned* by the State, this ownership, of itself, is sufficient justification for the Act's discrimination against nonresidents, and takes the Act totally without the scope of the Privileges and Immunities Clause." We concluded, however, that the State's interest in controlling those things it claims to own is not absolute. "Rather than placing a statute completely beyond the Clause, a State's ownership of the property with which the statute is concerned is a factor—although often the crucial factor—to be considered in evaluating whether the statute's discrimination against noncitizens violates the Clause." Much the same analysis, we think, is appropriate to a city's efforts to bias private employment decisions in favor of its residents on construction projects funded with public monies. The fact that Camden is expending its own funds or funds it administers in accordance with the terms of a grant is certainly a factor—perhaps the crucial factor—to be considered in evaluating whether the statute's discrimination violates the Privileges and Immunities Clause. But it does not remove the Camden ordinance completely from the purview of the Clause.

In sum, Camden may, without fear of violating the Commerce Clause, pressure private employers engaged in public works projects funded in whole or in part by the city to hire city residents. But that same exercise of power to bias the employment decisions of private contractors and subcontractors against out-of-state residents may be called to account under the Privileges and Immunities Clause. A determination of whether a privilege is "fundamental" for purposes of that Clause does not depend on whether the employees of private contractors and subcontractors engaged in public works projects can or cannot be said to be "working for the city." The opportunity to seek employment with such private employers is "sufficiently basic to the livelihood of the Nation," as to fall within the purview of the Privileges and Immunities Clause even though the contractors and subcontractors are themselves engaged in projects funded in whole or part by the city.

The conclusion that Camden's ordinance discriminates against a protected privilege does not, of course, end the inquiry. We have stressed in prior cases that "[l]ike many other constitutional provisions, the privileges and immunities clause is not an absolute." Toomer v. Witsell (1948). It does not preclude discrimination against citizens of other States where there is a "substantial reason" for the difference in treatment. "[T]he inquiry in each case must be concerned with whether such reasons do exist and whether the degree of discrimination bears a close relation to them." Ibid. As part of any justification offered for the discriminatory law, nonresidents must somehow be shown to "constitute a peculiar source of the evil at which the statute is aimed." Ibid.

The city of Camden contends that its ordinance is necessary to counteract grave economic and social ills. Spiraling unemployment, a sharp decline in population, and a dramatic reduction in the number of businesses located in the city have eroded property values and depleted the city's tax base. The resident hiring preference is designed, the city contends, to increase the number of employed persons living in Camden and to arrest the "middle class flight" currently plaguing the city. The city also argues that all non-Camden residents employed on city public works projects, whether they reside in New Jersey or Pennsylvania, constitute a "source of the evil at which the statute is aimed." That is, they "live off" Camden without "living in" Camden. Camden contends that the scope of the discrimination practiced in the ordinance, with its municipal residency requirement, is carefully tailored to alleviate this evil without unreasonably harming nonresidents, who still have access to 60% of the available positions.

Every inquiry under the Privileges and Immunities Clause "must ... be conducted with due regard for the principle that the states should have considerable leeway in analyzing local evils and in prescribing appropriate cures." Toomer v. Witsell (1948). This caution is particularly appropriate when a government body is merely setting conditions on the expenditure of funds it controls. See supra, at 1028. The Alaska Hire statute at issue in Hicklin, swept within its strictures not only contractors and subcontractors dealing directly with the State's oil and gas; it also covered suppliers who provided goods and services to those contractors and subcontractors. We invalidated the Act as "an attempt to force virtually all businesses that benefit in some way from the economic ripple effect of Alaska's decision to develop its oil and gas resources to bias their employment practices in favor of the State's residents." No similar "ripple effect" appears to infect the Camden ordinance. It is limited in scope to employees working directly on city public works projects.

Nonetheless, we find it impossible to evaluate Camden's justification on the record as it now stands. No trial has ever been held in the case. No findings of fact have been made. The Supreme Court of New Jersey certified the case for direct appeal after the brief administrative proceedings that led to approval of the ordinance by the State Treasurer. It would not be appropriate for this Court either to make factual determinations as an initial matter or to take judicial notice of Camden's decay. We, therefore, deem it wise to remand the case to the New Jersey Supreme Court. That court may decide, consistent with state procedures, on the best method for making the necessary findings. The judgment of the Supreme Court of New Jersey is reversed, and the case is remanded for proceedings not inconsistent with this opinion.

Exercise: Privileges and Immunities Clause

The State of Montana charges non-resident large game hunters significantly more for elk hunting license than it charges Montana residents. Out-of-state hunters challenge the differential pricing scheme under the Privileges and Immunities clause. Is their challenge likely to succeed?

D. Preemption

How are the courts supposed to resolve conflicts between federal and state law? The answer is supplied by the Supremacy Clause of the Constitution and the rule of federal preemption of state law. "Under the Supremacy Clause," the Court has said, "from which our pre-emption doctrine is derived, any state law, however clearly within a State's acknowledged power, which interferes with or is contrary to federal law, must yield." Gade v. National Solid Waste Management Assn., 505 U.S. 88, 108 (1992). The Supremacy Clause, Article VI, cl. 2, of the Constitution, provides:

> This Constitution, and the laws of the United States which shall be made in pursuance thereof; and all treaties made, or which shall be made, under the authority of the United States, shall be the supreme law of the land; and the judges in every state shall be bound thereby, anything in the Constitution or laws of any State to the contrary notwithstanding.

This provision has been interpreted as a kind of constitutional choice-of-law rule. When federal and state laws apply conflicting rules of decision to a case, the courts (both federal and state) are supposed to apply federal law. State law is deemed void for purposes of deciding the case; courts say in such cases that the state law is "superseded," or, more commonly, "preempted" by the federal law.

The black-letter preemption doctrine tells us that preemption, while constitutionally based in the Supremacy Clause, is an issue of Congressional intent. Assuming that federal legislation is within Congress's enumerated powers, its power to displace state law as part of that legislation is "plenary"—without any limit imposed by federalism principles. The question for courts in particular cases consequently becomes whether and to what extent Congress intended to preempt state law. This question is typically viewed as one of statutory interpretation and thus not really a constitutional question. Nevertheless, federalism principles may inform how the Court goes about interpreting the statute, as we will see in the cases below.

With ascertaining congressional intent as the goal, the courts have organized preemption doctrine into questions of "express" and "implied" preemption. Express preemption cases involve the interpretation of federal statutes with an express provision dealing with preemption. The Employee Retirement Income Security Act, 29 U.S.C. §§ 1001 et seq. (ERISA), for example, provides that it "shall supersede any and all State laws insofar as they may now or hereafter relate to any employee benefit plan[.]" 29 U.S.C. § 1144(a). Implied preemption cases involve statutes with no such preemptive language. In these cases, the courts try to determine the preemptive intent of Congress by examining other provisions of the statute or its legislative history.

Implied preemption is divided into further subcategories: field and conflict preemption. "Field" preemption is a finding by the Court that Congress intended to occupy a particular field of legislation to the exclusion of the states; any state law in the field will be preempted irrespective of whether the law is consistent with federal law. Nuclear energy regulation is an example of this.

Under "conflict" preemption, in contrast, a state law is void only if it conflicts with federal law. The notion of a conflict has been defined by yet two more categories. First, if the commands of federal and state law are so in conflict that it is impossible to comply with both, then the state law is void. Second, a conflict will also be found if the state law "stands as an obstacle" to the objectives of a federal law. This is by far the most common form of preemption case.

Figure 2.2. Preemption Doctrine

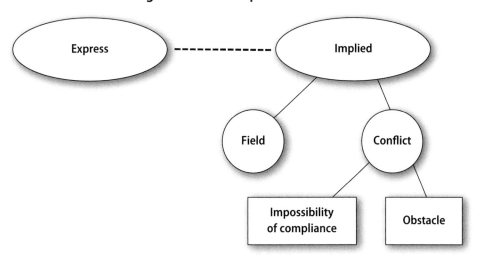

This black letter preemption taxonomy has been criticized frequently by commentators, and it is easy to see why. To begin with, the express/implied preemption distinction adds almost nothing to the analysis of specific preemption cases. The existence of an explicit preemption clause clearly makes it easier for a court to determine Congress's preemptive intent, but at the end of the day the court still has to decide if the state law is inconsistent with the federal law, whether the federal statute contains an express preemption clause or not. There is something to be said for a distinction between "conflict" and "field" pre-emption, since state laws consistent with a federal regulatory scheme are nevertheless pre-empted if Congress has occupied the field. However, even here the distinction blurs, depending on how one defines the field. There is case authority, for example, suggesting that Congress has preempted the field of immigration law, but more recent cases have seemed to allow some state regulation within that field and look instead for conflicts with existing federal statutes. Look for this in the *Geier* case that follows this introduction: is there really a true "conflict" between state tort law and federal regulation, or is the Court actually saying that Congress has preempted the "field" of automobile passive restraint regulation?

Finally, to the extent that "field" preemption makes sense as a concept, it makes little sense to deem it (as the Court has) a subcategory of "implied" rather than "express" preemption cases. Simply put, there is nothing to stop Congress from preempting a field with an express preemption clause. It did just that in ERISA, where the statute's "express" preemption clause has precluded the states from enforcing any laws regulating employee benefit plans.

Obstacle preemption — the second type of conflict preemption noted above — also has two aspects which courts frequently fail to distinguish. A state law could directly contradict a federal law, yet not create the other type of conflict: impossibility of compliance with both. For instance, California's medical marijuana law, which permits individuals to use marijuana for certain medical conditions, has been held to conflict with the federal Controlled Substances Act, which prohibits the individual use of marijuana for any purpose. But a person could technically "comply" with both laws at once by refraining from using marijuana. Another example might involve a state law that forbids, or at least penalizes, the assertion of a federal statutory right. A Florida law that denied unemployment compensation benefits to any fired worker who filed an unfair labor practice charge with the National Labor Relations Board was held to be preempted by the federal labor law. Conflicts of this type thus involve situations where state law *permits* something forbidden by federal law, or conversely, where state law *forbids or penalizes* something permitted by federal law. These situations are analyzed as obstacle preemption cases. Here, the state law contradicts the federal law, or is "repugnant" to it, to use the term famously employed by Chief Justice Marshall in the first conflict preemption case, *Gibbons v. Ogden.*

But modern preemption doctrine pushes the notion of obstacle preemption much further than did *Gibbons.* Obstacle preemption is used to nullify any state law that "stands as an obstacle to the accomplishment and execution of the full purposes of Congress." *E.g.,* Southland Corp. v. Keating, 465 U.S. 1 (1984). Federal courts have used this doctrine to preempt state laws not only in clear-cut "repugnance" situations, but also where the court defined the purpose of Congress in broader or fuzzier terms.

In addition to this specific challenge, there also are two overarching difficulties the courts face in determining congressional intent for preemptive purposes. First, is a congressional regulation intended to be a ceiling or a floor? If Congress sets the minimum wage at $7.50 is that a "floor" (employers cannot rely on lower state minimums to pay their employees less), or a "ceiling" (state laws will not be enforced if they require a higher pay rate)? Second, acts of Congress may reflect multiple purposes, or balance conflicting goals; maximum enforcement of a single "purpose" may not be the intention of most statutes. The idea of using preemption doctrine to advance the "full purposes of Congress" thus becomes problematic.

If preemption is a question of statutory interpretation (did Congress intended to supersede state law), why is it included in a Constitutional Law book? The answer is that preemption doctrine has two closely related constitutional dimensions. First, a decision by a court to hold that federal law preempts state law, in essence, voids that state law under the Supremacy Clause. It is functionally a kind of judicial review; the main difference is that the substantive contours of the federal law come from statute rather than from judicial interpretations of another constitutional provision. Second, preemption has huge consequences for state power. When a court voids a state law on the ground that it is preempted by federal law, it nullifies the policy choice of the state's legislature or its voters. Consider the example of medical marijuana: despite the laws of several states legalizing it, use of medical marijuana remains a crime *in all states* under the federal Controlled Substances Act. The early 1990s marked the beginning of what many observers considered to be a "federalism revival," with cases like *New York v. United States, Lopez,* and *Printz* (studied in Chapter 1) reasserting federalism limits that many thought had gone by the wayside. Even a recent case like *NFIB v. Sebelius* (the Affordable Care Act case) is filled with assertions about federalism limits. It is therefore striking that the Supreme Court has nullified about half as many state statutes on preemption grounds alone as it has under all other constitutional provisions combined!

Guided Reading Questions: *Geier v. American Honda Motor Co.*

1. What is the preemptive federal law and the preempted state law? Are either of them statutes? Does that make a difference to preemption doctrine?

2. Does the federal law set a ceiling or a floor? How can you tell? Is that point debated by the dissenters?

3. What is the "presumption against preemption"? Has it been applied here? Should it have been?

Geier v. American Honda Motor Co.

529 U.S. 861 (2000)

Majority: *Breyer*, Rehnquist (CJ), O'Connor, Scalia, Kennedy

Dissent: *Stevens*, Souter, Thomas, Ginsburg

JUSTICE BREYER delivered the opinion of the Court.

This case focuses on the 1984 version of a Federal Motor Vehicle Safety Standard promulgated by the Department of Transportation under the authority of the National Traffic and Motor Vehicle Safety Act of 1966, 15 U.S.C. § 1381 et seq. (1988 ed.). The standard, FMVSS 208, required auto manufacturers to equip some but not all of their 1987 vehicles with passive restraints. We ask whether the Act pre-empts a state common-law tort action in which the plaintiff claims that the defendant auto manufacturer, who was in compliance with the standard, should nonetheless have equipped a 1987 automobile with airbags. We conclude that the Act, taken together with FMVSS 208, pre-empts the lawsuit.

In 1992, petitioner Alexis Geier, driving a 1987 Honda Accord, collided with a tree and was seriously injured. The car was equipped with manual shoulder and lap belts which Geier had buckled up at the time. The car was not equipped with airbags or other passive restraint devices.

Geier and her parents, also petitioners, sued the car's manufacturer, American Honda Motor Company, Inc., and its affiliates (hereinafter American Honda), under District of Columbia tort law. They claimed, among other things, that American Honda had designed its car negligently and defectively because it lacked a driver's side airbag. The District Court dismissed the lawsuit.... The Court of Appeals agreed with the District Court's conclusion but on somewhat different reasoning....

Several state courts have held to the contrary, namely, that neither the Act's express pre-emption nor FMVSS 208 pre-empts a "no airbag" tort suit. All of the Federal Circuit Courts that have considered the question, however, have found pre-emption.... We granted certiorari to resolve these differences....

.... This Court, when describing conflict pre-emption, has spoken of pre-empting state law that "under the circumstances of the particular case ... stands as an obstacle to the accomplishment and execution of the full purposes and objectives of Congress" — whether that "obstacle" goes by the name of "conflicting; contrary to; ... repugnance; difference; irreconcilability; inconsistency; violation; curtailment; ... interference," or the like. Hines v. Davidowitz, 312 U.S. 52, 67 (1941).... "[C]onflicts" that prevent or frustrate the accomplishment of a federal objective and "conflicts" that make it "impossible" for private parties to comply with both state and federal law.... are [both] "nullified" by the Supremacy Clause, and [the Court] has assumed that Congress would not want either kind of conflict....

The basic question, then, is whether a common-law "no airbag" action like the one before us actually conflicts with FMVSS 208. We hold that it does.

In petitioners' and the dissent's view, FMVSS 208 sets a minimum airbag standard. As far as FMVSS 208 is concerned, the more airbags, and the sooner, the better. But that was not the Secretary's view. DOT's comments, which accompanied the promulgation of FMVSS 208, make clear that the standard deliberately provided the manufacturer with a range of choices among different passive restraint devices. Those choices would bring about a mix of different devices introduced gradually over time; and FMVSS 208 would thereby lower costs, overcome technical safety problems, encourage technological development, and win widespread consumer acceptance—all of which would promote FMVSS 208's safety objectives. See generally 49 Fed. Reg. 28962 (1984).

The history of FMVSS 208 helps explain why and how DOT sought these objectives. In 1967, DOT, understanding that seatbelts would save many lives, required manufacturers to install manual seat belts in all automobiles. It became apparent, however, that most occupants simply would not buckle up their belts. DOT then began to investigate the feasibility of requiring "passive restraints," such as airbags and automatic seatbelts.... Although the agency's focus was originally on airbags, at no point did FMVSS 208 formally require the use of airbags. From the start, as in 1984, it permitted passive restraint options.

.... [I]n 1974, when the agency approved the use of detachable automatic seatbelts, it conditioned that approval by providing that such systems must include an [ignition-blocking "interlock" system] and a continuous warning buzzer to encourage reattachment of the belt. But the interlock and buzzer devices were most unpopular with the public. And Congress, responding to public pressure, passed a law that forbade DOT from requiring, or permitting compliance by means of, such devices.

That experience influenced DOT's subsequent passive restraint initiatives. In 1976, DOT Secretary William Coleman, ... sought to win public acceptance for a variety of passive restraint devices through a demonstration project that would involve about half a million new automobiles. But his successor, Brock Adams, canceled the project, instead amending FMVSS 208 to require passive restraints, principally either airbags or passive seat belts.

Andrew Lewis, a new DOT Secretary in a new administration, rescinded the Adams requirements, primarily because DOT learned that the industry planned to satisfy those requirements almost exclusively through the installation of detachable automatic seatbelts. 46 Fed. Reg. 53419–53420 (1981). This Court held the rescission unlawful. And the stage was set for then-DOT Secretary, Elizabeth Dole, to amend FMVSS 208 once again, promulgating the version that is now before us.

Read in light of this history, DOT's own contemporaneous explanation of FMVSS 208 makes clear that the 1984 version of FMVSS 208 reflected [several] significant considerations ... Most importantly, that standard deliberately sought variety—a mix of several different passive restraint systems. It did so by setting a performance requirement for passive restraint devices and allowing manufacturers to choose among different passive restraint mechanisms, such as airbags, automatic belts, or other passive restraint technologies to satisfy that requirement. And DOT explained why FMVSS 208 sought the mix of devices that it expected its performance standard to produce. DOT wrote that it had rejected a proposed FMVSS 208 "all airbag" standard because of safety concerns (perceived or real) associated with airbags, which concerns threatened a "backlash" more easily overcome "if airbags" were "not the only way of complying." It added that a mix of devices would help develop data on comparative effectiveness, would allow the industry time to overcome the safety problems and the high production costs associated with airbags, and would facilitate the development of alternative, cheaper, and safer passive restraint systems....

The 1984 FMVSS 208 standard also deliberately sought a gradual phase-in of passive restraints. It required the manufacturers to equip only 10% of their car fleet manufactured after September 1, 1986, with passive restraints. It then increased the percentage in three annual stages, up to 100% of the new car fleet for cars manufactured after September 1, 1989. And it explained that the phased-in requirement would allow more time for manufacturers to develop airbags or other, better, safer passive restraint systems. It would help develop information about the comparative effectiveness of different systems, would lead to a mix in which airbags and other nonseatbelt passive restraint systems played a more prominent role than would otherwise result, and would promote public acceptance....

In sum, as DOT now tells us through the Solicitor General, the 1984 version of FMVSS 208 "embodies the Secretary's policy judgment that safety would best be promoted if manufacturers installed alternative protection systems in their fleets rather than one particular system in every car." Brief for United States as Amicus Curiae 25; see 49 Fed. Reg. 28997 (1984)....

... [P]etitioners' tort action depends upon its claim that manufacturers had a duty to install an airbag when they manufactured the 1987 Honda Accord. Such a state law—i.e., a rule of state tort law imposing such a duty—by its terms would have required manufacturers of all similar cars to install airbags rather than other passive restraint systems, such as automatic belts or passive interiors. It thereby would have presented an obstacle to the variety and mix of devices that the federal regulation sought. It would have required all manufacturers to have installed airbags in respect to the entire District-of-Columbia-related portion of their 1987 new car fleet, even though FMVSS 208 at that time required only that 10% of a manufacturer's nationwide fleet be equipped with any passive restraint device at all. It thereby also would have stood as an obstacle to the gradual passive restraint phase—in that the federal regulation deliberately imposed. In addition, it could have made less likely the adoption of a state mandatory buckle-up law. Because the rule of law for which petitioners contend would have stood "as an obstacle to the accomplishment and execution of" the important means-related federal objectives that we have just discussed, it is pre-empted....

One final point: We place some weight upon DOT's interpretation of FMVSS 208's objectives and its conclusion, as set forth in the Government's brief, that a tort suit such as this one would "stand as an obstacle to the accomplishment and execution" of those objectives. Congress has delegated to DOT authority to implement the statute; the subject matter is technical; and the relevant history and background are complex and extensive. The agency is likely to have a thorough understanding of its own regulation and its objectives and is "uniquely qualified" to comprehend the likely impact of state requirements.... In these circumstances, the agency's own views should make a difference....

Regardless, the language of FMVSS 208 and the contemporaneous 1984 DOT explanation is clear enough—even without giving DOT's own view special weight. FMVSS 208 sought a gradually developing mix of alternative passive restraint devices for safety-related reasons. The rule of state tort law for which petitioners argue would stand as an "obstacle" to the accomplishment of that objective. And the statute foresees the application of ordinary principles of pre-emption in cases of actual conflict. Hence, the tort action is pre-empted. The judgment of the Court of Appeals is affirmed.

JUSTICE STEVENS, with whom JUSTICE SOUTER, JUSTICE THOMAS, and JUSTICE GINSBURG join, dissenting.

Airbag technology has been available to automobile manufacturers for over 30 years. There is now general agreement on the proposition "that, to be safe, a car must have an airbag." Indeed, current federal law imposes that requirement on all automobile manufacturers. See 49 U.S.C. § 30127; 49 CFR § 571.208, S4.1.5.3 (1998). The question raised by petitioner's common-law tort action is whether that proposition was sufficiently obvious when Honda's 1987 Accord was manufactured to make the failure to install such a safety feature actionable under theories of negligence or defective design. The

Court holds that an interim regulation motivated by the Secretary of Transportation's desire to foster gradual development of a variety of passive restraint devices deprives state courts of jurisdiction to answer that question. I respectfully dissent from that holding, and especially from the Court's unprecedented extension of the doctrine of pre-emption....

"This is a case about federalism," Coleman v. Thompson, 501 U.S. 722, 726 (1991), that is, about respect for "the constitutional role of the States as sovereign entities." Alden v. Maine, 527 U.S. 706, 713 (1999). It raises important questions concerning the way in which the Federal Government may exercise its undoubted power to oust state courts of their traditional jurisdiction over common-law tort actions. The rule the Court enforces today was not enacted by Congress and is not to be found in the text of any Executive Order or regulation. It has a unique origin: it is the product of the Court's interpretation of the final commentary accompanying an interim administrative regulation and the history of airbag regulation generally. Like many other judge-made rules, its contours are not precisely defined....

.... [T]he objectives that the Secretary intended to achieve through the adoption of Federal Motor Vehicle Safety Standard 208 would not be frustrated one whit by allowing state courts to determine whether in 1987 the life-saving advantages of airbags had become sufficiently obvious that their omission might constitute a design defect in some new cars.

The question presented is whether either the National Traffic and Motor Vehicle Safety Act of 1966, or the version of Standard 208 promulgated by the Secretary of Transportation in 1984, pre-empts common-law tort claims that an automobile manufactured in 1987 was negligently and defectively designed because it lacked "an effective and safe passive restraint system, including, but not limited to, airbags." .... The purpose of the Act, as stated by Congress, was "to reduce traffic accidents and deaths and injuries to persons resulting from traffic accidents." 15 U.S.C. § 1381. The Act directed the Secretary of Trans-portation or his delegate to issue motor vehicle safety standards that "shall be practicable, shall meet the need for motor vehicle safety, and shall be stated in objective terms." § 1392(a). The Act defines the term "safety standard" as a "minimum standard for motor vehicle performance, or motor vehicle equipment performance." § 1391(2).

Standard 208 covers "occupant crash protection." Its purpose "is to reduce the number of deaths of vehicle occupants, and the severity of injuries, by specifying vehicle crash-worthiness requirements ... [and] equipment requirements for active and passive restraint systems." 49 CFR § 571.208, S2 (1998)....

Given that Secretary Dole promulgated the 1984 standard in response to our opinion invalidating her predecessor's rescission of the 1977 passive restraint requirement, she provided a full explanation for her decision not to require airbags in all cars and to phase in the new requirements....

Although the standard did not require airbags in all cars, it is clear that the Secretary did intend to encourage wider use of airbags. One of her basic conclusions was that "automatic occupant protection systems that do not totally rely upon belts, such as airbags..., offer significant additional potential for preventing fatalities and injuries, at least in part because the American public is likely to find them less intrusive; their development and availability should be encouraged through appropriate incentives." .... The Secretary therefore included a phase-in period in order to encourage manufacturers to comply with the standard by installing airbags and other (perhaps more effective) nonbelt technologies that they might develop, rather than by installing less expensive automatic seatbelts....

Before discussing the pre-emption issue, it is appropriate to note that there is a vast difference between a rejection of Honda's threshold arguments in favor of federal pre-emption and a conclusion that petitioners ultimately would prevail on their common-law tort claims. I express no opinion on the possible merit, or lack of merit, of those claims. I do observe, however, that even though good-faith compliance with the minimum requirements of Standard 208 would not provide Honda with a complete defense on the merits, I assume that such compliance would be admissible evidence tending to negate charges of negligent and defective design. In addition, if Honda were ultimately found liable, such compliance would presumably weigh against an award of punitive damages....

When a state statute, administrative rule, or common-law cause of action conflicts with a federal statute, it is axiomatic that the state law is without effect. U.S. Const., Art. VI, cl. 2; Cipollone v. Liggett Group, Inc., 505 U.S. 504, 516 (1992). On the other hand, it is equally clear that the Supremacy Clause does not give unelected federal judges carte blanche to use federal law as a means of imposing their own ideas of tort reform on the States. Because of the role of States as separate sovereigns in our federal system, we have long presumed that state laws—particularly those, such as the provision of tort remedies to compensate for personal injuries, that are within the scope of the States' historic police powers—are not to be pre-empted by a federal statute unless it is the clear and manifest purpose of Congress to do so.

When a federal statute contains an express pre-emption provision, "the task of statutory construction must in the first instance focus on the plain wording of [that provision], which necessarily contains the best evidence of Congress' pre-emptive intent.".... Even though the Safety Act does not expressly pre-empt common-law claims, Honda contends that Standard 208—of its own force—implicitly pre-empts the claims in this case.

"We have recognized that a federal statute implicitly overrides state law either when the scope of a statute indicates that Congress intended federal law to occupy a field exclusively, or when state law is in actual conflict with federal law. We have found implied conflict pre-emption where it is 'impossible for a private party to comply with both state and federal requirements,' or where state law 'stands as an obstacle to the accomplishment and execution of the full purposes and objectives of Congress.'"

In addition, we have concluded that regulations "intended to pre-empt state law" that are promulgated by an agency acting non-arbitrarily and within its congressionally delegated authority may also have pre-emptive force. In this case, Honda relies on the last of the implied pre-emption principles..., arguing that the imposition of common-law liability for failure to install an airbag would frustrate the purposes and objectives of Standard 208.

Both the text of the statute and the text of the standard provide persuasive reasons for rejecting this argument.... Honda argues, and the Court now agrees, that the risk of liability presented by common-law claims that vehicles without airbags are negligently and defectively designed would frustrate the policy decision that the Secretary made in promulgating Standard 208. This decision, in their view, was that safety—including a desire to encourage "public acceptance of the airbag technology and experimentation with better passive restraint systems,"—would best be promoted through gradual implementation of a passive restraint requirement making airbags only one of a variety of systems that a manufacturer could install in order to comply, rather than through a requirement mandating the use of one particular system in every vehicle. In its brief supporting Honda, the United States agreed with this submission. It argued that if the manufacturers had known in 1984 that they might later be held liable for failure to install airbags, that risk "would likely have led them to install airbags in all cars," thereby frustrating the Secretary's safety goals and interfering with the methods designed to achieve them.

There are at least three flaws in this argument that provide sufficient grounds for rejecting it. [First, manufacturers knew how to install airbags in 1987; if potential tort liability were a sufficient concern to induce them to put airbags in all their cars, they would have done so, and Standard 208 would have been unnecessary. In fact tort liability wasn't a big enough factor to make manufacturers go all out for airbags—therefore, it was not an "obstacle" to the purported goal of allowing various passage restraint systems.

[Second, tort law takes several years to produce liability judgments that shape behavior. By the time these would have occurred the phase-in period would have been long over: therefore, tort judgments would not have interfered with manufacturers decisions during the phase-in period. Moreover, such tort judgments would not have affected manufacturers' incentive to develop an alternative safer than the airbag—which would have prevented design defect liability for not using the airbag.]

Third, ... the Court completely ignores the important fact that by definition all of the standards established under the Safety Act—like the British regulations that governed the number and capacity of lifeboats aboard the Titanic—impose minimum, rather than fixed or maximum, requirements. The phase-in program authorized by Standard 208 thus set minimum percentage requirements for the installation of passive restraints, increasing in annual stages of 10, 25, 40, and 100%. Those requirements were not ceilings, and it is obvious that the Secretary favored a more rapid increase. The possibility that exposure to potential tort liability might accelerate the rate of increase would actually further the only goal explicitly mentioned in the standard itself: reducing the number of deaths and severity of injuries of vehicle occupants. Had gradualism been independently important as a method of achieving the Secretary's safety goals, presumably the Secretary would have put a ceiling as well as a floor on each annual increase in the required percentage of new passive restraint installations.... Moreover, ... there is nothing in the Standard, the accompanying commentary, or the history of airbag regulation to support the notion that the Secretary intended to advance those [claimed] purposes at all costs, without regard to the detrimental consequences that pre-emption of tort liability could have for the achievement of her avowed purpose of reducing vehicular injuries....

For these reasons, it is evident that Honda has not crossed the high threshold established by our decisions regarding pre-emption of state laws that allegedly frustrate federal purposes: it has not demonstrated that allowing a common-law no-airbag claim to go forward would impose an obligation on manufacturers that directly and irreconcilably contradicts any primary objective that the Secretary set forth with clarity in Standard 208. Furthermore, it is important to note that the text of Standard 208 (which the Court does not even bother to quote in its opinion), ... does not contain any expression of an intent to displace state law. Given our repeated emphasis on the importance of the presumption against pre-emption, this silence lends additional support to the conclusion that the continuation of whatever common-law liability may exist in a case like this poses no danger of frustrating any of the Secretary's primary purposes in promulgating Standard 208.

The Court apparently views the question of pre-emption in this case as a close one. Under "ordinary experience-proved principles of conflict pre-emption," therefore, the presumption against pre-emption should control. Instead, the Court simply ignores the presumption, preferring instead to put the burden on petitioners to show that their tort claim would not frustrate the Secretary's purposes In view of the important principles upon which the presumption is founded, however, rejecting it in this manner is profoundly unwise.

Our presumption against pre-emption is rooted in the concept of federalism. It recognizes that when Congress legislates "in a field which the States have traditionally occupied ... [,] we start with the assumption that the historic police powers of the States were not to be superseded by the Federal Act unless that was the clear and manifest purpose of Congress." Rice v. Santa Fe Elevator Corp., 331 U.S. at 230. The signal virtues of this presumption are its placement of the power of pre-emption squarely in the hands of Congress, which is far more suited than the Judiciary to strike the appropriate state/federal balance (particularly in areas of traditional state regulation), and its requirement that Congress speak clearly when exercising that power. In this way, the structural safeguards inherent in the normal operation of the legislative process operate to defend state interests from undue infringement. In addition, the presumption serves as a limiting principle that prevents federal judges from running amok with our potentially boundless (and perhaps inadequately considered) doctrine of implied conflict pre-emption based on frustration of purposes—i.e., that state law is pre-empted if it "stands as an obstacle to the accomplishment and execution of the full purposes and objectives of Congress." Hines v. Davidowitz, 312 U.S. at 67.

> FN22. Recently, one commentator has argued that our doctrine of frustration-of-purposes (or "obstacle") pre-emption is not supported by the text or history of the Supremacy Clause, and has suggested that we attempt to bring a measure of rationality to our pre-emption jurisprudence by eliminating it. Nelson, Preemption, 86 Va. L. Rev. 225, 231–232 (2000) ("Under the Supremacy Clause, preemption occurs if and only if state law contradicts a valid rule established by federal law, and the mere fact that the federal law serves certain purposes does not automatically mean that it contradicts everything that might get in the way of those purposes")....

While the presumption is important in assessing the pre-emptive reach of federal statutes, it becomes crucial when the pre-emptive effect of an administrative regulation is at issue. Unlike Congress, administrative agencies are clearly not designed to represent the interests of States, yet with relative ease they can promulgate comprehensive and detailed regulations that have broad pre-emption ramifications for state law. We have addressed the heightened federalism and nondelegation concerns that agency pre-emption raises by using the presumption to build a procedural bridge across the political accountability gap between States and administrative agencies. Thus, even in cases where implied regulatory pre-emption is at issue, we generally "expect an administrative regulation to declare any intention to pre-empt state law with some specificity." ...

Because neither the text of the statute nor the text of the regulation contains any indication of an intent to pre-empt petitioners' cause of action, and because I cannot agree with the Court's unprecedented use of inferences from regulatory history and commentary as a basis for implied pre-emption, I am convinced that Honda has not overcome the presumption against pre-emption in this case. I therefore respectfully dissent.

Review Questions and Explanations: *Geier*

1. Are you persuaded that Congress intended to set a ceiling on safety regulation? How clear should its intent have been in order to find preemption? Should the majority have at least discussed the presumption against preemption?

2. Regulations enacted by administrative agencies are designed to flesh out details of statutes in order to implement them. They have the force of law, in that they bind private parties. They also represent the agency's interpretation of

the statutes in question. A body of case law (that you can study in an Administrative Law course) has set out guidelines about how much deference a court should give to an agency's interpretation of a statute. Some agencies are deemed "expert" in the statute they administer, and their interpretations are given deference. Others are not. And in still other cases, agency flip-flopping on statutory interpretation is a strike against deferring to the agency's interpretation. Finally, note that agencies are headed by political appointees who presumably share the presidential administration's policy objectives.

Should regulations count as "laws of the United States" for Supremacy Clause purposes and be given full preemptive effect? How much deference should the agency interpretation have received in this case?

3. What is the net regulatory effect of the preemption ruling here? Is there more regulation or less regulation? And what kind of regulation?

4. Do you find it noteworthy that Justices Rehnquist, O'Connor, Kennedy, and Scalia (all of whom consistently voted for state autonomy in *Lopez, Morrison, New York,* and *Printz,* among other cases in Chapter 1) voted here to preempt—in essence, rejecting the pro-state-autonomy position? Why do you think they voted that way? Why do you think Justice Thomas didn't join them? And why did Justices Stevens, Souter, and Ginsburg vote *for* state autonomy?

PART TWO

SEPARATION OF POWERS

Separation of powers is the constitutional principle holding that the three branches of the federal government — legislative, executive and judicial — exercise powers limited to their own respective spheres. We have already seen that the powers of Congress vis-à-vis the states are limited by the Constitution's delegation of only enumerated powers to the federal government. This federalism-based division of power often is said to represent a "vertical" division of governmental power, insofar as the federal Constitution and federal laws enacted under it are "the supreme law of the land" (U.S. Const. Art. VI). The separation-of-powers concept, by comparison, represents a "horizontal" division of power, because the three branches of the federal government each exercise the sovereign power of the federal government in their respective spheres of authority. The three branches are thus "coordinate," in the sense of occupying the same level of a governmental hierarchy in which none is in theory superior over or inferior to the others.

Separation of powers in U.S. constitutional theory is another means by which the power of government is limited. The crucial division of legislative from executive authority — separating the power to make laws from the power to carry them out — was deemed by the framers as a necessary check against the tyranny of sovereigns who could wield both those attributes of governmental power. Similarly, the framers considered it to be a necessary safeguard against tyranny to separate the power to charge and prosecute alleged lawbreakers (a quintessential executive function) from the quintessentially judicial powers to apply the law to an individual case, to supervise determinations of guilt or innocence, to pass sentence and to hear challenges to the executive's authority to detain or imprison. The system of "checks and balances" familiar to you since grade school is an aspect of separation of powers, reflecting the various ways that each branch holds certain powers that effectively limit the powers of the others. The concept of separation of powers comprises not only these checks and balances, but also a principle that there are "boundaries" of authority between the branches that cannot, constitutionally, be crossed. Like the doctrine of enumerated powers, which limits the power of the federal government to that which is delegated to it by the Constitution, separation of powers is sometimes understood as protecting individual liberty by using the power held by the coordinate branches to check the power exercised by each.

These generalities are only a starting point, however, for a wide array of subtle, difficult and often insoluble constitutional problems. The difficulty stems in part from the relationship between two commonly expressed ideas: separation of powers and checks and balances. We speak of both of these as foundational concepts in our system of government. But they are in considerable tension: in order to "check" the power of a coordinate branch, an alternative branch must necessarily exercise power that is at least arguably within the sphere occupied by the branch being checked. Congress, for example, cannot check the executive's power over foreign affairs without involving itself in questions raising precisely those issues. Thus, while the three great powers of government—legislative, executive, and judicial—are separately delineated in our system, the ability to check the powers exercised by each branch depends on some subject-matter overlap. This type of overlap, we will see, recurs frequently throughout the Constitution. The difficult questions in separation-of-powers cases, consequently, often involve determining where "separation" ends and "checking" begins.

Consider this mid-twentieth century comment by a Supreme Court justice on the constitutional doctrine governing the powers of the President:

> Just what our forefathers did envision, or would have envisioned had they foreseen modern conditions, must be divined from materials almost as enigmatic as the dreams Joseph was called upon to interpret for Pharaoh. A century and a half of partisan debate and scholarly speculation yields no net result but only supplies more or less apt quotations from respected sources on each side of any question. They largely cancel each other out.

Youngstown Sheet & Tube Co. v. Sawyer, 343 U.S. 579, 634–35 (1952) (Jackson, J., concurring).

Separation-of-powers problems typically arise in situations where the limits of the powers of a branch of government are unclear, and where the relevant constitutional actors have made controversial and perhaps conflicting interpretations of their own constitutional authority. Not infrequently, these situations are politically charged and arise out of actual or perceived emergencies or crises. Controlling constitutional "law" in the form of binding Supreme Court precedent is, consequently, frequently thin or non-existent. Moreover, many separation-of-powers controversies take a form that is not "justiciable" as a legal case. (See Chapter 6, Justiciability.) Even when a separation-of-powers problem arises in justiciable form, the circumstances are typically so unique, highly contextual, or fact specific that prior precedents can be distinguished without great mental effort.

Finally, the majority of separation-of-powers controversies involve assertions of authority by the executive branch, in particular, the President, as against powers arguably held by Congress. For this reason, most constitutional law treatises and law school courses introduce the subject of separation of powers and the subject of executive power at the same time. And it is not entirely uncommon for legal commentators and even judges to use the term "separation of powers" to mean the powers of the executive branch vis-à-vis the legislative branch. However, the two concepts are not co-extensive or interchangeable. Although this book follows the convention of introducing executive power into a broader treatment of "separation of powers," it is important to keep the distinction between the two terms clearly in mind. "Executive power" refers specifically to the powers of the executive branch, vested primarily in the President but also in cabinet-level and lower-ranked officials within the executive branch. "Separation of powers" includes not only the boundaries of power between the executive and legislative branches, but also between the executive and judicial branches and even between the judicial and legislative branches.

We introduce the executive branch and executive power in Chapter 3. Much, probably most, of what we call "separation-of-powers doctrine" involves cases defining and limiting executive power. In Chapter 4, we turn to separation-of-powers questions that are not properly categorized as "executive power" issues.

Chapter 3

Executive Power

A. Overview

Why does the Presidency—the executive branch—raise so many separation-of-powers "problems"? The answer to that question is that the Constitution gives awesome powers and duties to the President. The President is invested with "The executive power," Art. II, § 1, cl. 1; and "shall be commander in chief of the Army and Navy of the United States," Art. II, § 2, cl. 1; and "shall take care that the laws be faithfully executed," Art. II, § 3, cl. 4. Other constitutional provisions relating to the President spell out, in somewhat more detail, specific powers and duties the President has when interacting with Congress—the veto power, for instance. But the three above-quoted powers are not further specified or defined. When you consider how much activity is involved in "executing the laws" and conducting foreign affairs on a day-to-day basis, how much detail remains to be filled in to cover gaps and flesh out general guidance in statutes and treaties, and how much initiative may be required to deal with sudden and unanticipated situations, you can see that there is much room for improvisation by the executive branch. And this is before we consider how a particular President may wish to get things done at times when Congress is unwilling or unable to act in concert—because it is politically opposed to the President, or stuck by its own internal political divisions, or not in session. Interpretation of the content of "executive power" thus leaves considerable room for creativity.

A second major contributor to separation-of-powers problems in the exercise of executive power comes from the nature of law itself. A clean and simple division of power among the three branches—Congress makes law, the President executes the law, and the Judiciary interprets and applies the law—becomes fuzzier on closer inspection. Every "execution" of a law necessarily involves an act of interpretation. If that interpretation is applied consistently from one instance to the next, it takes on a rule- or law-like character. So the separation between making and executing law is less like a line and more like a big gray smudge.

This latter problem is multiplied by the fact that the President does not "execute the laws" alone, but oversees a massive staff of executive branch employees. At present, there are over two million federal employees in the executive branch. While their numbers have greatly increased over time, the President has always had officials to whom to delegate executive functions. This structure itself raises separation-of-powers questions, for how is the President to supervise all these officials? The rules and policies that must be issued within the executive branch to "execute the laws" may themselves involve activities that look a lot like lawmaking and interpretation.

B. Foundational Doctrine

The following case, *Youngstown Sheet & Tube Co. v. Sawyer*, also known as "the Steel Seizure Case," is considered the leading case in the separation of powers area, at least where assertions of power by the President are concerned. In any legal inquiry into whether an action by the President exceeds his authority, *Youngstown* is almost invariably the starting point of the analysis.

During the Korean War, on April 8, 1952, President Truman ordered his Secretary of Commerce, Sawyer, to seize a number of steel mills inside the U.S. and operate them under government authority. The executive order to seize the mills came on the eve of a steelworkers' strike which Truman feared would jeopardize the production of steel necessary to supply the war effort. The steel companies brought suit in federal district court and won a preliminary injunction restraining the Secretary of Commerce from "continuing the seizure and possession of the plants" and "acting under the purported authority of" the executive order. The appeal went directly to the Supreme Court, where it was argued on May 12–13, 1952. The Court issued its decision just three weeks later, on June 2, upholding the injunction by a 6–3 vote. Due to hurried process, the justices apparently did not have the time to engage in the behind-the-scenes collaborating and negotiating that normally produces a more unified majority opinion. Thus, although Justice Black wrote an "opinion of the court," each of the four justices who joined that opinion issued an extensive concurring opinion. (With a sixth justice concurring in the judgment, there were six votes to overturn the President's seizure of the steel mills.) The dissenting justices all signed onto a single dissenting opinion by Chief Justice Vinson.

Guided Reading Questions: *Youngstown Sheet & Tube Co. v. Sawyer*

1. Try to articulate in one or two sentences the holding of Justice Black's opinion for the Court and the rationale for each of the concurring opinions.

2. The majority opinion says "the President's power to see that the laws are faithfully executed refutes the idea that he is to be a lawmaker." How is Truman "making laws" by ordering seizure of the steel mills?

3. The three main opinions — Black's for the Court, Frankfurter's and Jackson's — all rely heavily on a then-recent legislative episode in which Congress voted down a provision that would have authorized the President to seize war production industries in the event a strike threatened war supply. Why is this significant? Is voting down such a law equivalent to enacting a law prohibiting that seizure power?

4. Make sure you understand and can summarize the three-part framework in Jackson's concurrence.

Youngstown Sheet & Tube Co. v. Sawyer

["The Steel Seizure Case"]
343 U.S. 579 (1952)

Majority: *Black*, Frankfurter, Douglas, Jackson, Burton

Concurrences: *Frankfurter, Douglas, Jackson, Burton* (omitted)

Concurrence in the result: *Clark* (omitted)

Dissent: *Vinson* (CJ), Reed, Minton

MR. JUSTICE BLACK delivered the opinion of the Court.

We are asked to decide whether the President was acting within his constitutional power when he issued an order directing the Secretary of Commerce to take possession of and operate most of the Nation's steel mills. The mill owners argue that the President's order amounts to lawmaking, a legislative function which the Constitution has expressly confided to the Congress, and not to the President. The Government's position is that the order was made on findings of the President that his action was necessary to avert a national catastrophe which would inevitably result from a stoppage of steel production, and that, in meeting this grave emergency, the President was acting within the aggregate of his constitutional powers as the Nation's Chief Executive and the Commander in Chief of the Armed Forces of the United States. The issue emerges here from the following series of events:

In the latter part of 1951, a dispute arose between the steel companies and their employees over terms and conditions that should be included in new collective bargaining agreements. Long-continued conferences failed to resolve the dispute. On December 18, 1951, the employees' representative, United Steelworkers of America, CIO, gave notice of an intention to strike when the existing bargaining agreements expired on December 31. The Federal Mediation and Conciliation Service then intervened in an effort to get labor and management to agree. This failing, the President on December 22, 1951, referred the dispute to the Federal Wage Stabilization Board to investigate and make recommendations for fair and equitable terms of settlement. This Board's report resulted in no settlement. On April 4, 1952, the Union gave notice of a nationwide strike called to begin at 12:01 a.m. April 9. The indispensability of steel as a component of substantially all weapons and other war materials led the President to believe that the proposed work stoppage would immediately jeopardize our national defense and that governmental seizure of the steel mills was necessary in order to assure the continued availability of steel. Reciting these considerations for his action, the President, a few hours before the strike was to begin, issued Executive Order 10340. The order directed the Secretary of Commerce to take possession of most of the steel mills and keep them running. The Secretary immediately issued his own possessory orders, calling upon the presidents of the various seized companies to serve as operating managers for the United States. They were directed to carry on their activities in accordance with regulations and directions of the Secretary. The next morning the President sent a message to Congress reporting his action. Twelve days later, he sent a second message. Congress has taken no action.

Obeying the Secretary's orders under protest, the companies brought proceedings against him in the District Court. Their complaints charged that the seizure was not authorized by an act of Congress or by any constitutional provisions. The District Court was asked to declare the orders of the President and the Secretary invalid and to issue preliminary and permanent injunctions restraining their enforcement. Opposing the motion for preliminary injunction, the United States asserted that a strike disrupting steel production for even a brief period would so endanger the wellbeing and safety of the Nation that the President had "inherent power" to do what he had done — power "supported by the Constitution, by historical precedent, and by court decisions." .... [I]s the seizure order within the constitutional power of the President? .... The President's power, if any, to issue the order must stem either from an act of Congress or from the Constitution itself. There is no statute that expressly authorizes the President to take possession of property as he did here. Nor is there any act of Congress to which our attention has been directed from which such a power can fairly be implied. Indeed, we do not understand the Government to rely on statutory authorization for this seizure. There are two statutes which do authorize the President to take both personal and real property under certain conditions.

FN2. The Selective Service Act of 1948, 62 Stat. 604, 625–627, 50 U.S.C. App (Supp. IV) § 468; the Defense Production Act of 1950, Tit. II, 64 Stat. 798, as amended, 65 Stat. 132.

However, the Government admits that these conditions were not met, and that the President's order was not rooted in either of the statutes. The Government refers to the seizure provisions of one of these statutes (§ 201(b) of the Defense Production Act) as "much too cumbersome, involved, and time-consuming for the crisis which was at hand."

Moreover, the use of the seizure technique to solve labor disputes in order to prevent work stoppages was not only unauthorized by any congressional enactment; prior to this controversy, Congress had refused to adopt that method of settling labor disputes. When the Taft-Hartley Act was under consideration in 1947, Congress rejected an amendment which would have authorized such governmental seizures in cases of emergency. Apparently it was thought that the technique of seizure, like that of compulsory arbitration, would interfere with the process of collective bargaining. Consequently, the plan Congress adopted in that Act did not provide for seizure under any circumstances. Instead, the plan sought to bring about settlements by use of the customary devices of mediation, conciliation, investigation by boards of inquiry, and public reports. In some instances, temporary injunctions were authorized to provide cooling-off periods. All this failing, unions were left free to strike after a secret vote by employees as to whether they wished to accept their employers' final settlement offer....

It is clear that, if the President had authority to issue the order he did, it must be found in some provision of the Constitution.... The contention is that presidential power should be implied from the aggregate of his powers under the Constitution. Particular reliance is placed on provisions in Article II which say that "The executive Power shall be vested in a President ..."; that "he shall take Care that the Laws be faithfully executed," and that he "shall be Commander in Chief of the Army and Navy of the United States."

The order cannot properly be sustained as an exercise of the President's military power as Commander in Chief of the Armed Forces. The Government attempts to do so by citing a number of cases upholding broad powers in military commanders engaged in day-to-day fighting in a theater of war. Such cases need not concern us here. Even though "theater of war" is an expanding concept, we cannot with faithfulness to our constitutional system hold that the Commander in Chief of the Armed Forces has the ultimate power as such to take possession of private property in order to keep labor disputes from stopping production. This is a job for the Nation's lawmakers, not for its military authorities.

Nor can the seizure order be sustained because of the several constitutional provisions that grant executive power to the President. In the framework of our Constitution, the

President's power to see that the laws are faithfully executed refutes the idea that he is to be a lawmaker. The Constitution limits his functions in the lawmaking process to the recommending of laws he thinks wise and the vetoing of laws he thinks bad. And the Constitution is neither silent nor equivocal about who shall make laws which the President is to execute. The first section of the first article says that "All legislative Powers herein granted shall be vested in a Congress of the United States...." After granting many powers to the Congress, Article I goes on to provide that Congress may make all Laws which shall be necessary and proper for carrying into Execution the foregoing Powers, and all other Powers vested by this Constitution in the Government of the United States, or in any Department or Officer thereof.

The President's order does not direct that a congressional policy be executed in a manner prescribed by Congress — it directs that a presidential policy be executed in a manner prescribed by the President. The preamble of the order itself, like that of many statutes, sets out reasons why the President believes certain policies should be adopted, proclaims these policies as rules of conduct to be followed, and again, like a statute, authorizes a government official to promulgate additional rules and regulations consistent with the policy proclaimed and needed to carry that policy into execution. The power of Congress to adopt such public policies as those proclaimed by the order is beyond question. It can authorize the taking of private property for public use. It can make laws regulating the relationships between employers and employees, prescribing rules designed to settle labor disputes, and fixing wages and working conditions in certain fields of our economy. The Constitution does not subject this lawmaking power of Congress to presidential or military supervision or control.

It is said that other Presidents, without congressional authority, have taken possession of private business enterprises in order to settle labor disputes. But even if this be true, Congress has not thereby lost its exclusive constitutional authority to make laws necessary and proper to carry out the powers vested by the Constitution "in the Government of the United States, or any Department or Officer thereof."

The Founders of this Nation entrusted the lawmaking power to the Congress alone in both good and bad times. It would do no good to recall the historical events, the fears of power, and the hopes for freedom that lay behind their choice. Such a review would but confirm our holding that this seizure order cannot stand. The judgment of the District Court is affirmed.

MR. JUSTICE FRANKFURTER, concurring.

Although the considerations relevant to the legal enforcement of the principle of separation of powers seem to me more complicated and flexible than may appear from what MR. JUSTICE BLACK has written, I join his opinion....

The Founders of this Nation.... rested the structure of our central government on the system of checks and balances. For them, the doctrine of separation of powers was not mere theory; it was a felt necessity. Not so long ago, it was fashionable to find our system of checks and balances obstructive to effective government. It was easy to ridicule that system as outmoded — too easy. The experience through which the world has passed in our own day has made vivid the realization that the Framers of our Constitution were not inexperienced doctrinaires. These long-headed statesmen had no illusion that our people enjoyed biological or psychological or sociological immunities from the hazards of concentrated power. It is absurd to see a dictator in a representative product of the sturdy democratic traditions of the Mississippi Valley. The accretion of dangerous power does not come in a day. It does come, however slowly, from the generative force of unchecked disregard of the restrictions that fence in even the most disinterested assertion of authority.

The Framers, however, did not make the judiciary the overseer of our government.... Rigorous adherence to the narrow scope of the judicial function is especially demanded in controversies that arouse appeals to the Constitution. The attitude with which this Court must approach its duty when confronted with such issues is precisely the opposite of that normally manifested by the general public. So-called constitutional questions seem to exercise a mesmeric influence over the popular mind. This eagerness to settle — preferably forever — a specific problem on the basis of the broadest possible constitutional pronouncements may not unfairly be called one of our minor national traits.... It ought to be, but apparently is not, a matter of common understanding that clashes between different branches of the government should be avoided if a legal ground of less explosive potentialities is properly available. Constitutional adjudications are apt, by exposing differences, to exacerbate them.... [W]ith the utmost unwillingness, with every desire to avoid judicial inquiry into the powers and duties of the other two branches of the government, I cannot escape consideration of the legality of Executive Order No. 10340.

The pole-star for constitutional adjudications is John Marshall's greatest judicial utterance, that "it is a *constitution* we are expounding." McCulloch v. Maryland, 4 Wheat. 316, 407.... Not the least characteristic of great statesmanship which the Framers manifested was the extent to which they did not attempt to bind the future. It is no less incumbent upon this Court to avoid putting fetters upon the future by needless pronouncements today....

The issue before us can be met, and therefore should be, without attempting to define the President's powers comprehensively.... We must therefore put to one side consideration of what powers the President would have had if there had been no legislation whatever bearing on the authority asserted by the seizure, or if the seizure had been only for a short, explicitly temporary period, to be terminated automatically unless Congressional approval were given....

.... Congress has frequently — at least 16 times since 1916 — specifically provided for executive seizure of production, transportation, communications, or storage facilities. In every case, it has qualified this grant of power with limitations and safeguards. This body of enactments ... demonstrates that Congress deemed seizure so drastic a power as to require that it be carefully circumscribed whenever the President was vested with this extraordinary authority. The power to seize has uniformly been given only for a limited period or for a defined emergency, or has been repealed after a short period....

Congress, in 1947, was again called upon to consider whether governmental seizure should be used to avoid serious industrial shutdowns. Congress decided against conferring such power generally and in advance, without special Congressional enactment to meet each particular need. Under the urgency of telephone and coal strikes in the winter of 1946, Congress addressed itself to the problems raised by "national emergency" strikes and lockouts. The termination of wartime seizure powers on December 31, 1946, brought these matters to the attention of Congress with vivid impact. A proposal that the President be given powers to seize plants to avert a shutdown where the "health or safety" of the Nation was endangered was thoroughly canvassed by Congress, and rejected ... In adopting the provisions which it did, by the Labor Management Relations Act of 1947, for dealing with a "national emergency" arising out of a breakdown in peaceful industrial relations, Congress was very familiar with Governmental seizure as a protective measure. On a balance of considerations, Congress chose not to lodge this power in the President.... The President could not ignore the specific limitations of prior seizure statutes. No more could he act in disregard of the limitation put upon seizure by the 1947 Act.... The Defense Production Act [of 1950] affords no ground for the suggestion that the 1947 denial to the President of seizure powers has been impliedly repealed, and its legislative history contradicts such a suggestion. Although the proponents of that Act recognized that the President would have a choice of alternative methods of seeking a mediated settlement, they also recognized that Congress alone retained the ultimate coercive power to meet the threat of "any serious work stoppage." ...

It is one thing to draw an intention of Congress from general language and to say that Congress would have explicitly written what is inferred, where Congress has not addressed itself to a specific situation. It is quite impossible, however, when Congress did specifically address itself to a problem, as Congress did to that of seizure, to find secreted in the interstices of legislation the very grant of power which Congress consciously withheld....

.... The powers of the President are not as particularized as are those of Congress. But unenumerated powers do not mean undefined powers. The separation of powers built into our Constitution gives essential content to undefined provisions in the frame of our government.

To be sure, the content of the three authorities of government is not to be derived from an abstract analysis.... Deeply embedded traditional ways of conducting government cannot supplant the Constitution or legislation, but they give meaning to the words of a text or supply them. It is an inadmissibly narrow conception of American constitutional law to confine it to the words of the Constitution and to disregard the gloss which life has written upon them. In short, a systematic, unbroken, executive practice, long pursued to the knowledge of the Congress and never before questioned, engaged in by Presidents who have also sworn to uphold the Constitution, making as it were such exercise of power part of the structure of our government, may be treated as a gloss on "executive Power" vested in the President by § 1 of Art. II.

[However, no established] practice can be vouched for executive seizure of property at a time when this country was not at war, in the only constitutional way in which it can be at war.... [T]he list of executive assertions of the power of seizure in circumstances comparable to the present reduces to three in the six-month period from June to December of 1941. We need not split hairs in comparing those actions to the one before us, though much might be said by way of differentiation. Without passing on their validity, as we are not called upon to do, it suffices to say that these three isolated instances do not add up, either in number, scope, duration or contemporaneous legal justification, to the kind of executive construction of the Constitution [required]. Nor do they come to us sanctioned by long-continued acquiescence of Congress giving decisive weight to a construction by the Executive of its powers.

A scheme of government like ours no doubt at times feels the lack of power to act with complete, all-embracing, swiftly moving authority. No doubt a government with distributed authority, subject to be challenged in the courts of law, at least long enough to consider and adjudicate the challenge, labors under restrictions from which other governments are free. It has not been our tradition to envy such governments. In any event, our government was designed to have such restrictions. The price was deemed not too high in view of the safeguards which these restrictions afford....

MR. JUSTICE DOUGLAS, concurring.

.... As Mr. Justice Brandeis stated in his dissent in *Myers v. United States*, "The doctrine of the separation of powers was adopted by the Convention of 1787, not to promote efficiency but to preclude the exercise of arbitrary power...."

.... We therefore cannot decide this case by determining which branch of government can deal most expeditiously with the present crisis. The answer must depend on the allocation of powers under the Constitution.

The legislative nature of the action taken by the President seems to me to be clear. When the United States takes over an industrial plant to settle a labor controversy, it is condemning property.... But though the seizure is only for a week or a month, the condemnation is complete and the United States must pay compensation for the temporary possession.

.... The command of the Fifth Amendment is that no "private property be taken for public use, without just compensation." .... The President has no power to raise revenues. That power is in the Congress by Article I, Section 8 of the Constitution. The President might seize and the Congress by subsequent action might ratify the seizure. But until and unless Congress acted, no condemnation would be lawful. The branch of government that has the power to pay compensation for a seizure is the only one able to authorize a seizure or make lawful one that the President has effected. That seems to me to be the necessary result of the condemnation provision in the Fifth Amendment. It squares with the theory of checks and balances expounded by MR. JUSTICE BLACK in the opinion of the Court in which I join.

MR. JUSTICE JACKSON, concurring in the judgment and opinion of the Court.

That comprehensive and undefined presidential powers hold both practical advantages and grave dangers for the country will impress anyone who has served as legal adviser to a President in time of transition and public anxiety. While an interval of detached reflection may temper teachings of that experience, they probably are a more realistic influence on my views than the conventional materials of judicial decision which seem unduly to accentuate doctrine and legal fiction. But, as we approach the question of presidential power, we half overcome mental hazards by recognizing them. The opinions of judges, no less than executives and publicists, often suffer the infirmity of confusing the issue of a power's validity with the cause it is invoked to promote, of confounding the permanent executive office with its temporary occupant. The tendency is strong to emphasize transient results upon policies—such as wages or stabilization—and lose sight of enduring consequences upon the balanced power structure of our Republic.

A judge, like an executive adviser, may be surprised at the poverty of really useful and unambiguous authority applicable to concrete problems of executive power as they actually present themselves. Just what our forefathers did envision, or would have envisioned had they foreseen modern conditions, must be divined from materials almost as enigmatic as the dreams Joseph was called upon to interpret for Pharaoh. A century and a half of partisan debate and scholarly speculation yields no net result, but only supplies more or less apt quotations from respected sources on each side of any question. They largely cancel each other. And court decisions are indecisive because of the judicial practice of dealing with the largest questions in the most narrow way.

The actual art of governing under our Constitution does not, and cannot, conform to judicial definitions of the power of any of its branches based on isolated clauses, or even single Articles torn from context. While the Constitution diffuses power the better to secure liberty, it also contemplates that practice will integrate the dispersed powers into a workable government. It enjoins upon its branches separateness but interdependence, autonomy but reciprocity. Presidential powers are not fixed but fluctuate depending upon their disjunction or conjunction with those of Congress. We may well begin by a somewhat over-simplified grouping of practical situations in which a President may doubt, or others may challenge, his powers, and by distinguishing roughly the legal consequences of this factor of relativity.

1. When the President acts pursuant to an express or implied authorization of Congress, his authority is at its maximum, for it includes all that he possesses in his own right plus

all that Congress can delegate. In these circumstances, and in these only, may he be said (for what it may be worth) to personify the federal sovereignty. If his act is held unconstitutional under these circumstances, it usually means that the Federal Government, as an undivided whole, lacks power. A seizure executed by the President pursuant to an Act of Congress would be supported by the strongest of presumptions and the widest latitude of judicial interpretation, and the burden of persuasion would rest heavily upon any who might attack it.

2. When the President acts in absence of either a congressional grant or denial of authority, he can only rely upon his own independent powers, but there is a zone of twilight in which he and Congress may have concurrent authority, or in which its distribution is uncertain. Therefore, congressional inertia, indifference or quiescence may sometimes, at least, as a practical matter, enable, if not invite, measures on independent presidential responsibility. In this area, any actual test of power is likely to depend on the imperatives of events and contemporary imponderables, rather than on abstract theories of law.

3. When the President takes measures incompatible with the expressed or implied will of Congress, his power is at its lowest ebb, for then he can rely only upon his own constitutional powers minus any constitutional powers of Congress over the matter. Courts can sustain exclusive presidential control in such a case only by disabling the Congress from acting upon the subject. Presidential claim to a power at once so conclusive and preclusive must be scrutinized with caution, for what is at stake is the equilibrium established by our constitutional system.

Into which of these classifications does this executive seizure of the steel industry fit? It is eliminated from the first by admission, for it is conceded that no congressional authorization exists for this seizure. That takes away also the support of the many precedents and declarations which were made in relation, and must be confined, to this category.

Can it then be defended under flexible tests available to the second category? It seems clearly eliminated from that class, because Congress has not left seizure of private property an open field, but has covered it by three statutory policies inconsistent with this seizure … None of these were invoked. In choosing a different and inconsistent way of his own, the President cannot claim that it is necessitated or invited by failure of Congress to legislate upon the occasions, grounds and methods for seizure of industrial properties.

This leaves the current seizure to be justified only by the severe tests under the third grouping, where it can be supported only by any remainder of executive power after subtraction of such powers as Congress may have over the subject. In short, we can sustain the President only by holding that seizure of such strike-bound industries is within his domain and beyond control by Congress. Thus, this Court's first review of such seizures occurs under circumstances which leave presidential power most vulnerable to attack and in the least favorable of possible constitutional postures.

I did not suppose, and I am not persuaded, that history leaves it open to question, at least in the courts, that the executive branch, like the Federal Government as a whole, possesses only delegated powers. The purpose of the Constitution was not only to grant power, but to keep it from getting out of hand. However, because the President does not enjoy unmentioned powers does not mean that the mentioned ones should be narrowed by a niggardly construction. Some clauses could be made almost unworkable, as well as immutable, by refusal to indulge some latitude of interpretation for changing times. I have heretofore, and do now, give to the enumerated powers the scope and elasticity afforded by what seem to be reasonable, practical implications, instead of the rigidity dictated by a doctrinaire textualism.

The Solicitor General seeks the power of seizure in three clauses of the Executive Article, the first reading, "The executive Power shall be vested in a President of the United States of America." Lest I be thought to exaggerate, I quote the interpretation which his brief puts upon it: "In our view, this clause constitutes a grant of all the executive powers of which the Government is capable." If that be true, it is difficult to see why the forefathers bothered to add several specific items, including some trifling ones.

> FN9. " ... he may require the Opinion, in writing, of the principal Officer in each of the executive Departments, upon any Subject relating to the Duties of their respective Offices...." U.S.Const., Art. II, § 2. He " ... shall Commission all the Officers of the United States." U.S.Const., Art. II, § 3. Matters such as those would seem to be inherent in the Executive, if anything is.

The example of such unlimited executive power that must have most impressed the forefathers was the prerogative exercised by George III, and the description of its evils in the Declaration of Independence leads me to doubt that they were creating their new Executive in his image. Continental European examples were no more appealing. And, if we seek instruction from our own times, we can match it only from the executive powers in those governments we disparagingly describe as totalitarian. I cannot accept the view that this clause is a grant in bulk of all conceivable executive power, but regard it as an allocation to the presidential office of the generic powers thereafter stated.

The clause on which the Government next relies is that "The President shall be Commander in Chief of the Army and Navy of the United States...." These cryptic words have given rise to some of the most persistent controversies in our constitutional history. Of course, they imply something more than an empty title. But just what authority goes with the name has plagued presidential advisers who would not waive or narrow it by nonassertion, yet cannot say where it begins or ends. It undoubtedly puts the Nation's armed forces under presidential command. Hence, this loose appellation is sometimes advanced as support for any presidential action, internal or external, involving use of force, the idea being that it vests power to do anything, anywhere, that can be done with an army or navy.

That seems to be the logic of an argument tendered at our bar—that the President having, on his own responsibility, sent American troops abroad derives from that act "affirmative power" to seize the means of producing a supply of steel for them ... Thus, it is said, he has invested himself with "war powers."

I cannot foresee all that it might entail if the Court should indorse this argument. Nothing in our Constitution is plainer than that declaration of a war is entrusted only to Congress. Of course, a state of war may, in fact, exist without a formal declaration. But no doctrine that the Court could promulgate would seem to me more sinister and alarming than that a President whose conduct of foreign affairs is so largely uncontrolled, and often even is unknown, can vastly enlarge his mastery over the internal affairs of the country by his own commitment of the Nation's armed forces to some foreign venture. I do not, however, find it necessary or appropriate to consider the legal status of the Korean enterprise to discountenance argument based on it.

Assuming that we are in a war *de facto*, whether it is or is not a war *de jure*, does that empower the Commander in Chief to seize industries he thinks necessary to supply our army? The Constitution expressly places in Congress power "to raise and *support* Armies" and "to *provide* and *maintain* a Navy" (emphasis supplied). This certainly lays upon Congress primary responsibility for supplying the armed forces. Congress alone controls the raising of revenues and their appropriation, and may determine in what manner and by what means they shall be spent for military and naval procurement. I suppose no one would doubt that Congress can take over war supply as a Government enterprise. On the other hand, if Congress sees fit to rely on free private enterprise collectively bargaining with free labor for support and maintenance of our armed forces, can the Executive, because of lawful disagreements incidental to that process, seize the facility for operation upon Government-imposed terms?

There are indications that the Constitution did not contemplate that the title Commander in Chief *of the Army and Navy* will constitute him also Commander in Chief of the country, its industries and its inhabitants. He has no monopoly of "war powers," whatever they are. While Congress cannot deprive the President of the command of the army and navy, only Congress can provide him an army or navy to command. It is also empowered to make rules for the "Government and Regulation of land and naval Forces," by which it may, to some unknown extent, impinge upon even command functions.

That military powers of the Commander in Chief were not to supersede representative government of internal affairs seems obvious from the Constitution and from elementary American history. Time out of mind, and even now, in many parts of the world, a military commander can seize private housing to shelter his troops. Not so, however, in the United States, for the Third Amendment says,

No Soldier shall, in time of peace be quartered in any house, without the consent of the Owner, nor in time of war, but in a manner to be prescribed by law.

Thus, even in war time, his seizure of needed military housing must be authorized by Congress. It also was expressly left to Congress to "provide for calling forth the Militia to execute the Laws of the Union, suppress Insurrections and repel Invasions...." [U.S.Const., Art. I, §8, cl. 15.] Such a limitation on the command power, written at a time when the militia, rather than a standing army, was contemplated as the military weapon of the Republic, underscores the Constitution's policy that Congress, not the Executive, should control utilization of the war power as an instrument of domestic policy. Congress.... has forbidden him to use the army for the purpose of executing general laws except when *expressly* authorized by the Constitution or by Act of Congress....

We should not use this occasion to circumscribe, much less to contract, the lawful role of the President as Commander in Chief. I should indulge the widest latitude of interpretation to sustain his exclusive function to command the instruments of national force, at least when turned against the outside world for the security of our society. But, when it is turned inward not because of rebellion, but because of a lawful economic struggle between industry and labor, it should have no such indulgence. His command power is not such an absolute as might be implied from that office in a militaristic system, but is subject to limitations consistent with a constitutional Republic whose law and policymaking branch is a representative Congress. The purpose of lodging dual titles in one man was to insure that the civilian would control the military, not to enable the military to subordinate the presidential office. No penance would ever expiate the sin against free government of holding that a President can escape control of executive powers by law through assuming his military role. What the power of command may include I do not try to envision, but I think it is not a military prerogative, without support of law, to seize persons or property because they are important or even essential for the military and naval establishment.

The third clause in which the Solicitor General finds seizure powers is that "he shall take Care that the Laws be faithfully executed." U.S.Const., Art. II, §3. That authority must be matched against words of the Fifth Amendment that "No person shall be ...

deprived of life, liberty or property, without due process of law." One gives a governmental authority that reaches so far as there is law, the other gives a private right that authority shall go no farther. These signify about all there is of the principle that ours is a government of laws, not of men, and that we submit ourselves to rulers only if under rules.

The Solicitor General lastly grounds support of the seizure upon nebulous, inherent powers never expressly granted, but said to have accrued to the office from the customs and claims of preceding administrations. The plea is for a resulting power to deal with a crisis or an emergency according to the necessities of the case, the unarticulated assumption being that necessity knows no law.

Loose and irresponsible use of adjectives colors all nonlegal and much legal discussion of presidential powers. "Inherent" powers, "implied" powers, "incidental" powers, "plenary" powers, "war" powers and "emergency" powers are used, often interchangeably and without fixed or ascertainable meanings.

The vagueness and generality of the clauses that set forth presidential powers afford a plausible basis for pressures within and without an administration for presidential action beyond that supported by those whose responsibility it is to defend his actions in court. The claim of inherent and unrestricted presidential powers has long been a persuasive dialectical weapon in political controversy. While it is not surprising that counsel should grasp support from such unadjudicated claims of power, a judge cannot accept self-serving press statements of the attorney for one of the interested parties as authority in answering a constitutional question, even if the advocate was himself....

The appeal, however, that we declare the existence of inherent powers *ex necessitate* to meet an emergency asks us to do what many think would be wise, although it is something the forefathers omitted. They knew what emergencies were, knew the pressures they engender for authoritative action, knew, too, how they afford a ready pretext for usurpation. We may also suspect that they suspected that emergency powers would tend to kindle emergencies. Aside from suspension of the privilege of the writ of habeas corpus in time of rebellion or invasion, when the public safety may require it, they made no express provision for exercise of extraordinary authority because of a crisis. I do not think we rightfully may so amend their work....

In view of the ease, expedition and safety with which Congress can grant and has granted large emergency powers, certainly ample to embrace this crisis, I am quite unimpressed with the argument that we should affirm possession of them without statute. Such power either has no beginning or it has no end. If it exists, it need submit to no legal restraint. I am not alarmed that it would plunge us straightway into dictatorship, but it is at least a step in that wrong direction.

As to whether there is imperative necessity for such powers, it is relevant to note the gap that exists between the President's paper powers and his real powers. The Constitution does not disclose the measure of the actual controls wielded by the modern presidential office. That instrument must be understood as an Eighteenth-Century sketch of a government hoped for, not as a blueprint of the Government that is. Vast accretions of federal power, eroded from that reserved by the States, have magnified the scope of presidential activity. Subtle shifts take place in the centers of real power that do not show on the face of the Constitution.

Executive power has the advantage of concentration in a single head in whose choice the whole Nation has a part, making him the focus of public hopes and expectations. In drama, magnitude and finality, his decisions so far overshadow any others that, almost alone, he fills the public eye and ear. No other personality in public life can begin to compete with him in access to the public mind through modern methods of communications. By his prestige as head of state and his influence upon public opinion, he exerts a leverage upon those who are supposed to check and balance his power which often cancels their effectiveness.... I cannot be brought to believe that this country will suffer if the Court refuses further to aggrandize the presidential office, already so potent and so relatively immune from judicial review, at the expense of Congress.... With all its defects, delays and inconveniences, men have discovered no technique for long preserving free government except that the Executive be under the law, and that the law be made by parliamentary deliberations.

Such institutions may be destined to pass away. But it is the duty of the Court to be last, not first, to give them up.

MR. CHIEF JUSTICE VINSON, with whom MR. JUSTICE REED and MR. JUSTICE MINTON join, dissenting.

.... Those who suggest that this is a case involving extraordinary powers should be mindful that these are extraordinary times. A world not yet recovered from the devastation of World War II has been forced to face the threat of another and more terrifying global conflict.... In 1950, when the United Nations called upon member nations "to render every assistance" to repel aggression in Korea, the United States furnished its vigorous support. For almost two full years, our armed forces have been fighting in Korea, suffering casualties of over 108,000 men. Hostilities have not abated. The "determination of the United Nations to continue its action in Korea to meet the aggression" has been reaffirmed. Congressional support of the action in Korea has been manifested by provisions for increased military manpower and equipment and for economic stabilization, as hereinafter described.

Further efforts to protect the free world from aggression are found in the congressional enactments of the Truman Plan for assistance to Greece and Turkey and the Marshall Plan for economic aid needed to build up the strength of our friends in Western Europe ... The concept of mutual security recently has been extended by treaty to friends in the Pacific.

Our treaties represent not merely legal obligations, but show congressional recognition that mutual security for the free world is the best security against the threat of aggression on a global scale. The need for mutual security is shown by the very size of the armed forces outside the free world. Defendant's brief informs us that the Soviet Union maintains the largest air force in the world, and maintains ground forces much larger than those presently available to the United States and the countries joined with us in mutual security arrangements. Constant international tensions are cited to demonstrate how precarious is the peace.... Alert to our responsibilities, which coincide with our own self-preservation through mutual security, Congress has enacted a large body of implementing legislation. As an illustration of the magnitude of the over-all program, Congress has appropriated $130 billion for our own defense and for military assistance to our allies since the June, 1950, attack in Korea.

Congress recognized the impact of these defense programs upon the economy. Following the attack in Korea, the President asked for authority to requisition property and to allocate and fix priorities for scarce goods. In the Defense Production Act of 1950, Congress granted the powers requested and, *in addition,* granted power to stabilize prices and wages and to provide for settlement of labor disputes arising in the defense program. The Defense Production Act was extended in 1951, a Senate Committee noting that, in the dislocation caused by the programs for purchase of military equipment "lies the seed of an economic disaster that might well destroy the military might we are straining to build." ...

The President has the duty to execute the foregoing legislative programs. Their successful execution depends upon continued production of steel and stabilized prices for steel....

After bargaining had failed to avert the threatened shutdown of steel production, the President issued the [seizure] Executive Order....

The whole of the "executive Power" is vested in the President. Before entering office, the President swears that he "will faithfully execute the Office of President of the United States, and will to the best of [his] Ability, preserve, protect and defend the Constitution of the United States." Art. II, § 1.... [The] Presidency was deliberately fashioned as an office of power and independence. Of course, the Framers created no autocrat capable of arrogating any power unto himself at any time. But neither did they create an automaton impotent to exercise the powers of Government at a time when the survival of the Republic itself may be at stake....

.... With or without explicit statutory authorization, Presidents have ... dealt with national emergencies by acting promptly and resolutely to enforce legislative programs, at least to save those programs until Congress could act. Congress and the courts have responded to such executive initiative with consistent approval....

In an action furnishing a most apt precedent for this case, President Lincoln, without statutory authority, directed the seizure of rail and telegraph lines leading to Washington. Many months later, Congress recognized and confirmed the power of the President to seize railroads and telegraph lines and provided criminal penalties for interference with Government operation....

More recently, President Truman acted to repel aggression by employing our armed forces in Korea. Upon the intervention of the Chinese Communists, the President proclaimed the existence of an unlimited national emergency requiring the speedy build-up of our defense establishment. Congress responded by providing for increased manpower and weapons for our own armed forces, by increasing military aid under the Mutual Security Program, and by enacting economic stabilization measures, as previously described.

This is but a cursory summary of executive leadership. But it amply demonstrates that Presidents have taken prompt action to enforce the laws and protect the country whether or not Congress happened to provide in advance for the particular method of execution....

The absence of a specific statute authorizing seizure of the steel mills as a mode of executing the laws—both the military procurement program and the anti-inflation program—has not until today been thought to prevent the President from executing the laws.... There is no statute prohibiting seizure as a method of enforcing legislative programs....

.... Faced with the duty of executing the defense programs which Congress had enacted and the disastrous effects that any stoppage in steel production would have on those programs, the President acted to preserve those programs by seizing the steel mills. There is no question that the possession was other than temporary in character, and subject to congressional direction—either approving, disapproving, or regulating the manner in which the mills were to be administered and returned to the owners. The President immediately informed Congress of his action, and clearly stated his intention to abide by the legislative will. No basis for claims of arbitrary action, unlimited powers, or dictatorial usurpation of congressional power appears from the facts of this case. On the contrary, judicial, legislative and executive precedents throughout our history demonstrate that, in this case, the President acted in full conformity with his duties under the Constitution. Accordingly, we would reverse the order of the District Court.

Review Questions and Explanations: *Youngstown*

1. Is there an argument to be made that the President's actions should have been analyzed as falling with the "zone of twilight" in category 2 of Jackson's framework?

2. Over time, Justice Jackson's concurrence has emerged as the authoritative opinion in this case. It is Jackson's opinion that is cited, discussed, and used as the basis for subsequent separation-of-powers analyses. In contrast, Black's opinion has not been well-respected by subsequent courts and commentators. Why do you think this happened?

3. Justice Frankfurter's opinion has not been as influential as Jackson's, but expresses an insight that has won some adherents among constitutional scholars. Is his approach different from Jackson's, and if so how? Is it sound? Can you think of objections?

4. Do you think *Youngstown* was decided the right way? Do you think the Court would have reached the same decision in 1942, when the United States had just entered World War II, and the Court upheld the "exclusion order" against Japanese-Americans in *Korematsu v. United States*?

C. War and National Security

This section considers ways in which the Constitution assigns and divides powers concerning the conduct of war and national security. These issues have been made more complicated in the last half century by at least two developments. First, the practice of waging war based on a formal declaration of war has become less common. The last declarations of war by the United States were those against Japan, Germany and Italy in World War II. No declaration of war was made during what are commonly referred to as the Korean War and Vietnam War. The United States has committed troops to combat several other times since World War II without declarations of war. In the past 25 years alone it has done so in Iraq (twice), Afghanistan and Somalia.

Second, over the past 15 years, our national security focus has increasingly been placed on fighting terrorists and other enemy combatants who are not uniformed soldiers of a sovereign government. These sorts of foes make traditional concepts of war difficult to apply, and pose difficult tests of the constitutional assignments of powers.

Perhaps because of these developments, the use of the term "war" seems to have become looser. While President Johnson's "war on poverty," which was "declared" in 1965, was clearly used in a metaphorical sense and not literally intended to invoke "war powers," the "war on drugs" declared by President Reagan in the 1980s (and perhaps continuing to the present) is somewhat less clearly metaphorical: it has at times involved the use of armed forces abroad to combat drug operations, and perhaps more heavily armed conventional police forces at home, together with (some would say) the kind of erosion of civil liberties that wartime is known to bring about.

Even in the absence of these ambiguities about the "fact" of "war," constitutional issues also are created by the division of power between the three branches of government in cases, not only of war, but also, "rebellion," "invasion" and like emergency. It is worth identifying and reviewing the various constitutional provisions dealing with these issues at the outset.

There are at least six provisions in Article I giving Congress powers relevant to war and national security:

1. To declare war, grant letters of marque and reprisal, and make rules concerning captures on land and water, Art. I, § 8, cl. 11;

2. To raise and support armies, but no appropriation of money to that use shall be for a longer term than two years, Art. I, § 8, cl. 12;

3. To provide and maintain a navy, Art. I, § 8, cl. 13;

4. To make rules for the government and regulation of the land and naval forces, Art. I, § 8, cl. 14;

5. To provide for calling forth the militia to execute the laws of the union, suppress insurrections and repel invasions, Art. I, § 8, cl. 15;

6. To provide for organizing, arming, and disciplining, the militia, and for governing such part of them as may be employed in the service of the United States, reserving to the states respectively, the appointment of the officers, and the authority of training the militia according to the discipline prescribed by Congress, Art. I, § 8, cl. 16.

These are considerable and far-reaching powers over the nation's war-making capacity. A few historical explanations illustrate the point. "Letters of marque and reprisal" are government permissions to private ship-owners to conduct warlike activities at sea on behalf of the national sovereign—that is, to fire upon, board, capture or destroy ships of an enemy nation. In contrast, privately conducted warfare without such government authorization was (and is) deemed piracy in violation of the law of nations. "Rules regarding capture" refers to the pre-twentieth century practice of permitting members of the armed forces to receive "prize money" from valuable property they captured from the enemy in wartime; prize money was a significant incentive for naval officers and crew in particular. The two year limit on appropriations for an army (but not the navy), and the extensive references to militia forces stem from the founders' strongly held belief that standing national armies (but not navies) posed a significant threat to domestic liberty. The "rules for government and regulation of the [armed] forces" include the Uniform Code of Military Justice (formerly the "Articles of War").

There are two additional, highly relevant provisions in Article I:

> [The Congress shall have power] To define and punish piracies and felonies committed on the high seas, and offenses against the law of nations, Art. I, § 8, cl. 10.

> The privilege of the writ of habeas corpus shall not be suspended, unless when in cases of rebellion or invasion the public safety may require it. Art. I, § 9, cl. 2.

The first of these two provisions is highly relevant to the so-called "war on terrorism." Piracies, as mentioned, referred to the unauthorized conduct of war by persons who did not act on behalf of a sovereign government; it was and is deemed a violation of international law ("the law of nations"). Terrorism is essentially the same. While definitions vary, they commonly include the commission of acts of war by persons or groups not representing a sovereign government, in violation of international law.

The second provision, the habeas suspension clause, implies a role for the courts when the executive detains or imprisons persons, even for reasons of national security, if the threat giving rise to the detention doesn't rise to the level of "rebellion or invasion" and prompt a suspension of habeas corpus by the political branches. Habeas corpus is a centuries-old judicial procedure under which the legality of an individual's detention can be tested in court. The clause also suggests a role for Congress. The implication is that normal judicial processes, including habeas corpus, will be available unless the writ is "suspended." Who has that power, Congress or the President? The placement of the clause in Article I implies that it is Congress's role, but we will see below how the Supreme Court has approached that question.

In subsection 1, we examine cases which consider war powers of the President and Congress in general. There are very few such cases, for reasons that will become apparent. Subsection 2 focuses on the specific question of the suspension of habeas corpus. We will look at three principal historical contexts in which that issue has arisen: the Civil War, World War II, and the current so-called "war on terror."

1. Executive Powers over the Conduct of Hostilities

Abraham Lincoln was elected the sixteenth President of the United States on November 6, 1860. He had run on a platform of opposition to the extension of slavery to new territories and a vague intention to place slavery on a gradual and very long term "course of ultimate extinction." Dismayed by Lincoln's victory, South Carolina seceded from the Union on December 20, 1860. Seven other states followed between then and April 1861, and another three seceded by the end of May. When rebel forces fired on Fort Sumter on April 12, 1861, the United States Army consisted of approximately 16,000 troops scattered throughout the continental United States and its territories. Many of these soldiers hailed from southern states and would join the Confederate army. Although President Lincoln soon called upon the states to fill federal recruitment quotas by calling up state militias, it would be some time before an effective Union Army could take the field. Moreover, while public opinion strongly supported action to suppress the rebellion in the early months of the conflict, opinion—both in the public and within the military—was somewhat divided about the best way to do so. There was not initially strong support for waging a "war of conquest" against the southern states, even if that had been feasible. Instead, the initial strategy devised by General-in-Chief Winfield Scott, and embraced by President Lincoln, was built around an effort to subdue the rebel states economically by isolating them from foreign commerce. A key element of this strategy was to impose a blockade on southern ports.

Imposing a blockade presented a number of legal problems, however. To begin with, the newly elected Thirty-Seventh Congress was not scheduled to convene until December 1861. Strange as this now seems in an age when the new Congress convenes on January 3 of the year following the election (see Twentieth Amendment, § 2, adopted 1933), transportation to Washington remained comparatively rudimentary in the mid-nineteenth century, and Washington was thought of as a disease-ridden place to be avoided in the summer. Compounding the difficulties of convening Congress in Washington in 1861 was the fact that the Capital was surrounded by a rebel state (Virginia) to the south, and another slave state (Maryland) to the north. Although Maryland remained in the Union, secessionist sentiment in the southern part of that state, nearest Washington, ran high in the Spring of 1861. In the month of April alone, southern sympathizers rioted in Baltimore, blocked rail traffic, and cut telegraph wires to Washington.

Despite these obstacles, President Lincoln called Congress into emergency session, and Congress was able to convene in July 1861. The President, however, had already implemented the blockade of the southern ports. A blockade—including this one—is an assertion of power to turn back foreign neutral vessels or to seize foreign neutrals and enemy vessels and either destroy them or keep them and their cargoes as "prizes of war." To convert a captured vessel into a prize required proving to an admiralty court that the blockade was legal and that the captured vessel either belonged to an enemy or had violated the blockade. Because a blockade would affect foreign vessels as well as southern-owned ones, the Union blockade would have to be recognized as valid under international law. This required that reasonable notice be given to the nation from which the ship came, and that the blockade be effective.

Furthermore, a blockade is considered an act of war against the entity being blockaded. But under international law, "war" was a state of hostilities between two sovereign powers. Lincoln, a keenly sophisticated lawyer, was aware of this and recognized the dilemma it presented. To concede that the United States was "at war" with a sovereign entity called the Confederate States of America would be to recognize the sovereignty of the seceded states, encourage foreign countries to recognize the south as sovereign (a potential foreign policy disaster that loomed for the entire Civil War), and undermine the legal basis for fighting to restore the Union. Accordingly, Lincoln assiduously and consistently refused to refer to the conflict as a "war" or even a "Civil War," referring instead to the "insurrection" or "rebellion." This absence of a (legal) state of war, however, raised questions about the legality of the blockade.

In April and May 1861, several ships were seized by Union naval officers for violating the blockade. Some were owned by southern shipowners, others by foreign nationals. Four of these cases made their way to the Supreme Court: *The Brig Amy Warwick, The Schooner Crenshaw, The Barque Hiawatha,* and *The Schooner Brilliante.* (Admiralty cases for condemnation of a ship as prizes of war are captioned with the name of the ship in question.) The government sued to condemn these ships—one southern-owned, two British-owned and one Mexican-owned—as prizes. In each case, the district court sitting as an admiralty court, condemned the ships as prizes. The shipowners' appeals to the Supreme Court were consolidated into a single decision known as *The Prize Cases.* President Lincoln's proclamation of blockade of the southern ports is reprinted below, followed by the Supreme Court's decision in *The Prize Cases.*

President Lincoln's Proclamation of Blockade
April 19, 1861

Whereas an insurrection against the Government of the United States has broken out in the States of South Carolina, Georgia, Alabama, Florida, Mississippi, Louisiana, and Texas, and the laws of the United States for the collection of the revenue can not be effectually executed therein conformably to that provision of the Constitution which requires duties to be uniform throughout the United States; and

Whereas a combination of persons engaged in such insurrection have threatened to grant pretended letters of marque to authorize the bearers thereof to commit assaults on the lives, vessels, and property of good citizens of the country lawfully engaged in commerce on the high seas and in waters of the United States; and

Whereas an Executive proclamation has been already issued requiring the persons engaged in these disorderly proceedings to desist therefrom, calling out a militia force for the purpose of repressing the same, and convening Congress in extraordinary session to deliberate and determine thereon:

Now, therefore, I, Abraham Lincoln, President of the United States, with a view to the same purposes before mentioned and to the protection of the public peace and the lives and property of quiet and orderly citizens pursuing their lawful occupations until Congress shall have assembled and deliberated on the said unlawful proceedings or until the same shall have ceased, have further deemed it advisable to set on foot a blockade of the ports within the States aforesaid, in pursuance of the laws of the United States and of the law of nations in such case provided. For this purpose a competent force will be posted so as to prevent entrance and exit of vessels from the ports aforesaid. If, therefore, with a view to violate such blockade, a vessel shall approach or shall attempt to leave either of the said ports, she will be duly warned by the commander of one of the blockading vessels, who will indorse on her register the fact and date of such warning, and if the same vessel shall again attempt to enter or leave the blockaded port she will be captured and sent to the nearest convenient port for such proceedings against her and her cargo as prize as may be deemed advisable.

And I hereby proclaim and declare that if any person, under the pretended authority of the said States or under any other pretense, shall molest a vessel of the United States or the persons or cargo on board of her, such person will be held amenable to the laws of the United States for the prevention and punishment of piracy.

In witness whereof I have hereunto set my hand and caused the seal of the United States to be affixed.

Done at the city of Washington, this 19th day of April, A.D. 1861, and of the Independence of the United States the eighty-fifth.

ABRAHAM LINCOLN.

By the President:

WILLIAM H. SEWARD, Secretary of State

By proclamation of April 27, 1861, the blockade was extended to include Virginia and Tennessee.

Guided Reading Questions: *The Prize Cases*

1. The majority does not accept the view that the right of blockade can only occur only in a war between sovereign nations, but instead asserts that it can also be triggered by a civil war. What is the justification for this position? Does the dissent argue otherwise?

2. The dissent concedes that an armed rebellion is taking place, and that the President had the authority to meet it with force. So what is the main issue on which the majority and dissent disagree?

3. What role does the definition of "war" play in the legal analysis in the majority and dissent?

4. Does the majority say that the President can impose a blockade entirely on his own authority? More broadly, does the majority say that all constitutional

war powers devolve on the President so long as he is *responding* to military force rather than *initiating* a war?

The Prize Cases

67 U.S. 635 (1863)

Majority: *Grier*, Wayne, Swayne, Miller, Davis

Dissent: *Nelson*, Taney (CJ), Catron, Clifford

MR. JUSTICE GRIER.

.... Had the President a right to institute a blockade of ports in possession of persons in armed rebellion against the Government, on the principles of international law, as known and acknowledged among civilized States? ...

Neutrals have a right to challenge the existence of a blockade de facto, and also the authority of the party exercising the right to institute it. They have a right to enter the ports of a friendly nation for the purposes of trade and commerce, but are bound to recognize the rights of a belligerent engaged in actual war, to use this mode of coercion, for the purpose of subduing the enemy.

That a blockade de facto actually existed, and was formally declared and notified by the President on the 27th and 30th of April, 1861, is an admitted fact in these cases.

That the President, as the Executive Chief of the Government and Commander-in-chief of the Army and Navy, was the proper person to make such notification, has not been, and cannot be disputed.

The right of prize and capture has its origin in the "jus belli" [law of war], and is governed and adjudged under the law of nations. To legitimate the capture of a neutral vessel or property on the high seas, a war must exist de facto, and the neutral must have a knowledge or notice of the intention of one of the parties belligerent to use this mode of coercion against a port, city, or territory, in possession of the other.

Let us enquire whether, at the time this blockade was instituted, a state of war existed which would justify a resort to these means of subduing the hostile force.

War has been well defined to be, "That state in which a nation prosecutes its right by force."

The parties belligerent in a public war are independent nations. But it is not necessary to constitute war, that both parties should be acknowledged as independent nations or sovereign States. A war may exist where one of the belligerents, claims sovereign rights as against the other.

Insurrection against a government may or may not culminate in an organized rebellion, but a civil war always begins by insurrection against the lawful authority of the Government. A civil war is never solemnly declared; it becomes such by its accidents—the number, power, and organization of the persons who originate and carry it on. When the party in rebellion occupy and hold in a hostile manner a certain portion of territory; have declared their independence; have cast off their allegiance; have organized armies; have commenced hostilities against their former sovereign, the world acknowledges them as belligerents, and the contest a *war*. *They* claim to be in arms to establish their liberty and independence, in order to become a sovereign State, while the sovereign party treats them as insurgents and rebels who owe allegiance, and who should be punished with death for their treason.

The laws of war, as established among nations, have their foundation in reason, and all tend to mitigate the cruelties and misery produced by the scourge of war. Hence the parties to a civil war usually concede to each other belligerent rights. They exchange prisoners, and adopt the other courtesies and rules common to public or national wars.

"A civil war," says Vattel, "breaks the bands of society and government, or at least suspends their force and effect; it produces in the nation two independent parties, who consider each other as enemies, and acknowledge no common judge. Those two parties, therefore, must necessarily be considered as constituting, at least for a time, two separate bodies, two distinct societies. Having no common superior to judge between them, they stand in precisely the same predicament as two nations who engage in a contest and have recourse to arms.

"This being the case, it is very evident that the common laws of war — those maxims of humanity, moderation, and honor — ought to be observed by both parties in every civil war. Should the sovereign conceive he has a right to hang up his prisoners as rebels, the opposite party will make reprisals, &c., &c.; the war will become cruel, horrible, and every day more destructive to the nation."

As a civil war is never publicly proclaimed, eo nomine [by that name], against insurgents, its actual existence is a fact in our domestic history which the Court is bound to notice and to know.

The true test of its existence, as found in the writings of the sages of the common law, may be thus summarily stated: "When the regular course of justice is interrupted by revolt, rebellion, or insurrection, so that the Courts of Justice cannot be kept open, *civil war exists* and hostilities may be prosecuted on the same footing as if those opposing the Government were foreign enemies invading the land."

By the Constitution, Congress alone has the power to declare a national or foreign war. It cannot declare war against a State, or any number of States, by virtue of any clause in the Constitution. The Constitution confers on the President the whole Executive power. He is bound to take care that the laws be faithfully executed. He is Commander-in-chief of the Army and Navy of the United States, and of the militia of the several States when called into the actual service of the United States. He has no power to initiate or declare a war either against a foreign nation or a domestic State. But by the Acts of Congress of February 28th, 1795, and 3d of March, 1807, he is authorized to call out the militia and use the military and naval forces of the United States in case of invasion by foreign nations, and to suppress insurrection against the government of a State or of the United States.

If a war be made by invasion of a foreign nation, the President is not only authorized but bound to resist force by force. He does not initiate the war, but is bound to accept the challenge without waiting for any special legislative authority. And whether the hostile party be a foreign invader, or States organized in rebellion, it is none the less a war, although the declaration of it be "*unilateral.*" Lord Stowell (1 Dodson, 247) observes, "It is not the less a war on *that account*, for war may exist without a declaration on either side. It is so laid down by the best writers on the law of nations. A declaration of war by one country only, is not a mere challenge to be accepted or refused at pleasure by the other."

The battles of Palo Alto and Resaca de la Palma had been fought before the passage of the Act of Congress of May 13th, 1846, which recognized "*a state of war as existing by the act of the Republic of Mexico."* This act not only provided for the future prosecution of the war, but was itself a vindication and ratification of the Act of the President in accepting the challenge without a previous formal declaration of war by Congress.

This greatest of civil wars was not gradually developed by popular commotion, tumultuous assemblies, or local unorganized insurrections. However long may have been its previous conception, it nevertheless sprung forth suddenly from the parent brain, a Minerva in the full panoply of *war*. The President was bound to meet it in the shape it presented itself, without waiting for Congress to baptize it with a name; and no name given to it by him or them could change the fact.

It is not the less a civil war, with belligerent parties in hostile array, because it may be called an "insurrection" by one side, and the insurgents be considered as rebels or traitors. It is not necessary that the independence of the revolted province or State be acknowledged in order to constitute it a party belligerent in a war according to the law of nations. Foreign nations acknowledge it as war by a declaration of neutrality. The condition of neutrality cannot exist unless there be two belligerent parties....

As soon as the news of the attack on Fort Sumter, and the organization of a government by the seceding States, assuming to act as belligerents, could become known in Europe, to wit, on the 13th of May, 1861, the Queen of England issued her proclamation of neutrality, "recognizing hostilities as existing between the Government of the United States of American and *certain States* styling themselves the Confederate States of America." This was immediately followed by similar declarations or silent acquiescence by other nations.

After such an official recognition by the sovereign, a citizen of a foreign State is estopped to deny the existence of a war with all its consequences as regards neutrals. They cannot ask a Court to affect a technical ignorance of the existence of a war, which all the world acknowledges to be the greatest civil war known in the history of the human race, and thus cripple the arm of the Government and paralyze its power by subtle definitions and ingenious sophisms.

Whether the President in fulfilling his duties, as Commander-in-chief, in suppressing an insurrection, has met with such armed hostile resistance, and a civil war of such alarming proportions as will compel him to accord to them the character of belligerents, is a question to be decided *by him*, and this Court must be governed by the decisions and acts of the political department of the Government to which this power was entrusted. "He must determine what degree of force the crisis demands." The proclamation of blockade is itself official and conclusive evidence to the Court that a state of war existed which demanded and authorized a recourse to such a measure, under the circumstances peculiar to the case.

The correspondence of Lord Lyons [British minister to the United States] with the Secretary of State admits the fact and concludes the question.

If it were necessary to the technical existence of a war, that it should have a legislative sanction, we find it in almost every act passed at the extraordinary session of the Legislature of 1861, which was wholly employed in enacting laws to enable the Government to prosecute the war with vigor and efficiency. And finally, in 1861, we find Congress *"ex majore cautela"* [from an abundance of caution] and in anticipation of such astute objections, passing an act "approving, legalizing, and making valid all the acts, proclamations, and orders of the President, &c., as if they had been *issued and done under the previous express authority* and direction of the Congress of the United States."

Without admitting that such an act was necessary under the circumstances, it is plain that if the President had in any manner assumed powers which it was necessary should have the authority or sanction of Congress, that on the well known principle of law, "*omnis ratihabitio retrotrahitur et mandato equiparatur*" [every ratification is equal to an express prior command], this ratification has operated to perfectly cure the defect....

The objection made to this act of ratification, that it is *expost facto*, and therefore unconstitutional and void, might possibly have some weight on the trial of an indictment in a criminal Court. But precedents from that source cannot be received as authoritative in a tribunal administering public and international law.

... [T]herefore we are of the opinion that the President had a right, *jure belli* [under the law of war], to institute a blockade of ports in possession of the States in rebellion, which neutrals are bound to regard. [The Court affirmed the judgments of condemnation.]

MR. JUSTICE NELSON, dissenting.

.... It is remarkable, also, that both the President and the Secretary, in referring to the blockade, treat the measure, not as a blockade under the law of nations, but as a restraint upon commerce at the interdicted ports under the municipal laws of the Government.

Another objection taken to the seizure of this vessel and cargo is, that there was no existing war between the United States and the States in insurrection within the meaning of the law of nations, which drew after it the consequences of a public or civil war. A contest by force between independent sovereign States is called a public war; and, when duly commenced by proclamation or otherwise, it entitles both of the belligerent parties to all the rights of war against each other, and as respects neutral nations. Chancellor Kent observes, "Though a solemn declaration, or previous notice to the enemy, be now laid aside, it is essential that some formal public act, proceeding directly from the competent source, should announce to the people at home their new relations and duties growing out of a state of war, and which should equally apprize neutral nations of the fact, to enable them to conform their conduct to the rights belonging to the new state of things." "Such an official act operates from its date to legalize all hostile acts, in like manner as a treaty of peace operates from its date to annul them." He further observes, "as war cannot lawfully be commenced on the part of the United States without an act of Congress, such act is, of course, a formal notice to all the world, and equivalent to the most solemn declaration."

The legal consequences resulting from a state of war between two countries at this day are well understood, and will be found described in every approved work on the subject of international law. The people of the two countries become immediately the enemies of each other — all intercourse commercial or otherwise between them unlawful — all contracts existing at the commencement of the war suspended, and all made during its existence utterly void.... All the property of the people of the two countries on land or sea are subject to capture and confiscation by the adverse party as enemies' property, with certain qualifications as it respects property on land, all treaties between the belligerent parties are annulled. The ports of the respective countries may be blockaded, and letters of marque and reprisal granted as rights of war, and the law of prizes as defined by the law of nations comes into full and complete operation, resulting from maritime captures, jur belli. War also effects a change in the mutual relations of all States or countries, not directly, as in the case of the belligerents, but immediately and indirectly, though they take no part in the contest, but remain neutral.

.... [T]he same code which has annexed to the existence of a war all these disturbing consequences has declared that the right of making war belongs exclusively to the supreme or sovereign power of the State.... By our Constitution this power is lodged in Congress. Congress shall have power "to declare war, grant letters of marque and reprisal, and make rules concerning captures on land and water." ...

In the case of a rebellion or resistance of a portion of the people of a country against the established government, there is no doubt, if in its progress and enlargement the government thus sought to be overthrown sees fit, it may by the competent power recognize, or declare the existence of a state of civil war, which will draw after it all the consequences and rights of war between the contending parties as in the case of a public war.... It is not to be denied, therefor, that if a civil war existed between that portion of the people in organized insurrection to overthrow this Government at the time this vessel and cargo were seized, and if she was guilty of a violation of the blockade, she would be lawful prize of war. But before this insurrection against the established Government can be dealt with on the footing of a civil war, within the meaning of the law of nations and the Constitution of the United States, and which will draw after it belligerent rights, it must be recognized or declared by the war-making power of the Government. No power short of this can change the legal status of the Government or the relations of its citizens from that of peace to a state of war, or bring into existence all those duties and obligations to neutral third parties growing out of a state of war. The war power of the Government must be exercised before this changed condition of the Government and people and of neutral third parties can be admitted. There is no difference in this respect between a civil or a public war....

An idea seemed to be entertained that all that was necessary to constitute a war was organized hostility in the district of country in a state of rebellion—that conflicts on land and on sea—the taking of towns and capture of fleets—in fine, the magnitude and dimensions of the resistance against the Government—constituted war with all the belligerent rights belonging to civil war....

Now, in one sense, no doubt this is war, and may be a war of the most extensive and threatening dimensions and effects, but it is a statement simply of its existence in a material sense, and has no relevancy or weight when the question is what constitutes war in a legal sense, in the sense of the law of nations, and of the Constitution of the United States? ... For we find there that to constitute a civil war in the sense in which we are speaking, before it can exist, in contemplation of law, it must be recognized or declared by the sovereign power of the State, and which sovereign power by our Constitution is lodged in the Congress of the United States—civil war, therefore, under our system of government, can exist only by an act of Congress, which requires the assent of two of the great departments of the Government, the Executive and Legislative.

.... But we are asked, what would become of the peace and integrity of the Union in case of an insurrection at home or invasion from abroad if this power could not be exercised by the President in the recess of Congress, and until that body could be assembled?

The framers of the Constitution fully comprehended this question, and provided for the contingency.... The Constitution declares that Congress shall have power "to provide for calling forth the militia to execute the laws of the Union, suppress insurrections, and repel invasions." ... Congress passed laws on this subject in 1792 and 1795.

The [1795] Act provided that whenever the United States shall be invaded or be in imminent danger of invasion from a foreign nation, it shall be lawful for the President to call forth such number of the militia most convenient to the place of danger, and in case of insurrection in any State against the Government thereof, it shall be lawful for the

President, on the application of the Legislature of such State, if in session, or if not, of the Executive of the State, to call forth such number of militia of any other State or States as he may judge sufficient to suppress such insurrection.

The 2d section provides, that when the laws of the United States shall be opposed, or the execution obstructed in any State by combinations too powerful to be suppressed by the course of judicial proceedings, it shall be lawful for the President to call forth the militia of such State, or of any other State or States as may be necessary to suppress such combinations; and by the Act 3 March, 1807, it is provided that in case of insurrection or obstruction of the laws, either in the United States or of any State or Territory, where it is lawful for the President to call forth the militia for the purpose of suppressing such insurrection, and causing the laws to be executed, it shall be lawful to employ for the same purpose such part of the land and naval forces of the United States as shall be judged necessary.

It will be seen, therefore, that ample provision has been made under the Constitution and laws against any sudden and unexpected disturbance of the public peace from insurrection at home or invasion from abroad. The whole military and naval power of the country is put under the control of the President to meet the emergency.... It is the exercise of a power under the municipal laws of the country and not under the law of nations; and, as we see, furnishes the most ample means of repelling attacks from abroad or suppressing disturbances at home until the assembling of Congress, who can, if it be deemed necessary, bring into operation the war power, and thus change the nature and character of the contest....

It has been argued that the authority conferred on the President by the Act of 1795 invests him with the war power. But the obvious answer is, that it proceeds from a different clause in the Constitution and which is given for different purposes and objects, namely, to execute the laws and preserve the public order and tranquillity of the country in a time of peace by preventing or suppressing any public disorder or disturbance by foreign or domestic enemies. Certainly, if there is any force in this argument, then we are in a state of war with all the rights of war, and all the penal consequences attending it every time this power is exercised by calling out a military force to execute the laws or to suppress insurrection or rebellion.... The truth is, this idea of the existence of any necessity for clothing the President with the war power, under the Act of 1795, is simply a monstrous exaggeration; for, besides having the command of the whole of the army and navy, Congress can be assembled within any thirty days, if the safety of the country requires that the war power shall be brought into operation.

The Acts of 1795 and 1807 did not, and could not under the Constitution, confer on the President the power of declaring war against a State of this Union, or of deciding that war existed, and upon that ground authorize the capture and confiscation of the property of every citizen of the State whenever it was found on the waters. The laws of war, whether the war be civil or inter gentes, as we have seen, convert every citizen of the hostile State into a public enemy, and treat him accordingly, whatever may have been his previous conduct. This great power over the business and property of the citizen is reserved to the legislative department by the express words of the Constitution. It cannot be delegated or surrendered to the Executive. Congress alone can determine whether war exists or should be declared; and until they have acted, no citizen of the State can be punished in his person or property, unless he had committed some offence against a law of Congress passed before the act was committed, which made it a crime, and defined the punishment. The penalty of confiscation for the acts of others with which he had no concern cannot lawfully be inflicted.

In the breaking out of a rebellion against the established Government, the usage in all civilized countries, in its first stages, is to suppress it by confining the public forces and the operations of the Government against those in rebellion, and at the same time extending encouragement and support to the loyal people with a view to their cooperation in putting down the insurgents.... It is a personal war against the individuals engaged in resisting the authority of the Government. This was the character of the war of our Revolution till the passage of the Act of the Parliament of Great Britain of the 16th of George Third, 1776.... From this time the war became a territorial civil war between the contending parties, with all the rights of war known to the law of nations.... Until the passage of the act the American subjects were not regarded as enemies in the sense of the law of nations. The distinction between the loyal and rebel subjects was constantly observed....

So the war carried on by the President against the insurrectionary districts in the Southern States, as in the case of the King of Great Britain in the American Revolution, was a personal war against those in rebellion, ... until Congress assembled and acted upon this state of things.

Down to this period the only enemy recognized by the Government was the persons engaged in the rebellion, and others were peaceful citizens, entitled to all the privileges of citizens under the Constitution. Certainly it cannot rightfully be said that the President has the power to convert a loyal citizen into a belligerent enemy or confiscate his property as enemy's property.

Congress assembled on the call for an extra session the 4th of July, 1861, and among the first acts passed was one in which the President was authorized by proclamation to interdict all trade and intercourse between all the inhabitants of States in insurrection and the rest of the United States, subjecting vessel and cargo to capture and condemnation as prize, and also to direct the capture of any ship or vessel belonging in whole or in part to any inhabitant of a State whose inhabitants are declared by the proclamation to be in a state of insurrection, found at sea or in any part of the rest of the United States. Act of Congress of 13th of July, 1861, secs. 5, 6. The 4th section also authorized the President to close any port in a Collection District obstructed so that the revenue could not be collected, and provided for the capture and condemnation of any vessel attempting to enter.

The President's Proclamation was issued on the 16th of August following, and embraced Georgia, North and South Carolina, part of Virginia, Tennessee, Alabama, Louisiana, Texas, Arkansas, Mississippi and Florida.

This Act of Congress, we think, recognized a state of civil war between the Government and the Confederate States, and made it territorial.... Government in recognizing or declaring the existence of a civil war between itself and a portion of the people in insurrection usually modifies its effects with a view as far as practicable to favor the innocent and loyal citizens or subjects involved in the war. It is only the urgent necessities of the Government, arising from the magnitude of the resistance, that can excuse the conversion of the personal into a territorial war, and thus confound all distinction between guilt and innocence; ... We agree when such a war is recognized or declared to exist by the war-making power, but not otherwise, it is the duty of the Courts to follow the decision of the political power of the Government....

Congress on the 6th of August, 1862, passed an Act confirming all acts, proclamations, and orders of the President, after the 4th of March, 1861, respecting the army and navy, and legalizing them, so far as was competent for that body, and it has been suggested, but scarcely argued, that this legislation on the subject had the effect to bring into existence an ex post facto civil war with all the rights of capture and confiscation, jure belli, from the date referred to. An ex post facto law is defined, when, after an action, indifferent in itself, or lawful, is committed, the Legislature then, for the first time, declares it to have been a crime and inflicts punishment upon the person who committed it.... Here the captures were without any Constitutional authority, and void; and, on principle, no subsequent ratification could make them valid.

.... I am compelled to the conclusion that no civil war existed between this Government and the States in insurrection till recognized by the Act of Congress 13th of July, 1861; that the President does not possess the power under the Constitution to declare war or recognize its existence within the meaning of the law of nations, which carries with it belligerent rights, and thus change the country and all its citizens from a state of peace to a state of war; that this power belongs exclusively to the Congress of the United States, and, consequently, that the President had no power to set on foot a blockade under the law of nations, and that the capture of the vessel and cargo in this case, and in all cases before us in which the capture occurred before the 13th of July, 1861, for breach of blockade, or as enemies' property, are illegal and void, and that the decrees of condemnation should be reversed and the vessel and cargo restored.

Review Questions and Explanations: *The Prize Cases*

1. The blockade was ratified by Congress when it met in special session in July 1861. Was that ratification essential to the majority's conclusion? Do you agree or disagree with the dissent's argument that ratifying the blockade would be an unconstitutional "ex post facto" law?

2. "War" has implications for purposes of international law (triggering the law of war) and for constitutional purposes (a state of affairs to be declared by Congress). Are these two purposes the same in the majority opinion? What about the dissent?

3. The majority seems to define war in very practical and factual terms; the dissent tries to draw a distinction between a "public" war and a "private" or "personal" war. What are these two different approaches to defining war getting at?

4. Does the dissent's approach to war powers strike you as antiquated and inflexible? Or does it have modern relevance for civil liberties?

The next set of readings arises from the Vietnam War. Although American combat troops were engaged in fighting in Vietnam for more than ten years, suffering combat casualties of more than 58,000 dead and 300,000 wounded (with total civilian and military deaths of Vietnamese on both sides estimated in the low millions), no war was declared by Congress. Authorization for military action was based on the "Gulf of Tonkin Resolution." On August 5, 1964, President Lyndon Johnson issued a message to Congress requesting authorization for a military response to an exchange of fire between U.S. and North Vietnamese ships initiated by an alleged Vietnamese attack. The Resolution was passed by both Houses of Congress on August 7, and President Johnson issued a message of acknowledgment that same day. These documents follow.

President Johnson's Message to Congress

August 5, 1964

To the Congress of the United States:

Last night I announced to the American people that the North Vietnamese regime had conducted further deliberate attacks against U.S. naval vessels operating in international waters, and therefore directed air action against gunboats and supporting facilities used in these hostile operations. This air action has now been carried out with substantial damage to the boats and facilities. Two U.S. aircraft were lost in the action.

After consultation with the leaders of both parties in the Congress, I further announced a decision to ask the Congress for a resolution expressing the unity and determination of the United States in supporting freedom and in protecting peace in southeast Asia.

These latest actions of the North Vietnamese regime have given a new and grave turn to the already serious situation in southeast Asia. Our commitments in that area are well known to the Congress. They were first made in 1954 by President Eisenhower. They were further defined in the Southeast Asia Collective Defense Treaty approved by the Senate in February 1955.

This treaty with its accompanying protocol obligates the United States and other members to act in accordance with their constitutional processes to meet Communist aggression against any of the parties or protocol states....

As President of the United States I have concluded that I should now ask the Congress on its part, to join in affirming the national determination that all such attacks will be met, and that the United States will continue in its basic policy of assisting the free nations of the area to defend their freedom.

As I have repeatedly made clear, the United States intends no rashness, and seeks no wider war. We must make it clear to all that the United States is united in its determination to bring about the end of Communist subversion and aggression in the area. We seek the full and effective restoration of the international agreements signed in Geneva in 1954, with respect to South Vietnam, and again in Geneva in 1962, with respect to Laos.

I recommend a resolution expressing the support of the Congress for all necessary action to protect our Armed Forces and to assist nations covered by the SEATO Treaty. At the same time, I assure the Congress that we shall continue readily to explore any avenues of political solution that will effectively guarantee the removal of Communist subversion and the preservation of the independence of the nations of the area.

The resolution could well be based upon similar resolutions enacted by the Congress in the past—to meet the threat to Formosa in 1955, to meet the threat to the Middle East in 1957, and to meet the threat in Cuba in 1962. It could state in the simplest terms the resolve and support of the Congress for action to deal appropriately with attacks against our Armed Forces and to defend freedom and preserve peace in southeast Asia in accordance with the obligations of the United States under the Southeast Asia Treaty. I urge the Congress to enact such a resolution promptly and thus to give convincing evidence to the aggressive Communist nations, and to the world as a whole, that our policy in southeast Asia will be carried forward—and that the peace and security of the area will be preserved....

Lyndon B. Johnson

The Gulf of Tonkin Resolution

H.J. Res. 1145

Joint Resolution: To promote the maintenance of international peace and security in Southeast Asia.

Aug. 7, 1964

Whereas naval units of the Communist regime in Vietnam, in violation of the principles of the Charter of the United Nations and of international law, have deliberately and repeatedly attacked United States naval vessels lawfully present in international waters, and have thereby created a serious threat to international peace; and

Whereas these attacks are part of a deliberate and systematic campaign of aggression that the Communist regime in North Vietnam has been waging against its neighbors and the nations joined with them in the collective defense of their freedom; and

Whereas the United States is assisting the peoples of southeast Asia to protect their freedom and has no territorial, military or political ambitions in that area, but desires only that these peoples should be left in peace to work out their own destinies in their own way: Now, therefore, be it

Resolved by the Senate and House of Representatives of the United States of America in Congress assembled,

Sec. 1. That the Congress approves and supports the determination of the President, as Commander in Chief, to take all necessary measures to repel any armed attack against the forces of the United States and to prevent further aggression.

Sec. 2. The United States regards as vital to its national interest and to world peace the maintenance of international peace and security in southeast Asia. Consonant with the Constitution of the United States and the Charter of the United Nations and in accordance with its obligations under the Southeast Asia Collective Defense Treaty, the United States is, therefore, prepared, as the President determines, to take all necessary steps, including the use of armed force, to assist any member or protocol state of the Southeast Asia Collective Defense Treaty requesting assistance in defense of its freedom.

Sec. 3. This resolution shall expire when the President shall determine that the peace and security of the area is reasonably assured by international conditions created by action of the United Nations or otherwise, except that it may be terminated earlier by concurrent resolution of the Congress.

Speaker of the House of Representatives

President pro tempore of the Senate

Statement by the President on the Passage of the Joint Resolution on Southeast Asia

Aug. 7, 1964

The 414-to-nothing House vote and the 88-to-2 Senate vote on the passage of the Joint Resolution on Southeast Asia is a demonstration to all the world of the unity of all Americans. They prove our determination to defend our own forces, to prevent aggression, and to work firmly and steadily for peace and security in the area.

I am sure the American people join me in expressing the deepest appreciation to the leaders and Members of both parties, in both Houses of Congress, for their patriotic, resolute, and rapid action.

Lyndon B. Johnson

Subsequent investigations by Congress and historians after the war revealed that the reports of the Tonkin incident, as presented by President Johnson, were exaggerated and misleading. Although U.S. warships had been fired on prior to August 4, they had been engaged in surveillance activities, a belligerent act; and the alleged August 4 attack did not occur.

Several legal challenges were made to the Vietnam War in the lower courts, which reached inconsistent decisions. The Supreme Court never decided the issue of the constitutionality of the Vietnam War, or even whether that issue presented a non-justiciable political question. In at least two instances, individual justices had or assumed opportunities to issue opinions. The following is one such instance.

Massachusetts v. Laird

400 U.S. 886 (1970)

[The Commonwealth of Massachusetts attempted to bring suit against Secretary of Defense Melvin Laird for a declaration that the Vietnam War was unconstitutional and to enjoin the government from requiring Massachusetts residents to participate in combat or combat support roles in Vietnam. Pursuant to Art. III, § 2 cl. 3, which provides that "the Supreme Court shall have original jurisdiction" "in all cases … in which a state shall be a party," Massachusetts filed a motion for leave to file its initial complaint directly in the Supreme Court. The Supreme Court denied the motion, over the dissent of Justices Harlan and Douglas. Justice Douglas issued an opinion with his dissent.]

Mr. Justice DOUGLAS, dissenting.

This motion was filed by the Commonwealth of Massachusetts against the Secretary of Defense, a citizen of another State. It is brought pursuant to a mandate contained in an act of the Massachusetts Legislature. Massachusetts seeks to obtain an adjudication of the constitutionality of the United States' participation in the Indochina war. It requests that the United States' participation be declared 'unconstitutional in that it was not initially authorized or subsequently ratified by Congressional declaration'; it asks that the Secretary of Defense be enjoined 'from carrying out, issuing, or causing to be issued any further orders which would increase the present level of United States troops in Indochina'; and it asks that, if appropriate congressional action is not forthcoming within 90 days of this Court's decree, that the Secretary of Defense be enjoined 'from carrying out, issuing, or causing to be issued any further order directing any inhabitant of the Commonwealth of Massachusetts to Indochina for the purpose of participating in combat or supporting combat troops in the Vietnam war.' Today this Court denies leave to file the complaint. I dissent.

The threshold issues for granting leave to file a complaint in this case are standing and justiciability. I believe that Massachusetts has standing and the controversy is justiciable. At the very least, however, it is apparent that the issues are not so clearly foreclosed as to justify a summary denial of leave to file.

[Justice Douglas argued that the plaintiff had standing to sue, and he then considered the political question doctrine. Applying the 6-part framework of Baker v. Carr, he reasoned that the case did not present a non-justiciable political question.]

Marshal's admonition that "it is a *constitution* we are expounding," McCulloch v. Maryland, is especially relevant when the Court is required to give legal sanctions to an underlying principle of the Constitution — that of separation of powers.

It is far more important to be respectful to the Constitution than to a coordinate branch of government....

We have never ruled, I believe, that when the Federal Government takes a person by the neck and submits him to punishment, imprisonment, taxation, or submission to some ordeal, the complaining person may not be heard in court. The rationale in cases such as the present is that government cannot take life, liberty, or property of the individual and escape adjudication by the courts of the legality of its action.

That is the heart of this case. It does not concern the wisdom of fighting in Southeast Asia. Likewise no question of whether the conflict is either just or necessary is present. We are asked instead whether the Executive has power, absent a congressional declaration of war, to commit Massachusetts citizens in armed hostilities on foreign soil. Another way of putting the question is whether under our Constitution presidential wars are permissible? Should that question be answered in the negative we would then have to determine whether Congress has declared war. That question which Massachusetts presents is in my view justiciable.

"The war power of the United States like its other powers ... is subject to constitutional limitations." No less than the war power — the greatest leveler of them all — is the power of the Commander-in-Chief subject to constitutional limitations. That was the crux of the Steel Seizure Case. Concurring in that case, Mr. Justice Clark stated: "I conclude that where Congress has laid down specific procedures to deal with the type of crisis confronting the President, he must follow those procedures in meeting the crisis.... I cannot sustain the seizure in question because ... Congress had [sic] prescribed methods to be followed by the President...." If the President must follow procedures prescribed by Congress, it follows *a fortiori* that he must follow procedures prescribed by the Constitution.

This Court has previously faced issues of presidential war making. The legality of Lincoln's blockade was considered in the Prize Cases, and although the Court narrowly split in supporting the President's position, the split was on the merits, not on whether the claim was justiciable. And even though that war was the Civil War and not one involving an overseas expedition, the decision was 5 to 4.

In the Steel Seizure Case members of this Court wrote seven opinions and each reached the merits of the Executive's seizure. In that case, as here, the issue related to the President's powers as Commander-in-Chief and the fact that all nine Justices decided the case on the merits and construed the powers of a coordinate branch at a time of extreme emergency should be instructive.... If we determine that the Indochina conflict is unconstitutional because it lacks a congressional declaration of war, the Chief Executive is free to seek one, as was President Truman free to seek congressional approval after our *Steel Seizure* decision.

There is, of course, a difference between this case and the Prize Cases and the Steel Seizure Case. In those cases a private party was asserting a wrong to him: his property was being taken and he demanded a determination of the legality of the taking. Here the *lives* and *liberties* of Massachusetts citizens are in jeopardy. Certainly the Constitution gives no greater protection to *property* than to *life* and *liberty*. It might be argued that the authority in the Steel Seizure Case was not textually apparent in the Constitution, while the power of the Commander-in-Chief to commit troops is obvious and therefore a different determination on justiciability is needed. The Prize Cases, however, involved Lincoln's exercise of power in ordering a blockade by virtue of his powers as the Commander-in-Chief.

Since private parties — represented by Massachusetts as parens patriae are involved in this case — the teaching of the Prize Cases and the Steel Seizure Case is that their claims are justiciable.

The Solicitor General urges that no effective remedy can be formulated. He correctly points out enforcing or supervising injunctive relief would involve immense complexities and difficulties. But there is no requirement that we issue an injunction. Massachusetts seeks declaratory relief as well as injunctive relief. In Baker v. Carr we stated that we must determine whether "the duty asserted can be judicially identified and its breach judicially determined, and whether protection for the right asserted can be judicially molded." The Declaratory Judgment Act, 28 U.S.C. § 2201, provides that "any court of the United States may declare the rights ... of any interested party ... whether or not further relief is or could be sought." It may well be that even declaratory relief would be inappropriate respecting many of the numerous issues involved if the Court held that the war were unconstitutional. I restrict this opinion to the question of the propriety of a declaratory judgment that no Massachusetts man can be taken against his will and made to serve in that war....

Today we deny a hearing to a State which attempts to determine whether it is constitutional to require its citizens to fight in a foreign war absent a congressional declaration of war. Three years ago we refused to hear a case involving draftees who sought to prevent their shipment overseas. The question of an unconstitutional war is neither academic nor 'political.' These cases have raised the question in adversary settings. It should be settled here and now.

Review Questions and Explanations: Vietnam War Readings

1. *Massachusetts v. Laird* was one of several cases challenging the constitutionality of the Vietnam War. Most of these cases were decided in the lower courts; the Supreme Court did not render an opinion on the issue as a full court. Invariably, the courts declined to reach the merits. A common reason given for such decisions was the "political question" doctrine, essentially a ruling that there were no judicially cognizable criteria to decide the question. Do you agree? Or do you agree with Justice Douglas that decisions like *Youngstown* and *The Prize Cases* demonstrate the courts' capacity to decide such questions?

2. Do you think the Gulf of Tonkin Resolution was constitutionally sufficient authorization to the President to embark on a war of the duration and scope of the Vietnam War? Does it make a difference if you consider subsequent congressional actions, such as making appropriations in support of the war and passing a "selective service" (i.e., military draft) law?

The constitutional problem posed by the Vietnam War is a potentially recurring one. The President is expected to meet military emergencies swiftly, and this may at times require immediate deployment of military forces into combat situations without time for extensive consultations with Congress. But once armed forces are deployed, disengagement from combat may be extremely difficult; and the security of the deployed forces may depend on reinforcement. Hostilities, once begun may in many circumstances tend inexorably to escalate almost by their own logic.

Congress sought to address this problem in a pragmatic manner in October 1973, when it passed a bill entitled "The War Powers Act." The Act was designed to constrain the President's ability to commit United States armed forces to prolonged and large-scale combat without clear congressional authorization. It set time limits for the commitment of armed forces and created requirements for the President to consult with Congress. A key provision of the bill, section 8(a), stated that authorization for use of armed forces was not to be inferred from laws or treaties that did not expressly authorize military force. The legislative history explained the specific connection of this language to the Gulf of Tonkin Resolution:

> Section 8(a) states that authority to introduce armed forces is not to be inferred from any provision of law or treaty unless it specifically authorizes the introduction of armed forces into hostilities or potential hostilities and states that it is "intended to constitute specific statutory authorization within the meaning of this joint resolution." This language was derived from a Senate measure and was intended to prevent a security treaty or military appropriations act from being used to authorize the introduction of troops. It was also aimed against using a broad resolution like the Tonkin Gulf Resolution to justify hostilities abroad. This resolution had stated that the United States was prepared to take all necessary steps, including use of armed force, to assist certain nations, and it was cited by Presidents and many Members as congressional authorization for the Vietnam war.

The bill was presented to President Nixon, who vetoed it on October 24, 1973, claiming in his veto message that the bill unconstitutionally infringed on executive power. Two weeks later, on November 7, Congress voted by the required 2/3 majority to override the President's veto, 284–135 in the House, and 75–18 in the Senate. The bill thereby became law.

One technical note: a bill submitted to the President for signature might be styled an "Act," but it is better understood as a *proposed* Act. It only becomes an Act when signed by the President. A bill can nevertheless become a *law* if Congress votes to override the veto, but a law made through a veto override is styled a "resolution." Hence, the "War Powers Act" is what was vetoed; the "War Powers Resolution" is what became law, due to the veto override. It is now codified as 50 U.S.C. §§ 1541–48.

In the following pages, we reprint the War Powers Resolution, President Nixon's veto message, and the certification from Congress overriding the veto.

Guided Reading Questions: The War Powers Resolution

1. What constitutional powers authorize Congress to enact the War Powers Resolution?

2. Briefly summarize the key "operative" elements of this resolution: who is required to do what, when, and under what circumstances?

3. Carefully review the reasons President Nixon gives for his veto. What are they?

War Powers Resolution

Joint Resolution Concerning the War Powers of Congress and the President.

Resolved by the Senate and the House of Representatives of the United States of America in Congress assembled,

SHORT TITLE

SECTION 1. This joint resolution may be cited as the "War Powers Resolution."

PURPOSE AND POLICY

SEC. 2. (a) It is the purpose of this joint resolution to fulfill the intent of the framers of the Constitution of the United States and insure that the collective judgement of both the Congress and the President will apply to the introduction of United States Armed Forces into hostilities, or into situations where imminent involvement in hostilities is clearly indicated by the circumstances, and to the continued use of such forces in hostilities or in such situations.

(b) Under article I, section 8, of the Constitution, it is specifically provided that the Congress shall have the power to make all laws necessary and proper for carrying into execution, not only its own powers but also all other powers vested by the Constitution in the Government of the United States, or in any department or officer thereof.

(c) The constitutional powers of the President as Commander-in-Chief to introduce United States Armed Forces into hostilities, or into situations where imminent involvement in hostilities is clearly indicated by the circumstances, are exercised only pursuant to (1) a declaration of war, (2) specific statutory authorization, or (3) a national emergency created by attack upon the United States, its territories or possessions, or its armed forces.

CONSULTATION

SEC. 3. The President in every possible instance shall consult with Congress before introducing United States Armed Forces into hostilities or into situation where imminent involvement in hostilities is clearly indicated by the circumstances, and after every such introduction shall consult regularly with the Congress until United States Armed Forces are no longer engaged in hostilities or have been removed from such situations.

REPORTING

SEC. 4. (a) In the absence of a declaration of war, in any case in which United States Armed Forces are introduced—

(1) into hostilities or into situations where imminent involvement in hostilities is clearly indicated by the circumstances;

(2) into the territory, airspace or waters of a foreign nation, while equipped for combat, except for deployments which relate solely to supply, replacement, repair, or training of such forces; or

(3) in numbers which substantially enlarge United States Armed Forces equipped for combat already located in a foreign nation; the President shall submit within 48 hours to the Speaker of the House of Representatives and to the President pro tempore of the Senate a report, in writing, setting forth—

(A) the circumstances necessitating the introduction of United States Armed Forces;

(B) the constitutional and legislative authority under which such introduction took place; and

(C) the estimated scope and duration of the hostilities or involvement.

(b) The President shall provide such other information as the Congress may request in the fulfillment of its constitutional responsibilities with respect to committing the Nation to war and to the use of United States Armed Forces abroad.

(c) Whenever United States Armed Forces are introduced into hostilities or into any situation described in subsection (a) of this section, the President shall, so long as such armed forces continue to be engaged in such hostilities or situation, report to the Congress periodically on the status of such hostilities or situation as well as on the scope and duration of such hostilities or situation, but in no event shall he report to the Congress less often than once every six months.

CONGRESSIONAL ACTION

SEC. 5. (a) Each report submitted pursuant to section 4(a)(1) shall be transmitted to the Speaker of the House of Representatives and to the President pro tempore of the Senate on the same calendar day. Each report so transmitted shall be referred to the Committee on Foreign Affairs of the House of Representatives and to the Committee on Foreign Relations of the Senate for appropriate action. If, when the report is transmitted, the Congress has adjourned sine die or has adjourned for any period in excess of three calendar days, the Speaker of the House of Representatives and the President pro tempore of the Senate, if they deem it advisable (or if petitioned by at least 30 percent of the membership of their respective Houses) shall jointly request the President to convene Congress in order that it may consider the report and take appropriate action pursuant to this section.

(b) Within sixty calendar days after a report is submitted or is required to be submitted pursuant to section 4(a)(1), whichever is earlier, the President shall terminate any use of United States Armed Forces with respect to which such report was submitted (or required to be submitted), unless the Congress (1) has declared war or has enacted a specific authorization for such use of United States Armed Forces, (2) has extended by law such sixty-day period, or (3) is physically unable to meet as a result of an armed attack upon the United States. Such sixty-day period shall be extended for not more than an additional thirty days if the President determines and certifies to the Congress in writing that unavoidable military necessity respecting the safety of United States Armed Forces requires the continued use of such armed forces in the course of bringing about a prompt removal of such forces.

(c) Notwithstanding subsection (b), at any time that United States Armed Forces are engaged in hostilities outside the territory of the United States, its possessions and territories without a declaration of war or specific statutory authorization, such forces shall be removed by the President if the Congress so directs by concurrent resolution.

CONGRESSIONAL PRIORITY PROCEDURES FOR JOINT RESOLUTION OR BILL

SEC. 6. (a) Any joint resolution or bill introduced pursuant to section 5(b) at least thirty calendar days before the expiration of the sixty-day period specified in such section shall be referred to the Committee on Foreign Affairs of the House of Representatives or the Committee on Foreign Relations of the Senate, as the case may be, and such committee shall report one such joint resolution or bill, together with its recommendations, not later than twenty-four calendar days before the expiration of the sixty-day period specified in such section, unless such House shall otherwise determine by the yeas and nays.

(b) Any joint resolution or bill so reported shall become the pending business of the House in question (in the case of the Senate the time for debate shall be equally divided between the proponents and the opponents), and shall be voted on within three calendar days thereafter, unless such House shall otherwise determine by yeas and nays.

(c) Such a joint resolution or bill passed by one House shall be referred to the committee of the other House named in subsection (a) and shall be reported out not later than fourteen calendar days before the expiration of the sixty-day period specified in section 5(b). The joint resolution or bill so reported shall become the pending business of the House in question and shall be voted on within three calendar days after it has been reported, unless such House shall otherwise determine by yeas and nays.

(d) In the case of any disagreement between the two Houses of Congress with respect to a joint resolution or bill passed by both Houses, conferees shall be promptly appointed and the committee of conference shall make and file a report with respect to such resolution or bill not later than four calendar days before the expiration of the sixty-day period specified in section 5(b). In the event the conferees are unable to agree within 48 hours, they shall report back to their respective Houses in disagreement. Notwithstanding any rule in either House concerning the printing of conference reports in the Record or concerning any delay in the consideration of such reports, such report shall be acted on by both Houses not later than the expiration of such sixty-day period.

CONGRESSIONAL PRIORITY PROCEDURES FOR CONCURRENT RESOLUTION

SEC. 7. (a) Any concurrent resolution introduced pursuant to section 5(b) at least thirty calendar days before the expiration of the sixty-day period specified in such section shall be referred to the Committee on Foreign Affairs of the House of Representatives or the Committee on Foreign Relations of the Senate, as the case may be, and one such concurrent resolution shall be reported out by such committee together with its recommendations within fifteen calendar days, unless such House shall otherwise determine by the yeas and nays.

(b) Any concurrent resolution so reported shall become the pending business of the House in question (in the case of the Senate the time for debate shall be equally divided between the proponents and the opponents), and shall be voted on within three calendar days thereafter, unless such House shall otherwise determine by yeas and nays.

(c) Such a concurrent resolution passed by one House shall be referred to the committee of the other House named in subsection (a) and shall be reported out by such committee together with its recommendations within fifteen calendar days and shall thereupon become the pending business of such House and shall be voted on within three calendar days after it has been reported, unless such House shall otherwise determine by yeas and nays.

(d) In the case of any disagreement between the two Houses of Congress with respect to a concurrent resolution passed by both Houses, conferees shall be promptly appointed and the committee of conference shall make and file a report with respect to such concurrent resolution within six calendar days after the legislation is referred to the committee of conference. Notwithstanding any rule in either House concerning the printing of conference reports in the Record or concerning any delay in the consideration of such reports, such report shall be acted on by both Houses not later than six calendar days after the conference report is filed. In the event the conferees are unable to agree within 48 hours, they shall report back to their respective Houses in disagreement.

INTERPRETATION OF JOINT RESOLUTION

SEC. 8. (a) Authority to introduce United States Armed Forces into hostilities or into situations wherein involvement in hostilities is clearly indicated by the circumstances shall not be inferred—

(1) from any provision of law (whether or not in effect before the date of the en-actment of this joint resolution), including any provision contained in any appropriation Act, unless such provision specifically authorizes the introduction of United States Armed Forces into hostilities or into such situations and stating that it is intended to constitute specific statutory authorization within the meaning of this joint resolution; or

(2) from any treaty heretofore or hereafter ratified unless such treaty is implemented by legislation specifically authorizing the introduction of United States Armed Forces into hostilities or into such situations and stating that it is intended to constitute specific statutory authorization within the meaning of this joint resolution.

(b) Nothing in this joint resolution shall be construed to require any further specific statutory authorization to permit members of United States Armed Forces to participate jointly with members of the armed forces of one or more foreign countries in the headquarters operations of high-level military commands which were established prior to the date of enactment of this joint resolution and pursuant to the United Nations Charter or any treaty ratified by the United States prior to such date.

(c) For purposes of this joint resolution, the term "introduction of United States Armed Forces" includes the assignment of member of such armed forces to command, coordinate, participate in the movement of, or accompany the regular or irregular military forces of any foreign country or government when such military forces are engaged, or there exists an imminent threat that such forces will become engaged, in hostilities.

(d) Nothing in this joint resolution—

(1) is intended to alter the constitutional authority of the Congress or of the President, or the provision of existing treaties; or

(2) shall be construed as granting any authority to the President with respect to the introduction of United States Armed Forces into hostilities or into situations wherein involvement in hostilities is clearly indicated by the circumstances which authority he would not have had in the absence of this joint resolution.

SEPARABILITY CLAUSE

SEC. 9. If any provision of this joint resolution or the application thereof to any person or circumstance is held invalid, the remainder of the joint resolution and the application of such provision to any other person or circumstance shall not be affected thereby.

EFFECTIVE DATE

SEC. 10. This joint resolution shall take effect on the date of its enactment.

President Nixon's Veto of War Powers Resolution

October 24, 1973

To the House of Representatives:

I hereby return without my approval House Joint Resolution 542—the War Powers Resolution. While I am in accord with the desire of the Congress to assert its proper role in the conduct of our foreign affairs, the restrictions which this resolution would impose upon the authority of the President are both unconstitutional and dangerous to the best interests of our Nation.

The proper roles of the Congress and the Executive in the conduct of foreign affairs have been debated since the founding of our country. Only recently, however, has there been a serious challenge to the wisdom of the Founding Fathers in choosing not to draw a precise and detailed line of demarcation between the foreign policy powers of the two branches.

The Founding Fathers understood the impossibility of foreseeing every contingency that might arise in this complex area. They acknowledged the need for flexibility in responding to changing circumstances. They recognized that foreign policy decisions must be made through close cooperation between the two branches and not through rigidly codified procedures.

These principles remain as valid today as they were when our Constitution was written. Yet House Joint Resolution 542 would violate those principles by defining the President's powers in ways which would strictly limit his constitutional authority.

Clearly Unconstitutional

House Joint Resolution 542 would attempt to take away, by a mere legislative act, authorities which the President has properly exercised under the Constitution for almost 200 years. One of its provisions would automatically cut off certain authorities after sixty days unless the Congress extended them. Another would allow the Congress to eliminate certain authorities merely by the passage of a concurrent resolution—an action which does not normally have the force of law, since it denies the President his constitutional role in approving legislation.

I believe that both these provisions are unconstitutional. The only way in which the constitutional powers of a branch of the Government can be altered is by amending the Constitution—and any attempt to make such alterations by legislation alone is clearly without force.

Undermining Our Foreign Policy

While I firmly believe that a veto of House Joint Resolution 542 is warranted solely on constitutional grounds, I am also deeply disturbed by the practical consequences of this resolution. For it would seriously undermine this Nation's ability to act decisively and convincingly in times of international crisis. As a result, the confidence of our allies in our ability to assist them could be diminished and the respect of our adversaries for our deterrent posture could decline. A permanent and substantial element of unpredictability would be injected into the world's assessment of American behavior, further increasing the likelihood of miscalculation and war.

If this resolution had been in operation, America's effective response to a variety of challenges in recent years would have been vastly complicated or even made impossible. We may well have been unable to respond in the way we did during the Berlin crisis of 1961, the Cuban missile crisis of 1962, the Congo rescue operation in 1964, and the Jordanian crisis of 1970—to mention just a few examples. In addition, our recent actions to bring about a peaceful settlement of the hostilities in the Middle East would have been seriously impaired if this resolution had been in force.

While all the specific consequences of House Joint Resolution 542 cannot yet be predicted, it is clear that it would undercut the ability of the United States to act as an effective influence for peace. For example, the provision automatically cutting off certain authorities after 60 days unless they are extended by the Congress could work to prolong or intensify a crisis. Until the Congress suspended the deadline, there would be at least a chance of United States withdrawal and an adversary would be tempted therefore to postpone serious negotiations until the 60 days were up. Only after the Congress acted would there be a strong incentive for an adversary to negotiate. In addition, the very existence of a deadline could lead to an escalation of hostilities in order to achieve certain objectives before the 60 days expired.

The measure would jeopardize our role as a force for peace in other ways as well. It would, for example, strike from the President's hand a wide range of important peace-keeping tools by eliminating his ability to exercise quiet diplomacy backed by subtle shifts in our military deployments. It would also cast into doubt authorities which Presidents have used to undertake certain humanitarian relief missions in conflict areas, to protect fishing boats from seizure, to deal with ship or aircraft hijackings, and to respond to threats of attack. Not the least of the adverse consequences of this resolution would be the prohibition contained in section 8 against fulfilling our obligations under the NATO treaty as ratified by the Senate. Finally, since the bill is somewhat vague as to when the 60 day rule would apply, it could lead to extreme confusion and dangerous disagreements concerning the prerogatives of the two branches, seriously damaging our ability to respond to international crises.

Failure to Require Positive Congressional Action

I am particularly disturbed by the fact that certain of the President's constitutional powers as Commander in Chief of the Armed Forces would terminate automatically under this resolution 60 days after they were invoked. No overt Congressional action would be required to cut off these powers—they would disappear automatically unless the Congress extended them. In effect, the Congress is here attempting to increase its policy-making role through a provision which requires it to take absolutely no action at all.

In my view, the proper way for the Congress to make known its will on such foreign policy questions is through a positive action, with full debate on the merits of the issue and with each member taking the responsibility of casting a yes or no vote after considering those merits. The authorization and appropriations process represents one of the ways in which such influence can be exercised. I do not, however, believe that the Congress can responsibly contribute its considered, collective judgment on such grave questions without full debate and without a yes or no vote. Yet this is precisely what the joint resolution would allow. It would give every future Congress the ability to handcuff every future President merely by doing nothing and sitting still. In my view, one cannot become a responsible partner unless one is prepared to take responsible action.

Strengthening Cooperation Between the Congress and the Executive Branches

The responsible and effective exercise of the war powers requires the fullest cooperation between the Congress and the Executive and the prudent fulfillment by each branch of its constitutional responsibilities. House Joint Resolution 542 includes certain constructive measures which would foster this process by enhancing the flow of information from the executive branch to the Congress. Section 3, for example, calls for consultations with the Congress before and during the involvement of the United States forces in hostilities abroad. This provision is consistent with the desire of this Administration for regularized consultations with the Congress in an even wider range of circumstances.

I believe that full and cooperative participation in foreign policy matters by both the executive and the legislative branches could be enhanced by a careful and dispassionate study of their constitutional roles. Helpful proposals for such a study have already been made in the Congress. I would welcome the establishment of a non-partisan commission on the constitutional roles of the Congress and the President in the conduct of foreign affairs. This commission could make a thorough review of the principal constitutional issues in Executive-Congressional relations, including the war powers, the international agreement powers, and the question of Executive privilege, and then submit its recommendations to the President and the Congress. The members of such a commission could be drawn from both parties — and could represent many perspectives including those of the Congress, the executive branch, the legal profession, and the academic community.

This Administration is dedicated to strengthening cooperation between the Congress and the President in the conduct of foreign affairs and to preserving the constitutional prerogatives of both branches of our Government. I know that the Congress shares that goal. A commission on the constitutional roles of the Congress and the President would provide a useful opportunity for both branches to work together toward that common objective.

RICHARD NIXON

The White House

October 24, 1973

Certification of Congress Regarding Override of the War Powers Resolution Veto

In the House of Representatives, U.S., November 7, 1973.

The House of Representatives having proceeded to reconsider the resolution (H. J. Res. 542) entitled "Joint resolution concerning the war powers of Congress and the President," returned by the President of the United States with his objections, to the House of Representatives, in which it originated, it was

Resolved, That the said resolution pass, two-thirds of the House of Representatives agreeing to pass the same.

Attest: W. PAT JENNINGS, Clerk

I certify that this Joint Resolution originated in the House of Representatives.

W. PAT JENNINGS, Clerk.

In the Senate of the United States, November 7, 1973

The Senate having proceeded to reconsider the joint resolution (H. J. Res. 542) entitled "Joint resolution concerning the war powers of Congress and the President," returned by the President of the United States with his objections to the House of Representatives, in which it originate, it was

Resolved, That the said joint resolution pass, two-thirds of the Senators present having voted in the affirmative.

Attest: FRANCIS R. VALEO, Secretary.

Review Questions and Explanations: The War Powers Resolution

1. Does President Nixon object to the resolution in its entirety or only certain provisions? If the latter, what provisions?

2. Do you agree with the argument that the Resolution curtails the President's commander-in-chief authority "without congressional action"? (Note that there

are two parts to that argument—the curtailment of authority and the lack of congressional action.) If so, why is that unconstitutional?

3. Is there a different and less constitutionally objectionable way (if the Resolution is objectionable) for Congress to control the problem of what Justice Douglas called "presidential wars"?

4. President Nixon offers several arguments, that he denotes as "policy" arguments, against the Resolution. Is there a constitutional aspect to those policy arguments? In other words, could you recast them as constitutional arguments? (See *Curtiss-Wright* and *Dames & Moore*, in section D, "Foreign Affairs Power.")

Recap: The War Powers Resolution

Suppose the President initiates military action, and Congress quickly convenes and vigorously debates the issue. Suppose further that the House is evenly split and cannot pass a resolution; and in the Senate, 52 senators support a resolution terminating the military action, but the remaining 48 senators block the resolution by a filibuster.

1. Is this Congressional "inactivity" as President Nixon claims?

2. In the absence of the War Powers Resolution, would it constitute "acquiescence" or "tacit approval" of the President's actions under the Jackson analysis in *Youngstown*?

3. Does the War Powers Resolution itself constitute congressional disapproval (either express or implied) of the President's sustaining the military action beyond 60 days under Jackson's *Youngstown* analysis?

The constitutionality of the War Powers Resolution has not come before the courts. Most presidents since Nixon, while not conceding its constitutionality, have nevertheless attempted to abide by the Resolution, or at least its reporting provisions: over 100 reports have issued from Presidents to Congress pursuant to the Resolution. In a handful of cases, members of Congress have filed lawsuits to obtain judicial enforcement of the War Powers Resolution against presidents they claimed to have violated it. In each instance, the President's lawyers successfully moved to have the cases dismissed on technical grounds, without arguing against the constitutionality of the Resolution or otherwise addressing the merits. These technical grounds have invariably consisted of one or more "justiciability" doctrines (See Chapter 6), or the "doctrine of equitable discretion," in which a court declines to grant injunctive or declaratory relief for "prudential" reasons (such as a concern to avoid intruding on separation of powers). As will be explained in Chapter 6, cases may be held "non-justiciable" (not in a form suitable for judicial resolution) for any of several reasons, including a lack of standing or the presence of a "political question." *See Crockett v. Reagan*, 558 F. Supp. 893 (D.D.C. 1982), *aff'd* 720 F.2d 1355 (D.C. Cir. 1983) (suit by 29 members of Congress seeking declaration that sending of military advisors to El Salvador triggered War Powers Resolution dismissed as non-justiciable political question); *Sanchez-Espinoza v. Reagan*, 568 F. Supp. 596 (D.D.C. 1983), *aff'd*, 770 F.2d 202 (D.C. Cir. 1985) (suit by 12 members of Congress seeking declaratory and injunctive relief to stop military aid to Nicaraguan "Contra" rebels on grounds that it violated War Powers Resolution dismissed as non-justiciable political question; dismissal affirmed on mootness grounds); *Lowry v. Reagan*, 676 F. Supp. 333 (D.D.C. 1987) (suit by 110 members of Congress seeking declaration that military escorts of shipping in the Persian Gulf and strikes on Iranian warships triggered War Powers Resolution dismissed on political question and equitable discretion grounds).

These cases also typically involved a second, related claim: a violation to the "war powers *clause*" by the President, that is, Art. I, § 8, cl. 11, assigning to Congress (not the President) the power to declare war. The theory of the plaintiff members of Congress seems to be that the War Powers Resolution is a statutory specification regulating the delegation of certain war powers to the President; and that a violation of the Resolution also violates separation of powers by intruding on Congress's war power.

The most recent and extensive treatment of these issues by a court is presented in the following case.

Guided Reading Questions: *Campbell v. Clinton*

1. The doctrine of "standing" and the case of *Raines v. Byrd*, relied on heavily by the judges in *Campbell*, are presented in Chapter 6. For present purposes, all you need to know about "standing" is that it is the question of whether the plaintiff is entitled to have the court adjudicate the substantive "merits" of his claims. Standing is said to have separation-of-powers implications, which is the point you should focus on when reading the case. Specifically, what remedy are the plaintiffs seeking? Why would a court be reluctant to allow legislators who lost a vote in Congress to get such a remedy?

2. In the opinion for the court, Judge Silberman says that plaintiffs lack standing, i.e., they are not the proper persons to bring this type of claim. He then writes his own separate concurrence. Is he merely repeating himself, or is he making a different argument?

3. Do any of the judges say that President Clinton violated the War Powers Resolution? Do any of them say whether or not the War Powers Resolution is constitutional?

4. The debate between Judges Silberman and Tatel in their concurring opinions has to do with the findings a court would have to make determine to whether President Clinton violated the War Powers Resolution. Is a court in a position to make these kinds of findings? How does your answer to that question bear on how the court should decide this case?

Campbell v. Clinton

203 F.3d 19 (D.C. Cir. 2000)

[Thirty-one members of Congress, led by Tom Campbell of California, filed suit seeking a declaration that President Clinton violated the War Powers Clause of the Constitution and the War Powers Resolution by directing United States forces' participation in North Atlantic Treaty Organization (NATO) airstrikes against the

Federal Republic of Yugoslavia without congressional authorization. The United States District Court for the District of Columbia granted the President's motion to dismiss. The Court of Appeals affirmed. All three judges on the panel agreed, in an opinion for the court by Judge Silberman, that the plaintiffs lacked standing. But they did not entirely agree on why, and disagreed on related justiciability matters. Accordingly, each judge wrote a separate concurring opinion, including Judge Silberman, on points that did not command a two-judge majority.]

SILBERMAN, Circuit Judge.

.... The government does not respond to appellants' claim on the merits. Instead the government challenges the jurisdiction of the federal courts to adjudicate this claim on three separate grounds: the case is moot; appellants lack standing, as the district court concluded; and the case is non-justiciable. Since we agree with the district court that the congressmen lack standing it is not necessary to decide whether there are other jurisdictional defects.

The question whether congressmen have standing in federal court to challenge the lawfulness of actions of the executive was answered, at least in large part, in the Supreme Court's recent decision in Raines v. Byrd, 521 U.S. 811 (1997).... Individual congressmen claimed that under [the Line Item Veto] Act a President could veto (unconstitutionally) only part of a law and thereby diminish the institutional power of Congress. Observing it had never held that congressmen have standing to assert an institutional injury as against the executive, the Court held that petitioners in the case lacked "legislative standing" to challenge the Act. The Court observed that petitioners already possessed an adequate political remedy, since they could vote to have the Line Item Veto Act repealed, or to provide individual spending bills with a statutory exemption.

Thereafter in Chenoweth v. Clinton, 181 F.3d 112, 115 (D.C. Cir. 1999), emphasizing the separation-of-powers problems inherent in legislative standing, we held that congressmen had no standing to challenge the President's introduction of a program through executive order rather than statute. As in Raines, appellants contended that the President's action inflicted an institutional injury upon Congress, in this case by circumventing its legislative authority, but, we said,

> It is uncontested that the Congress could terminate the [contested program] were a sufficient number in each House so inclined. Because the parties' dispute is therefore fully susceptible to political resolution, we would [under circuit precedent] dismiss the complaint to avoid "meddling in the internal affairs of the legislative branch." Applying Raines, we would reach the same conclusion.

.... Congress certainly could have passed a law forbidding the use of U.S. forces in the Yugoslav campaign; indeed, there was a measure—albeit only a concurrent resolution—introduced to require the President to withdraw U.S. troops. Unfortunately, however, for those congressmen who, like appellants, desired an end to U.S. involvement in Yugoslavia, this measure was *defeated* by a 139 to 290 vote. Of course, Congress always retains appropriations authority and could have cut off funds for the American role in the conflict. Again there was an effort to do so but it failed; appropriations were authorized. And there always remains the possibility of impeachment should a President act in disregard of Congress' authority on these matters.

Appellants' constitutional claim stands on no firmer footing. Appellants argue that the War Powers Clause of the Constitution proscribes a President from using military force except as is necessary to repel a sudden attack. But they also argue that the [War Powers Resolution ("WPR")] "implements" or channels congressional authority under the Constitution. It may well be then that since we have determined that appellants lack standing to enforce the WPR there is nothing left of their constitutional claim. Assuming, however, that appellants' constitutional claim should be considered separately, the same logic dictates they do not have standing to bring such a challenge. That is to say Congress has a broad range of legislative authority it can use to stop a President's war making, and therefore under Raines congressmen may not challenge the President's war-making powers in federal court.

SILBERMAN, Circuit Judge, concurring.

Appellants argued that we should consider in our standing analysis that if congressmen lack standing only military personnel might be able to challenge a President's arguably unlawful use of force, and it would be undesirable to put the armed forces in such a position. Although that is not a consideration that bears on standing, see Schlesinger v. Reservists Comm. to Stop the War, 418 U.S. 208 (1974), that argument leads me to observe that, in my view, no one is able to bring this challenge because the two claims are not justiciable. We lack "judicially discoverable and manageable standards" for addressing them, and the War Powers Clause claim implicates the political question doctrine. See Baker v. Carr, 369 U.S. 186 (1962).

Prior litigation under the WPR has turned on the threshold test whether U.S. forces are engaged in hostilities or are in imminent danger of hostilities. But the question posed by appellants—whether the President's refusal to discontinue American activities in Yugoslavia violates the WPR—necessarily depends on the statute having been triggered in the first place. It has been held that the statutory threshold standard is not precise enough and too obviously calls for a political judgment to be one suitable for judicial determinations. I think that is correct. Appellants point to a House Report suggesting that hostilities for purposes of the WPR include all situations "where there is a reasonable expectation that American military personnel will be subject to hostile fire." See H.R. REP. NO. 287, 93rd Cong., 1st Sess. 7 (1973). That elaboration hardly helps. It could reasonably be thought that anytime American soldiers are confronted by armed or potentially armed forces of a non-ally there is a reasonable expectation that they will be subject to hostile fire. Certainly any competent military leader will assume that to be so.

Appellants argue that here there is no real problem of definition because this air war was so overwhelming and indisputable. It is asserted that the President implicitly conceded the applicability of the WPR by sending the report to Congress. In truth, the President only said the report was "consistent" with the WPR. In any event, I do not think it matters how clear it is in any particular case that "hostilities" were initiated if the statutory standard is one generally unsuited to judicial resolution.

Nor is the constitutional claim justiciable. Appellants contend this case is governed by Mitchell v. Laird, 488 F.2d 611, 614 (D.C. Cir. 1973), where we said that "there would be no insuperable difficulty in a court determining whether" the Vietnam conflict constituted a war in the Constitutional sense. See also Dellums v. Bush, 752 F. Supp. 1141, 1146 (D.D.C. 1990) ("The Court has no hesitation in concluding that an offensive entry into Iraq by several hundred thousand United States servicemen ... could be described as a 'war' within the meaning ... of the Constitution."). But a careful reading of both cases reveals that the language upon which appellants rely is only dicta. (In Laird the Court ultimately held that the resolution of the issues was a political question. See 488 F.2d at 616.)

Appellants cannot point to any constitutional test for what is war. Instead, appellants offer a rough definition of war provided in 1994 by an Assistant Attorney General to four Senators with respect to a planned intervention in Haiti, as well as a number of law review articles each containing its own definition of war. I do not think any of these sources, however, offers a coherent test for judges to apply to the question what constitutes war, a point only accentuated by the variances, for instance, between the numerous law review articles. For that reason, I disagree with Judge Tatel's assertion that we can decide appellants' constitutional claim because it is somehow obvious in this case that our country fought a war. Baker v. Carr speaks of a case involving "a lack of judicially discoverable and manageable standards for resolving" the issue presented, see 369 U.S. at 217, not just a case the facts of which are obscure; the focus is on the standards. Even if this court knows all there is to know about the Kosovo conflict, we still do not know what standards to apply to those facts.

Judge Tatel points to numerous cases in which a court has determined that our nation was at war, but none of these cases involved the question whether the President had "declared war" in violation of the Constitution. For instance, in Bas v. Tingy, 4 U.S. 37 (1800), the question whether there was a "war" was only relevant to determining whether France was an "enemy" within the meaning of a prize statute.... It is similarly irrelevant that courts have determined the existence of a war in cases involving insurance policies and other contracts, the Federal Tort Claims Act, and provisions of the military criminal code applicable in "time of war." None of these cases asked whether there was a war as the Constitution uses that word, but only whether a particular statutory or contractual provision was triggered by some instance of fighting. Comparing Bas v. Tingy's lengthy discussion whether our quarrel with France constituted a solemn or imperfect, general or limited war, with today's propensity to label any widespread conflict an undifferentiated war, it would not be surprising if an insurance contract's "war" provisions, or even a statute's for that matter, were triggered before the Constitution's.

Even assuming a court could determine what "war" is, it is important to remember that the Constitution grants Congress the power to declare war, which is not necessarily the same as the power to determine whether U.S. forces will fight in a war. This distinction was drawn in the Prize Cases, 67 U.S. 635 (1862). There, petitioners challenged the authority of the President to impose a blockade on the secessionist States, an act of war, where Congress had not declared war against the Confederacy. The Court, while recognizing that the President "has no power to initiate or declare a war," observed that "war may exist without a declaration on either side." In instances where war is declared against the United States by the actions of another country, the President "does not initiate the war, but is bound to accept the challenge without waiting for any special legislative authority." Importantly, the Court made clear that it would not dispute the President on measures necessary to repel foreign aggression. The President alone

> must determine what degree of force the crisis demands. The proclamation of blockade is itself official and conclusive evidence to the Court that a state of war existed which demanded and authorized a recourse to such a measure, under the circumstances peculiar to the case.

And, to confirm the independent authority of the President to meet foreign aggression, the Court noted that while Congress had authorized the war, it may not have been required to: "*If* it were necessary to the technical existence of a war, that it should have a legislative sanction, we find it...." Id. (emphasis added).

> FN2. Judge Tatel's reliance on the *Prize Cases* as an example of the Court concluding a war exists is misplaced because the Court itself did not label the Civil War such, but instead deferred to the President's determination that the country was at war. See 67 U.S. at 670 ("Whether the President in fulfilling his duties, as Commander-in-chief ... has met with such armed hostile resistance ... as will compel him to accord to them the

character of belligerents, is a question to be decided by *him*, and this Court must be governed by the decisions and acts of the political department of the Government to which this power was entrusted") (emphasis in original). Therefore, the Court's assertion that "it is bound to notice and to know" the war, *see id. at 667*, provides no support for the proposition that a court itself may decide when in fact there is one.

I read the *Prize Cases* to stand for the proposition that the President has independent authority to repel aggressive acts by third parties even without specific congressional authorization, and courts may not review the level of force selected. Therefore, I assume, arguendo, that appellants are correct and only Congress has authority to *initiate* "war." If the President may direct U.S. forces in response to third-party initiated war, then the question any plaintiff who challenges the constitutionality of a war must answer is, who started it? The question of who is responsible for a conflict is, as history reveals, rather difficult to answer, and we lack judicial standards for resolving it. Then there is the problem of actually discovering the necessary information to answer the question, when such information may be unavailable to the U.S. or its allies, or unavailable to courts due to its sensitivity. Perhaps Yugoslavia did pose a threat to a much wider region of Europe and to U.S. civilian and military interests and personnel there.

Judge Tatel does not take into account the *Prize Cases* when he concludes that the President was not exercising his independent authority to respond to foreign aggression because "in fact, the Kosovo issue had been festering for years." As quoted above the President alone "must determine what degree of force the crisis demands." Judge Tatel would substitute our judgment for the President's as to the point at which an intervention for reasons of national security is justified, after which point—when the crisis is no longer acute—the President must obtain a declaration of war. One should bear in mind that Kosovo's tensions antedate the creation of this republic.

In most cases this will also be an issue of the greatest sensitivity for our foreign relations. Here, the President claimed on national television that our country needed to respond to Yugoslav aggression to protect our trading interests in Europe, and to prevent a replay of World War I. A pronouncement by another branch of the U.S. government that U.S. participation in Kosovo was "unjustified" would no doubt cause strains within NATO.

In sum, there are no standards to determine either the statutory or constitutional questions raised in this case, and the question of whether the President has intruded on the war-declaring authority of Congress fits squarely within the political question doctrine. We therefore have another basis for our affirming the district court's dismissal of appellants' case.

RANDOLPH, Circuit Judge, concurring in the judgment.

.... I believe plaintiffs lack standing, at least to litigate their constitutional claim, but for reasons the majority opinion neglects.... The serious questions about the constitutionality of the War Powers Resolution must therefore be put off for still another day.

> FN2. I include as an Addendum to this opinion President Nixon's 1973 message to the House of Representatives explaining why he vetoed the War Powers Resolution on the grounds of its unconstitutionality.

The Constitution reserves the power to declare "war" to Congress and delegates the power to conduct war to the President. When President Clinton committed armed forces to the attack on the Federal Republic of Yugoslavia, he did so without a declaration of war from Congress. On April 28, 1999, after air operations and missile strikes were underway, the House of Representatives voted 427 to 2 against a declaration of war.

The War Powers Resolution, passed over President Nixon's veto in 1973, implements Congress's power to declare war under the Constitution. See 50 U.S.C. § 1541(a)–(b). It commands the President to "terminate any use of United States Armed Forces" within sixty days "unless the Congress (1) has declared war or has enacted a specific authorization for such use of United States Armed Forces, (2) has extended by law such sixty-day period, or (3) is physically unable to meet as a result of an armed attack upon the United States." 50 U.S.C. § 1544(b). The Senate, on March 23, 1999, passed a concurrent resolution providing that "the President of the United States is authorized to conduct military air operations and missile strikes in cooperation with our NATO allies against the Federal Republic of Yugoslavia." S. Con. Res. 21, 106th Cong. (1999); 145 CONG. REC. S3118 (daily ed. Mar. 23, 1999). The House rejected that measure by a tie vote on April 28, 1999. *See* 126 CONG. REC. H2451–52 (daily ed. Apr. 28, 1999).

The Members of Congress appearing as plaintiffs contend that President Clinton violated the Constitution and the War Powers Resolution and that they are entitled to a judicial declaration so stating. They have standing, they say, because President Clinton's prosecution of the war "completely nullified" their votes against declaring war and against authorizing a continuation of the hostilities.

The quoted phrase — "completely nullified" — is from Raines v. Byrd, 521 U.S. 811 (1997).... The heart of the *Raines* decision is this: "legislators whose votes would have been sufficient to defeat (or enact) a specific legislative act have standing to sue if that legislative action goes into effect (or does not go into effect), on the ground that their votes have been completely nullified." 521 U.S. at 823.

Here, plaintiffs had the votes "sufficient to defeat" "a specific legislative action" — they defeated a declaration of war (their constitutional claim) and they blocked a resolution approving the President's continuation of the war (their statutory claim). To follow precisely the formulation in *Raines*, they would have standing only if the legislative actions they defeated went "into effect." Obviously, this did not happen: war was not declared, and the President never maintained that he was prosecuting the war with the House's approval.

Plaintiffs' reply is that the President's military action against Yugoslavia without congressional authorization had the effect of completely nullifying their votes, of making their votes worthless. With respect to their vote against declaring war, that clearly is not true. A congressional declaration of war carries with it profound consequences. The United States Code is thick with laws expanding executive power "in time of war." Under these laws, the President's authority over industries, the use of land, and the terms and conditions of military employment is greatly enhanced. A declaration of war may also have the effect of decreasing commercial choices and curtailing civil liberties.

> **FN6.** Although the United States has committed its armed forces into combat more than a hundred times, Congress has declared war only five times: the War of 1812, the Mexican-American War of 1848, the Spanish-American War of 1898, World War I, and World War II.

The vote of the House on April 28, 1999, deprived President Clinton of these powers. The vote against declaring war followed immediately upon the vote not to require immediate withdrawal. Those who voted against a declaration of war did so to deprive the President of the authority to expand hostilities beyond the bombing campaign and, specifically, to deprive him of the authority to introduce ground troops into the conflict. *See* 145 CONG. REC. H2427–41 (daily ed. Apr. 28, 1999). There is no suggestion that despite the vote, President Clinton invaded Yugoslavia by land or took some other action authorized only during a declared war. It follows that plaintiffs' votes against declaring war were not for naught. For that reason, plaintiffs do not have standing to sue on their constitutional claim.

As to their claim under the War Powers Resolution, the beauty of this measure, or one of its defects (see the Addendum to this opinion), is in its automatic operation: unless a majority of both Houses declares war, or approves continuation of hostilities beyond 60 days, or Congress is "physically unable to meet as a result of an armed attack upon the United States," the Resolution requires the President to withdraw the troops. 50 U.S.C. § 1544(b). The President has nothing to veto. Congress may allow the time to run without taking any vote, or it may—as the House did here—take a vote and fail to muster a majority in favor of continuing the hostilities.

To put the matter in terms of *Raines* once again, plaintiffs had the votes "sufficient to defeat" "a specific legislative action"—they blocked a resolution authorizing the President's continuation of the war with Yugoslavia—but it is not true, in the language of *Raines*, that this "legislative action" nevertheless went "into effect." Congressional authorization simply did not occur. The President may have acted as if he had Congress's approval, or he may have acted as if he did not need it. Either way, plaintiffs' real complaint is not that the President ignored their votes; it is that he ignored the War Powers Resolution, and hence the votes of an earlier Congress, which enacted the law over President Nixon's veto. It is hard for me to see that this amounts to anything more than saying: "We, the members of Congress, have standing because the President violated one of our laws." To hold that Members of Congress may litigate on such a basis strikes me as highly problematic, not only because the principle is unconfined but also because it raises very serious separation-of-powers concerns. But because the case is moot, I need say no more.... [Judge Randolph argued that the case was moot because "All agree that the 'hostilities' ended by June 21, 1999, after NATO's Secretary General announced the official termination of the air campaign and Secretary of Defense Cohen announced the redeployment of more than 300 U.S. aircraft back to their home bases."]

TATEL, Circuit Judge, concurring.

Although I agree with Judge Silberman that Raines v. Byrd, 521 U.S. 811 (1997), as interpreted by this court in Chenoweth v. Clinton, 181 F.3d 112 (D.C. Cir. 1999), deprives plaintiffs of standing to bring this action, I do not share his view that the case poses a nonjusticiable political question. In my view, were this case brought by plaintiffs with standing, we could determine whether the President, in undertaking the air campaign in Yugoslavia, exceeded his authority under the Constitution or the War Powers Resolution.

To begin with, I do not agree that courts lack judicially discoverable and manageable standards for "determining the existence of a 'war.'" Whether the military activity in Yugoslavia amounted to "war" within the meaning of the Declare War Clause, Art. I, § 8, cl. 11, is no more standardless than any other question regarding the constitutionality of government action. Precisely what police conduct violates the Fourth Amendment guarantee "against unreasonable searches and seizures?" When does government action amount to "an establishment of religion" prohibited by the First Amendment? When is an election district so bizarrely shaped as to violate the Fourteenth Amendment guarantee of "equal protection of the laws?" Because such constitutional terms are not self-defining, standards for answering these questions have evolved, as legal standards always do, through years of judicial decisionmaking. Courts have proven no less capable of developing standards to resolve war powers challenges.

Since the earliest years of the nation, courts have not hesitated to determine when military action constitutes "war." In Bas v. Tingy, 4 U.S. 37 (1800), the Supreme Court had to decide whether hostilities between France and the United States amounted to a state of war in order to resolve disputes over captured ships. Because outright war had not been declared, the justices examined both the facts of the conflict ("the scene of bloodshed, depredation and confiscation, which has unhappily occurred"), and the acts of Congress that had authorized limited military action: "In March 1799, congress had raised an army; stopped all intercourse with France; dissolved our treaty; built and equip ships of war; and commissioned private armed ships; enjoining the former, and authorizing the latter, to defend themselves against the armed ships of France, to attack them on the high seas, to subdue and take them as prize, and to re-capture armed vessels found in their possession." Given these events, Justice Bushrod Washington concluded that France and the United States were at war both "in fact and in law." Id. at 42. "If they were not our enemies," he said, "I know not what constitutes an enemy." One year later, Chief Justice Marshall, focusing on the same conflict with France, said: "The whole powers of war being, by the constitution of the United States, vested in congress, the acts of that body can alone be resorted to as our guides in this enquiry.... To determine the real situation of America in regard to France, the acts of congress are to be inspected." Talbot v. Seeman, 5 U.S. 1, 28 (1801).

Half a century later, in The Prize Cases, 67 U.S. 635, 666 (1862), the Court had to determine whether a state of war, though undeclared, existed "de facto" between the United States and the confederacy, and if so, whether it justified the U.S. naval blockade of confederate ports. "As a civil war is never publicly proclaimed, ... its actual existence is a fact in our domestic history which the Court is bound to notice and to know." There was no formal declaration of war, the Court explained, because the Constitution does not permit Congress to "declare war against a State, or any number of States." Yet the Court, guided by the definition of war as "that state in which a nation prosecutes its right by force," determined that a state of war actually existed.... In making this determination, the Court looked to the facts of the conflict, to the acts of foreign governments recognizing the war and declaring their neutrality, and to congressional action authorizing the President's use of force....

More recent cases have also recognized the competence of courts to determine whether a state of war exists. Responding to a challenge to the constitutionality of the Vietnam War, this circuit confronted "the critical question ... whether the hostilities in Indo-China constitute *in the Constitutional sense* a 'war,' both within and beyond the meaning of that term in Article I, Section 8, Clause 11." Mitchell v. Laird, 488 F.2d 611, 614 (D.C. Cir. 1973) (emphasis added). The court found "no insuperable difficulty in a court determining whether," given the extent of the hostilities, "there has been a war in Indo-China." Id. Once the war was recognized as such, the court saw no problem in "facing up to the question as to whether because of the war's duration and magnitude the President is or was without power to continue the war without Congressional approval," or "whether Congress has given, in a Constitutionally satisfactory form, the approval requisite for a war of considerable duration and magnitude." Id. Nor did the court hesitate to determine that once the Gulf of Tonkin resolution had been repealed, later congressional actions appropriating funds for the war and extending the draft were insufficient to "serve as a valid assent to the Vietnam war." 488 F.2d at 615. Given this absence of congressional approval for the war's continuation, the President had a duty to try "in good faith and to the best of his ability, to bring the war to an end as promptly as was consistent with the safety of those fighting and with a profound concern for the durable interests of the na-tion—its defense, its honor, its morality." Id. at 616. Although the court ultimately declined to answer the question whether President Nixon was in fact fulfilling his duty to end the Vietnam War, it nonetheless made clear that courts are competent to adjudge the existence of war and the allocation of war powers between the President and Congress. Regardless of whether this language is dicta, see *supra* (Silberman, J., concurring), Mitchell supports my view that this court could resolve the war powers claims presented here. See also, e.g., Massachusetts v. Laird, 451 F.2d 26, 34 (1st Cir. 1971) ("The war in Vietnam is a product of the jointly supportive actions of the two branches to whom the congeries of the war powers have been committed. Because the branches are not in opposition, there is no necessity of determining boundaries. Should either branch be opposed to the continuance of hostilities, however, and present the issue in clear terms, a court might well take a different view."); Orlando v. Laird, 443 F.2d 1039, 1042 (2d Cir. 1971) ("The constitutional delegation of the war-declaring power to the Congress contains a discoverable and manageable standard imposing on the Congress a duty of mutual participation in the prosecution of war. Judicial scrutiny of that duty, therefore, is not foreclosed by the political question doctrine."); Berk v. Laird, 429 F.2d 302, 305 (2d Cir. 1970) ("History makes clear that the congressional power 'to declare War' conferred by Article I, section 8, of the Constitution was intended as an explicit restriction upon the power of the Executive to initiate war on his own prerogative which was enjoyed by the British sovereign.... Executive officers are under a threshold constitutional duty which can be judicially identified and its breach judicially determined.") (internal quotation marks and brackets omitted).

Without undue difficulty, courts have also determined whether hostilities amount to "war" in other contexts. These have included insurance policies and other contracts, the Federal Tort Claims Act, and provisions of military criminal law applicable "in time of war."

Although courts have thus determined the existence of war as defined by the Constitution, statutes, and contracts, in this case plaintiffs' War Powers Resolution claim would not even require that we do so. We would need to ask only whether, and at what time, "United States Armed Forces [were] introduced into hostilities or into situations where imminent involvement in hostilities [was] clearly indicated by the circumstances." 50 U.S.C. § 1543(a)(1). On this question, the record is clear. In his report to the Speaker of the House and the President pro tempore of the Senate, transmitted "consistent with the War Powers Resolution," President Clinton stated: "on March 24, 1999, U.S. military forces, at my direction ... began a series of air strikes in the Federal Republic of Yugoslavia...." 35 Weekly Comp. Pres. Doc. 527 (March 26, 1999), available at 1999 WL 12654381. Pursuant to the priority procedures of the War Powers Resolution, 50 U.S.C. §§ 1545–46, both houses of Congress responded by expediting consideration of resolutions to declare war, H.J. Res. 44, to authorize airstrikes, S.J. Res. 20, and to withdraw troops, H. Con. Res. 82. Defense Secretary William Cohen told the Senate Armed Services Committee: "We're certainly engaged in hostilities, we're engaged in combat." Hearing on Kosovo, Senate Armed Services Comm., 106th Cong., April 15, 1999, 1999 WL 221637 (testimony of William Cohen, Secretary of Defense). President Clinton issued an Executive Order designating the region a U.S. combat zone and March 24 as "the date of the commencement of combatant activities in such zone." Exec. Order No. 13,119, 64 Fed. Reg. 18797 (Apr. 13, 1999).

The undisputed facts of this case are equally compelling with respect to plaintiffs' constitutional claim. If in 1799 the Supreme Court could recognize that sporadic battles between American and French vessels amounted to a state of war, and if in 1862 it could examine the record of hostilities and conclude that a state of war existed with the confederacy, then surely we, looking to similar evidence, could determine whether months of daily airstrikes involving 800 U.S. aircraft flying more than 20,000 sorties and causing thousands of enemy casualties amounted to "war" within the meaning of Article I, section 8, clause 11.

Determining whether a state of war exists would certainly be more difficult in situations involving more limited military force over a shorter period of time. But just as we never shrink from deciding a First Amendment case simply because we can imagine a more difficult one, the fact that a challenge to a different military action might present a closer question would not justify abdicating our responsibility to construe the law and apply it to the facts of this case.

Nor is the question nonjusticiable because the President, as Commander in Chief, possesses emergency authority to use military force to defend the nation from attack without obtaining prior congressional approval. Judge Silberman's suggestion notwithstanding, President Clinton does not claim that the air campaign was necessary to protect the nation from imminent attack. In his report to Congress, the President explained that the military action was "in response to the [Federal Republic of Yugoslavia] government's continued campaign of violence and repression against the ethnic Albanian population in Kosovo." 35 Weekly Comp. Pres. Doc. 527 (Mar. 26, 1999). Although the President also said that military action would prevent an expanded war in Europe, *see* Radio Address of the President to the Nation, March 27, 1999, he never claimed that an emergency required him to act without congressional authorization; in fact, the Kosovo issue had been festering for years. *See* Declaration of Thomas Pickering, Undersecretary of State for Political Affairs.

The government also claims that this case is nonjusticiable because it "requires a political, not a judicial, judgment." The government has it backwards. Resolving the issue in this case would require us to decide not whether the air campaign was wise — a "policy choice[] and value determination[] constitutionally committed for resolution to the halls of Congress or the confines of the Executive Branch," — but whether the President possessed legal authority to conduct the military operation. Did the President exceed his constitutional authority as Commander in Chief? Did he intrude on Congress's power to declare war? Did he violate the War Powers Resolution? Presenting purely legal issues, these questions call on us to perform one of the most important functions of Article III courts: determining the proper constitutional allocation of power among the branches of government. Although our answer could well have political implications, "the presence of constitutional issues with significant political overtones does not auto- matically invoke the political question doctrine. Resolution of litigation challenging the constitutional authority of one of the three branches cannot be evaded by courts because the issues have political implications...." INS v. Chadha, 462 U.S. 919, 942–43 (1983). See also Baker v. Carr, 369 U.S. 186, 217 (1962) ("The doctrine ... is one of 'political questions,' not one of 'political cases.' The courts cannot reject as 'no law suit' a bona fide controversy as to whether some action denominated 'political' exceeds constitutional authority."). This is so even where, as here (and as in the other cases discussed above), the issue relates to foreign policy. See Baker, 369 U.S. at 211 ("It is error to suppose that every case or controversy which touches foreign relations lies beyond judicial cognizance"). If "we cannot shirk [our] responsibility" to decide whether an Act of Congress requires the President to impose economic sanctions on a foreign nation for diminishing the ef- fectiveness of an international treaty, a question rife with "political overtones," Japan Whaling Ass'n, 478 U.S. at 230, then surely we cannot shirk our responsibility to decide whether the President exceeded his constitutional or statutory authority by conducting the air campaign in Yugoslavia.

The Government's final argument—that entertaining a war powers challenge risks the government speaking with "multifarious voices" on a delicate issue of foreign policy—fails for similar reasons. Because courts are the final arbiters of the constitutionality of the President's actions, "there is no possibility of 'multifarious pronouncements' on this question." Chadha, 462 U.S. at 942. Any short-term confusion that judicial action might instill in the mind of an authoritarian enemy, or even an ally, is but a small price to pay for preserving the constitutional separation of powers and protecting the bedrock constitutional principle that "it is emphatically the province and duty of the judicial department to say what the law is." Marbury v. Madison, 5 U.S. 137 (1803).

Review Questions and Explanations: *Campbell v. Clinton*

1. There are two parallel disputes among the three judges in this case. Silberman and Randolph disagree on some fine points of legislative standing that are not pertinent here and are omitted from the excerpts. Silberman and Randolph agree that in this case, the legislators had political remedies available to them that precluded them from obtaining relief from a court. (Randolph's opinion is included here because it elaborates that theme, while also providing useful background information not included in Silberman's opinion for the court.) Silberman and Tatel disagree over whether the case presents a non-justiciable political question. Silberman says it does; Tatel says it doesn't: a court could adjudicate a claimed violation of the War Powers Resolution if a party had standing. Note that since the case was dismissed because these plaintiffs *did not* have standing, the entire discussion of the political question doctrine is dicta. But the Silberman and Tatel concurrences do a good job of articulating the arguments for and against a judicial role in deciding whether the War Powers Resolution has been violated.

2. Do you agree with the argument in the opinion of the Court and the Randolph concurrence that legislators who have lost a vote should not be allowed to go to court to obtain a judicial order giving them what they failed to accomplish in the legislature? Why or why not? Is your answer different in this context than it would be if legislators wanted to challenge a piece of domestic legislation, such as President Obama's Patient Protection and Affordable Care Act?

3. On what grounds does Silberman (in his concurrence) argue that a court cannot (or should not) determine whether the War Powers Resolution has been violated by the President? On what grounds does Tatel disagree? Who is right?

Recap: War Powers

1. Can federal courts ever decide whether a President's use of military force (a) violates a statute or (b) is unconstitutional? To answer this question, try to identify the relevant precedents and determine which way they point.

2. In "lining up the precedents" for question 1, should you rely only on judicial precedents, or can you use "historical" precedents (actual historical episodes of presidential and congressional action) as well? Does the Supreme Court have anything to say about the use of "historical precedents" in constitutional argument?

3. Should the Supreme Court have ruled on the legality of the Vietnam War, as Justice Douglas argued? If so, how should it have ruled? Would your answer differ if the War Powers Resolution had been in place at the time?

---

2. Suspension of Habeas Corpus

Article I, § 9, cl. 2 provides: "The privilege of the writ of habeas corpus shall not be suspended, unless when in cases of rebellion or invasion the public safety may require it." Issues regarding "war power" frequently arise in relation to this clause, because detention—imprisonment—and other punishments often are resorted to in the name of enhancing security. Prisoners of war, spies and saboteurs, "enemy aliens," suspected enemy sympathizers, and even, alas, pacifists, war protesters, and citizens ethnically descended from the enemy nation have been detained in wartime. A related problem arises because of the practice of resorting to military courts and tribunals during times of armed conflict, to try both combatants and non-combatants for alleged crimes.

Because habeas corpus is a traditional remedy to challenge the legality of detention, it contemplates a role for the courts, even in times of war, to hear the claims of detained persons. In addition, the legality of an effort by the President or Congress to substitute military justice procedures for the Article III (civilian) judiciary raises constitutional concerns that relate to the Suspension Clause. Significantly, by its own terms, the Suspension Clause is a war-related power, but is not necessarily triggered by all wars: the clause speaks only of "cases of rebellion and invasion."

The following cases and materials are not intended to be an exhaustive history the suspension of habeas corpus and challenges to the Article III courts in times of war or national security crisis. We do provide cases from what are arguably the three leading historical episodes in which these issues have arisen: the Civil War; World War II; and the contemporary "war on terrorism," including the related wars in Iraq and Afghanistan.

In reading the cases and materials on the suspension of habeas corpus, it is crucial as constitutional lawyers to keep in mind the important distinction between challenges to governmental action based on separation of powers, and challenges based on claims of individual rights—such as the rights to due process, equal protection, and trial upon indictment by a grand jury in the Fifth Amendment,[1] and the Sixth Amendment rights to counsel and trial by jury. To be sure, separation of powers is intended in part to protect the liberties of the people: Supreme Court opinions are filled with quotations to that effect from the Founders. Nevertheless, a separation-of-powers argument is based on the idea that a particular branch of government lacks the power to do what it did. An individual rights argument, in contrast, is based on the idea that no one in the federal government, regardless of the branch he or she is situated in, can do the thing objected to. One, the other, or both of these arguments may be present in any of the particular cases and historical examples that follow, but your attention at this point should remain firmly on the separation-of-powers issue.

---

1. The Fifth Amendment contains a due process clause, but unlike the Fourteenth, it has no "equal protection" clause. Nevertheless, the Supreme Court has held that the Fifth Amendment implicitly guarantees a right to equal protection of the laws. *See Bolling v. Sharp*, discussed in Chapter 8; *see also Korematsu v. United States* (Murphy, dissenting) (arguing that racial discrimination violated the Fifth Amendment guarantee of due process of law).

a. The Civil War

In the previous section, we briefly outline some of the circumstances present at the outbreak of the Civil War that led to President Lincoln's blockade proclamation. As we mentioned there, the Union military forces were seriously understaffed in April 1861, and Washington D.C. was threatened with being cut off from the loyal northern states, located as it was between Virginia and a vocally pro-secessionist population in southern Maryland. It is difficult to conceive of the anxiety President Lincoln and the government in Washington must have felt as they heard reports of pro-southern riots in Baltimore and sabotage of telegraph and rail lines running north from Washington. Lincoln's need to maintain order and open communications while awaiting the arrival of the first regiments of volunteers from Massachusetts and New York might help place in context his proclamation suspending habeas corpus. The suspension would allow federal authorities greater latitude to jail dissidents and suspected saboteurs in Maryland. Concern that local judges and juries might be in sympathy with the seceding states might help also explain Lincoln's resort to military tribunals to try offenders. Recall, too, that Congress was not in session and did not convene until July.

Regardless of the reasons, in April 1861, Lincoln issued a proclamation suspending habeas corpus in parts of Maryland and Pennsylvania. Unlike its response to Lincoln's blockade of the southern ports, Congress failed to ratify the president's action when it convened in July: A joint resolution that would have approved the President's suspension of habeas was filibustered by Democratic senators. The following February, 1862, Lincoln retracted the suspension and ordered the release of all "political prisoners." However, in September 1862, in the face of increasing incidents of interference with military conscription and recruitment, President Lincoln issued a new proclamation suspending habeas corpus for "all persons discouraging volunteer enlistments, resisting militia drafts, or guilty of any disloyal practice, affording aid and comfort to Rebels against the authority of the United States," and ordering that they "shall be subject to martial law and liable to trial and punishment by Courts Martial or Military Commission."

Congress did not take action on the question of habeas corpus suspension until it enacted a Habeas Corpus Suspension Act on March 3, 1863. Only a handful of Supreme Court decisions dealt with habeas corpus during the war. We first present the text of the Habeas Corpus Suspension Act, followed by President Lincoln's proclamation pursuant to that Act. It was this latter suspension of habeas corpus which was reviewed in *Ex Parte Milligan* (presented below), the most prominent habeas corpus case arising out of the Civil War.

An Act Relating to Habeas Corpus, and Regulating Judicial Proceedings in Certain Cases

March 3, 1863

Be it enacted by the Senate and House of Representatives of the United States of America in Congress assembled, That, during the present rebellion, the President of the United States, whenever, in his judgment, the public safety may require it, is authorized to suspend the privilege of the writ of habeas corpus in any case throughout the United States, or any part thereof. And whenever and wherever the said privilege shall be suspended, as aforesaid, no military or other officer shall be compelled, in answer to any writ of habeas corpus, to return the body of any person or persons detained by him by authority of the President; but upon the certificate, under oath, of the officer having charge of any one so detained that such person is detained by him as a prisoner under authority of the President, further proceedings under the writ of habeas corpus shall be suspended by the judge or court having issued the said writ, so long as said suspension by the President shall remain in force, and said rebellion continue.

Sec. 2. And be it further enacted, That the Secretary of State and the Secretary of War be, and they are hereby, directed, as soon as may be practicable, to furnish to the judges of the circuit and district courts of the United States and of the District of Columbia a list of the names of all persons, citizens of states in which the administration of the laws has continued unimpaired in the said Federal courts, who are now, or may hereafter be, held as prisoners of the United States, by order or authority of the President of the United States or either of said Secretaries, in any fort, arsenal, or other place, as state or political prisoners, or otherwise than as prisoners of war; the said list to contain the names of all those who reside in the respective jurisdictions of said judges, or who may be deemed by the said Secretaries, or either of them, to have violated any law of the United States in any of said jurisdictions, and also the date of each arrest; the Secretary of State to furnish a list of such persons as are imprisoned by the order or authority of the President, acting through the State Department, and the Secretary of War a list of such as are imprisoned by the order or authority of the President, acting through the Department of War. And in all cases where a grand jury, having attended any of said courts having jurisdiction in the premises, after the passage of this act, and after the furnishing of said list, as aforesaid, has terminated its session without finding an indictment or presentment, or other proceeding against any such person, it shall be the duty of the judge of said court forthwith to make an order that any such prisoner desiring a discharge from said imprisonment be brought before him to be discharged; and every officer of the United States having custody of such prisoner is hereby directed immediately to obey and execute said judge's order; and in case he shall delay or refuse so to do, he shall be subject to indictment for a misdemeanor, and be punished by a fine of not less than five hundred dollars and imprisonment in the common jail for a period not less than six months, in the discretion of the court: Provided, however, That no person shall be discharged by virtue of the provisions of this act until after he or she shall have taken an oath of allegiance to the Government of the United States, and to support the Constitution thereof; and that he or she will not hereafter in any way encourage or give aid and comfort to the present rebellion, or the supporters thereof: And provided, also, That the judge or court before whom such person may be brought, before discharging him or her from imprisonment, shall have power, on examination of the case, and, if the public safety shall require it, shall be required to cause him or her to enter into recognizance, with or without surety, in a sum to be fixed by said judge or court, to keep the peace and be of good behavior towards the United States and its citizens, and from time to time, and at such times as such judge or court may direct, appear before said judge or court to be further dealt with, according to law, as the circumstances may require. And it shall be the duty of the district attorney of the United States to attend such examination before the judge....

Sec. 4. And be it further enacted, That any order of the President, or under his authority, made at any time during the existence of the present rebellion, shall be a defence in all courts to any action or prosecution, civil or criminal, pending, or to be commenced, for any search, seizure, arrest, or imprisonment, made, done, or committed, or acts omitted to be done, under and by virtue of such order, or under color of any law of Congress, and such defence may be made by special plea, or under the general issue.

[Section 5 provided that any civil *or criminal* action against a federal officer for false arrest or related claims resulting under arrest or imprisonment pursuant to the a presidential suspension of habeas corpus could be removed to federal court.]

Lincoln's Proclamation Suspending Habeas Corpus throughout the United States, September 15, 1863

By the President of the United States of America.

A PROCLAMATION.

Whereas, the Constitution of the United States has ordained that the privilege of the Writ of Habeas Corpus shall not be suspended unless when, in cases of rebellion or invasion, the public safety may require it;

And Whereas, a rebellion was existing on the third day of March, 1863, which rebellion is still existing;

And Whereas, by a statute which was approved on that day, it was enacted by the Senate and House of Representatives of the United States, in Congress assembled, that during the present insurrection, the President of the United States, whenever in his judgment the public safety may require, is authorized to suspend the privilege of the Writ of Habeas Corpus in any case throughout the United States or any part thereof;

And Whereas, in the judgment of the President, the public safety does require that the privilege of the said Writ shall now be suspended throughout the United States in the cases where, by the authority of the President of the United States, military, naval, and civil officers of the United States, or any of them, hold persons under their command or in their custody, either as prisoners of war, spies, or aiders or abettors of the enemy, or officers, soldiers, or seamen enrolled or drafted or mustered or enlisted in or belonging to the land or naval forces of the United States, or as deserters therefrom, or otherwise amenable to military law or the rules and articles of war or the rules or regulations prescribed for the military or naval services by authority of the President of the United States, or for resisting a draft, or for any other offense against the military or naval service:

Now Therefore, I, Abraham Lincoln, President of the United States, do hereby proclaim and make known to all whom it may concern that the privilege of the Writ of Habeas Corpus is suspended throughout the United States in the several cases before mentioned, and that this suspension will continue throughout the duration of the said rebellion or until this proclamation shall, by a subsequent one to be issued by the President of the United States, be modified or revoked. And I do hereby require all magistrates, attorneys, and other civil officers within the United States and all officers and others in the military and naval services of the United States to take distinct notice of this suspension and to give it full effect, and all citizens of the United States to conduct and govern themselves accordingly and in conformity with the Constitution of the United States and the laws of Congress in such case made and provided.

IN TESTIMONY WHEREOF, I have hereunto set my hand, and caused the seal of the United States to be affixed, this fifteenth day of September, in the year of our Lord, one thousand, eight hundred and sixty-three, and of the Independence of the United States of America the eighty-eighth.

By the President:

[ABRAHAM LINCOLN]

WILLIAM H. SEWARD,

Secretary of State.

Guided Reading Questions: *Ex Parte Milligan*

1. The *Milligan* majority and President Lincoln, in his suspension proclamation, make different assumptions about what follows from a suspension of habeas corpus. The Court acknowledges that the writ of habeas corpus can be suspended under the Constitution. But then what? What does President Lincoln assume can be done with prisoners arrested pursuant to suspension of the writ? Is this consistent with the Suspension Act?

2. What does the majority mean by martial law, and how does that bear on the decision?

3. What is the rationale of the concurrence in the judgment in *Milligan*? Why does that opinion focus so much on the Suspension Act, and the majority focus so little on it?

4. The concurring opinion seems to argue that Milligan had to be released from military custody under the terms of the March 3, 1863 habeas corpus suspension act. What about the majority opinion? Does it hold that there are constitutional limits on the circumstances that justify suspension of habeas corpus? If so, what are those limits?

Ex Parte Milligan
71 U.S. 2 (1866)

Majority: *Davis*, Nelson, Grier, Clifford, Field

Concurrence in the judgment: *Chase* (CJ), Wayne, Swayne, Miller

[Lambdin Milligan became involved in a plot in 1864 to raid federal armories in Indiana and use the weapons to liberate confederate prisoners of war held in northern camps and conduct guerilla warfare in the North. The conspiracy fell apart before it accomplished anything, and Milligan was arrested and tried by military tribunal and sentenced to death. He petitioned for habeas corpus, and his case was heard by the Supreme Court the year after the war ended.]

MR. JUSTICE DAVIS delivered the opinion of the court.

.... During the late wicked Rebellion, the temper of the times did not allow that calmness in deliberation and discussion so necessary to a correct conclusion of a purely judicial question. Then, considerations of safety were mingled with the exercise of power; and feelings and interests prevailed which are happily terminated. Now that the public safety is assured, this question, as well as all others, can be discussed and decided without passion or the admixture of any element not required to form a legal judgment. We approach the investigation of this case, fully sensible of the magnitude of the inquiry and the necessity of full and cautious deliberation....

The controlling question in the case is this: Upon the facts stated in Milligan's petition, and the exhibits filed, had the military commission mentioned in it jurisdiction, legally, to try and sentence him? Milligan, not a resident of one of the rebellious states, or a prisoner of war, but a citizen of Indiana for twenty years past, and never in the military or naval service, is, while at his home, arrested by the military power of the United States, imprisoned, and, on certain criminal charges preferred against him, tried, convicted, and sentenced to be hanged by a military commission, organized under the direction of the military commander of the military district of Indiana. Had this tribunal the legal power and authority to try and punish this man?

No graver question was ever considered by this court, nor one which more nearly concerns the rights of the whole people; for it is the birthright of every American citizen when charged with crime, to be tried and punished according to law.... By the protection of the law human rights are secured; withdraw that protection, and they are at the mercy of wicked rulers, or the clamor of an excited people....

[The Founders] foresaw that troublous times would arise, when rules and people would become restive under restraint, and seek by sharp and decisive measures to accomplish ends deemed just and proper; and that the principles of constitutional liberty would be in peril, unless established by irrepealable law. The history of the world had taught them that what was done in the past might be attempted in the future. The Constitution of the United States is a law for rulers and people, equally in war and in peace, and covers with the shield of its protection all classes of men, at all times, and under all circumstances. No doctrine, involving more pernicious consequences, was ever invented by the wit of man than that any of its provisions can be suspended during any of the great exigencies of government. Such a doctrine leads directly to anarchy or despotism, but the theory of necessity on which it is based is false; for the government, within the Constitution, has all the powers granted to it, which are necessary to preserve its existence; as has been happily proved by the result of the great effort to throw off its just authority....

Every trial involves the exercise of judicial power; and from what source did the military commission that tried him derive their authority? Certainly no part of the judicial power of the country was conferred on them; because the Constitution expressly vests it "in one supreme court and such inferior courts as the Congress may from time to time ordain and establish," and it is not pretended that the commission was a court ordained and established by Congress. They cannot justify on the mandate of the President; because he is controlled by law, and has his appropriate sphere of duty, which is to execute, not to make, the laws; and there is "no unwritten criminal code to which resort can be had as a source of jurisdiction."

But it is said that the jurisdiction is complete under the "laws and usages of war."

It can serve no useful purpose to inquire what those laws and usages are, whence they originated, where found, and on whom they operate; they can never be applied to citizens in states which have upheld the authority of the government, and where the courts are open and their process unobstructed. This court has judicial knowledge that in Indiana the Federal authority was always unopposed, and its courts always open to hear criminal accusations and redress grievances; and no usage of war could sanction a military trial there for any offence whatever of a citizen in civil life, in nowise connected with the military service. Congress could grant no such power; and to the honor of our national legislature be it said, it has never been provoked by the state of the country even to attempt its exercise. One of the plainest constitutional provisions was, therefore, infringed when Milligan was tried by a court not ordained and established by Congress, and not composed of judges appointed during good behavior.

Why was he not delivered to the Circuit Court of Indiana to be proceeded against according to law? No reason of necessity could be urged against it; because Congress had declared penalties against the offences charged, provided for their punishment, and directed that court to hear and determine them. And soon after this military tribunal was ended, the Circuit Court met, peacefully transacted its business, and adjourned. It needed no bayonets to protect it, and required no military aid to execute its judgments. It was held in a state, eminently distinguished for patriotism, by judges commissioned during the Rebellion, who were provided with juries, upright, intelligent, and selected by a marshal appointed by the President. The government had no right to conclude that Milligan, if guilty, would not receive in that court merited punishment; for its records disclose that it was constantly engaged in the trial of similar offences, and was never interrupted in its administration of criminal justice....

The discipline necessary to the efficiency of the army and navy, required other and swifter modes of trial than are furnished by the common law courts; and, in pursuance of the power conferred by the Constitution, Congress has declared the kinds of trial, and the manner in which they shall be conducted, for offences committed while the party is in the military or naval service. Every one connected with these branches of the public service is amenable to the jurisdiction which Congress has created for their government, and, while thus serving, surrenders his right to be tried by the civil courts. All other persons, citizens of states where the courts are open, if charged with crime, are guaranteed the inestimable privilege of trial by jury....

It is claimed that.... when war exists, foreign or domestic, and the country is subdivided into military departments for mere convenience, the commander of one of them can, if he chooses, within his limits, on the plea of necessity, with the approval of the Executive, substitute military force for and to the exclusion of the laws, and punish all persons, as he thinks right and proper, without fixed or certain rules.

The statement of this proposition shows its importance; for, if true, republican government is a failure, and there is an end of liberty regulated by law. Martial law, established on such a basis, destroys every guarantee of the Constitution, and effectually renders the "military independent of and superior to the civil power"—the attempt to do which by the King of Great Britain was deemed by our fathers such an offence, that they assigned it to the world as one of the causes which impelled them to declare their independence. Civil liberty and this kind of martial law cannot endure together; the antagonism is irreconcilable; and, in the conflict, one or the other must perish....

It is essential to the safety of every government that, in a great crisis, like the one we have just passed through, there should be a power somewhere of suspending the writ of habeas corpus. In every war, there are men of previously good character, wicked enough to counsel their fellow-citizens to resist the measures deemed necessary by a good government to sustain its just authority and overthrow its enemies; and their influence may lead to dangerous combinations. In the emergency of the times, an immediate public investigation according to law may not be possible; and yet, the peril to the country may be too imminent to suffer such persons to go at large. Unquestionably, there is then an exigency which demands that the government, if it should see fit in the exercise of a proper discretion to make arrests, should not be required to produce the persons arrested in answer to a writ of habeas corpus. The Constitution goes no further. It does not say after a writ of habeas corpus is denied a citizen, that he shall be tried otherwise than by the course of the common law; if it had intended this result, it was easy by the use of direct words to have accomplished it. The illustrious men who framed that instrument were guarding the foundations of civil liberty against the abuses of unlimited power; they were full of wisdom, and the lessons of history informed them that a trial by an established court, assisted by an impartial jury, was the only sure way of protecting the citizen against oppression and wrong. Knowing this, they limited the suspension to one great right, and left the rest to remain forever inviolable....

It will be borne in mind that this is not a question of the power to proclaim martial law, when war exists in a community and the courts and civil authorities are overthrown. Nor is it a question what rule a military commander, at the head of his army, can impose on states in rebellion to cripple their resources and quell the insurrection.... If armies were collected in Indiana, they were to be employed in another locality, where the laws were obstructed and the national authority disputed. On her soil there was no hostile foot; if once invaded, that invasion was at an end, and with it all pretext for martial law. Martial law cannot arise from a threatened invasion. The necessity must be actual and present; the invasion real, such as effectually closes the courts and deposes the civil administration.

It is difficult to see how the safety of the country required martial law in Indiana. If any of her citizens were plotting treason, the power of arrest could secure them, until the government was prepared for their trial, when the courts were open and ready to try them....

.... If, in foreign invasion or civil war, the courts are actually closed, and it is impossible to administer criminal justice according to law, then, on the theatre of active military operations, where war really prevails, there is a necessity to furnish a substituted for the civil authority, thus overthrown, to preserve the safety of the army and society; and as no power is left but the military, it is allowed to govern by martial rule until the laws can have their free course. As necessity creates the rule, so it limits its duration; for, if this government is continued after the courts are reinstated, it is a gross usurpation of power. Martial rule can never exist where the courts are open, and in the proper and unobstructed exercise of their jurisdiction....

It is proper to say, although Milligan's trial and conviction by a military commission was illegal, yet, if guilty of the crimes imputed to him, and his guilt had been ascertained by an established court and impartial jury, he deserved severe punishment. Open resistance to the measures deemed necessary to subdue a great rebellion, by those who enjoy the protection of government, and have not the excuse even of prejudice of section to plead in their favor, is wicked; but that resistance becomes an enormous crime when it assumes the form of a secret political organization, armed to oppose the laws, and seeks by stealthy means to introduce the enemies of the country into peaceful communities, there to light the torch of civil war, and thus overthrow the power of the United States....

.... The suspension of the privilege of the writ of habeas corpus does not suspend the writ itself. The writ issues as a matter of course; and on the return made to it the court decides whether the party applying is denied the right of proceeding any further with it.

If the military trial of Milligan was contrary to law, then he was entitled, on the facts stated in his petition, to be discharged from custody by the terms of the act of Congress of March 3d, 1863....

The CHIEF JUSTICE delivered the following opinion.

Four members of the court, concurring with their brethren in the order heretofore made in this cause, but unable to concur in some important particulars with the opinion which has just been read, think it their duty to make a separate statement of their views of the whole case.

We do not doubt that the Circuit Court for the District of Indiana had jurisdiction of the petition of Milligan for the writ of habeas corpus....

The crimes with which Milligan was charged were of the gravest character, and the petition and exhibits in the record, which must here be taken as true, admit his guilt. But whatever his desert of punishment may be, it is more important to the country and to every citizen that he should not be punished under an illegal sentence, sanctioned by this court of last resort, than that he should be punished at all. The laws which protect the liberties of the whole people must not be violated or set aside in order to inflict, even upon the guilty, unauthorized though merited justice.

The trial and sentence of Milligan were by military commission convened in Indiana during the fall of 1864. The action of the commission had been under consideration by President Lincoln for some time, when he himself became the victim of an abhorred conspiracy. It was approved by his successor in May, 1865, and the sentence was ordered to be carried into execution. The proceedings, therefore, had the fullest sanction of the executive department of the government.

This sanction requires the most respectful and the most careful consideration of this court. The sentence which it supports must not be set aside except upon the clearest conviction that it cannot be reconciled with the Constitution and the constitutional legislation of Congress.

We must inquire, then, what constitutional or statutory provisions have relation to this military proceeding.

The act of Congress of March 3d, 1863, comprises all the legislation which seems to require consideration in this connection. The constitutionality of this act has not been questioned and is not doubted.

The first section authorized the suspension, during the Rebellion, of the writ of habeas corpus throughout the United States by the President. The two next sections limited this authority in important respects....

The holding of the Circuit and District Courts of the United States in Indiana had been uninterrupted. The administration of the laws in the Federal courts had remained unimpaired. Milligan was imprisoned under the authority of the President, and was not a prisoner of war. No list of prisoners had been furnished to the judges, either of the District or Circuit Courts, as required by the law. A grand jury had attended the Circuit Courts of the Indiana district, while Milligan was there imprisoned, and had closed its session without finding any indictment or presentment or otherwise proceeding against the prisoner.

His case was thus brought within the precise letter and intent of the act of Congress, unless it can be said that Milligan was not imprisoned by authority of the President; and nothing of this sort was claimed in argument on the part of the government.

It is clear upon this statement that the Circuit Court was bound to hear Milligan's petition for the writ of habeas corpus, called in the act an order to bring the prisoner before the judge or the court, and to issue the writ, or, in the language of the act, to make the order....

And it is equally clear that he was entitled to the discharge prayed for.

It must be borne in mind that the prayer of the petition was not for an absolute discharge, but to be delivered from military custody and imprisonment, and if found probably guilty of any offence, to be turned over to the proper tribunal for inquiry and punishment; or, if not found thus probably guilty, to be discharged altogether.

And the express terms of the act of Congress required this action of the court. The prisoner must be discharged on giving such recognizance as the court should require, not only for good behavior, but for appearance, as directed by the court, to answer and be further dealt with according to law....

The military commission could not have jurisdiction to try and sentence Milligan, if he could not be detained in prison under his original arrest or under sentence, after the close of a session of the grand jury without indictment or other proceeding against him.

Indeed, the act seems to have been framed on purpose to secure the trial of all offences of citizens by civil tribunals, in states where these tribunals were not interrupted in the regular exercise of their functions.

…. We do not think it necessary to look beyond these provisions [of the Act of March 3, 1863]. In them we find sufficient and controlling reasons for our conclusions.

But the [majority] opinion … goes further; and as we understand it, asserts not only that the military commission held in Indiana was not authorized by Congress, but that it was not in the power of Congress to authorize it; from which it may be thought to follow, that Congress has no power to indemnify the officers who composed the commission against liability in civil courts for acting as members of it.

We cannot agree to this…. We think that Congress had power, though not exercised, to authorize the military commission which was held in Indiana.

…. [W]hen the nation is involved in war, and some portions of the country are invaded, and all are exposed to invasion, it is within the power of Congress to determine in what states or districts such great and imminent public danger exists as justifies the authorization of military tribunals for the trial of crimes and offences against the discipline or security of the army or against the public safety.

Review Questions and Explanations: *Milligan*

1. What does the *Milligan* majority say about the power to suspend habeas corpus under the Suspension Clause? Does it address whether that power belongs to the President or Congress? Does it suggest that judgments about when a "rebellion or invasion" warrants suspension can be judicially reviewed? Does it express any views on the constitutionality of trying civilians in military tribunals?

2. On what basis do the justices concurring in the judgment disagree with the majority?

3. Does the opinion of Chief Justice Chase, concurring in the judgment, suggest that President Lincoln had exceeded his authority under the Suspension Act? If so, how?

4. The Chase opinion's statement about "indemnifying" officers reflected a concern that federal officials who participated in the arrest, detention, or military trial of persons under the Lincoln habeas suspension proclamation might be sued for damages in tort. Congress apparently tried to provide for this in sections 4 and 5 of the Suspension Act, by making obedience to presidential orders a defense in such cases and providing for removal of those cases to federal court.

---

b. World War II

Our inclusion of *Korematsu v. United States* in a habeas section of a casebook is unusual. The case is categorized in most Constitutional Law texts as an "equal protection" case about race discrimination. Moreover, it was argued and decided as an appeal from a criminal conviction in a federal (civilian) court, not as a habeas petition or a challenge to a military tribunal. Nevertheless, the case is highly relevant to the issue of Presidential war powers, since it was based on an "exclusion order" emanating from the President, pursuant to an act of Congress. As in other casebooks, you will read the majority opinion and Jackson dissent in the Equal Protection chapter of this book. You also will see the Jackson opinion in the discussion of justiciability in Chapter 6. Because the case does raise separation-of-powers concerns, we also include part of it here; specifically, the dissent of Justice Murphy.

Korematsu v. United States
323 U.S. 244 (1944)

MR. JUSTICE MURPHY, dissenting.

This exclusion of "all persons of Japanese ancestry, both alien and non-alien," from the Pacific Coast area on a plea of military necessity in the absence of martial law ought not to be approved. Such exclusion goes over "the very brink of constitutional power" and falls into the ugly abyss of racism.

In dealing with matters relating to the prosecution and progress of a war, we must accord great respect and consideration to the judgments of the military authorities who are on the scene and who have full knowledge of the military facts. The scope of their discretion must, as a matter of necessity and common sense, be wide. And their judgments ought not to be overruled lightly by those whose training and duties ill-equip them to deal intelligently with matters so vital to the physical security of the nation.

At the same time, however, it is essential that there be definite limits to military discretion, especially where martial law has not been declared. Individuals must not be left impoverished of their constitutional rights on a plea of military necessity that has neither substance nor support. Thus, like other claims conflicting with the asserted constitutional rights of the individual, the military claim must subject itself to the judicial process of having its reasonableness determined and its conflicts with other interests reconciled. "What are the allowable limits of military discretion, and whether or not they have been overstepped in a particular case, are judicial questions."

The judicial test of whether the Government, on a plea of military necessity, can validly deprive an individual of any of his constitutional rights is whether the deprivation is reasonably related to a public danger that is so "immediate, imminent, and impending" as not to admit of delay and not to permit the intervention of ordinary constitutional processes to alleviate the danger. Civilian Exclusion Order No. 34, banishing from a prescribed area of the Pacific Coast "all persons of Japanese ancestry, both alien and non-alien," clearly does not meet that test. Being an obvious racial discrimination, the order deprives all those within its scope of the equal protection of the laws as guaranteed by the Fifth Amendment. It further deprives these individuals of their constitutional rights to live and work where they will, to establish a home where they choose and to move about freely. In excommunicating them without benefit of hearings, this order also deprives them of all their constitutional rights to procedural due process. Yet no reasonable relation to an "immediate, imminent, and impending" public danger is evident to support this racial restriction which is one of the most sweeping and complete deprivations of constitutional rights in the history of this nation in the absence of martial law.

It must be conceded that the military and naval situation in the spring of 1942 was such as to generate a very real fear of invasion of the Pacific Coast, accompanied by fears of sabotage and espionage in that area. The military command was therefore justified in adopting all reasonable means necessary to combat these dangers. In adjudging the military action taken in light of the then apparent dangers, we must not erect too high or too meticulous standards; it is necessary only that the action have some reasonable relation to the removal of the dangers of invasion, sabotage and espionage. But the exclusion, either temporarily or permanently, of all persons with Japanese blood in their veins has no such reasonable relation. And that relation is lacking because the exclusion order necessarily must rely for its reasonableness upon the assumption that *all* persons of Japanese ancestry may have a dangerous tendency to commit sabotage and espionage and to aid our Japanese enemy in other ways. It is difficult to believe that reason, logic or experience could be marshaled in support of such an assumption.

That this forced exclusion was the result in good measure of this erroneous assumption of racial guilt rather than bona fide military necessity is evidenced by the Commanding General's Final Report on the evacuation from the Pacific Coast area. In it he refers to all individuals of Japanese descent as "subversive," as belonging to "an enemy race" whose "racial strains are undiluted," and as constituting "over 112,000 potential enemies ... at large today" along the Pacific Coast. In support of this blanket condemnation of all persons of Japanese descent, however, no reliable evidence is cited to show that such individuals were generally disloyal, or had generally so conducted themselves in this area as to constitute a special menace to defense installations or war industries, or had otherwise by their behavior furnished reasonable ground for their exclusion as a group.

Justification for the exclusion is sought, instead, mainly upon questionable racial and sociological grounds not ordinarily within the realm of expert military judgment, supplemented by certain semi-military conclusions drawn from an unwarranted use of circumstantial evidence. Individuals of Japanese ancestry are condemned because they are said to be "a large, unassimilated, tightly knit racial group, bound to an enemy nation by strong ties of race, culture, custom and religion." They are claimed to be given to "emperor worshipping ceremonies" and to "dual citizenship." Japanese language schools and allegedly pro-Japanese organizations are cited as evidence of possible group disloyalty, together with facts as to certain persons being educated and residing at length in Japan. It is intimated that many of these individuals deliberately resided "adjacent to strategic points," thus enabling them "to carry into execution a tremendous program of sabotage on a mass scale should any considerable number of them have been inclined to do so." The need for protective custody is also asserted....

The main reasons relied upon by those responsible for the forced evacuation, therefore, do not prove a reasonable relation between the group characteristics of Japanese Americans and the dangers of invasion, sabotage and espionage. The reasons appear, instead, to be largely an accumulation of much of the misinformation, half-truths and insinuations that for years have been directed against Japanese Americans by people with racial and economic prejudices—the same people who have been among the foremost advocates of the evacuation. A military judgment based upon such racial and sociological considerations is not entitled to the great weight ordinarily given the judgments based upon strictly military considerations. Especially is this so when every charge relative to race, religion, culture, geographical location, and legal and economic status has been substantially discredited by independent studies made by experts in these matters.

The military necessity which is essential to the validity of the evacuation order thus resolves itself into a few intimations that certain individuals actively aided the enemy, from which it is inferred that the entire group of Japanese Americans could not be trusted to be or remain loyal to the United States. No one denies, of course, that there were some disloyal persons of Japanese descent on the Pacific Coast who did all in their power to aid their ancestral land. Similar disloyal activities have been engaged in by many persons of German, Italian and even more pioneer stock in our country. But to infer that examples of individual disloyalty prove group disloyalty and justify discriminatory action against the entire group is to deny that under our system of law individual guilt is the sole basis for deprivation of rights. Moreover, this inference, which is at the very heart of the evacuation orders, has been used in support of the abhorrent and despicable treatment of minority groups by the dictatorial tyrannies which this nation is now pledged to destroy. To give constitutional sanction to that inference in this case, however well-intentioned may have been the military command on the Pacific Coast, is to adopt one of the cruelest of the rationales used by our enemies to destroy the dignity of the individual and to encourage and open the door to discriminatory actions against other minority groups in the passions of tomorrow.

No adequate reason is given for the failure to treat these Japanese Americans on an individual basis by holding investigations and hearings to separate the loyal from the disloyal, as was done in the case of persons of German and Italian ancestry. It is asserted merely that the loyalties of this group "were unknown and time was of the essence." Yet nearly four months elapsed after Pearl Harbor before the first exclusion order was issued; nearly eight months went by until the last order was issued; and the last of these "subversive" persons was not actually removed until almost eleven months had elapsed. Leisure and deliberation seem to have been more of the essence than speed. And the fact that conditions were not such as to warrant a declaration of martial law adds strength to the belief that the factors of time and military necessity were not as urgent as they have been represented to be.

Moreover, there was no adequate proof that the Federal Bureau of Investigation and the military and naval intelligence services did not have the espionage and sabotage situation well in hand during this long period. Nor is there any denial of the fact that not one person of Japanese ancestry was accused or convicted of espionage or sabotage after Pearl Harbor while they were still free, a fact which is some evidence of the loyalty of the vast majority of these individuals and of the effectiveness of the established methods of combatting these evils. It seems incredible that under these circumstances it would have been impossible to hold loyalty hearings for the mere 112,000 persons involved—or at least for the 70,000 American citizens—especially when a large part of this number represented children and elderly men and women. Any inconvenience that may have accompanied an attempt to conform to procedural due process cannot be said to justify violations of constitutional rights of individuals.

I dissent, therefore, from this legalization of racism. Racial discrimination in any form and in any degree has no justifiable part whatever in our democratic way of life. It is unattractive in any setting but it is utterly revolting among a free people who have embraced the principles set forth in the Constitution of the United States. All residents of this nation are kin in some way by blood or culture to a foreign land. Yet they are primarily and necessarily a part of the new and distinct civilization of the United States. They must accordingly be treated at all times as the heirs of the American experiment and as entitled to all the rights and freedoms guaranteed by the Constitution.

Review Questions and Explanations: *Korematsu v. United States*

1. If you have not read Justice Jackson's *Korematsu* dissent in Chapter 10, take a moment now to read the two-paragraph excerpt from that dissent presented

in section B of Chapter 6. Based on that excerpt, together with the Murphy dissent, what do you think of the proposition that the Court should have declined to rule on the case rather than placing a constitutional "stamp of approval" on the actions of the military authorities?

Try to write a short paragraph or bullet-point outline sketching out what an opinion taking such an approach should say. (You don't need to have studied the "political question" doctrine to have some ideas.)

2. Civilian Exclusion Order No. 34 was based on Executive Order No. 9066, issued by President Roosevelt on February 19, 1942. It provided for the exclusion and relocation of "any or all persons," including "residents," from "military areas" designated by the Secretary of War. The executive order claimed congressional authorization from federal criminal statutes prohibiting espionage and sabotage. No statute expressly authorized broad civilian exclusions from coastal areas. However, on March 21, 1942, Congress enacted the law under which Korematsu was charged, making it a crime to "enter, remain in, leave, or commit any act in any military area or military zone prescribed, under the authority of an Executive order of the President, by the Secretary of War, or by any military commander designated by the Secretary of War[.]" *Korematsu* was decided a decade before *Youngstown*; had *Youngstown* been on the books, which of Justice Jackson's three categories would have applied?

3. *Korematsu* is not technically a habeas case, but it in essence involved a massive detention order. Japanese-Americans were interned in camps away from the coast, and their freedom of movement was significantly restricted. Assuming that the exclusion order was authorized by Congress, is there nevertheless an argument that the Suspension Clause was violated?

4. Should the military situation, either at the time of the underlying events or the time of the judicial decision, affect the Court's constitutional rulings in wartime? Or should courts, given their insulation from politics, be able to look beyond (justified or excessive) wartime fears? The exclusion order had been issued in the Spring of 1942, when the United States was barely mobilized for war and Allied armed forces had experienced very little success. *Korematsu* was argued in October and decided on December 18, 1944, when (despite a temporary setback on December 16–19 in the opening days of the "Battle of the Bulge"), the Allied forces seemed headed for eventual victory.

5. German-Americans and Italian-Americans were not sent to internment camps. Does that call into question the rationale for the Japanese exclusion order? Coastal areas were not uniquely vulnerable to sabotage; one of the largest World War II munitions plants was in south-central Wisconsin, amidst a high-concentration of German-Americans. Note, too, that some German-Americans had formed outspoken pro-Nazi organizations before the U.S. entry into the war.

The next two cases, *Quirin* and *Eisentrager*, together with a third decision covered below in a case note, *Reid v. Covert*, have emerged as key precedents in the Supreme Court's recent decisions concerning detentions and military tribunals arising out of the armed conflicts in Iraq and Afghanistan, and the "war on terrorism."

When reading these cases, bear in mind a factual distinction between "courts martial" and "military commissions." The two are not identical: courts martial are more formal and employ the Federal Rules of Evidence, are presided over by legally trained judges, and follow many of the procedural safeguards used in federal criminal prosecutions. Military commissions may be composed and run in various ways, but do not follow strict evidence rules and may not have legally trained advocates or presiding judges. (Note: the term "military tribunal" is ambiguous. Sometimes it is used to mean a military commission; at other times, it appears to be used as a generic term encompassing both courts martial and military commissions.)

The following questions may be helpful both in understanding the two World War II era cases on their own terms as well as their impact as precedents in the present-day cases.

Guided Reading Questions: *Ex Parte Quirin; Eisentrager* and *Reid*

1. When reading *Quirin, Eisentrager,* and the *Reid* case note, keep track of the following elements of the decisions — indeed, you might want to try to array them in a chart.

    a) Are the habeas petitioners citizens or non-citizens? Military or civilian?

    b) Where were they arrested and imprisoned — in the United States or abroad? If abroad, what degree of control was exercised by United States authorities (e.g., was it a U.S. military base)?

    c) Were they tried by civilian authorities or military authorities? If they were United States military authorities, was the trial by court martial or by a military commission?

    d) Was there congressional authorization to try the person by military commission?

2. Try to articulate, if you can, the congressional authorization for a military commission in *Quirin*.

3. The "law of war" invoked in *Quirin* is the same concept that was discussed in *The Prize Cases* (the "ius belli"), a concept of customary international law. Why would this be relevant to the question of congressional authorization for a military commission?

Ex Parte Quirin
317 U.S. 1 (1942)

Unanimous decision: *Stone* (CJ), Roberts, Black, Reed, Frankfurter, Douglas, Byrnes, Jackson (Murphy did not participate)

[The *Quirin* case arises out of the trial by military commission of eight saboteurs who were landed in the United States by German submarines during World War II. Four of the saboteurs were landed on Amagansett Beach in New York on June 13 and the other four in Ponte Vedra Beach, Florida on June 17, 1942. All eight men had received training at a sabotage school near Berlin, were equipped with explosive devices, and were under orders from the German High Command to destroy various war-related industrial sites around the country. While the eight saboteurs had initially worn German military uniforms, they had immediately buried these and changed into civilian clothes upon landing. Shortly afterward, two of the saboteurs (Dasch and Burger) turned themselves in to the FBI, and within a few days all eight had been arrested by the FBI in New York or Chicago. Seven of the eight were German nationals who had lived in the United States for a time before the war, and the eighth, Herbert Haupt had immigrated to the United States from Germany as a child and become a U.S. citizen before returning to Germany to serve in the Nazi war effort.

[On July 2, 1942, President Roosevelt appointed a military commission to try the saboteurs, and the same day issued a proclamation that any person entering or attempting to enter the U.S. to commit sabotage or espionage on behalf on a nation at war with the U.S. "shall be subject to the law of war and to the jurisdiction of military tribunals." 7 Fed. Reg. 5101, 5103. Charges were filed by the Army Judge Advocate on July 3, accusing the eight men of spying and violation of the laws of war. Lawyers were appointed for the defendants and trial of the case began on July 8, with all proceedings completed except for closing arguments by July 27. During these proceedings, the prisoners filed petitions for habeas corpus in U.S. District Court for the District of Columbia. The district court denied the petitions on July 28. The prisoners immediately sought leave to file a petition for writ of habeas corpus in the U.S. Supreme Court, which heard full oral arguments at a special session of the court over the next two days, July 29–30.

[On July 31, 1942, the Supreme Court issued a 1-page decision briefly recounting the procedural background and setting out the following ruling:

> The Court has fully considered the questions raised in these cases and thoroughly argued at the bar, and has reached its conclusion upon them. It now announces its decision and enters its judgment in each case, in advance of the preparation of a full opinion which necessarily will require a considerable period of time for its preparation and which, when prepared, will be filed with the Clerk.

> The Court holds:

> (1) That the charges preferred against petitioners on which they are being tried by military commission appointed by the order of the President of July 2, 1942, allege an offense or offenses which the President is authorized to order tried before a military commission.

> (2) That the military commission was lawfully constituted.

> (3) That petitioners are held in lawful custody for trial before the military commission, and have not shown cause for being discharged by writ of habeas corpus.

> The motions for leave to file petitions for writs of habeas corpus are denied.

> The orders of the District Court are affirmed. The mandates are directed to issue forthwith.

[The Military Commission shortly thereafter found the eight prisoners guilty and sentenced them to death. President Roosevelt commuted the death sentences of Dasch and Burger, who had turned themselves in and cooperated with the authorities, to lengthy prison terms; but the other six convicted saboteurs were executed by electric chair on August 8, 1942.

[On October 29, 1942, the Court issued its full opinion.]

MR. CHIEF JUSTICE STONE delivered the opinion of the Court.

.... While it is the usual procedure on an application for a writ of habeas corpus in the federal courts for the court to issue the writ and on the return to hear and dispose of the case, it may without issuing the writ consider and determine whether the facts alleged by the petition, if proved, would warrant discharge of the prisoner....

Petitioners' main contention is that the President is without any statutory or constitutional authority to order the petitioners to be tried by military tribunal for offenses with which they are charged; that in consequence they are entitled to be tried in the civil courts with the safeguards, including trial by jury, which the Fifth and Sixth Amendments guarantee to all persons charged in such courts with criminal offenses....

The Government challenges ... these propositions. But regardless of their merits, it also insists that petitioners must be denied access to the courts, both because they are enemy aliens or have entered our territory as enemy belligerents, and because the President's Proclamation undertakes in terms to deny such access to the class of persons defined by the Proclamation, which aptly describes the character and conduct of petitioners. It is urged that if they are enemy aliens or if the Proclamation has force, no court may afford the petitioners a hearing. But there is certainly nothing in the Proclamation to preclude access to the courts for determining its applicability to the particular case. And neither the Proclamation nor the fact that they are enemy aliens forecloses consideration by the courts of petitioners' contentions that the Constitution and laws of the United States constitutionally enacted forbid their trial by military commission. As announced in our per curiam opinion, we have resolved those questions by our conclusion that the Commission has jurisdiction to try the charge preferred against petitioners....

.... [T]he detention and trial of petitioners—ordered by the President in the declared exercise of his powers as Commander in Chief of the Army in time of war and of grave public danger—are not to be set aside by the courts without the clear conviction that they are in conflict with the Constitution or laws of Congress constitutionally enacted....

The Constitution ... invests the President, as Commander in Chief, with the power to wage war which Congress has declared, and to carry into effect all laws passed by Congress for the conduct of war and for the government and regulation of the Armed Forces, and all laws defining and punishing offenses against the law of nations, including those which pertain to the conduct of war.

By the Articles of War, 10 U.S.C. §§ 1471–1593, Congress has provided rules for the government of the Army. It has provided for the trial and punishment, by courts martial, of violations of the Articles by members of the armed forces and by specified classes of persons associated or serving with the Army. Arts. 1, 2. But the Articles also recognize the "military commission" appointed by military command as an appropriate tribunal for the trial and punishment of offenses against the law of war not ordinarily tried by court martial.... Articles 81 and 82 authorize trial, either by court martial or military commission, of those charged with relieving, harboring or corresponding with the enemy and those charged with spying. And Article 15 declares that "the provisions of these articles conferring jurisdiction upon courts martial shall not be construed as depriving military commissions ... or other military tribunals of concurrent jurisdiction in respect of offenders or offenses that by statute or by the law of war may be triable by such military commissions ... or other military tribunals." Article 2 includes among those persons subject to military law the personnel of our own military establishment. But this, as Article 12 provides, does not exclude from that class "any other person who by the law of war is subject to trial by military tribunals" and who under Article 12 may be tried by court martial or under Article 15 by military commission....

From the very beginning of its history this Court has recognized and applied the law of war as including that part of the law of nations which prescribes, for the conduct of war, the status, rights and duties of enemy nations as well as of enemy individuals. By the Articles of War, and especially Article 15, Congress has explicitly provided, so far as it may constitutionally do so, that military tribunals shall have jurisdiction to try offenders or offenses against the law of war in appropriate cases. Congress, in addition to making rules for the government of our Armed Forces, has thus exercised its authority to define and punish offenses against the law of nations by sanctioning, within constitutional limitations, the jurisdiction of military commissions to try persons for offenses which, according to the rules and precepts of the law of nations, and more particularly the law of war, are cognizable by such tribunals. And the President, as Commander in Chief, by his Proclamation in time of war has invoked that law. By his Order creating the present Commission he has undertaken to exercise the authority conferred upon him by Congress, and also such authority as the Constitution itself gives the Commander in Chief, to direct the performance of those functions which may constitutionally be performed by the military arm of the nation in time of war.

An important incident to the conduct of war is the adoption of measures by the military command not only to repel and defeat the enemy, but to seize and subject to disciplinary measures those enemies who in their attempt to thwart or impede our military effort have violated the law of war. It is unnecessary for present purposes to determine to what extent the President as Commander in Chief has constitutional power to create military commissions without the support of Congressional legislation. For here Congress has authorized trial of offenses against the law of war before such commissions. We are concerned only with the question whether it is within the constitutional power of the National Government to place petitioners upon trial before a military commission for the offenses with which they are charged. We must therefore first inquire whether any of the acts charged is an offense against the law of war cognizable before a military tribunal, and if so whether the Constitution prohibits the trial....

It is no objection that Congress in providing for the trial of such offenses has not itself undertaken to codify that branch of international law or to mark its precise boundaries, or to enumerate or define by statute all the acts which that law condemns.... Congress had the choice of crystallizing in permanent form and in minute detail every offense against the law of war, or of adopting the system of common law applied by military tribunals so far as it should be recognized and deemed applicable by the courts. It chose the latter course.

By universal agreement and practice, the law of war draws a distinction between the armed forces and the peaceful populations of belligerent nations and also between those who are lawful and unlawful combatants. Lawful combatants are subject to capture and detention as prisoners of war by opposing military forces. Unlawful combatants are likewise subject to capture and detention, but in addition they are subject to trial and punishment by military tribunals for acts which render their belligerency unlawful. The spy who secretly and without uniform passes the military lines of a belligerent in time of war, seeking to gather military information and communicate it to the enemy, or an enemy combatant who without uniform comes secretly through the lines for the purpose of waging war by destruction of life or property, are familiar examples of belligerents who are generally deemed not to be entitled to the status of prisoners of war, but to be offenders against the law of war subject to trial and punishment by military tribunals....

Our Government, by thus defining lawful belligerents entitled to be treated as prisoners of war, has recognized that there is a class of unlawful belligerents not entitled to that privilege, including those who, though combatants, do not wear "fixed and distinctive emblems." And by Article 15 of the Articles of War Congress has made provision for their trial and punishment by military commission, according to "the law of war."

By a long course of practical administrative construction by its military authorities, our Government has likewise recognized that those who during time of war pass surreptitiously from enemy territory into our own, discarding their uniforms upon entry, for the commission of hostile acts involving destruction of life or property, have the status of unlawful combatants punishable as such by military commission. This precept of the law of war has been so recognized in practice both here and abroad, and has so generally been accepted as valid by authorities on international law that we think it must be regarded as a rule or principle of the law of war recognized by this Government by its enactment of the Fifteenth Article of War.

Specification 1 of the first charge is sufficient to charge all the petitioners with the offense of unlawful belligerency, trial of which is within the jurisdiction of the Commission, and the admitted facts affirmatively show that the charge is not merely colorable or without foundation.

Specification 1 states that petitioners, "being enemies of the United States and acting for ... the German Reich, a belligerent enemy nation, secretly and covertly passed, in civilian dress, contrary to the law of war, through the military and naval lines and defenses of the United States ... and went behind such lines, contrary to the law of war, in civilian dress ... for the purpose of committing ... hostile acts, and, in particular, to destroy certain war industries, war utilities and war materials within the United States."

This specification ... plainly alleges violation of the law of war.... By passing our boundaries for such purposes without uniform or other emblem signifying their belligerent status, or by discarding that means of identification after entry, such enemies become unlawful belligerents subject to trial and punishment.

Citizenship in the United States of an enemy belligerent does not relieve him from the consequences of a belligerency which is unlawful because in violation of the law of war. Citizens who associate themselves with the military arm of the enemy government, and with its aid, guidance and direction enter this country bent on hostile acts, are enemy belligerents within the meaning of the Hague Convention and the law of war. It is as an enemy belligerent that petitioner Haupt is charged with entering the United States, and unlawful belligerency is the gravamen of the offense of which he is accused.

Nor are petitioners any the less belligerents if, as they argue, they have not actually committed or attempted to commit any act of depredation or entered the theatre or zone of active military operations.... The offense was complete when with [a hostile] purpose they entered—or, having so entered, they remained upon—our territory in time of war without uniform or other appropriate means of identification. For that reason, even when committed by a citizen, the offense is distinct from the crime of treason defined in Article III, § 3 of the Constitution, since the absence of uniform essential to one is irrelevant to the other.

But petitioners insist that, even if the offenses with which they are charged are offenses against the law of war, their trial is subject to the requirement of the Fifth Amendment that no person shall be held to answer for a capital or otherwise infamous crime unless on a presentment or indictment of a grand jury, and that such trials by Article III, § 2, and the Sixth Amendment must be by jury in a civil court. Before the Amendments, § 2 of Article III, the Judiciary Article, had provided, "The Trial of all Crimes, except in Cases of Impeachment, shall be by Jury," and had directed that "such Trial shall be held in the State where the said Crimes shall have been committed."

Presentment by a grand jury and trial by a jury of the vicinage where the crime was committed were at the time of the adoption of the Constitution familiar parts of the machinery for criminal trials in the civil courts. But they were procedures unknown to military tribunals, which are not courts in the sense of the Judiciary Article, and which in the natural course of events are usually called upon to function under conditions precluding resort to such procedures.... The object [of Article III] was to preserve unimpaired trial by jury in all those cases in which it had been recognized by the common law and in all cases of a like nature as they might arise in the future, but not to bring within the sweep of the guaranty those cases in which it was then well understood that a jury trial could not be demanded as of right.

The Fifth and Sixth Amendments, while guaranteeing the continuance of certain incidents of trial by jury which Article III, § 2 had left unmentioned, did not enlarge the right to jury trial as it had been established by that Article....

.... In the light of ... long-continued and consistent interpretation we must conclude that § 2 of Article III and the Fifth and Sixth Amendments cannot be taken to have extended the right to demand a jury to trials by military commission, or to have required that offenses against the law of war not triable by jury at common law be tried only in the civil courts....

The exception from the Amendments of "cases arising in the land or naval forces" was not aimed at trials by military tribunals, without a jury, of such offenses against the law of war. Its objective was quite different—to authorize the trial by court martial of the members of our Armed Forces for all that class of crimes which under the Fifth and Sixth Amendments might otherwise have been deemed triable in the civil courts....

... [The amendments] present no greater obstacle to the trial in like manner of citizen enemies who have violated the law of war applicable to enemies. Under the original statute authorizing trial of alien spies by military tribunals, the offenders were outside the constitutional guaranty of trial by jury, not because they were aliens but only because they had violated the law of war by committing offenses constitutionally triable by military tribunal.

We cannot say that Congress in preparing the Fifth and Sixth Amendments intended to extend trial by jury to the cases of alien or citizen offenders against the law of war otherwise triable by military commission, while withholding it from members of our own armed forces charged with infractions of the Articles of War punishable by death.... We conclude that the Fifth and Sixth Amendments did not restrict whatever authority was conferred by the Constitution to try offenses against the law of war by military commission, and that petitioners, charged with such an offense not required to be tried by jury at common law, were lawfully placed on trial by the Commission without a jury.

Petitioners, and especially petitioner Haupt, stress the pronouncement of this Court in the *Milligan* case, that the law of war "can never be applied to citizens in states which have upheld the authority of the government, and where the courts are open and their process unobstructed." Elsewhere in its opinion, the Court was at pains to point out that Milligan, a citizen twenty years resident in Indiana, who had never been a resident of any of the states in rebellion, was not an enemy belligerent either entitled to the status of a prisoner of war or subject to the penalties imposed upon unlawful belligerents.... Milligan, not being a part of or associated with the armed forces of the enemy, was a non-belligerent, not subject to the law of war....

[*Milligan*] is inapplicable to the case presented by the present record. We have no occasion now to define with meticulous care the ultimate boundaries of the jurisdiction of military tribunals to try persons according to the law of war. It is enough that petitioners here, upon the conceded facts, were plainly within those boundaries, and were held in good faith for trial by military commission, charged with being enemies who, with the purpose of destroying war materials and utilities, entered, or after entry remained in, our territory without uniform—an offense against the law of war. We hold only that those particular acts constitute an offense against the law of war which the Constitution authorizes to be tried by military commission.

Review Questions and Explanations: *Quirin*

1. The *Quirin* decision is not a model of clarity. Its dense, confusing quality begins with its discussion of "The Articles of War" (which has been renamed the Uniform Code of Military Justice). The Court insists that Congress authorized the use of military commissions to try the saboteurs and that it therefore need not consider whether the President's commander-in-chief power itself authorized his employment of military commissions. If congressional authorization were clear, why is that section of the opinion so opaque? How exactly did Congress authorize the military commissions?

2. In *Quirin*, the government did not dispute Haupt's claim that he was a U.S. citizen. The Court brushes aside his claim to holding constitutional rights as a citizen by asserting that he teamed up with foreign belligerents and so could be treated like one. But if what Haupt did is not treason, what is? The Constitution has a very specific provision dealing with treason, Art. III, § 3:

> Treason against the United States, shall consist only in levying war against them, or in adhering to their enemies, giving them aid and comfort. No person shall be convicted of treason unless on the testimony of two witnesses to the same overt act, or on confession in open court. The Congress shall have power to declare the punishment of treason....

Can you make an argument that this provision is inconsistent with trial by military commission? The Court finessed this argument by saying, in essence, that Haupt's treasonous conduct could be charged as a different offense, one that came within the purview of the military commission (and for which he could be sentenced to death). Can the government constitutionally get around the treason clause by creating similar, substitute crimes and charging those instead of treason?[2]

3. The provisions of the Articles of War relied on by the *Quirin* court to justify the use of trial by military commission are still on the books, recodified in the U.S. Code of Military Justice. Does *Quirin* thereby support the idea of a standing justification for military commissions so long as these provisions are in effect?

4. In *Hamdi v. Rumsfeld*, 542 U.S. 507 (2004), presented below, Justice Scalia says, in his dissenting opinion, that *Quirin* "was not this Court's finest hour." He

---

2. This was a key (but unsuccessful) argument for the defendants in the *Rosenberg* case. In the early 1950s, Julius and Ethel Rosenberg were charged, convicted, and executed for giving nuclear secrets to the Soviet Union; the charged crime was violation of the Espionage Act of 1917, not treason.

goes on to say that *Quirin* "revise[d] *Milligan* rather than describe it." Recall that Lambdin Milligan was charged with conspiracy to raid U.S. military posts, obtain weapons, liberate Confederate POWs and wage guerilla war with them in northern states. Is it accurate to say the he was no enemy belligerent, while Haupt was? Milligan did not get very far, but neither did Haupt: and as the *Quirin* Court said, "Nor are petitioners any the less belligerents if, as they argue, they have not actually committed or attempted to commit any act of depredation[.]"

Johnson v. Eisentrager

339 U.S. 763 (1950)

Majority: *Jackson*, Vinson (CJ), Reed, Frankfurter, Clark, Minton

Dissent: *Black*, Douglas, Burton

MR. JUSTICE JACKSON delivered the opinion of the Court.

The ultimate question in this case is one of jurisdiction of civil courts of the United States vis-a-vis military authorities in dealing with enemy aliens overseas. The issues come here in this way:

Twenty-one German nationals petitioned the District Court of the District of Columbia for writs of habeas corpus.... These prisoners have been convicted of violating laws of war, by engaging in, permitting or ordering continued military activity against the United States after surrender of Germany and before surrender of Japan. Their hostile operations consisted principally of collecting and furnishing intelligence concerning American forces and their movements to the Japanese armed forces. They, with six others who were acquitted, were taken into custody by the United States Army after the Japanese surrender and were tried and convicted by a Military Commission constituted by our Commanding General at Nanking by delegation from the Commanding General, United States Forces, China Theatre, pursuant to authority specifically granted by the Joint Chiefs of Staff of the United States. The Commission sat in China, with express consent of the Chinese Government. The proceeding was conducted wholly under American auspices and involved no international participation. After conviction, the sentences were duly reviewed and, with immaterial modification, approved by military reviewing authority.

The prisoners were repatriated to Germany to serve their sentences. Their immediate custodian is Commandant of Landsberg Prison, an American Army officer under the Commanding General, Third United States Army and the Commanding General, European Command. He could not be reached by process from the District Court. Respondents named in the petition are Secretary of Defense, Secretary of the Army, Chief of Staff of the Army, and the Joint Chiefs of Staff of the United States.... The Court of Appeals assumed, and we do likewise, that, while prisoners are in immediate physical custody of an officer or officers not parties to the proceeding, respondents named in the petition have lawful authority to effect that release.

The petition prays an order that the prisoners be produced before the District Court, that it may inquire into their confinement and order them discharged from such offenses and confinement. It is claimed that their trial, conviction and imprisonment violate Articles I and III of the Constitution, and the Fifth Amendment thereto, and other provisions of the Constitution and laws of the United States and provisions of the Geneva Convention governing treatment of prisoners of war.

[The district court denied the petition on the ground that it lacked jurisdiction to review the decision of the military commission, and the Court of Appeals reversed.]

We are cited to no instance where a court, in this or any other country where the writ is known, has issued it on behalf of an alien enemy who, at no relevant time and in no stage of his captivity, has been within its territorial jurisdiction. Nothing in the text of the Constitution extends such a right, nor does anything in our statutes....

... [T]he privilege of litigation has been extended to aliens, whether friendly or enemy, only because permitting their presence in the country implied protection. No such basis can be invoked here, for these prisoners at no relevant time were within any territory over which the United States is sovereign, and the scenes of their offense, their capture, their trial and their punishment were all beyond the territorial jurisdiction of any court of the United States.

Another reason for a limited opening of our courts to resident aliens is that among them are many of friendly personal disposition to whom the status of enemy is only one imputed by law. But these prisoners were actual enemies, active in the hostile service of an enemy power. There is no fiction about their enmity....

A basic consideration in habeas corpus practice is that the prisoner will be produced before the court. This is the crux of the statutory scheme established by the Congress; indeed, it is inherent in the very term "habeas corpus".... To grant the writ to these prisoners might mean that our army must transport them across the seas for hearing. This would require allocation of shipping space, guarding personnel, billeting and rations. It might also require transportation for whatever witnesses the prisoners desired to call as well as transportation for those necessary to defend legality of the sentence. The writ, since it is held to be a matter of right, would be equally available to enemies during active hostilities as in the present twilight between war and peace. Such trials would hamper the war effort and bring aid and comfort to the enemy. They would diminish the prestige of our commanders, not only with enemies but with wavering neutrals. It would be difficult to devise more effective fettering of a field commander than to allow the very enemies he is ordered to reduce to submission to call him to account in his own civil courts and divert his efforts and attention from the military offensive abroad to the legal defensive at home. Nor is it unlikely that the result of such enemy litigiousness would be a conflict between judicial and military opinion highly comforting to enemies of the United States....

Despite this, the doors of our courts have not been summarily closed upon these prisoners. Three courts have considered their application and have provided their counsel opportunity to advance every argument in their support....

The Court of Appeals dispensed with all requirement of territorial jurisdiction based on place of residence, captivity, trial, offense, or confinement.... Instead, it gave our Constitution an extraterritorial application to embrace our enemies in arms.... [If the Fifth] Amendment invests enemy aliens in unlawful hostile action against us with immunity from military trial, it puts them in a more protected position than our own soldiers. American citizens conscripted into the military service are thereby stripped of their Fifth Amendment rights and as members of the military establishment are subject to its discipline, including military trials for offenses against aliens or Americans....

The decision below would extend coverage of our Constitution to nonresident alien enemies denied to resident alien enemies. The latter are entitled only to judicial hearing to determine what the petition of these prisoners admits: that they are really alien enemies. When that appears, those resident here may be deprived of liberty by Executive action without hearing. While this is preventive rather than punitive detention, no reason is apparent why an alien enemy charged with having committed a crime should have greater immunities from Executive action than one who it is only feared might at some future time commit a hostile act.

We hold that the Constitution does not confer a right of personal security or an immunity from military trial and punishment upon an alien enemy engaged in the hostile service of a government at war with the United States....

The jurisdiction of military authorities, during or following hostilities, to punish those guilty of offenses against the laws of war is long-established. By the Treaty of Versailles, "The German Government recognises the right of the Allied and Associated Powers to bring before military tribunals persons accused of having committed acts in violation of the laws and customs of war." Article 228. This Court has characterized as "well-established" the "power of the military to exercise jurisdiction over members of the armed forces, those directly connected with such forces, or enemy belligerents, prisoners of war, or others charged with violating the laws of war." And we have held in the Quirin and Yamashita cases, *supra*, that the Military Commission is a lawful tribunal to adjudge enemy offenses against the laws of war.

It is not for us to say whether these prisoners were or were not guilty of a war crime, or whether if we were to retry the case we would agree to the findings of fact or the application of the laws of war made by the Military Commission. The petition shows that these prisoners were formally accused of violating the laws of war and fully informed of particulars of these charges. As we observed in the Yamashita case, "If the military tribunals have lawful authority to hear, decide and condemn, their action is not subject to judicial review merely because they have made a wrong decision on disputed facts.... We consider here only the lawful power of the commission to try the petitioner for the offense charged."

That there is a basis in conventional and long-established law by which conduct ascribed to them might amount to a violation seems beyond question. Breach of the terms of an act of surrender is no novelty among war crimes. "That capitulations must be scrupulously adhered to is an old customary rule, since enacted by Article 35 of the Hague Regulations. Any act contrary to a capitulation would constitute an international delinquency if ordered by a belligerent Government, and a war crime if committed without such order. Such violation may be met by reprisals or punishment of the offenders as war criminals."....

[Petitioners may mean to argue] either that the presence of the military forces of the United States in China at the times in question was unconstitutional or, if lawfully there, that they had no right under the Constitution to set up a Military Commission on Chinese territory. But it can hardly be meant that it was unconstitutional for the Government of the United States to wage a war in foreign parts....

Certainly it is not the function of the Judiciary to entertain private litigation — even by a citizen — which challenges the legality, the wisdom, or the propriety of the Commander-in-Chief in sending our armed forces abroad or to any particular region. [The jurisdictional argument] involves a challenge to conduct of diplomatic and foreign affairs, for which the President is exclusively responsible. United States v. Curtiss-Wright Corp., 299 U.S. 304....

We are unable to find that the petition alleges any fact showing lack of jurisdiction in the military authorities to accuse, try and condemn these prisoners or that they acted in excess of their lawful powers.... For the reasons stated, the judgment of the Court of Appeals is reversed and the judgment of the District Court dismissing the petition is affirmed.

MR. JUSTICE BLACK, with whom MR. JUSTICE DOUGLAS and MR. JUSTICE BURTON concur, dissenting.

.... This case tests the power of courts to exercise habeas corpus jurisdiction on behalf of aliens, imprisoned in Germany, under sentences imposed by the executive through military tribunals. The trial court held that, because the persons involved are imprisoned overseas, it had no territorial jurisdiction even to consider their petitions. The Court of Appeals reversed.... I agree with the Court of Appeals.... Jurisdiction of a federal district court does not depend on whether the initial pleading sufficiently states a cause of action; if a court has jurisdiction of subject matter and parties, it should proceed to try the case, beginning with consideration of the pleadings....

Moreover, the question of whether the petition showed on its face that these prisoners had violated the laws of war, even if it were relevant, is not properly before this Court. The trial court did not reach that question because it concluded that their imprisonment outside its district barred it even from considering the petition; its doors were "summarily closed." And in reversing, the Court of Appeals specifically rejected requests that it consider the sufficiency of the petition, properly remanding the cause to the District Court for that determination.... The Government's petition for certiorari here presented no question except that of jurisdiction; and neither party has argued, orally or in briefs, that this Court should pass on the sufficiency of the petition. To decide this unargued question under these circumstances seems an unwarranted and highly improper deviation from ordinary judicial procedure....

Despite these objections, the Court now proceeds to find a "war crime" in the fact that after Germany had surrendered these prisoners gave certain information to Japanese military forces. I am not convinced that this unargued question is correctly decided. The petition alleges that when the information was given, the accused were "under the control of the armed forces of the Japanese Empire," in Japanese-occupied territory. Whether obedience to commands of their Japanese superiors would in itself constitute "unlawful" belligerency in violation of the laws of war is not so simple a question as the Court assumes. The alleged circumstances, if proven, would place these Germans in much the same position as patriotic French, Dutch, or Norwegian soldiers who fought on with the British after their homelands officially surrendered to Nazi Germany. There is not the slightest intimation that the accused were spies, or engaged in cruelty, torture, or any conduct other than that which soldiers or civilians might properly perform when entangled in their country's war. It must be remembered that legitimate "acts of warfare," however murderous, do not justify criminal conviction. In Ex parte Quirin, 317 U.S. 1, 30–31, we cautioned that military tribunals can punish only "unlawful" combatants; it is no "crime" to be a soldier. Certainly decisions by the trial court and the Court of Appeals concerning applicability of that principle to these facts would be helpful, as would briefs and arguments by the adversary parties. It should not be decided by this Court now without that assistance, particularly since failure to remand deprives these petitioners of any right to meet alleged deficiencies by amending their petitions.

.... [T]he Court apparently holds that no American court can even consider the jurisdiction of the military tribunal to convict and sentence these prisoners for the alleged crime.... [The holding appears to be] based on the facts that (1) they were enemy aliens who were belligerents when captured, and (2) they were captured, tried, and imprisoned outside our realm, never having been in the United States.

The contention that enemy alien belligerents have no standing whatever to contest conviction for war crimes by habeas corpus proceedings has twice been emphatically rejected by a unanimous Court. In Ex parte Quirin, 317 U.S. 1, we held that status as an enemy alien did not foreclose "consideration by the courts of petitioners' contentions that the Constitution and laws of the United States constitutionally enacted forbid their trial by military commission." This we did in the face of a presidential proclamation denying such prisoners access to our courts. Only after thus upholding jurisdiction of the courts to consider such habeas corpus petitions did we go on to deny those particular petitions upon a finding that the prisoners had been convicted by a military tribunal of competent jurisdiction for conduct that we found constituted an actual violation of the law of war. Similarly, in Yamashita v. United States, 327 U.S. 1, we held that courts could inquire whether a military commission, promptly after hostilities had ceased, had lawful authority to try and condemn a Japanese general charged with violating the law of war before hostilities had ceased. There we stated: "The Executive branch of the Government could not, unless there was suspension of the writ, withdraw from the courts the duty and power to make such inquiry into the authority of the commission as may be made by habeas corpus." Id. at 9. That we went on to deny the requested writ, as in the Quirin case, in no way detracts from the clear holding that habeas corpus jurisdiction is available even to belligerent aliens convicted by a military tribunal for an offense committed in actual acts of warfare.

Since the Court expressly disavows conflict with the Quirin or Yamashita decisions, it must be relying not on the status of these petitioners as alien enemy belligerents but rather on the fact that they were captured, tried and imprisoned outside our territory. The Court cannot, and despite its rhetoric on the point does not, deny that if they were imprisoned in the United States our courts would clearly have jurisdiction to hear their habeas corpus complaints. Does a prisoner's right to test legality of a sentence then depend on where the Government chooses to imprison him? Certainly the Quirin and Yamashita opinions lend no support to that conclusion, for in upholding jurisdiction they place no reliance whatever on territorial location. The Court is fashioning wholly indefensible doctrine if it permits the executive branch, by deciding where its prisoners will be tried and imprisoned, to deprive all federal courts of their power to protect against a federal executive's illegal incarcerations.

If the opinion thus means, and it apparently does, that these petitioners are deprived of the privilege of habeas corpus solely because they were convicted and imprisoned overseas, the Court is adopting a broad and dangerous principle. The range of that principle is underlined by the argument of the Government brief that habeas corpus is not even available for American citizens convicted and imprisoned in Germany by American military tribunals. While the Court wisely disclaims any such necessary effect for its holding, rejection of the Government's argument is certainly made difficult by the logic of today's opinion....

It has always been recognized that actual warfare can be conducted successfully only if those in command are left the most ample independence in the theatre of operations. Our Constitution is not so impractical or inflexible that it unduly restricts such necessary independence....

When a foreign enemy surrenders, the situation changes markedly. If our country decides to occupy conquered territory either temporarily or permanently, it assumes the problem of deciding how the subjugated people will be ruled, what laws will govern, who will promulgate them, and what governmental agency of ours will see that they are properly administered. This responsibility immediately raises questions concerning the extent to which our domestic laws, constitutional and statutory, are transplanted abroad. Probably no one would suggest, and certainly I would not, that this nation either must or should attempt to apply every constitutional provision of the Bill of Rights in controlling temporarily occupied countries. But that does not mean that the Constitution is wholly inapplicable in foreign territories that we occupy and govern.

The question here involves a far narrower issue. Springing from recognition that our government is composed of three separate and independent branches, it is whether the judiciary has power in habeas corpus proceedings to test the legality of criminal sentences imposed by the executive through military tribunals in a country which we have occupied for years.... We ask only whether the military tribunal was legally constituted and whether it had jurisdiction to impose punishment for the conduct charged. Such a limited habeas corpus review is the right of every citizen of the United States, civilian or soldier (unless the Court adopts the Government's argument that Americans imprisoned abroad have lost their right to habeas corpus). Any contention that a similarly limited use of habeas corpus for these prisoners would somehow give them a preferred position in the law cannot be taken seriously.

.... These prisoners were convicted by our own military tribunals under our own Articles of War, years after hostilities had ceased. However illegal their sentences might be, they can expect no relief from German courts or any other branch of the German Government we permit to function. Only our own courts can inquire into the legality of their imprisonment. Perhaps, as some nations believe, there is merit in leaving the administration of criminal laws to executive and military agencies completely free from judicial scrutiny. Our Constitution has emphatically expressed a contrary policy....

Conquest by the United States, unlike conquest by many other nations, does not mean tyranny. For our people "choose to maintain their greatness by justice rather than violence." Our constitutional principles are such that their mandate of equal justice under law should be applied as well when we occupy lands across the sea as when our flag flew only over thirteen colonies. Our nation proclaims a belief in the dignity of human beings as such, no matter what their nationality or where they happen to live. Habeas corpus, as an instrument to protect against illegal imprisonment, is written into the Constitution. Its use by courts cannot in my judgment be constitutionally abridged by Executive or by Congress. I would hold that our courts can exercise it whenever any United States official illegally imprisons any person in any land we govern. Courts should not for any reason abdicate this, the loftiest power with which the Constitution has endowed them.

CASE NOTE: *Reid v. Covert*, 354 U.S. 1 (1957). *Reid* involved two unrelated incidents in which the wives of active-duty U.S. serviceman murdered their husbands on overseas U.S. military bases (one in England, and one in Japan). In both cases, the defendants were charged and tried by court martial under the Uniform Code of Military Justice. The defendants petitioned for habeas corpus, claiming a right to be tried by the civilian courts of the United States. Six members of the Court agreed that civilian dependents of members of the Armed Forces overseas could not constitutionally be tried by a court-martial in times of peace for capital offenses committed abroad. The writ of habeas corpus was granted, and the petitioners were ordered released into civilian custody.

A four-justice plurality opinion by Justice Black, joined by Warren (CJ), Douglas and Brennan, concluded that the Constitution applied to government actions against U.S. citizens abroad, and held that the power of Congress under Art. I, § 8, cl. 14, "To make Rules for the Government and Regulation of the land and naval Forces," — the authority for the Uniform Code of Military Justice and for courts martial — does not extend to civilians, even though they may be dependents living with servicemen on a military base. Courts of law alone are given power to try civilians for their offenses against the United States. Justices Frankfurter and Harlan concurred in the result; although they appeared to agree that the Constitution applies to government action toward U.S. citizens abroad, they limited their judgment to capital cases and did not reach the question of how the result might differ in non-capital cases. Justices Clark and Burton dissented. (Whittaker did not participate.)

Review Questions and Explanations: *Quirin, Eisentrager* and *Reid*

1. *Quirin, Eisentrager* and *Reid* do not create the clearest line of precedent. See if you can articulate, in a few sentences, what they tell us about the jurisdiction of civilian courts in relation to military tribunals. The Supreme Court has itself struggled with the meaning of these cases in *Hamdi* and *Boumediene*, below.

2. *Quirin* and *Eisentrager* are both very focused on questions of jurisdiction, because the government's argument in both cases was that civilian courts lacked jurisdiction to issue a writ habeas corpus or decide anything on the merits. In a key passage, near the beginning of the opinion *Quirin* states:

> neither the Proclamation nor the fact that they are enemy aliens forecloses consideration by the courts of petitioners' contentions that the Constitution and laws of the United States constitutionally enacted forbid their trial by military commission.

This passage reflects a classic jurisdictional doctrine: a court always has jurisdiction to consider its own jurisdiction. It has the power to decide whether it has the authority to decide the merits of a case.

Significantly, both cases also involve jurisdictional challenges to the jurisdiction of military commissions. The question is whether a habeas court will resolve factual disputes going to the jurisdiction of the military commission. Sometimes these threshold factual issues are bound up with the merits. In both cases, the Court assumed that military commissions had authority to try violators of the law of war. In *Quirin*, that violation seemed to be undisputed; but not so in *Eisentrager*, where, the dissent argued, there were factual and legal questions about whether the petitioners were indeed war criminals. If the petitioners had not violated the laws of war, then arguably the military commission would have no jurisdiction over them. Thus the question becomes whether a military commission can assert unreviewable authority to decide its own jurisdiction, to the exclusion of the civilian court. The answer to that question remains murky after *Quirin* and *Eisentrager*.

3. *Quirin* and *Eisentrager* both remark caustically that, by demanding the Fifth and Sixth amendment rights to trial by indictment and jury, the enemy-unlawful-combatant petitioners seek more rights than are afforded U.S. service personnel, who are denied those rights. (See Fifth Amendment exception for "cases arising in the land and naval forces.") The argument seems to be that persons who have not served in the U.S. military are even less worthy of Fifth and Sixth Amendment protections than U.S. service personnel — who don't get those protections. Is that a proper argument? Most U.S. citizens accused of crimes haven't served in the military either — are they unworthy of Fifth and Sixth

Amendment protections? On the other hand, why *aren't* U.S. service personnel afforded those rights?

c. The "War on Terrorism"

The third set of cases and materials arises out of the "War on Terrorism" that took its current form in the aftermath of the September 11 attacks on the World Trade Center and other targets in the United States by foreign terrorists. The so-called "war on terrorism" has over the past decade brought issues of presidential power and the role of civilian courts once again to the forefront of separation-of-powers doctrine.

The history is undoubtedly familiar to you, and will not be recounted here. As you read these materials, it is worth considering the constitutional implications, if any, of making distinctions between the conduct of hostilities in Iraq and Afghanistan that were initiated in response to the 9/11 attacks, and counter-terrorism activities conducted outside of war zones both within and outside the United States.

Two major Supreme Court decisions arising out of detention of persons in the Iraq and Afghanistan conflicts and the related "war on terrorism" will be the focal point for studying these issues: *Hamdi v. Rumsfeld* (2004) and *Boumediene v. Bush* (2009). While there is much overlap between the two cases, there are also some important distinctions. The following chronology and key points are important in understanding the context of the cases:

1. *Hamdi* involved a U.S. citizen, while *Boumediene* involved non-citizens.

2. When *Hamdi* was decided in 2004, the primary legal basis for the military tribunals under which the Defense Department determined whether detainees were in fact "enemy combatants" was a 2001 executive order by President Bush. The administration claimed legal justification from the 2001 Authorization for Use of Military Force ("AUMF," presented below) against the perpetrators of the 9/11 attacks, although the AUMF says nothing about military tribunals. Since the enactment of the AUMF, Congress has enacted the Detainee Treatment Act of 2005 ("DTA") and the Military Commissions Act of 2006 ("MCA"), both of which more clearly authorize the type of military tribunals used.

3. The 2001 executive order purported to strip federal courts of habeas jurisdiction, raising serious separation-of-powers concerns (you will learn more about this issue when you study the Exceptions Clause in Chapter 5). The government took the position that the executive order merely followed *Johnson v. Eisentrager*, which (it claimed) held that the Constitution did not apply to non-citizen detainees outside the U.S. In *Rasul v. Bush* (2004), the Court rejected this argument on statutory (not constitutional grounds), holding that the federal habeas corpus statute applied to Guantanamo Bay.

4. The DTA, in 2005, amended the federal habeas corpus statute to deprive federal courts of jurisdiction to hear habeas petitions by Guantanamo Bay detainees, in effect overruling *Rasul*.

5. In *Hamdan v. Rumsfeld* (2006), the Supreme Court held that the DTA's jurisdiction-stripping amendment to the federal habeas statute did not apply to cases already pending (i.e., its effect would be prospective only, not retroactive).

6. Congress responded in 2006 by enacting the MCA, whose § 7 in effect overruled *Hamdan*, expressly providing that its revised jurisdiction-stripping provision applied to pending cases.

7. *Boumediene* thus considers the constitutional question to which the prior chain of events had been building: can Congress constitutionally strip federal courts of habeas corpus jurisdiction, or is there a constitutional right to habeas corpus (implicit in the suspension clause, Art. I, §9, cl. 2) irrespective of statute—and does it apply to non-citizens outside the formal territorial sovereignty of the U.S.?

When reading *Hamdi* and *Boumediene*, keep in mind the same set of questions we previously posed as Guided Reading Questions 1(a)–(d), just prior to the *Quirin* opinion, above.

Authorization for Use of Military Force

S.J.Res.23

One Hundred Seventh Congress of the United States of America

Joint Resolution

To authorize the use of United States Armed Forces against those responsible for the recent attacks launched against the United States.

Whereas, on September 11, 2001, acts of treacherous violence were committed against the United States and its citizens; and

Whereas, such acts render it both necessary and appropriate that the United States exercise its rights to self-defense and to protect United States citizens both at home and abroad; and

Whereas, in light of the threat to the national security and foreign policy of the United States posed by these grave acts of violence; and

Whereas, such acts continue to pose an unusual and extraordinary threat to the national security and foreign policy of the United States; and

Whereas, the President has authority under the Constitution to take action to deter and prevent acts of international terrorism against the United States: Now, therefore, be it

Resolved by the Senate and House of Representatives of the United States of America in Congress assembled,

SECTION 1. SHORT TITLE.

This joint resolution may be cited as the "Authorization for Use of Military Force."

SEC. 2. AUTHORIZATION FOR USE OF UNITED STATES ARMED FORCES.

(a) IN GENERAL. That the President is authorized to use all necessary and appropriate force against those nations, organizations, or persons he determines planned, authorized, committed, or aided the terrorist attacks that occurred on September 11, 2001, or harbored such organizations or persons, in order to prevent any future acts of international terrorism against the United States by such nations, organizations or persons.

(b) War Powers Resolution Requirements—

(1) SPECIFIC STATUTORY AUTHORIZATION—Consistent with section 8(a)(1) of the War Powers Resolution, the Congress declares that this section is intended to constitute specific statutory authorization within the meaning of section 5(b) of the War Powers Resolution.

(2) APPLICABILITY OF OTHER REQUIREMENTS—Nothing in this resolution supercedes any requirement of the War Powers Resolution.

Speaker of the House of Representatives.

Vice President of the United States and

President of the Senate.

Guided Reading Questions: *Hamdi v. Rumsfeld*

1. Who is Hamdi—where is he from, and what is he accused of? Where is he being detained? Is the government preparing to put him on trial, or does it intend to keep him locked up indefinitely?

2. What, if anything, do any of the opinions tell us about the Suspension Clause? In particular:

   (a) What conditions justify suspension?

   (b) What branch of government has power to suspend the clause?

   (c) What formalities, if any, are required to demonstrate that habeas has been suspended?

   (d) What are the consequences of suspension of habeas corpus—indefinite detentions? Military tribunals?

3. What does *Hamdi* actually decide? Justice Scalia's dissent attacks the plurality's "Mr. Fix-it mentality." What does he mean by that?

Hamdi v. Rumsfeld

542 U.S. 507 (2004)

Plurality: *O'Connor*, Rehnquist (CJ), Kennedy Breyer,

Concurrence in the judgment, partial dissent: *Souter*, Ginsburg

Dissents: *Scalia*, Stevens; *Thomas*

JUSTICE O'CONNOR announced the judgment of the Court....

At this difficult time in our Nation's history, we are called upon to consider the legality of the Government's detention of a United States citizen on United States soil as an "enemy combatant" and to address the process that is constitutionally owed to one who seeks to challenge his classification as such.... We hold that ... due process demands that a citizen held in the United States as an enemy combatant be given a meaningful opportunity to contest the factual basis for that detention before a neutral decisionmaker.

I

On September 11, 2001, the al Qaeda terrorist network used hijacked commercial airliners to attack prominent targets in the United States. Approximately 3,000 people were killed in those attacks. One week later, in response to these "acts of treacherous violence," Congress passed a resolution authorizing the President to "use all necessary and appropriate force against those nations, organizations, or persons he determines planned, authorized, committed, or aided the terrorist attacks" or "harbored such organizations or persons, in order to prevent any future acts of international terrorism against the United States by such nations, organizations or persons." Authorization for Use of Military Force (AUMF), 115 Stat. 224. Soon thereafter, the President ordered United States Armed Forces to Afghanistan, with a mission to subdue al Qaeda and quell the Taliban regime that was known to support it.

This case arises out of the detention of a man whom the Government alleges took up arms with the Taliban during this conflict. His name is Yaser Esam Hamdi. Born in Louisiana in 1980, Hamdi moved with his family to Saudi Arabia as a child. By 2001, the parties agree, he resided in Afghanistan. At some point that year, he was seized by members of the Northern Alliance, a coalition of military groups opposed to the Taliban government, and eventually was turned over to the United States military. The Government asserts that it initially detained and interrogated Hamdi in Afghanistan before transferring him to the United States Naval Base in Guantanamo Bay in January 2002. In April 2002, upon learning that Hamdi is an American citizen, authorities transferred him to a naval brig in Norfolk, Virginia, where he remained until a recent transfer to a brig in Charleston, South Carolina. The Government contends that Hamdi is an "enemy combatant," and that this status justifies holding him in the United States indefinitely—without formal charges or proceedings—unless and until it makes the determination that access to counsel or further process is warranted.

In June 2002, Hamdi's father, Esam Fouad Hamdi, filed the present petition for a writ of habeas corpus under 28 U.S.C. § 2241 in the Eastern District of Virginia, naming as petitioners his son and himself as next friend. The elder Hamdi alleges in the petition that he has had no contact with his son since the Government took custody of him in 2001, and that the Government has held his son "without access to legal counsel or notice of any charges pending against him." .... The District Court found that Hamdi's father was a proper next friend, appointed the federal public defender as counsel for the petitioners, and ordered that counsel be given access to Hamdi. The United States Court of Appeals for the Fourth Circuit reversed that order, holding that the District Court had failed to extend appropriate deference to the Government's security and intelligence interests. It directed the District Court to consider "the most cautious procedures first," and to conduct a deferential inquiry into Hamdi's status....

On remand, the Government filed a response and a motion to dismiss the petition. It attached to its response a declaration from one Michael Mobbs..., who identified himself as Special Advisor to the Under Secretary of Defense for Policy. Mobbs indicated that in this position, he has been "substantially involved with matters related to the detention of enemy combatants in the current war against the al Qaeda terrorists and those who support and harbor them (including the Taliban)." He expressed his "familiar[ity]" with Department of Defense and United States military policies and procedures applicable to the detention, control, and transfer of al Qaeda and Taliban personnel, and declared that "[b]ased upon my review of relevant records and reports, I am also familiar with the facts and circumstances related to the capture of ... Hamdi and his detention by U.S. military forces."

Mobbs then set forth what remains the sole evidentiary support that the Government has provided to the courts for Hamdi's detention. The declaration states that Hamdi "traveled to Afghanistan" in July or August 2001, and that he thereafter "affiliated with a Taliban military unit and received weapons training." It asserts that Hamdi "remained with his Taliban unit following the attacks of September 11" and that, during the time when Northern Alliance forces were "engaged in battle with the Taliban," "Hamdi's Taliban unit surrendered" to those forces, after which he "surrender[ed] his Kalishnikov assault rifle" to them. The Mobbs Declaration also states that, because al Qaeda and the Taliban "were and are hostile forces engaged in armed conflict with the armed forces of the United States," "individuals associated with" those groups "were and continue to be enemy combatants." Mobbs states that Hamdi was labeled an enemy combatant "[b]ased upon his interviews and in light of his association with the Taliban." According to the declaration, a series of "U.S. military screening team[s]" determined that Hamdi met "the criteria for enemy combatants," and "[a] subsequent interview of Hamdi has confirmed the fact that he surrendered and gave his firearm to Northern Alliance forces, which supports his classification as an enemy combatant."

.... The District Court found that the Mobbs Declaration fell "far short" of supporting Hamdi's detention. It criticized the generic and hearsay nature of the affidavit, calling it "little more than the government's 'say-so.'" It ordered the Government to turn over numerous materials for *in camera* review, including copies of all of Hamdi's statements and the notes taken from interviews with him that related to his reasons for going to Afghanistan and his activities therein; a list of all interrogators who had questioned Hamdi and their names and addresses; statements by members of the Northern Alliance regarding Hamdi's surrender and capture; a list of the dates and locations of his capture and subsequent detentions; and the names and titles of the United States Government officials who made the determinations that Hamdi was an enemy combatant and that he should be moved to a naval brig. The court indicated that all of these materials were necessary for "meaningful judicial review" of whether Hamdi's detention was legally authorized and whether Hamdi had received sufficient process to satisfy the Due Process Clause of the Constitution and relevant treaties or military regulations.

The Government sought to appeal the production order, and the District Court certified the question of whether the Mobbs Declaration, "standing alone, is sufficient as a matter of law to allow a meaningful judicial review of [Hamdi's] classification as an enemy combatant." The Fourth Circuit reversed, but did not squarely answer the certified question. It instead stressed that, because it was "undisputed that Hamdi was captured in a zone of active combat in a foreign theater of conflict," no factual inquiry or evidentiary hearing allowing Hamdi to be heard or to rebut the Government's assertions was necessary or proper. Concluding that the factual averments in the Mobbs Declaration, "if accurate," provided a sufficient basis upon which to conclude that the President had constitutionally detained Hamdi pursuant to the President's war powers, it ordered the habeas petition dismissed.... We now vacate the judgment below and remand.

II

The threshold question before us is whether the Executive has the authority to detain citizens who qualify as "enemy combatants." There is some debate as to the proper scope of this term, and the Government has never provided any court with the full criteria that it uses in classifying individuals as such. It has made clear, however, that, for purposes of this case, the "enemy combatant" that it is seeking to detain is an individual who, it alleges, was "part of or supporting forces hostile to the United States or coalition partners" in Afghanistan and who "engaged in an armed conflict against the United States" there. We therefore answer only the narrow question before us: whether the detention of citizens falling within that definition is authorized.

The Government maintains that no explicit congressional authorization is required, because the Executive possesses plenary authority to detain pursuant to Article II of the

Constitution. We do not reach the question whether Article II provides such authority, however, because we agree with the Government's alternative position, that Congress has in fact authorized Hamdi's detention, through the AUMF....

The AUMF authorizes the President to use "all necessary and appropriate force" against "nations, organizations, or persons" associated with the September 11, 2001, terrorist attacks. There can be no doubt that individuals who fought against the United States in Afghanistan as part of the Taliban, an organization known to have supported the al Qaeda terrorist network responsible for those attacks, are individuals Congress sought to target in passing the AUMF. We conclude that detention of individuals falling into the limited category we are considering, for the duration of the particular conflict in which they were captured, is so fundamental and accepted an incident to war as to be an exercise of the "necessary and appropriate force" Congress has authorized the President to use.

The capture and detention of lawful combatants and the capture, detention, and trial of unlawful combatants, by "universal agreement and practice," are "important incident[s] of war." Ex parte Quirin. The purpose of detention is to prevent captured individuals from returning to the field of battle and taking up arms once again.

There is no bar to this Nation's holding one of its own citizens as an enemy combatant. In Quirin, one of the detainees, Haupt, alleged that he was a naturalized United States citizen. We held that "[c]itizens who associate themselves with the military arm of the enemy government, and with its aid, guidance and direction enter this country bent on hostile acts, are enemy belligerents within the meaning of ... the law of war." While Haupt was tried for violations of the law of war, nothing in Quirin suggests that his citizenship would have precluded his mere detention for the duration of the relevant hostilities. Nor can we see any reason for drawing such a line here....

In light of these principles, it is of no moment that the AUMF does not use specific language of detention. Because detention to prevent a combatant's return to the battlefield is a fundamental incident of waging war, in permitting the use of "necessary and appropriate force," Congress has clearly and unmistakably authorized detention in the narrow circumstances considered here.

Hamdi objects, nevertheless, that Congress has not authorized the *indefinite* detention to which he is now subject. The Government responds that "the detention of enemy combatants during World War II was just as 'indefinite' while that war was being fought." We take Hamdi's objection to be not to the lack of certainty regarding the date on which the conflict will end, but to the substantial prospect of perpetual detention. We recognize that the national security underpinnings of the "war on terror," although crucially important, are broad and malleable. As the Government concedes, "given its unconventional nature, the current conflict is unlikely to end with a formal cease-fire agreement." The prospect Hamdi raises is therefore not farfetched. If the Government does not consider this unconventional war won for two generations, and if it maintains during that time that Hamdi might, if released, rejoin forces fighting against the United States, then the position it has taken throughout the litigation of this case suggests that Hamdi's detention could last for the rest of his life.

It is a clearly established principle of the law of war that detention may last no longer than active hostilities. Hamdi contends that the AUMF does not authorize indefinite or perpetual detention. Certainly, we agree that indefinite detention for the purpose of interrogation is not authorized. Further, we understand Congress' grant of authority for the use of "necessary and appropriate force" to include the authority to detain for the duration of the relevant conflict, and our understanding is based on longstanding law-of-war principles. If the practical circumstances of a given conflict are entirely unlike those of the conflicts that informed the development of the law of war, that understanding may unravel. But that is not the situation we face as of this date. Active combat operations against Taliban fighters apparently are ongoing in Afghanistan. The United States may detain, for the duration of these hostilities, individuals legitimately determined to be Taliban combatants who "engaged in an armed conflict against the United States." If the record establishes that United States troops are still involved in active combat in Afghanistan, those detentions are part of the exercise of "necessary and appropriate force," and therefore are authorized by the AUMF.

Ex parte Milligan does not undermine our holding about the Government's authority to seize enemy combatants, as we define that term today. In that case, the Court made repeated reference to the fact that its inquiry into whether the military tribunal had jurisdiction to try and punish Milligan turned in large part on the fact that Milligan was not a prisoner of war, but a resident of Indiana arrested while at home there. That fact was central to its conclusion. Had Milligan been captured while he was assisting Confederate soldiers by carrying a rifle against Union troops on a Confederate battlefield, the holding of the Court might well have been different....

Quirin was a unanimous opinion. It both postdates and clarifies Milligan, providing us with the most apposite precedent that we have on the question of whether citizens may be detained in such circumstances. Brushing aside such precedent—particularly when doing so gives rise to a host of new questions never dealt with by this Court—is unjustified and unwise....

III

Even in cases in which the detention of enemy combatants is legally authorized, there remains the question of what process is constitutionally due to a citizen who disputes his enemy-combatant status....

[The parties all] agree that, absent suspension, the writ of habeas corpus remains available to every individual detained within the United States. U.S. Const., Art. I, § 9, cl. 2. Only in the rarest of circumstances has Congress seen fit to suspend the writ. At all other times, it has remained a critical check on the Executive, ensuring that it does not detain individuals except in accordance with law. All agree suspension of the writ has not occurred here. Thus, it is undisputed that Hamdi was properly before an Article III court to challenge his detention under 28 U.S.C. § 2241. Further, all agree that § 2241 and its companion provisions provide at least a skeletal outline of the procedures to be afforded a petitioner in federal habeas review....

The simple outline of § 2241 makes clear both that Congress envisioned that habeas petitioners would have some opportunity to present and rebut facts and that courts in cases like this retain some ability to vary the ways in which they do so as mandated by due process. The Government [argues that] ... the presentation of the Mobbs Declaration to the habeas court completed the required factual development. It suggests two separate reasons for its position that no further process is due.

First, the Government [argues] that because it is "undisputed" that Hamdi's seizure took place in a combat zone, the habeas determination can be made purely as a matter of law, with no further hearing or factfinding necessary. This argument is easily rejected.... [T]he circumstances surrounding Hamdi's seizure cannot in any way be characterized as "undisputed," as "those circumstances are neither conceded in fact, nor susceptible to concession in law, because Hamdi has not been permitted to speak for himself or even through counsel as to those circumstances."…. Hamdi would need to be "part of or supporting forces hostile to the United States or coalition partners" and "engaged in an armed conflict against the United States" to justify his detention in the United States for the duration of the relevant conflict. [But Hamdi conceded] only that "[w]hen seized by the United States Government, Mr. Hamdi resided in Afghanistan."…. Accordingly, we reject any argument that Hamdi has made concessions that eliminate any right to further process.

The Government's second argument [is that]…. "[r]espect for separation of powers and the limited institutional capabilities of courts in matters of military decision-making in connection with an ongoing conflict" ought to eliminate entirely any individual process, restricting the courts to investigating only whether legal authorization exists for the broader detention scheme. At most, the Government argues, courts should review its determination that a citizen is an enemy combatant under a very deferential "some evidence" standard. Under this review, a court would assume the accuracy of the Government's articulated basis for Hamdi's detention, as set forth in the Mobbs Declaration, and assess only whether that articulated basis was a legitimate one.

In response, Hamdi emphasizes that this Court consistently has recognized that an individual challenging his detention may not be held at the will of the Executive without recourse to some proceeding before a neutral tribunal to determine whether the Executive's asserted justifications for that detention have basis in fact and warrant in law….

Both of these positions highlight legitimate concerns…. The ordinary mechanism that we use for balancing such serious competing interests, and for determining the procedures that are necessary to ensure that a citizen is not "deprived of life, liberty, or property, without due process of law," is the test that we articulated in Mathews v. Eldridge, 424 U.S. 319 (1976). Mathews dictates that the process due in any given instance is determined by weighing "the private interest that will be affected by the official action" against the Government's asserted interest, "including the function involved" and the burdens the Government would face in providing greater process. The Mathews calculus then contemplates a judicious balancing of these concerns, through an analysis of "the risk of an erroneous deprivation" of the private interest if the process were reduced and the "probable value, if any, of additional or substitute procedural safeguards."

…. [A]s critical as the Government's interest may be in detaining those who actually pose an immediate threat to the national security of the United States during ongoing international conflict, history and common sense teach us that an unchecked system of detention carries the potential to become a means for oppression and abuse of others who do not present that sort of threat. See Ex parte Milligan, 4 Wall., at 125…. [O]ur starting point for the Mathews v Eldridge analysis is unaltered by the allegations surrounding the particular detainee or the organizations with which he is alleged to have associated….

On the other side of the scale are the weighty and sensitive governmental interests in ensuring that those who have in fact fought with the enemy during a war do not return to battle against the United States…. The Government also argues at some length that its interests in reducing the process available to alleged enemy combatants are heightened by the practical difficulties that would accompany a system of trial-like process. In its view, military officers who are engaged in the serious work of waging battle would be unnecessarily and dangerously distracted by litigation half a world away, and discovery into military operations would both intrude on the sensitive secrets of national defense and result in a futile search for evidence buried under the rubble of war….

Striking the proper constitutional balance here is of great importance to the Nation during this period of ongoing combat. But it is equally vital that our calculus not give short shrift to the values that this country holds dear or to the privilege that is American citizenship. It is during our most challenging and uncertain moments that our Nation's commitment to due process is most severely tested; and it is in those times that we must preserve our commitment at home to the principles for which we fight abroad....

We therefore hold that a citizen-detainee seeking to challenge his classification as an enemy combatant must receive notice of the factual basis for his classification, and a fair opportunity to rebut the Government's factual assertions before a neutral decisionmaker....

At the same time, the exigencies of the circumstances may demand that, aside from these core elements, enemy-combatant proceedings may be tailored to alleviate their uncommon potential to burden the Executive at a time of ongoing military conflict. Hearsay, for example, may need to be accepted as the most reliable available evidence from the Government in such a proceeding. Likewise, the Constitution would not be offended by a presumption in favor of the Government's evidence, so long as that presumption remained a rebuttable one and fair opportunity for rebuttal were provided. Thus, once the Government puts forth credible evidence that the habeas petitioner meets the enemy-combatant criteria, the onus could shift to the petitioner to rebut that evidence with more persuasive evidence that he falls outside the criteria. A burden-shifting scheme of this sort would meet the goal of ensuring that the errant tourist, embedded journalist, or local aid worker has a chance to prove military error while giving due regard to the Executive once it has put forth meaningful support for its conclusion that the detainee is in fact an enemy combatant....

We think it unlikely that this basic process will have the dire impact on the central functions of warmaking that the Government forecasts. The parties agree that initial captures on the battlefield need not receive the process we have discussed here; that process is due only when the determination is made to *continue* to hold those who have been seized. The Government has made clear in its briefing that documentation regarding battlefield detainees already is kept in the ordinary course of military affairs. Any factfinding imposition created by requiring a knowledgeable affiant to summarize these records to an independent tribunal is a minimal one. Likewise, arguments that military officers ought not have to wage war under the threat of litigation lose much of their steam when factual disputes at enemy-combatant hearings are limited to the alleged combatant's acts. This focus meddles little, if at all, in the strategy or conduct of war, inquiring only into the appropriateness of continuing to detain an individual claimed to have taken up arms against the United States. While we accord the greatest respect and consideration to the judgments of military authorities in matters relating to the actual prosecution of a war, and recognize that the scope of that discretion necessarily is wide, it does not infringe on the core role of the military for the courts to exercise their own time-honored and constitutionally mandated roles of reviewing and resolving claims like those presented here. Cf. Korematsu v. United States, (1944) (Murphy, J., dissenting) ("[L]ike other claims conflicting with the asserted constitutional rights of the individual, the military claim must subject itself to the judicial process of having its reasonableness determined and its conflicts with other interests reconciled")....

In so holding, we necessarily reject the Government's assertion that separation-of-powers principles mandate a heavily circumscribed role for the courts in such circumstances.... [U]nless Congress acts to suspend it, the Great Writ of habeas corpus allows the Judicial Branch to play a necessary role in maintaining this delicate balance of governance, serving as an important judicial check on the Executive's discretion in the realm of detentions. Thus, while we do not question that our due process assessment must pay keen attention to the particular burdens faced by the Executive in the context of military action, it would turn our system of checks and balances on its head to suggest that a citizen could not make his way to court with a challenge to the factual basis for his detention by his Government, simply because the Executive opposes making available such a challenge. Absent suspension of the writ by Congress, a citizen detained as an enemy combatant is entitled to this process.

Because we conclude that due process demands some system for a citizen-detainee to refute his classification, the proposed "some evidence" standard is inadequate. Any process in which the Executive's factual assertions go wholly unchallenged or are simply presumed correct without any opportunity for the alleged combatant to demonstrate otherwise falls constitutionally short.... [Hamdi] has received no process. An interrogation by one's captor, however effective an intelligence-gathering tool, hardly constitutes a constitutionally adequate factfinding before a neutral decisionmaker....

There remains the possibility that the standards we have articulated could be met by an appropriately authorized and properly constituted military tribunal. Indeed, it is notable that military regulations already provide for such process in related instances, dictating that tribunals be made available to determine the status of enemy detainees who assert prisoner-of-war status under the Geneva Convention. See Headquarters Depts. Of Army, Navy, Air Force, and Marine Corps, Enemy Prisoners of War, Retained Personnel, Civilian Internees and Other Detainees, Army Regulation 190-8, ch. 1, §1-6 (1997). In the absence of such process, however, a court that receives a petition for a writ of habeas corpus from an alleged enemy combatant must itself ensure that the minimum requirements of due process are achieved.... As we have discussed, a habeas court in a case such as this may accept affidavit evidence like that contained in the Mobbs Declaration, so long as it also permits the alleged combatant to present his own factual case to rebut the Government's return. We anticipate that a District Court would proceed with the caution that we have indicated is necessary in this setting, engaging in a factfinding process that is both prudent and incremental. We have no reason to doubt that courts faced with these sensitive matters will pay proper heed both to the matters of national security that might arise in an individual case and to the constitutional limitations safeguarding essential liberties that remain vibrant even in times of security concerns....

The judgment of the United States Court of Appeals for the Fourth Circuit is vacated, and the case is remanded for further proceedings.

JUSTICE SCALIA, with whom JUSTICE STEVENS joins, dissenting.

Petitioner Yaser Hamdi, a presumed American citizen, has been imprisoned without charge or hearing in the Norfolk and Charleston Naval Brigs for more than two years, on the allegation that he is an enemy combatant who bore arms against his country for the Taliban. His father claims to the contrary, that he is an inexperienced aid worker caught in the wrong place at the wrong time. This case brings into conflict the competing demands of national security and our citizens' constitutional right to personal liberty. Although I share the plurality's evident unease as it seeks to reconcile the two, I do not agree with its resolution.

Where the Government accuses a citizen of waging war against it, our constitutional tradition has been to prosecute him in federal court for treason or some other crime. Where the exigencies of war prevent that, the Constitution's Suspension Clause, Art. I, §9, cl. 2, allows Congress to relax the usual protections temporarily. Absent suspension, however, the Executive's assertion of military exigency has not been thought sufficient to permit detention without charge. No one contends that the congressional Authorization for Use of Military Force, on which the Government relies to justify its actions here, is an implementation of the Suspension Clause. Accordingly, I would reverse the judgment below.

I

The very core of liberty secured by our Anglo-Saxon system of separated powers has been freedom from indefinite imprisonment at the will of the Executive....

The gist of the Due Process Clause, as understood at the founding and since, was to force the Government to follow those common-law procedures traditionally deemed necessary before depriving a person of life, liberty, or property. When a citizen was deprived of liberty because of alleged criminal conduct, those procedures typically required committal by a magistrate followed by indictment and trial....

To be sure, certain types of permissible *non*criminal detention—that is, those not dependent upon the contention that the citizen had committed a criminal act—did not require the protections of criminal procedure. However, these fell into a limited number of well-recognized exceptions—civil commitment of the mentally ill, for example, and temporary detention in quarantine of the infectious. It is unthinkable that the Executive could render otherwise criminal grounds for detention noncriminal merely by disclaiming an intent to prosecute, or by asserting that it was incapacitating dangerous offenders rather than punishing wrongdoing.

These due process rights have historically been vindicated by the writ of habeas corpus.... The writ of habeas corpus was preserved in the Constitution—the only common-law writ to be explicitly mentioned. See Art. I, § 9, cl. 2. Hamilton lauded "the establishment of the writ of *habeas corpus*" in his Federalist defense as a means to protect against "the practice of arbitrary imprisonments ... in all ages, [one of] the favourite and most formidable instruments of tyranny." The Federalist No. 84, at 444. Indeed, availability of the writ under the new Constitution (along with the requirement of trial by jury in criminal cases, see Art. III, § 2, cl. 3) was his basis for arguing that additional, explicit procedural protections were unnecessary. See The Federalist No. 83.

II

The allegations here, of course, are no ordinary accusations of criminal activity. Yaser Esam Hamdi has been imprisoned because the Government believes he participated in the waging of war against the United States. The relevant question, then, is whether there is a different, special procedure for imprisonment of a citizen accused of wrongdoing *by aiding the enemy in wartime*.

JUSTICE O'CONNOR, writing for a plurality of this Court, asserts that captured enemy combatants (other than those suspected of war crimes) have traditionally been detained until the cessation of hostilities and then released. That is probably an accurate description of wartime practice with respect to enemy *aliens*. The tradition with respect to American citizens, however, has been quite different. Citizens aiding the enemy have been treated as traitors subject to the criminal process.

[There] are times when military exigency renders resort to the traditional criminal process impracticable.... Where the Executive has not pursued the usual course of charge, committal, and conviction, it has historically secured the Legislature's explicit approval of a suspension.... Our Federal Constitution contains a provision explicitly permitting suspension, but limiting the situations in which it may be invoked: "The Privilege of the Writ of Habeas Corpus shall not be suspended, unless when in Cases of Rebellion or Invasion the public Safety may require it." Art. I, § 9, cl. 2. Although this provision does not state that suspension must be effected by, or authorized by, a legislative act, it has been so understood, consistent with English practice and the Clause's placement in Article I. See Ex parte Bollman, (1807); Ex parte Merryman, (CD Md. 1861) (Taney, C. J., rejecting Lincoln's unauthorized suspension).

The Suspension Clause was by design a safety valve, the Constitution's only "express provision for exercise of extraordinary authority because of a crisis," Youngstown Sheet & Tube Co. v. Sawyer (1952) (Jackson, J., concurring)....

[Writings] from the founding generation ... suggest that, without exception, the only constitutional alternatives are to charge the crime or suspend the writ.... The absence of military authority to imprison citizens indefinitely in wartime—whether or not a probability of treason had been established by means less than jury trial—was confirmed by three cases decided during and immediately after the War of 1812.... President Lincoln, when he purported to suspend habeas corpus without congressional authorization during the Civil War, apparently did not doubt that suspension was required if the prisoner was to be held without criminal trial....

Further evidence comes from this Court's decision in Ex parte Milligan. There, the Court issued the writ to an American citizen who had been tried by military commission for offenses that included conspiring to overthrow the Government, seize munitions, and liberate prisoners of war. The Court rejected in no uncertain terms the Government's assertion that military jurisdiction was proper "under the 'laws and usages of war.'"

> It can serve no useful purpose to inquire what those laws and usages are, whence they originated, where found, and on whom they operate; they can never be applied to citizens in states which have upheld the authority of the government, and where the courts are open and their process unobstructed[.]

.... The]Government justifies imprisonment of Hamdi on principles of the law of war and admits that, absent the war, it would have no such authority. But if the law of war cannot be applied to citizens where courts are open, then Hamdi's imprisonment without criminal trial is no less unlawful than Milligan's trial by military tribunal.... Thus, criminal process was viewed as the primary means—and the only means absent congressional action suspending the writ—not only to punish traitors, but to incapacitate them.

The proposition that the Executive lacks indefinite wartime detention authority over citizens is consistent with the Founders' general mistrust of military power permanently at the Executive's disposal. In the Founders' view, the "blessings of liberty" were threatened by "those military establishments which must gradually poison its very fountain." The Federalist No. 45, p. 238 (J. Madison). No fewer than 10 issues of the Federalist were devoted in whole or part to allaying fears of oppression from the proposed Constitution's authorization of standing armies in peacetime. Many safeguards in the Constitution reflect these concerns. Congress's authority "[t]o raise and support Armies" was hedged with the proviso that "no Appropriation of Money to that Use shall be for a longer Term than two Years." U.S. Const., Art. I, §8, cl. 12. Except for the actual command of military forces, all authorization for their maintenance and all explicit authorization for their use is placed in the control of Congress under Article I, rather than the President under Article II.... A view of the Constitution that gives the Executive authority to use military force rather than the force of law against citizens on American soil flies in the face of the mistrust that engendered these provisions.

III

The Government argues that our more recent jurisprudence ratifies its indefinite imprisonment of a citizen within the territorial jurisdiction of federal courts. It places primary reliance upon Ex parte Quirin (1942), a World War II case upholding the trial by military commission of eight German saboteurs, one of whom, Herbert Haupt, was a U.S. citizen. The case was not this Court's finest hour. The Court upheld the commission and denied relief in a brief per curiam issued the day after oral argument concluded; a week later the Government carried out the commission's death sentence upon six saboteurs, including Haupt. The Court eventually explained its reasoning in a written opinion issued several months later.

Only three paragraphs of the Court's lengthy opinion dealt with the particular circumstances of Haupt's case.... Quirin purported to interpret the language of Milligan quoted above ... [so as] to revise Milligan rather than describe it....

But even if Quirin gave a correct description of Milligan, or made an irrevocable revision of it, Quirin would still not justify denial of the writ here. In Quirin it was uncontested that the petitioners were members of enemy forces. They were "*admitted enemy invaders*," (emphasis added), and it was "undisputed" that they had landed in the United States in service of German forces. The specific holding of the Court was only that, "upon the *conceded* facts," the petitioners were "plainly within [the] boundaries" of military jurisdiction. But where those jurisdictional facts are *not* conceded—where the petitioner insists that he is *not* a belligerent—*Quirin* left the pre-existing law in place: Absent suspension of the writ, a citizen held where the courts are open is entitled either to criminal trial or to a judicial decree requiring his release.

IV

It follows from what I have said that Hamdi is entitled to a habeas decree requiring his release unless (1) criminal proceedings are promptly brought, or (2) Congress has suspended the writ of habeas corpus. A suspension of the writ could, of course, lay down conditions for continued detention, similar to those that today's opinion prescribes under the Due Process Clause. But there is a world of difference between the people's representatives' determining the need for that suspension (and prescribing the conditions for it), and this Court's doing so.

[The Authorization for Use of Military Force] is not remotely a congressional suspension of the writ, and no one claims that it is. Contrary to the plurality's view, I do not think this statute even authorizes detention of a citizen with the clarity necessary to satisfy the interpretive canon that statutes should be construed so as to avoid grave constitutional concerns, or with the clarity necessary to overcome the statutory prescription that "[n]o citizen shall be imprisoned or otherwise detained by the United States except pursuant to an Act of Congress." 18 U.S.C. §4001(a). But even if it did, I would not permit it to overcome Hamdi's entitlement to habeas corpus relief. The Suspension Clause of the Constitution, which carefully circumscribes the conditions under which the writ can be withheld, would be a sham if it could be evaded by congressional prescription of requirements *other than the common-law requirement of committal for criminal prosecution* that render the writ, though available, unavailing. If the Suspension Clause does not guarantee the citizen that he will either be tried or released, unless the conditions for suspending the writ exist and the grave action of suspending the writ has been taken; if it merely guarantees the citizen that he will not be detained unless Congress by ordinary legislation says he can be detained; it guarantees him very little indeed.

It should not be thought, however, that the plurality's evisceration of the Suspension Clause augments, principally, the power of Congress. As usual, the major effect of its constitutional improvisation is to increase the power of the Court. Having found a congressional authorization for detention of citizens where none clearly exists; and having discarded the categorical procedural protection of the Suspension Clause; the plurality then proceeds, under the guise of the Due Process Clause, to prescribe what procedural protections *it* thinks appropriate.... It claims authority to engage in this sort of "judicious balancing" from Mathews v. Eldridge, a case involving … *the withdrawal of disability benefits!* Whatever the merits of this technique when newly recognized property rights are at issue (and even there they are questionable), it has no place where the Constitution and the common law already supply an answer.

Having distorted the Suspension Clause, the plurality finishes up by transmogrifying the Great Writ—disposing of the present habeas petition by remanding for the District Court to "engag[e] in a factfinding process that is both prudent and incremental." "In the absence of [the Executive's prior provision of procedures that satisfy due process], … a court that receives a petition for a writ of habeas corpus from an alleged enemy combatant must itself ensure that the minimum requirements of due process are achieved." This judicial remediation of executive default is unheard of.… It is not the habeas court's function to make illegal detention legal by supplying a process that the Government could have provided, but chose not to. If Hamdi is being imprisoned in violation of the Constitution (because without due process of law), then his habeas petition should be granted; the Executive may then hand him over to the criminal authorities, whose detention for the purpose of prosecution will be lawful, or else must release him.

There is a certain harmony of approach in the plurality's making up for Congress's failure to invoke the Suspension Clause and its making up for the Executive's failure to apply what it says are needed procedures—an approach that reflects what might be called a Mr. Fix-it Mentality. The plurality seems to view it as its mission to Make Everything Come Out Right, rather than merely to decree the consequences, as far as individual rights are concerned, of the other two branches' actions and omissions. Has the Legislature failed to suspend the writ in the current dire emergency? Well, we will remedy that failure by prescribing the reasonable conditions that a suspension should have included. And has the Executive failed to live up to those reasonable conditions? Well, we will ourselves make that failure good, so that this dangerous fellow (if he is dangerous) need not be set free. The problem with this approach is not only that it steps out of the courts' modest and limited role in a democratic society; but that by repeatedly doing what it thinks the political branches ought to do it encourages their lassitude and saps the vitality of government by the people.

V

Several limitations give my views in this matter a relatively narrow compass. They apply only to citizens, accused of being enemy combatants, who are detained within the territorial jurisdiction of a federal court. This is not likely to be a numerous group; currently we know of only two, Hamdi and Jose Padilla. Where the citizen is captured outside and held outside the United States, the constitutional requirements may be different. Cf. Johnson v. Eisentrager, (1950); Rasul v. Bush, (SCALIA, J., dissenting). Moreover, even within the United States, the accused citizen-enemy combatant may lawfully be detained once prosecution is in progress or in contemplation. The Government has been notably successful in securing conviction, and hence long-term custody or execution, of those who have waged war against the state.

I frankly do not know whether these tools are sufficient to meet the Government's security needs, including the need to obtain intelligence through interrogation. It is far beyond my competence, or the Court's competence, to determine that. But it is not beyond Congress's. If the situation demands it, the Executive can ask Congress to authorize suspension of the writ—which can be made subject to whatever conditions Congress deems appropriate, including even the procedural novelties invented by the plurality today. To be sure, suspension is limited by the Constitution to cases of rebellion or invasion. But whether the attacks of September 11, 2001, constitute an "invasion," and whether those attacks still justify suspension several years later, are questions for Congress rather than this Court. If civil rights are to be curtailed during wartime, it must be done openly and democratically, as the Constitution requires, rather than by silent erosion through an opinion of this Court....

JUSTICE THOMAS, dissenting.

The Executive Branch, acting pursuant to the powers vested in the President by the Constitution and with explicit congressional approval, has determined that Yaser Hamdi is an enemy combatant and should be detained. This detention falls squarely within the Federal Government's war powers, and we lack the expertise and capacity to second-guess that decision. As such, petitioners' habeas challenge should fail.... I respectfully dissent....

JUSTICE SOUTER, with whom JUSTICE GINSBURG joins, concurring in part, dissenting in part, and concurring in the judgment.

.... The plurality rejects [the Government's proposed] limit on the exercise of habeas jurisdiction and so far I agree with its opinion. The plurality does, however, accept the Government's position that if Hamdi's designation as an enemy combatant is correct, his detention (at least as to some period) is authorized by an Act of Congress as required by § 4001(a), that is, by the Authorization for Use of Military Force (hereinafter Force Resolution). Here, I disagree and respectfully dissent. The Government has failed to demonstrate that the Force Resolution authorizes the detention complained of here even on the facts the Government claims. If the Government raises nothing further than the record now shows, the Non-Detention Act entitles Hamdi to be released....

The threshold issue is how broadly or narrowly to read the Non-Detention Act, the tone of which is severe: "No citizen shall be imprisoned or otherwise detained by the United States except pursuant to an Act of Congress." 18 U.S.C. § 4001(a)....

.... The provision superseded a cold-war statute, the Emergency Detention Act of 1950, which had authorized the Attorney General, in time of emergency, to detain anyone reasonably thought likely to engage in espionage or sabotage. That statute was repealed in 1971 out of fear that it could authorize a repetition of the World War II internment of citizens of Japanese ancestry; Congress meant to preclude another episode like the one described in Korematsu v. United States (1944)....

The fact that Congress intended to guard against a repetition of the World War II internments when it repealed the 1950 statute and gave us § 4001(a) provides a powerful reason to think that § 4001(a) was meant to require clear congressional authorization before any citizen can be placed in a cell....

.... In a government of separated powers, deciding finally on what is a reasonable degree of guaranteed liberty whether in peace or war (or some condition in between) is not well entrusted to the Executive Branch of Government, whose particular responsibility ... to maintain security.... will naturally amplify the claim that security legitimately raises. A reasonable balance is more likely to be reached on the judgment of a different branch, just as Madison said in remarking that "the constant aim is to divide and arrange the several offices in such a manner as that each may be a check on the other — that the private interest of every individual may be a sentinel over the public rights." The Federalist No. 51. Hence the need for an assessment by Congress before citizens are subject to lockup, and likewise the need for a clearly expressed congressional resolution of the competing claims.

.... [T]he Force Resolution.... never so much as uses the word detention, and there is no reason to think Congress might have perceived any need to augment Executive power to deal with dangerous citizens within the United States, given the well-stocked statutory arsenal of defined criminal offenses covering the gamut of actions that a citizen sympathetic to terrorists might commit.

.... Thirty-eight days after adopting the Force Resolution, Congress passed the statute entitled Uniting and Strengthening America by Providing Appropriate Tools Required to Intercept and Obstruct Terrorism Act of 2001 (USA PATRIOT ACT), 115 Stat. 272; that Act authorized the detention of alien terrorists for no more than seven days in the absence of criminal charges or deportation proceedings. It is very difficult to believe that the same Congress that carefully circumscribed Executive power over alien terrorists on home soil would not have meant to require the Government to justify clearly its detention of an American citizen held on home soil incommunicado.

Review Questions and Explanations: *Hamdi v. Rumsfeld*

1. *Hamdi* resulted in four opinions with no majority. It can be important to discern how many votes there are for each of the key propositions asserted in the various opinions.

   (a) Six justices, the plurality and the Scalia dissent, expressly agreed that habeas corpus had not been suspended in this case. The other three did not disagree. None directly explained what formalities are required to do so, but they seem to imply that there must be some explicit statement, as in the Civil War example.

   (b) Five justices—the plurality plus Thomas—agreed that the AUMF authorized detention of enemy combatants. Thomas suggested further that detention is an inherent executive "war power." Four justices disagreed: the Souter concurrence plainly; the Scalia dissent expressed "doubt."

   (c) Five justices—the plurality plus Thomas—seemed to agree that detention is warranted. Four justices would have ordered release, or at least release to civilian authorities: Scalia and Stevens on constitutional grounds, because habeas has not been suspended; Souter and Ginsburg in reliance on the Non-Detention Act.

   (d) Eight justices (all but Thomas) agreed that Hamdi's detention by military authorities was, at least under then-present circumstances, unlawful. The four-justice plurality would require a more robust hearing procedure than simple reliance on the Mobbs declaration, and would allow for the possibility of such a hearing being conducted by a military tribunal, with judicial habeas hearing as a default in the absence of such a procedure.

2. Is anything left of *Ex Parte Milligan*? Or does the modern Court read *Milligan* through the distorting lens of *Quirin*? The Court in *Quirin* had distinguished away *Milligan* by characterizing Lambdin Milligan as a harmless "resident of Indiana" rather than as a dangerous conspirator planning guerilla warfare in a time of national crisis. And what is the implication of distinguishing *Milligan* in this way: that the right to habeas corpus depends on the petitioner's dangerousness or lack thereof?

3. Are you satisfied with the plurality's apparent resolution of the problem that Hamdi could be detained for life ... or for a decade or more? (U.S. troops

are still fighting in Afghanistan as of mid-2012.) The plurality seems to say, if it seems to be going on too long, we'll deal with that question then.

4. Which of the four different resolutions of the case do you find most convincing?

Guided Reading Questions: *Boumediene v. Bush*

1. Who are Boumediene and the other petitioners—where are they from, and what are they accused of? Where are they being detained? Is the government preparing to put them on trial, or does it intend to keep them locked up indefinitely?

2. Try to identify the key elements of the Boumediene holding: (a) Do habeas corpus rights extend outside the territorial United States? (b) To alleged enemy combatants? (c) What sort of procedures do such rights entail? (d) What will the petitioners try to prove if they get hearings?

Boumediene v. Bush

553 U.S. 723 (2008)

Majority: *Kennedy*, Stevens, Souter, Ginsburg, Breyer

Concurrence: *Souter*, Ginsburg, Breyer

Dissents: *Roberts* (CJ), *Scalia*, Thomas, Alito

JUSTICE KENNEDY delivered the opinion of the Court.

Petitioners are aliens designated as enemy combatants and detained at the United States Naval Station at Guantanamo Bay, Cuba.... Petitioners present a question not resolved by our earlier cases relating to the detention of aliens at Guantanamo: whether they have the constitutional privilege of habeas corpus, a privilege not to be withdrawn except in conformance with the Suspension Clause, Art. I, § 9, cl. 2. We hold these petitioners do have the habeas corpus privilege. Congress has enacted a statute, the Detainee Treatment Act of 2005 (DTA), 119 Stat. 2739, that provides certain procedures for review of the detainees' status. We hold that those procedures are not an adequate and effective substitute for habeas corpus. Therefore § 7 of the Military Commissions Act of 2006 (MCA), 28 U.S.C. § 2241(e), operates as an unconstitutional suspension of the writ. We do not address whether the President has authority to detain these petitioners nor do we hold that the writ must issue. These and other questions regarding the legality of the detention are to be resolved in the first instance by the District Court.

I

.... In Hamdi v. Rumsfeld, five Members of the Court recognized that detention of individuals who fought against the United States in Afghanistan "for the duration of the particular conflict in which they were captured, is so fundamental and accepted an incident to war as to be an exercise of the 'necessary and appropriate force' Congress has authorized the President to use." (plurality opinion of O'Connor, J.), (Thomas, J., dissenting). After Hamdi, the Deputy Secretary of Defense established Combatant Status Review Tribunals (CSRTs) to determine whether individuals detained at Guantanamo were "enemy combatants," as the Department defines that term. A later memorandum established procedures to implement the CSRTs. The Government maintains these procedures were designed to comply with the due process requirements identified by the plurality in Hamdi.

Interpreting the AUMF, the Department of Defense ordered the detention of these petitioners, and they were transferred to Guantanamo. Some of these individuals were apprehended on the battlefield in Afghanistan, others in places as far away from there as Bosnia and Gambia. All are foreign nationals, but none is a citizen of a nation now at war with the United States. Each denies he is a member of the al Qaeda terrorist network that carried out the September 11 attacks or of the Taliban regime that provided sanctuary for al Qaeda. Each petitioner appeared before a separate CSRT; was determined to be an enemy combatant; and has sought a writ of habeas corpus in the United States District Court for the District of Columbia.

The first actions commenced in February 2002. The District Court ordered the cases dismissed for lack of jurisdiction because the naval station is outside the sovereign territory of the United States[, and the] Court of Appeals for the District of Columbia Circuit affirmed. We granted certiorari and reversed, holding that 28 U.S.C. § 2241 extended statutory habeas corpus jurisdiction to Guantanamo. See Rasul v. Bush (2004). The constitutional issue presented in the instant cases was not reached in Rasul.

After Rasul, petitioners' cases were consolidated and entertained in two separate proceedings. In the first set of cases, Judge Richard J. Leon granted the Government's motion to dismiss, holding that the detainees had no rights that could be vindicated in a habeas corpus action. In the second set of cases Judge Joyce Hens Green reached the opposite conclusion, holding the detainees had rights under the Due Process Clause of the Fifth Amendment.

While appeals were pending from the District Court decisions, Congress passed the DTA. Subsection (e) of § 1005 of the DTA amended 28 U.S.C. § 2241 to provide that "no court, justice, or judge shall have jurisdiction to hear or consider ... an application for a writ of habeas corpus filed by or on behalf of an alien detained by the Department of Defense at Guantanamo Bay, Cuba." Section 1005 further provides that the Court of Appeals for the District of Columbia Circuit shall have "exclusive" jurisdiction to review decisions of the CSRTs.

In Hamdan v. Rumsfeld (2006), the Court held this provision did not apply to cases (like petitioners') pending when the DTA was enacted. Congress responded by passing the MCA, 10 U.S.C. § 948a et seq., which again amended § 2241....

Petitioners' cases were consolidated on appeal, and the parties filed supplemental briefs in light of our decision in Hamdan. The Court of Appeals' ruling is the subject of our present review and today's decision.

The Court of Appeals concluded that MCA § 7 must be read to strip from it, and all federal courts, jurisdiction to consider petitioners' habeas corpus applications that petitioners are not entitled to the privilege of the writ or the protections of the Suspension Clause, and, as a result, that it was unnecessary to consider whether Congress provided an adequate and effective substitute for habeas corpus in the DTA.

We granted certiorari.

II

.... MCA § 7, 28 U.S.C. § 2241(e) now provides:

(1) No court, justice, or judge shall have jurisdiction to hear or consider an application for a writ of habeas corpus filed by or on behalf of an alien detained

by the United States who has been determined by the United States to have been properly detained as an enemy combatant or is awaiting such determination.

[Section] 7(b) of the MCA.... was a direct response to Hamdan's holding that the DTA's jurisdiction-stripping provision had no application to pending cases.... [Clearly,] the MCA deprives the federal courts of jurisdiction to entertain the habeas corpus actions now before us.

III

In deciding the constitutional questions now presented we must determine whether petitioners are barred from seeking the writ or invoking the protections of the Suspension Clause either because of their status, i.e., petitioners' designation by the Executive Branch as enemy combatants, or their physical location, i.e., their presence at Guantanamo Bay....

A

The Framers viewed freedom from unlawful restraint as a fundamental precept of liberty, and they understood the writ of habeas corpus as a vital instrument to secure that freedom.... [The history of habeas corpus in England] no doubt confirmed their view that pendular swings to and away from individual liberty were endemic to undivided, uncontrolled power. The Framers' inherent distrust of governmental power was the driving force behind the constitutional plan that allocated powers among three independent branches. This design serves not only to make Government accountable but also to secure individual liberty. Because the Constitution's separation-of-powers structure, like the substantive guarantees of the Fifth and Fourteenth Amendments, protects persons as well as citizens, foreign nationals who have the privilege of litigating in our courts can seek to enforce separation-of-powers principles, see, e.g., INS v. Chadha, 462 U.S. 919, 958–959 (1983).

That the Framers considered the writ a vital instrument for the protection of individual liberty is evident from the care taken to specify the limited grounds for its suspension: "The Privilege of the Writ of Habeas Corpus shall not be suspended, unless when in Cases of Rebellion or Invasion the public Safety may require it." Art. I, § 9, cl. 2....

Surviving accounts of the ratification debates provide additional evidence that the Framers deemed the writ to be an essential mechanism in the separation of powers scheme. In a critical exchange with Patrick Henry at the Virginia ratifying convention Edmund Randolph referred to the Suspension Clause as an "exception" to the "power given to Congress to regulate courts." See 3 Debates in the Several State Conventions on the Adoption of the Federal Constitution 460–464 (J. Elliot 2d ed. 1876) (hereinafter Elliot's Debates).... Alexander Hamilton likewise explained that by providing the detainee a judicial forum to challenge detention, the writ preserves limited government. As he explained in The Federalist No. 84:

> [T]he practice of arbitrary imprisonments, have been, in all ages, the favorite and most formidable instruments of tyranny. The observations of the judicious Blackstone ... are well worthy of recital: 'To bereave a man of life ... or by violence to confiscate his estate, without accusation or trial, would be so gross and notorious an act of despotism as must at once convey the alarm of tyranny throughout the whole nation; but confinement of the person, by secretly hurrying him to jail, where his sufferings are unknown or forgotten, is a less public, a less striking, and therefore a *more dangerous engine* of arbitrary government.' And as a remedy for this fatal evil he is everywhere peculiarly emphatical in his

encomiums on the *habeas corpus* act, which in one place he calls 'the bulwark of the British Constitution.'

... [T]he Suspension Clause is designed to protect against these cyclical abuses. The Clause.... ensures that, except during periods of formal suspension, the Judiciary will have a time-tested device, the writ, to maintain the "delicate balance of governance" that is itself the surest safeguard of liberty. See Hamdi (plurality opinion). The Clause protects the rights of the detained by affirming the duty and authority of the Judiciary to call the jailer to account....

B

[The Court considered extensive historical materials provided by the parties and amici on the question of whether foreign nationals detained outside the territorial United States had the right to the writ of habeas corpus, and found the historical arguments inconclusive.]

IV

Drawing from its position that at common law the writ ran only to territories over which the Crown was sovereign, the Government says the Suspension Clause affords petitioners no rights because the United States does not claim sovereignty over the place of detention.

Guantanamo Bay is not formally part of the United States. And under the terms of the lease between the United States and Cuba, Cuba retains "ultimate sovereignty" over the territory while the United States exercises "complete jurisdiction and control.".... [I]t is not altogether uncommon for a territory to be under the *de jure* sovereignty of one nation, while under the plenary control, or practical sovereignty, of another.... As we did in *Rasul*, ... we take notice of the obvious and uncontested fact that the United States, by virtue of its complete jurisdiction and control over the base, maintains *de facto* sovereignty over this territory....

A

The Court has discussed the issue of the Constitution's extraterritorial application on many occasions. These decisions undermine the Government's argument that, at least as applied to noncitizens, the Constitution necessarily stops where *de jure* sovereignty ends.

[Article IV, §3, cl. 2] grants Congress the "Power to dispose of and make all needful Rules and Regulations respecting the Territory or other Property belonging to the United States." ...

Fundamental questions regarding the Constitution's geographic scope first arose at the dawn of the 20th century when the Nation acquired noncontiguous Territories: Puerto Rico, Guam, and the Philippines—ceded to the United States by Spain at the conclusion of the Spanish-American War—and Hawaii—annexed by the United States in 1898. At this point Congress chose to discontinue its previous practice of extending constitutional rights to the territories by statute.

In a series of opinions later known as the Insular Cases, the Court addressed whether the Constitution, by its own force, applies in any territory that is not a State. The Court.... [created] the doctrine of territorial incorporation, under which the Constitution applies in full in incorporated Territories surely destined for statehood but only in part in unincorporated Territories.... Yet noting the inherent practical difficulties of enforcing all constitutional provisions "always and everywhere," the Court devised in the Insular Cases a doctrine that allowed it to use its power sparingly and where it would be most needed. This century-old doctrine informs our analysis in the present matter....

Practical considerations weighed heavily as well in Johnson v. Eisentrager, 339 U.S. 763 (1950), where the Court addressed whether habeas corpus jurisdiction extended to enemy aliens who had been convicted of violating the laws of war. The prisoners were detained at Landsberg Prison in Germany during the Allied Powers' postwar occupation. The Court stressed the difficulties of ordering the Government to produce the prisoners in a habeas corpus proceeding. It "would require allocation of shipping space, guarding personnel, billeting and rations" and would damage the prestige of military commanders at a sensitive time....

True, the Court in Eisentrager denied access to the writ, and it noted the prisoners "at no relevant time were within any territory over which the United States is sovereign, and [that] the scenes of their offense, their capture, their trial and their punishment were all beyond the territorial jurisdiction of any court of the United States." The Government seizes upon this language as proof positive that the Eisentrager Court adopted a formalistic, sovereignty-based test for determining the reach of the Suspension Clause.... We cannot accept the Government's view. Nothing in Eisentrager says that de jure sovereignty is or has ever been the only relevant consideration in determining the geographic reach of the Constitution or of habeas corpus.... A constricted reading of Eisentrager overlooks what we see as a common thread uniting the Insular Cases, Eisentrager, and Reid v. Covert: the idea that questions of extraterritoriality turn on objective factors and practical concerns, not formalism.

B

The Government's formal sovereignty-based test raises troubling separation-of-powers concerns as well.... The necessary implication of the [Government's] argument is that by surrendering formal sovereignty over any unincorporated territory to a third party, while at the same time entering into a lease that grants total control over the territory back to the United States, it would be possible for the political branches to govern without legal constraint.

Our basic charter cannot be contracted away like this. The Constitution grants Congress and the President the power to acquire, dispose of, and govern territory, not the power to decide when and where its terms apply.... Abstaining from questions involving formal sovereignty and territorial governance is one thing. To hold the political branches have the power to switch the Constitution on or off at will is quite another....

These concerns have particular bearing upon the Suspension Clause question in the cases now before us, for the writ of habeas corpus is itself an indispensable mechanism for monitoring the separation of powers. The test for determining the scope of this provision must not be subject to manipulation by those whose power it is designed to restrain.

C

.... [Based on Eisentrager], and the reasoning in our other extraterritoriality opinions, we conclude that at least three factors are relevant in determining the reach of the Suspension Clause: (1) the citizenship and status of the detainee and the adequacy of the process through which that status determination was made; (2) the nature of the sites where apprehension and then detention took place; and (3) the practical obstacles inherent in resolving the prisoner's entitlement to the writ.

Applying this framework, we note at the onset that the status of these detainees is a matter of dispute. The petitioners, like those in Eisentrager, are not American citizens. But the petitioners in Eisentrager did not contest, it seems, the Court's assertion that they were "enemy alien[s]." In the instant cases, by contrast, the detainees deny they are enemy combatants. They have been afforded some process in CSRT proceedings to determine their status; but, unlike in Eisentrager, there has been no trial by military commission for violations of the laws of war. The difference is not trivial. The records from the Eisentrager trials suggest that, well before the petitioners brought their case to this Court, there had been a rigorous adversarial process to test the legality of their detention. The Eisentrager petitioners were charged by a bill of particulars that made detailed factual allegations against them. See 14 United Nations War Crimes Commission, Law Reports of Trials of War Criminals 8–10 (1949) (reprint 1997). To rebut the accusations, they were entitled to representation by counsel, allowed to introduce evidence on their own behalf, and permitted to cross-examine the prosecution's witnesses.

In comparison the procedural protections afforded to the detainees in the CSRT hearings are far more limited, and, we conclude, fall well short of the procedures and adversarial mechanisms that would eliminate the need for habeas corpus review. Although the detainee is assigned a "Personal Representative" to assist him during CSRT proceedings, the Secretary of the Navy's memorandum makes clear that person is not the detainee's lawyer or even his "advocate." The Government's evidence is accorded a presumption of validity. The detainee is allowed to present "reasonably available" evidence, but his ability to rebut the Government's evidence against him is limited by the circumstances of his confinement and his lack of counsel at this stage. And although the detainee can seek review of his status determination in the Court of Appeals, that review process cannot cure all defects in the earlier proceedings.

As to the second factor...., there are critical differences between Landsberg Prison, circa 1950, and the United States Naval Station at Guantanamo Bay in 2008. Unlike its present control over the naval station, the United States' control over the prison in Germany was neither absolute nor indefinite. Like all parts of occupied Germany, the prison was under the jurisdiction of the combined Allied Forces.... The Allies had not planned a long-term occupation of Germany, nor did they intend to displace all German institutions even during the period of occupation. The Court's holding in Eisentrager was thus consistent with the Insular Cases, where it had held there was no need to extend full constitutional protections to territories the United States did not intend to govern indefinitely. Guantanamo Bay, on the other hand, is no transient possession. In every practical sense Guantanamo is not abroad; it is within the constant jurisdiction of the United States.

As to the third factor, we recognize, as the Court did in Eisentrager, that there are costs to holding the Suspension Clause applicable in a case of military detention abroad.... Yet civilian courts and the Armed Forces have functioned along side each other at various points in our history. The Government presents no credible arguments that the military mission at Guantanamo would be compromised if habeas corpus courts had jurisdiction to hear the detainees' claims. And in light of the plenary control the United States asserts over the base, none are apparent to us.

The situation in Eisentrager was far different, given the historical context and nature of the military's mission in post-War Germany. When hostilities in the European Theater came to an end, the United States became responsible for an occupation zone encompassing over 57,000 square miles with a population of 18 million. In addition to supervising massive reconstruction and aid efforts the American forces stationed in Germany faced potential security threats from a defeated enemy. In retrospect the post-War occupation may seem uneventful. But at the time Eisentrager was decided, the Court was right to be concerned about judicial interference with the military's efforts to contain "enemy elements, guerilla fighters, and 'were-wolves.'" 339 U.S., at 784.

Similar threats are not apparent here; nor does the Government argue that they are. The United States Naval Station at Guantanamo Bay consists of 45 square miles of land and water. The base has been used, at various points, to house migrants and refugees temporarily. At present, however, other than the detainees themselves, the only long-term residents are American military personnel, their families, and a small number of workers. The detainees have been deemed enemies of the United States. At present, dangerous as they may be if released, they are contained in a secure prison facility located on an isolated and heavily fortified military base.

.... Under the facts presented here, ... there are few practical barriers to the running of the writ. To the extent barriers arise, habeas corpus procedures likely can be modified to address them.

It is true that before today the Court has never held that noncitizens detained by our Government in territory over which another country maintains de jure sovereignty have any rights under our Constitution. But the cases before us lack any precise historical parallel. They involve individuals detained by executive order for the duration of a conflict that, if measured from September 11, 2001, to the present, is already among the longest wars in American history. The detainees, moreover, are held in a territory that, while technically not part of the United States, is under the complete and total control of our Government. Under these circumstances the lack of a precedent on point is no barrier to our holding.

We hold that Art. I, §9, cl. 2, of the Constitution has full effect at Guantanamo Bay. If the privilege of habeas corpus is to be denied to the detainees now before us, Congress must act in accordance with the requirements of the Suspension Clause. Cf. Hamdi, 542 U.S., at 564 (Scalia, J., dissenting) ("[I]ndefinite imprisonment on reasonable suspicion is not an available option of treatment for those accused of aiding the enemy, absent a suspension of the writ"). This Court may not impose a de facto suspension by abstaining from these controversies. The MCA does not purport to be a formal suspension of the writ; and the Government, in its submissions to us, has not argued that it is. Petitioners, therefore, are entitled to the privilege of habeas corpus to challenge the legality of their detention.

V

In light of this holding the question becomes whether the statute stripping jurisdiction to issue the writ avoids the Suspension Clause mandate because Congress has provided adequate substitute procedures for habeas corpus. The Government submits there has been compliance with the Suspension Clause because the DTA review process in the Court of Appeals, see DTA § 1005(e), provides an adequate substitute....

A

Our case law does not contain extensive discussion of standards defining suspension of the writ or of circumstances under which suspension has occurred. This simply confirms the care Congress has taken throughout our Nation's history to preserve the writ and its function. Indeed, most of the major legislative enactments pertaining to habeas corpus have acted not to contract the writ's protection but to expand it or to hasten resolution of prisoners' claims....

.... When Congress has intended to replace traditional habeas corpus with habeas-like substitutes, ... it has granted to the courts broad remedial powers to secure the historic office of the writ....

In contrast the DTA's jurisdictional grant is quite limited. The Court of Appeals has jurisdiction not to inquire into the legality of the detention generally but only to assess whether the CSRT complied with the "standards and procedures specified by the Secretary of Defense" and whether those standards and procedures are lawful. If Congress had envisioned DTA review as coextensive with traditional habeas corpus, it would not have drafted the statute in this manner.... [Moreover], there has been no effort to preserve habeas corpus review as an avenue of last resort....

.... Congress intended the Court of Appeals to have a more limited role in enemy combatant status determinations than a district court has in habeas corpus proceedings....

B

We do not endeavor to offer a comprehensive summary of the requisites for an adequate substitute for habeas corpus. We do consider it uncontroversial, however, that the privilege of habeas corpus entitles the prisoner to a meaningful opportunity to demonstrate that he is being held pursuant to "the erroneous application or interpretation" of relevant law. And the habeas court must have the power to order the conditional release of an individual unlawfully detained—though release need not be the exclusive remedy and is not the appropriate one in every case in which the writ is granted.... These are the easily identified attributes of any constitutionally adequate habeas corpus proceeding. But, depending on the circumstances, more may be required.

Indeed, common-law habeas corpus was, above all, an adaptable remedy. Its precise application and scope changed depending upon the circumstances....

Where a person is detained by executive order, rather than, say, after being tried and convicted in a court, the need for collateral review is most pressing. A criminal conviction in the usual course occurs after a judicial hearing before a tribunal disinterested in the outcome and committed to procedures designed to ensure its own independence. These dynamics are not inherent in executive detention orders or executive review procedures. In this context the need for habeas corpus is more urgent. The intended duration of the detention and the reasons for it bear upon the precise scope of the inquiry. Habeas corpus proceedings need not resemble a criminal trial, even when the detention is by executive order. But the writ must be effective. The habeas court must have sufficient authority to conduct a meaningful review of both the cause for detention and the Executive's power to detain....

[Here,] the detainee has limited means to find or present evidence to challenge the Government's case against him. He does not have the assistance of counsel and may not be aware of the most critical allegations that the Government relied upon to order his detention. The detainee can confront witnesses that testify during the CSRT proceedings. But given that there are in effect no limits on the admission of hearsay evidence—the only requirement is that the tribunal deem the evidence "relevant and helpful,"—the detainee's opportunity to question witnesses is likely to be more theoretical than real....

Although we make no judgment as to whether the CSRTs, as currently constituted, satisfy due process standards, we agree with petitioners that, even when all the parties involved in this process act with diligence and in good faith, there is considerable risk of error in the tribunal's findings of fact. This is a risk inherent in any process that, in the words of the former Chief Judge of the Court of Appeals, is "closed and accusatorial." And given that the consequence of error may be detention of persons for the duration of hostilities that may last a generation or more, this is a risk too significant to ignore.

For the writ of habeas corpus, or its substitute, to function as an effective and proper remedy in this context, the court that conducts the habeas proceeding must have the means to correct errors that occurred during the CSRT proceedings. This includes some authority to assess the sufficiency of the Government's evidence against the detainee. It also must have the authority to admit and consider relevant exculpatory evidence that was not introduced during the earlier proceeding. Federal habeas petitioners long have had the means to supplement the record on review, even in the postconviction habeas setting. Here that opportunity is constitutionally required.

Consistent with the historic function and province of the writ, habeas corpus review may be more circumscribed if the underlying detention proceedings are more thorough than they were here....

The extent of the showing required of the Government in these cases is a matter to be determined. We need not explore it further at this stage. We do hold that when the judicial power to issue habeas corpus properly is invoked the judicial officer must have adequate authority to make a determination in light of the relevant law and facts and to formulate and issue appropriate orders for relief, including, if necessary, an order directing the prisoner's release.

C

We now consider whether the DTA allows the Court of Appeals to conduct a proceeding meeting these standards. "[W]e are obligated to construe the statute to avoid [constitutional] problems" if it is "'fairly possible'" to do so. There are limits to this principle, however. The canon of constitutional avoidance does not supplant traditional modes of statutory interpretation. We cannot ignore the text and purpose of a statute in order to save it....

The DTA might be [construed] to allow the [the Court of Appeals to order release of a detainee, and to allow] petitioners to assert most, if not all, of the legal claims they seek to advance, including their most basic claim: that the President has no authority under the AUMF to detain them indefinitely....

.... The more difficult question is whether the DTA permits the Court of Appeals to make requisite findings of fact.... Assuming the DTA can be construed to allow the Court of Appeals to review or correct the CSRT's factual determinations, as opposed to merely certifying that the tribunal applied the correct standard of proof, we see no way to construe the statute to allow what is also constitutionally required in this context: an opportunity for the detainee to present relevant exculpatory evidence that was not made part of the record in the earlier proceedings.... There is no language in the DTA that can be construed to allow the Court of Appeals to admit and consider newly discovered evidence that could not have been made part of the CSRT record because it was unavailable to either the Government or the detainee when the CSRT made its findings. This evidence, however, may be critical to the detainee's argument that he is not an enemy combatant and there is no cause to detain him.

This is not a remote hypothetical. One of the petitioners, Mohamed Nechla, requested at his CSRT hearing that the Government contact his employer. The petitioner claimed the employer would corroborate Nechla's contention he had no affiliation with al Qaeda. Although the CSRT determined this testimony would be relevant, it also found the witness was not reasonably available to testify at the time of the hearing. Petitioner's counsel, however, now represents the witness is available to be heard. If a detainee can present reasonably available evidence demonstrating there is no basis for his continued detention, he must have the opportunity to present this evidence to a habeas corpus court. Even under the Court of Appeals' generous construction of the DTA, however, the evidence identified by Nechla would be inadmissible in a DTA review proceeding. The role of an Article III court in the exercise of its habeas corpus function cannot be circumscribed in this manner.

By foreclosing consideration of evidence not presented or reasonably available to the detainee at the CSRT proceedings, the DTA disadvantages the detainee by limiting the scope of collateral review to a record that may not be accurate or complete.... [W]here the underlying detention proceedings lack the necessary adversarial character, the detainee cannot be held responsible for all deficiencies in the record.

The Government ... does point out, however, that if a detainee obtains such evidence, he can request that the Deputy Secretary of Defense convene a new CSRT. Whatever the merits of this procedure, it is an insufficient replacement for the factual review these detainees are entitled to receive through habeas corpus. The Deputy Secretary's determination whether to initiate new proceedings is wholly a discretionary one.

.... [E]ven if it were possible, as a textual matter, to read into the statute each of the necessary procedures we have identified, we could not overlook the cumulative effect of our doing so. To hold that the detainees at Guantanamo may, under the DTA, challenge the President's legal authority to detain them, contest the CSRT's findings of fact, supplement the record on review with exculpatory evidence, and request an order of release would come close to reinstating the § 2241 habeas corpus process Congress sought to deny them. The language of the statute, read in light of Congress' reasons for enacting it, cannot bear this interpretation. Petitioners have met their burden of establishing that the DTA review process is, on its face, an inadequate substitute for habeas corpus.

Although we do not hold that an adequate substitute must duplicate § 2241 in all respects, it suffices that the Government has not established that the detainees' access to the statutory review provisions at issue is an adequate substitute for the writ of habeas corpus. MCA § 7 thus effects an unconstitutional suspension of the writ....

In light of our conclusion that there is no jurisdictional bar to the District Court's entertaining petitioners' claims the question remains whether there are prudential barriers to habeas corpus review under these circumstances....

The real risks, the real threats, of terrorist attacks are constant and not likely soon to abate. The ways to disrupt our life and laws are so many and unforeseen that the Court should not attempt even some general catalogue of crises that might occur. Certain principles are apparent, however. Practical considerations and exigent circumstances inform the definition and reach of the law's writs, including habeas corpus. The cases and our tradition reflect this precept.

In cases involving foreign citizens detained abroad by the Executive, it likely would be both an impractical and unprecedented extension of judicial power to assume that habeas corpus would be available at the moment the prisoner is taken into custody. If and when habeas corpus jurisdiction applies, as it does in these cases, then proper deference can be accorded to reasonable procedures for screening and initial detention under lawful and proper conditions of confinement and treatment for a reasonable period of time.... The cases before us, however, do not involve detainees who have been held for a short period of time while awaiting their CSRT determinations. Were that the case, or were it probable that the Court of Appeals could complete a prompt review of their applications, the case for requiring temporary abstention or exhaustion of alternative remedies would be much stronger. These qualifications no longer pertain here. In some of these cases six years have elapsed without the judicial oversight that habeas corpus or an adequate substitute demands. And there has been no showing that the Executive faces such onerous burdens that it cannot respond to habeas corpus actions. To require these detainees to complete DTA review before proceeding with their habeas corpus actions would be to require additional months, if not years, of delay. The first DTA review applications were filed over a year ago, but no decisions on the merits have been issued. While some delay in fashioning new procedures is unavoidable, the costs of delay can no longer be borne by those who are held in custody. The detainees in these cases are entitled to a prompt habeas corpus hearing.

Our decision today holds only that the petitioners before us are entitled to seek the writ; that the DTA review procedures are an inadequate substitute for habeas corpus; and that the petitioners in these cases need not exhaust the review procedures in the Court of Appeals before proceeding with their habeas actions in the District Court. The only law we identify as unconstitutional is MCA § 7. Accordingly, both the DTA and the CSRT process remain intact. Our holding with regard to exhaustion should not be read to imply that a habeas court should intervene the moment an enemy combatant steps foot in a territory where the writ runs. The Executive is entitled to a reasonable period of time to determine a detainee's status before a court entertains that detainee's habeas corpus petition. The CSRT process is the mechanism Congress and the President set up to deal with these issues. Except in cases of undue delay, federal courts should refrain from entertaining an enemy combatant's habeas corpus petition at least until after the Department, acting via the CSRT, has had a chance to review his status.

Although we hold that the DTA is not an adequate and effective substitute for habeas corpus, it does not follow that a habeas corpus court may disregard the dangers the detention in these cases was intended to prevent.... Certain accommodations can be made to reduce the burden habeas corpus proceedings will place on the military without impermissibly diluting the protections of the writ....

.... We make no attempt to anticipate all of the evidentiary and access-to-counsel issues that will arise during the course of the detainees' habeas corpus proceedings. We recognize, however, that the Government has a legitimate interest in protecting sources and methods of intelligence gathering; and we expect that the District Court will use its discretion to accommodate this interest to the greatest extent possible....

In considering both the procedural and substantive standards used to impose detention to prevent acts of terrorism, proper deference must be accorded to the political branches. See United States v. Curtiss-Wright Export Corp. (1936). Unlike the President and some designated Members of Congress, neither the Members of this Court nor most federal judges begin the day with briefings that may describe new and serious threats to our Nation and its people. The law must accord the Executive substantial authority to apprehend and detain those who pose a real danger to our security.

Officials charged with daily operational responsibility for our security may consider a judicial discourse on the history of the Habeas Corpus Act of 1679 and like matters to be far removed from the Nation's present, urgent concerns. Established legal doctrine, however, must be consulted for its teaching. Remote in time it may be; irrelevant to the present it is not. Security depends upon a sophisticated intelligence apparatus and the ability of our Armed Forces to act and to interdict. There are further considerations, however. Security subsists, too, in fidelity to freedom's first principles. Chief among these are freedom from arbitrary and unlawful restraint and the personal liberty that is secured by adherence to the separation of powers. It is from these principles that the judicial authority to consider petitions for habeas corpus relief derives.

Our opinion does not undermine the Executive's powers as Commander in Chief. On the contrary, the exercise of those powers is vindicated, not eroded, when confirmed by the Judicial Branch. Within the Constitution's separation-of-powers structure, few exercises of judicial power are as legitimate or as necessary as the responsibility to hear challenges to the authority of the Executive to imprison a person. Some of these petitioners have been in custody for six years with no definitive judicial determination as to the legality of their detention. Their access to the writ is a necessity to determine the lawfulness of their status, even if, in the end, they do not obtain the relief they seek.

Because our Nation's past military conflicts have been of limited duration, it has been possible to leave the outer boundaries of war powers undefined. If, as some fear, terrorism continues to pose dangerous threats to us for years to come, the Court might not have this luxury. This result is not inevitable, however. The political branches, consistent with their independent obligations to interpret and uphold the Constitution, can engage in a genuine debate about how best to preserve constitutional values while protecting the Nation from terrorism.

It bears repeating that our opinion does not address the content of the law that governs petitioners' detention. That is a matter yet to be determined. We hold that petitioners may invoke the fundamental procedural protections of habeas corpus. The laws and Constitution are designed to survive, and remain in force, in extraordinary times. Liberty and security can be reconciled; and in our system they are reconciled within the framework of the law. The Framers decided that habeas corpus, a right of first importance, must be a part of that framework, a part of that law.

The determination by the Court of Appeals that the Suspension Clause and its protections are inapplicable to petitioners was in error. The judgment of the Court of Appeals is reversed. The cases are remanded to the Court of Appeals with instructions that it remand the cases to the District Court for proceedings consistent with this opinion.

JUSTICE SOUTER, with whom JUSTICE GINSBURG and JUSTICE BREYER join, concurring.

I join the Court's opinion in its entirety and add this afterword only to emphasize two things one might overlook after reading the dissents.

Four years ago, this Court in Rasul v. Bush, 542 U.S. 466 (2004) held that statutory habeas jurisdiction extended to claims of foreign nationals imprisoned by the United States at Guantanamo Bay, "to determine the legality of the Executive's potentially indefinite detention" of them. Subsequent legislation eliminated the statutory habeas jurisdiction over these claims, so that now there must be constitutionally based jurisdiction or none at all. [N]o one who reads the Court's opinion in Rasul could seriously doubt that the jurisdictional question must be answered the same way in purely constitutional cases, given the Court's reliance on the historical background of habeas generally in answering the statutory question....

A second fact insufficiently appreciated by the dissents is the length of the disputed imprisonments, some of the prisoners represented here today having been locked up for six years. Hence the hollow ring when the dissenters suggest that the Court is somehow precipitating the judiciary into reviewing claims that the military (subject to appeal to the Court of Appeals for the District of Columbia Circuit) could handle within some reasonable period of time.... After six years of sustained executive detentions in Guantanamo, subject to habeas jurisdiction but without any actual habeas scrutiny, today's decision is no judicial victory, but an act of perseverance in trying to make habeas review, and the obligation of the courts to provide it, mean something of value both to prisoners and to the Nation.

CHIEF JUSTICE ROBERTS, with whom JUSTICE SCALIA, JUSTICE THOMAS, and JUSTICE ALITO join, dissenting.

Today the Court strikes down as inadequate the most generous set of procedural protections ever afforded aliens detained by this country as enemy combatants.... The majority merely replaces a review system designed by the people's representatives with a set of shapeless procedures to be defined by federal courts at some future date....

[The] critical threshold question in these cases, prior to any inquiry about the writ's scope, is whether the system the political branches designed protects whatever rights the detainees may possess. If so, there is no need for any additional process, whether called "habeas" or something else.... I believe the system the political branches constructed adequately protects any constitutional rights aliens captured abroad and detained as enemy combatants may enjoy....

JUSTICE SCALIA, with whom THE CHIEF JUSTICE, JUSTICE THOMAS, and JUSTICE ALITO join, dissenting.

Today, for the first time in our Nation's history, the Court confers a constitutional right to habeas corpus on alien enemies detained abroad by our military forces in the course of an ongoing war....

America is at war with radical Islamists. The enemy began by killing Americans and American allies abroad.... On September 11, 2001, the enemy brought the battle to American soil, killing 2,749 at the Twin Towers in New York City, 184 at the Pentagon in Washington, D. C., and 40 in Pennsylvania. It has threatened further attacks against our homeland; one need only walk about buttressed and barricaded Washington, or board a plane anywhere in the country, to know that the threat is a serious one. Our Armed Forces are now in the field against the enemy, in Afghanistan and Iraq. Last week, 13 of our countrymen in arms were killed.

The game of bait-and-switch that today's opinion plays upon the Nation's Commander in Chief will make the war harder on us. It will almost certainly cause more Americans to be killed. That consequence would be tolerable if necessary to preserve a time-honored legal principle vital to our constitutional Republic. But it is this Court's blatant *abandonment* of such a principle that produces the decision today. The President relied on our settled precedent in Johnson v. Eisentrager, 339 U.S. 763 (1950), when he established the prison at Guantanamo Bay for enemy aliens. Citing that case, the President's Office of Legal Counsel advised him "that the great weight of legal authority indicates that a federal district court could not properly exercise habeas jurisdiction over an alien detained at [Guantanamo Bay]." Had the law been otherwise, the military surely would not have transported prisoners there, but would have kept them in Afghanistan, transferred them to another of our foreign military bases, or turned them over to allies for detention. Those other facilities might well have been worse for the detainees themselves.

In the long term, then, the Court's decision today accomplishes little, except perhaps to reduce the well-being of enemy combatants that the Court ostensibly seeks to protect. In the short term, however, the decision is devastating. At least 30 of those prisoners hitherto released from Guantanamo Bay have returned to the battlefield. But others have succeeded in carrying on their atrocities against innocent civilians....

These, mind you, were detainees whom *the military* had concluded were not enemy combatants. Their return to the kill illustrates the incredible difficulty of assessing who is and who is not an enemy combatant in a foreign theater of operations where the environment does not lend itself to rigorous evidence collection. Astoundingly, the Court today raises the bar, requiring military officials to appear before civilian courts and defend their decisions under procedural and evidentiary rules that go beyond what Congress has specified....

But even when the military has evidence that it can bring forward, it is often foolhardy to release that evidence to the attorneys representing our enemies. And one escalation of procedures that the Court *is* clear about is affording the detainees increased access to witnesses (perhaps troops serving in Afghanistan?) and to classified information. During the 1995 prosecution of Omar Abdel Rahman, federal prosecutors gave the names of 200 unindicted co-conspirators to the "Blind Sheik's" defense lawyers; that information was in the hands of Osama Bin Laden within two weeks. See Minority Report 14–15. In another case, trial testimony revealed to the enemy that the United States had been monitoring their cellular network, whereupon they promptly stopped using it, enabling more of them to evade capture and continue their atrocities. See id., at 15....

... [T]he Military Commissions Act.... [makes] clear that Congress and the Executive—*both* political branches—have determined that limiting the role of civilian courts in adjudicating whether prisoners captured abroad are properly detained is important to success in the war that some 190,000 of our men and women are now fighting....

The Court today decrees that.... "The Government" ... "presents no credible arguments that the military mission at Guantanamo would be compromised if habeas corpus courts had jurisdiction to hear the detainees' claims." What competence does the Court have to second-guess the judgment of Congress and the President on such a point? None whatever. But the Court blunders in nonetheless. Henceforth, as today's opinion makes unnervingly clear, how to handle enemy prisoners in this war will ultimately lie with the branch that knows least about the national security concerns that the subject entails.

.... The Court admits that it cannot determine whether the writ historically extended to aliens held abroad, and it concedes (necessarily) that Guantanamo Bay lies outside the sovereign territory of the United States. Together, these two concessions establish that it is (in the Court's view) perfectly ambiguous whether the common-law writ would have provided a remedy for these petitioners. If that is so, the Court has no basis to strike down the Military Commissions Act, and must leave undisturbed the considered judgment of the coequal branches....

Putting aside the conclusive precedent of *Eisentrager*, it is clear that the original understanding of the Suspension Clause was that habeas corpus was not available to aliens abroad.... The nature of the writ of habeas corpus that cannot be suspended must be defined by the common-law writ that was available at the time of the founding....

.... [I]f the extraterritorial scope of habeas turned on flexible, "functional" considerations, as the Court holds, why would the Constitution limit its suspension almost entirely to instances of domestic crisis? Surely there is an even greater justification for suspension in foreign lands where the United States might hold prisoners of war during an ongoing conflict. And correspondingly, there is less threat to liberty when the Government suspends the writ's (supposed) application in foreign lands, where even on the most extreme view prisoners are entitled to fewer constitutional rights. It makes no sense, therefore, for the Constitution generally to forbid suspension of the writ abroad if indeed the writ has application there....

Today the Court.... most tragically, ... sets our military commanders the impossible task of proving to a civilian court, under whatever standards this Court devises in the future, that evidence supports the confinement of each and every enemy prisoner. The Nation will live to regret what the Court has done today. I dissent.

Review Questions and Explanations: *Boumediene v. Bush*

1. Does the majority resolve any of the unanswered questions about suspension of habeas corpus that arose in *Hamdi*?

2. *Boumediene* holds that the DTA/MCA procedures are not an "adequate substitute" for habeas corpus and that they therefore impose a "de facto" suspension of habeas corpus. This raises two related questions:

   (a) Why does the constitution permit substitutes for habeas corpus in the absence of suspension of the writ? This debate was at the heart of the plurality-vs.-Scalia debate in *Hamdi*.

   (b) Why doesn't the Court treat a de facto suspension of the writ as a proper one? Are there some formalities that need to be observed by Congress that are missing here?

3. What procedures are an adequate substitute for habeas corpus review in court? Is the Court being "Mr. Fix-it" again? If so, why exactly is this a problem?

4. What is the basis for the argument that habeas rights extend to the Guantanamo Bay detainees? Are you persuaded? Is the majority's effort to distinguish *Eisentrager* persuasive, or have they pulled a *Milligan* (i.e., misconstrued the facts or rationale in order to distinguish the case)? The *Eisentrager* petitioners may have conceded that they were "enemy aliens," as the *Boumediene* majority states, but wasn't the issue the disputed one of whether they were "enemy *unlawful combatants*"?

5. Consider Justice Scalia's dissent: (a) is it consistent or inconsistent with his position in his *Hamdi* dissent? (b) Is it entirely accurate to say, as he does at the end, that the majority opinion requires "our military commanders the impossible task of proving to a civilian court" that the detainees are each detainable enemy combatants? (c) What about his argument that the military authorities have mistakenly released dangerous terrorists? His implication is that civilian authorities are more likely to release dangerous terrorists. Does that follow? Or can we infer instead that the military procedures are more likely to produce erroneous determinations either way? Finally, the dangers Justice Scalia mentions in *Boumediene* did not surface in his *Hamdi* dissent; is that because suspected terrorists are more dangerous if they are aliens? Because there are numerically far fewer citizens in this category? Or what?

D. Foreign Affairs

In contrast to the numerous provisions in the Constitution relating to war and the use of military power, there are few clauses dealing with the power to conduct foreign affairs. Arguably, Congress's only general legislative power on non-military matters touching on foreign affairs is the power "to define and punish ... offenses against the law of nations." Art. I, § 8, cl. 10. The Senate has a more specifically defined role in foreign affairs: it confirms presidential appointments for "ambassadors, other public ministers and consuls," and it confirms treaties by a 2/3 vote (meaning that a number of senators consisting of 1/3 plus one of the total membership can reject a treaty). Art. II, §2, cl. 2.

The President's power "by and with the Advice and Consent of the Senate, to make treaties" seems to imply that the President has authority to initiate treaty negotiations. The President nominates "ambassadors, other public ministers and consuls," and he "receive(s) ambassadors and other public ministers" from foreign countries. Art. II, §3, cl. 3. Other considerations lend support to the idea that the President takes a primary role in foreign affairs, as the cases in this section suggest.

Guided Reading Questions: *United States v. Curtiss-Wright Export Corp.*

1. What is the precise issue in *Curtiss-Wright*? Was the lengthy paean to presidential power in foreign affairs necessary to the resolution in the case?

2. What is the theory underlying the contention that the president holds "the very delicate, plenary and exclusive power ... as the sole organ of the federal government in the field of international relations"?

3. Is the Court saying that the President could have banned the arms sales by proclamation in the *absence* of an authorizing act of Congress?

United States v. Curtiss-Wright Export Corp.
299 U.S. 304 (1936)

Majority: *Sutherland*, Hughes (CJ) Van Devanter, Brandeis, Butler, Roberts, Cardozo

Dissent: McReynolds (no opinion); (Stone took no part)

MR. JUSTICE SUTHERLAND delivered the opinion of the Court.

[A Joint Resolution approved by Congress on May 28, 1934, authorized the President to prohibit private arms to the belligerents, Bolivia and Paraguay, who were at war over control of the Chaco, a high-desert region between the two countries in which oil had recently been discovered. The Joint Resolution provided that the arms sale prohibition would take effect if and when the President made findings that an arms sale ban would contribute to peace and consulted with neighboring South American governments. Having met those two conditions, the President was authorized to issue a proclamation prohibiting the arms sales with whatever exceptions and conditions the President in his discretion might choose to establish. Violation of the arms sale prohibition was a felony punishable by a fine of up to $10,000 and up to two years imprisonment.

[On the same day the Joint Resolution was approved, President Roosevelt issued a proclamation banning the arms sales. Curtiss-Wright and three individuals allegedly conspired to sell 15 machine guns to Bolivia in violation of the law in July 1934. They were indicted on January 27, 1936. The District Court dismissed the indictment on the ground that the arms sale ban was unconstitutional, and the case went to the Supreme Court on direct appeal.

[The primary argument made by the defendants-appellees, both in the District Court and the Supreme Court, was that the delegation to the President to determine both whether the ban would go into effect, and with what exceptions and conditions, was an unconstitutional delegation of legislative authority to the executive. The so-called "non-delegation" doctrine, which still exists in some form today (and is an important topic in administrative law), had been applied by the Court to strike down certain acts of Congress in two cases the previous year.]

.... Assuming (but not deciding) that the challenged delegation, if it were confined to internal affairs, would be invalid, may it nevertheless be sustained on the ground that its exclusive aim is to afford a remedy for a hurtful condition within foreign territory?....

[We] first consider the differences between the powers of the federal government in respect of foreign or external affairs and those in respect of domestic or internal affairs.... [The] two classes of powers are different, both in respect of their origin and their nature. The broad statement that the federal government can exercise no powers except those specifically enumerated in the Constitution, and such implied powers as are necessary and proper to carry into effect the enumerated powers, is categorically true only in respect of our internal affairs. In that field, the primary purpose of the Constitution was to carve from the general mass of legislative powers *then possessed by the states* such portions as it was thought desirable to vest in the federal government, leaving those not included in the enumeration still in the states. Carter v. Carter Coal Co., 298 U.S. 238, 294. That this doctrine applies only to powers which the states had, is self evident. And since the states severally never possessed international powers, such powers could not have been carved from the mass of state powers but obviously were transmitted to the United States from some other source....

As a result of the separation from Great Britain by the colonies acting as a unit, the powers of external sovereignty passed from the Crown not to the colonies severally, but to the colonies in their collective and corporate capacity as the United States of America.... [The] Union existed before the Constitution, which was ordained and established among other things to form "a more perfect Union." Prior to that event, it is clear that the Union, declared by the Articles of Confederation to be "perpetual," was the sole possessor of external sovereignty and in the Union it remained without change save in so far as the Constitution in express terms qualified its exercise....

[It] results that the investment of the federal government with the powers of external sovereignty did not depend upon the affirmative grants of the Constitution. The powers to declare and wage war, to conclude peace, to make treaties, to maintain diplomatic relations with other sovereignties, if they had never been mentioned in the Constitution, would have vested in the federal government as necessary concomitants of nationality....

[Not] only, as we have shown, is the federal power over external affairs in origin and essential character different from that over internal affairs, but participation in the exercise of the power is significantly limited. In this vast external realm, with its important, complicated, delicate and manifold problems, the President alone has the power to speak or listen as a representative of the nation. He *makes* treaties with the advice and consent of the Senate; but he alone negotiates. Into the field of negotiation the Senate cannot intrude; and Congress itself is powerless to invade it. As Marshall said in his great argument of March 7, 1800, in the House of Representatives, "The President is the sole organ of the nation in its external relations, and its sole representative with foreign nations." Annals, 6th Cong., col. 613....

It is important to bear in mind that we are here dealing not alone with an authority vested in the President by an exertion of legislative power, but with such an authority plus the very delicate, plenary and exclusive power of the President as the sole organ of the federal government in the field of international relations—a power which does not require as a basis for its exercise an act of Congress, but which, of course, like every other governmental power, must be exercised in subordination to the applicable provisions of the Constitution. It is quite apparent that if, in the maintenance of our international relations, embarrassment—perhaps serious embarrassment—is to be avoided and success for our aims achieved, congressional legislation which is to be made effective through negotiation and inquiry within the international field must often accord to the President a degree of discretion and freedom from statutory restriction which would not be admissible were domestic affairs alone involved. Moreover, he, not Congress, has the better opportunity of knowing the conditions which prevail in foreign countries, and especially is this true in time of war. He has his confidential sources of information. He has his agents in the form of diplomatic, consular and other officials. Secrecy in respect of information gathered by them may be highly necessary, and the premature disclosure of it productive of harmful results. Indeed, so clearly is this true that the first President refused to accede to a request to lay before the House of Representatives the instructions, correspondence and documents relating to the negotiation of the Jay Treaty—a refusal the wisdom of which was recognized by the House itself and has never since been doubted. In his reply to the request, President Washington said:

> The nature of foreign negotiations requires caution, and their success must often depend on secrecy; and even when brought to a conclusion a full disclosure of all the measures, demands, or eventual concessions which may have been proposed or contemplated would be extremely impolitic; for this might have a pernicious influence on future negotiations, or produce immediate inconveniences, perhaps danger and mischief, in relation to other powers. The necessity of such caution and secrecy was one cogent reason for vesting the power of making treaties in the President, with the advice and consent of the Senate, the principle on which that body was formed confining it to a small number of members. To admit, then, a right in the House of Representatives to demand and to have as a matter of course all the papers respecting a negotiation with a foreign power would be to establish a dangerous precedent." 1 Messages and Papers of the Presidents, p. 194....

[When] the President is to be authorized by legislation to act in respect of a matter intended to affect a situation in foreign territory, the legislator properly bears in mind the important consideration that the form of the President's action—or, indeed, whether he shall act at all—may well depend, among other things, upon the nature of the confidential information which he has or may thereafter receive, or upon the effect which his action may have upon our foreign relations. This consideration, in connection with what we have already said on the subject, discloses the unwisdom of requiring Congress in this field of governmental power to lay down narrowly definite standards by which the President is to be governed....

In the light of the foregoing observations, it is evident that this court should not be in haste to apply a general rule which will have the effect of condemning legislation like that under review as constituting an unlawful delegation of legislative power. The principles which justify such legislation find overwhelming support in the unbroken legislative practice which has prevailed almost from the inception of the national government to the present day....

[Practically] every volume of the United States Statutes contains one or more acts or joint resolutions of Congress authorizing action by the President in respect of subjects affecting foreign relations, which either leave the exercise of the power to his unrestricted judgment, or provide a standard far more general than that which has always been considered requisite with regard to domestic affairs....

[The] uniform, long-continued and undisputed legislative practice just disclosed rests upon an admissible view of the Constitution which, even if the practice found far less support in principle than we think it does, we should not feel at liberty at this late day to disturb.

[We] conclude there is sufficient warrant for the broad discretion vested in the President to determine whether the enforcement of the statute will have a beneficial effect upon the reestablishment of peace in the affected countries; whether he shall make proclamation to bring the resolution into operation; whether and when the resolution shall cease to operate and to make proclamation accordingly; and to prescribe limitations and exceptions to which the enforcement of the resolution shall be subject....

[The] judgment of the court below must be reversed and the cause remanded for further proceedings in accordance with the foregoing opinion.

Review Questions and Explanations: *Curtiss-Wright*

1. Is *Curtiss-Wright* consistent with *Youngstown*? Despite the opinion's dwelling on foreign affairs powers, ultimately the presidential proclamation in question imposed criminal penalties on a U.S. company, thereby regulating domestic activities in significant part. If foreign affairs powers broaden the President's power over domestic affairs, wouldn't *Curtiss-Wright* have justified the opposite outcome in *Youngstown*? Put another way, could *Youngstown* have been recast as a foreign affairs case, since the domestic activity of steel production was claimed to have a major impact on the conduct of foreign affairs, i.e., waging the Korean War?

2. The Court probably felt some burden to justify the broad delegation of legislative discretion to the President in light of the fact that it had struck down two acts of Congress the previous year for purportedly excessive delegation of legislative discretion to the President. *See Schechter Poultry Corp. v. United States*, 295 U.S. 495, 538 (1935); *Panama Refining Co. v. Ryan*, 293 U.S. 388 (1935). But there has been a long history of authorizing the President to issue binding, law-like proclamations if he finds certain conditions; the Court even alludes to that history. So the suggestion that the President can act in foreign affairs without congressional authorization would seem to be dicta. And the Court's extreme deference is arguably superseded by *Youngstown*.

Nevertheless, the broad language in *Curtiss-Wright* has never been expressly disapproved by the Supreme Court, and the case continues to be cited by courts and commentators—particularly those looking for authority for sweeping presidential powers in the field of foreign affairs and war. Indeed, *Curtiss-Wright* and *Youngstown* can be seen as standing for sharply contrasting visions of presidential power and constitutional limits in this field.

CASE NOTE: *Dames & Moore v. Regan*, 453 U.S. 654 (1981). Here, a unanimous Court applied the Jackson *Youngstown* approach to uphold an assertion of executive power in the foreign affairs realm. From November 1979 to January 1981, Iranian militants held several American citizens hostage after storming the American Embassy in Tehran. On

January 20, 1981, the American hostages were released by Iran pursuant to an "executive agreement" entered into on January 19. (An "executive agreement" is an agreement entered into by the President with a foreign government that is not a treaty because it is not presented for ratification to the Senate.) The agreement provided for the termination of "all legal proceedings in United States courts involving claims of United States persons and institutions against Iran and its state enterprises." Such claims were to be transferred to a newly created Iran-United States Claims Tribunal. Iranian assets in the U.S., frozen by court orders pursuant to such legal proceedings, were to be transferred to a security account in the Bank of England, to the account of the Algerian Central Bank, and used to satisfy awards rendered against Iran by the Claims Tribunal.

In late June 1981, the Supreme Court granted expedited review of a case brought by petitioner Dames & Moore against the government of Iran claiming payment of $3.4 million plus interest for unpaid services it performed under a contract to conduct site studies for a proposed nuclear power plant in Iran. Dames & Moore had prevailed on the merits of its claim in a preliminary ruling by the district court, but could not obtain a final judgment in that court. The executive agreement issued by President Jimmy Carter and re-issued by President Ronald Reagan, and implemented by regulations issued by Treasury Secretary Donald Regan, suspended Dames & Moore's claims and ordered the Iranian assets transferred out of the country. Dames & Moore challenged the executive agreement and Treasury regulations as unconstitutional.

The Court concluded that there was specific statutory authorization for the President to nullify the freezing of Iranian assets. Although there was no specific statutory authorization to suspend litigation such as Dames & Moore's, the Court deemed that the "general tenor" of statutes granting emergency powers to the President were "relevant in the looser sense of indicating congressional acceptance of a broad scope for executive action in circumstances such as those presented in this case." The Court cited both *Curtiss-Wright* and *Youngstown*, in upholding the executive agreement and regulations. As to *Youngstown*, the Court cited Justice Frankfurter's concurrence to support its reliance in *Dames & Moore* on a congressional history of "implicitly approv[ing] the practice of claim settlement by executive agreement." Regarding the Jackson concurrence, the Court stated:

> Although we have in the past found and do today find Justice Jackson's classification of executive actions into three general categories analytically useful, ... Justice Jackson himself recognized that his three categories represented "a somewhat over-simplified grouping," 343 U.S., at 635, and it is doubtless the case that executive action in any particular instance falls, not neatly in one of three pigeonholes, but rather at some point along a spectrum running from explicit congressional authorization to explicit congressional prohibition. This is particularly true as respects cases such as the one before us, involving responses to international crises the nature of which Congress can hardly have been expected to anticipate in any detail....

Exercise: Foreign Affairs

(Re)consider President Roosevelt's proclamation making it a crime to sell arms to the belligerents in the armed conflict between Bolivia and Paraguay. Suppose there were no authorizing statute by Congress, but the proclamation is issued and Curtiss-Wright charged under the proclamation. With one or more classmates, assume the roles of attorneys for Curtiss-Wright and the government, and a presiding judge: make the arguments for and against the constitutionality of the proclamation.

E. Executive Privileges and Immunities

The cases in this section deal with assertions that the President cannot be subjected to judicial processes, such as civil suits, prosecutions, subpoenas, or other compelled disclosures. These claims have variously been labeled "executive [or Presidential] immunity" or "executive privilege." The meaning of these terms is unclear—in part, because their assertion by Presidents over time has varied in circumstances and the Court has rarely ruled on the matter. It is *probably* the case that "executive privilege" refers to a claim of a power to forbid disclosure of information from the executive branch to a coordinate branch or the public. The term "privilege" is thus used in largely the same manner as that term is used in evidence law. "Executive immunity," in contrast, means immunity from civil or criminal liability.

The Constitution identifies only one such "privilege" or "immunity," and it is for members of Congress, not for the President. The "speech or debate" clause, Art. I., §6, cl. 1, provides:

> The Senators and Representatives.... shall in all Cases, except Treason, Felony and Breach of the Peace, be privileged from Arrest during their Attendance at the Session of their respective Houses, and in going to and returning from the same; and for any Speech or Debate in either House, they shall not be questioned in any other Place.

This language is plainly intended to protect members of Congress from interference with their duties as legislators by executive branch or state officials—a safeguard against an executive coup d'etat. No similar language addresses presidential privilege or immunity. However, it is generally assumed that the President is immune from criminal processes—arrest and prosecution—while he holds office. The source for this assumption is not entirely clear. The "impeachment judgment" clause, Art. I., §3, cl. 7, can be read to imply that removal from office must occur before criminal process, at least for the President. (This is discussed further in the next chapter's subsection on impeachment.)

More likely, the source of presidential privileges and immunities comes from ideas about "inherent executive powers" and "sovereign immunity." The doctrine of "sovereign immunity" holds that a sovereign governmental entity cannot be sued without its consent. Sovereign immunity for state governments is encapsulated in the Eleventh Amendment and is discussed above in Chapter 1. Federal sovereign immunity has been recognized in numerous judicial decisions; generally speaking the federal government can be sued for monetary damages only under statutes that expressly waive sovereign immunity by permitting damages claims. *See, e.g.,* Federal Tort Claims Act, 28 U.S.C. §1346. Individual federal officials *other than* the President can be sued for damages for violating constitutional rights (so-called "constitutional torts") under the theory that, by violating the Constitution, they have exceeded their authority and have acted as individuals rather than as agents of the government. *See Bivens v. Six Unknown Named Agents of the FBI*, 403 U.S. 388 (1971).

"Sovereign immunity" is not mentioned in the Constitution, but the Supreme Court has repeatedly stated that it is a doctrine of common law that pre-dated the Constitution and was implicitly incorporated into it, along with other aspects of Anglo-American common law. The Court has said this despite the awkward fact that the English version of sovereign immunity was rooted in concepts of monarchical sovereignty holding that "the king could do no wrong" and therefore could not be sued without his consent. In monarchical theory, the connection between these concepts and sovereign immunity makes sense, because national sovereignty is vested in the person of the king. Assertions of executive privilege and executive immunity, vestiges of that monarchical theory, arguably make less sense in a constitutional regime such as ours. Nonetheless, the Court has held that the office of the President holds certain attributes of sovereign immunity that can be asserted by the individual office-holder. Once that person leaves office, however, most of those powers are left behind. Thus, the assumption is that the President is immune from criminal process, but only while in office.

Still, the nature and extent of sovereign-immunity-based concepts of executive privilege and executive immunity remain the subject of dispute. Chief Justice Marshall indicated, in *Marbury v. Madison*, that discretionary decisions by the President are only "politically examinable," meaning that the President is answerable to the electorate and the political process, not the Courts, for his actions. Clearly, that principle has its limits — *Youngstown* is a striking example. President Nixon, who tried to rely on assertions of executive privilege to fend off investigation into his actions around the Watergate scandal, famously made one of the most extreme statements regarding presidential immunity. In a television interview after his resignation from office, Nixon said: "if the President does it, it's not illegal." Current and even former presidents have an incentive to overstate the extent of executive privileges and immunities. The Court, not surprisingly, has been a bit more cautious.

Guided Reading Questions: *United States v. Nixon*

1. What is the precise issue before the Court in this case? To whom was the subpoena issued? On behalf of whom? To whose authority did Nixon's assertion of executive privilege object?

2. Does Nixon's assertion of executive privilege equate to an assertion that "the President is above the law," or can his claim be understood as asserting something more narrow?

3. On what grounds does the Court reject Nixon's privilege claim?

United States v. Nixon

418 U.S. 683 (1974)

Unanimous decision: *Burger* (CJ), Douglas, Brennan, Stewart, White, Marshall, Blackmun, Powell (Rehnquist took no part)

[On March 1, 1974, a federal grand jury indicted seven associates of President Richard M. Nixon with various offenses stemming from the cover-up of the 1972 "Watergate Break-in." The offenses included conspiracy to defraud the United States and to obstruct justice. In 1972, officials of Nixon's re-election campaign had orchestrated a burglary of the Democratic National Committee's headquarters in the Watergate office building. Certain of these officials, as well as White House staff members, subsequently participated in a campaign ultimately involving the President himself, to cover up the misdeeds. Although he was not designated as such in the indictment, the grand jury named the President, among others, as an unindicted co-conspirator. On April 18, 1974, on motion of Leon Jaworski, appointed as Special Prosecutor to investigate the Watergate scandal, a subpoena *duces tecum* was issued by the district court to the President requiring the President to turn over the infamous "Watergate tapes"—various recordings, transcripts, and other documents relating to certain meetings between the President and others discussing the cover-up. The subpoena required delivery of the documents to the district court by May 31, 1974. On April 30, the President publicly released edited transcripts of 43 conversations; portions of 20 conversations subject to subpoena in the present case were included. On May 1, 1974, the President's counsel filed a "special appearance" and a motion to quash the subpoena; but on May 20 the district court denied the motion and ordered production of the documents, including original, unedited versions of the tapes.

[On May 24, 1974, the President appealed the decision to the Court of Appeals for the District of Columbia Circuit. While that appeal was pending, the parties filed cross-petitions in the Supreme Court for writ of certiorari before judgment. These were granted on June 15, and the case went to the Supreme Court, skipping the intermediate appellate court. The Court heard arguments on July 8 and issued its decision on July 24. That schedule reflected the unusual and urgent nature of the case, since the Court rarely hears cases after April and usually issues all its opinions for the term by early July.

[It was assumed by observers and the general public that the content of the contested tapes and documents would be damaging to the President. Indeed, just over two weeks after the Supreme Court issued its decision affirming the District Court's order enforcing the subpoena, Richard Nixon resigned the presidency, on August 9, 1974.

[The Court first held that it had jurisdiction over the appeal, and then rejected the President's argument that a dispute between the Special Prosecutor and the Executive Branch was a non-justiciable "intra-branch" dispute over matters committed to prosecutorial discretion. The Court further determined that the Special Prosecutor had made a sufficient preliminary showing that the tapes and documents were likely to contain admissible evidence relevant to the charged crimes.]

MR. CHIEF JUSTICE BURGER delivered the opinion of the Court.

.... We turn to the claim that the subpoena should be quashed because it demands "confidential conversations between a President and his close advisors that it would be inconsistent with the public interest to produce." ...

In the performance of assigned constitutional duties each branch of the Government must initially interpret the Constitution, and the interpretation of its powers by any branch is due great respect from the others. The President's counsel, as we have noted, reads the Constitution as providing an absolute privilege of confidentiality for all Presidential communications. Many decisions of this Court, however, have unequivocally reaffirmed the holding of Marbury v. Madison, 1 Cranch 137 (1803), that "[it] is emphatically the province and duty of the judicial department to say what the law is."

Our system of government "requires that federal courts on occasion interpret the Constitution in a manner at variance with the construction given the document by another branch." Powell v. McCormack, supra. And in Baker v. Carr, 369 U.S., at 211, the Court stated:

> Deciding whether a matter has in any measure been committed by the Constitution to another branch of government, or whether the action of that branch exceeds whatever authority has been committed, is itself a delicate exercise in constitutional interpretation, and is a responsibility of this Court as ultimate interpreter of the Constitution.

Notwithstanding the deference each branch must accord the others, the "judicial Power of the United States" vested in the federal courts by Art. III, §1, of the Constitution can no more be shared with the Executive Branch than the Chief Executive, for example, can share with the Judiciary the veto power, or the Congress share with the Judiciary the power to override a Presidential veto. Any other conclusion would be contrary to the basic concept of separation of powers and the checks and balances that flow from the scheme of a tripartite government. We therefore reaffirm that it is the province and duty of this Court "to say what the law is" with respect to the claim of privilege presented in this case.

In support of his claim of absolute privilege, the President's counsel urges.... the valid need for protection of communications between high Government officials and those who advise and assist them in the performance of their manifold duties; the importance of this confidentiality is too plain to require further discussion. Human experience teaches that those who expect public dissemination of their remarks may well temper candor with a concern for appearances and for their own interests to the detriment of the decisionmaking process. Whatever the nature of the privilege of confidentiality of Presidential communications in the exercise of Art. II powers, the privilege can be said to derive from the supremacy of each branch within its own assigned area of constitutional duties. Certain powers and privileges flow from the nature of enumerated powers; the protection of the confidentiality of Presidential communications has similar constitutional underpinnings....

However, neither the doctrine of separation of powers, nor the need for confidentiality of high-level communications, without more, can sustain an absolute, unqualified Presidential privilege of immunity from judicial process under all circumstances.... Absent a claim of need to protect military, diplomatic, or sensitive national security secrets, we find it difficult to accept the argument that even the very important interest in confidentiality of Presidential communications is significantly diminished by production of such material for in camera inspection with all the protection that a district court will be obliged to provide.

The impediment that an absolute, unqualified privilege would place in the way of the primary constitutional duty of the Judicial Branch to do justice in criminal prosecutions would plainly conflict with the function of the courts under Art. III....

> While the Constitution diffuses power the better to secure liberty, it also contemplates that practice will integrate the dispersed powers into a workable government. It enjoins upon its branches separateness but interdependence, autonomy but reciprocity." Youngstown Sheet & Tube Co. v. Sawyer, 343 U.S., at 635 (Jackson, J., concurring).

.... Since we conclude that the legitimate needs of the judicial process may outweigh Presidential privilege, it is necessary to resolve those competing interests in a manner that preserves the essential functions of each branch....

[The President's] presumptive privilege must be considered in light of our historic commitment to the rule of law. This is nowhere more profoundly manifest than in our view that "the twofold aim [of criminal justice] is that guilt shall not escape or innocence suffer."…. The ends of criminal justice would be defeated if judgments were to be founded on a partial or speculative presentation of the facts. The very integrity of the judicial system and public confidence in the system depend on full disclosure of all the facts, within the framework of the rules of evidence. To ensure that justice is done, it is imperative to the function of courts that compulsory process be available for the production of evidence needed either by the prosecution or by the defense.

Whatever their origins, the [various testimonial privileges that are] exceptions to the demand for every man's evidence are not lightly created nor expansively construed, for they are in derogation of the search for truth…. [It] is the manifest duty of the courts to vindicate [the constitutional due process] guarantees, and to accomplish that it is essential that all relevant and admissible evidence be produced.

…. The interest in preserving confidentiality is weighty indeed and entitled to great respect. However, we cannot conclude that advisers will be moved to temper the candor of their remarks by the infrequent occasions of disclosure because of the possibility that such conversations will be called for in the context of a criminal prosecution….

On the other hand, the allowance of the privilege to withhold evidence that is demonstrably relevant in a criminal trial would cut deeply into the guarantee of due process of law and gravely impair the basic function of the courts. A President's acknowledged need for confidentiality in the communications of his office is general in nature, whereas the constitutional need for production of relevant evidence in a criminal proceeding is specific and central to the fair adjudication of a particular criminal case in the administration of justice. Without access to specific facts a criminal prosecution may be totally frustrated. The President's broad interest in confidentiality of communications will not be vitiated by disclosure of a limited number of conversations preliminarily shown to have some bearing on the pending criminal cases…. The generalized assertion of [executive] privilege must yield to the demonstrated, specific need for evidence in a pending criminal trial.

…. If a President concludes that compliance with a subpoena would be injurious to the public interest he may properly, as was done here, invoke a claim of privilege on the return of the subpoena. Upon receiving a claim of privilege from the Chief Executive, it became the further duty of the District Court to treat the subpoenaed material as presumptively privileged and to require the Special Prosecutor to demonstrate that the Presidential material was "essential to the justice of the [pending criminal] case." United States v. Burr, 25 F. Cas., at 192 (1807). Here the District Court treated the material as presumptively privileged, proceeded to find that the Special Prosecutor had made a sufficient showing to rebut the presumption, and ordered an in camera examination of the subpoenaed material. On the basis of our examination of the record we are unable to conclude that the District Court erred in ordering the inspection. Accordingly we affirm the order of the District Court that subpoenaed materials be transmitted to that court. We now turn to the important question of the District Court's responsibilities in conducting the in camera examination of Presidential materials or communications delivered under the compulsion of the subpoena duces tecum.

…. "[The] guard, furnished to [the President] to protect him from being harassed by vexatious and unnecessary subpoenas, is to be looked for in the conduct of a [district] court after those subpoenas have issued; not in any circumstance which is to precede their being issued." United States v. Burr, 25 F. Cas., at 34. Statements that meet the test of admissibility and relevance must be isolated; all other material must be excised. At this stage the District Court is not limited to representations of the Special Prosecutor as to the evidence sought by the subpoena; the material will be available to the District Court. It is elementary that in camera inspection of evidence is always a procedure calling for scrupulous protection against any release or publication of material not found by the court, at that stage, probably admissible in evidence and relevant to the issues of the trial for which it is sought. That being true of an ordinary situation, it is obvious that the District Court has a very heavy responsibility to see to it that Presidential conversations, which are either not relevant or not admissible, are accorded that high degree of respect due the President of the United States. Mr. Chief Justice Marshall, sitting as a trial judge in the Burr case, supra, was extraordinarily careful to point out that "[in] no case of this kind would a court be required to proceed against the President as against an ordinary individual." 25 F. Cas., at 192.... [A] President is [not] above the law, but.... a President's communications and activities encompass a vastly wider range of sensitive material than would be true of any "ordinary individual." It is therefore necessary in the public interest to afford Presidential confidentiality the greatest protection consistent with the fair administration of justice.... We have no doubt that the District Judge will at all times accord to Presidential records that high degree of deference suggested in United States v. Burr, supra, and will discharge his responsibility to see to it that until released to the Special Prosecutor no in camera material is revealed to anyone. This burden applies with even greater force to excised material; once the decision is made to excise, the material is restored to its privileged status and should be returned under seal to its lawful custodian.

Since this matter came before the Court during the pendency of a criminal prosecution, and on representations that time is of the essence, the mandate shall issue forthwith.

Review Questions and Explanations: *United States v. Nixon*

1. Does the Court hold that the President has no "executive privilege"? If not, what is the extent of that privilege? What is its constitutional basis?

2. *United States v. Burr* (1807), was a treason trial against Aaron Burr, a former U.S. Senator from New York and Vice President from 1801–1805, during Jefferson's first term. (Burr is most famous for killing Alexander Hamilton in a duel in July 1804.) Burr had fallen out of favor with Jefferson, and was replaced on the electoral ticket by another vice presidential candidate in the 1804 election. Subsequently, Burr busied himself trying to organize a "filibustering" expedition into Latin America. Such expeditions were private military adventures used to enlarge U.S. territory by conquest. They were not uncommon in the early 1800s, and often were undertaken with at least tacit governmental approval. Burr's political enemies claimed that the tiny force he assembled in Ohio (fewer than 100 men) was planning to march on Washington and overthrow the government. No expedition—to Washington or elsewhere—ever materialized, and Burr was arrested in Virginia, on his way back home to New York. He was put on trial for treason, and ultimately acquitted, after which he retired from politics and returned to his New York City law practice.

The trial was presided over by Chief Justice John Marshall in his capacity as circuit judge (Supreme Court justices in Marshall's era were required to act as traveling lower court judges). Marshall issued a series of rulings arising out of this trial, on evidentiary points as well as on the substantive law of treason. The ruling referred to by the *Nixon* Court was one in which Marshall upheld Burr's right to a subpoena demanding the production of documents in his defense from President Jefferson. Burr believed (rightly, as it turned out), that letters in

Jefferson's possession would exonerate him. Although an aged precedent, and technically one from a lower federal court, *Burr* came from an eminent authority and was very much on point.

Guided Reading Questions: *Nixon v. Fitzgerald; Clinton v. Jones*

1. What sort of privilege or immunity is the president asserting in the *Fitzgerald* and *Jones* cases, below? Is it the same as in *U.S. v. Nixon*? Is President Nixon's argument in *Fitzgerald* the same as or different from President Clinton's argument in *Jones*?

2. Identify the key factual distinctions between the *Fitzgerald* and *Jones* cases. Do these factual distinctions provide a convincing justification the different outcomes?

3. A key concept to understanding this case is the distinction between "absolute" and "qualified" immunity. See if you can find the relevant explanation of this distinction in the case and restate it in your own words.

Nixon v. Fitzgerald
457 U.S. 731 (1982)

Majority: *Powell*, Burger (CJ), Rehnquist, Stevens, O'Connor

Concurrence: *Burger* (CJ) (omitted)

Dissents: *White*, Brennan, Marshall, *Blackmun* (omitted)

JUSTICE POWELL delivered the opinion of the Court.

[Ernest Fitzgerald, a management analyst in the Air Force, became a high-profile "whistleblower" when he testified in Congress in November 1968 about a $2.3 billion cost-overrun in the Lockheed C-5 aircraft development contract. The testimony embarrassed the Pentagon and the Johnson administration. Animus toward Fitzgerald carried over into the administration of President Richard Nixon, who allegedly ordered Fitzgerald to be fired for "disloyalty" in early 1970. Fitzgerald's firing became a high profile matter, gaining attention in the press and from Congress. Fitzgerald filed a complaint with the federal Civil Service Commission, and in late 1973 won reinstatement to federal employment, successfully proving that his discharge violated federal whistleblower protection laws.

[In 1974, Fitzgerald filed suit in federal court against various federal officials and White House aides for conspiring to violate his statutory and constitutional rights; in 1978, after successfully appealing a dismissal of his complaint, and taking extensive discovery, he added former President Nixon as a defendant. In March 1980, the three remaining defendants—Nixon and two White House aides, Harlow and Butterfield—moved for summary judgment on grounds of presidential immunity. The District Court denied the motions and set the case for trial. The defendants appealed, and the court of appeals dismissed the appeals since no final judgment had been entered.

[The U.S. Supreme Court granted certiorari, in two companion cases, *Harlow v. Fitzgerald* and *Nixon v. Fitzgerald*. In both cases, the Court held that it had jurisdiction over the "interlocutory" appeal (i.e., it could decide the issue notwithstanding the absence of a final judgment). In *Harlow*, on the merits, the Court held that the presidential aides were entitled to qualified, but not absolute immunity from a civil damages suit: they could be held liable if they knew or should have known their actions violated "clearly established law." The *Nixon* decision was issued the same day, treating as a separate question whether the former President had absolute immunity from a damages suit.]

This Court consistently has recognized that government officials are entitled to some form of immunity from suits for civil damages....

.... To most executive officers, [we have] accorded qualified immunity. For them the scope of the defense varied in proportion to the nature of their official functions and the range of decisions that conceivably might be taken in "good faith." This "functional" approach also defined a second tier, however, at which the especially sensitive duties of certain officials — notably judges and prosecutors — required the continued recognition of absolute immunity....

[We have also] upheld a claim of absolute immunity for administrative officials engaged in functions analogous to those of judges and prosecutors. We also left open the question whether other federal officials could show that "public policy requires an exemption of that scope."

Our decisions concerning the immunity of government officials from civil damages liability have been guided by the Constitution, federal statutes, and history. Additionally, at least in the absence of explicit constitutional or congressional guidance, our immunity decisions have been informed by the common law....

This case now presents the claim that the President of the United States is shielded by absolute immunity from civil damages liability.... Because the Presidency did not exist through most of the development of common law, any historical analysis must draw its evidence primarily from our constitutional heritage and structure.... This inquiry involves policies and principles that may be considered implicit in the nature of the President's office in a system structured to achieve effective government under a constitutionally mandated separation of powers.

Here a former President asserts his immunity from civil damages claims of two kinds. He stands named as a defendant in a direct action under the Constitution and in two statutory actions under federal laws of general applicability. In neither case has Congress taken express legislative action to subject the President to civil liability for his official acts.

.... [W]e hold that petitioner, as a former President of the United States, is entitled to absolute immunity from damages liability predicated on his official acts. We consider this immunity a functionally mandated incident of the President's unique office, rooted in the constitutional tradition of the separation of powers and supported by our history.

The President occupies a unique position in the constitutional scheme. Article II, § 1.... establishes the President as the chief constitutional officer of the Executive Branch, entrusted with supervisory and policy responsibilities of utmost discretion and sensitivity....

Because of the singular importance of the President's duties, diversion of his energies by concern with private lawsuits would raise unique risks to the effective functioning of government. As is the case with prosecutors and judges — for whom absolute immunity now is established — a President must concern himself with matters likely to "arouse the most intense feelings." Yet, as our decisions have recognized, it is in precisely such cases that there exists the greatest public interest in providing an official "the maximum ability to deal fearlessly and impartially with" the duties of his office. This concern is compelling where the officeholder must make the most sensitive and far-reaching decisions entrusted to any official under our constitutional system. Nor can the sheer prominence of the President's office be ignored. In view of the visibility of his office and the effect of his actions on countless people, the President would be an easily identifiable target for suits for civil damages. Cognizance of this personal vulnerability frequently could distract a President from his public duties, to the detriment of not only the President and his office but also the Nation that the Presidency was designed to serve.

Courts traditionally have recognized the President's constitutional responsibilities and status as factors counseling judicial deference and restraint. For example, while courts generally have looked to the common law to determine the scope of an official's evidentiary privilege, we have recognized that the Presidential privilege is "rooted in the separation of powers under the Constitution." United States v. Nixon, 418 U.S. at 708. It is settled law that the separation-of-powers doctrine does not bar every exercise of jurisdiction over the President of the United States. See, e.g., United States v. Nixon, *supra*; United States v. Burr, 25 F.Cas. 187, 191, 196 (No. 14,694) (CC Va. 1807); cf. Youngstown Sheet & Tube Co. v. Sawyer, 343 U.S. 579 (1952). But our cases also have established that a court, before exercising jurisdiction, must balance the constitutional weight of the interest to be served against the dangers of intrusion on the authority and functions of the Executive Branch. When judicial action is needed to serve broad public interests—as when the Court acts not in derogation of the separation of powers, but to maintain their proper balance, cf. Youngstown Sheet & Tube Co. v. Sawyer, *supra*, or to vindicate the public interest in an ongoing criminal prosecution, see United States v. Nixon, *supra*—the exercise of jurisdiction has been held warranted. In the case of this merely private suit for damages based on a President's official acts, we hold it is not.

In defining the scope of an official's absolute privilege, this Court has recognized that the sphere of protected action must be related closely to the immunity's justifying purposes. Frequently our decisions have held that an official's absolute immunity should extend only to acts in performance of particular functions of his office.... In view of the special nature of the President's constitutional office and functions, we think it appropriate to recognize absolute Presidential immunity from damages liability for acts within the "outer perimeter" of his official responsibility.

Under the Constitution and laws of the United States, the President has discretionary responsibilities in a broad variety of areas, many of them highly sensitive. In many cases, it would be difficult to determine which of the President's innumerable "functions" encompassed a particular action. In this case, for example, respondent argues that he was dismissed in retaliation for his testimony to Congress—a violation of 5 U.S.C. §7211 and 18 U.S.C. §1505. The Air Force, however, has claimed that the underlying reorganization was undertaken to promote efficiency. Assuming that petitioner Nixon ordered the reorganization in which respondent lost his job, an inquiry into the President's motives could not be avoided under the kind of "functional" theory asserted both by respondent and the dissent. Inquiries of this kind could be highly intrusive.

Here, respondent argues that petitioner Nixon would have acted outside the outer perimeter of his duties by ordering the discharge of an employee who was lawfully entitled to retain his job in the absence of "'such cause as will promote the efficiency of the service.'" Because Congress has granted this legislative protection, respondent argues, no federal official could, within the outer perimeter of his duties of office, cause Fitzgerald to be dismissed without satisfying this standard in prescribed statutory proceedings.

This construction would subject the President to trial on virtually every allegation that an action was unlawful, or was taken for a forbidden purpose. Adoption of this construction thus would deprive absolute immunity of its intended effect. It clearly is within the President's constitutional and statutory authority to prescribe the manner in which the Secretary will conduct the business of the Air Force. (See 10 U.S.C. § 8012b.) Because this mandate of office must include the authority to prescribe reorganizations and reductions in force, we conclude that petitioner's alleged wrongful acts lay well within the outer perimeter of his authority.

A rule of absolute immunity for the President will not leave the Nation without sufficient protection against misconduct on the part of the Chief Executive. There remains the constitutional remedy of impeachment. In addition, there are formal and informal checks on Presidential action that do not apply with equal force to other executive officials. The President is subjected to constant scrutiny by the press. Vigilant oversight by Congress also may serve to deter Presidential abuses of office, as well as to make credible the threat of impeachment. Other incentives to avoid misconduct may include a desire to earn reelection, the need to maintain prestige as an element of Presidential influence, and a President's traditional concern for his historical stature.

The existence of alternative remedies and deterrents establishes that absolute immunity will not place the President "above the law." For the President, as for judges and prosecutors, absolute immunity merely precludes a particular private remedy for alleged misconduct in order to advance compelling public ends.

For the reasons stated in this opinion, the decision of the Court of Appeals is reversed, and the case is remanded for action consistent with this opinion.

JUSTICE WHITE, with whom JUSTICE BRENNAN, JUSTICE MARSHALL, and JUSTICE BLACKMUN join, dissenting.

.... Officials performing functions for which immunity is not absolute enjoy qualified immunity; they are liable in damages only if their conduct violated well-established law and if they should have realized that their conduct was illegal.

The Court now [holds that] a President, acting within the outer boundaries of what Presidents normally do, may, without liability, deliberately cause serious injury to any number of citizens even though he knows his conduct violates a statute or tramples on the constitutional rights of those who are injured.... He would be immune regardless of the damage he inflicts, regardless of how violative of the statute and of the Constitution he knew his conduct to be, and regardless of his purpose.

The Court intimates that its decision is grounded in the Constitution. If that is the case, Congress cannot provide a remedy against Presidential misconduct, and the criminal laws of the United States are wholly inapplicable to the President. I find this approach completely unacceptable. I do not agree that, if the Office of President is to operate effectively, the holder of that Office must be permitted, without fear of liability and regardless of the function he is performing, deliberately to inflict injury on others by conduct that he knows violates the law....

Attaching absolute immunity to the Office of the President, rather than to particular activities that the President might perform, places the President above the law. It is a reversion to the old notion that the King can do no wrong. Until now, this concept had survived in this country only in the form of sovereign immunity. That doctrine forecloses suit against the Government itself and against Government officials, but only when the suit against the latter actually seeks relief against the sovereign. Suit against an officer, however, may be maintained where it seeks specific relief against him for conduct contrary to his statutory authority or to the Constitution. Now, however, the Court clothes the Office of the President with sovereign immunity, placing it beyond the law.

.... While absolute immunity might maximize executive efficiency, and therefore be a worthwhile policy, lack of such immunity may not so disrupt the functioning of the Presidency as to violate the separation-of-powers doctrine. Insofar as liability in this case is of congressional origin, petitioner must demonstrate that subjecting the President to a private damages action will prevent him from "accomplishing [his] constitutionally assigned functions." ...

.... While the Speech or Debate Clause guarantees that, "for any Speech or Debate," Congressmen "shall not be questioned in any other Place," and, thus, assures that Congressmen, in their official capacity, shall not be the subject of the courts' injunctive powers, no such protection is afforded the Executive. Indeed, as the cases cited above indicate, it is the rule, not the exception, that executive actions—including those taken at the immediate direction of the President—are subject to judicial review. Regardless of the possibility of money damages against the President, then, the constitutionality of the President's actions or their legality under the applicable statutes can and will be subject to review. Indeed, in this very case, respondent Fitzgerald's dismissal was set aside by the Civil Service Commission as contrary to the applicable regulations issued pursuant to authority granted by Congress.

Nor can private damages actions be distinguished on the ground that such claims would involve the President personally in the litigation in a way not necessitated by suits seeking declaratory or injunctive relief against certain Presidential actions. ...

[Qualified immunity doctrine] makes clear that the President, were he subject to civil liability, could be held liable only for an action that he knew, or as an objective matter should have known, was illegal and a clear abuse of his authority and power. In such circumstances, the question that must be answered is who should bear the cost of the resulting injury—the wrongdoer or the victim. ...

The possibility of liability may, in some circumstances, distract officials from the performance of their duties and influence the performance of those duties in ways adverse to the public interest. ...

The Court's response, until today, to this problem has been to apply the argument to individual functions, not offices, and to evaluate the effect of liability on governmental decisionmaking within that function in light of the substantive ends that are to be encouraged or discouraged. In this case, therefore, the Court should examine the functions implicated by the causes of action at issue here and the effect of potential liability on the performance of those functions. ...

Absolute immunity is appropriate when the threat of liability may bias the decisionmaker in ways that are adverse to the public interest. But as the various regulations and statutes protecting civil servants from arbitrary executive action illustrate, this is an area in which the public interest is demonstrably on the side of encouraging less "vigor" and more "caution" on the part of decisionmakers. That is, the very steps that Congress has taken to assure that executive employees will be able freely to testify in Congress and to assure that they will not be subject to arbitrary adverse actions indicate that those policy arguments that have elsewhere justified absolute immunity are not applicable here. Absolute immunity would be nothing more than a judicial declaration of policy that directly contradicts the policy of protecting civil servants reflected in the statutes and regulations.

Review Questions and Explanations: *Nixon v. Fitzgerald*

1. Does the Court in *Fitzgerald* hold that the president enjoys "absolute immunity" from suits of any kind, by any party, for his official actions?

2. If the answer to that question is "no," can you think of doctrines other than presidential immunity that could be asserted by a president against claims for injunctive or declaratory relief?

3. *Nixon v. Fitzgerald* provides "absolute immunity" for the President from private damages suits. But the Court in *Butz v. Economou*, 438 U.S. 478 (1978), held that cabinet officials could be sued by private parties for damages for violating the Constitution (so-called *Bivens* suits); and this principle was extended to presidential advisors and other executive branch officials in *Harlow v. Fitzgerald*, 457 U.S. 800 (1982). Is it contradictory to hold that the President's functioning requires absolute immunity but that his advisors can be sued for damages for carrying out the President's orders? The issue is raised pointedly in the two *Fitzgerald* cases, where the plaintiff sued Nixon and his advisors for the same alleged injury.

The Court has explained its position in terms of a "balancing" of interests. The interest of claimants injured by unconstitutional official acts in seeking a judicial remedy is a powerful one, that is outweighed only in the President's case due to the uniqueness of his office. Do you agree with this argument? Does it make a difference whether your starting point is viewing immunity as an exception to a general rule of availability of judicial relief (rather than the other way around)?

Clinton v. Jones
520 U.S. 681 (1997)

Majority: *Stevens*, Rehnquist (CJ), O'Connor, Scalia, Kennedy, Souter, Thomas, Ginsburg,

Concurrence in the judgment: *Breyer*

JUSTICE STEVENS delivered the opinion of the Court.

.... Petitioner, William Jefferson Clinton, was elected to the Presidency in 1992, and re-elected in 1996. His term of office expires on January 20, 2001. In 1991 he was the Governor of the State of Arkansas. Respondent, Paula Corbin Jones, is a resident of California. In 1991 she lived in Arkansas, and was an employee of the Arkansas Industrial Development Commission.

On May 6, 1994, she commenced this action in the United States District Court for the Eastern District of Arkansas by filing a complaint naming petitioner and Danny Ferguson, a former Arkansas State Police officer, as defendants.... As the case comes to us, we are required to assume the truth of the detailed—but as yet untested—factual allegations in the complaint.

Those allegations principally describe events that are said to have occurred on the afternoon of May 8, 1991, during an official conference held at the Excelsior Hotel in Little Rock, Arkansas. The Governor delivered a speech at the conference; respondent— working as a state employee—staffed the registration desk. She alleges that Ferguson persuaded her to leave her desk and to visit the Governor in a business suite at the hotel, where he made "abhorrent" sexual advances that she vehemently rejected. She further claims that her superiors at work subsequently dealt with her in a hostile and rude manner, and changed her duties to punish her for rejecting those advances. Finally, she alleges that after petitioner was elected President, Ferguson defamed her by making a statement to a reporter that implied she had accepted petitioner's alleged overtures, and that various persons authorized to speak for the President publicly branded her a liar by denying that the incident had occurred.

Respondent seeks actual damages of $ 75,000, and punitive damages of $ 100,000 [based on various federal civil rights and state common law theories]…. With the exception of the [fourth cause of action, claiming that the President's agents defamed Jones], which arguably may involve conduct within the outer perimeter of the President's official responsibilities, it is perfectly clear that the alleged misconduct of petitioner was unrelated to any of his official duties as President of the United States and, indeed, occurred before he was elected to that office.

> FN3. … We do not address the question whether the President's immunity from damages liability for acts taken within the "outer perimeter" of his official responsibilities provides a defense to the fourth count of the complaint. See Nixon v. Fitzgerald, 457 U.S. 731, 756 (1982).

In response to the complaint, petitioner promptly advised the District Court that he intended to file a motion to dismiss on grounds of Presidential immunity, and requested the court to defer all other pleadings and motions until after the immunity issue was resolved…. The District Judge denied the motion to dismiss on immunity grounds and ruled that discovery in the case could go forward, but ordered any trial stayed until the end of petitioner's Presidency….

Both parties appealed. A divided panel of the Court of Appeals affirmed the denial of the motion to dismiss, but because it regarded the order postponing the trial until the President leaves office as the "functional equivalent" of a grant of temporary immunity, it reversed that order….

The President, represented by private counsel, filed a petition for certiorari. The Solicitor General, representing the United States, supported the petition, arguing that the decision of the Court of Appeals was "fundamentally mistaken" and created "serious risks for the institution of the Presidency."….

Petitioner's principal submission—that "in all but the most exceptional cases," the Constitution affords the President temporary immunity from civil damages litigation arising out of events that occurred before he took office—cannot be sustained on the basis of precedent.

Only three sitting Presidents have been defendants in civil litigation involving their actions prior to taking office. Complaints against Theodore Roosevelt and Harry Truman had been dismissed before they took office; the dismissals were affirmed after their respective inaugurations. Two companion cases arising out of an automobile accident were filed against John F. Kennedy in 1960 during the Presidential campaign. After taking office, he unsuccessfully argued that his status as Commander in Chief gave him a right to a stay under the Soldiers' and Sailors' Civil Relief Act of 1940. The motion for a stay was denied by the District Court, and the matter was settled out of court. Thus, none of those cases sheds any light on the constitutional issue before us.

The principal rationale for affording certain public servants immunity from suits for money damages arising out of their official acts is inapplicable to unofficial conduct. In cases involving prosecutors, legislators, and judges we have repeatedly explained that the immunity serves the public interest in enabling such officials to perform their designated functions effectively without fear that a particular decision may give rise to personal liability.... That rationale provided the principal basis for our holding that a former President of the United States was "entitled to absolute immunity from damages liability predicated on his official acts." Our central concern was to avoid rendering the President "unduly cautious in the discharge of his official duties."

This reasoning provides no support for an immunity for *unofficial* conduct. As we explained in Fitzgerald, "the sphere of protected action must be related closely to the immunity's justifying purposes." Because of the President's broad responsibilities, we recognized in that case an immunity from damages claims arising out of official acts extending to the "outer perimeter of his authority." But we have never suggested that the President, or any other official, has an immunity that extends beyond the scope of any action taken in an official capacity.

Moreover, when defining the scope of an immunity for acts clearly taken *within* an official capacity, we have applied a functional approach. "Frequently our decisions have held that an official's absolute immunity should extend only to acts in performance of particular functions of his office." Hence, for example, a judge's absolute immunity does not extend to actions performed in a purely administrative capacity. As our opinions have made clear, immunities are grounded in "the nature of the function performed, not the identity of the actor who performed it."....

Petitioner[] ... does not contend that the occupant of the Office of the President is "above the law," in the sense that his conduct is entirely immune from judicial scrutiny. The President argues merely for a postponement of the judicial proceedings that will determine whether he violated any law....

As a starting premise, petitioner contends that he occupies a unique office with powers and responsibilities so vast and important that the public interest demands that he devote his undivided time and attention to his public duties. He submits that—given the nature of the office—the doctrine of separation of powers places limits on the authority of the Federal Judiciary to interfere with the Executive Branch that would be transgressed by allowing this action to proceed....

... [P]etitioner contends that—as a by-product of an otherwise traditional exercise of judicial power—burdens will be placed on the President that will hamper the performance of his official duties. We have recognized that "even when a branch does not arrogate power to itself ... the separation-of-powers doctrine requires that a branch not impair another in the performance of its constitutional duties." As a factual matter, petitioner contends that this particular case—as well as the potential additional litigation that an affirmance of the Court of Appeals judgment might spawn—may impose an unacceptable burden on the President's time and energy, and thereby impair the effective performance of his office.

Petitioner's predictive judgment finds little support in either history or the relatively narrow compass of the issues raised in this particular case. As we have already noted, in the more than 200-year history of the Republic, only three sitting Presidents have been subjected to suits for their private actions. If the past is any indicator, it seems unlikely that a deluge of such litigation will ever engulf the Presidency. As for the case at hand, if properly managed by the District Court, it appears to us highly unlikely to occupy any substantial amount of petitioner's time.

Of greater significance.... [the] fact that a federal court's exercise of its traditional Article III jurisdiction may significantly burden the time and attention of the Chief

Executive is not sufficient to establish a violation of the Constitution. Two long-settled propositions, first announced by Chief Justice Marshall, support that conclusion.

First, we have long held that when the President takes official action, the Court has the authority to determine whether he has acted within the law. Perhaps the most dramatic example of such a case is our holding that President Truman exceeded his constitutional authority when he issued an order directing the Secretary of Commerce to take possession of and operate most of the Nation's steel mills in order to avert a national catastrophe. Youngstown Sheet & Tube Co. v. Sawyer, 343 U.S. 579 (1952). Despite the serious impact of that decision on the ability of the Executive Branch to accomplish its assigned mission, and the substantial time that the President must necessarily have devoted to the matter as a result of judicial involvement, we exercised our Article III jurisdiction to decide whether his official conduct conformed to the law. Our holding was an application of the principle established in Marbury v. Madison, 5 U.S. 137 (1803), that "it is emphatically the province and duty of the judicial department to say what the law is."

Second, it is also settled that the President is subject to judicial process in appropriate circumstances. Although Thomas Jefferson apparently thought otherwise, Chief Justice Marshall, when presiding in the treason trial of Aaron Burr, ruled that a subpoena *duces tecum* could be directed to the President. United States v. Burr, 25 F. Cas. 30 (No. 14,692d) (CC Va. 1807). We unequivocally and emphatically endorsed Marshall's position when we held that President Nixon was obligated to comply with a subpoena commanding him to produce certain tape recordings of his conversations with his aides. United States v. Nixon, 418 U.S. 683 (1974). As we explained, "neither the doctrine of separation of powers, nor the need for confidentiality of high-level communications, without more, can sustain an absolute, unqualified Presidential privilege of immunity from judicial process under all circumstances."

Sitting Presidents have responded to court orders to provide testimony and other information with sufficient frequency that such interactions between the Judicial and Executive Branches can scarcely be thought a novelty. President Monroe responded to written inter-rogatories, President Nixon—as noted above—produced tapes in response to a subpoena *duces tecum*, President Ford complied with an order to give a deposition in a criminal trial, and President Clinton has twice given videotaped testimony in criminal proceedings. Moreover, sitting Presidents have also voluntarily complied with judicial requests for testimony. President Grant gave a lengthy deposition in a criminal case under such circumstances, and President Carter similarly gave videotaped testimony for use at a criminal trial.

In sum, "it is settled law that the separation-of-powers doctrine does not bar every exercise of jurisdiction over the President of the United States." If the Judiciary may severely burden the Executive Branch by reviewing the legality of the President's official conduct, and if it may direct appropriate process to the President himself, it must follow that the federal courts have power to determine the legality of his unofficial conduct. The burden on the President's time and energy that is a mere by-product of such review surely cannot be considered as onerous as the direct burden imposed by judicial review and the occasional invalidation of his official actions. We therefore hold that the doctrine of separation of powers does not require federal courts to stay all private actions against the President until he leaves office.

The reasons for rejecting such a categorical rule apply as well to a rule that would require a stay "in all but the most exceptional cases." ...

Strictly speaking the stay was not the functional equivalent of the constitutional immunity.... The District Court has broad discretion to stay proceedings as an incident to its power to control its own docket.... Although we have rejected the argument that the potential burdens on the President violate separation-of-powers principles, those burdens are appropriate matters for the District Court to evaluate in its management of the case. The high respect that is owed to the office of the Chief Executive, though not justifying a rule of categorical immunity, is a matter that should inform the conduct of the entire proceeding, including the timing and scope of discovery.

Nevertheless, we are persuaded that it was an abuse of discretion for the District Court to defer the trial until after the President leaves office. Such a lengthy and categorical stay takes no account whatever of the respondent's interest in bringing the case to trial.... [D]elaying trial would increase the danger of prejudice resulting from the loss of evidence, including the inability of witnesses to recall specific facts, or the possible death of a party.

.... We think the District Court may have given undue weight to the concern that a trial might generate unrelated civil actions that could conceivably hamper the President in conducting the duties of his office. If and when that should occur, the court's discretion would permit it to manage those actions in such fashion (including deferral of trial) that interference with the President's duties would not occur. But no such impingement upon the President's conduct of his office was shown here.

We add a final comment on two matters that are discussed at length in the briefs: the risk that our decision will generate a large volume of politically motivated harassing and frivolous litigation, and the danger that national security concerns might prevent the President from explaining a legitimate need for a continuance.

We are not persuaded that either of these risks is serious. Most frivolous and vexatious litigation is terminated at the pleading stage or on summary judgment, with little if any personal involvement by the defendant. Moreover, the availability of sanctions provides a significant deterrent to litigation directed at the President in his unofficial capacity for purposes of political gain or harassment. History indicates that the likelihood that a significant number of such cases will be filed is remote. Although scheduling problems may arise,.... we have confidence in the ability of our federal judges to deal with ... these concerns.

If Congress deems it appropriate to afford the President stronger protection, it may respond with appropriate legislation. As petitioner notes in his brief, Congress has enacted more than one statute providing for the deferral of civil litigation to accommodate important public interests....

The Federal District Court has jurisdiction to decide this case. Like every other citizen who properly invokes that jurisdiction, respondent has a right to an orderly disposition of her claims. Accordingly, the judgment of the Court of Appeals is affirmed.

JUSTICE BREYER, concurring in the judgment.

I agree with the majority that the Constitution does not automatically grant the President an immunity from civil lawsuits based upon his private conduct. Nor does the "doctrine of separation of powers ... require federal courts to stay" virtually "all private actions against the President until he leaves office.".... To obtain a postponement the President must "bear the burden of establishing its need."

In my view, however, once the President sets forth and explains a conflict between judicial proceeding and public duties, the matter changes. At that point, the Constitution permits a judge to schedule a trial in an ordinary civil damages action (where postponement normally is possible without overwhelming damage to a plaintiff) only within the constraints of a constitutional principle—a principle that forbids a federal judge in such a case to interfere with the President's discharge of his public duties. I have no doubt that the Constitution contains such a principle applicable to civil suits, based upon Article II's vesting of the entire "executive Power" in a single individual, implemented through the Constitution's structural separation of powers, and revealed both by history and case precedent.

.... I also fear that the majority's description of the relevant precedents de-emphasizes the extent to which they support a principle of the President's independent authority to control his own time and energy. Further, if the majority is wrong in predicting the future infrequency of private civil litigation against sitting Presidents, acknowledgement and future delineation of the constitutional principle will prove a practically necessary institutional safeguard....

Review Questions and Explanations: *Nixon v. Fitzgerald; Clinton v. Jones*

1. Does President Clinton claim that the President is immune from damages suits for sexual harassment or other "private" misconduct unrelated to his official duties?

2. Try to articulate in a sentence or a short paragraph the doctrine of executive immunity from suit that can be derived from *Fitzgerald* and *Jones*. Don't simply state the rule or holding—try to incorporate the underlying policy rationale.

3. The Court stated that it found no "serious" risk that the President's performance of his duties would be hampered by civil litigation during his term in office. Did this concern receive due consideration from the Court? Consider the following: after the Supreme Court's ruling, the *Jones* litigation went forward and discovery proceedings were conducted, including the taking of President Clinton's deposition. President Clinton was subsequently impeached; the third Article of Impeachment (impeachment charge) was based entirely on charges that he gave false testimony at his deposition and supplied or encouraged false witness statements in discovery. It is not hard to imagine that a President, testifying under oath in a civil case against him, would weigh his words differently from a private citizen defendant in a similar kind of case, making a perjury allegation a predictable scenario.

There is little doubt that fallout from the *Jones* case and the resulting impeachment charges occupied significant time and attention of the President and his staff in Clinton's second term of office. There is also little doubt that the risk of political motivations underlying any private suit against a sitting president is very great indeed. Given these concerns, are you satisfied with the "safeguards" identified by the Court in *Jones*: the trial judge's "discretion" to manage the litigation and the power of Congress to enact legislation to require a stay of private lawsuits against a sitting President? Note that the trial judge's discretion is limited by the Court's holding that the litigation must go forward. And the hypothetical remedy from Congress would be cold comfort to a President if the congressional majority is from the opposing party (as it was in Clinton's second term).

4. There was no dissent in *Clinton v. Jones*—only Justice Breyer's concurrence in the judgment expressing some uneasiness on the President's behalf. In a

paragraph or bullet-point outline, try to sketch out the arguments for a dissenting opinion in this case. What should the President's remedy be — absolute immunity from suit, or simply the right to a stay while in office?

F. The Veto Power

Article I, § 7, cl. 2 of the Constitution provides:

> Every bill which shall have passed the House of Representatives and the Senate, shall, before it become a law, be presented to the President of the United States; if he approve he shall sign it, but if not he shall return it, with his objections to that House in which it shall have originated, who shall enter the objections at large on their journal, and proceed to reconsider it. If after such reconsideration two thirds of that House shall agree to pass the bill, it shall be sent, together with the objections, to the other House, by which it shall likewise be reconsidered, and if approved by two thirds of that House, it shall become a law.

This provision, sometimes referred to as the Presentment Clause (see *INS v. Chadha*, Chapter 4), delineates the President's "veto" power and the process for imposing and overriding a veto. The President can disapprove a bill by returning it "with his objections," and it will not become law unless each House votes by a 2/3 majority to "override the veto."

As you can see, the popular terminology "veto" and "override," are not written in the Constitution itself. "Veto" is Latin for "I forbid," and the concept of a veto power derives from the lawmaking process in the ancient Roman republic, in which laws passed by the Senate (a body representing the patrician class) could be nullified by one or more "tribunes," elected representatives of the lower (plebeian) class. The framers of the Constitution, who were great readers of Greek and Roman classics, knew this history well, and first used the informal appellation "veto." In formal debates and in the Federalist papers, the framers tended to speak of a power "to negative" bills passed by Congress.

The justification for reposing a veto or "negative" power over legislation in the President was argued by Hamilton in The Federalist, No. 73:

> The propensity of the legislative department to intrude upon the rights, and to absorb the powers, of the other departments has been already more than once suggested. The insufficiency of a mere parchment delineation of the boundaries of each has also been remarked upon; and the necessity of furnishing each with constitutional arms for its own defense has been inferred and proved. From these clear and indubitable principles results the propriety of a negative, either absolute or qualified, in the executive upon the acts of the legislative branches. (Rosseter ed. 1961, at 442.)

The framers opted for the "qualified" version of the veto, by providing for congressional override. Hamilton continued:

> But the power in question has a further use. It not only serves as a shield to the executive, but it furnishes an additional security against the enaction of improper laws. It establishes a salutary check upon the legislative body, calculated to guard the community against the effects of faction, precipitancy, or of any impulse

unfriendly to the public good, which may happen to influence the majority of that body.

.... The primary inducement to conferring the power in question upon the executive is to enable him to defend himself; the secondary one is to increase the chances in favor of the community against the passing of bad laws, through haste, inadvertence, or design. The oftener the measure is brought under examination, the greater the diversity in the situations of those who are to examine it, the less must be the danger of those errors which flow from the want of due deliberation, or of those missteps which proceed from the contagion of some common passion or interest. (*Id.* at 443.)

The veto power is not, and was not understood to be, a classic executive power; rather it was designed to give the President a limited but important role in the legislative process. *See, e.g., La Abra Silver Mining Co. v. United States*, 175 U.S. 423, 453 (1899) ("Undoubtedly the President when approving bills passed by Congress may be said to participate in the enactment of laws which the Constitution requires him to execute."); The Veto Power of the President, 12 F.R.D. 207 ("The exercise of the veto power is patently a legislative act"). This point is underscored by the placement of the veto power in Article I, in the section establishing the process for enacting a bill (proposed legislation) into law. Technically, and importantly, the President does not veto "a law"; rather, he vetoes "a bill" and thereby prevents it from ever becoming "a law" (unless his veto is overridden).

Debates have occasionally arisen over the question of whether there are any limits to the President's discretion to veto a bill. Certainly the constitution says nothing express on the subject. Questions about implied limits on the veto power might include: whether vetoes should be based on constitutional objections only, or if it is proper for the President to consider his own policy preferences to veto bills that are constitutionally permissible. If vetoes are based on the President's constitutional objections, to what extent may the President rely on his (and his advisors') own constitutional judgments, perhaps ignoring those of the Supreme Court? To what extent, if at all, should the President defer to the constitutional or policy judgments of Congress? (The President's authority to make independent constitutional judgments is discussed in section I, infra.)

Historical practice has evolved over time. Early presidents seemed to adhere to the view that vetoes should be used sparingly, and only where the President had constitutional objections to legislation. No President before Andrew Jackson vetoed more than six bills; Jackson, who saw his role as that of "tribune of the people" vetoed more bills than his six predecessors combined. Modern presidents veto more bills, which is not surprising given that Congress is probably more active in passing legislation.[3] Constitutionally based vetoes were the rule for vetoes by eighteenth and nineteenth century presidents, but have become the exception since the twentieth century. Scholars have estimated that until 1885, presidents relied on primarily constitutional grounds to veto proposed legislation more than 60%

---

3. Editors' note: Note that merely counting numbers of presidential vetoes can be somewhat misleading, because the nature of congressional activity has changed over time. At times in the past, Congress has been more active than in recent years in enacting "private bills"—bills affecting the rights of an individual. In the nineteenth century, for example, many military veterans or their widows had to apply to Congress for private bills to receive the award of a government pension. President Cleveland vetoed hundreds of these.

of the time; compared to 10% since 1897. Instead, modern Presidents cite the unsoundness of the bill on policy grounds.[4]

The Supreme Court has never ruled on the question of whether there are any substantive constitutional limits on the president's discretion to veto legislation. It is difficult to conceive that the modern Court would find the question justiciable; even before the rise of justiciability doctrines, it is likely that the Supreme Court would always have ruled that the President has non-reviewable discretion in exercising the veto power.

The Supreme Court has decided two cases relating to the veto power, both of which dealt with the technical question of the "pocket veto." *See The Pocket Veto Case*, 279 U.S. 655 (1929); *La Abra Silver Mining Co. v. United States*, 175 U.S. 423, 453 (1899). Article I, §7, cl. 2 continues, after the language quoted above, as follows:

> If any bill shall not be returned by the President within ten days (Sundays excepted) after it shall have been presented to him, the same shall be a law, in like manner as if he had signed it, unless the Congress by their adjournment prevent its return, in which case it shall not be a law.

In other words, where the President is presented a bill with fewer than ten non-Sunday days before adjournment of Congress, he may in effect veto the bill — it will not become law — simply by "putting it in his pocket," i.e., failing to sign the bill. The two Supreme Court cases upheld this "pocket veto" procedure, and *The Pocket Veto Case* held further that "adjournment" is not limited to the termination of the two-year congressional term, but includes recesses during the two-year term as well.

Exercise: The Veto Power

Does the Constitution place any implicit limits on the grounds on which a President can veto a bill? Consider the following two scenarios:

   a) The President returns a bill to the originating house of Congress with a "veto message" consisting entirely of the statement "I object to this bill" with no statement of reasons for the objection. Can the bill thereafter become law, without a 2/3 override vote, because the president failed to return the bill in the requisite time "with his objections"?

   b) The President returns a bill to the originating house of Congress with a veto message that concedes that the law is constitutional, but advancing several reasons why the law is unwise as a matter of policy. Can the bill thereafter become law, without a two-thirds override vote, because the President has failed to state constitutionally based objections?

With one or more fellow students, prepare and make a brief oral argument to the Supreme Court on these questions — one side representing members of Congress backing the bill, and the other side representing the President. (Feel free to skip over questions of standing and the political question doctrine for this exercise.)

---

4. *See* J. Richard Broughton, *Rethinking the Presidential Veto*, 42 Harv. J. on Legis. 91, 126–27 & nn. 239–46 (2005).

G. Executive Orders and Presidential Direct Action

1. Types of Presidential Direct Action

Over the course of U.S. history, presidents have developed several means of issuing directives that, at least to some extent, have the force of law: that is, they create binding rules and policies within the executive branch, or directly affect rights of private parties outside the government. They are issued by the President pursuant to claimed grants of authority given by statute or by the Constitution itself. The executive order is undoubtedly the most common and well known form of presidential directive, and the term is frequently overused to refer generically to all directives issued from the White House. Other recognized forms include executive agreements, presidential memoranda, presidential proclamations, national security orders and presidential signing statements. You have already encountered some of these: Truman's executive order seizing the steel mills reviewed in *Youngstown*; Lincoln's proclamations of an embargo on southern ports and of suspension of habeas corpus; the executive agreements and orders by Carter and Reagan in *Dames & Moore*; the Bush "military order" establishing military tribunals after September 11.

These and other modes of "presidential direct action"[5] are not provided for by the Constitution. They have been recognized in statutes, if at all, only long after they came into use by presidents. Their origins are in customary presidential practice, and they might serve as an example of how accepted historical practices can provide the type of "gloss" on constitutional meaning that Justice Frankfurter discussed in his *Youngstown* concurrence. Providing accurate, formal definitions of these modes of presidential direct action can be challenging because their uses and conventions may change over time: "Each administration seems to learn from its predecessors about how presidential power tools can be used, and each then seems to adapt the tools, applying those lessons, to new uses."[6] Sometimes presidents themselves have displayed confusion over what type of document they were signing. President Clinton, a trained lawyer, more than once referred to a presidential memorandum he had signed as an "executive order."[7]

a. Executive Orders and Proclamations

Executive orders and proclamations are the most formal tools of presidential direct action. According to a House of Representatives report in 1957, "Executive orders are written documents denominated as such.... [They] are generally directed to, and govern actions by, the Government officials and agencies. They usually affect private individuals only indirectly. Proclamations in most instances affect the activities of private individuals."[8]

---

5. The phrase was coined by Professor Phillip J. Cooper in his excellent study on this subject. Phillip J. Cooper, By Order of the President: the Use and Abuse of Executive Direct Action 4 (2002). This subsection is largely derived from that source. *See also* Tara L. Branum, *President or King? The Use and Abuse of Executive Orders in Modern-Day America*, 28 J. Legis. 1 (2002).

6. Cooper, *supra*, at 82.

7. Id. at 83–84.

8. H.R. Comm. On Government Operations, Executive Orders and Proclamations: a Study of the Use of Presidential Power, 85th Cong., 1st sess., 1 (1957).

In other words, it might be said in general that executive orders are tools for internal governance of the executive branch while proclamations are intended to have law-like effect extending outside of government. But inherent ambiguities in such labels, as well as changing presidential practice, make this seemingly useful definition somewhat unreliable. Truman's seizure order, for example, was directed to the Secretary of Commerce but certainly affected private rights outside the government. Likewise, Lincoln's blockade of southern ports and suspension of habeas corpus were styled "proclamations," but were directed in part to the government officials who would enforce them. To help you better understand this complex terminology, we will briefly summarize each type of direct action vehicle.

Executive Orders. President Grant in 1873 issued an executive order attempting, for the first time, to impose some sort of formal regularity on executive orders; prior to that time there was no formal requirement, and executive orders sometimes took the form of handwritten notes, perhaps even notes in the margins of documents proposing a course of action. Numbering of executive orders was started in 1907, but remained informal until the Federal Register Act of 1935. President Kennedy's Executive Order No. 11030 in 1962 attempted to impose further formalization, and subsequent presidents have imposed additional formalities on executive orders. These now require executive orders to be published in the Federal Register; and executive orders originating outside the White House must be submitted for approval to the Office of Management and Budget and thence to the Attorney General for a legal review before going to the President for signature.[9]

Executive orders have been used for a variety of purposes: to make binding pronouncements to the executive branch; to make policy in areas deemed to be within presidential control; to supervise and delegate authority to executive agencies and direct them to make regulations; to manage federal property and personnel; to reorganize federal agencies; and to direct military organization.[10]

Proclamations. "A Presidential proclamation is an instrument that states a condition, declares the law and requires obedience, recognizes an event, or triggers the implementation of a law[.]"[11] Lincoln's blockade of southern ports stated the condition of internal rebellion by the seceding states and declared law. Roosevelt's proclamation banning arms sales to Bolivia and Paraguay in *United States v. Curtiss-Wright Export Corp.* was an example of a proclamation that declared a condition (a presidential finding that the two countries were at war and that banning arms sales would contribute to peace), which in turn triggered implementation of a law (the arms sales ban). One of the earliest and most controversial proclamations was President Washington's 1793 declaration of neutrality in the war between Britain and France — controversial because it involved an assertion of presidential power to make foreign policy without an act of Congress. As suggested by the above examples, proclamations have been used historically by presidents to make foreign policy; to state conditions or make findings specified in acts of Congress that will trigger implementation of a law; and to make law binding on persons outside the government. Presidents have also used them to invoke emergency powers. Less controversially, presidents have used proclamations as the vehicle for exercising their constitutional power to grant pardons; and to make hortatory declarations, recognize individual achievements, or proclaim holidays. Like executive orders, proclamations are now numbered and published in the Federal Register.[12]

---

9. Cooper, *supra*, at 17–18; Branum, *supra*, at 8.
10. Cooper, *supra*, at 21–37.
11. Cooper, *supra*, at 117.
12. Cooper, *supra*, at 117–42.

b. Other Presidential Direct Action Devices

Presidential Memoranda. A presidential memorandum is a device developed by modern presidents to issue directives to executive branch officials. They have come over time to be used for the same purposes as executive orders. In addition, presidential veto messages in recent years have been styled "memoranda."

Presidential memoranda are not covered by the handful of formal requirements that govern executive orders: they are not numbered or indexed, and more importantly there is no requirement that any subordinates approve the memorandum before the President signs it. Nor is there any requirement that presidential memoranda be published, either in the federal Register or elsewhere. However, presidents sometimes instruct that a memorandum be published in the Federal Register, and most are published in the *Weekly Compilation of Presidential Documents* and *The Public Papers of the President.* It is probably the absence of these formal requirements that makes them a more attractive vehicle in certain circumstances than an executive order.[13]

National Security Directives. These are presidential directives intended to implement national security policy and coordinate government agencies with responsibility for aspects of national security. They are generally issued through the National Security Council. In essence, they are presidential memoranda that are intended to be shielded from public scrutiny, and are often classified and typically not published. Indeed, most presidential administrations have resisted inquiries by Congress into the existence or contents of specific NSDs. They have been given different names through different presidential administrations: NSC Policy Papers (Truman, Eisenhower); National Security Action Memoranda (Kennedy, Johnson); National Security Decision Memoranda (Nixon, Ford); Presidential Directives (Carter); National Security Decision Directives (Reagan); National Security Directives (Bush); Presidential Decision Directives (Clinton); and National Security Presidential Directives (G. W. Bush).[14]

Executive Agreements. The normal process for entering into treaties entails a negotiation under the direction of the President with one or more foreign governments, followed by submission of the proposed treaty to the Senate, for its approval by a two-thirds vote. Art. II, § 2, cl. 2. An "executive agreement" is an agreement between the United States and a foreign government that has not been presented to the Senate for ratification. The following analogy might be a helpful way of understanding the concept: an executive agreement is to a treaty as an executive order (or proclamation) is to an Act of Congress. Such an agreement underlay the decision in *Dames & Moore*, and the validity of the general practice of executive agreements did not seem to be seriously questioned.

Presidential Signing Statements. The Constitution expressly contemplates Presidential veto messages, but says nothing about presidential statements approving and signing a bill that passes both of Houses of Congress: "if he approve [the bill] he shall sign it, but if not he shall return it, with his objections to that House in which it shall have originated." Art. I, § 7, cl. 2. By longstanding tradition, presidents have made statements when signing a bill, using the opportunity to laud the policy of the new law or the process that led to its enactment.

But signing statements have in recent decades morphed into something more substantive. Beginning with President Reagan, signing statements have been used by

---

13. Cooper, *supra*, at 81–85.
14. Cooper, *supra*, at 143–46.

presidents to express *disapproval* and *concerns* with bills, or to offer contested interpretations of bills, that the President nevertheless then signs into law. The former practice may be an occasion to announce an intention to refuse to enforce the disapproved portion of the law. Both practices may be intended by the President to become part of the "legislative history" of the law and thereby influence subsequent judicial interpretations. To facilitate this latter purpose, Reagan's attorney general, Edwin Meese (who is credited with creating this more aggressive use of signing statements), reached an agreement in 1986 with West Publishing Company to include presidential signing statements in their legislative history volumes, *U.S. Code Congressional and Administrative News*.[15]

2. Legal and Constitutional Status

As a matter of form, presidential direct action documents typically begin by citing constitutional provisions and statutes that purportedly authorize the action. If taken at face value, these authorities would suggest that the President is simply doing his job to "take care that the laws be faithfully executed." Separation-of-powers problems would not arise if such presidential actions were always straightforward efforts to implement clear congressional or constitutional authorizations. But governance is not so tidy. The reality is that, in many instances, the President has identified the action he wishes to take and his legal advisors have stretched some constitutional and statutory provisions to argue that the action is authorized. The direct action documents then act as a vehicle allowing the President to explain why he thinks the actions is authorized.

The various modes of Presidential direct action are attractive precisely because of their adaptability, flexibility and informality. Compared to the legislative process, even the most formal version of the executive order is fast and simple. A presidential proclamation is faster and more direct than agency rulemaking, which requires a notice and comment period and provides for judicial review under the Administrative Procedure Act. 5 U.S.C. § 551 et seq. Whereas discretionary agency decisions are subject to judicial review and can be overruled by a court if they are "arbitrary, capricious, an abuse of discretion or otherwise not in accordance with law," 5 U.S.C. § 706, direct presidential actions appear not to be so reviewable, because the President has been held not to be an "agency" within the meaning of the Administrative Procedure Act; consequently, certain discretionary decisions by the President are unreviewable, at least on statutory grounds. *See Dalton v. Spector*, 511 U.S. 462 (1994); *Franklin v. Massachusetts*, 505 U.S. 788 (1992). So there may be circumstances where direct action is faster and easier than either legislation or administrative agency rulemaking.

Presidential executive orders and agreements, proclamations and presidential memoranda seem to be accorded the force of law. For example, it is acknowledged by longstanding practice that executive orders remain in effect from one presidential administration to the next unless rescinded by a subsequent executive order. The executive agreement at issue in *Dames & Moore* was deemed a sufficient basis to sustain administrative regulations that overrode the plaintiff's attempt to attach Iranian assets and that forced the plaintiff out of federal court and into the Iranian claims tribunal. The extent to which presidential direct action binds persons outside the government remains in a constitutional gray area.

---

15. Cooper, *supra*, at 201–03.

The historical practices of presidential direct action show that "the idea that [the President] is to be a lawmaker" has not exactly been "refuted." *Youngstown*, 343 U.S. at 587 (per Black, J.). The Supreme Court has never suggested that the various tools of presidential direct action are in themselves unconstitutional; indeed, it appears to be the Court's position that some mechanism for giving authoritative orders to subordinates is a functional necessity for the exercise of executive power.

Instead, the separation-of-powers question necessarily will be posed as whether a particular instance of executive direct action exceeds the President's powers and is therefore unconstitutional. And the starting point for such an analysis is likely to be the three-part framework set out in Justice Jackson's *Youngstown* opinion. *Youngstown* itself reviewed the constitutionality of President Truman's executive order without questioning the practice of issuing executive orders as such. As seen in *Dames & Moore*, the presidential practice of concluding an agreement with a foreign government that is not presented to the Senate for ratification appears to be treated as presumptively valid, subject to a *Youngstown*-type analysis. And of course, we are here only talking about *separation-of-powers problems* with presidential direct action; an executive order or proclamation that violated some other constitutional limit, such as the First Amendment, would be unconstitutional because it would exceed the power even of the President and Congress together.

There remain some general separation-of-powers problems with particular forms of presidential direct action. We said above that "an executive agreement is to a treaty as an executive order (or proclamation) is to an Act of Congress." Note that this analogy is not perfect, insofar as the courts seem to give greater deference to the President in conducting foreign affairs (see *Curtiss-Wright*) than in domestic affairs.

The practice of issuing presidential signing statements is the least well-established, and in some ways the most problematic, of the modes of presidential direct action. The Supreme Court has rarely cited presidential signing statements as authorities, and has never ruled on their constitutional status. As noted above, signing statements are sometimes intended by the President to influence subsequent judicial interpretations of the statute by being accepted as part of the statute's legislative history. To be sure, legislative history is frequently used by courts as an aid to understanding what Congress meant in drafting statutory language that proves to be ambiguous, in retrospect or in a particular application. But the President is, technically, not part of that drafting process: why should his interpretation of statutory language offer any insight into what the drafters of the statute intended?

To the extent that a presidential signing statement is intended to nullify a portion of a law which the President signs into law, it functions as a sort of "line item veto." The constitutionality of such a practice seems dubious, particularly in light of the Court's decision striking down the Line Item Veto Act in *Clinton v. City of New York*, 524 U.S. 417 (1998) (see Chapter 4).

H. Appointment and Removal
of Executive Officers

It was always assumed that the President would have assistance in executing the laws. Cabinet officers and staffs for three departments — Foreign Affairs, War and Treasury — were created by the first Congress in July 1789. (The departments were tiny compared to today's norms. The first Secretary of State, Thomas Jefferson, oversaw a staff of one chief clerk, three assistant clerks, a translator, and a messenger.) Congress intensively debated the questions of how these officers (and their chief clerks, who were also deemed officers of the United States) were to be appointed and removed from office. These debates are recounted at great length in *Myers v. United States*, 272 U.S. 52 (1926); although that account is edited out of the excerpt of Myers, below, it is a useful starting point for in-depth research into this history. They illuminate to some degree the persistent questions that have arisen about appointment and removal of government officials in the executive branch.

Why are appointment and removal questions important? Rules governing appointment and removal go a long way toward creating administrative structure of the executive branch. For example, an official appointed by the President alone and removable by the President at will (at any time, for any reason) is far more likely to be loyal to the President and to carry out the President's orders without resistance than an official whose appointment and removal is subject to congressional approval. Appointment and removal procedures and rules thus shape an official's accountability.

The Constitution provides in express terms for appointments, in Art. II, §2, cl. 2:

> ... he shall nominate, and by and with the advice and consent of the Senate, shall appoint ambassadors, other public ministers and consuls, judges of the Supreme Court, and all other officers of the United States, whose appointments are not herein otherwise provided for, and which shall be established by law: but the Congress may by law vest the appointment of such inferior officers, as they think proper, in the President alone, in the courts of law, or in the heads of departments.[16]

However, the Constitution mentions removals from office only in the "impeachment" clauses: since impeachment is an extraordinary remedy, the Constitution is essentially silent on the conditions for removal of federal officials in the ordinary course.

1. Appointment

The Appointments Clause, quoted above, raises two sets of questions by its plain terms. "[A]mbassadors, other public ministers and consuls" has been read as having a fixed meaning based on the understanding of the Framers, and refers to all emissaries representing the United States before foreign governments and international bodies. "Judges of the Supreme Court" is refreshingly unambiguous. Less clear is the scope of "all other officers of the United States, whose appointments are not herein otherwise provided for, and which shall be established by law[.]" This phrase has been traditionally understood to include cabinet officers and lower court judges. But what about sub-cabinet-level officials? Plainly, not every federal employee is subject to Senate confirmation.

Thus, the first question presented by the clause entails whether a federal official is "an officer of the United States," whose appointment must be the result of nomination by the President and confirmation by two-thirds of the Senate; or whether he is instead an

---

16. Editors' note: The clause goes on in the next sentence to state: "The President shall have power to fill up all vacancies that may happen during the recess of the Senate, by granting commissions which shall expire at the end of their next session." Such so-called "recess appointments," frequently relied on by presidents, thus require no Senate approval, but are temporary.

"inferior officer" whose appointment can either follow this same procedure—nomination by the President and Senate confirmation—or can be made through the alternative set of procedures: appointment by "the President alone, [by] the courts of law, or [by] the heads of departments" *without* Senate confirmation.[17]

Guided Reading Questions and Explanations: *Buckley v. Valeo*

1. What are the duties of the commission? How and why are these duties relevant to the question of whether the "appointments clause" has been violated?

2. How does the Court define an "officer of the United States"?

3. In what respects did the manner of appointing Federal Election commissioners violate the appointments clause? Be specific.

4. The appointments clause does not provide for appointments to be made by Congress. What sort of appointment power, if any, does the Court say that Congress has?

Buckley v. Valeo

424 U.S. 1 (1976)

[The Federal Election Campaign Act of 1971 made comprehensive reforms of federal election campaign finance law, and created the Federal Election Commission as an independent agency to oversee the law's ongoing regulatory functions. Several constitutional challenges were soon made both to the regulatory impact of the law and to the Commission, on both separation of powers and First Amendment grounds. The Court decided these challenges in a lengthy and complicated set of opinions that ran to over 90,000 words and well over 150 pages in the U.S. Reports. The following excerpt focuses on the separation-of-powers issues, relating to the manner in which Commission members were to be appointed. (The First Amendment portions of the opinions are present in the First Amendment chapter of this book.) Justice Brennan is now known to have been the author of the per curiam opinion. It was joined in this separation-of-powers portion by all seven other justices: Burger (CJ), Stewart, White, Marshall, Blackmun, Rehnquist and Powell. (Justice Stevens did not take part, because he did not take his seat on the Court until shortly after the case was argued.)]

PER CURIAM.

.... The 1974 Amendments to the Act create an eight-member Federal Election Commission (Commission) and vest in it primary and substantial responsibility for administering and enforcing the Act. The question that we address in this portion of the opinion is whether, in view of the manner in which a majority of its members are appointed, the Commission may under the Constitution exercise the powers conferred upon it....

---

17. Lower level federal employees who are neither "officers of the United States" nor "inferior officers" are not subject to the appointments clause at all. *See Buckley v. Valeo*, fn. 162, *infra*.

[The Act authorizes the Commission to make rules to carry out the provisions of the Act and "formulate general policy with respect to [its] administration"; to exercise "primary jurisdiction with respect to [the Act's] civil enforcement"; to render advisory opinions with respect to possible violations; and to authorize convention expenditures which exceed the statutory limits. The Commission is further authorized to institute civil enforcement action without requiring the concurrence of or participation by the Attorney General; or to require the Attorney General to do so. And the Commission can disqualify a candidate from future elections for failure to file the required disclosures and reports.]

The [Commission] consists of eight members. The Secretary of the Senate and the Clerk of the House of Representatives are ex officio members of the Commission without the right to vote. Two members are appointed by the President pro tempore of the Senate "upon the recommendations of the majority leader of the Senate and the minority leader of the Senate." Two more are to be appointed by the Speaker of the House of Representatives, likewise upon the recommendations of its respective majority and minority leaders. The remaining two members are appointed by the President. Each of the six voting members of the Commission must be confirmed by the majority of both Houses of Congress, and each of the three appointing authorities is forbidden to choose both of their appointees from the same political party. . . .

Appellants urge that since Congress has given the Commission wide-ranging rulemaking and enforcement powers with respect to the substantive provisions of the Act, Congress is precluded under the principle of separation of powers from vesting in itself the authority to appoint those who will exercise such authority. Their argument is based on the language of Art. II, § 2, cl. 2, of the Constitution. . . . We think its fair import is that any appointee exercising significant authority pursuant to the laws of the United States is an "Officer of the United States," and must, therefore, be appointed in the manner prescribed by § 2, cl. 2, of that Article.

. . . . If a Postmaster first class, Myers v. United States, 272 U.S. 52 (1926), and the clerk of a district court, Ex parte Hennen, 13 Pet. 230 (1839), are inferior officers of the United States within the meaning of the Appointments Clause, as they are, surely the Commissioners before us are at the very least such "inferior Officers" within the meaning of that Clause.

> FN162. "Officers of the United States" does not include all employees of the United States, but there is no claim made that the Commissioners are employees of the United States rather than officers. Employees are lesser functionaries subordinate to officers of the United States, whereas the Commissioners, appointed for a statutory term, are not subject to the control or direction of any other executive, judicial, or legislative authority.

Although two members of the Commission are initially selected by the President, his nominations are subject to confirmation not merely by the Senate, but by the House of Representatives as well. The remaining four voting members of the Commission are appointed by the President pro tempore of the Senate and by the Speaker of the House. While the second part of the Clause authorizes Congress to vest the appointment of the officers described in that part in "the Courts of Law, or in the Heads of Departments," neither the Speaker of the House nor the President pro tempore of the Senate comes within this language.

The phrase "Heads of Departments," used as it is in conjunction with the phrase "Courts of Law," suggests that the Departments referred to are themselves in the Executive Branch or at least have some connection with that branch. While the Clause expressly authorizes Congress to vest the appointment of certain officers in the "Courts of Law," the absence of similar language to include Congress must mean that neither Congress nor its officers were included within the language "Heads of Departments" in this part of cl. 2.

Thus with respect to four of the six voting members of the Commission, neither the President, the head of any department, nor the Judiciary has any voice in their selection.

The Appointments Clause specifies the method of appointment only for "Officers of the United States" whose appointment is not "otherwise provided for" in the Constitution. But there is no provision of the Constitution remotely providing any alternative means for the selection of the members of the Commission or for anybody like them. Appellee Commission has argued, and the Court of Appeals agreed, that the Appointments Clause of Art. II should not be read to exclude the "inherent power of Congress" to appoint its own officers to perform functions necessary to that body as an institution. But there is no need to read the Appointments Clause contrary to its plain language in order to [sustain the Commission]. Article I, §3, cl. 5, expressly authorizes the selection of the President pro tempore of the Senate, and §2, cl. 5, of that Article provides for the selection of the Speaker of the House. Ranking nonmembers, such as the Clerk of the House of Representatives, are elected under the internal rules of each House and are designated by statute as "officers of the Congress." There is no occasion for us to decide whether any of these member officers are "Officers of the United States" whose "appointment" is otherwise provided for within the meaning of the Appointments Clause, since even if they were such officers their appointees would not be. Contrary to the fears expressed by the majority of the Court of Appeals, nothing in our holding with respect to Art. II, §2, cl. 2, will deny to Congress "all power to appoint its own inferior officers to carry out appropriate legislative functions."

.... An interim version of the draft Constitution had vested in the Senate the authority to appoint Ambassadors, public Ministers, and Judges of the Supreme Court, and the language of Art. II as finally adopted is a distinct change in this regard. We believe that it was a deliberate change made by the Framers with the intent to deny Congress any authority itself to appoint those who were "Officers of the United States." ....

Appellee Commission and amici urge that because of what they conceive to be the extraordinary authority reposed in Congress to regulate elections, this case stands on a different footing than if Congress had exercised its legislative authority in another field. There is, of course, no doubt that Congress has express authority to regulate congressional elections, by virtue of the power conferred in Art. I, §4.... [But we] see no reason to believe that the authority of Congress over federal election practices is of such a wholly different nature from the other grants of authority to Congress that it may be employed in such a manner as to offend well-established constitutional restrictions stemming from the separation of powers.

.... Unless their selection is elsewhere provided for, all officers of the United States are to be appointed in accordance with the Clause. Principal officers are selected by the President with the advice and consent of the Senate. Inferior officers Congress may allow to be appointed by the President alone, by the heads of departments, or by the Judiciary. No class or type of officer is excluded because of its special functions. The President appoints judicial as well as executive officers. Neither has it been disputed — and apparently it is not now disputed — that the Clause controls the appointment of the members of a typical administrative agency even though its functions, as this Court recognized in Humphrey's Executor v. United States, 295 U.S. 602, 624 (1935), may be "predominantly quasi-judicial and quasi-legislative" rather than executive. The Court in that case carefully emphasized that although the members of such agencies were to be independent of the Executive in their day-to-day operations, the Executive was not excluded from selecting them. Id., at 625–626....

We are also told by appellees and amici that Congress had good reason for not vesting in a Commission composed wholly of Presidential appointees the authority to administer the Act, since the administration of the Act would undoubtedly have a bearing on any incumbent President's campaign for re-election. While one cannot dispute the basis for this sentiment as a practical matter, it would seem that those who sought to challenge incumbent Congressmen might have equally good reason to fear a Commission which was unduly responsive to Members of Congress whom they were seeking to unseat. But such fears, however rational, do not by themselves warrant a distortion of the Framers' work....

On the assumption that all of the powers granted in the statute may be exercised by an agency whose members have been appointed in accordance with the Appointments Clause, the ultimate question is which, if any, of those powers may be exercised by the present voting Commissioners, none of whom was appointed as provided by that Clause. Our previous description of the statutory provisions, disclosed that the Commission's powers fall generally into three categories: functions relating to the flow of necessary information—receipt, dissemination, and investigation; functions with respect to the Commission's task of fleshing out the statute—rulemaking and advisory opinions; and functions necessary to ensure compliance with the statute and rules—informal procedures, administrative determinations and hearings, and civil suits.

Insofar as the powers confided in the Commission are essentially of an investigative and informative nature, falling in the same general category as those powers which Congress might delegate to one of its own committees, there can be no question that the Commission as presently constituted may exercise them....

But when we go beyond this type of authority to the more substantial powers exercised by the Commission, we reach a different result. The Commission's enforcement power, exemplified by its discretionary power to seek judicial relief, is authority that cannot possibly be regarded as merely in aid of the legislative function of Congress. A lawsuit is the ultimate remedy for a breach of the law, and it is to the President, and not to the Congress, that the Constitution entrusts the responsibility to "take Care that the Laws be faithfully executed." Art. II, § 3.

Congress may undoubtedly under the Necessary and Proper Clause create "offices" in the generic sense and provide such method of appointment to those "offices" as it chooses. But Congress' power under that Clause is inevitably bounded by the express language of Art. II, § 2, cl. 2, and unless the method it provides comports with the latter, the holders of those offices will not be "Officers of the United States." They may, therefore, properly perform duties only in aid of those functions that Congress may carry out by itself, or in an area sufficiently removed from the administration and enforcement of the public law as to permit their being performed by persons not "Officers of the United States."....

"Not having the power of appointment, unless expressly granted or incidental to its powers, the legislature cannot engraft executive duties upon a legislative office, since that would be to usurp the power of appointment by indirection; though the case might be different if the additional duties were devolved upon an appointee of the executive."

We hold that these provisions of the Act, vesting in the Commission primary responsibility for conducting civil litigation in the courts of the United States for vindicating public rights, violate Art. II, § 2, cl. 2, of the Constitution. Such functions may be discharged only by persons who are "Officers of the United States" within the language of that section.

All aspects of the Act are brought within the Commission's broad administrative powers: rulemaking, advisory opinions, and determinations of eligibility for funds and even for federal elective office itself. These functions, exercised free from day-to-day supervision of either Congress or the Executive Branch, are more legislative and judicial in nature than are the Commission's enforcement powers, and are of kinds usually performed by independent regulatory agencies or by some department in the Executive Branch under the direction of an Act of Congress. Congress viewed these broad powers as essential to effective and impartial administration of the entire substantive framework of the Act. Yet each of these functions also represents the performance of a significant governmental duty exercised pursuant to a public law. While the President may not insist that such functions be delegated to an appointee of his removable at will, Humphrey's Executor v. United States, 295 U.S. 602 (1935), none of them operates merely in aid of congressional authority to legislate or is sufficiently removed from the administration and enforcement of public law to allow it to be performed by the present Commission. These administrative functions may therefore be exercised only by persons who are "Officers of the United States."

.... It is also our view that the Commission's inability to exercise certain powers because of the method by which its members have been selected should not affect the validity of the Commission's administrative actions and determinations to this date, including its administration of those provisions, upheld today, authorizing the public financing of federal elections. The past acts of the Commission are therefore accorded de facto validity, just as we have recognized should be the case with respect to legislative acts performed by legislators held to have been elected in accordance with an unconstitutional apportionment plan. We also draw on the Court's practice in the apportionment and voting rights cases and stay, for a period not to exceed 30 days, the Court's judgment insofar as it affects the authority of the Commission to exercise the duties and powers granted it under the Act. This limited stay will afford Congress an opportunity to reconstitute the Commission by law or to adopt other valid enforcement mechanisms without interrupting enforcement of the provisions the Court sustains, allowing the present Commission in the interim to function de facto in accordance with the substantive provisions of the Act.

Review Questions and Explanations: *Buckley*

1. Why do you think Congress created the complex and varied appointment system for federal election commissioners and gave itself a role in making appointments? Do those considerations bear on the constitutionality of the appointments procedure for the commissioners?

2. How do we know that the commissioners are "Officers of the United States"? Would it have made a difference if Congress had written into the statutory definitions that election commissioners were not "Officers of the United States"?

3. If the manner of appointing federal election commissioners was unconstitutional, why didn't the court strike down the entire statute?

2. Removal

The removal of federal officials from their jobs shares certain key attributes with employment termination in the private sector. The power of removal or termination "at will" means a right to fire the employee at any time, and for any reason or no reason. Job security doesn't mean an absolute right of an employee or government official to maintain their position for life, but rather that there are limited circumstances under which removal is permitted. (Even "life tenured" federal judges hold their judgeships on "good behavior," which is generally understood to mean subject only to removal by impeachment.) The most common limitation of "at will" terminations are rules restricting terminations to those justified by "good cause." Good-cause limitations involve fitness for the job or other merit-based considerations. They can be formulated in various ways, or even confined to specific grounds. Each of the removal cases below involved some sort of good-cause limitation on the President's power to fire the official in question.

Guided Reading Questions: *Myers v. United States, Humphrey's Executor v. United States*

1. What is the precise holding of *Myers* and its rationale?

2. Identify as clearly as you can what limits Congress sought to impose on removal of the officers in question in the two cases.

3. The idea that executive branch officials must be subject to unrestricted presidential direction and control if they are to assist the President in executing the laws seems fairly straightforward. Why is there a problem? Can you think of policy reasons why constitutional government would be well served by upholding congressionally imposed limits on the President's removal power?

4. *Humphreys' Executor* does uphold congressionally imposed limits on the President's removal power. But it claims not to overrule *Myers*. Is that claim correct—i.e., can you find a meaningful distinction between the two cases? Try to articulate, in a few sentences, the doctrinal rule that you derive from *Myers* and *Humphreys' Executor*.

Myers v. United States

272 U.S. 52 (1926)

Majority: *Taft* (CJ), Van Devanter, Sutherland, Butler, Sanford, Stone

Dissents: *Holmes, McReynolds, Brandeis*

MR. CHIEF JUSTICE TAFT delivered the opinion of the Court.

This case presents the question whether under the Constitution the President has the exclusive power of removing executive officers of the United States whom he has appointed by and with the advice and consent of the Senate.

[Frank S. Myers was nominated by President Wilson to a four-year term as "first class" postmaster of Portland, Oregon, and confirmed by the Senate on July 21,

1917. On February 2, 1920, after refusing a demand to resign the position, he was removed from office by order of the Postmaster General, acting by direction of the President, on February 2, 1920. Myers protested his removal and in April 1921, brought suit in the Court of Claims for his salary from the date of his removal. He died during the litigation, and the case was pursued by his widow as the administratrix of his estate.]

By the 6th section of the Act of Congress of July 12, 1876, under which Myers was appointed with the advice and consent of the Senate as a first-class postmaster, it is provided that

> Postmasters of the first, second and third classes shall be appointed and may be removed by the President by and with the advice and consent of the Senate and shall hold their offices for four years unless sooner removed or suspended according to law.

The Senate did not consent to the President's removal of Myers during his term. If this statute, in its requirement that his term should be four years unless sooner removed by the President by and with the consent of the Senate, is valid, the appellant, Myers' administratrix, is entitled to recover his unpaid salary for his full term, and the judgment of the Court of Claims must be reversed....

.... There is no express provision respecting removals in the Constitution, except as Section 4 of Article II, above quoted, provides for removal from office by impeachment. The subject was not discussed in the Constitutional Convention.... [But the] history of the clause by which the Senate was given a check upon the President's power of appointment makes it clear that it was not prompted by any desire to limit removals....

[Much of the opinion discusses legislation by the 1789 Congress creating the first three executive departments: State, War, and Treasury. The Court argues that the debates on this legislation manifested a congressional understanding that the Constitution did not permit limits on the President's power to remove cabinet officers.]

Mr. Madison and his associates in the discussion in the House dwelt at length upon the necessity there was for construing Article II to give the President the sole power of removal in his responsibility for the conduct of the executive branch, and enforced this by emphasizing his duty expressly declared in the third section of the Article to "take care that the laws be faithfully executed." Madison, 1 Annals of Congress, 496, 497.

The vesting of the executive power in the President was essentially a grant of the power to execute the laws. But the President alone and unaided could not execute the laws. He must execute them by the assistance of subordinates.... As he is charged specifically to take care that they be faithfully executed, the reasonable implication, even in the absence of express words, was that as part of his executive power he should select those who were to act for him under his direction in the execution of the laws. The further implication must be, in the absence of any express limitation respecting removals, that as his selection of administrative officers is essential to the execution of the laws by him, so must be his power of removing those for whom he can not continue to be responsible....

It was pointed out in this great debate that the power of removal, though equally essential to the executive power, is different in its nature from that of appointment. A veto by the Senate — a part of the legislative branch of the Government — upon removals is a much greater limitation upon the executive branch and a much more serious blending of the legislative with the executive than a rejection of a proposed appointment. It is not to be implied. The rejection of a nominee of the President for a particular office does not greatly embarrass him in the conscientious discharge of his high duties in the selection of those who are to aid him, because the President usually has an ample field from which to select for office, according to his preference, competent and capable men. The Senate has full power to reject newly proposed appointees whenever the President shall remove the incumbents. Such a check enables the Senate to prevent the filling of offices with bad or incompetent men or with those against whom there is tenable objection.

The power to prevent the removal of an officer who has served under the President is different from the authority to consent to or reject his appointment....

Made responsible under the Constitution for the effective enforcement of the law, the President needs as an indispensable aid to meet it the disciplinary influence upon those who act under him of a reserve power of removal.... Each head of a department is and must be the President's alter ego in the matters of that department where the President is required by law to exercise authority....

In all such cases, the discretion to be exercised is that of the President in determining the national public interest and in directing the action to be taken by his executive subordinates to protect it. In this field his cabinet officers must do his will. He must place in each member of his official family, and his chief executive subordinates, implicit faith. The moment that he loses confidence in the intelligence, ability, judgment or loyalty of any one of them he must have the power to remove him without delay. To require him to file charges and submit them to the consideration of the Senate might make impossible that unity and coordination in executive administration essential to effective action....

But this is not to say that there are not strong reasons why the President should have a like power to remove his appointees charged with other duties than those above described. The ordinary duties of officers prescribed by statute come under the general administrative control of the President by virtue of the general grant to him of the executive power, and he may properly supervise and guide their construction of the statutes under which they act in order to secure that unitary and uniform execution of the laws which Article II of the Constitution evidently contemplated in vesting general executive power in the President alone. Laws are often passed with specific provision for the adoption of regulations by a department or bureau head to make the law workable and effective. The ability and judgment manifested by the official thus empowered, as well as his energy and stimulation of his subordinates, are subjects which the President must consider and supervise in his administrative control. Finding such officers to be negligent and inefficient, the President should have the power to remove them. Of course there may be duties so peculiarly and specifically committed to the discretion of a particular officer as to raise a question whether the President may overrule or revise the officer's interpretation of his statutory duty in a particular instance.... But even in such a case he may consider the decision after its rendition as a reason for removing the officer, on the ground that the discretion regularly entrusted to that officer by statute has not been on the whole intelligently or wisely exercised. Otherwise he does not discharge his own constitutional duty of seeing that the laws be faithfully executed....

For the reasons given, we must therefore hold that the provision of the law of 1876, by which the unrestricted power of removal of first class postmasters is denied to the President, is in violation of the Constitution, and invalid. This leads to an affirmance of the judgment of the Court of Claims....

MR. JUSTICE HOLMES, dissenting.

... We have to deal with an office that owes its existence to Congress and that Congress may abolish tomorrow.... The duty of the President to see that the laws be executed is a duty that does not go beyond the laws or require him to achieve more than Congress sees fit to leave within his power.

The separate opinion of MR. JUSTICE McREYNOLDS.

.... The long struggle for civil service reform and the legislation designed to insure some security of official tenure ought not to be forgotten. Again and again Congress has enacted statutes prescribing restrictions on removals and by approving them many Presidents have affirmed its power therein....

Members of the Interstate Commerce Commission, Board of General Appraisers, Federal Reserve Board, Federal Trade Commission, Tariff Commission, Shipping Board, Federal Farm Loan Board, Railroad Labor Board; officers of the Army and Navy; Comptroller General; Postmaster General and his assistants; postmasters of the first, second and third classes; judge of the United States Court for China; judges of the Court of Claims, established in 1855, the judges to serve "during good behavior"; judges of Territorial (statutory) courts; judges of the Supreme Court and Court of Appeals for the District of Columbia (statutory courts), appointed to serve "during good behavior." Also members of the Board of Tax Appeals....

.... Generally, the actual ouster of an officer is executive action; but to prescribe the conditions under which this may be done is legislative.... The real question, therefore, comes to this—Does any constitutional provision definitely limit the otherwise plenary power of Congress over postmasters, when they are appointed by the President with consent of the Senate?.... If the framers of the Constitution had intended "the executive power," in Art. II, Sec. 1, to include all power of an executive nature, they would not have added the carefully defined grants of Sec. 2.... Why say, the President shall be commander-in-chief; may require opinions in writing of the principal officers in each of the executive departments; shall have power to grant reprieves and pardons; shall give information to Congress concerning the state of the union; shall receive ambassadors; shall take care that the laws be faithfully executed—if all of these things and more had already been vested in him by the general words?.... Judgment should go for the appellant.

MR. JUSTICE BRANDEIS, dissenting.

.... [P]ostmasters are inferior officers. Congress might have vested their appointment in the head of the department....

.... We need not consider what power the President, being Commander in Chief, has over officers in the Army and the Navy. We need not determine whether the President, acting alone, may remove high political officers.... The practice of Congress to control the exercise of the executive power of removal from inferior offices is evidenced by many statutes which restrict it in many ways besides the removal clause here in question. Each of these restrictive statutes became law with the approval of the President. Every President who has held office since 1861, except President Garfield, approved one or more of such statutes....

The separation of the powers of government did not make each branch completely autonomous. It left each, in some measure, dependent upon the others, as it left to each power to exercise, in some respects, functions in their nature executive, legislative and judicial. Obviously the President cannot secure full execution of the laws, if Congress denies to him adequate means of doing so. Full execution may be defeated because Congress declines to create offices indispensable for that purpose. Or, because Congress, having created the office, declines to make the indispensable appropriation. Or, because Congress, having both created the office and made the appropriation, prevents, by restrictions which it imposes, the appointment of officials who in quality and character are indispensable to the efficient execution of the law. If, in any such way, adequate means are denied to the President, the fault will lie with Congress. The President performs his full constitutional duty, if, with the means and instruments provided by Congress and within the limitations prescribed by it, he uses his best endeavors to secure the faithful execution of the laws enacted.

Humphrey's Executor v. United States

295 U.S. 602 (1935)

Unanimous decision: *Sutherland*, Hughes (CJ), Van Devanter, McReynolds, Brandeis, Butler, Stone, Roberts, Cardozo

MR. JUSTICE SUTHERLAND delivered the opinion of the Court.

.... William E. Humphrey, the decedent, on December 10, 1931, was nominated by President Hoover to succeed himself as a member of the Federal Trade Commission, and was confirmed by the United States Senate. He was duly commissioned for a term of seven years expiring September 25, 1938; and, after taking the required oath of office, entered upon his duties. On July 25, 1933, President Roosevelt addressed a letter to the commissioner asking for his resignation, on the ground "that the aims and purposes of the Administration with respect to the work of the Commission can be carried out most effectively with personnel of my own selection," but disclaiming any reflection upon the commissioner personally or upon his services. The commissioner replied, asking time to consult his friends. After some further correspondence upon the subject, the President on August 31, 1933, wrote the commissioner expressing the hope that the resignation would be forthcoming and saying:

> You will, I know, realize that I do not feel that your mind and my mind go along together on either the policies or the administering of the Federal Trade Commission, and, frankly, I think it is best for the people of this country that I should have a full confidence.

The commissioner declined to resign; and on October 7, 1933, the President wrote him: "Effective as of this date you are hereby removed from the office of Commissioner of the Federal Trade Commission."

[Humphrey sued in the Court of Claims to recover his salary of $10,000 per year through the end of his designated term. He died during the litigation, and the case was pursued by his estate.]

The Federal Trade Commission Act, 15 U.S.C. § 41, 42, creates a commission of five members to be appointed by the President by and with the advice and consent of the Senate, and § 1 provides:

> Not more than three of the commissioners shall be members of the same political party. The first commissioners appointed shall continue in office for terms of three, four, five, six, and seven years, respectively, from the date of the taking effect of this Act, the term of each to be designated by the President, but their successors shall be appointed for terms of seven years, except that any person chosen to fill a vacancy shall be appointed only for the unexpired term of the commissioner whom he shall succeed. The commission shall choose a chairman from its own membership. No commissioner shall engage in any other business, vocation, or employment. Any commissioner may be removed by the President for inefficiency, neglect of duty, or malfeasance in office....

.... The statute fixes a term of office.... subject to removal by the President for inefficiency, neglect of duty, or malfeasance in office. The words of the act are definite and unambiguous....

The commission is to be non-partisan; and it must, from the very nature of its duties, act with entire impartiality. It is charged with the enforcement of no policy except the policy of the law. Its duties are neither political nor executive, but predominantly quasi-judicial and quasi-legislative. Like the Interstate Commerce Commission, its members are called upon to exercise the trained judgment of a body of experts "appointed by law and informed by experience."

The legislative reports in both houses of Congress clearly reflect the view that a fixed term was necessary to the effective and fair administration of the law. [The] Senate Committee on Interstate Commerce [report said:] ... "It is manifestly desirable that the terms of the commissioners shall be long enough to give them an opportunity to acquire the expertness in dealing with these special questions concerning industry that comes from experience."

.... The debates in both houses demonstrate that the prevailing view was that the commission was not to be "subject to anybody in the government but ... only to the people of the United States"; free from "political domination or control" or the "probability or possibility of such a thing"; to be "separate and apart from any existing department of the government—not subject to the orders of the President."

.... [T]o hold that, nevertheless, the members of the commission continue in office at the mere will of the President, might be to thwart, in large measure, the very ends which Congress sought to realize by definitely fixing the term of office.

We conclude that the intent of the act is to limit the executive power of removal to the causes enumerated, the existence of none of which is claimed here; and we pass to the second question.

To support its contention that the removal provision of § 1, as we have just construed it, is an unconstitutional interference with the executive power of the President, the government's chief reliance is on Myers v. United States, 272 U.S. 52. That case has been so recently decided, and the prevailing and dissenting opinions so fully review the general subject of the power of executive removal, that further discussion would add little of value to the wealth of material there collected. These opinions examine at length the historical, legislative and judicial data bearing upon the question, beginning with what is called "the decision of 1789" in the first Congress and coming down almost to the day when the opinions were delivered. They occupy 243 pages of the volume in which they are printed. Nevertheless, the narrow point actually decided was only that the President had power to remove a postmaster of the first class, without the advice and consent of the Senate as required by act of Congress. In the course of the opinion of the court, expressions occur which tend to sustain the government's contention, but these are beyond the point involved and, therefore, do not come within the rule of stare decisis. In so far as they are out of harmony with the views here set forth, these expressions are disapproved....

The office of a postmaster is so essentially unlike the office now involved that the decision in the Myers case cannot be accepted as controlling our decision here. A postmaster is an executive officer restricted to the performance of executive functions. He is charged with no duty at all related to either the legislative or judicial power. The actual decision in the Myers case finds support in the theory that such an officer is merely one of the units in the executive department and, hence, inherently subject to the exclusive and illimitable power of removal by the Chief Executive, whose subordinate and aid he is. Putting aside dicta, which may be followed if sufficiently persuasive but which are not controlling, the necessary reach of the decision goes far enough to include all purely executive officers. It goes no farther; much less does it include an officer who occupies no place in the executive department and who exercises no part of the executive power vested by the Constitution in the President.

The Federal Trade Commission is an administrative body created by Congress to carry into effect legislative policies embodied in the statute in accordance with the legislative standard therein prescribed, and to perform other specified duties as a legislative or as a judicial aid. Such a body cannot in any proper sense be characterized as an arm or an eye of the executive. Its duties are performed without executive leave and, in the contemplation of the statute, must be free from executive control. In administering the provisions of the statute in respect of "unfair methods of competition"—that is to say in filling in and administering the details embodied by that general standard—the commission acts in part quasi-legislatively and in part quasi-judicially. In making investigations and reports thereon for the information of Congress under §6, in aid of the legislative power, it acts as a legislative agency. Under §7, which authorizes the commission to act as a master in chancery under rules prescribed by the court, it acts as an agency of the judiciary. To the extent that it exercises any executive function—as distinguished from executive power in the constitutional sense—it does so in the discharge and effectuation of its quasi-legislative or quasi-judicial powers, or as an agency of the legislative or judicial departments of the government....

We think it plain under the Constitution that illimitable power of removal is not possessed by the President in respect of officers of the character of those just named. The authority of Congress, in creating quasi-legislative or quasi-judicial agencies, to require them to act in discharge of their duties independently of executive control cannot well be doubted; and that authority includes, as an appropriate incident, power to fix the period during which they shall continue in office, and to forbid their removal except for cause in the meantime. For it is quite evident that one who holds his office only during the pleasure of another, cannot be depended upon to maintain an attitude of independence against the latter's will....

The power of removal here claimed for the President falls within this principle, since its coercive influence threatens the independence of a commission, which is not only wholly disconnected from the executive department, but which, as already fully appears, was created by Congress as a means of carrying into operation legislative and judicial powers, and as an agency of the legislative and judicial departments.

The result of what we now have said is this: Whether the power of the President to remove an officer shall prevail over the authority of Congress to condition the power by fixing a definite term and precluding a removal except for cause, will depend upon the character of the office; the Myers decision, affirming the power of the President alone to make the removal, is confined to purely executive officers; and as to officers of the kind here under consideration, we hold that no removal can be made during the prescribed term for which the officer is appointed, except for one or more of the causes named in the applicable statute.

To the extent that, between the decision in the Myers case, which sustains the unrestrictable power of the President to remove purely executive officers, and our present decision that such power does not extend to an office such as that here involved, there shall remain a field of doubt, we leave such cases as may fall within it for future consideration and determination as they may arise.

CASE NOTE: *Weiner v. United States*, 357 U.S. 349 (1958). Weiner was appointed by President Truman in 1950 to serve as one of three members of the "War Claims Commission," created by a 1948 Act of Congress to adjudicate compensation claims for bodily or property injuries suffered by internees, prisoners of war, and religious organizations, at the hands of the Axis powers during World War II. In 1953, President Eisenhower fired Weiner after Weiner refused the President's request for his resignation. Weiner filed suit in the U.S. Court of Claims for recovery of his back pay. The Court of Claims dismissed Weiner's suit, and the Supreme Court reversed. In a unanimous opinion by Justice Frankfurter, the Court reasoned that the functions of the War Claims Commission were not to carry out the policies of the President, but to render impartial adjudications of war claims. That function required the sort of independence recognized in *Humphrey's Executor*, even though the Act creating the War Claims Commission was silent about the conditions for removing commissioners. Considering "the claim that the President could remove a member of an adjudicatory body like the War Claims Commission merely because he wanted his own appointees on such a Commission, we are compelled to conclude that no such power is given to the President directly by the Constitution, and none is impliedly conferred upon him by statute simply because Congress said nothing about it. The philosophy of *Humphrey's Executor*, in its explicit language as well as its implications, precludes such a claim."

The *Weiner* decision reaches the same result as *Humphrey's Executor*, but by reasoning in reverse. *Humphrey's Executor* inferred independence of function from job security, and *Weiner* inferred job security from independence of function. The *Humphrey's* Court examined the "good cause" removal provisions protecting FTC commissioners, and inferred that the commissioners were intended to perform functions independent of the policy preferences of the President. *Weiner* examined the adjudicatory function of War Claims commissioners, concluded that these were independent of executive policy functions, and inferred that removal must be limited to "good cause" grounds.

CASE NOTE: *Bowsher v. Synar*, 478 U.S. 714 (1986). The idea that separation of powers requires an alignment of an official's functions with the manner of his removal—because removal provisions tell us in what branch the official is "located"—was developed further in *Bowsher v. Synar*. There, the Court considered a constitutional challenge to the Balanced Budget and Emergency Deficit Control Act of 1985, 2 U.S.C. § 901 et seq., popularly known as the "Gramm-Rudman-Hollings Act." The Act was designed to eliminate the federal budget deficit by delegating certain politically difficult budget-cutting decisions to an unelected official—the Comptroller General of the United States, who would make budget cutting recommendations to be implemented by the President.

The Comptroller General heads the General Accounting Office, "an instrumentality of the United States Government independent of the executive departments," 31 U.S.C. § 702(a), created by Congress in 1921 to monitor that public funds were being spent by the executive branch in conformity with Congressional appropriations decisions. The Comptroller General is nominated by the President from a list of three individuals recommended by the Speaker of the House of Representatives and the President pro tempore of the Senate, and confirmed by the Senate. He is removable only at the initiative of Congress, either by impeachment of by a joint resolution of Congress based on "permanent disability; inefficiency; neglect of duty; malfeasance; or a felony or conduct involving moral turpitude." 31 U.S.C. § 703(e). The Court concluded that the removal provisions established that the Comptroller General was an agent of Congress, and that as a member of the legislative branch, it was unconstitutional to assign him executive functions. Making binding recommendations of budget cuts to the President, according to the Court, was an executive function. The Court therefore held the law unconstitutional.

Review Questions and Explanations: Removal Powers

1. *Myers* has never been overruled, and it is still cited by the Supreme Court as authoritative. At the same time, it is clear that the *Myers* doctrine has been

significantly qualified by subsequent cases. Try to articulate, in few sentences, the constitutional doctrine of presidential removal powers, based on *Myers, Humphrey's, Weiner,* and *Bowsher.*

2. The dissenting justices in *Myers* express some concerns relating to "civil service reform." This issue had a long history. From the early days of the republic, but particularly beginning with the presidency of Andrew Jackson, presidents have used executive branch appointments as a means of doling out "patronage" jobs to repay political debts, to build individual and party loyalty, and to create or sustain a base of power. Throughout much of the 19th century, critics of the "patronage system" argued that the federal bureaucracy tended to be staffed by underqualified or incompetent party hacks. A "civil service reform" movement, with an avowed goal of promoting merit-based efficiency, gained momentum after the Civil War. It ultimately resulted in an overhaul of federal employment, insulating the majority of positions from political appointment and creating job security across changes in presidential administration.

We now have layers of federal officials who are deemed "political appointees" and those who are deemed "career civil servants" and are protected by these reform laws from politically motivated removal from office. But a tension remains: to what extent can a democratically expressed "mandate" in support of a new President's policies be undercut by holdover civil servants? Indeed, in recent years, a phrase has been coined for the appointment of an outgoing administration's political loyalists to protected "non-political" civil service posts: "burrowing in."

3. Chief Justice Taft's view in *Myers* that the President must have an unrestricted right to fire subordinates may have been informed by the fact that he served as President, from 1909–1913. We can wonder more about the views of Justices Van Devanter, Butler, and Sutherland, each of whom agreed with that doctrine in *Myers* but then, nine years later, voted to uphold limits on President Roosevelt's power to fire a Hoover-appointed Federal Trade Commissioner following an election in which Roosevelt was arguably given a mandate to make sweeping changes to economic policy. Historians have concluded that these justices were determined to resist what they perceived to be Roosevelt's assumption of excessive presidential powers; the conclusion that they were motivated by political concerns to switch their position between *Myers* and *Humphrey's Executor* is hard to resist. See Justice Scalia's dissent in *Morrison v. Olson,* below.

4. *Humphrey's Executor* is often credited as providing the constitutional foundation for so-called "independent administrative agencies," that is, agencies that are not part of the executive, legislative or judicial branches. The Federal Trade Commission is apparently one such agency; there are several others (e.g., the Federal Reserve Board of Governors). Their appointments have been held subject to the appointments clause, but not to the removal doctrine of *Myers.*

Does anything in the Constitution suggest the propriety of an agency independent of the three existing branches of government? Congress and the President are accountable to the people through elections. The chairman of the Federal Reserve Board, appointed for a ten-year term, is not; nor are officials of other "independent" agencies. Moreover, executive officials whom the President can remove from office at will have a line of political or electoral accountability, at least in theory: the President, knowing that he will be held accountable for their actions has an incentive to control their behavior to keep it within politically acceptable limits. Does *Humphrey's Executor* provide a persuasive constitutional foundation for independent agencies? Can you think of one?

3. Synthesis: Appointment and Removal Powers

Guided Reading Questions: *Morrison v. Olson*

1. *Morrison* involves two constitutional challenges to the office of special prosecutor, one based on violation of the appointments clause, and the second based on violation of the removal power doctrine. Identify the Court's holding on each issue.

2. The appointments power challenge turns on whether or not the special prosecutor is "an inferior officer." Why does that matter? Do you agree with the Court's resolution of that question?

3. Does the majority's resolution of the removal power question follow directly from the doctrine of *Myers, Humphrey's Executor, Weiner,* and *Bowsher*? If not, is it at least consistent with those precedents?

4. The special prosecutor law seems to place prosecutorial powers within what amounts to an independent agency. What is the advantage of doing that? What is the dissent's objection to such an arrangement? Is Justice Scalia simply being rigid, or does he have an underlying policy concern?

Morrison v. Olson

487 U.S. 654 (1988)

Majority: *Rehnquist* (CJ), Brennan, White, Marshall, Blackmun, Stevens, O'Connor

Dissent: *Scalia* (Kennedy took no part)

CHIEF JUSTICE REHNQUIST delivered the opinion of the Court.

This case presents us with a challenge to the independent counsel provisions of the Ethics in Government Act of 1978, 28 U.S.C. §§ 49, 591 et seq. We hold today that these provisions of the Act do not violate the Appointments Clause of the Constitution, Art. II, § 2, cl. 2, or the limitations of Article III, nor do they impermissibly interfere with the President's authority under Article II in violation of the constitutional principle of separation of powers.

I

Title VI of the Ethics in Government Act allows for the appointment of an "independent counsel" to investigate and, if appropriate, prosecute certain high-ranking Government officials for violations of federal criminal laws. The Act requires the Attorney General,

upon receipt of information that he determines is "sufficient to constitute grounds to investigate whether any person [covered by the Act] may have violated any Federal criminal
law," to conduct a preliminary investigation of the matter. When the Attorney General
has completed this investigation, or 90 days has elapsed, he is required to report to a
special court (the Special Division) created by the Act "for the purpose of appointing independent counsels." 28 U.S.C. § 49.

> FN3. The Special Division is a division of the United States Court of Appeals for the
> District of Columbia Circuit. The court consists of three circuit court judges or justices
> appointed by the Chief Justice of the United States. One of the judges must be a judge of
> the United States Court of Appeals for the District of Columbia Circuit, and no two of
> the judges may be named to the Special Division from a particular court. The judges are
> appointed for 2-year terms, with any vacancy being filled only for the remainder of the
> 2-year period.

If the Attorney General determines that "there are no reasonable grounds to believe that
further investigation is warranted," then he must notify the Special Division of this result.
In such a case, "the division of the court shall have no power to appoint an independent
counsel." § 592(b)(1). If, however, the Attorney General has determined that there are
"reasonable grounds to believe that further investigation or prosecution is warranted,"
then he "shall apply to the division of the court for the appointment of an independent
counsel."…. Upon receiving this application, the Special Division "shall appoint an
appropriate independent counsel and shall define that independent counsel's prosecutorial
jurisdiction." § 593(b). The functions of the independent counsel include conducting
grand jury proceedings and other investigations, participating in civil and criminal court
proceedings and litigation, and appealing any decision in any case in which the counsel
participates in an official capacity. §§ 594(a)(1)–(3). Under § 594(a)(9), the counsel's
powers include "initiating and conducting prosecutions in any court of competent
jurisdiction, framing and signing indictments, filing informations, and handling all aspects
of any case, in the name of the United States." The counsel may appoint employees,
§ 594(c), may request and obtain assistance from the Department of Justice, § 594(d),
and may accept referral of matters from the Attorney General if the matter falls within
the counsel's jurisdiction as defined by the Special Division, § 594(e). The Act also states
that an independent counsel "shall, except where not possible, comply with the written
or other established policies of the Department of Justice respecting enforcement of the
criminal laws." § 594(f).

Two statutory provisions govern the length of an independent counsel's tenure in office.
The first defines the procedure for removing an independent counsel. Section 596(a)(1)
provides:

> An independent counsel appointed under this chapter may be removed from
> office, other than by impeachment and conviction, only by the personal action
> of the Attorney General and only for good cause, physical disability, mental in-
> capacity, or any other condition that substantially impairs the performance of
> such independent counsel's duties.

…. The other provision governing the tenure of the independent counsel defines the
procedures for "terminating" the counsel's office. Under § 596(b)(1), the office of an independent counsel terminates when he or she notifies the Attorney General that he or
she has completed or substantially completed any investigations or prosecutions undertaken
pursuant to the Act. In addition, the Special Division, acting either on its own or on the
suggestion of the Attorney General, may terminate the office of an independent counsel
at any time if it finds that "the investigation of all matters within the prosecutorial

jurisdiction of such independent counsel ... have been completed or so substantially completed that it would be appropriate for the Department of Justice to complete such investigations and prosecutions." § 596(b)(2).

[In 1983, Theodore Olson, the Assistant Attorney General for the Office of Legal Counsel (OLC), testified before a House Subcommittee to explain the Reagan administration's refusal the previous year to comply with several Committee requests to produce certain documents relating to the conduct of the Environmental Protection Agency. In 1985, the House Judiciary Committee published a lengthy report on the Committee's investigation into the withholding of the documents, suggesting that Mr. Olson had given false and misleading testimony to the Subcommittee on March 10, 1983, thus obstructing the Committee's investigation. The Committee Chairman requested that the Attorney General investigate the allegations against Olson.

[The Attorney General directed the Public Integrity Section of the Criminal Division to conduct a preliminary investigation, which concluded that the appointment of an independent counsel was warranted. The Attorney General applied to the Special Division for the appointment of an independent counsel to investigate whether Olson had violated any federal criminal laws in obstructing a congressional inquiry. On April 23, 1986, the Special Division appointed James C. McKay as independent counsel to investigate "whether the testimony of ... Olson and his revision of such testimony on March 10, 1983, violated either 18 U.S.C. § 1505 or § 1001, or any other provision of federal law." McKay later resigned as independent counsel, and on May 29, 1986, the Division appointed appellant Antonia Morrison as his replacement, with the same jurisdiction. Morrison convened a grand jury and issued subpoenas for testimony and documents to Olson and two other OLC attorneys (the appellants). The appellants filed a motion in district court to quash the subpoenas, claiming, among other things, that the independent counsel provisions of the Act were unconstitutional and that appellant accordingly had no authority to proceed. On July 20, 1987, the District Court upheld the constitutionality of the Act and denied the motions to quash. A divided Court of Appeals reversed. Morrison then sought review in the Supreme Court.]

III

.... As we stated in Buckley v. Valeo, 424 U.S. 1, 132 (1976): "Principal officers are selected by the President with the advice and consent of the Senate. Inferior officers Congress may allow to be appointed by the President alone, by the heads of departments, or by the Judiciary." The initial question is, accordingly, whether appellant is an "inferior" or a "principal" officer. If she is the latter, as the Court of Appeals concluded, then the Act is in violation of the Appointments Clause.

[Although] the line between "inferior" and "principal" officers is one that is far from clear.... in our view appellant clearly falls on the "inferior officer" side of that line. Several factors lead to this conclusion.

First, appellant is subject to removal by a higher Executive Branch official. Although appellant may not be "subordinate" to the Attorney General (and the President) insofar as she possesses a degree of independent discretion to exercise the powers delegated to her under the Act, the fact that she can be removed by the Attorney General indicates that she is to some degree "inferior" in rank and authority. Second, ... [an] independent counsel's role is restricted primarily to investigation and, if appropriate, prosecution for certain federal crimes. Admittedly, the Act delegates to appellant "full power and independent authority to exercise all investigative and prosecutorial functions and powers of the Department of Justice," § 594(a), but this grant of authority does not include any authority to formulate policy for the Government or the Executive Branch.... The Act specifically provides that in policy matters appellant is to comply to the extent possible with the policies of the Department. § 594(f).

Third, ... an independent counsel can only act within the scope of the jurisdiction that has been granted by the Special Division pursuant to a request by the Attorney General. Finally.... the office of independent counsel is "temporary" in the sense that an independent counsel is appointed essentially to accomplish a single task, and when that task is over the office is terminated, either by the counsel herself or by action of the Special Division.... In our view, these factors ... are sufficient to establish that appellant is an "inferior" officer in the constitutional sense.

.... Appellees argue that even if appellant is an "inferior" officer, the Clause does not empower Congress to place the power to appoint such an officer outside the Executive Branch.... The relevant language of the Appointments Clause.... reads: " ... but the Congress may by Law vest the Appointment of such inferior Officers, as they think proper, in the President alone, in the courts of Law, or in the Heads of Departments." On its face, the language of this "excepting clause" admits of no limitation on interbranch appointments. Indeed, the inclusion of "as they think proper" seems clearly to give Congress significant discretion to determine whether it is "proper" to vest the appointment of, for example, executive officials in the "courts of Law."

.... We do not mean to say that Congress' power to provide for interbranch appointments of "inferior officers" is unlimited. In addition to separation-of-powers concerns, which would arise if such provisions for appointment had the potential to impair the constitutional functions assigned to one of the branches, ... Congress' decision to vest the appointment power in the courts would be improper if there was some "incongruity" between the functions normally performed by the courts and the performance of their duty to appoint. In this case, however, we do not think it impermissible for Congress to vest the power to appoint independent counsel in a specially created federal court.... We have recognized that courts may appoint private attorneys to act as prosecutor for judicial contempt judgments[,] we [have] approved court appointment of United States commissioners, who exercised certain limited prosecutorial powers[, and] we [have] indicated that judicial appointment of federal marshals, who are "executive officer[s]," would not be inappropriate....

[In Section III, the Court next rejected an argument that the Act vested the Special Division with supervisory authority in excess of Article III's limitation of the judicial power to "Cases" and "Controversies."]

IV

We now turn to consider whether the Act is invalid under the constitutional principle of separation of powers. Two related issues must be addressed: The first is whether the provision of the Act restricting the Attorney General's power to remove the independent counsel to only those instances in which he can show "good cause," taken by itself, impermissibly interferes with the President's exercise of his constitutionally appointed functions. The second is whether, taken as a whole, the Act violates the separation of powers by reducing the President's ability to control the prosecutorial powers wielded by the independent counsel.

A

.... Unlike both Bowsher [v. Synar] and Myers, this case does not involve an attempt by Congress itself to gain a role in the removal of executive officials other than its established powers of impeachment and conviction. The Act instead puts the removal power squarely in the hands of the Executive Branch; an independent counsel may be removed from office, "only by the personal action of the Attorney General, and only for good cause." ... In our view, the removal provisions of the Act make this case more analogous to Humphrey's Executor v. United States, 295 U.S. 602 (1935), and Wiener v. United States, 357 U.S. 349 (1958), than to Myers or Bowsher....

Appellees contend that Humphrey's Executor [is] distinguishable from this case because [it] did not involve officials who performed a "core executive function." ... In their view.... under Myers, the President must have absolute discretion to discharge "purely" executive officials at will.

We undoubtedly did rely on the terms "quasi-legislative" and "quasi-judicial" to distinguish the officials involved in Humphrey's Executor ... from those in Myers, but our present considered view is that the determination of whether the Constitution allows Congress to impose a "good cause"-type restriction on the President's power to remove an official cannot be made to turn on whether or not that official is classified as "purely executive." The analysis contained in our removal cases is designed not to define rigid categories of those officials who may or may not be removed at will by the President, but to ensure that Congress does not interfere with the President's exercise of the "executive power" and his constitutionally appointed duty to "take care that the laws be faithfully executed" under Article II. Myers was undoubtedly correct in its holding, and in its broader suggestion that there are some "purely executive" officials who must be removable by the President at will if he is to be able to accomplish his constitutional role.... At the other end of the spectrum from Myers, the characterization of the agencies in Humphrey's Executor ... as "quasi-legislative" or "quasi-judicial" in large part reflected our judgment that it was not essential to the President's proper execution of his Article II powers that these agencies be headed up by individuals who were removable at will. We do not mean to suggest that an analysis of the functions served by the officials at issue is irrelevant. But the real question is whether the removal restrictions are of such a nature that they impede the President's ability to perform his constitutional duty, and the functions of the officials in question must be analyzed in that light.

... [W]e cannot say that the imposition of a "good cause" standard for removal by itself unduly trammels on executive authority. There is no real dispute that the functions performed by the independent counsel are "executive" in the sense that they are law enforcement functions that typically have been undertaken by officials within the Executive Branch. As we noted above, however, the independent counsel is an inferior officer under the Appointments Clause, with limited jurisdiction and tenure and lacking policymaking or significant administrative authority. Although the counsel exercises no small amount of discretion and judgment in deciding how to carry out his or her duties under the Act, we simply do not see how the President's need to control the exercise of that discretion is so central to the functioning of the Executive Branch as to require as a matter of constitutional law that the counsel be terminable at will by the President.

Nor do we think that the "good cause" removal provision at issue here impermissibly burdens the President's power to control or supervise the independent counsel, as an executive official, in the execution of his or her duties under the Act. This is not a case in which the power to remove an executive official has been completely stripped from the President, thus providing no means for the President to ensure the "faithful execution" of the laws. Rather, because the independent counsel may be terminated for "good cause," the Executive, through the Attorney General, retains ample authority to assure that the counsel is competently performing his or her statutory responsibilities in a manner that comports with the provisions of the Act. Although we need not decide in this case exactly what is encompassed within the term "good cause" under the Act, the legislative history of the removal provision also makes clear that the Attorney General may remove an independent counsel for "misconduct." See H. R. Conf. Rep. No. 100-452, p. 37 (1987). Here, as with the provision of the Act conferring the appointment authority of the independent counsel on the special court, the congressional determination to limit the removal power of the Attorney General was essential, in the view of Congress, to establish the necessary independence of the office. We do not think that this limitation as it presently stands sufficiently deprives the President of control over the independent counsel to interfere impermissibly with his constitutional obligation to ensure the faithful execution of the laws....

B

The final question to be addressed is whether the Act, taken as a whole, violates the principle of separation of powers by unduly interfering with the role of the Executive Branch. Time and again we have reaffirmed the importance in our constitutional scheme of the separation of governmental powers into the three coordinate branches. We have not hesitated to invalidate provisions of law which violate this principle. On the other hand, we have never held that the Constitution requires that the three branches of Government "operate with absolute independence." United States v. Nixon, 418 U.S., at 707. In the often-quoted words of Justice Jackson:

> While the Constitution diffuses power the better to secure liberty, it also contemplates that practice will integrate the dispersed powers into a workable government. It enjoins upon its branches separateness but interdependence, autonomy but reciprocity." Youngstown Sheet & Tube Co. v. Sawyer, 343 U.S. 579, 635 (1952) (concurring opinion).

We observe first that this case does not involve an attempt by Congress to increase its own powers at the expense of the Executive Branch.... [With] the exception of the power of impeachment—which applies to all officers of the United States—Congress retained for itself no powers of control or supervision over an independent counsel. The Act does empower certain Members of Congress to request the Attorney General to apply for the appointment of an independent counsel, but the Attorney General has no duty to comply with the request, although he must respond within a certain time limit. § 592(g). Other than that, Congress' role under the Act is limited to receiving reports or other information and oversight of the independent counsel's activities, § 595(a), functions that we have recognized generally as being incidental to the legislative function of Congress.

Similarly, we do not think that the Act works any judicial usurpation of properly executive functions. As should be apparent from our discussion of the Appointments Clause above, the power to appoint inferior officers such as independent counsel is not in itself an "executive" function in the constitutional sense, at least when Congress has exercised its power to vest the appointment of an inferior office in the "courts of Law." We note nonetheless that under the Act the Special Division has no power to appoint an independent counsel sua sponte; it may only do so upon the specific request of the Attorney General, and the courts are specifically prevented from reviewing the Attorney General's decision not to seek appointment, § 592(f). In addition, once the court has appointed a counsel and defined his or her jurisdiction, it has no power to supervise or control the activities of the counsel....

Finally, we do not think that the Act "impermissibly undermine[s]" the powers of the Executive Branch, or "disrupts the proper balance between the coordinate branches [by]

prevent[ing] the Executive Branch from accomplishing its constitutionally assigned functions[.]" It is undeniable that the Act reduces the amount of control or supervision that
the Attorney General and, through him, the President exercises over the investigation
and prosecution of a certain class of alleged criminal activity. The Attorney General....
retains the power to remove the counsel for "good cause," a power that we have already
concluded provides the Executive with substantial ability to ensure that the laws are
"faithfully executed" by an independent counsel. No independent counsel may be appointed
without a specific request by the Attorney General, and the Attorney General's decision
not to request appointment if he finds "no reasonable grounds to believe that further investigation is warranted" is committed to his unreviewable discretion. The Act thus gives
the Executive a degree of control over the power to initiate an investigation by the
independent counsel. In addition, the jurisdiction of the independent counsel is defined
with reference to the facts submitted by the Attorney General, and once a counsel is
appointed, the Act requires that the counsel abide by Justice Department policy unless it
is not "possible" to do so....

V

In sum, we conclude today that it does not violate the Appointments Clause for
Congress to vest the appointment of independent counsel in the Special Division; that
the powers exercised by the Special Division under the Act do not violate Article III; and
that the Act does not violate the separation-of-powers principle by impermissibly
interfering with the functions of the Executive Branch. The decision of the Court of
Appeals is therefore Reversed.

JUSTICE SCALIA, dissenting.

It is the proud boast of our democracy that we have "a government of laws and not of
men." Many Americans are familiar with that phrase; not many know its derivation. It
comes from Part the First, Article XXX, of the Massachusetts Constitution of 1780, which
reads in full as follows:

> In the government of this Commonwealth, the legislative department shall never
> exercise the executive and judicial powers, or either of them: The executive shall
> never exercise the legislative and judicial powers, or either of them: The judicial
> shall never exercise the legislative and executive powers, or either of them: to the
> end it may be a government of laws and not of men.

The Framers of the Federal Constitution similarly viewed the principle of separation of
powers as the absolutely central guarantee of a just Government. In No. 47 of The Federalist,
Madison wrote that "[n]o political truth is certainly of greater intrinsic value, or is stamped
with the authority of more enlightened patrons of liberty." The Federalist No. 47, p. 301
(C. Rossiter ed. 1961) (hereinafter Federalist). Without a secure structure of separated
powers, our Bill of Rights would be worthless, as are the bills of rights of many nations
of the world that have adopted, or even improved upon, the mere words of ours....

But just as the mere words of a Bill of Rights are not self-effectuating, the Framers recognized "[t]he insufficiency of a mere parchment delineation of the boundaries" to achieve
the separation of powers. Federalist No. 73, p. 442 (A. Hamilton). "[T]he great security,"
wrote Madison, "against a gradual concentration of the several powers in the same
department consists in giving to those who administer each department the necessary
constitutional means and personal motives to resist encroachments of the others. The
provision for defense must in this, as in all other cases, be made commensurate to the
danger of attack." Federalist No. 51, pp. 321–322. Madison continued: "[In] republican

government, the legislative authority necessarily predominates. The remedy for this inconveniency is to divide the legislature into different branches.... As the weight of the legislative authority requires that it should be thus divided, the weakness of the executive may require, on the other hand, that it should be fortified." *Id.*, at 322–323.

The major "fortification" provided, of course, was the veto power. But in addition to providing fortification, the Founders conspicuously and very consciously declined to sap the Executive's strength in the same way they had weakened the Legislature: by dividing the executive power. Proposals to have multiple executives, or a council of advisers with separate authority were rejected. See 1 M. Farrand, Records of the Federal Convention of 1787, pp. 66, 71–74, 88, 91–92 (rev. ed. 1966). Thus, while "[a]ll legislative Powers herein granted shall be vested in a Congress of the United States, which shall consist of a Senate *and* House of Representatives," U.S. Const., Art. I, § 1 (emphasis added), "[t]he executive Power shall be vested in *a President of the United States*," Art. II, § 1, cl. 1 (emphasis added).

That is what this suit is about. Power. The allocation of power among Congress, the President, and the courts in such fashion as to preserve the equilibrium the Constitution sought to establish.... Frequently an issue of this sort will come before the Court clad, so to speak, in sheep's clothing: the potential of the asserted principle to effect important change in the equilibrium of power is not immediately evident, and must be discerned by a careful and perceptive analysis. But this wolf comes as a wolf.

.... [B]y the application of this statute in the present case, Congress has effectively compelled a criminal investigation of a high-level appointee of the President in connection with his actions arising out of a bitter power dispute between the President and the Legislative Branch. Mr. Olson may or may not be guilty of a crime; we do not know. But we do know that the investigation of him has been commenced, not necessarily because the President or his authorized subordinates believe it is in the interest of the United States, in the sense that it warrants the diversion of resources from other efforts, and is worth the cost in money and in possible damage to other governmental interests; and not even, leaving aside those normally considered factors, because the President or his authorized subordinates necessarily believe that an investigation is likely to unearth a violation worth prosecuting; but only because the Attorney General cannot affirm, as Congress demands, that there are *no reasonable grounds to believe* that further investigation is warranted. The decisions regarding the scope of that further investigation, its duration, and, finally, whether or not prosecution should ensue, are likewise beyond the control of the President and his subordinates.

II

.... To repeat, Article II, § 1, cl. 1, of the Constitution provides: "The executive Power shall be vested in a President of the United States." As I described at the outset of this opinion, this does not mean *some of* the executive power, but *all of* the executive power. It seems to me, therefore, that the decision of the Court of Appeals invalidating the present statute must be upheld on fundamental separation-of-powers principles if the following two questions are answered affirmatively: (1) Is the conduct of a criminal prosecution (and of an investigation to decide whether to prosecute) the exercise of purely executive power? (2) Does the statute deprive the President of the United States of exclusive control over the exercise of that power? Surprising to say, the Court appears to concede an affirmative answer to both questions, but seeks to avoid the inevitable conclusion that since the statute vests some purely executive power in a person who is not the President of the United States it is void.

.... There is no possible doubt that.... [governmental] investigation and prosecution of crimes is a quintessentially executive function.

As for the second question, whether the statute before us deprives the President of exclusive control over that quintessentially executive activity: The Court does not, and could not possibly, assert that it does not. That is indeed the whole object of the statute. Instead, the Court points out that the President, through his Attorney General, has at least *some* control. That concession is alone enough to invalidate the statute, but I cannot refrain from pointing out that the Court greatly exaggerates the extent of that "some" Presidential control. "Most importan[t]" among these controls, the Court asserts, is the Attorney General's "power to remove the counsel for 'good cause.'" This is somewhat like referring to shackles as an effective means of locomotion. As we recognized in Humphrey's Executor v. United States, 295 U.S. 602 (1935) — indeed, what Humphrey's Executor was all about — limiting removal power to "good cause" is an impediment to, not an effective grant of, Presidential control....

Moving on to the presumably "less important" controls that the President retains, the Court notes that no independent counsel may be appointed without a specific request from the Attorney General. [T]he condition that renders such a request mandatory (inability to find "no reasonable grounds to believe" that further investigation is warranted) is so insubstantial that the Attorney General's discretion is severely confined. And once the referral is made, it is for the Special Division to determine the scope and duration of the investigation. And in any event, the limited power over referral is irrelevant to the question whether, *once appointed*, the independent counsel exercises executive power free from the President's control....

.... The case is over when the Court acknowledges, as it must, that "[i]t is undeniable that the Act reduces the amount of control or supervision that the Attorney General and, through him, the President exercises over the investigation and prosecution of a certain class of alleged criminal activity.".... It is not for us to determine, and we have never presumed to determine, how much of the purely executive powers of government must be within the full control of the President. The Constitution prescribes that they *all* are....

Is it unthinkable that the President should have such exclusive power, even when alleged crimes by him or his close associates are at issue?.... A system of separate and coordinate powers necessarily involves an acceptance of exclusive power that can theoretically be abused.... While the separation of powers may prevent us from righting every wrong, it does so in order to ensure that we do not lose liberty. The checks against any branch's abuse of its exclusive powers are twofold: First, retaliation by one of the other branch's use of *its* exclusive powers: Congress, for example, can impeach the executive who willfully fails to enforce the laws; the executive can decline to prosecute under unconstitutional statutes, and the courts can dismiss malicious prosecutions. Second, and ultimately, there is the political check that the people will replace those in the political branches (the branches more "dangerous to the political rights of the Constitution," Federalist No. 78, p. 465) who are guilty of abuse. Political pressures produced special prosecutors — for Teapot Dome and for Watergate, for example — long before this statute created the independent counsel.

The Court has, nonetheless, replaced the clear constitutional prescription that the executive power belongs to the President with a "balancing test." What are the standards to determine how the balance is to be struck, that is, how much removal of Presidential power is too much?.... Once we depart from the text of the Constitution, just where short of that do we stop? The most amazing feature of the Court's opinion is that it does not even purport to give an answer. It simply *announces*, with no analysis, that the ability to control the decision whether to investigate and prosecute the President's closest advisers, and indeed the President himself, is not "so central to the functioning of the Executive Branch" as to be constitutionally required to be within the President's control.... Evidently, the governing standard is to be what might be called the unfettered wisdom of a majority of this Court, revealed to an obedient people on a case-by-case basis....

... [E]ven as an ad hoc, standardless judgment the Court's conclusion must be wrong.... Perhaps the boldness of the President himself will not be affected [by this statute] — though I am not even sure of that. (How much easier it is for Congress, instead of accepting the political damage attendant to the commencement of impeachment proceedings against the President on trivial grounds — or, for that matter, how easy it is for one of the President's political foes outside of Congress — simply to trigger a debilitating criminal investigation of the Chief Executive under this law.) But as for the President's high-level assistants, who typically have no political base of support, it is as utterly unrealistic to think that they will not be intimidated by th[e] prospect [of independent counsel investigations].... It deeply wounds the President, by substantially reducing the President's ability to protect himself and his staff. That is the whole object of the law, of course, and I cannot imagine why the Court believes it does not succeed....

II

.... Because appellant (who all parties and the Court agree is an officer of the United States) was not appointed by the President with the advice and consent of the Senate, but rather by the Special Division of the United States Court of Appeals, her appointment is constitutional only if (1) she is an "inferior" officer within the meaning of the above Clause, and (2) Congress may vest her appointment in a court of law.

The Court gives three reasons [for concluding the independent counsel is an "inferior officer"].... [but the] first of these lends no support to the [Court's] view.... Appellant is removable only for "good cause".... [But if] it were common usage to refer to someone as "inferior" who is subject to removal for cause by another, then one would say that the President is "inferior" to Congress.

The second reason offered by the Court — that appellant performs only certain, limited duties — may be relevant to whether she is an inferior officer, but it mischaracterizes the extent of her powers. As the Court states: "Admittedly, the Act delegates to appellant [the] '*full power and independent authority to exercise all investigative and prosecutorial functions and powers of the Department of Justice.*'".... Once all of this is "admitted," it seems to me impossible to maintain that appellant's authority is so "limited" as to render her an inferior officer....

The final set of reasons given by the Court for why the independent counsel clearly is an inferior officer emphasizes the limited nature of her jurisdiction and tenure. Taking the latter first, I find nothing unusually limited about the independent counsel's tenure. To the contrary, unlike most high ranking Executive Branch officials, she continues to serve until she (or the Special Division) decides that her work is substantially completed. This particular independent prosecutor has already served more than two years, which is at least as long as many Cabinet officials. As to the scope of her jurisdiction, there can be no doubt that is small (though far from unimportant). But within it she exercises more than the full power of the Attorney General. The Ambassador to Luxembourg is not anything less than a principal officer, simply because Luxembourg is small. And the federal judge who sits in a small district is not for that reason "inferior in rank and authority."....

More fundamentally,.... the text of the Constitution and the division of power that it establishes.... demonstrate, I think, that the independent counsel is not an inferior officer because she is not *subordinate* to any officer in the Executive Branch (indeed, not even to the President). Dictionaries in use at the time of the Constitutional Convention gave the word "inferiour" two meanings which it still bears today: (1) "[l]ower in place, ... station, ... rank of life, ... value or excellency," and (2) "[s]ubordinate." S. Johnson, Dictionary of the English Language (6th ed. 1785)....

That "inferior" means "subordinate" is also consistent with what little we know about the evolution of the Appointments Clause [:].... that it was intended merely to make clear (what Madison thought already was clear) that those officers appointed by the President with Senate approval could on their own appoint their subordinates, who would, of course, by chain of command still be under the direct control of the President....

To be sure, it is not a *sufficient* condition for "inferior" officer status that one be subordinate to a principal officer.... But it is surely a *necessary* condition for inferior officer status that the officer be subordinate to another officer.

The independent counsel is not even subordinate to the President....

Because appellant is not subordinate to another officer, she is not an "inferior" officer and her appointment other than by the President with the advice and consent of the Senate is unconstitutional.

IV

.... There is, of course, no provision in the Constitution stating who may remove executive officers, except the provisions for removal by impeachment. Before the present decision it was established, however, (1) that the President's power to remove principal officers who exercise purely executive powers could not be restricted, see Myers v. United States, 272 U.S. 52, 127 (1926), and (2) that his power to remove inferior officers who exercise purely executive powers, and whose appointment Congress had removed from the usual procedure of Presidential appointment with Senate consent, could be restricted, at least where the appointment had been made by an officer of the Executive Branch....

Since our 1935 decision in Humphrey's Executor v. United States, 295 U.S. 602 — which was considered by many at the time the product of an activist, anti-New Deal Court bent on reducing the power of President Franklin Roosevelt — it has been established that the line of permissible restriction upon removal of principal officers lies at the point at which the powers exercised by those officers are no longer purely executive. Thus, removal restrictions have been generally regarded as lawful for so-called "independent regulatory agencies," such as the Federal Trade Commission, the Interstate Commerce Commission, and the Consumer Product Safety Commission, which engage substantially in what has been called the "quasi-legislative activity" of rulemaking, and for members of Article I courts, such as the Court of Military Appeals, who engage in the "quasi-judicial" function of adjudication.... Today, however, Humphrey's Executor is swept into the dustbin of repudiated constitutional principles....

.... "[O]ur present considered view" is simply that *any* executive officer's removal can be restricted, so long as the President remains "able to accomplish his constitutional role." There are now no lines. If the removal of a prosecutor, the virtual embodiment of the power to "take care that the laws be faithfully executed," can be restricted, what officer's removal cannot? This is an open invitation for Congress to experiment....

V

.... Under our system of government, the primary check against prosecutorial abuse is a political one. The prosecutors who exercise this awesome discretion are selected and can be removed by a President, whom the people have trusted enough to elect. Moreover, when crimes are not investigated and prosecuted fairly, nonselectively, with a reasonable sense of proportion, the President pays the cost in political damage to his administration.... The President is directly dependent on the people, and since there is only *one* President, *he* is responsible. The people know whom to blame, whereas "one of the weightiest objections to a plurality in the executive ... is that it tends to conceal faults and destroy responsibility."

That is the system of justice the rest of us are entitled to, but what of that select class consisting of present or former high-level Executive Branch officials? ... [Once the statute is triggered, an] independent counsel is selected, and the scope of his or her authority prescribed, by a panel of judges. What if they are politically partisan, as judges have been known to be, and select a prosecutor antagonistic to the administration ... ? There is no remedy for that, not even a political one.... [Even] if it were entirely evident that unfairness was in fact the result—the judges hostile to the administration, the independent counsel an old foe of the President, the staff refugees from the recently defeated administration—*there would be no one accountable to the public to whom the blame could be assigned.*

CASE NOTE: *Free Enterprise Fund v. Public Company Accounting and Oversight Board*, 561 U.S. ___, 130 S. Ct. 3138 (2010). The flexible "functionalist" approach adopted by the majority in *Morrison v. Olson* has not meant that Congress has had unlimited flexibility in structuring administrative agencies to insulate them from political control of the executive branch. In *Free Enterprise Fund*, the Court considered a separation of powers/appointments clause challenge to the Public Company Accounting and Oversight Board (PCAOB), a board given broad regulatory oversight of accounting firms that participate in auditing public companies for compliance with federal securities laws. The PCAOB was created as part of the Sarbanes-Oxley Act, a 2002 statute enacted to tighten accounting regulations in the wake of a series of financial collapses of companies that had papered over their financial troubles with loose and misleading accounting practices, to the detriment of the investing public. Board members were to be appointed by the Securities and Exchange Commission (SEC), and removable by the SEC for limited "good cause" grounds defined in the statute. Since SEC members are themselves removable by the President only for good cause, the PCAOB was insulated from presidential control by "two layers" of good cause protection.

The Court struck down the good cause restriction on removal of PCAOB members. The Board, and the Sarbanes-Oxley Act, in all other respects were left intact: the net effect was simply that the SEC could thereafter remove PCAOB members at will, without the good cause restriction. (The petitioners' challenge to the provision allowing the SEC to appoint PCAOB members was rejected by the Court.) Despite certain statements by the Court about the need for presidential control over subordinates that are reminiscent of Justice Scalia's dissent in *Morrison*, the Court asserted that its holding was narrowly limited to striking down "a new type of restriction—two levels of protection for removal for those who nonetheless exercise significant executive power." The Court reaffirmed all its prior holdings on removal of executive officers, including *Myers*, *Humphrey's*, and *Morrison*.

Recap: Appointment and Removal Powers

1. Write a short paragraph summarizing current doctrine regarding the removal power. Incorporate the cases from *Myers* through *Morrison*. This task is made challenging by the fact that the Court itself has not drawn a straight doctrinal line.

2. Consider the approach to constitutional interpretation in the majority and dissenting opinions in *Morrison*. One is fairly characterized as "functionalist": a flexible strategy looking at whether the relevant government institutions will continue to function properly, in a manner consistent with constitutional language that creates a gray area. The other can be characterized as "formalist": a view that the Constitution sets out clearly applicable rules that should be rigorously applied. Which opinion is which? Is one approach preferable to the other, either in this case or in general?

3. Under the special prosecutor law, the special prosecutor could be removed by the Attorney General for specified good cause. Is that the same as removal by the President? The Attorney General would seem to be removable by the President "at pleasure" under *Myers*, and therefore, at least formally, an agent of the President's will. But, historically, many attorneys general have been appointed for reasons other than their loyalty to the President, and they may have a base of power outside the executive branch—such as strong Congressional support or public popularity—that would impose a high political cost to a president to fire the Attorney General. Clinton's Attorney General, Janet Reno, kept her position for the eight years of Clinton's presidency despite what is widely believed to have been the President's desire to replace her. Reno's engaging personality and her place in history as the first female Attorney General made her a popular figure in public opinion. Even if Reno would have followed a direction from the President to fire the special prosecutor, the political costs to the President of doing so might have been prohibitive.

The special prosecutor law, itself, was a response to a major chapter of the Watergate affair, known as the "Saturday Night Massacre." On Saturday, October 20, 1973, President Nixon ordered his Attorney General Elliott Richardson to fire Watergate Special Prosecutor Archibald Cox. Cox had been appointed special prosecutor under an ad hoc arrangement creating an office of special prosecutor directly subordinate to the Attorney General. (Note how this arrangement conforms more closely to the views later expressed by Justice Scalia in his *Morrison* dissent.) Richardson demurred, and the President immediately demanded his resignation. The President turned to Deputy Attorney General William Ruckelshaus, who likewise refused to fire Cox; he too was dismissed by the President. These firings/resignations, by law, made the Solicitor General, Robert Bork, acting Attorney General. Nixon directed Bork to fire Cox, and Bork complied. (The incident came back to haunt Bork when it resurfaced in Senate confirmation hearings as one of the objections to his ultimately unsuccessful nomination to the Supreme Court.) This history informed the structural "independence" guarantees under the special prosecutor law at issue in Morrison.

4. To the extent that you have read about independent agencies and the independent "special prosecutor," what do you think are the pros and cons of such an institutional arrangement? Is there a constitutional difference between an in-

dependent adjudicator (such as Weiner, on the War Claims Commission) and an independent prosecutor?

5. Many of Justice Scalia's concerns were played out, perhaps ironically, during the Clinton administration. A special prosecutor was called into being by a somewhat maverick Attorney General, to investigate the so-called "Whitewater" affair, allegations of illegality concerning the Clintons' investments prior to President Clinton's election. The special prosecutor was appointed by a "Special Branch" dominated by Republican-appointed judges, who selected Kenneth Starr, a former federal judge who was active in Republican politics. The "Special Branch" subsequently acceded to Starr's requests to broaden the scope of the investigation to include a wide range of alleged presidential misconduct, including the President's sexual liaison with a White House staffer. Ultimately the President was impeached, in part, for giving allegedly untruthful sworn answers to the special prosecutor on questions about the sexual liaison. No criminal charges were made against President or Mrs. Clinton relating to Whitewater, the matter for which the special prosecutor law was invoked, after an investigation lasting six years and costing over $40 million.

I. The Take Care Clause

In this section, we directly confront a question that has arisen implicitly throughout this chapter. To what extent, if at all, does the President have the power—or duty—to make and act upon his own, independent constitutional interpretations? Put another way, to what extent, if at all, does the Constitution suggest that the President should defer to constitutional judgments of co-ordinate branches—either in the form of explicit constitutional interpretations by the Supreme Court or by acts of Congress, which imply a constitutional judgment insofar as we presume that Congress would not intentionally exceed its constitutional powers.

We have named this section "The 'Take Care' Clause" more as a handy way to organize and label this set of questions than out of a considered opinion that the President's powers and duties in this regard are defined or enhanced by that phrase. Article II, § 3, cl. 4 states that the President "shall take care that the laws be faithfully executed." What does this provision mean? Looked at one way, it is an articulation of an idea that is plainly encompassed in the grant of "the executive power" to the President. Clearly, executive power means, in large part, "executing" or "tak[ing] care that the laws be ... executed." The addition of "faithfully" goes without saying as well; a President who was faithless toward duly enacted laws would be abusing the public trust and violating his oath of office.

But does "laws" mean statutes, or does the term include the Constitution itself? In some places, the Constitution and laws are referred to as two different things, suggesting that laws are statutes (acts of Congress). Bills signed by the President become "law," Art. I, § 7; the judicial power extends to cases "arising under this Constitution, [and] the laws of the United States[.]" Art. III, § 2. On the other hand, the Supremacy Clause suggests that the Constitution is "supreme law" binding on Courts at least: "This Constitution, and the laws of the United States which shall be made in pursuance thereof; and all treaties made, or which shall be made, under the authority of the United States, shall be the supreme law of the land[.]" Art. VI, cl. 2. *See also Marbury v. Madison* (Chapter 5) (treating the Constitution as "law"). Even if the Constitution were not one of the "laws" referred to explicitly in the "take care" clause, does "faithful execution" require faithfulness to statutes only, or to the Constitution as well? The Constitution, after all, does require the President to swear to "preserve, protect and defend the Constitution of the United States."

It is also worth noting that the President's obligation to consider the constitutionality of laws, to the extent there is such an obligation, can occur at two points. First, as we have seen in the material on the veto power (*supra*, section F), presidents have historically considered (or claimed to consider) the constitutionality of bills presented to them for signature. Second, the President may consider whether the Constitution might call into question the enforceability of a law on the books — should the President enforce an unconstitutional law? Note that here, the President considering such an action would be questioning not only the constitutional judgment of Congress, but also that of one of his predecessors: the former President who signed the bill into law, presumably agreeing with Congress that it was constitutional.

Very little legal authority exists relating to these questions. Perhaps this is not so surprising. A ruling on the President's duty to enforce the law would embroil the Court in an intractable separation-of-powers controversy, one going to the very core of executive power and involving second-guessing decisions that are likely to be deemed discretionary. Such issues are also likely to arise in non-justiciable form, raising standing problems if not non-justiciable "political questions." (See Chapter 6.)

In the subsections that follow, we consider non-judicial authorities as well as Supreme Court decisions relevant to these issues. In subsection 1, we look at statements by President Jackson, Senator Douglas and senatorial candidate and President Lincoln on the duty to adhere to Supreme Court interpretations. Subsection 2, presents an Office of Legal Counsel memorandum on the authority of the President to decline to enforce unconstitutional laws. Subsection 3 considers the related question of executive or prosecutorial discretion.

1. The Duty to Adhere to Supreme Court Constitutional Interpretations

In Chapter 5, examining judicial review, we will consider the question of judicial supremacy in constitutional interpretation, as that question has been raised in Supreme Court decisions. Here we look at that same question from the perspective of constitutional actors in the other branches, in particular, the President.

President Andrew Jackson's Message in Support of His Veto of the Re-Charter of the Bank of the United States

WASHINGTON, July 10, 1832.

To the Senate.

The bill "to modify and continue" the act entitled "An act to incorporate the subscribers to the Bank of the United States" was presented to me on the 4th July instant. Having considered it with that solemn regard to the principles of the Constitution which the day was calculated to inspire, and come to the conclusion that it ought not to become a law, I herewith return it to the Senate, in which it originated, with my objections.

A bank of the United States is in many respects convenient for the Government and useful to the people. Entertaining this opinion, and deeply impressed with the belief that some of the powers and privileges possessed by the existing bank are unauthorized by the Constitution, subversive of the rights of the States, and dangerous to the liberties of the people, I felt it my duty at an early period of my Administration to call the attention of Congress to the practicability of organizing an institution combining all its advantages and obviating these objections. I sincerely regret that in the act before me I can perceive none of those modifications of the bank charter which are necessary, in my opinion, to make it compatible with justice, with sound policy, or with the Constitution of our country.

[The veto message proceeded to make several policy arguments against the Bank. Among other points, Jackson objected that provisions in the law for selling stock to the public at less than market value will result in a large windfall to select, wealthy persons in a position to buy large blocks of shares. Jackson objected to significant foreign ownership interests in the bank as detrimental to national security. And he expressed concern that states would tax individual depositors because they could not, after *McCulloch v. Maryland*, tax the bank itself.]

It is maintained by the advocates of the bank that its constitutionality in all its features ought to be considered as settled by precedent and by the decision of the Supreme Court. To this conclusion I cannot assent. Mere precedent is a dangerous source of authority, and should not be regarded as deciding questions of constitutional power except where the acquiescence of the people and the States can be considered as well settled. So far from this being the case on this subject, an argument against the bank might be based on precedent. One Congress, in 1791, decided in favor of a bank; another, in 1811, decided against it. One Congress, in 1815, decided against a bank; another, in 1816, decided in its favor. Prior to the present Congress, therefore, the precedents drawn from that source were equal. If we resort to the States, the expressions of legislative, judicial, and executive opinions against the bank have been probably to those in its favor as 4 to 1. There is nothing in precedent, therefore, which, if its authority were admitted, ought to weigh in favor of the act before me.

If the opinion of the Supreme Court covered the whole ground of this act, it ought not to control the coordinate authorities of this Government. The Congress, the Executive, and the Court must each for itself be guided by its own opinion of the Constitution. Each public officer who takes an oath to support the Constitution swears that he will support it as he understands it, and not as it is understood by others. It is as much the duty of the House of Representatives, of the Senate, and of the President to decide upon the constitutionality of any bill or resolution which may be presented to them for passage or approval as it is of the supreme judges when it may be brought before them for judicial decision. The opinion of the judges has no more authority over Congress than the opinion of Congress has over the judges, and on that point the President is independent of both. The authority of the Supreme Court must not, therefore, be permitted to control the Congress or the Executive when acting in their legislative capacities, but to have only such influence as the force of their reasoning may deserve.

But in the case relied upon the Supreme Court have not decided that all the features of this corporation are compatible with the Constitution. It is true that the courts have said that the law incorporating the bank is a constitutional exercise of power by Congress; but taking into view the whole opinion of the court and the reasoning by which they have come to that conclusion, I understand them to have decided that inasmuch as a bank is an appropriate means for carrying into effect the enumerated powers of the General Government, therefore the law incorporating it is in accordance with that provision of the Constitution which declares that Congress shall have power "to make all laws which shall be necessary and proper for carrying those powers into execution." Having satisfied themselves that the word *"necessary"* in the Constitution means *"needful," "requisite," "essential," "conducive to,"* and that "a bank" is a convenient, a useful, and essential instrument in the prosecution of the Government's "fiscal operations," they conclude that to "use one must be within the discretion of Congress" and that "the act to incorporate the Bank of the United States is a law made in pursuance of the Constitution;" "but," say they, *"where the law is not prohibited and is really calculated to effect any of the objects intrusted to the Government, to undertake here to inquire into the degree of its necessity would be to pass the line which circumscribes the judicial department and to tread on legislative ground."*

The principle here affirmed is that the "degree of its necessity," involving all the details of a banking institution, is a question exclusively for legislative consideration. A bank is constitutional, but it is the province of the Legislature to determine whether this or that particular power, privilege, or exemption is "necessary and proper" to enable the bank to discharge its duties to the Government, and from their decision there is no appeal to the courts of justice. Under the decision of the Supreme Court, therefore, it is the exclusive province of Congress and the President to decide whether the particular features of this act are *necessary* and *proper* in order to enable the bank to perform conveniently and efficiently the public duties assigned to it as a fiscal agent, and therefore constitutional, or *unnecessary* and *improper*, and therefore unconstitutional.

.... It will be found that many of the powers and privileges conferred on [the Bank] cannot be supposed necessary for the purpose for which it is proposed to be created, and are not, therefore, means necessary to attain the end in view, and consequently not justified by the Constitution....

On two subjects only does the Constitution recognize in Congress the power to grant exclusive privileges or monopolies. It declares that "Congress shall have power to promote the progress of science and useful arts by securing for limited times to authors and inventors the exclusive right to their respective writings and discoveries." Out of this express delegation of power have grown our laws of patents and copyrights. As the Constitution expressly delegates to Congress the power to grant exclusive privileges in these cases as the means of executing the substantive power "to promote the progress of science and useful arts," it is consistent with the fair rules of construction to conclude that such a power was not intended to be granted as a means of accomplishing any other end.... Every act of Congress, therefore, which attempts by grants of monopolies or sale of exclusive privileges for a limited time, or a time without limit, to restrict or extinguish its own discretion in the choice of means to execute its delegated powers is equivalent to a legislative amendment of the Constitution, and palpably unconstitutional....

The principle is conceded that the States cannot rightfully tax the operations of the General Government. They cannot tax the money of the Government deposited in the State banks, nor the agency of those banks in remitting it; but will any man maintain that their mere selection to perform this public service for the General Government would exempt the State banks and their ordinary business from State taxation? Had the United States, instead of establishing a bank at Philadelphia, employed a private banker to keep and transmit their funds, would it have deprived Pennsylvania of the right to tax his bank and his usual banking operations? It will not be pretended. Upon what principal, then, are the banking establishments of the Bank of the United States and their usual banking operations to be exempted from taxation? ...

It cannot be *necessary* to the character of the bank as a fiscal agent of the Government that its private business should be exempted from that taxation to which all the State banks are liable, nor can I conceive it *"proper"* that the substantive and most essential powers reserved by the States shall be thus attacked and annihilated as a means of executing the powers delegated to the General Government. It may be safely assumed that none of those sages who had an agency in forming or adopting our Constitution ever imagined that any portion of the taxing power of the States not prohibited to them nor delegated to Congress was to be swept away and annihilated as a means of executing certain powers delegated to Congress.

If our power over means is so absolute that the Supreme Court will not call in question the constitutionality of an act of Congress the subject of which "is not prohibited, and is really calculated to effect any of the objects intrusted to the Government," although, as in the case before me, it takes away powers expressly granted to Congress and rights scrupulously reserved to the States, it becomes us to proceed in our legislation with the utmost caution. Though not directly, our own powers and the rights of the States may be indirectly legislated away in the use of means to execute substantive powers.... That a bank of the United States, competent to all the duties which may be required by the Government, might be so organized as not to infringe on our own delegated powers or the reserved rights of the States I do not entertain a doubt. Had the Executive been called upon to furnish the project of such an institution, the duty would have been cheerfully performed. In the absence of such a call it was obviously proper that he should confine himself to pointing out those prominent features in the act presented which in his opinion make it incompatible with the Constitution and sound policy....

It is to be regretted that the rich and powerful too often bend the acts of government to their selfish purposes. Distinctions in society will always exist under every just government. Equality of talents, of education, or of wealth cannot be produced by human institutions. In the full enjoyment of the gifts of Heaven and the fruits of superior industry, economy, and virtue, every man is equally entitled to protection by law; but when the laws undertake to add to these natural and just advantages artificial distinctions, to grant titles, gratuities, and exclusive privileges, to make the rich richer and the potent more powerful, the humble members of society—the farmers, mechanics, and laborers—who have neither the time nor the means of securing like favors to themselves, have a right to complain of the injustice of their Government. There are no necessary evils in government. Its evils exist only in its abuses. If it would confine itself to equal protection, and, as Heaven does its rains, shower its favors alike on the high and the low, the rich and the poor, it would be an unqualified blessing. In the act before me there seems to be a wide and unnecessary departure from these just principles.

ANDREW JACKSON.

Review Questions and Explanations: Jackson's Bank Veto

1. Andrew Jackson had a brief career as a lawyer and state court judge, but the bank veto message was written by his more legally sophisticated Attorney General, Roger B. Taney, whom Jackson later nominated to be the fifth Chief Justice of the United States. (In that role, Taney is best known for authoring the *Dred Scott*

decision.) At least one legal historian has contended that conclusive evidence suggests that, once on the Court, Taney and a majority of his colleagues were ready and willing to overrule *McCulloch v. Maryland* at the next opportunity — but an appropriate case never came before the Court.[18] The veto message may well stand as a blueprint for the decision that never was to overrule *McCulloch*.

2. The fourth and fifth paragraphs, starting "It is maintained by the advocates of the bank ..." lay out Jackson's argument regarding his independent interpretive power. Do you agree with it?

3. The veto message makes a number of policy arguments and casts several policy arguments as constitutional ones. The strategy for the latter was to argue that attributes of the bank that were not necessary to the core purpose of rationalizing national banking and government finance, and that raised constitutional questions, could not be deemed "necessary and proper," and therefore exceeded Congress's power. This discussion begins at the sixth paragraph of the veto message, beginning "But in the case relied upon the Supreme Court have not decided ...", and seems to consist of a lengthy argument distinguishing *McCulloch* — i.e., discussing constitutional problems with the bank not addressed in that opinion. Why spend so much time doing that?

Lincoln v. Douglas on Judicial Supremacy: The 1858 Illinois Senate Race

Although this next set of readings arises primarily from a race for the U.S. Senate, the views about the duty of the other branches to conform to Supreme Court opinions carries over into our discussion of the "take care" clause and the President's duty. Lincoln and Douglas both ran for President in 1860. The section concludes with an excerpt on this point from Lincoln's 1861 inaugural address.

On June 17, 1858, at the close of the Illinois Republican Party convention in Springfield, Abraham Lincoln received the nomination to run for the U.S. Senate against the incumbent, Democrat Stephen A. Douglas. His acceptance speech that evening, the famous "House Divided" speech, referred critically to the *Dred Scott* decision. Over the next few weeks, as Lincoln and Douglas campaigned around the state, their speeches staked out positions on various aspects of the slavery question, including the *Dred Scott* case. Their remarks touched on the role of the Supreme Court. The candidates had access to one another's speeches through verbatim transcripts published in the newspapers, and a debate of sorts occurred in July. By the end of the month, Lincoln and Douglas had agreed to the seven face-to-face debates around the state in September and October, known to history as "the Lincoln-Douglas debates." The following excerpts are from their pre-debate speeches in July 1858.

Douglas's speech at Chicago, July 9 1858:

.... The other proposition discussed by Mr. Lincoln in his speech consists in a crusade against the Supreme Court of the United States on account of the Dred Scott decision. On this question, also, I desire to say to you unequivocally, that I take direct and distinct issue

---

18. Mark Graber, *Naked Land Transfers and American Constitutional Development*, 53 Vand. L. Rev. 73 (2000).

with him. I have no warfare to make on the Supreme Court of the United States, either on account of that or any other decision which they have pronounced from that bench. The Constitution of the United States has provided that the powers of government (and the Constitution of each State has the same provision) shall be divided into three departments,—executive, legislative, and judicial. The right and the province of expounding the Constitution and constructing the law is vested in the judiciary established by the Constitution. As a lawyer, I feel at liberty to appear before the Court and controvert any principle of law while the question is pending before the tribunal; but when the decision is made, my private opinion, your opinion, all other opinions, must yield to the majesty of that authoritative adjudication. I wish you to bear in mind that this involves a great principle, upon which our rights, our liberty, and our property all depend. What security have you for your property, for your reputation, and for your personal rights, if the courts are not upheld, and their decisions respected when once fairly rendered by the highest tribunal known to the Constitution? I do not choose, therefore, to go into any argument with Mr. Lincoln in reviewing the various decisions which the Supreme Court has made, either upon the Dred Scott case or any other. I have no idea of appealing from the decision of the Supreme Court upon a Constitutional question to the decisions of a tumultuous town meeting.... It matters not with me who was on the bench, whether Mr. Lincoln or myself, whether a Lockwood or a Smith, a Taney or a Marshall; the decision of the highest tribunal known to the Constitution of the country must be final till it has been reversed by an equally high authority. Hence, I am opposed to this doctrine of Mr. Lincoln, by which he proposes to take an appeal from the decision of the Supreme Court of the United States, upon this high constitutional question, to a Republican caucus sitting in the country. Yes, or any other caucus or town meeting, whether it be Republican, American, or Democratic. I respect the decisions of that august tribunal; I shall always bow in deference to them. I am a law-abiding man. I will sustain the Constitution of my country as our fathers have made it. I will yield obedience to the laws, whether I like them or not, as I find them on the statute book. I will sustain the judicial tribunals and constituted authorities in all matters within the pale of their jurisdiction as defined by the Constitution....

Lincoln's Reply, at Chicago, July 10, 1858:

.... A little now on the other point—the Dred Scott decision. Another of the issues he says that is to be made with me, is upon his devotion to the Dred Scott decision, and my opposition to it. I have expressed heretofore, and I now repeat, my opposition to the Dred Scott decision; but I should be allowed to state the nature of that opposition, and I ask your indulgence while I do so. What is fairly implied by the term Judge Douglas[19] has used, "resistance to the decision?" I do not resist it. If I wanted to take Dred Scott from his master, I would be interfering with property, and that terrible difficulty that Judge Douglas speaks of, of interfering with property, would arise. But I am doing no such thing as that, but all that I am doing is refusing to obey it as a political rule. If I were in Congress, and a vote should come up on a question whether slavery should be prohibited in a new Territory, in spite of the Dred Scott decision, I would vote that it should. That is what I should do. Judge Douglas said last night, that before the decision he might advance his opinion, and it might be contrary to the decision when it was made; but after

---

19. Douglas had previously served for a short time on the Illinois Supreme Court, and it was and is customary to refer to both current and former judges with the honorific "judge." Lincoln consistently observed this custom during the Senate race, though he may have intended in part to drive home an ironic point: Douglas's appointment to the bench, as Lincoln did not hesitate to tell the audiences, had resulted from a court-packing scheme designed to overrule a state supreme court decision unpopular with Democrats.

it was made he would abide by it until it was reversed. Just so! We let this property abide by the decision, but we will try to reverse that decision. We will try to put it where Judge Douglas would not object, for he says he will obey it until it is reversed. Somebody has to reverse that decision, since it is made, and we mean to reverse it, and we mean to do it peaceably.

What are the uses of decisions of courts? They have two uses. As rules of property they have two uses. First, they decide upon the question before the court. They decide in this case that Dred Scott is a slave. Nobody resists that. Not only that, but they say to everybody else, that persons standing just as Dred Scott stands, is as he is. That is, they say that when a question comes up upon another person, it will be so decided again, unless the court decides in another way, unless the court overrules its decision. Well, we mean to do what we can to have the court decide the other way. That is one thing we mean to try to do.

The sacredness that Judge Douglas throws around this decision, is a degree of sacredness that has never been before thrown around any other decision. I have never heard of such a thing. Why, decisions apparently contrary to that decision, or that good lawyers thought were contrary to that decision, have been made by that very court before. It is the first of its kind; it is an astonisher in legal history. It is a new wonder of the world. It is based upon falsehood in the main as to the facts—allegations of facts upon which it stands are not facts at all in many instances, and no decision made on any question—the first instance of a decision made under so many unfavorable circumstances—thus placed, has ever been held by the profession as law, and it has always needed confirmation before the lawyers regarded it as settled law. But Judge Douglas will have it that all hands must take this extraordinary decision, made under these extraordinary circumstances, and give their vote in Congress in accordance with it, yield to it, and obey it in every possible sense. Circumstances alter cases. Do not gentlemen here remember the case of that same Supreme Court, some twenty-five or thirty years ago, deciding that a National Bank was constitutional? I ask, if somebody does not remember that a National Bank was declared to be constitutional? Such is the truth, whether it be remembered or not. The Bank charter ran out, and a re-charter was granted by Congress. That re-charter was laid before General Jackson. It was urged upon him, when he denied the constitutionality of the Bank, that the Supreme Court had decided that it was constitutional; and that General Jackson then said that the Supreme Court had no right to lay down a rule to govern a co-ordinate branch of the Government, the members of which had sworn to support the Constitution; that each member had sworn to support the Constitution as he understood it. I will venture here to say that I have heard Judge Douglas say that he approved of General Jackson for that act. What has now become of all his tirade about "resistance to the Supreme Court?" ...

Douglas's speech, July 16, at Bloomington:

.... Mr. Lincoln tells you that he is opposed to the decision of the Supreme Court in the Dred Scott case. Well, suppose he is; what is he going to do about it? I never got beat in a law suit in my life that I was not opposed to the decision, and if I had it before the Circuit Court I took it up to the Supreme Court, where, if I got beat again, I thought it better to say no more about it, as I did not know of any lawful mode of reversing the decision of the highest tribunal on earth.... Mr. Lincoln is going to appeal from that decision and reverse it. He does not intend to reverse it as to Dred Scott. Oh, no! But he will reverse it so that it shall not stand as a rule in the future. How will he do it? He says that if he is elected to the Senate, he will introduce and pass a law just like the Missouri Compromise, prohibiting slavery again in all the Territories. Suppose he does re-enact the same law which the Court has pronounced unconstitutional, will that make it constitutional? If the Act of 1820 was unconstitutional in consequence of Congress having no power to pass it, will Mr. Lincoln make it constitutional by passing it again? What clause of the Constitution of the United States provides for an appeal from the decision of the Supreme Court to Congress? If my reading of that instrument is correct, it is to the effect that that Constitution and all laws made in pursuance of it are of the supreme law of the land, anything in the Constitution or laws of a State to the contrary notwithstanding. Hence, you will find that only such acts of Congress are laws as are made in pursuance of the Constitution. When Congress has passed an Act, and put it on the statute book as law, who is to decide whether that Act is in conformity with the Constitution or not? The Constitution of the United States tells you. It has provided that the judicial power of the United States shall be vested in a Supreme Court, and such inferior Courts as Congress may from time to time ordain and establish. Thus, by the Constitution, the Supreme Court is declared, in so many words, to be the tribunal, and the only tribunal, which is competent to adjudicate upon the constitutionality of an Act of Congress. He tells you that that Court has adjudicated the question, and decided that an Act of Congress prohibiting slavery in the Territory is unconstitutional and void; and yet he says he is going to pass another like it. What for? Will it be any more valid? Will he be able to convince the Court that the second Act is valid when the first is invalid and void? What good does it do to pass a second Act? Why, it will have the effect to arraign the Supreme Court before the people, and to bring them into all the political discussions of the country. Will that do any good? Will it inspire any more confidence in the judicial tribunals of the country? What good can it do to wage this war upon the Court, arraying it against Congress, and Congress against the Court? The Constitution of the United States has said that this Government shall be divided into three separate and distinct branches, the executive, the legislative and the judicial, and of course each one is supreme and independent of the other within the circle of its own powers. The functions of Congress are to enact the statutes, the province of the Court is to pronounce upon their validity, and the duty of the Executive is to carry the decision into effect when rendered by the Court. And yet, notwithstanding the Constitution makes the decision of the Court final in regard to the validity of an Act of Congress, Mr. Lincoln is going to reverse that decision by passing another Act of Congress. When he has become convinced of the folly of the proposition, perhaps he will resort to the same subterfuge that I have found others of his party resort to, which is to agitate and agitate until he can change the Supreme Court and put other men in the places of the present incumbents.... I am afraid that my friend Lincoln would not accomplish this task during his own lifetime, and yet he wants to go to Congress to do it all in six years. Do you think that he can persuade nine Judges, or a majority of them, to die in that six years, just to accommodate him? ...

And by what process will he appoint them? He first looks for a man who has the legal qualifications, perhaps he takes Mr. Lincoln, and says, "Mr. Lincoln, would you not like to go on the Supreme bench?" "Yes," replies Mr. Lincoln. "Well," returns the Republican President, "I cannot appoint you until you give me a pledge as to how you will decide in the event of a particular question coming before you." What would you think of Mr. Lincoln if he would consent to give that pledge? And yet he is going to prosecute a war until he gets the present Judges out, and then catechise each man and require a pledge before his appointment as to how he will decide each question that may arise upon points affecting the Republican party. Now, my friends, suppose this scheme was practical, I ask you what confidence you would have in a Court thus constituted—a Court composed of partisan Judges, appointed on political grounds, selected with a view to the decision of questions in a particular way, and pledged in regard to a decision before the argument, and without reference to the peculiar state of the facts. Would such a Court command the respect of the country? If the Republican party cannot trust Democratic Judges, how can they expect us to trust Republican Judges, when they have been selected in advance for the purpose of packing a decision in the event of a case arising? My fellow-citizens, whenever partisan politics shall be carried on to the bench; whenever the Judges shall be arraigned upon the stump, and their judicial conduct reviewed in town meetings and caucuses; whenever the independence and integrity of the judiciary shall be tampered with to the extent of rendering them partial, blind and suppliant tools, what security will you have for your rights and your liberties? ...

Lincoln, July 17 at Springfield:

.... Now, as to the Dred Scott decision; for upon that he makes his last point at me. He boldly takes ground in favor of that decision.... I am opposed to that decision in a certain sense, but not in the sense which he puts on it.... He would have the citizen conform his vote to that decision; the member of Congress, his; the President, his use of the veto power. He would make it a rule of political action for the people and all the departments of the Government. I would not. By resisting it as a political rule, I disturb no right of property, create no disorder, excite no mobs.

.... I shall read from a letter written by Mr. Jefferson in 1820, and now to be found in the seventh volume of his correspondence, at page 177....

> You seem ... to consider the judges as the ultimate arbiters of all constitutional questions,—a very dangerous doctrine indeed, and one which would place us under the despotism of an oligarchy. Our judges are as honest as other men, and not more so. They have, with others, the same passions for party, for power, and the privilege of their corps. Their maxim is, 'boni judicis est ampliare juris-dictionem;'[20] and their power is the more dangerous as they are in office for life, and not responsible, as the other functionaries are, to the elective control. The Constitution has erected no such single tribunal, knowing that, to whatever hands confided, with the corruptions of time and party, its members would become despots. It has more wisely made all the departments co-equal and co-sovereign with themselves.

Thus we see the power claimed for the Supreme Court by Judge Douglas, Mr. Jefferson holds, would reduce us to the despotism of an oligarchy.

Now, I have said no more than this,—in fact, never quite so much as this; at least I am sustained by Mr. Jefferson.

Let us go a little further. You remember we once had a National Bank. Someone owed the bank a debt; he was sued, and sought to avoid payment on the ground that the bank was unconstitutional. The case went to the Supreme Court, and therein it was decided that the bank was constitutional. The whole Democratic party revolted against that decision. General Jackson himself asserted that he, as President, would not be bound to hold a National Bank to be constitutional, even though the court had decided it to be so. He fell in precisely with the view of Mr. Jefferson, and acted upon it under his official oath, in vetoing a charter for a National Bank. The declaration that Congress does not possess this constitutional power to charter a bank has gone into the Democratic platform, at their National Convention, and was brought forward and reaffirmed in their last Convention at Cincinnati. They have contended for that declaration, in the very teeth of

---

20. "It is the duty of a good judge to enlarge his jurisdiction."

the Supreme Court, for more than a quarter of a century. In fact, they have reduced the decision to an absolute nullity. That decision, I repeat, is repudiated in the Cincinnati platform; and still, as if to show that effrontery can go no further, Judge Douglas vaunts in the very speeches in which he denounces me for opposing the Dred Scott decision, that he stands on the Cincinnati platform....

Although Lincoln "won the popular vote" in the 1858 Senate race, in the sense that more votes were cast for Republican than Democratic state legislators, Douglas won retention of the Senate seat. Prior to the ratification of the Seventeenth Amendment in 1913, U.S. Senators were chosen by their state legislatures. Particularities of Illinois legislative districts in 1858 and the retention of Democratic seats not up for election preserved a Democratic state legislative majority that re-elected Douglas.

Lincoln faced Douglas again in the 1860 presidential election. This time, with the national Democratic party fractured between northern and southern wings, Lincoln defeated Douglas (and two other candidates) for the presidency. His inaugural address, which dealt primarily with the great questions of slavery and union, briefly referred again to the Supreme Court and, by implication, its *Dred Scott* decision. (Chief Justice Taney, the author of the *Dred Scott* decision, had just administered the oath of office to Lincoln and was on the dais during the address.)

Lincoln's First Inaugural Address, March, 1861:

.... I do not forget the position assumed by some, that constitutional questions are to be decided by the Supreme Court; nor do I deny that such decisions must be binding in any case, upon the parties to a suit, as to the object of that suit, while they are also entitled to very high respect and consideration in all parallel cases by all other departments of the government. And while it is obviously possible that such decision may be erroneous in any given case, still the evil effect following it, being limited to that particular case, with the chance that it may be over-ruled, and never become a precedent for other cases, can better be borne than could the evils of a different practice. At the same time, the candid citizen must confess that if the policy of the government upon vital questions, affecting the whole people, is to be irrevocably fixed by decisions of the Supreme Court, the instant they are made, in ordinary litigation between parties, in personal actions, the people will have ceased to be their own rulers, having to that extent practically resigned their government into the hands of that eminent tribunal. Nor is there in this view any assault upon the court or the judges. It is a duty from which they may not shrink, to decide cases properly brought before them; and it is no fault of theirs if others seek to turn their decisions to political purposes....

Review Questions and Explanations: Lincoln v. Douglas on Judicial Supremacy

1. Don't be too quick simply to write off the views of Lincoln and Douglas as opportunistic statements made during a political campaign. The positions they articulate speak to an issue of lasting importance: are members of Congress and the President obligated to adhere to Supreme Court rulings beyond the four corners of the particular case or not?

2. Lincoln suggests that treating the *Dred Scott* decision as a rule of law binding on Congress (or presumably the President) in the future is mistaken, in part because

the Supreme Court decision was wrong, and because the Court itself changes its constitutional doctrines from time to time. Are these valid justifications?

---

2. Faithful Execution: Does the President Have Power to Decline to Enforce Laws He Deems Unconstitutional?

The Office of Legal Counsel. This section presents a memorandum from Assistant Attorney General Walter Dellinger, the head of the Office of Legal Counsel in 1994 during the first Clinton administration. Before reading the memo, you should understand something about the OLC's function. The following description is taken from the OLC's website, http://www.justice.gov/olc/:

> By delegation from the Attorney General, the Assistant Attorney General in charge of the Office of Legal Counsel provides authoritative legal advice to the President and all the Executive Branch agencies. The Office drafts legal opinions of the Attorney General and also provides its own written opinions and oral advice in response to requests from the Counsel to the President, the various agencies of the Executive Branch, and offices within the Department. Such requests typically deal with legal issues of particular complexity and importance or about which two or more agencies are in disagreement. The Office also is responsible for providing legal advice to the Executive Branch on all constitutional questions and reviewing pending legislation for constitutionality.
>
> All executive orders and proclamations proposed to be issued by the President are reviewed by the Office of Legal Counsel for form and legality, as are various other matters that require the President's formal approval.
>
> In addition to serving as, in effect, outside counsel for the other agencies of the Executive Branch, the Office of Legal Counsel also plays a special role within the Department itself. It reviews all proposed orders of the Attorney General and all regulations requiring the Attorney General's approval. It also performs a variety of special assignments referred by the Attorney General or the Deputy Attorney General.

A July 16, 2010 internal "Memorandum for Attorneys of The Office [of Legal Counsel] Re: Best Practices for OLC Legal Advice and Written Opinions," laid out the following "Guiding Principles" for OLC opinions:

> OLC's central function is to provide, pursuant to the Attorney General's delegation, controlling legal advice to Executive Branch officials in furtherance of the President's constitutional duties to preserve, protect, and defend the Constitution, and to "take Care that the Laws be faithfully executed." To fulfill this function, OLC must provide advice based on its best understanding of what the law requires—not simply an advocate's defense of the contemplated action or position proposed by an agency or the Administration. Thus, in rendering legal advice, OLC seeks to provide an accurate and honest appraisal of applicable law, even if that appraisal will constrain the Administration's or an agency's pursuit of desired practices or policy objectives. This practice is critically important to the Office's effective performance of its assigned role, particularly because it is frequently asked to opine on issues of first impression that are unlikely to be

resolved by the courts—a circumstance in which OLC's advice may effectively be the final word on the controlling law.

In other words, OLC attorneys are manifestly not supposed to be "yes people" who tell their government clients what they want to hear or find legal justifications for whatever the President or executive branch officials wish to do. Indeed, the OLC came under intense criticism during the G.W. Bush administration for a series of memos purporting to find constitutional and legal justification for torture of suspected terrorists.

Opinion of the Office of Legal Counsel: Presidential Authority to Decline to Execute Unconstitutional Statutes

Memorandum for the Honorable Abner J. Mikva

Counsel To The President

I have reflected further on the difficult questions surrounding a President's decision to decline to execute statutory provisions that the President believes are unconstitutional, and I have a few thoughts to share with you. Let me start with a general proposition that I believe to be uncontroversial: there are circumstances in which the President may appropriately decline to enforce a statute that he views as unconstitutional.

First, there is significant judicial approval of this proposition. Most notable is the Court's decision in Myers v. United States, 272 U.S. 52 (1926). There the Court sustained the President's view that the statute at issue was unconstitutional without any member of the Court suggesting that the President had acted improperly in refusing to abide by the statute. More recently, in Freytag v. Commissioner, 501 U.S. 868 (1991), all four of the Justices who addressed the issue agreed that the President has "the power to veto encroaching laws ... or even to disregard them when they are unconstitutional." Id. at 906 (Scalia, J., concurring); see also Youngstown Sheet & Tube Co. v. Sawyer, 343 U.S. 579, 635–38 (1952) (Jackson, J., concurring) (recognizing existence of President's authority to act contrary to a statutory command).

Second, consistent and substantial executive practice also confirms this general proposition. Opinions dating to at least 1860 assert the President's authority to decline to effectuate enactments that the President views as unconstitutional. See, e.g., Memorial of Captain Meigs, 9 Op. Att'y Gen. 462, 469–70 (1860) (asserting that the President need not enforce a statute purporting to appoint an officer); see also annotations of attached Attorney General and Office of Legal Counsel opinions. Moreover, as we discuss more fully below, numerous Presidents have provided advance notice of their intention not to enforce specific statutory requirements that they have viewed as unconstitutional, and the Supreme Court has implicitly endorsed this practice. See INS v. Chadha, 462 U.S. 919, 942 n.13 (1983) (noting that Presidents often sign legislation containing constitutionally objectionable provisions and indicate that they will not comply with those provisions).

While the general proposition that in some situations the President may decline to enforce unconstitutional statutes is unassailable, it does not offer sufficient guidance as to the appropriate course in specific circumstances. To continue our conversation about these complex issues, I offer the following propositions for your consideration.

1. The President's office and authority are created and bounded by the Constitution; he is required to act within its terms. Put somewhat differently, in serving as the executive created by the Constitution, the President is required to act in accordance with the laws—including the Constitution, which takes precedence over other forms of law. This obligation is reflected in the Take Care Clause and in the President's oath of office.

2. When bills are under consideration by Congress, the executive branch should promptly identify unconstitutional provisions and communicate its concerns to Congress so that the provisions can be corrected. Although this may seem elementary, in practice there have been occasions in which the President has been presented with enrolled bills containing constitutional flaws that should have been corrected in the legislative process.

3. The President should presume that enactments are constitutional. There will be some occasions, however, when a statute appears to conflict with the Constitution. In such cases, the President can and should exercise his independent judgment to determine whether the statute is constitutional. In reaching a conclusion, the President should give great deference to the fact that Congress passed the statute and that Congress believed it was upholding its obligation to enact constitutional legislation. Where possible, the President should construe provisions to avoid constitutional problems.

4. The Supreme Court plays a special role in resolving disputes about the constitutionality of enactments. As a general matter, if the President believes that the Court would sustain a particular provision as constitutional, the President should execute the statute, notwithstanding his own beliefs about the constitutional issue. If, however, the President, exercising his independent judgment, determines both that a provision would violate the Constitution and that it is probable that the Court would agree with him, the President has the authority to decline to execute the statute.

5. Where the President's independent constitutional judgment and his determination of the Court's probable decision converge on a conclusion of unconstitutionality, the President must make a decision about whether or not to comply with the provision. That decision is necessarily specific to context, and it should be reached after careful weighing of the effect of compliance with the provision on the constitutional rights of affected individuals and on the executive branch's constitutional authority. Also relevant is the likelihood that compliance or non-compliance will permit judicial resolution of the issue. That is, the President may base his decision to comply (or decline to comply) in part on a desire to afford the Supreme Court an opportunity to review the constitutional judgment of the legislative branch.

6. The President has enhanced responsibility to resist unconstitutional provisions that encroach upon the constitutional powers of the Presidency. Where the President believes that an enactment unconstitutionally limits his powers, he has the authority to defend his office and decline to abide by it, unless he is convinced that the Court would disagree with his assessment. If the President does not challenge such provisions (i.e., by refusing to execute them), there often will be no occasion for judicial consideration of their constitutionality; a policy of consistent Presidential enforcement of statutes limiting his power thus would deny the Supreme Court the opportunity to review the limitations and thereby would allow for unconstitutional restrictions on the President's authority.

Some legislative encroachments on executive authority, however, will not be justiciable or are for other reasons unlikely to be resolved in court. If resolution in the courts is unlikely and the President cannot look to a judicial determination, he must shoulder the responsibility of protecting the constitutional role of the presidency. This is usually true, for example, of provisions limiting the President's authority as Commander in Chief. Where it is not possible to construe such provisions constitutionally, the President has the authority to act on his understanding of the Constitution.

One example of a Presidential challenge to a statute encroaching upon his powers that did result in litigation was Myers v. United States, 272 U.S. 52 (1926). In that case, President Wilson had defied a statute that prevented him from removing postmasters without Senate approval; the Supreme Court ultimately struck down the statute as an unconstitutional limitation on the President's removal power. Myers is particularly instructive because, at the time President Wilson acted, there was no Supreme Court precedent on point and the statute was not manifestly unconstitutional. In fact, the constitutionality of restrictions on the President's authority to remove executive branch officials had been debated since the passage of the Tenure of Office Act in 1867 over President Johnson's veto. The closeness of the question was underscored by the fact that three Justices, including Justices Holmes and Brandeis, dissented in Myers. Yet, despite the unsettled constitutionality of President Wilson's action, no member of the Court in Myers suggested that Wilson overstepped his constitutional authority—or even acted improperly—by refusing to comply with a statute he believed was unconstitutional. The Court in Myers can be seen to have implicitly vindicated the view that the President may refuse to comply with a statute that limits his constitutional powers if he believes it is unconstitutional. As Attorney General Civiletti stated in a 1980 opinion,

Myers is very nearly decisive of the issue [of presidential denial of the validity of statutes]. Myers holds that the President's constitutional duty does not require him to execute unconstitutional statutes; nor does it require him to execute them provisionally, against the day that they are declared unconstitutional by the courts. He cannot be required by statute to retain postmasters against his will unless and until a court says that he may lawfully let them go. If the statute is unconstitutional, it is unconstitutional from the start.

7. The fact that a sitting President signed the statute in question does not change this analysis. The text of the Constitution offers no basis for distinguishing bills based on who signed them; there is no constitutional analogue to the principles of waiver and estoppel. Moreover, every President since Eisenhower has issued signing statements in which he stated that he would refuse to execute unconstitutional provisions. See annotations of attached signing statements. As we noted in our memorandum on Presidential signing statements, the President "may properly announce to Congress and to the public that he will not enforce a provision of an enactment he is signing. If so, then a signing statement that challenges what the President determines to be an unconstitutional encroachment on his power, or that announces the President's unwillingness to enforce (or willingness to litigate) such a provision, can be a valid and reasonable exercise of Presidential authority." Memorandum for Bernard N. Nussbaum, Counsel to the President, from Walter Dellinger, Assistant Attorney General, Office of Legal Counsel at 4 (Nov. 3, 1993). (Of course, the President is not obligated to announce his reservations in a signing statement; he can convey his views in the time, manner, and form of his choosing.) Finally, the Supreme Court recognized this practice in INS v. Chadha, 462 U.S. 919 (1983): the Court stated that "it is not uncommon for Presidents to approve legislation containing parts which are objectionable on constitutional grounds" and then cited the example of President Franklin Roosevelt's memorandum to Attorney General Jackson, in which he indicated his intention not to implement an unconstitutional provision in a statute that he had just signed. Id. at 942 n.13. These sources suggest that the President's signing of a bill does not affect his authority to decline to enforce constitutionally objectionable provisions thereof.

In accordance with these propositions, we do not believe that a President is limited to choosing between vetoing, for example, the Defense Appropriations Act and executing an unconstitutional provision in it. In our view, the President has the authority to sign legislation containing desirable elements while refusing to execute a constitutionally defective provision.

We recognize that these issues are difficult ones. When the President's obligation to act in accord with the Constitution appears to be in tension with his duty to execute laws enacted by Congress, questions are raised that go to the heart of our constitutional structure. In these circumstances, a President should proceed with caution and with respect for the obligation that each of the branches shares for the maintenance of constitutional government.

Walter Dellinger

Assistant Attorney General

Review Questions and Explanations: The Dellinger Memo

How would you answer the question posed to Assistant Attorney General Dellinger?

---

3. Judicial Review of Executive Discretion

Cases seeking judicial review of discretionary decisions by the President are rare. In an early statement on the subject, Chief Justice Marshall, in *Marbury v. Madison*, opined that discretionary decisions (as opposed to mere ministerial or non-discretionary duties, like delivering a commission) are not subject to judicial review:

> [W]here the heads of departments are the political or confidential agents of the executive, merely to execute the will of the President, or rather to act in cases in which the executive possesses a constitutional or legal discretion, nothing can be more perfectly clear than that their acts are only politically examinable.

By "only politically examinable," Marshall meant that they are not "judicially examinable."

A classic and commonplace example of executive discretion is "prosecutorial discretion," which is described in the following case note.

CASE NOTE: *United States v. Armstrong*, 517 U.S. 456 (1996). Several African-American federal criminal defendants were indicted on drug conspiracy charges involving cocaine base ("crack"). The defendants filed a motion for discovery or for dismissal of the indictment, claiming that they had been selected for federal prosecution because they were Black. In support of this claim, they produced evidence that in every one of the 24 crack cocaine cases closed by a federal public defender's office during the prior year, the defendant had been Black. The district court granted the motion and ordered some discovery from the government in support of the selective-prosecution claim. On appeal, a panel of the United States Court of Appeals for the Ninth Circuit reversed. However, on rehearing en banc, the Court of Appeals affirmed the district court's order, ruling that

(1) for discovery purposes, a defendant is not required to demonstrate that the government has failed to prosecute others who are similarly situated, and (2) in the case at hand, the District Court judge's discovery order was within her discretion.

On certiorari, the Supreme Court reversed and remanded. In an opinion by Chief Justice Rehnquist, over one dissent (by Justice Stevens) the Court held that a criminal defendant could obtain discovery of government documents pertinent to a selective-prosecution claim only on a threshold showing that similarly situated defendants of other races have not been prosecuted. The Court determined that the defendants in the case at hand had failed to satisfy the threshold showing.

This case note is presented here for its statement of the law on prosecutorial discretion, with which the Court introduced its legal analysis of the claim. The Court said:

> A selective-prosecution claim asks a court to exercise judicial power over a "special province" of the Executive. The Attorney General and United States Attorneys retain "broad discretion" to enforce the Nation's criminal laws. Wayte v. United States, 470 U.S. 598, 607 (1985). They have this latitude because they are designated by statute as the President's delegates to help him discharge his constitutional responsibility to "take Care that the Laws be faithfully executed." U.S. Const., Art. II, § 3; see 28 U.S.C. §§ 516, 547. As a result, "the presumption of regularity supports" their prosecutorial decisions and, "in the absence of clear evidence to the contrary, courts presume that they have properly discharged their official duties." In the ordinary case, "so long as the prosecutor has probable cause to believe that the accused committed an offense defined by statute, the decision whether or not to prosecute, and what charge to file or bring before a grand jury, generally rests entirely in his discretion." Bordenkircher v. Hayes, 434 U.S. 357, 364 (1978).
>
> Of course, a prosecutor's discretion is "subject to constitutional constraints." One of these constraints, imposed by the equal protection component of the Due Process Clause of the Fifth Amendment, Bolling v. Sharpe, 347 U.S. 497 (1954), is that the decision whether to prosecute may not be based on "an unjustifiable standard such as race, religion, or other arbitrary classification." A defendant may demonstrate that the administration of a criminal law is "directed so exclusively against a particular class of persons ... with a mind so unequal and oppressive" that the system of prosecution amounts to "a practical denial" of equal protection of the law. Yick Wo v. Hopkins, 118 U.S. 356, 373 (1886).
>
> In order to dispel the presumption that a prosecutor has not violated equal protection, a criminal defendant must present "clear evidence to the contrary." We explained in Wayte why courts are "properly hesitant to examine the decision whether to prosecute." 470 U.S. at 608. Judicial deference to the decisions of these executive officers rests in part on an assessment of the relative competence of prosecutors and courts. "Such factors as the strength of the case, the prosecution's general deterrence value, the Government's enforcement priorities, and the case's relationship to the Government's overall enforcement plan are not readily susceptible to the kind of analysis the courts are competent to undertake." It also stems from a concern not to unnecessarily impair the performance of a core executive constitutional function. "Examining the basis of a prosecution delays the criminal proceeding, threatens to chill law enforcement by subjecting the prosecutor's motives and decisionmaking to outside inquiry, and may undermine prosecutorial effectiveness by revealing the Government's enforcement policy." Ibid.

Criminal prosecution is undoubtedly a function that lies at the very core of executive power, and so it is perhaps not surprising that reviewing courts will take a very deferential approach to challenges to prosecutorial discretion. Of course, executive discretionary decisions arise literally every day, as the President and subordinates within the executive branch make decisions about how to allocate enforcement resources and actually carry out the laws. The following two case notes illustrate approaches to judicial review of executive discretion outside the criminal law context.

———————

CASE NOTE: *Dalton v. Specter,* 511 U.S. 462 (1994). The Respondents — several shipyard employees, their unions, members of Congress from Pennsylvania and New Jersey (including Senator Arlen Specter, the lead respondent), and various city and state governments — sued to enjoin the Secretary of Defense John H. Dalton from carrying out a decision by President George H. W. Bush to close the Philadelphia Naval Shipyard. That decision was made pursuant to the Defense Base Closure and Realignment Act of 1990. The Act required the Secretary of Defense to recommend military base closures to a newly created, eight-member base closure commission, which in turn would recommend base closures to the President. The President then had to decide whether to approve or disapprove, in their entirety, the commission's base closure recommendations. Congress could thereafter reject the closures (again only in their entirety) by passing a joint resolution of disapproval. In July 1991, President Bush approved the commission's recommendations of various base closures, including the Philadelphia Naval Shipyard, and the House of Representatives rejected a proposed joint resolution of disapproval by a vote of 364 to 60. Respondents filed suit alleging that the substantive and procedural requirements of the 1990 Act had been violated in selecting the Philadelphia Naval Shipyard for closure.

The Supreme Court held that the claim was not judicially reviewable and ordered the case dismissed. The ultimate decision was that of the President, whose actions were not reviewable under the Administrative Procedure Act (a law providing generally for judicial review of executive agency decisions) because "the President is not an 'agency.'" Nor was the President's action reviewable on constitutional grounds. The Court of Appeals, relying primarily on *Youngstown,* had held that whenever the President acts in excess of his statutory authority, he also violates the constitutional separation-of-powers doctrine. A five-justice majority (*Rehnquist* (CJ), O'Connor, Scalia, Kennedy, Thomas), disagreed: "Our cases do not support the proposition that every action by the President, or by another executive official, in excess of his statutory authority is *ipso facto* in violation of the Constitution." The Court distinguished *Youngstown,* arguing that it "involved the conceded *absence* of *any* statutory authority, not a claim that the President acted in excess of such authority." The Court concluded:

> We may assume for the sake of argument that some claims that the President has violated a statutory mandate are judicially reviewable outside the framework of the APA. But longstanding authority holds that such review is not available when the statute in question commits the decision to the discretion of the President.... How the President chooses to exercise the discretion Congress has granted him is not a matter for our review.... "[N]o question of law is raised when the exercise of [the President's] discretion is challenged."

Justices *Blackmun, Souter,* Stevens and Ginsburg, concurred in the judgment on the ground that *this particular statute* "grants the President unfettered discretion to accept the Commission's base-closing report or to reject it, for a good reason, a bad reason, or no reason." The four justices endorsed neither the concept that the President's actions are unreviewable under the APA nor the suggestion that the President's discretion in enforcing statutes is inherently unreviewable as a general matter.

CASE NOTE: *Massachusetts v. Environmental Protection Agency*, 549 U.S. 497 (2007). Section 202(a)(1) of the Clean Air Act requires the EPA Administrator to issue regulations setting motor vehicle emissions standards. In 1999, the EPA in the Clinton administration began a notice-and-comment procedure for new vehicle emissions standards to address the problem of global warming. But the EPA under the Bush administration decided in 2003 to refrain from issuing any regulations, claiming: (1) that contrary to the opinions of its former general counsels, the Clean Air Act does not authorize EPA to issue mandatory regulations to address global climate change; and (2) that even if the Agency had the authority to set greenhouse gas emission standards, it would be unwise to do so because of political opposition. Several state and local government agencies sought review of the EPA's non-decision under the Administrative Procedure Act. The Court of Appeals upheld the EPA, but the Supreme Court reversed.

The five-justice majority (**Stevens**, Kennedy, Souter, Ginsburg, Breyer) acknowledged that an agency's "broad discretion to choose how best to marshal its limited resources.... is at its height when the agency decides not to bring an enforcement action. Therefore, ... an agency's refusal to initiate enforcement proceedings is not ordinarily subject to judicial review." In contrast, agencies' "[r]efusals to promulgate rules are ... susceptible to judicial review, though such review is 'extremely limited' and 'highly deferential.'" The Court went on to hold that the EPA did have a statutory power and duty to issue regulations under the Clean Air Act and that its rulemaking discretion did not extend to making a politically based policy judgment to decline to issue regulations: the EPA's "judgment" under the statute must relate to whether an air pollutant "cause[s], or contribute[s] to, air pollution which may reasonably be anticipated to endanger public health or welfare.... Under the clear terms of the Clean Air Act, EPA can avoid taking further action only if it determines that greenhouse gases do not contribute to climate change" or if it provides "a reasoned justification for declining to form a scientific judgment." The four dissenters (**Roberts** (CJ), **Scalia**, Thomas, Alito) argued that the agency's discretion allowed it to rely on political or policy-based factors to decline to issue regulations, and was not limited to scientific ones relating to the dangers posed by greenhouse gases.

Review Questions and Explanations: Executive Discretion

1. *Armstrong* dealt with review of prosecutorial discretion — the power to decide which cases to enforce — under the Equal Protection clause, and set an exceedingly high bar for such challenges. It may be even more difficult to challenge prosecutorial discretion on separation-of-powers or "take care clause" grounds — that is, by arguing that the executive is not properly or adequately enforcing the laws.

There are multitudes of federal laws on the books — both criminal and civil — that could occupy the full time and energies of countless federal officials. But enforcement resources are limited. In the criminal law field, for example, there are only so many FBI, DEA, and other federal agents; only so many federal prosecutors; and, indeed, only so many courts to hear cases. A major component of prosecutorial discretion involves resource allocation decisions: to what particular laws will law enforcement agencies devote their limited resources? The same kinds of questions face federal agencies charged with enforcing non-criminal, regulatory laws as well. Courts are extremely reluctant to involve themselves in second-guessing such decisions. Why might that be? Should courts be actively engaged in determining whether executive decisions about allocating enforcement resources have been made in a manner that "take[s[care that the laws [are being] faithfully executed"?

2. Some Supreme Court decisions contain language broadly suggesting that discretionary decisions by the President are not judicially reviewable, period. *Dalton*, and the quoted passage from *Marbury v. Madison* at the outset of this section, are just two examples. But that broad statement can't be true: *Youngstown* is a classic example of judicial review of a discretionary presidential act, and its continuing vitality is suggested by the fact that virtually every executive power decision by the Supreme Court since 1952 seems to cite it approvingly. How do you square a case like *Dalton*—or the *Marbury* language—with *Youngstown*? Is there a coherent doctrine here?

Exercise: The Take Care Clause and Related Matters

Suppose the President wishes to issue an executive order prohibiting federal law enforcement officials from "investigating, arresting, or prosecuting medical marijuana users or suppliers, or seizing or interdicting medical marijuana supplies of anyone who is conforming to state laws permitting medical use of marijuana."

The President is conscientious about her constitutional obligations, however, and will reconsider whether to issue the executive order if there are serious doubts about its constitutionality. You are an attorney in the Office of Legal Counsel in the Justice Department and have been asked to write a memo assessing the constitutionality of the executive order. You've been instructed specifically that "the President wants sound, objective advice. Don't just tell her what you think she wants to hear. Don't just write a one-sided advocacy piece."

This question will necessarily require you to draw on material you have studied in connection with the Controlled Substances Act and *Gonzales v. Raich* in Chapter 1.

Either by yourself, or as a collaboration with one or more fellow students, try your hand at writing this memo. At a minimum try to write at least a paragraph summarizing your argument plus a detailed outline.

Professional Development Reflection Questions

1. Consider the exercise above. Suppose you conclude that the proposed executive order is unconstitutional. A week after you submit your memo, your supervisor comes back to you and says, "the President read your memo and appreciates your candor. However, she disagrees with you. Please draft the Executive Order, and make sure to include supporting constitutional arguments with relevant authority." What should you do?

2. The Office of Legal Counsel under President George W. Bush was sharply criticized for a series of legal opinions it issued in 2002 and 2003 justifying the President's authorization of "enhanced interrogation techniques" by the CIA and the Department of Defense to question suspected terrorists. These techniques included several methods that were widely regarded by experts and by the human rights community as torture. The most controversial practice was "waterboarding," in which water is poured over the face of a restrained person to give him the sensation of drowning; victims of this practice have testified afterward that they were convinced they were being killed by drowning. Many medical experts contend that this practice creates a likelihood of causing serious and lasting physical and mental injury, even when "properly" conducted.

The memoranda from the OLC justifying this practice took the position that waterboarding and other "enhanced" techniques were not torture despite the following operative definition of torture, in 18 U.S.C. §2340:

> "torture" means an act committed by a person acting under the color of law specifically intended to inflict severe physical or mental pain or suffering (other than pain or suffering incidental to lawful sanctions) upon another person within his custody or physical control;
>
> (2) "severe mental pain or suffering" means the prolonged mental harm caused by or resulting from—
>
> > (A) the intentional infliction or threatened infliction of severe physical pain or suffering; ...
> >
> > (C) the threat of imminent death ...

Critics suggested that the OLC attorneys selectively presented the information regarding waterboarding by citing experts who disputed its risk of physical harm while ignoring contrary expert opinion.

In their constitutional analysis, the OLC memos asserted that the "enhanced interrogation techniques" were authorized by the President's commander-in-chief power. The memos acknowledged federal statutes prohibiting torture by U.S. government officials and agents. *See, e.g.,* 18 U.S.C. §2340. But they never cited *Youngstown* and, rather than considering the constitutional importance of congressional disapproval of torture, they baldly asserted that "Congress cannot interfere with the president's exercise of his authority as Commander in Chief to control the conduct of operations during a war." (OLC Memo of Mar. 14, 2003, p. 13.)

Was it ethical for lawyers in the OLC to provide this document as legal advice? What would you do if you were a government attorney and your supervisor expressly asked you to produce a legal analysis justifying the President's power to authorize actions widely considered to be torture? Does it matter that the OLC is expected to give independent advice? What if you were informed that some of the detainees under interrogation are believed to have information about impending terrorist attacks on the United States?

Chapter 4

Other Separation-of-Powers Issues

A. Overview

In Chapter 3, we looked at separation-of-powers issues through the lens of executive power, focusing on cases where the constitutional question centered on, or arose from, an assertion of power by the President—sometimes authorized by Congress, sometimes not. Here, we look at other separation-of-powers issues. In the cases and materials that follow, the constitutional question centers on, or arises from, assertions of power by Congress, and the way those assertions affect the powers of the Executive and Judicial branches, or the separation-of-powers scheme as a whole.

The cases in sections B and C of this chapter all have a common theme: they involve legislative efforts by Congress to tinker with the structure of government. The population of the United States has increased sixty-fold since the drafting of the Constitution—from around five million to about 300 million people. The size and complexity of the modern United States poses an ongoing challenge to efforts to govern in a rational and efficient way while staying within the guidelines set out in the Constitution. Ongoing tension exists (as you have already seen in the Executive Power chapter) between adhering strictly to a concept of precisely defined and separated legislative, executive, and judicial powers, and creating flexible structures that allow the federal government to adapt to changing circumstances while maintaining (it is hoped) fidelity to basic constitutional commands. This tension is expressed in the ongoing debate in separation-of-powers cases between "formalist" and "functionalist" judicial opinions. As you read the cases in this chapter, keep that debate in mind, and try to identify when an opinion is expressing a functionalist approach and when a formalist approach. You may also find it informative to keep an eye on whether particular justices tend to take one approach or the other.

The cases in section B involve legislation that arguably creates innovations in legislative processes. The question in these cases is whether the Constitution permits such innovation. Section C looks at the modern "administrative state"—a governmental regime in which agencies both within and outside the executive branch implement legislation and fill in its details by exercising authority that resembles not only executive powers, but legislative and judicial powers as well. Section C also considers the power of Congress to create courts that do not conform to the requirements of Article III. Section D wraps up the chapter by considering the impeachment power—a power vested in Congress to remove officials of the other two branches of government.

B. Integrity of the Legislative Process

Guided Reading Questions: *Immigration and Naturalization Service v. Chadha*

1. Be sure you understand both the procedure for enacting legislation arising out of the so-called "bicameralism" and "presentment" clauses, as well as the policy rationale of the framers which underlies the process. Try to summarize these in 3–5 sentences.

2. Describe the one-house veto procedure challenged in *Chadha*. In what ways does it violate the bicameralism and presentment requirements?

3. The answer to question 2 may be a bit more complicated than at first glance. In order to hold that bicameralism and presentment requirements were not followed, doesn't the Court have to decide that what the House did to Chadha was "legislation"? How is it "legislation" for the House to decide whether to deport Chadha but "execution of the laws" for the Attorney General to decide whether to deport Chadha?

4. How does Justice Powell's argument differ from the majority's?

5. Justice White begins with historical and pragmatic arguments. How do these bear on the constitutional question? What is his more specific argument as to why the one-house veto is constitutional?

Immigration and Naturalization Service v. Chadha
462 U.S. 919 (1983)

Majority: *Burger* (CJ), Brennan, Marshall, Blackmun, Stevens, O'Connor,

Concurrence in the judgment: *Powell*

Dissents: *White, Rehnquist*

CHIEF JUSTICE BURGER delivered the opinion of the Court.

[Chadha, a Kenya-born East Indian holding a British passport, was lawfully admitted to the United States in 1966 on a nonimmigrant student visa. When he overstayed the expiration of his visa, the Immigration and Naturalization Service commenced deportation proceedings. Chadha applied for "suspension of deportation," a statutory procedure by which an alien present in the United States for seven years or more can adjust his status to that of lawful permanent resident (that of a "Green Card" holder) by showing that deportation would "result in extreme hardship" to himself or to a citizen- (or lawful-permanent-resident-) spouse, parent, or child. "Suspension of deportation" was technically an exercise of discretion delegated to the Attorney General under the Immigration and Nationality Act (INA). The Attorney General, in turn, exercised his enforcement responsibilities through the former Immigration and Naturalization Service (formerly a division of the Department of Justice).[1] Suspension of

---

1. In 2003, the functions of INS were reconstituted and divided among three agencies within the newly created Department of Homeland Security. Deportation proceedings are now overseen by the United States Citizenship and Immigration Services.

deportation applications were decided at adversarial evidentiary hearings before an administrative law judge known as an "immigration judge." Prior to the creation of this suspension-of-deportation procedure, an immigrant could seek relief from deportation only by obtaining a "private bill" from Congress, basically a law waiving deportation in his or her individual case.

[In June 1974, based on evidence presented at his deportation hearing, the Immigration Judge ordered that Chadha's deportation be suspended. Pursuant to §244(c)(1) of the INA, a report of the suspension was transmitted to Congress. Section 244(c)(2) of the INA provided that Congress could review determinations by the Attorney General to suspend deportation, as follows:

> if during the session of the Congress at which a case is reported, or prior to the close of the session of the Congress next following the session at which a case is reported, either the Senate or the House of Representatives passes a resolution stating in substance that it does not favor the suspension of such deportation, the Attorney General shall thereupon deport such alien or authorize the alien's voluntary departure at his own expense under the order of deportation in the manner provided by law.

Otherwise, the Suspension of Deportation order would take permanent effect, terminating deportation proceedings.

[On December 12, 1975, Representative Eilberg, Chairman of the Judiciary Subcommittee on Immigration, Citizenship, and International Law, introduced a resolution opposing "the granting of permanent residence in the United States to [six] aliens," including Chadha. H. Res. 926, 94th Cong., 1st Sess.; 121 Cong Rec. 40247 (1975). The resolution was referred to the House Committee on the Judiciary. On December 16, 1975, the resolution was submitted to the full House for a vote. The House consideration of the resolution was based on Representative Eilberg's statement from the floor that

> [it] was the feeling of the committee, after reviewing 340 cases, that the aliens contained in the resolution [Chadha and five others] did not meet these statutory requirements, particularly as it relates to hardship; and it is the opinion of the committee that their deportation should not be suspended.

The resolution was passed without debate or recorded vote. Since the House action was pursuant to §244(c)(2), the resolution was not treated as an Art. I legislative act; it was not submitted to the Senate or presented to the President for his action.

[After the House veto of the Attorney General's decision to allow Chadha to remain in the United States, the Immigration Judge reopened the deportation proceedings and on November 8, 1976, ordered Chadha deported. Both the Immigration Judge and the Board of Immigration Appeals (an administrative review tribunal overseeing individual immigration judge decisions) rejected Chadha's constitutional challenge to the one-house legislative veto.

[Chadha filed a petition for review of the deportation order in the United States Court of Appeals for the Ninth Circuit, where INS agreed with Chadha's position that §244(c)(2) is unconstitutional. The Court of Appeals held that the House was without constitutional authority to order Chadha's deportation and ordered the Attorney General "to cease and desist from taking any steps to deport [Chadha] based upon the resolution enacted by the House of Representatives."

[The Supreme Court granted certiorari. Before the Court, the one-house veto provision was defended by the House and Senate, which had each appeared as parties before the Ninth Circuit and which both petitioned for certiorari. The Court rejected various jurisdictional and justiciability challenges raised by the House and Senate, and then proceeded to the merits.]

We turn now to the question whether action of one House of Congress under § 244(c)(2) violates strictures of the Constitution. We begin, of course, with the presumption that the challenged statute is valid. Its wisdom is not the concern of the courts; if a challenged action does not violate the Constitution, it must be sustained: "Once the meaning of an enactment is discerned and its constitutionality determined, the judicial process comes to an end. We do not sit as a committee of review, nor are we vested with the power of veto."

By the same token, the fact that a given law or procedure is efficient, convenient, and useful in facilitating functions of government, standing alone, will not save it if it is contrary to the Constitution.... [Our] inquiry is sharpened rather than blunted by the fact that congressional veto provisions are appearing with increasing frequency in statutes which delegate authority to executive and independent agencies:

> Since 1932, when the first veto provision was enacted into law, 295 congressional veto-type procedures have been inserted in 196 different statutes as follows: from 1932 to 1939, five statutes were affected; from 1940–49, nineteen statutes; between 1950–59, thirty-four statutes; and from 1960–69, forty-nine. From the year 1970 through 1975, at least one hundred sixty-three such provisions visions were included in eighty-nine laws. Abourezk, The Congressional Veto: A Contemporary Response to Executive Encroachment on Legislative Prerogatives, 52 Ind. L. Rev. 323, 324 (1977).

JUSTICE WHITE undertakes to make a case for the proposition that the one-House veto is a useful "political invention," and we need not challenge that assertion. We can even concede this utilitarian argument although the long-range political wisdom of this "invention" ... has been vigorously debated.... But policy arguments supporting even useful "political inventions" are subject to the demands of the Constitution which defines powers and, with respect to this subject, sets out just how those powers are to be exercised.

Explicit and unambiguous provisions of the Constitution prescribe and define the respective functions of the Congress and of the Executive in the legislative process.... The[] provisions of Art. I, [§§ 1, 7] are integral parts of the constitutional design for the separation of powers....

The records of the Constitutional Convention reveal that the requirement that all legislation be presented to the President before becoming law was uniformly accepted by the Framers. Presentment to the President and the Presidential veto were considered so imperative that the draftsmen took special pains to assure that these requirements could not be circumvented. During the final debate on Art. I, § 7, cl. 2, James Madison expressed concern that it might easily be evaded by the simple expedient of calling a proposed law a "resolution" or "vote" rather than a "bill." 2 Farrand 301–302. As a consequence, Art. I, § 7, cl. 3, was added....

The President's role in the lawmaking process also reflects the Framers' careful efforts to check whatever propensity a particular Congress might have to enact oppressive, improvident, or ill-considered measures. The President's veto role in the legislative process was described later during public debate on ratification:

It establishes a salutary check upon the legislative body, calculated to guard the community against the effects of faction, precipitancy, or of any impulse unfriendly to the public good, which may happen to influence a majority of that body.

... The primary inducement to conferring the power in question upon the Executive is, to enable him to defend himself; the secondary one is to increase the chances in favor of the community against the passing of bad laws, through haste, inadvertence, or design. The Federalist No. 73 (A. Hamilton).

The Court also has observed that the Presentment Clauses serve the important purpose of assuring that a "national" perspective is grafted on the legislative process:

The President is a representative of the people just as the members of the Senate and of the House are, and it may be, at some times, on some subjects, that the President elected by all the people is rather more representative of them all than are the members of either body of the Legislature whose constituencies are local and not countrywide ... *Myers v. United States, supra,* at 123.

The bicameral requirement of Art. I, §§ 1, 7, was of scarcely less concern to the Framers than was the Presidential veto and indeed the two concepts are interdependent. By providing that no law could take effect without the concurrence of the prescribed majority of the Members of both Houses, the Framers reemphasized their belief, already remarked upon in connection with the Presentment Clauses, that legislation should not be enacted unless it has been carefully and fully considered by the Nation's elected officials....

These observations are consistent with what many of the Framers expressed, none more cogently than Madison in pointing up the need to divide and disperse power in order to protect liberty:

In republican government, the legislative authority necessarily predominates. The remedy for this inconveniency is to divide the legislature into different branches; and to render them, by different modes of election and different principles of action, as little connected with each other as the nature of their common functions and their common dependence on the society will admit." The Federalist No. 51, p. 324 (H. Lodge ed. 1888) (sometimes attributed to "Hamilton or Madison" but now generally attributed to Madison).

.... It need hardly be repeated here that the Great Compromise, under which one House was viewed as representing the people and the other the states, allayed the fears of both the large and small states.

FN15. The Great Compromise was considered so important by the Framers that they inserted a special provision to ensure that it could not be altered, even by constitutional amendment, except with the consent of the states affected. See U.S. Const., Art V.

We see therefore that the Framers were acutely conscious that the bicameral requirement and the Presentment Clauses would serve essential constitutional functions. The President's participation in the legislative process was to protect the Executive Branch from Congress and to protect the whole people from improvident laws. The division of the Congress into two distinctive bodies assures that the legislative power would be exercised only after opportunity for full study and debate in separate settings. The President's unilateral veto power, in turn, was limited by the power of two-thirds of both Houses of Congress to overrule a veto thereby precluding final arbitrary action of one person. It emerges clearly that the prescription for legislative action in Art. I, §§ 1, 7, represents the Framers' decision that the legislative power of the Federal Government be exercised in accord with a single, finely wrought and exhaustively considered, procedure.

The Constitution sought to divide the delegated powers of the new Federal Government into three defined categories, Legislative, Executive, and Judicial, to assure, as nearly as possible, that each branch of government would confine itself to its assigned responsibility. The hydraulic pressure inherent within each of the separate Branches to exceed the outer limits of its power, even to accomplish desirable objectives, must be resisted.

Although not "hermetically" sealed from one another, Buckley v. Valeo, 424 U.S., at 121, the powers delegated to the three Branches are functionally identifiable....

Examination of the action taken here by one House pursuant to § 244(c)(2) reveals that it was essentially legislative in purpose and effect. In purporting to exercise power defined in Art. I, § 8, cl. 4, to "establish an uniform Rule of Naturalization," the House took action that had the purpose and effect of altering the legal rights, duties, and relations of persons, including the Attorney General, Executive Branch officials and Chadha, all outside the Legislative Branch. Section 244(c)(2) purports to authorize one House of Congress to require the Attorney General to deport an individual alien whose deportation otherwise would be canceled under § 244. The one-House veto operated in these cases to overrule the Attorney General and mandate Chadha's deportation; absent the House action, Chadha would remain in the United States. Congress has *acted* and its action has altered Chadha's status.

The legislative character of the one-House veto in these cases is confirmed by the character of the congressional action it supplants. Neither the House of Representatives nor the Senate contends that, absent the veto provision in § 244(c)(2), either of them, or both of them acting together, could effectively require the Attorney General to deport an alien once the Attorney General, in the exercise of legislatively delegated authority, had determined the alien should remain in the United States. Without the challenged provision in § 244(c)(2), this could have been achieved, if at all, only by legislation requiring deportation. Similarly, a veto by one House of Congress under § 244(c)(2) cannot be justified as an attempt at amending the standards set out in § 244(a)(1), or as a repeal of § 244 as applied to Chadha. Amendment and repeal of statutes, no less than enactment, must conform with Art. I.

The nature of the decision implemented by the one-House veto in these cases further manifests its legislative character. After long experience with the clumsy, time-consuming private bill procedure, Congress made a deliberate choice to delegate to the Executive Branch, and specifically to the Attorney General, the authority to allow deportable aliens to remain in this country in certain specified circumstances. It is not disputed that this choice to delegate authority is precisely the kind of decision that can be implemented only in accordance with the procedures set out in Art. I. Disagreement with the Attorney General's decision on Chadha's deportation—that is, Congress' decision to deport Chadha— no less than Congress' original choice to delegate to the Attorney General the authority to make that decision, involves determinations of policy that Congress can implement in only one way; bicameral passage followed by presentment to the President. Congress must abide by its delegation of authority until that delegation is legislatively altered or revoked.

> FN19. ... The Constitution provides Congress with abundant means to oversee and control its administrative creatures. Beyond the obvious fact that Congress ultimately controls administrative agencies in the legislation that creates them, other means of control, such as durational limits on authorizations and formal reporting requirements, lie well within Congress' constitutional power.

Finally, we see that when the Framers intended to authorize either House of Congress to act alone and.... independent of the other House, or of the President, they did so in explicit, unambiguous terms. These carefully defined exceptions from presentment and bicameralism [Art. I, § 2, cl. 5 (House's impeachment power); Art. I, § 3, cl. 6 (Senate's impeachment trial power); Art. II, §2, cl. 2 (Senate's approval of appointments and treaties)].... provide further support for the conclusion that congressional authority is not to be implied and for the conclusion that the veto provided for in §244(c)(2) is not authorized by the constitutional design of the powers of the Legislative Branch....

The veto authorized by §244(c)(2) doubtless has been in many respects a convenient shortcut; the "sharing" with the Executive by Congress of its authority over aliens in this manner is, on its face, an appealing compromise....

The choices we discern as having been made in the Constitutional Convention impose burdens on governmental processes that often seem clumsy, inefficient, even unworkable, but those hard choices were consciously made by men who had lived under a form of government that permitted arbitrary governmental acts to go unchecked. There is no support in the Constitution or decisions of this Court for the proposition that the cumbersomeness and delays often encountered in complying with explicit constitutional standards may be avoided, either by the Congress or by the President. See Youngstown Sheet & Tube Co. v. Sawyer, 343 U.S. 579 (1952). With all the obvious flaws of delay, untidiness, and potential for abuse, we have not yet found a better way to preserve freedom than by making the exercise of power subject to the carefully crafted restraints spelled out in the Constitution.

We hold that the congressional veto provision in §244(c)(2) is severable from the Act and that it is unconstitutional. Accordingly, the judgment of the Court of Appeals is affirmed.

JUSTICE POWELL, concurring in the judgment.

The Court's decision, based on the Presentment Clauses, Art. I, §7, cls. 2 and 3, apparently will invalidate every use of the legislative veto. The breadth of this holding gives one pause. Congress has included the veto in literally hundreds of statutes, dating back to the 1930s. Congress clearly views this procedure as essential to controlling the delegation of power to administrative agencies. One reasonably may disagree with Congress' assessment of the veto's utility, but the respect due its judgment as a coordinate branch of Government cautions that our holding should be no more extensive than necessary to decide these cases. In my view, the cases may be decided on a narrower ground. When Congress finds that a particular person does not satisfy the statutory criteria for permanent residence in this country it has assumed a judicial function in violation of the principle of separation of powers. Accordingly, I concur only in the judgment....

In addition to the report on Chadha, Congress had before it the names of 339 other persons whose deportations also had been suspended by the Service. The House Committee on the Judiciary decided that six of these persons, including Chadha, should not be allowed to remain in this country. Accordingly, it submitted a resolution to the House, which stated simply that "the House of Representatives does not approve the granting of permanent residence in the United States to the aliens hereinafter named." 121 Cong. Rec. 40800 (1975). The resolution was not distributed prior to the vote, but the Chairman of the Judiciary Subcommittee on Immigration, Citizenship, and International Law explained to the House:

> It was the feeling of the committee, after reviewing 340 cases, that the aliens contained in the resolution did not meet [the] statutory requirements, particularly as it relates to hardship; and it is the opinion of the committee that their deportation should not be suspended. (remarks of Rep. Eilberg).

Without further explanation and without a recorded vote, the House rejected the Service's determination that these six people met the statutory criteria.

On its face, the House's action appears clearly adjudicatory. The House did not enact a general rule; rather it made its own determination that six specific persons did not comply with certain statutory criteria. It thus undertook the type of decision that traditionally has been left to other branches....

The impropriety of the House's assumption of this function is confirmed by the fact that its action raises the very danger the Framers sought to avoid—the exercise of unchecked power. In deciding whether Chadha deserves to be deported, Congress is not subject to any internal constraints that prevent it from arbitrarily depriving him of the right to remain in this country. Unlike the judiciary or an administrative agency, Congress is not bound by established substantive rules. Nor is it subject to the procedural safeguards, such as the right to counsel and a hearing before an impartial tribunal, that are present when a court or an agency adjudicates individual rights. The only effective constraint on Congress' power is political, but Congress is most accountable politically when it prescribes rules of general applicability. When it decides rights of specific persons, those rights are subject to "the tyranny of a shifting majority."

.... In my view, when Congress undertook to apply its rules to Chadha, it exceeded the scope of its constitutionally prescribed authority. I would not reach the broader question whether legislative vetoes are invalid under the Presentment Clauses.

JUSTICE WHITE, dissenting.

.... The prominence of the legislative veto mechanism in our contemporary political system and its importance to Congress can hardly be overstated. It has become a central means by which Congress secures the accountability of executive and independent agencies. Without the legislative veto, Congress is faced with a Hobson's choice: either to refrain from delegating the necessary authority, leaving itself with a hopeless task of writing laws with the requisite specificity to cover endless special circumstances across the entire policy landscape, or in the alternative, to abdicate its law-making function to the Executive Branch and independent agencies. To choose the former leaves major national problems unresolved; to opt for the latter risks unaccountable policymaking by those not elected to fill that role. Accordingly, over the past five decades, the legislative veto has been placed in nearly 200 statutes. The device is known in every field of governmental concern: reorganization, budgets, foreign affairs, war powers, and regulation of trade, safety, energy, the environment, and the economy.

The legislative veto developed initially in response to the problems of reorganizing the sprawling Government structure created in response to the Depression. The Reorganization Acts established the chief model for the legislative veto. When President Hoover requested authority to reorganize the Government in 1929, he coupled his request that the "Congress be willing to delegate its authority over the problem (subject to defined principles) to the Executive" with a proposal for legislative review. He proposed that the Executive "should act upon approval of a joint committee of Congress or with the reservation of power of revision by Congress within some limited period adequate for its consideration." Public Papers of the Presidents, Herbert Hoover, 1929, p. 432 (1974). Congress followed President Hoover's suggestion and authorized reorganization subject to legislative review. Act of June 30, 1932. Although the reorganization authority reenacted in 1933 did not contain a legislative veto provision, the provision returned during the Roosevelt administration and has since been renewed numerous times. Over the years, the provision was used extensively. Presidents submitted 115 Reorganization Plans to Congress of which 23 were disapproved by Congress pursuant to legislative veto provisions

Shortly after adoption of the Reorganization Act of 1939, Congress and the President applied the legislative veto procedure to resolve the delegation problem for national security and foreign affairs. World War II occasioned the need to transfer greater authority to the President in these areas. The legislative veto offered the means by which Congress could confer additional authority while preserving its own constitutional role. During World War II, Congress enacted over 30 statutes conferring powers on the Executive with legislative veto provisions. President Roosevelt accepted the veto as the necessary price for obtaining exceptional authority.

Over the quarter century following World War II, Presidents continued to accept legislative vetoes by one or both Houses as constitutional, while regularly denouncing provisions by which congressional Committees reviewed Executive activity. The legislative veto balanced delegations of statutory authority in new areas of governmental involvement: the space program, international agreements on nuclear energy, tariff arrangements, and adjustment of federal pay rates.

During the 1970s the legislative veto was important in resolving a series of major constitutional disputes between the President and Congress over claims of the President to broad impoundment, war, and national emergency powers. The key provision of the War Powers Resolution, 50 U. S. C. § 1544(c), authorizes the termination by concurrent resolution of the use of armed forces in hostilities. A similar measure resolved the problem posed by Presidential claims of inherent power to impound appropriations. Congressional Budget and Impoundment Control Act of 1974, 31 U. S. C. § 1403. In conference, a compromise was achieved under which permanent impoundments, termed "rescissions," would require approval through enactment of legislation. In contrast, temporary impoundments, or "deferrals," would become effective unless disapproved by one House. This compromise provided the President with flexibility, while preserving ultimate congressional control over the budget....

> FN7. The Impoundment Control Act's provision for legislative review has been used extensively. Presidents have submitted hundreds of proposed budget deferrals, of which 65 have been disapproved by resolutions of the House or Senate with no protest by the Executive.

Even this brief review suffices to demonstrate that the legislative veto is more than "efficient, convenient, and useful." It is an important if not indispensable political invention that allows the President and Congress to resolve major constitutional and policy differences, assures the accountability of independent regulatory agencies, and preserves Congress' control over lawmaking. Perhaps there are other means of accommodation and accountability, but the increasing reliance of Congress upon the legislative veto suggests that the alternatives to which Congress must now turn are not entirely satisfactory.

The history of the legislative veto also makes clear that it has not been a sword with which Congress has struck out to aggrandize itself at the expense of the other branches — the concerns of Madison and Hamilton. Rather, the veto has been a means of defense, a reservation of ultimate authority necessary if Congress is to fulfill its designated role under Art. I as the Nation's lawmaker.... To be sure, the President may have preferred unrestricted power, but that could be precisely why Congress thought it essential to retain a check on the exercise of delegated authority.

For all these reasons, the apparent sweep of the Court's decision today is regrettable. The Court's Art. I analysis appears to invalidate all legislative vetoes irrespective of form or subject. Because the legislative veto is commonly found as a check upon rulemaking by administrative agencies and upon broad-based policy decisions of the Executive Branch, it is particularly unfortunate that the Court reaches its decision in cases involving the exercise of a veto over deportation decisions regarding particular individuals. Courts should always be wary of striking statutes as unconstitutional; to strike an entire class of statutes based on consideration of a somewhat atypical and more readily indictable exemplar of the class is irresponsible.

.... [T]he constitutionality of the legislative veto is anything but clear-cut. The issue divides scholars, courts, Attorneys General, and the two other branches of the National Government. If the veto devices so flagrantly disregarded the requirements of Art. I as the Court today suggests, I find it incomprehensible that Congress, whose Members are bound by oath to uphold the Constitution, would have placed these mechanisms in nearly 200 separate laws over a period of 50 years.

.... The Constitution does not directly authorize or prohibit the legislative veto. Thus, our task should be to determine whether the legislative veto is consistent with the purposes of Art. I and the principles of separation of powers which are reflected in that Article and throughout the Constitution. We should not find the lack of a specific constitutional authorization for the legislative veto surprising, and I would not infer disapproval of the mechanism from its absence. From the summer of 1787 to the present the Government of the United States has become an endeavor far beyond the contemplation of the Framers. Only within the last half century has the complexity and size of the Federal Government's responsibilities grown so greatly that the Congress must rely on the legislative veto as the most effective if not the only means to insure its role as the Nation's lawmaker. But the wisdom of the Framers was to anticipate that the Nation would grow and new problems of governance would require different solutions. Accordingly, our Federal Government was intentionally chartered with the flexibility to respond to contemporary needs without losing sight of fundamental democratic principles. This was the spirit in which Justice Jackson penned his influential concurrence in the Steel Seizure Case:

> The actual art of governing under our Constitution does not and cannot conform to judicial definitions of the power of any of its branches based on isolated clauses or even single Articles torn from context. While the Constitution diffuses power the better to secure liberty, it also contemplates that practice will integrate the dispersed powers into a workable government. Youngstown Sheet & Tube Co. v. Sawyer, 343 U.S. 579, 635 (1952).

This is the perspective from which we should approach the novel constitutional questions presented by the legislative veto. In my view, neither Art. I of the Constitution nor the doctrine of separation of powers is violated by this mechanism by which our elected Representatives preserve their voice in the governance of the Nation.

.... There is no question that a bill does not become a law until it is approved by both the House and the Senate, and presented to the President.... [That] does not, however, answer the constitutional question before us. The power to exercise a legislative veto is not the power to write new law without bicameral approval or Presidential consideration. The veto must be authorized by statute and may only negative what an Executive department or independent agency has proposed. On its face, the legislative veto no more allows one House of Congress to make law than does the Presidential veto confer such power upon the President....

.... [B]y virtue of congressional delegation, legislative power can be exercised by independent agencies and Executive departments without the passage of new legislation. For some time, the sheer amount of law—the substantive rules that regulate private conduct and direct the operation of government—made by the agencies has far outnumbered the lawmaking engaged in by Congress through the traditional process. There is no question but that agency rulemaking is lawmaking in any functional or realistic sense of the term....

If Congress may delegate lawmaking power to independent and Executive agencies, it is most difficult to understand Art. I as prohibiting Congress from also reserving a check on legislative power for itself. Absent the veto, the agencies receiving delegations of legislative or quasi-legislative power may issue regulations having the force of law without bicameral approval and without the President's signature. It is thus not apparent why the reservation of a veto over the exercise of that legislative power must be subject to a more exacting test. In both cases, it is enough that the initial statutory authorizations comply with the Art. I requirements.

.... Under the Court's analysis, the Executive Branch and the independent agencies may make rules with the effect of law while Congress, in whom the Framers confided the legislative power, Art. I, § 1, may not exercise a veto which precludes such rules from having operative force. If the effective functioning of a complex modern government requires the delegation of vast authority which, by virtue of its breadth, is legislative or "quasi-legislative" in character, I cannot accept that Art. I—which is, after all, the source of the nondelegation doctrine—should forbid Congress to qualify that grant with a legislative veto.

JUSTICE REHNQUIST, with whom JUSTICE WHITE joins, dissenting.

A severability clause creates a presumption that Congress intended the valid portion of the statute to remain in force when one part is found to be invalid. A severability clause does not, however, conclusively resolve the issue.... Because I believe that Congress did not intend the one-House veto provision of § 244(c)(2) to be severable, I dissent.

Review Questions and Explanations: *Chadha*

1. The "one-house veto" in this case essentially overruled the individualized administrative decisions to grant humanitarian waivers of deportation, and ordered several immigrants deported. There is something unseemly about Congress doing that, but what exactly? Would it have been better had both houses voted on the deportations and presented the bill for the President's signature? (Maybe the President would have signed—who knows?) Did the majority get to the nub of the problem in this case? Or did Justice Powell provide a more convincing way to resolve the case?

2. Justice White's main pragmatic argument is that, in modern times, Congress must make very extensive delegations of discretion to administrative agencies to fill in the details of complex laws. Congress necessarily paints with a broad brush, and has a limited ability to control its delegations of discretion in advance. Is there in fact a better way for Congress to do this, that does not involve a legislative veto? Or is the only option for Congress to continually amend statutes?

3. Which, if any, of the three main opinions—the majority's, Powell's and White's—is "formalistic" and which "functionalistic"? Based on this case, do you have a preference for "formalism" or "functionalism" as an approach to separation-of-powers questions?

4. The impact of *Chadha* is far from clear. The Supreme Court has not considered another legal challenge to a legislative veto law since *Chadha*, even though Congress has continued to enact laws employing the legislative veto technique. Post-*Chadha*, Congress has amended some legislative veto provisions, and enacted new ones, to impose a joint-resolution requirement rather than a

one-house veto (i.e., the legislative veto must be passed by both houses). In some instances, Congress has (as Justice White feared) restricted its delegation of discretion to the President. For example, certain laws authorizing the President to reorganize executive branch agencies now require a joint resolution of *approval*. This meets bicameralism and presentment requirements since such a resolution can be presented to the President, who will undoubtedly sign it into law, since it is the President's reorganization plan that has been voted on. This protocol replaces one in which the President's reorganization plan would be effective unless Congress voted to *disapprove* it.

5. In the aftermath of *Chadha*, many commentators worried that the case undermined the constitutional basis for the War Powers Resolution. Does it? Consider the exercise that follows.

Exercise: Legislative Veto and War Powers

You are an Attorney-Advisor on the staff of the Office of Legal Counsel. The President is contemplating deployment of U.S. armed forces in the Persian Gulf. The President's military advisors assert that the scope of the deployment necessarily depends on its projected duration. For a deployment of under sixty days, the President is advised only to rely on air and naval forces, not ground forces. The Secretary of Defense has asked the Office of Legal Counsel for an opinion on the constitutionality of two provisions of the War Powers Resolution. (See Chapter 3, section B.1, for the complete text.)

There is no question that the deployment is covered by the terms of the Resolution, because the forces will be combat-ready and hostilities are imminent. The specific provisions of concern are § 5(b), which requires the President to terminate the deployment in 60 days unless Congress has declared war or extended "by law" the 60-day period; and § 5(c), which provides that Congress can order the President to remove the armed forces from hostilities "at any time" by a "joint resolution" (a majority vote of both houses), so long as the hostilities have not been authorized by a declaration of War "or specific statutory authorization."

The Assistant Attorney General for the OLC has asked you to draft this memo, and instructed you to focus specifically on whether either of these provisions are unconstitutional under *Chadha*. She has also suggested that "obviously, you'll need to consider *Youngstown* and the doctrines around war powers generally."

Guided Reading Questions: *Clinton v. City of New York*

1. How does the Line Item Veto Act work and what is its purpose?

2. What is the basic constitutional problem with the Act? Although this is not a "legislative veto" case, the majority relies quite a bit on *Chadha*. What in *Chadha* supports the Court's holding here?

3. Both the Breyer and Scalia opinions argue that the spending cancellations authorized by the Act are no different in substance from constitutionally well-

established laws authorizing the President to withhold funds based on his discretionary finding of certain criteria or circumstances. How does the majority opinion respond to that argument?

Clinton v. City of New York
524 U.S. 417 (1998)

Majority: *Stevens*, Rehnquist (CJ), Kennedy, Souter, Thomas, Ginsburg

Concurrence: *Kennedy*

Dissents: *Scalia*, O'Connor, *Breyer*

JUSTICE STEVENS delivered the opinion of the Court.

[The Line Item Veto Act (Act), was enacted in April 1996 and became effective on January 1, 1997. The following day, six Members of Congress who had voted against the Act brought suit challenging its constitutionality. The District Court held the Act unconstitutional, but the Supreme Court vacated that decision and ordered dismissal of the case, holding that the Members of Congress lacked standing. *See Raines v. Byrd*, 521 U.S. 811 (1997), excerpted in chapter 6 of this book.

[Less than two months later, the President exercised his "line item veto" authority to cancel provisions in two laws:

(1) In Section 4722(c) of the Balanced Budget Act of 1997, Congress waived a reduction in the amount of the federal grant to be paid to the State of New York to help it finance its Medicaid (health care for the poor) program. This waiver amounted, in effect, to a subsidy to New York estimated to be worth as much as $2.6 billion.

(2) In § 968 of the Taxpayer Relief Act of 1997, Congress amended the Internal Revenue Code to permit owners of certain food refiners and processors to defer capital gains taxes on profits from selling its shares to eligible farmers' cooperatives. The stated purpose of the tax break was "to facilitate the transfer of refiners and processors to farmers' cooperatives."

[President Clinton "canceled" both of these federal budgetary expenditures on August 11, 1997, sending a notice to Congress that each "cancellation will reduce the Federal budget deficit." He argued, in essence, that each provision was costly special-interest legislation.

[Two separate suits were filed against the President and other federal officials challenging these two cancellations. The City of New York, two hospital associations, one hospital, and two health care workers' unions challenged the cancellation of the New York subsidy. The cancellation of the tax break was challenged by a farmers' cooperative consisting of about 30 potato growers in Idaho. The two cases were consolidated in the district court.

[The Supreme Court rejected challenges to jurisdiction and justiciability. In contrast to *Raines v. Byrd*, the President's exercise of his cancellation authority removed any concern about the ripeness of the dispute, and, moreover, the parties had alleged a "personal stake" in having an actual injury redressed rather than an "institutional injury" that is "abstract and widely dispersed." The loss of federal subsidies and tax benefits were concrete rather than speculative injuries, and gave the plaintiffs standing, according to the Court.]

The Line Item Veto Act gives the President the power to "cancel in whole" three types of provisions that have been signed into law: "(1) any dollar amount of discretionary budget authority; (2) any item of new direct spending; or (3) any limited tax benefit." It is undisputed that the New York case involves an "item of new direct spending" and that the Snake River [Idaho] case involves a "limited tax benefit" as those terms are defined in the Act. It is also undisputed that each of those provisions had been signed into law pursuant to Article I, § 7, of the Constitution before it was canceled.

The Act requires the President to adhere to precise procedures whenever he exercises his cancellation authority. In identifying items for cancellation he must consider the legislative history, the purposes, and other relevant information about the items. He must determine, with respect to each cancellation, that it will "(i) reduce the Federal budget deficit; (ii) not impair any essential Government functions; and (iii) not harm the national interest." § 691(a)(A). Moreover, he must transmit a special message to Congress notifying it of each cancellation within five calendar days (excluding Sundays) after the enactment of the canceled provision. It is undisputed that the President meticulously followed these procedures in these cases.

A cancellation takes effect upon receipt by Congress of the special message from the President. If, however, a "disapproval bill" pertaining to a special message is enacted into law, the cancellations set forth in that message become "null and void." The Act sets forth a detailed expedited procedure for the consideration of a "disapproval bill," but no such bill was passed for either of the cancellations involved in these cases. A majority vote of both Houses is sufficient to enact a disapproval bill. The Act does not grant the President the authority to cancel a disapproval bill, see § 691(c), but he does, of course, retain his constitutional authority to veto such a bill.

The effect of a cancellation is plainly stated in § 691e, which defines the principal terms used in the Act. With respect to both an item of new direct spending and a limited tax benefit, the cancellation prevents the item "from having legal force or effect." Thus, under the plain text of the statute, the two actions of the President that are challenged in these cases prevented one section of the Balanced Budget Act of 1997 and one section of the Taxpayer Relief Act of 1997 "from having legal force or effect." The remaining provisions of those statutes, with the exception of the second canceled item in the latter, continue to have the same force and effect as they had when signed into law.

In both legal and practical effect, the President has amended two Acts of Congress by repealing a portion of each. "Repeal of statutes, no less than enactment, must conform with Art. I." INS v. Chadha, 462 U.S. 919, 954 (1983). There is no provision in the Constitution that authorizes the President to enact, to amend, or to repeal statutes. Both Article I and Article II assign responsibilities to the President that directly relate to the lawmaking process, but neither addresses the issue presented by these cases. The President "shall from time to time give to the Congress Information on the State of the Union, and recommend to their Consideration such Measures as he shall judge necessary and expedient...." Art. II, § 3. Thus, he may initiate and influence legislative proposals. Moreover, after a bill has passed both Houses of Congress, but "before it becomes a Law," it must be presented to the President. If he approves it, "he shall sign it, but if not he shall return it, with his Objections to that House in which it shall have originated, who shall enter the Objections at large on their Journal, and proceed to reconsider it." Art. I, § 7, cl. 2.

His "return" of a bill, which is usually described as a "veto," is subject to being overridden by a two-thirds vote in each House.

There are important differences between the President's "return" of a bill pursuant to Article I, § 7, and the exercise of the President's cancellation authority pursuant to the Line Item Veto Act. The constitutional return takes place *before* the bill becomes law; the statutory cancellation occurs *after* the bill becomes law. The constitutional return is of the entire bill; the statutory cancellation is of only a part. Although the Constitution expressly authorizes the President to play a role in the process of enacting statutes, it is silent on the subject of unilateral Presidential action that either repeals or amends parts of duly enacted statutes.

There are powerful reasons for construing constitutional silence on this profoundly important issue as equivalent to an express prohibition. The procedures governing the enactment of statutes set forth in the text of Article I were the product of the great debates and compromises that produced the Constitution itself. Familiar historical materials provide abundant support for the conclusion that the power to enact statutes may only "be exercised in accord with a single, finely wrought and exhaustively considered, procedure." Chadha, 462 U.S. at 951. Our first President understood the text of the Presentment Clause as requiring that he either "approve all the parts of a Bill, or reject it in toto." What has emerged in these cases from the President's exercise of his statutory cancellation powers, however, are truncated versions of two bills that passed both Houses of Congress. They are not the product of the "finely wrought" procedure that the Framers designed.

.... [W]henever the President cancels an item of new direct spending or a limited tax benefit he is rejecting the policy judgment made by Congress and relying on his own policy judgment.... [C]ancellations pursuant to the Line Item Veto Act are the functional equivalent of partial repeals of Acts of Congress that fail to satisfy Article I, § 7....

[We are not] persuaded by the Government's contention that the President's authority to cancel new direct spending and tax benefit items is no greater than his traditional authority to decline to spend appropriated funds. The Government has reviewed in some detail the series of statutes in which.... the President was given wide discretion with respect to both the amounts to be spent and how the money would be allocated among different functions. It is argued that the Line Item Veto Act merely confers comparable discretionary authority over the expenditure of appropriated funds. The critical difference between this statute and all of its predecessors, however, is that unlike any of them, this Act gives the President the unilateral power to change the text of duly enacted statutes....

.... [O]ur decision rests on the narrow ground that the procedures authorized by the Line Item Veto Act are not authorized by the Constitution. The Balanced Budget Act of 1997 is a 500-page document that became "Public Law 105-33" after three procedural steps were taken: (1) a bill containing its exact text was approved by a majority of the Members of the House of Representatives; (2) the Senate approved precisely the same text; and (3) that text was signed into law by the President. The Constitution explicitly requires that each of those three steps be taken before a bill may "become a law." Art. I, § 7. If one paragraph of that text had been omitted at any one of those three stages, Public Law 105-33 would not have been validly enacted. If the Line Item Veto Act were valid, it would authorize the President to create a different law—one whose text was not voted on by either House of Congress or presented to the President for signature. Something that might be known as "Public Law 105-33 as modified by the President" may or may not be desirable, but it is surely not a document that may "become a law" pursuant to the procedures designed by the Framers of Article I, § 7, of the Constitution.... The judgment of the District Court is affirmed.

JUSTICE KENNEDY, concurring.

A nation cannot plunder its own treasury without putting its Constitution and its survival in peril. The statute before us, then, is of first importance, for it seems undeniable the Act will tend to restrain persistent excessive spending. Nevertheless, for the reasons given by Justice Stevens in the opinion for the Court, the statute must be found invalid. Failure of political will does not justify unconstitutional remedies.

I write to respond to my colleague Justice Breyer, who observes that the statute does not threaten the liberties of individual citizens, a point on which I disagree. The argument is related to his earlier suggestion that our role is lessened here because the two political branches are adjusting their own powers between themselves.... [But liberty] is always at stake when one or more of the branches seek to transgress the separation of powers.

[In] recent years, perhaps, we have come to think of liberty as defined by that word in the Fifth and Fourteenth Amendments and as illuminated by the other provisions of the Bill of Rights. The conception of liberty embraced by the Framers was not so confined. They used the principles of separation of powers and federalism to secure liberty in the fundamental political sense of the term, quite in addition to the idea of freedom from intrusive governmental acts.... [I]f a citizen who is taxed has the measure of the tax or the decision to spend determined by the Executive alone, without adequate control by the citizen's Representatives in Congress, liberty is threatened. Money is the instrument of policy and policy affects the lives of citizens. The individual loses liberty in a real sense if that instrument is not subject to traditional constitutional constraint....

JUSTICE BREYER, with whom JUSTICE O'CONNOR and JUSTICE SCALIA join as to Part III, dissenting.

.... [T]he Act represents a legislative effort to provide the President with the power to give effect to some, but not to all, of the expenditure and revenue-diminishing provisions contained in a single massive appropriations bill. And this objective is constitutionally proper.

When our Nation was founded, Congress could easily have provided the President with this kind of power. In that time period, our population was less than four million, federal employees numbered fewer than 5,000, annual federal budget outlays totaled approximately $ 4 million, and the entire operative text of Congress's first general appropriations law read as follows:

> Be it enacted ... that there be appropriated for the service of the present year, to be paid out of the monies which arise, either from the requisitions heretofore made upon the several states, or from the duties on import and tonnage, the following sums, viz. A sum not exceeding two hundred and sixteen thousand dollars for defraying the expenses of the civil list, under the late and present government; a sum not exceeding one hundred and thirty-seven thousand dollars for defraying the expenses of the department of war; a sum not exceeding one hundred and ninety thousand dollars for discharging the warrants issued by the late board of treasury, and remaining unsatisfied; and a sum not exceeding ninety-six thousand dollars for paying the pensions to invalids. Act of Sept. 29, 1789, ch. 23, § 1, 1 Stat. 95.

At that time, a Congress, wishing to give a President the power to select among appropriations, could simply have embodied each appropriation in a separate bill, each bill subject to a separate Presidential veto.

Today, however, our population is about 250 million, the Federal Government employs more than four million people, and a typical budget appropriations bill may have a dozen titles, hundreds of sections, and spread across more than 500 pages of the Statutes at Large. Congress cannot divide such a bill into thousands, or tens of thousands, of separate appropriations bills, each one of which the President would have to sign, or to veto, separately. Thus, the question is whether the Constitution permits Congress to choose a particular novel *means* to achieve this same, constitutionally legitimate, *end.*

... [T]he case in part requires us to focus upon the Constitution's generally phrased structural provisions, provisions that delegate all "legislative" power to Congress and vest all "executive" power in the President. The Court, when applying these provisions, has interpreted them generously in terms of the institutional arrangements that they permit.... Indeed, Chief Justice Marshall, in a well-known passage, explained,

> To have prescribed the means by which government should, in all future time, execute its powers, would have been to change, entirely, the character of the instrument, and give it the properties of a legal code. It would have been an unwise attempt to provide, by immutable rules, for exigencies which, if foreseen at all, must have been seen dimly, and which can be best provided for as they occur. McCulloch v. Maryland, 17 U.S. 316, 4 (1819).

This passage, like the cases I have just mentioned, calls attention to the genius of the Framers' pragmatic vision, which this Court has long recognized in cases that find constitutional room for necessary institutional innovation.

... [W]e need not here referee a dispute among the other two branches.... Cf. Youngstown Sheet and Tube Co., 343 U.S. at 635 (Jackson, J., concurring) ("Presidential powers are not fixed but fluctuate, depending on their disjunction or conjunction with those of Congress ... [and when] the President acts pursuant to an express or implied authorization of Congress, his authority is at its maximum").

.... [Thus], when one measures the *literal* words of the Act against the Constitution's *literal* commands, the fact that the Act may closely resemble a different, literally unconstitutional, arrangement is beside the point. To drive exactly 65 miles per hour on an interstate highway closely resembles an act that violates the speed limit. But it does not violate that limit, for small differences matter when the question is one of literal violation of law. No more does this Act literally violate the Constitution's words.

The background circumstances also mean that we are to interpret nonliteral Separation-of-powers principles in light of the need for "workable government." Youngstown Sheet and Tube Co., supra, at 635 (Jackson, J., concurring). If we apply those principles in light of that objective, as this Court has applied them in the past, the Act is constitutional.

III

The Court believes that the Act violates the literal text of the Constitution [because it falsely assumes that the Act authorizes the president to "repeal or amend" laws].... When the President "canceled" the two appropriation measures now before us, he did not *repeal* any law nor did he *amend* any law. He simply *followed* the law, leaving the statutes, as they are literally written, intact.

.... Imagine that the canceled New York health care tax provision at issue here had instead said the following:

> Section One. Taxes ... that were collected by the State of New York from a
> health care provider before June 1, 1997 and for which a waiver of provisions

[requiring payment] have been sought ... are deemed to be permissible health care related taxes ... *provided however that the President may prevent the just-mentioned provision from having legal force or effect if he determines x, y and z.* (Assume x, y and z to be the same determinations required by the Line Item Veto Act).

Whatever a person might say, or think, about the constitutionality of this imaginary law, there is one thing the English language would prevent one from saying. One could not say that a President who "prevents" the deeming language from "having legal force or effect," has either *repealed* or *amended* this particular hypothetical statute. Rather, the President has *followed* that law to the letter. He has exercised the power it explicitly delegates to him. He has executed the law, not repealed it.

It could make no significant difference to this linguistic point were the italicized proviso to appear, not as part of what I have called Section One, but, instead, at the bottom of the statute page, say referenced by an asterisk, with a statement that it applies to every spending provision in the act next to which a similar asterisk appears. And that being so, it could make no difference if that proviso appeared, instead, in a different, earlier-enacted law, along with legal language that makes it applicable to every future spending provision picked out according to a specified formula.

But, of course, this last-mentioned possibility is this very case. The earlier law, namely, the Line Item Veto Act, says that "the President may ... prevent such [future] budget authority from having legal force or effect." .... For that reason, one cannot dispose of this case through a purely literal analysis as the majority does. Literally speaking, the President has not "repealed" or "amended" anything. He has simply *executed* a power conferred upon him by Congress, which power is contained in laws that were enacted in compliance with the exclusive method set forth in the Constitution.

Nor can one dismiss this literal compliance as some kind of formal quibble, as if it were somehow "obvious" that what the President has done "amounts to," "comes close to," or is "analogous to" the repeal or amendment of a previously enacted law. That is because the power the Act grants the President (to render designated appropriations items without "legal force or effect") also "amounts to," "comes close to," or is "analogous to" a different legal animal, the delegation of a power to choose one legal path as opposed to another, such as a power to appoint....

In sum, I recognize that the Act before us is novel. In a sense, it skirts a constitutional edge. But that edge has to do with means, not ends. The means chosen do not amount literally to the enactment, repeal, or amendment of a law. Nor, for that matter, do they amount literally to the "line item veto" that the Act's title announces. Those means do not violate any basic Separation-of-powers principle. They do not improperly shift the constitutionally foreseen balance of power from Congress to the President. Nor, since they comply with Separation-of-powers principles, do they threaten the liberties of individual citizens. They represent an experiment that may, or may not, help representative government work better. The Constitution, in my view, authorizes Congress and the President to try novel methods in this way. Consequently, with respect, I dissent.

JUSTICE SCALIA, with whom JUSTICE O'CONNOR joins ... concurring in part and dissenting in part.

.... Article I, §7 of the Constitution obviously prevents the President from cancelling a law that Congress has not authorized him to cancel. Such action cannot possibly be considered part of his execution of the law.... But that is not this case. It was certainly arguable, as an original matter, that Art. I, §7 also prevents the President from cancelling a law which itself *authorizes* the President to cancel it. But as the Court acknowledges, that argument has long since been made and rejected. In 1809, Congress passed a law authorizing the President to cancel trade restrictions against Great Britain and France if either revoked edicts directed at the United States. Joseph Story regarded the conferral of that authority as entirely unremarkable in The Orono, 18 F. Cas. 830 (CCD Mass. 1812). The Tariff Act of 1890 authorized the President to "suspend, by proclamation to that effect" certain of its provisions if he determined that other countries were imposing "reciprocally unequal and unreasonable" duties. This Court upheld the constitutionality of that Act in Field v. Clark, 143 U.S. 649 (1892), reciting the history since 1798 of statutes conferring upon the President the power to, *inter alia*, "discontinue the prohibitions and restraints hereby enacted and declared," "suspend the operation of the aforesaid act," and "declare the provisions of this act to be inoperative."

... Art. I, §7, therefore, ... no more categorically prohibits the Executive *reduction* of congressional dispositions in the course of implementing statutes that authorize such reduction, than it categorically prohibits the Executive *augmentation* of congressional dispositions in the course of implementing statutes that authorize such augmentation — generally known as substantive rulemaking. There are, to be sure, limits upon the former just as there are limits upon the latter — and I am prepared to acknowledge that the limits upon the former may be much more severe. Those limits are established, however, not by some categorical prohibition of Art. I, §7, which our cases conclusively disprove, but by what has come to be known as the doctrine of unconstitutional delegation of legislative authority: When authorized Executive reduction or augmentation is allowed to go too far, it usurps the nondelegable function of Congress and violates the separation of powers....

Insofar as the degree of political, "law-making" power conferred upon the Executive is concerned, there is not a dime's worth of difference between Congress's authorizing the President to *cancel* a spending item, and Congress's authorizing money to be spent on a particular item at the President's discretion. And the latter has been done since the Founding of the Nation....

Certain Presidents have claimed Executive authority to withhold appropriated funds even *absent* an express conferral of discretion to do so. In 1876, for example, President Grant reported to Congress that he would not spend money appropriated for certain harbor and river improvements, because "under no circumstances [would he] allow expenditures upon works not clearly national," and in his view, the appropriations were for "works of purely private or local interest, in no sense national." President Franklin D. Roosevelt impounded funds appropriated for a flood control reservoir and levee in Oklahoma. President Truman ordered the impoundment of hundreds of millions of dollars that had been appropriated for military aircraft. President Nixon, the Mahatma Ghandi of all impounders, asserted at a press conference in 1973 that his "constitutional right" to impound appropriated funds was "absolutely clear." Our decision two years later in Train v. City of New York, 420 U.S. 35 (1975), proved him wrong, but it implicitly confirmed that Congress may confer discretion upon the executive to withhold appropriated funds, even funds appropriated for a specific purpose.

.... Had the Line Item Veto Act authorized the President to "decline to spend" any item of spending contained in the Balanced Budget Act of 1997, there is not the slightest doubt that authorization would have been constitutional. What the Line Item Veto Act does instead — authorizing the President to "cancel" an item of spending — is technically different. But the technical difference does *not* relate to the technicalities of the Presentment Clause, which have been fully complied with; and the doctrine of unconstitutional delegation, which *is* at issue here, is preeminently *not* a doctrine of technicalities. The title of the Line

Item Veto Act, which was perhaps designed to simplify for public comprehension, or perhaps merely to comply with the terms of a campaign pledge, has succeeded in faking out the Supreme Court. The President's action it authorizes in fact is not a line-item veto and thus does not offend Art. I, §7; and insofar as the substance of that action is concerned, it is no different from what Congress has permitted the President.

Review Questions and Explanations: *Clinton v. City of New York*

1. What is the basic constitutional problem with the Act? Note that there is no legislative veto issue here. The discretionary authority of the President to "cancel" a spending provision can, to be sure, be "nullified" by a joint resolution of Congress — which sounds like a legislative veto. But then the Court says the President "does, of course, retain his constitutional authority to veto such a [dis-approval] bill." If the President were to veto a disapproval bill, his "line item veto" would stand — which brings us right back to the original problem: is the line item veto unconstitutional?

2. Which argument do you find more persuasive, the majority opinion, or the Breyer or Scalia dissents? Before answering this question, it may be worth breaking the arguments down a bit. The majority argues that (1) cancelling a spending item, and thereby nullifying part of a law, rewrites the law and is therefore an exercise of legislative power that can't be delegated to the President; and (2) cancelling a spending item is not the same as acting under a legislative grant of discretion to decline to spend appropriated money, because it rewrites the text of a law.

Scalia and Breyer, in contrast, argue that (1) Art. I, §7 does not prohibit this type of delegation. Breyer then argues that (2) cancelling a spending item is not the same as acting under a legislative grant of discretion; and Scalia argues that (2) cancelling a spending item is virtually the same as acting under a legislative grant of discretion, and any difference is a question of whether too much discretion has been delegated, not whether the process for enacting laws has been complied with. And delegation, Scalia argues, is a highly flexible doctrine.

3. Consider Justice Breyer's hypothetical scenarios about spending laws that authorized the President to decline to spend the funds, at the beginning of section III of his dissent. He says these hypotheticals are all constitutional — are they? — and that the last one "is this very case." Is it? If those hypothetical laws are problematic, why are they? Is it because they somehow evade Art. I, §7, or because they give the President too much discretion?

4. Who is being formalistic and who functionalistic in this case? Do you find any inconsistency in judges switching from formalist to functionalist modes? Only Justices O'Connor, Rehnquist and Stevens were on the *Chadha* Court, but many of the *Clinton* justices were involved in cases involving formalist v. functionalist disputes over separation-of-powers questions, such as *Morrison v. Olson* (Chapter 3) and *Mistretta v. United States* (section C of this chapter).

Recap: *Chadha* and *Clinton v. New York*

1. Could the Line Item Veto Act have been upheld in *Clinton* without overruling *Chadha*?

2. Could we say that neither Congress nor the President were aggrandizing their power at the expense of the other (or of the Judiciary, for that matter) in either *Chadha* or *Clinton*? In *Chadha*, Congress was asserting a legislative (one-house) veto, but the alternative might well be to remove discretion from the executive entirely, or to provide that no deportations can become final unless Congress passes an approval bill (for the President's signature). In *Clinton*, the arrangement was plainly one of power-sharing: the President gained a line-item veto (more power), but Congress *authorized* that power. It seems that presidents and congresses have both been content with both the legislative and line-item vetoes. So what is the problem?

3. Can Congress pass a law giving the President discretion not to enforce some prior law on the books? Why or why not?

Exercise: *Chadha* and *Clinton v. New York*

Suppose Congress enacts a law called the Compassionate Drug Policy Act (CDPA). It authorizes the President or his designee to "suspend for a definite time or permanently repeal the Controlled Substances Act (CSA) to the extent, and only to the extent, that the CSA operates to criminalize the use or possession of marijuana for medical purposes, in any state (1) where the laws of that state legalize the use or possession of marijuana for medical purposes; and (2) as to which the President makes express written findings that such suspension or repeal of the CSA will not result in a substantial increase in otherwise illegal recreational use or possession of marijuana."

The President issues an executive order directing the Secretary of Health and Human Services and the U.S. Attorney General to issue regulations implementing a permanent repeal of the CSA in Colorado and a 5-year suspension of the CSA in California, to permit (only) use and possession of marijuana for medical purposes, after making the requisite findings.

The governor of Utah wishes to file a lawsuit against the Secretary of HHS and the U.S. Attorney General seeking declaratory and injunctive relief to rescind the suspension and repeal on the grounds that they are unconstitutional. The basic theory is that the suspension of the CSA will result in increased illegal drug traffic spilling over into Utah.

With one or more fellow students, assume the roles of attorneys for Utah and for the United States. For Utah, draft a short complaint. For the United States, draft the outline (in a page of prose or a bullet-point outline) of a motion to dismiss. For Utah, do the same for your opposition to the motion to dismiss. Try arguing the motion before one or more fellow students acting as district court judge or panel of appellate judges. (For purposes of this exercise, you should set aside questions about standing.)

[Note: This problem also raises a question under the "nondelegation doctrine." You could also try it after reading section B.1, "The Nondelegation Doctrine" or the *Mistretta* case in section C.]

C. The Administrative State

As you now know quite well, the Constitution vests "All legislative powers herein granted" in Congress (Art. I, § 1), "the executive power" in the President (Art. II, § 1, cl. 1), and "the judicial power" in the so-called Article III courts, "one Supreme Court and such inferior courts as Congress shall from time to time ordain and establish." Art. III, § 1, cl. 1.) Some of the more formalistic Supreme Court opinions seem to suggest that these powers are entirely distinct, *see, e.g., Youngstown Sheet & Tube v. Sawyer*, 343 U.S. 579, 588 (1952) (per Black, J.) ("the President's power to see that the laws are faithfully executed refutes the idea that he is to be a lawmaker"), while the less formalistic opinions admit "a hermetic sealing off of the three branches of Government from one another would preclude the establishment of a Nation capable of governing itself effectively." *Buckley v. Valeo*, 424 U.S. 1, 121 (1976); *see Youngstown Sheet & Tube v. Sawyer*, 343 U.S. 579, 588 (1952) (Jackson, J., concurring).

The basic idea of separated and divided powers neither describes nor accounts for the operations of the federal bureaucracy, sometimes referred to as the "administrative state." In 2006, there were approximately 2.7 million civilian federal government employees, of whom 97.6% worked in the executive branch.[2] If these federal employees were all engaged in "purely executive functions," assisting the President to "faithfully execute the laws," there might be no separation-of-powers issues raised by the administrative state. But things are not that simple, and the administrative state raises several perplexing separation-of-powers questions.

We can readily identify two broad sets of such questions. The first is that of locating the administrative agency within the branches of government; and the second is that of identifying and categorizing the functions performed. We considered the first set of questions in the previous chapter, under the headings of "appointment" and "removal." The cases involving those issues go some distance toward telling us what branch of government the administrative function has been located in. We have seen that the *Humphrey's Executor* case, for example, which upheld significant statutory limitations on the President's power to remove a federal officer, is viewed as providing the constitutional basis for so-called independent administrative agencies, not located clearly in any of the three branches.

In this section of this chapter, we will look at the second set of questions, those going to function. Using the Constitution's division of functions into legislative, executive and judicial, what is striking about the administrative state is how plainly and frequently all three functions are assigned by statute to officials in executive departments and independent administrative agencies. Administrative, investigative, and prosecutorial tasks are seemingly

---

2. U.S. Office of Personnel Management, Federal Civilian Workforce Statistics Fact Book 8 (2007), http://www.opm.gov/feddata/factbook/. Another approximately 1.4 million are on active duty in the armed forces. See http://www.usa.gov/Federal-Employees/Active-Military-Records.shtml#Data_and_Statistics.

unproblematic when assigned to executive branch officials, because they fit readily within our understanding of executive power. But executive branch officials and independent administrative agencies are also statutorily assigned lawmaking and judicial tasks. One of the most commonly assigned functions is that of "agency rulemaking," a process by which administrative agencies produce written rules and regulations fleshing out the details of statutes enacted by Congress. Such regulations have the force of law (and even preempt state law—see *Geier v. American Honda*, Chapter 2). In addition, Congress by statute has created numerous administrative hearing procedures of a plainly "judicial" character, in which disputed questions of fact and law in individual cases are decided by an "administrative law judge" based on (typically) adversarial presentation of evidence by the affected parties.

Much of an upper-level course on Administrative Law is occupied with the details about how administrative agencies (both those inside and outside the executive branch) perform these various functions. For present purposes, we are concerned with the separation-of-powers questions raised by laws that assign legislative, executive and judicial functions to other branches. How is it, for example, that separation-of-powers doctrine permits executive agencies to carry out lawmaking and adjudicative functions?

The assignment of legislative functions to the executive or judicial branch is typically analyzed as a question of delegation of legislative power under the so-called "nondelegation" doctrine. In another line of cases, the Supreme Court has considered challenges to the assignment of judicial functions to non-Article III courts.

1. Administrative Lawmaking Power: The Nondelegation Doctrine

Constitutional law does not—indeed cannot—prohibit all delegations of discretion by Congress to the executive branch.

> [A] certain degree of discretion, and thus of lawmaking, *inheres* in most executive or judicial action, and it is up to Congress, by the relative specificity or generality of its statutory commands, to determine—up to a point—how small or how large that degree shall be.

Mistretta v. United States, 488 U.S. 361 (1989) (Scalia, J., dissenting). The "nondelegation doctrine" is a rule asserting that there are limits on the extent to which Congress can delegate discretion to the executive branch to enforce a law. If those limits are exceeded, then Congress has unconstitutionally delegated its legislative power.

But the Court has struggled to distinguish "the delegation of power to make the law, which necessarily involves a discretion as to what it shall be, and conferring authority or discretion as to its execution, to be exercised under and in pursuance of the law." *Panama Refining Co. v. Ryan*, 293 U.S. 388 (1935). The line is so difficult to draw that the Court has only twice held that an act of Congress delegated excessive discretion to the executive. Both cases involved challenges to the National Industrial Recovery Act, a major piece of legislation enacted in the first 100 days of President Franklin Roosevelt's administration. The Act was designed to combat deflation, the steady depressing of prices and wages due to overproduction and cost-cutting competition, which was seen as a major contributor to the ongoing Great Depression. In *Panama Refining*, an eight-justice majority of the Court struck down a law authorizing the President to impose federal penalties on producers and shippers of "hot oil," that is, refined oil that exceeded state law limitations on oil production and shipment:

> Undoubtedly legislation must often be adapted to complex conditions involving a host of details with which the national legislature cannot deal directly. The Constitution has never been regarded as denying to the Congress the necessary resources of flexibility and practicality, which will enable it to perform its function in laying down policies and establishing standards, while leaving to selected instrumentalities the making of subordinate rules within prescribed limits and the determination of facts to which the policy as declared by the legislature is to apply.... But the constant recognition of the necessity and validity of such provisions, and the wide range of administrative authority which has been developed by means of them, cannot be allowed to obscure the limitations of the authority to delegate, if our constitutional system is to be maintained....

> .... As to the transportation of oil production in excess of state permission, the Congress has declared no policy, has established no standard, has laid down no rule. There is no requirement, no definition of circumstances and conditions in which the transportation is to be allowed or prohibited.

> .... To hold that [the President] is free to select as he chooses from the many and various objects generally described in the [statute], and then to act without making any finding with respect to any object that he does select, and the circumstances properly related to that object, would be in effect to make the conditions inoperative and to invest him with an uncontrolled legislative power.

Later the same year, in *A. L. A. Schechter Poultry Corp. v. United States*, 295 U.S. 495 (1935), the Court unanimously struck down NIRA provisions authorizing the President to create codes of fair competition upon recommendation of trade commissions on any matter within Congress's commerce power. (*Schechter* is excerpted in Chapter 1 for its Commerce Clause ruling.)

Note that both cases were decided at the height of the Supreme Court's resistance to the Roosevelt administration's domestic agenda. (*Schechter*, *Carter Coal* and *Humphreys' Executor* are all examples of the Court's rulings against such policies.) To the extent that *Panama Refining* sets out a standard for delegation at all, it is not clear how strictly the modern Court would adhere to it. Nevertheless, the nondelegation doctrine at a minimum stands as an outer limit to delegations of legislative power that the Court could, in theory, invoke to strike down "delegation running riot." *Schechter*, 295 U.S. at 552 (Cardozo, J., concurring).

2. Non-Article III Adjudicatory Power

The nondelegation doctrine examined in the previous section deals with the limits on the constitutional authority of Congress to delegate *legislative* functions to another branch, in the form of authorizing rule-making or broad interpretive discretion that may resemble the making of law.

What about Congress's power to assign *judicial* functions to a branch other than the Article III judiciary? The leading case in this area is *Crowell v. Benson*, 285 U.S. 22 (1932). There, the Court rejected a constitutional challenge by an employer to an administrative agency determination that an employee was entitled to an award under a federal workers' compensation statute. The challenger asserted that permitting an administrative agency to adjudicate such claims violated Article III by assigning judicial power to a non-Article III tribunal. The Court recognized the power of Congress to "establish 'legislative' courts (as distinguished from 'constitutional courts in which the judicial power conferred by the Constitution can be deposited')[.]" These Courts were permissible to adjudicate claims based on "public rights," defined as "matters, arising between the government and others, which from their nature do not require judicial determination and yet are susceptible of it." The immediate case, however, was "one of private right, that is, of the liability of one individual to another under the law as defined." But the Court went on to hold that it was constitutionally permissible to authorize administrative or "legislative" courts to make factual findings in "private rights" cases so long as a federal district court had "de novo" judicial review of questions of law and questions of fact going to the jurisdiction of the administrative agency. ("De novo" judicial review here meant review without restriction, in which a district court can redo the factfinding from scratch). Three justices dissented, arguing that the administrative agency should have the authority to make binding determinations on all factual questions, subject only to *appellate* review (which does not permit "de novo" review of factual findings). Thus, all nine justices agreed that legislative courts were permissible at least to some extent.

Crowell is viewed as a foundational case for the administrative state. It stands for the basic proposition that the assignment by Congress of adjudicatory powers to administrative tribunals and other legislative courts (e.g., bankruptcy courts) is, within limits, constitutional. What those limits are precisely is a question that has evolved over time; the details are covered in an Administrative Law course.

CASE NOTE: The Bankruptcy Court cases. The "bankruptcy clause" of the Constitution, Article I, § 8, cl. 4, empowers Congress "to establish … uniform laws on the subject of bankruptcies throughout the United States." Before 1978, federal district courts served as bankruptcy courts and appointed bankruptcy experts to act as "referees" or hearing officers, who would issue rulings that were fully appealable de novo to the district court. Congress comprehensively revised the bankruptcy system in 1978 to eliminate the referee system and establish "in each judicial district, as an adjunct to the district court for such district, a bankruptcy court which shall be a court of record known as the United States Bankruptcy Court for the district." Judges of the bankruptcy courts are appointed by the courts of appeals for the circuits in which their districts are located, and subject to removal by the "judicial council of the circuit" on account of "incompetency, misconduct, neglect of duty or physical or mental disability." In addition, the salaries of the bankruptcy judges are set by statute. Review by Article III courts is limited to appellate jurisdiction (i.e., excluding de novo review of factual findings).

It is undisputed that bankruptcy courts are not Article III courts, primarily because the bankruptcy judges lack the life tenure and salary protection of federal judges. The question becomes what kinds of matters bankruptcy judges can decide. While claims arising directly under the bankruptcy laws have been deemed "public rights" within the meaning of *Crowell v. Benson*, and thus delegable to a "legislative" court system like the bankruptcy courts, questions persist about "private rights" claims that are related to bankruptcy proceedings. The Supreme Court has addressed this particular issue twice.

In 1982, in *Northern Pipeline Construction Co. v. Marathon Pipe Line Co.*, 458 U.S. 50 (1982), six justices agreed that the 1978 Bankruptcy Act's authorization to the bankruptcy courts to decide state common law damages claims that "related to" a bankruptcy violated

Article III. There was no majority rationale: a four-justice plurality reasoned that Article III generally prohibited the assignment of judicial power to a non-Article III court, with three exceptions: courts in U.S. territories; military courts; and, citing *Crowell v. Benson,* claims involving "public rights." A state common-law damages claim was one of private, not public rights, the Court concluded.

More recently, in *Stern v. Marshall,* 131 S. Ct. 2594 (2011), the Court considered whether "private rights" cases could be fully adjudicated by a bankruptcy court if they were "core" proceedings—cases not merely "related to," but inextricably intertwined with the bankruptcy case. *Stern* arose out of a dispute between Vickie Lynn Marshall (known to the public as Anna Nicole Smith) and E. Pierce Marshall over the fortune of J. Howard Marshall II, a man believed to have been one of the richest people in Texas. Before J. Howard passed away, Vickie had filed suit in Texas state probate court, asserting that Pierce—J. Howard's younger son—fraudulently induced J. Howard to sign a living trust that did not include her, even though J. Howard meant to give her half his property. After J. Howard's death, Vickie petitioned for bankruptcy. In that bankruptcy proceeding, Pierce filed a complaint contending that Vickie had defamed him by her fraud charge. Vickie responded to Pierce's complaint by filing a counterclaim for tortious interference with the gift she expected from J. Howard. The bankruptcy court issued a judgment on Vickie's counterclaim in her favor for over $425 million.

In post-trial proceedings, Pierce argued that the Bankruptcy Court lacked jurisdiction over Vickie's counterclaim. A five-justice majority of the Supreme Court agreed. In an opinion by Chief Justice Roberts, the Court held that although Vickie's counterclaim was indeed a "core proceeding," it was nevertheless a "private right" that could not be delegated to a non-Article III court for a binding adjudication:

> Article III is "an inseparable element of the constitutional system of checks and balances" that "both defines the power and protects the independence of the Judicial Branch." ...

> Vickie's counterclaim cannot be deemed a matter of "public right" that can be decided outside the Judicial Branch. ... [W]hat makes a right "public" rather than private is that the right is integrally related to particular federal government action. ... Vickie's counterclaim ... does not fall within any of the varied formulations of the public rights exception in this Court's cases.

> ... [T]his case involves the most prototypical exercise of judicial power: the entry of a final, binding judgment *by a court* with broad substantive jurisdiction, on a common law cause of action, when the action neither derives from nor depends upon any agency regulatory regime. If such an exercise of judicial power may nonetheless be taken from the Article III Judiciary simply by deeming it part of some amorphous "public right," then Article III would be transformed from the guardian of individual liberty and separation of powers we have long recognized into mere wishful thinking. ...

In dissent, Justice Breyer (joined by Justices Ginsburg, Sotomayor, and Kagan) argued that the delegation of compulsory state-law counterclaims to bankruptcy courts was supported by a flexible approach derived from several cases upholding non-Article III courts, based on balancing several factors, including 1) the risk of encroachment on the Federal Judiciary; 2) the nature of the non-Article III tribunal; 3) the control exercised by Article III judges over the non-Article III proceedings; 4) whether the parties have consented to non-Article III court jurisdiction; and 5) the nature and importance of the legislative purpose served by the non-Article III court. The dissenters observed that the 1.6 million bankruptcy cases filed each year very typically involve numerous compulsory counterclaims:

> Consider a typical case: A tenant files for bankruptcy. The landlord files a claim for unpaid rent. The tenant asserts a counterclaim for damages suffered by the landlord's (1) failing to fulfill his obligations as lessor, and (2) improperly recovering possession of the premises by misrepresenting the facts in housing court.

The dissenters argued that requiring federal district courts, rather than bankruptcy courts, to hear such matters, will bog down federal courts and lead to "increased cost, delay, and needless additional suffering among those faced with bankruptcy."

3. Synthesis: Delegation of Legislative and Judicial Power

The next case combines principles from the prior two sub-sections. Specifically, the constitutionality of the U.S. Sentencing Commission was challenged on the grounds that Congress had *both* improperly delegated legislative functions outside the legislative branch, *and* had intruded on the Article III judicial power.

Guided Reading Questions: *Mistretta v. United States*

1. What is the basis of the argument that the nondelegation doctrine has been violated, and how does the majority answer it? Does the dissent disagree?

2. To address the separation-of-powers challenge—the argument that Article III power has been intruded upon—the majority first considers the "location" of the Commission. Why is there a need to fix the Commission's location and how does the Court decide where in the three branches it is located?

3. What sort of powers does the majority say the Commission is exercising?

4. The rest of the separation-of-powers analysis considers two further questions: (a) whether it is proper for judges to serve on the Commission given the tasks it is assigned to perform (a question that seems to overlap or even repeat the "location" part of the opinion); and (b) whether the judges' Article III power is diminished by serving on a politically appointed body that is not a court. What are the Court's answers?

5. Justice Scalia's dissent is worth careful study. What sort of power does he assume is exercised by the Sentencing Commission—legislative, executive, or judicial? Does he maintain this assumption consistently throughout his dissent, or does he subtly change grounds?

Mistretta v. United States

488 U.S. 361 (1989)

Majority: *Blackmun*, Rehnquist (CJ), White, Marshall, Stevens, O'Connor, Kennedy, Brennan

Dissent: *Scalia*

JUSTICE BLACKMUN delivered the opinion of the Court.

[This litigation considered a constitutional challenge to the United States Sentencing Commission, created under the Sentencing Reform Act of 1984. The Commission was assigned by the Act to study federal sentencing policies and practices and to promulgate a set of federal sentencing guidelines that would be binding on federal courts in criminal cases. The Commission issued the Federal Sentencing Guidelines, which were formally adopted in 1987. These replaced a century-old system of "indeterminate sentencing," under which criminal statutes authorized judges to decide the length of a prison term within a wide range of discretion, and whether to impose probation instead of imprisonment or fine. Increasing dissatisfaction and criticism of indeterminate sentencing focused on two sets of issues: (1) inconsistency or disparity in sentences for similar offenders and offenses, due to wide variation in practice by individual judges; and (2) a lack of transparency or "truth" in sentencing, insofar as nominally lengthy sentences tended in practice to be cut significantly short by early release on parole. The Sentencing Guidelines are far more determinate than sentences under the "indeterminate" system, providing narrow ranges of sentencing discretion and spelling out limited factors that allow departures from the Guidelines. Sentences can be reversed for failing to conform to the Guidelines.]

Historically, federal sentencing—the function of determining the scope and extent of punishment—never has been thought to be assigned by the Constitution to the exclusive jurisdiction of any one of the three Branches of Government. Congress, of course, has the power to fix the sentence for a federal crime, and the scope of judicial discretion with respect to a sentence is subject to congressional control. Congress early abandoned fixed-sentence rigidity, however, and put in place a system of ranges within which the sentencer could choose the precise punishment. Congress delegated almost unfettered discretion to the sentencing judge to determine what the sentence should be within the customarily wide range so selected. This broad discretion was further enhanced by the power later granted the judge to suspend the sentence and by the resulting growth of an elaborate probation system. Also, with the advent of parole, Congress moved toward a "three-way sharing" of sentencing responsibility by granting corrections personnel in the Executive Branch the discretion to release a prisoner before the expiration of the sentence imposed by the judge. Thus, under the indeterminate-sentence system, Congress defined the maximum, the judge imposed a sentence within the statutory range (which he usually could replace with probation), and the Executive Branch's parole official eventually determined the actual duration of imprisonment....

[The Sentencing Commission] is established "as an independent commission in the judicial branch of the United States." § 991(a). It has seven voting members (one of whom is the Chairman) appointed by the President "by and with the advice and consent of the Senate." "At least three of the members shall be Federal judges selected after considering a list of six judges recommended to the President by the Judicial Conference of the United

States." No more than four members of the Commission shall be members of the same political party. The Attorney General, or his designee, is an ex officio nonvoting member. The Chairman and other members of the Commission are subject to removal by the President "only for neglect of duty or malfeasance in office or for other good cause shown." Ibid. Except for initial staggering of terms, a voting member serves for six years and may not serve more than two full terms. §§ 992(a) and (b)....

[Petitioner John M. Mistretta pleaded guilty to federal charges for selling cocaine, but challenged his sentence on the grounds that the Sentencing Commission and Guidelines were unconstitutional. The district court rejected the arguments and imposed sentence. The Supreme Court granted certiorari before judgment in the Court of Appeals because of the "imperative public importance" of resolving "disarray among the Federal District Courts."]

Petitioner argues that in delegating the power to promulgate sentencing guidelines for every federal criminal offense to an independent Sentencing Commission, Congress has granted the Commission excessive legislative discretion in violation of the constitutionally based nondelegation doctrine. We do not agree.

The nondelegation doctrine is rooted in the principle of separation of powers that underlies our tripartite system of Government. The Constitution provides that "[a]ll legislative Powers herein granted shall be vested in a Congress of the United States," U.S. Const., Art. I, § 1, and we long have insisted that "the integrity and maintenance of the system of government ordained by the Constitution" mandate that Congress generally cannot delegate its legislative power to another Branch. We also have recognized, however, that the separation-of-powers principle, and the nondelegation doctrine in particular, do not prevent Congress from obtaining the assistance of its coordinate Branches. In a passage now enshrined in our jurisprudence, Chief Justice Taft, writing for the Court, explained our approach to such cooperative ventures: "In determining what [Congress] may do in seeking assistance from another branch, the extent and character of that assistance must be fixed according to common sense and the inherent necessities of the government co-ordination." J. W. Hampton, Jr., & Co. v. United States, 276 U.S. 394, 406 (1928). So long as Congress "shall lay down by legislative act an intelligible principle to which the person or body authorized to [exercise the delegated authority] is directed to conform, such legislative action is not a forbidden delegation of legislative power." Id., at 409.

Applying this "intelligible principle" test to congressional delegations, our jurisprudence has been driven by a practical understanding that in our increasingly complex society, replete with ever changing and more technical problems, Congress simply cannot do its job absent an ability to delegate power under broad general directives. "The Constitution has never been regarded as denying to the Congress the necessary resources of flexibility and practicality, which will enable it to perform its function." Panama Refining Co. v. Ryan, 293 U.S. 388, 421 (1935). Accordingly, this Court has deemed it "constitutionally sufficient if Congress clearly delineates the general policy, the public agency which is to apply it, and the boundaries of this delegated authority." American Power & Light Co. v. SEC, 329 U.S. 90, 105 (1946).

Until 1935, this Court never struck down a challenged statute on delegation grounds. After invalidating in 1935 two statutes as excessive delegations, see A. L. A. Schechter Poultry Corp. v. United States, 295 U.S. 495, and Panama Refining Co. v. Ryan, supra, we have upheld, again without deviation, Congress' ability to delegate power under broad standards.

In light of our approval of these broad delegations, we harbor no doubt that Congress' delegation of authority to the Sentencing Commission is sufficiently specific and detailed to meet constitutional requirements. Congress charged the Commission with three goals: to "assure the meeting of the purposes of sentencing as set forth" in the Act; to "provide certainty and fairness in meeting the purposes of sentencing, avoiding unwarranted sentencing disparities among defendants with similar records ... while maintaining sufficient flexibility to permit individualized sentences," where appropriate; and to "reflect, to the extent practicable, advancement in knowledge of human behavior as it relates to the criminal justice process." 28 U. S. C. § 991(b)(1). Congress further specified four "purposes" of sentencing that the Commission must pursue in carrying out its mandate: "to reflect the seriousness of the offense, to promote respect for the law, and to provide just punishment for the offense"; "to afford adequate deterrence to criminal conduct"; "to protect the public from further crimes of the defendant"; and "to provide the defendant with needed ... correctional treatment." 18 U. S. C. § 3553(a)(2).

In addition, Congress prescribed the specific tool—the guidelines system—for the Commission to use in regulating sentencing. More particularly, Congress directed the Commission to develop a system of "sentencing ranges" applicable "for each category of offense involving each category of defendant." 28 U. S. C. § 994(b). Congress instructed the Commission that these sentencing ranges must be consistent with pertinent provisions of Title 18 of the United States Code and could not include sentences in excess of the statutory maxima. Congress also required that for sentences of imprisonment, "the maximum of the range established for such a term shall not exceed the minimum of that range by more than the greater of 25 percent or 6 months, except that, if the minimum term of the range is 30 years or more, the maximum may be life imprisonment." § 994(b)(2). Moreover, Congress directed the Commission to use current average sentences "as a starting point" for its structuring of the sentencing ranges. § 994(m).

To guide the Commission in its formulation of offense categories, Congress directed it to consider seven factors: the grade of the offense; the aggravating and mitigating circumstances of the crime; the nature and degree of the harm caused by the crime; the community view of the gravity of the offense; the public concern generated by the crime; the deterrent effect that a particular sentence may have on others; and the current incidence of the offense. §§ 994(c)(1)–(7). Congress set forth 11 factors for the Commission to consider in establishing categories of defendants. These include the offender's age, education, vocational skills, mental and emotional condition, physical condition (including drug dependence), previous employment record, family ties and responsibilities, community ties, role in the offense, criminal history, and degree of dependence upon crime for a livelihood. § 994(d)(1)–(11). Congress also prohibited the Commission from considering the "race, sex, national origin, creed, and socioeconomic status of offenders," § 994(d), and instructed that the guidelines should reflect the "general inappropriateness" of considering certain other factors, such as current unemployment, that might serve as proxies for forbidden factors, § 994(e).

In addition to these overarching constraints, Congress provided even more detailed guidance to the Commission about categories of offenses and offender characteristics. Congress directed that guidelines require a term of confinement at or near the statutory maximum for certain crimes of violence and for drug offenses, particularly when committed by recidivists. § 994(h). Congress further directed that the Commission assure a substantial term of imprisonment for an offense constituting a third felony conviction, for a career felon, for one convicted of a managerial role in a racketeering enterprise, for a crime of violence by an offender on release from a prior felony conviction, and for an offense involving a substantial quantity of narcotics. § 994(i). Congress also instructed "that the guidelines reflect ... the general appropriateness of imposing a term of imprisonment" for a crime of violence that resulted in serious bodily injury. On the other hand, Congress directed that guidelines reflect the general inappropriateness of imposing a sentence of imprisonment "in cases in which the defendant is a first offender who has not been convicted of a crime of violence or an otherwise serious offense." §994(j). Congress also enumerated various aggravating and mitigating circumstances, such as, respectively, multiple offenses or substantial assistance to the Government, to be reflected in the guidelines. §§994(l) and (n). In other words, although Congress granted the Commission substantial discretion in formulating guidelines, in actuality it legislated a full hierarchy of punishment—from near maximum imprisonment, to substantial imprisonment, to some imprisonment, to alternatives—and stipulated the most important offense and offender characteristics to place defendants within these categories.

We cannot dispute petitioner's contention that the Commission enjoys significant discretion in formulating guidelines. The Commission does have discretionary authority to determine the relative severity of federal crimes and to assess the relative weight of the offender characteristics that Congress listed for the Commission to consider. The Commission also has significant discretion to determine which crimes have been punished too leniently, and which too severely. Congress has called upon the Commission to exercise its judgment about which types of crimes and which types of criminals are to be considered similar for the purposes of sentencing.

But our cases do not at all suggest that delegations of this type may not carry with them the need to exercise judgment on matters of policy.... :

> It is no objection that the determination of facts and the inferences to be drawn from them in the light of the statutory standards and declaration of policy call for the exercise of judgment, and for the formulation of subsidiary administrative policy within the prescribed statutory framework.... Only if we could say that there is an absence of standards for the guidance of the Administrator's action, so that it would be impossible in a proper proceeding to ascertain whether the will of Congress has been obeyed, would we be justified in overriding its choice of means for effecting its declared purpose.... Yakus v. United States, 321 U.S., at 425–426.

Congress has met that standard here. The Act sets forth more than merely an "intelligible principle" or minimal standards. One court has aptly put it: "The statute outlines the policies which prompted establishment of the Commission, explains what the Commission should do and how it should do it, and sets out specific directives to govern particular situations."

Developing proportionate penalties for hundreds of different crimes by a virtually limitless array of offenders is precisely the sort of intricate, labor-intensive task for which delegation to an expert body is especially appropriate. Although Congress has delegated significant discretion to the Commission to draw judgments from its analysis of existing sentencing practice and alternative sentencing models, "Congress is not confined to that method of executing its policy which involves the least possible delegation of discretion to administrative officers." We have no doubt that in the hands of the Commission "the criteria which Congress has supplied are wholly adequate for carrying out the general policy and purpose" of the Act.

... [W]e turn to Mistretta's claim that the Act violates the constitutional principle of separation of powers.

This Court consistently has given voice to, and has reaffirmed, the central judgment of the Framers of the Constitution that, within our political scheme, the separation of governmental powers into three coordinate Branches is essential to the preservation of liberty. Madison, in writing about the principle of separated powers, said: "No political truth is certainly of greater intrinsic value or is stamped with the authority of more enlightened patrons of liberty." The Federalist No. 47, p. 324 (J. Cooke ed. 1961).

... [W]hile our Constitution mandates that "each of the three general departments of government [must remain] entirely free from the control or coercive influence, direct or indirect, of either of the others," Humphrey's Executor v. United States, 295 U.S. 602, 629 (1935), the Framers did not require—and indeed rejected—the notion that the three Branches must be entirely separate and distinct.... Madison recognized that our constitutional system imposes upon the Branches a degree of overlapping responsibility, a duty of interdependence as well as independence the absence of which "would preclude the establishment of a Nation capable of governing itself effectively." Buckley v. Valeo, 424 U.S. 1, 121 (1976). In a passage now commonplace in our cases, Justice Jackson summarized the pragmatic, flexible view of differentiated governmental power to which we are heir:

> While the Constitution diffuses power the better to secure liberty, it also contemplates that practice will integrate the dispersed powers into a workable government. It enjoins upon its branches separateness but interdependence, autonomy but reciprocity. Youngstown Sheet & Tube Co. v. Sawyer, 343 U.S. 579, 635 (1952) (concurring opinion).

In adopting this flexible understanding of separation of powers, we simply have recognized Madison's teaching that the greatest security against tyranny—the accumulation of excessive authority in a single Branch—lies not in a hermetic division among the Branches, but in a carefully crafted system of checked and balanced power within each Branch....

It is this concern of encroachment and aggrandizement that has animated our separation-of-powers jurisprudence and aroused our vigilance against the "hydraulic pressure inherent within each of the separate Branches to exceed the outer limits of its power." INS v. Chadha, 462 U.S. 919, 951 (1983). Accordingly, we have not hesitated to strike down provisions of law that either accrete to a single Branch powers more appropriately diffused among separate Branches or that undermine the authority and independence of one or another coordinate Branch.... By the same token, we have upheld statutory provisions that to some degree commingle the functions of the Branches, but that pose no danger of either aggrandizement or encroachment. Morrison v. Olson, 487 U.S. 654 (1988) (upholding judicial appointment of independent counsel); Commodity Futures Trading Comm'n v. Schor, 478 U.S. 833 (1986) (upholding agency's assumption of jurisdiction over state-law counterclaims).

In Nixon v. Administrator of General Services, supra, upholding, against a separation-of-powers challenge, legislation providing for the General Services Administration to control Presidential papers after resignation, we described our separation-of-powers inquiry as focusing "on the extent to which [a provision of law] prevents the Executive Branch from accomplishing its constitutionally assigned functions." 433 U.S., at 443. In cases specifically involving the Judicial Branch, we have expressed our vigilance against two dangers: first, that the Judicial Branch neither be assigned nor allowed "tasks that are more properly accomplished by [other] branches," Morrison v. Olson, 487 U.S., at 680–681, and, second, that no provision of law "impermissibly threatens the institutional integrity of the Judicial Branch." Commodity Futures Trading Comm'n v. Schor, 478 U.S., at 851.

Mistretta argues.... that in delegating to an independent agency within the Judicial Branch the power to promulgate sentencing guidelines, Congress unconstitutionally has required the Branch, and individual Article III judges, to exercise not only their judicial authority, but legislative authority—the making of sentencing policy—as well. Such rulemaking authority, petitioner contends, may be exercised by Congress, or delegated by Congress to the Executive, but may not be delegated to or exercised by the Judiciary.

At the same time, petitioner asserts, Congress unconstitutionally eroded the integrity and independence of the Judiciary by.... by co-opting federal judges into the quintessentially political work of establishing sentencing guidelines, by subjecting those judges to the political whims of the Chief Executive, and by forcing judges to share their power with nonjudges.

.... Although the unique composition and responsibilities of the Sentencing Commission give rise to serious concerns about a disruption of the appropriate balance of governmental power among the coordinate Branches, we conclude, upon close inspection, that petitioner's fears for the fundamental structural protections of the Constitution prove, at least in this case, to be "more smoke than fire," and do not compel us to invalidate Congress' considered scheme for resolving the seemingly intractable dilemma of excessive disparity in criminal sentencing....

The Sentencing Commission unquestionably is a peculiar institution within the framework of our Government. Although placed by the Act in the Judicial Branch, it is not a court and does not exercise judicial power. Rather, the Commission is an "independent" body comprised of seven voting members including at least three federal judges, entrusted by Congress with the primary task of promulgating sentencing guidelines. Our constitutional principles of separated powers are not violated, however, by mere anomaly or innovation. Setting to one side, for the moment, the question whether the composition of the Sentencing Commission violates the separation of powers, we observe that Congress' decision to create an independent rulemaking body to promulgate sentencing guidelines and to locate that body within the Judicial Branch is not unconstitutional unless Congress has vested in the Commission powers that are more appropriately performed by the other Branches or that undermine the integrity of the Judiciary.

According to express provision of Article III, the judicial power of the United States is limited to "Cases" and "Controversies." In implementing this limited grant of power, we have refused to issue advisory opinions or to resolve disputes that are not justiciable. These doctrines help to ensure the independence of the Judicial Branch by precluding debilitating entanglements between the Judiciary and the two political Branches, and prevent the Judiciary from encroaching into areas reserved for the other Branches by extending judicial power to matters beyond those disputes "traditionally thought to be capable of resolution through the judicial process." As a general principle, we stated as recently as last Term that "executive or administrative duties of a nonjudicial nature may not be imposed on judges holding office under Art. III of the Constitution." Morrison v. Olson, 487 U.S., at 677.

Nonetheless, we have recognized significant exceptions to this general rule and have approved the assumption of some nonadjudicatory activities by the Judicial Branch.... In his dissent in Myers v. United States, 272 U.S. 52 (1926), Justice Brandeis explained that the separation of powers "left to each [Branch] power to exercise, in some respects, functions in their nature executive, legislative and judicial." Id., at 291.

That judicial rulemaking, at least with respect to some subjects, falls within this twilight area is no longer an issue for dispute.... [W]e specifically have held that Congress, in some circumstances, may confer rulemaking authority on the Judicial Branch. In Sibbach v. Wilson & Co., 312 U.S. 1 (1941), we.... observed: "Congress has undoubted power to regulate the practice and procedure of federal courts, and may exercise that power by delegating to this or other federal courts authority to make rules not inconsistent with the statutes or constitution of the United States." ... [In] Wayman v. Southard, 10 Wheat. 1, 43 (1825), decided more than a century earlier, ... Chief Justice Marshall wrote for the Court that rulemaking power pertaining to the Judicial Branch may be "conferred on the judicial department." .... Pursuant to this power to delegate rulemaking authority to the Judicial Branch, Congress expressly has authorized this Court to establish rules for the conduct of its own business and to prescribe rules of procedure for lower federal courts in bankruptcy cases, in other civil cases, and in criminal cases, and to revise the Federal Rules of Evidence.

... [W]e specifically have upheld ... Congress' power to ... to vest in judicial councils authority to "make 'all necessary orders for the effective and expeditious administration of the business of the courts.'" ... [B]y established practice we have recognized Congress' power to create the Judicial Conference of the United States, the Rules Advisory Committees that it oversees, and the Administrative Office of the United States Courts whose myriad responsibilities include the administration of the entire probation service.

> FN 15. The Judicial Conference of the United States is charged with "promot[ing] uniformity of management procedures and the expeditious conduct of court business," in part by "a continuous study of the operation and effect of the general rules of practice and procedure," and recommending changes "to promote simplicity in procedure, fairness in administration, the just determination of litigation, and the elimination of unjustifiable expense and delay." 28 U. S. C. § 331. Similarly, the Administrative Office of the United States Courts handles the administrative and personnel matters of the courts, matters essential to the effective and efficient operation of the judicial system. § 604 (1982 ed. and Supp. IV). Congress also has established the Federal Judicial Center which studies improvements in judicial administration. §§ 620–628.

These entities, some of which are comprised of judges, others of judges and nonjudges, still others of nonjudges only, do not exercise judicial power in the constitutional sense of deciding cases and controversies, but they share the common purpose of providing for the fair and efficient fulfillment of responsibilities that are properly the province of the Judiciary.... Because of their close relation to the central mission of the Judicial Branch, such extrajudicial activities are consonant with the integrity of the Branch and are not more appropriate for another Branch.

In light of this precedent and practice, we can discern no separation-of-powers impediment to the placement of the Sentencing Commission within the Judicial Branch. As we described at the outset, the sentencing function long has been a peculiarly shared responsibility among the Branches of Government and has never been thought of as the exclusive constitutional province of any one Branch. For more than a century, federal judges have enjoyed wide discretion to determine the appropriate sentence in individual cases and have exercised special authority to determine the sentencing factors to be applied in any given case. Indeed, the legislative history of the Act makes clear that Congress' decision to place the Commission within the Judicial Branch reflected Congress' "strong feeling" that sentencing has been and should remain "primarily a judicial function." Report, at 159. That Congress should vest such rulemaking in the Judicial Branch, far from being "incongruous" or vesting within the Judiciary responsibilities that more appropriately belong to another Branch, simply acknowledges the role that the Judiciary always has played, and continues to play, in sentencing.

> FN 17. Indeed, had Congress decided to confer responsibility for promulgating sentencing guidelines on the Executive Branch, we might face the constitutional questions whether Congress unconstitutionally had assigned judicial responsibilities to the Executive or unconstitutionally had united the power to prosecute and the power to sentence within one Branch....

... [T]he role of the Commission in promulgating guidelines for the exercise of that judicial function bears considerable similarity to the role of this Court in establishing rules of procedure under the various enabling Acts.... Just as the rules of procedure bind judges and courts in the proper management of the cases before them, so the Guidelines bind judges and courts in the exercise of their uncontested responsibility to pass sentence in criminal cases. In other words, the Commission's functions, like this Court's function in promulgating procedural rules, are clearly attendant to a central element of the historically acknowledged mission of the Judicial Branch.

Petitioner nonetheless objects that ... [a]lthough the Judicial Branch may participate in rulemaking and administrative work that is "procedural" in nature, ... the "substantive" authority over sentencing policy ... entangles the Judicial Branch in essentially political work of the other Branches and unites both judicial and legislative power in the Judicial Branch.

.... Although we are loath to enter the logical morass of distinguishing between substantive and procedural rules, see Sun Oil Co. v. Wortman, 486 U.S. 717 (1988) (distinction between substance and procedure depends on context), and although we have recognized that the Federal Rules of Civil Procedure regulate matters "falling within the uncertain area between substance and procedure, [and] are rationally capable of classification as either," Hanna v. Plumer, 380 U.S., at 472, we recognize that the task of promulgating rules regulating practice and pleading before federal courts does not involve the degree of political judgment integral to the Commission's formulation of sentencing guidelines....

We do not believe, however, that the significantly political nature of the Commission's work renders unconstitutional its placement within the Judicial Branch.... In this case, the "practical consequences" of locating the Commission within the Judicial Branch pose no threat of undermining the integrity of the Judicial Branch or of expanding the powers of the Judiciary beyond constitutional bounds....

First, although the Commission is located in the Judicial Branch, its powers are not united with the powers of the Judiciary in a way that has meaning for separation-of-powers analysis. Whatever constitutional problems might arise if the powers of the Commission were vested in a court, the Commission is not a court, does not exercise judicial power, and is not controlled by or accountable to members of the Judicial Branch. The Commission, on which members of the Judiciary may be a minority, is an independent agency in every relevant sense. In contrast to a court's exercising judicial power, the Commission is fully accountable to Congress, which can revoke or amend any or all of the Guidelines as it sees fit either within the 180-day waiting period, see § 235(a)(1)(B)(ii)(III) of the Act, or at any time. In contrast to a court, the Commission's members are subject to the President's limited powers of removal. In contrast to a court, its rulemaking is subject to the notice and comment requirements of the Administrative Procedure Act, 28 U. S. C. § 994(x).... [B]ecause Congress vested the power to promulgate sentencing guidelines in an independent agency, not a court, there can be no serious argument that Congress combined legislative and judicial power within the Judicial Branch.

Second, although the Commission wields rulemaking power and not the adjudicatory power exercised by individual judges when passing sentence, the placement of the Sentencing Commission in the Judicial Branch has not increased the Branch's authority. Prior to the passage of the Act, the Judicial Branch, as an aggregate, decided precisely the questions assigned to the Commission: what sentence is appropriate to what criminal conduct under what circumstances. It was the everyday business of judges, taken collectively, to evaluate and weigh the various aims of sentencing and to apply those aims to the individual cases that came before them. The Sentencing Commission does no more than this, albeit basically through the methodology of sentencing guidelines, rather than entirely individualized sentencing determinations. Accordingly, in placing the Commission in the Judicial Branch, Congress cannot be said to have aggrandized the authority of that Branch or to have deprived the Executive Branch of a power it once possessed. Indeed, because the Guidelines have the effect of promoting sentencing within a narrower range than was previously applied, the power of the Judicial Branch is, if anything, somewhat diminished by the Act. And, since Congress did not unconstitutionally delegate its own authority, the Act does not unconstitutionally diminish Congress' authority. Thus, although Congress has authorized the Commission to exercise a greater degree of political judgment than has been exercised in the past by any one entity within the Judicial Branch, in the unique context of sentencing, this authorization does nothing to upset the balance of power among the Branches.

What Mistretta's argument comes down to, then, is not that the substantive responsibilities of the Commission aggrandize the Judicial Branch, but that that Branch is inevitably weakened by its participation in policymaking. We do not believe, however, that the placement within the Judicial Branch of an independent agency charged with the promulgation of sentencing guidelines can possibly be construed as preventing the Judicial Branch "from accomplishing its constitutionally assigned functions." Despite the substantive nature of its work, the Commission is not incongruous or inappropriate to the Branch. As already noted, sentencing is a field in which the Judicial Branch long has exercised substantive or political judgment.... Congress placed the Commission in the Judicial Branch precisely because of the Judiciary's special knowledge and expertise.

Nor do the Guidelines, though substantive, involve a degree of political authority inappropriate for a nonpolitical Branch. Although the Guidelines are intended to have substantive effects on public behavior (as do the rules of procedure), they do not bind or regulate the primary conduct of the public or vest in the Judicial Branch the legislative responsibility for establishing minimum and maximum penalties for every crime. They do no more than fetter the discretion of sentencing judges to do what they have done for generations—impose sentences within the broad limits established by Congress. Given their limited reach, the special role of the Judicial Branch in the field of sentencing, and the fact that the Guidelines are promulgated by an independent agency and not a court, it follows that as a matter of "practical consequences" the location of the Sentencing Commission within the Judicial Branch simply leaves with the Judiciary what long has belonged to it....

The Act provides in part: "At least three of [the Commission's] members shall be Federal judges selected [by the President] after considering a list of six judges recommended to the President by the Judicial Conference of the United States." 28 U. S. C. § 991(a). Petitioner urges us to strike down the Act on the ground that its requirement of judicial participation on the Commission unconstitutionally conscripts individual federal judges for political service and thereby undermines the essential impartiality of the Judicial Branch....

.... The Constitution does include an Incompatibility Clause applicable to national legislators:

> No Senator or Representative shall, during the Time for which he was elected, be appointed to any civil Office under the Authority of the United States, which shall have been created, or the Emoluments whereof shall have been encreased during such time; and no Person holding any Office under the United States,

shall be a Member of either House during his Continuance in Office. U.S. Const., Art. I, §6, cl. 2.

No comparable restriction applies to judges, and we find it at least inferentially meaningful that at the Constitutional Convention two prohibitions against plural officeholding by members of the Judiciary were proposed, but did not reach the floor of the Convention for a vote.

.... Our early history indicates that the Framers themselves did not read the Constitution as forbidding extrajudicial service by federal judges. The first Chief Justice, John Jay, served simultaneously as Chief Justice and as Ambassador to England, where he negotiated the treaty that bears his name. Oliver Ellsworth served simultaneously as Chief Justice and as Minister to France. While he was Chief Justice, John Marshall served briefly as Secretary of State and was a member of the Sinking Fund Commission with responsibility for refunding the Revolutionary War debt.

All these appointments were made by the President with the "Advice and Consent" of the Senate. Thus, at a minimum, both the Executive and Legislative Branches acquiesced in the assumption of extrajudicial duties by judges.... This contemporaneous practice by the Founders themselves is significant evidence that the constitutional principle of separation of powers does not absolutely prohibit extrajudicial service.

Subsequent history, moreover, reveals a frequent and continuing, albeit controversial, practice of extrajudicial service. In 1877, five Justices served on the Election Commission that resolved the hotly contested Presidential election of 1876, where Samuel J. Tilden and Rutherford B. Hayes were the contenders. Justices Nelson, Fuller, Brewer, Hughes, Day, Roberts, and Van Devanter served on various arbitral commissions. Justice Roberts was a member of the commission organized to investigate the attack on Pearl Harbor. Justice Jackson was one of the prosecutors at the Nuremberg trials; and Chief Justice Warren presided over the commission investigating the assassination of President Kennedy. Such service has been no less a practice among lower court federal judges. While these extrajudicial activities spawned spirited discussion and frequent criticism, and although some of the judges who undertook these duties sometimes did so with reservation and may have looked back on their service with regret, "traditional ways of conducting government ... give meaning" to the Constitution. Youngstown Sheet & Tube Co. v. Sawyer, 343 U.S., at 610 (concurring opinion). Our 200-year tradition of extrajudicial service is additional evidence that the doctrine of separated powers does not prohibit judicial participation in certain extrajudicial activity.

.... [W]e conclude that the principle of separation of powers does not absolutely prohibit Article III judges from serving on commissions such as that created by the Act.... [This] does not mean that every extrajudicial service would be compatible with, or appropriate to, continuing service on the bench; nor does it mean that Congress may require a federal judge to assume extrajudicial duties as long as the judge is assigned those duties in an individual, not judicial, capacity. The ultimate inquiry remains whether a particular extrajudicial assignment undermines the integrity of the Judicial Branch.

.... The Act does not conscript judges for the Commission. No Commission member to date has been appointed without his consent and we have no reason to believe that the Act confers upon the President any authority to force a judge to serve on the Commission against his will.... [A]bsent a more specific threat to judicial independence, the fact that Congress has included federal judges on the Commission does not itself threaten the integrity of the Judicial Branch.

Moreover, we cannot see how the service of federal judges on the Commission will have a constitutionally significant practical effect on the operation of the Judicial Branch. We see no reason why service on the Commission should result in widespread judicial recusals. That federal judges participate in the promulgation of guidelines does not affect their or other judges' ability impartially to adjudicate sentencing issues. While in the abstract a proliferation of commissions with congressionally mandated judiciary participation might threaten judicial independence by exhausting the resources of the Judicial Branch, that danger is far too remote for consideration here....

Although it is a judgment that is not without difficulty, we [also] conclude that the participation of federal judges on the Sentencing Commission does not threaten, either in fact or in appearance, the impartiality of the Judicial Branch. We are drawn to this conclusion by one paramount consideration: that the Sentencing Commission is devoted exclusively to the development of rules to rationalize a process that has been and will continue to be performed exclusively by the Judicial Branch. In our view, this is an essentially neutral endeavor and one in which judicial participation is peculiarly appropriate....

Finally, we reject petitioner's argument that the mixed nature of the Commission violates the Constitution by requiring Article III judges to share judicial power with nonjudges. As noted earlier, the Commission is not a court and exercises no judicial power. Thus, the Act does not vest Article III power in nonjudges or require Article III judges to share their power with nonjudges.

The Act empowers the President to appoint all seven members of the Commission with the advice and consent of the Senate. The Act further provides that the President shall make his choice of judicial appointees to the Commission after considering a list of six judges recommended by the Judicial Conference of the United States. The Act also grants the President authority to remove members of the Commission, although "only for neglect of duty or malfeasance in office or for other good cause shown." 28 U. S. C. § 991(a).

.... [W]e do not believe that the President's appointment and removal powers over the Commission afford him influence over the functions of the Judicial Branch or undue sway over its members.

> FN 30. Petitioner does not raise the issue central to our most recent opinions discussing removal power, namely, whether Congress unconstitutionally has limited the President's authority to remove officials engaged in executive functions or has reserved for itself excessive removal power over such officials. See Morrison v. Olson, 487 U.S. 654 (1988); Bowsher v. Synar, 478 U.S. 714 (1986).

The notion that the President's power to appoint federal judges to the Commission somehow gives him influence over the Judicial Branch or prevents, even potentially, the Judicial Branch from performing its constitutionally assigned functions is fanciful. We have never considered it incompatible with the functioning of the Judicial Branch that the President has the power to elevate federal judges from one level to another or to tempt judges away from the bench with Executive Branch positions. The mere fact that the President within his appointment portfolio has positions that may be attractive to federal judges does not, of itself, corrupt the integrity of the Judiciary. Were the impartiality of the Judicial Branch so easily subverted, our constitutional system of tripartite Government would have failed long ago....

The President's removal power over Commission members poses a similarly negligible threat to judicial independence. The Act does not, and could not under the Constitution, authorize the President to remove, or in any way diminish the status of Article III judges, as judges. Even if removed from the Commission, a federal judge appointed to the Commission would continue, absent impeachment, to enjoy tenure "during good Behaviour" and a full judicial salary. U.S. Const., Art. III, § 1. Also, the President's removal power under the Act is limited.... [to removal] only for good cause..., [thereby preventing] the President from exercising "coercive influence" over independent agencies....

We conclude that in creating the Sentencing Commission—an unusual hybrid in structure and authority—Congress neither delegated excessive legislative power nor upset the constitutionally mandated balance of powers among the coordinate Branches.... The judgment of United States District Court for the Western District of Missouri is affirmed.

JUSTICE SCALIA, dissenting.

While the products of the Sentencing Commission's labors have been given the modest name "Guidelines," they have the force and effect of laws, prescribing the sentences criminal defendants are to receive. A judge who disregards them will be reversed, 18 U. S. C. § 3742. I dissent from today's decision because I can find no place within our constitutional system for an agency created by Congress to exercise no governmental power other than the making of laws.

I

There is no doubt that the Sentencing Commission has established significant, legally binding prescriptions governing application of governmental power against private individuals—indeed, application of the ultimate governmental power, short of capital punishment. Statutorily permissible sentences for particular crimes cover as broad a range as zero years to life, see, and within those ranges the Commission was given broad discretion to prescribe the "correct" sentence, 28 U. S. C. § 994(b)(2). Average prior sentences were to be a starting point for the Commission's inquiry, § 994(m), but it could and regularly did deviate from those averages as it thought appropriate....

The Commission also determined when probation was permissible, imposing a strict system of controls because of its judgment that probation had been used for an "inappropriately high percentage of offenders guilty of certain economic crimes." Moreover, the Commission had free rein in determining whether statutorily authorized fines should be imposed in addition to imprisonment, and if so, in what amounts. It ultimately decided that every nonindigent offender should pay a fine according to a schedule devised by the Commission. Congress also gave the Commission discretion to determine whether 7 specified characteristics of offenses, and 11 specified characteristics of offenders, "have any relevance," and should be included among the factors varying the sentence. 28 U. S. C. §§ 994(c), (d). Of the latter, it included only three among the factors required to be considered, and declared the remainder not ordinarily relevant. Guidelines, at 5.29–5.31.

It should be apparent from the above that the decisions made by the Commission are far from technical, but are heavily laden (or ought to be) with value judgments and policy assessments....

Petitioner's most fundamental and far-reaching challenge to the Commission is that Congress' commitment of such broad policy responsibility to any institution is an unconstitutional delegation of legislative power. It is difficult to imagine a principle more essential to democratic government than that upon which the doctrine of unconstitutional delegation is founded: Except in a few areas constitutionally committed to the Executive Branch, the basic policy decisions governing society are to be made by the Legislature.

Our Members of Congress could not, even if they wished, vote all power to the President and adjourn sine die.

But while the doctrine of unconstitutional delegation is unquestionably a fundamental element of our constitutional system, it is not an element readily enforceable by the courts. Once it is conceded, as it must be, that no statute can be entirely precise, and that some judgments, even some judgments involving policy considerations, must be left to the officers executing the law and to the judges applying it, the debate over unconstitutional delegation becomes a debate not over a point of principle but over a question of degree. As Chief Justice Taft expressed the point for the Court in the landmark case of J. W. Hampton, Jr., & Co. v. United States, 276 U.S. 394, 406 (1928), the limits of delegation "must be fixed according to common sense and the inherent necessities of the governmental co-ordination." Since Congress is no less endowed with common sense than we are, and better equipped to inform itself of the "necessities" of government; and since the factors bearing upon those necessities are both multifarious and (in the nonpartisan sense) highly political—including, for example, whether the Nation is at war, see Yakus v. United States, 321 U.S. 414 (1944), or whether for other reasons "emergency is instinct in the situation," Amalgamated Meat Cutters and Butcher Workmen of North America v. Connally, 337 F. Supp. 737, 752 (DC 1971) (three-judge court)—it is small wonder that we have almost never felt qualified to second-guess Congress regarding the permissible degree of policy judgment that can be left to those executing or applying the law. As the Court points out, we have invoked the doctrine of unconstitutional delegation to invalidate a law only twice in our history, over half a century ago. See Panama Refining Co. v. Ryan, 293 U.S. 388 (1935); A. L. A. Schechter Poultry Corp. v. United States, 295 U.S. 495 (1935). What legislated standard, one must wonder, can possibly be too vague to survive judicial scrutiny, when we have repeatedly upheld, in various contexts, a "public interest" standard?

In short, I fully agree with the Court's rejection of petitioner's contention that the doctrine of unconstitutional delegation of legislative authority has been violated because of the lack of intelligible, congressionally prescribed standards to guide the Commission.

Precisely because the scope of delegation is largely uncontrollable by the courts, we must be particularly rigorous in preserving the Constitution's structural restrictions that deter excessive delegation. The major one, it seems to me, is that the power to make law cannot be exercised by anyone other than Congress, except in conjunction with the lawful exercise of executive or judicial power.

The whole theory of *lawful* congressional "delegation" is not that Congress is sometimes too busy or too divided and can therefore assign its responsibility of making law to someone else; but rather that a certain degree of discretion, and thus of lawmaking, *inheres* in most executive or judicial action, and it is up to Congress, by the relative specificity or generality of its statutory commands, to determine—up to a point—how small or how large that degree shall be. Thus, the courts could be given the power to say precisely what constitutes a "restraint of trade," see Standard Oil Co. of New Jersey v. United States, 221 U.S. 1 (1911), or to adopt rules of procedure, see Sibbach v. Wilson & Co., 312 U.S. 1, 22 (1941), or to prescribe by rule the manner in which their officers shall execute their judgments, because that "lawmaking" was ancillary to their exercise of judicial powers. And the Executive could be given the power to adopt policies and rules specifying in detail what radio and television licenses will be in the "public interest, convenience or necessity," because that was ancillary to the exercise of its executive powers in granting and policing licenses and making a "fair and equitable allocation" of the electromagnetic spectrum. Or to take examples closer to the case before us: Trial judges could be given the power to determine what factors justify a greater or lesser sentence within the statutorily prescribed limits because that was ancillary to their exercise of the judicial power of pronouncing sentence upon individual defendants. And the President, through the Parole Commission subject to his appointment and removal, could be given the power to issue Guidelines specifying when parole would be available, because that was ancillary to the President's exercise of the executive power to hold and release federal prisoners.

The focus of controversy, in the long line of our so-called excessive delegation cases, has been whether the *degree* of generality contained in the authorization for exercise of executive or judicial powers in a particular field is so unacceptably high as to *amount to* a delegation of legislative powers. I say "so-called excessive delegation" because although that convenient terminology is often used, what is really at issue is whether there has been *any* delegation of legislative power, which occurs (rarely) when Congress authorizes the exercise of executive or judicial power without adequate standards. Strictly speaking, there is *no* acceptable delegation of legislative power.... In the present case, however, a pure delegation of legislative power is precisely what we have before us. It is irrelevant whether the standards are adequate, because they are not standards related to the exercise of executive or judicial powers; they are, plainly and simply, standards for further legislation.

The lawmaking function of the Sentencing Commission is completely divorced from any responsibility for execution of the law or adjudication of private rights under the law. It is divorced from responsibility for execution of the law not only because the Commission is not said to be "located in the Executive Branch" (as I shall discuss presently, I doubt whether Congress can "locate" an entity within one Branch or another for constitutional purposes by merely saying so); but, more importantly, because the Commission neither exercises any executive power on its own, nor is subject to the control of the President who does. The only functions it performs, apart from prescribing the law, conducting the investigations useful and necessary for prescribing the law, and clarifying the intended application of the law that it prescribes are data collection and intragovernmental advice giving and education. These latter activities—similar to functions performed by congressional agencies and even congressional staff—neither determine nor affect private rights, and do not constitute an exercise of governmental power. See Humphrey's Executor v. United States, 295 U.S. 602, 628 (1935). And the Commission's lawmaking is completely divorced from the exercise of judicial powers since, not being a court, it has no judicial powers itself, nor is it subject to the control of any other body with judicial powers. The power to make law at issue here, in other words, is not ancillary but quite naked....

The delegation of lawmaking authority to the Commission is, in short, unsupported by any legitimating theory to explain why it is not a delegation of legislative power. To disregard structural legitimacy is wrong in itself—but since structure has purpose, the disregard also has adverse practical consequences....

By reason of today's decision, I anticipate that Congress will find delegation of its law-making powers much more attractive in the future. If rulemaking can be entirely unrelated to the exercise of judicial or executive powers, I foresee all manner of "expert" bodies, insulated from the political process, to which Congress will delegate various portions of its lawmaking responsibility. How tempting to create an expert Medical Commission (mostly M.D.'s, with perhaps a few Ph.D.'s in moral philosophy) to dispose of such thorny, "nowin" political issues as the withholding of life-support systems in federally funded hospitals, or the use of fetal tissue for research. This is an undemocratic precedent that we set—not because of the scope of the delegated power, but because its recipient is not one of the three Branches of Government. The only governmental power the Commission possesses is the power to make law; and it is not the Congress.

The strange character of the body that the Court today approves, and its incompatibility with our constitutional institutions, is apparent from that portion of the Court's opinion entitled "Location of the Commission."…. Separation-of-powers problems are dismissed, however, on the ground that "[the Commission's] powers are not united with the powers of the Judiciary in a way that has meaning for separation-of-powers analysis," since the Commission "is not a court, does not exercise judicial power, and is not controlled by or accountable to members of the Judicial Branch." In light of the latter concession, I am at a loss to understand why the Commission is "within the Judicial Branch" in any sense that has relevance to today's discussion. I am sure that Congress can divide up the Government any way it wishes, and employ whatever terminology it desires, for nonconstitutional pur-poses—for example, perhaps the statutory designation that the Commission is "within the Judicial Branch" places it outside the coverage of certain laws which say they are inapplicable to that Branch, such as the Freedom of Information Act, see 5 U. S. C. §552(f). For such statutory purposes, Congress can define the term as it pleases. But since our subject here is the Constitution, to admit that that congressional designation "has [no] meaning for separation-of-powers analysis" is to admit that the Court must therefore decide for itself where the Commission *is* located for purposes of separation-of-powers analysis.

It would seem logical to decide the question of which Branch an agency belongs to on the basis of who controls its actions…. In Humphrey's Executor v. United States, 295 U.S. 602 (1935), we approved the concept of an agency that was controlled by (and thus within) none of the Branches. We seem to have assumed, however, that that agency (the old Federal Trade Commission, before it acquired many of its current functions) exercised no governmental power whatever, but merely assisted Congress and the courts in the performance of their functions. Where no governmental power is at issue, there is no strict constitutional impediment to a "branchless" agency, since it is only "[a]ll legislative Powers," Art. I, §1, "[t]he executive Power," Art. II, §1, and "[t]he judicial Power," Art. III, §1, which the Con-stitution divides into three departments. (As an example of a "branchless" agency exercising no governmental powers, one can conceive of an Advisory Commission charged with reporting to all three Branches, whose members are removable only for cause and are thus subject to the control of none of the Branches.) Over the years, however, Humphrey's Executor has come in general contemplation to stand for something quite different—not an "independent agency" in the sense of an agency independent of all three Branches, but an "independent agency" in the sense of an agency *within* the Executive Branch (and thus authorized to exercise executive powers) independent of the control of the President.

We approved that concept last Term in Morrison. I dissented in that case, essentially because I thought that concept illogical and destructive of the structure of the Constitution. I must admit, however, that today's next step—recognition of an independent agency in the Judicial Branch—makes Morrison seem, by comparison, rigorously logical. "The Commission," we are told, "is an independent agency in every relevant sense." There are several problems with this. First, once it is acknowledged that an "independent agency" may be within *any* of the three Branches, and not merely within the Executive, then there really *is* no basis for determining what Branch such an agency belongs to, and thus what governmental powers it may constitutionally be given, except (what the Court today uses) Congress' say-so. More importantly, however, the concept of an "independent agency" simply does not translate into the legislative or judicial spheres. Although the Constitution says that "[t]he executive Power shall be vested in a President of the United States of America," Art. II, §1, it was never thought that the President would have to exercise that power *personally*. He may generally authorize others to exercise executive powers, with full effect of law, in his place. It is already a leap from the proposition that a person who is not the President may exercise executive powers to the proposition we accepted in *Morrison* that a person who is *neither* the President *nor* subject to the President's control may exercise executive powers. But with respect to the exercise of judicial powers (the business of the Judicial Branch) the platform for such a leap does not even exist. For unlike executive power, judicial and legislative powers have never been thought delegable. A judge may not leave the decision to his law clerk, or to a master. Senators and Members of the House may not send delegates to consider and vote upon bills in their place. Thus, however well established may be the "independent agencies" of the Executive Branch, here we have an anomaly beyond equal: an independent agency exercising governmental power on behalf of a Branch where all governmental power is supposed to be exercised personally by the judges of courts.

Today's decision may aptly be described as the Humphrey's Executor of the Judicial Branch, and I think we will live to regret it. Henceforth there may be agencies "within the Judicial Branch" (whatever that means), exercising governmental powers, that are neither courts nor controlled by courts, nor even controlled by judges. If an "independent agency" such as this can be given the power to fix sentences previously exercised by district courts, I must assume that a similar agency can be given the powers to adopt rules of procedure and rules of evidence previously exercised by this Court. The bases for distinction would be thin indeed.

Today's decision follows the regrettable tendency of our recent separation-of-powers jurisprudence to treat the Constitution as though it were no more than a generalized prescription that the functions of the Branches should not be commingled too much—how much is too much to be determined, case-by-case, by this Court. The Constitution is not that. Rather, as its name suggests, it is a prescribed structure, a framework, for the conduct of government. In designing that structure, the Framers *themselves* considered how much commingling was, in the generality of things, acceptable, and set forth their conclusions in the document. That is the meaning of the statements concerning acceptable commingling made by Madison in defense of the proposed Constitution, and now routinely used as an excuse for disregarding it. When he said, as the Court correctly quotes, that separation of powers "'d[oes] not mean that these [three] departments ought to have no *partial agency* in, or no *control* over the acts of each other,'" quoting The Federalist No. 47, his point was that the commingling specifically provided for in the structure that he and his colleagues had designed—the Presidential veto over legislation, the Senate's confirmation of executive and judicial officers, the Senate's ratification of treaties, the Congress' power to impeach and remove executive and judicial officers—did not violate a proper understanding of separation of powers. He would be aghast, I think, to hear those words used as justification for ignoring that carefully designed structure so long as, in the changing view of the Supreme Court from time to time, "too much commingling" does not occur. Consideration of the degree of commingling that a particular disposition produces may be appropriate at the margins, where the outline of the framework itself is not clear; but it seems to me far from a marginal question whether our constitutional structure allows for a body which is not the Congress, and yet exercises no governmental powers except the making of rules that have the effect of laws.

I think the Court errs, in other words, not so much because it mistakes the degree of commingling, but because it fails to recognize that this case is not about commingling, but about the creation of a new Branch altogether, a sort of junior varsity Congress. It may well be that in some circumstances such a Branch would be desirable; perhaps the agency before us here will prove to be so. But there are many desirable dispositions that do not accord with the constitutional structure we live under. And in the long run the improvisation of a constitutional structure on the basis of currently perceived utility will be disastrous.

I respectfully dissent from the Court's decision, and would reverse the judgment of the District Court.

Review Questions and Explanations: *Mistretta*

1. Have you noticed how some of the same choice quotations, e.g., from Justice Jackson's *Youngstown* concurrence, are repeatedly recited in functionalist separation-of-powers opinions? What is the bottom-line test for separation of powers employed by the majority (hint: you've seen it before, e.g., in *Morrison v. Olson*). Is it a formalist or functionalist test?

2. Absent the statute's express statement that the Commission is located in the Judicial Branch, what about the Commission locates it there? The fact that judges serve on it? Did you get the sense that the Commission would have been unconstitutional if it were deemed an independent agency not located in any particular branch, like the Federal Trade Commission in *Humprey's Executor* or the independent counsel in *Morrison*?

3. Perhaps what makes this case so complicated is that sentencing has always been a function with legislative and judicial powers so intermingled that the respective roles of those two branches can't be meaningfully distinguished. Consider the alternatives: huge, virtually unbounded discretion to trial judges in individual cases; or rigid rules based on very general statutory criteria that will prevent sentencers from taking varied individual circumstances into account and thereby creating significant unfairness in individual cases. Are either of these alternatives required or even preferable from a separation-of-powers point of view?

4. The default—the existing system of indeterminate sentencing—leaves it all up to judges in the individual case. An unspoken argument is that *that* system may represent an excessive delegation of legislative authority—not to mention the problem of unlawlike variations in results between individual offenders and judges. Are those flaws with the existing sentencing system the ketchup that covers all separation-of-powers objections?

5. Justice Scalia's dissent makes some good points—at least on the surface. He argues that failure to adhere to the structural requirements of separation of powers undermines democratic accountability: Congress can avoid necessary decisions on "no win" political issues by fobbing them off on independent commissions. This argument has some force, especially if the issue would clearly be resolved by Congress or the executive branch under strict adherence to separation of powers. But are all three branches politically accountable? Congress can already fob off difficult questions to unelected judges, like Scalia himself, by writing ambiguous statutes. Arguably, Congress did exactly that with the pre-Guidelines system of indeterminate sentencing. At the end of the day, does Justice Scalia resolve the conundrum of whether sentencing is a legislative or judicial power?

6. Perhaps Scalia's real objection to the Sentencing Commission is excessive delegation after all—despite his claim to agree that the nondelegation doctrine has not been violated. But if the Sentencing Commission is constitutionally objectionable, how should federal sentencing be properly handled?

Exercises: *Other Separation-of-Powers Questions*

With two or more classmates, try to brainstorm about societal problems that could benefit from some sort of government solution but that are not being well handled by the current political system or existing institutional arrangements. Try to create a list of two or three such problems. With that list in front of you, try your hand at legislative design. In a bullet point outline, a half-page description, or some sort of chart, try to map out a structure to address the substantive problem while resolving the associated political problems. Consider whether the nitty-gritty details of the problem can be fully dealt with in the statute, or whether some kind of commission or other administrative body would be preferable to flesh out details.

If you are not successful in generating your own list, try addressing one of the following:

1) **Sentencing**: Try to address the problems of federal criminal sentences without relying on a commission located in the judicial branch.

2) **Medical Marijuana**: The Controlled Substances Act currently lists marijuana as a "schedule I" drug, meaning that its use is illegal and that it has no valid medical use. Although the medical community has disputed that characterization, removal of marijuana from schedule I (to schedules II, III or IV, which permit controlled medical use) requires that a decision be made by the Attorney General. (Congress could, of course, itself amend the law.) Politically, for the Attorney General to adopt the prevailing view of the medical community would probably result in adverse political consequences for the presidential administration. Can you address this issue by assigning it to a commission?

3) **Global warming**: Reduction of greenhouse gases to address the problem of global warming has become a politicized issue. Under the Bush administration, the EPA declined to exercise its regulatory authority on this issue, for largely political reasons. (*See Massachusetts v. EPA*, Chapter 3.) Under the Obama administration, Senate filibuster and a Republican House majority have been capable of blocking EPA regulations. Can you think of a way to address this problem outside of the "political" branches?

4) **"War on terrorism."** Can you create a statutory scheme that would allow for impartial review of claims by prisoners at Guantanamo Bay that they are not unlawful enemy combatants or terrorist threats, by a tribunal that is not under the control of the President (i.e., in the executive branch), the same authority that has detained the prisoners—yet, at the same time, that does not resort to the civilian federal courts, with their procedural formalities and heavy presumption in favor of access to the public?

D. Impeachment

"Impeachment" is the power of Congress to remove members of the executive and judicial branches from their offices. This straightforward definition is not itself stated in the Constitution, but is inferable from various sources, historical practices, and cases.

The basic structure of the impeachment process is outlined in three places in the Constitution. Article I, § 2, cl. 5 provides, "The House of Representatives ... shall have the sole power of impeachment." The Senate's role is specified in Art. I, § 2, cls. 6, 7:

> The Senate shall have the sole power to try all impeachments. When sitting for that purpose, they shall be on oath or affirmation. When the President of the United States is tried, the Chief Justice shall preside: And no person shall be convicted without the concurrence of two thirds of the members present.

> Judgment in cases of impeachment shall not extend further than to removal from office, and disqualification to hold and enjoy any office of honor, trust or profit under the United States: but the party convicted shall nevertheless be liable and subject to indictment, trial, judgment and punishment, according to law.

Finally, under Art. II, § 4, "The President, Vice President and all civil officers of the United States, shall be removed from office on impeachment for, and conviction of, treason, bribery, or other high crimes and misdemeanors."

These provisions tell us that impeachment is, in effect, a charge that is made by the House of Representatives against either the President, the Vice President or a "civil officer of United States," alleging that that official has committed "treason, bribery, or other high crimes and misdemeanors." Impeachment is not itself a removal from office — it is just a charge — and removal results only after a conviction by a two-thirds Senate vote following a "trial" in the Senate. The only express procedural requirement for the Senate's trial is that the Chief Justice must preside when the President is impeached.

Several questions are left unanswered by these provisions. Who is responsible for creating the procedures for impeachment and trial? Can Supreme Court justices, lower court judges, or members of Congress be impeached? And perhaps most importantly, what are the "other high crimes and misdemeanors," that fill out the understanding of impeachable offenses beyond treason and bribery?

The quoted constitutional provisions imply that the House is responsible for creating procedural rules for impeachments and the Senate for impeachment trials. This understanding was confirmed by the Supreme Court in *Nixon v. United States*, 506 U.S. 224 (1993) (presented in Chapter 6), which involved an impeachment trial of federal district judge Walter L. Nixon. Nixon had been convicted and imprisoned for bribery. The Court held, in essence, that the Senate had unreviewable discretion to set up trial procedures, at least for someone other than the President. (The exact nature of the Chief Justice's role in a presidential impeachment, and in particular his authority to make evidentiary and procedural rules and rulings, has not been authoritatively answered.) The House has proceeded in impeachments by drawing up Articles of Impeachment under the usual procedures for a bill or resolution, and submitting them to a majority vote. Before the Senate, individual House members act as "managers" to present the case for impeachment.

Can judges and justices be impeached? Supreme Court justices are listed between ambassadors and "all other officers of the United States" in the Appointments Clause. Lower court judges appear to be "officers of the United States" within the meaning of the Appointments Clause, Art. II, § 2, cl. 2. Presumably "officers" would not have a different meaning in the Art. II, § 4 impeachment clause. (There, the modifier "civil" before "officers" undoubtedly means that military officers are removable on grounds, and by procedures, other than impeachment.) The prevailing understanding seems to be that the "good behavior" condition on judicial life tenure contemplates impeachment as the means of removing judges and justices for a failure of "good behavior." The *Walter L. Nixon* case also seems to confirm this, at least as to lower court judges. The premise of his impeachment proceeding was that removal from office by impeachment was the only way to stop the embarrassment of continuing to pay his salary while he was in prison serving his sentence for bribery.

No Supreme Court justices have been removed by impeachment. Justice Samuel Chase is the only Justice ever to be impeached. An ardent Federalist appointed to the Court by President Washington in 1796, Chase was charged by the Republican-dominated House in 1804 in articles of impeachment that cited his alleged numerous procedural errors, and "inflammatory and indecent" behavior, including making highly politicized attacks on the administration from the bench as a circuit judge. He was acquitted by the Senate. In 1969–1970, impeachments of liberal Justices Abe Fortas and William O. Douglas were debated in the House. Fortas, who was also involved in alleged financial improprieties, resigned; the impeachment talk concerning Douglas blew over.

It would appear that impeachment does not apply to members of Congress (though apparently this was attempted before 1800). They are expressly excluded from the category of "civil officers of the United States." The "incompatibility clause", Art. I, § 6, cl. 2, provides:

> No Senator or Representative shall, during the time for which he was elected, be appointed to any civil office under the authority of the United States, which shall have been created, or the emoluments whereof shall have been increased during such time: and no person holding any office under the United States, shall be a member of either House during his continuance in office.

Furthermore, officers of the United States are appointed by the President pursuant to Art. II, § 2, cl. 2, which is manifestly inconsistent with how members of Congress obtain their positions. Finally, the manner of removal of members of Congress from office is expressly provided for, by means other than impeachment, in Art. I, § 5, cl. 2: "Each House may determine the rules of its proceedings, punish its members for disorderly behavior, and, with the concurrence of two thirds, expel a member."

The question of what constitutes "high crimes and misdemeanors" remains unresolved. Arguably, defining the term is up to the House of Representatives. In a floor speech in the House advocating the impeachment of Justice Douglas, Rep. Gerald R. Ford (later, the 38th President) said:

> What, then, is an impeachable offense? The only honest answer is whatever a majority of the House of Representatives considers to be at a given moment in history; conviction results from whatever offense or offenses two-thirds of the other body considers to be sufficiently serious to require removal of the accused from office. Again, the historical context and political climate are important; there are few fixed principles among the handful of precedents.

> I think it is fair to come to one conclusion, however, from our history of impeachments: a higher standard *is* expected of Federal judges than of any other "civil officers" of the United States. The President and Vice President, and all

persons holding office at the pleasure of the President, can be thrown out of office by the voters at least every four years....

Ford went on to argue that "good behavior" in Article III imposed a higher standard on judicial conduct than for executive branch officials; and, conversely, that violating good behavior on the part of a judge could be something less than "high crimes and misdemeanors."[3]

Three Presidents have faced impeachment. President Andrew Johnson was impeached in 1866 under eleven articles of impeachment; the vote to convict and remove him from office fell one vote short in the Senate. President Bill Clinton was impeached in 1998–99. The House drew up four articles of impeachment, and sent two for trial in the Senate, where the vote was far short of the two thirds required to remove him from office (45 out of 100 votes to impeach on a charge of perjury; and 50 votes on a charge of obstruction of justice). The Senate did vote to "censure" the President—a strong statement of disapproval that was unusual but not unprecedented. President Richard Nixon came close to being impeached. From July 27 to 30, 1974, a House subcommittee approved by wide margins three articles of impeachment against President Nixon for "obstruction of justice," "abuse of power" and "contempt of Congress." Nixon resigned the presidency on August 9, before the articles came up for a vote of the full House. One of three articles of impeachment against President Richard Nixon is reprinted here.

Articles of Impeachment [of Richard Nixon]

RESOLVED, That Richard M. Nixon, President of the United States, is impeached for high crimes and misdemeanors, and that the following articles of impeachment to be exhibited to the Senate....

Article 2: Abuse of Power.

Using the powers of the office of President of the United States, Richard M. Nixon, in violation of his constitutional oath faithfully to execute the office of President of the United States and, to the best of his ability, preserve, protect, and defend the Constitution of the United States, and in disregard of his constitutional duty to take care that the laws be faithfully executed, has repeatedly engaged in conduct violating the constitutional rights of citizens, imparting the due and proper administration of justice and the conduct of lawful inquiries, or contravening the laws governing agencies of the executive branch and the purposes of these agencies.

This conduct has included one or more of the following:

(1) He has, acting personally and through his subordinated and agents, endeavored to obtain from the Internal Revenue Service, in violation of the constitutional rights of citizens, confidential information contained in income tax returns for purposes not authorized by law, and to cause, in violation of the constitutional rights of citizens, income tax audits or other income tax investigation to be initiated or conducted in a discriminatory manner.

(2) He misused the Federal Bureau of Investigation, the Secret Service, and other executive personnel, in violation or disregard of the constitutional rights of citizens, by directing or authorizing such agencies or personnel to conduct or continue electronic

---

3. House Floor Speech, April 1970: Impeach Justice Douglas, Box D29, Gerald R. Ford Congressional Papers, Gerald R. Ford Library.

surveillance or other investigations for purposes unrelated to national security, the enforcement of laws, or any other lawful function of his office; he did direct, authorize, or permit the use of information obtained thereby for purposes unrelated to national security, the enforcement of laws, or any other lawful function of his office; and he did direct the concealment of certain records made by the Federal Bureau of Investigation of electronic surveillance.

(3) He has, acting personally and through his subordinates and agents, in violation or disregard of the constitutional rights of citizens, authorized and permitted to be maintained a secret investigative unit within the office of the President, financed in part with money derived from campaign contributions to him, which unlawfully utilized the resources of the Central Intelligence Agency, engaged in covert and unlawful activities, and attempted to prejudice the constitutional right of an accused to a fair trial.

(4) He has failed to take care that the laws were faithfully executed by failing to act when he knew or had reason to know that his close subordinates endeavored to impede and frustrate lawful inquiries by duly constituted executive; judicial and legislative entities concerning the unlawful entry into the headquarters of the Democratic National Committee, and the cover-up thereof, and concerning other unlawful activities including those relating to the confirmation of Richard Kleindienst as attorney general of the United States, the electronic surveillance of private citizens, the break-in into the office of Dr. Lewis Fielding, and the campaign financing practices of the Committee to Re-elect the President.

(5) In disregard of the rule of law: he knowingly misused the executive power by interfering with agencies of the executive branch: including the Federal Bureau of Investigation, the Criminal Division and the Office of Watergate Special Prosecution Force of the Department of Justice, in violation of his duty to take care that the laws by faithfully executed.

In all of this, Richard M. Nixon has acted in a manner contrary to his trust as President and subversive of constitutional government, to the great prejudice of the cause of law and justice and to the manifest injury of the people of the United States.

Wherefore Richard M. Nixon, by such conduct, warrants impeachment and trial, and removal from office.

On December 19, 1998, the House of Representatives passed two of four articles of impeachment (each voted on separately) against President Bill Clinton. The first article, adopted by a vote of 228–206, follows:

Resolution Impeaching William Jefferson Clinton, President of the United States, for High Crimes and Misdemeanors

Resolved, That William Jefferson Clinton, President of the United States, is impeached for high crimes and misdemeanors and that the following articles of impeachment be exhibited to the United States Senate:

Articles of impeachment exhibited by the House of Representatives of the United States of America in the name of itself and of the people of the United States of America, against William Jefferson Clinton, President of the United States of America, in maintenance and support of its impeachment against him for high crimes and misdemeanors.

Article I

In his conduct while President of the United States, William Jefferson Clinton, in violation of his constitutional oath faithfully to execute the office of President of the United States and, to the best of his ability, preserve, protect and defend the Constitution of the United States, and in violation of his constitutional duty to take care that the laws be faithfully executed, has willfully corrupted and manipulated the judicial process of the United States for his personal gain and exoneration, impeding the administration of justice, in that:

On August 17, 1998, William Jefferson Clinton swore to tell the truth, the whole truth and nothing but the truth before a Federal grand jury of the United States. Contrary to that oath, William Jefferson Clinton willfully provided perjurious, false and misleading testimony to the grand jury concerning one or more of the following: (1) the nature and details of his relationship with a subordinate Government employee; (2) prior perjurious, false and misleading testimony he gave in a Federal civil rights action brought against him; (3) prior false and misleading statements he allowed his attorney to make to a Federal judge in that civil rights action; and (4) his corrupt efforts to influence the testimony of witnesses and to impede the discovery of evidence in that civil rights action.

In doing this, William Jefferson Clinton has undermined the integrity of his office, has brought disrepute on the Presidency, has betrayed his trust as President and has acted in a manner subversive of the rule of law and justice, to the manifest injury of the people of the United States.

Wherefore, William Jefferson Clinton, by such conduct, warrants impeachment and trial, and removal from office and disqualification to hold and enjoy any office of honor, trust or profit under the United States.

Exercise: Impeachment

A majority in the House of Representatives, consisting of the opposition political party to that of the President, votes to impeach the President, under the following Article of Impeachment:

> In her conduct while President of the United States, Elizabeth Tudor has, in violation of her constitutional oath faithfully to execute the office of President of the United States, made federal judicial nominations on the basis of rewarding political friends and loyalists without due regard for the qualifications of such nominees to serve on the lower federal judicial and Supreme Court benches.

The White House counsel has announced that he will file a motion, on behalf of the President, to dismiss the Article of Impeachment on the ground that it is a constitutionally insufficient ground for impeachment.

With one or more fellow classmates, assume the roles of White House counsel and counsel to the House of Representatives. Draft the motion and an opposition, briefly summarizing (or outlining) your constitutional arguments. The first question you may need to resolve is: with whom, or in what body, do you "file" this motion? Choose another fellow student (or students) to play the role of whomever you think needs to decide it.

PART THREE

Judicial Power

This Part examines the power of the federal courts, particularly the Supreme Court, in our governing system. Chapter 5 explores the power of "judicial review," while Chapter 6 introduces you to various "justiciability" doctrines. Judicial review—the power of courts to declare laws unconstitutional—lies at the core of every basic Constitutional Law course taught in the United States. It is a practice that allows the courts, and again particularly the Supreme Court, to exercise extraordinary power. Justiciability doctrines, in contrast, are mechanisms, some constitutionally based and some more pragmatic, that *limit* the power of the courts.

Most Constitutional Law casebooks begin with these concepts. This book, obviously, does not. This is not because we think they are unimportant. Quite to the contrary; the Supreme Court's exercise of the power of judicial review, for example, has shaped our history in deeply important ways. Rather, we ordered the casebook the way we did for four reasons.

First, constitutional law (and law school in general) can too often leave students with the impression that only courts matter in constitutional law making. This is plainly not true. As powerful as the Supreme Court is, its primary role is to react to the actions of others. Consequently, the actions of state and federal executives and legislatures necessarily shape the nature of the Court's decisions. The founders were certainly aware of this. The big fights at the constitutional convention were not about the Supreme Court; rather, they were about the make up of the federal legislature and the division of power between the federal government and state governments.

Second, beginning a casebook with an examination of judicial power can too easily lead students to imagine that the Supreme Court stands separate from the other branches of government. In fact, the Court is integrated into our Constitution's system of checks and balances in many ways. Justices, for example, are nominated by the President and confirmed by the Senate. Moreover, the Court's ability to exercise the very power discussed in Chapter 5, the power of judicial review, is ultimately possible only through the political acquiesces of the elected branches. As Professor Mark Graber argues, "Constitutional casebooks promote the jurocentric view that Justices, acting without outside political support, successfully established judicial review when they declared in judicial opinions that Justices have the power to declare laws unconstitutional." But the Supreme Court, he continues, "tends to declare laws unconstitutional only after receiving fairly explicit invitations to do so by members of the dominant national coalition." Graber concludes by noting that as a matter of "jurisprudential logic and historical practice" courts can exercise power over the long run only with the cooperation of elected officials.[1]

Third, we have found that students are better equipped to critically evaluate the Court's use of its power after spending some time seeing how things like judicial review work in practice. Studying examples of the Court's work "in action" before turning to the question of Article III judicial power facilitates this.

Finally, we note that the Constitution itself proceeds in the same way as does this casebook. Article I deals with the powers of Congress and Article II describes the presidency, but the judiciary has to wait for its turn until Article III. If this ordering is good enough for the Constitution, we figure it is good enough for us as well.

---

1. Mark A. Graber, *Establishing Judicial Review: Marbury and the Judicial Act of 1789*, 38 TULSA L. REV. 609 (2003).

Chapter 5

Judicial Review

A. Overview

Before we can examine the power of judicial review we first must define it. In the introduction to this Part, we described judicial review as "the power of courts to declare laws unconstitutional." Most new law students could probably supply this definition even before beginning a law school course in constitutional law. But viewed in these simple terms, "judicial review" glosses over several important issues.

"Judicial review," for example, isn't limited to review of "laws," in the sense of statutes or legislative enactments. These of course can be judicially reviewed — that is, challenged as unconstitutional — but so can actions of the President and other executive branch agents. So a better definition of "judicial review" is the courts' power to declare the *actions* of other branches of government unconstitutional.

There also are important federalism aspects of judicial review. Courts have the power to review the constitutionality of laws and executive actions of both the federal government and state governments, and the "courts" exercising that review are not just federal courts, but state courts as well. Article VI, §2 of the Constitution — the Supremacy Clause — provides not only that the U.S. Constitution is "the supreme law of the land," but goes on to say that "the judges in every state shall be bound thereby." This language serves as both an obligation and a source of power: state judges have the power to declare, not only state, but in most cases even federal laws, unconstitutional pursuant to the U.S. Constitution.[2] While most constitutional law textbooks include only U.S. Supreme Court decisions, that Court's decisions are emphasized not because it is the only court exercising judicial review, but rather because it is the court with the final say over judicial interpretations of the U.S. Constitution.

There also is a set of difficult and controversial questions that lie just below the broad acceptance of the courts' exercise of judicial review. These questions form a major theme in this or any constitutional law course: what are the sources of and limitations to the power of judicial review? After all, no clause of the Constitution specifically authorizes courts to declare actions of the other branches unconstitutional, and the Constitution also binds members of the legislative and executive branches. Doesn't that imply that those governmental actors themselves have a duty — and corresponding power — to interpret the Constitution for themselves? If so, what is it about courts that gives them the *final* say over constitutional interpretation? Should having "the final say" even be considered a necessary or appropriate part of judicial review?

---

2. This is a rare occurrence due to jurisdictional rules which make it unlikely, as a practical matter, that constitutional challenges to federal laws would reach the merits in state courts. Some federal statutes give exclusive jurisdiction to federal courts, so that cases involving those statutes cannot be heard in state court. In other instances, parties will choose to have federal courts hear the cases by invoking federal question jurisdiction.

The traditional starting point for studying judicial review (and thinking about the answers to these questions) is the famous decision issued by the Marshall Court in *Marbury v. Madison* (1803). The orthodox understanding is that *Marbury* "established" judicial review by declaring an act of Congress unconstitutional and, in doing so, explaining why the power of judicial review is, in Chief Justice John Marshall's view, necessarily implied in the Constitution. Judicial review is thus recognized by *stare decisis* even though it is not an express part of the judicial power given to the federal courts in Article III.

Some scholars have questioned whether the *Marbury* decision did establish—or could have established—judicial review. (Recall Professor Graber's comments, above.) Even if one accepts the broad outlines of the orthodox understanding, however, it remains somewhat controversial whether *Marbury* supports pushing the concept of judicial review as far as do courts today. As you read the cases in the following section, consider whether *Marbury* goes as far as do modern courts in exercising their power of judicial review.

Before we turn to *Marbury*, however, it is important to understand the historical, political and legal context in which the case was decided. The following materials provide that context. Reading them will help you better understand what the Court did in *Marbury*, and why. The first piece is a historical summary of the political situation underlying the *Marbury* decision. The second is an excerpt of the Judiciary Act of 1789. Enacted by the first Congress, the Judiciary Act of 1789 is a landmark piece of legislation, in that it established the federal judicial system. Although the Act has been frequently amended, the basic structure of the judicial system it created remains intact. A provision of that law becomes a central issue of *Marbury*, as you will see.

B. Historical Antecedents

1. The Political "Revolution" of 1800 and *Marbury v. Madison*

Marbury v. Madison was decided in an atmosphere of intense partisan politics in which the Supreme Court's institutional survival was at risk.[3] The hopes of the framers of the Constitution for a system of government that would discourage the dominance of "factions" had been dashed by the time of the Adams administration (1797–1801). Factions in the form of two competing political parties—Federalists and Republicans[4]—had emerged

---

3. The following account is drawn from numerous sources. In particular, see Cliff Sloan and David McKean, The Great Decision: Jefferson, Adams, Marshall, and the Battle for the Supreme Court (2009); John E. Ferling, Adams vs. Jefferson: The Tumultuous Election of 1800 (2004); William W. Van Alstyne, *A Critical Guide to Marbury v. Madison*, 18 Duke L. J. 1 (1969).

4. We refer here to the Jeffersonian Republican Party, sometimes called the Democratic Republican party. Jefferson's party became so dominant that it was not seriously challenged for control of Congress and the presidency for the two decades after Jefferson's election. But internal divisions over issues relating to federalism created a split by the 1820s into the "National" and the "Democratic" wings of the party. The National Republicans eventually became the Whigs, and the Democratic Republicans became the Democratic party of President Jackson and his successors. Today's Republican party is distinct from both of these, and is generally considered to have its origins in the pre-Civil War era. *See generally* Daniel Walker Howe, What Hath God Wrought: the Transformation of America, 1815–1848 (2007).

as dominant forces in national politics. Roughly speaking, Federalists (the party of John Adams and Alexander Hamilton) tended to favor manufacturing and financial interests, tariffs, centralized banking, normalization of relations with Britain, and a robust role for the federal government in economic development. Republicans (the party of Thomas Jefferson and James Madison) tended to favor agrarian interests, to favor France over Britain in foreign relations, to oppose tariffs and central banks, and to favor state sovereignty and a relatively small role for the national government.

Prior to the 1800 elections, Federalists controlled the presidency and held majorities in both houses of Congress. The outcome of the 1800 elections, often referred to by historians as a "revolution" in party politics, saw the Republicans sweep into the presidency and gain majorities in both houses of Congress. The Republican Party remained dominant for the next generation, while the Federalists never again won the presidency or a congressional majority, and ultimately disbanded in the early 1820s.

But the Federalists did not go down without a fight. Stung by their defeat in the 1800 election, they used the time period between the election and the inauguration of the President-elect to install party loyalists in key positions throughout the federal government. Thus, in the waning days of the Adams administration, the lame duck Congress finally acted on a judicial reform bill that President Adams had been advocating for more than a year. The bill, subsequently known as the Judiciary Act of 1801, was enacted just three weeks before Jefferson's March 4th inauguration. It significantly reorganized the federal judiciary and, did so in ways that favored the Federalist Party.

While there were numerous detailed provisions in its 35 sections, the 1801 Judiciary Act made three major changes to the federal court system established by the earlier Judiciary Act of 1789. First, it eliminated the duty of Supreme Court justices to "ride circuit." Under the 1789 Act, the federal district courts were organized into three judicial circuits; each circuit had one circuit court which had original jurisdiction over some matters and appellate jurisdiction over district court judgments. But no circuit court judgeships were created: instead, the circuit court would consist of two Supreme Court justices plus the local district court judge. In order to sit as circuit judges, the Justices thus had to travel each spring to various district court locations in their assigned circuits. Not only did this cut significantly into the time that the justices could work on Supreme Court matters, it also required the middle-aged justices to travel hundreds or even thousands of miles, at the speed of a horse, in bone-jarring carriages over muddy or corduroyed dirt roads. These physical rigors should not be minimized. Circuit riding duty in the years prior to 1801 had caused judges to suffer health problems, resign from the Supreme Court, or refuse nominations to it. The 1801 Act ended this obligation. It also expanded the number of circuits (from three to six), staffed these circuits with 16 new full-time circuit judges, and reduced the number of Supreme Court justices from six to five, the change to take effect after the next vacancy.

In context, these changes were not politically neutral. The Supreme Court was dominated by Federalists. Strengthening the Court by relieving it of circuit riding and increasing its capacity to hear cases would work in the Federalists' favor—particularly in light of the extra fillip of eliminating the Republican's opportunity to fill the next vacancy by eliminating the seat. The 16 new circuit judgeships, which Adams planned to appoint before leaving office, would further entrench Federalists through life-tenured judicial appointments, a feature not lost on Republicans. And indeed, Adams moved quickly to nominate judges to fill these appointments, and the Senate promptly confirmed them. Both the Republicans and subsequent historians came to call these eleventh-hour judicial appointments "the midnight judges."

Two central figures in the drama of *Marbury v. Madison* emerged from this flurry of activity. John Marshall, who held the position of Secretary of State in the Adams administration, was nominated by President Adams to fill the position of Chief Justice, which had been vacated by the resignation of Oliver Ellsworth in fall 1800. Marshall was confirmed at the beginning of February, but continued to fulfill his role as Secretary of State right up until Jefferson's March 4th inauguration, thereby holding posts in the executive and judicial branches throughout that time period. One of Marshall's duties as Secretary of State was to place the official seal of the United States on public documents, including judicial "commissions"—the papers signifying the appointment of a person to a federal judgeship. Physical receipt of the commission was seen by many as necessary to finalize a judicial appointment. However, Secretary of State Marshall, aided in his work by only one or two clerks and a single messenger, did not quite manage to send out all of the judicial commissions on his desk prior to Jefferson's assumption of office. Fatefully, one of those that did not go out was William Marbury's.

Marbury had been among the midnight judges appointed not to a life-tenured circuit judgeship, but to the much lesser position of justice of the peace for the District of Columbia.[5] Although nominated by the President, confirmed by the Senate, and with a sealed commission sitting on the desk of the Secretary of State, Marbury's appointment was stymied when the new President's Secretary of State, James Madison, refused to deliver the undelivered commissions to Marbury and other Federalist appointees.

In late 1801, Marbury filed suit directly in the U.S. Supreme Court seeking a writ of mandamus, a sort of injunction directed to government officials to perform non-discretionary acts. Marbury's argument was that withholding the commission was not within the executive's discretion, and its delivery could therefore be compelled by court order. Marbury's jurisdictional basis for filing suit directly in the U.S. Supreme Court (rather than starting in a lower federal court) was Section 13 of the Judiciary Act of 1789, which authorized the Supreme Court to issue writs of mandamus. Section 13 was ambiguous, insofar as it could be construed to provide for "original jurisdiction" in the Supreme Court in mandamus cases. ("Original jurisdiction" means that the case can be initiated in that court; appellate jurisdiction means that a case can be heard in that court only on appeal from a lower court.) We might speculate that Marbury filed in the high Court because he believed that the Supreme Court would have more institutional confidence than a lower court to issue a mandamus to an official as highly placed as James Madison.

Although *Marbury v. Madison* is seen now as a significant legal drama, it may have been somewhat of a sideshow in 1801. The political energies of the parties at the time were more likely focused on a much bigger battle: the attempt by the new Republican Congress to repeal the Judiciary Act of 1801. The question of whether Marbury would or would not receive his commission to the minor judgeship was trivial compared to the issue of whether the 16 new circuit judges created by the Act—who had taken their oaths of office and begun hearing cases—could be removed from office and their positions abolished by repeal of the Act. The Federalists in Congress argued that it was unconstitutional to abolish the newly created circuit judgeships because life-tenured Article III judges could be removed from office only by impeachment.[6] They further questioned

---

5. Another last minute piece of Federalist judicial legislation in February 1801 had created 42 of these District of Columbia "justice of the peace" positions, which were limited to five-year terms and were roughly analogous to federal "magistrate judges" today.

6. In fact, contrary to popular belief, the Constitution does not specifically say that Article III judges have "life tenure." Rather, "they shall hold their offices during good behavior," Art. III, § 1. "Good behavior" is not defined in the Constitution.

the constitutionality of requiring Supreme Court justices to sit both as members of the Supreme Court and of lower courts, and thus of requiring circuit-riding duty.

The Republican-dominated elected branches did not share these concerns, and on March 8, 1802, they passed the Repeal Act, which repealed the Judiciary Act of 1801. On April 29, they enacted the Judiciary Act of 1802, which kept the number of federal judicial circuits at six, but required the Supreme Court justices once again to ride circuit. The federal circuit judgeships, which were in effect abolished by the Repeal Act, were not restored by the 1802 Judiciary Act: instead, the latter act reconstituted the circuit courts as two-judge courts consisting of one Supreme Court justice (riding circuit) plus the local district court judge. Finally, the 1802 Act in effect abolished the Supreme Court's 1802 term. Under the Act, the Supreme Court would hold just one session, beginning in February each year, and would ride circuit in the late spring and fall. Since it was already the end of April, it was time to begin Circuit riding. The Supreme Court, consequently, did not sit in 1802.

The constitutionality of both the repeal of the Judiciary Act of 1801 and of the Judiciary Act of 1802 was tested in the Supreme Court in a case called *Stuart v. Laird*. The plaintiff, Laird, had won a damages judgment against Stuart in various proceedings in the Circuit Court in Virginia. The court that had awarded Laird's judgment was constituted by circuit judges appointed pursuant to the 1801 Judiciary Act. In December 1802, Laird sought a court order executing the judgment in the circuit court in Virginia. That court was now constituted under the 1802 Judiciary Act and consisted of the local district judge and a circuit-riding Supreme Court justice—none other than John Marshall himself. The defendants argued that the currently constituted circuit court had no power to execute the judgment because its creation by the 1802 Judiciary Act, and the abolition of the prior circuit court on which the new court was based, was unconstitutional.

Marshall, as circuit judge, rejected these arguments and entered judgment for the plaintiff, despite what scholars now agree was his view that the 1802 Repeal and Judiciary Acts were indeed unconstitutional. The defendant Stuart sought review in the Supreme Court. It is against this backdrop that the Supreme Court, in its February 1803 term, heard *Marbury v. Madison* and *Stuart v. Laird*.

2. Judiciary Act of 1789

The Judiciary Act of 1789 had 35 sections, establishing and laying out a procedural code for the federal courts. We excerpt sections 1, 13 and 25. Section 1 establishes the number of justices and their term for hearing cases; Section 13 specifies the Supreme Court's jurisdiction, and is discussed in *Marbury*; and Section 25 establishes Supreme Court review of federal law questions decided in state courts, and is examined in *Martin v. Hunters' Lessee*, which appears later in this chapter.

The Judiciary Act of 1789

Congress of the United States, begun and held at the City of New York on Wednesday the fourth of March one thousand seven hundred and eighty nine.

CHAP. XX.—An Act to establish the Judicial Courts of the United States.

SECTION 1. Be it enacted by the Senate and House of Representatives of the United States of America in Congress assembled, That the supreme court of the United States shall consist of a chief justice and five associate justices, any four of whom shall be a quorum, and shall hold annually at the seat of government two sessions, the one commencing the first Monday of February, and the other the first Monday of August. That the associate justices shall have precedence according to the date of their commissions, or when the commissions of two or more of them bear date on the same day, according to their respective ages....

SEC. 13. And be it further enacted, That the Supreme Court shall have exclusive jurisdiction of all controversies of a civil nature, where a state is a party, except between a state and its citizens; and except also between a state and citizens of other states, or aliens, in which latter case it shall have original but not exclusive jurisdiction. And shall have exclusively all such jurisdiction of suits or proceedings against ambassadors, or other public ministers, or their domestics, or domestic servants, as a court of law can have or exercise consistently with the law of nations; and original, but not exclusive jurisdiction of all suits brought by ambassadors, or other public ministers, or in which a consul, or vice consul, shall be a party. And the trial of issues in fact in the Supreme Court, in all actions at law against citizens of the United States, shall be by jury. The Supreme Court shall also have appellate jurisdiction from the circuit courts and courts of the several states, in the cases herein after specially provided for; and shall have power to issue writs of prohibition to the district courts, when proceeding as courts of admiralty and maritime jurisdiction, and writs of mandamus, in cases warranted by the principles and usages of law, to any courts appointed, or persons holding office, under the authority of the United States....

SEC. 25. And be it further enacted, That a final judgment or decree in any suit, in the highest court of law or equity of a State in which a decision in the suit could be had, where is drawn in question the validity of a treaty or statute of, or an authority exercised under the United States, and the decision is against their validity; or where is drawn in question the validity of a statute of, or an authority exercised under any State, on the ground of their being repugnant to the constitution, treaties or laws of the United States, and the decision is in favour of such their validity, or where is drawn in question the construction of any clause of the constitution, or of a treaty, or statute of, or commission held under the United States, and the decision is against the title, right, privilege or exemption specially set up or claimed by either party, under such clause of the said Constitution, treaty, statute or commission, may be re-examined and reversed or affirmed in the Supreme Court of the United States upon a writ of error, the citation being signed by the chief justice, or judge or chancellor of the court rendering or passing the judgment or decree complained of, or by a justice of the Supreme Court of the United States, in the same manner and under the same regulations, and the writ shall have the same effect, as if the judgment or decree complained of had been rendered or passed in a circuit court, and the proceeding upon the reversal shall also be the same, except that the Supreme Court, instead of remanding the cause for a final decision as before provided, may at their discretion, if the cause shall have been once remanded before, proceed to a final decision of the same, and award execution. But no other error shall be assigned or regarded as a ground of reversal in any such case as aforesaid, than such as appears on the face of the record, and immediately respects the before mentioned questions of validity or construction of the said constitution, treaties, statutes, commissions, or authorities in dispute....

Frederick Augustus Muhlenberg, Speaker of the House of Representatives

John Adams, Vice-President of the United States, and President of the Senate

APPROVED, September the Twenty fourth, 1789.

George Washington, President of the United States.

Guided Reading Questions

1. Why did Mr. Marbury think he could file his case directly in the Supreme Court? When reading the case, reconstruct his arguments in your own words.

2. Look at Article III of the Constitution. When reading the case, think about what Article III says about the "original" and the "appellate" jurisdiction of the Supreme Court. Now read § 13 of the Judiciary Act (printed above). Do you see any inconsistencies between Article III and § 13? John Marshall does.

3. Chief Justice Marshall's *Marbury* opinion gives several reasons for Marshall's claim that the Supreme Court must have the power to declare federal legislation inconsistent with the Constitution. Spend some time identifying these reasons, and thinking about whether you agree with them. Your professor is likely to discuss them at length in class.

4. *Marbury* draws a distinction between "political acts," which lie solely within the discretion of the executive and are not reviewable by the judiciary; and acts involving questions of individual rights, which are reviewable. How helpful is this distinction?

5. What was the immediate practical outcome of the *Marbury* opinion?

Marbury v. Madison

5 U.S. (1 Cranch) 137 (1803)

Unanimous decision: *Marshall* (CJ), Paterson, Chase, Washington (Cushing and Moore did not participate)

CHIEF JUSTICE MARSHALL delivered the opinion of the court.

At the last term on the affidavits then read and filed with the clerk, a rule was granted in this case, requiring the secretary of state to shew cause why a mandamus should not issue, directing him to deliver to William Marbury his commission as a justice of the peace of the county of Washington, in the district of Columbia....

In the order in which the court has viewed this subject, the following questions have been considered and decided.

1st. Has the applicant a right to the commission he demands?

2dly. If he has a right, and that right has been violated, do the laws of his country afford him a remedy?

3dly. If they do afford him a remedy, is it a mandamus issuing from this court?

The first object of enquiry is,

1st. Has the applicant a right to the commission he demands?

His right originates in an act of congress passed in February, 1801, concerning the district of Columbia.... It appears, from the affidavits, that in compliance with this law, a commission for William Marbury as a justice of peace for the county of Washington, was signed by John Adams, then president of the United States; after which the seal of the United States was affixed to it; but the commission has never reached the person for whom it was made out....

The last act to be done by the President, is the signature of the commission. He has then acted on the advice and consent of the senate to his own nomination. The time for deliberations has then passed. He has decided. His judgment, on the advice and consent of the senate concurring with his nomination, has been made, and the officer is appointed. This appointment is evidenced by an open, unequivocal act; and being the last act required from the person making it, necessarily excludes the idea of its being, so far as respects the appointment, an inchoate and incomplete transaction.... The transmission of the commission, is a practice directed by convenience, but not by law. It cannot therefore be necessary to constitute the appointment which must precede it, and which is the mere act of the President.... A commission is transmitted to a person already appointed; not to a person to be appointed or not, as the letter enclosing the commission should happen to get into the post-office and reach him in safety, or to miscarry....

Mr. Marbury, then, since his commission was signed by the President, and sealed by the secretary of state, was appointed; and as the law creating the office, gave the officer a right to hold for five years, independent of the executive, the appointment was not revocable; but vested in the officer legal rights, which are protected by the laws of his country. To withhold his commission, therefore, is an act deemed by the court not warranted by law, but violative of a vested legal right.

This brings us to the second enquiry; which is,

2dly. If he has a right, and that right has been violated, do the laws of his country afford him a remedy?

The very essence of civil liberty certainly consists in the right of every individual to claim the protection of the laws, whenever he receives an injury. One of the first duties of government is to afford that protection....

The government of the United States has been emphatically termed a government of laws, and not of men. It will certainly cease to deserve this high appellation, if the laws furnish no remedy for the violation of a vested legal right.... It behooves us then to enquire whether there be in its composition any ingredient which shall exempt it from legal investigation, or exclude the injured party from legal redress.... Is the act of delivering or withholding a commission to be considered as a mere political act, belonging to the executive department alone, for the performance of which, entire confidence is placed by our constitution in the supreme executive; and for any misconduct respecting which, the injured individual has no remedy. That there may be such cases is not to be questioned; but that every act of duty, to be performed in any of the great departments of government, constitutes such a case is not to be admitted....

It follows then that the question, whether the legality of an act of the head of a department be examinable in a court of justice or not, must always depend on the nature of that act. If some acts be examinable, and others not, there must be some rule of law to guide the court in the exercise of its jurisdiction. In some instances there may be difficulty in applying the rule to particular cases; but there cannot, it is believed, be much difficulty in laying down the rule. By the constitution of the United States, the President is invested with certain important political powers, in the exercise of which he is to use his own discretion, and is accountable only to his country in his political character, and to his own conscience. To aid him in the performance of these duties, he is authorized to appoint certain officers, who act by his authority and in conformity with his orders.

In such cases, their acts are his acts; and whatever opinion may be entertained of the manner in which executive discretion may be used, still there exists, and can exist, no power to control that discretion. The subjects are political. They respect the nation, not individual rights, and being entrusted to the executive, the decision of the executive is conclusive. The application of this remark will be perceived by adverting to the act of congress for establishing the department of foreign affairs. This office, as his duties were prescribed by that act, is to conform precisely to the will of the President. He is the mere organ by whom that will is communicated. The acts of such an officer, as an officer, can never be examinable by the courts.

But when the legislature proceeds to impose on that officer other duties; when he is directed peremptorily to perform certain acts; when the rights of individuals are dependent on the performance of those acts; he is so far the officer of the law; is amenable to the laws for his conduct; and cannot at his discretion sport away the vested rights of others.

The conclusion from this reasoning is, that where the heads of departments are the political or confidential agents of the executive, merely to execute the will of the President, or rather to act in cases in which the executive possesses a constitutional or legal discretion, nothing can be more perfectly clear than that their acts are only politically examinable. But where a specific duty is assigned by law, and individual rights depend upon the performance of that duty, it seems equally clear that the individual who considers himself injured, has a right to resort to the laws of his country for a remedy.

If this be the rule, let us enquire how it applies to the case under the consideration of the court. The power of nominating to the senate, and the power of appointing the person nominated, are political powers, to be exercised by the President according to his own discretion. When he has made an appointment, he has exercised his whole power, and his discretion has been completely applied to the case. If, by law, the officer be removable at the will of the President, then a new appointment may be immediately made, and the rights of the officer are terminated. But as a fact which has existed cannot be made never to have existed, the appointment cannot be annihilated; and consequently if the officer is by law not removable at the will of the President; the rights he has acquired are protected by the law, and are not resumeable by the President. They cannot be extinguished by executive authority, and he has the privilege of asserting them in like manner as if they had been derived from any other source.

The question whether a right has vested or not, is, in its nature, judicial, and must be tried by the judicial authority.... That question has been discussed, and the opinion is, that the latest point of time which can be taken as that at which the appointment was complete, and evidenced, was when, after the signature of the president, the seal of the United States was affixed to the commission.

It is then the opinion of the court,

1st. That by signing the commission of Mr. Marbury, the president of the United States appointed him a justice of peace, for the county of Washington in the district of Columbia; and that the seal of the United States, affixed thereto by the secretary of state, is conclusive testimony of the verity of the signature, and of the completion of the appointment; and that the appointment conferred on him a legal right to the office for the space of five years.

2dly. That, having this legal title to the office, he has a consequent right to the commission; a refusal to deliver which, is a plain violation of that right, for which the laws of his country afford him a remedy.

It remains to be enquired whether,

3dly. He is entitled to the remedy for which he applies. This depends on,

1st. The nature of the writ applied for, and,

2dly. The power of this court.

1st. The nature of the writ.

This writ, if awarded, would be directed to an officer of government, and its mandate to him would be, to use the words of Blackstone, "to do a particular thing therein specified, which appertains to his office and duty and which the court has previously determined, or at least supposes, to be consonant to right and justice." Or, in the words of Lord Mansfield, the applicant, in this case, has a right to execute an office of public concern, and is kept out of possession of that right.

These circumstances certainly concur in this case.

Still, to render the mandamus a proper remedy, the officer to whom it is directed, must be one to whom, on legal principles, such writ may be directed; and the person applying for it must be without any other specific and legal remedy.

1st. With respect to the officer to whom it would be directed. The intimate political relation, subsisting between the president of the United States and the heads of departments, necessarily renders any legal investigation of the acts of one of those high officers peculiarly irksome, as well as delicate; and excites some hesitation with respect to the propriety of entering into such investigation....

The province of the court is, solely, to decide on the rights of individuals, not to enquire how the executive, or executive officers, perform duties in which they have a discretion. Questions, in their nature political, or which are, by the constitution and laws, submitted to the executive, can never be made in this court.... Where the head of a department acts in a case, in which executive discretion is to be exercised; in which he is the mere organ of executive will; it is again repeated, that any application to a court to control, in any respect, his conduct, would be rejected without hesitation.

But where he is directed by law to do a certain act affecting the absolute rights of individuals, in the performance of which he is not placed under the particular direction of the President, and the performance of which, the President cannot lawfully forbid, and therefore is never presumed to have forbidden; as for example, to record a commission, or a patent for land, which has received all the legal solemnities; or to give a copy of such record; in such cases, it is not perceived on what ground the courts of the country are further excused from the duty of giving judgment, that right be done to an injured individual, than if the same services were to be performed by a person not the head of a department....

It is true that the mandamus, now moved for, is not for the performance of an act expressly enjoined by statute. It is to deliver a commission; on which subject the acts of Congress are silent. This difference is not considered as affecting the case. It has already been stated that the applicant has, to that commission, a vested legal right, of which the executive cannot deprive him. He has been appointed to an office, from which he is not removable at the will of the executive; and being so appointed, he has a right to the commission which the secretary has received from the president for his use. The act of congress does not indeed order the secretary of state to send it to him, but it is placed in his hands for the person entitled to it; and cannot be more lawfully withheld by him, than by any other person.... This, then, is a plain case for a mandamus, either to deliver the commission, or a copy of it from the record; and it only remains to be enquired, whether it can issue from this court.

The act to establish the judicial courts of the United States authorizes the supreme court "to issue writs of mandamus, in cases warranted by the principles and usages of law, to any courts appointed, or persons holding office, under the authority of the United States." The secretary of state, being a person holding an office under the authority of the United States, is precisely within the letter of the description; and if this court is not authorized to issue a writ of mandamus to such an officer, it must be because the law is unconstitutional, and therefore absolutely incapable of conferring the authority, and assigning the duties which its words purport to confer and assign.

The constitution vests the whole judicial power of the United States in one supreme court, and such inferior courts as congress shall, from time to time, ordain and establish. This power is expressly extended to all cases arising under the laws of the United States; and consequently, in some form, may be exercised over the present case; because the right claimed is given by a law of the United States.

In the distribution of this power it is declared that "the supreme court shall have original jurisdiction in all cases affecting ambassadors, other public ministers and consuls, and those in which a state shall be a party. In all other cases, the supreme court shall have appellate jurisdiction."

It has been insisted, at the bar, that as the original grant of jurisdiction, to the supreme and inferior courts, is general, and the clause, assigning original jurisdiction to the supreme court, contains no negative or restrictive words; the power remains to the legislature, to assign original jurisdiction to that court in other cases than those specified in the article which has been recited; provided those cases belong to the judicial power of the United States.

If it had been intended to leave it to the discretion of the legislature to apportion the judicial power between the supreme and inferior courts according to the will of that body, it would certainly have been useless to have proceeded further than to have defined the judicial powers, and the tribunals in which it should be vested. The subsequent part of the section is mere surplusage, is entirely without meaning, if such is to be the construction. If congress remains at liberty to give this court appellate jurisdiction, where the constitution has declared their jurisdiction shall be original; and original jurisdiction where the constitution has declared it shall be appellate; the distribution of jurisdiction, made in the constitution, is form without substance.

Affirmative words are often, in their operation, negative of other objects than those affirmed; and in this case, a negative or exclusive sense must be given to them or they have no operation at all. It cannot be presumed that any clause in the constitution is intended to be without effect; and therefore such a construction is inadmissible, unless the words require it....

When an instrument organizing fundamentally a judicial system, divides it into one supreme, and so many inferior courts as the legislature may ordain and establish; then enumerates its powers, and proceeds so far to distribute them, as to define the jurisdiction of the supreme court by declaring the cases in which it shall take original jurisdiction, and that in others it shall take appellate jurisdiction; the plain import of the words seems to be, that in one class of cases its jurisdiction is original, and not appellate; in the other it is appellate, and not original. If any other construction would render the clause inoperative, that is an additional reason for rejecting such other construction, and for adhering to their obvious meaning. To enable this court then to issue a mandamus, it must be shown to be an exercise of appellate jurisdiction, or to be necessary to enable them to exercise appellate jurisdiction....

It is the essential criterion of appellate jurisdiction, that it revises and corrects the proceedings in a cause already instituted, and does not create that cause. Although, therefore, a mandamus may be directed to courts, yet to issue such a writ to an officer for the delivery of a paper, is in effect the same as to sustain an original action for that paper, and therefore seems not to belong to appellate, but to original jurisdiction. Neither is it necessary in such a case as this, to enable the court to exercise its appellate jurisdiction.

The authority, therefore, given to the supreme court, by the act establishing the judicial courts of the United States, to issue writs of mandamus to public officers, appears not to be warranted by the constitution; and it becomes necessary to enquire whether a jurisdiction, so conferred, can be exercised.

The question, whether an act, repugnant to the constitution, can become the law of the land, is a question deeply interesting to the United States; but, happily, not of an intricacy proportioned to its interest. It seems only necessary to recognize certain principles, supposed to have been long and well established, to decide it.

That the people have an original right to establish, for their future government, such principles as, in their opinion, shall most conduce to their own happiness, is the basis, on which the whole American fabric has been erected. The exercise of this original right is a very great exertion; nor can it, nor ought it to be frequently repeated. The principles, therefore, so established, are deemed fundamental. And as the authority, from which they proceed, is supreme, and can seldom act, they are designed to be permanent.

This original and supreme will organizes the government, and assigns, to different departments, their respective powers. It may either stop here; or establish certain limits not to be transcended by those departments. The government of the United States is of the latter description. The powers of the legislature are defined, and limited; and that those limits may not be mistaken, or forgotten, the constitution is written. To what purpose are powers limited, and to what purpose is that limitation committed to writing, if these limits may, at any time, be passed by those intended to be restrained? The distinction, between a government with limited and unlimited powers, is abolished, if those limits do not confine the persons on whom they are imposed, and if acts prohibited and acts allowed, are of equal obligation. It is a proposition too plain to be contested, that the constitution controls any legislative act repugnant to it; or, that the legislature may alter the constitution by an ordinary act.

Between these alternatives there is no middle ground. The constitution is either a superior, paramount law, unchangeable by ordinary means, or it is on a level with ordinary legislative acts, and like other acts, is alterable when the legislature shall please to alter it. If the former part of the alternative be true, then a legislative act contrary to the constitution is not law: if the latter part be true, then written constitutions are absurd attempts, on the part of the people, to limit a power, in its own nature illimitable.

Certainly all those who have framed written constitutions contemplate them as forming the fundamental and paramount law of the nation, and consequently the theory of every such government must be, that an act of the legislature, repugnant to the constitution, is void. This theory is essentially attached to a written constitution, and is consequently to be considered, by this court, as one of the fundamental principles of our society. It is not therefore to be lost sight of in the further consideration of this subject.

If an act of the legislature, repugnant to the constitution, is void, does it, notwithstanding its invalidity, bind the courts, and oblige them to give it effect? Or, in other words, though it be not law, does it constitute a rule as operative as if it was a law? This would be to overthrow in fact what was established in theory; and would seem, at first view, an absurdity too gross to be insisted on. It shall, however, receive a more attentive consideration.

It is emphatically the province and duty of the judicial department to say what the law is. Those who apply the rule to particular cases, must of necessity expound and interpret that rule. If two laws conflict with each other, the courts must decide on the operation of each. So if a law be in opposition to the constitution; if both the law and the constitution apply to a particular case, so that the court must either decide that case conformably to the law, disregarding the constitution; or conformably to the constitution, disregarding the law; the court must determine which of these conflicting rules governs the case. This is of the very essence of judicial duty.

If then the courts are to regard the constitution; and the constitution is superior to any ordinary act of the legislature; the constitution, and not such ordinary act, must govern the case to which they both apply. Those then who controvert the principle that the constitution is to be considered, in court, as a paramount law, are reduced to the necessity of maintaining that courts must close their eyes on the constitution, and see only the law. This doctrine would subvert the very foundation of all written constitutions. It would declare that an act, which, according to the principles and theory of our government, is entirely void; is yet, in practice, completely obligatory. It would declare, that if the legislature shall do what is expressly forbidden, such act, notwithstanding the express prohibition, is in reality effectual. It would be giving to the legislature a practical and real omnipotence, with the same breath which professes to restrict their powers within narrow limits. It is prescribing limits, and declaring that those limits may be passed at pleasure.

That it thus reduces to nothing what we have deemed the greatest improvement on political institutions—a written constitution—would of itself be sufficient, in America, where written constitutions have been viewed with so much reverence, for rejecting the construction. But the peculiar expressions of the constitution of the United States furnish additional arguments in favor of its rejection.

The judicial power of the United States is extended to all cases arising under the constitution. Could it be the intention of those who gave this power, to say that, in using it, the constitution should not be looked into? That a case arising under the constitution should be decided without examining the instrument under which it arises? This is too extravagant to be maintained. In some cases then, the constitution must be looked into by the judges. And if they can open it at all, what part of it are they forbidden to read, or to obey?

There are many other parts of the constitution which serve to illustrate this subject. It is declared that "no tax or duty shall be laid on articles exported from any state." Suppose a duty on the export of cotton, of tobacco, or of flour; and a suit instituted to recover it. Ought judgment to be rendered in such a case? ought the judges to close their eyes on the constitution, and only see the law. The constitution declares that "no bill of attainder or ex post facto law shall be passed." If, however, such a bill should be passed and a person should be prosecuted under it; must the court condemn to death those victims whom the constitution endeavors to preserve? "No person," says the constitution, "shall be convicted of treason unless on the testimony of two witnesses to the fame overt act, or on confession in open court." Here the language of the constitution is addressed especially to the courts. It prescribes, directly for them, a rule of evidence not to be departed from. If the legislature should change that rule, and declare one witness, or a confession out of court, sufficient for conviction, must the constitutional principle yield to the legislative act?

From these, and many other selections which might be made, it is apparent, that the framers of the constitution contemplated that instrument, as a rule for the government of courts, as well as of the legislature.

Why otherwise does it direct the judges to take an oath to support it? This oath certainly applies, in an especial manner, to their conduct in their official character. How immoral to impose it on them, if they were to be used as the instruments, and the knowing instruments, for violating what they swear to support?

The oath of office, too, imposed by the legislature, is completely demonstrative of the legislative opinion on the subject. It is in these words, "I do solemnly swear that I will administer justice without respect to persons, and do equal right to the poor and to the rich; and that I will faithfully and impartially discharge all the duties incumbent on me as according to the best of my abilities and understanding, agreeably to the constitution, and laws of the United States."

Why does a judge swear to discharge his duties agreeably to the constitution of the United States, if that constitution forms no rule for his government? if it is closed upon him, and cannot be inspected by him? If such be the real state of things, this is worse than solemn mockery. To prescribe, or to take this oath, becomes equally a crime. It is also not entirely unworthy of observation, that in declaring what shall be the supreme law of the land, the constitution itself is first mentioned; and not the laws of the United States generally, but those only which shall be made in pursuance of the constitution, have that rank.

Thus, the particular phraseology of the constitution of the United States confirms and strengthens the principle, supposed to be essential to all written constitutions, that a law repugnant to the constitution is void; and that courts, as well as other departments, are bound by that instrument.

The rule must be discharged.

* * *

The opinion in *Stuart v. Laird* was issued a week after *Marbury*. Marshall decided to recuse himself from *Laird* on the ground that he had written the lower court opinion as circuit justice; significantly, that ground for recusal was unusual throughout the Marshall Court era, when Justices (including Marshall) routinely participated in Supreme Court review of their own circuit court decisions. Interestingly, Marshall's recusal tended to offset somewhat one of the arguments offered on behalf of Stewart: that it was unconstitutional to require Supreme Court justices to perform double-duty as circuit justices, in part because it would put them in the position of reviewing their own decisions.[7] In contrast to the extended reasoning offered in *Marbury*, the opinion in *Stuart v. Laird* was cursory, consisting of one paragraph of facts and three short paragraphs of legal analysis.

Stuart v. Laird

5 U.S. (1 Cranch) 299 (1803)

Unanimous decision: *Paterson*, Cushing, Chase, Washington, Moore (Chief Justice Marshall took no part)

JUSTICE PATERSON (Judge Cushing being absent on account of ill health,) delivered the opinion of the court.

On an action instituted by John Laird against Hugh Stuart, a judgment was entered in a court for the fourth circuit in the eastern district of Virginia, in December term 1801.

---

7. Given his recusal from *Laird,* it is even more striking that Marshall did *not* recuse himself from *Marbury*. As the former Secretary of State, Marshall had relevant firsthand knowledge that Marbury's commission was in fact signed and sealed—a fact that Marbury had some difficulty in proving in an evidentiary hearing before the Supreme Court prior to the issuance of the *Marbury* decision. Today, it would be unthinkable for a judge to sit on a case in which he was a potential material witness.

On this judgment, an execution was issued, returnable to April term 1802, in the same court. In the term of December 1802, John Laird obtained judgment at a court for the fifth circuit in the Virginia district, against Hugh Stuart and Charles L. Carter, upon their bond for the forthcoming and delivery of certain property therein mentioned, which had been levied upon by virtue of the above execution against the said Hugh Stuart.

Two reasons have been assigned by counsel for reversing the judgment on the forthcoming bond. 1. That as the bond was given for the delivery of property levied on by virtue of an execution issuing out of, and returnable to a court for the fourth circuit, no other court could legally proceed upon the said bond. This is true, if there be no statutable provision to direct and authorize such proceeding. Congress have constitutional authority to establish from time to time such inferior tribunals as they may think proper; and to transfer a cause from one such tribunal to another. In this last particular, there are no words in the constitution to prohibit or restrain the exercise of legislative power.

The present is a case of this kind. It is noting more than the removal of the suit brought by Stuart against Laird from the court of the fourth circuit to the court of the fifth circuit, which is authorized to proceed upon and carry it into full effect. This is apparent from the ninth section of the act entitled, "an act to amend the judicial system of the United States," passed the 29th of April, 1802. The forthcoming bond is an appendage to the cause, or rather a component part of the proceedings.

2d. Another reason for reversal is, that the judges of the supreme court have no right to sit as judges, not being appointed as such, or in other words, that they ought to have distinct commissions for that purpose. To this objection, which is of recent date, it is sufficient to observe, that practice and acquiescence under it for a period of several years, commencing with the organization of the judicial system, affords an irresistable answer, and has indeed fixed the construction. It is a contemporary interpretation of the most forcible nature. This practical exposition is too strong and obstinate to be shaken or controlled. Of course, the question is a rest, and ought not now to be disturbed. Judgment affirmed.

* * *

The traditional account of the *Marbury* decision is that Chief Justice Marshall executed a brilliant strategic ploy in which he successfully and greatly expanded the Court's power by establishing a solid precedential foundation for judicial review, while seeming on the surface to concede defeat by declining to provoke a confrontation with the Jefferson administration by ordering it to deliver Marbury's commission. That point is debatable, and remains much debated.

Less debatable are the historical facts. At the time *Marbury* was decided, the Federalist-dominated Supreme Court was under heavy attack from the Republican-dominated elected branches. Talk of judicial impeachments was in the air. As noted above, Congress had abolished existing judgeships, turning 16 Federalist circuit judges out of office; and the Supreme Court justices had been in effect ordered by Congress to ride circuit in the late Spring and Fall of 1802, thereby requiring them to sit as lower court judges and *not* as Supreme Court justices during that time.

The significant historical point is that Chief Justice Marshall and his Court backed away from every one of these confrontations. They meekly submitted to their circuit riding duties, which continued for the rest of Marshall's life. They made no objection to the abolition of the lower court justices despite having the opportunity to do so in *Stuart v. Laird*, nor did they attempt to challenge the elimination of their 1802 term. If anything, the events of 1802–03 set a precedent, later confirmed in Court rulings, upholding the constitutional authority of Congress to decide some of the most important structural questions about the federal courts, including how the lower courts would be organized, how many justices would sit, and when and in what capacity.

Marshall's decision to beat a strategic retreat may have well-served the Court's institutional health. In the short run, it probably took the edge off the impeachment furor. One Supreme Court justice, Samuel Chase, was impeached by the House, but he was not convicted by the Senate and kept his seat on the Court. No other Justices were impeached. More importantly, further congressional efforts to reduce the Court's powers receded. The most noteworthy, a bill to repeal the Court's power to review state court decisions on issues of federal law (a power discussed below) died in the House of Representatives in 1831.[8]

Seen from this vantage point, *Marbury* was arguably a modest assertion of judicial review in a low-stakes case in which the holding backed away from a confrontation with the elected branches.[9] And while subsequent decisions of the Marshall Court may have been controversial, that Court never again held an act of Congress unconstitutional. In fact, the next occasion on which the Supreme Court struck down an act of Congress came more than 50 years later, in *Scott v. Sandford* (1857) — a case more commonly known as *Dred Scott*.

C. Judicial Review and Judicial Supremacy

Guided Reading Questions: *Scott v. Sandford*

1. *Dred Scott* is one of the most reviled decisions ever issued by the Supreme Court. Like *Plessy v. Ferguson*, *Korematsu v. United States,* and *Lochner v. New York*, it sits at the heart of our constitutional "anti-cannon" — the cases we think of today as grotesque missteps in our constitutional history. The challenge as a contemporary reader of the case is to take the *legal* arguments presented in the case seriously. This is difficult to do, but we believe it is important. Writing off repulsive cases as "obviously" legally wrong oversimplifies what is a much more complex story about the intersections of history, social movements and constitutional law. Understanding how these things have in fact shaped our constitutional history will enable us better able to understand the constitutional conflicts of our own era.

2. *Dred Scott* is sometimes said to have "started" the Civil War. The Court, of course, could no more start a war than it could end one. What the Court did do in *Dred Scott* is invalidate the Missouri Compromise, an 1820 law that had attempted to create a politically sustainable balance of power between slave and free states. The law provided that slavery would be prohibited in territories formed out of the Louisiana Purchase region north of 36° 30 latitude, and permitted in territories south of that line (with the exception of Missouri, where slavery would be permitted even though it was north of the line). The Missouri Compromise

---

8. Section 25 of the 1789 Judiciary Act.
9. *See* Graber, *supra* note 1.

had been repealed in 1854 by the Kansas-Nebraska Act, but the underlying question of whether Congress had the power to prohibit slavery in the territories remained a point of significant controversy. As Mark Graber has written, the position taken by the *Dred Scott* majority probably sat at about the center of the antebellum political spectrum (at least among those who could vote and participate in the debate).[10] The justices, consequently, are unlikely to have thought of themselves as doing something radical in the case. The difficulty was that by the time the decision was issued, the political center could no longer hold. More extreme elements had taken control of both sides of the debate, and war was probably inevitable.

3. There were two issues presented in *Dred Scott*: whether Mr. Scott was a citizen of the United States and therefore entitled to sue in federal court under its "diversity of citizenship" jurisdiction; and whether Congress had power under the Constitution to prohibit slavery north of the Missouri Compromise line. The latter issue arose because Mr. Scott claimed that he became free by virtue his having been brought to live, for a time, on "free soil" — the upper Louisiana territory in what is now Minnesota. (The 1854 repeal of the Missouri Compromise was apparently assumed to be prospective, and not retroactive in its effect.) Despite holding that Mr. Scott was not a citizen and that the Court therefore did not have jurisdiction of the case, the majority went on to also decide the second question presented. Recall that John Marshall did something similar in *Marbury v. Madison*.

4. The congressional power holding turns on a dispute about the nature of the laws deeming slaves "property." The majority argues that slaves are recognized as property by the Constitution and that the Constitution thereby protects a slave holder's "property" interest in the same way it protects other rights. Justice McLean, writing in dissent, argues that the property laws governing slavery are merely "municipal" laws and thus need not be recognized outside of the jurisdictions in which they are passed. This was not a new debate, and both positions had vocal advocates at the time the case was decided.

Scott v. Sandford
60 U.S. 393 (1857)

Majority: *Taney* (CJ), Wayne, Catron, Daniel, Nelson, Grier, Campbell

Concurrences: *Wayne; Catron; Daniel; Nelson, Grier; Campbell* (all omitted)

Dissents: *McLean; Curtis*

MR. CHIEF JUSTICE TANEY delivered the opinion of the court.

There are two leading questions presented by the record:

1. Had the Circuit Court of the United States jurisdiction to hear and determine the case between these parties? And

---

10. Mark A. Graber, Dred Scott and the Problem of Constitutional Evil (2006).

2. If it had jurisdiction, is the judgment it has given erroneous or not?

The plaintiff in error, who was also the plaintiff in the court below, was, with his wife and children, held as slaves by the defendant, in the State of Missouri; and he brought this action in the Circuit Court of the United States for that district, to assert the title of himself and his family to freedom.

The declaration is in the form usually adopted in that State to try questions of this description, and contains the averment necessary to give the court jurisdiction; that he and the defendant are citizens of different States; that is, that he is a citizen of Missouri, and the defendant & citizen of New York.

The defendant pleaded in abatement to the jurisdiction of the court, that the plaintiff was not a citizen of the State of Missouri, as alleged in his declaration, being a negro of African descent, whose ancestors were of pure African blood, and who were brought into this country and sold as slaves....

The [first question presented] is simply this: Can a negro, whose ancestors were imported into this country, and sold as slaves, become a member of the political community formed and brought into existence by the Constitution of the United States, and as such become entitled to all the rights, and privileges, and immunities, guaranteed by that instrument to the citizen? One of which rights is the privilege of suing in a court of the United States in the cases specified in the Constitution.

> [The Court holds that former slaves could not become citizens of the United States because they would not have been recognized as part of the political community at the time the Constitution was enacted (a holding that was overturned after the Civil War by the Fourteenth Amendment), and that therefore the Court did not have jurisdiction to decide the case. The Court nonetheless went on to answer the second question presented: whether Congress had authority under the Constitution to enact the "Missouri Compromise" prohibiting slavery in the northern territories.]

[B]efore we proceed to [the second question], it may be proper to notice an objection taken to the judicial authority of this court to decide it; and it has been said, that as this court has decided against the jurisdiction of the Circuit Court on the plea in abatement, it has no right to examine any question presented by the exception; and that anything it may say upon that part of the case will be extra-judicial, and mere obiter dicta.

This is a manifest mistake; there can be no doubt as to the jurisdiction of this court to revise the judgment of a Circuit Court, and to reverse it for any error apparent on the record, whether it be the error of giving judgment in a case over which it had no jurisdiction, or any other material error; and this, too, whether there is a plea in abatement or not.... The correction of one error in the court below does not deprive the appellate court of the power of examining further into the record, and correcting any other material errors which may have been committed by the inferior court....

We proceed, therefore, to inquire whether the facts relied on by the plaintiff entitled him to his freedom.

The case, as he himself states it, on the record brought here by his writ of error, it this:

The plaintiff was a negro slave, belonging to Dr. Emerson, who was a surgeon in the army of the United States. In the year 1834, he took the plaintiff from the State of Missouri to the military post at Rock Island, in the State of Illinois, and held him there as a slave until the month of April or May, 1836. At the time last mentioned, said Dr. Emerson removed the plaintiff from said military post at Rock Island to the military post at Fort Snelling, situate on the west bank of the Mississippi river, in the Territory known as Upper Louisiana, acquired by the United States of France, and situate north of the latitude of thirty-six degrees thirty minutes north, and north of the State of Missouri. Said Dr. Emerson held the plaintiff in slavery at said Fort Snelling, from said last-mentioned date until the year 1838....

In the year 1838, said Dr. Emerson removed the plaintiff and said Harriet [also a slave, whom Scott had married], and their said daughter Eliza, from said Fort Snelling to the State of Missouri, where they have ever since resided. Before the commencement of this suit, said Dr. Emerson sold and conveyed the plaintiff, and Harriet, Eliza, and Lizzie, to the defendant, as slaves, and the defendant has ever since claimed to hold them, and each of them, as slaves.

In considering this part of the controversy, two questions arise: 1. Was he, together with his family, free in Missouri by reason of the stay in the territory of the United States hereinbefore mentioned? And 2. If they were not, is Scott himself free by reason of his removal to Rock Island, in the State of Illinois, as stated in the above admissions?

We proceed to examine the first question.

The act of Congress, upon which the plaintiff relies, declares that slavery and involuntary servitude, except as a punishment for crime, shall be forever prohibited in all that part of the territory ceded by France, under the name of Louisiana, which lies north of thirty-six degrees thirty minutes north latitude, and not included within the limits of Missouri. And the difficulty which meets us at the threshold of this part of the inquiry is, whether Congress was authorized to pass this law under any of the powers granted to it by the Constitution; for if the authority is not given by that instrument, it is the duty of this court to declare it void and inoperative, and incapable of conferring freedom upon any one who is held as a slave under the laws of any one of the States.

The counsel for the plaintiff has laid much stress upon that article in the Constitution which confers on Congress the power "to dispose of and make all needful rules and regulations respecting the territory or other property belonging to the United States"; but, in the judgment of the court, that provision had no bearing on the present controversy, and the power there given, whatever it may be, is confined, and was intended to be confined, to the territory which at that time belonged to, or was claimed by, the United States, and was within their boundaries as settled by the treaty with Great Britain, and can have no influence upon a territory afterwards acquired from a foreign Government. It was a special provision for a known and particular territory, and to meet a present emergency, and nothing more....

This brings us to examine by what provision of the Constitution the present Federal Government, under its delegated and restricted powers, is authorized to acquire territory outside of the original limits of the United States, and what powers it may exercise therein over the person or property of a citizen of the United States, while it remains a Territory, and until it shall be admitted as one of the States of the Union.... We do not mean [to question the power of Congress to acquire territories]. The power to expand the territory of the United States by the admission of new States is plainly given; and in the construction of this power by all the departments of the Government, it has been held to authorize the acquisition of territory, not fit for admission at the time, but to be admitted as soon as its population and situation would entitle it to admission.... All we mean to say on this point is, that, as there is no express regulation in the Constitution defining the power which the General Government may exercise over the person or property of a citizen in a Territory thus acquired, the court must necessarily look to the provisions and principles of the Constitution, and its distribution of powers, for the rules and principles by which its decision must be governed.

Taking this rule to guide us, it may be safely assumed that citizens of the United States who migrate to a Territory belonging to the people of the United States, cannot be ruled as mere colonists, dependent upon the will of the General Government, and to be governed by any laws it may think proper to impose. The principle upon which our Governments rest, and upon which alone they continue to exist, is the union of States, sovereign and independent within their own limits in their internal and domestic concerns, and bound together as one people by a General Government, possessing certain enumerated and restricted powers, delegated to it by the people of the several States, and exercising supreme authority within the scope of the powers granted to it, throughout the dominion of the United States. A power, therefore, in the General Government to obtain and hold colonies and dependent territories, over which they might legislate without restriction, would be inconsistent with its own existence in its present form. Whatever it acquires, it acquires for the benefit of the people of the several states who created it. It is their trustee acting for them, and charged with the duty of promoting the interests of the whole people of the Union in the exercise of the powers specifically granted....

[Until a Territory becomes a state], it is undoubtedly necessary that some Government should be established, in order to organize society, and to protect the inhabitants in their persons and property; and as the people of the United States could act in this matter only through the Government which represented them, and through which they spoke and acted when the Territory was obtained, it was not only within the scope of its powers, but it was its duty to pass such laws and establish such a Government as would enable those by whose authority they acted to reap the advantages anticipated from its acquisition, and to gather there a population which would enable it to assume the position to which it was destined among the States of the Union. The power to acquire necessarily carries with it the power to preserve and apply to the purposes for which it was acquired. The form of government to be established necessarily rested in the discretion of Congress. It was their duty to establish the one that would be best suited for the protection and security of the citizens of the United States, and other inhabitants who might be authorized to take up their abode there, and that must always depend upon the existing condition of the Territory, as to the number and character of its inhabitants, and their situation in the Territory. In some cases a Government, consisting of persons appointed by the Federal Government, would best subserve the interests of the Territory, when the inhabitants were few and scattered, and new to one another. In other instances, it would be more advisable to commit the powers of self-government to the people who had settled in the Territory, as being the most competent to determine what was best for their own interests. But some form of civil authority would be absolutely necessary to organize and preserve civilized society, and prepare it to become a State; and what is the best form must always depend on the condition of the Territory at the time, and the choice of the mode must depend upon the exercise of a discretionary power by Congress, acting within the scope of its constitutional authority, and not infringing upon the rights of person or rights of property of the citizen who might go there to reside, or for any other lawful purpose. It was acquired by the exercise of this discretion, and it must be held and governed in like manner, until it is fitted to be a State.

But the power of Congress over the person or property of a citizen can never be a mere discretionary power under our Constitution and form of Government. The powers of the Government and the rights and privileges of the citizen are regulated and plainly defined by the Constitution itself. And when the Territory becomes a part of the United States, the Federal Government enters into possession in the character impressed upon it by those who created it. It enters upon it with its powers over the citizen strictly defined, and limited by the Constitution, from which it derives its own existence, and by virtue of which alone it continues to exist and act as a Government and sovereignty. It has no power of any kind beyond it; and it cannot, when it enters a Territory of the United States, put off its character, and assume discretionary or despotic powers which the Constitution has denied to it. It cannot create for itself a new character separated from the citizens of the United States, and the duties it owes them under of the United States, the Government and the citizen both enter it under the authority of the Constitution, with their respective rights defined and marked out; and the Federal Government can exercise no power over his person or property, beyond what that instrument confers, nor lawfully deny any right which it has reserved.

A reference to a few of the provisions of the Constitution will illustrate this proposition. For example, no one, we presume, will contend that Congress can make any law in a Territory respecting that establishment of religion, or the free exercise thereof, or abridging the freedom of speech or of the press, or the right of the people of the Territory peaceably to assemble, and to petition the Government for the redress of grievances. . . .

These powers, and others, in relation to rights of person, which it is not necessary here to enumerate, are, in express and positive terms, denied to the General Government; and the rights of private property have been guarded with equal care. Thus the rights of property are united with the rights of person, and placed on the same ground by the *fifth amendment to the Constitution*, which provides that no person shall be deprived of life, liberty, and property, without due process of law. And an act of Congress which deprives a citizen of the United States of his liberty or property, merely because he came himself or brought his property into a particular Territory of the United States, and who had committed no offence against the laws, could hardly be dignified with the name of due process of law. . . .

The powers over person and property of which we speak are not only not granted to Congress, but are in express terms denied, and they are forbidden to exercise them. And this prohibition is not confined to the States, but the words are general, and extend to the whole territory over which the Constitution gives it power to legislate, including those portions of it remaining under Territorial Government, as well as that covered by States. It is a total absence of power everywhere within the dominion of the United States, and places the citizens of a Territory, so far as these rights are concerned, on the same footing with citizens of the States, and guards them as firmly and plainly against any inroads which the General Government might attempt, under the plea of implied or incidental powers. And if Congress itself cannot do this—if it is beyond the powers conferred on the Federal Government—it will be admitted, we presume, that it could not authorize a Territorial Government to exercise them. It could confer no power on any local Government, established by its authority, to violate the provisions of the Constitution.

It seems, however, to be supposed, that there is a difference between property in a slave and other property, and that different rules may be applied to it in expounding the Constitution of the United States. . . . [I]f the Constitution recognizes the right of property of the master in a slave, and makes no distinction between that description of property and other property owned by a citizen, no tribunal, acting under the authority of the United States, whether it be legislative, executive, or judicial, has a right to draw such a distinction, or deny to it the benefit of the provisions and guarantees which have been provided for the protection of private property against the encroachments of the Government.

Now, as we have already said in an earlier part of this opinion, upon a different point, the right of property in a slave is distinctly and expressly affirmed in the Constitution. The right to traffic in it, like an ordinary article of merchandise and property, was guarantied to the citizens of the United States, in every State that might desire it, for twenty years. And the Government in express terms is pledged to protect it in all future time, if the slave escapes from his owner. This is done in plain words — too plain to be misunderstood. And no word can be found in the Constitution which gives Congress a greater power over slave property, or which entitles property of that kind to less protection than property of any other description. The only power conferred is the power coupled with the duty of guarding and protecting the owner in his rights.

Upon these considerations, it is the opinion of the court that the act of Congress which prohibited a citizen from holding and owning property of this kind in the territory of the United States north of the line therein mentioned, is not warranted by the Constitution, and is therefore void; and that neither Dred Scott himself, nor any of his family, were made free by being carried into this territory; even if they had been carried there by the owner, with the intention of becoming a permanent resident....

And as the Circuit court had no jurisdiction, either in the case stated in the plea in abatement, or in the one stated in the exception, its judgment in favor of the defendant is erroneous, and must be reversed.

MR. JUSTICE McLEAN dissenting.

[Justice McLean first disputes the assertion by the majority that historical practice disproves Mr. Scott's claim to U.S. citizenship.]

The power of Congress to establish Territorial Governments, and to prohibit the introduction of slavery therein, is the next point to be considered....

The prohibition of slavery north of thirty-six degrees thirty minutes, and of the State of Missouri, contained in the act admitting that State into the Union, was passed by a vote of 134, in the House of Representatives, to 42. Before Mr. Monroe signed the act, it was submitted by him to his Cabinet, and they held the restriction of slavery in a Territory to be within the constitutional powers of Congress. It would be singular, if in 1804 Congress had power to prohibit the introduction of slaves in Orleans Territory from any other part of the Union, under the penalty of freedom to the slave, if the same power, embodied in the Missouri compromise, could not be exercised in 1820.

But this law of Congress, which prohibits slavery north of Missouri and of thirty-six degrees thirty minutes, is declared to have been null and void by my brethren. And this opinion is founded mainly, as I understand, on the distinction drawn between the ordinance of 1787 and the Missouri compromise line. In what does the distinction consist? ... I am unable to perceive the force of this distinction. That the ordinance was intended for the government of the Northwestern Territory, and was limited to such Territory, is admitted. It was extended to Southern Territories, with modifications, by acts of Congress, and to some Northern Territories. But the ordinance was made valid by the act of Congress, and without such act could have been of no force. It rested for its validity on the act of Congress, the same, in my opinion, as the Missouri compromise line. If Congress may establish a Territorial Government in the exercise of its discretion, it is a clear principle that a court cannot control that discretion. This being the case, I do not see on what ground the act is held to be void. It did not purport to forfeit property, or take it for public purposes. It only prohibited slavery; in doing which, it followed the ordinance of 1787.

I will now consider … "The effect of taking slaves into a State or Territory, and so holding them, where slavery is prohibited."

If the principle laid down in the case of Prigg v. The State of Pennsylvania is to be maintained, and it is certainly to be maintained until overruled, as the law of this court, there can be no difficulty on this point. In that case, the court says: "The state of slavery is deemed to be a mere municipal regulation, founded upon and limited to the range of the territorial laws." If this be so, slavery can exist nowhere except under the authority of law, founded on usage having the force of law, or by statutory recognition…. [I]f slavery be limited to the range of the territorial laws, how can the slave be coerced to serve in a State or Territory, not only without the authority of law, but against its express provisions? What gives the master the right to control the will of his slave? The local law, which exists in some form. But where there is no such law, can the master control the will of the slave by force? Where no slavery exists, the presumption, without regard to color, is in favor of freedom. Under such a jurisdiction, may the colored man be levied on as the property of his master by a creditor? On the decease of the master, does the slave descend to his heirs as property? Can the master sell him? Any one or all of these acts may be done to the slave, where he is legally held to service. But where the law does not confer this power, it cannot be exercised.

I think the judgment of the court below should be reversed.

MR. JUSTICE CURTIS dissenting.

I dissent from the opinion pronounced by the Chief Justice, and from the judgment which the majority of the Court think it proper to render in this case….

If [the Territorial Clause] does contain a power to legislate respecting the territory, what art the limits of that power?

To this I answer, that, in common with all the other legislative powers of Congress, it finds limits in the express prohibitions on Congress not to do certain things; that, in the exercise of the legislative power, Congress cannot pass an ex post facto law or bill of attainder; and so in respect to each of the other prohibitions contained in the Constitution.

Besides this, the rules and regulations must be needful. But undoubtedly the question whether a particular rule or regulation be needful, must be finally determined by Congress itself. Whether a law be needful, is a legislative or political, not a judicial, question. Whatever Congress deems needful is so, under the grant of power.

Nor am I aware that it has ever been questioned that laws providing for the temporary government of the settlers on the public lands are needful, not only to prepare them for admission to the Union as States, but even to enable the United States to dispose of the lands.

Without government and social order, there can be no property; for without law, its ownership, its use, and the power of disposing of it, cease to exist, in the sense in which those words are used and understood in all civilized States.

Since, then, this power was manifestly conferred to enable the United States to dispose of its public lands to settlers, and to admit them into the Union as States, when in the judgment of Congress they should be fitted therefor, since these were the needs provided for, since it is confessed that Government is indispensable to provide for those needs, and the power is, to make all needful rules and regulations respecting the territory, I cannot doubt that this is a power to govern the inhabitants of the territory, by such laws as Congress deems needful, until they obtain admission as States.

Review Questions and Explanations: *Dred Scott*

1. Why is *Dred Scott* legally wrong? Did the Court misinterpret the Constitution? Historical research has revealed that the majority justices believed that their decision would settle the question of whether slavery could be prohibited in the territories—one of the foremost points of dispute between pro- and anti-slavery politicians, and a controversy that seemed incapable of settlement through normal political processes. Southern leaders had already threatened to secede from the union if John C. Fremont, the anti-slavery Republican candidate, defeated Democrat James Buchanan in the 1856 presidential election (he did not). By constitutionalizing the pro-slavery position, the justices believed they were preserving the union. Is that what is wrong with the decision—meddling in politics? Judicial hubris?

2. Law students often have a highly celebratory view of judicial review. We have intentionally juxtaposed *Marbury* with *Dred Scott* in order to challenge that view. The same Court that gave us *Marbury* (as well as *Brown v. Board of Education* and other great cases) also gave us *Dred Scott*. Does this change your thinking about the value of deciding important issues through judicial review versus ordinary politics?

3. One way to reconcile a celebratory view of judicial review with dreadful decisions is to say that the Court just got the Constitution wrong in those cases. Law professor Jamal Greene has argued that we use cases in the "anti-cannon" in just this way, to construct self-affirming constitutional narratives.[11] But, as Greene and others point out, legions of scholars have shown that the arguments put forth in the anti-cannon cases are almost always supported by what were considered at the time to be reasonable legal arguments. Courts, in other words, don't just make this stuff up. What does that tell us about judicial review and, indeed, about constitutional law making itself? Can our constitutional system live with the fact that a morally reprehensible decision may be legally reasonable? Can it live with the possibility that there may well be more than one legally reasonable answer to difficult constitutional questions?

4. Consider the above question in the context of today's constitutional controversies. Most law students can see that there are reasonable legal arguments on both sides of contemporary constitutional disputes, even if they believe that one side is better reasoned than the other. Will future generations look back on these decisions the way we back on *Dred Scott*? In other words, will they take seriously the legal arguments on both sides of today's hard cases, or will they write off the losing side's arguments as self-evidently wrong? If they do deem one side's arguments simply wrong, will it be because they are better lawyers than we are? If not that, to what would you attribute their response?

5. Many, if not most, legal scholars accept that the tools of legal reasoning are under-determinate in at least some constitutional cases. Yet public officials and judges seem exceptionally reluctant to admit this openly. Consider the type of dialogue that occurs at most Supreme Court confirmation hearings. Over and over again, senators ask the nominees if they are going to "apply the law" or whether instead they are going to impose their "personal preferences" when deciding constitutional cases. And over and over again the nominees swear to follow the law and nothing but the law, thank you very much.

---

11. Jamal Greene, *The Anti Cannon*, 125 Harv. L. Rev. 379 (2011).

This is a remarkably shallow narrative. It assumes that *either* there are legally determinative answers to constitutional questions, *or* that the Court's constitutional choices turn on the purely political preferences of the justices. As you probably recognize by this point in your legal studies, both of these positions are caricatures of a more complex reality. Constitutional law making is not a mechanical process — judges cannot just input data and generate a constitutionally correct answer. Nor, though, do most judges believe that they are imposing their own personal preferences in lieu of law. Rather, they recognize that judges acting in good faith will often disagree about what the best answer to a hard legal question is, and that those disagreements will often reflect conflicting views about constitutional values, approaches to interpretation, and the appropriate institutional roles of courts and legislatures.

Why do you think our public discourse on this point is so cramped? What would courts, elected officials, and the public each gain or lose by a more frank discussion of the reality of judicial decisionmaking?

Exercise: Judicial Review and Constitutional Interpretation

You are a legislative aide to the Chair of the Senate Judiciary Committee. The President, who is a member of the same party as your boss, has just announced that she is nominating Vince Chin to a recently vacated Supreme Court seat. You have been charged with preparing Judge Chin for the confirmation hearings, which will be held before the Judiciary Committee next month. You know he will be asked questions, like those noted above, about how Supreme Court justices should decide hard cases. Both Judge Chin and your boss believe that the hearings are an opportunity to help educate the public about the proper role of the Supreme Court in our governing system. They have asked you to prepare a three or four paragraph statement, to be included in Judge Chin's opening statement to the Committee, explaining how justices should decide constitutional cases. Work with two or three of your classmates to prepare the statement.

Cooper v. Aaron, our next case, was argued on September 11, 1958. The next day the Court issued a brief per curiam opinion that unanimously affirmed the Court of Appeals judgment that the state defendants were bound by the Supreme Court's previous desegregation orders. The Court issued its decision quickly "[i]n order that the School Board might know, without doubt, its duty in this regard before the opening of school, which had been set for the following Monday, September 15, 1958." The full opinion, excerpted below, was announced on September 29. In an unusual step, intended to place particular emphasis on the Court's unanimity, all nine justices signed the opinion. (Justice Frankfurter added a concurrence.)

Cooper v. Aaron

358 U.S. 1 (1958)

Opinion of the Court by THE CHIEF JUSTICE [WARREN], MR. JUSTICE BLACK, MR. JUSTICE FRANKFURTER, MR. JUSTICE DOUGLAS, MR. JUSTICE BURTON,

MR. JUSTICE CLARK, MR. JUSTICE HARLAN, MR. JUSTICE BRENNAN, and MR. JUSTICE WHITTAKER.

As this case reaches us it raises questions of the highest importance to the maintenance of our federal system of government. It necessarily involves a claim by the Governor and Legislature of a State that there is no duty on state officials to obey federal court orders resting on this Court's considered interpretation of the United States Constitution. Specifically it involves actions by the Governor and Legislature of Arkansas upon the premise that they are not bound by our holding in Brown v. Board of Education. That holding was that the Fourteenth Amendment forbids States to use their governmental powers to bar children on racial grounds from attending schools where there is state participation through any arrangement, management, funds or property. We are urged to uphold a suspension of the Little Rock School Board's plan to do away with segregated public schools in Little Rock until state laws and efforts to upset and nullify our holding in Brown v. Board of Education have been further challenged and tested in the courts. We reject these contentions.

On May 17, 1954, this Court decided that enforced racial segregation in the public schools of a State is a denial of the equal protection of the laws enjoined by the *Fourteenth Amendment*. Brown v. Board of Education. The Court postponed, pending further argument, formulation of a decree to effectuate this decision. That decree was rendered May 31, 1955. Brown v. Board of Education, 349 U.S. 294. In the formulation of that decree the Court recognized that good faith compliance with the principles declared in Brown might in some situations "call for elimination of a variety of obstacles in making the transition to school systems operated in accordance with the constitutional principles set forth in our May 17, 1954, decision." ...

On May 20, 1954, three days after the first Brown opinion, the Little Rock District School Board adopted, and on May 23, 1954, made public, a statement of policy entitled "Supreme Court Decision — Segregation in Public Schools." In this statement the Board recognized that

"It is our responsibility to comply with Federal Constitutional Requirements and we intend to do so when the Supreme Court of the United States outlines the method to be followed."

Thereafter the Board undertook studies of the administrative problems confronting the transition to a desegregated public school system at Little Rock.... While the School Board was thus going forward with its preparation for desegregating the Little Rock school system, other state authorities, in contrast, were actively pursuing a program designed to perpetuate in Arkansas the system of racial segregation which this Court had held violated the Fourteenth Amendment. First came, in November 1956, an amendment to the State Constitution flatly commanding the Arkansas General Assembly to oppose "in every Constitutional manner the Un-constitutional desegregation decisions of May 17, 1954 and May 31, 1955 of the United States Supreme Court," Ark. Const., Amend. 44, and, through the initiative, a pupil assignment law, Ark. Stat. 80-1519 to 80-1524. Pursuant to this state constitutional command, a law relieving school children from compulsory attendance at racially mixed schools, Ark. Stat. 80-1525, and a law establishing a State Sovereignty Commission, Ark. Stat. 6-801 to 6-824, were enacted by the General Assembly in February 1957....

On September 2, 1957, the day before these Negro students were to enter Central High, the school authorities were met with drastic opposing action on the part of the Governor of Arkansas who dispatched units of the Arkansas National Guard to the Central High

School grounds and placed the school "off limits" to colored students. As found by the District Court in subsequent proceedings, the Governor's action had not been requested by the school authorities, and was entirely unheralded.... On the morning of the next day, September 4, 1957, the Negro children attempted to enter the high school but, as the District Court later found, units of the Arkansas National Guard "acting pursuant to the Governor's order, stood shoulder to shoulder at the school grounds and thereby forcibly prevented the 9 Negro students ... from entering," as they continued to do every school day during the following three weeks.

That same day, September 4, 1957, the United States Attorney for the Eastern District of Arkansas was requested by the District Court to begin an immediate investigation in order to fix responsibility for the interference with the orderly implementation of the District Court's direction to carry out the desegregation program. Three days later, September 7, the District Court denied a petition of the School Board and the Superintendent of Schools for an order temporarily suspending continuance of the program.

Upon completion of the United States Attorney's investigation, he and the Attorney General of the United States, at the District Court's request, entered the proceedings and filed a petition on behalf of the United States, as *amicus curiae*, to enjoin the Governor of Arkansas and officers of the Arkansas National Guard from further attempts to prevent obedience to the court's order. After hearings on the petition, the District Court found that the School Board's plan had been obstructed by the Governor through the use of National Guard troops, and granted a preliminary injunction on September 20, 1957, enjoining the Governor and the officers of the Guard from preventing the attendance of Negro children at Central High School, and from otherwise obstructing or interfering with the orders of the court in connection with the plan. The National Guard was then withdrawn from the school.

The next school day was Monday, September 23, 1957. The Negro children entered the high school that morning under the protection of the Little Rock Police Department and members of the Arkansas State Police. But the officers caused the children to be removed from the school during the morning because they had difficulty controlling a large and demonstrating crowd which had gathered at the high school. On September 25, however, the President of the United States dispatched federal troops to Central High School and admission of the Negro students to the school was thereby effected. Regular army troops continued at the high school until November 27, 1957. They were then replaced by federalized National Guardsmen who remained throughout the balance of the school year. Eight of the Negro students remained in attendance at the school throughout the school year.

We come now to the aspect of the proceedings presently before us. On February 20, 1958, the School Board and the Superintendent of Schools filed a petition in the District Court seeking a postponement of their program for desegregation. Their position in essence was that because of extreme public hostility, which they stated had been engendered largely by the official attitudes and actions of the Governor and the Legislature, the maintenance of a sound educational program at Central High School, with the Negro students in attendance, would be impossible. The Board therefore proposed that the Negro students already admitted to the school be withdrawn and sent to segregated schools, and that all further steps to carry out the Board's desegregation program be postponed for a period later suggested by the Board to be two and one-half years.

After a hearing the District Court granted the relief requested by the Board. Among other things the court found that the past year at Central High School had been attended by conditions of "chaos, bedlam and turmoil"; that there were "repeated incidents of more or less serious violence directed against the Negro students and their property"; that there was "tension and unrest among the school administrators, the class-room teachers, the pupils, and the latters' parents, which inevitably had an adverse effect upon the educational program"; that a school official was threatened with violence; that a "serious financial burden" had been cast on the School District; that the education of the students had suffered "and under existing conditions will continue to suffer"; that the Board would continue to need "military assistance or its equivalent"; that the local police department would not be able "to detail enough men to afford the necessary protection"; and that the situation was "intolerable." ...

The significance of [the lower courts' findings that the School Board and the Superintendent of Schools acted in good faith] is to be considered in light of the fact, indisputably revealed by the record before us, that the conditions they depict are directly traceable to the actions of legislators and executive officials of the State of Arkansas, taken in their official capacities, which reflect their own determination to resist this Court's decision in the *Brown* case and which have brought about violent resistance to that decision in Arkansas. In its petition for certiorari filed in this Court, the School Board itself describes the situation in this language: "The legislative, executive, and judicial departments of the state government opposed the desegregation of Little Rock schools by enacting laws, calling out troops, making statements villifying federal law and federal courts, and failing to utilize state law enforcement agencies and judicial processes to maintain public peace." ...

The constitutional rights of respondents are not to be sacrificed or yielded to the violence and disorder which have followed upon the actions of the Governor and Legislature.... Law and order are not here to be preserved by depriving the Negro children of their constitutional rights....

The controlling legal principles are plain. The command of the Fourteenth Amendment is that no "State" shall deny to any person within its jurisdiction the equal protection of the laws. "A State acts by its legislative, its executive, or its judicial authorities. It can act in no other way. The constitutional provision, therefore, must mean that no agency of the State, or of the officers or agents by whom its powers are exerted, shall deny to any person within its jurisdiction the equal protection of the laws." ...

What has been said, in the light of the facts developed, is enough to dispose of the case. However, we should answer the premise of the actions of the Governor and Legislature that they are not bound by our holding in the Brown case. It is necessary only to recall some basic constitutional propositions which are settled doctrine.

Article VI of the Constitution makes the Constitution the "supreme Law of the Land." In 1803, Chief Justice Marshall, speaking for a unanimous Court, referring to the Constitution as "the fundamental and paramount law of the nation," declared in the notable case of Marbury v. Madison, that "It is emphatically the province and duty of the judicial department to say what the law is." This decision declared the basic principle that the federal judiciary is supreme in the exposition of the law of the Constitution, and that principle has ever since been respected by this Court and the Country as a permanent and indispensable feature of our constitutional system. It follows that the interpretation of the Fourteenth Amendment enunciated by this Court in the Brown case is the supreme law of the land, and Art. VI of the Constitution makes it of binding effect on the States "any Thing in the Constitution or Laws of any State to the Contrary notwithstanding." Every state legislator and executive and judicial officer is solemnly committed by oath taken pursuant to Art. VI, cl. 3, "to support this Constitution." Chief Justice Taney, speaking for a unanimous Court in 1859, said that this requirement reflected the framers' "anxiety to preserve it [the Constitution] in full force, in all its powers, and to guard against resistance to or evasion of its authority, on the part of a State...." Ableman v. Booth, 21 How. 506, 524.[12]

No state legislator or executive or judicial officer can war against the Constitution without violating his undertaking to support it. Chief Justice Marshall spoke for a unanimous Court in saying that: "If the legislatures of the several states may, at will, annul the judgments of the courts of the United States, and destroy the rights acquired under those judgments, the constitution itself becomes a solemn mockery...." United States v. Peters, 5 Cranch 115, 136. A Governor who asserts a power to nullify a federal court order is similarly restrained. If he had such power, said Chief Justice Hughes, in 1932, also for a unanimous Court, "it is manifest that the fiat of a state Governor, and not the Constitution of the United States, would be the supreme law of the land; that the restrictions of the Federal Constitution upon the exercise of state power would be but impotent phrases...."

It is, of course, quite true that the responsibility for public education is primarily the concern of the States, but it is equally true that such responsibilities, like all other state activity, must be exercised consistently with federal constitutional requirements as they apply to state action. The Constitution created a government dedicated to equal justice under law. The Fourteenth Amendment embodied and emphasized that ideal. State support of segregated schools through any arrangement, management, funds, or property cannot be squared with the Amendment's command that no State shall deny to any person within its jurisdiction the equal protection of the laws. The right of a student not to be segregated on racial grounds in schools so maintained is indeed so fundamental and pervasive that it is embraced in the concept of due process of law. The basic decision in Brown was unanimously reached by this Court only after the case had been briefed and twice argued and the issues had been given the most serious consideration. Since the first Brown opinion three new Justices have come to the Court. They are at one with the Justices still on the Court who participated in that basic decision as to its correctness, and that decision is now unanimously reaffirmed. The principles announced in that decision and the obedience of the States to them, according to the command of the Constitution, are indispensable for the protection of the freedoms guaranteed by our fundamental charter for all of us. Our constitutional ideal of equal justice under law is thus made a living truth.... Judgment accordingly.

* * *

CASE NOTES: *Boerne, Dickerson,* and Judicial Supremacy

Cooper v. Aaron shows the Court's reaction to a claim by state officials that they were entitled to interpret the Constitution in a manner diverging from Supreme Court rulings. Two more recent cases address the same claim as asserted by Congress. In *City of Boerne v. Flores,* 521 U.S. 507 (1997), presented in Chapter 1, the Court held, in essence, that Congress's power to enforce the Fourteenth Amendment did not include the power to interpret the Constitution independently of the courts by creating or expanding judicially recognized Fourteenth Amendment rights:

---

12. Editors' note: *Ableman v. Booth* involved a constitutional challenge to a state "personal freedom law," designed to protect fugitive slaves captured in free states against forced return to slavery. The Court held the state law preempted by the federal Fugitive Slave Act of 1850, which established streamlined federal procedures for forced return of fugitive slaves. Is there an unintended irony here?

There is language in our opinion in Katzenbach v. Morgan which could be interpreted as acknowledging a power in Congress to enact legislation that expands
the rights contained in § 1 of the Fourteenth Amendment. This is not a necessary
interpretation, however, or even the best one....

If Congress could define its own powers by altering the Fourteenth Amendment's
meaning, no longer would the Constitution be "superior paramount law, unchangeable by ordinary means." It would be "on a level with ordinary legislative
acts, and, like other acts, ... alterable when the legislature shall please to alter
it." Marbury v. Madison. Under this approach, it is difficult to conceive of a
principle that would limit congressional power.... Shifting legislative majorities
could change the Constitution and effectively circumvent the difficult and detailed
amendment process contained in Article V.

In *Dickerson v. United States* (2000), the Court considered the constitutionality of a
1968 federal statute that purported to overrule the Court's famous 1966 decision in
Miranda v. Arizona (1966). *Miranda* held that statements by an accused made in the
absence of notification of the right to remain silent and right to counsel (the so-called
"*Miranda* warning") were generally inadmissible against an accused. But a provision of
the Omnibus Crime Control and Safe Streets Act of 1968 purported to overrule *Miranda*
by providing statements by an accused were admissible notwithstanding the absence of
a "Miranda warning," so long as they were otherwise voluntarily made. *See* 18 U.S.C.
§ 3501. For three decades, courts assumed that the statute was ineffective because of
Miranda. But in the late 1990s, a handful of courts and commentators began to argue
that, because the Supreme Court had consistently described *Miranda* as a "prophylactic"
or pragmatic rule to protect constitutional rights, but one that was not itself constitutionally
required, it was subject to being legislatively overruled. Therefore, the argument went,
the 1968 statute superseded *Miranda*.

The Supreme Court in *Dickerson* responded to this argument as follows:

Congress retains the ultimate authority to modify or set aside any judicially
created rules of evidence and procedure that are not required by the
Constitution.... But Congress may not legislatively supersede our decisions interpreting and applying the Constitution. See, e.g., City of Boerne v. Flores
(1997). This case therefore turns on whether the Miranda Court announced a
constitutional rule or merely exercised its supervisory authority to regulate
evidence in the absence of congressional direction.

By a 7–2 majority, the Court held that *Miranda* was indeed a constitutional rule and the
congressional attempt to overrule it in 18 U.S.C. § 3501 was, therefore, unconstitutional.
Of note for present purposes is the assertion that Congress cannot supersede the Court's
constitutional decisions by legislation, and the citation to *Boerne* for that proposition.

Review Questions and Explanations: Judicial Review and Judicial Supremacy

1. We asked you at the beginning of this chapter to consider whether *Marbury*'s
assertion of the Court's power of judicial review went as far as that of later
decisions. The argument that it did not rests on a distinction between judicial
review and judicial supremacy. Judicial review is the power of courts to declare
that acts of other governmental bodies violate the Constitution. Judicial supremacy

is the idea that the Court gets the final word on the question, and that all other branches must comply with the Court's decision. Under a system of judicial review, the Court could—consistent with *Marbury*—refuse to enforce what it sees as unconstitutional laws. Other branches could then decide whether or not they agreed with the Court's decision, and could react accordingly.

2. The decisions in *City of Boerne, Cooper v. Aaron,* and *Dickerson v. United States* illustrate this distinction in different ways. In *Boerne,* the Court aggressively slaps down a congressional effort to expand the religious freedom protections of the First and Fourteenth Amendments beyond that approved by the Court. In *Cooper,* Arkansas asserts the right to make its own determination about the meaning of the Equal Protection clause. In *Dickerson,* Congress attempts to limit the rights given in *Miranda.* These challenges to judicial supremacy raise distinct issues. *Boerne* involves an effort to *expand* the scope of a constitutional right beyond that recognized by the Court, while *Cooper* and *Dickerson* involve efforts to do the opposite. Second, in *Boerne* and *Dickerson,* it is Congress that wants a say in constitutional interpretation, while in *Cooper* it is a state. What differences do these distinctions make in the cases? Should they make a difference?

3. The next case, *Martin v. Hunter's Lessee,* talks about the Court's power to review constitutional decisions issued by state supreme courts. The power to review decisions of state courts is arguably more important than the power to review federal legislation. Why might that be? Read the opinion with this question in mind.

D. Supreme Court Review of State Court Opinions

Guided Reading Questions: *Martin v. Hunter's Lessee*

1. As is the case in many of the Court's older decisions, it can be hard to sort out the facts in *Martin v. Hunter's Lessee.* When reading the case, pay attention to the source in which each party has staked his claim to the disputed property. Understanding this will help you understand the Court's decision.

2. You should review Article III of the Constitution, and section 25 of the 1789 Judiciary Act (printed before the *Marbury* case) before reading *Martin.* The losing party in the Virginia Supreme Court appealed that court's decision to the U.S. Supreme Court. What was the basis for claiming that the U.S. Supreme Court had appellate jurisdiction in this case?

3. There is a similarity between the argument made by Virginia in *Martin* and John Marshall's decision in *Marbury.* See if you can spot it.

4. In rebutting the Virginia court's claims, Justice Story makes three distinct arguments. Two of them are text based and one is grounded in policy. Can you identify each argument? Which do you think are the strongest and weakest of them?

Martin v. Hunter's Lessee

14 U.S. (1 Wheat.) 304 (1816)

Unanimous decision: *Story*, Washington, Johnson, Livingston, Todd, Duvall

Concurrence: *Johnson* (omitted) (Marshall did not participate)

JUSTICE STORY delivered the opinion of the court.

[This case involved a land dispute in Virginia. Mr. Martin based his claim to the land on a title granted by the British Crown prior to the Revolutionary War. Mr. Hunter's lessee based his claim on a Virginia state law that divested property rights of British citizens who had not renounced their loyalty to the British crown. The U.S. Supreme Court had earlier held that the Treaty of 1783, entered into by the United States and Great Britain after the war, preserved Mr. Martin's title. The U.S. Supreme Court then remanded the case to the Virginia Supreme Court with instructions to enter judgment accordingly. The Virginia Supreme Court refused, asserting that the U.S. Supreme Court did not have authority to overturn the final decision of a state supreme court, even on questions involving federal law. The decision below is the U.S. Supreme Court's response.]

This is a writ of error from the court of appeals of Virginia, founded upon the refusal of that court to obey the mandate of this court, requiring the judgment rendered in this very cause, at February term, 1813, to be carried into due execution. The following is the judgment of the court of appeals rendered on the mandate: 'The court is unanimously of opinion, that the appellate power of the supreme court of the United States does not extend to this court, under a sound construction of the constitution of the United States; that so much of the 25th section of the act of congress to establish the judicial courts of the United States, as extends the appellate jurisdiction of the supreme court to this court, is not in pursuance of the constitution of the United States; that the writ of error, in this cause, was improvidently allowed under the authority of that act; that the proceedings thereon in the supreme court were, *coram non judice*, in relation to this court, and that obedience to its mandate be declined by the court.'

The questions involved in this judgment are of great importance and delicacy. Perhaps it is not too much to affirm, that, upon their right decision, rest some of the most solid principles which have hitherto been supposed to sustain and protect the constitution itself. The great respectability, too, of the court whose decisions we are called upon to review, and the entire deference which we entertain for the learning and ability of that court, add much to the difficulty of the task which has so unwelcomely fallen upon us. It is, however, a source of consolation, that we have had the assistance of most able and learned arguments to aid our inquiries; and that the opinion which is now to be pronounced has been weighed with every solicitude to come to a correct result, and matured after solemn deliberation.

Before proceeding to the principal questions, it may not be unfit to dispose of some preliminary considerations which have grown out of the arguments at the bar.

The constitution of the United States was ordained and established, not by the states in their sovereign capacities, but emphatically, as the preamble of the constitution declares, by 'the people of the United States.' There can be no doubt that it was competent to the people to invest the general government with all the powers which they might deem proper and necessary; to extend or restrain these powers according to their own good pleasure, and to give them a paramount and supreme authority. As little doubt can there be, that the people had a right to prohibit to the states the exercise of any powers which were, in their judgment, incompatible with the objects of the general compact; to make the powers of the state governments, in given cases, subordinate to those of the nation, or to reserve to themselves those sovereign authorities which they might not choose to delegate to either. The constitution was not, therefore, necessarily carved out of existing state sovereignties, nor a surrender of powers already existing in state institutions, for the powers of the states depend upon their own constitutions; and the people of every state had the right to modify and restrain them, according to their own views of the policy or principle. On the other hand, it is perfectly clear that the sovereign powers vested in the state governments, by their respective constitutions, remained unaltered and unimpaired, except so far as they were granted to the government of the United States.

These deductions do not rest upon general reasoning, plain and obvious as they seem to be. They have been positively recognized by one of the articles in amendment of the constitution, which declares, that 'the powers not delegated to the United States by the constitution, nor prohibited by it to the states, are reserved to the *states* respectively, or *to the people.*' The government, then, of the United States, can claim no powers which are not granted to it by the constitution, and the powers actually granted, must be such as are expressly given, or given by necessary implication. On the other hand, this instrument, like every other grant, is to have a reasonable construction, according to the import of its terms; and where a power is expressly given in general terms, it is not to be restrained to particular cases, unless that construction grow out of the context expressly, or by necessary implication. The words are to be taken in their natural and obvious sense, and not in a sense unreasonably restricted or enlarged.

The constitution unavoidably deals in general language. It did not suit the purposes of the people, in framing this great charter of our liberties, to provide for minute specifications of its powers, or to declare the means by which those powers should be carried into execution. It was foreseen that this would be a perilous and difficult, if not an impracticable, task. The instrument was not intended to provide merely for the exigencies of a few years, but was to endure through a long lapse of ages, the events of which were locked up in the inscrutable purposes of Providence. It could not be foreseen what new changes and modifications of power might be indispensable to effectuate the general objects of the charter; and restrictions and specifications, which, at the present, might seem salutary, might, in the end, prove the overthrow of the system itself. Hence its powers are expressed in general terms, leaving to the legislature, from time to time, to adopt its own means to effectuate legitimate objects, and to mould and model the exercise of its powers, as its own wisdom, and the public interests, should require.

With these principles in view, principles in respect to which no difference of opinion ought to be indulged, let us now proceed to the interpretation of the constitution, so far as regards the great points in controversy.

The third article of the constitution is that which must principally attract our attention. The 1st. section declares, 'the judicial power of the United States shall be vested in one supreme court, and in such other inferior courts as the congress may, from time to time, ordain and establish.' The 2d section declares, that 'the judicial power shall extend to all cases in law or equity, arising under this constitution, the laws of the United States, and the treaties made, or which shall be made, under their authority; to all cases affecting ambassadors, other public ministers and consuls; to all cases of admiralty and maritime jurisdiction; to controversies to which the United States shall be a party; to controversies between two or more states; between a state and citizens of another state; between citizens of different states; between citizens of the same state, claiming lands under the grants of different states; and between a state or the citizens thereof, and foreign states, citizens, or subjects.' It then proceeds to declare, that 'in all cases affecting ambassadors, other public ministers and consuls, and those in which a state shall be a party, the supreme court shall have *original jurisdiction*. In all the other cases before mentioned the supreme court shall have *appellate jurisdiction*, both as to law and fact, with such exceptions, and under such regulations, as the congress shall make.'

Such is the language of the article creating and defining the judicial power of the United States. It is the voice of the whole American people solemnly declared, in establishing one great department of that government which was, in many respects, national, and in all, supreme. It is a part of the very same instrument which was to act not merely upon individuals, but upon states; and to deprive them altogether of the exercise of some powers of sovereignty, and to restrain and regulate them in the exercise of others.

Let this article be carefully weighed and considered. The language of the article throughout is manifestly designed to be mandatory upon the legislature. Its obligatory force is so imperative, that congress could not, without a violation of its duty, have refused to carry it into operation. The judicial power of the United States *shall be vested* (not may be vested) in one supreme court, and in such inferior courts as congress may, from time to time, ordain and establish. Could congress have lawfully refused to create a supreme court, or to vest in it the constitutional jurisdiction? 'The judges, both of the supreme and inferior courts, *shall hold* their offices' during good behavior ... and '*shall*, at stated times, receive, for their services, a compensation which shall not be diminished during their continuance in office.' Could congress create or limit any other tenure of the judicial office? Could they refuse to pay, at stated times, the stipulated salary, or diminish it during the continuance in office? But one answer can be given to these questions: it must be in the negative. The object of the constitution was to establish three great departments of government; the legislative, the executive, and the judicial departments. The first was to pass laws, the second to approve and execute them, and the third to expound and enforce them. Without the latter, it would be impossible to carry into effect some of the express provisions of the constitution. How, otherwise, could crimes against the United States be tried and punished? How could causes between two states be heard and determined? The judicial power must, therefore, be vested in some court, by congress; and to suppose that it was not an obligation binding on them, but might, at their pleasure, be admitted or declined, is to suppose that, under the sanction of the constitution, they might defeat the constitution itself; a construction which would lead to such a result cannot be sound.

The same expression, 'shall be vested,' occurs in other parts of the constitution, in defining the powers of the other co-ordinate branches of the government. The first article declares that 'all legislative powers herein granted *shall be vested* in a congress of the United States.' Will it be contended that the legislative power is not absolutely vested? That the words merely refer to some future act, and mean only that the legislative power may be thereafter be vested? The second article declares that 'the executive power *shall be vested* in a president of the United States of America.' Could congress vest it in any other person; or, is it to await their good pleasure, whether it is to vest at all? It is apparent that such a construction, in either case, would be utterly inadmissible. Why, then, is it entitled to a better support in reference to the judicial department?

If, then, it is a duty of congress to vest the judicial power of the United States, it is a duty to vest the *whole judicial power*. The language, if imperative as to one part, is imperative as to all. If it were otherwise, this anomaly would exist, that congress might successively refuse to vest the jurisdiction in any one class of cases enumerated in the constitution, and thereby defeat the jurisdiction as to all; for the constitution has not singled out any class on which congress are bound to act in preference to others.

The next consideration is as to the courts in which the judicial power shall be vested. It is manifest that a supreme court must be established; but whether it be equally obligatory to establish inferior courts, is a question of some difficulty. If congress may lawfully omit to establish inferior courts, it might follow, that in some of the enumerated cases the judicial power could nowhere exist. The supreme court can have original jurisdiction in two classes of cases only, viz. in cases affecting ambassadors, other public ministers and consuls, and in cases in which a state is a party. Congress cannot vest any portion of the judicial power of the United States, except in courts ordained and established by itself; and if in any of the cases enumerated in the constitution, the state courts did not then possess jurisdiction, the appellate jurisdiction of the supreme court (admitting that it could act on state courts) could not reach those cases, and, consequently, the injunction of the constitution, that the judicial power 'shall be vested,' would be disobeyed. It would seem, therefore, to follow, that congress are bound to create some inferior courts, in which to vest all that jurisdiction which, under the constitution, is exclusively vested in the United States, and of which the supreme court cannot take original cognizance. They might establish one or more inferior courts; they might parcel out the jurisdiction among such courts, from time to time, at their own pleasure. But the whole judicial power of the United States should be, at all times, vested either in an original or appellate form, in some courts created under its authority....

It being, then, established that the language of this clause is imperative, the next question is as to the cases to which it shall apply. The answer is found in the constitution itself. The judicial power shall extend to all the cases enumerated in the constitution. As the mode is not limited, it may extend to all such cases, in any form, in which judicial power may be exercised. It may, therefore, extend to them in the shape of original or appellate jurisdiction, or both; for there is nothing in the nature of the cases which binds to the exercise of the one in preference to the other. But even admitting that the language of the constitution is not mandatory...

This leads us to the consideration of the great question as to the nature and extent of the appellate jurisdiction of the United States. We have already seen that appellate jurisdiction is given by the constitution to the supreme court in all cases where it has not original jurisdiction; subject, however, to such exceptions and regulations as congress may prescribe. It is, therefore, capable of embracing every case enumerated in the constitution, which is not exclusively to be decided by way of original jurisdiction. But the exercise of appellate jurisdiction is far from being limited by the terms of the constitution to the supreme court. There can be no doubt that congress may create a succession of inferior tribunals, in each of which it may vest appellate as well as original jurisdiction. The judicial power is delegated by the constitution in the most general terms, and may, therefore, be exercised by congress under every variety of form, of appellate or original jurisdiction. And as there is nothing in the constitution which restrains or limits this power, it must, therefore, in all other cases, subsist in the utmost latitude of which, in its own nature, it is susceptible.

As, then, by the terms of the constitution, the appellate jurisdiction is not limited as to the supreme court, and as to this court it may be exercised in all other cases than those of which it has original cognizance, what is there to restrain its exercise over state tribunals in the enumerated cases? The appellate power is not limited by the terms of the third article to any particular courts. The words are, 'the judicial power (which includes appellate power) shall extend to all cases,' &c., and 'in all other cases before mentioned the supreme court shall have appellate jurisdiction.' It is the case, then, and not the court, that gives the jurisdiction. If the judicial power extends to the case, it will be in vain to search in the letter of the constitution for any qualification as to the tribunal where it depends. It is incumbent, then, upon those who assert such a qualification to show its existence by necessary implication. If the text be clear and distinct, no restriction upon its plain and obvious import ought to be admitted, unless the inference be irresistible.

If the constitution meant to limit the appellate jurisdiction to cases pending in the courts of the United States, it would necessarily follow that the jurisdiction of these courts would, in all the cases enumerated in the constitution, be exclusive of state tribunals. How otherwise could the jurisdiction extend to *all* cases arising under the constitution, laws, and treaties of the United States, or *to all cases* of admiralty and maritime jurisdiction? If some of these cases might be entertained by state tribunals, and no appellate jurisdiction as to them should exist, then the appellate power would not extend to *all*, but to *some*, cases. If state tribunals might exercise concurrent jurisdiction over all or some of the other classes of cases in the constitution without control, then the appellate jurisdiction of the United States might, as to such cases, have no real existence, contrary to the manifest intent of the constitution. Under such circumstances, to give effect to the judicial power, it must be construed to be exclusive; and this not only when the *casus foederis* should arise directly, but when it should arise, incidentally, in cases pending in state courts. This construction would abridge the jurisdiction of such court far more than has been ever contemplated in any act of congress.

On the other hand, if, as has been contended, a discretion be vested in congress to establish, or not to establish, inferior courts at their own pleasure, and congress should not establish such courts, the appellate jurisdiction of the supreme Court would have nothing to act upon, unless it could act upon cases pending in the state courts. Under such circumstances it must be held that the appellate power would extend to state courts; for the constitution is peremptory that it shall extend to certain enumerated cases, which cases could exist in no other courts. Any other construction, upon this supposition, would involve this strange contradiction, that a discretionary power vested in congress, and which they might rightfully omit to exercise, would defeat the absolute injunctions of the constitution in relation to the whole appellate power.

But it is plain that the framers of the constitution did contemplate that cases within the judicial cognizance of the United States not only might but would arise in the state courts, in the exercise of their ordinary jurisdiction. With this view the sixth article declares, that 'this constitution, and the laws of the United States which shall be made in pursuance thereof, and all treaties made, or which shall be made, under the authority of the United States, shall be the supreme law of the land, and the judges in every state shall be bound thereby, any thing in the constitution or laws of any state to the contrary notwith-standing.' It is obvious that this obligation is imperative upon the state judges in their official, and not merely in their private, capacities. From the very nature of their judicial duties they would be called upon to pronounce the law applicable to the case in judgment. They were not to decide merely according to the laws or constitution of the state, but according to the constitution, laws and treaties of the United States — 'the supreme law of the land.' . . .

It must, therefore, be conceded that the constitution not only contemplated, but meant to provide for cases within the scope of the judicial power of the United States, which might yet depend before state tribunals. It was foreseen that in the exercise of their ordinary jurisdiction, state courts would incidentally take cognizance of cases arising under the constitution, the laws, and treaties of the United States. Yet to all these cases the judicial power, by the very terms of the constitution, is to extend. It cannot extend by original jurisdiction if that was already rightfully and exclusively attached in the state courts, which (as has been already shown) may occur; it must, therefore, extend by appellate jurisdiction, or not at all. It would seem to follow that the appellate power of the United States must, in such cases, extend to state tribunals; and if in such cases, there is no reason why it should not equally attach upon all others within the purview of the constitution.

It has been argued that such an appellate jurisdiction over state courts is inconsistent with the genius of our governments, and the spirit of the constitution. That the latter was never designed to act upon state sovereignties, but only upon the people, and that if the power exists, it will materially impair the sovereignty of the states, and the independence of their courts. We cannot yield to the force of this reasoning; it assumes principles which we cannot admit, and draws conclusions to which we do not yield our assent.

It is a mistake that the constitution was not designed to operate upon states, in their corporate capacities. It is crowded with provisions which restrain or annul the sovereignty of the states in some of the highest branches of their prerogatives. The tenth section of the first article contains a long list of disabilities and prohibitions imposed upon the states. Surely, when such essential portions of state sovereignty are taken away, or prohibited to be exercised, it cannot be correctly asserted that the constitution does not act upon the states. The language of the constitution is also imperative upon the states as to the performance of many duties. It is imperative upon the state legislatures to make laws prescribing the time, places, and manner of holding elections for senators and representatives, and for electors of president and vice-president. And in these, as well as some other cases, congress have a right to revise, amend, or supercede the laws which may be passed by state legislatures. When, therefore, the states are stripped of some of the highest attributes of sovereignty, and the same are given to the United States; when the legislatures of the states are, in some respects, under the control of congress, and in every case are, under the constitution, bound by the paramount authority of the United States; it is certainly difficult to support the argument that the appellate power over the decisions of state courts is contrary to the genius of our institutions. The courts of the United States can, without question, revise the proceedings of the executive and legislative authorities of the states, and if they are found to be contrary to the constitution, may declare them to be of no legal validity. Surely the exercise of the same right over judicial tribunals is not a higher or more dangerous act of sovereign power....

This is not all. A motive of another kind, perfectly compatible with the most sincere respect for state tribunals, might induce the grant of appellate power over their decisions. That motive is the importance, and even necessity of *uniformity* of decisions throughout the whole United States, upon all subjects within the purview of the constitution. Judges of equal learning and integrity, in different states, might differently interpret a statute, or a treaty of the United States, or even the constitution itself: If there were no revising authority to control these jarring and discordant judgments, and harmonize them into uniformity, the laws, the treaties, and the constitution of the United States would be different in different states, and might, perhaps, never have precisely the same construction, obligation, or efficacy, in any two states. The public mischiefs that would attend such a state of things would be truly deplorable; and it cannot be believed that they could have escaped the enlightened convention which formed the constitution. What, indeed, might then have been only prophecy, has now become fact; and the appellate jurisdiction must continue to be the only adequate remedy for such evils....

On the whole, the court are of opinion, that the appellate power of the United States does extend to cases pending in the state courts; and that the 25th section of the judiciary act, which authorizes the exercise of this jurisdiction in the specified cases, by a writ of error, is supported by the letter and spirit of the constitution. We find no clause in that instrument which limits this power; and we dare not interpose a limitation where the people have not been disposed to create one.... Judgment affirmed.

Review Questions and Explanations: *Martin v. Hunter's Lessee*

1. At the time *Martin* was decided, the Virginia Supreme Court had been operating in one form or another for more than 200 years. It obviously did not take kindly to having its decisions being overturned by a young and presumptuous court like the U.S. Supreme Court.

2. The Virginia Supreme Court ruled that Section 25 of the Judiciary Act of 1789 was unconstitutional. Like Congress in *City of Boerne* and Arkansas in *Cooper v. Aaron*, the Virginia court was disputing the power of the U.S. Supreme Court to override its own understanding of what the federal Constitution requires. Of these three entities—Congress, a state government, and a state Supreme Court—which has the strongest case against the Supreme Court's claim of judicial supremacy?

3. Many people consider *Martin v. Hunter's Lessee* as or more important of a case as *Marbury v. Madison*. Do you understand why?

4. In one of his more famous quotations, Justice Oliver Wendell Holmes, Jr., wrote "I do not think the United States would come to an end if we lost our power to declare an act of Congress void. I do think the Union would be imperilled if we could not make that declaration as to the laws of the several States." O. Holmes, *Law and the Court*, in Collected Legal Papers 291, 295–296 (1952). What do you think he meant? Do you agree?

Like *Martin v. Hunter's Lessee*, the next case, *Michigan v. Long*, also raises questions about federal court review of state court decisions. Before reading *Long*, it is worth reviewing some basic concepts involving the interaction between the federal Constitution and state constitutions. State constitutions often protect the same types of rights as are protected in the federal Constitution. Most state constitutions, for example, include a bill of rights protecting such things as freedom of speech and religion. These constitutions often use the same language found in the federal Bill of Rights. But they are *state* constitutions. As such, they need not define those rights in exactly (or even remotely) the same way they are defined by the federal Constitution. This is true even when the rights are identically worded. Furthermore, state courts are the final interpreters of state laws, including state constitutions. A state law or state constitutional provisions that deprives someone of a federally protected right will be *pre-empted* by federal law, but it is the state court that gets to decide what the state law means, even if its decision about the meaning of the law subjects the state law to federal override.

Because state courts have the final say about the meaning of state laws, federal courts rarely agree to hear cases in which state courts used state constitutions to protect *more* rights than those granted by the federal Constitution. Unless the expansion of state rights intrudes on the federally protected rights of others, the Court traditionally has seen little need to evaluate these cases, because its decision would not change the outcome: the greater protection offered by the relevant state constitution (again presuming it did not infringe on any other federal rights) would stand. Federal review of such cases consequently risks becoming merely "advisory." Advisory decisions—decisions that offer opinions on federal law but do not change outcomes in actual cases—raise constitutional concerns because of Article III's requirement that the Court limit its jurisdiction to "cases and controversies" (discussed in the next chapter).

But the significant overlap between state and federal constitutional texts means that state supreme court decisions often discuss *both* state and federal rights. Unfortunately, these decisions are not always clear about which right, the state or the federal, the court is basing its decision on. In other words, it can be difficult in these cases to tell whether the state court is basing its decision on the state right, the federal right, or both. The question presented in *Michigan v. Long* is whether the Court should exercise its power to review state court decisions in cases in which the state court decision is muddled in this way.

Prior to *Long*, the Court rarely heard such cases. *Long*, however, expands the circumstances under which the Court will do so. The key to understanding *Long* is to figure out why the Court would do this.

Michigan v. Long
463 U.S. 1032 (1983)

Majority: *O'Connor*, Burger (CJ), White, Powell, Rehnquist, Blackmun

Concurrence: *Blackmun* (omitted)

Dissents: *Brennan*, Marshall (omitted); *Stevens*

JUSTICE O'CONNOR delivered the opinion of the Court.

In Terry v. Ohio, we upheld the validity of a protective search for weapons in the absence of probable cause to arrest because it is unreasonable to deny a police officer the right "to neutralize the threat of physical harm," ... when he possesses an articulable suspicion that an individual is armed and dangerous. We did not, however, expressly address whether such a protective search for weapons could extend to an area beyond the person in the absence of probable cause to arrest. In the present case, respondent David Long was convicted for possession of marijuana found by police in the passenger compartment and trunk of the automobile that he was driving. The police searched the passenger compartment because they had reason to believe that the vehicle contained weapons potentially dangerous to the officers. We hold that the protective search of the passenger compartment was reasonable under the principles articulated in Terry and other decisions of this Court. We also examine Long's argument that the decision below rests upon an adequate and independent state ground, and we decide in favor of our jurisdiction....

Before reaching the merits, we must consider Long's argument that we are without jurisdiction to decide this case because the decision below rests on an adequate and independent state ground. The court below referred twice to the state constitution in its opinion, but otherwise relied exclusively on federal law. Long argues that the Michigan courts have provided greater protection from searches and seizures under the state constitution than is afforded under the Fourth Amendment, and the references to the state constitution therefore establish an adequate and independent ground for the decision below.

It is, of course, "incumbent upon this Court ... to ascertain for itself ... whether the asserted non-federal ground independently and adequately supports the judgment." ... Although we have announced a number of principles in order to help us determine whether various forms of references to state law constitute adequate and independent state grounds, we openly admit that we have thus far not developed a satisfying and consistent approach for resolving this vexing issue. In some instances, we have taken the strict view that if the ground of decision was at all unclear, we would dismiss the case.... In more recent cases, we have ourselves examined state law to determine whether state courts have used federal law to guide their application of state law or to provide the actual basis for the decision that was reached.... In Oregon v. Kennedy, we rejected an invitation to remand to the state court for clarification even when the decision rested in part on a case from the state court, because we determined that the state case itself rested upon federal grounds. We added that "[e]ven if the case admitted of more doubt as to whether federal and state grounds for decision were intermixed, the fact that the state court relied to the extent it did on federal grounds requires us to reach the merits." ...

This *ad hoc* method of dealing with cases that involve possible adequate and independent state grounds is antithetical to the doctrinal consistency that is required when sensitive issues of federal-state relations are involved. Moreover, none of the various methods of disposition that we have employed thus far recommends itself as the preferred method that we should apply to the exclusion of others, and we therefore determine that it is appropriate to reexamine our treatment of this jurisdictional issue in order to achieve the consistency that is necessary.

The process of examining state law is unsatisfactory because it requires us to interpret state laws with which we are generally unfamiliar, and which often, as in this case, have not been discussed at length by the parties. Vacation and continuance for clarification have also been unsatisfactory both because of the delay and decrease in efficiency of judicial administration, ... and, more important, because these methods of disposition place significant burdens on state courts to demonstrate the presence or absence of our jurisdiction.... Finally, outright dismissal of cases is clearly not a panacea because it cannot be doubted that there is an important need for uniformity in federal law, and that this need goes unsatisfied when we fail to review an opinion that rests primarily upon federal grounds and where the *independence* of an alleged state ground is not apparent from the four corners of the opinion. We have long recognized that dismissal is inappropriate "where there is strong indication ... that the federal constitution as judicially construed controlled the decision below." ...

Respect for the independence of state courts, as well as avoidance of rendering advisory opinions, have been the cornerstones of this Court's refusal to decide cases where there is an adequate and independent state ground. It is precisely because of this respect for state courts, and this desire to avoid advisory opinions, that we do not wish to continue to decide issues of state law that go beyond the opinion that we review, or to require state courts to reconsider cases to clarify the grounds of their decisions. Accordingly, when, as in this case, a state court decision fairly appears to rest primarily on federal law, or to be interwoven with the federal law, and when the adequacy and independence of any possible state law ground is not clear from the face of the opinion, we will accept as the most reasonable explanation that the state court decided the case the way it did because it believed that federal law required it to do so. If a state court chooses merely to rely on federal precedents as it would on the precedents of all other jurisdictions, then it need only make clear by a plain statement in its judgment or opinion that the federal cases are being used only for the purpose of guidance, and do not themselves compel the result that the court has reached. In this way, both justice and judicial administration will be greatly improved. If the state court decision indicates clearly and expressly that it is alternatively based on bona fide separate, adequate, and independent grounds, we, of course, will not undertake to review the decision.

This approach obviates in most instances the need to examine state law in order to decide the nature of the state court decision, and will at the same time avoid the danger of our rendering advisory opinions. It also avoids the unsatisfactory and intrusive practice of requiring state courts to clarify their decisions to the satisfaction of this Court. We believe that such an approach will provide state judges with a clearer opportunity to develop state jurisprudence unimpeded by federal interference, and yet will preserve the integrity of federal law. "It is fundamental that state courts be left free and unfettered by us in interpreting their state constitutions. But it is equally important that ambiguous or obscure adjudications by state courts do not stand as barriers to a determination by this Court of the validity under the federal constitution of state action." ...

The principle that we will not review judgments of state courts that rest on adequate and independent state grounds is based, in part, on "the limitations of our own jurisdiction." Herb v. Pitcairn (1945). The jurisdictional concern is that we not "render an advisory opinion, and if the same judgment would be rendered by the state court after we corrected its views of federal laws, our review could amount to nothing more than an advisory opinion." ... Our requirement of a "plain statement" that a decision rests upon adequate and independent state grounds does not in any way authorize the rendering of advisory opinions. Rather, in determining, as we must, whether we have jurisdiction to review a case that is alleged to rest on adequate and independent state grounds, see Abie State Bank v. Bryan, we merely assume that there are no such grounds when it is not clear from the opinion itself that the state court relied upon an adequate and independent state ground and when it fairly appears that the state court rested its decision primarily on federal law.

Our review of the decision below under this framework leaves us unconvinced that it rests upon an independent state ground. Apart from its two citations to the state constitution, the court below relied *exclusively* on its understanding of Terry and other federal cases. Not a single state case was cited to support the state court's holding that the search of the passenger compartment was unconstitutional. Indeed, the court declared that the search in this case was unconstitutional because "[t]he Court of Appeals erroneously applied the principles of Terry v. Ohio ... to the search of the interior of the vehicle in this case." ... The references to the state constitution in no way indicate that the decision below rested on grounds in any way *independent* from the state court's interpretation of federal law. Even if we accept that the Michigan constitution has been interpreted to provide independent protection for certain rights also secured under the Fourth Amendment, it fairly appears in this case that the Michigan Supreme Court rested its decision primarily on federal law.... Reversed and Remanded.

JUSTICE STEVENS, dissenting.

The jurisprudential questions presented in this case are far more important than the question whether the Michigan police officer's search of respondent's car violated the Fourth Amendment. The case raises profoundly significant questions concerning the relationship between two sovereigns—the State of Michigan and the United States of America.

The Supreme Court of the State of Michigan expressly held "that the deputies' search of the vehicle was proscribed by the Fourth Amendment of the United States Constitution and art. 1, § 11 of the Michigan Constitution." ... The state law ground is clearly adequate to support the judgment, but the question whether it is independent of the Michigan Supreme Court's understanding of federal law is more difficult. Four possible ways of resolving that question present themselves: (1) asking the Michigan Supreme Court directly, (2) attempting to infer from all possible sources of state law what the Michigan Supreme Court meant, (3) presuming that adequate state grounds are independent unless it clearly appears otherwise, or (4) presuming that adequate state grounds are *not* independent unless it clearly appears otherwise. This Court has, on different occasions, employed each of the first three approaches; never until today has it even hinted at the fourth. In order to "achieve the consistency that is necessary," the Court today undertakes a reexamination of all the possibilities. It rejects the first approach as inefficient and unduly burdensome for state courts, and rejects the second approach as an inappropriate expenditure of our resources. Although I find both of those decisions defensible in themselves, I cannot accept the Court's decision to choose the fourth approach over the third — to presume that adequate state grounds are intended to be dependent on federal law unless the record plainly shows otherwise. I must therefore dissent.

If we reject the intermediate approaches, we are left with a choice between two presumptions: one in favor of our taking jurisdiction, and one against it. Historically, the latter presumption has always prevailed.... The rule, as succinctly stated in Lynch, was as follows:

> Where the judgment of the state court rests on two grounds, one involving a federal question and the other not, or if it does not appear upon which of two grounds the judgment was based, and the ground independent of a federal question is sufficient in itself to sustain it, this Court will not take jurisdiction.

The Court today points out that in several cases we have weakened the traditional presumption by using the other two intermediate approaches identified above. Since those two approaches are now to be rejected, however, I would think that *stare decisis* would call for a return to historical principle. Instead, the Court seems to conclude that because some precedents are to be rejected, we must overrule them all.

Even if I agreed with the Court that we are free to consider as a fresh proposition whether we may take presumptive jurisdiction over the decisions of sovereign states, I could not agree that an expansive attitude makes good sense. It appears to be common ground that any rule we adopt should show "respect for state courts, and [a] desire to avoid advisory opinions." ... And I am confident that all members of this Court agree that there is a vital interest in the sound management of scarce federal judicial resources. All of those policies counsel against the exercise of federal jurisdiction. They are fortified by my belief that a policy of judicial restraint — one that allows other decisional bodies to have the last word in legal interpretation until it is truly necessary for this Court to intervene — enables this Court to make its most effective contribution to our federal system of government.

The nature of the case before us hardly compels a departure from tradition. These are not cases in which an American citizen has been deprived of a right secured by the United States Constitution or a federal statute. Rather, they are cases in which a state court has upheld a citizen's assertion of a right, finding the citizen to be protected under both federal and state law. The complaining party is an officer of the state itself, who asks us to rule that the state court interpreted federal rights too broadly and "overprotected" the citizen....

In this case the State of Michigan has arrested one of its citizens and the Michigan Supreme Court has decided to turn him loose. The respondent is a United States citizen as well as a Michigan citizen, but since there is no claim that he has been mistreated by the State of Michigan, the final outcome of the state processes offended no federal interest whatever. Michigan simply provided greater protection to one of its citizens than some other State might provide or, indeed, than this Court might require throughout the country....

Until recently we had virtually no interest in cases of this type.... The Court offers only one reason for asserting authority over cases such as the one presented today: "an important need for uniformity in federal law [that] goes unsatisfied when we fail to review an opinion that rests primarily upon federal grounds and where the independence of an alleged state ground is not apparent from the four corners of the opinion." ... Of course, the supposed need to "review an opinion" clashes directly with our oft-repeated reminder that "our power is to correct wrong judgments, not to revise opinions." ... The clash is not merely one of form: the "need for uniformity in federal law" is truly an ungovernable engine. That same need is no less present when it is perfectly clear that a state ground is both independent and adequate. In fact, it is equally present if a state prosecutor announces that he believes a certain policy of nonenforcement is commanded by federal law. Yet we have never claimed jurisdiction to correct such errors, no matter how egregious they may be, and no matter how much they may thwart the desires of the state electorate. We do not sit to expound our understanding of the Constitution to interested listeners in the legal community; we sit to resolve disputes. If it is not apparent that our views would affect the outcome of a particular case, we cannot presume to interfere. I respectfully dissent.

Review Questions and Explanations: *Michigan v. Long*

1. Why does the majority think it is important for the Court to review decisions like that presented in this case? Why does Justice Stevens disagree?

2. Test your understanding of *Michigan v. Long*: if a state court decision satisfies the adequate and independent state grounds test, will the Supreme Court be likely to review the decision?

Exercises: Supreme Court Review of State Court Decisions

1. How would a state court wishing to avoid federal review of its decision satisfy the adequate and independent state ground test? Pretend you are a justice on the Michigan Supreme Court. Using the facts of the underlying case in *Michigan v. Long*, write one or two sentences geared toward meeting the Court's test.

2. Imagine that the Arkansas legislature passes a law restricting the ability of corporations doing business in Arkansas to spend general corporate revenue on political advertising advocating the election or defeat of a candidate for public office. Prior to enactment of this state law, the U.S. Supreme Court had held that corporations had a federal First Amendment right to use their general revenue funds to buy such advertising. A corporation doing business in Arkansas challenges the state law in state court. The state supreme court hears the case, and rules against the corporation. Mindful of *Michigan v. Long*, the state high court is careful to insert a plain statement into its decision clarifying that it is basing its decisions solely on the Arkansas constitution, which it expressly states provides an adequate and independent ground for its holding. Under *Michigan v. Long*, is the U.S. Supreme Court likely to review the state court's decision?

With one or more classmates, outline the arguments for a petition for certiorari and an opposition to the petition. Then sit as a group of Supreme Court justices and discuss whether to grant certiorari.

E. Judicial Review in Practice

The above materials illustrate the development of judicial review and explore the theoretical and historical underpinnings of the practice. A full understanding of how judicial review functions in our system of government, however, requires some awareness of how the power actually has been used by the justices of the Supreme Court. One of the authors of this casebook, Lori Ringhand, took advantage of the extraordinary 12 year period between 1994 and 2005, when there were no changes of personnel on the high Court, to examine this question. The length of this "natural court" period meant that there were an unusually large number of decisions in which the choices made by the justices could be compared on an "apples to apples" basis: with just a few exceptions for recusals, each of the nine justices for more than a decade had heard and issued decisions in exactly the same cases. This allowed for a detailed look at how the different justices exercised their powers of judicial review.

Using a large database compiled by political scientists, Ringhand found that both "liberal" and "conservatives" justices on the Rehnquist Court used their power of judicial review at about the same rates, and that both groups did so in ideologically predictable ways.[13] More conservative justices, she found, were likely to use that power to invalidate federal laws, while the more liberal justices were more likely to strike down state laws. For example, Justice Thomas, one of the most conservative members of the Rehnquist Court, cast the most votes to declare a federal statute unconstitutional, while Justice Stevens, one of the Rehnquist Court's more liberal members, cast the most votes to invalidate a state law on constitutional grounds.

The liberal and conservatives justices also used their power of judicial review in different issues areas. Figure 5.1 shows the issue areas in which each of the nine Rehnquist Court justices cast their votes to invalidate federal laws. Figure 5.2 provides the same information for votes to invalidate state laws.

Figure 5.1. Votes by Justice and Issue Area to Declare Federal Laws Unconstitutional: 1994–2004 Term

	Crim Pro	Civil Rights	1st Am	Due Process	Feder-alism	Fed Tax	Misc	Total
Thomas	2	0	15	2	13	1	1	34
Scalia	1	0	15	2	11	1	1	31
Kennedy	1	0	15	2	10	1	1	30
Rehnquist	1	0	10	2	10	1	1	25
O'Connor	1	0	9	2	10	1	1	24
Souter	3	0	14	2	0	1	1	21
Ginsburg	3	0	11	2	0	1	0	17
Stevens	3	0	12	1	0	1	0	17
Breyer	2	0	8	2	0	1	1	14

---

13. For the full study, see Lori A. Ringhand, *The Changing Face of Judicial Activism: An Empirical Examination of Voting Behavior on the Rehnquist Natural Court*, 24 Const. Comment. 43 (2007).

**Figure 5.2. Votes by Justice and Issue Area to Declare
State Laws Unconstitutional: 1994–2004 Term**

	Crim Pro	Civil Rights	1st Am	Due Process	Privacy	Economic Activity	Federalism	Total
Stevens	11	7	11	4	4	7	2	46
Souter	8	7	11	4	5	7	3	45
Breyer	9	7	8	4	4	8	4	44
Ginsburg	9	7	10	3	5	5	2	41
O'Connor	4	9	7	4	5	7	3	39
Kennedy	4	9	9	3	2	6	3	36
Scalia	2	7	7	3	1	6	1	27
Thomas	2	6	8	3	2	5	1	27
Rehnquist	1	6	4	3	1	4	2	21

As these Figures show, the conservative justices sitting on the Rehnquist Court used their power of judicial review primarily in cases involving federalism and First Amendment issues, while the liberal justices use their power to invalidate laws involving criminal procedure, civil rights, and different First Amendment issues.

To the extent that criticisms about judicial review are driven by principled concerns about majoritarian democracy and self-governance, Ringhand's work shows that both liberal and conservative justices are willing to overturn duly enacted laws; they just do so in different issues areas and at different levels of government. Do you find these results surprising? Do they change your thoughts about the value of judicial review?

F. The Exceptions Clause

This chapter has examined the Supreme Court's use of its power of judicial review to invalidate the actions of the other branches of government. Having worked through these materials, you should have a crisp understanding of the origins of the power of judicial review, the justifications for it, and the ways in which it has been used by the justices of the high Court.

In lieu of traditional review questions, we would like at this point to challenge you to think harder about what you have learned about judicial review by introducing you to a constitutional provision you may not have heard of: the Exceptions Clause.

Article III, § 2[2] of the Constitution sets forth the appellate jurisdiction of the Supreme Court. It includes the following language:

> In all other Cases before mentioned, the Supreme Court shall have appellate Jurisdiction, both as to law and Fact, with such Exceptions and under such Regulations as the Congress shall make.

What does the final phrase of this clause mean? Read literally, it appears to allow Congress to limit by statute the jurisdiction of the Supreme Court to hear cases, even if those cases would otherwise be within the constitutional jurisdiction of the Court. What would the consequences of such a limitation be?

Although many bills invoking the Exceptions Clause power have been introduced in Congress, few have become law. Consequently, not many cases involving the Clause have made it to the Supreme Court. The Court has further contributed to the lack of on-point decisions in the area by avoiding issuing comprehensive interpretations of the Clause even when it has had the opportunity (you saw examples of this in Chapter 3). What follows are two cases in which the Court did directly address the meaning of the Exceptions Clause. These materials are followed by questions about the Exceptions Clause. Use the questions to review what you have learned about judicial review.

Ex parte McCardle

74 U.S. 506 (1868)

Unanimous decision: *Chase* (CJ), Nelson, Grier, Clifford, Swayne, Miller, Davis, Field

> [This case was decided after the Civil War. Mr. McCardle was a former Confederate soldier and a newspaper man. After the war, his newspaper published numerous articles questioning the legality of the Military Reconstruction Act of 1867 (the Act under which Northern troops occupied and governed the South after the war). McCardle was arrested and tried by a military court. He appealed to the Supreme Court under the Habeas Corpus Act of 1867, which authorized such appeals. After the case had been argued, but before the Supreme Court issued its decision, Congress passed a law repealing the Act. Although the "repealer act" was written in general language, it was widely understood that the purpose of the repeal was to end the *McCardle* case and thereby deprive the Supreme Court of an opportunity to rule on the constitutionality of Military Reconstruction Act.]

CHIEF JUSTICE CHASE delivered the opinion of the court.

... It is quite true, as was argued by the counsel for the petitioner, that the appellate jurisdiction of this court is not derived from acts of Congress. It is, strictly speaking, conferred by the Constitution. But it is conferred 'with such exceptions and under such regulations as Congress shall make.'

It is unnecessary to consider whether, if Congress had made no exceptions and no regulations, this court might not have exercised general appellate jurisdiction under rules prescribed by itself. For among the earliest acts of the first Congress, at its first session, was the act of September 24th, 1789, to establish the judicial courts of the United States. That act provided for the organization of this court, and prescribed regulations for the exercise of its jurisdiction.

The source of that jurisdiction, and the limitations of it by the Constitution and by statute, have been on several occasions subjects of consideration here. In the case of Durousseau v. The United States, particularly, the whole matter was carefully examined, and the court held, that while 'the appellate powers of this court are not given by the judicial act, but are given by the Constitution,' they are, nevertheless, 'limited and regulated by that act, and by such other acts as have been passed on the subject.' The court said, further, that the judicial act was an exercise of the power given by the Constitution to Congress 'of making exceptions to the appellate jurisdiction of the Supreme Court.' 'They have described affirmatively,' said the court, 'its jurisdiction, and this affirmative description has been understood to imply a negation of the exercise of such appellate power as is not comprehended within it.'

The principle that the affirmation of appellate jurisdiction implies the negation of all such jurisdiction not affirmed having been thus established, it was an almost necessary consequence that acts of Congress, providing for the exercise of jurisdiction, should come to be spoken of as acts granting jurisdiction, and not as acts making exceptions to the constitutional grant of it.

The exception to appellate jurisdiction in the case before us, however, is not an inference from the affirmation of other appellate jurisdiction. It is made in terms. The provision of the act of 1867, affirming the appellate jurisdiction of this court in cases of habeas corpus is expressly repealed. It is hardly possible to imagine a plainer instance of positive exception.

We are not at liberty to inquire into the motives of the legislature. We can only examine into its power under the Constitution; and the power to make exceptions to the appellate jurisdiction of this court is given by express words.

What, then, is the effect of the repealing act upon the case before us? We cannot doubt as to this. Without jurisdiction the court cannot proceed at all in any cause. Jurisdiction is power to declare the law, and when it ceases to exist, the only function remaining to the court is that of announcing the fact and dismissing the cause. And this is not less clear upon authority than upon principle.... It is quite clear, therefore, that this court cannot proceed to pronounce judgment in this case, for it has no longer jurisdiction of the appeal; and judicial duty is not less fitly performed by declining ungranted jurisdiction than in exercising firmly that which the Constitution and the laws confer.

Counsel seem to have supposed, if effect be given to the repealing act in question, that the whole appellate power of the court, in cases of habeas corpus, is denied. But this is an error. The act of 1868 does not except from that jurisdiction any cases but appeals from Circuit Courts under the act of 1867. It does not affect the jurisdiction which was previously exercised. Dismissed for want of jurisdiction.

United States v. Klein

80 U.S. 128 (1872)

Majority: *Chase* (CJ), Nelson, Clifford, Swayne, Davis, Field, Strong

Dissent: *Miller*, Bradley (omitted)

CHIEF JUSTICE CHASE delivered the opinion of the Court.

[Like *McCardle*, *Klein* was decided in the aftermath of the Civil War. A congressional law authorized the confiscation and sale of property owned or abandoned by those engaged in armed insurrection against the Union. The law allowed the owner of confiscated property to be compensated for it upon proof that the owner had not aided or supported the Confederacy. Mr. Klein was the estate administrator of a Mr. Wilson, who had given aid to the Confederacy but who had been pardoned by the President under a post-War proclamation granting amnesty to former Confederates who took an oath to uphold and support the Union. Since Mr. Wilson had received his presidential pardon before his death, Mr. Klein sued on behalf of the estate for compensation for the confiscated property. While the case was pending, Congress passed a law declaring that a

Presidential pardon could not be used under the compensation law as proof that the owner had not aided or supported the Confederacy and that in fact such a pardon was to be treated as conclusive evidence that the owner had done exactly that. The law further required that any case presenting such a situation be immediately dismissed for want of jurisdiction. The question presented to the Court was whether the Exceptions Clause allowed Congress to control the Court's jurisdiction in this way.]

The [Congressional law dictating the legal effect of a Presidential pardon] declares in substance that no pardon, acceptance, oath, or other act performed in pursuance, or as a condition of pardon, shall be admissible in evidence in support of any claim against the United States in the Court of Claims, or to establish the right of any claimant to bring suit in that court; nor, if already put in evidence, shall be used or considered on behalf of the claimant, by said court, or by the appellate court on appeal.... It is further provided that whenever any pardon, granted to any suitor in the Court of Claims, for the proceeds of captured and abandoned property, shall recite in substance that the person pardoned took part in the late rebellion, or was guilty of any act of rebellion or disloyalty, and shall have been accepted in writing without express disclaimer and protestation against the fact so recited, such pardon or acceptance shall be taken as conclusive evidence in the Court of Claims, and on appeal, that the claimant did give aid to the rebellion; and on proof of such pardon, or acceptance, which proof may be made summarily on motion or otherwise, the jurisdiction of the court shall cease, and the suit shall be forthwith dismissed.

The substance of this enactment is that an acceptance of a pardon, without disclaimer, shall be conclusive evidence of the acts pardoned, but shall be null and void as evidence of the rights conferred by it, both in the Court of Claims and in this court on appeal....

The Court of Claims is ... one of those inferior courts which Congress authorizes, and has jurisdiction of contracts between the government and the citizen, from which appeal regularly lies to this court. Undoubtedly the legislature has complete control over the organization and existence of that court and may confer or withhold the right of appeal from its decisions. And if this act did nothing more, it would be our duty to give it effect. If it simply denied the right of appeal in a particular class of cases, there could be no doubt that it must be regarded as an exercise of the power of Congress to make 'such exceptions from the appellate jurisdiction' as should seem to it expedient.

But the language of the proviso shows plainly that it does not intend to withhold appellate jurisdiction except as a means to an end. Its great and controlling purpose is to deny to pardons granted by the President the effect which this court had adjudged them to have. The proviso declares that pardons shall not be considered by this court on appeal. We had already decided that it was our duty to consider them and give them effect, in cases like the present, as equivalent to proof of loyalty. It provides that whenever it shall appear that any judgment of the Court of Claims shall have been founded on such pardons, without other proof of loyalty, the Supreme Court shall have no further jurisdiction of the case and shall dismiss the same for want of jurisdiction. The proviso further declares that every pardon granted to any suitor in the Court of Claims and reciting that the person pardoned has been guilty of any act of rebellion or disloyalty, shall, if accepted in writing without disclaimer of the fact recited, be taken as conclusive evidence in that court and on appeal, of the act recited; and on proof of pardon or acceptance, summarily made on motion or otherwise, the jurisdiction of the court shall cease and the suit shall be forthwith dismissed.

It is evident from this statement that the denial of jurisdiction to this court, as well as to the Court of Claims, is founded solely on the application of a rule of decision, in causes pending, prescribed by Congress. The court has jurisdiction of the cause to a given point; but when it ascertains that a certain state of things exists, its jurisdiction is to cease and it is required to dismiss the cause for want of jurisdiction.

It seems to us that this is not an exercise of the acknowledged power of Congress to make exceptions and prescribe regulations to the appellate power.

The court is required to ascertain the existence of certain facts and thereupon to declare that its jurisdiction on appeal has ceased, by dismissing the bill. What is this but to prescribe a rule for the decision of a cause in a particular way? In the case before us, the Court of Claims has rendered judgment for the claimant and an appeal has been taken to this court. We are directed to dismiss the appeal, if we find that the judgment must be affirmed, because of a pardon granted to the intestate of the claimants. Can we do so without allowing one party to the controversy to decide it in its own favor? Can we do so without allowing that the legislature may prescribe rules of decision to the Judicial Department of the government in cases pending before it? ...

We must think that Congress has inadvertently passed the limit which separates the legislative from the judicial power. It is of vital importance that these powers be kept distinct. The Constitution provides that the judicial power of the United States shall be vested in one Supreme Court and such inferior courts as the Congress shall from time to time ordain and establish. The same instrument, in the last clause of the same article, provides that in all cases other than those of original jurisdiction, 'the Supreme Court shall have appellate jurisdiction both as to law and fact, with such exceptions and under such regulations as the Congress shall make.' Congress has already provided that the Supreme Court shall have jurisdiction of the judgments of the Court of Claims on appeal. Can it prescribe a rule in conformity with which the court must deny to itself the jurisdiction thus conferred, because and only because its decision, in accordance with settled law, must be adverse to the government and favorable to the suitor? This question seems to us to answer itself.

The rule prescribed is also liable to just exception as impairing the effect of a pardon, and thus infringing the constitutional power of the Executive.

It is the intention of the Constitution that each of the great co-ordinate departments of the government—the Legislative, the Executive, and the Judicial—shall be, in its sphere, independent of the others. To the executive alone is entrusted the power of pardon; and it is granted without limit. Pardon includes amnesty. It blots out the offence pardoned and removes all its penal consequences. It may be granted on conditions. In these particular pardons, that no doubt might exist as to their character, restoration of property was expressly pledged, and the pardon was granted on condition that the person who availed himself of it should take and keep a prescribed oath. We repeat that it is impossible to believe that this provision was not inserted in the appropriation bill through inadvertence; and that we shall not best fulfill the deliberate will of the legislature by DENYING the motion to dismiss and AFFIRMING the judgment of the Court of Claims; which is ACCORDINGLY DONE.

Review Questions and Explanations: *McCardle* and *Klein*

1. Are *McCardle* and *Klein* distinguishable and thereby reconcilable? Or did the Court just change its position? Try to identify all the distinguishing factors in the cases and see whether you think they are sufficiently weighty to dictate different outcomes.

2. Professor Lawrence Tribe offers a third way of understanding the Exceptions Clause. Tribe argues that whatever else the Exception Clause means, its scope is limited by other constraints the Constitution puts on Congress. Consequently, Tribe (and others) argues that that clause, like all other congressional powers, cannot be exercised in ways that violate other provisions of the Constitution. To illustrate: Article 1 gives Congress the power to regulate commerce among the states, but that does not mean that Congress can use that power in a way that violates the First Amendment—by, for example, prohibiting the interstate transport of books critical of the President. In the same way, Congress cannot use its Exceptions Clause power in ways that violate other constitutional provisions by, for example, eliminating the Court's jurisdiction to hear free exercise cases brought by Muslims but not by Protestants. Under this view, other provisions of the Constitution impose "external limitations" on the meaning of the Exceptions Clause.

McCardle, *Klein*, and the "external limitations" view thus illustrate three distinct approaches to interpreting the Exceptions Clause. Which approach to you prefer? What implications does each approach have for judicial review, as practiced today by the Supreme Court?

Exercises: The Exceptions Clause

1. The Marriage Protection Act of 2003 was passed in the House of Representatives. The purpose of the Act was to deny federal courts power to hear challenges to the Federal Defense of Marriage Act, or to the MPA itself. It included the following provision:

> Sec. 1632. Limitation on jurisdiction. No court created by Act of Congress shall have any jurisdiction, and the Supreme Court shall have no appellate jurisdiction, to hear or determine any question pertaining to the interpretation of section 1738c of this title or of this section. Neither the Supreme Court nor any court created by Act of Congress shall have any appellate jurisdiction to hear or determine any question pertaining to the interpretation of section 7 of title 1.

Is this a constitutional exercise of Congress's Exceptions Clause power?

2. After a series of financial fraud cases were dismissed from federal court for being brought outside of the statute of limitations, Congress passed a new section, section 27A, to the Securities Exchange Act. The amendment extended the statute of limitations in a well-defined category of cases. It also provided for the "reinstatement" of causes of action within that category of cases that had been dismissed on statute of limitations grounds during the two years preceding the passage of the amendment. You are a law clerk to a judge hearing a previously dismissed case that has recently been refiled under the authority granted by the amended statute. Write a short memo addressing whether the amendment is a constitutional exercise of Congress's power to alter the jurisdiction of the federal courts.

Recap: Judicial Review

1. What does the presence of the Exceptions Clause tell us about the balance of power envisioned by the authors and ratifiers of the Constitution? What does

its relative lack of use tell us about the point made by Mark Graber at the beginning of this Part?

2. Constitutional courts across the world differ significantly in the extent to which they are authorized to invalidate legislation as inconsistent with their nations' fundamental laws. British courts, for example, are famously not empowered to invalidate acts of Parliament, even when they think such legislation violates Britain's constitutional norms or international obligations. While the interplay between domestic law and Britain's obligations under various European human rights treaties has complicated this picture, it remains true that British courts do not exercise the type of judicial review enjoyed by the U.S. Supreme Court. Canada's constitution sets up a system by which federal and provincial legislatures can by ordinary legislation pass laws "notwithstanding" the fact the laws infringe upon things that Canada's courts have found violate certain rights protected by the Canadian Charter of Rights and Freedoms. Do you think British or Canadian citizens in practice enjoy significantly fewer rights then do Americans?

3. If you were writing a constitution from scratch, what type of judicial review powers would you give to the high court?

4. Revisit the "take care clause" exercise at the end of Chapter 3. Can the President justify issuing the executive order on the ground that, contrary to the Supreme Court's decision in *Raich*, Congress lacks the constitutional authority under the commerce power to prohibit medical use of marijuana in states that have legalized it?

Professional Development Reflection Questions

1. The Assistant Attorney General in charge of the Office of Legal Counsel has asked you to write a memo in support of an executive order in which the President directs the Department of Justice not to prosecute users or distributors of marijuana who are in compliance with state medical marijuana laws. She has expressly instructed you that the *Raich* decision was wrong, and does not bind the President. She directs you to write the memo accordingly. You are an "attorney advisor" working under the supervision of the Assistant Attorney General. How do you respond?

Chapter 6

Justiciability

A. Overview

"Justiciability" refers to a set of doctrines limiting the power of federal courts to hear cases. Article III, §2 extends the judicial power to "cases" and "controversies." The Supreme Court has interpreted the term "cases ... and ... controversies" to impose a set of requirements and limitations on what sorts of cases are "justiciable," meaning suitable in form for judicial resolution. According to the Supreme Court, the "'cases' and 'controversies' requirement" limits federal courts to deciding only "questions presented in an adversary context and in a form historically viewed as capable of resolution through the judicial process." *Flast v. Cohen*, 392 U.S. 83, 95 (1968). These requirements are organized into the set of doctrines known collectively as justiciability.

The justiciability doctrines are grouped under five labels: standing, political question, ripeness, mootness and advisory opinions. "Standing" refers to the question of whether a litigant is the proper party to assert a claim or defense. The "political question" doctrine prohibits federal courts from deciding issues committed to the political branches of government or that cannot be resolved based on "judicially manageable" criteria. The requirement of "ripeness" means that the dispute underlying the case must have fully arisen and is not merely a future, speculative dispute uncertain to arise. Cases also may be deemed non-justiciable due to "mootness," meaning that the dispute underlying the case is no longer ongoing. The rule against "advisory opinions" prohibits the courts from issuing counseling-type legal opinions to other branches of government.

B. Foundational Doctrine

In theory, the various justiciability limitations make courts stick to what they're good at: resolving concrete (not abstract) legal and factual disputes between adverse parties, at least one of whose rights has allegedly been violated. Justiciability limitations are also justified on separation-of-powers grounds, in that they are said to help keep the courts from performing functions better left to the legislative and judicial branches.

Justiciability doctrines resemble, but are distinct from, jurisdictional issues. Like jurisdiction, they are threshold requirements going to the federal courts' power to hear cases. Justiciability doctrines can be applied, as can jurisdictional doctrines, to dismiss cases on "technical" grounds, i.e., for reasons that do not go to the substantive merits of the case. (A dismissal on justiciability grounds ends the case without conclusively determining whether the plaintiff's rights were violated.) Finally, like jurisdiction, justiciability questions go to the court's power to hear a case; are normally considered prior to reaching the merits; and are non-waivable, meaning that the court can and indeed must consider apparent objections to justiciability even if not raised by the parties.

Nonetheless, justiciability is analytically distinct from jurisdiction. Jurisdiction is the court's power over parties and substantive legal issues. But cases can be dismissed as non-justiciable even where personal and subject-matter jurisdictional requirements are met. Moreover, justiciability doctrines are, in practice if not in theory, far more flexible than jurisdictional doctrines. A federal court with subject matter jurisdiction has no discretion to decline to hear the case on jurisdictional grounds. In contrast, federal courts seem freer to exercise discretion when it comes to justiciability doctrines. This may be simply another way of saying that justiciability doctrines are sufficiently complex, exception-ridden, and malleable to allow the federal courts relatively greater latitude to pick and choose when to apply them to dismiss cases.

Justiciability issues have a way of arising in certain kinds of cases, including environmental protection claims, civil rights and "good government" cases, and disputes involving potential or actual clashes between coordinate branches of government. Since justiciability doctrines are applied as a limit on judicial power—that is, as a way of dismissing cases—their use has been frequently criticized by commentators who argue that the federal courts use them to dodge difficult issues or to restrict environmental and civil rights claims. Other commentators criticize justiciability doctrines for their frequently confusing or incoherent quality. There is undoubtedly some truth to these criticisms.

At the same time, these apparent defects in justiciability doctrine may in fact present certain advantages. By providing technical ways out of deciding cases that are politically loaded or that might lead to unwinnable conflicts with coordinate branches of government, justiciability doctrines allow the federal courts to avoid damaging their prestige. In a classic defense of strategic use of justiciability doctrines, law professor Alexander Bickel argued that the Supreme Court should, at times, dismiss cases on justiciability grounds when deciding the case on the merits would require the Court to endorse a bad principle or an explosively unpopular one. Alexander Bickel, *The Passive Virtues*, 75 Harv. L. Rev. 40 (1961). Presumably, endorsing a bad principle weakens the Court's legitimacy, while taking an explosively unpopular stand exposes the Court to being ignored or overruled by other political actors. Either way, its authority can be damaged. By practicing the "passive virtues" at key times—that is, by dismissing dangerous cases on arcane, technical justiciability grounds—the federal courts can act prudently by giving the so-called "political" branches (the elected ones) their sway and keeping out of politics when the going gets rough.

A classic example of the danger of failing to practice passive virtues is the case of *Korematsu v. United States*, 323 U.S. 214 (1944), which upheld the internment of American citizens of Japanese ancestry during World War II. Justice Jackson's dissent makes the point eloquently:

> In the very nature of things, military decisions are not susceptible of intelligent judicial appraisal. They do not pretend to rest on evidence, but are made on information that often would not be admissible and on assumptions that could not be proved. Information in support of an order could not be disclosed to courts without danger that it would reach the enemy. Neither can courts act on communications made in confidence. Hence courts can never have any real alternative to accepting the mere declaration of the authority that issued the order that it was reasonably necessary from a military viewpoint.
>
> [A] judicial construction of the due process clause that will sustain this order is a far more subtle blow to liberty than the promulgation of the order itself. A military order, however unconstitutional, is not apt to last longer than the military

emergency. [But] once a judicial opinion rationalizes such an order to show that it conforms to the Constitution, or rationalizes the Constitution to show that the Constitution sanctions such an order, the Court for all times has validated the principle of racial discrimination.... The principle then lies about like a loaded weapon ready for the hand of any authority that can bring forward a plausible claim of an urgent need. [A] military commander may overstep the bounds of constitutionality, and it becomes an incident. But if we review and approve, that passing incident becomes a doctrine of the Constitution. 323 U.S. at 245–46 (Jackson, J., dissenting).

One can read Jackson's dissent as suggesting that the Court would have done better to decline the constitutional ruling in *Korematsu* on "political question" grounds.

C. Standing

The doctrine of "standing" is probably the most important of the justiciability doctrines; standing issues are certainly the most commonly occurring of all the justiciability problems. Standing—the sufficiency of a litigant's connection to the substantive claims or defenses he asserts—is potentially an issue in every case. In most cases, the issue is not raised because standing is obvious. A party claiming damages for an injury that the law expressly recognizes as compensable, such as a breach of contract, a tort, a trademark infringement, virtually always has standing. Standing problems tend to arise where the claim is for something other than compensation for an expressly compensable right. Enforcement of environmental laws presents a recurring example, as illustrated by the *Lujan* case in the next Section.

1. Basic Doctrine

Guided Reading Questions: *Allen v. Wright*

1. What are the two injuries alleged by the plaintiffs?

2. Why aren't these injuries sufficient to confer standing?

3. What does the majority mean by "causation" in the context of this case? How, if at all, does the majority's understanding differ from the dissenters'?

Allen v. Wright
468 U.S. 737 (1984)

Majority: *O'Connor*, Burger (CJ), White, Powell, Rehnquist

Dissents: *Brennan; Stevens*, Blackmun

(Marshall took no part in the decision)

JUSTICE O'CONNOR delivered the opinion of the Court.

[The Internal Revenue Code requires the IRS to deny tax-exempt status to racially discriminatory private schools, in order to promote a federal policy against racially discriminatory schools. Denial of tax exempt status would deprive the discriminatory private schools of their eligibility to receive tax-deductible contributions. Several parents of black children attending public schools in districts undergoing desegregation brought a nationwide class action against the IRS, claiming that the agency had not adopted sufficient standards and procedures to enforce the policy. According to plaintiffs—the respondents in the Supreme Court—many racially segregated private schools had received tax exemptions despite the IRS policy; these unlawful tax exemptions harmed plaintiffs by assisting in the ensuing creation or expansion of segregated private schools in desegregation districts, thereby undermining desegregation by promoting "white flight," tending to deprive the plaintiffs' children of their right to attend desegregated schools, and harming the quality of the public schools. Plaintiffs sought declaratory and injunctive relief.

[The District Court dismissed the complaint at the pleading stage on the ground that respondents lacked standing to bring the suit. The Court of Appeals reversed, and the Supreme Court granted certiorari.]

... "In essence the question of standing is whether the litigant is entitled to have the court decide the merits of the dispute or of particular issues." Standing doctrine embraces several judicially self-imposed limits on the exercise of federal jurisdiction, such as the general prohibition on a litigant's raising another person's legal rights, the rule barring adjudication of generalized grievances more appropriately addressed in the representative branches, and the requirement that a plaintiff's complaint fall within the zone of interests protected by the law invoked. The requirement of standing, however, has a core component derived directly from the Constitution. A plaintiff must allege personal injury fairly traceable to the defendant's allegedly unlawful conduct and likely to be redressed by the requested relief.

... [T]he constitutional component of standing doctrine incorporates concepts concededly not susceptible of precise definition. The injury alleged must be, for example, "distinct and palpable," and not "abstract" or "conjectural" or "hypothetical[.]" The injury must be "fairly" traceable to the challenged action, and relief from the injury must be "likely" to follow from a favorable decision. These terms cannot be defined so as to make application of the constitutional standing requirement a mechanical exercise....

Respondents allege two injuries in their complaint to support their standing to bring this lawsuit. First, they say that they are harmed directly by the mere fact of Government financial aid to discriminatory private schools. Second, they say that the federal tax exemptions to racially discriminatory private schools in their communities impair their ability to have their public schools desegregated....

... [A]n asserted right to have the Government act in accordance with law is not sufficient ... to confer [standing].... There can be no doubt that this sort of noneconomic injury [racial stigma] is one of the most serious consequences of discriminatory government action and is sufficient in some circumstances to support standing. Our cases make clear, however, that such injury accords a basis for standing only to "those persons who are personally denied equal treatment" by the challenged discriminatory conduct.

... [R]espondents' second claim of injury cannot support standing because the injury alleged is not fairly traceable to the Government conduct respondents challenge as unlawful.... The illegal conduct challenged by respondents is the IRS's grant of tax exemptions to some racially discriminatory schools. The line of causation between that conduct and desegregation of respondents' schools is attenuated at best. From the perspective of the IRS, the injury to respondents is highly indirect and "results from the independent action of some third party not before the court." ... [I]t is entirely speculative ... whether withdrawal of a tax exemption from any particular school would lead the school to change its policies. It is just as speculative whether any given parent of a child attending such a private school would decide to transfer the child to public school as a result of any changes in educational or financial policy made by the private school once it was threatened with loss of tax-exempt status. It is also pure speculation whether, in a particular community, a large enough number of the numerous relevant school officials and parents would reach decisions that collectively would have a significant impact on the racial composition of the public schools.

The links in the chain of causation between the challenged Government conduct and the asserted injury are far too weak for the chain as a whole to sustain respondents' standing.... The judgment of the Court of Appeals is accordingly reversed, and the injunction issued by that court is vacated.

JUSTICE BRENNAN, dissenting.

.... [T]he respondents have alleged a direct causal relationship between the Government action they challenge and the injury they suffer: their inability to receive an education in a racially integrated school is directly and adversely affected by the tax-exempt status granted by the IRS to racially discriminatory schools in their respective school districts. Common sense alone would recognize that the elimination of tax-exempt status for racially discriminatory private schools would serve to lessen the impact that those institutions have in defeating efforts to desegregate the public schools.

.... [R]espondents specifically refer by name to at least 32 private schools that discriminate on the basis of race and yet continue to benefit illegally from tax-exempt status. Eighteen of those schools—including at least 14 elementary schools, 2 junior high schools, and 1 high school—are located in the city of Memphis, Tenn., which has been the subject of several court orders to desegregate. See Complaint paras. 24–27, 45. Similarly, the respondents cite two private schools in Orangeburg, S. C. that continue to benefit from federal tax exemptions even though they practice race discrimination in school districts that are desegregating pursuant to judicial and administrative orders. See Complaint paras. 29, 46. At least with respect to these school districts, as well as the others specifically mentioned in the complaint, there can be little doubt that the respondents have identified communities containing "enough racially discriminatory private schools receiving tax exemptions ... to make an appreciable difference in public school integration." ...

More than one commentator has noted that the causation component of the Court's standing inquiry is no more than a poor disguise for the Court's view of the merits of the underlying claims....

JUSTICE STEVENS, with whom JUSTICE BLACKMUN joins, dissenting.

.... [T]he wrong respondents allege that the Government has committed is to subsidize the exodus of white children from schools that would otherwise be racially integrated.... If the granting of preferential tax treatment would "encourage" private segregated schools to conduct their "charitable" activities, it must follow that the withdrawal of the treatment would "discourage" them, and hence promote the process of desegregation.

We have held that when a subsidy makes a given activity more or less expensive, injury can be fairly traced to the subsidy for purposes of standing analysis because of the resulting increase or decrease in the ability to engage in the activity. Indeed, we have employed exactly this causation analysis in the same context at issue here—subsidies given private schools that practice racial discrimination.... Considerations of tax policy, economics, and pure logic all confirm the conclusion that respondents' injury in fact is fairly traceable to the Government's allegedly wrongful conduct.... I respectfully dissent.

Guided Reading Questions: *Lujan v. Defenders of Wildlife*

1. In *Lujan*, what was the substantive remedy available to plaintiffs hoping to protect the endangered species' habitats in Sri Lanka and Egypt? Could they have obtained damages for destruction of the habitat, or an injunction preventing the projects from going forward?

2. How does your answer to question 1 factor into the standing analysis?

3. Standing is supposed to be a threshold issue that does not go to the substance or "merits" of the legal claim. But critics of standing decisions sometimes argue that such decisions pre-judge, or at least "peek at," the merits of the case. Did that occur in *Lujan*? If so, how?

4. What is the procedural injury claimed by the plaintiffs in *Lujan*? Why didn't it give the plaintiffs standing?

Lujan v. Defenders of Wildlife
504 U.S. 555 (1992)

Majority (Except part III-B): *Scalia*, Rehnquist (CJ), White, Kennedy, Souter, Thomas

Plurality (Part III-B): *Scalia*, Rehnquist (CJ), White, Thomas

Concurrence in part (except part III-B): *Kennedy*, Souter

Concurrence in the Judgment: *Stevens*

Dissent: *Blackmun*, O'Connor

JUSTICE SCALIA delivered the opinion of the Court.

.... This case involves a challenge to a rule promulgated by the Secretary of the Interior interpreting §7 of the Endangered Species Act of 1973 (ESA) ... to render it applicable only to actions within the United States or on the high seas. The preliminary issue, and the only one we reach, is whether respondents here, plaintiffs below, have standing to seek judicial review of the rule.

The ESA, 16 U. S. C. §1531 et seq., seeks to protect species of animals against threats to their continuing existence caused by man. The ESA instructs the Secretary of the Interior to promulgate by regulation a list of those species which are either endangered or threatened under enumerated criteria, and to define the critical habitat of these species. Section 7(a)(2) of the Act then provides, in pertinent part:

> Each Federal agency shall, in consultation with and with the assistance of the Secretary [of the Interior], insure that any action authorized, funded, or carried out by such agency ... is not likely to jeopardize the continued existence of any endangered species or threatened species or result in the destruction or adverse modification of habitat of such species which is determined by the Secretary,

after consultation as appropriate with affected States, to be critical. 16 U. S. C. § 1536(a)(2).

In 1978, the Fish and Wildlife Service (FWS) and the National Marine Fisheries Service (NMFS), on behalf of the Secretary of the Interior and the Secretary of Commerce respectively, promulgated a joint regulation stating that the obligations imposed by § 7(a)(2) extend to actions taken in foreign nations. 43 Fed. Reg. 874 (1978). The next year, however, the Interior Department began to reexamine its position. A revised joint regulation, reinterpreting § 7(a)(2) to require consultation only for actions taken in the United States or on the high seas, was proposed in 1983, and promulgated in 1986, 51 Fed. Reg. 19926; 50 CFR 402.01 (1991).

Shortly thereafter, respondents, organizations dedicated to wildlife conservation and other environmental causes, filed this action against the Secretary of the Interior, seeking a declaratory judgment that the new regulation is in error as to the geographic scope of § 7(a)(2) and an injunction requiring the Secretary to promulgate a new regulation restoring the initial interpretation. The District Court granted the Secretary's motion to dismiss for lack of standing. The Court of Appeals for the Eighth Circuit reversed by a divided vote. Defenders of Wildlife v. Hodel, 851 F.2d 1035 (1988). On remand, the Secretary moved for summary judgment on the standing issue, and respondents moved for summary judgment on the merits. The District Court denied the Secretary's motion, on the ground that the Eighth Circuit had already determined the standing question in this case; it granted respondents' merits motion, and ordered the Secretary to publish a revised regulation. The Eighth Circuit affirmed. We granted certiorari.

While the Constitution of the United States divides all power conferred upon the Federal Government into "legislative Powers," Art. I, § 1, "the executive Power," Art. II, § 1, and "the judicial Power," Art. III, § 1, it does not attempt to define those terms. To be sure, it limits the jurisdiction of federal courts to "Cases" and "Controversies," but an executive inquiry can bear the name "case" (the Hoffa case) and a legislative dispute can bear the name "controversy" (the Smoot-Hawley controversy). Obviously, then, the Constitution's central mechanism of separation of powers depends largely upon common understanding of what activities are appropriate to legislatures, to executives, and to courts. In The Federalist No. 48, Madison expressed the view that "it is not infrequently a question of real nicety in legislative bodies whether the operation of a particular measure will, or will not, extend beyond the legislative sphere," whereas "the executive power [is] restrained within a narrower compass and ... more simple in its nature," and "the judiciary [is] described by landmarks still less uncertain." The Federalist No. 48, p. 256 (Carey and McClellan eds. 1990). One of those landmarks, setting apart the "Cases" and "Controversies" that are of the justiciable sort referred to in Article III — "serving to identify those disputes which are appropriately resolved through the judicial process" — is the doctrine of standing. Though some of its elements express merely prudential considerations that are part of judicial self-government, the core component of standing is an essential and unchanging part of the case-or-controversy requirement of Article III. See, e.g., Allen v. Wright, 468 U.S. 737, 751 (1984). Over the years, our cases have established that the irreducible constitutional minimum of standing contains three elements. First, the plaintiff must have suffered an "injury in fact" — an invasion of a legally protected interest which is (a) concrete and particularized, see id., at 756; Warth v. Seldin, 422 U.S. 490 (1975);

> FN1. By particularized, we mean that the injury must affect the plaintiff in a personal and individual way.

and (b) "actual or imminent, not conjectural or hypothetical." Second, there must be a causal connection between the injury and the conduct complained of — the injury has to be "fairly ... trace[able] to the challenged action of the defendant, and not ... the result [of] the independent action of some third party not before the court." Simon v. Eastern Ky. Welfare Rights Organization, 426 U.S. 26, 41–42 (1976). Third, it must be "likely," as opposed to merely "speculative," that the injury will be "redressed by a favorable decision." Id., at 38, 43.

The party invoking federal jurisdiction bears the burden of establishing these elements. Since they are not mere pleading requirements but rather an indispensable part of the plaintiff's case, each element must be supported in the same way as any other matter on which the plaintiff bears the burden of proof, i. e., with the manner and degree of evidence required at the successive stages of the litigation. At the pleading stage, general factual allegations of injury resulting from the defendant's conduct may suffice, for on a motion to dismiss we "presume that general allegations embrace those specific facts that are necessary to support the claim." In response to a summary judgment motion, however, the plaintiff can no longer rest on such "mere allegations," but must "set forth" by affidavit or other evidence "specific facts," Fed. Rule Civ. Proc. 56(e), which for purposes of the summary judgment motion will be taken to be true. And at the final stage, those facts (if controverted) must be "supported adequately by the evidence adduced at trial." When.... the plaintiff is himself an object of [a governmental] action (or forgone action)..., there is ordinarily little question that the action or inaction has caused him injury, and that a judgment preventing or requiring the action will redress it. When, however, as in this case, a plaintiff's asserted injury arises from the government's allegedly unlawful regulation (or lack of regulation) of someone else, much more is needed. In that circumstance, causation and redressability ordinarily hinge on the response of the regulated (or regulable) third party to the government action or inaction—and perhaps on the response of others as well. The existence of one or more of the essential elements of standing "depends on the unfettered choices made by independent actors not before the courts and whose exercise of broad and legitimate discretion the courts cannot presume either to control or to predict," and it becomes the burden of the plaintiff to adduce facts showing that those choices have been or will be made in such manner as to produce causation and permit redressability of injury. Thus, when the plaintiff is not himself the object of the government action or inaction he challenges, standing is not precluded, but it is ordinarily "substantially more difficult" to establish. Allen, supra, at 758; Simon, supra, at 44–45; Warth, supra, at 505...

III[-A]

Respondents' claim to injury is that the lack of consultation with respect to certain funded activities abroad "increas[es] the rate of extinction of endangered and threatened species." Complaint P5. Of course, the desire to use or observe an animal species, even for purely esthetic purposes, is undeniably a cognizable interest for purpose of standing. See, e.g., Sierra Club v. Morton, 405 U.S. at 734. "But the 'injury in fact' test requires more than an injury to a cognizable interest. It requires that the party seeking review be himself among the injured." Id. To survive the Secretary's summary judgment motion, respondents had to submit affidavits or other evidence showing, through specific facts, not only that listed species were in fact being threatened by funded activities abroad, but also that one or more of respondents' members would thereby be "directly" affected apart from their "special interest in the subject." With respect to this aspect of the case, the Court of Appeals focused on the affidavits of two Defenders' members—Joyce Kelly and Amy Skilbred. Ms. Kelly stated that she traveled to Egypt in 1986 and "observed the traditional habitat of the endangered Nile crocodile there and intend[s] to do so again, and hope[s] to observe the crocodile directly," and that she "will suffer harm in fact as the result of [the] American ... role ... in overseeing the rehabilitation of the Aswan High Dam on the Nile ... and [in] developing ... Egypt's ... Master Water Plan." App. 101. Ms. Skilbred averred that she traveled to Sri Lanka in 1981 and "observed the habitat" of "endangered species such as the Asian elephant and the leopard" at what is now the site of the Mahaweli project funded by the Agency for International Development (AID), although she "was unable to see any of the endangered species"; "this development project," she continued, "will seriously reduce endangered, threatened, and endemic species habitat including areas that I visited ... [, which] may severely shorten the future of these species"; that threat, she concluded, harmed her because she "intend[s] to return to Sri Lanka in the future and hope[s] to be more fortunate in spotting at least the endangered elephant and leopard." Id., at 145–146. When Ms. Skilbred was asked at a subsequent deposition if and when she had any plans to return to Sri Lanka, she reiterated that "I intend to go back to Sri Lanka," but confessed that she had no current plans: "I don't know [when]. There is a civil war going on right now. I don't know. Not next year, I will say. In the future." Id., at 318.c

We shall assume for the sake of argument that these affidavits contain facts showing that certain agency-funded projects threaten listed species—though that is questionable. They plainly contain no facts, however, showing how damage to the species will produce "imminent" injury to Mses. Kelly and Skilbred. That the women "had visited" the areas of the projects before the projects commenced proves nothing. As we have said in a related context, "Past exposure to illegal conduct does not in itself show a present case or controversy regarding injunctive relief ... if unaccompanied by any continuing, present adverse effects." Los Angeles v. Lyons, 461 U.S. at 102. And the affiants' profession of an "intent" to return to the places they had visited before—where they will presumably, this time, be deprived of the opportunity to observe animals of the endangered species—is simply not enough. Such "some day" intentions—without any description of concrete plans, or indeed even any specification of when the some day will be—do not support a finding of the "actual or imminent" injury that our cases require.

> FN2. The dissent acknowledges the settled requirement that the injury complained of be, if not actual, then at least imminent, but it contends that respondents could get past summary judgment because "a reasonable finder of fact could conclude ... that ... Kelly or Skilbred will soon return to the project sites." This analysis suffers either from a factual or from a legal defect, depending on what the "soon" is supposed to mean. If "soon" refers to the standard mandated by our precedents—that the injury be "imminent"—we are at a loss to see how, as a factual matter, the standard can be met by respondents' mere profession of an intent, some day, to return. But if, as we suspect, "soon" means nothing more than "in this lifetime," then the dissent has undertaken quite a departure from our precedents. Although "imminence" is concededly a somewhat elastic concept, it cannot be stretched beyond its purpose, which is to ensure that the alleged injury is not too speculative for Article III purposes—that the injury is "certainly impending." It has been stretched beyond the breaking point when, as here, the plaintiff alleges only an injury at some indefinite future time, and the acts necessary to make the injury happen are at least partly within the plaintiff's own control....

Besides relying upon the Kelly and Skilbred affidavits, respondents propose a series of novel standing theories. The first, inelegantly styled "ecosystem nexus," proposes that any person who uses any part of a "contiguous ecosystem" adversely affected by a funded activity has standing even if the activity is located a great distance away. This approach ... is inconsistent with our opinion in National Wildlife Federation, which held that a plaintiff claiming injury from environmental damage must use the area affected by the challenged activity and not an area roughly "in the vicinity" of it....

Respondents' other theories are called, alas, the "animal nexus" approach, whereby anyone who has an interest in studying or seeing the endangered animals anywhere on the globe has standing; and the "vocational nexus" approach, under which anyone with a professional interest in such animals can sue. Under these theories, anyone who goes to see Asian elephants in the Bronx Zoo, and anyone who is a keeper of Asian elephants in the Bronx Zoo, has standing to sue because the Director of the Agency for International Development (AID) did not consult with the Secretary regarding the AID-funded project in Sri Lanka. This is beyond all reason. Standing is not "an ingenious academic exercise in the conceivable," but as we have said requires, at the summary judgment stage, a factual showing of perceptible harm. It is clear that the person who observes or works with a particular animal threatened by a federal decision is facing perceptible harm, since the very subject of his interest will no longer exist. It is even plausible—though it goes to the outermost limit of plausibility—to think that a person who observes or works with animals of a particular species in the very area of the world where that species is threatened by a federal decision is facing such harm, since some animals that might have been the subject of his interest will no longer exist. It goes beyond the limit, however, and into pure speculation and fantasy, to say that anyone who observes or works with an endangered species, anywhere in the world, is appreciably harmed by a single project affecting some portion of that species with which he has no more specific connection.

B

Besides failing to show injury, respondents failed to demonstrate redressability.... Since the agencies funding the projects were not parties to the case, the District Court could accord relief only against the Secretary: He could be ordered to revise his regulation to require consultation for foreign projects. But this would not remedy respondents' alleged injury unless the funding agencies were bound by the Secretary's regulation, which is very much an open question. Whereas in other contexts the ESA is quite explicit as to the Secretary's controlling authority, see, e.g., 16 U. S. C. § 1533(a)(1)("The Secretary shall" promulgate regulations determining endangered species), with respect to consultation the initiative, and hence arguably the initial responsibility for determining statutory necessity, lies with the agencies, see § 1536(a)(2) (*"Each Federal agency shall*, in consultation with and with the assistance of the Secretary, insure that any" funded action is not likely to jeopardize endangered or threatened species) (emphasis added).... [T]he short of the matter is that redress of the only injury in fact respondents complain of requires action (termination of funding until consultation) by the individual funding agencies; and any relief the District Court could have provided in this suit against the Secretary was not likely to produce that action....

A further impediment to redressability is the fact that the agencies generally supply only a fraction of the funding for a foreign project. AID, for example, has provided less than 10% of the funding for the Mahaweli project. Respondents have produced nothing to indicate that the projects they have named will either be suspended, or do less harm to listed species, if that fraction is eliminated.... [I]t is entirely conjectural whether the non-agency activity that affects respondents will be altered or affected by the agency activity they seek to achieve. There is no standing.

IV

The Court of Appeals found that respondents had standing for an additional reason: because they had suffered a "procedural injury." The so-called "citizen-suit" provision of the ESA provides, in pertinent part, that "any person may commence a civil suit on his own behalf (A) to enjoin any person, including the United States and any other governmental instrumentality or agency ... who is alleged to be in violation of any provision of this chapter." 16 U. S. C. § 1540(g). The court held that, because § 7(a)(2) requires interagency consultation, the citizen-suit provision creates a "procedural right" to consultation in all "persons"—so that anyone can file suit in federal court to challenge the Secretary's (or presumably any other official's) failure to follow the assertedly correct consultative procedure, notwithstanding his or her inability to allege any discrete injury flowing from that failure. To understand the remarkable nature of this holding one must be clear about what it does not rest upon: This is not a case where plaintiffs are seeking to enforce a procedural requirement the disregard of which could impair a separate concrete interest of theirs (e.g., the procedural requirement for a hearing prior to denial of their license application, or the procedural requirement for an environmental impact statement before a federal facility is constructed next door to them).

> FN7. There is this much truth to the assertion that "procedural rights" are special: The person who has been accorded a procedural right to protect his concrete interests can assert that right without meeting all the normal standards for redressability and immediacy. Thus, under our case law, one living adjacent to the site for proposed construction of a federally licensed dam has standing to challenge the licensing agency's failure to prepare an environmental impact statement, even though he cannot establish with any certainty that the statement will cause the license to be withheld or altered, and even though the dam will not be completed for many years. (That is why we do not rely, in the present case, upon the Government's argument that, even if the other agencies were obliged to consult with the Secretary, they might not have followed his advice.) What respondents' "procedural rights" argument seeks, however, is quite different from this: standing for persons who have no concrete interests affected—persons who live (and propose to live) at the other end of the country from the dam.

Nor is it simply a case where concrete injury has been suffered by many persons, as in mass fraud or mass tort situations. Nor, finally, is it the unusual case in which Congress has created a concrete private interest in the outcome of a suit against a private party for the Government's benefit, by providing a cash bounty for the victorious plaintiff. Rather, the court held that the injury-in-fact requirement had been satisfied by congressional conferral upon all persons of an abstract, self-contained, noninstrumental "right" to have the Executive observe the procedures required by law. We reject this view.

We have consistently held that a plaintiff raising only a generally available grievance about government—claiming only harm to his and every citizen's interest in proper application of the Constitution and laws, and seeking relief that no more directly and tangibly benefits him than it does the public at large—does not state an Article III case or controversy. For example, in Fairchild v. Hughes, 258 U.S. 126, 129–130 (1922), we dismissed a suit challenging the propriety of the process by which the Nineteenth Amendment was ratified. Justice Brandeis wrote for the Court:

> [This is] not a case within the meaning of ... Article III.... Plaintiff has [asserted] only the right, possessed by every citizen, to require that the Government be administered according to law and that the public moneys be not wasted. Obviously this general right does not entitle a private citizen to institute in the federal courts a suit...."

.... More recent cases are to the same effect. In United States v. Richardson, 418 U.S. 166 (1974), we dismissed for lack of standing a taxpayer suit challenging the Government's failure to disclose the expenditures of the Central Intelligence Agency, in alleged violation of the constitutional requirement, Art. I, § 9, cl. 7, that "a regular Statement and Account of the Receipts and Expenditures of all public Money shall be published from time to time." We held that such a suit rested upon an impermissible "generalized grievance," and was inconsistent with "the framework of Article III" because "the impact on [plaintiff] is plainly undifferentiated and 'common to all members of the public.'" And in Schlesinger v. Reservists Comm. to Stop the War, 418 U.S. 208 (1974), we dismissed for the same reasons a citizen-taxpayer suit contending that it was a violation of the Incompatibility Clause, Art. I, § 6, cl. 2, for Members of Congress to hold commissions in the military Reserves.... And only two Terms ago, we rejected the notion that Article III permits a citizen suit to prevent a condemned criminal's execution on the basis of "the public interest protections of the Eighth Amendment"....

To be sure, our generalized-grievance cases have typically involved Government violation of procedures assertedly ordained by the Constitution rather than the Congress. But there is absolutely no basis for making the Article III inquiry turn on the source of the asserted right. Whether the courts were to act on their own, or at the invitation of Congress, in ignoring the concrete injury requirement described in our cases, they would be discarding a principle fundamental to the separate and distinct constitutional role of the Third Branch—one of the essential elements that identifies those "Cases" and "Controversies" that are the business of the courts rather than of the political branches. "The province of the court," as Chief Justice Marshall said in Marbury v. Madison, 5 U.S. (1 Cranch) 137 (1803), "is, solely, to decide on the rights of individuals." Vindicating the public interest (including the public interest in Government observance of the Constitution and laws) is the function of Congress and the Chief Executive. The question presented here is whether the public interest in proper administration of the laws (specifically, in agencies' observance of a particular, statutorily prescribed procedure) can be converted into an individual right by a statute that denominates it as such, and that permits all citizens (or, for that matter, a subclass of citizens who suffer no distinctive concrete harm) to sue. If the concrete injury requirement has the separation-of-powers significance we have always said, the answer must be obvious: To permit Congress to convert the undifferentiated public interest in executive officers' compliance with the law into an "individual right" vindicable in the courts is to permit Congress to transfer from the President to the courts the Chief Executive's most important constitutional duty, to "take Care that the Laws be faithfully executed," Art. II, § 3. It would enable the courts, with the permission of Congress, "to assume a position of authority over the governmental acts of another and co-equal department," and to become "virtually continuing monitors of the wisdom and soundness of Executive action." Allen, supra, at 760. We have always rejected that vision of our role....

Nothing in this contradicts the principle that "the ... injury required by Art. III may exist solely by virtue of statutes creating legal rights, the invasion of which creates standing." Warth, 422 U.S. at 500.... As we said in Sierra Club, "[Statutory] broadening [of] the categories of injury that may be alleged in support of standing is a different matter from abandoning the requirement that the party seeking review must himself have suffered an injury." 405 U.S. at 738....

We hold that respondents lack standing to bring this action and that the Court of Appeals erred in denying the summary judgment motion filed by the United States. The opinion of the Court of Appeals is hereby reversed, and the cause is remanded for proceedings consistent with this opinion.

JUSTICE KENNEDY, with whom JUSTICE SOUTER joins, concurring in part and concurring in the judgment.

...I agree with the Court's conclusion in Part III-A that, on the record before us, respondents have failed to demonstrate that they themselves are "among the injured." ... While it may seem trivial to require that Mses. Kelly and Skilbred acquire airline tickets to the project sites or announce a date certain upon which they will return, this is not a case where it is reasonable to assume that the affiants will be using the sites on a regular basis, nor do the affiants claim to have visited the sites since the projects commenced.... I am not willing to foreclose the possibility, however, that in different circumstances a nexus theory similar to those proffered here might support a claim to standing....

In light of the conclusion that respondents have not demonstrated a concrete injury here sufficient to support standing under our precedents, I would not reach the issue of redressability that is discussed by the plurality in Part III-B.

I also join Part IV of the Court's opinion with the following observations. As Government programs and policies become more complex and far reaching, we must be sensitive to the articulation of new rights of action that do not have clear analogs in our common-law tradition. Modern litigation has progressed far from the paradigm of Marbury suing Madison to get his commission, or Ogden seeking an injunction to halt Gibbons' steamboat operations, Gibbons v. Ogden, 22 U.S. (9 Wheat.) 1 (1824). In my view, Congress has the power to define injuries and articulate chains of causation that will give rise to a case or controversy where none existed before, and I do not read the Court's opinion to suggest a contrary view. In exercising this power, however, Congress must at the very least identify the injury it seeks to vindicate and relate the injury to the class of persons entitled to bring suit. The citizen-suit provision of the Endangered Species Act does not meet these minimal requirements, because while the statute purports to confer a right on "any person ... to enjoin ... the United States and any other governmental instrumentality or agency ... who is alleged to be in violation of any provision of this chapter," it does not of its own force establish that there is an injury in "any person" by virtue of any "violation." 16 U. S. C. §1540(g)(1)(A).

The Court's holding that there is an outer limit to the power of Congress to confer rights of action is a direct and necessary consequence of the case and controversy limitations found in Article III. I agree that it would exceed those limitations if, at the behest of Congress and in the absence of any showing of concrete injury, we were to entertain citizen suits to vindicate the public's nonconcrete interest in the proper administration of the laws....

JUSTICE STEVENS, concurring in the judgment.

Because I am not persuaded that Congress intended the consultation requirement in §7(a)(2) of the Endangered Species Act of 1973 (ESA), 16 U. S. C. §1536(a)(2), to apply to activities in foreign countries, I concur in the judgment of reversal. I do not, however, agree with the Court's conclusion that respondents lack standing because the threatened injury to their interest in protecting the environment and studying endangered species is not "imminent." Nor do I agree with the plurality's additional conclusion that respondents' injury is not "redressable" in this litigation.

In my opinion a person who has visited the critical habitat of an endangered species has a professional interest in preserving the species and its habitat, and intends to revisit them in the future has standing to challenge agency action that threatens their destruction. Congress has found that a wide variety of endangered species of fish, wildlife, and plants are of "aesthetic, ecological, educational, historical, recreational, and scientific value to the Nation and its people." 16 U. S. C. §1531(a)(3). Given that finding, we have no license to demean the importance of the interest that particular individuals may have in observing any species or its habitat, whether those individuals are motivated by esthetic enjoyment, an interest in professional research, or an economic interest in preservation of the species. Indeed, this Court has often held that injuries to such interests are sufficient to confer standing, and the Court reiterates that holding today. The Court nevertheless concludes that respondents have not suffered "injury in fact" because they have not shown that the harm to the endangered species will produce "imminent" injury to them. I disagree. An injury to an individual's interest in studying or enjoying a species and its natural habitat occurs when someone (whether it be the Government or a private party) takes action that harms that species and habitat. In my judgment, therefore, the "imminence" of such an injury should be measured by the timing and likelihood of the threatened environmental harm, rather than — as the Court seems to suggest — by the time that might elapse between the present and the time when the individuals would visit the area if no such injury should occur.... [T]he likelihood that respondents will be injured by the destruction of the endangered species is not speculative. If respondents are genuinely interested in the preservation of the endangered species and intend to study or observe these animals in the future, their injury will occur as soon as the animals are destroyed. Thus the only potential source of "speculation" in this case is whether respondents' intent to study or observe the animals is genuine. In my view, Joyce Kelly and Amy Skilbred have introduced sufficient evidence to negate petitioner's contention that their claims of injury are "speculative" or "conjectural."... [A] reasonable finder of fact could conclude, from their past visits, their professional backgrounds, and their affidavits and deposition testimony, that Ms. Kelly and Ms. Skilbred will return to the project sites and, consequently, will be injured by the destruction of the endangered species and critical habitat.

The plurality also concludes that respondents' injuries are not redressable in this litigation for two reasons. First.... the plurality opines, even if respondents succeed and a new regulation is promulgated, there is no guarantee that federal agencies that are not parties to this case will actually consult with the Secretary. Furthermore, the plurality continues, respondents have not demonstrated that federal agencies can influence the behavior of the foreign governments where the affected projects are located....

We must presume that if this Court holds that § 7(a)(2) requires consultation, all affected agencies would abide by that interpretation and engage in the requisite consultations. Certainly the Executive Branch cannot be heard to argue that an authoritative construction of the governing statute by this Court may simply be ignored by any agency head. Moreover, if Congress has required consultation between agencies, we must presume that such consultation will have a serious purpose that is likely to produce tangible results.... [I]t is not mere speculation to think that foreign governments, when faced with the threatened withdrawal of United States assistance, will modify their projects to mitigate the harm to endangered species....

JUSTICE BLACKMUN, with whom JUSTICE O'CONNOR joins, dissenting.

.... [T]he sworn affidavits and deposition testimony of Joyce Kelly and Amy Skilbred advance sufficient facts to create a genuine issue for trial concerning whether one or both would be imminently harmed by the Aswan and Mahaweli projects. In the first instance, as the Court itself concedes, the affidavits contained facts making it at least "questionable" (and therefore within the province of the factfinder) that certain agency funded projects threaten listed species.

> FN1. The record is replete with genuine issues of fact about the harm to endangered species from the Aswan and Mahaweli projects....

The only remaining issue, then, is whether Kelly and Skilbred have shown that they personally would suffer imminent harm.

.... A reasonable finder of fact could conclude, based not only upon their statements of intent to return, but upon their past visits to the project sites, as well as their professional backgrounds, that it was likely that Kelly and Skilbred would make a return trip to the project areas. Contrary to the Court's contention that Kelly's and Skilbred's past visits "prove nothing," the fact of their past visits could demonstrate to a reasonable factfinder that Kelly and Skilbred have the requisite resources and personal interest in the preservation of the species endangered by the Aswan and Mahaweli projects to make good on their intention to return again. Similarly, Kelly's and Skilbred's professional backgrounds in wildlife preservation, also make it likely—at least far more likely than for the average citizen—that they would choose to visit these areas of the world where species are vanishing.

By requiring a "description of concrete plans" or "specification of when the some day [for a return visit] will be," the Court, in my view, demands what is likely an empty formality. No substantial barriers prevent Kelly or Skilbred from simply purchasing plane tickets to return to the Aswan and Mahaweli projects....

The Court also concludes that injury is lacking, because respondents' allegations of "ecosystem nexus" failed to demonstrate sufficient proximity to the site of the environmental harm.... Many environmental injuries, however, cause harm distant from the area immediately affected by the challenged action. Environmental destruction may affect animals traveling over vast geographical ranges, or rivers running long geographical courses. It cannot seriously be contended that a litigant's failure to use the precise or exact site where animals are slaughtered or where toxic waste is dumped into a river means he or she cannot show injury.

The Court also rejects respondents' claim of vocational or professional injury. The Court says that it is "beyond all reason" that a zoo "keeper" of Asian elephants would have standing to contest his Government's participation in the eradication of all the Asian elephants in another part of the world. I am unable to see how the distant location of the destruction necessarily (for purposes of ruling at summary judgment) mitigates the harm to the elephant keeper. If there is no more access to a future supply of the animal that sustains a keeper's livelihood, surely there is harm....

A plurality of the Court suggests that respondents have not demonstrated redressability: a likelihood that a court ruling in their favor would remedy their injury. The plurality identifies two obstacles. The first is that the "action agencies" (e.g., AID) cannot be required to undertake consultation with petitioner Secretary, because they are not directly bound as parties to the suit and are otherwise not indirectly bound by being subject to petitioner Secretary's regulation. Petitioner, however, officially and publicly has taken the position that his regulations regarding consultation under § 7 of the Act are binding on action agencies. 50 CFR § 402.14(a) (1991). And he has previously taken the same position in this very litigation, having stated in his answer to the complaint that petitioner "admits the Fish and Wildlife Service (FWS) was designated the lead agency for the formulation of regulations concerning section 7 of the [Endangered Species Act]." App. 246. I cannot agree with the plurality that the Secretary (or the Solicitor General) is now free, for the convenience of this appeal, to disavow his prior public and litigation positions. More generally, I cannot agree that the Government is free to play "Three-Card Monte" with its description of agencies' authority to defeat standing against the agency given the lead in administering a statutory scheme.... The second redressability obstacle relied on by the plurality is that "the [action] agencies generally supply only a fraction of the funding for a foreign project." What this Court might "generally" take to be true does not eliminate the existence of a genuine issue of fact to withstand summary judgment. Even if the action agencies supply only a fraction of the funding for a particular foreign project, it remains at least a question for the finder of fact whether threatened withdrawal of that fraction would affect foreign government conduct sufficiently to avoid harm to listed species.... I do not share the plurality's astonishing confidence that, on the record here, a factfinder could only conclude that AID was powerless to ensure the protection of listed species at the [projects].

The Court concludes that any "procedural injury" suffered by respondents is insufficient to confer standing.... The Court expresses concern that allowing judicial enforcement of "agencies' observance of a particular, statutorily prescribed procedure" would "transfer from the President to the courts the Chief Executive's most important constitutional duty, to 'take Care that the Laws be faithfully executed,' Art. II, § 3." In fact, the principal effect of foreclosing judicial enforcement of such procedures is to transfer power into the hands of the Executive at the expense — not of the courts — but of Congress, from which that power originates and emanates.

Under the Court's anachronistically formal view of the separation of powers, Congress legislates pure, substantive mandates and has no business structuring the procedural manner in which the Executive implements these mandates....

The consultation requirement of § 7 of the Endangered Species Act.... is designed as an integral check on federal agency action, ensuring that such action does not go forward without full consideration of its effects on listed species. Once consultation is initiated, the Secretary is under a duty to provide to the action agency "a written statement setting forth the Secretary's opinion, and a summary of the information on which the opinion is based, detailing how the agency action affects the species or its critical habitat." 16 U. S. C. § 1536(b)(3)(A). The Secretary is also obligated to suggest "reasonable and prudent alternatives" to prevent jeopardy to listed species. The action agency must undertake as well its own "biological assessment for the purpose of identifying any endangered species or threatened species" likely to be affected by agency action. § 1536(c)(1). After the initiation of consultation, the action agency "shall not make any irreversible or irretrievable commitment of resources" which would foreclose the "formulation or implementation of any reasonable and prudent alternative measures" to avoid jeopardizing listed species. § 1536(d). These action-forcing procedures are "designed to protect some threatened concrete interest," of persons who observe and work with endangered or threatened species. That is why I am mystified by the Court's unsupported conclusion that "this is not a case where plaintiffs are seeking to enforce a procedural requirement the disregard of which could impair a separate concrete interest of theirs."

Congress legislates in procedural shades of gray not to aggrandize its own power but to allow maximum Executive discretion in the attainment of Congress' legislative goals. Congress could simply impose a substantive prohibition on Executive conduct; it could say that no agency action shall result in the loss of more than 5% of any listed species. Instead, Congress sets forth substantive guidelines and allows the Executive, within certain procedural constraints, to decide how best to effectuate the ultimate goal. The Court never has questioned Congress' authority to impose such procedural constraints on Executive power. Just as Congress does not violate separation of powers by structuring the procedural manner in which the Executive shall carry out the laws, surely the federal courts do not violate separation of powers when, at the very instruction and command of Congress, they enforce these procedures.... Here Congress seeks not to delegate "executive" power but only to strengthen the procedures it has legislatively mandated. "We have long recognized that the nondelegation doctrine does not prevent Congress from seeking assistance, within proper limits, from its coordinate Branches." Touby v. United States, 500 U.S. 160, 165. "Congress does not violate the Constitution merely because it legislates in broad terms, leaving a certain degree of discretion to executive *or judicial actors*" Ibid. (emphasis added).

Ironically, this Court has previously justified a relaxed review of congressional delegation to the Executive on grounds that Congress, in turn, has subjected the exercise of that power to judicial review. The Court's intimation today that procedural injuries are not constitutionally cognizable threatens this understanding upon which Congress has undoubtedly relied. In no sense is the Court's suggestion compelled by our "common understanding of what activities are appropriate to legislatures, to executives, and to courts." In my view, it reflects an unseemly solicitude for an expansion of power of the Executive Branch.

.... There may be factual circumstances in which a congressionally imposed procedural requirement is so insubstantially connected to the prevention of a substantive harm that it cannot be said to work any conceivable injury to an individual litigant. But, as a general matter, the courts owe substantial deference to Congress' substantive purpose in imposing a certain procedural requirement.... There is no room for a per se rule or presumption excluding injuries labeled "procedural" in nature.

In conclusion, I cannot join the Court on what amounts to a slash-and-burn expedition through the law of environmental standing.... I dissent.

Review Questions and Explanations: *Lujan*

1. Kelly and Skilbred did not have specific plans to return to the animal habitats in question. Should that have made a difference as to their standing? Did their lack of plane tickets put them into the same position as the mass of citizens with a generalized interest in endangered species?

2. Congress has the power to create causes of action, giving potential plaintiffs the right to sue in federal court. The citizen suit provision of the Endangered Species Act purported to give such a cause of action to the plaintiffs in this case — indeed, to "any person" — to sue to enforce the Endangered Species Act. *See* 16 U.S.C. § 1540(g). Why wasn't that enough to confer standing on the plaintiffs?

3. How, if at all, might Congress amend the citizen suit provision of the Endangered Species Act, to meet the constitutional requirements for standing? (Note: there is some suggestive language in Section IV of the majority opinion.)

4. There is considerable attention given by the majority and dissenting opinions to litigation procedure. You should think about what you learned (or are learning) in your basic Civil Procedure course about Rule 12 motions to dismiss and Rule 56 summary judgment motions. Both motions can deal with the same legal issues: in *Lujan*, for example, whether plaintiffs had standing. Motions under Rules 12 and 56 differ primarily over where the court gets the case facts on which it makes its legal ruling. Rule 12 motions rely for their facts entirely on the allegations of the complaint; summary judgment motions, in contrast, are based on testimony and other evidence presented to the court through affidavits, as well as depositions and other discovery responses.

Lujan is fundamentally the Supreme Court's review of a summary judgment ruling. In ruling on summary judgment motions, a court is supposed to draw all reasonable inferences in favor of the non-moving party (here, the Defenders of Wildlife) — ultimately to allow the "trier of fact" to decide between competing reasonable inferences. Justice Blackmun argues, in essence, that the majority has given short shrift to a reasonable inference that Kelly and Skilbred will return to the respective animal habitats. Is that a valid point?

5. Consider the two "redressability" questions: whether inter-agency consultation on endangered species impact is likely to protect the species, and whether withdrawal of U.S. funding would affect the foreign projects threatening the species. Are these

factual questions about which a reasonable factfinder could decide either way? If so, summary judgment should have been denied on this issue.

2. Organizational and Representational Standing

While the basic standing doctrine discussed above speaks of standing in terms of concrete injuries to "individuals," organizations also can have standing to sue. In many cases, the organization itself has suffered an injury of some sort, and its standing to sue will not be problematic. In addition, "[a]n association has standing to bring suit on behalf of its members when [1] its members would otherwise have standing to sue in their own right, [2] the interests at stake are germane to the organization's purpose, and [3] neither the claim asserted nor the relief requested requires the participation of individual members in the lawsuit." *Friends of the Earth v. Laidlaw*, 528 U.S. 167, 181 (2000).

In some, but not all circumstances, states are deemed to have standing to sue in Federal Court. *See, e.g., Massachusetts v. EPA*, 549 U.S. 497 (2007) (state had standing to sue for enforcement of environmental law to prevent harm to its coastline).

The standing of legislators to sue—either individually or as a body—is somewhat unclear, and may depend on the capacity in which they are attempting to bring suit. In *Powell v. McCormack*, discussed below in the political question context, the Court recognized the standing of an individual member of Congress to sue to enforce his personal right to assume his seat in the House of Representatives. We have also seen that citizens don't have standing to sue to correct procedural failures of government that do not injure them particularly. But can legislators sue to enforce legislative procedures? The next case considers that issue.

Guided Reading Questions: *Raines v. Byrd*

1. Why does the Court conclude the plaintiffs-appellees (the members of Congress challenging the statute) lack standing? Put another way, which of the three elements of standing identified in *Wright* and *Lujan* are missing here?

2. The Line Item Veto Act itself authorizes members of Congress to challenge the constitutionality of the act in federal court. Why doesn't that provision confer standing on the plaintiffs-appellees?

Raines v. Byrd

521 U.S. 811 (1997)

Majority: *Rehnquist* (CJ), O'Connor, Scalia, Kennedy, Thomas

Concurrence in the judgment: *Souter*, Ginsburg

Dissent: *Stevens*, Breyer

CHIEF JUSTICE REHNQUIST delivered the opinion of the Court.

[Appellees, six Members of the 104th Congress (1995–1996)—Senators Robert Byrd, Carl Levin, Daniel Patrick Moynihan and Mark Hatfield, and Congressmen

David Skaggs and Henry Waxman—filed suit in federal court to challenge the constitutionality of the Line Item Veto Act. On March 27, 1996, the Senate passed the bill by a vote of 69–31; the next day, the House of Representatives passed the identical bill by a vote of 232–177. All six appellees had voted "nay." On April 4, 1996, President Clinton signed the Line Item Veto Act into law. The Act went into effect on January 1, 1997, and the appellees filed suit in the District Court for the District of Columbia the next day. The suit named the Secretary of the Treasury and the Director of the Office of Management and Budget as defendants.

[The Line Item Veto Act gave the President authority to "cancel" certain spending and tax benefit measures after he has signed them into law, based on his determination that "such cancellation will — (i) reduce the Federal budget deficit; (ii) not impair any essential Government functions; and (iii) not harm the national interest." He must then "notify the Congress of such cancellation by transmitting a special message ... within five calendar days (excluding Sundays) after the enactment of the law." The Act provided that "any Member of Congress or any individual adversely affected by [this Act] may bring an action, in the United States District Court for the District of Columbia, for declaratory judgment and injunctive relief on the ground that any provision of this part violates the Constitution." Appellees brought suit under this provision, claiming that "the Act violates Article I" of the Constitution.

[On April 10, 1997, the district court (i) denied appellants' motion to dismiss, holding that appellees had standing to bring this suit and that their claim was ripe, and (ii) granted appellees' summary judgment motion, holding that the Act is unconstitutional. The Supreme Court noted probable jurisdiction under a provision of the Act providing for a direct, expedited appeal to the Supreme Court.]

.... "No principle is more fundamental to the judiciary's proper role in our system of government than the constitutional limitation of federal-court jurisdiction to actual cases or controversies." One element of the case-or-controversy requirement is that appellees, based on their complaint, must establish that they have standing to sue.... We have consistently stressed that a plaintiff's complaint must establish that he has a "personal stake" in the alleged dispute, and that the alleged injury suffered is particularized as to him.... [T]he plaintiff have suffered "an invasion of a legally protected interest which is ... concrete and particularized," Lujan, 504 U.S. at 560, and that the dispute is "traditionally thought to be capable of resolution through the judicial process," Flast v. Cohen, 392 U.S. 83, 97 (1968).

We have always insisted on strict compliance with this jurisdictional standing requirement. And our standing inquiry has been especially rigorous when reaching the merits of the dispute would force us to decide whether an action taken by one of the other two branches of the Federal Government was unconstitutional....

> FN3. It is settled that Congress cannot erase Article III's standing requirements by statutorily granting the right to sue to a plaintiff who would not otherwise have standing.

We have never had occasion to rule on the question of legislative standing presented here. In Powell v. McCormack, 395 U.S. 486, 496 (1969), we held that a Member of Congress' constitutional challenge to his exclusion from the House of Representatives (and his consequent loss of salary) presented an Article III case or controversy. But Powell does not help appellees. First, appellees have not been singled out for specially unfavorable treatment as opposed to other Members of their respective bodies. Their claim is that the Act causes a type of institutional injury (the diminution of legislative power), which necessarily damages all Members of Congress and both Houses of Congress equally. Second, appellees do not claim that they have been deprived of something to which they personally are entitled — such as their seats as Members of Congress after their constituents had elected them. Rather, appellees' claim of standing is based on a loss of political power, not loss of any private right, which would make the injury more concrete. Unlike the injury claimed by Congressman Adam Clayton Powell, the injury claimed by the Members of Congress here is not claimed in any private capacity but solely because they are Members of Congress. If one of the Members were to retire tomorrow, he would no longer have a claim; the claim would be possessed by his successor instead. The claimed injury thus runs (in a sense) with the Member's seat, a seat which the Member holds (it may quite arguably be said) as trustee for his constituents, not as a prerogative of personal power. See The Federalist No. 62, p. 378 (J. Madison) (C. Rossiter ed. 1961) ("It is a misfortune incident to republican government, though in a less degree than to other governments, that those who administer it may forget their obligations to their constituents and prove unfaithful to their important trust").

The one case in which we have upheld standing for legislators (albeit state legislators) claiming an institutional injury is Coleman v. Miller, 307 U.S. 433 (1939). Appellees, relying heavily on this case, claim that they, like the state legislators in Coleman, "have a plain, direct and adequate interest in maintaining the effectiveness of their votes," sufficient to establish standing. In Coleman, 20 of Kansas' 40 State Senators voted not to ratify the proposed "Child Labor Amendment" to the Federal Constitution. With the vote deadlocked 20–20, the amendment ordinarily would not have been ratified. However, the State's Lieutenant Governor, the presiding officer of the State Senate, cast a deciding vote in favor of the amendment, and it was deemed ratified (after the State House of Representatives voted to ratify it). The 20 State Senators who had voted against the amendment, joined by a 21st State Senator and three State House Members, filed an action in the Kansas Supreme Court seeking a writ of mandamus that would compel the appropriate state officials to recognize that the legislature had not in fact ratified the amendment. That court held that the members of the legislature had standing to bring their mandamus action, but ruled against them on the merits.

This Court affirmed. By a vote of 5–4, we held that the members of the legislature had standing. In explaining our holding, we repeatedly emphasized that if these legislators (who were suing as a bloc) were correct on the merits, then their votes not to ratify the amendment were deprived of all validity:

> Here, the plaintiffs include twenty senators, whose votes against ratification have been *overridden* and *virtually held for naught* although if they are right in their contentions *their votes would have been sufficient to defeat ratification....*

> We find no departure from principle in recognizing in the instant case that at least the twenty senators whose votes, if their contention were sustained, *would have been sufficient to defeat the resolution* ratifying the proposed constitutional amendment, have an interest in the controversy which, treated by the state court as a basis for entertaining and deciding the federal questions, is sufficient to give the Court jurisdiction to review that decision." Id., at 446 (emphasis added).

It is obvious, then, that our holding in Coleman stands for the proposition that legislators whose votes would have been sufficient to defeat (or enact) a specific legislative act have standing to sue if that legislative action goes into effect (or does not go into effect), on the ground that their votes have been completely nullified.

It should be equally obvious that appellees' claim does not fall within our holding in Coleman, as thus understood. They have not alleged that they voted for a specific bill, that there were sufficient votes to pass the bill, and that the bill was nonetheless deemed defeated. In the vote on the Line Item Veto Act, their votes were given full effect. They simply lost that vote.

> **FN7.** Just as appellees cannot show that their vote was denied or nullified as in Coleman (in the sense that a bill they voted for would have become law if their vote had not been stripped of its validity), so are they unable to show that their vote was denied or nullified in a discriminatory manner (in the sense that their vote was denied its full validity in relation to the votes of their colleagues). Thus, the various hypotheticals offered by appellees in their briefs and discussed during oral argument have no applicability to this case ... Nor can they allege that the Act will nullify their votes in the future in the same way that the votes of the Coleman legislators had been nullified. In the future, a majority of Senators and Congressman can pass or reject appropriations bills; the Act has no effect on this process. In addition, a majority of Senators and Congressman can vote to repeal the Act, or to exempt a given appropriations bill (or a given provision in an appropriations bill) from the Act; again, the Act has no effect on this process. Coleman thus provides little meaningful precedent for appellees' argument.

> **FN8.** Since we hold that Coleman may be distinguished from the instant case on this ground, we need not decide whether Coleman may also be distinguished in other ways. For instance, appellants have argued that.... Coleman has no applicability to a similar suit brought by federal legislators, since the separation-of-powers concerns present in such a suit were not present in Coleman, and since any federalism concerns were eliminated by the Kansas Supreme Court's decision to take jurisdiction over the case.

Nevertheless, appellees rely heavily on our statement in Coleman that the Kansas senators had "a plain, direct, and adequate interest in maintaining the effectiveness of their votes." Appellees claim that ... their votes on future appropriations bills ... will be less "effective" than before.... Before the Act.... a vote for the appropriations bill meant a vote for a package of projects that were inextricably linked. After the Act, however, a vote for an appropriations bill that includes Project X means ... [that a] bill will become law and then the President [may] "cancel" Project X.... Appellees' use of the word "effectiveness" to link their argument to Coleman stretches the word far beyond the sense in which the Coleman opinion used it. There is a vast difference between the level of vote nullification at issue in Coleman and the abstract dilution of institutional legislative power that is alleged here. To uphold standing here would require a drastic extension of Coleman. We are unwilling to take that step....

In sum, appellees have alleged no injury to themselves as individuals (contra Powell), the institutional injury they allege is wholly abstract and widely dispersed (contra Coleman), and their attempt to litigate this dispute at this time and in this form is contrary to historical experience. We attach some importance to the fact that appellees have not been authorized to represent their respective Houses of Congress in this action, and indeed both Houses actively oppose their suit. We also note that our conclusion neither deprives Members of Congress of an adequate remedy (since they may repeal the Act or exempt appropriations bills from its reach), nor forecloses the Act from constitutional challenge (by someone who suffers judicially cognizable injury as a result of the Act)....

We therefore hold that these individual members of Congress do not have a sufficient "personal stake" in this dispute and have not alleged a sufficiently concrete injury to have established Article III standing.

> **FN11.** In addition, it is far from clear that this injury is "fairly traceable" to appellants, as our precedents require, since the alleged cause of appellees's injury is not appellants' exercise of legislative power but the actions of their own colleagues in Congress in passing the Act.

The judgment of the District Court is vacated, and the case is remanded with instructions to dismiss the complaint for lack of jurisdiction.

JUSTICE SOUTER, concurring in the judgment, with whom JUSTICE GINSBURG joins, concurring.

.... Appellees allege that the Act deprives them of an element of their legislative power; as a factual matter they have a more direct and tangible interest in the preservation of that power than the general citizenry has. On the other hand, the alleged, continuing deprivation of federal legislative power is not as specific or limited as the nullification of the decisive votes of a group of legislators in connection with a specific item of legislative consideration in Coleman, being instead shared by all the members of the official class who could suffer that injury, the Members of Congress. Because it is fairly debatable whether appellees' injury is sufficiently personal and concrete to give them standing, it behooves us to resolve the question under more general separation-of-powers principles underlying our standing requirements.... Although the contest here is not formally between the political branches (since Congress passed the bill augmenting Presidential power and the President signed it), it is in substance an interbranch controversy about calibrating the legislative and executive powers, as well as an intrabranch dispute between segments of Congress itself. Intervention in such a controversy would risk damaging the public confidence that is vital to the functioning of the Judicial Branch by embroiling the federal courts in a power contest nearly at the height of its political tension.

While it is true that a suit challenging the constitutionality of this Act brought by a party from outside the Federal Government would also involve the Court in resolving the dispute over the allocation of power between the political branches, it would expose the Judicial Branch to a lesser risk. Deciding a suit to vindicate an interest outside the Government raises no specter of judicial readiness to enlist on one side of a political tug-of-war, since "the propriety of such action by a federal court has been recognized since Marbury v. Madison." Valley Forge Christian College, supra, at 473–474....

The virtue of waiting for a private suit is only confirmed by the certainty that another suit can come to us. The parties agree, and I see no reason to question, that if the President "cancels" a conventional spending or tax provision pursuant to the Act, the putative beneficiaries of that provision will likely suffer a cognizable injury and thereby have standing under Article III....

JUSTICE STEVENS, dissenting.

The Line Item Veto Act purports to establish a procedure for the creation of laws that are truncated versions of bills that have been passed by the Congress and presented to the President for signature. If the procedure were valid, it would deny every Senator and every Representative any opportunity to vote for or against the truncated measure that survives the exercise of the President's cancellation authority. Because the opportunity to cast such votes is a right guaranteed by the text of the Constitution, I think it clear that the persons who are deprived of that right by the Act have standing to challenge its constitutionality. Moreover, because the impairment of that constitutional right has an immediate impact on their official powers, in my judgment they need not wait until after the President has exercised his cancellation authority to bring suit. Finally, the same reason that the respondents have standing provides a sufficient basis for concluding that the statute is unconstitutional.... In my judgment, the deprivation of this right—essential to the legislator's office—constitutes a sufficient injury to provide every Member of Congress with standing to challenge the constitutionality of the statute. If the dilution of an individual voter's power to elect representatives provides that voter with standing—

as it surely does, see, e.g., Baker v. Carr, 369 U.S. 186, 204–208 (1962)—the deprivation of the right possessed by each Senator and Representative to vote for or against the precise text of any bill before it becomes law must also be a sufficient injury to create Article III standing for them....

> FN2. The respondents' assertion of their right to vote on legislation is not simply a generalized interest in the proper administration of government....

Accordingly, I would affirm the judgment of the District Court.

JUSTICE BREYER, dissenting.

.... [T]he dispute before us, when compared to Coleman, presents a much stronger claim, not a weaker claim, for constitutional justiciability. The lawmakers in Coleman complained of a lawmaking procedure that, at worst, improperly counted Kansas as having ratified one proposed constitutional amendment, which had been ratified by only 5 other States, and rejected by 26, making it unlikely that it would ever become law. The lawmakers in this case complain of a lawmaking procedure that threatens the validity of many laws (for example, all appropriations laws) that Congress regularly and frequently enacts. The systematic nature of the harm immediately affects the legislators' ability to do their jobs. The harms here are more serious, more pervasive, and more immediate than the harm at issue in Coleman.... [S]ince many of the present plaintiffs will likely vote in the majority for at least some appropriations bills that are then subject to presidential cancellation, I think that—on their view of the law—their votes are threatened with nullification [as in Coleman].... While I recognize the existence of potential differences between state and federal legislators, I do not believe that those differences would be determinative here.... In sum, I do not believe that the Court can find this case nonjusticiable without overruling Coleman.... I can and would find this case justiciable on Coleman's authority....

Review Questions and Explanations: *Raines*

1. Does the majority opinion present a self-contained argument against legislative standing, or does it simply argue that none of the precedents recognizing legislative standing apply to the case? Suppose the Court were writing on a clean slate with no precedent dealing specifically with legislator's standing. (Arguably it was!) Can you make an argument that the three elements of standing were present?

2. Does *Raines v. Byrd* stand for the proposition that members of Congress *never* have standing to challenge an action by one or both houses of Congress? Or can you articulate an affirmative rule derived from *Raines* suggesting when members of Congress might have standing?

3. Suppose the Court recognized the standing of legislators to bring a constitutional challenge to any statute they opposed in the legislative voting process. What practical problems, or problems of constitutional theory might, arise under such a legal regime? Do these problems create arguments against legislative standing?

4. As anticipated in the majority and concurring opinions, shortly after *Raines* was decided, a case arose in which parties were adversely affected by a spending cancellation ordered by the President. Their standing was recognized and the case decided on the merits; and the Court, in an opinion by Justice Stevens, struck down the Line Item Veto Act. *See Clinton v. City of New York*, 524 U.S. 417 (1998), excerpted in Chapter 4.

D. Advisory Opinions

The case-or-controversy requirement of Article III bars federal courts from rendering so-called "advisory opinions"—decisions on abstract, hypothetical, or contingent questions. An advisory opinion is a paradigm "not-case": it refers to a legal opinion on an issue that is presented as a hypothetical dispute that could arise rather than an actual legal dispute between identified parties. The rule against advisory opinions is based on the idea that the judicial function is to decide concrete disputes. The adversaries' positions in such disputes sharpen the issues to be decided. Imagined, hypothetical cases often have a half-baked quality compared to real ones; real cases often raise issues the hypothetical might have overlooked. Moreover, consonant with separation of powers, a court's decision rendered in a specific case, at least in theory, has an immediate and narrow scope, in contrast to an advisory opinion, which has the forward-reaching generality of legislation.

The Supreme Court early on established the rule against advisory opinions. In 1793, Thomas Jefferson, as Secretary of State in the Washington administration, sent a letter to the Supreme Court asking for legal opinions on 29 specific questions relating to U.S. neutrality in the ongoing war between France and Great Britain. The letter began:

> The war which has taken place among the powers of Europe produces frequent transactions within our ports and limits, on which questions arise of considerable difficulty, and of greater importance to the peace of the United States. Their questions depend for their solution on the construction of our treaties, on the laws of nature and nations, and on the laws of the land, and are often presented under circumstances which do not give a cognizance of them to the tribunals of the country.... The President therefore would be much relieved if he found himself free to refer questions of this description to the opinions of the judges of the Supreme Court[.]

The Court responded by letter to President Washington:

> We have considered the previous question stated in a letter written by your direction to us by the Secretary of State on the 18th of last month.... [T]he lines of separation drawn by the Constitution between the three departments of the government.... being in certain respects checks upon each other, and our being judges of a court in the last resort, are considerations which afford strong arguments against the propriety of our extra-judicially deciding the questions alluded to, especially as the power given by the Constitution to the President, of calling on the heads of departments for opinions, seems to have been purposely as well as expressly united to the executive departments.

> We exceedingly regret every event that may cause embarrassment to your administration, but we derive consolation from the reflection that your judgment will discern what is right, and that your usual prudence, decision, and firmness will surmount every obstacle to the preservation of the rights, peace, and dignity of the United States.

In contrast to this historical precedent, there is no clear example of the Supreme Court dismissing a case as a non-justiciable request for advisory opinion. *Hayburn's Case*, 2 U.S. (2 Dall.) 409 (1792), is routinely cited by courts and commentators as the source of the proposition that the federal courts will not render advisory opinions. *See, e.g., Massachusetts v. Environmental Protection Agency* ("no justiciable 'controversy' exists when parties ... ask for an advisory opinion[.] *Hayburn's Case*"); Laurence H. Tribe, American Constitutional Law 328–39 & n. 5 (3d ed. 2000) ("The ban on advisory opinions traces [in part] from" *Hayburn's Case*). There, the Court was asked to review a decision by a circuit court refusing to determine one Hayburn's entitlement to veterans' pension benefits. In the Act of March 23, 1792, Congress provided that Revolutionary War veterans disabled by wounds suffered in the war, were entitled to receive pensions by presenting proof of their service wounds and disability to a federal circuit court. The court was to forward its findings and recommendations to the Secretary of War, who would enroll the veteran on the pension list, unless "the said Secretary shall have cause to suspect imposition or mistake," in which case he could withhold the pension and report that fact to Congress. The Supreme Court dismissed the case as moot, because Congress amended the 1792 Act and changed the pension procedure before the Court rendered a decision. Nevertheless, the Court impliedly approved the lower court decision, reproducing it and two other circuit court decisions which had all reached the same conclusion that there was no justiciable case or controversy:

> Upon due consideration, we have been unanimously of opinion that under this act, the circuit court held for the Pennsylvania District could not proceed, 1st. Because the business directed by this act is not of a judicial nature. It forms no part of the power vested by the Constitution in the courts of the United States....
>
> 2d. Because if, upon that business, the court had proceeded, its judgments (for its opinions are its judgments) might, under the same act, have been revised and controlled by the legislature, and by an officer in the executive department. Such revision and control we deemed radically inconsistent with the independence of that judicial power which is vested in the courts ...

In other words, the 1792 Act was unconstitutional, in that it assigned a function to the courts that was not "judicial" in two respects: first, it was non-adversarial, requiring no resolution of a dispute between opposing parties; and second, it was subject to being overruled by the other branches.

Did the statute thus seek an "advisory opinion"? Perhaps a decision in any non-adversarial setting is "advisory." But in another sense not: the veterans were not seeking legal advice from a court (like President Washington did), but rather an individualized determination based on specific facts. Did the non-final aspect of the court's decision also make it "advisory"? Again, perhaps: advice is by its nature non-binding. At the same time, trial court decisions are not rendered non-binding or "advisory" simply because they may be overturned on appeal. If the problem is that the "appeal" lies to the Secretary of War or Congress rather than a higher court, that seems less a question of assigning non-judicial "advisory opinions" to a court than one of assigning a judicial function outside the judicial branch. Either way, a separation-of-powers problem is raised. So whether *Hayburn's Case* truly involved an advisory opinion or not, it does illustrate to some degree the connection between the "case or controversy" requirement and separation of powers. As a practical matter, assigning routine, high-volume administrative duties to courts could undermine their ability to execute their judicial functions.

E. Ripeness

Closely related to the ban on advisory opinions, the doctrine of "ripeness" prevents courts from deciding controversies that have not yet really materialized. A case is not "ripe," and thus not justiciable, if the suit seeks to prevent a future injury that may not occur.

For example, suppose Congress has just passed a statute prohibiting burning the American flag, and a would-be protester seeks a declaratory judgment that the law is unconstitutional, claiming that she may wish to burn a flag someday in protest of government policies.

The court might well dismiss such a claim as unripe. The fact that the plaintiff has not yet burned the flag leaves too many questions unanswered. For instance, would the flag-burning be done in a context (political, artistic, or whatever) that would make it "protected speech" under the First Amendment? Would the government enforce the statute in such a way as to infringe the First Amendment? Will the protester ever actually burn a flag?

In practice, ripeness is far from a rigorous doctrine, and the Supreme Court has allowed numerous suits seeking to prevent speculative future harms, including enforcement of unconstitutional laws. Instead, it appears that ripeness is largely a doctrine of prudence and practicality. The court wants to decide cases based on a factual record or allegations that make the issues sufficiently definite. Legal challenges that were arguably premature have nevertheless been held to be ripe for adjudication where either 1) contemplation of the future challenged event (such as enforcement of an unconstitutional law) produces a significant injury in the present; or 2) the legal questions can be resolved without a well-developed factual background.

F. Mootness

A case is moot if the passage of time and events has ended the live controversy. For example, a lawsuit against a school district seeking to prohibit school prayer would become moot if the state passed a law prohibiting school prayer and the school complied. A plaintiff's claim for reinstatement in a job becomes moot if the plaintiff dies. A mootness issue was considered in *Roe v. Wade*, in which a pregnant woman's constitutional challenge to the state's anti-abortion law reached the Supreme Court after the woman gave birth.

Mootness problems usually focus on whether a case will be heard *in spite of* facts suggesting the controversy has become moot. There are a number of exceptions to the doctrine of dismissing cases for mootness. An issue will not be dismissed as moot if it is "capable of repetition, yet evading review." In other words, if the wrong complained of could happen repeatedly, but predictably would become technically moot each time, the court will not dismiss such a claim as moot. *Roe v. Wade* provided a classic example of such a case (and was thus held not moot) because "Pregnancy often comes more than once to the same woman[.]"

Courts have also held that a case will not be mooted simply because the defendant voluntarily ceases the conduct for which he is being sued, if there is a possibility that the defendant might revert to his old ways.

G. Political Question

The "political question doctrine" considers whether a particular constitutional issue can be resolved by the courts or must instead be left for resolution by the so-called "political branches" or the political process. The mere fact that a legal issue has political implications—even significant ones—doesn't make it a non-justiciable political question. Numerous cases involving the propriety of voting districts, for example, have been held justiciable. *NFIB v. Sebelius*, the ACA case, involved high profile political issues, but there was no question of its being non-justiciable. Instead, a political question is one that invokes constitutional provisions that cannot be construed to protect judicially enforceable rights.

The Supreme Court's definitive statement says that political questions reveal at least one of the following traits:

> [1] a textually demonstrable constitutional commitment to a coordinate political department; [2] a lack of judicially discoverable and manageable standards for resolving it; [3] the impossibility of deciding without an initial policy determination of a kind clearly for nonjudicial discretion; [4] the impossibility of a court's undertaking independent resolution without expressing lack of the respect due coordinate branches of government; [5] an unusual need for unquestioning adherence to a political decision already made; [6] the potentiality of embarrassment from multifarious pronouncements by various departments [i.e., branches of government] on one question.

Baker v. Carr, 369 U.S. 186, 217 (1962). Each of these factors reflects in some way a concern about the limits of the court's proper role and competence in constitutional adjudication. The first factor straightforwardly holds that questions which the Constitution says must be decided by another branch are non-justiciable political questions. An example of this would be a lawsuit challenging the failure of the President to nominate a representative number of women and minorities to federal judgeships: the Constitution clearly commits the nomination of federal judges to the President, precluding judicial review of the content of appointment decisions.

The second and third factors suggest a "functional" approach in which the Court considers its own competence to decide the type of issue: both whether there are any legal standards, and whether the court can get the type of information it needs to decide. These factors were present in *Gilligan v. Morgan*, 413 U.S. 1 (1973), in which the plaintiffs challenged the training procedures used by the Ohio National Guard in the aftermath of the shooting death of four anti-war student protesters by national guardsmen at Kent State University. The Court dismissed the suit as a nonjusticiable political question, noting that courts have no competence to evaluate the "control of a military force."

The last three factors suggest a "prudential" view of the courts' role. Although not strictly required by the Constitution, the courts find it advisable to avoid confrontations with the other branches where possible. An example of the sixth factor was presented in *Luther v. Borden*, 48 U.S. (7 How.) 1 (1849), in which the Court was asked to decide during an armed populist rebellion which of two competing governments of Rhode Island was the lawful one. The Court declined to do so, on the ground that the "guaranty clause," Art. IV, §4, gave Congress the power to decide that issue, and it would be inadvisable for the Court to take a shot at the question and reach a possibly conflicting answer.

The political question doctrine, more than other justiciability doctrines, seems designed for use in dismissing sensitive issues whose judicial resolution could produce a backlash against the courts' authority. Yet dismissals of cases on political question grounds are relatively infrequent. Instead, standing seems to have emerged as the merits-avoiding doctrine of choice for the modern Court, perhaps because it is more arcane and technical. Only rarely has a majority of the Court voted to dismiss a case as presenting a non-justiciable political question.

Guided Reading Questions: *Powell v. McCormack*

1. *Powell v. McCormack* involves a constitutional challenge to a decision by the House of Representatives to exclude one of its members. Be sure to review the first two clauses of Art. I, § 5 before reading the case. Why don't these two clauses reflect a "textually demonstrable commitment" to the House of Representatives of the question of a House member's fitness to assume his seat?

2. See if you can articulate the difference between "jurisdiction" and "justiciability," which is discussed in the opinion.

Powell v. McCormack

395 U.S. 486 (1969)

Majority: *Warren* (CJ), Black, Douglas, Harlan, Brennan, White, Marshall*

Concurrence: *Douglas*

Dissent: *Stewart*

[*Editors' note: No appointment had been made to the seat vacated by the resignation of Justice Fortas.]

CHIEF JUSTICE WARREN delivered the opinion of the Court.

[Adam Clayton Powell, Jr., was an outspoken and controversial Democratic congressman representing the Eighteenth Congressional district, comprising the Harlem section of New York City. First elected in 1944, Powell was only the second black member of Congress since reconstruction. During the Eighty-ninth Congress (1965–66), Powell was investigated by a congressional subcommittee which concluded that he had misappropriated funds and illegally directed salary payments to his wife while he was Chairman of the House Committee on Education and Labor.

[Powell was duly re-elected to the Ninetieth Congress in November 1966, but the House passed a resolution in January 1967 refusing to swear Powell in and allow him to assume his seat. The House held further hearings into Powell's alleged misconduct in early 1967, concluding that he had wrongfully diverted House funds for the use of others and himself, and had made false reports on expenditures. On March 1, 1967, the House voted 307 to 116 to adopt House Resolution No. 278, which excluded Powell from the House and directed the House Speaker to notify the Governor of New York that the seat for the 18th Congressional District was vacant.

[Powell and 13 voters filed suit in the United States District Court for the District of Columbia. Five members of the House of Representatives were named as defendants, including John W. McCormack, named in his official capacity as Speaker, along with three House officials. The complaint alleged that House Resolution No. 278 violated the Constitution, specifically Art. I, § 2, cl. 1, because the resolution was inconsistent with the mandate that the members of the House shall be elected by the people of each State, and Art. I, § 2, cl. 2, which, petitioners alleged, sets forth the exclusive qualifications for membership: 25 years of age, seven years a citizen of the United States, and a resident of the state in which he is elected. The complaint sought a declaratory judgment that Powell's exclusion was unconstitutional and an injunction restoring him to his seat and paying his unpaid salary.

[The District Court dismissed the complaint for lack of subject matter jurisdiction, and the Court of Appeals affirmed. The Supreme Court granted certiorari.]

.... On January 3, 1969, the House of Representatives of the 90th Congress officially terminated, and petitioner Powell was seated as a member of the 91st Congress. Respondents insist that the gravamen of petitioners' complaint was the failure of the 90th Congress to seat petitioner Powell and that, since the House of Representatives is not a continuing body and Powell has now been seated, his claims are moot.... We conclude that Powell's claim for back salary remains viable even though he has been seated in the 91st Congress and thus find it unnecessary to determine whether the other issues have become moot.

Simply stated, a case is moot when the issues presented are no longer "live" or the parties lack a legally cognizable interest in the outcome. Where one of the several issues presented becomes moot, the remaining live issues supply the constitutional requirement of a case or controversy....

[The Court went on to reject the argument that the House has unreviewable discretion to expel a member "with the Concurrence of two thirds." Art. I, § 5. The Court deemed it significant that Powell was not "expelled," but was rather "excluded" from the 90th Congress: he was not administered the oath of office and was prevented from taking his seat. The Court cited substantial circumstantial evidence that the House sees exclusion and expulsion as different and thought they were doing the former in their vote on Powell.]

As we pointed out in Baker v. Carr, 369 U.S. 186, 198 (1962), there is a significant difference between determining whether a federal court has "jurisdiction of the subject matter" and determining whether a cause over which a court has subject matter jurisdiction is "justiciable." The District Court determined that "to decide this case on the merits ... would constitute a clear violation of the doctrine of separation of powers" and then dismissed the complaint "for want of jurisdiction of the subject matter." However, as the Court of Appeals correctly recognized, the doctrine of separation of powers is more properly considered in determining whether the case is "justiciable." We agree with the unanimous conclusion of the Court of Appeals that the District Court had jurisdiction over the subject matter of this case.... [T]his case clearly is one "arising under" the Constitution as the Court has interpreted that phrase. Any bar to federal courts reviewing the judgments made by the House or Senate in excluding a member arises from the allocation of powers between the two branches of the Federal Government (a question of justiciability), and not from the petitioners' failure to state a claim based on federal law....

Respondents [argue] ... that this case is not justiciable because, they assert, it is impossible for a federal court to "mold effective relief for resolving this case." Respondents emphasize that petitioners asked for coercive relief against the officers of the House, and, they contend, federal courts cannot issue mandamus or injunctions compelling officers or employees of the House to perform specific official acts. Respondents rely primarily on the Speech or Debate Clause to support this contention.

We need express no opinion about the appropriateness of coercive relief in this case, for petitioners sought a declaratory judgment, a form of relief the District Court could have issued. The Declaratory Judgment Act, 28 U. S. C. § 2201, provides that a district court may "declare the rights ... of any interested party ... whether or not further relief is or could be sought." … [A] request for declaratory relief may be considered independently of whether other forms of relief are appropriate. …

Respondents maintain that even if this case is otherwise justiciable, it presents only a political question. … because under Art. I, § 5, there has been a "textually demonstrable constitutional commitment" to the House of the "adjudicatory power" to determine Powell's qualifications. Thus it is argued that the House, and the House alone, has power to determine who is qualified to be a member. …

If examination of § 5 disclosed that the Constitution gives the House judicially unreviewable power to set qualifications for membership and to judge whether prospective members meet those qualifications, further review of the House determination might well be barred by the political question doctrine. On the other hand, if the Constitution gives the House power to judge only whether elected members possess the three standing qualifications set forth in the Constitution, further consideration would be necessary to determine whether any of the other formulations of the political question doctrine are "inextricable from the case at bar." Baker v. Carr, supra, at 217.

> FN41. In addition to the three qualifications set forth in Art. I, § 2, Art. I, § 3, cl. 7, authorizes the disqualification of any person convicted in an impeachment proceeding from "any Office of honor, Trust or Profit under the United States"; Art. I, § 6, cl. 2, provides that "no Person holding any Office under the United States, shall be a Member of either House during his Continuance in Office"; and § 3 of the 14th Amendment disqualifies any person "who, having previously taken an oath … to support the Constitution of the United States, shall have engaged in insurrection or rebellion against the same, or given aid or comfort to the enemies thereof." … [B]oth sides agree that Powell was not ineligible under any of these provisions.

… . In order to determine the scope of any "textual commitment" under Art. I, § 5, we necessarily must determine the meaning of the phrase to "be the Judge of the Qualifications of its own Members." … [Respondents argue] that the "qualifications" expressly set forth in the Constitution were not meant to limit the long-recognized legislative power to exclude or expel at will, but merely to establish "standing incapacities," which could be altered only by a constitutional amendment. Our examination of the relevant historical materials leads us to the conclusion that petitioners are correct and that the Constitution leaves the House without authority to *exclude* any person, duly elected by his constituents, who meets all the requirements for membership expressly prescribed in the Constitution.

[After a lengthy historical analysis of English historical precedents likely known to the Framers, and second, the ratification debates on the Constitution, the Court concluded that members of parliament, and later, of Congress, could be excluded only on failure to meet limited and specific qualifications.]

… . [Respondents] suggest that far more relevant is Congress' own understanding of its power to judge qualifications as manifested in post-ratification exclusion cases. Unquestionably, both the House and the Senate have excluded members-elect for reasons other than their failure to meet the Constitution's standing qualifications. For almost the first 100 years of its existence, however, Congress strictly limited its power to judge the qualifications of its members to those enumerated in the Constitution.

Congress was first confronted with the issue in 1807, when the eligibility of William McCreery was challenged because he did not meet additional residency requirements imposed by the State of Maryland. … [D]uring the ensuing debate the chairman [of the House Committee of Elections] explained … : "The Committee of Elections considered the qualifications of members to have been unalterably determined by the Federal

Convention, unless changed by an authority equal to that which framed the Constitution at first;.... Congress, by the Federal Constitution, are not authorized to prescribe the qualifications of their own members, but they are authorized to judge of their qualifications; in doing so, however, they must be governed by the rules prescribed by the Federal Constitution, and by them only ..." The chairman emphasized that the committee's narrow construction of the power of the House to judge qualifications was compelled by the "fundamental principle in a free government," id., at 873, that restrictions upon the people to choose their own representatives must be limited to those "absolutely necessary for the safety of the society." Id., at 874....

[The Court considered several more recent exclusions by the House and Senate.]

Had these congressional exclusion precedents been more consistent, their precedential value still would be quite limited. That an unconstitutional action has been taken before surely does not render that same action any less unconstitutional at a later date. Particularly in view of the Congress' own doubts in those few cases where it did exclude members-elect, we are not inclined to give its precedents controlling weight. The relevancy of prior exclusion cases is limited largely to the insight they afford in correctly ascertaining the draftsmen's intent. Obviously, therefore, the precedential value of these cases tends to increase in proportion to their proximity to the Convention in 1787. See Myers v. United States, 272 U.S. 52, 175 (1926). And, what evidence we have of Congress' early understanding confirms our conclusion that the House is without power to exclude any member-elect who meets the Constitution's requirements for membership.

Had the intent of the Framers emerged from these materials with less clarity, we would nevertheless have been compelled to resolve any ambiguity in favor of a narrow construction of the scope of Congress' power to exclude members-elect. A fundamental principle of our representative democracy is, in Hamilton's words, "that the people should choose whom they please to govern them." 2 Elliot's Debates 257. As Madison pointed out at the Convention, this principle is undermined as much by limiting whom the people can select as by limiting the franchise itself. In apparent agreement with this basic philosophy, the Convention adopted his suggestion limiting the power to expel. To allow essentially that same power to be exercised under the guise of judging qualifications, would be to ignore Madison's warning.... For these reasons, we have concluded that Art. I, §5, is at most a "textually demonstrable commitment" to Congress to judge only the qualifications expressly set forth in the Constitution. Therefore, the "textual commitment" formulation of the political question doctrine does not bar federal courts from adjudicating petitioners' claims.

Respondents' alternate contention is that the case presents a political question because judicial resolution of petitioners' claim would produce a "potentially embarrassing confrontation between coordinate branches" of the Federal Government. But, as our interpretation of Art. I, §5, discloses, a determination of petitioner Powell's right to sit would require no more than an interpretation of the Constitution. Such a determination falls within the traditional role accorded courts to interpret the law, and does not involve a "lack of the respect due [a] coordinate [branch] of government," nor does it involve an "initial policy determination of a kind clearly for nonjudicial discretion." Baker v. Carr, 369 U.S. 186, at 217. Our system of government requires that federal courts on occasion interpret the Constitution in a manner at variance with the construction given the document by another branch. The alleged conflict that such an adjudication may cause cannot justify the courts' avoiding their constitutional responsibility. See Youngstown Sheet & Tube Co. v. Sawyer, 343 U.S. 579, 613–614 (1952) (Frankfurter, J., concurring).

Nor are any of the other formulations of a political question "inextricable from the case at bar." Baker v. Carr, supra, at 217. Petitioners seek a determination that the House was without power to exclude Powell from the 90th Congress, which, we have seen, requires an interpretation of the Constitution—a determination for which clearly there arc "judicially ... manageable standards." Finally, a judicial resolution of petitioners' claim will not result in "multifarious pronouncements by various departments on one question." For, as we noted in Baker v. Carr, supra, at 211, it is the responsibility of this Court to act as the ultimate interpreter of the Constitution. Marbury v. Madison, 1 Cranch 137 (1803). Thus, we conclude that petitioners' claim is not barred by the political question doctrine, and, having determined that the claim is otherwise generally justiciable, we hold that the case is justiciable.

.... [A]nalysis of the "textual commitment" under Art. I, §5 (see Part VI, B (1)), has demonstrated that in judging the qualifications of its members Congress is limited to the standing qualifications prescribed in the Constitution. Respondents concede that Powell met these. Thus, there is no need to remand this case to determine whether he was entitled to be seated in the 90th Congress. Therefore, we hold that, since Adam Clayton Powell, Jr., was duly elected by the voters of the 18th Congressional District of New York and was not ineligible to serve under any provision of the Constitution, the House was without power to exclude him from its membership.

Petitioners seek additional forms of equitable relief, including mandamus for the release of petitioner Powell's back pay. The propriety of such remedies, however, is more appropriately considered in the first instance by the courts below. Therefore.... the case is remanded to the United States District Court for the District of Columbia with instructions to enter a declaratory judgment and for further proceedings consistent with this opinion.

MR. JUSTICE DOUGLAS.

While I join the opinion of the Court, I add a few words. As the Court says, the important constitutional question is whether the Congress has the power to deviate from or alter the qualifications for membership as a Representative contained in Art. I, §2, cl. 2, of the Constitution. Up to now the understanding has been quite clear to the effect that such authority does not exist. To be sure, Art. I, §5, provides that: "Each House shall be the Judge of the Elections, Returns and Qualifications of its own Members...." Contests may arise over whether an elected official meets the "qualifications" of the Constitution, in which event the House is the sole judge. But the House is not the sole judge when "qualifications" are added which are not specified in the Constitution....

A man is not seated because he is a Socialist or a Communist.

Another is not seated because in his district members of a minority are systematically excluded from voting.

Another is not seated because he has spoken out in opposition to the war in Vietnam.

The possible list is long. Some cases will have the racist overtones of the present one.

Others may reflect religious or ideological clashes.

At the root of all these cases, however, is the basic integrity of the electoral process. Today we proclaim the constitutional principle of "one man, one vote." When that principle is followed and the electors choose a person who is repulsive to the Establishment in Congress, by what constitutional authority can that group of electors be disenfranchised?

MR. JUSTICE STEWART, dissenting.

I believe that events which have taken place since certiorari was granted in this case on November 18, 1968, have rendered it moot, and that the Court should therefore refrain from deciding the novel, difficult, and delicate constitutional questions which the case presented at its inception.

Review Questions and Explanations: *Powell*

1. Do you agree with the Court's decision to consider the case on the merits rather than dismissing it on political question grounds?

2. The Douglas concurrence, as well as language in the majority opinion, speak of this case as though it involved voting rights of Rep. Powell's constituents. Do you think voting rights somehow factored into the decision to decline to apply the political question doctrine? Note that *Baker v. Carr*, the leading case on political question doctrine, rejected a political question argument and held that a voting rights controversy was justiciable.

3. Consider the difference between declaratory and injunctive ("coercive") relief issued by a court. Injunctive relief orders the defendant to do something (or refrain from doing something). A declaratory judgment pronounces legal rights without ordering the defendant to do anything as a result: the hope is that the defendant will voluntarily comply with the declaratory judgment. Would injunctive relief ordering the House of Representatives to seat Rep. Powell have raised justiciability issues that were not raised by a declaratory judgment?

The following case involves a challenge by an impeached federal judge, Walter L. Nixon, to his conviction by the Senate. (We include his full name in the case caption to avoid confusion with cases involving former President Richard M. Nixon.)

Guided Reading Questions: *Nixon v. United States*

1. Try to articulate the precise argument made on behalf of Judge Nixon in this case.

2. The main rationale for the Court's decision seems to turn on the words "try" and "sole" in the impeachment trial clause. How do these words form the basis for an argument that Nixon's claim presents a non-justiciable political question?

3. See if you can identify any other grounds—even ones that may be implicit or subtle—for the Court's decision aside from reliance on the words "try" and "sole."

4. Try to articulate the arguments against the majority's decision. Does the White opinion make any arguments that seem not to have been made by Nixon's lawyers (those reflected in the majority opinion's rebuttals of the "petitioner's" arguments)?

Walter L. Nixon v. United States

506 U.S. 224 (1993)

Majority: *Rehnquist* (CJ), Stevens, O'Connor, Scalia, Kennedy, Thomas

Concurrence: *Stevens*

Concurrences in the judgment: *White*, Blackmun; *Souter*

CHIEF JUSTICE REHNQUIST delivered the opinion of the Court.

Petitioner Walter L. Nixon, Jr., asks this Court to decide whether Senate Rule XI, which allows a committee of Senators to hear evidence against an individual who has been impeached and to report that evidence to the full Senate, violates the Impeachment Trial Clause, Art. I, §3, cl. 6. That Clause provides that the "Senate shall have the sole Power to try all Impeachments." But before we reach the merits of such a claim, we must decide whether it is "justiciable," that is, whether it is a claim that may be resolved by the courts. We conclude that it is not.

Nixon, a former Chief Judge of the United States District Court for the Southern District of Mississippi, was convicted by a jury of two counts of making false statements before a federal grand jury and sentenced to prison. The grand jury investigation stemmed from reports that Nixon had accepted a gratuity from a Mississippi businessman in exchange for asking a local district attorney to halt the prosecution of the businessman's son. Because Nixon refused to resign from his office as a United States District Judge, he continued to collect his judicial salary while serving out his prison sentence. See H. R. Rep. No. 101-36, p. 13 (1989).

On May 10, 1989, the House of Representatives adopted three articles of impeachment for high crimes and misdemeanors. The first two articles charged Nixon with giving false testimony before the grand jury and the third article charged him with bringing disrepute on the Federal Judiciary. See 135 Cong. Rec. H1811.

After the House presented the articles to the Senate, the Senate voted to invoke its own Impeachment Rule XI, under which the presiding officer appoints a committee of Senators to "receive evidence and take testimony." Senate Impeachment Rule XI.

> FN1. Specifically, Rule XI provides: "In the trial of any impeachment the Presiding Officer of the Senate, if the Senate so orders, shall appoint a committee of Senators to receive evidence and take testimony at such times and places as the committee may determine, and for such purpose the committee so appointed and the chairman thereof, to be elected by the committee, shall (unless otherwise ordered by the Senate) exercise all the powers and functions conferred upon the Senate and the Presiding Officer of the Senate, respectively, under the rules of procedure and practice in the Senate when sitting on impeachment trials...."

The Senate committee held four days of hearings, during which 10 witnesses, including Nixon. Pursuant to Rule XI, the committee presented the full Senate with a complete transcript of the proceeding and a Report stating the uncontested facts and summarizing the evidence on the contested facts. Nixon and the House impeachment managers submitted extensive final briefs to the full Senate and delivered arguments from the Senate floor during the three hours set aside for oral argument in front of that body. Nixon himself gave a personal appeal, and several Senators posed questions directly to both parties. 135 Cong. Rec. S14493–14517 (Nov. 1, 1989). The Senate voted by more than the constitutionally required two-thirds majority to convict Nixon on the first two articles. Id., at S14635 (Nov. 3, 1989). The presiding officer then entered judgment removing Nixon from his office as United States District Judge.

Nixon thereafter commenced the present suit, arguing that Senate Rule XI violates the constitutional grant of authority to the Senate to "try" all impeachments because it prohibits the whole Senate from taking part in the evidentiary hearings. See Art. I, § 3, cl. 6. Nixon sought a declaratory judgment that his impeachment conviction was void and that his judicial salary and privileges should be reinstated. The District Court held that his claim was nonjusticiable, and the Court of Appeals for the District of Columbia Circuit agreed. We granted certiorari.

A controversy is nonjusticiable—i.e., involves a political question—where there is "a textually demonstrable constitutional commitment of the issue to a coordinate political department; or a lack of judicially discoverable and manageable standards for resolving it...." Baker v. Carr, 369 U.S. 186, 217 (1962). But the courts must, in the first instance, interpret the text in question and determine whether and to what extent the issue is textually committed. See ibid.; Powell v. McCormack, 395 U.S. 486, 519 (1969). As the discussion that follows makes clear, the concept of a textual commitment to a coordinate political department is not completely separate from the concept of a lack of judicially discoverable and manageable standards for resolving it; the lack of judicially manageable standards may strengthen the conclusion that there is a textually demonstrable commitment to a coordinate branch.

In this case, we must examine Art. I, § 3, cl. 6, to determine the scope of authority conferred upon the Senate by the Framers regarding impeachment. It provides:

> The Senate shall have the sole Power to try all Impeachments. When sitting for that Purpose, they shall be on Oath or Affirmation. When the President of the United States is tried, the Chief Justice shall preside: And no Person shall be convicted without the Concurrence of two thirds of the Members present.

The language and structure of this Clause are revealing. The first sentence is a grant of authority to the Senate, and the word "sole" indicates that this authority is reposed in the Senate and nowhere else. The next two sentences specify requirements to which the Senate proceedings shall conform: The Senate shall be on oath or affirmation, a two-thirds vote is required to convict, and when the President is tried the Chief Justice shall preside.

Petitioner argues that the word "try" in the first sentence imposes by implication an additional requirement on the Senate in that the proceedings must be in the nature of a judicial trial. From there petitioner goes on to argue that this limitation precludes the Senate from delegating to a select committee the task of hearing the testimony of witnesses, as was done pursuant to Senate Rule XI. "'Try' means more than simply 'vote on' or 'review' or 'judge.' In 1787 and today, trying a case means hearing the evidence, not scanning a cold record." Brief for Petitioner 25. Petitioner concludes from this that courts may review whether or not the Senate "tried" him before convicting him.

There are several difficulties with this position which lead us ultimately to reject it. The word "try," both in 1787 and later, has considerably broader meanings than those to which petitioner would limit it. Older dictionaries define try as "to examine" or "to examine as a judge." See 2 S. Johnson, A Dictionary of the English Language (1785). In more modern usage the term has various meanings. For example, try can mean "to examine or investigate judicially," "to conduct the trial of," or "to put to the test by experiment, investigation, or trial." Webster's Third New International Dictionary 2457 (1971). Petitioner submits that "try," as contained in T. Sheridan, Dictionary of the English Language (1796), means "to examine as a judge; to bring before a judicial tribunal." Based on the variety of definitions, however, we cannot say that the Framers used the word "try" as an implied limitation on the method by which the Senate might proceed in trying impeachments. "As a rule the

Constitution speaks in general terms, leaving Congress to deal with subsidiary matters of detail as the public interests and changing conditions may require   "

The conclusion that the use of the word "try" in the first sentence of the Impeachment Trial Clause lacks sufficient precision to afford any judicially manageable standard of review of the Senate's actions is fortified by the existence of the three very specific requirements that the Constitution does impose on the Senate when trying impeachments: The Members must be under oath, a two-thirds vote is required to convict, and the Chief Justice presides when the President is tried. These limitations are quite precise, and their nature suggests that the Framers did not intend to impose additional limitations on the form of the Senate proceedings by the use of the word "try" in the first sentence.

.... [T]he first sentence of Clause 6 ... provides that "the Senate shall have the sole Power to try all Impeachments." We think that the word "sole" is of considerable significance. Indeed, the word "sole" appears only one other time in the Constitution—with respect to the House of Representatives' "*sole* Power of Impeachment." Art. I, § 2, cl. 5 (emphasis added). The commonsense meaning of the word "sole" is that the Senate alone shall have authority to determine whether an individual should be acquitted or convicted. The dictionary definition bears this out. "Sole" is defined as "having no companion," "solitary," "being the only one," and "functioning ... independently and without assistance or interference." Webster's Third New International Dictionary 2168 (1971). If the courts may review the actions of the Senate in order to determine whether that body "tried" an impeached official, it is difficult to see how the Senate would be "functioning ... independently and without assistance or interference."

Nixon asserts that the word "sole" has no substantive meaning. To support this contention, he argues that the word is nothing more than a mere "cosmetic edit" added by the Committee of Style after the delegates had approved the substance of the Impeachment Trial Clause. There are two difficulties with this argument. First, accepting as we must the proposition that the Committee of Style had no authority from the Convention to alter the meaning of the Clause, see 2 Records of the Federal Convention of 1787, p. 553 (M. Farrand ed. 1966) (hereinafter Farrand), we must presume that the Committee's reorganization or rephrasing accurately captured what the Framers meant in their unadorned language. That is, we must presume that the Committee did its job. This presumption is buttressed by the fact that the Constitutional Convention voted on, and accepted, the Committee of Style's linguistic version. See 2 Farrand 663–667. We agree with the Government that "the word 'sole' is entitled to no less weight than any other word of the text, because the Committee revision perfected what 'had been agreed to.'" Brief for Respondents 25. Second, carrying Nixon's argument to its logical conclusion would constrain us to say that the *second to last draft* would govern in every instance where the Committee of Style added an arguably substantive word. Such a result is at odds with the fact that the Convention passed the Committee's version, and with the well-established rule that the plain language of the enacted text is the best indicator of intent.

Petitioner also contends that the word "sole" should not bear on the question of justiciability because Art. II, § 2, cl. 1, of the Constitution grants the President pardon authority "except in Cases of Impeachment." He argues that such a limitation on the President's pardon power would not have been necessary if the Framers thought that the Senate alone had authority to deal with such questions. But the granting of a pardon is in no sense an overturning of a judgment of conviction by some other tribunal; it is "an executive action that mitigates or sets aside *punishment* for a crime." Black's Law Dictionary 1113 (6th ed. 1990) (emphasis added). Authority in the Senate to determine procedures for trying an impeached official, unreviewable by the courts, is therefore not at all inconsistent with authority in the President to grant a pardon to the convicted official. The exception from the President's pardon authority of cases of impeachment was a separate determination by the Framers that executive clemency should not be available in such cases.

Petitioner finally argues that even if significance be attributed to the word "sole" in the first sentence of the Clause, the authority granted is to the Senate, and this means that "the Senate — not the courts, not a lay jury, not a Senate Committee — shall try impeachments." Brief for Petitioner 42. It would be possible to read the first sentence of the Clause this way, but it is not a natural reading. Petitioner's interpretation would bring into judicial purview not merely the sort of claim made by petitioner, but other similar claims based on the conclusion that the word "Senate" has imposed by implication limitations on procedures which the Senate might adopt. Such limitations would be inconsistent with the construction of the Clause as a whole, which, as we have noted, sets out three express limitations in separate sentences.

The history and contemporary understanding of the impeachment provisions support our reading of the constitutional language. The parties do not offer evidence of a single word in the history of the Constitutional Convention or in contemporary commentary that even alludes to the possibility of judicial review in the context of the impeachment powers. This silence is quite meaningful in light of the several explicit references to the availability of judicial review as a check on the Legislature's power with respect to bills of attainder, ex post facto laws, and statutes. See The Federalist No. 78, p. 524 (J. Cooke ed. 1961) ("Limitations ... can be preserved in practice no other way than through the medium of the courts of justice").

The Framers labored over the question of where the impeachment power should lie. Significantly, in at least two considered scenarios the power was placed with the Federal Judiciary. See 1 Farrand 21–22 (Virginia Plan); id., at 244 (New Jersey Plan). Indeed, James Madison and the Committee of Detail proposed that the Supreme Court should have the power to determine impeachments. Despite these proposals, the Convention ultimately decided that the Senate would have "the sole Power to try all Impeachments." Art. I, §3, cl. 6. According to Alexander Hamilton, the Senate was the "most fit depositary of this important trust" because its Members are representatives of the people. See The Federalist No. 65, p. 440 (J. Cooke ed. 1961). The Supreme Court was not the proper body because the Framers "doubted whether the members of that tribunal would, at all times, be endowed with so eminent a portion of fortitude as would be called for in the execution of so difficult a task" or whether the Court "would possess the degree of credit and authority" to carry out its judgment if it conflicted with the accusation brought by the Legislature — the people's representative. See id., at 441. In addition, the Framers believed the Court was too small in number: "The awful discretion, which a court of impeachments must necessarily have, to doom to honor or to infamy the most confidential and the most distinguished characters of the community, forbids the commitment of the trust to a small number of persons." Id., at 441–442.

There are two additional reasons why the Judiciary, and the Supreme Court in particular, were not chosen to have any role in impeachments. First, the Framers recognized that most likely there would be two sets of proceedings for individuals who commit impeachable offenses — the impeachment trial and a separate criminal trial. In fact, the Constitution explicitly provides for two separate proceedings. See Art. I, §3, cl. 7. The Framers deliberately separated the two forums to avoid raising the specter of bias and to ensure independent judgments:

> Would it be proper that the persons, who had disposed of his fame and his most valuable rights as a citizen in one trial, should in another trial, for the same offence, be also the disposers of his life and his fortune? Would there not be the greatest reason to apprehend, that error in the first sentence would be the parent of error in the second sentence? That the strong bias of one decision would be apt to overrule the influence of any new lights, which might be brought to vary the complexion of another decision? The Federalist No. 65, p. 442 (J. Cooke ed. 1961).

Certainly judicial review of the Senate's "trial" would introduce the same risk of bias as would participation in the trial itself.

Second, judicial review would be inconsistent with the Framers' insistence that our system be one of checks and balances. In our constitutional system, impeachment was designed to be the *only* check on the Judicial Branch by the Legislature. [The Federalist, No. 79 (Hamilton).] ... Judicial involvement in impeachment proceedings, even if only for purposes of judicial review, is counterintuitive because it would eviscerate the "important constitutional check" placed on the Judiciary by the Framers. See id., No. 81. Nixon's argument would place final reviewing authority with respect to impeachments in the hands of the same body that the impeachment process is meant to regulate.

Nevertheless, Nixon argues that judicial review is necessary in order to place a check on the Legislature. Nixon fears that if the Senate is given unreviewable authority to interpret the Impeachment Trial Clause, there is a grave risk that the Senate will usurp judicial power. The Framers anticipated this objection and created two constitutional safeguards to keep the Senate in check. The first safeguard is that the whole of the impeachment power is divided between the two legislative bodies, with the House given the right to accuse and the Senate given the right to judge. Id., No. 66, at 446. This split of authority "avoids the inconvenience of making the same persons both accusers and judges; and guards against the danger of persecution from the prevalency of a factious spirit in either of those branches." The second safeguard is the two-thirds supermajority vote requirement. Hamilton explained that "as the concurrence of two-thirds of the senate will be requisite to a condemnation, the security to innocence, from this additional circumstance, will be as complete as itself can desire." Ibid.

In addition to the textual commitment argument, we are persuaded that the lack of finality and the difficulty of fashioning relief counsel against justiciability. See Baker v. Carr, 369 U.S. at 210. We agree with the Court of Appeals that opening the door of judicial review to the procedures used by the Senate in trying impeachments would "expose the political life of the country to months, or perhaps years, of chaos." 938 F.2d at 246. This lack of finality would manifest itself most dramatically if the President were impeached. The legitimacy of any successor, and hence his effectiveness, would be impaired severely, not merely while the judicial process was running its course, but during any retrial that a differently constituted Senate might conduct if its first judgment of conviction were invalidated. Equally uncertain is the question of what relief a court may give other than simply setting aside the judgment of conviction. Could it order the reinstatement of a convicted federal judge, or order Congress to create an additional judgeship if the seat had been filled in the interim?

Petitioner finally contends that a holding of nonjusticiability cannot be reconciled with our opinion in Powell v. McCormack, 395 U.S. 486 (1969).... Our conclusion in Powell was based on the fixed meaning of "qualifications" set forth in Art. I, §2. The claim by the House that its power to "be the Judge of the Elections, Returns and Qualifications of its own Members" was a textual commitment of unreviewable authority was defeated by the existence of this separate provision specifying the only qualifications which might be imposed for House membership. The decision as to whether a Member satisfied these qualifications *was* placed with the House, but the decision as to what these qualifications consisted of was not.

In the case before us, there is no separate provision of the Constitution that could be defeated by allowing the Senate final authority to determine the meaning of the word "try" in the Impeachment Trial Clause. We agree with Nixon that courts possess power to review either legislative or executive action that transgresses identifiable textual limits. As we have made clear, "whether the action of [either the Legislative or Executive Branch] exceeds whatever authority has been committed, is itself a delicate exercise in constitutional interpretation, and is a responsibility of this Court as ultimate interpreter of the Constitution." Baker v. Carr, supra, at 211; accord, Powell, supra, at 521.But we conclude, after exercising that delicate responsibility, that the word "try" in the Impeachment Trial Clause does not provide an identifiable textual limit on the authority which is committed to the Senate.

For the foregoing reasons, the judgment of the Court of Appeals is affirmed.

JUSTICE STEVENS, concurring.

For me, the debate about the strength of the inferences to be drawn from the use of the words "sole" and "try" is far less significant than the central fact that the Framers decided to assign the impeachment power to the Legislative Branch. The disposition of the impeachment of Samuel Chase in 1805 demonstrated that the Senate is fully conscious of the profound importance of that assignment, and nothing in the subsequent history of the Senate's exercise of this extraordinary power suggests otherwise. Respect for a coordinate branch of the Government forecloses any assumption that improbable hypotheticals like those mentioned by JUSTICE WHITE and JUSTICE SOUTER will ever occur. Accordingly, the wise policy of judicial restraint, coupled with the potential anomalies associated with a contrary view, provide a sufficient justification for my agreement with the views of THE CHIEF JUSTICE.

JUSTICE WHITE, with whom JUSTICE BLACKMUN joins, concurring in the judgment.

Petitioner contends that the method by which the Senate convicted him on two articles of impeachment violates Art. I, § 3, cl. 6, of the Constitution, which mandates that the Senate "try" impeachments. The Court is of the view that the Constitution forbids us even to consider his contention. I find no such prohibition and would therefore reach the merits of the claim. I concur in the judgment because the Senate fulfilled its constitutional obligation to "try" petitioner.

It should be said at the outset that, as a practical matter, it will likely make little difference whether the Court's or my view controls this case. This is so because the Senate has very wide discretion in specifying impeachment trial procedures and because it is extremely unlikely that the Senate would abuse its discretion and insist on a procedure that could not be deemed a trial by reasonable judges.... I would not issue an invitation to the Senate to find an excuse, in the name of other pressing business, to be dismissive of its critical role in the impeachment process....

.... [T]he issue in the political question doctrine is *not* whether the constitutional text commits exclusive responsibility for a particular governmental function to one of the political branches. There are numerous instances of this sort of textual commitment, e.g., Art. I, § 8, and it is not thought that disputes implicating these provisions are non-justiciable. Rather, the issue is whether the Constitution has given one of the political branches final responsibility for interpreting the scope and nature of such a power.

Although Baker directs the Court to search for "a textually demonstrable constitutional commitment" of such responsibility, there are few, if any, explicit and unequivocal instances in the Constitution of this sort of textual commitment.... The courts therefore are usually left to infer the presence of a political question from the text and structure of the Constitution. In drawing the inference that the Constitution has committed final interpretive authority to one of the political branches, courts are sometimes aided by textual evidence that the Judiciary was not meant to exercise judicial review—a coordinate inquiry expressed in Baker's "lack of judicially discoverable and manageable standards" criterion....

The historical evidence reveals above all else that the Framers were deeply concerned about placing in any branch the "awful discretion, which a court of impeachments must necessarily have." The Federalist No. 65. Viewed against this history, the discord between the majority's position and the basic principles of checks and balances underlying the Constitution's separation of powers is clear. In essence, the majority suggests that the Framers' conferred upon Congress a potential tool of legislative dominance yet at the same time rendered Congress' exercise of that power one of the very few areas of legislative authority immune from any judicial review....

The majority also contends that the term "try" does not present a judicially manageable standard.... [But] one would intuitively expect that, in defining the power of a political body to conduct an inquiry into official wrongdoing, the Framers used "try" in its legal sense. That intuition is borne out by reflection on the alternatives. The third Clause of Art. I, § 3, cannot seriously be read to mean that the Senate shall "attempt" or "experiment with" impeachments. It is equally implausible to say that the Senate is charged with "investigating" impeachments given that this description would substantially overlap with the House of Representatives' "sole" power to draw up articles of impeachment. Art. I, § 2, cl. 5. That these alternatives are not realistic possibilities is finally evidenced by the use of "tried" in the third sentence of the Impeachment Trial Clause ("when the President of the United States is tried ..."), and by Art. III, § 2, cl. 3 ("the Trial of all Crimes, except in Cases of Impeachment ...").

The other variant of the majority position focuses not on which sense of "try" is employed in the Impeachment Trial Clause, but on whether the legal sense of that term creates a judicially manageable standard. The majority concludes that the term provides no "identifiable textual limit." Yet, as the Government itself conceded at oral argument, the term "try" is hardly so elusive as the majority would have it. See Tr. of Oral Arg. 51–52. Were the Senate, for example, to adopt the practice of automatically entering a judgment of conviction whenever articles of impeachment were delivered from the House, it is quite clear that the Senate will have failed to "try" impeachments. Indeed in this respect, "try" presents no greater, and perhaps fewer, interpretive difficulties than some other constitutional standards that have been found amenable to familiar techniques of judicial construction, including, for example, "Commerce ... among the several States," and "due process of law." ...

The majority's conclusion that "try" is incapable of meaningful judicial construction is not without irony. One might think that if any class of concepts would fall within the definitional abilities of the Judiciary, it would be that class having to do with procedural justice....

[Nevertheless, the] fact that Art. III, § 2, cl. 3, specifically exempts impeachment trials from the jury requirement provides some evidence that the Framers were anxious not to have additional specific procedural requirements read into the term "try." Contemporaneous commentary further supports this view. Hamilton, for example, stressed that a trial by so large a body as the Senate (which at the time promised to boast 26 members) necessitated that the proceedings not "be tied down to ... strict rules, either in the delineation of the offence by the prosecutors, or in the construction of it by the Judges...." The Federalist No. 65....

In short, textual and historical evidence reveals that the Impeachment Trial Clause was not meant to bind the hands of the Senate beyond establishing a set of minimal procedures. Without identifying the exact contours of these procedures, it is sufficient to say that the Senate's use of a fact-finding committee under Rule XI is entirely compatible with the Constitution's command that the Senate "try all impeachments." Petitioner's challenge to his conviction must therefore fail.

Petitioner has not asked the Court to conduct his impeachment trial; he has asked instead that it determine whether his impeachment was tried by the Senate. The majority refuses to reach this determination out of a laudable desire to respect the authority of the Legislature. Regrettably, this concern is manifested in a manner that does needless violence to the Constitution....

JUSTICE SOUTER, concurring in the judgment.

.... [T]he political question doctrine is "essentially a function of the separation of powers," existing to restrain courts "from inappropriate interference in the business of the other branches of Government," and deriving in large part from prudential concerns about the respect we owe the political departments. Not all interference is inappropriate or disrespectful, however, and application of the doctrine ultimately turns, as Learned Hand put it, on "how importunately the occasion demands an answer." L. Hand, The Bill of Rights 15 (1958).

This occasion does not demand an answer. The Impeachment Trial Clause commits to the Senate "the sole Power to try all Impeachments," subject to three procedural requirements: the Senate shall be on oath or affirmation; the Chief Justice shall preside when the President is tried; and conviction shall be upon the concurrence of two-thirds of the Members present. U.S. Const., Art. I, § 3, cl. 6. It seems fair to conclude that the Clause contemplates that the Senate may determine, within broad boundaries, such subsidiary issues as the procedures for receipt and consideration of evidence necessary to satisfy its duty to "try" impeachments. Other significant considerations confirm a conclusion that this case presents a nonjusticiable political question: the "unusual need for unquestioning adherence to a political decision already made," as well as "the potentiality of embarrassment from multifarious pronouncements by various departments on one question." Baker, supra, at 217. As the Court observes, judicial review of an impeachment trial would under the best of circumstances entail significant disruption of government.

One can, nevertheless, envision different and unusual circumstances that might justify a more searching review of impeachment proceedings. If the Senate were to act in a manner seriously threatening the integrity of its results, convicting, say, upon a coin toss, or upon a summary determination that an officer of the United States was simply " 'a bad guy,' " judicial interference might well be appropriate. In such circumstances, the Senate's action might be so far beyond the scope of its constitutional authority, and the consequent impact on the Republic so great, as to merit a judicial response despite the prudential concerns that would ordinarily counsel silence. "The political question doctrine, a tool for maintenance of governmental order, will not be so applied as to promote only disorder." Baker, supra, at 215.

Review Questions and Explanations: *Nixon v. United States*

1. How convincing is the majority's reliance on the word "sole" in the impeachment trial clause? Does a grant of power in the Constitution not using the word "sole" imply the absence of a "textually demonstrable commitment" to that branch? Or is it also important to conclude that there is no plain language prohibiting the Senate from delegating the factfinding process to a committee? Consider how the Court might decide the following cases:

   a)   the Senate purports to "convict" an impeached official on a simple majority vote (rather than two-thirds);

   b)   the Senate convicts with a two-thirds vote but allows absent Senators to vote (raising questions about the meaning of "present" in the impeachment clause).

Would a challenge by the impeached and convicted official be non-justiciable in these cases, based on *Nixon*?

2. Justice White's separate opinion seems to argue that there is a difference between a "textually demonstrable commitment" of a *power* to a branch of government and a commitment of the question of *interpreting the meaning or limits of that power*. Do you agree? Can you think of other instances where this distinction applies where the Court does *not* seem to see a non-justiciable political question?

3. Is the meaning of the word "sole" truly determinative of the decision in this case, or are there any pragmatic grounds, wholly apart from the word "sole," that justify the Court's decision to find a non-justiciable political question?

4. A dismissal on political question grounds, as the majority says at the very beginning, is supposed to forestall consideration of the merits of the dispute. Does the majority "take a peek at the merits," as it is sometimes said to do when deciding that a plaintiff lacks standing?

Recap: Political Question Doctrine

1. On the surface, *Powell* and *Nixon* reach opposing results on the question of "textually demonstrable commitment." One distinction is the presence of the word "sole" in the impeachment trial clause. Is that a convincing distinction? What other grounds can you think of to distinguish the two cases and harmonize their results?

2. The three basic elements of standing (injury-in-fact, causation, redressability) are deemed to be constitutional requirements imposed by Article III for a justiciable controversy that cannot, according to *Lujan*, be bypassed by an act of Congress. Is the political question doctrine, similarly, a constitutional requirement? Or is it merely a "prudential" doctrine that can be overcome by statute? For example, would it be constitutional for Congress to enact a statute authorizing the Court to review the constitutionality of Senate Rule XI, its committee-based impeachment trial procedure?

Exercises: Justiciability

1. With one or more classmates, try brainstorming to create a list of four or five "generalized grievances" that at least one of you has about public policy or governmental choices that affect your general interest as a citizen.

Now choose one or more of these grievances, and try to draft a law that would provide for citizen enforcement in federal court. You can write up the purpose and the operative provision in broad outline; focus instead on the enforcement aspect. See if you can get around the restriction in section IV of *Lujan* that a citizen suit provision is not by itself enough to confer standing to sue for a generalized grievance.

2. Gordon Chu is a 51-year-old law professor and former civil rights lawyer who has been nominated by the President (a Democrat) to the U.S. Court of Appeals for the 10th Circuit. His nomination was approved by the Senate Judiciary Committee on a straight party-line vote, six Democrats voting yes and five Republicans voting no. The 53 Democratic senators have all stated that they will vote to approve Chu, who received the American Bar Association's highest rating for judicial nominee qualifications. The Senate minority leader has stated publicly that "Chu's ultra-liberal approach to the law is out of step with the views of the American people," and announced a filibuster of the nomination. After a failure of the cloture vote to end the filibuster (45 of the 47 Republican senators voting against cloture), Chu's nomination has been permanently tabled.

Consider whether any or all of the following plaintiffs could overcome standing and political question objections to a lawsuit against the U.S. Senate, and seek an adjudication on the merits to obtain the following remedies: a judicial declaration that the filibuster is unconstitutional, and an injunction ordering the Senate to vote on the nomination.

1) Gordon Chu;
2) Citizens for a Democratic Judiciary, a liberal advocacy group that focuses on public education and advocacy relating to judicial appointments;
3) the President;
4) a Democratic Senator.

The plaintiffs wish to challenge the filibuster — U.S. Senate Rule 22, which provides that debate on a matter before the Senate can be extended indefinitely unless 60 Senators vote to close debate ("cloture"). The constitutional challenge would be based on the argument that the "Vice President clause" (Art. I, § 3, cl. 4) implies that Senate decisions must be by simple majority vote unless otherwise expressly provided. (By comparison, the impeachment conviction clause, Art. I, § 3, cl. 6, and the veto override clause, Art. I, § 7, cl. 2, both expressly require two-thirds votes.) Senate Rule 22 unconstitutionally imposes, in effect, a 60-vote supermajority requirement on all matters — so the argument goes.

Given what you know about standing and political question doctrines, will a federal court reach the merits in either of these cases?

With one or more fellow students, assume the roles of lawyers for the plaintiffs and the defendant Senate, and judge(s). Outline the arguments for your client —

do the plaintiffs have standing? Does the political question doctrine bar adjudication on the merits? — and present them in a mock oral argument against your opposing counsel.

Professional Development Reflection Questions

1. Suppose you are a lawyer in the Justice Department assigned to represent the Internal Revenue Service in a case like *Allen v. Wright*, and feel the evidence indeed shows that the IRS was failing to enforce its policy of denying tax-exempt status to racially discriminatory private schools. The standing argument, if successful, will lead to the case being dismissed without any decision on the merits — with the possible result that an illegal governmental practice will continue. Is your duty as a public servant well-served by making that standing argument? Are your obligations the same as, or different from, those of a lawyer in a private firm hired to represent the allegedly discriminatory private schools?

2. In *Lujan*, government lawyers argued that the citizen suit provision of the Endangered Species Act was unconstitutional. *See Lujan*, Brief of Petitioner, at 55 (citizen suit provision "cannot overcome standing deficiencies under Article III"). Is there any ethical problem with a lawyer for the government (an executive branch employee) challenging a validly enacted federal law? What about the duty of the President to "take care that the laws be faithfully executed"? If the answer is somehow based on the Constitution, does that imply a belief that the President and executive branch are entitled to second-guess the constitutional judgments of Congress — and of whatever President signed the bill into law (assuming the law passed without the override of a veto)? Does it matter that the argument against the constitutionality of the citizen suit provision was novel — i.e., is it ethical for executive branch lawyers to come up with new and innovative ways to persuade a court to strike down acts of Congress that the current President doesn't like?

What would you do as a lawyer for the Environmental Protection Agency in a case like this?

PART FOUR

Due Process, Fundamental Rights, and Equal Protection

The materials presented in the first three Parts of this casebook involve separation of powers issues arising out of Articles I, II and III of the Constitution. The cases studied in this and the next Part are different, in that they involve questions of individual rights. They nonetheless do present a similar type of issue. Generally speaking, U.S. constitutional rights restrict the actions of both federal and state governments. To the extent the federal Constitution imposes restrictions on what state governments can do to state residents, they in effect impose a federal limitation on state action. Like the materials presented earlier in the book, these materials thus address the division of power between governmental actors: when federal rights restrain state actors, they move decision making power over issues involving those rights from the state to the federal realm.

The following two chapters examine individual rights under the Due Process clauses of the Fifth and Fourteenth Amendments, and the Equal Protection and Privileges or Immunities clauses of the Fourteenth Amendment. The Fifth Amendment provides:

> **No person shall** be held to answer for a capital, or otherwise infamous crime, unless on a presentment or indictment of a grand jury, except in cases arising in the land or naval forces, or in the militia, when in actual service in time of war or public danger; nor shall any person be subject for the same offense to be twice put in jeopardy of life or limb; nor shall be compelled in any criminal case to be a witness against himself, nor **be deprived of life, liberty, or property, without due process of law**; nor shall private property be taken for public use, without just compensation.

Within this Amendment, our focus will be on the Due Process clause, highlighted in bold. (The provision before the Due Process clause are considered "constitutional criminal law" and are generally covered in a Criminal Procedure course.)

The first section of the Fourteenth Amendment reads as follows:

> All persons born or naturalized in the United States, and subject to the jurisdiction thereof, are citizens of the United States and of the State wherein they reside. No State shall make or enforce any law which shall abridge the privileges or im-

munities of citizens of the United States; nor shall any State deprive any person of life, liberty, or property, without due process of law; nor deny to any person within its jurisdiction the equal protection of the laws.

Within this Amendment, we will examine the Privileges or Immunities clause, the Due Process clause, and the Equal Protection clause.

These two Amendments (the Fifth and the Fourteenth) form the basis for what has become a complex web of individual rights doctrines involving the concepts of "liberty," "equal protection," "due process," and fundamental rights. Chapter 7 looks at the Due Process clauses found in the two Amendments, the concept of "liberty" embodied by these clauses, and the application of that concept as a protection against federal and state governmental action. Chapter 8 focuses on the last clause of the Fourteenth Amendment, and the concept of "equal protection of the laws." In doing so, both Chapters engage the idea of "fundamental rights."

We will save a more detailed overview of these concepts for their respective Chapters. For now, however, it is worthwhile setting out a basic road map of the ideas that underlie both Chapters. Because these ideas may be difficult to make sense of in the abstract, we suggest that you look at the road map now and return to it as you work through Chapters 7 and 8.

Figure IV.1 is a conceptual road map of individual rights: their sources in the Constitution and the levels of government against which the rights may be asserted.

Figure IV.1. Rights Roadmap

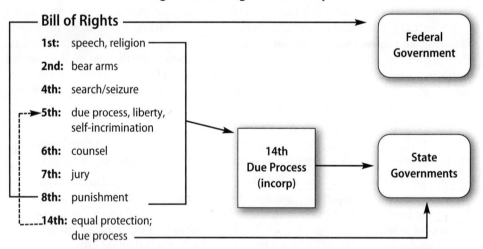

In a nutshell, Figure IV.1 illustrates the current state of constitutional doctrine, in which the Bill of Rights (the first ten amendments) apply directly to the federal government and, with certain exceptions, apply to the states by "incorporation" into the Fourteenth Amendment's Due Process clause. The Equal Protection clause in contrast, was designed to apply to the states directly. The Supreme Court also has held that the Fifth Amendment's due process clause includes an equal protection-type guarantee against federal government action, even though the Fifth Amendment lacks an explicit Equal Protection clause.

These clauses provide the starting point for many individual rights-based challenges to the constitutionality of governmental action. Governmental acts, whether laws or executive actions, regulate behavior or re-distribute resources, or both. In doing so, they affect individuals in at least two ways that can provoke these types of claims. First, they *affect "liberty"* in that they restrict behavior or re-direct resources from one person or group to another. Second, they *create classifications* for differential or unequal treatment: some group is identified by some criteria and is subject to regulation, while another group is regulated differently, or not at all. The Due Process clause is the basis for challenging the "liberty" effect of governmental actions, and the Equal Protection clause is the basis for challenging the "differential treatment" effect. These clauses thus represent two analytically distinct ways of formulating individual rights claims, although some governmental actions, it is worth noting, raise both types of questions and can be reviewed under either — or both — clauses.

Perhaps not surprisingly, courts do not consider all restrictions of liberty or differences in treatment as equally deserving of stringent judicial protection. The judicial inquiry under the Due Process and Equal Protection clauses, therefore, varies depending on what liberty is being infringed upon or what classification is being drawn. These variations are reflected in the degree of deference that courts give to governmental acts infringing on different types of liberty or drawing different types of classifications. Current doctrine captures this idea in what are commonly called "levels of scrutiny." We illustrate this in Figure IV.2.

Figure IV.2. Levels of Scrutiny

Level of scrutiny	Required nexus	Required governmental interest	Subject matter
Strict	Narrowly tailored to further ...	a *compelling* interest	Race-based distinctions; laws limiting fundamental rights
Intermediate	Substantially related to ...	an *important* interest	Sex-based distinctions; affirmative action (former view)
Minimal (a/k/a "rational basis test" or "mere rationality" review)	Rationally related to ...	a *legitimate* interest	Economic and property regulation; almost all other subjects of legislation

Most laws challenged under the Due Process or Equal Protection clauses are reviewed deferentially by the courts under the so-called "rational basis" test: as long as the law is reasonably related to a legitimate governmental objective, it will be upheld against a due process or equal protection challenge. At the other extreme, there are a handful of circumstances under which the courts will apply non-deferential review, known as "strict scrutiny": the law will be upheld only if it is "narrowly tailored to achieve a compelling governmental interest." Laws are frequently struck down when reviewed under this demanding standard. A middle form of heightened judicial scrutiny, "intermediate scrutiny," lies between these two poles. Much of what you will study in the next two Chapters concerns the criteria for determining what level of scrutiny a court should apply in a particular case. Generally speaking, laws that infringe "fundamental rights" or that draw classification on the basis of race, ethnicity or nationality, receive strict scrutiny, while other laws are reviewed more deferentially.

Figure IV.3 illustrates the idea of deference. "Deference" in this context means an unwillingness of courts to second guess the decisions made by the legislative and executive branches.

Figure IV.3. Levels of Deference

• Strict scrutiny

• Intermediate scrutiny

Less deferential, more likely to find unconstitutional

• Rational basis, rational relationship, "mere rationality"

More deferential, less likely to find unconstitutional

All of these concepts—due process, fundamental rights, equal protection, suspect classifications, and judicial deference—are discussed in detail in the next two Chapters. This summary is intended merely to introduce you to the basic concepts, in order to facilitate your study of the following materials.

Chapter 7

Substantive Due Process

A. Overview

Most of the remainder of this casebook is devoted to understanding the substantive scope of the individual rights protected by the Bill of Rights and the Fourteenth Amendment. The first section of this chapter, however, asks why the Bill of Rights constrains the actions of states at all. As you will see in the first case below, under the original Constitution they did not. The rights included in the federal Bill of Rights—including things like the speech and religious rights found in the First Amendment—did not run against the states. Only the Federal Government could violate your U.S. constitutional rights because only the Federal Government was constrained by the Bill of Rights. Other than the few specific limitations imposed on states under the original Constitution—such as the provision prohibiting states from passing *ex post facto* laws—individuals had rights against states only if given them by their state constitutions.

The Civil War Amendments, most importantly the Fourteenth Amendment, changed that. The first section of the Fourteenth Amendment reads as follows:

> All persons born or naturalized in the United States, and subject to the jurisdiction thereof, are citizens of the United States and of the State wherein they reside. No State shall make or enforce any law which shall abridge the privileges or immunities of citizens of the United States; nor shall any State deprive any person of life, liberty, or property, without due process of law; nor deny to any person within its jurisdiction the equal protection of the laws.

By its own terms, the Fourteenth Amendment imposes federal restrictions on what states can do to their inhabitants. The question addressed in the first set of cases below is just what those limits are and precisely how the text of the Fourteenth Amendment imposes them. As we will see, the doctrinal mechanism—the way the Fourteenth Amendment "incorporates" federal constitutional rights against state actors—is not just of historical interest. The incorporation of the Bill of Rights against the states, something which generates very little controversy today, turns out to rest on one of the Court's most contested doctrines, the "substantive due process" doctrine. Thus, while most of this chapter deals directly with that doctrine, and the controversial cases decided under it, we find it worthwhile to first explore the doctrine's relationship to incorporation. The mechanics of incorporation also are important to understand because some members of the current Court, most notably Justice Thomas, seem interested in revisiting some of the early (and arguably unwise) choices made by the Court in this area.

Consequently, this chapter proceeds as follows. First, after briefly considering the antebellum understanding of the Bill of Rights, we examine the status of the Bill of Rights immediately after the Civil War, and consider the various ways in which the then newly minted Fourteenth Amendment could have been read to make those rights binding on the states. We then look in depth at the path actually taken by the Court: the incorporation of most of the rights found in the Bill of Rights through the Fourteenth Amendment's Due Process clause, and the doctrine of "fundamental rights" developed under that clause. Next, we explore the Court's struggle to define "fundamental rights" in a judicially manageable way. In doing so, we consider the different tests preferred by different justices over time. Finally, we examine the various things the Court has protected under the fundamental rights doctrine, including its movement from using the doctrine to protect economic rights to the current practice of using it to provide more robust protection to individual liberties.

Throughout the chapter, we focus on one of the core questions at the heart of these materials: when faced with broad or open-textured constitutional provisions, when should the Court defer to legislative judgments and when should it assert its own power to protect individual rights? As you will see, different justices (and different Courts) have answered this question differently. These differences drive much of the debate about judicial "activism" explored in Part Three. As illustrated in the charts in Chapter 5, very few justices believe it is their job to always defer to the elected branches. Rather, different justices believe that deference is appropriate in different situations for different reasons. The uncertainty inherent in terms like "due process" and "liberty," magnify those differences—an issue we will explore throughout this chapter, as well as the next.

We begin by examining the text of the Fourteenth Amendment. Section 1 of the Amendment has four distinct clauses: the Citizenship Clause (the first sentence); the Privileges or Immunities clause (the second sentence); the Due Process clause (the first part of the third sentence); and the Equal Protection clause (the last part of the third sentence). The Citizenship Clause was added to the Fourteenth Amendment specifically to overturn the Supreme Court's decision, in *Dred Scott v. Sanford*, that even free people of African descent could not be citizens of the United States. The Equal Protection clause, which you were introduced to in Chapter 1, governs when and how state actors can treat different groups of people differently. There are many similarities between the Court's equal protection doctrine and the doctrines developed under the Due Process clause. Indeed, claims can be—and often are—brought under both clauses. We explore the Equal Protection clause in the next chapter.

The analysis in this chapter focuses on the remaining two clauses of the Fourteenth Amendment: the Privileges or Immunities clause and the Due Process clause. Both of these clauses explicitly restrict the power of the states in ways that did not exist before the Civil War Amendments were added to the Constitution. The Privileges or Immunities clause prohibits states from abridging citizens' "privileges or immunities," while the Due Process clause prohibits states from depriving people within their jurisdiction of "life, liberty or property" without "due process" of law. The challenge in this chapter is to determine just what these prohibitions include.

It may be helpful before reading the cases to consider the various ways this question *could* have been answered. One possible answer is to interpret the Privileges or Immunities clause as protecting *all* the rights recognized as essential to citizenship in a free and democratic society—i.e., the privileges and immunities of citizenship. This may have been the most textually coherent interpretation, and was the interpretation flirted with by some members of the Court in the early cases in this area. As you will see in the *Slaughterhouse Cases*, however, it is not the path taken by majority of those early justices.

Another route would be to read either the Privileges or Immunities clause or the Due Process clause as incorporating against the states the specific rights set out in the Bill of

Rights. This reading would define either "privileges or immunities" or the "liberty" protected by the Due Process clause as synonymous with the first eight amendments to the Constitution. Under this reading, the rights contained in those amendments would be, by definition, the rights protected by the Fourteenth Amendment against state intrusion. John Bingham, a Republican congressman from Ohio who was the primary author of the Fourteenth Amendment, appears to have intended this result in regard to the Privileges or Immunities clause. But the *Slaughterhouse Cases* also ruled this option out in relation to that clause. This understanding of the Due Process clause, however, has been advocated by several justices, most notably Justice Black (whose thoughts on the subject you will read in *Adamson v. California*).

The third option is that the liberties protected by either the Privileges or Immunities clause or the Due Process clause could be defined in some other way, not directly tied to or restricted by the rights articulated in the Bill of Rights, but resting instead on an independent determination of what rights are so fundamental that the deprivation of them without sufficient reason would violate the requirements of due process. As you will see in *Twining v. New Jersey* and *Palko v. Connecticut*, this is the path the Court has taken under the Due Process clause (although it is worth noting that in doing so it has effectively incorporated most of the Bill of Rights). The best argument for this approach may, somewhat surprisingly, be textual. The text prohibits deprivations of liberty, life and property without due process of law. It does not expressly incorporate the Bill of Rights against the states, something that would have been easy enough to do textually if that was in fact what was intended. The disadvantage, pointed out by Justice Black and many, many others, is that this method requires the Court to independently determine which rights are so fundamental that they warrant extra judicial protection. As you will see below, the Court has articulated numerous different ways in which it makes this determination, none of which, we posit, are entirely satisfying.

Before moving on to the cases it is worth pausing to consider one additional issue. A commonly heard critique of the Court's reasoning in this line of cases is that the Court erred from the very beginning in reading a *substantive* component into a *procedural* clause. In this view, the Court's view of the Due Process clause as protecting fundamental rights is not textually supported at all. What these critics mean by this is that the due *process* clause—note that "process" means "procedure"—should not be read as including any substantive limits on governmental action, but rather as speaking to only purely procedural protections, things like notice and an opportunity to be heard, that a state must provide before depriving someone of a protected liberty or property right.

This criticism has some validity. It is not, however, quite as self-evidently true as it may at first appear. First, a purely procedural reading of the clause would defeat not just the controversial "fundamental rights" approach developed by the Court in *Twining*, but the relatively uncontroversial Bill of Rights incorporation approach preferred by Justice Black: after all, many of the most prized rights protected by the Bill of Rights are substantive, not procedural protections.

Second, the Due Process clause may offer a better textual foundation for incorporation of the Bill of Rights than either of the two other most likely candidates—the Privileges or Immunities clause (discussed above) and the Ninth Amendment.[1] Certainly, the Supreme Court ultimately seemed to think so. If there is to be any judicial recognition of fundamental substantive rights aside from those expressly mentioned in the Constitution (a point that perhaps should not be taken for granted), it is worth

---

1. The Ninth Amendment provides: "The enumeration in the Constitution, of certain rights, shall not be construed to deny or disparage others retained by the people."

considering whether the Due Process clause, despite its flaws, may nevertheless be the best way to do it.

Third, the separation between "substance" and "procedure" is not nearly as clear as critics of the doctrine imply. Even purely procedural due process is at least in part about reason-giving. Star Chambers and kangaroo courts are considered illegitimate precisely because we care about process not merely for its own sake, but because process done right requires the state to adequately *justify* what it is doing to people within its control. We would hardly think sufficient process had been provided, for example, if the state could take your client's children away from her simply by giving her notice and an opportunity to be heard before doing so. We would want the state to also have to explain *why* it is doing what it is doing, and we would want those reasons to justify the state's action in some meaningful way. Fair process requires more than merely going through the motions. In this sense, all process has a substantive component in that a "due" process is one that requires the state to explain and defend its actions. The substantive due process doctrine developed in these cases is likewise about reason-giving. As you will see when you read the final set of cases, a judicial declaration that something is a "fundamental right" does not automatically mean the state cannot deprive you of it. Rather, it means a state must give very important ("compelling") reasons before it can do so, and the way in which it deprives you of the right must be narrowly tailored to further those reasons.

The actual legal debate in this area, consequently, is not really about whether there is a substantive component to due process. Most jurists, as you will see in the below cases, agree that there is. They also agree that at least some rights are indeed so fundamental that a deprivation of them must be justified by compelling reasons. The real fight, therefore, is more about what role the courts should play in determining *what types* of reasons are sufficient to justify *what types* of deprivations—a point Justice Scalia makes forcefully in his dissent in *Lawrence v. Texas*, a case you will read toward the end of this chapter.

B. Foundational Doctrine

1. The Privileges or Immunities Clause

Guided Reading Questions: *Barron v. Baltimore* and *The Slaughterhouse Cases*

1. What is the precise question presented in *Barron* and how does the Court answer it? Does this holding surprise you?

2. *The Slaughterhouse Cases* are responsible for rendering the Privileges or Immunities clause largely a constitutional non-starter. When reading the cases, think about why they had that result.

3. When reading *The Slaughterhouse Cases*, pay close attention to the distinction the Court is drawing between the rights of state citizenship and the rights of federal citizenship. Why is this distinction important to the Court, and what types of rights does the Court put in each category?

Barron v. Baltimore

32 U.S. (7 Pet.) 243 (1833)

Unanimous decision: *Marshall* (CJ), Johnson, Duvall, Story, Thompson, McLean, Baldwin

CHIEF JUSTICE MARSHALL delivered the opinion of the Court.

[This case was instituted by the plaintiff in error, against the city of Baltimore ... to recover damages for injuries to the wharf-property of the plaintiff, arising from the acts of the city.]

The plaintiff in error contends, that [this case] comes within that clause in the fifth amendment to the constitution, which inhibits the taking of private property for public use, without just compensation. He insists, that this amendment being in favor of the liberty of the citizen, ought to be so construed as to restrain the legislative power of a state, as well as that of the United States. If this proposition be untrue, the court can take no jurisdiction of the cause. The question thus presented is, we think, of great importance, but not of much difficulty.

The constitution was ordained and established by the people of the United States for themselves, for their own government, and not for the government of the individual states. Each state established a constitution for itself, and in that constitution, provided such limitations and restrictions on the powers of its particular government, as its judgment dictated. The people of the United States framed such a government for the United States as they supposed best adapted to their situation and best calculated to promote their interests. The powers they conferred on this government were to be exercised by itself; and the limitations on power, if expressed in general terms, are naturally, and, we think, necessarily, applicable to the government created by the instrument. They are limitations of power granted in the instrument itself; not of distinct governments, framed by different persons and for different purposes.

If these propositions be correct, the Fifth Amendment must be understood as restraining the power of the general government, not as applicable to the states. In their several constitutions, they have imposed such restrictions on their respective governments, as their own wisdom suggested; such as they deemed most proper for themselves. It is a subject on which they judge exclusively, and with which others interfere no further than they are supposed to have a common interest....

A state is forbidden [under the Constitution] to enter into any treaty, alliance or confederation. If these compacts are with foreign nations, they interfere with the treaty-making power, which is conferred entirely on the general government; if with each other, for political purposes, they can scarcely fail to interfere with the general purpose and intent of the constitution. To grant letters of marque and reprisal, would lead directly to war; the power of declaring which is expressly given to congress. To coin money is also the exercise of a power conferred on congress. It would be tedious to recapitulate the several limitations on the powers of the states which are contained in this section. They will be found, generally, to restrain state legislation on subjects entrusted to the government of the Union, in which the citizens of all the states are interested. In these alone, were the whole people concerned. The question of their application to states is not left to construction. It is averred in positive words.

If the original constitution draws this plain and marked line of discrimination between the limitations it imposes on the powers of the general government, and on those of the state; if, in every inhibition intended to act on state power, words are employed, which directly express that intent; some strong reason must be assigned for departing from this safe and judicious course, in framing the amendments, before that departure can be assumed.

We search in vain for that reason.

Had the people of the several states, or any of them, required changes in their constitutions; had they required additional safe-guards to liberty from the apprehended encroachments of their particular governments; the remedy was in their own hands, and could have been applied by themselves. A convention could have been assembled by the discontented state, and the required improvements could have been made by itself. The unwieldy and cumbrous machinery of procuring a recommendation from two-thirds of congress, and the assent of three-fourths of their sister states, could never have occurred to any human being, as a mode of doing that which might be effected by the state itself. Had the framers of these amendments intended them to be limitations on the powers of the state governments, they would have imitated the framers of the original constitution, and have expressed that intention. Had congress engaged in the extraordinary occupation of improving the constitutions of the several states, by affording the people additional protection from the exercise of power by their own governments, in matters which concerned themselves alone, they would have declared this purpose in plain and intelligible language.

But it is universally understood, it is a part of the history of the day, that the great revolution which established the constitution of the United States, was not affected without immense opposition. Serious fears were extensively entertained, that those powers which the patriot statesmen, who then watched over the interests of our country, deemed essential to union, and to the attainment of those invaluable objects for which union was sought, might be exercised in a manner dangerous to liberty. In almost every convention by which the constitution was adopted, amendments to guard against the abuse of power were rec-ommended. These amendments demanded security against the apprehended encroachments of the general government not against those of the local governments.

In compliance with a sentiment thus generally expressed, to quiet fears thus extensively entertained, amendments were proposed by the required majority in congress, and adopted by the states. These amendments contain no expression indicating an intention to apply them to the state governments. This court cannot so apply them.

We are of opinion, that the provision in the Fifth Amendment to the constitution, declaring that private property shall not be taken for public use, without just compensation, is intended solely as a limitation on the exercise of power by the government of the United States, and is not applicable to the legislation of the states. We are, therefore, of opinion, that there is no repugnancy between the several acts of the general assembly of Maryland, given in evidence by the defendants at the trial of this cause, in the court of that state, and the constitution of the United States. This court, therefore, has no jurisdiction of the cause, and it is dismissed.

The Slaughterhouse Cases

83 U.S. (16 Wall.) 36 (1873)

Majority: *Miller*, Clifford, Strong, Hunt, Davis

Dissents: *Field* (omitted), Chase (CJ), *Bradley, Swayne*

MR. JUSTICE MILLER delivered the opinion of the Court.

These cases are brought here by writs of error to the Supreme Court of the State of Louisiana. They arise out of the efforts of the butchers of New Orleans to resist the

Crescent City Live-Stock Landing and Slaughter-House Company in the exercise of certain powers conferred by the charter which created it, and which was granted by the legislature of that State....

The statute thus assailed as unconstitutional was passed March 8th, 1869, and is entitled 'An act to protect the health of the city of New Orleans, to locate the stock-landings and slaughter-houses, and to incorporate the Crescent City Live-Stock Landing and Slaughter-House Company.'

The first section forbids the landing or slaughtering of animals whose flesh is intended for food, within the city of New Orleans and other parishes and boundaries named and defined, or the keeping or establishing any slaughter-houses or *abattoirs* within those limits except by the corporation thereby created, which is also limited to certain places afterwards mentioned. Suitable penalties are enacted for violations of this prohibition....

Section five orders the closing up of all other stock-landings and slaughter-houses after the first day of June, in the parishes of Orleans, Jefferson, and St. Bernard, and makes it the duty of the company to permit any person to slaughter animals in their slaughter-houses under a heavy penalty for each refusal....

It cannot be denied that the statute under consideration is aptly framed to remove from the more densely populated part of the city, the noxious slaughter-houses, and large and offensive collections of animals necessarily incident to the slaughtering business of a large city, and to locate them where the convenience, health, and comfort of the people require they shall be located. And it must be conceded that the means adopted by the act for this purpose are appropriate, are stringent, and effectual. But it is said that in creating a corporation for this purpose, and conferring upon it exclusive privileges—privileges which it is said constitute a monopoly—the legislature has exceeded its power.... The proposition is, therefore, reduced to these terms: Can any exclusive privileges be granted to any of its citizens, or to a corporation, by the legislature of a State? ...

The plaintiffs in error accepting this issue, allege that the statute is a violation of the Constitution of the United States in these several particulars:

That it abridges the privileges and immunities of citizens of the United States;

That it denies to the plaintiffs the equal protection of the laws; and,

That it deprives them of their property without due process of law; contrary to the provisions of the first section of the fourteenth article of amendment.

This court is thus called upon for the first time to give construction to [the Fourteenth Amendment].

We do not conceal from ourselves the great responsibility which this duty devolves upon us. No questions so far-reaching and pervading in their consequences, so profoundly interesting to the people of this country, and so important in their bearing upon the relations of the United States, and of the several States to each other and to the citizens of the States and of the United States, have been before this court during the official life of any of its present members. We have given every opportunity for a full hearing at the bar; we have discussed it freely and compared views among ourselves; we have taken ample time for careful deliberation, and we now propose to announce the judgments which we have formed in the construction of those articles, so far as we have found them necessary to the decision of the cases before us, and beyond that we have neither the inclination nor the right to go.

Twelve articles of amendment were added to the Federal Constitution soon after the original organization of the government under it in 1789. Of these all but the last were adopted so soon afterwards as to justify the statement that they were practically contemporaneous with the adoption of the original; and the twelfth, adopted in eighteen hundred and three, was so nearly so as to have become, like all the others, historical and of another age. But within the last eight years three other articles of amendment of vast importance have been added by the voice of the people to that now venerable instrument.

The most cursory glance at these articles discloses a unity of purpose, when taken in connection with the history of the times, which cannot fail to have an important bearing on any question of doubt concerning their true meaning. Nor can such doubts, when any reasonably exist, be safely and rationally solved without a reference to that history; for in it is found the occasion and the necessity for recurring again to the great source of power in this country, the people of the States, for additional guarantees of human rights; additional powers to the Federal government; additional restraints upon those of the States. Fortunately that history is fresh within the memory of us all, and its leading features, as they bear upon the matter before us, free from doubt.

The institution of African slavery, as it existed in about half the States of the Union, and the contests pervading the public mind for many years, between those who desired its curtailment and ultimate extinction and those who desired additional safeguards for its security and perpetuation, culminated in the effort, on the part of most of the States in which slavery existed, to separate from the Federal government, and to resist its authority. This constituted the war of the rebellion, and whatever auxiliary causes may have contributed to bring about this war, undoubtedly the overshadowing and efficient cause was African slavery....

The process of restoring to their proper relations with the Federal government and with the other States those which had sided with the rebellion, undertaken under the proclamation of President Johnson in 1865, and before the assembling of Congress, developed the fact that, notwithstanding the formal recognition by those States of the abolition of slavery, the condition of the slave race would, without further protection of the Federal government, be almost as bad as it was before. Among the first acts of legislation adopted by several of the States in the legislative bodies which claimed to be in their normal relations with the Federal government, were laws which imposed upon the colored race onerous disabilities and burdens, and curtailed their rights in the pursuit of life, liberty, and property to such an extent that their freedom was of little value, while they had lost the protection which they had received from their former owners from motives both of interest and humanity.

They were in some States forbidden to appear in the towns in any other character than menial servants. They were required to reside on and cultivate the soil without the right to purchase or own it. They were excluded from many occupations of gain, and were not permitted to give testimony in the courts in any case where a white man was a party. It was said that their lives were at the mercy of bad men, either because the laws for their protection were insufficient or were not enforced.

These circumstances, whatever of falsehood or misconception may have been mingled with their presentation, forced upon the statesmen who had conducted the Federal government in safety through the crisis of the rebellion, and who supposed that by the thirteenth article of amendment they had secured the result of their labors, the conviction that something more was necessary in the way of constitutional protection to the unfortunate race who had suffered so much. They accordingly passed through Congress the proposition for the fourteenth amendment, and they declined to treat as restored to their full participation in the government of the Union the States which had been in insurrection, until they ratified that article by a formal vote of their legislative bodies.

The first section of the fourteenth article opens with a definition of citizenship—not only citizenship of the United States, but citizenship of the States. No such definition was previously found in the Constitution, nor had any attempt been made to define it by act of Congress. It had been the occasion of much discussion in the courts, by the executive departments, and in the public journals. It had been said by eminent judges that no man was a citizen of the United States, except as he was a citizen of one of the States composing the Union. Those, therefore, who had been born and resided always in the District of Columbia or in the Territories, though within the United States, were not citizens. Whether this proposition was sound or not had never been judicially decided. But it had been held by this court, in the celebrated Dred Scott case, only a few years before the outbreak of the civil war, that a man of African descent, whether a slave or not, was not and could not be a citizen of a State or of the United States. This decision, while it met the condemnation of some of the ablest statesmen and constitutional lawyers of the country, had never been overruled; and if it was to be accepted as a constitutional limitation of the right of citizenship, then all the negro race who had recently been made freemen, were still, not only not citizens, but were incapable of becoming so by anything short of an amendment to the Constitution.

To remove this difficulty primarily, and to establish a clear and comprehensive definition of citizenship which should declare what should constitute citizenship of the United States, and also citizenship of a State, the first clause of the first section was framed.

'All persons born or naturalized in the United States, and subject to the jurisdiction thereof, are citizens of the United States and of the State wherein they reside.'

The first observation we have to make on this clause is, that it puts at rest both the questions which we stated to have been the subject of differences of opinion. It declares that persons may be citizens of the United States without regard to their citizenship of a particular State, and it overturns the Dred Scott decision by making *all persons* born within the United States and subject to its jurisdiction citizens of the United States. That its main purpose was to establish the citizenship of the negro can admit of no doubt.... The next observation is more important in view of the arguments of counsel in the present case. It is, that the distinction between citizenship of the United States and citizenship of a State is clearly recognized and established. Not only may a man be a citizen of the United States without being a citizen of a State, but an important element is necessary to convert the former into the latter. He must reside within the State to make him a citizen of it, but it is only necessary that he should be born or naturalized in the United States to be a citizen of the Union.

It is quite clear, then, that there is a citizenship of the United States, and a citizenship of a State, which are distinct from each other, and which depend upon different characteristics or circumstances in the individual.

We think this distinction and its explicit recognition in this amendment of great weight in this argument, because the next paragraph of this same section, which is the one mainly relied on by the plaintiffs in error, speaks only of privileges and immunities of citizens of the United States, and does not speak of those of citizens of the several States. The argument, however, in favor of the plaintiffs rests wholly on the assumption that the citizenship is the same, and the privileges and immunities guaranteed by the clause are the same.

The language is, 'No State shall make or enforce any law which shall abridge the privileges or immunities of citizens of *the United States.*' It is a little remarkable, if this clause was intended as a protection to the citizen of a State against the legislative power of his own State, that the word citizen of the State should be left out when it is so carefully used, and used in contradistinction to citizens of the United States, in the very sentence which precedes it. It is too clear for argument that the change in phraseology was adopted understandingly and with a purpose.

Of the privileges and immunities of the citizen of the United States, and of the privileges and immunities of the citizen of the State, and what they respectively are, we will presently consider; but we wish to state here that it is only the former which are placed by this clause under the protection of the Federal Constitution, and that the latter, whatever they may be, are not intended to have any additional protection by this paragraph of the amendment.

If, then, there is a difference between the privileges and immunities belonging to a citizen of the United States as such, and those belonging to the citizen of the State as such the latter must rest for their security and protection where they have heretofore rested; for they are not embraced by this paragraph of the amendment....

In the Constitution of the United States, which superseded the Articles of Confederation, the corresponding provision is found in section two of the fourth article, in the following words: 'The citizens of each State shall be entitled to all the privileges and immunities of citizens of the several States.' ... Fortunately we are not without judicial construction of this clause of the Constitution. The first and the leading case on the subject is that of Corfield v. Coryell, decided by Mr. Justice Washington in the Circuit Court for the District of Pennsylvania in 1823. 'The inquiry,' he says, 'is, what are the privileges and immunities of citizens of the several States? We feel no hesitation in confining these expressions to those privileges and immunities which are *fundamental;* which belong of right to the citizens of all free governments, and which have at all times been enjoyed by citizens of the several States which compose this Union, from the time of their becoming free, independent, and sovereign. What these fundamental principles are, it would be more tedious than difficult to enumerate. They may all, however, be comprehended under the following general heads: protection by the government, with the right to acquire and possess property of every kind, and to pursue and obtain happiness and safety, subject, nevertheless, to such restraints as the government may prescribe for the general good of the whole.'

This definition of the privileges and immunities of citizens of the States ... embraces nearly every civil right for the establishment and protection of which organized government is instituted. They are, in the language of Judge Washington, those rights which the fundamental. Throughout his opinion, they are spoken of as rights belonging to the individual as a citizen of a State. They are so spoken of in the constitutional provision which he was construing. And they have always been held to be the class of rights which the State governments were created to establish and secure....

It would be the vainest show of learning to attempt to prove by citations of authority, that up to the adoption of the recent amendments, no claim or pretence was set up that those rights depended on the Federal government for their existence or protection.... Was it the purpose of the fourteenth amendment, by the simple declaration that no State should make or enforce any law which shall abridge the privileges and immunities of *citizens of the United States,* to transfer the security and protection of all the civil rights which we have mentioned, from the States to the Federal government? And where it is declared that Congress shall have the power to enforce that article, was it intended to bring within the power of Congress the entire domain of civil rights heretofore belonging exclusively to the States?

All this and more must follow, if the proposition of the plaintiffs in error be sound. For not only are these rights subject to the control of Congress whenever in its discretion any of them are supposed to be abridged by State legislation, but that body may also pass laws in advance, limiting and restricting the exercise of legislative power by the States, in their most ordinary and usual functions, as in its judgment it may think proper on all such subjects. And still further, such a construction followed by the reversal of the judgments of the Supreme Court of Louisiana in these cases, would constitute this court a perpetual censor upon all legislation of the States, on the civil rights of their own citizens, with authority to nullify such as it did not approve as consistent with those rights, as they existed at the time of the adoption of this amendment.

The argument we admit is not always the most conclusive which is drawn from the consequences urged against the adoption of a particular construction of an instrument. But when, as in the case before us, these consequences are so serious, so far-reaching and pervading, so great a departure from the structure and spirit of our institutions; when the effect is to fetter and degrade the State governments by subjecting them to the control of Congress, in the exercise of powers heretofore universally conceded to them of the most ordinary and fundamental character; when in fact it radically changes the whole theory of the relations of the State and Federal governments to each other and of both these governments to the people; the argument has a force that is irresistible, in the absence of language which expresses such a purpose too clearly to admit of doubt.

We are convinced that no such results were intended by the Congress which proposed these amendments, nor by the legislatures of the States which ratified them.

Having shown that the privileges and immunities relied on in the argument are those which belong to citizens of the States as such, and that they are left to the State governments for security and protection, and not by this article placed under the special care of the Federal government, we may hold ourselves excused from defining the privileges and immunities of citizens of the United States which no State can abridge, until some case involving those privileges may make it necessary to do so.

But lest it should be said that no such privileges and immunities are to be found if those we have been considering are excluded, we venture to suggest some which own their existence to the Federal government, its National character, its Constitution, or its laws.

One of these is well described in the case of Crandall v. Nevada. It is said to be the right of the citizen of this great country, protected by implied guarantees of its Constitution, 'to come to the seat of government to assert any claim he may have upon that government, to transact any business he may have with it, to seek its protection, to share its offices, to engage in administering its functions. He has the right of free access to its seaports, through which all operations of foreign commerce are conducted, to the subtreasuries, land offices, and courts of justice in the several States.' And quoting from the language of Chief Justice Taney in another case, it is said 'that *for all the great purposes for which the Federal government* was established, we are one people, with one common country, *we are all citizens of the United States;*' and it is, as such citizens, that their rights are supported in this court in Crandall v. Nevada.

Another privilege of a citizen of the United States is to demand the care and protection of the Federal government over his life, liberty, and property when on the high seas or within the jurisdiction of a foreign government. Of this there can be no doubt, nor that the right depends upon his character as a citizen of the United States. The right to peaceably assemble and petition for redress of grievances, the privilege of the writ of habeas corpus, are rights of the citizen guaranteed by the Federal Constitution. The right to use the navigable waters of the United States, however they may penetrate the territory of the several States, all rights secured to our citizens by treaties with foreign nations, are dependent upon citizenship of the United States, and not citizenship of a State. One of these privileges is conferred by the very article under consideration. It is that a citizen of the United States can, of his own volition, become a citizen of any State of the Union by a bonâ fide residence therein, with the same rights as other citizens of that State. To these may be added the rights secured by the thirteenth and fifteenth articles of amendment, and by the other clause of the fourteenth, next to be considered.

But it is useless to pursue this branch of the inquiry, since we are of opinion that the rights claimed by these plaintiffs in error, if they have any existence, are not privileges and immunities of citizens of the United States within the meaning of the clause of the fourteenth amendment under consideration....

The adoption of the first eleven amendments to the Constitution so soon after the original instrument was accepted, shows a prevailing sense of danger at that time from the Federal power. And it cannot be denied that such a jealousy continued to exist with many patriotic men until the breaking out of the late civil war. It was then discovered that the true danger to the perpetuity of the Union was in the capacity of the State or- ganizations to combine and concentrate all the powers of the State, and of contiguous States, for a determined resistance to the General Government.

Unquestionably this has given great force to the argument, and added largely to the number of those who believe in the necessity of a strong National government. But, however pervading this sentiment, and however it may have contributed to the adoption of the amendments we have been considering, we do not see in those amendments any purpose to destroy the main features of the general system. Under the pressure of all the excited feeling growing out of the war, our statesmen have still believed that the existence of the State with powers for domestic and local government, including the regulation of civil rights—the rights of person and of property—was essential to the perfect working of our complex form of government, though they have thought proper to impose additional limitations on the States, and to confer additional power on that of the Nation.

But whatever fluctuations may be seen in the history of public opinion on this subject during the period of our national existence, we think it will be found that this court, so far as its functions required, has always held with a steady and an even hand the balance between State and Federal power, and we trust that such may continue to be the history of its relation to that subject so long as it shall have duties to perform which demand of it a construction of the Constitution, or of any of its parts. The judgments of the Supreme Court of Louisiana in these cases are AFFIRMED.

MR. JUSTICE BRADLEY, dissenting.

The fourteenth amendment to the Constitution of the United States, section 1, declares that no State shall make or enforce any law which shall abridge the privileges and immunities of citizens of the United States.... It is contended that this prohibition abridges the privileges and immunities of citizens of the United States, especially of the plaintiffs in error, who were particularly affected thereby; and whether it does so or not is the simple question in this case. And the solution of this question depends upon the solution of two other questions, to wit:

First. Is it one of the rights and privileges of a citizen of the United States to pursue such civil employment as he may choose to adopt, subject to such reasonable regulations as may be prescribed by law?

Secondly. Is a monopoly, or exclusive right, given to one person to the exclusion of all others, to keep slaughter-houses, in a district of nearly twelve hundred square miles, for the supply of meat for a large city, a reasonable regulation of that employment which the legislature has a right to impose?

The first of these questions is one of vast importance, and lies at the very foundations of our government. The question is now settled by the fourteenth amendment itself, that citizenship of the United States is the primary citizenship in this country; and that State citizenship is secondary and derivative, depending upon citizenship of the United States and the citizen's place of residence. The States have not now, if they ever had, any power to restrict their citizenship to any classes or persons. A citizen of the United States has a perfect constitutional right to go to and reside in any State he chooses, and to claim citizenship therein, and an equality of rights with every other citizen; and the whole power of the nation is pledged to sustain him in that right. He is not bound to cringe to any superior, or to pray for any act of grace, as a means of enjoying all the rights and privileges enjoyed by other citizens. And when the spirit of lawlessness, mob violence, and sectional hate can be so completely repressed as to give full practical effect to this right, we shall be a happier nation, and a more prosperous one than we now are. Citizenship of the United States ought to be, and, according to the Constitution, is, a sure and undoubted title to equal rights in any and every States in this Union, subject to such regulations as the legislature may rightfully prescribe. If a man be denied full equality before the law, he is denied one of the essential rights of citizenship as a citizen of the United States.

Every citizen, then, being primarily a citizen of the United States, and, secondarily, a citizen of the State where he resides, what, in general, are the privileges and immunities of a citizen of the United States? Is the right, liberty, or privilege of choosing any lawful employment one of them? ...

This seems to me to be the essential question before us for consideration. And, in my judgment, the right of any citizen to follow whatever lawful employment he chooses to adopt (submitting himself to all lawful regulations) is one of his most valuable rights, and one which the legislature of a State cannot invade, whether restrained by its own constitution or not.

The right of a State to regulate the conduct of its citizens is undoubtedly a very broad and extensive one, and not to be lightly restricted. But there are certain fundamental rights which this right of regulation cannot infringe. It may prescribe the manner of their exercise, but it cannot subvert the rights themselves. I speak now of the rights of citizens of any free government. Granting for the present that the citizens of one government cannot claim the privileges of citizens in another government; that prior to the union of our North American States the citizens of one State could not claim the privileges of citizens in another State; or, that after the union was formed the citizens of the United States, as such, could not claim the privileges of citizens in any particular State; yet the citizens of each of the States and the citizens of the United States would be entitled to certain privileges and immunities as citizens, at the hands of their own government-privileges and immunities which their own governments respectively would be bound to respect and maintain. In this free country, the people of which inherited certain traditional rights and privileges from their ancestors, citizenship means something. It has certain privileges and immunities attached to it which the government, whether restricted by express or implied limitations, cannot take away or impair. It may do so temporarily by force, but it cannot do so by right. And these privileges and immunities attach as well to citizenship of the United States as to citizenship of the States.

The people of this country brought with them to its shores the rights of Englishmen; the rights which had been wrested from English sovereigns at various periods of the nation's history. One of these fundamental rights was expressed in these words, found in Magna Charta: 'No freeman shall be taken or imprisoned, or be disseized of his freehold or liberties or free customs, or be outlawed or exiled, or any otherwise destroyed; nor will we pass upon him or condemn him but by lawful judgment of his peers or by the law of the land.' English constitutional writers expound this article as rendering life, liberty, and property inviolable, except by due process of law. This is the very right which the plaintiffs in error claim in this case....

I think sufficient has been said to show that citizenship is not an empty name, but that, in this country at least, it has connected with it certain incidental rights, privileges, and immunities of the greatest importance. And to say that these rights and immunities attach only to State citizenship, and not to citizenship of the United States, appears to me to evince a very narrow and insufficient estimate of constitutional history and the rights of men, not to say the rights of the American people.

On this point the often-quoted language of Mr. Justice Washington, in Corfield v. Coryell, is very instructive. Being called upon to expound that clause in the fourth article of the Constitution, which declares that 'the citizens of each State shall be entitled to all the privileges and immunities of citizens in the several States,' he says: 'The inquiry is, what are the privileges and immunities of citizens in the several States? We feel no hesitation in confining these expressions to those privileges and immunities which are, in their nature, *fundamental;* which belong, of right, to the citizens of all free governments, and which have at all times been enjoyed by the citizens of the several States which compose this Union from the time of their becoming free, independent, and sovereign. What these fundamental privileges are it would perhaps be more tedious than difficult to enumerate. They may, however, be all comprehended under the following general heads: Protection by the government; the enjoyment of life and liberty, with the right to acquire and possess property of every kind, and to pursue and obtain happiness and safety, subject, nevertheless, to such restraints as the government may justly prescribe for the general good of the whole; the right of a citizen of one State to pass through, or to reside in, any other State for purposes of trade, agriculture, professional pursuits, or otherwise; to claim the benefit of the writ of *habeas corpus;* to institute and maintain actions of any kind in the courts of the State; to take, hold, and dispose of property, either real or personal; and an exemption from higher taxes or impositions than are paid by the other citizens of the State, may be mentioned as some of the particular privileges and immunities of citizens which are clearly embraced by the general description of privileges deemed to be fundamental.'

The mischief to be remedied [by the Civil War Amendments] was not merely slavery and its incidents and consequences; but that spirit of insubordination and disloyalty to the National government which had troubled the country for so many years in some of the States, and that intolerance of free speech and free discussion which often rendered life and property insecure, and led to much unequal legislation. The amendment was an attempt to give voice to the strong National yearning for that time and that condition of things, in which American citizenship should be a sure guaranty of safety, and in which every citizen of the United States might stand erect on every portion of its soil, in the full enjoyment of every right and privilege belonging to a freeman, without fear of violence or molestation.

MR. JUSTICE SWAYNE, dissenting:

I concur in the dissent in these cases and in the views expressed by my brethren, Mr. Justice Field and Mr. Justice Bradley. I desire, however, to submit a few additional remarks.

The thirteenth amendment was proposed by Congress on the 1st of February, 1865, the fourteenth on the 16th of June, 1866, and the fifteenth on the 27th of February, 1869. These amendments are a new departure, and mark an important epoch in the constitutional history of the country. They trench directly upon the power of the States, and deeply affect those bodies. They are, in this respect, at the opposite pole from the first eleven.... These amendments are all consequences of the late civil war. The prejudices and apprehension as to the central government which prevailed when the Constitution was adopted were dispelled by the light of experience. The public mind became satisfied that there was less danger of tyranny in the head than of anarchy and tyranny in the members. The provisions of this section are all eminently conservative in their character. They are a bulwark of defense, and can never be made an engine of oppression. The language employed is unqualified in its scope. There is no exception in its terms, and there can be properly none in their application. By the language 'citizens of the United States' was meant *all* such citizens; and by 'any person' was meant *all* persons within the jurisdiction of the State. No distinction is intimated on account of race or color. This court has no authority to interpolate a limitation that is neither expressed nor implied. Our duty is to execute the law, not to make it. The protection provided was not intended to be confined to those of any particular race or class, but to embrace equally all races, classes, and conditions of men.

It is objected that the power conferred is novel and large. The answer is that the novelty was known and the measure deliberately adopted. The power is beneficent in its nature, and cannot be abused. It is such as should exist in every well-ordered system of polity. Where could it be more appropriately lodged than in the hands to which it is confided? It is necessary to enable the government of the nation to secure to every one within its jurisdiction the rights and privileges enumerated, which, according to the plainest considerations of reason and justice and the fundamental principles of the social compact, all are entitled to enjoy. Without such authority any government claiming to be national is glaringly defective.

The construction adopted by the majority of my brethren is, in my judgment, much too narrow. It defeats, by a limitation not anticipated, the intent of those by whom the instrument was framed and of those by whom it was adopted. To the extent of that limitation it turns, as it were, what was meant for bread into a stone. By the Constitution, as it stood before the war, ample protection was given against oppression by the Union, but little was given against wrong and oppression by the States. That want was intended to be supplied by this amendment. Against the former this court has been called upon more than once to interpose. Authority of the same amplitude was intended to be conferred as to the latter. But this arm of our jurisdiction is, in these cases, stricken down by the judgment just given. Nowhere, than in this court, ought the will of the nation, as thus expressed, to be more liberally construed or more cordially executed. This determination of the majority seems to me to lie far in the other direction.

I earnestly hope that the consequences to follow may prove less serious and far-reaching than the minority fear they will be.

Review Questions and Explanations: *Barron* and *Slaughterhouse*

1. What is the point of Justice Bradley's dissent in *Slaughterhouse*? What interests do you think he was concerned about protecting? What about Justice Swayne?

2. Note that *Slaughterhouse*—the first and most important of the Supreme Court's cases interpreting a key Civil War amendment—involved the property

rights of commercial actors, not the civil rights of the recently freed slaves. What effect might this have had on the Court's interpretation of the new amendment?

3. Note this line from Justice Bradley's dissent: "We feel no hesitation in confining these expressions to those privileges and immunities which are, in their nature, *fundamental;* which belong, of right, to the citizens of all free governments, and which have at all times been enjoyed by the citizens of the several States which compose this Union from the time of their becoming free, independent, and sovereign. What these fundamental privileges are it would perhaps be more tedious than difficult to enumerate." Justice Bradley then goes on to list several general categories of rights he sees as fundamental, including the "enjoyment of life and liberty" and the right to "pursue and obtain happiness and safety" subject to such restraints as the government may justly prescribe for the "general good of the whole." How would a court go about defining and protecting such rights? Does the difficulty in doing so mean that fundamental rights do not exist, or should not be protected by the Court? If you agree with that, does that mean you agree with the majority opinion? While Justice Bradley was, obviously, writing in relation to the Privileges or Immunities clause, the same issues arise, as we will see, in applying the Due Process clause.

4. Justice Bradley also writes that the "mischief" the Civil War amendments sought to remedy was not merely slavery, but national disunity. The Fourteenth Amendment, he said, therefore "was an attempt to give voice to the strong National yearning for that time and that condition of things, in which American citizenship should be a sure guaranty of safety, and in which every citizen of the United States might stand erect on every portion of its soil, in the full enjoyment of every right and privilege belonging to a freeman, without fear of violence or molestation." This idea of the Fourteenth Amendment as a mechanism to promote a common set of rights, and thereby a common national identify, is important and remains relevant in today's world. Consider, for example, arguments that contested issues like abortion or gun rights should be left to the states. Leaving such issues to the states signals that we do not consider them constitutive of our national identity. Should this be relevant to constitutional analysis? If not, what normative arguments do support incorporating the Bill of Rights against the states?

---

2. Incorporation and Due Process

In deciding the *The Slaughterhouse Cases* the way it did, the Court shut down one path toward incorporating the Bill of Rights against the states: under *Slaughterhouse*, the privileges or immunities of national citizenship do not include the rights set forth in the Bill of Rights. This part of the decision has never been overturned. *Slaughterhouse*, consequently, turned the path of incorporation away from the Privileges or Immunities clause. This left the Court struggling to determine whether, and how, incorporation should be accomplished. *Twining v. New Jersey* shows the Court groping its way toward using the Due Process clause as a vehicle for incorporation. It is an important case, in that it bridges the analytical gap between the *Slaughterhouse* Court's refusal to incorporate the Bill of Rights via the Privileges and Immunities clause, and the cases presented in the next subsection, in which the justices argue about *what* should be incorporated through the Due Process clause, rather than whether that clause is the correct vehicle for incorporation.

Brown v. Mississippi, the case following *Twining*, is not in itself a further development of incorporation doctrine. What it does do—and does vividly—is illustrate the types of facts underlying the incorporation debate. The justices on the Court at the time would have been well aware of facts like these, and had to make their doctrinal choices against the backdrop presented by them. *Brown* thus puts the debate in the larger social and political context in which the justices themselves would have confronted it.

Guided Reading Questions: *Twining v. New Jersey* and *Brown v. Mississippi*

1. The Court in *Twining* addresses three distinct questions: whether the right against self incrimination is a right of national citizenship; whether the right against self incrimination is a "fundamental right"; and the methods by which the Court should make that determination. Pay attention to how the Court answers each of them.

2. Why does the Court ask whether the right against self incrimination is "fundamental"? Doctrinally, how does that question fit into the Court's analysis?

3. As noted above, *Brown v. Mississippi* is included here to remind us of the types of facts that lay just beneath the surface of the Court's decisions in this area. What role should facts like this play in constitutional interpretation? Should the Court attempt to ignore them, or intentionally build a constitutional jurisprudence that is responsive to them? What are the pros and cons of each approach? Consider again Justice Bradley's statement in *Slaughterhouse* about fundamental rights and national unity.

Twining v. New Jersey
211 U.S. 78 (1908)

Majority: *Moody*, Fuller (CJ), Brewer, White, Peckham, McKenna, Holmes, Day
Dissent: *Harlan* (omitted)

MR. JUSTICE MOODY, delivered the opinion of the Court.

[Two defendants in a bank fraud case did not take the stand to defend themselves after evidence had been submitted showing that they had knowledge of the fraudulent transactions in questions. In closing arguments, the state argued that the jury should infer their guilt from their silence. The law of New Jersey allowed such arguments to be made. The defendants argued that the federal constitutional right against self-incrimination prohibited such arguments, and should be binding on the state court procedure through the Privileges or Immunities and Due Process clauses of the Fourteenth Amendment.]

... The general question, therefore, is, whether such a law violates the Fourteenth Amendment, either by abridging the privileges or immunities of citizens of the United States, or by depriving persons of their life, liberty, or property without due process of law. In order to bring themselves within the protection of the Constitution it is incumbent on the defendants to prove two propositions: First, that the exemption from compulsory self-incrimination is guaranteed by the Federal Constitution against impairment by the states; and, second, if it be so guaranteed, that the exemption was in fact impaired in the case at bar....

The exemption from testimonial compulsion, that is, from disclosure as a witness of evidence against oneself, forced by any form of legal process, is universal in American law, though there may be differences as to its exact scope and limits. At the time of the formation of the Union the principle that no person could be compelled to be a witness against himself had become embodied in the common law and distinguished it from all other systems of jurisprudence. It was generally regarded then, as now, as a privilege of great value, a protection to the innocent, though a shelter to the guilty, and a safeguard against heedless, unfounded, or tyrannical prosecutions. Five of the original thirteen states ... had then guarded the principle from legislative or judicial change by including it in Constitutions or Bills of Right; Maryland had provided in her Constitution (1776) that 'no man ought to be compelled to give evidence against himself, in a common court of law, or in any other court, but in such cases as have been usually practiced in this state or may hereafter be directed by the legislature;' and in the remainder of those states there seems to be no doubt that it was recognized by the courts....

It is obvious from this short statement that it has been supposed by the states that, so far as the state courts are concerned, the privilege had its origin in the Constitutions and laws of the states, and that persons appealing to it must look to the state for their protection. Indeed, since, by the unvarying decisions of this court, the first ten Amendments of the Federal Constitution are restrictive only of national action, there was nowhere else to look up to the time of the adoption of the Fourteenth Amendment, and the state, at least until then, might give, modify, or withhold the privilege at its will. The Fourteenth Amendment withdrew from the states powers theretofore enjoyed by them to an extent not yet fully ascertained, or rather, to speak more accurately, limited those powers and restrained their exercise. There is no doubt of the duty of this court to enforce the limitations and restraints whenever they exist, and there has been no hesitation in the performance of the duty.

But, whenever a new limitation or restriction is declared, it is a matter of grave import, since, to that extent, it diminishes the authority of the state, so necessary to the perpetuity of our dual form of government, and changes its relation to its people and to the Union.... The defendants contend, in the first place, that the exemption from self-incrimination is one of the privileges and immunities of citizens of the United States which the Fourteenth Amendment forbids the states to abridge. It is not argued that the defendants are protected by that part of the Fifth Amendment which provides that 'no person ... shall be compelled in any criminal case to be a witness against himself,' for it is recognized by counsel that, by a long line of decisions, the first ten Amendments are not operative on the states. Barron v. Baltimore. But it is argued that this privilege is one of the fundamental rights of national citizenship, placed under national protection by the Fourteenth Amendment, and it is specifically argued that the 'privileges and immunities of citizens of the United States,' protected against state action by that Amendment, include those fundamental personal rights which were protected against national action by the first eight Amendments; that this was the intention of the framers of the Fourteenth Amendment, and that this part of it would otherwise have little or no meaning and effect.

These arguments are not new to this court and the answer to them is found in its decisions. The meaning of the phrase 'privileges and immunities of citizens of the United

States,' as used in the Fourteenth Amendment, came under early consideration in the Slaughter-House Cases.... The Fourteenth Amendment, it is observed by Mr. Justice Miller, delivering the opinion of the court, removed the doubt whether there could be a citizenship of the United States independent of citizenship of the state, by recognizing or creating and defining the former. 'It is quite clear, then,' he proceeds to say, 'that there is a citizenship of the United States and a citizenship of a state, which are distinct from each other and which depend upon different characteristics or circumstances in the individual.'

The description of the privileges and immunities of state citizenship, given by Mr. Justice Washington in Corfield v. Coryell is then quoted, approved, and said to include 'those rights which are fundamental,' to embrace 'nearly every civil right for the establishment and protection of which organized government is instituted,' and 'to be the class of rights which the state governments were created to establish and secure.' This part of the opinion then concludes with the holding that the rights relied upon in the case are those which belong to the citizens of states, as such, and are under the sole care and protection of the state governments. The conclusion is preceded by the important declaration that the civil rights theretofore appertaining to citizenship of the states and under the protection of the states were not given the security of national protection by this clause of the Fourteenth Amendment. The exact scope and the momentous consequence of this decision are brought into clear light by the dissenting opinions. The view of Mr. Justice Field, concurred in by Chief Justice Chase and Justices Swayne and Bradley, was that the fundamental rights of citizenship, which, by the opinion of the court, were held to be rights of state citizenship, protected only by the state government, became, as the result of the Fourteenth Amendment, rights of national citizenship, protected by the national Constitution....

There can be no doubt, so far as the decision in the Slaughter-House Cases has determined the question, that the civil rights sometimes described as fundamental and inalienable, which, before the War Amendments, were enjoyed by state citizenship and protected by state government, were left untouched by this clause of the Fourteenth Amendment. Criticism of this case has never entirely ceased, nor has it ever received universal assent by members of this court. Undoubtedly, it gave much less effect to the Fourteenth Amendment than some of the public men active in framing it intended, and disappointed many others. On the other hand, if the views of the minority had prevailed, it is easy to see how far the authority and independence of the states would have been diminished, by subjecting all their legislative and judicial acts to correction by the legislative and review by the judicial branch of the national government. But we need not now inquire into the merits of the original dispute. This part, at least, of the Slaughter-House Cases, has been steadily adhered to by this court....

Privileges and immunities of citizens of the United States ... are only such as arise out of the nature and essential character of the national government, or are specifically granted or secured to all citizens or persons by the Constitution of the United States. Slaughter-House Cases. Thus, among the rights and privileges of national citizenship recognized by this court are the right to pass freely from state to state ...; the right to petition Congress for a redress of grievances ...; the right to vote for national officers ...; the right to enter the public lands ...; the right to be protected against violence while in the lawful custody of a United States marshal ...; and the right to inform the United States authorities of violation of its laws....

The defendants, however, do not stop here. They appeal to another clause of the Fourteenth Amendment, and insist that the self-incrimination which they allege the instruction to the jury compelled was a denial of due process of law. This contention requires separate consideration, for it is possible that some of the personal rights safeguarded by the first eight Amendments against national action may also be safeguarded against state action, because a denial of them would be a denial of due process of law.... If this is so, it is not because those rights are enumerated in the first eight Amendments, but because they are of such a nature that they are included in the conception of due process of law.

Few phrases of the law are so elusive of exact apprehension as this. Doubtless the difficulties of ascertaining its connotation have been increased in American jurisprudence, where it has been embodied in constitutions and put to new uses as a limit on legislative power. This court has always declined to give a comprehensive definition of it, and has preferred that its full meaning should be gradually ascertained by the process of inclusion and exclusion in the course of the decisions of cases as they arise. There are certain general principles, well settled, however, which narrow the field of discussion, and may serve as helps to correct conclusions.... From the consideration of the meaning of the words in the light of their historical origin this court has drawn the following conclusions:

First. What is due process of law may be ascertained by an examination of those settled usages and modes of proceedings existing in the common and statute law of England before the emigration of our ancestors, and shown not to have been unsuited to their civil and political condition by having been acted on by them after the settlement of this country....

Second. It does not follow, however, that a procedure settled in English law at the time of the emigration, and brought to this country and practiced by our ancestors, is an essential element of due process of law. If that were so, the procedure of the first half of the seventeenth century would be fastened upon the American jurisprudence like a straight jacket, only to be unloosed by constitutional amendment. That, said Mr. Justice Matthews, 'would be to deny every quality of the law but its age, and to render it incapable of progress or improvement.'

Third. But, consistently with the requirements of due process, no change in ancient procedure can be made which disregards those fundamental principles, to be ascertained from time to time by judicial action, which have relation to process of law, and protect the citizen in his private right, and guard him against the arbitrary action of government. This idea has been many times expressed in differing words by this court, and it seems well to cite some expressions of it. The words 'due process of law' 'were intended to secure the individual from the arbitrary exercise of the powers of government, unrestrained by the established principles of private rights and distributive justice.'

'This court has never attempted to define with precision the words 'due process of law.' ... It is sufficient to say that there are certain immutable principles of justice which inhere in the very idea of free government which no member of the Union may disregard.' Holden v. Hardy. 'The same words refer to that law of the land in each state, which derives its authority from the inherent and reserved powers of the state, exerted within the limits of those fundamental principles of liberty and justice which lie at the base of all our civil and political institutions.' ... 'The limit of the full control which the state has in the proceedings of its courts, both in civil and criminal cases, is subject only to the qualification that such procedure must not work a denial of fundamental rights or conflict with specific and applicable provisions of the Federal Constitution.'

The question under consideration may first be tested by the application of these settled doctrines of this court. If the statement of Mr. Justice Curtis, as elucidated in Hurtado v. California, is to be taken literally, that alone might almost be decisive. For nothing is more certain, in point of historical fact, than that the practice of compulsory self-incrimination in the courts and elsewhere existed for four hundred years after the granting of Magna Charta, continued throughout the reign of Charles I.... But ... we prefer to rest our decision on broader grounds, and inquire whether the exemption from self-incrimination is of such a nature that it must be included in the conception of due process. Is it a fundamental principle of liberty and justice which inheres in the very idea of free government and is the inalienable right of a citizen of such a government? If it is, and if it is of a nature that pertains to process of law, this court has declared it to be essential to due process of law.

In approaching such a question it must not be forgotten that in a free representative government nothing is more fundamental than the right of the people, through their appointed servants, to govern themselves in accordance with their own will, except so far as they have restrained themselves by constitutional limits specifically established, and that, in our peculiar dual form of government, nothing is more fundamental than the full power of the state to order its own affairs and govern its own people, except so far as the Federal Constitution, expressly or by fair implication, has withdrawn that power. The power of the people of the states to make and alter their laws at pleasure is the greatest security for liberty and justice.... We are not invested with the jurisdiction to pass upon the expediency, wisdom, or justice of the laws of the states as declared by their courts, but only to determine their conformity with the Federal Constitution and the paramount laws enacted pursuant to it. Under the guise of interpreting the Constitution we must take care that we do not import into the discussion our own personal views of what would be wise, just, and fitting rules of government to be adopted by a free people, and confound them with constitutional limitations.

The question before us is the meaning of a constitutional provision which forbids the states to deny to any person due process of law. In the decision of this question we have the authority to take into account only those fundamental rights which are expressed in that provision; not the rights fundamental in citizenship, state or national, for they are secured otherwise; but the rights fundamental in due process, and therefore an essential part of it. We have to consider whether the right is so fundamental in due process that a refusal of the right is a denial of due process. One aid to the solution of the question is to inquire how the right was rated during the time when the meaning of due process was in a formative state, and before it was incorporated in American constitutional law. Did those who then were formulating and insisting upon the rights of the people entertain the view that the right was so fundamental that there could be no due process without it?

It has already appeared that, prior to the formation of the American Constitutions, in which the exemption from compulsory self-incrimination was specifically secured, separately, independently, and side by side with the requirement of due process, the doctrine was formed, as other doctrines of the law of evidence have been formed, by the course of decision in the courts, covering a long period of time. Searching further, we find nothing to show that it was then thought to be other than a just and useful principle of law. None of the great instruments in which we are accustomed to look for the declaration of the fundamental rights made reference to it....

We are not here concerned with the effect of due process in restraining substantive laws, as, for example, that which forbids the taking of private property for public use without compensation. We need notice now only those cases which deal with the principles which must be observed in the trial of criminal and civil causes. Due process requires that the court which assumes to determine the rights of parties shall have jurisdiction ... and that there shall be notice and opportunity for hearing given the parties.... Subject to these two fundamental conditions, which seem to be universally prescribed in all systems of law established by civilized countries, this court has, up to this time, sustained all state laws, statutory or judicially declared, regulating procedure, evidence, and methods of trial, and held them to be consistent with due process of law....

Even if the historical meaning of due process of law and the decisions of this court did not exclude the privilege from it, it would be going far to rate it as an immutable principle of justice which is the inalienable possession of every citizen of a free government. Salutary as the principle may seem to the great majority, it cannot be ranked with the right to hearing before condemnation, the immunity from arbitrary power not acting by general laws, and the inviolability of private property.... It has no place in the jurisprudence of civilized and free countries outside the domain of the common law, and it is nowhere observed among our own people in the search for truth outside the administration of the law. It should, must, and will be rigidly observed where it is secured by specific constitutional safeguards, but there is nothing in it which gives it a sanctity above and before constitutions themselves.

Much might be said in favor of the view that the privilege was guaranteed against state impairment as a privilege and immunity of national citizenship, but, as has been shown, the decisions of this court have foreclosed that view. There seems to be no reason whatever, however, for straining the meaning of due process of law to include this privilege within it, because, perhaps, we may think it of great value. The states had guarded the privilege to the satisfaction of their own people up to the adoption of the Fourteenth Amendment. No reason is perceived why they cannot continue to do so. The power of their people ought not to be fettered, their sense of responsibility lessened, and their capacity for sober and restrained self-government weakened, by forced construction of the Federal Constitution. If the people of New Jersey are not content with the law as declared in repeated decisions of their courts, the remedy is in their own hands. They may, if they choose, alter it by legislation, as the people of Maine did when the courts of that state made the same ruling.... Judgment affirmed.

Brown v. Mississippi
297 U.S. 278 (1936)

Unanimous decision: *Hughes* (CJ), Van Devanter, McReynolds, Brandeis, Sutherland, Butler, Stone, Roberts, Cardozo

MR. CHIEF JUSTICE HUGHES delivered the opinion of the Court.

The question in this case is whether convictions, which rest solely upon confessions shown to have been extorted by officers of the state by brutality and violence, are consistent with the due process of law required by the Fourteenth Amendment of the Constitution of the United States.

Petitioners were indicted for the murder of one Raymond Stewart, whose death occurred on March 30, 1934. They were indicted on April 4, 1934, and were then arraigned and pleaded not guilty. Counsel were appointed by the court to defend them. Trial was begun the next morning and was concluded on the following day, when they were found guilty and sentenced to death.

Aside from the confessions, there was no evidence sufficient to warrant the submission of the case to the jury. After a preliminary inquiry, testimony as to the confessions was received over the objection of defendants' counsel. Defendants then testified that the confessions were false and had been procured by physical torture....

The opinion of the state court did not set forth the evidence as to the circumstances in which the confessions were procured. That the evidence established that they were procured by coercion was not questioned. The state court said: 'After the state closed its case on the merits, the appellants, for the first time, introduced evidence from which it appears that the confessions were not made voluntarily but were coerced.'... There is no dispute as to the facts upon this point, and as they are clearly and adequately stated in the dissenting opinion of Judge Griffith (with whom Judge Anderson concurred), showing both the extreme brutality of the measures to extort the confessions and the participation of the state authorities, we quote this part of his opinion in full, as follows:

'The crime with which these defendants, all ignorant negroes, are charged, was discovered about 1 o'clock p.m. on Friday, March 30, 1934. On that night one Dial, a deputy sheriff, accompanied by others, came to the home of Ellington, one of the defendants, and requested him to accompany them to the house of the deceased, and there a number of white men were gathered, who began to accuse the defendant of the crime. Upon his denial they seized him, and with the participation of the deputy they hanged him by a rope to the limb of a tree, and, having let him down, they hung him again, and when he was let down the second time, and he still protested his innocence, he was tied to a tree and whipped, and, still declining to accede to the demands that he confess, he was finally released, and he returned with some difficulty to his home, suffering intense pain and agony. The record of the testimony shows that the signs of the rope on his neck were plainly visible during the so-called trial. A day or two thereafter the said deputy, accompanied by another, returned to the home of the said defendant and arrested him, and departed with the prisoner towards the jail in an adjoining county, but went by a route which led into the state of Alabama; and while on the way, in that state, the deputy stopped and again severely whipped the defendant, declaring that he would continue the whipping until he confessed, and the defendant then agreed to confess to such a statement as the deputy would dictate, and he did so, after which he was delivered to jail.

'The other two defendants, Ed Brown and Henry Shields, were also arrested and taken to the same jail. On Sunday night, April 1, 1934, the same deputy, accompanied by a number of white men, one of whom was also an officer, and by the jailer, came to the jail, and the two last named defendants were made to strip and they were laid over chairs and their backs were cut to pieces with a leather strap with buckles on it, and they were likewise made by the said deputy definitely to understand that the whipping would be continued unless and until they confessed, and not only confessed, but confessed in every matter of detail as demanded by those present; and in this manner the defendants confessed the crime, and, as the whippings progressed and were repeated, they changed or adjusted their confession in all particulars of detail so as to conform to the demands of their torturers. When the confessions had been obtained in the exact form and contents as desired by the mob, they left with the parting admonition and warning that, if the defendants changed their story at any time in any respect from that last stated, the perpetrators of the outrage would administer the same or equally effective treatment.

'Further details of the brutal treatment to which these helpless prisoners were subjected need not be pursued. It is sufficient to say that in pertinent respects the transcript reads more like pages torn from some medieval account than a record made within the confines of a modern civilization which aspires to an enlightened constitutional government.

'All this having been accomplished, on the next day, that is, on Monday, April 2, when the defendants had been given time to recuperate somewhat from the tortures to which they had been subjected, the two sheriffs, one of the county where the crime was committed, and the other of the county of the jail in which the prisoners were confined, came to the jail, accompanied by eight other persons, some of them deputies, there to hear the free and voluntary confession of these miserable and abject defendants. The sheriff of the county of the crime admitted that he had heard of the whipping, but averred that he had no personal knowledge of it. He admitted that one of the defendants, when brought before him to confess, was limping and did not sit down, and that this particular defendant then and there stated that he had been strapped so severely that he could not sit down, and, as already stated, the signs of the rope on the neck of another of the defendants were plainly visible to all. Nevertheless the solemn farce of hearing the free and voluntary confessions was gone through with, and these two sheriffs and one other person then present were the three witnesses used in court to establish the so-called confessions, which were received by the court and admitted in evidence over the objections of the defendants duly entered of record as each of the said three witnesses delivered their alleged testimony. There was thus enough before the court when these confessions were first offered to make known to the court that they were not, beyond all reasonable doubt, free and voluntary; and the failure of the court then to exclude the confessions is sufficient to reverse the judgment, under every rule of procedure that has heretofore been prescribed, and hence it was not necessary subsequently to renew the objections by motion or otherwise.

The state stresses the statement in Twining v. New Jersey that 'exemption from compulsory self-incrimination in the courts of the states is not secured by any part of the Federal Constitution.' ... But the question of the right of the state to withdraw the privilege against self-incrimination is not here involved. The compulsion to which the quoted statements refer is that of the processes of justice by which the accused may be called as a witness and required to testify. Compulsion by torture to extort a confession is a different matter.

The state is free to regulate the procedure of its courts in accordance with its own conceptions of policy, unless in so doing it 'offends some principle of justice so rooted in the traditions and conscience of our people as to be ranked as fundamental.' Snyder v. Massachusetts. ... The due process clause requires 'that state action, whether through one agency or another, shall be consistent with the fundamental principles of liberty and justice which lie at the base of all our civil and political institutions.' Hebert v. Louisiana. It would be difficult to conceive of methods more revolting to the sense of justice than those taken to procure the confessions of these petitioners, and the use of the confessions thus obtained as the basis for conviction and sentence was a clear denial of due process. ... Judgment reversed.

Review Questions and Explanations: *Twining* and *Brown*

1. The *Twining* Court follows the *The Slaughterhouse Cases* and refuses to deem the right against self-incrimination a right of national citizenship protected by the Privileges or Immunities clause. In doing so, it notes that the right is one that had traditionally been protected by the states. Therefore, under *Slaughterhouse*,

is was a right of state, not national, citizenship. Remember this when reading the cases in the next section. These cases, as you will see, often ask whether a particular practice is part of our collective "tradition." If so, this increases rather than decreases the likelihood that it will be deemed fundamental for due process purposes.

2. Although the Court in *Twining* refuses to find that the right against self in-crimination is a fundamental right protected by the Due Process clause, the decision recognizes that some things would be so protected. The Court also attempts to define what those rights might be by listing several "general principles" governing the question. Can you articulate those principles in your own words? Do you agree with the Court's list? What would you add or exclude?

3. *Brown* distinguishes *Twining* by saying that the case at bar involves a right against torture, not against self-incrimination. Are you persuaded by this distinction? If it is correct, is that a tacit recognition by the Court that substantive rights, not just procedural rights, can be deemed fundamental for Due Process purposes?

4. *Brown* says that the rights protected as fundamental under the Due Process clause are those which are "so rooted in the traditions and conscience of our people as to be ranked as fundamental." Is this consistent with the "general principles" listed in *Twining*?

Professional Development Reflection Question

You are a deputy Attorney General in the Alabama Attorney General's office at the time the *Brown* case was argued. It is your job to defend the constitutionality of the state court's decision. You are appalled by the decision of the state court, and aware that if the Supreme Court finds that no federal right was violated, the defendants in the underlying litigation will find no relief in state court. You also are aware that the doctrine of incorporation via the Due Process clause is still evolving, and that there is no clear on point precedent governing the case. What would you do?

CASE NOTE: *Gitlow v. New York* (1925). The right against self-incrimination at issue in *Twining* (and arguably in *Brown*) can easily be described as a "procedural" right in that it involves the rules governing a trial: what evidence can be used against a defendant. Many of the Court's early due process cases involved this type of right. One of the earliest cases in which the Court applied a substantive right against the states was in a First Amendment case, *Gitlow v. New York* (1925). The Court did not elaborate on the distinction, which later commentators have deemed important, between procedural rights and substantive rights. In fact, the Court's entire reasoning on this point was this: "The precise question presented, and the only question which we can consider under this writ of error, then is, whether the statute, as construed and applied in this case, by the State courts, deprived the defendant of his liberty of expression in violation of the due process clause of the Fourteenth Amendment.... For present purposes we may and do assume that freedom of speech and of the press — which are protected by the First Amendment from abridgment by Congress — are among the fundamental personal rights and 'liberties' protected by the due process clause of the Fourteenth Amendment from impairment by the States. We do not regard the incidental statement in [prior cases] that the Fourteenth Amendment imposes no restrictions on the States concerning freedom of speech, as determinative of this question."

3. Selective or Total Incorporation?

Cases like *Twining* and *Gitlow* established the Due Process clause as the doctrinal mechanism the Court would use to protect some set of individual rights from encroachment by state (as opposed to federal) actors. But just *what* rights would be protected, and *why*, remained open questions. The debate concerned how the Court should determine what rights were "fundamental" and therefore protected under the Due Process clause. As you will see below, the justices—most famously Justice Frankfurter and Justice Black— disagreed about this. Justice Frankfurter argued that what is and is not a "fundamental" right is an issue the Court must decide for itself, using a variety of criteria. Justice Black, in contrast, argued that the only rights that should be considered "fundamental" were those laid out in the first eight amendments to the Constitution. Consider the strengths and weaknesses of each of these positions as you read the following cases.

Guided Reading Questions: *Palko, Adamson*, and *Rochin*

1. When reading the following cases, make a list of all the different words the Court uses to describe what constitutes a "fundamental right." Your list will help you tease out the various tests the Court has developed in this area.

2. When reading *Adamson* and *Rochin*, pay particular attention to the debate, noted above, between Justices Black (writing in dissent in *Adamson*) and Frankfurter (writing the majority opinion in *Rochin*). Whose side are you on?

Palko v. Connecticut
302 U.S. 319 (1937)

Majority: *Cardozo*, McReynolds, Brandeis, Sutherland, Stone (CJ), Roberts, Black

Dissent: *Butler* (omitted)

MR. JUSTICE CARDOZO delivered the opinion of the Court.

A statute of Connecticut permitting appeals in criminal cases to be taken by the state is challenged by appellant as an infringement of the Fourteenth Amendment of the Constitution of the United States. Whether the challenge should be upheld is now to be determined....

The argument for appellant is that whatever is forbidden by the Fifth Amendment is forbidden by the Fourteenth also. The Fifth Amendment, which is not directed to the States, but solely to the federal government, creates immunity from double jeopardy. No person shall be 'subject for the same offense to be twice put in jeopardy of life or limb.' The Fourteenth Amendment ordains, 'nor shall any State deprive any person of life, liberty, or property, without due process of law.' To retry a defendant, though under one indictment and only one, subjects him, it is said, to double jeopardy in violation of the Fifth Amendment, if the prosecution is one on behalf of the United States. From this the consequence is said to follow that there is a denial of life or liberty without due process of law, if the prosecution is one on behalf of the people of a state....

We have said that in appellant's view the Fourteenth Amendment is to be taken as embodying the prohibitions of the Fifth. His thesis is even broader. Whatever would be a violation of the original bill of rights if done by the federal government is now equally unlawful by force of the Fourteenth Amendment if done by a state. There is no such general rule.

... [T]he due process clause of the Fourteenth Amendment may make it unlawful for a state to abridge by its statutes the freedom of speech which the First Amendment safeguards against encroachment by the Congress, or the like freedom of the press, or the free exercise of religion, or the right of peaceable assembly, without which speech would be unduly trammeled, or the right of one accused of crime to the benefit of counsel.[2] In these and other situations immunities that are valid as against the federal government by force of the specific pledges of particular amendments have been found to be implicit in the concept of ordered liberty, and thus, through the Fourteenth Amendment, become valid as against the states.

The line of division may seem to be wavering and broken if there is a hasty catalogue of the cases on the one side and the other. Reflection and analysis will induce a different view. There emerges the perception of a rationalizing principle which gives to discrete instances a proper order and coherence. The right to trial by jury and the immunity from prosecution except as the result of an indictment may have value and importance. Even so, they are not of the very essence of a scheme of ordered liberty. To abolish them is not to violate a 'principle of justice so rooted in the traditions and conscience of our people as to be ranked as fundamental.'... Few would be so narrow or provincial as to maintain that a fair and enlightened system of justice would be impossible without them. What is true of jury trials and indictments is true also, as the cases show, of the immunity from compulsory self-incrimination. Twining v. New Jersey. This too might be lost, and justice still be done. Indeed, today as in the past there are students of our penal system who look upon the immunity as a mischief rather than a benefit, and who would limit its scope, or destroy it altogether. No doubt there would remain the need to give protection against torture, physical or mental. Brown v. Mississippi....

We reach a different plane of social and moral values when we pass to the privileges and immunities that have been taken over from the earlier articles of the Federal Bill of Rights and brought within the Fourteenth Amendment by a process of absorption. These in their origin were effective against the federal government alone. If the Fourteenth Amendment has absorbed them, the process of absorption has had its source in the belief that neither liberty nor justice would exist if they were sacrificed. Twining. This is true, for illustration, of freedom of thought and speech. Of that freedom one may say that it is the matrix, the indispensable condition, of nearly every other form of freedom. With rare aberrations a pervasive recognition of that truth can be traced in our history, political and legal. So it has come about that the domain of liberty, withdrawn by the Fourteenth Amendment from encroachment by the states, has been enlarged by latter-day judgments to include liberty of the mind as well as liberty of action. The extension became, indeed,

---

2. Editors' note: Each of these examples was supported by citation to a Supreme Court decision dating back only as far as the 1920s or 1930s.

a logical imperative when once it was recognized, as long ago it was, that liberty is something more than exemption from physical restraint, and that even in the field of substantive rights and duties the legislative judgment, if oppressive and arbitrary, may be overridden by the courts.... Fundamental too in the concept of due process, and so in that of liberty, is the thought that condemnation shall be rendered only after trial.... The hearing, moreover, must be a real one, not a sham or a pretense.... For that reason, ignorant defendants in a capital case were held to have been condemned unlawfully when in truth, though not in form, they were refused the aid of counsel....

The conviction of appellant is not in derogation of any privileges or immunities that belong to him as a citizen of the United States. The judgment is affirmed.

Adamson v. California
332 U.S. 46 (1947)

Majority: *Reed*, Vinson (CJ), Frankfurter, Jackson, Burton (omitted)

Concurrence: *Frankfurter* (omitted)

Dissents: *Black*, Douglas; *Murphy*, Rutledge (omitted)

[The majority opinion affirms the holding of *Twining*, acknowledging that the Due Process clause of the Fourteenth Amendment requires states to respect certain "fundamental rights" but finding that the right against self-incrimination is not such a right. What follows is Justice Black's dissenting opinion.]

MR. JUSTICE BLACK, dissenting.

This decision reasserts a constitutional theory spelled out in Twining v. New Jersey that this Court is endowed by the Constitution with boundless power under 'natural law' periodically to expand and contract constitutional standards to conform to the Court's conception of what at a particular time constitutes 'civilized decency' and 'fundamental principles of liberty and justice.' Invoking this Twining rule, the Court concludes that although comment upon testimony in a federal court would violate the Fifth Amendment, identical comment in a state court does not violate today's fashion in civilized decency and fundamentals and is therefore not prohibited by the Federal Constitution as amended.

The Twining case was the first, as it is the only decision of this Court, which has squarely held that states were free, notwithstanding to Fifth and Fourteenth Amendments, to extort evidence from one accused of crime. I agree that if Twining be reaffirmed, the result reached might appropriately follow. But I would not reaffirm the Twining decision. I think that decision and the 'natural law' theory of the Constitution upon which it relies, degrade the constitutional safeguards of the Bill of Rights and simultaneously appropriate for this Court a broad power which we are not authorized by the Constitution to exercise....

The first ten amendments were proposed and adopted largely because of fear that Government might unduly interfere with prized individual liberties. The people wanted and demanded a Bill of Rights written into their Constitution. The amendments embodying the Bill of Rights were intended to curb all branches of the Federal Government in the fields touched by the amendments—Legislative, Executive, and Judicial. The Fifth, Sixth, and Eighth Amendments were pointedly aimed at confining exercise of power by courts and judges within precise boundaries, particularly in the procedure used for the trial of criminal cases. Past history provided strong reasons for the apprehensions which brought these procedural amendments into being and attest the wisdom of their adoption. For the fears of arbitrary court action sprang largely from the past use of courts in the imposition of criminal punishments to suppress speech, press, and religion. Hence the constitutional limitations of courts' powers were, in the view of the Founders, essential supplements to the First Amendment, which was itself designed to protect the widest scope for all people to believe and to express the most divergent political, religious, and other views.

But these limitations were not expressly imposed upon state court action. In 1833, Barron v. Baltimore, was decided by this Court. It specifically held inapplicable to the states that provision of the Fifth Amendment which declares: 'nor shall private property be taken for public use, without just compensation.' In deciding the particular point raised, the Court there said that it could not hold that the first eight amendments applied to the states. This was the controlling constitutional rule when the Fourteenth Amendment was proposed in 1866.

My study of the historical events that culminated in the Fourteenth Amendment, and the expressions of those who sponsored and favored, as well as those who opposed its submission and passage, persuades me that one of the chief objects that the provisions of the Amendment's first section, separately, and as a whole, were intended to accomplish was to make the Bill of Rights, applicable to the states. With full knowledge of the import of the Barron decision, the framers and backers of the Fourteenth Amendment proclaimed its purpose to be to overturn the constitutional rule that case had announced. This historical purpose has never received full consideration or exposition in any opinion of this Court interpreting the Amendment....

In my judgment [history] conclusively demonstrates that the language of the first section of the Fourteenth Amendment, taken as a whole, was thought by those responsible for its submission to the people, and by those who opposed its submission, sufficiently explicit to guarantee that thereafter no state could deprive its citizens of the privileges and protections of the Bill of Rights.... I further contend that the 'natural law' formula which the Court uses to reach its conclusion in this case should be abandoned as an incongruous excrescence on our Constitution. I believe that formula to be itself a violation of our Constitution, in that it subtly conveys to courts, at the expense of legislatures, ultimate power over public policies in fields where no specific provision of the Constitution limits legislative power. And my belief seems to be in accord with the views expressed by this Court, at least for the first two decades after the Fourteenth Amendment was adopted....

In Palko v. Connecticut ... a case which involved former jeopardy only, this Court re-examined the path it had traveled in interpreting the Fourteenth Amendment since the Twining opinion was written. In Twining the Court had declared that none of the rights enumerated in the first eight amendments were protected against state invasion because they were incorporated in the Bill of Rights. But the Court in Palko answered a contention that all eight applied with the more guarded statement ... that 'there is no such general rule.' Implicit in this statement, and in the cases decided in the interim between Twining and Palko and since, is the understanding that some of the eight amendments do apply by their very terms....

In the Twining case fundamental liberties were things apart from the Bill of Rights.... I cannot consider the Bill of Rights to be an outworn 18th Century 'strait jacket' as the Twining opinion did. Its provisions may be thought outdated abstractions by some. And it is true that they were designed to meet ancient evils. But they are the same kind of human evils that have emerged from century to century wherever excessive power is sought by the few at the expense of the many. In my judgment the people of no nation can lose their liberty so long as a Bill of Rights like ours survives and its basic purposes are conscientiously interpreted, enforced and respected so as to afford continuous protection against old, as well as new, devices and practices which might thwart those purposes.

I fear to see the consequences of the Court's practice of substituting its own concepts of decency and fundamental justice for the language of the Bill of Rights as its point of departure in interpreting and enforcing that Bill of Rights. If the choice must be between the selective process of the Palko decision applying some of the Bill of Rights to the States, or the Twining rule applying none of them, I would choose the Palko selective process. But rather than accept either of these choices. I would follow what I believe was the original purpose of the Fourteenth Amendment — to extend to all the people of the nation the complete protection of the Bill of Rights. To hold that this Court can determine what, if any, provisions of the Bill of Rights will be enforced, and if so to what degree, is to frustrate the great design of a written Constitution.... Affirmed.

Rochin v. California

342 U.S. 165 (1952)

Majority: *Frankfurter*, Reed, Jackson, Burton, Vinson (CJ), Clark

Concurrences: *Black; Douglas* (both omitted)

> [Mr. Rochin was convicted in state court for the possession of morphine in violation of state law. The police had entered Mr. Rochin's apartment, forced open the door to his bedroom, and forcibly attempted to extract capsules he had swallowed. When they could not, Mr. Rochin was taken to a hospital at which a physician was ordered to force an emetic solution through a tube in his stomach, against his will, and "pump" his stomach to induce vomiting. Two morphine capsules were found in the vomit. On the basis of that evidence, Mr. Rochin was convicted and sentenced to sixty days' imprisonment. The District Court of Appeal affirmed the conviction, despite the finding that the officers were guilty of unlawfully breaking into and entering Mr. Rochin's room, and of unlawfully assaulting, battering, torturing and falsely imprisoning him. Mr. Rochin challenged his conviction on the ground that the police conduct violated his federal Due Process rights.]

MR. JUSTICE FRANKFURTER delivered the opinion of the Court.

In our federal system the administration of criminal justice is predominantly committed to the care of the States. The power to define crimes belongs to Congress only as an appropriate means of carrying into execution its limited grant of legislative powers. Broadly speaking, crimes in the United States are what the laws of the individual States make them, subject to the limitations ... in the original Constitution, prohibiting bills of attainder and ex post facto laws, and of the Thirteenth and Fourteenth Amendments.

These limitations, in the main, concern not restrictions upon the powers of the States to define crime, except in the restricted area where federal authority has pre-empted the field, but restrictions upon the manner in which the States may enforce their penal codes. Accordingly, in reviewing a State criminal conviction under a claim of right guaranteed by the Due Process Clause of the Fourteenth Amendment, from which is derived the most far reaching and most frequent federal basis of challenging State criminal justice, 'we must be deeply mindful of the responsibilities of the States for the enforcement of criminal laws, and exercise with due humility our merely negative function in subjecting convictions from state courts to the very narrow scrutiny which the Due Process Clause of the Fourteenth Amendment authorizes.' Due process of law, 'itself a historical product,' is not to be turned into a destructive dogma against the States in the administration of their systems of criminal justice.

However, this Court too has its responsibility. Regard for the requirements of the Due Process Clause 'inescapably imposes upon this Court an exercise of judgment upon the whole course of the proceedings (resulting in a conviction) in order to ascertain whether they offend those canons of decency and fairness which express the notions of justice of English-speaking peoples even toward those charged with the most heinous offenses.' ... These standards of justice are not authoritatively formulated anywhere as though they were specifics. Due process of law is a summarized constitutional guarantee of respect for those personal immunities which, as Mr. Justice Cardozo twice wrote for the Court, are 'so rooted in the traditions and conscience of our people as to be ranked as fundamental', ... or are 'implicit in the concept of ordered liberty.' Palko v. State of Connecticut.

The Court's function in the observance of this settled conception of the Due Process Clause does not leave us without adequate guides in subjecting State criminal procedures to constitutional judgment. In dealing not with the machinery of government but with human rights, the absence of formal exactitude, or want of fixity of meaning, is not an unusual or even regrettable attribute of constitutional provisions. Words being symbols do not speak without a gloss.... [T]he gloss of some of the verbal symbols of the Constitution does not give them a fixed technical content. It exacts a continuing process of application.

When the gloss has thus not been fixed but is a function of the process of judgment, the judgment is bound to fall differently at different times and differently at the same time through different judges. Even more specific provisions, such as the guaranty of freedom of speech and the detailed protection against unreasonable searches and seizures, have inevitably evoked as sharp divisions in this Court as the least specific and most comprehensive protection of liberties, the Due Process Clause.

The vague contours of the Due Process Clause do not leave judges at large. We may not draw on our merely personal and private notions and disregard the limits that bind judges in their judicial function. Even though the concept of due process of law is not final and fixed, these limits are derived from considerations that are fused in the whole nature of or judicial process.... These are considerations deeply rooted in reason and in the compelling traditions of the legal profession. The Due Process Clause places upon this Court the duty of exercising a judgment, within the narrow confines of judicial power in reviewing State convictions, upon interests of society pushing in opposite directions.

Due process of law thus conceived is not to be derided as resort to a revival of 'natural law.' To believe that this judicial exercise of judgment could be avoided by freezing 'due process of law' at some fixed stage of time or thought is to suggest that the most important aspect of constitutional adjudication is a function for inanimate machines and not for judges, for whom the independence safeguarded by Article III of the Constitution was designed and who are presumably guided by established standards of judicial behavior. Even cybernetics has not yet made that haughty claim. To practice the requisite detachment and to achieve sufficient objectivity no doubt demands of judges the habit of self-discipline and self-criticism, incertitude that one's own views are incontestable and alert tolerance toward views not shared. But these are precisely the presuppositions of our judicial process. They are precisely the qualities society has a right to expect from those entrusted with ultimate judicial power....

Applying these general considerations to the circumstances of the present case, we are compelled to conclude that the proceedings by which this conviction was obtained do more than offend some fastidious squeamishness or private sentimentalism about combating crime too energetically. This is conduct that shocks the conscience. Illegally breaking into the privacy of the petitioner, the struggle to open his mouth and remove what was there, the forcible extraction of his stomach's contents — this course of proceeding by agents of government to obtain evidence is bound to offend even hardened sensibilities. They are methods too close to the rack and the screw to permit of constitutional differentiation.

It has long since ceased to be true that due process of law is heedless of the means by which otherwise relevant and credible evidence is obtained. This was not true even before the series of recent cases enforced the constitutional principle that the States may not base convictions upon confessions, however much verified, obtained by coercion. These decisions are not arbitrary exceptions to the comprehensive right of States to fashion their own rules of evidence for criminal trials. They are not sports in our constitutional law but applications of a general principle. They are only instances of the general requirement that States in their prosecutions respect certain decencies of civilized conduct. Due process of law, as a historic and generative principle, precludes defining, and thereby confining, these standards of conduct more precisely than to say that convictions cannot be brought about by methods that offend 'a sense of justice.' See Mr. Chief Justice Hughes, speaking for a unanimous Court in Brown v. State of Mississippi, 297 U.S. 278. It would be a stultification of the responsibility which the course of constitutional history has cast upon this Court to hold that in order to convict a man the police cannot extract by force what is in his mind but can extract what is in his stomach. Judgment reversed.

Review Questions and Explanations: *Palko, Adamson,* and *Rochin*

1. Review the list you made of words used by the justices to define what constitutes a fundamental right for due process purposes. Choose your most and least favorite and try formulating a test that captures the essence of each of them.

2. You should at this point be able to anticipate the difficulties the Court will have in applying its "tests" to contemporary problems. Consider three issues that arise in this area: abortion rights, marriage equality, and a requirement to buy health insurance (we are aware that this last item was not argued in the Affordable Care Act case as a substantive due process issue but, as noted in Part One, much of the public debate about the "mandate" found in the Act sounded in the substantive due process rhetoric of liberty and freedom from governmental intrusion on private choices). Apply your most and least favorite tests to each of these areas. How do they turn out? What questions arose when you tried to apply your tests?

C. Fundamental Rights and Economic Regulation

As you will recall from your study of the Commerce Clause and the Tenth Amendment, the early twentieth century Court frequently used its power of judicial review to restrict, sometimes dramatically, the power of Congress to enact economic regulations. Perhaps not surprisingly, the Court during this same era also was using its evolving due process doctrine to similarly restrict the regulatory power of the states. This development was foreshadowed in the dissenting opinions in *The Slaughterhouse Cases*. Those justices, you may recall, wanted to use the Privileges or Immunities clause to invalidate state legislation regulating slaughterhouses.

This section explores this use of the Due Process clause. The first case below, *Lochner v. New York*, illustrates the type of review the pre-1937 Court frequently engaged in when evaluating the constitutionality of state legislation regulating economic issues. As you know, *Lochner* and the doctrine it embraced have since been rejected by the Court; the Due Process clause today is rarely used to protect the type of economic liberty embraced by that Court. The two cases following *Lochner* are *Meyer v. Nebraska* and *Pierce v. Society of Sisters*. These cases illustrate the close connection the Court saw between economic liberty and personal liberty. They also form the foundation of the modern substantive due process doctrine.

West Coast Hotel v. Parrish and *U.S. v. Carolene Products* come next. These cases show the Court's famous withdrawal from the practice of policing economic regulation. They also show the Court's early efforts to do what it had not done in *Meyer* and *Pierce*: draw a principled distinction between its approach to economic regulation (which it would subsequently review with a light hand) and its approach to regulations infringing on personal rights and liberties (which it would go on to review with increasing rigor). In doing so, these cases introduce a doctrinal methodology that we will see throughout the remainder of the book, that of tiered review or levels of scrutiny. You saw this idea in Part One when we studied congressional powers under Section 5 of the Fourteenth Amendment; it also was discussed in the Introduction to this Part. We will examine it in greater detail here. Finally, the section closes with a case, *Ferguson v. Skrupa*, which illustrates just how far the Court has retreated from the assertive review of economic legislation seen in *Lochner*.

Combined, these cases show how the substantive due process doctrine grew in fits and starts from a mechanism used to incorporate most of the Bill of Rights against the states, to a judicial hammer used to quash economic regulation, to a system of tiered judicial review dependant on the type of regulation being challenged. In doing so, they prepare you to study the modern disputes that form the battleground of today's substantive due process doctrine. These disputes, which include deeply contested issues such as abortion rights, end of life autonomy, and gay rights, are addressed in the final section of this chapter.

Guided Reading Questions: *Lochner v. New York*

1. The Court calls the liberty interest it is protecting in *Lochner* the "right to contract." When reading the case, think about how the Court defines this right, and what it sees it as protecting. Be precise.

2. The *Lochner* Court is, today, routinely criticized for inappropriately intervening with the power of the elected legislature to govern. When reading the case, think about what it is about this use of judicial power that seems particularly inappropriate. What, specifically, does the Court do in *Lochner* that is different (or appears to be different) than what it does in more celebrated cases like *Brown v. Board of Education,* or any number of free speech cases?

3. The majority acknowledges that states may regulate contracts under their "police powers," which are understood to include regulation of "health, safety,

and morals." Does the majority see the regulation of the working hours of bakers as a regulation of "health, safety, and morals"? If not, what is it?

4. Justice Holmes dissent in *Lochner* is considered by many to be a judicial classic. Read it carefully. Which of his arguments do you find the most and least persuasive?

Lochner v. New York

198 U.S. 45 (1905)

Majority: *Peckham*, Fuller (CJ), Brewer, Brown, McKenna

Dissents: *Harlan*, White, Day; *Holmes*

MR. JUSTICE PECKHAM, delivered the opinion of the court.

The indictment, it will be seen, charges that the plaintiff in error violated ... the labor law of the state of New York, in that he wrongfully and unlawfully required and permitted an employee working for him to work more than sixty hours in one week.... The mandate of the statute, that 'no employee shall be required or permitted to work,' is the substantial equivalent of an enactment that 'no employee shall contract or agree to work,' more than ten hours per day....

The statute necessarily interferes with the right of contract between the employer and employees, concerning the number of hours in which the latter may labor in the bakery of the employer. The general right to make a contract in relation to his business is part of the liberty of the individual protected by the Fourteenth Amendment of the Federal Constitution. Allgeyer v. Louisiana. Under that provision no state can deprive any person of life, liberty, or property without due process of law. The right to purchase or to sell labor is part of the liberty protected by this amendment ... There are, however, certain powers, existing in the sovereignty of each state in the Union, somewhat vaguely termed police powers, the exact description and limitation of which have not been attempted by the courts. Those powers, broadly stated, and without, at present, any attempt at a more specific limitation, relate to the safety, health, morals, and general welfare of the public. Both property and liberty are held on such reasonable conditions as may be imposed by the governing power of the state in the exercise of those powers, and with such conditions the Fourteenth Amendment was not designed to interfere.

The state, therefore, has power to prevent the individual from making certain kinds of contracts, and in regard to them the Federal Constitution offers no protection. If the contract be one which the state, in the legitimate exercise of its police power, has the right to prohibit, it is not prevented from prohibiting it by the 14th Amendment. Contracts in violation of a statute, either of the Federal or state government, or a contract to let one's property for immoral purposes, or to do any other unlawful act, could obtain no protection from the Federal Constitution, as coming under the liberty of person or of free contract. Therefore, when the state, by its legislature, in the assumed exercise of its police powers, has passed an act which seriously limits the right to labor or the right of contract in regard to their means of livelihood between persons who are *sui juris* (both employer and employee), it becomes of great importance to determine which shall prevail,—the right of the individual to labor for such time as he may choose, or the right of the state to prevent the individual from laboring, or from entering into any contract to labor, beyond a certain time prescribed by the state.

This court has recognized the existence and upheld the exercise of the police powers of the states in many cases which might fairly be considered as border ones, and it has, in the course of its determination of questions regarding the asserted invalidity of such statutes, on the ground of their violation of the rights secured by the Federal Constitution, been guided by rules of a very liberal nature, the application of which has resulted, in numerous instances, in upholding the validity of state statutes thus assailed. Among the later cases where the state law has been upheld by this court is that of *Holden* v. *Hardy*, 169 U. S. 366. A provision in the act of the legislature of Utah was there under consideration, the act limiting the employment of workmen in all underground mines or workings, to eight hours per day, 'except in cases of emergency, where life or property is in imminent danger.' It also limited the hours of labor in smelting and other institutions for the reduction or refining of ores or metals to eight hours per day, except in like cases of emergency. The act was held to be a valid exercise of the police powers of the state. A review of many of the cases on the subject, decided by this and other courts, is given in the opinion. It was held that the kind of employment, mining, smelting, etc., and the character of the employees in such kinds of labor, were such as to make it reasonable and proper for the state to interfere to prevent the employees from being constrained by the rules laid down by the proprietors in regard to labor. The following citation from the observations of the supreme court of Utah in that case was made by the judge writing the opinion of this court, and approved: 'The law in question is confined to the protection of that class of people engaged in labor in underground mines, and in smelters and other works wherein ores are reduced and refined. This law applies only to the classes subjected by their employment to the peculiar conditions and effects attending underground mining and work in smelters, and other works for the reduction and refining of ores. Therefore it is not necessary to discuss or decide whether the legislature can fix the hours of labor in other employments.' ...

It must, of course, be conceded that there is a limit to the valid exercise of the police power by the state. There is no dispute concerning this general proposition. Otherwise the Fourteenth Amendment would have no efficacy and the legislatures of the states would have unbounded power, and it would be enough to say that any piece of legislation was enacted to conserve the morals, the health, or the safety of the people; such legislation would be valid, no matter how absolutely without foundation the claim might be. The claim of the police power would be a mere pretext, become another and delusive name for the supreme sovereignty of the state to be exercised free from constitutional restraint. This is not contended for. In every case that comes before this court, therefore, where legislation of this character is concerned, and where the protection of the Federal Constitution is sought, the question necessarily arises: Is this a fair, reasonable, and appropriate exercise of the police power of the state, or is it an unreasonable, unnecessary, and arbitrary interference with the right of the individual to his personal liberty, or to enter into those contracts in relation to labor which may seem to him appropriate or necessary for the support of himself and his family? Of course the liberty of contract relating to labor includes both parties to it. The one has as much right to purchase as the other to sell labor.

This is not a question of substituting the judgment of the court for that of the legislature. If the act be within the power of the state it is valid, although the judgment of the court might be totally opposed to the enactment of such a law. But the question would still remain: Is it within the police power of the state? And that question must be answered by the court.

The question whether this act is valid as a labor law, pure and simple, may be dismissed in a few words. There is no reasonable ground for interfering with the liberty of person or the right of free contract, by determining the hours of labor, in the occupation of a baker. There is no contention that bakers as a class are not equal in intelligence and capacity to men in other trades or manual occupations, or that they are not able to assert their rights and care for themselves without the protecting arm of the state, interfering with their independence of judgment and of action. They are in no sense wards of the state. Viewed in the light of a purely labor law, with no reference whatever to the question of health, we think that a law like the one before us involves neither the safety, the morals, nor the welfare, of the public, and that the interest of the public is not in the slightest degree affected by such an act. The law must be upheld, if at all, as a law pertaining to the health of the individual engaged in the occupation of a baker. It does not affect any other portion of the public than those who are engaged in that occupation. Clean and wholesome bread does not depend upon whether the baker works but ten hours per day or only sixty hours a week. The limitation of the hours of labor does not come within the police power on that ground.

It is a question of which of two powers or rights shall prevail, the power of the state to legislate or the right of the individual to liberty of person and freedom of contract. The mere assertion that the subject relates, though but in a remote degree, to the public health, does not necessarily render the enactment valid. The act must have a more direct relation, as a means to an end, and the end itself must be appropriate and legitimate, before an act can be held to be valid which interferes with the general right of an individual to be free in his person and in his power to contract in relation to his own labor.

This case has caused much diversity of opinion in the state courts. In the supreme court two of the five judges composing the court dissented from the judgment affirming the validity of the act. In the court of appeals three of the seven judges also dissented from the judgment upholding the statute. Although found in what is called a labor law of the state, the court of appeals has upheld the act as one relating to the public health, — in other words, as a health law. One of the judges of the court of appeals, in upholding the law, stated that, in his opinion, the regulation in question could not be sustained unless they were able to say, from common knowledge, that working in a bakery and candy factory was an unhealthy employment. The judge held that, while the evidence was not uniform, it still led him to the conclusion that the occupation of a baker or confectioner was unhealthy and tended to result in diseases of the respiratory organs. Three of the judges dissented from that view, and they thought the occupation of a baker was not to such an extent unhealthy as to warrant the interference of the legislature with the liberty of the individual.

We think the limit of the police power has been reached and passed in this case. There is, in our judgment, no reasonable foundation for holding this to be necessary or appropriate as a health law to safeguard the public health, or the health of the individuals who are following the trade of a baker. If this statute be valid, and if, therefore, a proper case is made out in which to deny the right of an individual, sui juris, as employer or employee, to make contracts for the labor of the latter under the protection of the provisions of the Federal Constitution, there would seem to be no length to which legislation of this nature might not go.

We think that there can be no fair doubt that the trade of a baker, in and of itself, is not an unhealthy one to that degree which would authorize the legislature to interfere with the right to labor, and with the right of free contract on the part of the individual, either as employer or employee In looking through statistics regarding all trades and occupations, it may be true that the trade of a baker does not appear to be as healthy as some other trades, and is also vastly more healthy than still others. To the common understanding the trade of a baker has never been regarded as an unhealthy one. Very likely physicians would not recommend the exercise of that or of any other trade as a remedy for ill health.

Some occupations are more healthy than others, but we think there are none which might not come under the power of the legislature to supervise and control the hours of working therein, if the mere fact that the occupation is not absolutely and perfectly healthy is to confer that right upon the legislative department of the government. It might be safely affirmed that almost all occupations more or less affect the health. There must be more than the mere fact of the possible existence of some small amount of unhealthiness to warrant legislative interference with liberty. It is unfortunately true that labor, even in any department, may possibly carry with it the seeds of unhealthiness. But are we all, on that account, at the mercy of legislative majorities? A printer, a tinsmith, a locksmith, a carpenter, a cabinetmaker, a dry goods clerk, a bank's, a lawyer's, or a physician's clerk, or a clerk in almost any kind of business, would all come under the power of the legislature, on this assumption. No trade, no occupation, no mode of earning one's living, could escape this all-pervading power, and the acts of the legislature in limiting the hours of labor in all employments would be valid, although such limitation might seriously cripple the ability of the laborer to support himself and his family. In our large cities there are many buildings into which the sun penetrates for but a short time in each day, and these buildings are occupied by people carrying on the business of bankers, brokers, lawyers, real estate, and many other kinds of business, aided by many clerks, messengers, and other employees.

Upon the assumption of the validity of this act under review, it is not possible to say that an act, prohibiting lawyers' or bank clerks, or others, from contracting to labor for their employers more than eight hours a day would be invalid. It might be said that it is unhealthy to work more than that number of hours in an apartment lighted by artificial light during the working hours of the day; that the occupation of the bank clerk, the lawyer's clerk, the real estate clerk, or the broker's clerk, in such offices is therefore unhealthy, and the legislature, in its paternal wisdom, must, therefore, have the right to legislate on the subject of, and to limit, the hours for such labor; and, if it exercises that power, and its validity be questioned, it is sufficient to say, it has reference to the public health; it has reference to the health of the employees condemned to labor day after day in buildings where the sun never shines; it is a health law, and therefore it is valid, and cannot be questioned by the courts.

It is also urged, pursuing the same line of argument, that it is to the interest of the state that its population should be strong and robust, and therefore any legislation which may be said to tend to make people healthy must be valid as health laws, enacted under the police power. If this be a valid argument and a justification for this kind of legislation, it follows that the protection of the Federal Constitution from undue interference with liberty of person and freedom of contract is visionary, wherever the law is sought to be justified as a valid exercise of the police power. Scarcely any law but might find shelter under such assumptions, and conduct, properly so called, as well as contract, would come under the restrictive sway of the legislature. Not only the hours of employees, but the hours of employers, could be regulated, and doctors, lawyers, scientists, all professional men, as well as athletes and artisans, could be forbidden to fatigue their brains and bodies by prolonged hours of exercise, lest the fighting strength of the state be impaired. We mention these extreme cases because the contention is extreme. We do not believe in the soundness of the views which uphold this law....

The act is not, within any fair meaning of the term, a health law, but is an illegal interference with the rights of individuals, both employers and employees, to make contracts regarding labor upon such terms as they may think best, or which they may agree upon with the other parties to such contracts. Statutes of the nature of that under review, limiting the hours in which grown and intelligent men may labor to earn their living, are mere meddlesome interferences with the rights of the individual, and they are not saved from condemnation by the claim that they are passed in the exercise of the police power and upon the subject of the health of the individual whose rights are interfered with, unless there be some fair ground, reasonable in and of itself, to say that there is material danger to the public health, or to the health of the employees, if the hours of labor are not curtailed. If this be not clearly the case, the individuals whose rights are thus made the subject of legislative interference are under the protection of the Federal Constitution regarding their liberty of contract as well as of person; and the legislature of the state has no power to limit their right as proposed in this statute....

In our judgment it is not possible in fact to discover the connection between the number of hours a baker may work in the bakery and the healthful quality of the bread made by the workman. The connection, if any exist, is too shadowy and thin to build any argument for the interference of the legislature. If the man works ten hours a day it is all right, but if ten and a half or eleven his health is in danger and his bread may be unhealthy, and, therefore, he shall not be permitted to do it. This, we think, is unreasonable and entirely arbitrary. When assertions such as we have adverted to become necessary in order to give, if possible, a plausible foundation for the contention that the law is a 'health law,' it gives rise to at least a suspicion that there was some other motive dominating the legislature than the purpose to subserve the public health or welfare....

It is impossible for us to shut our eyes to the fact that many of the laws of this character, while passed under what is claimed to be the police power for the purpose of protecting the public health or welfare, are, in reality, passed from other motives. We are justified in saying so when, from the character of the law and the subject upon which it legislates, it is apparent that the public health or welfare bears but the most remote relation to the law. The purpose of a statute must be determined from the natural and legal effect of the language employed; and whether it is or is not repugnant to the Constitution of the United States must be determined from the natural effect of such statutes when put into operation, and not from their proclaimed purpose.... The court looks beyond the mere letter of the law in such cases. Yick Wo v. Hopkins.... Reversed.

MR. JUSTICE HARLAN, with whom MR. JUSTICE WHITE and MR. JUSTICE DAY concurred, dissenting.

.... I take it to be firmly established that what is called the liberty of contract may, within certain limits, be subjected to regulations designed and calculated to promote the general welfare or to guard the public health, the public morals or the public safety.... [W]hat are the conditions under which the judiciary may declare such regulations to be in excess of legislative authority and void? Upon this point there is no room for dispute; for, the rule is universal that a legislative enactment, Federal or state, is never to be disregarded or held invalid unless it be, beyond question, plainly and palpably in excess of legislative power.... If there be doubt as to the validity of the statute, that doubt must therefore be resolved in favor of its validity, and the courts must keep their hands off, leaving the legislature to meet the responsibility for unwise legislation. If the end which the legislature seeks to accomplish be one to which is power extends, and if the means employed to that end, although not the wisest or best, are yet not plainly and palpably unauthorized by law, then the court cannot interfere.... McCulloch v. Maryland, 4 Wheat. 316, 421....

It is plain that this statute was enacted in order to protect the physical well-being of those who work in bakery and confectionery establishments. It may be that the statute had its origin, in part, in the belief that employers and employes in such establishments were not upon an equal footing, and that the necessities of the latter often compelled them to submit to such exactions as unduly taxed their strength. Be this as it may, the statute must be taken as expressing the belief of the people of New York that, as a general rule, and in the case of the average man, labor in excess of sixty hours during a week in such establishments may endanger the health of those who thus labor. Whether or not this be wise legislation it is not the province of the court to inquire. Under our systems of government the courts are not concerned with the wisdom or policy of legislation. So that in determining the question of power to interfere with liberty of contract, the court may inquire whether the means devised by the State are germane to an end which may be lawfully accomplished and have a real or substantial relation to the protection of health, as involved in the daily work of the persons, male and female, engaged in bakery and confectionery establishments. But when this inquiry is entered upon I find it impossible, in view of common experience, to say that there is here no real or substantial relation between the means employed by the State and the end sought to be accomplished by its legislation.... It must be remembered that this statute does not apply to all kinds of business. It applies only to work in bakery and confectionery establishments, in which, as all know, the air constantly breathed by workmen is not as pure and healthful as that to be found in some other establishments or out of doors.

Professor Hirt in his treatise on the "Diseases of the Workers" has said: "The labor of the bakers is among the hardest and most laborious imaginable, because it has to be performed under conditions injurious to the health of those engaged in it...." Another writer says: "The constant inhaling of flour dust causes inflammation of the lungs and of the bronchial tubes.... [Bakers] seldom live over their fiftieth year, most of them dying between the ages of forty and fifty. During periods of epidemic diseases the bakers are generally the first to succumb to the disease, and the number swept away during such periods far exceeds the number of other crafts in comparison to the men employed in the respective industries...."

We ... judicially know that the number of hours that should constitute a day's labor in particular occupations involving the physical strength and safety of workmen has been the subject of enactments by Congress and by nearly all of the States. Many, if not most, of those enactments fix eight hours as the proper basis of a day's labor.

I do not stop to consider whether any particular view of this economic question presents the sounder theory.... It is enough for the determination of this case, and it is enough for this court to know, that the question is one about which there is room for debate and for an honest difference of opinion. There are many reasons of a weighty, substantial character, based upon the experience of mankind, in support of the theory that, all things considered, more than ten hours' steady work each day, from week to week, in a bakery or confectionery establishment, may endanger the health, and shorten the lives of the workmen, thereby diminishing their physical and mental capacity to serve the State, and to provide for those dependent upon them.

If such reasons exist that ought to be the end of this case.... The judgment in my opinion should be affirmed.

MR. JUSTICE HOLMES, dissenting.

I regret sincerely that I am unable to agree with the judgment in this case, and that I think it my duty to express my dissent.

This case is decided upon an economic theory which a large part of the country does not entertain. If it were a question whether I agreed with that theory, I should desire to study it further and long before making up my mind. But I do not conceive that to be my duty, because I strongly believe that my agreement or disagreement has nothing to do with the right of a majority to embody their opinions in law. It is settled by various decisions of this court that state constitutions and state laws may regulate life in many ways which we as legislators might think as injudicious, or if you like as tyrannical, as this, and which, equally with this, interfere with the liberty to contract. Sunday laws and usury laws are ancient examples. A more modern one is the prohibition of lotteries.

The liberty of the citizen to do as he likes so long as he does not interfere with the liberty of others to do the same, which has been a shibboleth for some well-known writers, is interfered with by school laws, by the Post Office, by every state or municipal institution which takes his money for purposes thought desirable, whether he likes it or not. The Fourteenth Amendment does not enact Mr. Herbert Spencer's Social Statics.... But a Constitution is not intended to embody a particular economic theory, whether of paternalism and the organic relation of the citizen to the state or of laissez faire. It is made for people of fundamentally differing views, and the accident of our finding certain opinions natural and familiar, or novel, and even shocking, ought not to conclude our judgment upon the question whether statutes embodying them conflict with the Constitution of the United States.

General propositions do not decide concrete cases. The decision will depend on a judgment or intuition more subtle than any articulate major premise. But I think that the proposition just stated, if it is accepted, will carry us far toward the end. Every opinion tends to become a law. I think that the word 'liberty,' in the Fourteenth Amendment, is perverted when it is held to prevent the natural outcome of a dominant opinion, unless it can be said that a rational and fair man necessarily would admit that the statute proposed would infringe fundamental principles as they have been understood by the traditions of our people and our law. It does not need research to show that no such sweeping condemnation can be passed upon the statute before us. A reasonable man might think it a proper measure on the score of health. Men whom I certainly could not pronounce unreasonable would uphold it as a first instalment of a general regulation of the hours of work. Whether in the latter aspect it would be open to the charge of inequality I think it unnecessary to discuss.

Review Questions and Explanations: *Lochner*

1. The Court in *Lochner* is not very deferential (to say the least) to the decision made by the state legislature that working long hours in a bakery was harmful to the worker's health. Should it have been?

2. In explaining its opinion, the Court states that "It is impossible for us to shut our eyes to the fact that many of the laws of this character, while passed under what is claimed to be the police power for the purpose of protecting the public health or welfare, are, in reality, passed from other motives." The "other motive" of course was legislative concern about the enormous imbalance of economic bargaining power between workers and employers. Earlier decisions of the Court had made clear that legislation based on this type of concern would be struck down. So the state argued its case in terms of the physical, rather than economic, health of the workers. Assume for the moment that this was pretextual: does that explain the Court's lack of deference? Should the Court "look[] beyond the mere letter of the law" in such situations?

3. Justice Holmes argues that the Court errs in not deferring to legislative judgment and upholding the statute. Why does he think deference is appropriate in this case? When would deference not be appropriate?

4. How does Justice Harlan's dissent differ from Holmes'? The majority assumes that there is a fundamental right to enter into contracts, but that those contracts can nevertheless be regulated to promote "health, safety, and morals." It then holds, however, that "labor laws" fall outside the realm of "health, safety, and morals." Does Harlan disagree with that view? What about Holmes?

Guided Reading Questions: *Meyer v. Nebraska* and *Pierce v. Society of Sisters*

1. As will be discussed below, the Court today reviews legislation interfering with personal liberty much more aggressively (less deferentially) than it reviews legislation interfering with economic liberties like those asserted in *Lochner*. This distinction, however, is of relatively recent origin; it stems from a footnote in *U.S. v. Carolene Products*, decided in 1938 and discussed below. When reading *Meyer* and *Pierce*, think about how this distinction would have been applied in these cases: do the cases address economic or personal liberties?

2. Regardless of the answer to the above question, *Meyer* and *Pierce* are seen today as setting the foundation for contemporary substantive due process cases protecting personal liberties. When reading the cases, see if you can spot the language these future cases build on.

3. Argument by analogy is grounded in rule of law concerns about treating like things alike. Are the liberties at issue in *Lochner*, *Meyer*, and *Pierce* "like" each other? If not, how do they differ?

Meyer v. Nebraska

262 U.S. 390 (1923)

Majority: McReynolds, Taft (CJ), McKenna, Van Devanter, Brandeis, Butler, Sanford

Dissents: *Holmes; Sutherland* (both omitted)

MR. JUSTICE McREYNOLDS delivered the opinion of the Court.

Plaintiff in error was tried and convicted in the district court for Hamilton county, Nebraska, under an information which charged that on May 25, 1920, while an instructor in Zion Parochial School he unlawfully taught the subject of reading in the German language to Raymond Parpart, a child of 10 years, who had not attained and successfully passed the eighth grade. The information is based upon 'An act relating to the teaching of foreign languages in the state of Nebraska,' ... which follows:

> Section 1. No person, individually or as a teacher, shall, in any private, denominational, parochial or public school, teach any subject to any person in any language than the English language.

The problem for our determination is whether the statute as construed and applied unreasonably infringes the liberty guaranteed to the plaintiff in error by the Fourteenth

Amendment: "No state ... shall deprive any person of life, liberty or property without due process of law."

While this court has not attempted to define with exactness the liberty thus guaranteed, the term has received much consideration and some of the included things have been definitely stated. Without doubt, it denotes not merely freedom from bodily restraint but also the right of the individual to contract, to engage in any of the common occupations of life, to acquire useful knowledge, to marry, establish a home and bring up children, to worship God according to the dictates of his own conscience, and generally to enjoy those privileges long recognized at common law as essential to the orderly pursuit of happiness by free men. Slaughter-House Cases. The established doctrine is that this liberty may not be interfered with, under the guise of protecting the public interest, by legislative action which is arbitrary or without reasonable relation to some purpose within the competency of the state to effect. Determination by the Legislature of what constitutes proper exercise of police power is not final or conclusive but is subject to supervision by the courts.

.... Mere knowledge of the German language cannot reasonable be regarded as harmful. Heretofore it has been commonly looked upon as helpful and desirable. Plaintiff in error taught this language in school as part of his occupation. His right thus to teach and the right of parents to engage him so to instruct their children, we think, are within the liberty of the [Fourteenth] Amendment.

The challenged statute forbids the teaching in school of any subject except in English; also the teaching of any other language until the pupil has attained and successfully passed the eighth grade, which is not usually accomplished before the age of twelve. The Supreme Court of the State has held that "the so-called ancient or dead languages" are not "within the spirit or the purpose of the act." Latin, Greek, Hebrew are not proscribed; but German, French, Spanish, Italian and every other alien speech are within the ban. Evidently the legislature has attempted materially to interfere with the calling of modern language teachers, with the opportunities of pupils to acquire knowledge, and with the power of parents to control the education of their own.

It is said the purpose of the legislation was to promote civic development by inhibiting training and education of the immature in foreign tongues and ideals before they could learn English and acquire American ideals, and 'that the English language should be and become the mother tongue of all children reared in this state.' It is also affirmed that the foreign born population is very large, that certain communities commonly use foreign words, follow foreign leaders, move in a foreign atmosphere, and that the children are thereby hindered from becoming citizens of the most useful type and the public safety is imperiled.

That the state may do much, go very far, indeed, in order to improve the quality of its citizens, physically, mentally and morally, is clear; but the individual has certain fundamental rights which must be respected. The protection of the Constitution extends to all, to those who speak other languages as well as to those born with English on the tongue. Perhaps it would be highly advantageous if all had ready understanding of our ordinary speech, but this cannot be coerced by methods which conflict with the Constitution — a desirable end cannot be promoted by prohibited means.... The power of the state to compel attendance at some school and to make reasonable regulations for all schools, including a requirement that they shall give instructions in English, is not questioned. Nor has challenge been made of the state's power to prescribe a curriculum for institutions which it supports. Those matters are not within the present controversy. Our concern is with the prohibition approved by the Supreme Court.... No emergency has arisen which renders knowledge by a child of some language other than English so clearly harmful as to justify its inhibition with the consequent infringement of rights long freely enjoyed. We are constrained to conclude that the statute as applied is arbitrary and without reasonable relation to any end within the competency of the state.... Reversed and remanded.

Pierce v. Society of Sisters

268 U.S. 510 (1925)

Unanimous decision: *McReynolds*, Taft (CJ), Holmes, Van Devanter, Brandeis, Sutherland, Butler, Sanford, Stone

MR. JUSTICE McREYNOLDS delivered the opinion of the Court.

These appeals are from decrees, based upon undenied allegations, which granted preliminary orders restraining appellants from threatening or attempting to enforce the Compulsory Education Act adopted ... under the initiative provision of her Constitution by the voters of Oregon. They present the same points of law; there are no controverted questions of fact. Rights said to be guaranteed by the federal Constitution were specially set up, and appropriate prayers asked for their protection.

The challenged act, effective September 1, 1926, requires every parent, guardian, or other person having control or charge or custody of a child between 8 and 16 years to send him 'to a public school for the period of time a public school shall be held during the current year' in the district where the child resides; and failure so to do is declared a misdemeanor. There are exemptions—not specially important here—for children who are not normal, or who have completed the eighth grade, or whose parents or private teachers reside at considerable distances from any public school, or who hold special permits from the county superintendent. The manifest purpose is to compel general attendance at public schools by normal children, between 8 and 16, who have not completed the eight grade. And without doubt enforcement of the statute would seriously impair, perhaps destroy, the profitable features of appellees' business and greatly diminish the value of their property.

Appellee the Society of Sisters is an Oregon corporation, organized in 1880, with power to care for orphans, educate and instruct the youth, establish and maintain academies or schools, and acquire necessary real and personal property. It has long devoted its property and effort to the secular and religious education and care of children, and has acquired the valuable good will of many parents and guardians. It conducts interdependent primary and high schools and junior colleges, and maintains orphanages for the custody and control of children between 8 and 16. In its primary schools many children between those ages are taught the subjects usually pursued in Oregon public schools during the first eight years. Systematic religious instruction and moral training according to the tenets of the Roman Catholic Church are also regularly provided. All courses of study, both temporal and religious, contemplate continuity of training under appellee's charge; the primary schools are essential to the system and the most profitable. It owns valuable buildings, especially constructed and equipped for school purposes. The business is remunerative—the annual income from primary schools exceeds $30,000—and the successful conduct of this requires long time contracts with teachers and parents. The Compulsory Education Act of 1922 has already caused the withdrawal from its schools of children who would otherwise continue, and their income has steadily declined. The appellants, public officers, have proclaimed their purpose strictly to enforce the statute.

After setting out the above facts, the Society's bill alleges that the enactment conflicts with the right of parents to choose schools where their children will receive appropriate mental and religious training, the right of the child to influence the parents' choice of a school, the right of schools and teachers therein to engage in a useful business or profession, and is accordingly repugnant to the Constitution and void. And, further, that unless enforcement of the measure is enjoined the corporation's business and property will suffer irreparable injury.

Appellee Hill Military Academy is a private corporation organized in 1908 under the laws of Oregon, engaged in owning, operating, and conducting for profit an elementary, college preparatory, and military training school for boys between the ages of 5 and 21 years. The average attendance is 100, and the annual fees received for each student amount to some $800. The elementary department is divided into eight grades, as in the public schools; the college preparatory department has four grades, similar to those of the public high schools; the courses of study conform to the requirements of the state board of education. Military instruction and training are also given, under the supervision of an army officer. It owns considerable real and personal property, some useful only for school purposes. The business and incident good will are very valuable. In order to conduct its affairs, long time contracts must be made for supplies, equipment, teachers, and pupils. Appellants, law officers of the state and county, have publicly announced that the Act of November 7, 1922, is valid and have declared their intention to enforce it. By reason of the statute and threat of enforcement appellee's business is being destroyed and its property depreciated; parents and guardians are refusing to make contracts for the future instruction of their sons, and some are being withdrawn.

The Academy's bill states the foregoing facts and then alleges that the challenged act contravenes the corporation's rights guaranteed by the Fourteenth Amendment and that unless appellants are restrained from proclaiming its validity and threatening to enforce it irreparable injury will result. The prayer is for an appropriate injunction....

The inevitable practical result of enforcing the act under consideration would be destruction of appellees' primary schools, and perhaps all other private primary schools for normal children within the state of Oregon. Appellees are engaged in a kind of undertaking not inherently harmful, but long regarded as useful and meritorious. Certainly there is nothing in the present records to indicate that they have failed to discharge their obligations to patrons, students, or the state. And there are no peculiar circumstances or present emergencies which demand extraordinary measures relative to primary education.

Under the doctrine of Meyer v. Nebraska, we think it entirely plain that the Act of 1922 unreasonably interferes with the liberty of parents and guardians to direct the upbringing and education of children under their control. As often heretofore pointed out, rights guaranteed by the Constitution may not be abridged by legislation which has no reasonable relation to some purpose within the competency of the state. The fundamental theory of liberty upon which all governments in this Union repose excludes any general power of the state to standardize its children by forcing them to accept instruction from public teachers only. The child is not the mere creature of the state; those who nurture him and direct his destiny have the right, coupled with the high duty, to recognize and prepare him for additional obligations....

Generally, it is entirely true, as urged by counsel, that no person in any business has such an interest in possible customers as to enable him to restrain exercise of proper power of the state upon the ground that he will be deprived of patronage. But the injunctions here sought are not against the exercise of any proper power. Appellees asked protection against arbitrary, unreasonable, and unlawful interference with their patrons and the consequent destruction of their business and property. Their interest is clear and immediate, within the rule approved in … many other cases where injunctions have issued to protect business enterprises against interference with the freedom of patrons or customers.… The decrees below are affirmed.

Review Questions and Explanations: *Meyer* and *Pierce*

1. What is the right being protected in *Meyer*, and who holds it? What about in *Pierce*? As noted above, *Meyer* and *Pierce* frequently are cited by modern courts and commentators for the proposition that there is a fundamental privacy right protecting parents' educational choices for their children. Do you read the cases that way?

2. Does it matter whether the justices who decided these early cases anticipated the way these cases would be used, or is the only relevant question whether the reasoning of the cases supports the cases that follow? When answering this question, think about the pros and cons of common law reasoning, and the relationship between this type of reasoning, constitutionalism, and the rule of law.

3. Why do you think the Nebraska state legislatures banned teaching German? [Hint: look at the date of the case]. If a state today banned the teaching of a foreign language on the grounds that it posed a danger to national security, do you think the Supreme Court would interfere? Should it?

Recap: Early Fundamental Rights Doctrine

1. Pause at this point in your reading and go back and identify all the variations of the test the Court has used to identify fundamental rights. What do the tests have in common? What are the key differences between them?

2. Take a shot at devising your own test. What considerations are important in developing such a test? Think about doctrinal, practical, and institutional considerations as you create your test.

The three cases below, *West Coast Hotel v. Parrish, U.S. v. Carolene Products,* and *Ferguson v. Skrupa,* illustrate the Court's current approach to substantive due process in the area of economic regulation. As you will see, the Court has stopped using substantive due process and the doctrine of fundamental rights to strike down economic regulations. When reading these cases, consider the reasons the Court gives for retreating from this realm.

Also pay close attention to footnote 4 in *Carolene Products.* It is one of the most famous footnotes in Supreme Court history. In it, the Court, probably seeing a need to distinguish cases like *Pierce* and *Meyer* from *Lochner,* and possibly seeing the Civil Rights Movement on its horizon, attempts to articulate a principled reason for reviewing state laws restricting personal liberties more aggressively than laws restricting economic liberties. When pondering this, consider again the question asked before *Meyer* about treating like things alike.

Finally, take note of the language the Court uses when reviewing these different types of laws. As noted above, laws infringing on fundamental rights (now limited to rights involving personal liberties) are subject to various forms of heightened scrutiny, while laws involving economic regulations are reviewed under a much more deferential standard. The Court in these early cases had not yet fully articulated these different standards of review, but the language reflecting them is in the cases. Watch for it.

West Coast Hotel Co. v. Parrish

300 U.S. 379 (1937)

Majority: *Hughes* (CJ), Brandeis, Stone, Roberts, Cardozo

Dissent: *Sutherland*, Van Devanter, McReynolds, Butler

[Appellee Elsie Parrish was employed as a chambermaid at the West Coast Hotel. Parrish, with her husband, sued the hotel to recover the difference between what she was paid and the minimum wage required by the state law (the minimum wage was $14.50 per 48 hour work week). West Coast Hotel defended the suit by asserting that the state law violated the Due Process clause of the Fourteenth Amendment. The trial court ruled in favor of the hotel, but the Washington Supreme Court, reversed and directed judgment for Parrish.]

MR. CHIEF JUSTICE HUGHES delivered the opinion of the Court.

This case presents the question of the constitutional validity of the minimum wage law of the state of Washington.... The Supreme Court of Washington has upheld the minimum wage statute of that state. It has decided that the statute is a reasonable exercise of the police power of the state. In reaching that conclusion, the state court has invoked principles long established by this Court in the application of the Fourteenth Amendment.... The importance of the question, in which many states having similar laws are concerned, the close division by which the decision in the Adkins Case [an earlier Supreme Court case striking down a minimum wage law for women] was reached, and the economic conditions which have supervened, and in the light of which the reasonableness of the exercise of the protective power of the state must be considered, make it not only appropriate, but we think imperative, that in deciding the present case the subject should receive fresh consideration....

The principle which must control our decision is not in doubt. The constitutional provision invoked is the due process clause of the Fourteenth Amendment governing the states, as the due process clause invoked in the Adkins Case governed Congress. In each case the violation alleged by those attacking minimum wage regulation for women is deprivation of freedom of contract. What is this freedom? The Constitution does not speak of freedom of contract. It speaks of liberty and prohibits the deprivation of liberty without due process of law. In prohibiting that deprivation, the Constitution does not recognize an absolute and uncontrollable liberty. Liberty in each of its phases has its history and connotation. But the liberty safeguarded is liberty in a social organization which requires the protection of law against the evils which menace the health, safety, morals, and welfare of the people. Liberty under the Constitution is thus necessarily subject to the restraints of due process, and regulation which is reasonable in relation to its subject and is adopted in the interests of the community is due process....

With full recognition of the earnestness and vigor which characterize the prevailing opinion in the Adkins Case, we find it impossible to reconcile that ruling with these well-

considered declarations. What can be closer to the public interest than the health of
women and their protection from unscrupulous and overreaching employers? And if the
protection of women is a legitimate end of the exercise of state power, how can it be said
that the requirement of the payment of a minimum wage fairly fixed in order to meet the
very necessities of existence is not an admissible means to that end? The Legislature of
the state was clearly entitled to consider the situation of women in employment, the fact
that they are in the class receiving the least pay, that their bargaining power is relatively
weak, and that they are the ready victims of those who would take advantage of their ne-
cessitous circumstances. The Legislature was entitled to adopt measures to reduce the
evils of the 'sweating system,' the exploiting of workers at wages so low as to be insufficient
to meet the bare cost of living, thus making their very helplessness the occasion of a most
injurious competition. The Legislature had the right to consider that its minimum wage
requirements would be an important aid in carrying out its policy of protection. The
adoption of similar requirements by many states evidences a deep seated conviction both
as to the presence of the evil and as to the means adapted to check it. Legislative response
to that conviction cannot be regarded as arbitrary or capricious and that is all we have to
decide. Even if the wisdom of the policy be regarded as debatable and its effects uncertain,
still the Legislature is entitled to its judgment....

The judgment of the Supreme Court of the state of Washington is affirmed.

MR. JUSTICE SUTHERLAND, with whom MR. JUSTICE VAN DEVANTER, MR.
JUSTICE McREYNOLDS, MR. JUSTICE BUTLER agree, dissenting.

Under our form of government, where the written Constitution, by its own terms, is
the supreme law, some agency, of necessity, must have the power to say the final word as
to the validity of a statute assailed as unconstitutional. The Constitution makes it clear
that the power has been entrusted to this court when the question arises in a controversy
within its jurisdiction; and so long as the power remains there, its exercise cannot be
avoided without betrayal of the trust.

It has been pointed out many times, as in the Adkins Case, that this judicial duty is
one of gravity and delicacy; and that rational doubts must be resolved in favor of the constitutionality of the statute. But whose doubts, and by whom resolved? Undoubtedly it
is the duty of a member of the court, in the process of reaching a right conclusion, to
give due weight to the opposing views of his associates; but in the end, the question which
he must answer is not whether such views seem sound to those who entertain them, but
whether they convince him that the statute is constitutional or engender in his mind a
rational doubt upon that issue. The oath which he takes as a judge is not a composite
oath, but an individual one. And in passing upon the validity of a statute, he discharges
a duty imposed upon him, which cannot be consummated justly by an automatic acceptance
of the views of others which have neither convinced, nor created a reasonable doubt in,
his mind. If upon a question so important he thus surrender his deliberate judgment, he
stands forsworn. He cannot subordinate his convictions to that extent and keep faith with
his oath or retain his judicial and moral independence.

The suggestion that the only check upon the exercise of the judicial power, when
properly invoked, to declare a constitutional right superior to an unconstitutional statute
is the judge's own faculty of self-restraint, is both ill considered and mischievous. Self-
restraint belongs in the domain of will and not of judgment. The check upon the judge
is that imposed by his oath of office, by the Constitution, and by his own conscientious
and informed convictions; and since he has the duty to make up his own mind and adjudge
accordingly, it is hard to see how there could be any other restraint. This Court acts as a

unit. It cannot act in any other way; and the majority (whether a bare majority or a majority of all but one of its members), therefore, establishes the controlling rule as the decision of the court, binding, so long as it remains unchanged, equally upon those who disagree and upon those who subscribe to it. Otherwise, orderly administration of justice would cease. But it is the right of those in the minority to disagree, and sometimes, in matters of grave importance, their imperative duty to voice their disagreement at such length as the occasion demands — always, of course, in terms which, however forceful, do not offend the proprieties or impugn the good faith of those who think otherwise.

[handwritten: Didn't reckon on Scalia]

It is urged that the question involved should now receive fresh consideration, among other reasons, because of 'the economic conditions which have supervened'; but the meaning of the Constitution does not change with the ebb and flow of economic events. We frequently are told in more general words that the Constitution must be construed in the light of the present. If by that it is meant that the Constitution is made up of living words that apply to every new condition which they include, the statement is quite true. But to say, if that be intended, that the words of the Constitution mean today what they did not mean when written — that is, that they do not apply to a situation now to which they would have applied then — is to rob that instrument of the essential element which continues it in force as the people have made it until they, and not their official agents, have made it otherwise.

[handwritten: Great Depression]

Review Questions and Explanations: *West Coast Hotel*

1. What reasons does the majority give for overturning the *Adkins Case*?

2. Justice Sutherland writes a vigorous dissent. Consider his argument in relation to the materials about judicial review and judicial supremacy you read in Chapter 5. Is Justice Southerland's understanding of judicial power any different than that expressed by Justice Kennedy in *City of Boerne v. Flores*? Is it different from that asserted by the Court in *Marbury v. Madison*? What about in *Brown v. Mississippi*? Can you draw a principled distinction between these uses of judicial power?

Guided Reading Questions: *U.S. v. Carolene Products* and *Ferguson v. Skrupa*

1. *Carolene Products* is most famous for the footnote, discussed above, in which the Court attempts to justify a tiered system of judicial review. The case also, however, is a striking example of the deference the Court was giving to legislative judgments about economic regulations after *West Coast Hotel* and the 1937 judicial reversal on all things economic. When reading the case, pay attention to the underlying statute. What did it do and why do you think Congress enacted it?

2. The law being challenged in *Carolene Products* is a federal statute. The Court's analysis, consequently, takes place under the Due Process clause of the Fifth Amendment, not the Fourteenth Amendment. As you know, this is because the Fifth Amendment, as part of the original Bill of Rights, constrains the federal government while the Fourteenth Amendment, by its own terms, only applies to state governments. Does this make any difference in the Court's analysis?

3. Note the string of cases cited in footnote 4. You've read several of these. Do you agree with Justice Stone that the cases stand for the proposition he is citing them for?

4. In *Carolene Products,* the Court began reviewing economic regulations under what came to be called the "rational basis test." As you will see in *Ferguson v. Skrupa,* the rational basis test, particularly when used to review economic regulations, is exceptionally deferential to legislative judgments. Is this deference appropriate?

United States v. Carolene Products Co.

304 U.S. 144 (1938)

Majority: *Stone,* Hughes (CJ), Brandeis, Roberts, Black

Concurrence: *Butler* (omitted)

Dissent: *McReynolds* (omitted)

MR. JUSTICE STONE delivered the opinion of the Court.

The question for decision is whether the 'Filled Milk Act' of Congress of March 4, 1923 ... which prohibits the shipment in interstate commerce of skimmed milk compounded with any fat or oil other than milk fat, so as to resemble milk or cream, transcends the power of Congress to regulate interstate commerce or infringes the Fifth Amendment.... [in that it] deprives it of its property without due process of law, particularly in that the statute purports to make binding and conclusive upon appellee the legislative declaration that appellee's product 'is an adulterated article of food, injurious to the public health, and its sale constitutes a fraud on the public.'

Appellee was indicted in the District Court for Southern Illinois for violation of the act by the shipment in interstate commerce of certain packages of 'Milnut,' a compound of condensed skimmed milk and coconut oil made in imitation or semblance of condensed milk or cream. The indictment states ... that Milnut 'is an adulterated article of food, injurious to the public health,' and that it is not a prepared food product of the type excepted from the prohibition of the act. The case was brought here on appeal under the Criminal Appeals Act of March 2, 1907, 34 Stat. 1246.

Appellee [argues that the law] deprives it of its property without due process of law, particularly in that the statute purports to make binding and conclusive upon appellee the legislative declaration that appellee's product 'is an adulterated article of food, injurious to the public health, and its sale constitutes a fraud on the public.'

In twenty years evidence has steadily accumulated of the danger to the public health from the general consumption of foods which have been stripped of elements essential to the maintenance of health. The Filled Milk Act was adopted by Congress after committee hearings, in the course of which eminent scientists and health experts testified. An extensive investigation was made of the commerce in milk compounds in which vegetable oils have been substituted for natural milk fat, and of the effect upon the public health of the use of such compounds as a food substitute for milk. The conclusions drawn from evidence presented at the hearings were embodied in reports of the House Committee on Agriculture.... Both committees concluded, as the statute itself declares, that the use of filled milk as a substitute for pure milk is generally injurious to health and facilitates fraud on the public.

There is nothing in the Constitution which compels a Legislature, either national or state, to ignore such evidence, nor need it disregard the other evidence which amply supports the conclusions of the Congressional committees that the danger is greatly enhanced where an inferior product, like appellee's, is indistinguishable from a valuable food of almost universal use, thus making fraudulent distribution easy and protection of the consumer difficult....

Here the prohibition of the statute is inoperative unless the product is 'in imitation or semblance of milk, cream, or skimmed milk, whether or not condensed.' Whether in such circumstance the public would be adequately protected by the prohibition of false labels and false branding imposed by the Pure Food and Drugs Act, or whether it was necessary to go farther and prohibit a substitute food product thought to be injurious to health if used as a substitute when the two are not distinguishable, was a matter for the legislative judgment and not that of courts....

We may assume for present purposes that no pronouncement of a Legislature can forestall attack upon the constitutionality of the prohibition which it enacts by applying opprobrious epithets to the prohibited act, and that a statute would deny due process which precluded the disproof in judicial proceedings of all facts which would show or tend to show that a statute depriving the suitor of life, liberty, or property had a rational basis.

But such we think is not the purpose or construction of the statutory characterization of filled milk as injurious to health and as a fraud upon the public. There is no need to consider it here as more than a declaration of the legislative findings deemed to support and justify the action taken as a constitutional exertion of the legislative power, aiding informed judicial review, as do the reports of legislative committees, by revealing the rationale of the legislation. Even in the absence of such aids, the existence of facts supporting the legislative judgment is to be presumed, for regulatory legislation affecting ordinary commercial transactions is not to be pronounced unconstitutional unless in the light of the facts made known or generally assumed it is of such a character as to preclude the assumption that it rests upon some rational basis within the knowledge and experience of the legislators.

> **FN4.** There may be narrower scope for operation of the presumption of constitutionality when legislation appears on its face to be within a specific prohibition of the Constitution, such as those of the first ten Amendments, which are deemed equally specific when held to be embraced within the Fourteenth. See Stromberg v. California; Lovell v. Griffin (1938). It is unnecessary to consider now whether legislation which restricts those political processes which can ordinarily be expected to bring about repeal of undesirable legislation, is to be subjected to more exacting judicial scrutiny under the general prohibitions of the Fourteenth Amendment than are most other types of legislation. On restrictions upon the right to vote, see Nixon v. Herndon; Nixon v. Condon; on restraints upon the dissemination of information, see Near v. Minnesota; Grosjean v. American Press Co.; Lovell v. Griffin, supra; on interferences with political organizations, see Stromberg v. California, Whitney v. California; Herndon v. Lowry; and see Holmes, J., in Gitlow v. New York; as to prohibition of peaceable assembly, see De Jonge v. Oregon. Nor need we enquire whether similar considerations enter into the review of statutes directed at particular religious, Pierce v. Society of Sisters; or national, Meyer v. Nebraska; Bartels v. Iowa; Farrington v. Tokushige; or racial minorities. Nixon v. Herndon; Nixon v. Condon; whether prejudice against discrete and insular minorities may be a special condition, which tends seriously to curtail the operation of those political processes ordinarily to be relied upon to protect minorities, and which may call for a correspondingly more searching judicial inquiry. Compare McCulloch v. Maryland; South Carolina State Highway Department v. Barnwell Bros.

Reversed.

Ferguson v. Skrupa

372 U.S. 726 (1963)

Majority: *Black*, Warren (CJ), Douglas, Clark, Brennan, Stewart, White, Goldberg

Concurrence: *Harlan* (omitted)

MR. JUSTICE BLACK delivered the opinion of the Court.

[A Kansas statute made it a misdemeanor for any person to help another person make a "debt adjustment" contract—i.e., an agreement to renegotiate a debt or make a payment plan. The statute deemed this to be the unauthorized practice of law. Skrupa, a non-lawyer operating a "debt adjustment" business, sued to enjoin the statute as being a violation of the Due Process Clause of the Fourteenth Amendment. The district court enjoined the statute, relying on Adams v. Tanner, 244 U.S. 590 (1917), which had held that the Due Process clause forbids a State from prohibiting a business which is "useful" and not "inherently immoral or dangerous to public welfare."]

…. Under the system of government created by our Constitution, it is up to legislatures, not courts, to decide on the wisdom and utility of legislation. There was a time when the Due Process Clause was used by this Court to strike down laws which were thought unreasonable, that is, unwise or incompatible with some particular economic or social philosophy. In this manner the Due Process Clause was used, for example, to nullify laws prescribing maximum hours for work in bakeries, Lochner v. New York, 198 U.S. 45 (1905), outlawing "yellow dog" contracts, Coppage v. Kansas, 236 U.S. 1 (1915), setting minimum wages for women, Adkins v. Children's Hospital, 261 U.S. 525 (1923), and fixing the weight of loaves of bread, Jay Burns Baking Co. v. Bryan, 264 U.S. 504 (1924). This intrusion by the judiciary into the realm of legislative value judgments was strongly objected to at the time, particularly by Mr. Justice Holmes and Mr. Justice Brandeis. Dissenting [in Adkins, Justice Holmes said:] "The criterion of constitutionality is not whether we believe the law to be for the public good."

The doctrine that prevailed in Lochner, Coppage, Adkins, Burns, and like cases—that due process authorizes courts to hold laws unconstitutional when they believe the legislature has acted unwisely—has long since been discarded. We have returned to the original constitutional proposition that courts do not substitute their social and economic beliefs for the judgment of legislative bodies, who are elected to pass laws. As this Court stated in a unanimous opinion in 1941, "We are not concerned … with the wisdom, need, or appropriateness of the legislation." Legislative bodies have broad scope to experiment with economic problems, and this Court does not sit to "subject the State to an intolerable supervision hostile to the basic principles of our Government and wholly beyond the protection which the general clause of the Fourteenth Amendment was intended to secure." …

In the face of our abandonment of the use of the "vague contours" [Holmes, dissenting in Adkins] of the Due Process Clause to nullify laws which a majority of the Court believed to be economically unwise, reliance on Adams v. Tanner is as mistaken as would be adherence to Adkins v. Children's Hospital, overruled by West Coast Hotel Co. v. Parrish, 300 U.S. 379 (1937). Not only has the philosophy of Adams been abandoned, but also this Court almost 15 years ago expressly pointed to another opinion of this Court as having "clearly undermined" Adams. We conclude that the Kansas Legislature was free to decide for itself that legislation was needed to deal with the business of debt adjusting. Unquestionably, there are arguments showing that the business of debt adjusting has social utility, but such arguments are properly addressed to the legislature, not to us. We refuse to sit as a "superlegislature to weigh the wisdom of legislation," and we emphatically refuse to go back to the time when courts used the Due Process Clause "to strike down state laws, regulatory of business and industrial conditions, because they may be unwise, improvident, or out of harmony with a particular school of thought." ... Whether the legislature takes for its textbook Adam Smith, Herbert Spencer, Lord Keynes, or some other is no concern of ours. The Kansas debt adjusting statute may be wise or unwise. But relief, if any be needed, lies not with us but with the body constituted to pass laws for the State of Kansas.... Reversed.

Review Questions and Explanations: *Carolene Products* and *Ferguson*

1. What do the laws at issue in *Carolene Products* and *Ferguson* actually do? To borrow a question from our dormant Commerce Clause studies, whom do they help and whom do they hurt? What is the best argument for subjecting such statutes to something more than rational basis review?

2. The *Carolene Products* Court recited the congressional fact-finding on filled milk, but then at the end of the opinion stated "Even in the absence of such [evidentiary] aids, the existence of facts supporting the legislative judgment is to be presumed ..." What is the significance of that for rational basis review?

3. *Carolene Products* footnote 4 identifies two distinct situations in which heightened judicial review may be justified. What are they? What is the justification for each?

4. Using the rationale of footnote 4, make a list of three laws the Court should review rigorously and three it should review deferentially. If you can, use real world laws—legislation actually being discussed and debated today.

5. Figure IV.2 (in the introduction to this Part of the casebook) illustrates the system of tiered review the Court has developed since 1937. Note that economic regulations receive the lowest level of review. Yet, as Justice Holmes noted in *Lochner,* the "liberty of the citizen to do as he likes so long as he does not interfere with the liberty of others to do the same," is interfered with by innumerable rules and regulations. This means that virtually all regulation *can* be challenged as offending the liberty provision of the Fourteenth Amendment. Such challenges are rarely brought, however, because they almost inevitably fail under rational basis review. What would happen if the Court reviewed all such legislation more vigorously?

Exercise: Substantive Due Process and Economic Regulation

Suppose Congress passes a law regulating the sale of vegetable-based beverages, such as soy milk, oat milk, etc. in the following manner: (1) the beverage cannot be produced to be opaque and white or off white in color; (2) it cannot be called "milk"; and (3) it cannot be advertised as a "milk substitute." Congressional findings state that these beverages are far less healthy than animal milk, and the use of the terms "milk" or "milk substitute" and the beverages' milk-like appearance are misleading and deceptive. Suppose there is irrefutable evidence that the dairy industry was a major force behind the enactment of the law. Setting any First

Amendment issues aside, what are the substantive due process arguments that can be made for and against the constitutionality of this law? With one or more classmates, outline arguments challenging and supporting the law, and present the arguments to another classmate acting as district court judge.

D. Fundamental Rights and Personal Liberties

The cases you have read so far in this chapter constitute the foundation of the Court's current substantive due process doctrine. At this point, you should understand and be able to explain the mechanism through which the Due Process clause incorporates some of the rights found in the Bill of Rights, the role the concept of "fundamental rights" plays in that process, the debate about how the Court should determine what rights are or are not fundamental, the way the Court used the concept of fundamental rights during the *Lochner* era, the reasons that use was controversial, the distinction the Court has since drawn between economic and personal liberties, and (finally!) the deferential review given to economic regulation today.

As you have seen, the Court has struggled in these cases to balance the need to give meaning to the liberty provision of the Due Process clause with a sensitively to its own role in a democratic society. That struggle continues today, and raises complex questions of the appropriate role of the judiciary in dealing with some of the most contested social issues of our era.[3] Before moving on to those contemporary cases, however, it is worth taking a moment to set the stage by exploring the different perspectives justices have brought to these cases over the years.

The excerpts below illustrate four distinct approaches that have been used by the Court or by individual justices to define the "fundamental rights" given greater judicial protection under the Due Process clause. The first is from Justice Harlan's dissent in *Poe v. Ullman* (1961). *Poe* involved an early challenge to a state law prohibiting married couples from using contraception. The majority refused to hear the case on jurisdictional grounds; Justice Harlan dissented and addressed the issue on the merits. The second excerpt is from an opinion written by Justice Scalia in *Michael H. v. Gerald D.* (1989), a case involving a biological father's attempt to claim parental rights to his child. It also includes a lengthy footnote in which Justice Scalia addresses arguments raised by Justice Brennan, who was writing in dissent. The excerpt thus provides two views of how the Court should proceed in such cases.

The final excerpt is written by Justice Kennedy, and comes from *Lawrence v. Texas* (2003), a case you will read later in this chapter. *Lawrence* involved a state law criminalizing consensual sodomy between consenting adults. As in the above excerpts, the question presented by the underlying case is whether the legislation being challenged unconstitutionally infringes upon a right protected as fundamental under the Due Process clause.

When reading the excerpts, try to restate each justice's test in your own words. Also, see if you can identify what, if anything, the justices actually *agree* on — is there a core idea about fundamental rights that is shared by all of them?

---

3. We note that the difference between the Court's earlier cases and those which stymie it today is not that today's Court is leaping into deeply contested political issues; rather, what has changed is which issues are politically contested.

Justice Harlan: *Poe v. Ullman*
367 U.S. 497 (1961)

[The majority held that a Connecticut couple did not have standing to challenge a state law making it a crime for married couples to use contraception. The decision rested on the fact that the law was not being enforced and that therefore no one risked suffering a cognizable injury because of it. Justice Harlan dissented, and addressed the substantive due process issue raised in the challenge.]

I believe that a statute making it a criminal offense for married couples to use contraceptives is an intolerable and unjustifiable invasion of privacy in the conduct of the most intimate concerns of an individual's personal life.... Since [this contention draws its] basis from no explicit language of the Constitution, and [has] yet to find expression in any decision of this Court, I feel it desirable at the outset to state the framework of Constitutional principles in which I think the issue must be judged....

As to the Fourteenth [Amendment] which is involved here, the history of the Amendment also sheds little light on the meaning of the [due process] provision. It is important to note, however, that two views of the Amendment have not been accepted by this Court as delineating its scope. One view, which was ably and insistently argued in response to what were felt to be abuses by this Court of its reviewing power, sought to limit the provision to a guarantee of procedural fairness. The other view which has been rejected would have it that the Fourteenth Amendment, whether by way of the Privileges and Immunities Clause or the Due Process Clause, applied against the States only and precisely those restraints which had prior to the Amendment been applicable merely to federal action. However, 'due process' in the consistent view of this Court has even been a broader concept than the first view and more flexible than the second.

Were due process merely a procedural safeguard it would fail to reach those situations where the deprivation of life, liberty or property was accomplished by legislation which by operating in the future could, given even the fairest possible procedure in application to individuals, nevertheless destroy the enjoyment of all three. Thus the guaranties of due process, though having their roots in Magna Carta's 'per legem terrae' and considered as procedural safeguards 'against executive usurpation and tyranny,' have in this country 'become bulwarks also against arbitrary legislation.'

However it is not the particular enumeration of rights in the first eight Amendments which spells out the reach of Fourteenth Amendment due process, but rather, as was suggested in another context long before the adoption of that Amendment, those concepts which are considered to embrace those rights 'which are fundamental; which belong to the citizens of all free governments,' for 'the purposes (of securing) which men enter into society.' Calder v. Bull (1798). Again and again this Court has resisted the notion that the Fourteenth Amendment is no more than a shorthand reference to what is explicitly set out elsewhere in the Bill of Rights. Indeed the fact that an identical provision limiting federal action is found among the first eight Amendments, applying to the Federal Government, suggests that due process is a discrete concept which subsists as an independent guaranty of liberty and procedural fairness, more general and inclusive than the specific prohibitions.

Due process has not been reduced to any formula; its content cannot be determined by reference to any code. The best that can be said is that through the course of this Court's decisions it has represented the balance which our Nation, built upon postulates of respect for the liberty of the individual, has struck between that liberty and the demands of organized society. If the supplying of content to this Constitutional concept has of necessity been a rational process, it certainly has not been one where judges have felt free to roam where unguided speculation might take them. The balance of which I speak is the balance struck by this country, having regard to what history teaches are the traditions from which it developed as well as the traditions from which it broke. That tradition is a living thing. A decision of this Court which radically departs from it could not long survive, while a decision which builds on what has survived is likely to be sound. No formula could serve as a substitute, in this area, for judgment and restraint.

It is this outlook which has led the Court continuingly to perceive distinctions in the imperative character of Constitutional provisions, since that character must be discerned from a particular provision's larger context. And inasmuch as this context is one not of words, but of history and purposes, the full scope of the liberty guaranteed by the Due Process Clause cannot be found in or limited by the precise terms of the specific guarantees elsewhere provided in the Constitution. This 'liberty' is not a series of isolated points pricked out in terms of the taking of property; the freedom of speech, press, and religion; the right to keep and bear arms; the freedom from unreasonable searches and seizures; and so on. It is a rational continuum which, broadly speaking, includes a freedom from all substantial arbitrary impositions and purposeless restraints, and which also recognizes, what a reasonable and sensitive judgment must, that certain interests require particularly careful scrutiny of the state needs asserted to justify their abridgment.

As was said in *Meyer v. Nebraska*, 'this court has not attempted to define with exactness the liberty thus guaranteed. Without doubt, it denotes, not merely freedom from bodily restraint.' Thus, for instance, when in that case and in *Pierce* that the Court struck down laws which sought not to require what children must learn in schools, but to prescribe, in the first case, what they must not learn, and in the second, where they must acquire their learning, I do not think it was wrong to put those decisions on 'the right of the individual to … establish a home and bring up children,' *Meyer v. State of Nebraska*, or on the basis that 'The fundamental theory of liberty upon which all governments in this Union repose excludes any general power of the State to standardize its children by forcing them to accept instruction from public teachers only,' *Pierce*. I consider this so, even though today those decisions would probably have gone by reference to the concepts of freedom of expression and conscience assured against state action by the Fourteenth Amendment, concepts that are derived from the explicit guarantees of the First Amendment against federal encroachment upon freedom of speech and belief. For it is the purposes of those guarantees and not their text, the reasons for their statement by the Framers and not the statement itself, see *Palko v. Connecticut*; *United States v. Carolene Products Co.*, which have led to their present status in the compendious notion of 'liberty' embraced in the Fourteenth Amendment.

Each new claim to constitutional protection must be considered against a background of constitutional purposes, as they have been rationally perceived and historically developed. Though we exercise limited and sharply restrained judgment, yet there is no 'mechanical yard-stick,' no 'mechanical answer.' The decision of an apparently novel claim must depend on grounds which follow closely on well-accepted principles and criteria. The new decision must take 'its place in relation to what went before and further (cut) a channel for what is to come.'

'The vague contours of the Due Process Clause do not leave judges at large. We may not draw on our merely personal and private notions and disregard the limits that bind judges in their judicial function. Even though the concept of due process of law is not final and fixed, these limits are derived from considerations that are fused in the whole nature of our judicial process.... These are considerations deeply rooted in reason and in the compelling traditions of the legal profession.'

Justice Scalia: *Michael H. v. Gerald D.*
491 U.S. 110 (1989)

Under California law, a child born to a married woman living with her husband is presumed to be a child of the marriage. The presumption of legitimacy may be rebutted only by the husband or wife, and then only in limited circumstances. The instant appeal presents the claim that this presumption infringes upon the due process rights of a man who wishes to establish his paternity of a child born to the wife of another man....

The facts of this case are, we must hope, extraordinary. On May 9, 1976, in Las Vegas, Nevada, Carole D., an international model, and Gerald D., a top executive in a French oil company, were married. The couple established a home in Playa del Rey, California, in which they resided as husband and wife when one or the other was not out of the country on business. In the summer of 1978, Carole became involved in an adulterous affair with a neighbor, Michael H. In September 1980, she conceived a child, Victoria D., who was born on May 11, 1981. Gerald was listed as father on the birth certificate and has always held Victoria out to the world as his daughter. Soon after delivery of the child, however, Carole informed Michael that she believed he might be the father.... Carole and Michael had blood tests of themselves and Victoria, which showed a 98.07% probability that Michael was Victoria's father....

Michael contends as a matter of substantive due process that ... that [he] has a constitutionally protected liberty interest in his relationship with Victoria.

It is an established part of our constitutional jurisprudence that the term "liberty" in the Due Process Clause extends beyond freedom from physical restraint. See, *e.g.* Pierce v. Society of Sisters (1925); Meyer v. Nebraska (1923). Without that core textual meaning as a limitation, defining the scope of the Due Process Clause "has at times been a treacherous field for this Court," giving "reason for concern lest the only limits to ... judicial intervention become the predilections of those who happen at the time to be Members of this Court." Moore v. East Cleveland (1977).

In an attempt to limit and guide interpretation of the Clause, we have insisted not merely that the interest denominated as a "liberty" be "fundamental" (a concept that, in isolation, is hard to objectify), but also that it be an interest traditionally protected by our society. As we have put it, the Due Process Clause affords only those protections "so rooted in the traditions and conscience of our people as to be ranked as fundamental." Our cases reflect "continual insistence upon respect for the teachings of history [and] solid recognition of the basic values that underlie our society...." Griswold v. Connecticut....

We have found nothing in the older sources, nor in the older cases, addressing specifically the power of the natural father to assert parental rights over a child born into a woman's existing marriage with another man.... What Michael [must establish] is not that our society has traditionally allowed a natural father in his circumstances to establish paternity, but that it has traditionally accorded such a father parental rights, or at least has not traditionally denied them. Even if the law in all States had always been that the entire world could challenge the marital presumption and obtain a declaration as to who was the natural father, that would not advance Michael's claim. Thus, it is ultimately irrelevant, even for purposes of determining *current* social attitudes towards the alleged substantive right Michael asserts, that the present law in a number of States appears to allow the natural father—including the natural father who has not established a relationship with the child—the theoretical power to rebut the marital presumption. What counts is whether the States in fact award substantive parental rights to the natural father of a child conceived within, and born into, an extant marital union that wishes to embrace the child. We are not aware of a single case, old or new, that has done so. This is not the stuff of which fundamental rights qualifying as liberty interests are made.

> FN6. Justice Brennan criticizes our methodology in using historical traditions specifically relating to the rights of an adulterous natural father, rather than inquiring more generally "whether parenthood is an interest that historically has received our attention and protection." There seems to us no basis for the contention that this methodology is "nove[l]." For example, in Bowers v. Hardwick (1986), we noted that at the time the Fourteenth Amendment was ratified all but 5 of the 37 States had criminal sodomy laws, that all 50 of the States had such laws prior to 1961, and that 24 States and the District of Columbia continued to have them; and we concluded from that record, regarding that very specific aspect of sexual conduct, that "to claim that a right to engage in such conduct is 'deeply rooted in this Nation's history and tradition' or 'implicit in the concept of ordered liberty' is, at best, facetious." Id. In Roe v. Wade, we spent about a fifth of our opinion negating the proposition that there was a longstanding tradition of laws proscribing abortion.
>
> We do not understand why, having rejected our focus upon the societal tradition regarding the natural father's rights vis-à-vis a child whose mother is married to another man, Justice Brennan would choose to focus instead upon "parenthood." Why should the relevant category not be even more general—perhaps "family relationships"; or "personal relationships"; or even "emotional attachments in general"? Though the dissent has no basis for the level of generality it would select, we do: We refer to the most specific level at which a relevant tradition protecting, or denying protection to, the asserted right can be identified. If, for example, there were no societal tradition, either way, regarding the rights of the natural father of a child adulterously conceived, we would have to consult, and (if possible) reason from, the traditions regarding natural fathers in general. But there is such a more specific tradition, and it unqualifiedly denies protection to such a parent.
>
> One would think that Justice Brennan would appreciate the value of consulting the most specific tradition available, since he acknowledges that "[e]ven if we can agree … that 'family' and 'parenthood' are part of the good life, it is absurd to assume that we can agree on the content of those terms and destructive to pretend that we do." Because such general traditions provide such imprecise guidance, they permit judges to dictate rather than discern the society's views. The need, if arbitrary decisionmaking is to be avoided, to adopt the most specific tradition as the point of reference—or at least to announce, as Justice Brennan declines to do, some other criterion for selecting among the innumerable relevant traditions that could be consulted—is well enough exemplified by the fact that in the present case Justice Brennan's opinion and Justice O'Connor's opinion, which disapproves this footnote, *both* appeal to tradition, but on the basis of the tradition they select reach opposite results. Although assuredly having the virtue (if it be that) of leaving judges free to decide as they think best when the unanticipated occurs, a rule of law that binds neither by text nor by any particular, identifiable tradition is no rule of law at all.[4]

---

4. Editors' note: Chief Justice Rehnquist joined Justice Scalia's majority opinion but did not join this footnote. Think about this when answering the question about judicial styles posed in the Guided Reading Questions before *Planned Parenthood v. Casey*.

Justice Kennedy: *Lawrence v. Texas*
539 U.S. 558 (2003)

Liberty protects the person from unwarranted government intrusions into a dwelling or other private places. In our tradition the State is not omnipresent in the home. And there are other spheres of our lives and existence, outside the home, where the State should not be a dominant presence. Freedom extends beyond spatial bounds. Liberty presumes an autonomy of self that includes freedom of thought, belief, expression, and certain intimate conduct. The instant case involves liberty of the person both in its spatial and in its more transcendent dimensions.

The question before the Court is the validity of a Texas statute making it a crime for two persons of the same sex to engage in certain intimate sexual conduct.... We conclude the case should be resolved by determining whether the petitioners were free as adults to engage in the private conduct in the exercise of their liberty under the Due Process Clause of the Fourteenth Amendment to the Constitution....

The issue is whether the majority may use the power of the State to enforce these views on the whole society through operation of the criminal law. "Our obligation is to define the liberty of all, not to mandate our own moral code."... In all events we think that our laws and traditions in the past half century are of most relevance here. These references show an emerging awareness that liberty gives substantial protection to adult persons in deciding how to conduct their private lives in matters pertaining to sex. "[H]istory and tradition are the starting point but not in all cases the ending point of the substantive due process inquiry."... The Casey decision again confirmed that our laws and tradition afford constitutional protection to personal decisions relating to marriage, procreation, contraception, family relationships, child rearing, and education.

Guided Reading Questions: *Griswold v. Connecticut* and *Roe v. Wade*

1. The following cases show the contemporary Court's efforts to define the liberty interest protected by the Due Process clause. Before reading the cases, reconsider the tests articulated by the Court in the foundational cases set forth above. Do the contemporary cases necessarily follow from the Court's earlier decisions or are they doing something different than those cases did?

2. As noted earlier, *Meyer* and *Pierce* are often cited as precedent for the recognition of the constitutional right to privacy articulated in *Griswold* and *Roe*. Review those cases after reading *Griswold* and *Roe*, and consider whether you agree with this assessment.

3. Is *Roe* dictated by the result in *Griswold*? Why or why not? Be precise—if you agree with *Griswold* but disagree with *Roe*, what test are you using and what distinction are you drawing between the two cases?

4. The basic question presented in these cases is the same as it was in the pre-1937 cases: what rights are so "fundamental" that they are entitled to greater protection under the Due Process clause? Nonetheless, the Court's language in these cases moves from "liberty" (the term used in the clause itself) to "privacy" (a term, as oft noted, that does not appear in the Constitution). Why do you think the justices make this move?

5. *Griswold, Roe, Casey* and *Lawrence* are well known cases. As such, everyone thinks they know what they say. Whether you think you agree with them or think you disagree with them, take the time to read them carefully. Does the actual content of these cases surprise you in any way?

Griswold v. Connecticut

381 U.S. 479 (1965)

Majority: *Douglas,* Warren (CJ), Clark, Brennan, Goldberg

Concurrence: *Goldberg,* Warren, Brennan; *Harlan; White* (omitted)

Disssents: *Black; Stewart* (omitted)

MR. JUSTICE DOUGLAS delivered the opinion of the Court.

Appellant Griswold is Executive Director of the Planned Parenthood League of Connecticut. Appellant Buxton is a licensed physician and a professor at the Yale Medical School who served as Medical Director for the League at its Center in New Haven—a center open and operating from November 1 to November 10, 1961, when appellants were arrested. They gave information, instruction, and medical advice to *married persons* as to the means of preventing conception. They examined the wife and prescribed the best contraceptive device or material for her use. Fees were usually charged, although some couples were serviced free.

The statutes whose constitutionality is involved in this appeal ... provide[]:

> Any person who uses any drug, medicinal article or instrument for the purpose of preventing conception shall be fined not less than fifty dollars or imprisoned not less than sixty days nor more than one year or be both fined and imprisoned.

> Any person who assists, abets, counsels, causes, hires or commands another to commit any offense may be prosecuted and punished as if he were the principal offender.

We think that appellants have standing to raise the constitutional rights of the married people with whom they had a professional relationship.... This case is more akin to ... Pierce v. Society of Sisters, where the owners of private schools were entitled to assert the rights of potential pupils and their parents.... The rights of husband and wife, pressed here, are likely to be diluted or adversely affected unless those rights are considered in a suit involving those who have this kind of confidential relation to them.

Coming to the merits, we are met with a wide range of questions that implicate the Due Process Clause of the Fourteenth Amendment. Overtones of some arguments suggest that Lochner v. New York should be our guide. But we decline that invitation ... We do not sit as a super-legislature to determine the wisdom, need, and propriety of laws that touch economic problems, business affairs, or social conditions. This law, however, operates directly on an intimate relation of husband and wife and their physician's role in one aspect of that relation.

The association of people is not mentioned in the Constitution nor in the Bill of Rights. The right to educate a child in a school of the parents' choice—whether public or private or parochial—is also not mentioned. Nor is the right to study any particular subject or any foreign language. Yet the First Amendment has been construed to include certain of those rights.

By Pierce v. Society of Sisters ... the right to educate one's children as one chooses is made applicable to the States by the force of the First and Fourteenth Amendments. By Meyer v. State of Nebraska ... the same dignity is given the right to study the German language in a private school. In other words, the State may not, consistently with the spirit of the First Amendment, contract the spectrum of available knowledge. The right of freedom of speech and press includes not only the right to utter or to print, but the right to distribute, the right to receive, the right to read ... and freedom of inquiry, freedom of thought, and freedom to teach ... indeed the freedom of the entire university community.... Without those peripheral rights the specific rights would be less secure. And so we reaffirm the principle of the Pierce and the Meyer cases.

In NAACP v. Alabama we protected the 'freedom to associate and privacy in one's associations,' noting that freedom of association was a peripheral First Amendment right. Disclosure of membership lists of a constitutionally valid association, we held, was invalid 'as entailing the likelihood of a substantial restraint upon the exercise by petitioner's members of their right to freedom of association.' ... In other words, the First Amendment has a penumbra where privacy is protected from governmental intrusion. In like context, we have protected forms of 'association' that are not political in the customary sense but pertain to the social, legal, and economic benefit of the members. NAACP v. Button. In Schware v. Board of Bar Examiners we held it not permissible to bar a lawyer from practice, because he had once been a member of the Communist Party....

Those cases involved more than the 'right of assembly' — a right that extends to all irrespective of their race or ideology. The right of 'association,' like the right of belief, is more than the right to attend a meeting; it includes the right to express one's attitudes or philosophies by membership in a group or by affiliation with it or by other lawful means. Association in that context is a form of expression of opinion; and while it is not expressly included in the First Amendment its existence is necessary in making the express guarantees fully meaningful.

The foregoing cases suggest that specific guarantees in the Bill of Rights have penumbras, formed by emanations from those guarantees that help give them life and substance. Various guarantees create zones of privacy. The right of association contained in the penumbra of the First Amendment is one, as we have seen. The Third Amendment in its prohibition against the quartering of soldiers 'in any house' in time of peace without the consent of the owner is another facet of that privacy. The Fourth Amendment explicitly affirms the 'right of the people to be secure in their persons, houses, papers, and effects, against unreasonable searches and seizures.' The Fifth Amendment in its Self-Incrimination Clause enables the citizen to create a zone of privacy which government may not force him to surrender to his detriment. The Ninth Amendment provides: 'The enumeration in the Constitution, of certain rights, shall not be construed to deny or disparage others retained by the people.' ...

The Fourth and Fifth Amendments were described [by the Court] as protection against all governmental invasions 'of the sanctity of a man's home and the privacies of life.' We recently referred in Mapp v. Ohio to the Fourth Amendment as creating a 'right to privacy, no less important than any other right carefully and particularly reserved to the people.' ...

The present case, then, concerns a relationship lying within the zone of privacy created by several fundamental constitutional guarantees. And it concerns a law which, in forbidding the use of contraceptives rather than regulating their manufacture or sale, seeks to achieve its goals by means having a maximum destructive impact upon that relationship. Such a law cannot stand in light of the familiar principle, so often applied by this Court, that a 'governmental purpose to control or prevent activities constitutionally subject to state regulation may not be achieved by means which sweep unnecessarily broadly and thereby invade the area of protected freedoms.'... Would we allow the police to search the sacred precincts of marital bedrooms for telltale signs of the use of contraceptives? The very idea is repulsive to the notions of privacy surrounding the marriage relationship.

We deal with a right of privacy older than the Bill of Rights — older than our political parties, older than our school system. Marriage is a coming together for better or for worse, hopefully enduring, and intimate to the degree of being sacred. It is an association that promotes a way of life, not causes; a harmony in living, not political faiths; a bilateral loyalty, not commercial or social projects. Yet it is an association for as noble a purpose as any involved in our prior decisions. Reversed.

MR. JUSTICE GOLDBERG, whom THE CHIEF JUSTICE and MR. JUSTICE BRENNAN join, concurring.

I agree with the Court that Connecticut's birth-control law unconstitutionally intrudes upon the right of marital privacy, and I join in its opinion and judgment. Although I have not accepted the view that 'due process' as used in the Fourteenth Amendment includes all of the first eight Amendments..., I do agree that the concept of liberty protects those personal rights that are fundamental, and is not confined to the specific terms of the Bill of Rights. My conclusion that the concept of liberty is not so restricted and that it embraces the right of marital privacy though that right is not mentioned explicitly in the Constitution is supported both by numerous decisions of this Court, referred to in the Court's opinion, and by the language and history of the Ninth Amendment. In reaching the conclusion that the right of marital privacy is protected, as being within the protected penumbra of specific guarantees of the Bill of Rights, the Court refers to the Ninth Amendment. I add these words to emphasize the relevance of that Amendment to the Court's holding.

> FN1. My Brother STEWART dissents on the ground that he 'can find no ... general right of privacy in the Bill of Rights, in any other part of the Constitution, or in any case ever before decided by this Court.'... He would require a more explicit guarantee than the one which the Court derives from several constitutional amendments. This Court, however, has never held that the Bill of Rights or the Fourteenth Amendment protects only those rights that the Constitution specifically mentions by name.

The Court stated many years ago that the Due Process Clause protects those liberties that are 'so rooted in the traditions and conscience of our people as to be ranked as fundamental.' In Gitlow, the Court said:

> For present purposes we may and do assume that freedom of speech and of the press — which are protected by the First Amendment from abridgment by Congress — are among the fundamental personal rights and 'liberties' protected by the due process clause of the Fourteenth Amendment from impairment by the States.

And in Meyer v. Nebraska the Court, referring to the Fourteenth Amendment, stated:

> While this court has not attempted to define with exactness the liberty thus guaranteed, the term has received much consideration and some of the included things have been definitely stated. Without doubt, it denotes not merely freedom from bodily restraint but also (for example,) the right ... to marry, establish a home and bring up children.

This Court, in a series of decisions, has held that the Fourteenth Amendment absorbs and applies to the States those specifics of the first eight amendments which express fundamental personal rights. The language and history of the Ninth Amendment reveal that the Framers of the Constitution believed that there are additional fundamental rights, protected from governmental infringement, which exist alongside those fundamental rights specifically mentioned in the first eight constitutional amendments.

The Ninth Amendment reads, 'The enumeration in the Constitution, of certain rights, shall not be construed to deny or disparage others retained by the people.' The Amendment is almost entirely the work of James Madison. It was introduced in Congress by him and passed the House and Senate with little or no debate and virtually no change in language. It was proffered to quiet expressed fears that a bill of specifically enumerated rights could not be sufficiently broad to cover all essential rights and that the specific mention of certain rights would be interpreted as a denial that others were protected....

A dissenting opinion suggests that my interpretation of the Ninth Amendment somehow 'broaden(s) the powers of this Court.' With all due respect, I believe that it misses the import of what I am saying. I do not take the position of my Brother Black in his dissent in Adamson that the entire Bill of Rights is incorporated in the Fourteenth Amendment, and I do not mean to imply that the Ninth Amendment is applied against the States by the Fourteenth. Nor do I mean to state that the Ninth Amendment constitutes an independent source of rights protected from infringement by either the States or the Federal Government. Rather, the Ninth Amendment shows a belief of the Constitution's authors that fundamental rights exist that are not expressly enumerated in the first eight amendments and an intent that the list of rights included there not be deemed exhaustive. As any student of this Court's opinions knows, this Court has held, often unanimously, that the Fifth and Fourteenth Amendments protect certain fundamental personal liberties from abridgment by the Federal Government or the States. The Ninth Amendment simply shows the intent of the Constitution's authors that other fundamental personal rights should not be denied such protection or disparaged in any other way simply because they are not specifically listed in the first eight constitutional amendments. I do not see how this broadens the authority of the Court; rather it serves to support what this Court has been doing in protecting fundamental rights.

Nor am I turning somersaults with history in arguing that the Ninth Amendment is relevant in a case dealing with a State's infringement of a fundamental right. While the Ninth Amendment—and indeed the entire Bill of Rights—originally concerned restrictions upon federal power, the subsequently enacted Fourteenth Amendment prohibits the States as well from abridging fundamental personal liberties. And, the Ninth Amendment, in indicating that not all such liberties are specifically mentioned in the first eight amendments, is surely relevant in showing the existence of other fundamental personal rights, now protected from state, as well as federal, infringement. In sum, the Ninth Amendment simply lends strong support to the view that the 'liberty' protected by the Fifth And Fourteenth Amendments from infringement by the Federal Government or the States is not restricted to rights specifically mentioned in the first eight amendments....

In determining which rights are fundamental, judges are not left at large to decide cases in light of their personal and private notions. Rather, they must look to the 'traditions and (collective) conscience of our people' to determine whether a principle is 'so rooted (there) ... as to be ranked as fundamental.' ... The inquiry is whether a right involved 'is of such a character that it cannot be denied without violating those 'fundamental principles of liberty and justice which lie at the base of all our civil and political institutions' .... 'Liberty' also 'gains content from the emanations of ... specific (constitutional) guarantees' and 'from experience with the requirements of a free society.' Poe v. Ullman (J. Douglas, dissenting).

I agree fully with the Court that, applying these tests, the right of privacy is a fundamental personal right, emanating 'from the totality of the constitutional scheme under which we live.'... Mr. Justice Brandeis, dissenting in Olmstead v. U.S., comprehensively summarized the principles underlying the Constitution's guarantees of privacy:

> The protection guaranteed by the (Fourth and Fifth) amendments is much broader in scope. The makers of our Constitution undertook to secure conditions favorable to the pursuit of happiness. They recognized the significance of man's spiritual nature, of his feelings and of his intellect. They knew that only a part of the pain, pleasure and satisfactions of life are to be found in material things. They sought to protect Americans in their beliefs, their thoughts, their emotions and their sensations. They conferred, as against the government, the right to be let alone — the most comprehensive of rights and the right most valued by civilized men.

The Connecticut statutes here involved deal with a particularly important and sensitive area of privacy — that of the marital relation and the marital home. This Court recognized in Meyer v. Nebraska that the right 'to marry, establish a home and bring up children' was an essential part of the liberty guaranteed by the Fourteenth Amendment. In Pierce v. Society of Sisters, the Court held unconstitutional an Oregon Act which forbade parents from sending their children to private schools because such an act 'unreasonably interferes with the liberty of parents and guardians to direct the upbringing and education of children under their control.'... As this Court said in Prince v. Massachusetts, the Meyer and Pierce decisions 'have respected the private realm of family life which the state cannot enter.'

I agree with Mr. Justice Harlan's statement in his dissenting opinion in Poe, 'Certainly the safeguarding of the home does not follow merely from the sanctity of property rights. The home derives its pre-eminence as the seat of family life. And the integrity of that life is something so fundamental that it has been found to draw to its protection the principles of more than one explicitly granted Constitutional right.... Of this whole 'private realm of family life' it is difficult to imagine what is more private or more intimate than a husband and wife's marital relations.'

The entire fabric of the Constitution and the purposes that clearly underlie its specific guarantees demonstrate that the rights to marital privacy and to marry and raise a family are of similar order and magnitude as the fundamental rights specifically protected.

Although the Constitution does not speak in so many words of the right of privacy in marriage, I cannot believe that it offers these fundamental rights no protection. The fact that no particular provision of the Constitution explicitly forbids the State from disrupting the traditional relation of the family — a relation as old and as fundamental as our entire civilization — surely does not show that the Government was meant to have the power to do so. Rather, as the Ninth Amendment expressly recognizes, there are fundamental personal rights such as this one, which are protected from abridgment by the Government though not specifically mentioned in the Constitution....

The logic of the dissents would sanction federal or state legislation that seems to me even more plainly unconstitutional than the statute before us. Surely the Government, absent a showing of a compelling subordinating state interest, could not decree that all husbands and wives must be sterilized after two children have been born to them. Yet by their reasoning such an invasion of marital privacy would not be subject to constitutional challenge because, while it might be 'silly,' no provision of the Constitution specifically prevents the Government from curtailing the marital right to bear children and raise a family. While it may shock some of my Brethren that the Court today holds that the Constitution protects the right of marital privacy, in my view it is far more shocking to believe that the personal liberty guaranteed by the Constitution does not include protection against such totalitarian limitation of family size, which is at complete variance with our constitutional concepts. Yet, if upon a showing of a slender basis of rationality, a law outlawing voluntary birth control by married persons is valid, then, by the same reasoning, a law requiring compulsory birth control also would seem to be valid. In my view, however, both types of law would unjustifiably intrude upon rights of marital privacy which are constitutionally protected.

In a long series of cases this Court has held that where fundamental personal liberties are involved, they may not be abridged by the States simply on a showing that a regulatory statute has some rational relationship to the effectuation of a proper state purpose. 'Where there is a significant encroachment upon personal liberty, the State may prevail only upon showing a subordinating interest which is compelling,' ... The law must be shown 'necessary, and not merely rationally related to, the accomplishment of a permissible state policy.' ... [Justice Goldberg then determines that Connecticut has made no such showing in this case].

MR. JUSTICE HARLAN, concurring in the judgment.

I fully agree with the judgment of reversal, but find myself unable to join the Court's opinion. The reason is that it seems to me to evince an approach to this case very much like that taken by my Brothers Black and Stewart in dissent, namely: the Due Process Clause of the Fourteenth Amendment does not touch this Connecticut statute unless the enactment is found to violate some right assured by the letter or penumbra of the Bill of Rights.

In other words, what I find implicit in the Court's opinion is that the 'incorporation' doctrine may be used to restrict the reach of Fourteenth Amendment Due Process. For me this is just as unacceptable constitutional doctrine as is the use of the 'incorporation' approach to impose upon the States all the requirements of the Bill of Rights as found in the provisions of the first eight amendments and in the decisions of this Court interpreting them....

In my view, the proper constitutional inquiry in this case is whether this Connecticut statute infringes the Due Process Clause of the Fourteenth Amendment because the enactment violates basic values 'implicit in the concept of ordered liberty,' Palko. For reasons stated at length in my dissenting opinion in Poe v. Ullman, I believe that it does. While the relevant inquiry may be aided by resort to one or more of the provisions of the Bill of Rights, it is not dependent on them or any of their radiations. The Due Process Clause of the Fourteenth Amendment stands, in my opinion, on its own bottom.

A further observation seems in order respecting the justification of my Brothers BLACK and STEWART for their 'incorporation' approach to this case. Their approach does not rest on historical reasons, which are of course wholly lacking..., but on the thesis that by limiting the content of the Due Process Clause of the Fourteenth Amendment to the protection of rights which can be found elsewhere in the Constitution, in this instance in the Bill of Rights, judges will thus be confined to 'interpretation' of specific constitutional provisions, and will thereby be restrained from introducing their own notions of constitutional right and wrong into the 'vague contours of the Due Process Clause.' ...

While I could not more heartily agree that judicial 'self restraint' is an indispensable ingredient of sound constitutional adjudication, I do submit that the formula suggested for achieving it is more hollow than real. 'Specific' provisions of the Constitution, no less than 'due process,' lend themselves as readily to 'personal' interpretations by judges whose constitutional outlook is simply to keep the Constitution in supposed 'tune with the times'.... Need one go further than to recall last Term's reapportionment cases ... where a majority of the Court 'interpreted' 'by the People' (Art. I, § 2) and 'equal protection' (Amdt. 14) to command 'one person, one vote,' an interpretation that was made in the face of irrefutable and still unanswered history to the contrary? ...

Judicial self-restraint will not, I suggest, be brought about in the 'due process' area by the historically unfounded incorporation formula long advanced by my Brother Black, and now in part espoused by my Brother Stewart. It will be achieved in this area, as in other constitutional areas, only by continual insistence upon respect for the teachings of history, solid recognition of the basic values that underlie our society, and wise appreciation of the great roles that the doctrines of federalism and separation of powers have played in establishing and preserving American freedoms.... Adherence to these principles will not, of course, obviate all constitutional differences of opinion among judges, nor should it. Their continued recognition will, however, go farther toward keeping most judges from roaming at large in the constitutional field than will the interpolation into the Constitution of an artificial and largely illusory restriction on the content of the Due Process Clause.

MR. JUSTICE BLACK, with whom MR. JUSTICE STEWART joins, dissenting.

... The Court talks about a constitutional 'right of privacy' as though there is some constitutional provision or provisions forbidding any law ever to be passed which might abridge the 'privacy' of individuals. But there is not. There are, of course, guarantees in certain specific constitutional provisions which are designed in part to protect privacy at certain times and places with respect to certain activities. Such, for example, is the Fourth Amendment's guarantee against 'unreasonable searches and seizures.' But I think it belittles that Amendment to talk about it as though it protects nothing but 'privacy.' To treat it that way is to give it a niggardly interpretation, not the kind of liberal reading I think any Bill of Rights provision should be given. The average man would very likely not have his feelings soothed any more by having his property seized openly than by having it seized privately and by stealth. He simply wants his property left alone. And a person can be just as much, if not more, irritated, annoyed and injured by an unceremonious public arrest by a policeman as he is by a seizure in the privacy of his office or home.

One of the most effective ways of diluting or expanding a constitutionally guaranteed right is to substitute for the crucial word or words of a constitutional guarantee another word or words, more or less flexible and more or less restricted in meaning. This fact is well illustrated by the use of the term 'right of privacy' as a comprehensive substitute for the Fourth Amendment's guarantee against 'unreasonable searches and seizures.' 'Privacy' is a broad, abstract and ambiguous concept which can easily be shrunken in meaning but which can also, on the other hand, easily be interpreted as a constitutional ban against many things other than searches and seizures. I have expressed the view many times that First Amendment freedoms, for example, have suffered from a failure of the courts to stick to the simple language of the First Amendment in construing it, instead of invoking multitudes of words substituted for those the Framers used.... For these reasons I get nowhere in this case by talk about a constitutional 'right or privacy' as an emanation from one or more constitutional provisions. I like my privacy as well as the next one, but I am nevertheless compelled to admit that government has a right to invade it unless prohibited by some specific constitutional provision. For these reasons I cannot agree with the Court's judgment and the reasons it gives for holding this Connecticut law unconstitutional....

The due process argument which my Brothers Harlan and White adopt here is based, as their opinions indicate, on the premise that this Court is vested with power to invalidate all state laws that it consider to be arbitrary, capricious, unreasonable, or oppressive, or this

Court's belief that a particular state law under scrutiny has no 'rational or justifying' purpose, or is offensive to a 'sense of fairness and justice.' If these formulas based on 'natural justice,' or others which mean the same thing, are to prevail, they require judges to determine what is or is not constitutional on the basis of their own appraisal of what laws are unwise or unnecessary. The power to make such decisions is of course that of a legislative body. Surely it has to be admitted that no provision of the Constitution specifically gives such blanket power to courts to exercise such a supervisory veto over the wisdom and value of legislative policies and to hold unconstitutional those laws which they believe unwise or dangerous. I readily admit that no legislative body, state or national, should pass laws that can justly be given any of the invidious labels invoked as constitutional excuses to strike down state laws. But perhaps it is not too much to say that no legislative body ever does pass laws without believing that they will accomplish a sane, rational, wise and justifiable purpose.

While I completely subscribe to the holding of Marbury v. Madison and subsequent cases, that our Court has constitutional power to strike down statutes, state or federal, that violate commands of the Federal Constitution, I do not believe that we are granted power by the Due Process Clause or any other constitutional provision or provisions to measure constitutionality by our belief that legislation is arbitrary, capricious or unreasonable, or accomplishes no justifiable purpose, or is offensive to our own notions of 'civilized standards of conduct.' Such an appraisal of the wisdom of legislation is an attribute of the power to make laws, not of the power to interpret them. The use by federal courts of such a formula or doctrine or whatnot to veto federal or state laws simply takes away from Congress and States the power to make laws based on their own judgment of fairness and wisdom and transfers that power to this Court for ultimate determination—a power which was specifically denied to federal courts by the convention that framed the Constitution....

I realize that many good and able men have eloquently spoken and written, sometimes in rhapsodical strains, about the duty of this Court to keep the Constitution in tune with the times. The idea is that the Constitution must be changed from time to time and that this Court is charged with a duty to make those changes. For myself, I must with all deference reject that philosophy. The Constitution makers knew the need for change and provided for it. Amendments suggested by the people's elected representatives can be submitted to the people or their selected agents for ratification. That method of change was good for our Fathers, and being somewhat old fashioned I must add it is good enough for me. And so, I cannot rely on the Due Process Clause or the Ninth Amendment or any mysterious and uncertain natural law concept as a reason for striking down this state law. The Due Process Clause with an 'arbitrary and capricious' or 'shocking to the conscience' formula was liberally used by this Court to strike down economic legislation in the early decades of this century, threatening, many people thought, the tranquility and stability of the Nation.... That formula, based on subjective considerations of 'natural justice,' is no less dangerous when used to enforce this Court's views about personal rights than those about economic rights. I had thought that we had laid that formula, as a means for striking down state legislation, to rest once and for all in cases like [the post-1937 economic regulation cases] and many other opinions.

Review Questions and Explanations: *Griswold*

1. Justice Douglas's opinion states that the "specific guarantees in the Bill of Rights have penumbras, formed by emanations from those guarantees that help give them life and substance." These penumbras and emanations, according to

the majority, work together to create a zone of constitutionally protected privacy. Although, as noted by the Court, this type of language also has been used in the First Amendment context to construct a textually non-existent association right, its use in *Griswold* has been harshly criticized. The concept, consequently, has all but disappeared from the Court's jurisprudence. But the idea of a constitutionally protected zone of privacy has not. What is the core idea the Court is groping toward with this language? Does the majority opinion need the language about "penumbras" in order to support its constitutional argument?

2. Justice Black says that the Bill of Rights should be given a liberal reading, yet he refuses to read it as including a right of privacy. Why?

3. Justice Goldberg's concurring opinion sources the privacy right in the Ninth Amendment. The Ninth Amendment states that "The enumeration in the Constitution, of certain rights, shall not be construed to deny or disparage others retained by the people." Judges throughout our history have been leery of using the Ninth Amendment as a source of judicially protected rights. Judge Robert Bork, who was nominated but not confirmed to the Supreme Court in 1987, famously referred to it as an "ink blot" on the Constitution. Why might courts be reluctant to source judicially protected rights in the Ninth Amendment? How would a court "enforce" the Ninth Amendment? Would the problems involved in doing so be meaningfully different than the problems the Court encounters in its substantive due process cases?

Roe v. Wade

410 U.S. 113 (1973)

Majority: *Blackmun,* Burger (CJ), Douglas, Brennan, Stewart, Marshall, Powell

Concurrences: *Burger; Douglas* (both omitted); *Stewart*

Dissents: *White* (omitted), *Rehnquist*

MR. JUSTICE BLACKMUN delivered the opinion of the Court.

This Texas federal appeal and its Georgia companion ... present constitutional challenges to state criminal abortion legislation. The Texas statutes under attack here are typical of those that have been in effect in many States for approximately a century. The Georgia statutes, in contrast, have a modern cast and are a legislative product that, to an extent at least, obviously reflects the influences of recent attitudinal change, of advancing medical knowledge and techniques, and of new thinking about an old issue.

We forthwith acknowledge our awareness of the sensitive and emotional nature of the abortion controversy, of the vigorous opposing views, even among physicians, and of the deep and seemingly absolute convictions that the subject inspires. One's philosophy, one's experiences, one's exposure to the raw edges of human existence, one's religious training, one's attitudes toward life and family and their values, and the moral standards one establishes and seeks to observe, are all likely to influence and to color one's thinking and conclusions about abortion....

The Texas statutes that concern us here make it a crime to 'procure an abortion,' as therein defined, or to attempt one, except with respect to 'an abortion procured or attempted by medical advice for the purpose of saving the life of the mother.' Similar statutes are in existence in a majority of the States. Texas first enacted a criminal abortion statute in 1854....

The principal thrust of appellant's attack on the Texas statutes is that they improperly invade a right, said to be possessed by the pregnant woman, to choose to terminate her pregnancy. Appellant would discover this right in the concept of personal 'liberty' embodied in the Fourteenth Amendment's Due Process Clause; or in personal marital, familial, and sexual privacy said to be protected by the Bill of Rights or its penumbras, see Griswold v. Connecticut, or among those rights reserved to the people by the Ninth Amendment (Griswold, Goldberg, J., concurring). Before addressing this claim, we feel it desirable briefly to survey, in several aspects, the history of abortion, for such insight as that history may afford us, and then to examine the state purposes and interests behind the criminal abortion laws.

It perhaps is not generally appreciated that the restrictive criminal abortion laws in effect in a majority of States today are of relatively recent vintage. Those laws, generally proscribing abortion or its attempt at any time during pregnancy except when necessary to preserve the pregnant woman's life, are not of ancient or even of common-law origin. Instead, they derive from statutory changes effected, for the most part, in the latter half of the 19th century.

1. Ancient attitudes. [Justice Blackmun reviews the history of abortion regulations in Greek and Roman times, and determines that abortion was widely practiced in these eras. He also notes that what abortion prosecutions did exist seemed to have been based on a father's 'right to his offspring.']

2. The Hippocratic Oath. [Justice Blackmun note that the Hippocratic oath condemns abortion and that this part of the oath has been contested throughout its history.]

3. The common law. [Justice Blackmun reviews the history of the common law regulation of abortion and determines that abortion performed before 'quickening' — the first recognizable movement of the fetus in utero, which usually occurs between the 16th to the 18th week of pregnancy, was not an indictable offense. He then notes that it is disputed whether the abortion of a 'quick' fetus was a common law crime or not.]

4. The English statutory law. [Justice Blackmun notes that English common law in 1803 made it a felony to abort a quick fetus, but had lesser penalties for abortions undertaken before quickening.]

5. The American law. In this country, the law in effect in all but a few States until mid-19th century was the pre-existing English common law. Connecticut, the first State to enact abortion legislation, adopted in 1821 that part of Lord Ellenborough's Act that related to a woman 'quick with child.' The death penalty was not imposed. Abortion before quickening was made a crime in that State only in 1860. In 1828, New York enacted legislation that, in two respects, was to serve as a model for early anti-abortion statutes. First, while barring destruction of an unquickened fetus as well as a quick fetus, it made the former only a misdemeanor, but the latter second-degree manslaughter. Second, it incorporated a concept of therapeutic abortion by providing that an abortion was excused if it 'shall have been necessary to preserve the life of such mother, or shall have been advised by two physicians to be necessary for such purpose.' By 1840, when Texas had received the common law, only eight American States had statutes dealing with abortion. It was not until after the War Between the States that legislation began generally to replace the common law. Most of these initial statutes dealt severely with abortion after quickening but were lenient with it before quickening. Most punished attempts equally with completed abortions. While many statutes included the exception for an abortion thought by one or more physicians to be necessary to save the mother's life, that provision soon disappeared and the typical law required that the procedure actually be necessary for that purpose.

Gradually, in the middle and late 19th century the quickening distinction disappeared from the statutory law of most States and the degree of the offense and the penalties were increased. By the end of the 1950s a large majority of the jurisdictions banned abortion, however and whenever performed, unless done to save or preserve the life of the mother.…

It is thus apparent that at common law, at the time of the adoption of our Constitution, and throughout the major portion of the 19th century, abortion was viewed with less disfavor than under most American statutes currently in effect. Phrasing it another way, a woman enjoyed a substantially broader right to terminate a pregnancy than she does in most States today. At least with respect to the early stage of pregnancy, and very possibly without such a limitation, the opportunity to make this choice was present in this country well into the 19th century. Even later, the law continued for some time to treat less punitively an abortion procured in early pregnancy.…

Three reasons have been advanced to explain historically the enactment of criminal abortion laws in the 19th century and to justify their continued existence.

It has been argued occasionally that these laws were the product of a Victorian social concern to discourage illicit sexual conduct. Texas, however, does not advance this justification in the present case, and it appears that no court or commentator has taken the argument seriously. The appellants and amici contend, moreover, that this is not a proper state purpose at all and suggest that, if it were, the Texas statutes are overbroad in protecting it since the law fails to distinguish between married and unwed mothers.…

A second reason is concerned with abortion as a medical procedure. When most criminal abortion laws were first enacted, the procedure was a hazardous one for the woman. This was particularly true prior to the development of antisepsis.… Thus, it has been argued that a State's real concern in enacting a criminal abortion law was to protect the pregnant woman, that is, to restrain her from submitting to a procedure that placed her life in serious jeopardy.

Modern medical techniques have altered this situation. Appellants and various amici refer to medical data indicating that abortion in early pregnancy, that is, prior to the end of the first trimester, although not without its risk, is now relatively safe. Mortality rates for women undergoing early abortions, where the procedure is legal, appear to be as low as or lower than the rates for normal childbirth. Consequently, any interest of the State in protecting the woman from an inherently hazardous procedure, except when it would be equally dangerous for her to forgo it, has largely disappeared. Of course, important state interests in the areas of health and medical standards do remain. The State has a legitimate interest in seeing to it that abortion, like any other medical procedure, is performed under circumstances that insure maximum safety for the patient. This interest obviously extends at least to the performing physician and his staff, to the facilities involved, to the availability of after-care, and to adequate provision for any complication or emergency that might arise. The prevalence of high mortality rates at illegal 'abortion mills' strengthens, rather than weakens, the State's interest in regulating the conditions under which abortions are performed. Moreover, the risk to the woman increases as her pregnancy continues. Thus, the State retains a definite interest in protecting the woman's own health and safety when an abortion is proposed at a late stage of pregnancy.

The third reason is the State's interest—some phrase it in terms of duty—in protecting prenatal life. Some of the argument for this justification rests on the theory that a new human life is present from the moment of conception. The State's interest and general obligation to protect life then extends, it is argued, to prenatal life. Only when the life of the pregnant mother herself is at stake, balanced against the life she carries within her, should the interest of the embryo or fetus not prevail. Logically, of course, a legitimate state interest in this area need not stand or fall on acceptance of the belief that life begins at conception or at some other point prior to life birth. In assessing the State's interest, recognition may be given to the less rigid claim that as long as at least potential life is involved, the State may assert interests beyond the protection of the pregnant woman alone....

The Constitution does not explicitly mention any right of privacy. In a line of decisions, however, going back perhaps as far as [1891], the Court has recognized that a right of personal privacy, or a guarantee of certain areas or zones of privacy, does exist under the Constitution. In varying contexts, the Court or individual Justices have, indeed, found at least the roots of that right in the First Amendment, Stanley v. Georgia, in the Fourth and Fifth Amendments, Terry v. Ohio, in the penumbras of the Bill of Rights, Griswold v. Connecticut; in the Ninth Amendment, Griswold (Goldberg, J., concurring); or in the concept of liberty guaranteed by the first section of the Fourteenth Amendment, Meyer v. Nebraska. These decisions make it clear that only personal rights that can be deemed 'fundamental' or 'implicit in the concept of ordered liberty,' Palko v. Connecticut, are included in this guarantee of personal privacy. They also make it clear that the right has some extension to activities relating to marriage, Loving v. Virginia; procreation, Skinner v. Oklahoma; contraception, Eisenstadt v. Baird; family relationships, Prince v. Massachusetts; and child rearing and education, Pierce v. Society of Sisters; Meyer v. Nebraska.

This right of privacy, whether it be founded in the Fourteenth Amendment's concept of personal liberty and restrictions upon state action, as we feel it is, or, as the District Court determined, in the Ninth Amendment's reservation of rights to the people, is broad enough to encompass a woman's decision whether or not to terminate her pregnancy. The detriment that the State would impose upon the pregnant woman by denying this choice altogether is apparent. Specific and direct harm medically diagnosable even in early pregnancy may be involved. Maternity, or additional offspring, may force upon the woman a distressful life and future. Psychological harm may be imminent. Mental and physical health may be taxed by child care. There is also the distress, for all concerned, associated with the unwanted child, and there is the problem of bringing a child into a family already unable, psychologically and otherwise, to care for it. In other cases, as in this one, the additional difficulties and continuing stigma of unwed motherhood may be involved. All these are factors the woman and her responsible physician necessarily will consider in consultation.

On the basis of elements such as these, appellant and some amici argue that the woman's right is absolute and that she is entitled to terminate her pregnancy at whatever time, in whatever way, and for whatever reason she alone chooses. With this we do not agree. Appellant's arguments that Texas either has no valid interest at all in regulating the abortion decision, or no interest strong enough to support any limitation upon the woman's sole determination, are unpersuasive. The Court's decisions recognizing a right of privacy also acknowledge that some state regulation in areas protected by that right is appropriate. As noted above, a State may properly assert important interests in safeguarding health, in maintaining medical standards, and in protecting potential life. At some point in pregnancy, these respective interests become sufficiently compelling to sustain regulation of the factors that govern the abortion decision. The privacy right involved, therefore, cannot be said to be absolute. In fact, it is not clear to us that the claim asserted by some amici that one has an unlimited right to do with one's body as one pleases bears a close relationship to the right of privacy previously articulated in the Court's decisions. The Court has refused to recognize an unlimited right of this kind in the past. Buck v. Bell.

We, therefore, conclude that the right of personal privacy includes the abortion decision, *Holding* but that this right is not unqualified and must be considered against important state interests in regulation.... [a]t some point the state interests as to protection of health, medical standards, and prenatal life, become dominant. We agree with this approach.

Where certain 'fundamental rights' are involved, the Court has held that regulation limiting these rights may be justified only by a 'compelling state interest'... and that legislative enactments must be narrowly drawn to express only the legitimate state interests at stake.... In the recent abortion cases, cited above, courts have recognized these principles. Those striking down state laws have generally scrutinized the State's interests in protecting health and potential life, and have concluded that neither interest justified broad limitations on the reasons for which a physician and his pregnant patient might decide that she should have an abortion in the early stages of pregnancy. Courts sustaining state laws have held that the State's determinations to protect health or prenatal life are dominant and constitutionally justifiable....

Appellant, as has been indicated, claims an absolute right that bars any state imposition of criminal penalties in the area. Appellee argues that the State's determination to recognize and protect prenatal life from and after conception constitutes a compelling state interest. As noted above, we do not agree fully with either formulation....

The pregnant woman cannot be isolated in her privacy. She carries an embryo and, later, a fetus, if one accepts the medical definitions of the developing young in the human uterus.... The situation therefore is inherently different from marital intimacy, or bedroom possession of obscene material, or marriage, or procreation, or education, with which Eisenstadt and Griswold, Stanley, Loving, Skinner and Pierce and Meyer were respectively concerned. As we have intimated above, it is reasonable and appropriate for a State to decide that at some point in time another interest, that of health of the mother or that of potential human life, becomes significantly involved. The woman's privacy is no longer sole and any right of privacy she possesses must be measured accordingly.

Texas urges that, apart from the Fourteenth Amendment, life begins at conception and is present throughout pregnancy, and that, therefore, the State has a compelling interest in protecting that life from and after conception. We need not resolve the difficult question of when life begins. When those trained in the respective disciplines of medicine, philosophy, and theology are unable to arrive at any consensus, the judiciary, at this point in the development of man's knowledge, is not in a position to speculate as to the answer.

It should be sufficient to note briefly the wide divergence of thinking on this most sensitive and difficult question. There has always been strong support for the view that life does not begin until live birth.... In areas other than criminal abortion, the law has been reluctant to endorse any theory that life, as we recognize it, begins before life birth or to accord legal rights to the unborn except in narrowly defined situations and except when the rights are contingent upon life birth. For example, the traditional rule of tort law denied recovery for prenatal injuries even though the child was born alive. That rule has been changed in almost every jurisdiction. In most States, recovery is said to be permitted only if the fetus was viable, or at least quick, when the injuries were sustained, though few courts have squarely so held.

In a recent development, generally opposed by the commentators, some States permit the parents of a stillborn child to maintain an action for wrongful death because of prenatal injuries. Such an action, however, would appear to be one to vindicate the parents' interest and is thus consistent with the view that the fetus, at most, represents only the potentiality of life. Similarly, unborn children have been recognized as acquiring rights or interests by way of inheritance or other devolution of property, and have been represented by guardians ad litem. Perfection of the interests involved, again, has generally been contingent upon live birth. In short, the unborn have never been recognized in the law as persons in the whole sense.

In view of all this, we do not agree that, by adopting one theory of life, Texas may override the rights of the pregnant woman that are at stake. We repeat, however, that the State does have an important and legitimate interest in preserving and protecting the health of the pregnant woman, whether she be a resident of the State or a non-resident who seeks medical consultation and treatment there, and that it has still another important and legitimate interest in protecting the potentiality of human life. These interests are separate and distinct. Each grows in substantiality as the woman approaches term and, at a point during pregnancy, each becomes 'compelling.'

With respect to the State's important and legitimate interest in the health of the mother, the 'compelling' point, in the light of present medical knowledge, is at approximately the end of the first trimester. This is so because of the now-established medical fact, referred to above that until the end of the first trimester mortality in abortion may be less than mortality in normal childbirth. It follows that, from and after this point, a State may regulate the abortion procedure to the extent that the regulation reasonably relates to the preservation and protection of maternal health. Examples of permissible state regulation in this area are requirements as to the qualifications of the person who is to perform the abortion; as to the licensure of that person; as to the facility in which the procedure is to be performed, that is, whether it must be a hospital or may be a clinic or some other place of less-than-hospital status; as to the licensing of the facility; and the like.

This means, on the other hand, that, for the period of pregnancy prior to this 'compelling' point, the attending physician, in consultation with his patient, is free to determine, without regulation by the State, that, in his medical judgment, the patient's pregnancy should be terminated. If that decision is reached, the judgment may be effectuated by an abortion free of interference by the State.

With respect to the State's important and legitimate interest in potential life, the 'compelling' point is at viability. This is so because the fetus then presumably has the capability of meaningful life outside the mother's womb. State regulation protective of fetal life after viability thus has both logical and biological justifications. If the State is interested in protecting fetal life after viability, it may go so far as to proscribe abortion during that period, except when it is necessary to preserve the life or health of the mother.

Measured against these standards, Art. 1196 of the Texas Penal Code, in restricting legal abortions to those 'procured or attempted by medical advice for the purpose of saving the life of the mother,' sweeps too broadly. The statute makes no distinction between abortions performed early in pregnancy and those performed later, and it limits to a single reason, 'saving' the mother's life, the legal justification for the procedure. The statute, therefore, cannot survive the constitutional attack made upon it here....

Affirmed in part and reversed in part.

MR. JUSTICE STEWART, concurring.

... Griswold [] can be rationally understood only as a holding that the Connecticut statute substantively invaded the 'liberty' that is protected by the Due Process Clause of the Fourteenth Amendment.... There is no constitutional right of privacy, as such. '(The Fourth) Amendment protects individual privacy against certain kinds of governmental intrusion, but its protections go further, and often have nothing to do with privacy at all. Other provisions of the Constitution protect personal privacy from other forms of governmental invasion. But the protection of a person's general right to privacy—his right to be let alone by other people—is like the protection of his property and of his very life, left largely to the law of the individual States.'... This was also clear to Mr. Justice Black, (dissenting opinion); to Mr. Justice Harlan, (opinion concurring in the judgment); and to Mr. Justice White, (opinion concurring in the judgment)....

'In a Constitution for a free people, there can be no doubt that the meaning of 'liberty' must be broad indeed.' The Constitution nowhere mentions a specific right of personal choice in matters of marriage and family life, but the 'liberty' protected by the Due Process Clause of the Fourteenth Amendment covers more than those freedoms explicitly named in the Bill of Rights. As Mr. Justice Harlan once wrote: '(T)he full scope of the liberty guaranteed by the Due Process Clause cannot be found in or limited by the precise terms of the specific guarantees elsewhere provided in the Constitution. This 'liberty' is not a series of isolated points priced out in terms of the taking of property; the freedom of speech, press, and religion; the right to keep and bear arms; the freedom from unreasonable searches and seizures; and so on. It is a rational continuum which, broadly speaking, includes a freedom from all substantial arbitrary impositions and purposeless restraints ... and which also recognizes, what a reasonable and sensitive judgment must, that certain interests require particularly careful scrutiny of the state needs asserted to justify their abridgment.' Poe v. Ullman (opinion dissenting from dismissal of appeal). In the words of Mr. Justice Frankfurter, 'Great concepts like ... 'liberty' ... were purposely left to gather meaning from experience. For they relate to the whole domain of social and economic fact, and the statesmen who founded this Nation knew too well that only a stagnant society remains unchanged.'...

Several decisions of this Court make clear that freedom of personal choice in matters of marriage and family life is one of the liberties protected by the Due Process Clause of the Fourteenth Amendment. Loving v. Virginia; Griswold v. Connecticut; Pierce v. Society of Sisters; Meyer v. Nebraska. As recently as last Term, we recognized 'the right of the individual, married or single, to be free from unwarranted governmental intrusion into matters so fundamentally affecting a person as the decision whether to bear or beget a child.' That right necessarily includes the right of a woman to decide whether or not to terminate her pregnancy. 'Certainly the interests of a woman in giving of her physical and emotional self during pregnancy and the interests that will be affected throughout her life by the birth and raising of a child are of a far greater degree of significance and personal intimacy than the right to send a child to private school protected in Pierce v. Society of Sisters or the right to teach a foreign language protected in Meyer v. Nebraska....

Clearly, therefore, the Court today is correct in holding that the right asserted by Jane Roe is embraced within the personal liberty protected by the Due Process Clause of the Fourteenth Amendment.

It is evident that the Texas abortion statute infringes that right directly. Indeed, it is difficult to imagine a more complete abridgment of a constitutional freedom than that worked by the inflexible criminal statute now in force in Texas. The question then becomes whether the state interests advanced to justify this abridgment can survive the 'particularly careful scrutiny' that the Fourteenth Amendment here requires.

The asserted state interests are protection of the health and safety of the pregnant woman, and protection of the potential future human life within her. These are legitimate objectives, amply sufficient to permit a State to regulate abortions as it does other surgical procedures, and perhaps sufficient to permit a State to regulate abortions more stringently or even to prohibit them in the late stages of pregnancy. But such legislation is not before us, and I think the Court today has thoroughly demonstrated that these state interests cannot constitutionally support the broad abridgment of personal liberty worked by the existing Texas law. Accordingly, I join the Court's opinion holding that that law is invalid under the Due Process Clause of the Fourteenth Amendment.

MR. JUSTICE REHNQUIST, dissenting.

The Court's opinion brings to the decision of this troubling question both extensive historical fact and a wealth of legal scholarship. While the opinion thus commands my respect, I find myself nonetheless in fundamental disagreement with those parts of it that invalidate the Texas statute in question, and therefore dissent....

I have difficulty in concluding, as the Court does, that the right of 'privacy' is involved in this case. Texas, by the statute here challenged, bars the performance of a medical abortion by a licensed physician on a plaintiff such as Roe. A transaction resulting in an operation such as this is not 'private' in the ordinary usage of that word. Nor is the 'privacy' that the Court finds here even a distant relative of the freedom from searches and seizures protected by the Fourth Amendment to the Constitution, which the Court has referred to as embodying a right to privacy....

If the Court means by the term 'privacy' no more than that the claim of a person to be free from unwanted state regulation of consensual transactions may be a form of 'liberty' protected by the Fourteenth Amendment, there is no doubt that similar claims have been upheld in our earlier decisions on the basis of that liberty. I agree with the statement of Mr. Justice STEWART in his concurring opinion that the 'liberty,' against deprivation of which without due process the Fourteenth Amendment protects, embraces more than the rights found in the Bill of Rights. But that liberty is not guaranteed absolutely against deprivation, only against deprivation without due process of law. The test traditionally applied in the area of social and economic legislation is whether or not a law such as that challenged has a rational relation to a valid state objective.)...

The Due Process Clause of the Fourteenth Amendment undoubtedly does place a limit, albeit a broad one, on legislative power to enact laws such as this. If the Texas statute were to prohibit an abortion even where the mother's life is in jeopardy, I have little doubt that such a statute would lack a rational relation to a valid state objective under the test stated in Williamson ... But the Court's sweeping invalidation of any restrictions on abortion during the first trimester is impossible to justify under that standard, and the conscious weighing of competing factors that the Court's opinion apparently substitutes for the established test is far more appropriate to a legislative judgment than to a judicial one....

While the Court's opinion quotes from the dissent of Mr. Justice Holmes in Lochner, the result it reaches is more closely attuned to the majority opinion of Mr. Justice Peckham in that case. As in Lochner and similar cases applying substantive due process standards to economic and social welfare legislation, the adoption of the compelling state interest standard will inevitably require this Court to examine the legislative policies and pass on the wisdom of these policies in the very process of deciding whether a particular state interest put forward may or may not be 'compelling.' The decision here to break pregnancy into three distinct terms and to outline the permissible restrictions the State may impose in each one, for example, partakes more of judicial legislation than it does of a determination of the intent of the drafters of the Fourteenth Amendment.

The fact that a majority of the States reflecting, after all the majority sentiment in those States, have had restrictions on abortions for at least a century is a strong indication, it seems to me, that the asserted right to an abortion is not 'so rooted in the traditions and conscience of our people as to be ranked as fundamental.' Even today, when society's views on abortion are changing, the very existence of the debate is evidence that the 'right' to an abortion is not so universally accepted as the appellant would have us believe.

To reach its result, the Court necessarily has had to find within the Scope of the Fourteenth Amendment a right that was apparently completely unknown to the drafters of the Amendment. As early as 1821, the first state law dealing directly with abortion was enacted by the Connecticut Legislature. By the time of the adoption of the Fourteenth Amendment in 1868, there were at least 36 laws enacted by state or territorial legislatures limiting abortion. While many States have amended or updated their laws, 21 of the laws on the books in 1868 remain in effect today. Indeed, the Texas statute struck down today was, as the majority notes, first enacted in 1857 and 'has remained substantially unchanged to the present time.'...

There apparently was no question concerning the validity of this provision or of any of the other state statutes when the Fourteenth Amendment was adopted. The only conclusion possible from this history is that the drafters did not intend to have the Fourteenth Amendment withdraw from the States the power to legislate with respect to this matter.

Review Questions and Explanations: *Roe*

1. *Roe* is now thought of as one of the most controversial decisions ever issued by the Supreme Court. It did not begin that way, however. The case was decided by a 7 to 2 vote, and was not even mentioned at the first confirmation hearing (that of Justice Stevens in 1975) held after it was issued. Does this tell us anything meaningful about the wisdom of the Court's decision?

2. Recall the Affordable Care Act, discussed in Part One of this book. As we have already noted, while the legal debate over the law hinged on Congress's Article 1 powers, much of the public debate about it sounded in ideas about personal liberty and a right to be left alone. Can you use *Griswold* and *Roe* to construct an argument that the decision to purchase health insurance is part of the privacy right protected by the Due Process clause?

3. Also recall the arguments made in the Affordable Care Act case about structural federalism. The four-justice opinion signed by Justices Scalia, Thomas, Kennedy and Alito asserted that the structural division of power in the original Constitution exists to protect "personal freedom" and that it is the "responsibility of the Court to ... remind our people" of that. Is this any different than arguing, as the majority does in *Roe*, that the Bill of Rights exists to protect "liberty" and it is the job of the Court to protect those liberties?

Guided Reading Questions: *Planned Parenthood v. Casey*

1. How is the test set out in *Casey* different than that found in *Roe*? Identify each test, and then consider the effect the different tests may have on the ability to obtain abortions. In other words, what effect does the switch from *Roe* to *Casey* have in the real world?

2. Chief Justice Rehnquist and Justice Scalia each write a dissenting opinion in *Casey*. Both justices appear to disagree deeply with the plurality, but the two opinions differ dramatically in style and tone. One of the things you should think about as a lawyer is how you talk to and about people who disagree with you. Lawyers often are leaders in both their professional and personal communities. Which style of leadership do you want to emulate, Rehnquist's or Scalia's?

Undue burden

Planned Parenthood v. Casey

505 U.S. 833 (1992)

Plurality: *O'Connor*, Kennedy, Souter

Concurrences/Dissents: *Stevens* (omitted)*; Blackmun; Rehnquist* (CJ), White, *Scalia*, Thomas

JUSTICE O'CONNOR, JUSTICE KENNEDY, and JUSTICE SOUTER delivered the opinion of the Court.

Liberty finds no refuge in a jurisprudence of doubt. Yet 19 years after our holding that the Constitution protects a woman's right to terminate her pregnancy in its early stages, Roe v. Wade (1973), that definition of liberty is still questioned. Joining the respondents as *amicus curiae*, the United States, as it has done in five other cases in the last decade, again asks us to overrule Roe....

At issue in these cases are five provisions of the Pennsylvania Abortion Control Act of 1982, as amended in 1988 and 1989. The Act requires that a woman seeking an abortion give her informed consent prior to the abortion procedure, and specifies that she be provided with certain information at least 24 hours before the abortion is performed.... For a minor to obtain an abortion, the Act requires the informed consent of one of her parents, but provides for a judicial bypass option if the minor does not wish to or cannot obtain a parent's consent.... Another provision of the Act requires that, unless certain exceptions apply, a married woman seeking an abortion must sign a statement indicating that she has notified her husband of her intended abortion.... The Act exempts compliance with these three requirements in the event of a "medical emergency," which is defined in ... of the Act.... In addition to the above provisions regulating the performance of abortions, the Act imposes certain reporting requirements on facilities that provide abortion services.... After considering the fundamental constitutional questions resolved by Roe, principles of institutional integrity, and the rule of *stare decisis*, we are led to conclude this: the essential holding of Roe v. Wade should be retained and once again reaffirmed.

It must be stated at the outset and with clarity that Roe's essential holding, the holding we reaffirm, has three parts. First is a recognition of the right of the woman to choose to have an abortion before viability and to obtain it without undue interference from the State. Before viability, the State's interests are not strong enough to support a prohibition of abortion or the imposition of a substantial obstacle to the woman's effective right to elect the procedure. Second is a confirmation of the State's power to restrict abortions after fetal viability, if the law contains exceptions for pregnancies which endanger the woman's life or health. And third is the principle that the State has legitimate interests from the outset of the pregnancy in protecting the health of the woman and the life of the fetus that may become a child. These principles do not contradict one another; and we adhere to each.

Constitutional protection of the woman's decision to terminate her pregnancy derives from the Due Process Clause of the Fourteenth Amendment. It declares that no State shall "deprive any person of life, liberty, or property, without due process of law." The controlling word in the cases before us is "liberty." Although a literal reading of the Clause might suggest that it governs only the procedures by which a State may deprive persons of liberty, for at least 105 years, since Mugler v. Kansas (1887), the Clause has been understood to contain a substantive component as well, one "barring certain government actions regardless of the fairness of the procedures used to implement them." As Justice Brandeis (joined by Justice Holmes) observed, "[d]espite arguments to the contrary which had seemed to me persuasive, it is settled that the due process clause of the Fourteenth Amendment applies to matters of substantive law as well as to matters of procedure. Thus all fundamental rights comprised within the term liberty are protected by the Federal Constitution from invasion by the States." Whitney v. California. "[T]he guaranties of due process, though having their roots in Magna Carta's *per legem terrae* and considered as procedural safeguards 'against executive usurpation and tyranny,' have in this country 'become bulwarks also against arbitrary legislation.'" Poe v. Ullman.

The most familiar of the substantive liberties protected by the Fourteenth Amendment are those recognized by the Bill of Rights. We have held that the Due Process Clause of the Fourteenth Amendment incorporates most of the Bill of Rights against the States.... It is tempting, as a means of curbing the discretion of federal judges, to suppose that liberty encompasses no more than those rights already guaranteed to the individual against federal interference by the express provisions of the first eight Amendments to the Constitution. See Adamson v. California, (1947) (Black, J., dissenting). But of course this Court has never accepted that view.

It is also tempting, for the same reason, to suppose that the Due Process Clause protects only those practices, defined at the most specific level, that were protected against government interference by other rules of law when the Fourteenth Amendment was ratified. See Michael H. v. Gerald D. (1989) (opinion of SCALIA, J.). But such a view would be inconsistent with our law. It is a promise of the Constitution that there is a realm of personal liberty which the government may not enter. We have vindicated this principle before. Marriage is mentioned nowhere in the Bill of Rights and interracial marriage was illegal in most States in the 19th century, but the Court was no doubt correct in finding it to be an aspect of liberty protected against state interference by the substantive component of the Due Process Clause in Loving v. Virginia (1967) (relying, in an opinion for eight Justices, on the Due Process Clause)....

Neither the Bill of Rights nor the specific practices of States at the time of the adoption of the Fourteenth Amendment marks the outer limits of the substantive sphere of liberty which the Fourteenth Amendment protects.... The inescapable fact is that adjudication of substantive due process claims may call upon the Court in interpreting the Constitution to exercise that same capacity which by tradition courts always have exercised: reasoned judgment. Its boundaries are not susceptible of expression as a simple rule. That does not mean we are free to invalidate state policy choices with which we disagree; yet neither does it permit us to shrink from the duties of our office....

Men and women of good conscience can disagree, and we suppose some always shall disagree, about the profound moral and spiritual implications of terminating a pregnancy, even in its earliest stage. Some of us as individuals find abortion offensive to our most basic principles of morality, but that cannot control our decision. Our obligation is to define the liberty of all, not to mandate our own moral code. The underlying constitutional issue is whether the State can resolve these philosophic questions in such a definitive way that a woman lacks all choice in the matter, except perhaps in those rare circumstances in which the pregnancy is itself a danger to her own life or health, or is the result of rape or incest.

It is conventional constitutional doctrine that where reasonable people disagree the government can adopt one position or the other.... That theorem, however, assumes a state of affairs in which the choice does not intrude upon a protected liberty. Thus, while some people might disagree about whether or not the flag should be saluted, or disagree about the proposition that it may not be defiled, we have ruled that a State may not compel or enforce one view or the other.... Our law affords constitutional protection to personal decisions relating to marriage, procreation, contraception, family relationships, child rearing, and education.... Our cases recognize "the right of the *individual,* married or single, to be free from unwarranted governmental intrusion into matters so fundamentally affecting a person as the decision whether to bear or beget a child." Eisenstadt v. Baird. Our precedents "have respected the private realm of family life which the state cannot enter." Prince v. Massachusetts (1944). These matters, involving the most intimate and personal choices a person may make in a lifetime, choices central to personal dignity and autonomy, are central to the liberty protected by the Fourteenth Amendment. At the heart of liberty is the right to define one's own concept of existence, of meaning, of the universe, and of the mystery of human life. Beliefs about these matters could not define the attributes of personhood were they formed under compulsion of the State.

These considerations begin our analysis of the woman's interest in terminating her pregnancy but cannot end it, for this reason: though the abortion decision may originate within the zone of conscience and belief, it is more than a philosophic exercise. Abortion is a unique act. It is an act fraught with consequences for others: for the woman who must live with the implications of her decision; for the persons who perform and assist in the procedure; for the spouse, family, and society which must confront the knowledge that these procedures exist, procedures some deem nothing short of an act of violence against innocent human life; and, depending on one's beliefs, for the life or potential life that is aborted. Though abortion is conduct, it does not follow that the State is entitled to proscribe it in all instances. That is because the liberty of the woman is at stake in a sense unique to the human condition and so unique to the law. The mother who carries a child to full term is subject to anxieties, to physical constraints, to pain that only she must bear. That these sacrifices have from the beginning of the human race been endured by woman with a pride that ennobles her in the eyes of others and gives to the infant a bond of love cannot alone be grounds for the State to insist she make the sacrifice. Her suffering is too intimate and personal for the State to insist, without more, upon its own vision of the woman's role, however dominant that vision has been in the course of our history and our culture. The destiny of the woman must be shaped to a large extent on her own conception of her spiritual imperatives and her place in society.

It should be recognized, moreover, that in some critical respects the abortion decision is of the same character as the decision to use contraception.... We have no doubt as to the correctness of those decisions. They support the reasoning in Roe relating to the woman's liberty because they involve personal decisions concerning not only the meaning of procreation but also human responsibility and respect for it. As with abortion, reasonable people will have differences of opinion about these matters. One view is based on such reverence for the wonder of creation that any pregnancy ought to be welcomed and carried to full term no matter how difficult it will be to provide for the child and ensure its well-being. Another is that the inability to provide for the nurture and care of the infant is a cruelty to the child and an anguish to the parent. These are intimate views with infinite variations, and their deep, personal character underlay our decisions in Griswold.... The same concerns are present when the woman confronts the reality that, perhaps despite her attempts to avoid it, she has become pregnant. It was this dimension of personal liberty that Roe sought to protect, and its holding invoked the reasoning and the tradition of the precedents we have discussed, granting protection to substantive liberties of the person....

Even when the decision to overrule a prior case is not, as in the rare, latter instance, virtually foreordained, it is common wisdom that the rule of *stare decisis* is not an "inexorable command," and certainly it is not such in every constitutional case.... Rather, when this Court reexamines a prior holding, its judgment is customarily informed by a series of prudential and pragmatic considerations designed to test the consistency of overruling a prior decision with the ideal of the rule of law, and to gauge the respective costs of reaffirming and overruling a prior case. Thus, for example, we may ask whether the rule has proven to be intolerable simply in defying practical workability ... whether the rule is subject to a kind of reliance that would lend a special hardship to the consequences of overruling and add inequity to the cost of repudiation ... whether related principles of law have so far developed as to have left the old rule no more than a remnant of abandoned doctrine ... or whether facts have so changed, or come to be seen so differently, as to have robbed the old rule of significant application or justification....

So in this case we may enquire whether Roe central rule has been found unworkable; whether the rule's limitation on state power could be removed without serious inequity to those who have relied upon it or significant damage to the stability of the society governed by it; whether the law's growth in the intervening years has left Roe central rule a doctrinal anachronism discounted by society; and whether Roe's premises of fact have so far changed in the ensuing two decades as to render its central holding somehow irrelevant or unjustifiable in dealing with the issue it addressed....

The sum of the precedential enquiry to this point shows Roe's underpinnings unweakened in any way affecting its central holding. While it has engendered disapproval, it has not been unworkable. An entire generation has come of age free to assume Roe's concept of liberty in defining the capacity of women to act in society, and to make reproductive decisions; no erosion of principle going to liberty or personal autonomy has left Roe's central holding a doctrinal remnant; Roe portends no developments at odds with other precedent for the analysis of personal liberty; and no changes of fact have rendered viability more or less appropriate as the point at which the balance of interests tips. Within the bounds of normal *stare decisis* analysis, then, and subject to the considerations on which it customarily turns, the stronger argument is for affirming Roe's central holding, with whatever degree of personal reluctance any of us may have, not for overruling it....

From what we have said so far it follows that it is a constitutional liberty of the woman to have some freedom to terminate her pregnancy. We conclude that the basic decision in Roe was based on a constitutional analysis which we cannot now repudiate. The woman's liberty is not so unlimited, however, that from the outset the State cannot show its concern for the life of the unborn, and at a later point in fetal development the State's interest in life has sufficient force so that the right of the woman to terminate the pregnancy can be restricted.... That brings us, of course, to the point where much criticism has been directed at Roe, a criticism that always inheres when the Court draws a specific rule from what in the Constitution is but a general standard. We conclude, however, that the urgent claims of the woman to retain the ultimate control over her destiny and her body, claims implicit in the meaning of liberty, require us to perform that function.

Liberty must not be extinguished for want of a line that is clear. And it falls to us to give some real substance to the woman's liberty to determine whether to carry her pregnancy to full term.

We conclude the line should be drawn at viability, so that before that time the woman has a right to choose to terminate her pregnancy. We adhere to this principle for two reasons. First, as we have said, is the doctrine of *stare decisis.* Any judicial act of line-drawing may seem somewhat arbitrary, but Roe was a reasoned statement, elaborated with great care.... It is that premise which we reaffirm today. The second reason is that the concept of viability, as we noted in Roe is the time at which there is a realistic possibility of maintaining and nourishing a life outside the womb, so that the independent existence of the second life can in reason and all fairness be the object of state protection that now overrides the rights of the woman.... The woman's right to terminate her pregnancy before viability is the most central principle of Roe v. Wade. It is a rule of law and a component of liberty we cannot renounce....

Yet it must be remembered that Roe v. Wade speaks with clarity in establishing not only the woman's liberty but also the State's "important and legitimate interest in potential life." ... That portion of the decision in Roe has been given too little acknowledgment and implementation by the Court in its subsequent cases. Those cases decided that any regulation touching upon the abortion decision must survive strict scrutiny, to be sustained only if drawn in narrow terms to further a compelling state interest.... Not all of the cases decided under that formulation can be reconciled with the holding in Roe itself that the State has legitimate interests in the health of the woman and in protecting the potential life within her.... Roe established a trimester framework to govern abortion regulations. Under this elaborate but rigid construct, almost no regulation at all is permitted during the first trimester of pregnancy; regulations designed to protect the woman's health, but not to further the State's interest in potential life, are permitted during the second trimester; and during the third trimester, when the fetus is viable, prohibitions are permitted provided the life or health of the mother is not at stake.... The trimester framework no doubt was erected to ensure that the woman's right to choose not become so subordinate to the State's interest in promoting fetal life that her choice exists in theory but not in fact. We do not agree, however, that the trimester approach is necessary to accomplish this objective. A framework of this rigidity was unnecessary and in its later interpretation sometimes contradicted the State's permissible exercise of its powers.

Though the woman has a right to choose to terminate or continue her pregnancy before viability, it does not at all follow that the State is prohibited from taking steps to ensure that this choice is thoughtful and informed. Even in the earliest stages of pregnancy, the State may enact rules and regulations designed to encourage her to know that there are philosophic and social arguments of great weight that can be brought to bear in favor of continuing the pregnancy to full term and that there are procedures and institutions to allow adoption of unwanted children as well as a certain degree of state assistance if the mother chooses to raise the child herself. "'[T]he Constitution does not forbid a State or city, pursuant to democratic processes, from expressing a preference for normal childbirth.'" ... It follows that States are free to enact laws to provide a reasonable framework for a woman to make a decision that has such profound and lasting meaning. This, too, we find consistent with Roe's central premises, and indeed the inevitable consequence of our holding that the State has an interest in protecting the life of the unborn.

We reject the trimester framework, which we do not consider to be part of the essential holding of Roe.... Measures aimed at ensuring that a woman's choice contemplates the consequences for the fetus do not necessarily interfere with the right recognized in Roe although those measures have been found to be inconsistent with the rigid trimester framework announced in that case. A logical reading of the central holding in Roe itself, and a necessary reconciliation of the liberty of the woman and the interest of the State in promoting prenatal life, require, in our view, that we abandon the trimester framework as a rigid prohibition on all previability regulation aimed at the protection of fetal life. The trimester framework suffers from these basic flaws: in its formulation it misconceives the nature of the pregnant woman's interest; and in practice it undervalues the State's interest in potential life, as recognized in Roe.

As our jurisprudence relating to all liberties save perhaps abortion has recognized, not every law which makes a right more difficult to exercise is, *ipso facto*, an infringement of that right.... The abortion right is similar. Numerous forms of state regulation might have the incidental effect of increasing the cost or decreasing the availability of medical care, whether for abortion or any other medical procedure. The fact that a law which serves a valid purpose, one not designed to strike at the right itself, has the incidental effect of making it more difficult or more expensive to procure an abortion cannot be enough to invalidate it. Only where state regulation imposes an undue burden on a woman's ability to make this decision does the power of the State reach into the heart of the liberty protected by the Due Process Clause....

The very notion that the State has a substantial interest in potential life leads to the conclusion that not all regulations must be deemed unwarranted. Not all burdens on the right to decide whether to terminate a pregnancy will be undue. In our view, the undue burden standard is the appropriate means of reconciling the State's interest with the woman's constitutionally protected liberty.... What is at stake is the woman's right to make the ultimate decision, not a right to be insulated from all others in doing so. Regulations which do no more than create a structural mechanism by which the State, or the parent or guardian of a minor, may express profound respect for the life of the unborn are permitted, if they are not a substantial obstacle to the woman's exercise of the right to choose.... Unless it has that effect on her right of choice, a state measure designed to persuade her to choose childbirth over abortion will be upheld if reasonably related to that goal. Regulations designed to foster the health of a woman seeking an abortion are valid if they do not constitute an undue burden.... We now consider the separate statutory sections at issue.

Because it is central to the operation of various other requirements, we begin with the statute's definition of medical emergency.... Petitioners argue that the definition is too narrow, contending that it forecloses the possibility of an immediate abortion despite some significant health risks ... While the definition could be interpreted in an unconstitutional manner, the Court of Appeals construed the phrase [as follows]: "[W]e read the medical emergency exception as intended by the Pennsylvania legislature to assure that compliance with its abortion regulations would not in any way pose a significant threat to the life or health of a woman." ... We adhere to that course today, and conclude that, as construed by the Court of Appeals, the medical emergency definition imposes no undue burden on a woman's abortion right....

We next consider the informed consent requirement.... Our prior decisions establish that as with any medical procedure, the State may require a woman to give her written informed consent to an abortion.... In this respect, the statute is unexceptional. Petitioners challenge the statute's definition of informed consent because it includes the provision of specific information by the doctor and the mandatory 24-hour waiting period.... To the extent [that our earlier cases] find a constitutional violation when the government requires, as it does here, the giving of truthful, nonmisleading information about the nature of the procedure, the attendant health risks and those of childbirth, and the "probable gestational age" of the fetus, those cases go too far, are inconsistent with Roe's acknowledgment of an important interest in potential life, and are overruled.... It cannot be questioned that psychological well-being is a facet of health. Nor can it be doubted that most women considering an abortion would deem the impact on the fetus relevant, if not dispositive, to the decision. In attempting to ensure that a woman apprehend the full consequences of her decision, the State furthers the legitimate purpose of reducing the risk that a woman may elect an abortion, only to discover later, with devastating psychological consequences, that her decision was not fully informed. If the information the State requires to be made available to the woman is truthful and not misleading, the requirement may be permissible.... This requirement cannot be considered a substantial obstacle to obtaining an abortion, and, it follows, there is no undue burden....

Whether the mandatory 24-hour waiting period is nonetheless invalid because in practice it is a substantial obstacle to a woman's choice to terminate her pregnancy is a closer question. The findings of fact by the District Court indicate that because of the distances many women must travel to reach an abortion provider, the practical effect will often be a delay of much more than a day because the waiting period requires that a woman seeking an abortion make at least two visits to the doctor. The District Court also found that in many instances this will increase the exposure of women seeking abortions to "the harassment and hostility of anti-abortion protestors demonstrating outside a clinic."... As a result, the District Court found that for those women who have the fewest financial resources, those who must travel long distances, and those who have difficulty explaining their whereabouts to husbands, employers, or others, the 24-hour waiting period will be "particularly burdensome."...

These findings are troubling in some respects, but they do not demonstrate that the waiting period constitutes an undue burden. We do not doubt that, as the District Court held, the waiting period has the effect of "increasing the cost and risk of delay of abortions,"... but the District Court did not conclude that the increased costs and potential delays amount to substantial obstacles. Rather, applying the trimester framework's strict prohibition of all regulation designed to promote the State's interest in potential life before viability, ... the District Court concluded that the waiting period does not further the state "interest in maternal health" and "infringes the physician's discretion to exercise sound medical judgment".... Yet, as we have stated, under the undue burden standard a State is permitted to enact persuasive measures which favor childbirth over abortion, even if those measures do not further a health interest. And while the waiting period does limit a physician's discretion, that is not, standing alone, a reason to invalidate it. In light of the construction given the statute's definition of medical emergency by the Court of Appeals, and the District Court's findings, we cannot say that the waiting period imposes a real health risk....

The spousal notification requirement [imposed by the statute on married women] is ... likely to prevent a significant number of women from obtaining an abortion. [The Court based this decision on detailed findings about domestic violence made by the lower court.] It does not merely make abortions a little more difficult or expensive to obtain; for many women, it will impose a substantial obstacle. We must not blind ourselves to the fact that the significant number of women who fear for their safety and the safety of their children are likely to be deterred from procuring an abortion as surely as if the Commonwealth had outlawed abortion in all cases.... There was a time, not so long ago, when a different understanding of the family and of the Constitution prevailed. In Bradwell v. State (1873) three Members of this Court reaffirmed the common-law principle that "a woman had no legal existence separate from her husband, who was regarded as her head and representative in the social state; and, notwithstanding some recent modifications of this civil status, many of the special rules of law flowing from and dependent upon this cardinal principle still exist in full force in most States." ... Only one generation has passed since this Court observed that "woman is still regarded as the center of home and family life," with attendant "special responsibilities" that precluded full and independent legal status under the Constitution.... These views, of course, are no longer consistent with our understanding of the family, the individual, or the Constitution....

We next consider the parental consent provision. Except in a medical emergency, an unemancipated young woman under 18 may not obtain an abortion unless she and one of her parents (or guardian) provides informed consent as defined above. If neither a parent nor a guardian provides consent, a court may authorize the performance of an abortion upon a determination that the young woman is mature and capable of giving informed consent and has in fact given her informed consent, or that an abortion would be in her best interests.

We have been over most of this ground before. Our cases establish, and we reaffirm today, that a State may require a minor seeking an abortion to obtain the consent of a parent or guardian, provided that there is an adequate judicial bypass procedure....

Affirmed in part, reversed in part, and remanded.

JUSTICE BLACKMUN, concurring in part, concurring in the judgment in part, and dissenting in part.

Three years ago, in Webster v. Reproductive Health Services (1989), four Members of this Court appeared poised to "cas[t] into darkness the hopes and visions of every woman in this country" who had come to believe that the Constitution guaranteed her the right to reproductive choice.... All that remained between the promise of Roe and the darkness of the plurality was a single, flickering flame. Decisions since Webster gave little reason to hope that this flame would cast much light. But now, just when so many expected the darkness to fall, the flame has grown bright. I do not underestimate the significance of today's joint opinion. Yet I remain steadfast in my belief that the right to reproductive choice is entitled to the full protection afforded by this Court before Webster. And I fear for the darkness as four Justices anxiously await the single vote necessary to extinguish the light....

At long last, the Chief Justice and those who have joined him admit it. Gone are the contentions that the issue need not be (or has not been) considered. There, on the first page, for all to see, is what was expected: "We believe that Roe was wrongly decided, and that it can and should be overruled consistently with our traditional approach to *stare decisis* in constitutional cases." ... The chief Justice's criticism of Roe follows from his stunted conception of individual liberty. While recognizing that the Due Process Clause protects more than simple physical liberty, he then goes on to construe this Court's personal-liberty cases as establishing only a laundry list of particular rights, rather than a principled account of how these particular rights are grounded in a more general right of privacy.... This constricted view is reinforced by the Chief Justice's exclusive reliance on tradition as a source of fundamental rights.... Even more shocking than the Chief Justice's cramped notion of individual liberty is his complete omission of any discussion of the effects that compelled childbirth and motherhood have on women's lives. The only expression of concern with women's health is purely instrumental—for the Chief Justice, only women's *psychological* health is a concern, and only to the extent that he assumes that every woman who decides to have an abortion does so without serious consideration of the moral implications of their decision.... The Chief Justice's narrow conception of individual liberty and *stare decisis* leads him to propose the same standard of review proposed by the plurality in Webster. "States may regulate abortion procedures in ways rationally related to a legitimate state interest."....

In one sense, the Court's approach is worlds apart from that of the Chief Justice and Justice Scalia. And yet, in another sense, the distance between the two approaches is short—the distance is but a single vote. I am 83 years old. I cannot remain on this Court forever, and when I do step down, the confirmation process for my successor well may focus on the issue before us today. That, I regret, may be exactly where the choice between the two worlds will be made.

CHIEF JUSTICE REHNQUIST, with whom JUSTICE WHITE, JUSTICE SCALIA, and JUSTICE THOMAS join, concurring in the judgment in part and dissenting in part.

The joint opinion, following its newly minted variation on *stare decisis,* retains the outer shell of Roe v. Wade, but beats a wholesale retreat from the substance of that case. We believe that Roe was wrongly decided, and that it can and should be overruled consistently with our traditional approach to *stare decisis* in constitutional cases....

We have held that a liberty interest protected under the Due Process Clause of the Fourteenth Amendment will be deemed fundamental if it is "implicit in the concept of ordered liberty." Palko v. Connecticut (1937). Three years earlier, in Snyder v. Massachusetts, we referred to a "principle of justice so rooted in the traditions and conscience of our people as to be ranked as fundamental." ... These expressions are admittedly not precise, but our decisions implementing this notion of "fundamental" rights do not afford any more elaborate basis on which to base such a classification.

In construing the phrase "liberty" incorporated in the Due Process Clause of the Fourteenth Amendment, we have recognized that its meaning extends beyond freedom from physical restraint. In Pierce v. Society of Sisters (1925), we held that it included a parent's right to send a child to private school; in Meyer v. Nebraska (1923), we held that it included a right to teach a foreign language in a parochial school. Building on these cases, we have held that the term "liberty" includes a right to marry, Loving v. Virginia (1967); a right to procreate, Skinner v. Oklahoma (1942); and a right to use contraceptives, Griswold v. Connecticut (1965). But a reading of these opinions makes clear that they do not endorse any all-encompassing "right of privacy."

In Roe v. Wade, the Court recognized a "guarantee of personal privacy" which "is broad enough to encompass a woman's decision whether or not to terminate her pregnancy." ... We are now of the view that, in terming this right fundamental, the Court in Roe read the earlier opinions upon which it based its decision much too broadly. Unlike marriage, procreation, and contraception, abortion "involves the purposeful termination of a potential life." ... The abortion decision must therefore "be recognized as *sui generis,* different in kind from the others that the Court has protected under the rubric of personal or family privacy and autonomy." ...

Nor do the historical traditions of the American people support the view that the right to terminate one's pregnancy is "fundamental." The common law which we inherited from England made abortion after "quickening" an offense. At the time of the adoption of the Fourteenth Amendment, statutory prohibitions or restrictions on abortion were commonplace; in 1868, at least 28 of the then-37 States and 8 Territories had statutes banning or limiting abortion. J. Mohr, Abortion in America 200 (1978). By the turn of the century virtually every State had a law prohibiting or restricting abortion on its books. By the middle of the present century, a liberalization trend had set in. But 21 of the restrictive abortion laws in effect in 1868 were still in effect in 1973 when Roe was decided, and an overwhelming majority of the States prohibited abortion unless necessary to preserve the life or health of the mother.... On this record, it can scarcely be said that any deeply rooted tradition of relatively unrestricted abortion in our history supported the classification of the right to abortion as "fundamental" under the Due Process Clause of the Fourteenth Amendment.

[handwritten margin note: Abortion not "deeply rooted" tradition.]

JUSTICE SCALIA, with whom THE CHIEF JUSTICE, JUSTICE WHITE, and JUSTICE THOMAS join, concurring in the judgment in part and dissenting in part.

The Imperial Judiciary lives. It is instructive to compare this Nietzschean vision of us unelected, life-tenured judges—leading a Volk who will be "tested by following," and whose very "belief in themselves" is mystically bound up in their "understanding" of a Court that "speak[s] before all others for their constitutional ideals"—with the somewhat more modest role envisioned for these lawyers by the Founders.

> The judiciary ... has ... no direction either of the strength or of the wealth of the society, and can take no active resolution whatever. It may truly be said to have neither Force nor Will, but merely judgment.

Or, again, to compare this ecstasy of a Supreme Court in which there is, especially on controversial matters, no shadow of change or hint of alteration ... with the more democratic views of a more humble man:

> [T]he candid citizen must confess that if the policy of the Government upon vital questions affecting the whole people is to be irrevocably fixed by decisions of the Supreme Court, ... the people will have ceased to be their own rulers, having to that extent practically resigned their Government into the hands of that eminent tribunal.

It is particularly difficult, in the circumstances of the present decision, to sit still for the Court's lengthy lecture upon the virtues of "constancy," ... of "remain[ing] steadfast," ... of adhering to "principle...." Among the five Justices who purportedly adhere to Roe, at most three agree upon the *principle* that constitutes adherence (the joint opinion's "undue burden" standard)—and that principle is inconsistent with Roe.... To make matters worse, two of the three, in order thus to remain steadfast, had to abandon previously stated positions.... It is beyond me how the Court expects these accommodations to be accepted "as grounded truly in principle, not as compromises with social and political pressures having, as such, no bearing on the principled choices that the Court is obliged to make." ... The only principle the Court "adheres" to, it seems to me, is the principle that the Court must be seen as standing by Roe. That is not a principle of law (which is what I thought the Court was talking about), but a principle of *Realpolitik*—and a wrong one at that.

I cannot agree with, indeed I am appalled by, the Court's suggestion that the decision whether to stand by an erroneous constitutional decision must be strongly influenced—*against* overruling, no less—by the substantial and continuing public opposition the decision has generated. The Court's judgment that any other course would "subvert the Court's legitimacy" must be another consequence of reading the error-filled history book that described the deeply divided country brought together by Roe. In my history-book, the Court was covered with dishonor and deprived of legitimacy by Dred Scott v. Sanford, an erroneous (and widely opposed) opinion that it did not abandon, rather than by West Coast Hotel v. Parrish, which produced the famous "switch in time" from the Court's erroneous (and widely opposed) constitutional opposition to the social measures of the New Deal....

But whether it would "subvert the Court's legitimacy" or not, the notion that we would decide a case differently from the way we otherwise would have in order to show that we can stand firm against public disapproval is frightening. It is a bad enough idea, even in the head of someone like me, who believes that the text of the Constitution, and our traditions, say what they say and there is no fiddling with them. But when it is in the mind of a Court that believes the Constitution has an evolving meaning, ... that the Ninth Amendment's reference to "othe [r]" rights is not a disclaimer, but a charter for action ... and that the function of this Court is to "speak before all others for [the people's] constitutional ideals" unrestrained by meaningful text or tradition—then the notion that the Court must adhere to a decision for as long as the decision faces "great opposition" and the Court is "under fire" acquires a character of almost czarist arrogance. We are offended by these marchers who descend upon us, every year on the anniversary of Roe, to protest our saying that the Constitution requires what our society has never thought the Constitution requires. These people who refuse to be "tested by following" must be taught a lesson. We have no Cossacks, but at least we can stubbornly refuse to abandon an erroneous opinion that we might otherwise change—to show how little they intimidate us.

Of course, as the Chief Justice points out, we have been subjected to what the Court calls "'political pressure'" by *both* sides of this issue.... Maybe today's decision *not* to overrule Roe will be seen as buckling to pressure from *that* direction. Instead of engaging in the hopeless task of predicting public perception—a job not for lawyers but for political campaign managers—the Justices should do what is *legally* right by asking two questions: (1) Was Roe correctly decided? (2) Has Roe succeeded in producing a settled body of law? If the answer to both questions is no, Roe should undoubtedly be overruled.

In truth, I am as distressed as the Court is—and expressed my distress several years ago ... about the "political pressure" directed to the Court: the marches, the mail, the protests aimed at inducing us to change our opinions. How upsetting it is, that so many of our citizens (good people, not lawless ones, on both sides of this abortion issue, and on various sides of other issues as well) think that we Justices should properly take into account their views, as though we were engaged not in ascertaining an objective law but in determining some kind of social consensus. The Court would profit, I think, from giving less attention to the *fact* of this distressing phenomenon, and more attention to the *cause* of it. That cause permeates today's opinion: a new mode of constitutional adjudication that relies not upon text and traditional practice to determine the law, but upon what the Court calls "reasoned judgment," ... which turns out to be nothing but philosophical predilection and moral intuition. All manner of "liberties," the Court tells us, inhere in the Constitution and are enforceable by this Court—not just those mentioned in the text or established in the traditions of our society.... Why even the Ninth Amendment—which says only that "[t]he enumeration in the Constitution, of certain rights, shall not be construed to deny or disparage others retained by the people"—is, despite our contrary understanding for almost 200 years, a literally boundless source of additional, unnamed, unhinted—at "rights," definable and enforceable by us, through "reasoned judgment." ...

What makes all this relevant to the bothersome application of "political pressure" against the Court are the twin facts that the American people love democracy and the American people are not fools. As long as this Court thought (and the people thought) that we Justices were doing essentially lawyers' work up here—reading text and discerning our society's traditional understanding of that text—the public pretty much left us alone. Texts and traditions are facts to study, not convictions to demonstrate about. But if in reality our process of constitutional adjudication consists primarily of making *value judgments*; if we can ignore a long and clear tradition clarifying an ambiguous text ... then a free and intelligent people's attitude towards us can be expected to be (*ought* to be) quite different. The people know that their value judgments are quite as good as those taught in any law school — maybe better. If, indeed, the "liberties" protected by the Constitution are, as the Court says, undefined and unbounded, then the people *should* demonstrate, to protest that we do not implement *their* values instead of *ours*. Not only that, but confirmation hearings for new Justices *should* deteriorate into question-and-answer sessions in which Senators go through a list of their constituents' most favored and most disfavored alleged constitutional rights, and seek the nominee's commitment to support or oppose them. Value judgments, after all, should be voted on, not dictated; and if our Constitution has somehow accidently committed them to the Supreme Court, at least we can have a sort of plebiscite each time a new nominee to that body is put forward. Justice Blackmun not only regards this prospect with equanimity, he solicits it....

We should get out of this area, where we have no right to be, and where we do neither ourselves nor the country any good by remaining.

Review Questions and Explanations: *Casey*

1. *Planned Parenthood v. Casey* was decided in 1992, shortly after Justice Souter joined the Court. Souter was appointed by the first President Bush, a Republican. The Republican Party's position on abortion was still evolving at the time, and Souter's position on the question was unclear. Thus, while no one was really sure how he would vote, *Casey* was widely seen as the vehicle a new majority, one including Justice Souter, might use to strike down *Roe*. His decision to instead join the plurality opinion reaffirming the core holding of *Roe* infuriated many people, and may have contributed to the passion found in some of the dissents.

2. Reflect upon what Justice Scalia says in *Casey* about the Court and public opinion. Should the court be completely isolated from public opinion? If so, why? Should it be responsive to it? If so, in what ways? Recall that the Constitution itself sets up a confirmation process that makes the membership of the Court dependant on the preferences of elected officials. What, if anything, does this tell us about what the founders thought about the relationship between the Court and the public?

Professional Development Reflection Question

As a lawyer, how you talk about the Constitution will influence what the non-lawyers in your life think about it. How should this power influence how you talk about controversial cases? Smart lawyers can use their knowledge to craft arguments that appear unassailable to those without legal training, or they can use that knowledge to give non-lawyers better tools with which to form their own opinions. If you were conversing with someone about an issue outside of your area of expertise, such as talking about a medical issue with a doctor, which approach would you want her to take?

CASE NOTE: In 2007, the Court decided *Gonzales v. Carhart*. *Gonzales* involved a challenge to a federal law that completely prohibited a certain type of abortion procedure. Medically, the prohibited procedure is known as an "intact D&E" (or a "D&X", for dilation and extraction). Opponents of the procedure refer to it as "partial birth abortion." A doctor performing an intact D&E extracts the fetus part way out of the woman's vagina before dismantling it. The ban was different than much of the legislation the Court had examined since *Roe*, in that it did not include an exception to protect either the life or health of the woman. The Court, in an emotional decision written by Justice Kennedy, sustained the federal law against a Fourteenth Amendment challenge, making it the first abortion restriction not including a life or health exception ever to be upheld by the Court.

Like all of the Court's decisions in this area, *Gonzales* was, and remains, controversial. Justice Ginsburg's dissent accuses the majority of writing its own version of morality into the Constitution by allowing the legislature to completely ban a particular *type* of abortion procedure even when a doctor believed it would be the safer option for his or her patient. Justice Kennedy's opinion, on the other hand, argues that the state interest in "preserving and promoting fetal life" allows Congress to ban a procedure that it believed would "coarsen society to the humanity of not only newborns, but all vulnerable and innocent human life," even if the number of abortions is itself not reduced by banning a given procedure. This same issue—the extent to which moral judgments can, without more, constitute a sufficient reason for governmental actions infringing on personal liberties—is at issue in the following case. It also is debated at length in *Lawrence v. Texas*, which follows *Washington v. Glucksberg*.

Washington v. Glucksberg
521 U.S. 702 (1997)

Majority: *Rehnquist* (CJ), O'Connor, Scalia, Kennedy, Thomas

Concurrence/concurrences in the judgment: *O'Connor, Ginsburg, Breyer; Stevens; Souter* (all but Souter omitted)

CHIEF JUSTICE REHNQUIST delivered the opinion of the Court.

The question presented in this case is whether Washington's prohibition against "caus[ing]" or "aid[ing]" a suicide offends the Fourteenth Amendment to the United States Constitution. We hold that it does not....

Petitioners in this case are the State of Washington and its Attorney General. Respondents Harold Glucksberg, M. D., Abigail Halperin, M. D., Thomas A. Preston, M. D., and Peter Shalit, M. D., are physicians who practice in Washington. These doctors occasionally treat terminally ill, suffering patients, and declare that they would assist these patients in ending their lives if not for Washington's assisted-suicide ban. In January 1994, respondents, along with three gravely ill, pseudonymous plaintiffs who have since died and Compassion in Dying, a nonprofit organization that counsels people considering physician-assisted suicide, sued in the United States District Court, seeking a declaration that Wash.Rev.Code § 9A.36.060(1) (1994) is, on its face, unconstitutional....

The plaintiffs asserted "the existence of a liberty interest protected by the Fourteenth Amendment which extends to a personal choice by a mentally competent, terminally ill adult to commit physician-assisted suicide." ... We begin, as we do in all due process cases, by examining our Nation's history, legal traditions, and practices.... In almost every State—

indeed, in almost every western democracy—it is a crime to assist a suicide. The States' assisted-suicide bans are not innovations. Rather, they are longstanding expressions of the States' commitment to the protection and preservation of all human life....

More specifically, for over 700 years, the Anglo-American common-law tradition has punished or otherwise disapproved of both suicide and assisting suicide.... In the 13th century, Henry de Bracton, one of the first legal-treatise writers, observed that "[j]ust as a man may commit felony by slaying another so may he do so by slaying himself."... The real and personal property of one who killed himself to avoid conviction and punishment for a crime were forfeit to the King; however, thought Bracton, "if a man slays himself in weariness of life or because he is unwilling to endure further bodily pain ... [only] his movable goods [were] confiscated."... Thus, "[t]he principle that suicide of a sane person, for whatever reason, was a punishable felony was ... introduced into English common law." Centuries later, Sir William Blackstone, whose Commentaries on the Laws of England not only provided a definitive summary of the common law but was also a primary legal authority for 18th- and 19th-century American lawyers, referred to suicide as "self-murder" and "the pretended heroism, but real cowardice, of the Stoic philosophers, who destroyed themselves to avoid those ills which they had not the fortitude to endure...." 4 W. Blackstone, Commentaries. Blackstone emphasized that "the law has ... ranked [suicide] among the highest crimes,"... although, anticipating later developments, he conceded that the harsh and shameful punishments imposed for suicide "borde[r] a little upon severity."...

For the most part, the early American Colonies adopted the common-law approach. For example, the legislators of the Providence Plantations, which would later become Rhode Island, declared, in 1647, that "[s]elf-murder is by all agreed to be the most unnatural, and it is by this present Assembly declared, to be that, wherein he that doth it, kills himself out of a premeditated hatred against his own life or other humor: ... his goods and chattels are the king's custom, but not his debts nor lands; but in case he be an infant, a lunatic, mad or distracted man, he forfeits nothing."... Over time, however, the American Colonies abolished these harsh common-law penalties. William Penn abandoned the criminal-forfeiture sanction in Pennsylvania in 1701, and the other Colonies (and later, the other States) eventually followed this example.... Zephaniah Swift, who would later become Chief Justice of Connecticut, wrote in 1796:

> There can be no act more contemptible, than to attempt to punish an offender for a crime, by exercising a mean act of revenge upon lifeless clay, that is insensible of the punishment. There can be no greater cruelty, than the inflicting [of] a punishment, as the forfeiture of goods, which must fall solely on the innocent offspring of the offender.... [Suicide] is so abhorrent to the feelings of mankind, and that strong love of life which is implanted in the human heart, that it cannot be so frequently committed, as to become dangerous to society. There can of course be no necessity of any punishment.

This statement makes it clear, however, that the movement away from the common law's harsh sanctions did not represent an acceptance of suicide; rather, as Chief Justice Swift observed, this change reflected the growing consensus that it was unfair to punish the suicide's family for his wrongdoing.... The earliest American statute explicitly to outlaw assisting suicide was enacted in New York in 1828 ... and many of the new States and Territories followed New York's example....

Though deeply rooted, the States' assisted-suicide bans have in recent years been re-examined and, generally, reaffirmed. Because of advances in medicine and technology, Americans today are increasingly likely to die in institutions, from chronic illnesses....

Public concern and democratic action are therefore sharply focused on how best to protect dignity and independence at the end of life, with the result that there have been many significant changes in state laws and in the attitudes these laws reflect.... Thus, the States are currently engaged in serious, thoughtful examinations of physician-assisted suicide and other similar issues.... Against this backdrop of history, tradition, and practice, we now turn to respondents' constitutional claim.

The Due Process Clause guarantees more than fair process, and the "liberty" it protects includes more than the absence of physical restraint.... The Clause also provides heightened protection against government interference with certain fundamental rights and liberty interests.... In a long line of cases, we have held that, in addition to the specific freedoms protected by the Bill of Rights, the "liberty" specially protected by the Due Process Clause includes the rights to marry ... to have children ... to direct the education and upbringing of one's children ... to marital privacy ... to use contraception ... to bodily integrity ... and to abortion.... We have also assumed, and strongly suggested, that the Due Process Clause protects the traditional right to refuse unwanted lifesaving medical treatment....

But we "ha[ve] always been reluctant to expand the concept of substantive due process because guideposts for responsible decisionmaking in this unchartered area are scarce and open-ended." By extending constitutional protection to an asserted right or liberty interest, we, to a great extent, place the matter outside the arena of public debate and legislative action. We must therefore "exercise the utmost care whenever we are asked to break new ground in this field," ... lest the liberty protected by the Due Process Clause be subtly transformed into the policy preferences of the Members of this Court....

Our established method of substantive-due-process analysis has two primary features: First, we have regularly observed that the Due Process Clause specially protects those fundamental rights and liberties which are, objectively, "deeply rooted in this Nation's history and tradition," ... and "implicit in the concept of ordered liberty," such that "neither liberty nor justice would exist if they were sacrificed," Palko v. Connecticut (1937). Second, we have required in substantive-due-process cases a "careful description" of the asserted fundamental liberty interest. Our Nation's history, legal traditions, and practices thus provide the crucial "guideposts for responsible decisionmaking" ... that direct and restrain our exposition of the Due Process Clause. As we stated recently ... the Fourteenth Amendment "forbids the government to infringe ... 'fundamental' liberty interests *at all,* no matter what process is provided, unless the infringement is narrowly tailored to serve a compelling state interest." ...

Justice Souter, relying on Justice Harlan's dissenting opinion in Poe v. Ullman, would largely abandon this restrained methodology, and instead ask "whether [Washington's] statute sets up one of those 'arbitrary impositions' or 'purposeless restraints' at odds with the Due Process Clause of the Fourteenth Amendment...." In our view, however, the development of this Court's substantive-due-process jurisprudence ... has been a process whereby the outlines of the "liberty" specially protected by the Fourteenth Amendment — never fully clarified, to be sure, and perhaps not capable of being fully clarified — have at least been carefully refined by concrete examples involving fundamental rights found to be deeply rooted in our legal tradition. This approach tends to rein in the subjective elements that are necessarily present in due-process judicial review. In addition, by establishing a threshold requirement — that a challenged state action implicate a fundamental right — before requiring more than a reasonable relation to a legitimate state interest to justify the action, it avoids the need for complex balancing of competing interests in every case.

Turning to the claim at issue here, the Court of Appeals stated that "[p]roperly analyzed, the first issue to be resolved is whether there is a liberty interest in determining the time and manner of one's death,"... or, in other words, "[i]s there a right to die?"... Similarly, respondents assert a "liberty to choose how to die" and a right to "control of one's final days,"... and describe the asserted liberty as "the right to choose a humane, dignified death,"... and "the liberty to shape death...." As noted above, we have a tradition of carefully formulating the interest at stake in substantive-due-process cases. The Washington statute at issue in this case prohibits "aid[ing] another person to attempt suicide," and, thus, the question before us is whether the "liberty" specially protected by the Due Process Clause includes a right to commit suicide which itself includes a right to assistance in doing so.

We now inquire whether this asserted right has any place in our Nation's traditions. Here... we are confronted with a consistent and almost universal tradition that has long rejected the asserted right, and continues explicitly to reject it today, even for terminally ill, mentally competent adults. To hold for respondents, we would have to reverse centuries of legal doctrine and practice, and strike down the considered policy choice of almost every State....

Respondents also rely on Casey. There, the Court's opinion concluded that "the essential holding of Roe v. Wade should be retained and once again reaffirmed." In reaching [its] conclusion, the opinion discussed in some detail this Court's substantive-due-process tradition of interpreting the Due Process Clause to protect certain fundamental rights and "personal decisions relating to marriage, procreation, contraception, family relationships, child rearing, and education," and noted that many of those rights and liberties "involv[e] the most intimate and personal choices a person may make in a lifetime."... "At the heart of liberty is the right to define one's own concept of existence, of meaning, of the universe, and of the mystery of human life. Beliefs about these matters could not define the attributes of personhood were they formed under compulsion of the State."...

By choosing this language, the Court's opinion in Casey described, in a general way and in light of our prior cases, those personal activities and decisions that this Court has identified as so deeply rooted in our history and traditions, or so fundamental to our concept of constitutionally ordered liberty, that they are protected by the Fourteenth Amendment. The opinion moved from the recognition that liberty necessarily includes freedom of conscience and belief about ultimate considerations to the observation that "though the abortion decision may originate within the zone of conscience and belief, it is *more than a philosophic exercise*." That many of the rights and liberties protected by the Due Process Clause sound in personal autonomy does not warrant the sweeping conclusion that any and all important, intimate, and personal decisions are so protected, ... and Casey did not suggest otherwise.

The history of the law's treatment of assisted suicide in this country has been and continues to be one of the rejection of nearly all efforts to permit it. That being the case, our decisions lead us to conclude that the asserted "right" to assistance in committing suicide is not a fundamental liberty interest protected by the Due Process Clause. The Constitution also requires, however, that Washington's assisted-suicide ban be rationally related to legitimate government interests.... This requirement is unquestionably met here. As the court below recognized, Washington's assisted-suicide ban implicates a number of state interests. [The Court goes on to hold that the statute is rationally related to Washington's interest in preserving human life, protecting the integrity of the medical profession, protecting the vulnerable from coercion and harmful stereotypes, and avoiding a slippery slope leading to euthanasia.]...

Reversed and remanded.

JUSTICE SOUTER, concurring in the judgment.

When the physicians claim that the Washington law deprives them of a right falling within the scope of liberty that the Fourteenth Amendment guarantees against denial without due process of law, they are not claiming some sort of procedural defect in the process through which the statute has been enacted or is administered. Their claim, rather, is that the State has no substantively adequate justification for barring the assistance sought by the patient and sought to be offered by the physician. Thus, we are dealing with a claim to one of those rights sometimes described as rights of substantive due process and sometimes as unenumerated rights, in view of the breadth and indeterminacy of the "due process" serving as the claim's textual basis. The doctors accordingly arouse the skepticism of those who find the Due Process Clause an unduly vague or oxymoronic warrant for judicial review of substantive state law, just as they also invoke two centuries of American constitutional practice in recognizing unenumerated, substantive limits on governmental action. Although this practice has neither rested on any single textual basis nor expressed a consistent theory (or, before Poe v. Ullman, a much articulated one), a brief overview of its history is instructive on two counts. The persistence of substantive due process in our cases points to the legitimacy of the modern justification for such judicial review found in Justice Harlan's dissent in Poe, on which I will dwell further on, while the acknowledged failures of some of these cases point with caution to the difficulty raised by the present claim.

Before the ratification of the Fourteenth Amendment, substantive constitutional review resting on a theory of unenumerated rights occurred largely in the state courts applying state constitutions that commonly contained either due process clauses like that of the Fifth Amendment (and later the Fourteenth) or the textual antecedents of such clauses, repeating Magna Carta's guarantee of "the law of the land." On the basis of such clauses, or of general principles untethered to specific constitutional language, state courts evaluated the constitutionality of a wide range of statutes. Thus, a Connecticut court approved a statute legitimating a class of previous illegitimate marriages, as falling within the terms of the "social compact," while making clear its power to review constitutionality in those terms.... In the same period, a specialized court of equity, created under a Tennessee statute solely to hear cases brought by the state bank against its debtors, found its own authorization unconstitutional as "partial" legislation violating the State Constitution's "law of the land" clause.... And the middle of the 19th century brought the famous Wynehamer case, invalidating a statute purporting to render possession of liquor immediately illegal except when kept for narrow, specified purposes, the state court finding the statute inconsistent with the State's due process clause. The statute was deemed an excessive threat to the "fundamental rights of the citizen" to property....

Even in this early period, however, this Court anticipated the developments that would presage both the Civil War and the ratification of the Fourteenth Amendment, by making it clear on several occasions that it too had no doubt of the judiciary's power to strike down legislation that conflicted with important but unenumerated principles of American government. In most such instances, after declaring its power to invalidate what it might find inconsistent with rights of liberty and property, the Court nevertheless went on to uphold the legislative Acts under review....

After the ratification of the Fourteenth Amendment, with its guarantee of due process protection against the States, interpretation of the words "liberty" and "property" as used in Due Process Clauses became a sustained enterprise, with the Court generally describing the due process criterion in converse terms of reasonableness or arbitrariness. That standard is fairly traceable to Justice Bradley's dissent in the Slaughter-House Cases, in which he said that a person's right to choose a calling was an element of liberty (as the calling, once chosen, was an aspect of property) and declared that the liberty and property protected by due process are not truly recognized if such rights may be "arbitrarily assailed." ... After that, opinions comparable to those that preceded Dred Scott expressed willingness to review legislative action for consistency with the Due Process Clause even as they upheld the laws in question....

The theory became serious, however, beginning with Allgeyer v. Louisiana (1897), where the Court invalidated a Louisiana statute for excessive interference with Fourteenth Amendment liberty to contract, ... and offered a substantive interpretation of "liberty," that in the aftermath of the so-called Lochner Era has been scaled back in some respects, but expanded in others, and never repudiated in principle. The Court said that Fourteenth Amendment liberty includes "the right of the citizen to be free in the enjoyment of all his faculties; to be free to use them in all lawful ways; to live and work where he will; to earn his livelihood by any lawful calling; to pursue any livelihood or avocation; and for that purpose to enter into all contracts which may be proper, necessary and essential to his carrying out to a successful conclusion the purposes above mentioned." ...

Although this principle was unobjectionable, what followed for a season was, in the realm of economic legislation, the echo of Dred Scott. Allegeyer was succeeded within a decade by Lochner v. New York, and the era to which that case gave its name, famous now for striking down as arbitrary various sorts of economic regulations that post-New Deal courts have uniformly thought constitutionally sound.... As the parentheticals here suggest, while the cases in the Lochner line routinely invoked a correct standard of constitutional arbitrariness review, they harbored the spirit of Dred Scott in their absolutist implementation of the standard they espoused.

Even before the deviant economic due process cases had been repudiated, however, the more durable precursors of modern substantive due process were reaffirming this Court's obligation to conduct arbitrariness review, beginning with Meyer v. Nebraska. Without referring to any specific guarantee of the Bill of Rights, the Court invoked precedents from the Slaughter-House Cases through Adkins to declare that the Fourteenth Amendment protected "the right of the individual to contract, to engage in any of the common occupations of life, to acquire useful knowledge, to marry, establish a home and bring up children, to worship God according to the dictates of his own conscience, and generally to enjoy those privileges long recognized at common law as essential to the orderly pursuit of happiness by free men." The Court then held that the same Fourteenth Amendment liberty included a teacher's right to teach and the rights of parents to direct their children's education without unreasonable interference by the States, with the result that Nebraska's prohibition on the teaching of foreign languages in the lower grades was "arbitrary and without reasonable relation to any end within the competency of the State ..." See also Pierce v. Society of Sisters.... After Meyer and Pierce, two further opinions took the major steps that lead to the modern law. The first was not even in a due process case but one about equal protection, Skinner v. Oklahoma ex rel. Williamson (1942), where the Court emphasized the "fundamental" nature of individual choice about procreation and so foreshadowed not only the later prominence of procreation as a subject of liberty protection, but the corresponding standard of "strict scrutiny," in this Court's Fourteenth Amendment law.... Skinner, that is, added decisions regarding procreation to the list of liberties recognized in Meyer and Pierce and loosely suggested, as a gloss on their standard of arbitrariness, a judicial obligation to scrutinize any impingement on such an important interest with heightened care. In so doing, it suggested a point that

Justice Harlan would develop, that the kind and degree of justification that a sensitive judge would demand of a State would depend on the importance of the interest being asserted by the individual. Poe.

[Justice Harlan's dissent in Poe] is important for three things that point to our responsibilities today. The first is Justice Harlan's respect for the tradition of substantive due process review itself, and his acknowledgment of the Judiciary's obligation to carry it on. For two centuries American courts, and for much of that time this Court, have thought it necessary to provide some degree of review over the substantive content of legislation under constitutional standards of textual breadth. The obligation was understood before Dred Scott and has continued after the repudiation of Lochner's progeny, most notably on the subjects of segregation in public education.... This enduring tradition of American constitutional practice is, in Justice Harlan's view, nothing more than what is required by the judicial authority and obligation to construe constitutional text and review legislation for conformity to that text.... Like many judges who preceded him and many who followed, he found it impossible to construe the text of due process without recognizing substantive, and not merely procedural, limitations. "Were due process merely a procedural safeguard it would fail to reach those situations where the deprivation of life, liberty or property was accomplished by legislation which by operating in the future could, given even the fairest possible procedure in application to individuals, nevertheless destroy the enjoyment of all three." ... The text of the Due Process Clause thus imposes nothing less than an obligation to give substantive content to the words "liberty" and "due process of law."

Following the first point of the Poe dissent, on the necessity to engage in the sort of examination we conduct today, the dissent's second and third implicitly address those cases, already noted, that are now condemned with virtual unanimity as disastrous mistakes of substantive due process review. The second of the dissent's lessons is a reminder that the business of such review is not the identification of extratextual absolutes but scrutiny of a legislative resolution (perhaps unconscious) of clashing principles, each quite possibly worthy in and of itself, but each to be weighed within the history of our values as a people. It is a comparison of the relative strengths of opposing claims that informs the judicial task, not a deduction from some first premise. Thus informed, judicial review still has no warrant to substitute one reasonable resolution of the contending positions for another, but authority to supplant the balance already struck between the contenders only when it falls outside the realm of the reasonable. Part III, below, deals with this second point, and also with the dissent's third, which takes the form of an object lesson in the explicit attention to detail that is no less essential to the intellectual discipline of substantive due process review than an understanding of the basic need to account for the two sides in the controversy and to respect legislation within the zone of reasonableness.

My understanding of unenumerated rights in the wake of the Poe dissent and subsequent cases avoids the absolutist failing of many older cases without embracing the opposite pole of equating reasonableness with past practice described at a very specific level.... This approach calls for a court to assess the relative "weights" or dignities of the contending interests, and to this extent the judicial method is familiar to the common law. Common-law method is subject, however, to two important constraints in the hands of a court engaged in substantive due process review. First, such a court is bound to confine the values that it recognizes to those truly deserving constitutional stature, either to those expressed in constitutional text, or those exemplified by "the traditions from which [the Nation] developed," or revealed by contrast with "the traditions from which it broke." Poe

(Harlan, J., dissenting). "'We may not draw on our merely personal and private notions and disregard the limits ... derived from considerations that are fused in the whole nature of our judicial process ... [,] considerations deeply rooted in reason and in the compelling traditions of the legal profession.'" ...

The second constraint, again, simply reflects the fact that constitutional review, not judicial lawmaking, is a court's business here. The weighing or valuing of contending interests in this sphere is only the first step, forming the basis for determining whether the statute in question falls inside or outside the zone of what is reasonable in the way it resolves the conflict between the interests of state and individual.... It is no justification for judicial intervention merely to identify a reasonable resolution of contending values that differs from the terms of the legislation under review. It is only when the legislation's justifying principle, critically valued, is so far from being commensurate with the individual interest as to be arbitrarily or pointlessly applied that the statute must give way. Only if this standard points against the statute can the individual claimant be said to have a constitutional right....

Just as results in substantive due process cases are tied to the selections of statements of the competing interests, the acceptability of the results is a function of the good reasons for the selections made. It is here that the value of common-law method becomes apparent, for the usual thinking of the common law is suspicious of the all-or-nothing analysis that tends to produce legal petrification instead of an evolving boundary between the domains of old principles. Common-law method tends to pay respect instead to detail, seeking to understand old principles afresh by new examples and new counterexamples. The "tradition is a living thing," Poe, (Harlan, J., dissenting), albeit one that moves by moderate steps carefully taken. "The decision of an apparently novel claim must depend on grounds which follow closely on well-accepted principles and criteria. The new decision must take its place in relation to what went before and further [cut] a channel for what is to come." ...

The argument supporting respondents' position thus progresses through three steps of increasing forcefulness. First, it emphasizes the decriminalization of suicide. Reliance on this fact is sanctioned under the standard that looks not only to the tradition retained, but to society's occasional choices to reject traditions of the legal past.... While the common law prohibited both suicide and aiding a suicide, with the prohibition on aiding largely justified by the primary prohibition on self-inflicted death itself ... the State's rejection of the traditional treatment of the one leaves the criminality of the other open to questioning that previously would not have been appropriate. The second step in the argument is to emphasize that the State's own act of decriminalization gives a freedom of choice much like the individual's option in recognized instances of bodily autonomy. One of these, abortion, is a legal right to choose in spite of the interest a State may legitimately invoke in discouraging the practice, just as suicide is now subject to choice, despite a state interest in discouraging it. The third step is to emphasize that respondents claim a right to assistance not on the basis of some broad principle that would be subject to exceptions if that continuing interest of the State's in discouraging suicide were to be recognized at all. Respondents base their claim on the traditional right to medical care and counsel, subject to the limiting conditions of informed, responsible choice when death is imminent, conditions that support a strong analogy to rights of care in other situations in which medical counsel and assistance have been available as a matter of course. There can be no stronger claim to a physician's assistance than at the time when death is imminent, a moral judgment implied by the State's own recognition of the legitimacy of medical procedures necessarily hastening the moment of impending death.

In my judgment, the importance of the individual interest here, as within that class of "certain interests" demanding careful scrutiny of the State's contrary claim, ... cannot be gainsaid. Whether that interest might in some circumstances, or at some time, be seen as "fundamental" to the degree entitled to prevail is not, however, a conclusion that I need draw here, for I am satisfied that the State's interests described in the following section are sufficiently serious to defeat the present claim that its law is arbitrary or purposeless....

One must bear in mind that the nature of the right claimed, if recognized as one constitutionally required, would differ in no essential way from other constitutional rights guaranteed by enumeration or derived from some more definite textual source than "due process." An unenumerated right should not therefore be recognized, with the effect of displacing the legislative ordering of things, without the assurance that its recognition would prove as durable as the recognition of those other rights differently derived. To recognize a right of lesser promise would simply create a constitutional regime too uncertain to bring with it the expectation of finality that is one of this Court's central obligations in making constitutional decisions.

Legislatures, however, are not so constrained. The experimentation that should be out of the question in constitutional adjudication displacing legislative judgments is entirely proper, as well as highly desirable, when the legislative power addresses an emerging issue like assisted suicide. The Court should accordingly stay its hand to allow reasonable legislative consideration. While I do not decide for all time that respondents' claim should not be recognized, I acknowledge the legislative institutional competence as the better one to deal with that claim at this time.

Review Questions and Explanations: *Glucksberg*

1. The physicians challenging the law in *Glucksberg* claim there is a fundamental right for terminally ill, mentally competent individuals to commit suicide with the assistance of a physician. The majority rejects this argument, finding no such right in our "history, legal traditions, and practices." The majority defends this statement by pointing to a long practice in Western nations of criminalizing suicide. Given that, as the Court acknowledges, dying in hospitals is a relatively recent trend, can you think of any other traditions or practices that might counter the majority's narrative? How, if at all, should these competing traditions have influenced the Court's decision?

2. In framing the tradition it is looking for, the majority states that the Court has "a tradition of carefully formulating the interest at stake in substantive due process cases" and that it has "required in substantive due process cases a 'careful description' of the asserted fundamental liberty interest." Is this an accurate description of what the Court has done in the cases you have read?

3. The majority says that it must "exercise the utmost care [when] we are asked to break new ground in this field ... lest the liberty protected by the Due Process Clause be subtly transformed into the policy preferences of the Members of this Court." Does Justice Souter's concurrence adequately address this concern?

4. Justice Souter's concurrence is steeped in history, yet he rejects the majority's approach, which claims to be tightly grounded in history and tradition. What do you make of this?

Lawrence v. Texas

539 U.S. 558 (2003)

Majority: *Kennedy,* Stevens, Souter, Ginsburg, Breyer

Concurrence: *O'Connor* (reprinted in Chapter 8)

Dissents: *Scalia,* Rehnquist (CJ), *Thomas* (omitted)

JUSTICE KENNEDY delivered the opinion of the Court.

Liberty protects the person from unwarranted government intrusions into a dwelling or other private places. In our tradition the State is not omnipresent in the home. And there are other spheres of our lives and existence, outside the home, where the State should not be a dominant presence. Freedom extends beyond spatial bounds. Liberty presumes an autonomy of self that includes freedom of thought, belief, expression, and certain intimate conduct. The instant case involves liberty of the person both in its spatial and in its more transcendent dimensions.

The question before the Court is the validity of a Texas statute making it a crime for two persons of the same sex to engage in certain intimate sexual conduct.... We conclude the case should be resolved by determining whether the petitioners were free as adults to engage in the private conduct in the exercise of their liberty under the Due Process Clause of the Fourteenth Amendment to the Constitution....

There are broad statements of the substantive reach of liberty under the Due Process Clause in earlier cases, including Pierce v. Society of Sisters, and Meyer v. Nebraska; but the most pertinent beginning point is our decision in Griswold v. Connecticut.

In Griswold the Court invalidated a state law prohibiting the use of drugs or devices of contraception and counseling or aiding and abetting the use of contraceptives. The Court described the protected interest as a right to privacy and placed emphasis on the marriage relation and the protected space of the marital bedroom....

After Griswold it was established that the right to make certain decisions regarding sexual conduct extends beyond the marital relationship. In Eisenstadt v. Baird, the Court invalidated a law prohibiting the distribution of contraceptives to unmarried persons. The case was decided under the Equal Protection Clause, ... but with respect to unmarried persons, the Court went on to state the fundamental proposition that the law impaired the exercise of their personal rights.... It quoted from the statement of the Court of Appeals finding the law to be in conflict with fundamental human rights, and it followed with this statement of its own:

> It is true that in Griswold the right of privacy in question inhered in the marital relationship.... If the right of privacy means anything, it is the right of the individual, married or single, to be free from unwarranted governmental intrusion into matters so fundamentally affecting a person as the decision whether to bear or beget a child.

The opinions in Griswold and Eisenstadt were part of the background for the decision in Roe v. Wade. As is well known, the case involved a challenge to the Texas law prohibiting abortions, but the laws of other States were affected as well. Although the Court held the woman's rights were not absolute, her right to elect an abortion did have real and substantial protection as an exercise of her liberty under the Due Process Clause. The Court cited cases that protect spatial freedom and cases that go well beyond it. Roe recognized the right of a woman to make certain fundamental decisions affecting her destiny and confirmed once more that the protection of liberty under the Due Process Clause has a substantive dimension of fundamental significance in defining the rights of the person....

This was the state of the law with respect to some of the most relevant cases when the Court considered Bowers v. Hardwick. The facts in Bowers had some similarities to the instant case.... The Court, in an opinion by Justice White, sustained the Georgia law. Chief Justice Burger and Justice Powell joined the opinion of the Court and filed separate, concurring opinions.... The Court began its substantive discussion in Bowers as follows: "The issue presented is whether the Federal Constitution confers a fundamental right upon homosexuals to engage in sodomy and hence invalidates the laws of the many States that still make such conduct illegal and have done so for a very long time."... That statement, we now conclude, discloses the Court's own failure to appreciate the extent of the liberty at stake.

To say that the issue in Bowers was simply the right to engage in certain sexual conduct demeans the claim the individual put forward, just as it would demean a married couple were it to be said marriage is simply about the right to have sexual intercourse. The laws involved in Bowers and here are, to be sure, statutes that purport to do no more than prohibit a particular sexual act. Their penalties and purposes, though, have more far-reaching consequences, touching upon the most private human conduct, sexual behavior, and in the most private of places, the home. The statutes do seek to control a personal relationship that, whether or not entitled to formal recognition in the law, is within the liberty of persons to choose without being punished as criminals.

This, as a general rule, should counsel against attempts by the State, or a court, to define the meaning of the relationship or to set its boundaries absent injury to a person or abuse of an institution the law protects. It suffices for us to acknowledge that adults may choose to enter upon this relationship in the confines of their homes and their own private lives and still retain their dignity as free persons. When sexuality finds overt expression in intimate conduct with another person, the conduct can be but one element in a personal bond that is more enduring. The liberty protected by the Constitution allows homosexual persons the right to make this choice.

> [Justice Kennedy next questions the historical arguments made in Bowers purporting to show that sexual relations between members of the same sex have historically been prohibited by law. He notes that the history is more complex than Bowers recognized, and that prosecutions against consenting adults engaged in private, same-sex, intimate relations have been rare.]

These considerations do not answer the question before us, however. The issue is whether the majority may use the power of the State to enforce these views on the whole society through operation of the criminal law. "Our obligation is to define the liberty of all, not to mandate our own moral code."... In all events we think that our laws and traditions in the past half century are of most relevance here. These references show an emerging awareness that liberty gives substantial protection to adult persons in deciding how to conduct their private lives in matters pertaining to sex. "[H]istory and tradition are the starting point but not in all cases the ending point of the substantive due process inquiry."... In Planned Parenthood of Southeastern Pa. v. Casey, the Court reaffirmed the substantive force of the liberty protected by the Due Process Clause. The Casey decision again confirmed that our laws and tradition afford constitutional protection to personal decisions relating to marriage, procreation, contraception, family relationships, child rearing, and education.... In explaining the respect the Constitution demands for the autonomy of the person in making these choices, we stated as follows:

These matters, involving the most intimate and personal choices a person may make in a lifetime, choices central to personal dignity and autonomy, are central to the liberty protected by the Fourteenth Amendment. At the heart of liberty is the right to define one's own concept of existence, of meaning, of the universe, and of the mystery of human life. Beliefs about these matters could not define the attributes of personhood were they formed under compulsion of the State.

Persons in a homosexual relationship may seek autonomy for these purposes, just as heterosexual persons do. The decision in Bowers would deny them this right....

The rationale of Bowers does not withstand careful analysis. In his dissenting opinion in Bowers Justice Stevens came to these conclusions:

Our prior cases make two propositions abundantly clear. First, the fact that the governing majority in a State has traditionally viewed a particular practice as immoral is not a sufficient reason for upholding a law prohibiting the practice; neither history nor tradition could save a law prohibiting miscegenation from constitutional attack. Second, individual decisions by married persons, concerning the intimacies of their physical relationship, even when not intended to produce offspring, are a form of 'liberty' protected by the Due Process Clause of the Fourteenth Amendment. Moreover, this protection extends to intimate choices by unmarried as well as married persons.

Justice Stevens' analysis, in our view, should have been controlling in Bowers and should control here.... The present case does not involve minors. It does not involve persons who might be injured or coerced or who are situated in relationships where consent might not easily be refused. It does not involve public conduct or prostitution. It does not involve whether the government must give formal recognition to any relationship that homosexual persons seek to enter. The case does involve two adults who, with full and mutual consent from each other, engaged in sexual practices common to a homosexual lifestyle. The petitioners are entitled to respect for their private lives. The State cannot demean their existence or control their destiny by making their private sexual conduct a crime. Their right to liberty under the Due Process Clause gives them the full right to engage in their conduct without intervention of the government. "It is a promise of the Constitution that there is a realm of personal liberty which the government may not enter." Casey. The Texas statute furthers no legitimate state interest which can justify its intrusion into the personal and private life of the individual.

Had those who drew and ratified the Due Process Clauses of the Fifth Amendment or the Fourteenth Amendment known the components of liberty in its manifold possibilities, they might have been more specific. They did not presume to have this insight. They knew times can blind us to certain truths and later generations can see that laws once thought necessary and proper in fact serve only to oppress. As the Constitution endures, persons in every generation can invoke its principles in their own search for greater freedom.

The judgment of the Court of Appeals for the Texas Fourteenth District is reversed, and the case is remanded for further proceedings not inconsistent with this opinion.

JUSTICE SCALIA, with whom THE CHIEF JUSTICE and JUSTICE THOMAS join, dissenting.

[Justice Scalia begins his dissent by criticizing the Court's disregard of precedent in its overruling of Bowers.]

Having decided that it need not adhere to *stare decisis,* the Court still must establish that Bowers was wrongly decided and that the Texas statute, as applied to petitioners, is unconstitutional.

[The Texas law] undoubtedly imposes constraints on liberty. So do laws prohibiting prostitution, recreational use of heroin, and, for that matter, working more than 60 hours per week in a bakery. But there is no right to "liberty" under the Due Process Clause, though today's opinion repeatedly makes that claim.... ("The liberty protected by the Constitution allows homosexual persons the right to make this choice"; "These matters ... are central to the liberty protected by the Fourteenth Amendment" ... "Their right to liberty under the Due Process Clause gives them the full right to engage in their conduct without intervention of the government"). The Fourteenth Amendment *expressly allows* States to deprive their citizens of "liberty," *so long as "due process of law" is provided:*

> No state shall ... deprive any person of life, liberty, or property, *without due process of law.*

Our opinions applying the doctrine known as "substantive due process" hold that the Due Process Clause prohibits States from infringing *fundamental* liberty interests, unless the infringement is narrowly tailored to serve a compelling state interest. Washington v. Glucksberg. We have held repeatedly, in cases the Court today does not overrule, that *only* fundamental rights qualify for this so-called "heightened scrutiny" protection—that is, rights which are "'deeply rooted in this Nation's history and tradition'" ... Reno v. Flores, (1993) (fundamental liberty interests must be "so rooted in the traditions and conscience of our people as to be ranked as fundamental"); United States v. Salerno (1987) (same). See also Michael H. v. Gerald D (1989) ("[W]e have insisted not merely that the interest denominated as a 'liberty' be 'fundamental' ... but also that it be an interest traditionally protected by our society"); Moore v. East Cleveland (1977) (plurality opinion); Meyer v. Nebraska, (1923) (Fourteenth Amendment protects "those privileges *long recognized at common law* as essential to the orderly pursuit of happiness by free men" (emphasis added)). All other liberty interests may be abridged or abrogated pursuant to a validly enacted state law if that law is rationally related to a legitimate state interest.

Bowers held, first, that criminal prohibitions of homosexual sodomy are not subject to heightened scrutiny because they do not implicate a "fundamental right" under the Due Process Clause ... The Court today does not overrule this holding. Not once does it describe homosexual sodomy as a "fundamental right" or a "fundamental liberty interest," nor does it subject the Texas statute to strict scrutiny. Instead, having failed to establish that the right to homosexual sodomy is "'deeply rooted in this Nation's history and tradition,'" the Court concludes that the application of Texas's statute to petitioners' conduct fails the rational-basis test, and overrules Bowers' holding to the contrary.... "The Texas statute furthers no legitimate state interest which can justify its intrusion into the personal and private life of the individual." ...

Next the Court makes the claim, again unsupported by any citations, that "[l]aws prohibiting sodomy do not seem to have been enforced against consenting adults acting in private." ... The key qualifier here is "acting in private"—since the Court admits that sodomy laws *were* enforced against consenting adults (although the Court contends that prosecutions were "infrequen[t]," ...). I do not know what "acting in private" means; surely consensual sodomy, like heterosexual intercourse, is rarely performed on stage. If all the Court means by "acting in private" is "on private premises, with the doors closed and windows covered," it is entirely unsurprising that evidence of enforcement would be hard to come by.... Surely that lack of evidence would not sustain the proposition that consensual sodomy on private premises with the doors closed and windows covered was regarded as a "fundamental right," even though all other consensual sodomy was criminalized.... Bowers' conclusion that homosexual sodomy is not a fundamental right "deeply rooted in this Nation's history and tradition" is utterly unassailable....

I turn now to the ground on which the Court squarely rests its holding: the contention that there is no rational basis for the law here under attack. This proposition is so out of accord with our jurisprudence—indeed, with the jurisprudence of *any* society we know—that it requires little discussion.

The Texas statute undeniably seeks to further the belief of its citizens that certain forms of sexual behavior are "immoral and unacceptable "... the same interest furthered by criminal laws against fornication, bigamy, adultery, adult incest, bestiality, and obscenity. Bowers held that this *was* a legitimate state interest. The Court today reaches the opposite conclusion. The Texas statute, it says, "furthers *no legitimate state interest* which can justify its intrusion into the personal and private life of the individual".... The Court embraces instead Justice Stevens' declaration in his Bowers dissent, that "the fact that the governing majority in a State has traditionally viewed a particular practice as immoral is not a sufficient reason for upholding a law prohibiting the practice." ... This effectively decrees the end of all morals legislation. If, as the Court asserts, the promotion of majoritarian sexual morality is not even a *legitimate* state interest, none of the above-mentioned laws can survive rational-basis review....

One of the most revealing statements in today's opinion is the Court's grim warning that the criminalization of homosexual conduct is "an invitation to subject homosexual persons to discrimination both in the public and in the private spheres." ... Many Americans do not want persons who openly engage in homosexual conduct as partners in their business, as scoutmasters for their children, as teachers in their children's schools, or as boarders in their home. They view this as protecting themselves and their families from a lifestyle that they believe to be immoral and destructive. The Court views it as "discrimination" which it is the function of our judgments to deter. So imbued is the Court with the law profession's anti-anti-homosexual culture, that it is seemingly unaware that the attitudes of that culture are not obviously "mainstream"; that in most States what the Court calls "discrimination" against those who engage in homosexual acts is perfectly legal; that proposals to ban such "discrimination" under Title VII have repeatedly been rejected by Congress ... that in some cases such "discrimination" is *mandated* by federal statute ... (mandating discharge from the Armed Forces of any service member who engages in or intends to engage in homosexual acts); and that in some cases such "discrimination" is a constitutional right, see Boy Scouts of America v. Dale (2000).

Let me be clear that I have nothing against homosexuals, or any other group, promoting their agenda through normal democratic means. Social perceptions of sexual and other morality change over time, and every group has the right to persuade its fellow citizens that its view of such matters is the best.... One of the benefits of leaving regulation of this matter to the people rather than to the courts is that the people, unlike judges, need not carry things to their logical conclusion. The people may feel that their disapprobation of homosexual conduct is strong enough to disallow homosexual marriage, but not strong enough to criminalize private homosexual acts—and may legislate accordingly....

At the end of its opinion—after having laid waste the foundations of our rational-basis jurisprudence—the Court says that the present case "does not involve whether the government must give formal recognition to any relationship that homosexual persons seek to enter." ... Do not believe it. More illuminating than this bald, unreasoned disclaimer is the progression of thought displayed by an earlier passage in the Court's opinion, which notes the constitutional protections afforded to "personal decisions relating to *marriage,* procreation, contraception, family relationships, child rearing, and education," and then declares that "[p]ersons in a homosexual relationship may seek autonomy for these purposes, just as heterosexual persons do." ...

Today's opinion dismantles the structure of constitutional law that has permitted a distinction to be made between heterosexual and homosexual unions, insofar as formal recognition in marriage is concerned. If moral disapprobation of homosexual conduct is "no legitimate state interest" for purposes of proscribing that conduct ... and if, as the Court coos (casting aside all pretense of neutrality), "[w]hen sexuality finds overt expression in intimate conduct with another person, the conduct can be but one element in a personal bond that is more enduring," ... what justification could there possibly be for denying the benefits of marriage to homosexual couples exercising "[t]he liberty protected by the Constitution," ... ? Surely not the encouragement of procreation, since the sterile and the elderly are allowed to marry. This case "does not involve" the issue of homosexual marriage only if one entertains the belief that principle and logic have nothing to do with the decisions of this Court. Many will hope that, as the Court comfortingly assures us, this is so.

Review Questions and Explanations: Fundamental Rights and Personal Liberties

1. In what ways are *Griswold, Roe* and *Lawrence* similar to and different from the *Meyer* and *Pierce*? In what ways are they similar and different from *Lochner*?

2. If you agree with some of the earlier cases studied in this chapter, but disagree with the recent cases, what is the constitutional line you are relying on in doing so?

3. The majority in *Roe* sees the case as largely an extension of *Griswold,* as well as the earlier privacy/liberty cases. Do you agree?

4. The dissenting justices do not seem to want to overturn *Meyer, Pierce, Buck, Skinner,* and or even *Griswold.* How are they distinguishing these cases? Do you find their distinction persuasive?

CASE NOTE: In 1967, the Supreme Court decided *Loving v. Virginia. Loving,* which is cited in several of the cases you have read in this chapter, involved a challenge to a Virginia law prohibiting interracial marriages. Mildred and Richard Loving, who had been married in the District of Columbia but lived in Virginia, were indicted for violating the Virginia law. The trial judge upheld the ban, stating that:

Almighty God created the races white, black, yellow, malay and red, and he placed them on separate continents. And but for the interference with his arrangement there would be no cause for such marriages. The fact that he separated the races shows that he did not intend for the races to mix.

The order issued by the trial judge suspended the Lovings' sentences on the condition that they agree to leave Virginia and not return together for 25 years. The Lovings left, but filed an appeal to vacate the trial court's order. The Supreme Court of Appeals of Virginia refused to do so. Instead, it upheld the trial court's decision, referencing a 1955 state court decision defending the state's anti-miscegenation laws as necessary to protect the state's ability to "to preserve the racial integrity of its citizens," and to prevent "the corruption of blood," the creation of "a mongrel breed of citizens," and "the obliteration of racial pride." The court also noted that marriage has traditionally been subject to state regulation without federal intervention.

The Lovings then challenged the decision in federal court, arguing that Virginia's law violated their rights under both the Equal Protection and the Due Process clauses of the Fourteenth Amendment. Writing for a unanimous Court, Justice Warren agreed with the Lovings on both counts. In regard to their Due Process argument, Justice Warren wrote this:

> The freedom to marry has long been recognized as one of the vital personal rights essential to the orderly pursuit of happiness by free men. Marriage is one of the 'basic civil rights of man,' fundamental to our very existence and survival. Skinner v. Oklahoma (1942). To deny this fundamental freedom on so unsupportable a basis as the racial classifications embodied in these statutes, classifications so directly subversive of the principle of equality at the heart of the Fourteenth Amendment, is surely to deprive all the State's citizens of liberty without due process of law. The Fourteenth Amendment requires that the freedom of choice to marry not be restricted by invidious racial discriminations. Under our Constitution, the freedom to marry or not marry, a person of another race resides with the individual and cannot be infringed by the State.

Recall the excerpts from Justices Harlan, Scalia, and Kennedy explaining different ways to evaluate fundamental rights claims in substantive due process cases. How would *Loving* come out under each approach? Which approach does Justice Warren use?

Exercise: Due Process and Marriage Equality

Do state laws prohibiting same-sex couples from legally marrying violate the Due Process clause? Working with two or three classmates, use the cases studied in this chapter to prepare the best argument possible for and against the constitutionality, under the Due Process clause, of same-sex restrictions on the right to marry. [Note that this question also raises Equal Protection concerns. We address Equal Protection in the next chapter. Your analysis here should focus on the due process issue.]

Recap: Fundamental Rights and Personal Liberties

We mentioned in the introduction to this chapter that Justice Thomas was keen to overturn *The Slaughterhouse Cases* and resurrect the Privileges or Immunities clause. What follows is an excerpt from *McDonald v. Chicago*, in which the justices debate exactly this question. You should use these materials to review what you have learned in this chapter. Based on what you now know about substantive due process, do you think Justice Thomas' approach would change the nature of the debate about fundamental rights, or merely relocate it? Regardless of your answer to this question, do you agree with Justice Thomas that it is a project the Court should undertake?

McDonald v. City of Chicago

561 U.S. ___, 130 S. Ct. 3020 (2010)

Majority: *Alito*, Roberts (CJ), Kennedy

Concurrences: *Scalia* (omitted), *Thomas*

Dissents: *Stevens*, *Breyer*, Ginsburg, Sotomayor (both omitted)

[The question presented to the Court was whether the individual right to keep and bear arms, established by the Court a year earlier in *District of Columbia v. Heller*, was incorporated against the states through the Fourteenth Amendment. A case decided shortly after the Fourteenth Amendment was ratified, *U.S. v. Cruikshank*, had declined to do so. *McDonald* overturns *Cruikshank* and incorporates the Second Amendment against the states. The first part of the majority opinion, excerpted below, discusses *The Slaughterhouse Cases* and their effect on the Privileges or Immunities clause. Justice Thomas, concurring, encourages the Court to overturn *Slaughterhouse* and revisit its Privileges or Immunities clause jurisprudence.]

Four years after the adoption of the Fourteenth Amendment, this Court was asked to interpret the Amendment's reference to "the privileges or immunities of citizens of the United States." The *Slaughter-House Cases*, involved challenges to a Louisiana law permitting the creation of a state-sanctioned monopoly on the butchering of animals within the city of New Orleans. Justice Samuel Miller's opinion for the Court concluded that the Privileges or Immunities Clause protects only those rights "which owe their existence to the Federal government, its National character, its Constitution, or its laws." The Court held that other fundamental rights — rights that predated the creation of the Federal Government and that "the State governments were created to establish and secure" — were not protected by the Clause.

In drawing a sharp distinction between the rights of federal and state citizenship, the Court relied on two principal arguments. First, the Court emphasized that the Fourteenth Amendment's Privileges or Immunities Clause spoke of "the privileges or immunities of *citizens of the United States*," and the Court contrasted this phrasing with the wording in the first sentence of the Fourteenth Amendment and in the Privileges and Immunities Clause of Article IV, both of which refer to *state* citizenship (emphasis added). Second, the Court stated that a contrary reading would "radically chang[e] the whole theory of the relations of the State and Federal governments to each other and of both these governments to the people," and the Court refused to conclude that such a change had been made "in the absence of language which expresses such a purpose too clearly to admit of doubt." Finding the phrase "privileges or immunities of citizens of the United States" lacking by this high standard, the Court reasoned that the phrase must mean something more limited.

Under the Court's narrow reading, the Privileges or Immunities Clause protects such things as the right "to come to the seat of government to assert any claim [a citizen] may have upon that government, to transact any business he may have with it, to seek its protection, to share its offices, to engage in administering its functions ... [and to] become a citizen of any State of the Union by a *bonafide* residence therein, with the same rights as other citizens of that State."

Finding no constitutional protection against state intrusion of the kind envisioned by the Louisiana statute, the Court upheld the statute. Four Justices dissented. Justice Field, joined by Chief Justice Chase and Justices Swayne and Bradley, criticized the majority for reducing the Fourteenth Amendment's Privileges or Immunities Clause to "a vain and idle enactment, which accomplished nothing, and most unnecessarily excited Congress and the people on its passage." Justice Field opined that the Privileges or Immunities Clause protects rights that are "in their nature ... fundamental," including the right of every man to pursue his profession without the imposition of unequal or discriminatory restrictions. Justice Bradley's dissent observed that "we are not bound to resort to implication ... to find an authoritative declaration of some of the most important privileges and immunities of citizens of the United States. It is in the Constitution itself." Justice Bradley would have construed the Privileges or Immunities Clause to include those rights enumerated in the Constitution as well as some unenumerated rights. Justice Swayne described the majority's narrow reading of the Privileges or Immunities Clause as "turn[ing] ... what was meant for bread into a stone."

Today, many legal scholars dispute the correctness of the narrow *Slaughter-House* interpretation. ("Virtually no serious modern scholar—left, right, and center—thinks that this [interpretation] is a plausible reading of the Amendment"); Brief for Constitutional Law Professors as *Amici Curiae* 33 (claiming an "overwhelming consensus among leading constitutional scholars" that the opinion is "egregiously wrong"); C. Black, A New Birth of Freedom 74–75 (1997).

We see no need to reconsider that interpretation here. For many decades, the question of the rights protected by the Fourteenth Amendment against state infringement has been analyzed under the Due Process Clause of that Amendment and not under the Privileges or Immunities Clause. We therefore decline to disturb the *Slaughter-House* holding.

At the same time, however, this Court's decisions in *Cruikshank, Presser,* and *Miller* do not preclude us from considering whether the Due Process Clause of the Fourteenth Amendment makes the Second Amendment right binding on the States. None of those cases "engage[d] in the sort of Fourteenth Amendment inquiry required by our later cases." As explained more fully below, *Cruikshank, Presser,* and *Miller* all preceded the era in which the Court began the process of "selective incorporation" under the Due Process Clause, and we have never previously addressed the question whether the right to keep and bear arms applies to the States under that theory....

Reversed and remanded.

Justice THOMAS, concurring in part and concurring in the judgment.

Applying what is now a well-settled test, the plurality opinion concludes that the right to keep and bear arms applies to the States through the Fourteenth Amendment's Due Process Clause because it is "fundamental" to the American "scheme of ordered liberty," and "'deeply rooted in this Nation's history and tradition.'" I agree with that description of the right. But I cannot agree that it is enforceable against the States through a clause that speaks only to "process." Instead, the right to keep and bear arms is a privilege of American citizenship that applies to the States through the Fourteenth Amendment's Privileges or Immunities Clause....

As the Court explains, if this case were litigated before the Fourteenth Amendment's adoption in 1868, the answer to that question would be simple. In *Barron v. Baltimore,* this Court held that the Bill of Rights applied only to the Federal Government. Writing for the Court, Chief Justice Marshall recalled that the founding generation added the first eight Amendments to the Constitution in response to Antifederalist concerns regarding the extent of federal—not state—power, and held that if "the framers of these amendments [had] intended them to be limitations on the powers of the state governments," "they would have declared this purpose in plain and intelligible language." Finding no such language in the Bill, Chief Justice Marshall held that it did not in any way restrict state authority.

Nearly three decades after *Barron,* the Nation was splintered by a civil war fought principally over the question of slavery. As was evident to many throughout our Nation's early history, slavery, and the measures designed to protect it, were irreconcilable with the principles of equality, government by consent, and inalienable rights proclaimed by the Declaration of Independence and embedded in our constitutional structure.... After the war, a series of constitutional amendments were adopted to repair the Nation from the damage slavery had caused. The provision at issue here, § 1 of the Fourteenth Amendment, significantly altered our system of government.

The meaning of § 1's next sentence has divided this Court for many years. That sentence begins with the command that "[n]o State shall make or enforce any law which shall abridge the privileges or immunities of citizens of the United States." On its face, this appears to grant the persons just made United States citizens a certain collection of rights — *i.e.,* privileges or immunities — attributable to that status.

This Court's precedents accept that point, but define the relevant collection of rights quite narrowly. In *The Slaughter-House Cases,* decided just five years after the Fourteenth Amendment's adoption, the Court interpreted this text, now known as the Privileges or Immunities Clause, for the first time. In a closely divided decision, the Court drew a sharp distinction between the privileges and immunities of state citizenship and those of federal citizenship, and held that the Privileges or Immunities Clause protected only the latter category of rights from state abridgment. The Court defined that category to include only those rights "which owe their existence to the Federal government, its National character, its Constitution, or its laws." This arguably left open the possibility that certain individual rights enumerated in the Constitution could be considered privileges or immunities of federal citizenship. But the Court soon rejected that proposition, interpreting the Privileges or Immunities Clause even more narrowly in its later cases.

Chief among those cases is United States v. Cruikshank (1876). There, the Court held that members of a white militia who had brutally murdered as many as 165 black Louisianians congregating outside a courthouse had not deprived the victims of their privileges as American citizens to peaceably assemble or to keep and bear arms. See L. Keith, The Colfax Massacre 109 (2008). According to the Court, the right to peaceably assemble codified in the First Amendment was not a privilege of United States citizenship because "[t]he right ... existed long *before* the adoption of the Constitution" (emphasis added). Similarly, the Court held that the right to keep and bear arms was not a privilege of United States citizenship because it was not "in any manner dependent upon that instrument for its existence." In other words, the reason the Framers codified the right to bear arms in the Second Amendment — its nature as an inalienable right that pre-existed the Constitution's adoption — was the very reason citizens could not enforce it against States through the Fourteenth.

That circular reasoning effectively has been the Court's last word on the Privileges or Immunities Clause. In the intervening years, the Court has held that the Clause prevents state abridgment of only a handful of rights, such as the right to travel, that are not readily described as essential to liberty.

As a consequence of this Court's marginalization of the Clause, litigants seeking federal protection of fundamental rights turned to the remainder of § 1 in search of an alternative fount of such rights. They found one in a most curious place — that section's command that every State guarantee "due process" to any person before depriving him of "life, liberty, or property." At first, litigants argued that this Due Process Clause "incorporated" certain procedural rights codified in the Bill of Rights against the States. The Court generally rejected those claims, however, on the theory that the rights in question were not sufficiently "fundamental" to warrant such treatment.

That changed with time. The Court came to conclude that certain Bill of Rights guarantees *were* sufficiently fundamental to fall within § 1's guarantee of "due process."

While this Court has at times concluded that a right gains "fundamental" status only if it is essential to the American "scheme of ordered liberty" or " 'deeply rooted in this Nation's history and tradition' " (plurality opinion) (quoting *Glucksberg)* the Court has just as often held that a right warrants Due Process Clause protection if it satisfies a far less measurable range of criteria, see *Lawrence v. Texas* (concluding that the Due Process Clause protects "liberty of the person both in its spatial and in its more transcendent dimensions"). Using the latter approach, the Court has determined that the Due Process Clause applies rights against the States that are not mentioned in the Constitution at all, even without seriously arguing that the Clause was originally understood to protect such rights. See, *e.g.,* Lochner v. New York (1905); Roe v. Wade (1973); Lawrence.

All of this is a legal fiction. The notion that a constitutional provision that guarantees only "process" before a person is deprived of life, liberty, or property could define the substance of those rights strains credulity for even the most casual user of words. Moreover, this fiction is a particularly dangerous one. The one theme that links the Court's substantive due process precedents together is their lack of a guiding principle to distinguish "fundamental" rights that warrant protection from nonfundamental rights that do not. Today's decision illustrates the point. Replaying a debate that has endured from the inception of the Court's substantive due process jurisprudence, the dissents laud the "flexibility" in this Court's substantive due process doctrine (STEVENS, J., dissenting); see *post,* at 3122–3123 (BREYER, J., dissenting), while the plurality makes yet another effort to impose principled restraints on its exercise. But neither side argues that the meaning they attribute to the Due Process Clause was consistent with public understanding at the time of its ratification.

To be sure, the plurality's effort to cabin the exercise of judicial discretion under the Due Process Clause by focusing its inquiry on those rights deeply rooted in American history and tradition invites less opportunity for abuse than the alternatives. See *post,* at 3123 (BREYER, J., dissenting) (arguing that rights should be incorporated against the States through the Due Process Clause if they are "well-suited to the carrying out of … constitutional promises"); *post,* at 3100 (STEVENS, J., dissenting) (warning that there is no "all-purpose, top-down, totalizing theory of 'liberty' " protected by the Due Process Clause). But any serious argument over the scope of the Due Process Clause must acknowledge that neither its text nor its history suggests that it protects the many substantive rights this Court's cases now claim it does.

I cannot accept a theory of constitutional interpretation that rests on such tenuous footing. This Court's substantive due process framework fails to account for both the text of the Fourteenth Amendment and the history that led to its adoption, filling that gap with a jurisprudence devoid of a guiding principle. I believe the original meaning of the Fourteenth Amendment offers a superior alternative, and that a return to that meaning would allow this Court to enforce the rights the Fourteenth Amendment is designed to protect with greater clarity and predictability than the substantive due process framework has so far managed.

Chapter 8

Equal Protection

A. Overview

The Equal Protection clause is part of the Fourteenth Amendment, which reads as follows:

> All persons born or naturalized in the United States, and subject to the jurisdiction thereof, are citizens of the United States and of the State wherein they reside. **No State shall** make or enforce any law which shall abridge the privileges or immunities of citizens of the United States; nor shall any State deprive any person of life, liberty, or property, without due process of law; nor **deny to any person within its jurisdiction the equal protection of the laws.**

The Equal Protection clause, highlighted in bold, is the part that reads "No State shall ... deny to any person within its jurisdiction the equal protection of the laws." But what does it mean to deny someone the equal protection of the laws? It cannot mean that law cannot draw distinctions between groups of people. After all, law does this all the time. For example, people who park illegally get parking tickets while people who park in legal spaces do not. Creating classifications that distinguish between people and then treating them differently based on the classification they fit into is, quite simply, what law does.

The question in equal protection cases, consequently, is not *whether* law can classify people in different ways, but rather how they can be classified, and for what reasons. Consider four different laws. The first creates a classification distinguishing between people who smoke marijuana for recreational purposes and those who smoke it for medical purposes, criminalizing the conduct of the former group but not the latter. The second law distinguishes medical doctors and chiropractors, allowing medical doctors to prescribe a wide array of medications which chiropractors can not. The third law classifies people based on their age. People who are 21 years old or older can legally buy alcohol, while those younger than 21 cannot. The fourth distinguishes people on the basis of their race, and requires people deemed white to go to different schools than those attended by people deemed black.

How might we begin working through which, if any, of these classifications violate the Equal Protection clause? We would, as always, start with the text of the clause. As we have seen, the clause can't sensibly be interpreted literally to mean that it is always unconstitutional for laws to classify and treat people differently. The text, therefore, is written at a level of generality that provides little practical guidance. But a bit of thinking may generate some ideas about how to proceed. Take a moment to consider the parking and medical marijuana examples. These examples raise the possibility that the idea of "equal protection" might reasonably be construed to mean not that all people must be treated the same no matter what, but that the law must "treat like cases alike" or must "treat *similarly situated* people equally." This begins to make more sense out of the clause, reading it as a principle requiring legal classifications to be drawn in a way that requires fair and equal application of legally imposed differential treatment.

This is progress. But the idea only takes us so far, because it begs the question of what makes it appropriate to identify a case as "unlike" another, or a person as "differently situated" from someone else. Comparing the race-based classification to the other classifications listed above suggests that some distinctions form less proper grounds for classification than do others. But which ones?

To answer *this* question, we might look to the history of the clause. As part of the Fourteenth Amendment, the Equal Protection clause was enacted after the Civil War. The ratifiers of the Equal Protection clause obviously, then, were concerned with issues of slavery and race. But unlike the Thirteenth Amendment, the Fourteenth does not mention slavery or previous condition of servitude, and unlike the Fifteenth Amendment, the Equal Protection clause is not textually restricted to classifications drawn on the basis of race or color.

One next might try thinking about the nature of the classification itself. Is there any reason why the Court should be *suspicious* of a legislative decision to treat medical doctors differently from chiropractors, or 21-year-olds differently than younger people, or people of one racial group differently from people of other racial groups? We also might consider the *reason for the distinction* drawn by the law. The 21-year age limit for buying alcohol might be intended to protect young people from the dangers of binge drinking, or to protect third parties from drunken drivers. Is this something that it is legitimate or important for the state to do? Finally, we might think about the *fit* between the classification and the state's goal: even if the goal is a good one, is the law an appropriate way to accomplish it? If the law is intended to protect young people, why is the line drawn at age 21? If the law is intended to reduce drunk driving, how well does the age-limit serve that purpose?

We now have a list of considerations that includes the type of classification drawn, the state's reason for drawing it, and the fit between that reason and the law itself. Applying these considerations to our four laws, one might conclude that there is little reason for courts to be suspicious of legislative judgments about marijuana use, or how to license doctors or chiropractors, but that perhaps there are reasons to be suspicious of legislative distinctions drawn on the basis of race. (We'll come back to age.) While people choose to become doctors or chiropractors, very few people choose their race. Moreover, race is a characteristic that has historically been used to exclude and discriminate against disfavored groups.

We may conclude, therefore, that classifications based on immutable characteristics or characteristics that are related to a history of discrimination warrant a higher degree of judicial scrutiny than do other types of classifications. Drawing on the language of *Carolene Products* footnote 4, which you studied in Chapter 7, we might therefore decide to focus on characteristics that define a "discrete and insular minority" as triggering heightened scrutiny, when those characteristics are made the basis of a legislative classification. While footnote 4 has not formally been embraced as controlling doctrine by the Supreme Court, its framework is analytically useful and has influenced many commentators and some justices. For convenience, we repeat it here:

> It is unnecessary to consider now whether legislation which restricts those political processes which can ordinarily be expected to bring about repeal of undesirable legislation, is to be subjected to more exacting judicial scrutiny under the general

prohibitions of the Fourteenth Amendment than are most other types of legislation. On restrictions upon the right to vote, on restraints upon the dissemination of information, see Near v. Minnesota ex rel. Olson, 283 U.S. 697, 713–714, 718–720, 722; Grosjean v. American Press Co., 297 U.S. 233; Lovell v. Griffin, supra; on interferences with political organizations, see Stromberg v. California, supra, 369; Fiske v. Kansas, 274 U.S. 380; Whitney v. California, 274 U.S. 357, 373–378; Herndon v. Lowry, 301 U.S. 242; and see Holmes, J., in Gitlow v. New York, 268 U.S. 652, 673; as to prohibition of peaceable assembly, see De Jonge v. Oregon, 299 U.S. 353, 365.

Nor need we enquire whether similar considerations enter into the review of statutes directed at particular religious, or racial minorities; whether prejudice against discrete and insular minorities may be a special condition, which tends seriously to curtail the operation of those political processes ordinarily to be relied upon to protect minorities, and which may call for a correspondingly more searching judicial inquiry.

These considerations, in turn, might lead us to formulate a legal rule that would encourage courts to generally defer to legislative judgments in regard to laws such as those differentiating between medical professionals, but to more rigorously scrutinize the laws classifying people on the basis of race. But what would we do with age, under this regime? Age does not fit neatly into the analyses we have developed so far. Age is an inherent trait: no one chooses their age. But we all know what it is like to be younger than we are, and we know (or, more accurately, hope) that we will "age in" to any classification we make affecting those older than ourselves. Consequently, age is not, perhaps, as unknowable to or isolating from others as is sex or race. So we may need to think harder about how rigorously we want courts to review age-based classifications.

Even after all of this, however, our work is not done. Even if we decide to give more rigorous review to classifications based on certain types of traits, that review surely must still take into account the importance of the state's interest in the law, and the extent to which the law furthers that interest (the issue of "fit" mentioned above). Consider a law requiring separate men's and women's restrooms in government buildings. If, in accordance with the reasoning above, we develop a legal rule that gives more searching judicial scrutiny to classifications based on sex (as a characteristic not generally thought of as chosen by individuals), does that mean this law would be unconstitutional? You haven't read any equal protection cases yet, but you can probably guess that the answer is likely to be "no."

To understand why, we have to consider not just the suspect nature of the classification drawn by the law, but also the state's interest in enacting it, and the fit between that interest and the differential treatment it creates. If we asked the state why it enacted a law requiring men and women to use separate restrooms, the state might well respond that it did so in order to protect the modesty and privacy of its citizens, and that it thought separate restrooms were a good way to do that in most situations. We would then have to decide whether we agreed that this reason was sufficient to justify the classification in this situation.

As we will see below, during the past few decades the Court has organized this cluster of concerns into a system of tiered review which it uses to evaluate equal protection claims. You have already studied this concept in Chapter 7 and the introduction to Part Four. To refresh your recollection: laws drawing "suspect" classifications or involving "fundamental rights" are subject to strict scrutiny, meaning the state must show both that the law is supported by a "compelling" state interest and that the law is "narrowly tailored" to advance that interest. Laws drawing somewhat less suspect classifications are subject to an intermediate scrutiny. Laws evaluated under this level of scrutiny must be supported by an "important" state interest and must be "substantially related" to that interest. Laws drawing other types of classifications—like our law regulating medical doctors and chiropractors—need only advance a "legitimate" state interest in a "reasonable" or "rational" way.

There are a lot of unpopped kernels in this Crackerjack box, however. We saw in the last chapter how difficult it has been for the Court to determine what rights are sufficiently fundamental to trigger heightened review under the Due Process clause. The same types of issues permeate Equal Protection clause cases. How does the Court decide what is a "suspect" classification? Does age count? How about sexual orientation? And what does it mean for a state interest to be "compelling"? Is avoiding de facto segregation or creating racial diversity in the classroom compelling? What about protecting traditional community values? Can a state interest that seemed sufficient in 1896 be insufficient in 1954? If so, why? Did the earlier Court get the law wrong or does the law incorporate changed norms and understandings about appropriate classifications? Even more fundamentally, does a tiered system of review make sense? Does such a system obscure rather than illuminate what the Court is really doing in these cases? (As we will see, several justices over the years have thought so.) And finally, just how vigorously should the Court review classifications that do *not* warrant any sort of heightened review?

These are the issues we will explore in this chapter. We begin with the last of the questions set out above: what does equal protection review look like in most cases? We start here to reinforce a simple but often forgotten point. Even though most of the interesting contemporary disputes in this area are about whether and how to apply heightened review to particular classifications, *all* classifications can, in theory, be subjected to an equal protection analysis. Cases not involving suspect or quasi-suspect classes, or fundamental rights, are rarely brought, however, for the simple reason that they are almost always upheld under rational basis review. The first three cases below illustrate the type of judicial deference typical under rational basis review.

We then move to *The Civil Rights Cases.* In *The Civil Rights Cases,* the Supreme Court for the first time construed the Equal Protection clause. Among other things, the case introduces us to the "state action" doctrine, an important component of equal protection analysis. The three cases that come next—*Plessy v. Ferguson, Brown v. Board of Education,* and *Korematsu v. United States*—provide an overview of the various ways in which the Court has understood the substantive guarantee found in the Equal Protection clause. Note that the earliest of these cases do not use the tiered system of review we outlined above. Nor do all of these cases remain good law. *Plessy,* famously, was nullified by *Brown,* and today both it and *Korematsu* are firmly in the constitutional anti-canon.[1] We feel strongly, however, that these cases are worth reading. They are some of the Court's most famous (or infamous) decisions and should stimulate your thinking about the various ways one can construe the phrase "equal protection of the laws." These cases also have lot to teach us about how we think about the very process of constitutional law making. As such, they provide a helpful framework through which to consider the more contemporary cases.

The materials following *Korematsu* illustrate the Court's more recent struggles to construct the Equal Protection clause. These first of these sections addresses three doctrinal issues

---

1. See Jamal Greene, *The Anticanon,* 125 Harv. L. Rev. 379 (2011).

the Court has had to work through when applying strict scrutiny in race cases. Later sections explore other areas in which heightened review has been applied or considered.

B. Foundational Doctrine

This section examines three ideas at the core of equal protection doctrine: the constitutional "default" of deferential review; the "state action" requirement; and the conceptual possibilities in the term "equal protection." The first of these ideas — the default rule of deference — illustrates the important point that in almost all modern cases the Court will take a deferential approach toward legislative classifications. The second, the state action requirement, explains the constitutionally significant difference between in-equalities perpetrated by governmental actors from those created or aggravated by private actors. And the third explores different ways in which we can think about the idea of equal protection itself: what concepts of equality are embodied in this term? To illustrate this last idea, we explore the various ideas of equal protection deployed by the Court in the three paradigm race cases noted above (*Plessy, Brown* and *Korematsu*).

1. Rational Basis Review

All laws classify in some way. All laws, therefore, could in theory generate equal protection challenges. Outside the context of suspect classifications giving rise to heightened judicial scrutiny, however, legal classifications (excepting some situations involving fundamental rights, discussed below) are subject only to rational basis review by the courts. The practical reality is that since all laws create classifications, broad, non-deferential equal protection review of *all* legislative classifications would overwhelm courts and have serious implications for self-governance.

It is sometimes said that rational basis review in the equal protection context is used in cases involving economic regulation (just as it is under the Due Process clause, at least since the New Deal jurisprudential shift). This is true as far as it goes, but rational basis review is not *confined* to economic regulation. Rather, economic regulation is one subcategory (albeit a very significant one), within the broader category of laws that would be reviewed under the rational basis test if subjected to an equal protection challenge. But that category is best defined as all laws that are not based on suspect classifications or do not infringe upon fundamental rights.

In this chapter, only a handful of the cases we present are rational basis cases. One reason for that is that relatively few such cases are litigated. Because "rational basis" is such a deferential standard, a rational-basis challenge is extremely unlikely to succeed. Consequently, few such challenges are brought — they are rarely worth your time or your client's money. A second reason we include relatively few rational basis cases is because they tend to be doctrinally straightforward enough that you don't need to study a lot of them to get the idea. Yet we start with these cases because the core idea remains fundamental (if easily forgotten): of the mass of federal and state laws and government actions governing day to day life, vanishingly few of them are vulnerable to a viable equal protection challenge. So although most of your study of the Equal Protection clause will involve issues related to heightened scrutiny, keep in mind that in sheer numbers of laws, rational basis is the rule and heightened scrutiny the exception.

Guided Reading Questions: *Railway Express v. New York* and *Williamson v. Lee Optical*

1. Identify the structure of the equal protection problem in both *Railway Express* and *Williamson*: (1) what is the legislative distinction or classification being drawn; (2) what does the regulation require or prohibit; (3) what is the governmental objective or interest in imposing the requirement or prohibition on the regulated class; and (4) how strong is the connection — the fit — between the regulation of the class (1 and 2) and the governmental objective (3)?

2. What are the weak links, if any, in the analysis you mapped out when answering the above question? Is the governmental interest weak or dubious? Is the connection between the regulation and the objective weak or dubious?

3. Would you characterize the majority opinion as rigorous in examining the strength of the governmental objectives and the closeness of "fit" of the regulation? Try to articulate the reasons for your answer.

4. How does Justice Jackson's concurrence differ from the opinion of the Court in *Railway Express*?

Railway Express Agency v. New York
336 U.S. 106 (1949)

Unanimous decision: *Douglas*, Vinson (CJ), Black, Frankfurter, Murphy, Jackson, Rutledge, Burton

Concurrence: *Jackson*

MR. JUSTICE DOUGLAS delivered the opinion of the Court.

[Appellant Railway Express, a trucking company that operated 1,900 trucks in New York City and sold advertizing space on the exterior sides of these trucks, was convicted and fined in a city magistrate's court for violating a municipal ordinance that barred advertising on commercial vehicles unconnected to the vehicle's business. Appellant challenged the conviction arguing that the law violated equal protection.]

.... It is pointed out that the regulation draws the line between advertisements of products sold by the owner of the truck and general advertisements. It is argued that unequal treatment on the basis of such a distinction is not justified by the aim and purpose of the regulation. It is said, for example, that one of appellant's trucks carrying the advertisement of a commercial house would not cause any greater distraction of pedestrians and vehicle drivers than if the commercial house carried the same advertisement on its own truck. Yet the regulation allows the latter to do what the former is forbidden from doing. It is therefore contended that the classification which the regulation makes has no relation to the traffic problem since a violation turns not on what kind of advertisements are carried on trucks but on whose trucks they are carried.

That, however, is a superficial way of analyzing the problem.... The local authorities may well have concluded that those who advertise their own wares on their trucks do not present the same traffic problem in view of the nature or extent of the advertising which they use. It would take a degree of omniscience which we lack to say that such is not the case. If that judgment is correct, the advertising displays that are exempt have less incidence on traffic than those of appellants.

.... It is by such practical considerations based on experience rather than by theoretical inconsistencies that the question of equal protection is to be answered. And the fact that New York City sees fit to eliminate from traffic this kind of distraction but does not touch what may be even greater ones in a different category, such as the vivid displays on Times Square, is immaterial. It is no requirement of equal protection that all evils of the same genus be eradicated or none at all. Affirmed.

MR. JUSTICE JACKSON, concurring.

.... Invocation of the equal protection clause [unlike the due process clause], does not disable any governmental body from dealing with the subject at hand. It merely means that the prohibition or regulation must have a broader impact. I regard it as a salutary doctrine that cities, states and the Federal Government must exercise their powers so as not to discriminate between their inhabitants except upon some reasonable differentiation fairly related to the object of regulation.... [T]here is no more effective practical guaranty against arbitrary and unreasonable government than to require that the principles of law which officials would impose upon a minority must be imposed generally. Conversely, nothing opens the door to arbitrary action so effectively as to allow those officials to pick and choose only a few to whom they will apply legislation and thus to escape the political retribution that might be visited upon them if larger numbers were affected. Courts can take no better measure to assure that laws will be just than to require that laws be equal in operation.

This case affords an illustration. Even casual observations from the sidewalks of New York will show that an ordinance which would forbid all advertising on vehicles would run into conflict with many interests, including some, if not all, of the great metropolitan newspapers, which use that advertising extensively. Their blandishment of the latest sensations is not less a cause of diverted attention and traffic hazard than the commonplace cigarette advertisement which this truck-owner is forbidden to display. But any regulation applicable to all such advertising would require much clearer justification in local conditions to enable its enactment than does some regulation applicable to a few. I do not mention this to criticize the motives of those who enacted this ordinance, but it dramatizes the point that we are much more likely to find arbitrariness in the regulation of the few than of the many. Hence, for my part, I am more receptive to attack on local ordinances for denial of equal protection than for denial of due process, while the Court has more often used the latter clause.

In this case, if the City of New York should assume that display of any advertising on vehicles tends and intends to distract the attention of persons using the highways and to increase the dangers of its traffic, I should think it fully within its constitutional powers to forbid it all. The same would be true if the City should undertake to eliminate or minimize the hazard by any generally applicable restraint, such as limiting the size, color, shape or perhaps to some extent the contents of vehicular advertising. Instead of such general regulation of advertising, however, the City seeks to reduce the hazard only by saying that while some may, others may not exhibit such appeals. The same display, for example, advertising cigarettes, which this appellant is forbidden to carry on its trucks, may be carried on the trucks of a cigarette dealer and might on the trucks of this appellant if it dealt in cigarettes. And almost an identical advertisement, certainly one of equal size, shape, color and appearance, may be carried by this appellant if it proclaims its own offer to transport cigarettes. But it may not be carried so long as the message is not its own but a cigarette dealer's offer to sell the same cigarettes.

The City urges that.... while this [regulation] does not eliminate vehicular advertising, it does eliminate such advertising for hire and to this extent cuts down the hazard sought to be controlled....

As a matter of principle and in view of my attitude toward the equal protection clause, I do not think differences of treatment under law should be approved on classification because of differences unrelated to the legislative purpose. The equal protection clause ceases to assure either equality or protection if it is avoided by any conceivable difference that can be pointed out between those bound and those left free....

The question in my mind comes to this. Where individuals contribute to an evil or danger in the same way and to the same degree, may those who do so for hire be prohibited, while those who do so for their own commercial ends but not for hire be allowed to continue? I think the answer has to be that the hireling may be put in a class by himself and may be dealt with differently than those who act on their own....

Of course, this appellant did not hold itself out to carry or display everybody's advertising, and its rental of space on the sides of its trucks was only incidental to the main business which brought its trucks into the streets. But it is not difficult to see that, in a day of extravagant advertising more or less subsidized by tax deduction, the rental of truck space could become an obnoxious enterprise. While I do not think highly of this type of regulation, that is not my business, and in view of the control I would concede to cities to protect citizens in quiet and orderly use for their proper purposes of the highways and public places, I think the judgment below must be affirmed.

CASE NOTE: *Williamson v. Lee Optical of Oklahoma*, 348 U.S. 483 (1955). An Oklahoma statute made it unlawful to fit and sell corrective lenses or replace lenses in eyeglass frames without a prescription from an Oklahoma licensed ophthalmologist or optometrist. Ophthalmologists are physicians who specialize in the care of the eyes. Optometrists examine eyes for refractive error and diagnose eye. The law distinguished these professions from opticians, who are artisans qualified to grind lenses, fill prescriptions, and fit frames. The law exempted sellers of "ready to wear" refractive lenses, which presumably included department stores and chain pharmacies. The district court held that the law failed to meet rational basis review under both the Due Process and Equal Protection clauses.

In a unanimous decision (*Douglas*, Warren (CJ), Black, Reed, Frankfurter, Douglas, Burton, Clark, Minton), the Supreme Court reversed. The Court first rejected a substantive due process challenge to the law ("The day is gone when this Court uses the Due Process clause of the Fourteenth Amendment to strike down state laws, regulatory of business and industrial conditions, because they may be unwise, improvident, or out of harmony with a particular school of thought"). The Court went on to reject the equal protection challenge, made on the ground that the purported health rationale did not support the restriction against opticians while allowing the sale of corrective "ready to wear" glasses. The Court said:

> The problem of legislative classification is a perennial one, admitting of no doctrinaire definition. Evils in the same field may be of different dimensions and proportions, requiring different remedies. Or so the legislature may think. Or

the reform may take one step at a time, addressing itself to the phase of the problem which seems most acute to the legislative mind. The legislature may select one phase of one field and apply a remedy there, neglecting the others. The prohibition of the Equal Protection Clause goes no further than the invidious discrimination. We cannot say that that point has been reached here. For all this record shows, the ready-to-wear branch of this business may not loom large in Oklahoma or may present problems of regulation distinct from the other branch.

[handwritten margin note: Why can the States reform one step at a time for certain problem but not for race-related laws & remedial laws?]

Review Questions and Explanations: *Railway Express* and *Williamson*

1. We are left to speculate why New York City drew the distinction it did in *Railway Express*. Did businesses who advertized on their own trucks have some common interest that gave them greater clout in the legislative process? Was it a "divide and conquer" strategy in which the legislative body could take on a definable subgroup of truck advertisers but not all of them at once? *Williamson*, on the other hand, more clearly smacks of special interest legislation: the most plausible explanation to exempt "ready-to-wear" glasses sellers from the prescription requirement (a requirement that itself promotes the interests of ophthalmologists and optometrists at the expense of opticians) is that they had more clout in the legislature than did opticians, perhaps because such glasses were sold by large chain stores.

2. Is Justice Jackson's concurrence consistent with *Carolene Products* footnote 4? Who is Jackson trying to protect? Many, if not most laws, result from a legislative contest that creates winners and losers: is Justice Jackson trying to protect all the losers? Or just some of them? Which legislative losers deserve protection from the courts?

3. Both *Railway Express* and *Williamson* pose a problem of underinclusiveness. As explained in the Jackson concurrence in *Railway Express*, laws that attack a legitimate problem in piecemeal fashion may be strategic ploys to foist the cost of regulation onto politically weaker groups. Do you agree with Jackson that equal protection doctrine should disfavor narrowly drawn laws that arguably should have been drawn more broadly? Would this, as Jackson argues, act as a check on unwise or unfair laws? Does the majority in either case adopt this view?

4. It is not unusual for a legislative classification challenged as irrational on equal protection grounds to be challenged as irrational on due process grounds as well. Both tests examine the strength of the governmental interest and the fit between the means and ends of the law. *Carolene Products* from Chapter 7 was a due process challenge to a law prohibiting the sale of beverages made to resemble milk and called "milk," but containing vegetable rather than milk fats. Can you reframe the challengers' argument in that case as an equal protection argument?

Guided Reading Questions: *Central State University v. Am. Assoc. of Univ. Profs.*

1. Identify the structure of the equal protection problem: what is the legislative classification or distinction; what conduct is required or forbidden; what is the government interest; and what is the fit between the regulation and the interest.

2. The Court spends time going through a factual question about whether collective bargaining has resulted in diminution of teaching loads. Where in the equal protection analysis does this factual question fit?

3. The U.S. Supreme Court, after focusing on that factual question, reverses the Ohio Supreme Court. Do the justices disagree with the Ohio court's factual findings? If not, how do they deal with the finding that there was no evidence presented in the case to show that collective bargaining has caused diminished teaching loads?

Central State University v. American Association of University Professors
526 U.S. 124 (1999)

Unanimous decision (per curiam): Rehnquist (CJ), Stevens, O'Connor, Scalia, Kennedy, Souter, Thomas, Ginsburg, Breyer.

Concurrence: *Ginsburg*, Breyer (omitted)

PER CURIAM.

Petitioner Central State University challenges a ruling of the Ohio Supreme Court striking down on equal protection grounds a state law requiring public universities to develop standards for professors' instructional workloads and exempting those standards from collective bargaining. We grant the petition and reverse the judgment of the Ohio Supreme Court....

In 1994, petitioner Central State University adopted a workload policy pursuant to [state law] and notified respondent, the certified collective-bargaining agent for Central State's professors, that it would not bargain over the issue of faculty workload. Respondent subsequently filed a complaint in Ohio state court for declaratory and injunctive relief, alleging that [the state law] created a class of public employees not entitled to bargain regarding their workload and that this classification violated the Equal Protection Clauses of the Ohio and United States Constitutions.

By a divided vote, the Ohio Supreme Court agreed with respondent that [the state law] deprived public university professors the equal protection of the laws. The court acknowledged that Ohio's purpose in enacting the statute was legitimate and that all legislative enactments enjoy a strong presumption of constitutionality. Nonetheless, the court held that § 3345's collective-bargaining exemption bore no rational relationship to the State's interest in correcting the imbalance between research and teaching at its public universities. The State had argued that achieving uniformity, consistency, and equity in faculty workload was necessary to recapture the decline in teaching, and that collective bargaining produced variation in workloads across universities in departments having the same academic mission. Reviewing evidence that the State had submitted in support of this contention, the Ohio Supreme Court held that "there is not a shred of evidence in the entire record which links collective bargaining with the decline in teaching over the last decade, or in any way purports to establish that collective bargaining contributed in the slightest to the lost faculty time devoted to undergraduate teaching." Based on this determination, the court concluded that the State had failed to show "any rational basis for singling out university faculty members as the only public employees ... precluded from bargaining over their workload."

The dissenting justices pointed out that the majority's methodology and conclusion conflicted with this Court's standards for rational-basis review of equal protection challenges. In their view, "that collective bargaining has not *caused* the decline in teaching proves nothing in assessing whether the faculty workload standards imposed pursuant to [the statute] legitimately relate to that statute's purpose of restoring losses in undergraduate teaching activity." The majority's review of the State's evidence was therefore "inconsequential" to the only question in the case: whether the challenged legislative action was arbitrary or irrational. Answering this question, the dissent concluded that imposing uniform workload standards via the exemption "is not an irrational means of effecting an increasing in teaching activity. In fact, it was probably the most direct means of accomplishing that objective available to the General Assembly."

We agree that the Ohio Supreme Court's holding cannot be reconciled with the requirements of the Equal Protection Clause. We have repeatedly held that "a classification neither involving fundamental rights nor proceeding along suspect lines ... cannot run afoul of the Equal Protection Clause if there is a rational relationship between disparity of treatment and some legitimate governmental purpose." The legislative classification created by [the statute] passes this test. One of the statute's objectives was to increase the time spent by faculty in the classroom; the imposition of a faculty workload policy not subject to collective bargaining was an entirely rational step to accomplish this objective. The legislature could quite reasonably have concluded that the policy animating the law would have been undercut and likely varied if it were subject to collective bargaining. The State, in effect, decided that the attainment of this goal was more important than the system of collective bargaining that had previously included university professors.

The fact that the record before the Ohio courts did not show that collective bargaining in the past had led to the decline in classroom time for faculty does not detract from the rationality of the legislative decision. The legislature wanted a uniform workload policy to be in place by a certain date. It could properly conclude that collective bargaining about that policy in the future would interfere with the attainment of this end. Under our precedent, this is sufficient to sustain the exclusion of university professors from the otherwise general collective-bargaining scheme for public employees.

The petition for a writ of certiorari is granted, the judgment of the Supreme Court of Ohio is reversed, and the case is remanded for further proceedings not inconsistent with this opinion.

Review Questions and Explanations: *Central State University*

1. A general rule of appellate review is to defer to trial court fact-finding, and reject only those findings that are "clearly erroneous." Here, we don't know exactly what the trial court found. The opinion focuses on the Ohio Supreme Court's review of the evidence in the record, but the U.S. Supreme Court never addresses that evidence directly. Suppose the Ohio Supreme Court was right—that there was no evidence presented in the litigation to show that collective bargaining has caused teaching load reductions. Would that have affected the outcome in the U.S. Supreme Court?

2. Why do you think the Court agrees with the Ohio Supreme Court dissenters in saying that the evidence on this question is "inconsequential"? In other words,

what is the connection between this point about factfinding being "inconsequential" and the idea of deferential review under the rational basis test?

3. Is *Central State University* consistent with *Railway Express* and *Williamson*? Explain.

---

2. The Fourteenth Amendment's State Action Requirement

The next case you will read, *The Civil Rights Cases,* involved a challenge to a major piece of civil rights legislation passed by Congress after the end of the Civil War. The legislation prohibited race-based discrimination in privately owned places of public accommodation, such as restaurants and hotels. If enforced, the federal law would have prohibited the "Jim Crow" system of legalized racial separation that took hold in the South shortly after these cases were decided. Instead, the Court struck the legislation down. Congress would not enact similar legislation until the Civil Rights Act of 1964—almost a hundred years later. Moreover, it would pass this later legislation under its Commerce Clause powers, not the powers given it under the Fourteenth and Fifteenth Amendments. When reading the case, think about why the Court's decision made that necessary—and whether it was right in doing so.

Doctrinally, the *Civil Rights Cases* introduce you to the "state action" doctrine. The state action doctrine limits the reach of constitutional rights and duties. Generally speaking, the doctrine holds that only governmental actors can violate the Constitution. Thus, while a public entity must not violate your right to freedom of speech or your right to equal protection, a private actor is under no such constitutional constraints. Prohibitions on things like race or sex discrimination in interactions between private actors do exist, but they are statutory, not constitutional, restrictions.

The first requirement in this area of law, consequently, is determining when something is and is not state action. Limiting the reach of constitutional obligations to encompass only state actions has the presumptively beneficial effect of leaving a zone of liberty for private decisionmaking. The Court, however, (also understandably) has been reluctant to let this limitation be used in ways that allow states to circumvent their constitutional duties by delegating them to private actors, or that systemically deprive people of substantive rights.

Guided Reading Questions: *The Civil Rights Cases*

1. What does it mean for a "state" to "deny" someone the "equal protection of the laws"? When reading the case, pay close attention to how both the majority and the dissent are interpreting this phrase.

2. The Court in *The Civil Rights Cases* says that Congress does not have power under the Fourteenth Amendment to regulate the conduct of private, as opposed to governmental, actors. Why not? Consider whether you agree with the Court that either the text or history of the Equal Protection clause mandate this result.

3. *The Civil Rights Cases* are important, in that they severely constrain the reach of the Fourteenth Amendment and Congress's power under it. When

reading the case, consider the arguments about judicial review discussed in Part
Three of this book.

The Civil Rights Cases

109 U.S. 3 (1883)

Majority: *Bradley*, Waite (CJ), Miller, Field, Woods, Matthews, Gray, Blatchford
Dissent: *Harlan*

JUSTICE BRADLEY delivered the opinion of the Court.

These cases are all founded on the first and second sections of the act of congress known
as the 'Civil Rights Act,' passed March 1, 1875, entitled 'An act to protect all citizens in
their civil and legal rights.' 18 St. 335. It is obvious that the primary and important question
in all the cases is the constitutionality of the law; for if the law is unconstitutional none of
the prosecutions can stand. The sections of the law referred to provide as follows:

> Section 1. That all persons within the jurisdiction of the United States shall be
> entitled to the full and equal enjoyment of the accommodations, advantages, fa-
> cilities, and privileges of inns, public conveyances on land or water, theaters,
> and other places of public amusement; subject only to the conditions and
> limitations established by law, and applicable alike to citizens of every race and
> color, regardless of any previous condition of servitude.

> Sec. 2. That any person who shall violate the foregoing section by denying to
> any citizen, except for reasons by law applicable to citizens of every race and
> color, and regardless of any previous condition of servitude, the full enjoyment
> of any of the accommodations, advantages, facilities, or privileges in said section
> enumerated, or by aiding or inciting such denial, shall, for every such offense,
> forfeit and pay the sum of $500 to the person aggrieved thereby, to be recovered
> in an action of debt, with full costs; and shall, also, for every such offense, be
> deemed guilty of a misdemeanor, and upon conviction thereof shall be fined not
> less than $500 nor more than $1,000, or shall be imprisoned not less than 30
> days nor more than one year.

Are these sections constitutional? The first section, which is the principal one, cannot
be fairly understood without attending to the last clause, which qualifies the preceding part.
The essence of the law is, not to declare broadly that all persons shall be entitled to the full
and equal enjoyment of the accommodations, advantages, facilities, and privileges of inns,
public conveyances, and theaters; but that such enjoyment shall not be subject to any
conditions applicable only to citizens of a particular race or color, or who had been in a
previous condition of servitude. In other words, it is the purpose of the law to declare that,
in the enjoyment of the accommodations and privileges of inns, public conveyances, theaters,
and other places of public amusement, no distinction shall be made between citizens of
different race or color, or between those who have, and those who have not, been slaves.
Its effect is to declare that in all inns, public conveyances, and places of amusement, colored
citizens, whether formerly slaves or not, and citizens of other races, shall have the same
accommodations and privileges in all inns, public conveyances, and places of amusement,
as are enjoyed by white citizens; and *vice versa*. The second section makes it a penal offense
in any person to deny to any citizen of any race or color, regardless of previous servitude,
any of the accommodations or privileges mentioned in the first section.

Has congress constitutional power to make such a law? Of course, no one will contend that the power to pass it was contained in the constitution before the adoption of the last three amendments. The power is sought, first, in the fourteenth amendment, and the views and arguments of distinguished senators, advanced while the law was under consideration, claiming authority to pass it by virtue of that amendment, are the principal arguments adduced in favor of the power. We have carefully considered those arguments, as was due to the eminent ability of those who put them forward, and have felt, in all its force, the weight of authority which always invests a law that congress deems itself competent to pass. But the responsibility of an independent judgment is now thrown upon this court; and we are bound to exercise it according to the best lights we have.

The first section of the fourteenth amendment, which is the one relied on, after declaring who shall be citizens of the United States, and of the several states, is prohibitory in its character, and prohibitory upon the states. It declares that no state shall make or enforce any law which shall abridge the privileges or immunities of citizens of the United States; nor shall any state deprive any person of life, liberty, or property without due process of law; nor deny to any person within its jurisdiction the equal protection of the laws.' It is state action of a particular character that is prohibited. Individual invasion of individual rights is not the subject-matter of the amendment. It has a deeper and broader scope. It nullifies and makes void all state legislation, and state action of every kind, which impairs the privileges and immunities of citizens of the United States, or which injures them in life, liberty, or property without due process of law, or which denies to any of them the equal protection of the laws.

It not only does this, but, in order that the national will, thus declared, may not be a mere *brutum fulmen*, the last section of the amendment invests congress with power to enforce it by appropriate legislation. To enforce what? To enforce the prohibition. To adopt appropriate legislation for correcting the effects of such prohibited state law and state acts, and thus to render them effectually null, void, and innocuous. This is the legislative power conferred upon congress, and this is the whole of it. It does not invest congress with power to legislate upon subjects which are within the domain of state legislation; but to provide modes of relief against state legislation, or state action, of the kind referred to. It does not authorize congress to create a code of municipal law for the regulation of private rights; but to provide modes of redress against the operation of state laws, and the action of state officers, executive or judicial, when these are subversive of the fundamental rights specified in the amendment.

Positive rights and privileges are undoubtedly secured by the fourteenth amendment; but they are secured by way of prohibition against state laws and state proceedings affecting those rights and privileges, and by power given to congress to legislate for the purpose of carrying such prohibition into effect; and such legislation must necessarily be predicated upon such supposed state laws or state proceedings, and be directed to the correction of their operation and effect....

And so in the present case, until some state law has been passed, or some state action through its officers or agents has been taken, adverse to the rights of citizens sought to be protected by the fourteenth amendment, no legislation of the United States under said amendment, nor any proceeding under such legislation, can be called into activity, for the prohibitions of the amendment are against state laws and acts done under state authority. Of course, legislation may and should be provided in advance to meet the exigency when it arises, but it should be adapted to the mischief and wrong which the amendment was intended to provide against; and that is, state laws or state action of some kind adverse to the rights of the citizen secured by the amendment.

Such legislation cannot properly cover the whole domain of rights appertaining to life, liberty, and property, defining them and providing for their vindication. That would be to establish a code of municipal law regulative of all private rights between man and man in society. It would be to make congress take the place of the state legislatures and to supersede them. It is absurd to affirm that, because the rights of life, liberty, and property (which include all civil rights that men have) are by the amendment sought to be protected against invasion on the part of the state without due process of law, congress may, therefore, provide due process of law for their vindication in every case; and that, because the denial by a state to any persons of the equal protection of the laws is prohibited by the amendment, therefore congress may establish laws for their equal protection. In fine, the legislation which congress is authorized to adopt in this behalf is not general legislation upon the rights of the citizen, but corrective legislation; that is, such as may be necessary and proper for counteracting such laws as the states may adopt or enforce, and which by the amendment they are prohibited from making or enforcing, or such acts and proceedings as the states may commit or take, and which by the amendment they are prohibited from committing or taking. It is not necessary for us to state, if we could, what legislation would be proper for congress to adopt. It is sufficient for us to examine whether the law in question is of that character.

An inspection of the law shows that it makes no reference whatever to any supposed or apprehended violation of the fourteenth amendment on the part of the states. It is not predicated on any such view. It proceeds *ex directo* to declare that certain acts committed by individuals shall be deemed offenses, and shall be prosecuted and punished by proceedings in the courts of the United States. It does not profess to be corrective of any constitutional wrong committed by the states; it does not make its operation to depend upon any such wrong committed. It applies equally to cases arising in states which have the justest laws respecting the personal rights of citizens, and whose authorities are ever ready to enforce such laws as to those which arise in states that may have violated the prohibition of the amendment. In other words, it steps into the domain of local jurisprudence, and lays down rules for the conduct of individuals is society towards each other, and imposes sanctions for the enforcement of those rules, without referring in any manner to any supposed action of the state or its authorities.

If this legislation is appropriate for enforcing the prohibitions of the amendment, it is difficult to see where it is to stop. Why may not congress, with equal show of authority, enact a code of laws for the enforcement and vindication of all rights of life, liberty, and property? If it is supposable that the states may deprive persons of life, liberty, and property without due process of law, (and the amendment itself does suppose this,) why should not congress proceed at once to prescribe due process of law for the protection of every one of these fundamental rights, in every possible case, as well as to prescribe equal privileges in inns, public conveyances, and theaters. The truth is that the implication of a power to legislate in this manner is based upon the assumption that if the states are forbidden to legislate or act in a particular way on a particular subject, and power is conferred upon congress to enforce the prohibition, this gives congress power to legislate generally upon that subject, and not merely power to provide modes of redress against such state legislation or action. The assumption is certainly unsound. It is repugnant to the tenth amendment of the constitution, which declares that powers not delegated to the United States by the constitution, nor prohibited by it to the states, are reserved to the states respectively or to the people....

In this connection it is proper to state that civil rights, such as are guaranteed by the constitution against state aggression, cannot be impaired by the wrongful acts of individuals, unsupported by state authority in the shape of laws, customs, or judicial or executive proceedings. The wrongful act of an individual, unsupported by any such authority, is simply a private wrong, or a crime of that individual; an invasion of the rights of the injured party, it is true, whether they affect his person, his property, or his reputation; but if not sanctioned in some way by the state, or not done under state authority, his rights remain in full force, and may presumably be vindicated by resort to the laws of the state for redress.... Hence, in all those cases where the constitution seeks to protect the rights of the citizen against discriminative and unjust laws of the state by prohibiting such laws, it is not individual offenses, but abrogation and denial of rights, which it denounces, and for which it clothes the congress with power to provide a remedy. This abrogation and denial of rights, for which the states alone were or could be responsible, was the great seminal and fundamental wrong which was intended to be remedied. And the remedy to be provided must necessarily be predicated upon that wrong. It must assume that in the cases provided for, the evil or wrong actually committed rests upon some state law or state authority for its excuse and perpetration....

On the whole, we are of opinion that no countenance of authority for the passage of the law in question can be found in either the thirteenth or fourteenth amendment of the constitution; and no other ground of authority for its passage being suggested, it must necessarily be declared void, at least so far as its operation in the several states is concerned.

This conclusion disposes of the cases now under consideration.... [T]he answer to be given will be, that the first and second sections of the act of congress of March 1, 1875, entitled 'An act to protect all citizens in their civil and legal rights,' are unconstitutional and void, and that judgment should be rendered upon the several indictments in those cases accordingly. And it is so ordered.

JUSTICE HARLAN, dissenting.

The opinion in these cases proceeds, as it seems to me, upon grounds entirely too narrow and artificial. The substance and spirit of the recent amendments of the constitution have been sacrificed by a subtle and ingenious verbal criticism. 'It is not the words of the law but the internal sense of it that makes the law. The letter of the law is the body; the sense and reason of the law is the soul.' Constitutional provisions, adopted in the interest of liberty, and for the purpose of securing, through national legislation, if need be, rights inhering in a state of freedom, and belonging to American citizenship, have been so construed as to defeat the ends the people desired to accomplish, which they attempted to accomplish, and which they supposed they had accomplished by changes in their fundamental law. By this I do not mean that the determination of these cases should have been materially controlled by considerations of mere expediency or policy. I mean only, in this form, to express an earnest conviction that the court has departed from the familiar rule requiring, in the interpretation of constitutional provisions, that full effect be given to the intent with which they were adopted.

The purpose of the first section of the act of congress of March 1, 1875, was to prevent *race* discrimination. It does not assume to define the general conditions and limitations under which inns, public conveyances, and places of public amusement may be conducted, but only declares that such conditions and limitations, whatever they may be, shall not be applied, by way of discrimination, *on account of race, color, or previous condition of servitude.* The second section provides a penalty against any one denying, or aiding or inciting the denial, to any citizen that equality of right given by the first section, except for reasons by law applicable to citizens of every race or color, and regardless of any previous condition of servitude.

There seems to be no substantial difference between my brethren and myself as to what was the purpose of congress; for they say that the essence of the law is, not to declare broadly that all persons shall be entitled to the full and equal enjoyment of the accommodations, advantages, facilities, and privileges of inns, public conveyances, and theaters, but that such enjoyment shall not be subject to any conditions applicable only to citizens of a particular race or color, or who had been in a previous condition of servitude. The effect of the statute, the court says, is that colored citizens, whether formerly slaves or not, and citizens of other races, shall have the same accommodations and privileges in all inns, public conveyances, and places of amusement as are enjoyed by white persons, and *vice versa*.

The court adjudges that congress is without power, under either the thirteenth or fourteenth amendment, to establish such regulations, and that the first and second sections of the statute are, in all their parts, unconstitutional and void.

Before considering the particular language and scope of these amendments it will be proper to recall the relations which, prior to their adoption, subsisted between the national government and the institution of slavery, as indicated by the provisions of the constitution, the legislation of congress, and the decisions of this court. In this mode we may obtain keys with which to open the mind of the people, and discover the thought intended to be expressed.

In section 2 of article 4 of the constitution it was provided that 'no person held to service or labor in one state, under the laws thereof, escaping into another, shall, in consequence of any law or regulation therein, be discharged from such service or labor, but shall be delivered up on claim of the party to whom such service or labor may be due.' Under the authority of that clause congress passed the fugitive slave law of 1793, establishing the mode for the recovery of a fugitive slave, and prescribing a penalty against any person knowingly and willingly obstructing or hindering the master, his agent or attorney, in seizing, arresting, and recovering the fugitive, or who should rescue the fugitive from him, or who should harbor or conceal the slave after notice that he was a fugitive.

In Prigg v. Com., this court had occasion to define the powers and duties of congress in reference to fugitives from labor. Speaking by Mr. Justice STORY, the court laid down these propositions: That a clause of the constitution conferring a right should not be so construed as to make it shadowy, or unsubstantial, or leave the citizen without a remedial power adequate for its protection, when another mode, equally accordant with the words and the sense in which they were used, would enforce and protect the right so granted; that congress is not restricted to legislation for the exertion of its powers expressly granted; but, for the protection of rights guaranteed by the constitution, it may employ, through legislation, such means, not prohibited, as are necessary and proper, or such as are appropriate, to attain the ends proposed; that the constitution recognized the master's right of property in his fugitive slave, and, as incidental thereto, the right of seizing and recovering him, regardless of any state law, or regulation, or local custom whatsoever; and that the right of the master to have his slave, so escaping, delivered up on claim, being guaranteed by the constitution, the fair implication was that the national government was clothed with appropriate authority and functions to enforce it.

The court said:

> The fundamental principle, applicable to all cases of this sort, would seem to be that when the end is required the means are given, and when the duty is enjoined the ability to perform it is contemplated to exist on the part of the functionary to whom it is entrusted.

Again:

> It would be a strange anomaly and forced construction to suppose that the
> national government meant to rely for the due fulfillment of its own proper
> duties, and the rights which it intended to secure, upon state legislation, and
> not upon that of the Union. *A fortiori*, it would be more objectionable to suppose
> that a power which was to be the same throughout the Union should be confided
> to state sovereignty, which could not rightfully act beyond its own territorial
> limits.

The act of 1793 was, upon these grounds, adjudged to be a constitutional exercise of
the powers of congress....

It remains now to consider these cases with reference to the power congress has possessed
since the adoption of the fourteenth amendment.

Before the adoption of the recent amendments it had become, as we have seen, the
established doctrine of this court that negroes, whose ancestors had been imported and
sold as slaves, could not become citizens of a state, or even of the United States, with the
rights and privileges guarantied to citizens by the national constitution; further, that one
might have all the rights and privileges of a citizen of a state without being a citizen in
the sense in which that word was used in the national constitution, and without being
entitled to the privileges and immunities of citizens of the several states.... It was openly
announced that whatever rights persons of that race might have as freemen, under the
guaranties of the national constitution, they could not become citizens of a state, with
the rights belonging to citizens, except by the consent of such state; consequently, that
their civil rights, as citizens of the state, depended entirely upon state legislation. To meet
this new peril to the black race, that the purposes of the nation might not be doubted or
defeated, and by way of further enlargement of the power of congress, the fourteenth
amendment was proposed for adoption.

Remembering that this court, in the Slaughter-house Cases, declared that the one
pervading purpose found in all the recent amendments, lying at the foundation of each,
and without which none of them would have been suggested, was 'the freedom of the
slave race, the security and firm establishment of that freedom, and the protection of the
newly made freeman and citizen from the oppression of those who had formerly exercised
unlimited dominion over him;' that each amendment was addressed primarily to the
grievances of that race,—let us proceed to consider the language of the fourteenth amendment. Its first and fifth sections are in these words:

> Section 1. All persons born or naturalized in the United States, and subject to
> the jurisdiction thereof, are citizens of the United States and of the state wherein
> they reside. No state shall make or enforce any law which shall abridge the
> privileges or immunities of citizens of the United States; nor shall any state
> deprive any person of life, liberty, or property without due process of law; nor
> deny to any person within its jurisdiction the equal protection of the laws.

> Sec. 5. That congress shall have power to enforce, by appropriate legislation, the
> provisions of this article.

It is, therefore, an essential inquiry what, if any, right, privilege, or immunity was
given by the nation to colored persons when they were made citizens of the state in which
they reside? Did the national grant of state citizenship to that race, of its own force, invest
them with any rights, privileges, and immunities whatever? That they became entitled,
upon the adoption of the fourteenth amendment, 'to all privileges and immunities of

citizens in the several states,' within the meaning of section 2 of article 4 of the constitution, no one, I suppose, will for a moment question. What are the privileges and immunities to which, by that clause of the constitution, they became entitled? To this it may be answered, generally, upon the authority of the adjudged cases, that they are those which are fundamental in citizenship in a free government, 'common to the citizens in the latter states under their constitutions and laws by virtue of their being citizens.' Of that provision it has been said, with the approval of this court, that no other one in the constitution has tended so strongly to constitute the citizens of the United States one people....

But what was secured to colored citizens of the United States—as between them and their respective states—by the grant to them of state citizenship? With what rights, privileges, or immunities did this grant from the nation invest them? There is one, if there be no others—exemption from race discrimination in respect of any civil right belonging to citizens of the white race in the same state. That, surely, is their constitutional privilege when within the jurisdiction of other states. And such must be their constitutional right, in their own state, unless the recent amendments be 'splendid baubles,' thrown out to delude those who deserved fair and generous treatment at the hands of the nation. Citizenship in this country necessarily imports equality of civil rights among citizens of every race in the same state. It is fundamental in American citizenship that, in respect of such rights, there shall be no discrimination by the state, or its officers, or by individuals, or corporations exercising public functions or authority, against any citizen because of his race or previous condition of servitude....

It can hardly be claimed that exemption from race discrimination, in respect of civil rights, against those to whom state citizenship was granted by the nation, is any less for the colored race a new constitutional right, derived from and secured by the national constitution, than is exemption from such discrimination in the exercise of the elective franchise. It cannot be that the latter is an attribute of national citizenship, while the other is not essential in national citizenship, or fundamental in state citizenship.

If, then, exemption from discrimination in respect of civil rights is a new constitutional right, secured by the grant of state citizenship to colored citizens of the United States, why may not the nation, by means of its own legislation of a primary direct character, guard, protect, and enforce that right? It is a right and privilege which the nation conferred. It did not come from the states in which those colored citizens reside. It has been the established doctrine of this court during all its history, accepted as vital to the national supremacy, that congress, in the absence of a positive delegation of power to the state legislatures, may by legislation enforce and protect any right derived from or created by the national constitution.... Will any one claim, in view of the declarations of this court in former cases, or even without them, that exemption of colored citizens within their states from race discrimination, in respect of the civil rights of citizens, is not an immunity created or derived from the national constitution?

This court has always given a broad and liberal construction to the constitution, so as to enable congress, by legislation, to enforce rights secured by that instrument. The legislation congress may enact, in execution of its power to enforce the provisions of this amendment, is that which is appropriate to protect the right granted. Under given circumstances, that which the court characterizes as corrective legislation might be sufficient. Under other circumstances primary direct legislation may be required. But it is for congress, not the judiciary, to say which is best adapted to the end to be attained. In U.S. v. Fisher this court said that 'congress must possess the choice of means, and must be empowered to use any means which are in fact conducive to the exercise of a power granted by the constitution.' 'The sound construction of the constitution,' said Chief Justice Marshall, 'must allow to the national legislature that discretion, with respect to the means by which the powers it confers are to be carried into execution, which will enable that body to perform the high duties assigned to it in the manner most beneficial to the people. Let the end be legitimate,—let it be within the scope of the constitution,—and all means which are appropriate, which are plainly adapted to that end, which are not prohibited, but consistent with the letter and spirit of the constitution, are constitutional.' McCulloch v. Maryland.

Must these rules of construction be now abandoned? Are the powers of the national legislature to be restrained in proportion as the rights and privileges, derived from the nation, are more valuable? Are constitutional provisions, enacted to secure the dearest rights of freemen and citizens, to be subjected to that rule of construction, applicable to private instruments, which requires that the words to be interpreted must be taken most strongly against those who employ them? Or shall it be remembered that 'a constitution of government, founded by the people for themselves and their posterity, and for objects of the most momentous nature,—for perpetual union, for the establishment of justice, for the general welfare, and for a perpetuation of the blessings of liberty,—necessarily requires that every interpretation of its powers should have a constant reference to these objects? No interpretation of the words in which those powers are granted can be a sound one which narrows down their ordinary import so as to defeat those objects.'...

Exemption from race discrimination in respect of the civil rights which are fundamental in *citizenship* in a republican government, is, as we have seen, a new constitutional right, created by the nation, with express power in congress, by legislation, to enforce the constitutional provision from which it is derived. If, in some sense, such race discrimination is a denial of the equal protection of the laws, within the letter of the last clause of the first section, it cannot be possible that a mere prohibition upon state denial of such equal protection to persons within its jurisdiction, or a prohibition upon state laws abridging the privileges and immunities of citizens of the United States, takes from the nation the power which it has uniformly exercised of protecting, by primary direct legislation, those privileges and immunities which existed under the constitution before the adoption of the fourteenth amendment, or which have been created by that amendment in behalf of those thereby made *citizens* of their respective states.

It was said of Dred Scott v. Sandford that this court in that case overruled the action of two generations, virtually inserted a new clause in the constitution, changed its character, and made a new departure in the workings of the federal government. I may be permitted to say that if the recent amendments are so construed that congress may not, in its own discretion, and independently of the action or non-action of the states, provide, by legislation of a primary and direct character, for the security of rights created by the national constitution; if it be adjudged that the obligation to protect the fundamental privileges and immunities granted by the fourteenth amendment to citizens residing in the several states, rests, primarily, not on the nation, but on the states; if it be further adjudged that individuals and corporations exercising public functions may, without liability to direct primary legislation on the part of congress, make the race of citizens the ground for denying them that equality of civil rights which the constitution ordains as a principle of republican citizenship,—then, not only the foundations upon which the national supremacy has always securely rested will be materially disturbed, but we shall enter upon an era of constitutional law when the rights of freedom and American citizenship cannot receive from the nation that efficient protection which heretofore was accorded to slavery and the rights of the master....

Review Questions and Explanations: *The Civil Rights Cases*

1. The majority states that "Positive rights and privileges are undoubtedly secured by the fourteenth amendment; but they are secured by way of prohibition against state laws and state proceedings affecting those rights and privileges." Does this assertion follow directly from the text? If not, how does the Court defend it?

2. The majority also makes this statement: "Of course, no one will contend that the power to pass [the law] was contained in the constitution before the adoption of the last three amendments." If correct, does that mean the Civil Rights Act of 1964 also is unconstitutional?

3. Regardless of the statement quoted above, does the Court's holding about state action mean that Congress cannot use its Commerce Clause power to prohibit race discrimination in privately owned restaurants and other places of public accommodation? Why or why not?

4. By this point in your study of constitutional law, you are familiar with the various tools of constitutional interpretation used by the courts. The majority and the dissent emphasize different interpretive tools. Which tools are the justices using in the majority and dissenting opinions, and how are they using them?

Exercise: The State Action Doctrine

Imagine that your syllabus includes a rule stating that class participation accounts for 25 percent of your final grade. Imagine also that the syllabus further states that each student shall be allowed the equal opportunity to participate in class discussion. Your professor is in charge of enforcing this rule. If one of your classmates repeatedly interrupts you and everyone else, and dominates the classroom discussion, who has denied your opportunity to participate equally in the discussion, your classmate or your professor? Prepare to defend your conclusion in class.

The Court's decision limiting the reach of the Fourteenth Amendment to "state action" has never been overturned. The following Case Note explains the Court's work in this area.

CASE NOTE: The "White Primary" cases. The most famous series of cases in this area involve the so-called "White Primary" cases coming out of Texas in the first half of the twentieth century. The Jaybird Democrats were, formally speaking, a private association in Texas. During the time period relevant here, the group worked, often in cooperation with state officials, to avoid the Fourteenth and Fifteenth Amendments' prohibition on racial discrimination in voting. These amendments prohibited states from engaging in racial discrimination in voting matters. This irritated the Texas Democratic Party, which did not want to let African Americans vote in its primary. The Texas Legislature, controlled by Texas Democrats, was accommodating, passing a law prohibiting African-Americans from voting in the Democratic Primary. Given that the discrimination was expressly authorized by state law, the Court had little difficulty finding state action and striking the law down as a violation of the Fourteenth Amendment. *Nixon v. Herdon*, 273 U.S. 536 (1927).

The state legislature then repealed the direct prohibition, but went on to pass a law authorizing the party's executive committee to determine for itself the qualifications of its primary voters. The committee immediately passed a resolution restricting primary voting to whites. The Court invalidated this as well, finding state action in the decision of the state to delegate its authority to the executive committee. *Nixon v. Condon*, 286 U.S. 73 (1932). A few years later, the Court also invalidated a system in which the executive committee imposed the same restrictions, but without explicit authorization from the state to do so. In that case, *Smith v. Allwright*, 321 U.S. 649 (1944), the Court held that state's involvement in regulating and operating the primary election made the primary itself a state function and therefore was sufficient to satisfy the state action doctrine.

The Texas Democrats were not yet done, however. Their next move was to rely on a "pre-primary primary" held by the Jaybird Democrats. The Jaybirds choose their candidate and then voted in accordance with the "club's" selection in the state sponsored primary. Candidates who won the Jaybird primary would inevitably win the Democratic nomination, which in the post-Civil War, single-party South, meant that the Jaybird's preferred candidate would win the general election as well. It also just so happened that membership of the Jaybirds automatically included all white Democrats registered in the jurisdiction. The club's primary also followed all the rules used in the official party primary, and the club was governed by the same officers who led the local Democratic Party. For all intents and purposes, then, the Jaybird Democrats Club was the local Democratic Party stripped of its African American members.

This arrangement was challenged in *Terry v. Adams*, 345 U.S. 461 (1953). The Court found this a much harder case than the ones preceding it. Justice Rehnquist, in memo he wrote while working as a law clerk for Justice Jackson, wrote this of the case:

> The Constitution does not prevent the majority from banding together, nor does it attaint success in the effort. It is about time the Court faced the fact that the white people of the south do not like the colored people: the constitution restrains them from effecting this dislike through state action but it most assuredly did not appoint the Court as a sociological watchdog to rear up every time private discrimination raises its admittedly ugly head.

The Constitution, as clerk-Rehnquist pointed out, does not generally restrict the conduct of private clubs. Nor, however, has the Court been eager to allow states to "contract out" their obligations to comply with constitutional requirements. In *Terry*, the Court found sufficient state action to strike down the discriminatory practice. The Jaybird primary, the Court held, had become an integral part of the process of choosing elected officials. As such, it was undertaking a traditional state function and was subject to constitutional prohibitions on racial discrimination.

The Court continues to struggle with the scope of the state action doctrine. In *Shelley v. Kraemer*, 334 U.S. 1 (1948), the Court found state action in the participation of local police and court officials in enforcing private contracts restricting the sale of real property to non-white buyers. More recently, the Court has found state action in the decisions made by the governing boards of high school athletic associations comprised of public and private school members. In that case, *Brentwood Academy v. Tennessee Secondary School Athletic Association*, 531 U.S. 288 (2001), the Court held that the athletic association's conduct constituted state action when its actions and history were sufficiently "entangled" with the State. The majority held that "[t]he nominally private character of the Association is overborne by the pervasive entwinement of public institutions and public officials in its composition and workings, and there is no substantial reason to claim unfairness in applying constitutional standards to it." Justice Thomas, writing in dissent, complained that the majority's "entwinement" standard was both unclear and too expansive to protect purely private conduct from constitutional scrutiny.

3. Competing Concepts of Equality: *Plessy, Brown,* and *Korematsu*

The next three cases, *Plessy v. Ferguson, Brown v. Board of Education*, and *Korematsu v. United States,* each involve racial classifications challenged under the Equal Protection clause. These cases were issued before the Court had fully articulated the system of tiered review discussed above. The decisions do not, therefore, use the tidy language of "suspect classifications" and "strict scrutiny." What they do instead is present various ways of thinking about what the term "equal protection" might mean and how it is to be implemented in our constitutional law.

Plessy and *Korematsu* are among the most reviled decisions ever issued by the U.S. Supreme Court. And with good reason: the Court in *Plessy* gave legal sanction to the "separate but equal" doctrine eventually struck down in *Brown v. Board of Education,* while the *Korematsu* Court upheld an order authorizing the blanket incarceration of Japanese Americans.

It would be a mistake, however, to create and critique cartoon caricatures of these cases. Justices rarely construct bad decisions out of thin air. The justices in these cases, as in all cases, used the tools of legal reasoning generally accepted in their time and place. The distinction between "political" and "social" equality used in *Plessy*, for example, dated back many decades and had been used by Abraham Lincoln in his famous debates with Stephen A. Douglas in the 1858 Illinois Senate race: Lincoln, like Douglas, said he did not favor social equality or "intermingling" of the races. And the effort to recast the exclusion order at issue in *Korematsu* as aimed at something other than race is echoed in arguments made today about same-sex marriage: it is not beyond the limits of accepted political discourse to argue today that prohibitions on same-sex marriage do not discriminate on the basis of sexual orientation because gay men and woman, like straight men and women, are free to marry members of the opposite sex.

Plessy, Brown, and *Korematsu* each, then, present ways of thinking about equal protection that are not alien, for better or worse, to our political and legal systems. We present the cases as a group here to encourage you to think deeply about the different visions of "equal" protection they represent.

Guided Reading Questions: *Plessy v. Ferguson*

1. *Plessy* distinguishes political equality from what the Court sees as "merely" social equality. What work is this distinction doing in the majority opinion? What vision of equal protection does this distinction support?

2. Note the passage in the majority opinion where the Court says that it would enforce state laws prohibiting segregated public accommodations. Given this, what is the precise constitutional holding of the case?

3. Justice Harlan's dissent in *Plessy* criticizes the majority's reasoning in four distinct ways. Identify each of them, and then critique his critique. Which of his criticisms do you find the most (and least) persuasive?

Plessy v. Ferguson

163 U.S. 537 (1896)

Majority: *Brown*, Fuller (CJ), Field, Gray, Shiras, White, Peckham

Dissent: *Harlan*

MR. JUSTICE BROWN delivered the opinion of the court.

[A]n act of the General Assembly of the State of Louisiana, passed in 1890 ... enacts "that all railway companies carrying passengers in their coaches in this State, shall provide equal but separate accommodations for the white, and colored races ... and should any passenger refuse to occupy the coach or compartment to which he or she is assigned by the officer of such railway, said officer shall have power to refuse to carry such passenger on his train ..."

The third section provides ... that "nothing in this act shall be construed as applying to nurses attending children of the other race." ... The information filed in the criminal District Court charged in substance that Plessy, being a passenger between two stations within the State of Louisiana, was assigned by officers of the company to the coach used for the race to which he belonged, but he insisted upon going into a coach used by the race to which he did not belong. Neither in the information nor plea was his particular race or color averred.

The petition for the writ of prohibition averred that petitioner was seven-eighths Caucasian and one-eighth African blood; that the mixture of colored blood was not discernible in him, and that he was entitled to every right, privilege and immunity secured to citizens of the United States of the white race; and that, upon such theory, he took possession of a vacant seat in a coach where passengers of the white race were accommodated, and was ordered by the conductor to vacate said coach and take a seat in another assigned to persons of the colored race, and having refused to comply with such demand he was forcibly ejected with the aid of a police officer, and imprisoned in the parish jail to answer a charge of having violated the above act.

The constitutionality of this act is attacked upon the ground that it conflicts both with the *Thirteenth Amendment of the Constitution*, abolishing slavery, and the *Fourteenth Amendment*, which prohibits certain restrictive legislation on the part of the States....

A statute which implies merely a legal distinction between the white and colored races— a distinction which is founded in the color of the two races, and which must always exist so long as white men are distinguished from the other race by color—has no tendency to destroy the legal equality of the two races, or reestablish a state of involuntary servitude....

The object of the [Fourteenth Amendment] was undoubtedly to enforce the absolute equality of the two races before the law, but in the nature of things it could not have been intended to abolish distinctions based upon color, or to enforce social, as distinguished from political equality, or a commingling of the two races upon terms unsatisfactory to either. Laws permitting, and even requiring, their separation in places where they are liable to be brought into contact do not necessarily imply the inferiority of either race to the other, and have been generally, if not universally, recognized as within the competency of the state legislatures in the exercise of their police power. The most common instance of this is connected with the establishment of separate schools for white and colored children, which has been held to be a valid exercise of the legislative power even by courts of States where the political rights of the colored race have been longest and most earnestly enforced....

Laws forbidding the intermarriage of the two races may be said in a technical sense to interfere with the freedom of contract, and yet have been universally recognized as within the police power of the State....

The distinction between laws interfering with the political equality of the negro and those requiring the separation of the two races in schools, theatres and railway carriages has been frequently drawn by this court. Thus in Strauder v. West Virginia, it was held that a law of West Virginia limiting to white male persons, 21 years of age and citizens of the State, the right to sit upon juries, was a discrimination which implied a legal inferiority in civil society, which lessened the security of the right of the colored race, and was a step toward reducing them to a condition of servility....

[W]here the laws of a particular locality or the charter of a particular railway corporation has provided that no person shall be excluded from the cars on account of color, we have held that this meant that persons of color should travel in the same car as white ones, and that the enactment was not satisfied by the company's providing cars assigned exclusively to people of color, though they were as good as those which they assigned exclusively to white persons....

It is claimed by the plaintiff in error that, in any mixed community, the reputation of belonging to the dominant race, in this instance the white race, is property, in the same sense that a right of action, or of inheritance, is property. Conceding this to be so, for the purposes of this case, we are unable to see how this statute deprives him of, or in any way affects his right to, such property. If he be a white man and assigned to a colored coach, he may have his action for damages against the company for being deprived of his so called property. Upon the other hand, if he be a colored man and be so assigned, he has been deprived of no property, since he is not lawfully entitled to the reputation of being a white man.

In this connection, it is also suggested by the learned counsel for the plaintiff in error that the same argument that will justify the state legislature in requiring railways to provide separate accommodations for the two races will also authorize them to require separate cars to be provided for people whose hair is of a certain color, or who are aliens, or who belong to certain nationalities, or to enact laws requiring colored people to walk upon one side of the street, and white people upon the other, or requiring white men's houses to be painted white, and colored men's black, or their vehicles or business signs to be of different colors, upon the theory that one side of the street is as good as the other, or that a house or vehicle of one color is as good as one of another color. The reply to all this is that every exercise of the police power must be reasonable, and extend only to such laws as are enacted in good faith for the promotion for the public good, and not for the annoyance or oppression of a particular class. Thus in Yick Wo v. Hopkins, it was held by this court that a municipal ordinance of the city of San Francisco, to regulate the carrying on the public laundries within the limits of the municipality, violated the provisions of the Constitution of the United States, if it conferred upon the municipal authorities arbitrary power, at their own will, and without regard to discretion, in the legal sense of the term....

In determining the question of reasonableness it is at liberty to act with reference to the established usages, customs and traditions of the people, and with a view to the promotion of their comfort, and the preservation of the public peace and good order. Gauged by this standard, we cannot say that a law which authorizes or even requires the separation of the two races in public conveyances is unreasonable, or more obnoxious to the Fourteenth Amendment than the acts of Congress requiring separate schools for colored children in the District of Columbia, the constitutionality of which does not seem to have been questioned, or the corresponding acts of state legislatures.

We consider the underlying fallacy of the plaintiff's argument to consist in the assumption that the enforced separation of the two races stamps the colored race with a badge of inferiority. If this be so, it is not by reason of anything found in the act, but solely because the colored race chooses to put that construction upon it. The argument necessarily assumes that if, as has been more than once the case, and is not unlikely to be so again, the colored race should become the dominant power in the state legislature, and should enact a law in precisely similar terms, it would thereby relegate the white race to an inferior position. We imagine that the white race, at least, would not acquiesce in this assumption. The argument also assumes that social prejudices may be overcome by legislation, and that equal rights cannot be secured to the negro except by an enforced commingling of the two races. We cannot accept this proposition. If the two races are to meet upon terms of social equality, it must be the result of natural affinities, a mutual appreciation of each other's merits and a voluntary consent of individuals....

Legislation is powerless to eradicate racial instincts or to abolish distinctions based upon physical differences, and the attempt to do so can only result in accentuating the difficulties of the present situation. If the civil and political rights of both races be equal one cannot be inferior to the other civilly or politically. If one race be inferior to the other socially, the Constitution of the United States cannot put them upon the same plane.

It is true that the question of the proportion of colored blood necessary to constitute a colored person, as distinguished from a white person, is one upon which there is a difference of opinion in the different States, some holding that any visible admixture of black blood stamps the person as belonging to the colored race ... others that it depends upon the preponderance of blood ... and still others that the predominance of white blood must only be in the proportion of three-fourths.... But these are question to be determined under the laws of each State and are not properly put in issue in this case. Under the allegations of his petition it may undoubtedly become a question of importance whether, under the laws of Louisiana, the petitioner belongs to the white or colored race.

The judgment of the court below is therefore affirmed.

MR. JUSTICE HARLAN dissenting.

Every true man has pride of race, and under appropriate circumstances when the rights of others, his equals before the law, are not to be affected, it is his privilege to express such pride and to take such action based upon it as to him seems proper. But I deny that any legislative body or judicial tribunal may have regard to the race of citizens when the civil rights of those citizens are involved. Indeed, such legislation, as that here in question, is inconsistent not only with that equality of rights which pertains to citizenship, National and State, but with the personal liberty enjoyed by every one within the United States.

The Thirteenth Amendment does not permit the withholding or the deprivation of any right necessarily inhering in freedom. It not only struck down the institution of slavery as previously existing in the United States, but it prevents the imposition of any burdens or disabilities that constitute badges of slavery or servitude. It decreed universal civil freedom in this country. This court has so adjudged. But that amendment having been found inadequate to the protection of the rights of those who had been in slavery, it was followed by the Fourteenth Amendment, which added greatly to the dignity and glory of American citizenship.... These two amendments, if enforced according to their true intent and meaning, will protect all the civil rights that pertain to freedom and citizenship. Finally, and to the end that no citizen should be denied, on account of his race, the privilege of participating in the political control of his country, it was declared by the Fifteenth Amendment that "the right of citizens of the United States to vote shall not be denied or abridged by the United States or by any State on account of race, color or previous condition of servitude."

These notable additions to the fundamental law were welcomed by the friends of liberty throughout the world. They removed the race line from our governmental systems.... They declared, in legal effect, this court has further said, "that the law in the States shall be the same for the black as for the white; that all persons, whether colored or white, shall stand equal before the laws of the States, and, in regard to the colored race, for whose protection the amendment was primarily designed, that no discrimination shall be made against them by law because of their color." ...

It was said in argument that the statute of Louisiana does not discriminate against either race, but prescribes a rule applicable alike to white and colored citizens. But this argument does not meet the difficulty. Every one knows that the statute in question had its origin in the purpose, not so much to exclude white persons from railroad cars occupied by blacks, as to exclude colored people from coaches occupied by or assigned to white persons.... The thing to accomplish was, under the guise of giving equal accommodation for whites and blacks, to compel the latter to keep to themselves while travelling in railroad passenger coaches. No one would be so wanting in candor as to assert the contrary. The fundamental objection, therefore, to the statute is that it interferes with the personal freedom of citizens.... If a white man and a black man choose to occupy the same public conveyance on a public highway, it is their right to do so, and no government, proceeding alone on grounds of race, can prevent it without infringing the personal liberty of each....

If a State can prescribe, as a rule of civil conduct, that whites and blacks shall not travel as passengers in the same railroad coach, why may it not so regulate the use of the streets of its cities and towns as to compel white citizens to keep on one side of a street and black citizens to keep on the other?.... Why may it not require sheriffs to assign whites to one side of a court-room and blacks to the other? And why may it not also prohibit the commingling of the two races in the galleries of legislative halls or in public assemblages convened for the considerations of the political questions of the day? Further, if this statute of Louisiana is consistent with the personal liberty of citizens, why may not the State require the separation in railroad coaches of native and naturalized citizens of the United States, or of Protestants and Roman Catholics?

The answer given at the argument to these questions was that regulations of the kind they suggest would be unreasonable, and could not, therefore, stand before the law. Is it meant that the determination of questions of legislative power depends upon the inquiry whether the statute whose validity is questioned is, in the judgment of the courts, a reasonable one, taking all the circumstances into consideration? A statute may be unreasonable merely because a sound public policy forbade its enactment. But I do not understand that the courts have anything to do with the policy or expediency of legislation.... There is a dangerous tendency in these latter days to enlarge the functions of the courts, by means of judicial interference with the will of the people as expressed by the legislature.... If the power exists to enact a statute, that ends the matter so far as the courts are concerned. The adjudged cases in which statutes have been held to be void, because unreasonable, are those in which the means employed by the legislature were not at all germane to the end to which the legislature was competent.

The white race deems itself to be the dominant race in this country. And so it is, in prestige, in achievements, in education, in wealth and in power. So, I doubt not, it will continue to be for all time, if it remains true to its great heritage and holds fast to the principles of constitutional liberty. But in view of the Constitution, in the eye of the law, there is in this country no superior, dominant, ruling class of citizens. There is no caste here. Our Constitution is color-blind, and neither knows nor tolerates classes among citizens. In respect of civil rights, all citizens are equal before the law. The humblest is the peer of the most powerful. The law regards man as man, and takes no account of his surroundings or of his color when his civil rights as guaranteed by the supreme law of the land are involved. It is, therefore, to be regretted that this high tribunal, the final expositor of the fundamental law of the land, has reached the conclusion that it is competent for a State to regulate the enjoyment by citizens of their civil rights solely upon the basis of race.

In my opinion, the judgment this day rendered will, in time, prove to be quite as pernicious as the decision made by this tribunal in the Dred Scott case. It was adjudged in that case that the descendants of Africans who were imported into this country, and sold as slaves, were.... "considered as a subordinate and inferior class of beings, who had been subjugated by the dominant race, and, whether emancipated or not, yet remained subject to their authority, and had no rights or privileges but such as those who held the power and the government might choose to grant them." ... The recent amendments of the Constitution, it was supposed, had eradicated these principles from our institutions. But it seems that we have yet, in some of the States, a dominant race—a superior class of citizens, which assumes to regulate the enjoyment of civil rights, common to all citizens, upon the basis of race.... Sixty millions of whites are in no danger from the presence here of eight millions of blacks. The destinies of the two races, in this country, are indissolubly linked together, and the interests of both require that the common government of all shall not permit the seeds of race hate to be planted under the sanction of law....

The arbitrary separation of citizens, on the basis of race, while they are on a public highway, is a badge of servitude wholly inconsistent with the civil freedom and the equality before the law established by the Constitution....

For the reasons stated, I am constrained to withhold my assent from the opinion and judgment of the majority.

Review Questions and Explanations: *Plessy*

1. Justice Harlan's dissent has become a common citation for the idea that the Constitution requires that state action be "colorblind." What does it mean for the state to be colorblind? Is the effect of a colorblind reading of the Equal Protection clause different today than it would have been in the era in which Justice Harlan was writing?

2. Is Justice Harlan saying that any state use or consideration of or race is virtually *per se* unconstitutional? His opinion often has been read this way; do you agree with that reading? Would such a requirement be likely to generate more or less substantive equality?

3. Notice how both the majority and dissent in *Plessy* assume that judicial review under the Equal Protection clause, even in a case alleging racial discrimination, is limited to the application of a "rational basis" or "reasonableness" test. The majority appears to hold that the law bears a rational relationship to a legitimate governmental end (separation of the races is within the "police power"). The dissent doesn't apply a different test, but rather views the governmental end being pursued as prohibited by the Equal Protection clause. Review footnote 4 in *Carolene Products*, and think again about the arguments for and against heightened review in racial classification cases.

4. The assertion made above that *Plessy* was reasonably well-grounded in then-existing law does not mean the decision was not reprehensible — among other things, the Court obviously failed to see how social inequality can undermine political equality. But it does mean that we need to grapple with what made the decision legally, as opposed to morally or ethically, wrong. If it is wrong because it rests on a formalistic, non-substantive notion of equality that we have since come to reject, what does that tell us how we should approach today's equal protection disputes? Indeed, what, if anything, does it tell us about the very task of constitutional interpretation?

Guided Reading Questions: *Brown v. Board of Education*

1. The Court in *Brown* embraces a different vision of equality than did the *Plessy* Court. Just what vision that is, however, is deeply contested. As you will see later in this chapter in *Parents Involved v. Seattle Schools* (a case involving racial integration efforts voluntarily undertaken in two school districts) advocates on both sides of contemporary debates claim to be the true heirs of *Brown's* legacy. When reading the case, try to articulate with some precision the vision(s) of equality embraced in the case. Is it the right to not be classified on the basis of race for any purpose, or is it the right to not have racial classifications used for purposes of class-based subordination?

2. When reading the case, consider whether *Brown* embraces the same notion of equal protection Justice Harlan did in his dissent in *Plessy*.

Brown v. Board of Education

347 U.S. 483 (1954)

Unanimous decision: *Warren* (CJ), Black, Reed, Frankfurter, Douglas, Jackson, Burton, Clark, Minton

MR. CHIEF JUSTICE WARREN delivered the opinion of the Court.

These cases come to us from the States of Kansas, South Carolina, Virginia, and Delaware. They are premised on different facts and different local conditions, but a common legal question justifies their consideration together in this consolidated opinion.

In each of the cases, minors of the Negro race, through their legal representatives, seek the aid of the courts in obtaining admission to the public schools of their community on a nonsegregated basis. In each instance, they have been denied admission to schools attended by white children under laws requiring or permitting segregation according to race. This segregation was alleged to deprive the plaintiffs of the equal protection of the laws under the Fourteenth Amendment. In each of the cases other than the Delaware case, a three-judge federal district court denied relief to the plaintiffs on the so-called 'separate but equal' doctrine announced by this Court in Plessy v. Ferguson. Under that doctrine, equality of treatment is accorded when the races are provided substantially equal facilities, even though these facilities be separate. In the Delaware case, the Supreme Court of Delaware adhered to that doctrine, but ordered that the plaintiffs be admitted to the white schools because of their superiority to the Negro schools.

The plaintiffs contend that segregated public schools are not 'equal' and cannot be made 'equal,' and that hence they are deprived of the equal protection of the laws. Because of the obvious importance of the question presented, the Court took jurisdiction Argument was heard in the 1952 Term, and reargument was heard this Term on certain questions propounded by the Court.

Reargument was largely devoted to the circumstances surrounding the adoption of the Fourteenth Amendment in 1868. It covered exhaustively consideration of the Amendment in Congress, ratification by the states, then existing practices in racial segregation, and the views of proponents and opponents of the Amendment. This discussion and our own investigation convince us that, although these sources cast some light, it is not enough to resolve the problem with which we are faced. At best, they are inconclusive. The most avid proponents of the post-War Amendments undoubtedly intended them to remove all legal distinctions among 'all persons born or naturalized in the United States.' Their opponents, just as certainly, were antagonistic to both the letter and the spirit of the Amendments and wished them to have the most limited effect. What others in Congress and the state legislatures had in mind cannot be determined with any degree of certainty.

An additional reason for the inconclusive nature of the Amendment's history, with respect to segregated schools, is the status of public education at that time. In the South, the movement toward free common schools, supported by general taxation, had not yet taken hold. Education of white children was largely in the hands of private groups. Education of Negroes was almost nonexistent, and practically all of the race were illiterate. In fact, any education of Negroes was forbidden by law in some states. Today, in contrast, many Negroes have achieved outstanding success in the arts and sciences as well as in the business and professional world. It is true that public school education at the time of the Amendment had advanced further in the North, but the effect of the Amendment on Northern States was generally ignored in the congressional debates. Even in the North, the conditions of public education did not approximate those existing today. The curriculum was usually rudimentary; ungraded schools were common in rural areas; the school term was but three months a year in many states; and compulsory school attendance was virtually unknown. As a consequence, it is not surprising that there should be so little in the history of the Fourteenth Amendment relating to its intended effect on public education.

FN4. For a general study of the development of public education prior to the Amendment, see Butts and Cremin, A History of Education in American Culture (1953) (additional citations omitted). Although the demand for free public schools followed substantially the same pattern in both the North and the South, the development in the South did not begin to gain momentum until about 1850, some twenty years after that in the North. The reasons for the somewhat slower development in the South (e.g., the rural character of the South and the different regional attitudes toward state assistance) are well explained in Cubberley, supra, at 408–423. In the country as a whole, but particularly in the South, the War virtually stopped all progress in public education. Id., at 427–428. The low status of Negro education in all sections of the country, both before and immediately after the War, is described in Beale, A History of Freedom of Teaching in American Schools (1941), 112–132, 175–195. Compulsory school attendance laws were not generally adopted until after the ratification of the Fourteenth Amendment, and it was not until 1918 that such laws were in force in all the states. Cubberley, supra, at 563–565.

In the first cases in this Court construing the Fourteenth Amendment, decided shortly after its adoption, the Court interpreted it as proscribing all state-imposed discriminations against the Negro race. The doctrine of "separate but equal" did not make its appearance in this court until 1896 in the case of Plessy v. Ferguson, supra, involving not education but transportation. American courts have since labored with the doctrine for over half a century. In this Court, there have been six cases involving the 'separate but equal' doctrine in the field of public education. In Cumming v. Board of Education of Richmond County, and Gong Lum v. Rice, the validity of the doctrine itself was not challenged. In more recent cases, all on the graduate school level, inequality was found in that specific benefits enjoyed by white students were denied to Negro students of the same educational qualifications.... In none of these cases was it necessary to re-examine the doctrine to grant relief to the Negro plaintiff. And in Sweatt v. Painter, supra, the Court expressly reserved decision on the question whether Plessy v. Ferguson should be held inapplicable to public education.

> FN5. In re Slaughter-House Cases, 1873; Strauder v. West Virginia, 'It ordains that no State shall deprive any person of life, liberty, or property, without due process of law, or deny to any person within its jurisdiction the equal protection of the laws. What is this but declaring that the law in the States shall be the same for the black as for the white; that all persons, whether colored or white, shall stand equal before the laws of the States, and, in regard to the colored race, for whose protection the amendment was primarily designed, that no discrimination shall be made against them by law because of their color? The words of the amendment, it is true, are prohibitory, but they contain a necessary implication of a positive immunity, or right, most valuable to the colored race,—the right to exemption from unfriendly legislation against them distinctively as colored,—exemption from legal discriminations, implying inferiority in civil society, lessening the security of their enjoyment of the rights which others enjoy, and discriminations which are steps towards reducing them to the condition of a subject race.'

In the instant cases, that question is directly presented. Here, unlike Sweatt v. Painter, there are findings below that the Negro and white schools involved have been equalized, or are being equalized, with respect to buildings, curricula, qualifications and salaries of teachers, and other 'tangible' factors. Our decision, therefore, cannot turn on merely a comparison of these tangible factors in the Negro and white schools involved in each of the cases. We must look instead to the effect of segregation itself on public education.

In approaching this problem, we cannot turn the clock back to 1868 when the Amendment was adopted, or even to 1896 when Plessy v. Ferguson was written. We must consider public education in the light of its full development and its present place in American life throughout the Nation. Only in this way can it be determined if segregation in public schools deprives these plaintiffs of the equal protection of the laws.

Today, education is perhaps the most important function of state and local governments. Compulsory school attendance laws and the great expenditures for education both demonstrate our recognition of the importance of education to our democratic society. It is required in the performance of our most basic public responsibilities, even service in the armed forces. It is the very foundation of good citizenship. Today it is a principal instrument in awakening the child to cultural values, in preparing him for later professional training, and in helping him to adjust normally to his environment. In these days, it is doubtful that any child may reasonably be expected to succeed in life if he is denied the opportunity of an education. Such an opportunity, where the state has undertaken to provide it, is a right which must be made available to all on equal terms.

We come then to the question presented: Does segregation of children in public schools solely on the basis of race, even though the physical facilities and other 'tangible' factors may be equal, deprive the children of the minority group of equal educational opportunities? We believe that it does.

In Sweatt v. Painter ... in finding that a segregated law school for Negroes could not provide them equal educational opportunities, this Court relied in large part on 'those qualities which are incapable of objective measurement but which make for greatness in a law school.' In McLaurin v. Oklahoma State Regents, the Court, in requiring that a Negro admitted to a white graduate school be treated like all other students, again resorted to intangible considerations; '... his ability to study, to engage in discussions and exchange views with other students, and, in general, to learn his profession. Such considerations apply with added force to children in grade and high schools. To separate them from others of similar age and qualifications solely because of their race generates a feeling of inferiority as to their status in the community that may affect their hearts and minds in a way unlikely ever to be undone. The effect of this separation on their educational opportunities was well stated by a finding in the Kansas case by a court which nevertheless felt compelled to rule against the Negro plaintiffs:

> Segregation of white and colored children in public schools has a detrimental effect upon the colored children. The impact is greater when it has the sanction of the law; for the policy of separating the races is usually interpreted as denoting the inferiority of the Negro group. A sense of inferiority affects the motivation of a child to learn. Segregation with the sanction of law, therefore, has a tendency to (retard) the educational and mental development of Negro children and to deprive them of some of the benefits they would receive in a racial(ly) integrated school system.

We conclude that in the field of public education the doctrine of 'separate but equal' has no place. Separate educational facilities are inherently unequal. Therefore, we hold that the plaintiffs and others similarly situated for whom the actions have been brought are, by reason of the segregation complained of, deprived of the equal protection of the laws guaranteed by the Fourteenth Amendment. This disposition makes unnecessary any discussion whether such segregation also violates the Due Process Clause of the Fourteenth Amendment.

Because these are class actions, because of the wide applicability of this decision, and because of the great variety of local conditions, the formulation of decrees in these cases presents problems of considerable complexity. On reargument, the consideration of appropriate relief was necessarily subordinated to the primary question—the constitutionality of segregation in public education. We have now announced that such segregation is a denial of the equal protection of the laws. In order that we may have the full assistance of the parties in formulating decrees, the cases will be restored to the docket, and the parties are requested to present further argument on Questions 4 and 5 previously propounded by the Court for the reargument this Term. The Attorney General of the United States is again invited to participate. The Attorneys General of the states requiring or permitting segregation in public education will also be permitted to appear as amici curiae upon request to do so by September 15, 1954, and submission of briefs by October 1, 1954....

Review Questions and Explanations: *Brown*

1. Does the Court in *Brown* apply strict scrutiny?

2. Do you agree or disagree with the below statement, made by the Court in *Brown*?

> In approaching this problem, we cannot turn the clock back to 1868 when the Amendment was adopted, or even to 1896 when *Plessy v. Ferguson* was written. We must consider public education in the light of its full development and its present place in American life throughout the Nation. Only in this way can it be determined if segregation in public schools deprives these plaintiffs of the equal protection of the laws.

How would the Court's reasoning in this statement apply to an assertion that the equal protection clause prohibits discrimination in civil marriage on the basis of sexual orientation?

3. Was the problem in *Brown* the fact of separation, or the effects of it? Consider again the question of sex segregated restrooms. Are such restrooms as offensive as race segregated restrooms? If not, why not?

4. *Brown* was the culmination of a long legal battle led by NAACP lawyer (and future Supreme Court justice) Thurgood Marshall. Marshall and the NAACP had previously litigated a series of cases challenging racial segregation in graduate and professional programs by arguing that the separate programs did not meet *Plessy's* "separate but equal" test because options available to black Americans were in fact not equal to those offered to whites. The Supreme Court agreed with Marshall in *Sweatt v. Painter*, 339 U.S. 626 (1950), holding that the facilities provided to a black student at the University Texas Law School were not equal to those provided to white students. These cases, as well as the emerging Civil Rights Movement happening on the streets, set the stage for the Court's decision in *Brown*.

5. The Fourteenth Amendment, and therefore the Equal Protection clause, does not bind the federal government. In substantive due process cases (see Chapter 7) this does not matter much because there is a due process clause in the Fifth Amendment which, as part of the original Bill of Rights, *does* bind the federal government. But the Fifth Amendment has no Equal Protection clause. This left no clear mechanism by which to prohibit racially segregated schools in the District of Columbia. The Court resolved this in *Bolling v. Sharpe*, 347 U.S. 497 (1954). Justice Warren, speaking for the Court in *Bolling*, wrote that "the concepts of equal protection and due process, both stemming from our American ideal of fairness, are not mutually exclusive" and that racial "discrimination may be so unjustifiable as to be violative of due process" even though the Fifth Amendment lacked an Equal Protection clause. *Bolling* was handed down the same day as *Brown*. What does *Bolling* tell us about the vision of equality the Court was advancing in *Brown*? The *Bolling* opinion also states: "Classifications based solely upon race must be scrutinized with particular care, since they are contrary to

our traditions and hence constitutionally suspect." Does this language of heightened scrutiny and "suspect" classifications appear in *Brown*?

NOTE: The Rehnquist Memo on *Brown*

Future Chief Justice William H. Rehnquist was a law clerk for Justice Robert Jackson when *Brown* was argued and decided. Below is a memo the future justice wrote for Justice Jackson about the then-pending *Brown* case. Contrast the argument made in the memo to *Carolene Product's* footnote 4. The memo was entered into the record during the Senate Judiciary Committee hearings on Rehnquist's promotion to Chief Justice. The copy below is from the transcript of that hearing. It should be noted that Justice Rehnquist maintained at his hearing that, while he wrote the memo, the views within it reflected Justice Jackson's position, not his own. Many senators at the hearing were skeptical of this, and recent scholarship has questioned Rehnquist's assertion.[2] (Justice Jackson voted with the unanimous majority in *Brown*.) Read clerk Rehnquist's argument. How would you respond to his argument that the Court should no more intervene in *Brown* than it should have in *Lochner*? Does *Carolene Products* footnote 4 help you here?

A Random Thought on the Segregation Cases

One-hundred fifty years ago this Court held that it was the ultimate judge of the restrictions which the Constitution imposed on the various branches of the national and state government. Marbury v. Madison. This was presumably on the basis that there are standards to be applied other than the personal predilections of the Justices. As applied to questions of inter-state or state-federal relations, as well as to inter-departmental disputes within the federal government, this doctrine of judicial review has worked well. Where theoretically co-ordinate bodies of government are disputing, the Court is well suited to its role as arbiter. This is because these problems involve much less emotionally charged subject matter than do those discussed below.

In effect, they determine the skeletal relations of the governments to each other without influencing the substantive business of those governments.

As applied to relations between the individual and the state, the system has worked much less well. The Constitution, of course, deals with individual rights, particularly in the first Ten and the fourteenth Amendments. But as I read the history of this Court, it has seldom been out of hot water when attempting to interpret these individual rights. Fletcher v. Peck, in 1810, represented an attempt by Chief Justice Marshall to extend the protection of the contract clause to infant business. Scott v. Sanford was the result of Taney's effort to protect slaveholders from legislative interference. After the Civil War, business interest came to dominate the court, and they in turn ventured into the deep water of protecting certain types of individuals against legislative interference. Championed first by

---

2. Brad Snyder & John Q. Barrett, *Rehnquist's Missing Letter: A Former Law Clerk's 1955 Thoughts on Justice Jackson And Brown*, 53 B.C.L.Rev. 631 (2012).

Field, then by Peckham and Brewer, the high water mark of the trend in protecting the majority opinion in that case, Holmes replied that the fourteenth Amendment did not enact Herbert Spencer's Social Statics. Other cases coming later in a similar vein were Adkins v. Children's Hospital, Hammer v. Dagenhart, Tyson v. Banton, Ribnik v. McBride. But eventually the Court called a halt to this reading of its own economic views into the Constitution. Apparently it recognized that where a legislature was dealing with its own citizens, it was not part of the judicial function to thwart public opinion except in extreme cases. In these cases now before the Court, the Court is, as Davis suggested, being asked to read its own sociological views into the Constitution. Urging a view palpably at variance with precedent and probably with legislative history, appellants seek to convince the Court of the moral wrongness of the treatment they are receiving.

I would suggest that this is a question the Court need never reach; for regardless of the Justice's individual views on the merits of segregation, it quite clearly is not one of those extreme cases which commands intervention from one of any conviction. If this Court, because its members individually are "liberal" and dislike segregation, now chooses to strike it down, it differs from the McReynolds court only in the kinds of litigants it favors and the kinds of special claims it protects. To those who would argue that "personal" rights are more sacrosanct than "property" rights, the short answer is that the Constitution makes no such distinction. To the argument made by Thurgood Marshall that a majority may not deprive a minority of its constitutional right, the answer must be made that while this is sound in theory, in the long run it is the majority who will determine what the constitutional rights of the minority are. One hundred and fifty years of attempts on the part of this Court to protect minority rights of any kind — whether those of business, slaveholders, or Jehovah's Witnesses — have been sloughed off, and crept silently to rest. If the present Court is unable to profit by this example it must be prepared to see its work fade in time, too, as embodying only the sentiments of a transient majority of nine men. I realize that it is an unpopular and unhumanitarian position, for which I have been excoriated by "liberal" colleagues, but I think Plessy v. Ferguson was right and should be re-affirmed. If the fourteenth Amendment did not enact Spencer's Social Statics, it just as surely did not enact Myrddahl's American Dilemma.

WHR

Guided Reading Question: *Korematsu v. United States*

1. As noted above, the idea that racial classifications may be subject to a more rigorous level of scrutiny than other classifications appears to arise first in *Carolene Products* footnote 4. The doctrinal articulation of "strict scrutiny" as a standard of review, however, makes its first definite appearance in *Korematsu*. Today, we treat the decision of whether or not to apply strict scrutiny to a particular classification as quite consequential, but the Court's initial use of the language of tiered review should perhaps make us wonder whether its importance is substantive or symbolic. In other words, is "strict scrutiny" doing any substantive work in deciding cases, or is it merely a label we apply *after* deciding that certain types of classifications should almost never be tolerated? Consider how much help the designation of strict scrutiny was to Mr. Korematsu.

2. Does the Court, either implicitly or explicitly, apply strict scrutiny in a way that would be recognizable under current doctrine? (Refer to Chapter 7 and the Introduction to Part IV to review the analytical framework now used in strict scrutiny cases.) What role does the Court see itself playing here in the guarantee of equal protection of the laws?

3. Like *Plessy*, *Korematsu* is one of those cases we use to tell a narrative of constitutional error and redemption. As with *Plessy*, we should be skeptical of efforts to dismiss the case too quickly as "obviously" legally wrong. There are better and worse legal arguments, of course, but as noted above, it is rare for the Supreme Court to issue decisions with absolutely no legal foundation underlying them. When reading *Korematsu*, think about which of the majority's arguments are the strongest. Does the dissent fully answer them?

Korematsu v. United States

323 U.S. 214 (1944)

Majority: *Black*, Stone (CJ), Reed, Douglas, Rutledge, Frankfurter

Concurrence: *Frankfurter* (omitted)

Dissents: *Roberts; Murphy* (both omitted); *Jackson*

MR. JUSTICE BLACK delivered the opinion of the Court.

The petitioner, an American citizen of Japanese descent, was convicted in a federal district court for remaining in San Leandro, California, a 'Military Area', contrary to Civilian Exclusion Order No. 34 of the Commanding General of the Western Command, U.S. Army, which directed that after May 9, 1942, all persons of Japanese ancestry should be excluded from that area. [Editors' note: the "Military Area" defined by Order 34 included the entire state of California as well as the costal areas of Washington and Oregon and most of southern Arizona.] No question was raised as to petitioner's loyalty to the United States. The Circuit Court of Appeals affirmed and the importance of the constitutional question involved caused us to grant certiorari.

It should be noted, to begin with, that all legal restrictions which curtail the civil rights of a single racial group are immediately suspect. That is not to say that all such restrictions are unconstitutional. It is to say that courts must subject them to the most rigid scrutiny. Pressing public necessity may sometimes justify the existence of such restrictions; racial antagonism never can.... *never justify curtailment of civil rights of single racial group*

Exclusion Order No. 34, which the petitioner knowingly and admittedly violated was one of a number of military orders and proclamations, all of which were substantially based upon Executive Order No. 9066.... That order, issued after we were at war with Japan, declared that "the successful prosecution of the war requires every possible protection against espionage and against sabotage to national-defense material, national-defense premises, and national-defense utilities...."

One of the series of orders and proclamations, a curfew order, which like the exclusion order here was promulgated pursuant to Executive Order 9066, subjected all persons of Japanese ancestry in prescribed West Coast military areas to remain in their residences from 8 p.m. to 6 a.m. As is the case with the exclusion order here, that prior curfew order was designed as a "protection against espionage and against sabotage." In Kiyoshi Hirabayashi

v. United States, we sustained a conviction obtained for violation of the curfew order. The Hirabayashi conviction and this one thus rest on the same 1942 Congressional Act and the same basic executive and military orders, all of which orders were aimed at the twin dangers of espionage and sabotage.

The 1942 Act was attacked in the Hirabayashi case as an unconstitutional delegation of power; it was contended that the curfew order and other orders on which it rested were beyond the war powers of the Congress, the military authorities and of the President, as Commander in Chief of the Army; and finally that to apply the curfew order against none but citizens of Japanese ancestry amounted to a constitutionally prohibited discrimination solely on account of race. To these questions, we gave the serious consideration which their importance justified. We upheld the curfew order as an exercise of the power of the government to take steps necessary to prevent espionage and sabotage in an area threatened by Japanese attack.

In the light of the principles we announced in the Hirabayashi case, we are unable to conclude that it was beyond the war power of Congress and the Executive to exclude those of Japanese ancestry from the West Coast war area at the time they did. True, exclusion from the area in which one's home is located is a far greater deprivation than constant confinement to the home from 8 p.m. to 6 a.m. Nothing short of apprehension by the proper military authorities of the gravest imminent danger to the public safety can constitutionally justify either. But exclusion from a threatened area, no less than curfew, has a definite and close relationship to the prevention of espionage and sabotage. The military authorities, charged with the primary responsibility of defending our shores, concluded that curfew provided inadequate protection and ordered exclusion. They did so, as pointed out in our Hirabayashi opinion, in accordance with Congressional authority to the military to say who should, and who should not, remain in the threatened areas.

In this case the petitioner challenges the assumptions upon which we rested our conclusions in the Hirabayashi case. He also urges that by May 1942, when Order No. 34 was promulgated, all danger of Japanese invasion of the West Coast had disappeared. After careful consideration of these contentions we are compelled to reject them.

Here, as in the Hirabayashi case, "... we cannot reject as unfounded the judgment of the military authorities and of Congress that there were disloyal members of that population, whose number and strength could not be precisely and quickly ascertained. We cannot say that the war-making branches of the Government did not have ground for believing that in a critical hour such persons could not readily be isolated and separately dealt with, and constituted a menace to the national defense and safety, which demanded that prompt and adequate measures be taken to guard against it."

Like curfew, exclusion of those of Japanese origin was deemed necessary because of the presence of an unascertained number of disloyal members of the group, most of whom we have no doubt were loyal to this country. It was because we could not reject the finding of the military authorities that it was impossible to bring about an immediate segregation of the disloyal from the loyal that we sustained the validity of the curfew order as applying to the whole group. In the instant case, temporary exclusion of the entire group was rested by the military on the same ground. The judgment that exclusion of the whole group was for the same reason a military imperative answers the contention that the exclusion was in the nature of group punishment based on antagonism to those of Japanese origin. That there were members of the group who retained loyalties to Japan has been confirmed by investigations made subsequent to the exclusion. Approximately five thousand American citizens of Japanese ancestry refused to swear unqualified allegiance to the United States and to renounce allegiance to the Japanese Emperor, and several thousand evacuees requested repatriation to Japan.

We uphold the exclusion order as of the time it was made and when the petitioner violated it.... In doing so, we are not unmindful of the hardships imposed by it upon a large group of American citizens.... But hardships are part of war, and war is an aggregation of hardships. All citizens alike, both in and out of uniform, feel the impact of war in greater or lesser measure. Citizenship has its responsibilities as well as its privileges, and in time of war the burden is always heavier. Compulsory exclusion of large groups of citizens from their homes, except under circumstances of direst emergency and peril, is inconsistent with our basic governmental institutions. But when under conditions of modern warfare our shores are threatened by hostile forces, the power to protect must be commensurate with the threatened danger....

Some of the members of the Court are of the view that evacuation and detention in an Assembly Center were inseparable. After May 3, 1942, the date of Exclusion Order No. 34, Korematsu was under compulsion to leave the area not as he would choose but via an Assembly Center. The Assembly Center was conceived as a part of the machinery for group evacuation. The power to exclude includes the power to do it by force if necessary. And any forcible measure must necessarily entail some degree of detention or restraint whatever method of removal is selected. But whichever view is taken, it results in holding that the order under which petitioner was convicted was valid.

It is said that we are dealing here with the case of imprisonment of a citizen in a concentration camp solely because of his ancestry, without evidence or inquiry concerning his loyalty and good disposition towards the United States. Our task would be simple, our duty clear, were this a case involving the imprisonment of a loyal citizen in a concentration camp because of racial prejudice. Regardless of the true nature of the assembly and relocation centers—and we deem it unjustifiable to call them concentration camps with all the ugly connotations that term implies—we are dealing specifically with nothing but an exclusion order. To cast this case into outlines of racial prejudice, without reference to the real military dangers which were presented, merely confuses the issue. Korematsu was not excluded from the Military Area because of hostility to him or his race. He was excluded because we are at war with the Japanese Empire, because the properly constituted military authorities feared an invasion of our West Coast and felt constrained to take proper security measures, because they decided that the military urgency of the situation demanded that all citizens of Japanese ancestry be segregated from the West Coast temporarily, and finally, because Congress, reposing its confidence in this time of war in our military leaders—as inevitably it must—determined that they should have the power to do just this. There was evidence of disloyalty on the part of some, the military authorities considered that the need for action was great, and time was short. We cannot—by availing ourselves of the calm perspective of hindsight—now say that at that time these actions were unjustified.

Affirmed.

MR. JUSTICE JACKSON, dissenting.

Korematsu was born on our soil, of parents born in Japan. The Constitution makes him a citizen of the United States by nativity and a citizen of California by residence. No claim is made that he is not loyal to this country. There is no suggestion that apart from the matter involved here he is not law-abiding and well disposed. Korematsu, however, has been convicted of an act not commonly a crime. It consists merely of being present in the state whereof he is a citizen, near the place where he was born, and where all his life he has lived.

Even more unusual is the series of military orders which made this conduct a crime. They forbid such a one to remain, and they also forbid him to leave. They were so drawn that the only way Korematsu could avoid violation was to give himself up to the military authority. This meant submission to custody, examination, and transportation out of the territory, to be followed by indeterminate confinement in detention camps.

A citizen's presence in the locality, however, was made a crime only if his parents were of Japanese birth. Had Korematsu been one of four—the others being, say, a German alien enemy, an Italian alien enemy, and a citizen of American-born ancestors, convicted of treason but out on parole—only Korematsu's presence would have violated the order. The difference between their innocence and his crime would result, not from anything he did, said, or thought, different than they, but only in that he was born of different racial stock.

Now, if any fundamental assumption underlies our system, it is that guilt is personal and not inheritable. Even if all of one's antecedents had been convicted of treason, the Constitution forbids its penalties to be visited upon him, for it provides that "no Attainder of Treason shall work Corruption of Blood, or Forfeiture except during the Life of the Person attained." Article 3, §3, cl. 2. But here is an attempt to make an otherwise innocent act a crime merely because this prisoner is the son of parents as to whom he had no choice, and belongs to a race from which there is no way to resign. If Congress in peace-time legislation should enact such a criminal law, I should suppose this Court would refuse to enforce it.

But the 'law' which this prisoner is convicted of disregarding is not found in an act of Congress, but in a military order. Neither the Act of Congress nor the Executive Order of the President, nor both together, would afford a basis for this conviction. It rests on the orders of General DeWitt. And it is said that if the military commander had reasonable military grounds for promulgating the orders, they are constitutional and become law, and the Court is required to enforce them. There are several reasons why I cannot subscribe to this doctrine.

It would be impracticable and dangerous idealism to expect or insist that each specific military command in an area of probable operations will conform to conventional tests of constitutionality. When an area is so beset that it must be put under military control at all, the paramount consideration is that its measures be successful, rather than legal. The armed services must protect a society, not merely its Constitution. The very essence of the military job is to marshal physical force, to remove every obstacle to its effectiveness, to give it every strategic advantage. Defense measures will not, and often should not, be held within the limits that bind civil authority in peace. No court can require such a commander in such circumstances to act as a reasonable man; he may be unreasonably cautious and exacting. Perhaps he should be. But a commander in temporarily focusing the life of a community on defense is carrying out a military program; he is not making law in the sense the courts know the term. He issues orders, and they may have a certain authority as military commands, although they may be very bad as constitutional law.

But if we cannot confine military expedients by the Constitution, neither would I distort the Constitution to approve all that the military may deem expedient. This is what the Court appears to be doing, whether consciously or not. I cannot say, from any evidence before me, that the orders of General DeWitt were not reasonably expedient military precautions, nor could I say that they were. But even if they were permissible military procedures, I deny that it follows that they are constitutional. If, as the Court holds, it does follow, then we may as well say that any military order will be constitutional and have done with it.

The limitation under which courts always will labor in examining the necessity for a military order are illustrated by this case. How does the Court know that these orders have a reasonable basis in necessity? No evidence whatever on that subject has been taken by this or any other court. There is sharp controversy as to the credibility of the DeWitt report. So the Court, having no real evidence before it, has no choice but to accept General DeWitt's own unsworn, self serving statement, untested by any cross-examination, that what he did was reasonable. And thus it will always be when courts try to look into the reasonableness of a military order.

In the very nature of things military decisions are not susceptible of intelligent judicial appraisal. They do not pretend to rest on evidence, but are made on information that often would not be admissible and on assumptions that could not be proved. Information in support of an order could not be disclosed to courts without danger that it would reach the enemy. Neither can courts act on communications made in confidence. Hence courts can never have any real alternative to accepting the mere declaration of the authority that issued the order that it was reasonably necessary from a military viewpoint.

Much is said of the danger to liberty from the Army program for deporting and detaining these citizens of Japanese extraction. But a judicial construction of the due process clause that will sustain this order is a far more subtle blow to liberty than the promulgation of the order itself. A military order, however unconstitutional, is not apt to last longer than the military emergency. Even during that period a succeeding commander may revoke it all. But once a judicial opinion rationalizes such an order to show that it conforms to the Constitution, or rather rationalizes the Constitution to show that the Constitution sanctions such an order, the Court for all time has validated the principle of racial discrimination in criminal procedure and of transplanting American citizens. The principle then lies about like a loaded weapon ready for the hand of any authority that can bring forward a plausible claim of an urgent need. Every repetition imbeds that principle more deeply in our law and thinking and expands it to new purposes. All who observe the work of courts are familiar with what Judge Cardozo described as "the tendency of a principle to expand itself to the limit of its logic." A military commander may overstep the bounds of constitutionality, and it is an incident. But if we review and approve, that passing incident becomes the doctrine of the Constitution. There it has a generative power of its own, and all that it creates will be in its own image. Nothing better illustrates this danger than does the Court's opinion in this case....

In that case we were urged to consider only that curfew feature, that being all that technically was involved, because it was the only count necessary to sustain Hirabayashi's conviction and sentence. We yielded, and the Chief Justice guarded the opinion as carefully as language will do. He said: "Our investigation here does not go beyond the inquiry whether, in the light of all the relevant circumstances preceding and attending their promulgation, the challenged orders and statute afforded a reasonable basis for the action taken in imposing the curfew." ... "We decide only the issue as we have defined it—we decide only that the curfew order as applied, and at the time it was applied, was within the boundaries of the war power." ... And again: "It is unnecessary to consider whether or to what extent such findings would support orders differing from the curfew order." ... However, in spite of our limiting words we did validate a discrimination of the basis of ancestry for mild and temporary deprivation of liberty. Now the principle of racial discrimination is pushed from support of mild measures to very harsh ones, and from temporary deprivations to indeterminate ones. And the precedent which it is said requires us to do so is Hirabayashi. The Court is now saying that in Hirabayashi we did decide the very things we there said we were not deciding. Because we said that these citizens could be made to stay in their homes during the hours of dark, it is said we must require them to leave home entirely; and if that, we are told they may also be taken into custody for deportation; and if that, it is argued they may also be held for some undetermined time in detention camps. How far the principle of this case would be extended before plausible reasons would play out, I do not know.

I should hold that a civil court cannot be made to enforce an order which violates constitutional limitations even if it is a reasonable exercise of military authority. The courts can exercise only the judicial power, can apply only law, and must abide by the Constitution, or they cease to be civil courts and become instruments of military policy.

Of course the existence of a military power resting on force, so vagrant, so centralized, so necessarily heedless of the individual, is an inherent threat to liberty. But I would not lead people to rely on this Court for a review that seems to me wholly delusive. The military reasonableness of these orders can only be determined by military superiors. If the people ever let command of the war power fall into irresponsible and unscrupulous hands, the courts wield no power equal to its restraint. The chief restraint upon those who command the physical forces of the country, in the future as in the past, must be their responsibility to the political judgments of their contemporaries and to the moral judgments of history.

My duties as a justice as I see them do not require me to make a military judgment as to whether General DeWitt's evacuation and detention program was a reasonable military necessity. I do not suggest that the courts should have attempted to interfere with the Army in carrying out its task. But I do not think they may be asked to execute a military expedient that has no place in law under the Constitution. I would reverse the judgment and discharge the prisoner.

Review Questions and Explanations: *Korematsu*

1. Justice Black's majority opinion says that *Korematsu* does not involve a racial classification because Mr. Korematsu was not detained because of "hostility" to his race, but because the United States was at war with the Japanese Empire. Justice Black was not a foolish man; what do you think he meant by this? What concept of equal protection is evidenced by it?

2. After the September 11th terrorist attacks, there were calls to detain or question American Muslims. Imagine that American Muslims or persons of Arab descent had been sent to detention camps, as happened to Japanese Americans in World War II. What, if anything, would or could the Supreme Court have done about it? Consider this question when reading the case.

Recap: Concepts of Equality

1. You have now read three major equal protection cases: *Plessy v. Ferguson, Brown v. Board of Education* and *Korematsu*. You also have read Justice Harlan's dissent in *Plessy* and William Rehnquist's *Plessy* memo. Each of these readings expresses or implies an idea about equal protection and equality, and about the role of the courts in enforcing that idea. Try to articulate what these are in each of the readings so far.

2. *Korematsu* and *Brown* show the early stages of the Court's effort to create a tiered system of review under which to analyze equal protection cases. The cases below will more fully develop that system. For now, you should understand the basic outlines of tiered review sketched out in these cases, and consider why the Court decided to follow this path of analysis.

3. After identifying each of the concepts of equal protection illustrated by the above decisions, try resolving the question of marriage equality using each of

them. Which, if any, of the above approaches to the Equal Protection clause would prohibit states from discriminating on the basis of sexual orientation in state civil marriage laws?

4. Reconsider the standards of review used in *Brown*, *Plessy*, and *Korematsu*. Could segregation have been struck down using a rational basis test? Is that what *Brown* in fact did?

C. Strict Scrutiny and Race Discrimination

Under now well established doctrine, governmental classifications based on race are deemed "suspect" and are reviewed under strict scrutiny. Early articulations of the concept of "strict scrutiny" appeared, as we have seen, in *Korematsu* (1944) and *Bolling v. Sharpe* (1955) (although strangely not in *Brown* itself). By the 1960s, the Court had made clear that "the Equal Protection Clause demands that racial classifications ... be subjected to the 'most rigid scrutiny[.]'" Loving v. Virginia, 388 U.S. 1, 11 (1967) (quoting *Korematsu* and striking down a law prohibiting interracial marriage).

This seemingly straightforward idea requires several explanations and qualifications, however. To begin with, our use of the term "race"—and to some extent, the term as it is used in constitutional law—represents a simplification of a much more complex reality. "Race" is less a scientific or biological fact than it is a social construction, and how it has been construed has changed over time. Fortunately, constitutional doctrine at least arguably spares us from having to resolve some of the thorny questions this raises, insofar as it treats discrimination based on race, ethnicity, or national origin as more or less the same: all are treated as classifications that are "inherently suspect" and subjected to strict scrutiny.

Regardless of how it is labeled, race-based discrimination in the United States has a long and complex history. There is no question that the dominant story of race discrimination in this country is that of the social and political discrimination by whites against blacks stemming from slavery and its legacy. The prominence of this history of white-black discrimination should not, however, cause us to lose sight of the histories of discrimination suffered by Hispanic-Americans, *see, e.g.,* Hernandez v. Texas, 347 U.S. 475 (1954), Asian-Americans, *see, e.g., Yick Wo* and *Korematsu*, and Native Americans, among others. There is also a history in the United States of discrimination by White Anglo-Saxon protestants against various immigrant groups or non-protestant religious groups, although this type of discrimination has proven less intractable than race-based conflict appears to be.

A versatile, but imprecise name we tend to use outside legal discourse to refer to groups that have been discriminated against is "minorities." But "minorities" are not always subject to political and social subordination; in many times and places, a minority group may have been politically dominant (e.g., whites in South Africa under apartheid). The Federalist Papers speak of constitutional safeguards against both majority *and* minority tyranny. Thus, the term "minority" begs a question that we should keep in mind when considering the Equal Protection clause: what is it about being a minority that merits the protection of the courts, exercising judicial review under the Equal Protection clause, against discriminatory governmental action?

Further complicating the inquiry, legislative classifications can have a racial effect without being explicitly race-based. A "Jim Crow" law, such as that challenged in *Plessy*, or the law against interracial marriage struck down in *Loving*, presents what would now be an easy case: the intent to discriminate on the basis of race is explicit and the racial classification is based in racial bias and prejudice. But harder cases are presented where the law does not on its face draw racial distinctions, or where it does so but the distinction is intended to help rather than harm racial minorities who have been subjected to a history of discrimination. These issues are considered in the following two sections.

1. The Intentional Discrimination Requirement

Guided Reading Questions: *Yick Wo v. Hopkins* and *Palmer v. Thompson*

1. As the Court began applying more rigorous scrutiny to racial classifications, it found itself confronted with a new question: how should it determine whether a classification is in fact based on race? *Yick Wo* is an early case in which the Court addressed this issue. When reading the case, pay attention to how the Court answers this question. Note the arguments in favor and against deeming the state action here a racial classification.

2. Determining whether a facially neutral classification should trigger strict scrutiny because of its racial salience requires deciding whether the law should be concerned with a law's discriminatory *purpose*, its discriminatory *effect*, both, or neither. How one answers this question has important consequences. One can imagine a law passed for discriminatory reasons that nonetheless has no discriminatory effect (this is how the majority in *Palmer v. Thomson*, below, appears to see the facts of that case). One also can imagine a rule enacted for non-racial reasons that none the less has a disproportionate affect on racial minorities. Finally, one can imagine state actions, like those undertaken in affirmative action programs, that are enacted with a keen awareness of race, but which are not based on racial hostility or prejudice. Does the Equal Protection clause require courts to be equally suspicious of each of these types of laws?

Yick Wo v. Hopkins

118 U.S. 356 (1886)

Unanimous decision: Matthews, Waite (CJ), Miller, Field, Bradley, Harlan, Woods, Gray, Blatchford

MR. JUSTICE MATTHEWS delivered the opinion of the court.

The plaintiff in error, Yick Wo, on August 24, 1885, petitioned the Supreme Court of California for the writ of habeas corpus, alleging that he was illegally deprived of his personal liberty by the defendant as sheriff of the city and county of San Francisco.... The ordinances for the violation of which he had been found guilty are set out as follows:

Order No. 1,569, passed May 26, 1880, prescribing the kind of buildings in which laundries may be located.

'The people of the city and county of San Francisco do ordain as follows:

'Section 1. It shall be unlawful, from and after the passage of this order, for any person or persons to establish, maintain, or carry on a laundry, within the corporate limits of the city and county of San Francisco, without having first obtained the consent of the board of supervisors, except the same be located in a building constructed either of brick or stone.

'Sec. 2. It shall be unlawful for any person to erect, build, or maintain, or cause to be erected, built, or maintained, over or upon the roof of any building now erected, or which may hereafter be erected, within the limits of said city and county, any scaffolding, without first obtaining the written permission of the board of supervisors, which permit shall state fully for what purpose said scaffolding is to be erected and used, and such scaffolding shall not be used for any other purpose than that designated in such permit.

'Sec. 3. Any person who shall violate any of the provisions of this order shall be deemed guilty of a misdemeanor, and upon conviction thereof shall be punished by a fine of not more than one thousand dollars, or by imprisonment in the county jail not more than six months, or by both such fine and imprisonment.'

Order No. 1,587, passed July 28, 1880, the following section:

'Sec. 68. It shall be unlawful, from and after the passage of this order, for any person or persons to establish, maintain, or carry on a laundry within the corporate limits of the city and county of San Francisco without having first obtained the consent of the board of supervisors, except the same be located in a building constructed either of brick or stone'

The following facts are also admitted on the record: That petitioner is a native of China, and came to California in 1861, and is still a subject of the emperor of China; that he has been engaged in the laundry business in the same premises and building for 22 years last past; that he had a license from the board of fire-wardens, dated March 3, 1884, from which it appeared 'that the above-described premises have been inspected by the board of fire-wardens, and upon such inspection said board found all proper arrangements for carrying on the business; that the stoves, washing and drying apparatus, and the appliances for heating smoothing-irons, are in good condition, and that their use is not dangerous to the surrounding property from fire, and that all proper precautions have been taken to comply with the provisions of order No. 1,617, defining 'the fire limits of the city and county of San Francisco, and making regulations concerning the erection and use of buildings in said city and county,' and of order No. 1,670, 'prohibiting the kindling, maintenance, and use of open fires in houses'; that he had a certificate from the health officer that the same premises had been inspected by him, and that he found that they were properly and sufficiently drained, and that all proper arrangements for carrying on the business of a laundry, without injury to the sanitary condition of the neighborhood, had been complied with; that the city license of the petitioner was in force, and expired October 1, 1885; and that the petitioner applied to the board of supervisors, June 1, 1885, for consent of said board to maintain and carry on his laundry, but that said board, on July 1, 1885, refused said consent.'

It is also admitted to be true, as alleged in the petition, that on February 24, 1880, 'there were about 320 laundries in the city and county of San Francisco, of which about 240 were owned and conducted by subjects of China, and of the whole number, viz., 320, about 310 were constructed of wood, the same material that constitutes nine tenths of the houses in the city of San Francisco. The capital thus invested by the subjects of China was not less than two hundred thousand dollars, and they paid annually for rent, license, taxes, gas, and water about one hundred and eighty thousand dollars.' It is alleged in the petition that 'your petitioner, and more than one hundred and fifty of his countrymen, have been arrested upon the charge of carrying on business without having such special consent, while those who are not subjects of China, and who are conducting eighty odd laundries under similar conditions, are left unmolested, and free to enjoy the enhanced trade and profits arising from this hurtful and unfair discrimination. The business of your petitioners, and of those of his countrymen similarly situated, is greatly impaired, and in many cases practically ruined, by this system of oppression to one kind of men, and favoritism to all others.' ... It is also admitted 'that petitioner and 200 of his countrymen similarly situated petitioned the board of supervisors for permission to continue their business in the various houses which they had been occupying and using for laundries for more than twenty years, and such petitions were denied, and all the petitions of those who were not Chinese, with one exception of Mrs. Mary Meagles, were granted.' ...

In the case of the petitioner, brought here by writ of error to the supreme court of California, our jurisdiction is limited to the question whether the plaintiff in error has been denied a right in violation of the constitution, laws, or treaties of the United States....

We are consequently constrained, at the outset, to differ from the supreme court of California upon the real meaning of the ordinances in question. That court considered these ordinances as vesting in the board of supervisors a not unusual discretion in granting or withholding their assent to the use of wooden buildings as laundries, to be exercised in reference to the circumstances of each case, with a view to the protection of the public against the dangers of fire. We are not able to concur in that interpretation of the power conferred upon the supervisors. There is nothing in the ordinances which points to such a regulation of the business of keeping and conducting laundries. They seem intended to confer, and actually to confer, not a discretion to be exercised upon a consideration of the circumstances of each case, but a naked and arbitrary power to give or withhold consent, not only as to places, but as to persons; so that, if an applicant for such consent, being in every way a competent and qualified person, and having complied with every reasonable condition demanded by any public interest, should, failing to obtain the requisite consent of the supervisors to the prosecution of his business, apply for redress by the judicial process of mandamus to require the supervisors to consider and act upon his case, it would be a sufficient answer for them to say that the law had conferred upon them authority to withhold their assent, without reason and without responsibility. The power given to them is not confided to their discretion in the legal sense of that term, but is granted to their mere will. It is purely arbitrary, and acknowledges neither guidance nor restraint.

This erroneous view of the ordinances in question led the supreme court of California into the further error of holding that they were justified by the decisions of this court in the cases of Barbier v. Connelly and Soon Hing v. Crowley. In both of these cases the ordinance involved was simply a prohibition to carry on the washing and ironing of clothes in public laundries and wash houses, within certain prescribed limits of the city and county of San Francisco, from 10 o'clock at night until 6 o'clock in the morning of the following day. This provision was held to be purely a police regulation, within the competency of any municipality possessed of the ordinary powers belonging to such bodies, — a necessary measure of precaution in a city composed largely of wooden buildings, like San Francisco, in the application of which there was no invidious discrimination against any one within the prescribed limits; all persons engaged in the same business being treated alike, and subject to the same restrictions, and entitled to the same privileges, under similar conditions. For these reasons that ordinance was adjudged not to be within the prohibitions of the fourteenth amendment to the constitution of the United States, which, it was said in the first case cited, 'undoubtedly intended, not only that there should be no arbitrary deprivation of life or liberty, or arbitrary spoliation of property, but that equal protection and security should be given to all under like circumstances in the enjoyment of their personal and civil rights; that all persons should be equally entitled to pursue their happiness, and acquire and enjoy property; that they should have like access to the courts of the country for the protection of their persons and property, the prevention and redress of wrongs, and the enforcement of contracts; that no impediment should be interposed to the pursuits of any one, except as applied to the same pursuits by others under like circumstances; that no greater burdens should be laid upon one than are laid upon others in the same calling and condition; and that, in the administration of criminal justice, no different or higher punishment should be imposed upon one than such as is prescribed to all for like offenses.... Class legislation, discriminating against some and favoring others, is prohibited; but legislation which, in carrying out a public purpose, is limited in its application, if, within the sphere of its operation, it affects alike all persons similarly situated, is not within the amendment.'

The ordinance drawn in question in the present case is of a very different character. It does not prescribe a rule and conditions, for the regulation of the use of property for laundry purposes, to which all similarly situated may conform. It allows, without restriction, the use for such purposes of buildings of brick or stone; but, as to wooden buildings, constituting nearly all those in previous use, it divides the owners or occupiers into two classes, not having respect to their personal character and qualifications for the business, nor the situation and nature and adaptation of the buildings themselves, but merely by an arbitrary line, on one side of which are those who are permitted to pursue their industry by the mere will and consent of the supervisors, and on the other those from whom that consent is withheld, at their mere will and pleasure. And both classes are alike only in this: that they are tenants at will, under the supervisors, of their means of living. The ordinance, therefore, also differs from the not unusual case where discretion is lodged by law in public officers or bodies to grant or withhold licenses to keep taverns, or places for the sale of spirituous liquors, and the like, when one of the conditions is that the applicant shall be a fit person for the exercise of the privilege, because in such cases the fact of fitness is submitted to the judgment of the officer, and calls for the exercise of a discretion of a judicial nature.

The rights of the petitioners, as affected by the proceedings of which they complain, are not less because they are aliens and subjects of the emperor of China.... The fourteenth amendment to the constitution is not confined to the protection of citizens. It says: 'Nor shall any state deprive any person of life, liberty, or property without due process of law; nor deny to any person within its jurisdiction the equal protection of the laws.' These provisions are universal in their application, to all persons within the territorial jurisdiction, without regard to any differences of race, of color, or of nationality; and the equal protection of the laws is a pledge of the protection of equal laws. It is accordingly enacted by section 1977 of the Revised Statutes that 'all persons within the jurisdiction of the United States shall have the same right, in every state and territory, to make and enforce contracts, to sue, be parties, give evidence, and to the full and equal benefit of all laws and proceedings for the security of persons and property as is enjoyed by white citizens, and shall be subject to like punishment, pains, penalties, taxes, licenses, and exactions of every kind, and to no other.' The questions we have to consider and decide in these cases, therefore, are to be treated as involving the rights of every citizen of the United States equally with those of the strangers and aliens who now invoke the jurisdiction of the court....

When we consider the nature and the theory of our institutions of government, the principles upon which they are supposed to rest, and review the history of their development, we are constrained to conclude that they do not mean to leave room for the play and action of purely personal and arbitrary power.... [T]he law is the definition and limitation of power. It is, indeed, quite true that there must always be lodged somewhere, and in some person or body, the authority of final decision; and in many cases of mere administration, the responsibility is purely political, no appeal lying except to the ultimate tribunal of the public judgment, exercised either in the pressure of opinion, or by means of the suffrage. But the fundamental rights to life, liberty, and the pursuit of happiness, considered as individual possessions, are secured by those maxims of constitutional law which are the monuments showing the victorious progress of the race in securing to men the blessings of civilization under the reign of just and equal laws, so that, in the famous language of the Massachusetts bill of rights, the government of the commonwealth 'may be a government of laws and not of men.' For the very idea that one man may be compelled to hold his life, or the means of living, or any material right essential to the enjoyment of life, at the mere will of another, seems to be intolerable in any country where freedom prevails, as being the essence of slavery itself....

There are many illustrations that might be given of this truth, which would make manifest that it was self-evident in the light of our system of jurisprudence. The case of the political franchise of voting is one. Though not regarded strictly as a natural right, but as a privilege merely conceded by society, according to its will, under certain conditions, nevertheless it is regarded as a fundamental political right, because preservative of all rights. In reference to that right, it was declared by the supreme judicial court of Massachusetts, in Capen v. Foster ... 'that in all cases where the constitution has conferred a political right or privilege, and where the constitution has not particularly designated the manner in which that right is to be exercised, it is clearly within the just and constitutional limits of the legislative power to adopt any reasonable and uniform regulations, in regard to the time and mode of exercising that right, which are designed to secure and facilitate the exercise of such right in a prompt, orderly, and convenient manner;' nevertheless, 'such a construction would afford no warrant for such an exercise of legislative power as, under the pretense and color of regulating, should subvert or injuriously restrain, the right itself.' It has accordingly been held generally in the states that whether the particular provisions of an act of legislation establishing means for ascertaining the qualifications of those entitled to vote, and making previous registration in lists of such, a condition precedent to the exercise of the right, were or were not reasonable regulations, and accordingly valid or void, was always open to inquiry, as a judicial question....

In the present cases, we are not obliged to reason from the probable to the actual, and pass upon the validity of the ordinances complained of, as tried merely by the opportunities which their terms afford, of unequal and unjust discrimination in their administration; for the cases present the ordinances in actual operation, and the facts shown establish an administration directed so exclusively against a particular class of persons as to warrant and require the conclusion that, whatever may have been the intent of the ordinances as adopted, they are applied by the public authorities charged with their administration, and thus representing the state itself, with a mind so unequal and oppressive as to amount to a practical denial by the state of that equal protection of the laws which is secured to the petitioners, as to all other persons, by the broad and benign provisions of the fourteenth amendment to the constitution of the United States. Though the law itself be fair on its face, and impartial in appearance, yet, if it is applied and administered by public authority with an evil eye and an unequal hand, so as practically to make unjust and illegal discriminations between persons in similar circumstances, material to their rights, the denial of equal justice is still within the prohibition of the constitution....

The present cases, as shown by the facts disclosed in the record, are within this class. It appears that both petitioners have complied with every requisite deemed by the law, or by the public officers charged with its administration, necessary for the protection of neighboring property from fire, or as a precaution against injury to the public health. No reason whatever, except the will of the supervisors, is assigned why they should not be permitted to carry on, in the accustomed manner, their harmless and useful occupation, on which they depend for a livelihood; and while this consent of the supervisors is withheld from them, and from 200 others who have also petitioned, all of whom happen to be Chinese subjects, 80 others, not Chinese subjects, are permitted to carry on the same business under similar conditions. The fact of this discrimination is admitted. No reason for it is shown, and the conclusion cannot be resisted that no reason for it exists except hostility to the race and nationality to which the petitioners belong, and which, in the eye of the law, is not justified. The discrimination is therefore illegal, and the public administration which enforces it is a denial of the equal protection of the laws, and a violation of the fourteenth amendment of the constitution. The imprisonment of the petitioners is therefore illegal, and they must be discharged.

Palmer v. Thompson
403 U.S. 217 (1971)

Majority: *Black*, Burger (CJ), Harlan, Stewart, Blackmun

Concurrences: *Burger* (CJ); *Blackmun* (both omitted)

Dissents: *Douglas* (omitted); *White*, Brennan, *Marshall* (omitted)

MR. JUSTICE BLACK delivered the opinion of the Court.

In 1962 the city of Jackson, Mississippi, was maintaining five public parks along with swimming pools, golf links, and other facilities for use by the public on a racially segregated basis. Four of the swimming pools were used by whites only and one by Negroes only. Plaintiffs brought an action in the United States District Court seeking a declaratory judgment that this state-enforced segregation of the races was a violation of the Thirteenth and Fourteenth Amendments, and asking an injunction to forbid such practices. After hearings the District Court entered a judgment declaring that enforced segregation denied equal protection of the laws but it declined to issue an injunction. The Court of Appeals affirmed, and we denied certiorari. The city proceeded to desegregate its public parks, auditoriums, golf courses, and the city zoo. However, the city council decided not to try to operate the public swimming pools on a desegregated basis. Acting in its legislative capacity, the council surrendered its lease on one pool and closed four which the city owned. A number of Negro citizens of Jackson then filed this suit to force the city to reopen the pools and operate them on a desegregated basis. The District Court found that the closing was justified to preserve peace and order and because the pools could not be operated economically on an integrated basis. It held the city's action did not deny black citizens equal protection of the laws. The Court of Appeals sitting en banc affirmed, six out of 13 judges dissenting. That court rejected the contention that since the pools had been closed either in whole or in part to avoid desegregation the city council's action was a denial of equal protection of the laws. We granted certiorari to decide that question. We affirm.

Petitioners rely chiefly on the first section of the Fourteenth Amendment which forbids any State to 'deny to any person within its jurisdiction the equal protection of the laws.' There can be no doubt that a major purpose of this amendment was to safeguard

Negroes against discriminatory state laws — state laws that fail to give Negroes protection equal to that afforded white people. History shows that the achievement of equality for Negroes was the urgent purpose not only for passage of the Fourteenth Amendment but for the Thirteenth and Fifteenth Amendments as well. See, e.g. Slaughterhouse Cases.... There can be no doubt that a major purpose of ... the Equal Protection Clause was principally designed to protect Negroes against discriminatory action by the States. Here there has unquestionably been 'state action' because the official local government legislature, the city council, has closed the public swimming pools of Jackson. The question, however, is whether this closing of the pools is state action that denies 'the equal protection of the laws' to Negroes. It should be noted first that neither the Fourteenth Amendment nor any Act of Congress purports to impose an affirmative duty on a State to begin to operate or to continue to operate swimming pools. Furthermore, this is not a case where whites are permitted to use public facilities while blacks are denied access. It is not a case where a city is maintaining different sets of facilities for blacks and whites and forcing the races to remain separate in recreational or educational activities....

Petitioners have also argued that respondents' action violates the Equal Protection Clause because the decision to close the pools was motivated by a desire to avoid integration of the races. But no case in this Court has held that a legislative act may violate equal protection solely because of the motivations of the men who voted for it.... A similar contention that illicit motivation should lead to a finding of unconstitutionality was advanced in United States v. O'Brien (1968), where this Court rejected the argument that a defendant could not be punished for burning his draft card because Congress had allegedly passed the statute to stifle dissent. That opinion explained well the hazards of declaring a law unconstitutional because of the motivations of its sponsors. First, it is extremely difficult for a court to ascertain the motivation, or collection of different motivations, that lie behind a legislative enactment.... Here, for example, petitioners have argued that the Jackson pools were closed because of ideological opposition to racial integration in swimming pools. Some evidence in the record appears to support this argument. On the other hand the courts below found that the pools were closed because the city council felt they could not be operated safely and economically on an integrated basis. There is substantial evidence in the record to support this conclusion. It is difficult or impossible for any court to determine the 'sole' or 'dominant' motivation behind the choices of a group of legislators. Furthermore, there is an element of futility in a judicial attempt to invalidate a law because of the bad motives of its supporters. If the law is struck down for this reason, rather than because of its facial content or effect, it would presumably be valid as soon as the legislature or relevant governing body re-passed it for different reasons.

It is true there is language in some of our cases interpreting the Fourteenth and Fifteenth Amendments which may suggest that the motive or purpose behind a law is relevant to its constitutionality.... But the focus in those cases was on the actual effect of the enactments, not upon the motivation which led the States to behave as they did. In Griffin, as discussed supra, the State was in fact perpetuating a segregated public school system by financing segregated 'private' academies. And in Gomillion the Alabama Legislature's gerrymander of the boundaries of Tuskegee excluded virtually all Negroes from voting in town elections. Here the record indicates only that Jackson once ran segregated public swimming pools and that no public pools are now maintained by the city. Moreover, there is no evidence in this record to show that the city is now covertly aiding the maintenance and operation of pools which are private in name only. It shows no state action affecting blacks differently from whites.

MR. JUSTICE WHITE, with whom MR. JUSTICE BRENNAN and MR. JUSTICE MARSHALL join, dissenting.

I agree with the majority that the central purpose of the Fourteenth Amendment is to protect Negroes from invidious discrimination. Consistent with this view, I had thought official policies forbidding or discouraging joint use of public facilities by Negroes and whites were at war with the Equal Protection Clause. Our cases make it unquestionably clear, as all of us agree, that a city or State may not enforce such a policy by maintaining officially separate facilities for the two races. It is also my view, but apparently not that of the majority, that a State may not have an official stance against desegregating public facilities and implement it by closing those facilities in response to a desegregation order.

Let us assume a city has been maintaining segregated swimming pools and is ordered to desegregate them. Its express response is an official resolution declaring desegregation to be contrary to the city's policy and ordering the facilities closed rather than continued in service on a desegregated basis. To me it is beyond cavil that on such facts the city is adhering to an unconstitutional policy and is implementing it by abandoning the facilities. It will not do in such circumstances to say that whites and Negroes are being treated alike because both are denied use of public services. The fact is that closing the pools is an expression of official policy that Negroes are unfit to associate with whites. Closing pools to prevent interracial swimming is little different from laws or customs forbidding Negroes and whites from eating together or from co-habiting or intermarrying.... The Equal Protection Clause is a hollow promise if it does not forbid such official denigrations of the race the Fourteenth Amendment was designed to protect.

The case before us is little, if any, different from the case just described. Jackson, Mississippi, closed its swimming pools when a district judge struck down the city's tradition of segregation in municipal services and made clear his expectation that public facilities would be integrated. The circumstances surrounding this action and the absence of other credible reasons for the closings leave little doubt that shutting down the pools was nothing more or less than a most effective expression of official policy that Negroes and whites must not be permitted to mingle together when using the services provided by the city.

I am quite unpersuaded by the majority's assertion that it is impermissible to impeach the otherwise valid act of closing municipal swimming pools by resort to evidence of invidious purpose or motive. Congress has long provided civil and criminal remedies for a variety of official and private conduct. In various situations these statutes and our interpretations of them provide that such conduct falls within the federal proscription only upon proof of forbidden racial motive or animus. An otherwise valid refusal to contract the sale of real estate falls within the ban of 42 U.S.C. § 1982 upon proof that the refusal was racially motivated. Jones v. Alfred H. Mayer Co. (1968). A restaurant's refusal to serve a white customer is actionable under 42 U.S.C. § 1983 where the evidence shows that refusal occurred because the white was accompanied by Negroes and was pursuant to a state-enforced custom of racial segregation. Just last week in Griffin v. Breckenridge, we construed 42 U.S.C. § 1985(3) to reach wholly private conspiracies—in that case to commit assault on Negroes—where sufficient evidence of 'racial ... animus' or 'invidiously discriminatory motivation' accompanied the conspirators' actions.... In rejecting the argument that § 1985(3) was subject to an implied state action limitation, we indicated that racially motivated conspiracies or activities would be actionable under § 1983 if done under color of law.... Official conduct is no more immune to characterization based on its motivation than is private conduct, and we have so held many times. The police are vulnerable under § 1983 if they subject a person 'to false arrest for vagrancy for the purpose of harassing and punishing (him) for attempting to eat with black people,' ... or if they 'intentionally tolerate violence or threats of violence directed toward those who violated the practice of segregating the races at restaurants.'"

The city of Jackson was one of many places where the consistent line of decisions following from Brown had little or no effect. Public recreational facilities were not desegregated although it had become clear that such action was required by the Constitution. As respondents state in their brief in this case: ... 'In 1963 the City of Jackson was operating equal but separate recreational facilities such as parks and golf links, including swimming pools. A suit was brought in the Southern District of Mississippi to enjoin the segregated operation of these facilities. The City of Jackson took the position in that litigation that the segregation of recreational facilities, if separate but equal recreational facilities were provided and if citizens voluntarily used segregated facilities, was constitutional.' ... This was nearly nine years after Brown. ...

There is no dispute that the closing of the pools constituted state action. Similarly, there can be no disagreement that the desegregation ruling in Clark v. Thompson was the event that precipitated the city's decision to cease furnishing public swimming facilities to its citizens. Although the secondary evidence of what the city officials thought and believed about the wisdom of desegregation is relevant, it is not necessary to rely on it to establish the causal link between Clark v. Thompson and the closings. The officials' sworn affidavits, accepted by the courts below, stated that loss of revenue and danger to the citizens would obviously result from operating the pools on an integrated basis. Desegregation, and desegregation alone, was the catalyst that would produce these undesirable consequences. Implicit in this official judgment were assumptions that the citizens of Jackson were of such a mind that they would no longer pay the 10- or 20-cent fee imposed by the city if their swimming and wading had to be done with their neighbors of another race, that some citizens would direct violence against their neighbors for using pools previously closed to them, and that the anticipated violence would not be controllable by the authorities. Stated more simply, although the city officials knew what the Constitution required after Clark v. Thompson became final, their judgment was that compliance with that mandate, at least with respect to swimming pools, would be intolerable to Jackson's citizens. ...

With all due respect, I am quite unable to agree with the majority's assertion that there is 'substantial evidence in the record' to support the conclusion of the lower courts that the pools could not be operated safely and economically on an integrated basis. Officials may take effective action to control violence or to prevent it when it is reasonably imminent. But the anticipation of violence in this case rested only on unsupported assertion, to which the permanent closing of swimming pools was a wholly unjustified response. The city seems to fear that even if some or all of the pools suffered a sharp decline in revenues from the levels pertaining before 1963 because Negro and white neighbors refused to use integrated facilities, the city could never close the pools for that reason. I need only observe that such a case, if documented by objective record evidence, would present different considerations. As Judge Wisdom stated below, 'We do not say that a city may never abandon a previously rendered municipal service. If the facts show that the city has acted in good faith for economic or other nonracial reasons, the action would have no overtones of racial degradation, and would therefore not offend the Constitution.' ... It is enough for the present case to re-emphasize that the only evidence in this record is the conclusions of the officials themselves, unsupported by even a scintilla of added proof.

Watson counsels us to reject the vague speculation that the citizens of Jackson will not obey the law, as well as the correlative assumption that they would prefer no public pools to pools open to all residents who come in peace. The argument based on economy is no more than a claim that a major portion of the city's population will not observe constitutional norms. The argument based on potential violence, as counsel for the city indicated at oral argument, unfortunately reflects the views of a few immoderates who purport to speak for the white population of the city of Jackson.... Perhaps it could have been presented, but there is no evidence now before us that there exists any group among the citizens of Jackson that would employ lawless violence to prevent use of swimming pools by Negroes and whites together. In my view, the Fourteenth Amendment does not permit any official act—whether in the form of open refusal to desegregate facilities that continue to operate, decisions to delay complete desegregation, or closure of facilities— to be predicated on so weak a reed. Public officials sworn to uphold the Constitution may not avoid a constitutional duty by bowing to the hypothetical effects of private racial prejudice that they assume to be both widely and deeply held. Surely the promise of the Fourteenth Amendment demands more than nihilistic surrender. As Mr. Justice Frankfurter observed more than 12 years ago:

> The process of ending unconstitutional exclusion of pupils from the common school system—'common' meaning shared alike—solely because of color is no doubt not an easy, overnight task in a few States where a drastic alteration in the ways of communities is involved. Deep emotions have, no doubt, been stirred. They will not be calmed by letting violence loose—violence and defiance employed and encouraged by those upon whom the duty of law observance should have the strongest claim—nor by submitting to it under whatever guise employed. Only the constructive use of time will achieve what an advanced civilization demands and the Constitution confirms.

I thus arrive at the question of whether closing public facilities to citizens of both races, whatever the reasons for such action, is a special kind of state action somehow insulated from scrutiny under the Fourteenth Amendment.... Here, too, the reality is that the impact of the city's act falls on the minority. Quite apart from the question whether the white citizens of Jackson have a better chance to swim than do their Negro neighbors absent city pools, there are deep and troubling effects on the racial minority that should give us all pause. As stated at the outset of this opinion, by closing the pools solely because of the order to desegregate, the city is expressing its official view that Negroes are so inferior that they are unfit to share with whites this particular type of public facility, though pools were long a feature of the city's segregated recreation program. But such an official position may not be enforced by designating certain pools for use by whites and others for the use of Negroes. Closing the pools without a colorable nondiscriminatory reason was every bit as much an official endorsement of the notion that Negroes are not equal to whites as was the use of state National Guard troops in 1957 to bar the entry of nine Negro students into Little Rock's Central High School, a public facility that was ordered desegregated in the wake of Brown.... These considerations were not abandoned as Brown was applied in other contexts, and it is untenable to suggest that the closing of the swimming pools—a pronouncement that Negroes are somehow unfit to swim with whites—operates equally on Negroes and whites. Whites feel nothing but disappointment and perhaps anger at the loss of the facilities. Negroes feel that and more. They are stigmatized by official implementation of a policy that the Fourteenth Amendment condemns as illegal. And the closed pools stand as mute reminders to the community of the official view of Negro inferiority.

Review Questions and Explanations: *Yick Wo* and *Palmer*

1. Did the Court in *Palmer v. Thomson* apply the rule it had developed in *Yick Wo*?

2. In *Palmer*, the majority is uninterested in whether the legislature acted with discriminatory purpose. Instead, it focuses on what it sees as a lack of discriminatory effect: under the city's actions, neither black nor white residents will be able to swim in public pools. Because this effect is, to the majority, not racially discriminatory, the Court declines to apply strict scrutiny. Is this consistent with *Yick Wo*?

3. Justice White disagrees that closing the pools has a non-discriminatory effect. Whites, he says, will feel nothing but "disappointment and perhaps anger," but blacks will feel stigmatized. This type of subordinating message is the same type of reasoning that the Court used in *Brown*. If the message of inferiority was constitutionally relevant in *Brown*, why isn't it relevant here? This issue will come up again. Justice Thomas repeatedly argues in affirmative action cases that race based admission preferences are unconstitutional in part because they stigmatize African Americans. Is the Court simply inconsistent with how it is weighing this fact? Or is the disagreement itself a factual one about whether or not such stigmatization occurs? If it is a factual dispute, what should the Court's role be in resolving it?

4. Justice White posits a situation where the city of Jackson coupled its closure of the pools with an announcement that it was closing them because it disapproved of and refused to operate racially integrated pools. He believes the majority would have agreed with him that this would undoubtedly be seen as a race-based decision and would be subjected to strict scrutiny. The majority does not dispute this point. If Justice White is correct about this, then is the majority correct to assert that legislative motive is irrelevant to the constitutional question presented, or does the majority simply disagree about whether a discriminatory motive has been shown here?

Exercise: Discriminatory Purpose

You are a clerk to federal appellate judge. You have been asked to review a decision issued by a state court in a custody dispute. The dispute involved a child born to two white parents. Custody was awarded to the child's mother at the time of the parents' divorce. One year later, the mother began living with an African American man. The child's father petitioned the court to re-open the custody case and award him custody of the child. The state court judge agreed, and granted custody of the child to the father. In doing so, the state court judge reasoned that leaving the child in the mother's custody would expose the child to the "social stigma" and racial hostility that still attached to mixed race couples in the community in which the mother lived. Consequently, the judge held that it was in the best interest of the child (the governing legal standard under state law) to be transferred to her father's custody. Using *Yick Wo* and *Palmer* as your controlling precedents, decide whether the state court's actions violate the Equal Protection clause.

Guided Reading Questions: *Washington v. Davis*

1. The issue in *Yick Wo* and *Palmer* was how (and if) the Court will consider the legislative purpose and the actual effect of the state's actions when determining whether to treat a facially neutral statute as a racial classification. *Wick Yo* looked at the actual and racialized effect of the laundry licensing process and struck it down as a violation of the Equal Protection clause. *Palmer,* in contrast, saw no discriminatory effect in Jackson's decision to close the pools rather than integrate them, and seemed both skeptical and uninterested in the city's allegedly discriminatory purpose in doing so. *Washington v. Davis* is the Court's effort to reconcile these cases. When reading the case, consider whether you think the Court succeeded in doing so.

Washington v. Davis

426 U.S. 229 (1976)

Majority: *White*, Burger (CJ), Blackmun, Powell, Rehnquist, Stevens, Stewart

Concurrence: *Stevens* (omitted)

Dissent: *Brennan*, Marshall (omitted)

MR. JUSTICE WHITE delivered the opinion of the Court.

This case involves the validity of a qualifying test administered to applicants for positions as police officers in the District of Columbia Metropolitan Police Department.... This action began on April 10, 1970, when two Negro police officers filed suit against the then Commissioner of the District of Columbia ... An amended complaint ... alleged that the promotion policies of the Department were racially discriminatory and sought a declaratory judgment and an injunction.... [The] amended complaint assert[ed] that their applications to become officers in the Department had been rejected, and that the Department's recruiting procedures discriminated on the basis of race against black applicants by a series of practices including, but not limited to, a written personnel test which excluded a disproportionately high number of Negro applicants....

The central purpose of the Equal Protection Clause of the Fourteenth Amendment is the prevention of official conduct discriminating on the basis of race. It is also true that the Due Process Clause of the Fifth Amendment contains an equal protection component prohibiting the United States from invidiously discriminating between individuals or groups. Bolling v. Sharpe (1954). But our cases have not embraced the proposition that a law or other official act, without regard to whether it reflects a racially discriminatory purpose, is unconstitutional solely because it has a racially disproportionate impact.

Almost 100 years ago, Strauder v. West Virginia (1880), established that the exclusion of Negroes from grand and petit juries in criminal proceedings violated the Equal Protection Clause, but the fact that a particular jury or a series of juries does not statistically reflect the racial composition of the community does not in itself make out an invidious discrimination forbidden by the Clause. "A purpose to discriminate must be present which may be proven by systematic exclusion of eligible jurymen of the proscribed race or by unequal application of the law to such an extent as to show intentional discrimination." Akins v. Texas, (1945). A defendant in a criminal case is entitled "to require that the State not deliberately and systematically deny to members of his race the right to participate as jurors in the administration of justice." Alexander v. Louisiana, (1972)....

The school desegregation cases have also adhered to the basic equal protection principle that the invidious quality of a law claimed to be racially discriminatory must ultimately be traced to a racially discriminatory purpose. That there are both predominantly black and predominantly white schools in a community is not alone violative of the Equal Protection Clause. The essential element of De jure segregation is "a current condition of segregation resulting from intentional state action.... The differentiating factor between De jure segregation and so-called De facto segregation ... is Purpose or Intent to segregate." ... The Court has also recently rejected allegations of racial discrimination based solely on the statistically disproportionate racial impact of various provisions of the Social Security Act because "(t)he acceptance of appellants' constitutional theory would render suspect each difference in treatment among the grant classes, however lacking in racial motivation and however otherwise rational the treatment might be." ...

This is not to say that the necessary discriminatory racial purpose must be express or appear on the face of the statute, or that a law's disproportionate impact is irrelevant in cases involving Constitution-based claims of racial discrimination. A statute, otherwise neutral on its face, must not be applied so as invidiously to discriminate on the basis of race. Yick Wo v. Hopkins (1886). It is also clear from the cases dealing with racial discrimination in the selection of juries that the systematic exclusion of Negroes is itself such an "unequal application of the law ... as to show intentional discrimination." ... A prima facie case of discriminatory purpose may be proved as well by the absence of Negroes on a particular jury combined with the failure of the jury commissioners to be informed of eligible Negro jurors in a community ... or with racially non-neutral selection procedures.... With a prima facie case made out, "the burden of proof shifts to the State to rebut the *2-steps* presumption of unconstitutional action by showing that permissible racially neutral selection criteria and procedures have produced the monochromatic result." ...

Necessarily, an invidious discriminatory purpose may often be inferred from the totality of the relevant facts, including the fact, if it is true, that the law bears more heavily on one race than another. It is also not infrequently true that the discriminatory impact in the jury cases for example, the total or seriously disproportionate exclusion of Negroes from jury venires may for all practical purposes demonstrate unconstitutionality because in various circumstances the discrimination is very difficult to explain on nonracial grounds. Nevertheless, we have not held that a law, neutral on its face and serving ends otherwise within the power of government to pursue, is invalid under the Equal Protection Clause simply because it may affect a greater proportion of one race than of another. Disproportionate impact is not irrelevant, but it is not the sole touchstone of an invidious racial discrimination forbidden by the Constitution. Standing alone, it does not trigger the rule ... that racial classifications are to be subjected to the strictest scrutiny and are justifiable only by the weightiest of considerations.

There are some indications to the contrary in our cases. In Palmer v. Thompson (1971), the city of Jackson, Miss., following a court decree to this effect, desegregated all of its public facilities save five swimming pools which had been operated by the city and which, following the decree, were closed by ordinance pursuant to a determination by the city council that closure was necessary to preserve peace and order and that integrated pools could not be economically operated. Accepting the finding that the pools were closed to avoid violence and economic loss, this Court rejected the argument that the abandonment of this service was inconsistent with the outstanding desegregation decree and that the otherwise seemingly permissible ends served by the ordinance could be impeached by demonstrating that racially invidious motivations had prompted the city council's action. The holding was that the city was not overtly or covertly operating segregated pools and was extending identical treatment to both whites and Negroes. The opinion warned against grounding decision on legislative purpose or motivation, thereby lending support for the proposition that the operative effect of the law rather than its purpose is the paramount factor. But the holding of the case was that the legitimate purposes of the ordinance to preserve peace and avoid deficits were not open to impeachment by evidence that the councilmen were actually motivated by racial considerations. Whatever dicta the opinion may contain, the decision did not involve, much less invalidate, a statute or ordinary having neutral purposes but disproportionate racial consequences.

Wright v. Council of City of Emporia (1972), also indicates that in proper circumstances, the racial impact of a law, rather than its discriminatory purpose, is the critical factor. That case involved the division of a school district. The issue was whether the division was consistent with an outstanding order of a federal court to desegregate the dual school system found to have existed in the area. The constitutional predicate for the District Court's invalidation of the divided district was "the enforcement until 1969 of racial segregation in a public school system of which Emporia had always been a part." ... There was thus no need to find "an independent constitutional violation." ... citing Palmer v. Thompson, we agreed with the District Court that the division of the district had the effect of interfering with the federal decree and should be set aside.

That neither Palmer nor Wright was understood to have changed the prevailing rule is apparent from Keyes v. School Dist. No. 1 ... where the principal issue in litigation was whether to what extent there had been purposeful discrimination resulting in a partially or wholly segregated school system. Nor did other later cases, Alexander v. Louisiana, supra, and Jefferson v. Hackney, supra, indicate that either Palmer or Wright had worked a fundamental change in equal protection law.

> FN11. To the extent that Palmer suggests a generally applicable proposition that legislative purpose is irrelevant in constitutional adjudication, our prior cases as indicated in the text are to the contrary; and very shortly after Palmer, all Members of the Court majority in that case joined the Court's opinion in Lemon v. Kurtzman (1971), which dealt with the issue of public financing for private schools and which announced, as the Court had several times before, that the validity of public aid to church-related schools includes close inquiry into the purpose of the challenged statute.

Both before and after Palmer v. Thompson, however, various Courts of Appeals have held in several contexts, including public employment, that the substantially disproportionate racial impact of a statute or official practice standing alone and without regard to discriminatory purpose, suffices to prove racial discrimination violating the Equal Protection Clause absent some justification going substantially beyond what would be necessary to validate most other legislative classifications. The cases impressively demonstrate that there is another side to the issue; but, with all due respect, to the extent that those cases rested on or expressed the view that proof of discriminatory racial purpose is unnecessary in making out an equal protection violation, we are in disagreement.

Review Questions and Explanations: *Washington v. Davis*

1. After *Washington v. Davis* what is the legal relevance of a law's racially discriminatory purpose? What is the legal relevance of a law's racially discriminatory effect?

2. *Washington* interpreted *Yick Wo* as standing for the proposition that a law's discriminatory *purpose* can at times be ascertained from its discriminatory *effect*. It is the discriminatory purpose, though, that is legally relevant. How does the Court square this with *Palmer*?

3. What type of evidence showing discriminatory purpose would persuade the Court to apply strict scrutiny to the type of law challenged in *Washington*?

2. Affirmative Action

This next set of cases review governmental efforts to remedy or ameliorate the lingering effects of past discrimination through affirmative action. Governmental affirmative action programs emerged in the late 1960s offering preferences to racial and ethnic minorities, and to women, in employment, government contracts, and admission to higher education. Starting with the *Bakke* case (presented below) in 1978, the Supreme Court has heard numerous challenges to such programs, and appears to have reviewed them with increasing stringency. In the cases that follow, we trace this development, focusing on affirmative action in the context of race.[3]

Affirmative action has sometimes been called "benign discrimination." The word "discrimination" in itself means "distinction" or "differentiation," something that, as we have seen, virtually all laws do. Thus, despite how we tend to use the term, not all "discrimination" is bad. "Benign" discrimination is the term used by proponents of affirmative action to distinguish what they see as acceptable *differentiation* from invidious *discrimination*. Invidious, which means "calculated to give offense, hateful," is a term courts used frequently in early race cases — the justices in those cases would talk about using heightened review to ferret out invidious discrimination and prejudice. The question in affirmative action cases is whether such review is appropriate in the absence of these things.

These cases thus force us to confront the very core of what we mean by equality, or denial of equal protection of the laws. They also force us to think precisely about why race discrimination is wrong. In the context of higher education, for example, why is it constitutionally problematic to have a race-based quota but not, for example, quotas requiring admitting a certain number of lacrosse players, alumni children, or applicants from Nebraska? Does it promote or hinder the purpose of the Equal Protection clause to allow preferences for these groups while subjecting race- (or sex-) based preferences to heightened judicial review? As you will see, even Supreme Court justices sometimes fail to answer that question clearly.

---

3. Affirmative action programs exist in the private sector — private employers and universities — as well as in the government sector. The Court has been actively, albeit somewhat less so, reviewing these kinds of affirmative action plans as well. But they are not included here because race-based decisions by private actors don't constitute "state action" and therefore do not directly implicate the Equal Protection clause. Instead, they are regulated by statutes, such as the Civil Rights Act of 1964.

Guided Reading Questions: *Regents of the University of California v. Bakke*

1. *Bakke* is a long and difficult opinion, and its voting breakdown is unusual. As explained in the editors' note at the beginning of the case, the governing opinion, that of Justice Powell, was not joined by any other justices. Instead, two sharply opposed blocs of four justices concurred in the result with one of the two key holdings in the Powell opinion. Although initially representing only Justice Powell's views, Powell's *Bakke* opinion has become the authoritative, foundational opinion for the law on affirmative action. Because of the complexity of the opinion, we have provided a breakdown at the start of the case of the judicial alignments on each of the Court's major holdings. It will be helpful to you to review this carefully before reading the case.

2. When reading the Powell opinion, ask why he insists on applying strict scrutiny to a voluntarily enacted affirmative action program. Is doing so dictated by *Brown* or any prior race case that you have read?

3. Justices Brennan, White, Marshall and Blackmun argue in *Bakke* that intermediate scrutiny is appropriate. What is their argument? (Note that these justices label their standard of review "strict," but they describe the test that has come to be known as "intermediate scrutiny," borrowed as we will see later in this chapter from the sex discrimination context.)

Regents of the University of California v. Bakke
438 U.S. 265 (1978)

[Editors' note: because of an unusual breakdown of votes, the judgment of the Court was announced by Justice Powell in an opinion that was not joined in its entirety by any other justice. However, key points of Powell's opinion were joined by one of two opposing 4-justice blocs: (1) Brennan, White, Marshall and Blackmun; or (2) Burger (CJ), Stewart, Rehnquist, and Stevens. Other aspects of the Powell opinion represented only his own views. Nevertheless, in subsequent cases, the Powell opinion came to be viewed as the authoritative opinion on those points as well.

Holdings (as expressed in the Powell opinion):

1. *The Davis minority set-aside program for medical school admissions is unlawful.* (5–4: Powell, Burger (CJ), Stewart, Rehnquist, and Stevens)

Note: there was no majority rationale for this ruling.

Powell opinion: the Davis set-aside (or quota) violated equal protection because it was not narrowly tailored to meet a compelling state interest.

Stevens, Burger, Stewart, Rehnquist: Title VI of the Civil Rights Act of 1964 prohibits any use of race whatever by federally funded educational institutions.

2. *Title VI of the Civil Rights Act of 1964 prohibits only those racial classifications that would violate the Equal Protection clause.* (5–4: *Powell*; concurrence by *Brennan*, White, Marshall and Blackmun; dissent by *Stevens*, Burger, Stewart, Rehnquist.)

3. *The Fourteenth Amendment (and Title VI, pursuant to holding 2), permits "benign" use of race in governmental decisions (affirmative action) if it meets the appropriate level of heightened judicial scrutiny.*(5–4: *Powell*; **concurrence** by *Brennan*, White, Marshall and Blackmun; **dissent** by *Stevens*, Burger, Stewart, Rehnquist.)

Powell opinion: traditional strict scrutiny must be applied, the race-based classification must be "narrowly tailored to achieve a compelling state interest." **Note:** only Powell adopted this position in Bakke, but his view subsequently prevailed.

Brennan, White, Marshall and Blackmun **partial concurrence:** modified "strict" scrutiny (i.e., what later came to be called "intermediate scrutiny") should apply: the race-based classification must be "substantially related to achievement of an important state interest."]

4. *A university's First Amendment interest in academic freedom and providing education in a diverse society makes the diversity of the student body a compelling governmental interest.*(5–4: *Powell*; **concurrence** by *Brennan*, White, Marshall and Blackmun; **not joined** by *Stevens*, Burger, (CJ), Stewart, Rehnquist.)

5. *Remedying past "societal discrimination" (i.e., without express findings suggesting that the university has itself discriminated in the past) is NOT a compelling governmental interest.* *Powell* opinion. **Note:** only Powell adopted this position in *Bakke*, but his view subsequently prevailed.

MR. JUSTICE POWELL announced the judgment of the Court.

This case presents a challenge to the special admissions program of the petitioner, the Medical School of the University of California at Davis, which is designed to assure the admission of a specified number of students from certain minority groups....

[In 1970, University of California at Davis Medical School created a "special admissions" program for minority applicants. Out of an entering class 100 students, 16 places were set aside for the "special admissions" program, which was open to members of a "minority group," which the Medical School apparently viewed as "Blacks," "Chicanos," "Asians," and "American Indians." The special admissions program was operated by an admissions committee, a majority of whom were themselves members of minority groups. Minority applicants could be considered for the general and the special admissions programs, but whites would only apply for the 84 slots in the general admissions program. Applicants to either program had to have a GPA of at least 2.5 on a scale of 4.0. It was undisputed that students admitted through the special admissions program had, on average, a lower GPA and lower scores on the MCAT (medical school entrance exam). From 1971 through 1974, the special program resulted in the admission of 21 black students, 30 Mexican-Americans, and 12 Asians, for a total of 63 minority students. Over the same period, the regular admissions program produced 1 black, 6 Mexican-Americans, and 37 Asians, for a total of 44 minority students. Allan Bakke, a white male, was rejected by the Davis Medical School in 1973 and 1974. In both years, Bakke's grade point average, MCAT scores, and "benchmark scores" (numerical ratings assigned by the Davis admissions committee) were lower than the average applicant in the general admissions process but higher than average for those admitted under the special admissions program. After the second rejection, Bakke filed suit in California state court seeking an compelling his admission to the Medical School, claiming that the admissions system violated the Fourteenth Amendment, the state constitution and Title VI.

[Powell, with the concurrence of Brennan, White, Marshall and Blackmun, concluded that Title VI of the Civil Rights Act of 1964 did not offer an independent basis for deciding the case.]

In view of the clear legislative intent, Title VI must be held to proscribe only those racial classifications that would violate the Equal Protection clause or the Fifth Amendment....

En route to this crucial battle over the scope of judicial review, the parties fight a sharp preliminary action over the proper characterization of the special admissions program. Petitioner prefers to view it as establishing a "goal" of minority representation in the Medical School. Respondent, echoing the courts below, labels it a racial quota.

This semantic distinction is beside the point: The special admissions program is undeniably a classification based on race and ethnic background. To the extent that there existed a pool of at least minimally qualified minority applicants to fill the 16 special admissions seats, white applicants could compete only for 84 seats in the entering class, rather than the 100 open to minority applicants. Whether this limitation is described as a quota or a goal, it is a line drawn on the basis of race and ethnic status.

The guarantees of the Fourteenth Amendment extend to all persons. Its language is explicit: "No State shall ... deny to any person within its jurisdiction the equal protection of the laws." ... The guarantee of equal protection cannot mean one thing when applied to one individual and something else when applied to a person of another color. If both are not accorded the same protection, then it is not equal.

Nevertheless, petitioner argues that the court below erred in applying strict scrutiny to the special admissions program because white males, such as respondent, are not a "discrete and insular minority" requiring extraordinary protection from the majoritarian political process. Carolene Products Co. This rationale, however, has never been invoked in our decisions as a prerequisite to subjecting racial or ethnic distinctions to strict scrutiny. Nor has this Court held that discreteness and insularity constitute necessary preconditions to a holding that a particular classification is invidious.... These characteristics may be relevant in deciding whether or not to add new types of classifications to the list of "suspect" categories or whether a particular classification survives close examination.... Racial and ethnic classifications, however, are subject to stringent examination without regard to these additional characteristics....

Although many of the Framers of the Fourteenth Amendment conceived of its primary function as bridging the vast distance between members of the Negro race and the white "majority," Slaughter-House Cases, the Amendment itself was framed in universal terms, without reference to color, ethnic origin, or condition of prior servitude....

Petitioner urges us to adopt for the first time a more restrictive view of the Equal Protection Clause and hold that discrimination against members of the white "majority" cannot be suspect if its purpose can be characterized as "benign." The clock of our liberties, however, cannot be turned back to 1868.... It is far too late to argue that the guarantee of equal protection to *all* persons permits the recognition of special wards entitled to a degree of protection greater than that accorded others....

Once the artificial line of a "two-class theory" of the Fourteenth Amendment is put aside, the difficulties entailed in varying the level of judicial review according to a perceived "preferred" status of a particular racial or ethnic minority are intractable. The concepts of "majority" and "minority" necessarily reflect temporary arrangements and political judgments. As observed above, the white "majority" itself is composed of various minority groups, most of which can lay claim to a history of prior discrimination at the hands of the State and private individuals. Not all of these groups can receive preferential treatment and corresponding judicial tolerance of distinctions drawn in terms of race and nationality, for then the only "majority" left would be a new minority of white Anglo-Saxon Protestants. There is no principled basis for deciding which groups would merit "heightened judicial solicitude" and which would not. Courts would be asked to evaluate the extent of the prejudice and consequent harm suffered by various minority groups. Those whose societal injury is thought to exceed some arbitrary level of tolerability then would be entitled to preferential classifications at the expense of individuals belonging to other groups. Those classifications would be free from exacting judicial scrutiny. As these preferences began to have their desired effect, and the consequences of past discrimination were undone, new judicial rankings would be necessary. The kind of variable sociological and political analysis necessary to produce such rankings simply does not lie within the judicial competence—even if they otherwise were politically feasible and socially desirable.

Moreover, there are serious problems of justice connected with the idea of preference itself. First, it may not always be clear that a so-called preference is in fact benign. Courts may be asked to validate burdens imposed upon individual members of a particular group in order to advance the group's general interest.... Nothing in the Constitution supports the notion that individuals may be asked to suffer otherwise impermissible burdens in order to enhance the societal standing of their ethnic groups. Second, preferential programs may only reinforce common stereotypes holding that certain groups are unable to achieve success without special protection based on a factor having no relationship to individual worth.... Third, there is a measure of inequity in forcing innocent persons in respondent's position to bear the burdens of redressing grievances not of their making.

By hitching the meaning of the Equal Protection Clause to these transitory considerations, we would be holding, as a constitutional principle, that judicial scrutiny of classifications touching on racial and ethnic background may vary with the ebb and flow of political forces. Disparate constitutional tolerance of such classifications well may serve to exacerbate racial and ethnic antagonisms rather than alleviate them.... Also, the mutability of a constitutional principle, based upon shifting political and social judgments, undermines the chances for consistent application of the Constitution from one generation to the next, a critical feature of its coherent interpretation.... In expounding the Constitution, the Court's role is to discern "principles sufficiently absolute to give them roots throughout the community and continuity over significant periods of time, and to lift them above the level of the pragmatic political judgments of a particular time and place."...

If it is the individual who is entitled to judicial protection against classifications based upon his racial or ethnic background because such distinctions impinge upon personal rights, rather than the individual only because of his membership in a particular group, then constitutional standards may be applied consistently. Political judgments regarding the necessity for the particular classification may be weighed in the constitutional balance, Korematsu v. United States, but the standard of justification will remain constant. This is as it should be, since those political judgments are the product of rough compromise struck by contending groups within the democratic process. When they touch upon an individual's race or ethnic background, he is entitled to a judicial determination that the burden he is asked to bear on that basis is precisely tailored to serve a compelling governmental interest. The Constitutional guarantees that right to every person regardless of his background....

The special admissions program purports to serve the purposes of: (i) "reducing the historic deficit of traditionally disfavored minorities in medical schools and in the medical profession," (ii) countering the effects of societal discrimination; (iii) increasing the number of physicians who will practice in communities currently underserved; and (iv) obtaining the educational benefits that flow from an ethnically diverse student body. It is necessary to decide which, if any, of these purposes is substantial enough to support the use of a suspect classification.

If petitioner's purpose is to assure within its student body some specified percentage of a particular group merely because of its race or ethnic origin, such a preferential purpose must be rejected not as insubstantial but as facially invalid. Preferring members of any one group for no reason other than race or ethnic origin is discrimination for its own sake. This the Constitution forbids....

The State certainly has a legitimate and substantial interest in ameliorating, or eliminating where feasible, the disabling effects of identified discrimination.... In the school [deseg-regation] cases, the States were required by court order to redress the wrongs worked by specific instances of racial discrimination. That goal was far more focused than the remedying of the effects of "societal discrimination," an amorphous concept of injury that may be ageless in its reach into the past.

We have never approved a classification that aids persons perceived as members of relatively victimized groups at the expense of other innocent individuals in the absence of judicial, legislative, or administrative findings of constitutional or statutory violations.... After such findings have been made, the governmental interest in preferring members of the injured groups at the expense of others is substantial, since the legal rights of the victims must be vindicated. In such a case, the extent of the injury and the consequent remedy will have been judicially, legislatively, or administratively defined. Also, the remedial action usually remains subject to continuing oversight to assure that it will work the least harm possible to other innocent persons competing for the benefit. Without such findings of constitutional or statutory violations, it cannot be said that the government has any greater interest in helping one individual than in refraining from harming another. Thus, the government has no compelling justification for inflicting such harm.

Petitioner does not purport to have made, and is in no position to make, such findings. Its broad mission is education, not the formulation of any legislative policy or the adjudication of particular claims of illegality.... [Isolated] segments of our vast governmental structures are not competent to make those decisions, at least in the absence of legislative mandates and legislatively determined criteria.... Before relying upon these sorts of findings in establishing a racial classification, a governmental body must have the authority and capability to establish, in the record, that the classification is responsive to identified discrimination....

It may be assumed that in some situations a State's interest in facilitating the health care of its citizens is sufficiently compelling to support the use of a suspect classification. But there is virtually no evidence in the record indicating that petitioner's special admissions program is either needed or geared to promote that goal. The court below addressed this failure of proof:

> The University concedes it cannot assure that minority doctors who entered under the program, all of whom expressed an 'interest' in practicing in a disad-vantaged community, will actually do so. It may be correct to assume that some of them will carry out this intention, and that it is more likely they will practice in minority communities than the average white doctor.... Nevertheless, there

are more precise and reliable ways to identify applicants who are genuinely interested in the medical problems of minorities than by race.

.... The fourth goal asserted by petitioner is the attainment of a diverse student body. This clearly is a constitutionally permissible goal for an institution of higher education. Academic freedom, though not a specifically enumerated constitutional right, long has been viewed as a special concern of the First Amendment. The freedom of a university to make its own judgments as to education includes the selection of its student body....

The atmosphere of "speculation, experiment and creation"—so essential to the quality of higher education—is widely believed to be promoted by a diverse student body. As the Court noted in Keyishian, it is not too much to say that the "nation's future depends upon leaders trained through wide exposure" to the ideas and mores of students as diverse as this Nation of many peoples....

Physicians serve a heterogeneous population. An otherwise qualified medical student with a particular background—whether it be ethnic, geographic, culturally advantaged or disadvantaged—may bring to a professional school of medicine experiences, outlooks, and ideas that enrich the training of its student body and better equip its graduates to render with understanding their vital service to humanity.

Ethnic diversity, however, is only one element in a range of factors a university properly may consider in attaining the goal of a heterogeneous student body. Although a university must have wide discretion in making the sensitive judgments as to who should be admitted, constitutional limitations protecting individual rights may not be disregarded....

.... The diversity that furthers a compelling state interest encompasses a far broader array of qualifications and characteristics of which racial or ethnic origin is but a single though important element. Petitioner's special admissions program, focused *solely* on ethnic diversity, would hinder rather than further attainment of genuine diversity....

The experience of other university admissions programs, which take race into account in achieving the educational diversity valued by the First Amendment, demonstrates that the assignment of a fixed number of places to a minority group is not a necessary means toward that end. An illuminating example is found in the Harvard College program:

> .... When the Committee on Admissions reviews the large middle group of applicants who are 'admissible' and deemed capable of doing good work in their courses, the race of an applicant may tip the balance in his favor just as geographic origin or a life spent on a farm may tip the balance in other candidates' cases. A farm boy from Idaho can bring something to Harvard College that a Bostonian cannot offer. Similarly, a black student can usually bring something that a white person cannot offer.
>
> In Harvard College admissions the Committee has not set target-quotas for the number of blacks, or of musicians, football players, physicists or Californians to be admitted in a given year.... [I]n choosing among thousands of applicants who are not only 'admissible' academically but have other strong qualities, the Committee, with a number of criteria in mind, pays some attention to distribution among many types and categories of students.

In such an admissions program, race or ethnic background may be deemed a "plus" in a particular applicant's file, yet it does not insulate the individual from comparison with all other candidates for the available seats. The file of a particular black applicant may be examined for his potential contribution to diversity without the factor of race being decisive when compared, for example, with that of an applicant identified as an Italian-American if the latter is thought to exhibit qualities more likely to promote beneficial educational pluralism. Such qualities could include exceptional personal talents, unique work or service experience, leadership potential, maturity, demonstrated compassion, a history of overcoming disadvantage, ability to communicate with the poor, or other qualifications deemed important.... [T]he weight attributed to a particular quality may vary from year to year depending upon the "mix" both of the student body and the applicants for the incoming class.

This kind of program treats each applicant as an individual in the admissions process. The applicant who loses out on the last available seat to another candidate receiving a "plus" on the basis of ethnic background will not have been foreclosed from all consideration for that seat simply because he was not the right color or had the wrong surname. It would mean only that his combined qualifications, which may have included similar nonobjective factors, did not outweigh those of the other applicant. His qualifications would have been weighed fairly and competitively, and he would have no basis to complain of unequal treatment under the Fourteenth Amendment.

It has been suggested that an admissions program which considers race only as one factor is simply a subtle and more sophisticated—but no less effective—means of according racial preference than the Davis program. A facial intent to discriminate, however, is evident in petitioner's preference program and not denied in this case. No such facial infirmity exists in an admissions program where race or ethnic background is simply one element—to be weighed fairly against other elements—in the selection process. "A boundary line," as Mr. Justice Frankfurter remarked in another connection, "is none the worse for being narrow." ... And a court would not assume that a university, professing to employ a facially nondiscriminatory admissions policy, would operate it as a cover for the functional equivalent of a quota system. In short, good faith would be presumed in the absence of a showing to the contrary in the manner permitted by our cases....

.... [W]hen a State's distribution of benefits or imposition of burdens hinges on ancestry or the color of a person's skin, that individual is entitled to a demonstration that the challenged classification is necessary to promote a substantial state interest. Petitioner has failed to carry this burden. For this reason, that portion of the California court's judgment holding petitioner's special admissions program invalid under the Fourteenth Amendment must be affirmed.

In enjoining petitioner from ever considering the race of any applicant, however, the courts below failed to recognize that the State has a substantial interest that legitimately may be served by a properly devised admissions program involving the competitive consideration of race and ethnic origin. For this reason, so much of the California court's judgment as enjoins petitioner from any consideration of the race of any applicant must be reversed.

With respect to respondent's entitlement to an injunction directing his admission to the Medical School, petitioner has conceded that it could not carry its burden of proving that, but for the existence of its unlawful special admissions program, respondent still would not have been admitted. Hence, respondent is entitled to the injunction, and that portion of the judgment must be affirmed.

MR. JUSTICE BRENNAN, MR. JUSTICE WHITE, MR. JUSTICE MARSHALL, and MR. JUSTICE BLACKMUN, concurring in the judgment in part and dissenting in part.

... The difficulty of the issue presented—whether government may use race-conscious programs to redress the continuing effects of past discrimination—and the mature consideration which each of our Brethren has brought to it have resulted in many opinions, no single one speaking for the Court. But this should not and must not mask the central meaning of today's opinions: Government may take race into account when it acts not to demean or insult any racial group, but to remedy disadvantages cast on minorities by past racial prejudice, at least when appropriate findings have been made by judicial, legislative, or administrative bodies with competence to act in this area....

.... Since we conclude that the affirmative admissions program at the Davis Medical School is constitutional, we would reverse the judgment below in all respects. MR. JUSTICE POWELL agrees that some uses of race in university admissions are permissible and, therefore, he joins with us to make five votes reversing the judgment below insofar as it prohibits the University from establishing race-conscious programs in the future.

... [T]he Framers of our Constitution, to forge the 13 Colonies into one Nation, openly compromised this principle of equality with its antithesis: slavery. The consequences of this compromise are well known and have aptly been called our "American Dilemma." ...

The Fourteenth Amendment, the embodiment in the Constitution of our abiding belief in human equality, has been the law of our land for only slightly more than half its 200 years. And for half of that half, the Equal Protection Clause of the Amendment was largely moribund so that, as late as 1927, Mr. Justice Holmes could sum up the importance of that Clause by remarking that it was the "last resort of constitutional arguments." Buck v. Bell, (1927). Worse than desuetude, the Clause was early turned against those whom it was intended to set free, condemning them to a "separate but equal" status before the law, a status always separate but seldom equal. Not until 1954—only 24 years ago—was this odious doctrine interred by our decision in Brown v. Board of Education....

Against this background, claims that law must be "colorblind" or that the datum of race is no longer relevant to public policy must be seen as aspiration rather than as description of reality.... Yet we cannot—and, as we shall demonstrate, need not under our Constitution or Title VI, which merely extends the constraints of the Fourteenth Amendment to private parties who receive federal funds—let color blindness become myopia which masks the reality that many "created equal" have been treated within our lifetimes as inferior both by the law and by their fellow citizens....

In our view, Title VI prohibits only those uses of racial criteria that would violate the Fourteenth Amendment if employed by a State or its agencies; it does not bar the preferential treatment of racial minorities as a means of remedying past societal discrimination to the extent that such action is consistent with the Fourteenth Amendment....

Our cases have always implied that.... racial classifications are not *per se* invalid under the Fourteenth Amendment. Accordingly, we turn to the problem of articulating what our role should be in reviewing state action that expressly classifies by race....

Unquestionably we have held that a government practice or statute which restricts "fundamental rights" or which contains "suspect classifications" is to be subjected to "strict scrutiny" and can be justified only if it furthers a compelling government purpose and, even then, only if no less restrictive alternative is available.

But no fundamental right is involved here.... Nor do whites as a class have any of the "traditional indicia of suspectness: the class is not saddled with such disabilities, or subjected to such a history of purposeful unequal treatment, or relegated to such a position of political powerlessness as to command extraordinary protection from the majoritarian political process." ...

- No fundamental rights issue
- No indicia of suspectness
- No political powerlessness requiring extraordinary protections

The fact that this case does not fit neatly into our prior analytic framework for race cases does not mean that it should be analyzed by applying the very loose rational-basis standard of review that is the very least that is always applied in equal protection cases.... Instead, a number of considerations—developed in gender-discrimination cases but which carry even more force when applied to racial classifications—lead us to conclude that racial classifications designed to further remedial purposes "must serve important governmental objectives and must be substantially related to achievement of those objectives."...

Because of the significant risk that racial classifications established for ostensibly benign purposes can be misused, causing effects not unlike those created by invidious classifications,.... our review under the Fourteenth Amendment should be strict—not "'strict' in theory and fatal in fact," because it is stigma that causes fatality—but strict and searching nonetheless.

Davis' articulated purpose of remedying the effects of past societal discrimination is, under our cases, sufficiently important to justify the use of race-conscious admissions programs where there is a sound basis for concluding that minority underrepresentation is substantial and chronic, and that the handicap of past discrimination is impeding access of minorities to the Medical School....

Davis had very good reason to believe that the national pattern of underrepresentation of minorities in medicine would be perpetuated if it retained a single admissions standard. For example, the entering classes in 1968 and 1969, the years in which such a standard was used, included only 1 Chicano and 2 Negroes out of the 50 admittees for each year. Nor is there any relief from this pattern of underrepresentation in the statistics for the regular admissions program in later years....

Moreover ... the Department of Health, Education, and Welfare, the expert agency charged by Congress with promulgating regulations enforcing Title VI of the Civil Rights Act of 1964, ... has also reached the conclusion that race may be taken into account in situations where a failure to do so would limit participation by minorities in federally funded programs.... In these circumstances, the conclusion implicit in the regulations—that the lingering effects of past discrimination continue to make race-conscious remedial programs appropriate means for ensuring equal educational opportunity in universities—deserves considerable judicial deference....

The second prong of our test—whether the Davis program stigmatizes any discrete group or individual and whether race is reasonably used in light of the program's objectives—is clearly satisfied by the Davis program. It is not even claimed that Davis' program in any way operates to stigmatize or single out any discrete and insular, or even any identifiable, nonminority group. Nor will harm comparable to that imposed upon racial minorities by exclusion or separation on grounds of race be the likely result of the program. It does not, for example, establish an exclusive preserve for minority students apart from and exclusive of whites. Rather, its purpose is to overcome the effects of segregation by bringing the races together. True, whites are excluded from participation in the special admissions program, but this fact only operates to reduce the number of whites to be admitted in the regular admissions program in order to permit admission of a reasonable percentage—less than their proportion of the California population—of otherwise underrepresented qualified minority applicants.

Nor was Bakke in any sense stamped as inferior by the Medical School's rejection of him. Indeed, it is conceded by all that he satisfied those criteria regarded by the school as generally relevant to academic performance better than most of the minority members who were admitted. Moreover, there is absolutely no basis for concluding that Bakke's rejection as a result of Davis' use of racial preference will affect him throughout his life in the same way as the segregation of the Negro schoolchildren in Brown I would have affected them. Unlike discrimination against racial minorities, the use of racial preferences for remedial purposes does not inflict a pervasive injury upon individual whites in the sense that wherever they go or whatever they do there is a significant likelihood that they will be treated as second-class citizens because of their color....

Finally, Davis' special admissions program cannot be said to violate the Constitution simply because it has set aside a predetermined number of places for qualified minority applicants rather than using minority status as a positive factor to be considered in evaluating the applications of disadvantaged minority applicants. For purposes of constitutional adjudication, there is no difference between the two approaches. In any admissions program which accords special consideration to disadvantaged racial minorities, a determination of the degree of preference to be given is unavoidable, and any given preference that results in the exclusion of a white candidate is no more or less constitutionally acceptable than a program such as that at Davis.

MR. JUSTICE MARSHALL, concurring in the judgment.

I agree with the judgment of the Court only insofar as it permits a university to consider the race of an applicant in making admissions decisions. I do not agree that petitioner's admissions program violates the Constitution....

The position of the Negro today in America is the tragic but inevitable consequence of centuries of unequal treatment. Measured by any benchmark of comfort or achievement, meaningful equality remains a distant dream for the Negro.

A Negro child today has a life expectancy which is shorter by more than five years than that of a white child. The Negro child's mother is over three times more likely to die of complications in childbirth, and the infant mortality rate for Negroes is nearly twice that for whites. The median income of the Negro family is only 60% that of the median of a white family, and the percentage of Negroes who live in families with incomes below the poverty line is nearly four times greater than that of whites....

The relationship between those figures and the history of unequal treatment afforded to the Negro cannot be denied. At every point from birth to death the impact of the past is reflected in the still disfavored position of the Negro.

In light of the sorry history of discrimination and its devastating impact on the lives of Negroes, bringing the Negro into the mainstream of American life should be a state interest of the highest order. To fail to do so is to ensure that America will forever remain a divided society.

I do not believe that the Fourteenth Amendment requires us to accept that fate. Neither its history nor our past cases lend any support to the conclusion that a university may not remedy the cumulative effects of society's discrimination by giving consideration to race in an effort to increase the number and percentage of Negro doctors....

While I applaud the judgment of the Court that a university may consider race in its admissions process, it is more than a little ironic that, after several hundred years of class-based discrimination against Negroes, the Court is unwilling to hold that a class-based remedy for that discrimination is permissible. In declining to so hold, today's judgment ignores the fact that for several hundred years Negroes have been discriminated against, not as individuals, but rather solely because of the color of their skins. It is unnecessary in 20th-century America to have individual Negroes demonstrate that they have been victims of racial discrimination; the racism of our society has been so pervasive that none, regardless of wealth or position, has managed to escape its impact. The experience of Negroes in America has been different in kind, not just in degree, from that of other ethnic groups. It is not merely the history of slavery alone but also that a whole people were marked as inferior by the law. And that mark has endured. The dream of America as the great melting pot has not been realized for the Negro; because of his skin color he never even made it into the pot.

.... In the Civil Rights Cases, supra, the Court wrote that the Negro emerging from slavery must cease "to be the special favorite of the laws." ... We cannot in light of the history of the last century yield to that view....

It is because of a legacy of unequal treatment that we now must permit the institutions of this society to give consideration to race in making decisions about who will hold the positions of influence, affluence, and prestige in America. For far too long, the doors to those positions have been shut to Negroes. If we are ever to become a fully integrated society, one in which the color of a person's skin will not determine the opportunities available to him or her, we must be willing to take steps to open those doors. I do not believe that anyone can truly look into America's past and still find that a remedy for the effects of that past is impermissible....

I fear that we have come full circle. After the Civil War our Government started several "affirmative action" programs. This Court in the Civil Rights Cases and Plessy v. Ferguson destroyed the movement toward complete equality. For almost a century no action was taken, and this nonaction was with the tacit approval of the courts. Then we had Brown v. Board of Education and the Civil Rights Acts of Congress, followed by numerous affirmative-action programs. *Now*, we have this Court again stepping in, this time to stop affirmative-action programs of the type used by the University of California.

MR. JUSTICE BLACKMUN, concurring in the judgment.

.... At least until the early 1970s, apparently only a very small number, less than 2%, of the physicians, attorneys, and medical and law students in the United States were members of what we now refer to as minority groups. In addition, approximately three-fourths of our Negro physicians were trained at only two medical schools. If ways are not found to remedy that situation, the country can never achieve its professed goal of a society that is not race conscious....

It is somewhat ironic to have us so deeply disturbed over a program where race is an element of consciousness, and yet to be aware of the fact, as we are, that institutions of higher learning, albeit more on the undergraduate than the graduate level, have given conceded preferences up to a point to those possessed of athletic skills, to the children of alumni, to the affluent who may bestow their largess on the institutions, and to those having connections with celebrities, the famous, and the powerful.... I suspect that it would be impossible to arrange an affirmative-action program in a racially neutral way and have it successful. To ask that this be so is to demand the impossible. In order to get beyond racism, we must first take account of race. There is no other way. And in order to treat some persons equally, we must treat them differently. We cannot—we dare not—let the Equal Protection Clause perpetuate racial supremacy....

MR. JUSTICE STEVENS, with whom THE CHIEF JUSTICE, MR. JUSTICE STEWART, and MR. JUSTICE REHNQUIST join, concurring in the judgment in part and dissenting in part.

[Title VI] of the Civil Rights Act of 1964, 42 U. S. C. § 2000d, provides:

No person in the United States shall, on the ground of race, color, or national origin, be excluded from participation in, be denied the benefits of, or be subjected to discrimination under any program or activity receiving Federal financial assistance.

The University, through its special admissions policy, excluded Bakke from participation in its program of medical education because of his race. The University also acknowledges that it was, and still is, receiving federal financial assistance. The plain language of the statute therefore requires affirmance of the judgment below....

Title VI is an integral part of the far-reaching Civil Rights Act of 1964.... The opponents feared that the term "discrimination" would be read as mandating racial quotas and "racially balanced" colleges and universities, and they pressed for a specific definition of the term in order to avoid this possibility. In response, the proponents of the legislation gave repeated assurances that the Act would be "colorblind" in its application.... it seems clear that the proponents of Title VI assumed that the Constitution itself required a colorblind standard on the part of government....

Review Questions and Explanations: *Bakke*

1. Is affirmative action "invidious" discrimination against whites? If voluntary affirmative action programs were upheld by the courts, what other, non judicial, checks would there be on the creation or maintenance of such programs?

2. Consider footnote 4 of *Carolene Products*, and the various arguments discussed above for heightened judicial review of some types of cases. Which of those arguments support judicial intervention on behalf of white majorities?

3. Under *Bakke*, what state interests are sufficiently compelling to pass strict scrutiny review? Why is remedying past "societal discrimination" not sufficient? Do you agree with Justice Powell about what interests are more or less compelling?

4. Is the discrimination at issue in *Bakke* just as bad as that involved in *Plessy*, *Korematsu* or *Brown*? Why or why not? Consider whether intermediate scrutiny would suffice to protect someone in Alan Bakke's position.

5. For that matter, why do we need strict scrutiny at all? Reconsider *Brown* and *Plessy*, and the standards of review. Could segregation have been struck down as failing the rational basis test? (Was it in *Brown*?) Note that discrimination against gays and lesbians was struck down under rational basis in *Romer v. Evans* (presented later in this chapter).

Justice Powell's controlling opinion in *Bakke* subjected even "benign" racial classifications to strict scrutiny, but then held that diversity in educational settings was a sufficiently compelling state interest to pass strict scrutiny. It was unclear, however, whether the Court would apply strict scrutiny to all classifications based on race. In a 1980 opinion, *Fullilove v. Klutznick* 448 U.S. 448 (1980), the Court considered whether Congress could, for the purpose of remedying prior discrimination, engage in a minority "set-aside" program guaranteeing a certain percentage of governmental contracts would go to minority-owned businesses. The Court declined to apply strict scrutiny and upheld the program, but the opinion was deeply divided, with no single opinion gaining the support of more than three justices. The following case, *Richmond v. J.A. Croson, Co.*, addresses the question of whether, and how, to apply strict scrutiny in such cases.

Guided Reading Questions: *City of Richmond v. J.A. Croson Co.*

1. The majority opinion draws a distinction between "remedial" affirmative action or remedying past specific discrimination, which can be a compelling interest, and addressing the effects of "societal discrimination," which the majority says is not compelling. The distinction is critical: make sure you understand it.

2. What sort of evidence does a governmental actor need to compile in order to show a compelling interest? What barriers might there be to a governmental entity putting together a convincing case that it, or its constituents, have engaged in intentional race discrimination in the past?

3. Pay attention to Justice Stevens' concurring opinion: what is his objection to the system of tiered review being developed by the Court?

City of Richmond v. J. A. Croson Co.

488 U.S. 469 (1989)

Majority (except parts II, III-A, V): *O'Connor*, Rehnquist (CJ), White, Stevens, Kennedy

Concurrences: *Stevens; Kennedy* (omitted)

Concurrence in the judgment: *Scalia*

Dissent: *Marshall*, Brennan, *Blackmun* (omitted)

JUSTICE O'CONNOR delivered the opinion of the Court.

In this case, we confront once again the tension between the Fourteenth Amendment's guarantee of equal treatment to all citizens, and the use of race-based measures to ameliorate the effects of past discrimination on the opportunities enjoyed by members of minority groups in our society....

On April 11, 1983, the Richmond City Council adopted the Minority Business Utilization Plan (the Plan). The Plan required prime contractors to whom the city awarded construction contracts to subcontract at least 30% of the dollar amount of the contract to one or more Minority Business Enterprises (MBE's).... The 30% set-aside did not apply to city contracts awarded to minority-owned prime contractors....

The Plan defined an MBE as "[a] business at least fifty-one (51) percent of which is owned and controlled ... by minority group members." ... "Minority group members" were defined as "[c]itizens of the United States who are Blacks, Spanish-speaking, Orientals, Indians, Eskimos, or Aleuts." ... There was no geographic limit to the Plan; an otherwise qualified MBE from anywhere in the United States could avail itself of the 30% set-aside. The Plan declared that it was "remedial" in nature, and enacted "for the purpose of promoting wider participation by minority business enterprises in the construction of public projects." ... The Plan expired on June 30, 1988, and was in effect for approximately five years....

The Plan was adopted by the Richmond City Council after a public hearing.... Seven members of the public spoke to the merits of the ordinance: five were in opposition, two in favor. Proponents of the set-aside provision relied on a study which indicated that, while the general population of Richmond was 50% black, only 0.67% of the city's prime construction contracts had been awarded to minority businesses in the 5-year period from 1978 to 1983. It was also established that a variety of contractors' associations, whose representatives appeared in opposition to the ordinance, had virtually no minority businesses within their membership....

II

.... [A] a state or local subdivision (if delegated the authority from the State) has the authority to eradicate the effects of private discrimination within its own legislative jurisdiction. This authority must, of course, be exercised within the constraints of.... the Equal Protection Clause [which] require[s] "some showing of prior discrimination by the governmental unit involved." As a matter of state law, the city of Richmond has legislative authority over its procurement policies, and can use its spending powers to remedy private discrimination, if it identifies that discrimination with the particularity required by the Fourteenth Amendment....

[margin note: Not approved by O'Connor, Rehnquist, White, Stevens, Kennedy + Marshall, Brennan, Blackmun (dissenting) in whole]

Thus, if the city could show that it had essentially become a "passive participant" in a system of racial exclusion practiced by elements of the local construction industry, we think it clear that the city could take affirmative steps to dismantle such a system. It is beyond dispute that any public entity, state or federal, has a compelling interest in assuring that public dollars, drawn from the tax contributions of all citizens, do not serve to finance the evil of private prejudice....

III

A

The Equal Protection Clause of the Fourteenth Amendment provides that "[n]o State shall ... deny to any person within its jurisdiction the equal protection of the laws." ... As this Court has noted in the past, the "rights created by the first section of the Fourteenth Amendment are, by its terms, guaranteed to the individual. The rights established are personal rights." ... The Richmond Plan denies certain citizens the opportunity to compete for a fixed percentage of public contracts based solely upon their race. To whatever racial group these citizens belong, their "personal rights" to be treated with equal dignity and respect are implicated by a rigid rule erecting race as the sole criterion in an aspect of public decisionmaking.

Absent searching judicial inquiry into the justification for such race-based measures, there is simply no way of determining what classifications are "benign" or "remedial" and what classifications are in fact motivated by illegitimate notions of racial inferiority or simple racial politics. Indeed, the purpose of strict scrutiny is to "smoke out" illegitimate uses of race by assuring that the legislative body is pursuing a goal important enough to warrant use of a highly suspect tool. The test also ensures that the means chosen "fit" this compelling goal so closely that there is little or no possibility that the motive for the classification was illegitimate racial prejudice or stereotype.

Classifications based on race carry a danger of stigmatic harm. Unless they are strictly reserved for remedial settings, they may in fact promote notions of racial inferiority and lead to a politics of racial hostility.... We thus reaffirm the view expressed by the plurality in Wygant that the standard of review under the Equal Protection Clause is not dependent on the race of those burdened or benefited by a particular classification.... Under the standard proposed by Justice MARSHALL's dissent, "race-conscious classifications designed to further remedial goals," ... are forthwith subject to a relaxed standard of review. How the dissent arrives at the legal conclusion that a racial classification is "designed to further remedial goals," without first engaging in an examination of the factual basis for its enactment and the nexus between its scope and that factual basis, we are not told. However, once the "remedial" conclusion is reached, the dissent's standard is singularly deferential, and bears little resemblance to the close examination of legislative purpose we have engaged in when reviewing classifications based either on race or gender. ... The dissent's watered-down version of equal protection review effectively assures that race will always be relevant in American life, and that the "ultimate goal" of "eliminat[ing] entirely from governmental decisionmaking such irrelevant factors as a human being's race," ... will never be achieved.

Even were we to accept a reading of the guarantee of equal protection under which the level of scrutiny varies according to the ability of different groups to defend their interests in the representative process, heightened scrutiny would still be appropriate in the circumstances of this case. One of the central arguments for applying a less exacting standard to "benign" racial classifications is that such measures essentially involve a choice made by dominant racial groups to disadvantage themselves. If one aspect of the judiciary's role under the Equal Protection Clause is to protect "discrete and insular minorities" from majoritarian prejudice or indifference, see United States v. Carolene Products Co. (1938), some maintain that these concerns are not implicated when the "white majority" places burdens upon itself.

In this case, blacks constitute approximately 50% of the population of the city of Richmond. Five of the nine seats on the city council are held by blacks. The concern that a political majority will more easily act to the disadvantage of a minority based on unwarranted assumptions or incomplete facts would seem to militate for, not against, the application of heightened judicial scrutiny in this case.

B

We think it clear that.... a generalized assertion that there has been past discrimination in an entire industry provides no guidance for a legislative body to determine the precise scope of the injury it seeks to remedy. It "has no logical stopping point." "Relief" for such an ill-defined wrong could extend until the percentage of public contracts awarded to MBE's in Richmond mirrored the percentage of minorities in the population as a whole....

While there is no doubt that the sorry history of both private and public discrimination in this country has contributed to a lack of opportunities for black entrepreneurs, this observation, standing alone, cannot justify a rigid racial quota in the awarding of public contracts in Richmond, Virginia. Like the claim that discrimination in primary and secondary schooling justifies a rigid racial preference in medical school admissions, an amorphous claim that there has been past discrimination in a particular industry cannot justify the use of an unyielding racial quota.

It is sheer speculation how many minority firms there would be in Richmond absent past societal discrimination, just as it was sheer speculation how many minority medical students would have been admitted to the medical school at Davis absent past discrimination in educational opportunities. Defining these sorts of injuries as "identified discrimination" would give local governments license to create a patchwork of racial preferences based on statistical generalizations about any particular field of endeavor.

IV

As noted by the court below, it is almost impossible to assess whether the Richmond Plan is narrowly tailored to remedy prior discrimination since it is not linked to identified discrimination in any way. We limit ourselves to two observations in this regard.

First, there does not appear to have been any consideration of the use of race-neutral means to increase minority business participation in city contracting.... Second, the 30% quota cannot be said to be narrowly tailored to any goal, except perhaps outright racial balancing. It rests upon the "completely unrealistic" assumption that minorities will choose a particular trade in lockstep proportion to their representation in the local population....

.... [T]he city's only interest in maintaining a quota system rather than investigating the need for remedial action in particular cases would seem to be simple administrative convenience.... We think it obvious that such a program is not narrowly tailored to remedy the effects of prior discrimination.

V

Nothing we say today precludes a state or local entity from taking action to rectify the effects of identified discrimination within its jurisdiction. If the city of Richmond had evidence before it that nonminority contractors were systematically excluding minority businesses from subcontracting opportunities, it could take action to end the discriminatory exclusion. Where there is a significant statistical disparity between the number of qualified minority contractors willing and able to perform a particular service and the number of such contractors actually engaged by the locality or the locality's prime contractors, an inference of discriminatory exclusion could arise. Under such circumstances, the city could act to dismantle the closed business system by taking appropriate measures against those who discriminate on the basis of race or other illegitimate criteria. In the extreme case, some form of narrowly tailored racial preference might be necessary to break down patterns of deliberate exclusion....

Even in the absence of evidence of discrimination, the city has at its disposal a whole array of race-neutral devices to increase the accessibility of city contracting opportunities to small entrepreneurs of all races. Simplification of bidding procedures, relaxation of bonding requirements, and training and financial aid for disadvantaged entrepreneurs of all races would open the public contracting market to all those who have suffered the effects of past societal discrimination or neglect. Many of the formal barriers to new entrants may be the product of bureaucratic inertia more than actual necessity, and may have a disproportionate effect on the opportunities open to new minority firms....

In the case at hand, the city has not ascertained how many minority enterprises are present in the local construction market nor the level of their participation in city construction projects. The city points to no evidence that qualified minority contractors have been passed over for city contracts or subcontracts, either as a group or in any individual case. Under such circumstances, it is simply impossible to say that the city has demonstrated "a strong basis in evidence for its conclusion that remedial action was necessary."

Proper findings in this regard are necessary to define both the scope of the injury and the extent of the remedy necessary to cure its effects. Such findings also serve to assure all citizens that the deviation from the norm of equal treatment of all racial and ethnic groups is a temporary matter, a measure taken in the service of the goal of equality itself. Absent such findings, there is a danger that a racial classification is merely the product of unthinking stereotypes or a form of racial politics.... Because the city of Richmond has failed to identify the need for remedial action in the awarding of its public construction contracts, its treatment of its citizens on a racial basis violates the dictates of the Equal Protection Clause. Accordingly, the judgment of the Court of Appeals for the Fourth Circuit is Affirmed.

JUSTICE STEVENS, concurring in part and concurring in the judgment.

A central purpose of the Fourteenth Amendment is to further the national goal of equal opportunity for all our citizens. In order to achieve that goal we must learn from our past mistakes, but I believe the Constitution requires us to evaluate our policy decisions—including those that govern the relationships among different racial and ethnic groups—primarily by studying their probable impact on the future. I therefore do not agree with the premise that seems to underlie today's decision, as well as the decision in Wygant v. Jackson Board of Education (1986), that a governmental decision that rests on a racial classification is never permissible except as a remedy for a past wrong.... In my view the Court's approach to this case gives unwarranted deference to race-based legislative action that purports to serve a purely remedial goal, and overlooks the potential value of race-based determinations that may serve other valid purposes.... I think it unfortunate that the Court in neither Wygant nor this case seems prepared to acknowledge that some race-based policy decisions may serve a legitimate public purpose. I agree, of course, that race is so seldom relevant to legislative decisions on how best to foster the public good that legitimate justifications for race-based legislation will usually not be available. But unlike the Court, I would not totally discount the legitimacy of race-based decisions that may produce tangible and fully justified future benefits....

[T]he city makes no claim that the public interest in the efficient performance of its construction contracts will be served by granting a preference to minority-business enterprises. This case is therefore completely unlike Wygant, in which I thought it quite obvious that the school board had reasonably concluded that an integrated faculty could provide educational benefits to the entire student body that could not be provided by an all-white, or nearly all-white, faculty. As I pointed out in my dissent in that case, even if we completely disregard our history of racial injustice, race is not always irrelevant to sound governmental decisionmaking....

[I]nstead of engaging in a debate over the proper standard of review to apply in affirmative-action litigation, I believe it is more constructive to try to identify the characteristics of the advantaged and disadvantaged classes that may justify their disparate treatment.... In this case that approach convinces me that, instead of carefully identifying the characteristics of the two classes of contractors that are respectively favored and disfavored by its ordinance, the Richmond City Council has merely engaged in the type of stereotypical analysis that is a hallmark of violations of the Equal Protection Clause. Whether we look at the class of persons benefited by the ordinance or at the disadvantaged class, the same conclusion emerges.

> FN5. "There is only one Equal Protection Clause. It requires every State to govern impartially. It does not direct the courts to apply one standard of review in some cases and a different standard in other cases." Craig v. Boren (1976) (STEVENS, J., concurring).

> FN6. "I have always asked myself whether I could find a 'rational basis' for the classification at issue. The term 'rational,' of course, includes a requirement that an impartial lawmaker could logically believe that the classification would serve a legitimate public purpose that transcends the harm to the members of the disadvantaged class. Thus, the word 'rational'—for me at least—includes elements of legitimacy and neutrality that must always characterize the performance of the sovereign's duty to govern impartially."

"In every equal protection case, we have to ask certain basic questions. What class is harmed by the legislation, and has it been subjected to a 'tradition of disfavor' by our laws? What is the public purpose that is being served by the law? What is the characteristic of the disadvantaged class that justifies the disparate treatment? In most cases the answer to these questions will tell us whether the statute has a 'rational basis.'"

JUSTICE SCALIA, concurring in the judgment.

I agree with much of the Court's opinion, and, in particular, with JUSTICE O'CONNOR's conclusion that strict scrutiny must be applied to all governmental classification by race, whether or not its asserted purpose is "remedial" or "benign." I do not agree, however, with JUSTICE O'CONNOR's dictum suggesting that, despite the Fourteenth Amendment, state and local governments may in some circumstances discriminate on the basis of race in order (in a broad sense) "to ameliorate the effects of past discrimination." The benign purpose of compensating for social disadvantages, whether they have been acquired by reason of prior discrimination or otherwise, can no more be pursued by the illegitimate means of racial discrimination than can other assertedly benign purposes we have repeatedly rejected. The difficulty of overcoming the effects of past discrimination is as nothing compared with the difficulty of eradicating from our society the source of those effects, which is the tendency—fatal to a Nation such as ours—to classify and judge men and women on the basis of their country of origin or the color of their skin.

JUSTICE MARSHALL, with whom JUSTICE BRENNAN and JUSTICE BLACKMUN join, dissenting.

It is a welcome symbol of racial progress when the former capital of the Confederacy acts forthrightly to confront the effects of racial discrimination in its midst. In my view, nothing in the Constitution can be construed to prevent Richmond, Virginia, from allocating a portion of its contracting dollars for businesses owned or controlled by members of minority groups.... A majority of this Court holds today, however, that the Equal Protection Clause of the Fourteenth Amendment blocks Richmond's initiative. The essence of the majority's position is that Richmond has failed to catalog adequate findings to prove that past discrimination has impeded minorities from joining or participating fully in Richmond's construction contracting industry. I find deep irony in second-guessing Richmond's judgment on this point. As much as any municipality in the United States, Richmond knows what racial discrimination is; a century of decisions by this and other federal courts has richly documented the city's disgraceful history of public and private racial discrimination....

More fundamentally, today's decision marks a deliberate and giant step backward in this Court's affirmative-action jurisprudence. Cynical of one municipality's attempt to redress the effects of past racial discrimination in a particular industry, the majority launches a grapeshot attack on race-conscious remedies in general. The majority's unnecessary pronouncements will inevitably discourage or prevent governmental entities, particularly States and localities, from acting to rectify the scourge of past discrimination. This is the harsh reality of the majority's decision, but it is not the Constitution's command....

Today, for the first time, a majority of this Court has adopted strict scrutiny as its standard of Equal Protection Clause review of race-conscious remedial measures.... This is an unwelcome development. A profound difference separates governmental actions that themselves are racist, and governmental actions that seek to remedy the effects of prior racism or to prevent neutral governmental activity from perpetuating the effects of such racism.

Racial classifications "drawn on the presumption that one race is inferior to another or because they put the weight of government behind racial hatred and separatism" warrant the strictest judicial scrutiny because of the very irrelevance of these rationales.... By contrast, racial classifications drawn for the purpose of remedying the effects of discrimination that itself was race based have a highly pertinent basis: the tragic and indelible fact that discrimination against blacks and other racial minorities in this Nation has pervaded our Nation's history and continues to scar our society. As I stated in Fullilove: "Because the consideration of race is relevant to remedying the continuing effects of past racial discrimination, and because governmental programs employing racial classifications for remedial purposes can be crafted to avoid stigmatization, ... such programs should not be subjected to conventional 'strict scrutiny'—scrutiny that is strict in theory, but fatal in fact." Fullilove.

In concluding that remedial classifications warrant no different standard of review under the Constitution than the most brutal and repugnant forms of state-sponsored racism, a majority of this Court signals that it regards racial discrimination as largely a phenomenon of the past, and that government bodies need no longer preoccupy themselves with rectifying racial injustice. I, however, do not believe this Nation is anywhere close to eradicating racial discrimination or its vestiges. In constitutionalizing its wishful thinking, the majority today does a grave disservice not only to those victims of past and present racial discrimination in this Nation whom government has sought to assist, but also to this Court's long tradition of approaching issues of race with the utmost sensitivity.

I am also troubled by the majority's assertion that, even if it did not believe generally in strict scrutiny of race-based remedial measures, "the circumstances of this case" require this Court to look upon the Richmond City Council's measure with the strictest scrutiny.... The sole such circumstance which the majority cites, however, is the fact that blacks in Richmond are a "dominant racial grou[p]" in the city.... In support of this characterization of dominance, the majority observes that "blacks constitute approximately 50% of the population of the city of Richmond" and that "[f]ive of the nine seats on the City Council are held by blacks." ...

While I agree that the numerical and political supremacy of a given racial group is a factor bearing upon the level of scrutiny to be applied, this Court has never held that numerical inferiority, standing alone, makes a racial group "suspect" and thus entitled to strict scrutiny review. Rather, we have identified other "traditional indicia of suspectness": whether a group has been "saddled with such disabilities, or subjected to such a history of purposeful unequal treatment, or relegated to such a position of political powerlessness as to command extraordinary protection from the majoritarian political process." ...

It cannot seriously be suggested that nonminorities in Richmond have any "history of purposeful unequal treatment." ... Nor is there any indication that they have any of the disabilities that have characteristically afflicted those groups this Court has deemed suspect. Indeed, the numerical and political dominance of nonminorities within the State of Virginia and the Nation as a whole provides an enormous political check against the "simple racial politics" at the municipal level which the majority fears.... If the majority really believes that groups like Richmond's nonminorities, which constitute approximately half the population but which are outnumbered even marginally in political fora, are deserving of suspect class status for these reasons alone, this Court's decisions denying suspect status to women, see Craig v. Boren (1976), and to persons with below-average incomes, stand on extremely shaky ground....

In my view, the "circumstances of this case," ... underscore the importance of not subjecting to a strict scrutiny straitjacket the increasing number of cities which have recently come under minority leadership and are eager to rectify, or at least prevent the perpetuation of, past racial discrimination. In many cases, these cities will be the ones with the most in the way of prior discrimination to rectify. Richmond's leaders had just witnessed decades of publicly sanctioned racial discrimination in virtually all walks of life—discrimination amply documented in the decisions of the federal judiciary.... This history of "purposefully unequal treatment" forced upon minorities, not imposed by them, should raise an inference that minorities in Richmond had much to remedy—and that the 1983 set-aside was undertaken with sincere remedial goals in mind, not "simple racial politics."

Richmond's own recent political history underscores the facile nature of the majority's assumption that elected officials' voting decisions are based on the color of their skins. In recent years, white and black councilmembers in Richmond have increasingly joined hands on controversial matters. When the Richmond City Council elected a black man mayor in 1982, for example, his victory was won with the support of the city council's four white members.... The vote on the set-aside plan a year later also was not purely along racial lines. Of the four white councilmembers, one voted for the measure and another abstained.... The majority's view that remedial measures undertaken by municipalities with black leadership must face a stiffer test of Equal Protection Clause scrutiny than remedial measures undertaken by municipalities with white leadership implies a lack of political maturity on the part of this Nation's elected minority officials that is totally unwarranted. Such insulting judgments have no place in constitutional jurisprudence.

Review Questions and Explanations: *Croson*

1. Justice O'Connor's opinion says that "absent searching judicial inquiry into the justification for such race-based measures, there is simply no way of determining what classifications are 'benign' or 'remedial' and what classifications are in fact motivated by illegitimate notions of racial inferiority or simple racial politics." Justice Marshall implies the opposite, saying that: "A profound difference separates governmental actions that themselves are racist, and governmental actions that seek to remedy the effects of prior racism or to prevent neutral governmental activity from perpetuating the effects of such racism." Neither O'Connor nor Marshall is claiming that any type of race-based distinction is "racist." Rather, they disagree on the constitutional relevance of the state's reason for drawing a race-based classification. Should all racial classifications trigger strict scrutiny? Why or why not?

2. The first sentence of Justice White's dissent in *Palmer v. Thompson* says this: "I agree with the majority that the central purpose of the Fourteenth Amendment is to protect Negroes from invidious discrimination." Justice O'Connor's majority opinion in *Richmond v. Croson* says this: "The central purpose of the Equal Protection clause of the Fourteenth Amendment is the prevention of official conduct discriminating on the basis of race." Which of these statements is more consistent with the various opinions you have read so far? Which is more consistent with the text and history of the Fourteenth Amendment, as presented in the earlier cases?

3. Justice Stevens' dissent suggests that the Court's system of tiered review in equal protection cases is fundamentally flawed. Do you agree? How would you analyze the *Croson* case using his proposed test?

4. Justice Scalia and Justice Thomas frequently have repeated the position that race-conscious remedies are never justified outside the context of a judicial finding of discrimination. Do you agree?

Guided Reading Questions: *Grutter v. Bollinger*

1. Articulate the specific application of strict scrutiny by the majority to the Michigan Law School admissions plan: what is the governmental interest, why is it compelling, and how is the plan narrowly tailored?

2. Read the majority and separate opinions carefully. Which of the justices accept the Powell opinion in *Bakke* as authoritative?

3. Justice Powell in *Bakke* considered "diversity" a compelling interest; here, the Court considers both "diversity" and "critical mass." What is the relationship between these concepts?

4. Does the Court "hold" (as Justice Thomas says) that affirmative action will be illegal as of 2028 (i.e., 25 years after *Grutter*)?

Grutter v. Bollinger

539 U.S. 306 (2003)

Majority: *O'Connor*, Stevens, Souter, Ginsburg, Breyer

Concurrence: *Ginsburg*, Breyer

Dissents: *Rehnquist (CJ)*, *Scalia*, *Kennedy*, *Thomas*

JUSTICE O'CONNOR delivered the opinion of the Court.

This case requires us to decide whether the use of race as a factor in student admissions by the University of Michigan Law School (Law School) is unlawful.

The Law School ranks among the Nation's top law schools. It receives more than 3,500 applications each year for a class of around 350 students. Seeking to "admit a group of students who individually and collectively are among the most capable," the Law School looks for individuals with "substantial promise for success in law school" and "a strong likelihood of succeeding in the practice of law and contributing in diverse ways to the well-being of others." More broadly, the Law School seeks "a mix of students with varying backgrounds and experiences who will respect and learn from each other." Ibid. In 1992, the dean of the Law School charged a faculty committee with crafting a written admissions policy to implement these goals. In particular, the Law School sought to ensure that its efforts to achieve student body diversity complied with this Court's most recent ruling on the use of race in university admissions....

The hallmark of that policy is its focus on academic ability coupled with a flexible assessment of applicants' talents, experiences, and potential "to contribute to the learning of those around them." The policy requires admissions officials to evaluate each applicant based on all the information available in the file, including a personal statement, letters of recommendation, and an essay describing the ways in which the applicant will contribute to the life and diversity of the Law School.... The policy makes clear, however, that even the highest possible score does not guarantee admission to the Law School. Nor does a low score automatically disqualify an applicant. Rather, the policy requires admissions officials to look beyond grades and test scores to other criteria that are important to the Law School's educational objectives.

.... The policy does not restrict the types of diversity contributions eligible for "substantial weight" in the admissions process, but instead recognizes "many possible bases for diversity admissions." The policy does, however, reaffirm the Law School's longstanding commitment to "one particular type of diversity," that is, "racial and ethnic diversity with special reference to the inclusion of students from groups which have been historically discriminated against, like African-Americans, Hispanics and Native Americans, who without this commitment might not be represented in our student body in meaningful numbers." By enrolling a "'critical mass' of [underrepresented] minority students," the Law School seeks to "ensure their ability to make unique contributions to the character of the Law School." ...

Petitioner Barbara Grutter is a white Michigan resident who applied to the Law School in 1996 with a 3.8 grade point average and 161 LSAT score. The Law School initially placed petitioner on a waiting list, but subsequently rejected her application. [Grutter filed suit in district court naming as defendants Lee Bollinger (Dean of the Law School from 1987 to 1994, and President of the University of Michigan from 1996 to 2002), the Law School, the University Regents and others. She alleged race discrimination under in violation of the Fourteenth Amendment, Title VI of the Civil Rights Act of 1964, and 42 USC § 1981. The district court granted class certification and conducted a 15-day bench trial, concluding that the Law School's use of race as a factor in admissions decisions was unlawful. The District Court enjoined the Law School from using race as a factor in its admissions decisions. Sitting en banc, the Court of Appeals reversed the District Court's judgment and vacated the injunction.]

We granted certiorari to resolve the disagreement among the Courts of Appeals on a question of national importance: Whether diversity is a compelling interest that can justify the narrowly tailored use of race in selecting applicants for admission to public universities.

II

We last addressed the use of race in public higher education over 25 years ago[, in] the landmark Bakke case.... Since this Court's splintered decision in Bakke, Justice Powell's opinion announcing the judgment of the Court has served as the touchstone for constitutional analysis of race-conscious admissions policies. Public and private universities across the Nation have modeled their own admissions programs on Justice Powell's views on permissible race-conscious policies.

Justice Powell approved the university's use of race to further only one interest: "the attainment of a diverse student body." [...] Justice Powell was, however, careful to emphasize that in his view race "is only one element in a range of factors a university properly may consider in attaining the goal of a heterogeneous student body." ... Rather, "the diversity that furthers a compelling state interest encompasses a far broader array of qualifications and characteristics of which racial or ethnic origin is but a single though important element."

.... [F]or the reasons set out below, today we endorse Justice Powell's view that student body diversity is a compelling state interest that can justify the use of race in university admissions.

.... We have held that all racial classifications imposed by government "must be analyzed by a reviewing court under strict scrutiny." This means that such classifications are con-stitutional only if they are narrowly tailored to further compelling governmental interests.... Strict scrutiny is not "strict in theory, but fatal in fact." Although all governmental uses of race are subject to strict scrutiny, not all are invalidated by it....

III
A

.... [T]he Law School asks us to recognize, in the context of higher education, a compelling state interest in student body diversity.

We first wish to dispel the notion that the Law School's argument has been foreclosed, either expressly or implicitly, by our affirmative-action cases decided since Bakke. It is true that some language in those opinions might be read to suggest that remedying past discrimination is the only permissible justification for race-based governmental action. See, e.g., Richmond v. J. A. Croson Co., (plurality opinion). But we have never held that the only governmental use of race that can survive strict scrutiny is remedying past discrimination. Nor, since Bakke, have we directly addressed the use of race in the context of public higher education. Today, we hold that the Law School has a compelling interest in attaining a diverse student body.

The Law School's educational judgment that such diversity is essential to its educational mission is one to which we defer. The Law School's assessment that diversity will, in fact, yield educational benefits is substantiated by respondents and their amici. Our scrutiny of the interest asserted by the Law School is no less strict for taking into account complex educational judgments in an area that lies primarily within the expertise of the university....

We have long recognized that, given the important purpose of public education and the expansive freedoms of speech and thought associated with the university environment, universities occupy a special niche in our constitutional tradition. In announcing the principle of student body diversity as a compelling state interest, Justice Powell invoked our cases recognizing a constitutional dimension, grounded in the First Amendment, of educational autonomy.... From this premise, Justice Powell reasoned that by claiming "the right to select those students who will contribute the most to the 'robust exchange of ideas,'" a university "seeks to achieve a goal that is of paramount importance in the fulfillment of its mission." Our conclusion that the Law School has a compelling interest in a diverse student body is informed by our view that attaining a diverse student body is at the heart of the Law School's proper institutional mission, and that "good faith" on the part of a university is "presumed" absent "a showing to the contrary."

As part of its goal of "assembling a class that is both exceptionally academically qualified and broadly diverse," the Law School seeks to "enroll a 'critical mass' of minority students." Brief for Respondents Bollinger et al. 13. The Law School's interest is not simply "to assure within its student body some specified percentage of a particular group merely because of its race or ethnic origin." Bakke, 438 U.S., at 307 (opinion of Powell, J.). That would amount to outright racial balancing, which is patently unconstitutional. Rather, the Law School's concept of critical mass is defined by reference to the educational benefits that diversity is designed to produce.

These benefits are substantial.... [T]he Law School's admissions policy promotes "cross-racial understanding," helps to break down racial stereotypes, and "enables [students] to better understand persons of different races." These benefits are "important and laudable," because "classroom discussion is livelier, more spirited, and simply more enlightening and interesting" when the students have "the greatest possible variety of backgrounds."

The Law School's claim of a compelling interest is further bolstered by its amici, who point to the educational benefits that flow from student body diversity. In addition to the expert studies and reports entered into evidence at trial, numerous studies show that student body diversity promotes learning outcomes, and "better prepares students for an increasingly diverse workforce and society, and better prepares them as professionals."

These benefits are not theoretical but real, as major American businesses have made clear that the skills needed in today's increasingly global marketplace can only be developed through exposure to widely diverse people, cultures, ideas, and viewpoints. Brief for 3M et al. as Amici Curiae 5; Brief for General Motors Corp. as Amicus Curiae 3–4. What is more, high-ranking retired officers and civilian leaders of the United States military assert that, "based on [their] decades of experience," a "highly qualified, racially diverse officer corps ... is essential to the military's ability to fulfill its principle mission to provide national security." Brief for Julius W. Becton, Jr. et al. as Amici Curiae 27....

Moreover, universities, and in particular, law schools, represent the training ground for a large number of our Nation's leaders. Individuals with law degrees occupy roughly half the state governorships, more than half the seats in the United States Senate, and more than a third of the seats in the United States House of Representatives. The pattern is even more striking when it comes to highly selective law schools. A handful of these schools accounts for 25 of the 100 United States Senators, 74 United States Courts of Appeals judges, and nearly 200 of the more than 600 United States District Court judges.

In order to cultivate a set of leaders with legitimacy in the eyes of the citizenry, it is necessary that the path to leadership be visibly open to talented and qualified individuals of every race and ethnicity....

The Law School does not premise its need for critical mass on "any belief that minority students always (or even consistently) express some characteristic minority viewpoint on any issue." To the contrary, diminishing the force of such stereotypes is both a crucial part of the Law School's mission, and one that it cannot accomplish with only token numbers of minority students. Just as growing up in a particular region or having particular professional experiences is likely to affect an individual's views, so too is one's own, unique experience of being a racial minority in a society, like our own, in which race unfortunately still matters. The Law School has determined, based on its experience and expertise, that a "critical mass" of underrepresented minorities is necessary to further its compelling interest in securing the educational benefits of a diverse student body.

B

.... To be narrowly tailored, a race-conscious admissions program cannot use a quota system — it cannot "insulate each category of applicants with certain desired qualifications from competition with all other applicants." Bakke, supra, (opinion of Powell, J.). Instead, a university may consider race or ethnicity only as a "'plus' in a particular applicant's file," without "insulating the individual from comparison with all other candidates for the available seats." In other words, an admissions program must be "flexible enough to consider all pertinent elements of diversity in light of the particular qualifications of each applicant, and to place them on the same footing for consideration, although not necessarily according them the same weight." Ibid.

We are satisfied that the Law School's admissions program, like the Harvard plan described by Justice Powell, does not operate as a quota. Properly understood, a "quota" is a program in which a certain fixed number or proportion of opportunities are "reserved exclusively for certain minority groups." Richmond v. J. A. Croson Co., supra.... In contrast, "a permissible goal ... requires only a good-faith effort ... to come within a range demarcated by the goal itself," and permits consideration of race as a "plus" factor in any given case while still ensuring that each candidate "competes with all other qualified applicants." ...

The Law School's goal of attaining a critical mass of underrepresented minority students does not transform its program into a quota. As the Harvard plan described by Justice Powell recognized, there is of course "some relationship between numbers and achieving the benefits to be derived from a diverse student body, and between numbers and providing a reasonable environment for those students admitted." "Some attention to numbers," without more, does not transform a flexible admissions system into a rigid quota. Nor, as Justice Kennedy posits, does the Law School's consultation of the "daily reports," which keep track of the racial and ethnic composition of the class (as well as of residency and gender), "suggest[] there was no further attempt at individual review save for race itself" during the final stages of the admissions process. To the contrary, the Law School's admissions officers testified without contradiction that they never gave race any more or less weight based on the information contained in these reports. Moreover, as Justice Kennedy concedes, between 1993 and 2000, the number of African-American, Latino, and Native-American students in each class at the Law School varied from 13.5 to 20.1 percent, a range inconsistent with a quota.

The Chief Justice believes that the Law School's policy conceals an attempt to achieve racial balancing, and cites admissions data to contend that the Law School discriminates among different groups within the critical mass. But, as the Chief Justice concedes, the number of underrepresented minority students who ultimately enroll in the Law School differs substantially from their representation in the applicant pool and varies considerably for each group from year to year.

That a race-conscious admissions program does not operate as a quota does not, by itself, satisfy the requirement of individualized consideration. When using race as a "plus" factor in university admissions, a university's admissions program must remain flexible enough to ensure that each applicant is evaluated as an individual and not in a way that makes an applicant's race or ethnicity the defining feature of his or her application. The importance of this individualized consideration in the context of a race-conscious admissions program is paramount.

Here, the Law School engages in a highly individualized, holistic review of each applicant's file, giving serious consideration to all the ways an applicant might contribute to a diverse educational environment. The Law School affords this individualized consideration to applicants of all races. There is no policy, either de jure or de facto, of automatic acceptance or rejection based on any single "soft" variable.... [T]he Law School awards no mechanical, predetermined diversity "bonuses" based on race or ethnicity. Like the Harvard plan, the Law School's admissions policy "is flexible enough to consider all pertinent elements of diversity in light of the particular qualifications of each applicant, and to place them on the same footing for consideration, although not necessarily according them the same weight."

We also find that, like the Harvard plan Justice Powell referenced in Bakke, the Law School's race-conscious admissions program adequately ensures that all factors that may contribute to student body diversity are meaningfully considered alongside race in admissions decisions. With respect to the use of race itself, all underrepresented minority students admitted by the Law School have been deemed qualified. By virtue of our Nation's struggle with racial inequality, such students are both likely to have experiences of particular importance to the Law School's mission, and less likely to be admitted in meaningful numbers on criteria that ignore those experiences.

The Law School does not, however, limit in any way the broad range of qualities and experiences that may be considered valuable contributions to student body diversity. To the contrary, the 1992 policy makes clear "there are many possible bases for diversity admissions," and provides examples of admittees who have lived or traveled widely abroad, are fluent in several languages, have overcome personal adversity and family hardship, have exceptional records of extensive community service, and have had successful careers in other fields. The Law School seriously considers each "applicant's promise of making a notable contribution to the class by way of a particular strength, attainment, or characteristic—e.g., an unusual intellectual achievement, employment experience, nonacademic performance, or personal background." All applicants have the opportunity to highlight their own potential diversity contributions through the submission of a personal statement, letters of recommendation, and an essay describing the ways in which the applicant will contribute to the life and diversity of the Law School.

What is more, the Law School actually gives substantial weight to diversity factors besides race. The Law School frequently accepts nonminority applicants with grades and test scores lower than underrepresented minority applicants (and other nonminority applicants) who are rejected. This shows that the Law School seriously weighs many other diversity factors besides race that can make a real and dispositive difference for nonminority applicants as well. By this flexible approach, the Law School sufficiently takes into account, in practice as well as in theory, a wide variety of characteristics besides race and ethnicity that contribute to a diverse student body. Justice Kennedy speculates that "race is likely outcome determinative for many members of minority groups" who do not fall within the upper range of LSAT scores and grades. But the same could be said of the Harvard plan discussed approvingly by Justice Powell in Bakke, and indeed of any plan that uses race as one of many factors.

Petitioner and the United States argue that the Law School's plan is not narrowly tailored because race-neutral means exist to obtain the educational benefits of student body diversity that the Law School seeks. We disagree. Narrow tailoring does not require exhaustion of every conceivable race-neutral alternative. Nor does it require a university to choose between maintaining a reputation for excellence or fulfilling a commitment to provide educational opportunities to members of all racial groups. Narrow tailoring does, however, require serious, good faith consideration of workable race-neutral alternatives that will achieve the diversity the university seeks.

We agree with the Court of Appeals that the Law School sufficiently considered workable race-neutral alternatives. The District Court took the Law School to task for failing to consider race-neutral alternatives such as "using a lottery system" or "decreasing the emphasis for all applicants on undergraduate GPA and LSAT scores." But these alternatives would require a dramatic sacrifice of diversity, the academic quality of all admitted students, or both.

The Law School's current admissions program considers race as one factor among many, in an effort to assemble a student body that is diverse in ways broader than race. Because a lottery would make that kind of nuanced judgment impossible, it would effectively sacrifice all other educational values, not to mention every other kind of diversity. So too with the suggestion that the Law School simply lower admissions standards for all students, a drastic remedy that would require the Law School to become a much different institution and sacrifice a vital component of its educational mission. The United States advocates "percentage plans," recently adopted by public undergraduate institutions in Texas, Florida, and California to guarantee admission to all students above a certain class-rank threshold in every high school in the State. Brief for United States as Amicus Curiae 14–18. The United States does not, however, explain how such plans could work for graduate and professional schools. Moreover, even assuming such plans are race-neutral, they may preclude the university from conducting the individualized assessments necessary to assemble a student body that is not just racially diverse, but diverse along all the qualities valued by the university. We are satisfied that the Law School adequately considered race-neutral alternatives currently capable of producing a critical mass without forcing the Law School to abandon the academic selectivity that is the cornerstone of its educational mission.

.... To be narrowly tailored, a race-conscious admissions program must not "unduly burden individuals who are not members of the favored racial and ethnic groups."

We are satisfied that the Law School's admissions program does not. Because the Law School considers "all pertinent elements of diversity," it can (and does) select nonminority applicants who have greater potential to enhance student body diversity over underrepresented minority applicants. As Justice Powell recognized in Bakke, so long as a race-conscious admissions program uses race as a "plus" factor in the context of individualized consideration, a rejected applicant "will not have been foreclosed from all consideration for that seat simply because he was not the right color or had the wrong surname...." We agree that, in the context of its individualized inquiry into the possible diversity contributions of all applicants, the Law School's race-conscious admissions program does not unduly harm nonminority applicants.

.... [R]ace-conscious admissions policies must be limited in time. This requirement reflects that racial classifications, however compelling their goals, are potentially so dangerous that they may be employed no more broadly than the interest demands. Enshrining a permanent justification for racial preferences would offend this fundamental equal protection principle ...

We take the Law School at its word that it would "like nothing better than to find a race-neutral admissions formula" and will terminate its race-conscious admissions program as soon as practicable. It has been 25 years since Justice Powell first approved the use of race to further an interest in student body diversity in the context of public higher education. Since that time, the number of minority applicants with high grades and test scores has indeed increased. We expect that 25 years from now, the use of racial preferences will no longer be necessary to further the interest approved today.

IV

In summary, the Equal Protection Clause does not prohibit the Law School's narrowly tailored use of race in admissions decisions to further a compelling interest in obtaining the educational benefits that flow from a diverse student body.... The judgment of the Court of Appeals for the Sixth Circuit, accordingly, is affirmed.

JUSTICE GINSBURG, with whom JUSTICE BREYER joins, concurring.

[The Court] observes that "it has been 25 years since Justice Powell [in Bakke] first approved the use of race to further an interest in student body diversity in the context of public higher education." For at least part of that time, however, the law could not fairly be described as "settled," and in some regions of the Nation, overtly race-conscious admissions policies have been proscribed. Moreover, it was only 25 years before Bakke that this Court declared public school segregation unconstitutional, a declaration that, after prolonged resistance, yielded an end to a law-enforced racial caste system, itself the legacy of centuries of slavery.

It is well documented that conscious and unconscious race bias, even rank discrimination based on race, remain alive in our land, impeding realization of our highest values and ideals. As to public education, data for the years 2000–2001 show that 71.6% of African-American children and 76.3% of Hispanic children attended a school in which minorities made up a majority of the student body. And schools in predominantly minority communities lag far behind others measured by the educational resources available to them.

However strong the public's desire for improved education systems may be, it remains the current reality that many minority students encounter markedly inadequate and unequal educational opportunities. Despite these inequalities, some minority students are able to meet the high threshold requirements set for admission to the country's finest undergraduate and graduate educational institutions. As lower school education in minority communities improves, an increase in the number of such students may be anticipated. From today's vantage point, one may hope, but not firmly forecast, that over the next generation's span, progress toward nondiscrimination and genuinely equal opportunity will make it safe to sunset affirmative action.

CHIEF JUSTICE REHNQUIST, with whom JUSTICE SCALIA, JUSTICE KENNEDY, and JUSTICE THOMAS join, dissenting.

I agree with the Court that, "in the limited circumstance when drawing racial distinctions is permissible," the government must ensure that its means are narrowly tailored to achieve a compelling state interest. I do not believe, however, that the University of Michigan Law School's (Law School) means are narrowly tailored to the interest it asserts.... Stripped of its "critical mass" veil, the Law School's program is revealed as a naked effort to achieve racial balancing....

.... In practice, the Law School's program bears little or no relation to its asserted goal of achieving "critical mass." ... From 1995 through 2000, the Law School admitted between 1,130 and 1,310 students. Of those, between 13 and 19 were Native American, between 91 and 108 were African-Americans, and between 47 and 56 were Hispanic. If the Law School is admitting between 91 and 108 African-Americans in order to achieve "critical mass," thereby preventing African-American students from feeling "isolated or like spokespersons for their race," one would think that a number of the same order of magnitude would be necessary to accomplish the same purpose for Hispanics and Native Americans. Similarly, even if all of the Native American applicants admitted in a given year matriculate, which the record demonstrates is not at all the case, how can this possibly constitute a "critical mass" of Native Americans in a class of over 350 students? In order for this pattern of admission to be consistent with the Law School's explanation of "critical mass," one would have to believe that the objectives of "critical mass" offered by respondents are achieved with only half the number of Hispanics and one-sixth the number of Native Americans as compared to African-Americans. But respondents offer no race-specific reasons for such disparities. Instead, they simply emphasize the importance of achieving "critical mass," without any explanation of why that concept is applied differently among the three underrepresented minority groups.

.... The correlation between the percentage of the Law School's pool of applicants who are members of the three minority groups and the percentage of the admitted applicants who are members of these same groups is far too precise to be dismissed as merely the result of the school paying "some attention to [the] numbers." ... For example, in 1995, when 9.7% of the applicant pool was African-American, 9.4% of the admitted class was African-American. By 2000, only 7.5% of the applicant pool was African-American, and 7.3% of the admitted class was African-American.... The tight correlation between the percentage of applicants and admittees of a given race, therefore, must result from careful race based planning by the Law School. It suggests a formula for admission based on the aspirational assumption that all applicants are equally qualified academically, and therefore that the proportion of each group admitted should be the same as the proportion of that group in the applicant pool.... I do not believe that the Constitution gives the Law School such free rein in the use of race....

[handwritten margin note: This is one % of #s. How many total app? Unqualified apps?]

Finally, I believe that the Law School's program fails strict scrutiny because it is devoid of any reasonably precise time limit on the Law School's use of race in admissions....

JUSTICE KENNEDY, dissenting.

The separate opinion by Justice Powell in [Bakke].... in my view, states the correct rule for resolving this case. The Court, however, does not apply strict scrutiny. By trying to say otherwise, it undermines both the test and its own controlling precedents.

.... The dissenting opinion by The Chief Justice, which I join in full, demonstrates beyond question why the concept of critical mass is a delusion used by the Law School to mask its attempt to make race an automatic factor in most instances and to achieve numerical goals indistinguishable from quotas.... About 80 to 85 percent of the places in the entering class are given to applicants in the upper range of Law School Admissions Test scores and grades. An applicant with these credentials likely will be admitted without consideration of race or ethnicity. With respect to the remaining 15 to 20 percent of the seats, race is likely outcome determinative for many members of minority groups. That is where the competition becomes tight and where any given applicant's chance of admission is far smaller if he or she lacks minority status. At this point the numerical concept of critical mass has the real potential to compromise individual review.

The Law School has not demonstrated how individual consideration is, or can be, preserved at this stage of the application process given the instruction to attain what it calls critical mass. In fact the evidence shows otherwise. There was little deviation among admitted minority students during the years from 1995 to 1998. The percentage of enrolled minorities fluctuated only by 0.3%, from 13.5% to 13.8%. The number of minority students to whom offers were extended varied by just a slightly greater magnitude of 2.2%, from the high of 15.6% in 1995 to the low of 13.4% in 1998.... The narrow fluctuation band raises an inference that the Law School subverted individual determination....

The Law School has the burden of proving, in conformance with the standard of strict scrutiny, that it did not utilize race in an unconstitutional way. At the very least, the constancy of admitted minority students and the close correlation between the racial breakdown of admitted minorities and the composition of the applicant pool, require the Law School either to produce a convincing explanation or to show it has taken adequate steps to ensure individual assessment.... There is no constitutional objection to the goal of considering race as one modest factor among many others to achieve diversity, but an educational institution must ensure, through sufficient procedures, that each applicant receives individual consideration and that race does not become a predominant factor in the admissions decisionmaking. The Law School failed to comply with this requirement, and by no means has it carried its burden to show otherwise by the test of strict scrutiny.

JUSTICE SCALIA, with whom JUSTICE THOMAS joins, [dissenting]:

.... The "educational benefit" that the University of Michigan seeks to achieve by racial discrimination consists, according to the Court, of "'cross-racial understanding,'" and "'better prepar[ation of] students for an increasingly diverse workforce and society,'" all of which is necessary not only for work, but also for good "citizenship." This is not, of course, an "educational benefit" on which students will be graded on their Law School transcript (Works and Plays Well with Others: B+) or tested by the bar examiners (Q: Describe in 500 words or less your cross-racial understanding). For it is a lesson of life rather than law—essentially the same lesson taught to (or rather learned by, for it cannot be "taught" in the usual sense) people three feet shorter and twenty years younger than the full-grown adults at the University of Michigan Law School, in institutions ranging from Boy Scout troops to public-school kindergartens. If properly considered an "educational benefit" at all, it is surely not one that is either uniquely relevant to law school or uniquely "teachable" in a formal educational setting. And therefore: If it is appropriate for the University of Michigan Law School to use racial discrimination for the purpose of putting together a "critical mass" that will convey generic lessons in socialization and good citizenship, surely it is no less appropriate—indeed, particularly appropriate— for the civil service system of the State of Michigan to do so. There, also, those exposed to "critical masses" of certain races will presumably become better Americans, better Michiganders, better civil servants. And surely private employers cannot be criticized— indeed, should be praised—if they also "teach" good citizenship to their adult employees through a patriotic, all-American system of racial discrimination in hiring. The nonminority individuals who are deprived of a legal education, a civil service job, or any job at all by reason of their skin color will surely understand.

Unlike a clear constitutional holding that racial preferences in state educational institutions are impermissible, or even a clear anticonstitutional holding that racial preferences in state educational institutions are OK, today's Grutter-Gratz split double header seems perversely designed to prolong the controversy and the litigation.setting at issue, any educational benefits flow from racial diversity....

JUSTICE THOMAS, with whom JUSTICE SCALIA joins, [dissenting].

Frederick Douglass, speaking to a group of abolitionists almost 140 years ago, delivered a message lost on today's majority:

> In regard to the colored people, there is always more that is benevolent, I perceive, than just, manifested towards us. What I ask for the negro is not benevolence, not pity, not sympathy, but simply justice. The American people have always been anxious to know what they shall do with us.... I have had but one answer from the beginning. Do nothing with us! Your doing with us has already played the mischief with us. Do nothing with us! If the apples will not remain on the tree of their own strength, if they are worm-eaten at the core, if they are early ripe and disposed to fall, let them fall! ... And if the negro cannot stand on his own legs, let him fall also. All I ask is, give him a chance to stand on his own legs! Let him alone! ... Your interference is doing him positive injury.

What the Black Man Wants: An Address Delivered in Boston, Massachusetts, on 26 January 1865, reprinted in 4 The Frederick Douglass Papers 59, 68 (J. Blassingame & J. McKivigan eds. 1991) (emphasis in original).

Like Douglass, I believe blacks can achieve in every avenue of American life without the meddling of university administrators. Because I wish to see all students succeed whatever their color, I share, in some respect, the sympathies of those who sponsor the type of discrimination advanced by the University of Michigan Law School (Law School). The Constitution does not, however, tolerate institutional devotion to the status quo in admissions policies when such devotion ripens into racial discrimination....

No one would argue that a university could set up a lower general admission standard and then impose heightened requirements only on black applicants. Similarly, a university may not maintain a high admission standard and grant exemptions to favored races. The Law School, of its own choosing, and for its own purposes, maintains an exclusionary admissions system that it knows produces racially disproportionate results. Racial discrimination is not a permissible solution to the self-inflicted wounds of this elitist admissions policy.

The majority upholds the Law School's racial discrimination not by interpreting the people's Constitution, but by responding to a faddish slogan of the cognoscenti. Nevertheless, I concur in part in the Court's opinion. First, I agree with the Court insofar as its decision, which approves of only one racial classification, confirms that further use of race in admissions remains unlawful. Second, I agree with the Court's holding that racial discrimination in higher education admissions will be illegal in 25 years. I respectfully dissent from the remainder of the Court's opinion and the judgment, however, because

I believe that the Law School's current use of race violates the Equal Protection Clause and that the Constitution means the same thing today as it will in 300 months....

The strict scrutiny standard that the Court purports to apply in this case was first enunciated in Korematsu v. United States, [w]here the Court held that "pressing public necessity may sometimes justify the existence of [racial discrimination]; racial antagonism never can." This standard of "pressing public necessity" has more frequently been termed "compelling governmental interest." A majority of the Court has validated only two circumstances where "pressing public necessity" or a "compelling state interest" can possibly justify racial discrimination by state actors. First, the lesson of Korematsu is that national security constitutes a "pressing public necessity," though the government's use of race to advance that objective must be narrowly tailored. Second, the Court has recognized as a compelling state interest a government's effort to remedy past discrimination for which it is responsible. Richmond v. J. A. Croson Co....

Where the Court has accepted only national security, and rejected even the best interests of a child, as a justification for racial discrimination, I conclude that only those measures the State must take to provide a bulwark against anarchy, or to prevent violence, will constitute a "pressing public necessity."...

The Constitution abhors classifications based on race, not only because those classifications can harm favored races or are based on illegitimate motives, but also because every time the government places citizens on racial registers and makes race relevant to the provision of burdens or benefits, it demeans us all....

.... Michigan has no compelling interest in having a law school at all, much less an elite one.... The Law School's decision to be an elite institution does little to advance the welfare of the people of Michigan or any cognizable interest of the State of Michigan....

With the adoption of different admissions methods, such as accepting all students who meet minimum qualifications, the Law School could achieve its vision of the racially aesthetic student body without the use of racial discrimination. The Law School concedes this, but the Court holds, implicitly and under the guise of narrow tailoring, that the Law School has a compelling state interest in doing what it wants to do. I cannot agree.... For those who believe that every racial disproportionality in our society is caused by some kind of racial discrimination, there can be no distinction between remedying societal discrimination and erasing racial disproportionalities in the country's leadership caste. And if the lack of proportional racial representation among our leaders is not caused by societal discrimination, then "fixing" it is even less of a pressing public necessity.

.... The majority appears to believe that broader utopian goals justify the Law School's use of race, but "the Equal Protection Clause commands the elimination of racial barriers, not their creation in order to satisfy our theory as to how society ought to be organized."...

CASE NOTE: *Gratz v. Bollinger*, 539 U.S. 244 (2003). The same day it decided *Grutter*, the Court in *Gratz* struck down the affirmative action plan in the University of Michigan's undergraduate admissions program. The undergraduate admissions plan relied on a system in which points were awarded for a variety of applicant criteria, and 100 cumulative points would guarantee admission. The affirmative action part of the plan automatically awarded 20 points to every "underrepresented minority" applicant. In contrast to *Grutter*, the majority (*Rehnquist* (CJ), O'Connor, Scalia, Kennedy, Thomas; *Breyer* concurring in the judgment) concluded that the point system, and the size of the point-award to minority applicants, gave too much weight to race and did not sufficiently allow for individualized consideration of each applicant. (In the relevant year, according to the district court, the University received about 13,500 undergraduate applications for admission to the LSA in 1997, from which it offered admission to about 4,000.) In dissent, Justices *Stevens*, Souter and Ginsburg argued that the plaintiffs did not have standing for prospective (injunctive and declaratory) relief, because they had gone to other universities and no longer had an intent to enroll in Michigan. The majority rejected this argument. Significantly, even the dissenters agreed that the plaintiffs "have standing to seek damages as compensation for the alleged wrongful denial of their respective applications under Michigan's old freshman admissions system." Justices *Ginsburg* and Souter would have upheld the plan, noting that "If honesty is the best policy, surely Michigan's accurately described, fully disclosed College affirmative action program is preferable to achieving similar numbers through winks, nods, and disguises."

Review Questions and Explanations: *Grutter* and *Gratz*

1. Barbara Grutter's GPA/LSAT combination would have placed her very low in the applicant pool at Michigan Law School. On the one hand, there was evidence that minority applicants with lower GPA/LSAT scores were admitted; on the other hand, it is clear that Grutter would have been unable to prove by a preponderance of the evidence that in the absence of the affirmative plan, she would have been admitted. In other words, she could not establish "but for" cause that she was denied admission on account of her race. None of the nine justices considered that a problem with Grutter's case. Denial of admission, therefore, cannot have been her injury; so what was it? And why should she have had standing?

2. The majority opinions in *Grutter* states: "Our scrutiny of the interest asserted by the Law School is no less strict for taking into account complex educational judgments in an area that lies primarily within the expertise of the university." Do you agree? The dissenters charge that the majority has applied less than strict scrutiny. Was it on this point, or other aspects of the majority opinion?

3. Who has the burden of proof? The majority says that a university's good faith is "presumed." Justices Rehnquist and Kennedy say that the University has the burden of proving that its plan is narrowly tailored to meet a compelling state interest—specifically, that it is not engaging in "racial balancing." Are these views reconcilable? What is at stake in adopting one view rather than the other?

4. Justices Rehnquist and Kennedy purport to agree with Powell's *Bakke* opinion that diversity is a compelling interest, but argue that the Michigan plan was not narrowly tailored. As a practical matter, could any affirmative action plan meet their test for narrow tailoring?

5. Rehnquist and Kennedy conclude that race is given too much weight in admissions decisions in large part because the admissions numbers are consistent from year to year. Is that a logical inference? Law school admissions data shows that the applicant pools—number of applicants, average GPAs and LSAT scores, etc.—are very consistent from year to year. The consistent percentages of minority admissions thus tells us only that the weight given to race is also consistent from year to year—not that the weights are juggled to keep the admissions percentages consistent. If that is true, then the "too much weight to race" argument boils

down to an argument, not about consistency, but about the percentage itself: too many minorities are admitted. Is that the Rehnquist-Kennedy criticism? If so, why don't they just come out and say so?

6. The majority argues that given the role elite law schools play as springboards for political and social leadership positions, their student body diversity is a compelling interest. Justice Thomas's dissent responds, in essence, that Michigan Law School has no right to maintain its status as an elite law school: it should choose between its elite admissions standards and its commitment to diversity. The Thomas dissent seems anti-elitist at first blush, but is it really attacking the idea of the elite law schools in our society in general? Justice Thomas himself graduated from Yale Law School, and was appointed to the Supreme Court to fill the seat vacated by Thurgood Marshall, the first African-American Supreme Court Justice.

Recap: Affirmative Action

1. Professor John Hart Ely criticized the Court's opinion in *Roe v. Wade*, for among other things, drafting "a sort of guidebook, addressing questions not before the Court and drawing lines with an apparent precision one generally associates with a commissioner's regulations." If this is an error, does Powell (and, by extension, the *Grutter/Gratz* Court) also commit it by going into such detail about how university admissions committees can and cannot incorporate race into their decisions? Does applying strict scrutiny compel the Court to get into that level of detail?

2. Is the undergraduate point system meaningfully different from the "soft variable" system used by the law school? Justice O'Connor apparently thought so, and her vote was decisive. Is it constitutionally preferable to use a numberless system like the Harvard plan and the Michigan Law School plan, in which, presumably, race can be weighted differently for similarly situated applicants? Note, too, that Michigan reviewed 13,500 undergraduate applications. How "individualized" can the consideration of these applications really be?

3. What compelling interests do Justices Scalia and Thomas recognize? Do they view the Powell opinion in *Bakke* as authoritative?

4. Why aren't the interests that are adversely affected by affirmative action sufficiently protected by intermediate scrutiny?

---

3. School Integration

One of the more recent equal protection disputes to come to the Supreme Court involves a situation that may well have been inconceivable to the Court in 1954: to what extent can an elected school board (and the country) voluntarily use race to integrate its public schools? As with affirmative action, this scenario forces us to evaluate just what the purpose of the Equal Protection clause is. Is it to promote a "colorblind" government? To prohibit government sanctioned, race-based subordination? To protect insular and historically discriminated against minority groups? To create a more fully integrated society?

The Court did not have to answer this question in early cases like *Brown*, because each of these purposes pointed to the same result. But that is no longer true. The next case, *Parents Involved in Community Schools v. Seattle School Districts,* shows just how difficult the question has been for the Court to answer in today's changed circumstances.

Guided Reading Questions: *Parents Involved v. Seattle Schools*

1. The placement programs being challenged in *Parents Involved* are complicated. Pay attention to how they actually work, and the way race is used in each of them. Then consider how each of the justices uses those facts. Pay particular attention to how much of a role each justice thinks race places in student placements, and how the justices defend the positions they take on this point.

2. The majority opinion uses language developed in the affirmative action cases. The dissent disputes whether this is appropriate. When reading the case, consider the ways in which the facts presented are like and unlike those arising under affirmative action programs.

3. The Court in *Bakke* held that promoting diversity in educational settings was a compelling state interest for strict scrutiny purposes. Does the diversity interest justify the program at issue here? Does the school district assert other interests that are—or should be—considered as or more compelling?

4. Justice Kennedy votes with the majority, but also writes a concurrence. How does the legal analysis set forth in his concurring opinion differ from that found in the majority opinion? Watch for the key differences.

Parents Involved in Community Schools v. Seattle School District

551 U.S. 701 (2007)

Majority: *Roberts* (CJ), Scalia, Kennedy, Thomas, Alito

Concurrences: *Roberts* (omitted); *Thomas*; *Kennedy*

Dissents: *Stevens*, *Breyer*, Souter, Ginsburg

CHIEF JUSTICE ROBERTS delivered the opinion of the Court.

The school districts in these cases voluntarily adopted student assignment plans that rely upon race to determine which public schools certain children may attend. The Seattle school district classifies children as white or nonwhite; the Jefferson County school district as black or "other." In Seattle, this racial classification is used to allocate slots in oversubscribed high schools. In Jefferson County, it is used to make certain elementary school assignments and to rule on transfer requests. In each case, the school district relies upon an individual student's race in assigning that student to a particular school, so that the racial balance at the school falls within a predetermined range based on the racial composition of the school district as a whole. Parents of students denied assignment to particular schools under these plans solely because of their race brought suit, contending that allocating children to different public schools on the basis of race violated the

Fourteenth Amendment guarantee of equal protection. The Courts of Appeals below upheld the plans. We granted certiorari, and now reverse.

Both cases present the same underlying legal question—whether a public school that had not operated legally segregated schools or has been found to be unitary may choose to classify students by race and rely upon that classification in making school assignments. Although we examine the plans under the same legal framework, the specifics of the two plans, and the circumstances surrounding their adoption, are in some respects quite different.

Seattle School District No. 1 operates 10 regular public high schools. In 1998, it adopted the plan at issue in this case for assigning students to these schools.... The plan allows incoming ninth graders to choose from among any of the district's high schools, ranking however many schools they wish in order of preference.

Some schools are more popular than others. If too many students list the same school as their first choice, the district employs a series of "tiebreakers" to determine who will fill the open slots at the oversubscribed school. The first tiebreaker selects for admission students who have a sibling currently enrolled in the chosen school. The next tiebreaker depends upon the racial composition of the particular school and the race of the individual student. In the district's public schools approximately 41 percent of enrolled students are white; the remaining 59 percent, comprising all other racial groups, are classified by Seattle for assignment purposes as nonwhite.... If an oversubscribed school is not within 10 percentage points of the district's overall white/nonwhite racial balance, it is what the district calls "integration positive," and the district employs a tiebreaker that selects for assignment students whose race "will serve to bring the school into balance." ... If it is still necessary to select students for the school after using the racial tiebreaker, the next tiebreaker is the geographic proximity of the school to the student's residence....

Seattle has never operated segregated schools—legally separate schools for students of different races—nor has it ever been subject to court-ordered desegregation. It nonetheless employs the racial tiebreaker in an attempt to address the effects of racially identifiable housing patterns on school assignments. Most white students live in the northern part of Seattle, most students of other racial backgrounds in the southern part.... Four of Seattle's high schools are located in the north—Ballard, Nathan Hale, Ingraham, and Roosevelt—and five in the south—Rainier Beach, Cleveland, West Seattle, Chief Sealth, and Franklin. One school—Garfield—is more or less in the center of Seattle....

For the 2000–2001 school year, five of these schools were oversubscribed—Ballard, Nathan Hale, Roosevelt, Garfield, and Franklin—so much so that 82 percent of incoming ninth graders ranked one of these schools as their first choice.... Three of the oversubscribed schools were "integration positive" because the school's white enrollment the previous school year was greater than 51 percent-Ballard, Nathan Hale, and Roosevelt. Thus, more nonwhite students (107, 27, and 82, respectively) who selected one of these three schools as a top choice received placement at the school than would have been the case had race not been considered, and proximity been the next tiebreaker.... Franklin was "integration positive" because its nonwhite enrollment the previous school year was greater than 69 percent; 89 more white students were assigned to Franklin by operation of the racial tiebreaker in the 2000–2001 school year than otherwise would have been.... Garfield was the only oversubscribed school whose composition during the 1999–2000 school year was within the racial guidelines, although in previous years Garfield's enrollment had been predominantly nonwhite, and the racial tiebreaker had been used to give preference to white students....

Petitioner Parents Involved in Community Schools (Parents Involved) is a nonprofit corporation comprising the parents of children who have been or may be denied assignment to their chosen high school in the district because of their race. The concerns of Parents Involved are illustrated by Jill Kurfirst, who sought to enroll her ninth-grade son, Andy Meeks, in Ballard High School's special Biotechnology Career Academy. Andy suffered from attention deficit hyperactivity disorder and dyslexia, but had made good progress with hands-on instruction, and his mother and middle school teachers thought that the smaller biotechnology program held the most promise for his continued success. Andy was accepted into this selective program but, because of the racial tiebreaker, was denied assignment to Ballard High School.... Parents Involved commenced this suit in the Western District of Washington, alleging that Seattle's use of race in assignments violated the Equal Protection Clause of the Fourteenth Amendment.... [The Court's discussion of standing is omitted.]

It is well established that when the government distributes burdens or benefits on the basis of individual racial classifications, that action is reviewed under strict scrutiny. Gruter v. Bollinger. As the Court recently reaffirmed, "'racial classifications are simply too pernicious to permit any but the most exact connection between justification and classification.'"... In order to satisfy this searching standard of review, the school districts must demonstrate that the use of individual racial classifications in the assignment plans here under review is "narrowly tailored" to achieve a "compelling" government interest....

Without attempting in these cases to set forth all the interests a school district might assert, it suffices to note that our prior cases, in evaluating the use of racial classifications in the school context, have recognized two interests that qualify as compelling. The first is the compelling interest of remedying the effects of past intentional discrimination.... Yet the Seattle public schools have not shown that they were ever segregated by law, and were not subject to court-ordered desegregation decrees. The Jefferson County public schools were previously segregated by law and were subject to a desegregation decree entered in 1975. In 2000, the District Court that entered that decree dissolved it, finding that Jefferson County had "eliminated the vestiges associated with the former policy of segregation and its pernicious effects," and thus had achieved "unitary" status.... Jefferson County accordingly does not rely upon an interest in remedying the effects of past intentional discrimination in defending its present use of race in assigning students....

Nor could it. We have emphasized that the harm being remedied by mandatory desegregation plans is the harm that is traceable to segregation, and that "the Constitution is not violated by racial imbalance in the schools, without more."... Once Jefferson County achieved unitary status, it had remedied the constitutional wrong that allowed race-based assignments. Any continued use of race must be justified on some other basis.

The second government interest we have recognized as compelling for purposes of strict scrutiny is the interest in diversity in higher education upheld in Gruter. The specific interest found compelling in Grutter was student body diversity "in the context of higher education."... The diversity interest was not focused on race alone but encompassed "all factors that may contribute to student body diversity."...

The entire gist of the analysis in Grutter was that the admissions program at issue there focused on each applicant as an individual, and not simply as a member of a particular racial group. The classification of applicants by race upheld in Grutter was only as part of a "highly individualized, holistic review."... As the Court explained, "[t]he importance of this individualized consideration in the context of a race-conscious admissions program is paramount."... The point of the narrow tailoring analysis in which the Grutter Court engaged was to ensure that the use of racial classifications was indeed part of a broader assessment of diversity, and not simply an effort to achieve racial balance, which the Court explained would be "patently unconstitutional." ...

In the present cases, by contrast, race is not considered as part of a broader effort to achieve "exposure to widely diverse people, cultures, ideas, and viewpoints," ... race, for some students, is determinative standing alone. The districts argue that other factors, such as student preferences, affect assignment decisions under their plans, but under each plan when race comes into play, it is decisive by itself. It is not simply one factor weighed with others in reaching a decision, as in Grutter; it is the factor. Like the University of Michigan undergraduate plan struck down in Gratz, the plans here "do not provide for a meaningful individualized review of applicants" but instead rely on racial classifications in a "nonindividualized, mechanical" way....

Even when it comes to race, the plans here employ only a limited notion of diversity, viewing race exclusively in white/nonwhite terms in Seattle and black/"other" terms in Jefferson County.... The Seattle "Board Statement Reaffirming Diversity Rationale" speaks of the "inherent educational value" in "[p]roviding students the opportunity to attend schools with diverse student enrollment".... But under the Seattle plan, a school with 50 percent Asian-American students and 50 percent white students but no African-American, Native-American, or Latino students would qualify as balanced, while a school with 30 percent Asian-American, 25 percent African-American, 25 percent Latino, and 20 percent white students would not. It is hard to understand how a plan that could allow these results can be viewed as being concerned with achieving enrollment that is "broadly diverse." ...

In upholding the admissions plan in Grutter, though, this Court relied upon considerations unique to institutions of higher education, noting that in light of "the expansive freedoms of speech and thought associated with the university environment, universities occupy a special niche in our constitutional tradition." See also Bakke, (opinion of Powell, J.).... The present cases are not governed by Grutter.

Perhaps recognizing that reliance on Grutter cannot sustain their plans, both school districts assert additional interests, distinct from the interest upheld in Grutter, to justify their race-based assignments. In briefing and argument before this Court, Seattle contends that its use of race helps to reduce racial concentration in schools and to ensure that racially concentrated housing patterns do not prevent nonwhite students from having access to the most desirable schools.... Jefferson County has articulated a similar goal, phrasing its interest in terms of educating its students "in a racially integrated environment." ... Each school district argues that educational and broader socialization benefits flow from a racially diverse learning environment, and each contends that because the diversity they seek is racial diversity — not the broader diversity at issue in Grutter — it makes sense to promote that interest directly by relying on race alone.

The parties and their amici dispute whether racial diversity in schools in fact has a marked impact on test scores and other objective yardsticks or achieves intangible socialization benefits. The debate is not one we need to resolve, however, because it is clear that the racial classifications employed by the districts are not narrowly tailored to the goal of achieving the educational and social benefits asserted to flow from racial diversity. In design and operation, the plans are directed only to racial balance, pure and simple, an objective this Court has repeatedly condemned as illegitimate.

The plans are tied to each district's specific racial demographics, rather than to any pedagogic concept of the level of diversity needed to obtain the asserted educational benefits. In Seattle, the district seeks white enrollment of between 31 and 51 percent (within 10 percent of "the district white average" of 41 percent), and nonwhite enrollment of between 49 and 69 percent (within 10 percent of "the district minority average" of 59 percent).... In Jefferson County, by contrast, the district seeks black enrollment of no less than 15 or more than 50 percent, a range designed to be "equally above and below Black student enrollment systemwide," ... based on the objective of achieving at "all schools ... an African-American enrollment equivalent to the average district-wide African-American enrollment" of 34 percent.... In Seattle, then, the benefits of racial diversity require enrollment of at least 31 percent white students; in Jefferson County, at least 50 percent. There must be at least 15 percent nonwhite students under Jefferson County's plan; in Seattle, more than three times that figure. This comparison makes clear that the racial demographics in each district—whatever they happen to be—drive the required "diversity" numbers. The plans here are not tailored to achieving a degree of diversity necessary to realize the asserted educational benefits; instead the plans are tailored, in the words of Seattle's Manager of Enrollment Planning, Technical Support, and Demographics, to "the goal established by the school board of attaining a level of diversity within the schools that approximates the district's overall demographics." ...

The districts offer no evidence that the level of racial diversity necessary to achieve the asserted educational benefits happens to coincide with the racial demographics of the respective school districts—or rather the white/nonwhite or black/"other" balance of the districts, since that is the only diversity addressed by the plans....

In fact, in each case the extreme measure of relying on race in assignments is unnecessary to achieve the stated goals, even as defined by the districts. For example, at Franklin High School in Seattle, the racial tiebreaker was applied because nonwhite enrollment exceeded 69 percent, and resulted in an incoming ninth-grade class in 2000–2001 that was 30.3 percent Asian-American, 21.9 percent African-American, 6.8 percent Latino, 0.5 percent Native-American, and 40.5 percent Caucasian. Without the racial tiebreaker, the class would have been 39.6 percent Asian-American, 30.2 percent African-American, 8.3 percent Latino, 1.1 percent Native-American, and 20.8 percent Caucasian.... When the actual racial breakdown is considered, enrolling students without regard to their race yields a substantially diverse student body under any definition of diversity....

In Grutter, the number of minority students the school sought to admit was an undefined "meaningful number" necessary to achieve a genuinely diverse student body.... Although the matter was the subject of disagreement on the Court, ... the majority concluded that the law school did not count back from its applicant pool to arrive at the "meaningful number" it regarded as necessary to diversify its student body.... Here the racial balance the districts seek is a defined range set solely by reference to the demographics of the respective school districts.

This working backward to achieve a particular type of racial balance, rather than working forward from some demonstration of the level of diversity that provides the purported benefits, is a fatal flaw under our existing precedent. We have many times over reaffirmed that "[r]acial balance is not to be achieved for its own sake." ... Grutter itself reiterated that "outright racial balancing" is "patently unconstitutional." ...

Accepting racial balancing as a compelling state interest would justify the imposition of racial proportionality throughout American society, contrary to our repeated recognition that "[a]t the heart of the Constitution's guarantee of equal protection lies the simple command that the Government must treat citizens as individuals, not as simply components of a racial, religious, sexual or national class." ... Allowing racial balancing as a compelling end in itself would "effectively assur[e] that race will always be relevant in American life, and that the 'ultimate goal' of 'eliminating entirely from governmental decisionmaking such irrelevant factors as a human being's race' will never be achieved." Croson (plurality opinion of O'Connor, J.). An interest "linked to nothing other than proportional representation of various races ... would support indefinite use of racial classifications, employed first to obtain the appropriate mixture of racial views and then to ensure that the [program] continues to reflect that mixture." ... However closely related race-based assignments may be to achieving racial balance, that itself cannot be the goal, whether labeled "racial diversity" or anything else. To the extent the objective is sufficient diversity so that students see fellow students as individuals rather than solely as members of a racial group, using means that treat students solely as members of a racial group is fundamentally at cross-purposes with that end....

The districts assert, as they must, that the way in which they have employed individual racial classifications is necessary to achieve their stated ends. The minimal effect these classifications have on student assignments, however, suggests that other means would be effective. Seattle's racial tiebreaker results, in the end, only in shifting a small number of students between schools. Approximately 307 student assignments were affected by the racial tiebreaker in 2000–2001; the district was able to track the enrollment status of 293 of these students.... Of these, 209 were assigned to a school that was one of their choices, 87 of whom were assigned to the same school to which they would have been assigned without the racial tiebreaker. Eighty-four students were assigned to schools that they did not list as a choice, but 29 of those students would have been assigned to their respective school without the racial tiebreaker, and 3 were able to attend one of the over-subscribed schools due to waitlist and capacity adjustments.... In over one-third of the assignments affected by the racial tiebreaker, then, the use of race in the end made no difference, and the district could identify only 52 students who were ultimately affected adversely by the racial tiebreaker in that it resulted in assignment to a school they had not listed as a preference and to which they would not otherwise have been assigned.

As the panel majority in Parents Involved VI concluded:

> [T]he tiebreaker's annual effect is thus merely to shuffle a few handfuls of different minority students between a few schools—about a dozen additional Latinos into Ballard, a dozen black students into Nathan Hale, perhaps two dozen Asians into Roosevelt, and so on. The District has not met its burden of proving these marginal changes ... outweigh the cost of subjecting hundreds of students to disparate treatment based solely upon the color of their skin.

While we do not suggest that greater use of race would be preferable, the minimal impact of the districts' racial classifications on school enrollment casts doubt on the necessity of using racial classifications. In Grutter, the consideration of race was viewed as indispensable in more than tripling minority representation at the law school—from 4 to 14.5 percent.... Here the most Jefferson County itself claims is that "because the guidelines provide a firm definition of the Board's goal of racially integrated schools, they 'provide administrators with the authority to facilitate, negotiate and collaborate with principals and staff to maintain schools within the 15–50% range.'" ... Classifying and assigning schoolchildren according to a binary conception of race is an extreme approach in light of our precedents and our Nation's history of using race in public schools, and requires more than such an amorphous end to justify it.

The districts have also failed to show that they considered methods other than explicit racial classifications to achieve their stated goals. Narrow tailoring requires "serious, good faith consideration of workable race-neutral alternatives," Grutter, and yet in Seattle several alternative assignment plans—many of which would not have used express racial classi-fications—were rejected with little or no consideration.... Compare Croson, (KENNEDY, J., concurring in part and concurring in judgment) (racial classifications permitted only "as a last resort")....

If the need for the racial classifications embraced by the school districts is unclear, even on the districts' own terms, the costs are undeniable. "[D]istinctions between citizens solely because of their ancestry are by their very nature odious to a free people whose in-stitutions are founded upon the doctrine of equality." Adarand. Government action dividing us by race is inherently suspect because such classifications promote "notions of racial inferiority and lead to a politics of racial hostility," Croson, "reinforce the belief, held by too many for too much of our history, that individuals should be judged by the color of their skin," ... and "endorse race-based reasoning and the conception of a Nation divided into racial blocs, thus contributing to an escalation of racial hostility and conflict." ... As the Court explained in Rice v. Cayetano, "[o]ne of the principal reasons race is treated as a forbidden classification is that it demeans the dignity and worth of a person to be judged by ancestry instead of by his or her own merit and essential qualities."

All this is true enough in the contexts in which these statements were made—government contracting, voting districts, allocation of broadcast licenses, and electing state officers—but when it comes to using race to assign children to schools, history will be heard. In Brown v. Board of Education, we held that segregation deprived black children of equal educational opportunities regardless of whether school facilities and other tangible factors were equal, because government classification and separation on grounds of race themselves denoted inferiority.... It was not the inequality of the facilities but the fact of legally separating children on the basis of race on which the Court relied to find a con-stitutional violation in 1954.... The next Term, we accordingly stated that "full compliance" with Brown I required school districts "to achieve a system of determining admission to the public schools on a nonracial basis." Brown II....

Before Brown, schoolchildren were told where they could and could not go to school based on the color of their skin. The school districts in these cases have not carried the heavy burden of demonstrating that we should allow this once again—even for very different reasons. For schools that never segregated on the basis of race, such as Seattle, or that have removed the vestiges of past segregation, such as Jefferson County, the way "to achieve a system of determining admission to the public schools on a nonracial basis," Brown II, is to stop assigning students on a racial basis. The way to stop discrimination on the basis of race is to stop discriminating on the basis of race.

The judgments of the Courts of Appeals for the Sixth and Ninth Circuits are reversed, and the cases are remanded for further proceedings.

JUSTICE THOMAS, concurring

... Even supposing it mattered to the constitutional analysis, the race-based student-assignment programs before us are not as benign as the dissent believes...."[R]acial paternalism and its unintended consequences can be as poisonous and pernicious as any other form of discrimination." Adarand. (opinion of THOMAS, J.). As these programs demonstrate, every time the government uses racial criteria to "bring the races together," ... someone gets excluded, and the person excluded suffers an injury solely because of his or her race. The petitioner in the Louisville case received a letter from the school board informing her that her *kindergartner* would not be allowed to attend the school of petitioner's choosing because of the child's race.... Doubtless, hundreds of letters like this went out from both school boards every year these race-based assignment plans were in operation.

This type of exclusion, solely on the basis of race, is precisely the sort of government action that pits the races against one another, exacerbates racial tension, and "provoke[s] resentment among those who believe that they have been wronged by the government's use of race." Adarand (opinion of THOMAS, J.). Accordingly, these plans are simply one more variation on the government race-based decisionmaking we have consistently held must be subjected to strict scrutiny. Grutter.

Though the dissent admits to discomfort in applying strict scrutiny to these plans, it claims to have nonetheless applied that exacting standard. But in its search for a compelling interest, the dissent casually accepts even the most tenuous interests asserted on behalf of the plans, grouping them all under the term "'integration.'" ... "'[I]ntegration,'" we are told, has "three essential elements." ... None of these elements is compelling. And the combination of the three unsubstantiated elements does not produce an interest any more compelling than that represented by each element independently.

According to the dissent, integration involves "an interest in setting right the consequences of prior conditions of segregation." For the reasons explained above, the records in these cases do not demonstrate that either school board's plan is supported by an interest in remedying past discrimination....

Moreover, the school boards have no interest in remedying the sundry consequences of prior segregation unrelated to schooling, such as "housing patterns, employment practices, economic conditions, and social attitudes." ... General claims that past school segregation affected such varied societal trends are "too amorphous a basis for imposing a racially classified remedy".... Consequently, school boards seeking to remedy those societal problems with race-based measures in schools today would have no way to gauge the proper scope of the remedy.... Indeed, remedial measures geared toward such broad and unrelated societal ills have "'no logical stopping point,'"... and threaten to become "ageless in their reach into the past, and timeless in their ability to affect the future,"... See Grutter (stating the "requirement that all governmental use of race must have a logical end point").

Because the school boards lack any further interest in remedying segregation, this element offers no support for the purported interest in "integration." ...

The segregationists in Brown embraced the arguments the Court endorsed in Plessy. Though Brown decisively rejected those arguments, today's dissent replicates them to a distressing extent. Thus, the dissent argues that "[e]ach plan embodies the results of local experience and community consultation." ... Similarly, the segregationists made repeated appeals to societal practice and expectation.... The dissent argues that "weight [must be given] to a local school board's knowledge, expertise, and concerns," ... and with equal vigor, the segregationists argued for deference to local authorities.... The dissent argues that today's decision "threatens to substitute for present calm a disruptive round of race-related litigation," ... and claims that today's decision "risks serious harm to the law and for the Nation".... The segregationists also relied upon the likely practical consequences of ending the state-imposed system of racial separation.... And foreshadowing today's dissent, the segregationists most heavily relied upon judicial precedent....

JUSTICE KENNEDY, concurring in part and concurring in the judgment.

The Nation's schools strive to teach that our strength comes from people of different races, creeds, and cultures uniting in commitment to the freedom of all. In these cases two school districts in different parts of the country seek to teach that principle by having classrooms that reflect the racial makeup of the surrounding community. That the school districts consider these plans to be necessary should remind us our highest aspirations are yet unfulfilled. But the solutions mandated by these school districts must themselves be lawful. To make race matter now so that it might not matter later may entrench the very prejudices we seek to overcome. In my view the state-mandated racial classifications at issue, official labels proclaiming the race of all persons in a broad class of citizens—elementary school students in one case, high school students in another—are unconstitutional as the cases now come to us. . . .

Our Nation from the inception has sought to preserve and expand the promise of liberty and equality on which it was founded. Today we enjoy a society that is remarkable in its openness and opportunity. Yet our tradition is to go beyond present achievements, however significant, and to recognize and confront the flaws and injustices that remain. This is especially true when we seek assurance that opportunity is not denied on account of race. The enduring hope is that race should not matter; the reality is that too often it does.

This is by way of preface to my respectful submission that parts of the opinion by the Chief Justice imply an all-too-unyielding insistence that race cannot be a factor in instances when, in my view, it may be taken into account. The plurality opinion is too dismissive of the legitimate interest government has in ensuring all people have equal opportunity regardless of their race. The plurality's postulate that "[t]he way to stop discrimination on the basis of race is to stop discriminating on the basis of race," . . . is not sufficient to decide these cases. Fifty years of experience since Brown v. Board of Education (1954), should teach us that the problem before us defies so easy a solution. School districts can seek to reach Brown's objective of equal educational opportunity. The plurality opinion is at least open to the interpretation that the Constitution requires school districts to ignore the problem of de facto resegregation in schooling. I cannot endorse that conclusion. To the extent the plurality opinion suggests the Constitution mandates that state and local school authorities must accept the status quo of racial isolation in schools, it is, in my view, profoundly mistaken.

The statement by Justice Harlan that "[o]ur Constitution is color-blind" was most certainly justified in the context of his dissent in Plessy v. Ferguson (1896). The Court's decision in that case was a grievous error it took far too long to overrule. Plessy, of course, concerned official classification by race applicable to all persons who sought to use railway carriages. And, as an aspiration, Justice Harlan's axiom must command our assent. In the real world, it is regrettable to say, it cannot be a universal constitutional principle.

In the administration of public schools by the state and local authorities it is permissible to consider the racial makeup of schools and to adopt general policies to encourage a diverse student body, one aspect of which is its racial composition. Cf. Grutter v. Bollinger, (Kennedy, J., dissenting). If school authorities are concerned that the student-body compositions of certain schools interfere with the objective of offering an equal educational opportunity to all of their students, they are free to devise race-conscious measures to address the problem in a general way and without treating each student in different fashion solely on the basis of a systematic, individual typing by race.

School boards may pursue the goal of bringing together students of diverse backgrounds and races through other means, including strategic site selection of new schools; drawing attendance zones with general recognition of the demographics of neighborhoods; allocating resources for special programs; recruiting students and faculty in a targeted fashion; and tracking enrollments, performance, and other statistics by race. These mechanisms are race conscious but do not lead to different treatment based on a classification that tells each student he or she is to be defined by race, so it is unlikely any of them would demand strict scrutiny to be found permissible. . . . Executive and legislative branches, which for generations now have considered these types of policies and procedures, should be permitted to employ them with candor and with confidence that a constitutional violation does not occur whenever a decisionmaker considers the impact a given approach might have on students of different races. Assigning to each student a personal designation according to a crude system of individual racial classifications is quite a different matter; and the legal analysis changes accordingly.

Each respondent has asserted that its assignment of individual students by race is permissible because there is no other way to avoid racial isolation in the school districts. Yet, as explained, each has failed to provide the support necessary for that proposition. Cf. Croson. ("The history of racial classifications in this country suggests that blind judicial deference to legislative or executive pronouncements of necessity has no place in equal protection analysis"). And individual racial classifications employed in this manner may be considered legitimate only if they are a last resort to achieve a compelling interest....

In the cases before us it is noteworthy that the number of students whose assignment depends on express racial classifications is limited. I join Part III-C of the Court's opinion because I agree that in the context of these plans, the small number of assignments affected suggests that the schools could have achieved their stated ends through different means. These include the facially race-neutral means set forth above or, if necessary, a more nuanced, individual evaluation of school needs and student characteristics that might include race as a component. The latter approach would be informed by Grutter though of course the criteria relevant to student placement would differ based on the age of the students, the needs of the parents, and the role of the schools.

JUSTICE STEVENS, dissenting.

While I join Justice Breyer's eloquent and unanswerable dissent in its entirety, it is appropriate to add these words.

There is a cruel irony in the Chief Justice's reliance on our decision in Brown v. Board of Education. The first sentence in the concluding paragraph of his opinion states: "Before Brown, schoolchildren were told where they could and could not go to school based on the color of their skin." ... This sentence reminds me of Anatole France's observation: "[T]he majestic equality of the la[w], forbid[s] rich and poor alike to sleep under bridges, to beg in the streets, and to steal their bread." The Chief Justice fails to note that it was only black schoolchildren who were so ordered; indeed, the history books do not tell stories of white children struggling to attend black schools. In this and other ways, the Chief Justice rewrites the history of one of this Court's most important decisions....

The Chief Justice rejects the conclusion that the racial classifications at issue here should be viewed differently than others, because they do not impose burdens on one race alone and do not stigmatize or exclude. The only justification for refusing to acknowledge the obvious importance of that difference is the citation of a few recent opinions—none of which even approached unanimity—grandly proclaiming that all racial classifications must be analyzed under "strict scrutiny." See, e.g., Adarand. Even today, two of our wisest federal judges have rejected such a wooden reading of the Equal Protection Clause in the context of school integration.... The Court's misuse of the three-tiered approach to Equal Protection analysis merely reconfirms my own view that there is only one such Clause in the Constitution. See Craig v. Boren (concurring opinion).

If we look at cases decided during the interim between Brown and Adarand, we can see how a rigid adherence to tiers of scrutiny obscures Brown's clear message. Perhaps the best example is provided by our approval of the decision of the Supreme Judicial Court of Massachusetts in 1967 upholding a state statute mandating racial integration in that State's school system.... Rejecting arguments comparable to those that the plurality accepts today, that court noted: "It would be the height of irony if the racial imbalance act, enacted as it was with the laudable purpose of achieving equal educational opportunities, should, by prescribing school pupil allocations based on race, founder on unsuspected shoals in the Fourteenth Amendment." ...

The Court has changed significantly since it decided School Comm. of Boston in 1968. It was then more faithful to Brown and more respectful of our precedent than it is today. It is my firm conviction that no Member of the Court that I joined in 1975 would have agreed with today's decision.

JUSTICE BREYER, with whom JUSTICE STEVENS, JUSTICE SOUTER, and JUSTICE GINSBURG join, dissenting.

These cases consider the longstanding efforts of two local school boards to integrate their public schools. The school board plans before us resemble many others adopted in the last 50 years by primary and secondary schools throughout the Nation. All of those plans represent local efforts to bring about the kind of racially integrated education that Brown v. Board of Education, long ago promised — efforts that this Court has repeatedly required, permitted, and encouraged local authorities to undertake. This Court has recognized that the public interests at stake in such cases are "compelling." We have approved of "narrowly tailored" plans that are no less race-conscious than the plans before us. And we have understood that the Constitution permits local communities to adopt desegregation plans even where it does not require them to do so.

The plurality pays inadequate attention to this law, to past opinions' rationales, their language, and the contexts in which they arise. As a result, it reverses course and reaches the wrong conclusion. In doing so, it distorts precedent, it misapplies the relevant constitutional principles, it announces legal rules that will obstruct efforts by state and local governments to deal effectively with the growing resegregation of public schools, it threatens to substitute for present calm a disruptive round of race-related litigation, and it undermines Brown's promise of integrated primary and secondary education that local communities have sought to make a reality. This cannot be justified in the name of the Equal Protection Clause.

The historical and factual context in which these cases arise is critical. In Brown, this Court held that the government's segregation of schoolchildren by race violates the Constitution's promise of equal protection. The Court emphasized that "education is perhaps the most important function of state and local governments." ... And it thereby set the Nation on a path toward public school integration.

In dozens of subsequent cases, this Court told school districts previously segregated by law what they must do at a minimum to comply with Brown's constitutional holding. The measures required by those cases often included race-conscious practices, such as mandatory busing and race-based restrictions on voluntary transfers....

Beyond those minimum requirements, the Court left much of the determination of how to achieve integration to the judgment of local communities. Thus, in respect to race-conscious desegregation measures that the Constitution permitted, but did not require (measures similar to those at issue here), this Court unanimously stated:

> School authorities are traditionally charged with broad power to formulate and implement educational policy and might well conclude, for example, that in order to prepare students to live in a pluralistic society each school should have a prescribed ratio of Negro to white students reflecting the proportion for the

district as a whole. To do this as an educational policy is within the broad discretionary powers of school authorities.

As a result, different districts—some acting under court decree, some acting in order to avoid threatened lawsuits, some seeking to comply with federal administrative orders, some acting purely voluntarily, some acting after federal courts had dissolved earlier orders—adopted, modified, and experimented with hosts of different kinds of plans, including race-conscious plans, all with a similar objective: greater racial integration of public schools.... I describe those histories at length in order to highlight three important features of these cases. First, the school districts' plans serve "compelling interests" and are "narrowly tailored" on any reasonable definition of those terms. Second, the distinction between de jure segregation (caused by school systems) and de facto segregation (caused, e.g., by housing patterns or generalized societal discrimination) is meaningless in the present context, thereby dooming the plurality's endeavor to find support for its views in that distinction. Third, real-world efforts to substitute racially diverse for racially segregated schools (however caused) are complex, to the point where the Constitution cannot plausibly be interpreted to rule out categorically all local efforts to use means that are "conscious" of the race of individuals.

[Justice Breyer's discussion of the history of de facto racial segregation in the Seattle and Louisville school districts, and the districts efforts to integrate the schools, has been deleted.]

The histories I have set forth describe the extensive and ongoing efforts of two school districts to bring about greater racial integration of their public schools. In both cases the efforts were in part remedial. Louisville began its integration efforts in earnest when a federal court in 1975 entered a school desegregation order. Seattle undertook its integration efforts in response to the filing of a federal lawsuit and as a result of its settlement of a segregation complaint filed with the federal OCR....

The plans in both Louisville and Seattle grow out of these earlier remedial efforts. Both districts faced problems that reflected initial periods of severe racial segregation, followed by such remedial efforts as busing, followed by evidence of resegregation, followed by a need to end busing and encourage the return of, *e.g.,* suburban students through increased student choice. When formulating the plans under review, both districts drew upon their considerable experience with earlier plans, having revised their policies periodically in light of that experience. Both districts rethought their methods over time and explored a wide range of other means, including non-race-conscious policies. Both districts also considered elaborate studies and consulted widely within their communities.

Both districts sought greater racial integration for educational and democratic, as well as for remedial, reasons. Both sought to achieve these objectives while preserving their commitment to other educational goals, *e.g.,* district wide commitment to high quality public schools, increased pupil assignment to neighborhood schools, diminished use of busing, greater student choice, reduced risk of white flight, and so forth. Consequently, the present plans expand student choice; they limit the burdens (including busing) that earlier plans had imposed upon students and their families; and they use race-conscious criteria in limited and gradually diminishing ways. In particular, they use race-conscious criteria only to mark the outer bounds of broad population-related ranges.

The histories also make clear the futility of looking simply to whether earlier school segregation was *de jure* or *de facto* in order to draw firm lines separating the constitutionally permissible from the constitutionally forbidden use of "race-conscious" criteria. Justice THOMAS suggests that it will be easy to identify *de jure* segregation because "[i]n most cases, there either will or will not have been a state constitutional amendment, state statute, local ordinance, or local administrative policy explicitly requiring separation of the races." ... But our precedent has recognized that *de jure* discrimination can be present even in the absence of racially explicit laws. See Yick Wo v. Hopkins.

No one here disputes that Louisville's segregation was *de jure*. But what about Seattle's? Was it *de facto*? *De jure*? A mixture? Opinions differed. Or is it that a prior federal court had not adjudicated the matter? Does that make a difference? Is Seattle free on remand to say that its schools were *de jure* segregated, just as in 1956 a memo for the School Board admitted? The plurality does not seem confident as to the answer. Compare ... ("[T]he Seattle public schools *have never shown* that they were ever segregated by law" ...), with ... (assuming "the Seattle school district was never segregated by law," but seeming to concede that a school district with *de jure* segregation need not be subject to a court order to be allowed to engage in race-based remedial measures).

A court finding of *de jure* segregation cannot be the crucial variable. After all, a number of school districts in the South that the Government or private plaintiffs challenged as segregated *by law* voluntarily desegregated their schools *without a court order*—just as Seattle did....

The histories also indicate the complexity of the tasks and the practical difficulties that local school boards face when they seek to achieve greater racial integration.... These facts and circumstances help explain why in this context, as to means, the law often leaves legislatures, city councils, school boards, and voters with a broad range of choice, thereby giving "different communities" the opportunity to "try different solutions to common problems and gravitate toward those that prove most successful or seem to them best to suit their individual needs." ...

With this factual background in mind, I turn to the legal question: Does the United States Constitution prohibit these school boards from using race-conscious criteria in the limited ways at issue here?

A longstanding and unbroken line of legal authority tells us that the Equal Protection Clause permits local school boards to use race-conscious criteria to achieve positive race-related goals, even when the Constitution does not compel it. Because of its importance, I shall repeat what this Court said about the matter in Swann. Chief Justice Burger, on behalf of a unanimous Court in a case of exceptional importance, wrote:

> School authorities are traditionally charged with broad power to formulate and implement educational policy and might well conclude, for example, that in order to prepare students to live in a society each school should have a prescribed ratio of Negro to white students reflecting the proportion for the district as a whole. To do this as an educational policy is within the broad discretionary powers of school authorities.

The statement was not a technical holding in the case. But the Court set forth in Swann a basic principle of constitutional law—a principle of law that has found "wide acceptance in the legal culture." ... Then-Justice Rehnquist echoed this view in Bustop, Inc. v. Los Angelos Bd. Of Ed (1978) (opinion in chambers), making clear that he too believed that Swann's statement reflected settled law: "While I have the gravest doubts that [a state supreme court] was *required* by the United States Constitution to take the [desegregation] action that it has taken in this case, I have very little doubt that it was *permitted* by that Constitution to take such action." ...

These statements nowhere suggest that this freedom is limited to school districts where court-ordered desegregation measures are also in effect....

That Swann's legal statement should find such broad acceptance is not surprising. For *Swann* is predicated upon a well-established legal view of the Fourteenth Amendment. That view understands the basic objective of those who wrote the Equal Protection Clause as forbidding practices that lead to racial exclusion. The Amendment sought to bring into American society as full members those whom the Nation had previously held in slavery. See Slaughterhouse Cases ("[N]o one can fail to be impressed with the one pervading purpose found in [all the Reconstruction amendments] ... we mean the freedom of the slave race")....

There is reason to believe that those who drafted an Amendment with this basic purpose in mind would have understood the legal and practical difference between the use of race-conscious criteria in defiance of that purpose, namely to keep the races apart, and the use of race-conscious criteria to further that purpose, namely to bring the races together.... Sometimes Members of this Court have disagreed about the degree of leniency that the Clause affords to programs designed to include.... But I can find no case in which this Court has followed Justice Thomas' "colorblind" approach. And I have found no case that otherwise repudiated this constitutional asymmetry between that which seeks to *exclude* and that which seeks to *include* members of minority races.

What does the plurality say in response? First, it seeks to distinguish Swann and other similar cases on the ground that those cases involved remedial plans in response to *judicial findings* of *de jure* segregation. As McDaniel and Harris show, that is historically untrue.... Second, the plurality downplays the importance of Swann and related cases by frequently describing their relevant statements as "dicta." These criticisms, however, miss the main point. *Swann* did not hide its understanding of the law in a corner of an obscure opinion or in a footnote, unread but by experts. It set forth its view prominently in an important opinion joined by all nine Justices, knowing that it would be read and followed throughout the Nation. The basic problem with the plurality's technical "dicta"-based response lies in its overly theoretical approach to case law, an approach that emphasizes rigid distinctions between holdings and dicta in a way that serves to mask the radical nature of today's decision. Law is not an exercise in mathematical logic. And statements of a legal rule set forth in a judicial opinion do not always divide neatly into "holdings" and "dicta." (Consider the legal "status" of Justice Powell's separate opinion in Regents of Univ. of Cal. v. Bakke.) The constitutional principle enunciated in Swann, reiterated in subsequent cases, and relied upon over many years, provides, and has widely been thought to provide, authoritative legal guidance. And if the plurality now chooses to reject that principle, it cannot adequately justify its retreat simply by affixing the label "dicta" to reasoning with which it disagrees. Rather, it must explain to the courts and to the Nation *why* it would abandon guidance set forth many years before, guidance that countless others have built upon over time, and which the law has continuously embodied.

Third, a more important response is the plurality's claim that later cases — in particular Johnson, Adarand and Grutter — supplanted Swann.... The plurality says that cases such as Swann and the others I have described all "were decided before this Court definitively determined that 'all racial classifications ... must be analyzed by a reviewing court under strict scrutiny.' " ... Several of these cases were significantly more restrictive than Swann in respect to the degree of leniency the Fourteenth Amendment grants to programs designed to *include* people of all races.... But that legal circumstance cannot make a critical difference here for two separate reasons.

First, no case — not Adarand, Gratz, Grutter, or any other — has ever held that the test of "strict scrutiny" means that all racial classifications — no matter whether they seek to include or exclude — must in practice be treated the same. The Court did not say in

Adarand or in Johnson or in Grutter that it was overturning *Swann* or its central constitutional principle.

Indeed, in its more recent opinions, the Court recognized that the "fundamental purpose" of strict scrutiny review is to "take relevant differences" between "fundamentally different situations ... into account." Adarand. The Court made clear that "[s]trict scrutiny does not trea[t] dissimilar race-based decisions as though they were equally objectionable." ... It added that the fact that a law "treats [a person] unequally because of his or her race ... says nothing about the ultimate validity of any particular law." ... And the Court, using the very phrase that Justice Marshall had used to describe strict scrutiny's application to any *exclusionary* use of racial criteria, sought to "*dispel the notion that strict scrutiny*" is as likely to condemn *inclusive* uses of "race-conscious" criteria as it is to invalidate *exclusionary* uses. That is, it is *not* in all circumstances "'strict in theory, but fatal in fact.'" ...

The Court's holding in Grutter demonstrates that the Court meant what it said, for the Court upheld an elite law school's race-conscious admissions program.

The upshot is that the cases to which the plurality refers, though all applying strict scrutiny, do not treat exclusive and inclusive uses the same. Rather, they apply the strict scrutiny test in a manner that is "fatal in fact" only to racial classifications that harmfully *exclude;* they apply the test in a manner that is *not* fatal in fact to racial classifications that seek to *include.*

The plurality cannot avoid this simple fact.... Today's opinion reveals that the plurality would rewrite this Court's prior jurisprudence, at least in practical application, transforming the "strict scrutiny" test into a rule that is fatal in fact across the board. In doing so, the plurality parts company from this Court's prior cases, and it takes from local government the longstanding legal right to use race-conscious criteria for inclusive purposes in limited ways.

Second, as Grutter specified, "[c]ontext matters when reviewing race-based governmental action under the Equal Protection Clause." ... And contexts differ dramatically one from the other. Governmental use of race-based criteria can arise in the context of, for example, census forms, research expenditures for diseases, assignments of police officers patrolling predominantly minority-race neighborhoods, efforts to de-segregate racially segregated schools, policies that favor minorities when distributing goods or services in short supply, actions that create majority-minority electoral districts, peremptory strikes that remove potential jurors on the basis of race, and others. Given the significant differences among these contexts, it would be surprising if the law required an identically strict legal test for evaluating the constitutionality of race-based criteria as to each of them.

Here, the context is one in which school districts seek to advance or to maintain racial integration in primary and secondary schools. It is a context, as Swann makes clear, where history has required special administrative remedies. And it is a context in which the school boards' plans simply set race-conscious limits at the outer boundaries of a broad range.

This context is *not* a context that involves the use of race to decide who will receive goods or services that are normally distributed on the basis of merit and which are in short supply. It is not one in which race-conscious limits stigmatize or exclude; the limits at issue do not pit the races against each other or otherwise significantly exacerbate racial tensions. They do not impose burdens unfairly upon members of one race alone but instead seek benefits for members of all races alike. The context here is one of racial limits that seek, not to keep the races apart, but to bring them together....

The view that a more lenient standard than "strict scrutiny" should apply in the present context would not imply abandonment of judicial efforts carefully to determine the need for race-conscious criteria and the criteria's tailoring in light of the need. And the present context requires a court to examine carefully the race-conscious program at issue. In doing so, a reviewing judge must be fully aware of the potential dangers and pitfalls that Justice THOMAS and Justice KENNEDY mention....

But unlike the plurality, such a judge would also be aware that a legislature or school administrators, ultimately accountable to the electorate, could *nonetheless* properly conclude that a racial classification sometimes serves a purpose important enough to overcome the risks they mention, for example, helping to end racial isolation or to achieve a diverse student body in public schools.... Where that is so, the judge would carefully examine the program's details to determine whether the use of race-conscious criteria is proportionate to the important ends it serves.

In my view, this contextual approach to scrutiny is altogether fitting. I believe that the law requires application here of a standard of review that is not "strict" in the traditional sense of that word, although it does require the careful review I have just described.... Nonetheless, in light of Grutter and other precedents, see, e.g., Bakke, (opinion of Powell, J.), I shall adopt the first alternative. I shall apply the version of strict scrutiny that those cases embody. I shall consequently ask whether the school boards in Seattle and Louisville adopted these plans to serve a "compelling governmental interest" and, if so, whether the plans are "narrowly tailored" to achieve that interest....

The principal interest advanced in these cases to justify the use of race-based criteria goes by various names. Sometimes a court refers to it as an interest in achieving racial "diversity." Other times a court, like the plurality here, refers to it as an interest in racial "balancing." I have used more general terms to signify that interest, describing it, for example, as an interest in promoting or preserving greater racial "integration" of public schools. By this term, I mean the school districts' interest in eliminating school-by-school racial isolation and increasing the degree to which racial mixture characterizes each of the district's schools and each individual student's public school experience.

Regardless of its name, however, the interest at stake possesses three essential elements. First, there is a historical and remedial element: an interest in setting right the consequences of prior conditions of segregation. This refers back to a time when public schools were highly segregated, often as a result of legal or administrative policies that facilitated racial segregation in public schools. It is an interest in continuing to combat the remnants of segregation caused in whole or in part by these school-related policies, which have often affected not only schools, but also housing patterns, employment practices, economic conditions, and social attitudes. It is an interest in maintaining hard-won gains. And it has its roots in preventing what gradually may become the *de facto* resegregation of America's public schools....

Second, there is an educational element: an interest in overcoming the adverse educational effects produced by and associated with highly segregated schools. Cf. Grutter (Ginsburg, J., concurring). Studies suggest that children taken from those schools and placed in integrated settings often show positive academic gains.... Other studies reach different conclusions.... But the evidence supporting an educational interest in racially integrated schools is well established and strong enough to permit a democratically elected school board reasonably to determine that this interest is a compelling one....

Third, there is a democratic element: an interest in producing an educational environment that reflects the "pluralistic society" in which our children will live. Swann.

It is an interest in helping our children learn to work and play together with children of different racial backgrounds. It is an interest in teaching children to engage in the kind of cooperation among Americans of all races that is necessary to make a land of three hundred million people one Nation.... There are again studies that offer contrary conclusions.... Again, however, the evidence supporting a democratic interest in racially integrated schools is firmly established and sufficiently strong to permit a school board to determine, as this Court has itself often found, that this interest is compelling....

In light of this Court's conclusions in Grutter, the "compelling" nature of these interests in the context of primary and secondary public education follows here *a fortiori*. Primary and secondary schools are where the education of this Nation's children begins, where each of us begins to absorb those values we carry with us to the end of our days. As Justice Marshall said, "unless our children begin to learn together, there is little hope that our people will ever learn to live together." ... The compelling interest at issue here, then, includes an effort to eradicate the remnants, not of general "societal discrimination," ... but of primary and secondary school segregation ... ; it includes an effort to create school environments that provide better educational opportunities for all children; it includes an effort to help create citizens better prepared to know, to understand, and to work with people of all races and backgrounds, thereby furthering the kind of democratic government our Constitution foresees. If an educational interest that combines these three elements is not "compelling," what is? ...

For his part, Justice Thomas faults my citation of various studies supporting the view that school districts can find compelling educational and civic interests in integrating their public schools.... He is entitled of course to his own opinion as to which studies he finds convincing—although it bears mention that even the author of some of Justice Thomas' preferred studies has found *some* evidence linking integrated learning environments to increased academic achievement.... If we are to insist upon unanimity in the social science literature before finding a compelling interest, we might never find one. I believe only that the Constitution allows democratically elected school boards to make up their own minds as to how best to include people of all races in one America.

I next ask whether the plans before us are "narrowly tailored" to achieve these "compelling" objectives.... First, the race-conscious criteria at issue only help set the outer bounds of *broad* ranges.... They constitute but one part of plans that depend primarily upon other, nonracial elements. To use race in this way is not to set a forbidden "quota." ... In fact, the defining feature of both plans is greater emphasis upon student choice. In Seattle, for example, in more than 80% of all cases, that choice alone determines which high schools Seattle's ninth graders will attend. After ninth grade, students can decide voluntarily to transfer to a preferred district high school (without any consideration of race-conscious criteria). *Choice*, therefore, is the "predominant factor" in these plans. *Race* is not....

Second, broad-range limits on voluntary school choice plans are less burdensome, and hence more narrowly tailored, see Grutter, than other race-conscious restrictions this Court has previously approved. See, *e.g.*, Swann. Indeed, the plans before us are *more narrowly tailored* than the race-conscious admission plans that this Court approved in Grutter. Here, race becomes a factor only in a fraction of students' non-merit-based assignments—not in large numbers of students' merit-based applications. Moreover, the effect of applying race-conscious criteria here affects potentially disadvantaged students *less severely*, not more severely, than the criteria at issue in Grutter. Disappointed students are not rejected from a State's flagship graduate program; they simply attend a different one of the district's many public schools, which in aspiration and in fact are substantially equal.... And, in Seattle, the disadvantaged student loses at most one year at the high school of his choice. One will search Grutter in vain for similarly persuasive evidence of narrow tailoring as the school districts have presented here.

Third, the manner in which the school boards developed these plans itself reflects "narrow tailoring." Each plan was devised to overcome a history of segregated public schools. Each plan embodies the results of local experience and community consultation. Each plan is the product of a process that has sought to enhance student choice, while diminishing the need for mandatory busing. And each plan's use of race-conscious elements is *diminished* compared to the use of race in preceding integration plans....

Moreover, giving some degree of weight to a local school board's knowledge, expertise, and concerns in these particular matters is not inconsistent with rigorous judicial scrutiny. It simply recognizes that judges are not well suited to act as school administrators. Indeed, in the context of school desegregation, this Court has repeatedly stressed the importance of acknowledging that local school boards better understand their own communities and have a better knowledge of what in practice will best meet the educational needs of their pupils....

The Founders meant the Constitution as a practical document that would transmit its basic values to future generations through principles that remained workable over time. Hence it is important to consider the potential consequences of the plurality's approach, as measured against the Constitution's objectives. To do so provides further reason to believe that the plurality's approach is legally unsound....

The wide variety of different integration plans that school districts use throughout the Nation suggests that the problem of racial segregation in schools, including *de facto* segregation, is difficult to solve. The fact that many such plans have used explicitly racial criteria suggests that such criteria have an important, sometimes necessary, role to play. The fact that the controlling opinion would make a school district's use of such criteria often unlawful (and the plurality's "colorblind" view would make such use always unlawful) suggests that today's opinion will require setting aside the laws of several States and many local communities.

As I have pointed out, ... *de facto* resegregation is on the rise.... It is reasonable to conclude that such resegregation can create serious educational, social, and civic problems.... Given the conditions in which school boards work to set policy, ... they may need all of the means presently at their disposal to combat those problems. Yet the plurality would deprive them of at least one tool that some districts now consider vital — the limited use of broad race-conscious student population ranges.

I use the words "may need" here deliberately. The plurality, or at least those who follow Justice Thomas' "'color-blind'" approach ... may feel confident that, to end invidious discrimination, one must end *all* governmental use of race-conscious criteria including those with inclusive objectives.... By way of contrast, I do not claim to know how best to stop harmful discrimination; how best to create a society that includes all Americans; how best to overcome our serious problems of increasing *de facto* segregation, troubled inner city schooling, and poverty correlated with race. But, as a judge, I do know that the Constitution does not authorize judges to dictate solutions to these problems. Rather, the Constitution creates a democratic political system through which the people themselves must together find answers. And it is for them to debate how best to educate the Nation's children and how best to administer America's schools to achieve that aim. The Court should leave them to their work. And it is for them to decide, to quote the plurality's slogan, whether the best "way to stop discrimination on the basis of race is to stop discriminating on the basis of race." ... See also Parents Involved VII, 426 F.3d, at 1222 (Bea, J., dissenting) ("The way to end racial discrimination is to stop discriminating by race"). That is why the Equal Protection Clause outlaws invidious discrimination, but does not similarly forbid all use of race-conscious criteria....

And what of the long history and moral vision that the Fourteenth Amendment itself embodies? The plurality cites in support those who argued in *Brown* against segregation, and Justice Thomas likens the approach that I have taken to that of segregation's defenders.... (comparing Jim Crow segregation to Seattle and Louisville's integration polices).... But segregation policies did not simply tell schoolchildren "where they could and could not go to school based on the color of their skin," ... they perpetuated a caste system rooted in the institutions of slavery and 80 years of legalized subordination. The lesson of history ... is not that efforts to continue racial segregation are constitutionally indistinguishable from efforts to achieve racial integration. Indeed, it is a cruel distortion of history to compare Topeka, Kansas, in the 1950s to Louisville and Seattle in the modern day—to equate the plight of Linda Brown (who was ordered to attend a Jim Crow school) to the circumstances of Joshua McDonald (whose request to transfer to a school closer to home was initially declined). This is not to deny that there is a cost in applying "a state-mandated racial label." ... But that cost does not approach, in degree or in kind, the terrible harms of slavery, the resulting caste system, and 80 years of legal racial segregation.

Finally, what of the hope and promise of Brown? For much of this Nation's history, the races remained divided. It was not long ago that people of different races drank from separate fountains, rode on separate buses, and studied in separate schools. In this Court's finest hour, Brown v. Board of Education challenged this history and helped to change it. For Brown held out a promise. It was a promise embodied in three Amendments designed to make citizens of slaves. It was the promise of true racial equality—not as a matter of fine words on paper, but as a matter of everyday life in the Nation's cities and schools. It was about the nature of a democracy that must work for all Americans. It sought one law, one Nation, one people, not simply as a matter of legal principle but in terms of how we actually live.

Not everyone welcomed this Court's decision in Brown. Three years after that decision was handed down, the Governor of Arkansas ordered state militia to block the doors of a white schoolhouse so that black children could not enter. The President of the United States dispatched the 101st Airborne Division to Little Rock, Arkansas, and federal troops were needed to enforce a desegregation decree.... Today, almost 50 years later, attitudes toward race in this Nation have changed dramatically. Many parents, white and black alike, want their children to attend schools with children of different races. Indeed, the very school districts that once spurned integration now strive for it. The long history of their efforts reveals the complexities and difficulties they have faced. And in light of those challenges, they have asked us not to take from their hands the instruments they have used to rid their schools of racial segregation, instruments that they believe are needed to overcome the problems of cities divided by race and poverty. The plurality would decline their modest request.

The plurality is wrong to do so. The last half-century has witnessed great strides toward racial equality, but we have not yet realized the promise of Brown. To invalidate the plans under review is to threaten the promise of Brown. The plurality's position, I fear, would break that promise. This is a decision that the Court and the Nation will come to regret.

I must dissent.

Review Questions and Explanations: *Parents Involved*

1. You have read the Court's important affirmative action cases. Is *Parents Involved* an affirmative action case? Why or why not?

2. What is Justice Breyer's point about *de jure* and *de facto* segregation? Articulate it in your own words, and consider how it influences his decision. Assume for the moment that it is possible to more crisply distinguish between these two types of segregation: how would that influence Justice Breyer's position?

3. Does race play a decisive (as asserted by the majority) or an insignificant (as claimed by the dissenters) role in student placements in the two programs being reviewed? How can the justices disagree on such a basic point? Make the best case you can for each position.

4. What state interests do the school districts assert? Do these interests seem more or less compelling to you than the diversity interest accepted in *Bakke*? What legal test does the Court use to determine if an interest is sufficiently compelling?

Exercise: School Integration

You are the staff attorney for the Seattle School System. You have been tasked with outlining a school integration plan that will satisfy the criteria set forth in Justice Kennedy's concurring opinion. Working with a partner, sketch out such a program. Then take turns arguing for and against its constitutionality, with one of you acting as advocate and the other as Justice Kennedy.

D. Sex Discrimination

This section explores the application of the Equal Protection clause outside of the race context. One of the first things we must consider is why non-racial classifications are governed by the Equal Protection clause at all. The clause, after all, is embedded in the Fourteenth Amendment, one of the Civil War Amendments. But the text of the Fourteenth Amendment is not restricted to racial classifications. It simply says that no state shall deny to any person within its jurisdiction the equal protection of the laws. Consequently, there is no textual reason to limit its reach to racial classifications.

Sex[4] and most other types of classifications have not, however, enjoyed the same degree of scrutiny the Court employs when evaluating the constitutionality of racial classifications. The first set of cases below show the evolution of the Court's jurisprudence regarding the level of scrutiny appropriate in cases involving sex. In the first case, *Bradwell v. Illinois*, the Court refused to seriously consider a constitutional challenge to a sex-based classification.

---

4. As with race, it is increasingly clear that "sex" is a biologically squishy concept. Sex is the term used in the Court's decisions in this area, so we use it here as well.

In *Reed v. Reed*, the Court struck down a sex-based distinction, but did so using rational basis review. In *Frontiero v. Richardson*, a plurality of the Court applied strict scrutiny to invalidate the classification at issue, but then in *Craig v. Boren*, the Court reverted to an intermediate type of review. And in the Court's most recent significant case in this area, *Virginia Military Institute v. U.S.*, the Court applied that intermediate test in a suspiciously strict way.

As you will see in these cases, the Court's understanding of what is and is not a sufficiently important state interest justifying sex-based distinctions has varied over time. *Bradwell v. Illinois* helps illustrate this point. *Bradwell* was decided in 1873. It was issued just after *The Slaughterhouse Cases*. *Bradwell*, like *Slaughterhouse*, was decided under the Privileges or Immunities clause, not the Equal Protection clause. Nonetheless, the reasoning set out in Justice Bradley's concurring opinion (which is the opinion excerpted below) readily demonstrates how the Court in that era evaluated the state interest in drawing distinctions barring women from participating in many areas of public and civil life. The case thus provides an interesting contrast to Justice Brennan's opinion, written a century later, in *Frontiero v. Richardson*. The point to think about is this: both Justice Bradley and Justice Brennan rely on social norms when evaluating the states' justifications for treating men and women differently, yet they reach radically different constitutional conclusions, based on the norms of the era in which they each were writing. What implications does that have for equal protection doctrine?

Bradwell v. Illinois

83 U.S. 130 (1873)

Majority: *Miller*, Clifford, Davis, Strong, Hunt (omitted)

Concurrence: *Bradley*, Field, Swayne

Dissent: *Chase* (CJ) (omitted)

MR. JUSTICE BRADLEY, concurring.

I concur in the judgment of the court in this case, by which the judgment of the Supreme Court of Illinois is affirmed, but not for the reasons specified in the opinion just read.

The claim of the plaintiff, who is a married woman, to be admitted to practice as an attorney and counsellor-at-law, is based upon the supposed right of every person, man or woman, to engage in any lawful employment for a livelihood. The Supreme Court of Illinois denied the application on the ground that, by the common law, which is the basis of the laws of Illinois, only men were admitted to the bar, and the legislature had not made any change in this respect, but had simply provided that no person should be admitted to practice as attorney or counsellor without having previously obtained a license for that purpose from two justices of the Supreme Court, and that no person should receive a license without first obtaining a certificate from the court of some county of his good moral character. In other respects it was left to the discretion of the court to establish the rules by which admission to the profession should be determined. The court, however, regarded itself as bound by at least two limitations. One was that it should establish such terms of admission as would promote the proper administration of justice, and the other that it should not admit any persons, or class of persons, not intended by the legislature to be admitted, even though not expressly excluded by statute. In view of this latter limitation the court felt compelled to deny the application of females to be admitted as members of the bar. Being contrary to the rules of the common law and the usages of Westminster Hall from time immemorial, it could not be supposed that the legislature had intended to adopt any different rule.

The claim that, under the fourteenth amendment of the Constitution, which declares that no State shall make or enforce any law which shall abridge the privileges and immunities of citizens of the United States, the statute law of Illinois, or the common law prevailing in that State, can no longer be set up as a barrier against the right of females to pursue any lawful employment for a livelihood (the practice of law included), assumes that it is one of the privileges and immunities of women as citizens to engage in any and every profession, occupation, or employment in civil life.

It certainly cannot be affirmed, as an historical fact, that this has ever been established as one of the fundamental privileges and immunities of the sex. On the contrary, the civil law, as well as nature herself, has always recognized a wide difference in the respective spheres and destinies of man and woman. Man is, or should be, woman's protector and defender. The natural and proper timidity and delicacy which belongs to the female sex evidently unfits it for many of the occupations of civil life. The constitution of the family organization, which is founded in the divine ordinance, as well as in the nature of things, indicates the domestic sphere as that which properly belongs to the domain and functions of womanhood. The harmony, not to say identity, of interest and views which belong, or should belong, to the family institution is repugnant to the idea of a woman adopting a distinct and independent career from that of her husband. So firmly fixed was this sentiment in the founders of the common law that it became a maxim of that system of jurisprudence that a woman had no legal existence separate from her husband, who was regarded as her head and representative in the social state; and, notwithstanding some recent modifications of this civil status, many of the special rules of law flowing from and dependent upon this cardinal principle still exist in full force in most States. One of these is, that a married woman is incapable, without her husband's consent, of making contracts which shall be binding on her or him. This very incapacity was one circumstance which the Supreme Court of Illinois deemed important in rendering a married woman incompetent fully to perform the duties and trusts that belong to the office of an attorney and counsellor.

It is true that many women are unmarried and not affected by any of the duties, complications, and incapacities arising out of the married state, but these are exceptions to the general rule. The paramount destiny and mission of woman are to fulfill the noble and benign offices of wife and mother. This is the law of the Creator. And the rules of civil society must be adapted to the general constitution of things, and cannot be based upon exceptional cases.

The humane movements of modern society, which have for their object the multiplication of avenues for woman's advancement, and of occupations adapted to her condition and sex, have my heartiest concurrence. But I am not prepared to say that it is one of her fundamental rights and privileges to be admitted into every office and position, including those which require highly special qualifications and demanding special responsibilities. In the nature of things it is not every citizen of every age, sex, and condition that is qualified for every calling and position. It is the prerogative of the legislator to prescribe regulations founded on nature, reason, and experience for the due admission of qualified persons to professions and callings demanding special skill and confidence. This fairly belongs to the police power of the State; and, in my opinion, in view of the peculiar characteristics, destiny, and mission of woman, it is within the province of the legislature to ordain what offices, positions, and callings shall be filled and discharged by men, and shall receive the benefit of those energies and responsibilities, and that decision and firmness which are presumed to predominate in the sterner sex.

For these reasons I think that the laws of Illinois now complained of are not obnoxious to the charge of abridging any of the privileges and immunities of citizens of the United States.

Guided Reading Questions: *Reed, Frontiero,* and *Craig*

1. In the following cases, the justices debate whether any form of heightened review should be applied to state actions that classify people on the basis of sex. What are the arguments for and against heightened scrutiny of such actions? Consider *Carolene Products* footnote 4, as well as the race discrimination materials just studied.

2. Is expanding constitutional protection to match changing social norms likely to give the Court (and the Constitution) more or less legitimacy? This is a difficult question to answer, in that it requires us to consider a counterfactual: would the Court (and the Constitution) be perceived as more or less legitimate if cases like *Brown* and *Craig* had come out the opposite way?

Reed v. Reed

404 U.S. 71 (1971)

Unanimous decision: *Burger* (CJ), Black, Douglas, Harlan, Brennan, Stewart, White, Marshall, Blackmun

MR. CHIEF JUSTICE BURGER delivered the opinion for a unanimous Court.

Richard Lynn Reed, a minor, died intestate in Ada County, Idaho, on March 29, 1967. His adoptive parents, who had separated sometime prior to his death, are the parties to this appeal.... Section 15-312 [of the Idaho Code] designates the persons who are entitled to administer the estate of one who dies intestate. In making these designations, that section lists 11 classes of persons who are so entitled and provides, in substance, hat the order in which those classes are listed in the section shall be determinative of the relative rights of competing applicants for letters of administration. One of the 11 classes so enumerated is '(t)he father or mother' of the person dying intestate. Under this section then appellant and appellee, being members of the same entitlement class, would seem to have been equally entitled to administer their son's estate. Section 15-314 provides, however, that '(o)f several persons claiming and equally entitled (under s 15-312) to administer, males must be preferred to females, and relatives of the whole to those of the half blood.'

In issuing its order, the probate court implicitly recognized the equality of entitlement of the two applicants under § 15-312 and noted that neither of the applicants was under any legal disability; the court ruled, however, that appellee, being a male, was to be preferred to the female appellant 'by reason of Section 15-314 of the Idaho Code.' In stating this conclusion, the probate judge gave no indication that he had attempted to determine the relative capabilities of the competing applicants to perform the functions incident to the administration of an estate. It seems clear the probate judge considered himself bound by statute to give preference to the male candidate over the female, each being otherwise 'equally entitled.'

Sally Reed appealed from the probate court order, and her appeal was treated by the District Court of the Fourth Judicial District of Idaho as a constitutional attack on § 15-314. In dealing with the attack, that court held that the challenged section violated the Equal Protection Clause of the Fourteenth Amendment and was, therefore, void; the matter was ordered 'returned to the Probate Court for its determination of which of the two parties' was better qualified to administer the estate.

This order was never carried out, however, for Cecil Reed took a further appeal to the Idaho Supreme Court, which reversed the District Court and reinstated the original order naming the father administrator of the estate. In reaching this result, the Idaho Supreme Court first dealt with the governing statutory law and held that under § 15-312 'a father and mother are "equally entitled" to letters of administration,' but the preference given to males by § 15-314 is 'mandatory' and leaves no room for the exercise of a probate court's discretion in the appointment of administrators. Having thus definitively and authoritatively interpreted the statutory provisions involved, the Idaho Supreme Court then proceeded to examine, and reject, Sally Reed's contention that § 15-314 violates the Equal Protection Clause by giving a mandatory preference to males over females, without regard to their individual qualifications as potential estate administrators....

Sally Reed thereupon appealed for review by this Court pursuant to 28 U.S.C. § 1257(2), and we noted probable jurisdiction.... Having examined the record and considered the briefs and oral arguments of the parties, we have concluded that the arbitrary preference established in favor of males by § 15-314 of the Idaho Code cannot stand in the face of the Fourteenth Amendment's command that no State deny the equal protection of the laws to any person within its jurisdiction.

Idaho does not, of course, deny letters of administration to women altogether. Indeed, under § 15-312, a woman whose spouse dies intestate has a preference over a son, father, brother, or any other male relative of the decedent. Moreover, we can judicially notice that in this country, presumably due to the greater longevity of women, a large proportion of estates, both intestate and under wills of decedents, are administered by surviving widows.

Section 15-314 is restricted in its operation to those situations where competing applications for letters of administration have been filed by both male and female members of the same entitlement class established by § 15-312. In such situations, § 15-314 provides that different treatment be accorded to the applicants on the basis of their sex; it thus establishes a classification subject to scrutiny under the Equal Protection Clause.

In applying that clause, this Court has consistently recognized that the Fourteenth Amendment does not deny to States the power to treat different classes of persons in different ways.... The Equal Protection Clause of that amendment does, however, deny to States the power to legislate that different treatment be accorded to persons placed by a statute into different classes on the basis of criteria wholly unrelated to the objective of that statute. A classification 'must be reasonable, not arbitrary, and must rest upon some ground of difference having a fair and substantial relation to the object of the legislation, so that all persons similarly circumstanced shall be treated alike.' Royster Guano Co. v. Virginia (1920). The question presented by this case, then, is whether a difference in the sex of competing applicants for letters of administration bears a rational relationship to a state objective that is sought to be advanced by the operation of §§ 15-312 and 15-314.

In upholding the latter section, the Idaho Supreme Court concluded that its objective was to eliminate one area of controversy when two or more persons, equally entitled under § 15-312, seek letters of administration and thereby present the probate court 'with the issue of which one should be named.' The court also concluded that where such persons are not of the same sex, the elimination of females from consideration 'is neither an illogical nor arbitrary method devised by the legislature to resolve an issue that would otherwise require a hearing as to the relative merits ... of the two or more petitioning relatives ...'.

Clearly the objective of reducing the workload on probate courts by eliminating one class of contests is not without some legitimacy. The crucial question, however, is whether § 15-314 advances that objective in a manner consistent with the command of the Equal Protection Clause. We hold that it does not. To give a mandatory preference to members of either sex over members of the other, merely to accomplish the elimination of hearings on the merits, is to make the very kind of arbitrary legislative choice forbidden by the Equal Protection Clause of the Fourteenth Amendment; and whatever may be said as to the positive values of avoiding intrafamily controversy, the choice in this context may not lawfully be mandated solely on the basis of sex....

The judgment of the Idaho Supreme Court is reversed and the case remanded for further proceedings not inconsistent with this opinion.

Review Questions and Explanations: *Reed*

1. What justifications does the state offer for its sex-based classification? What test does the Court use to determine whether these justifications are sufficiently compelling? In other words, what standard of review does the Court apply to the question presented?

2. Legally, how does the standard of review the Court used in *Reed* differ from that used by Justice Bradley in *Bradwell*?

Frontiero v. Richardson

411 U.S. 677 (1973)

Plurality: *Brennan*, Douglas, White, Marshall

Concurrences in the judgment: *Stewart* (omitted)*; Powell*, Burger (CJ), Blackmun

Dissent: *Rehnquist* (omitted)

MR. JUSTICE BRENNAN delivered the opinion of the Court.

The question before us concerns the right of a female member of the uniformed services to claim her spouse as a 'dependent' for the purposes of obtaining increased quarters allowances and medical and dental benefits under 37 U.S.C. §§ 401, 403, and 10 U.S.C. §§ 1072, 1076, on an equal footing with male members. Under these statutes, a serviceman may claim his wife as a 'dependent' without regard to whether she is in fact dependent upon him for any part of her support.... A servicewoman, on the other hand, may not claim her husband as a 'dependent' under these programs unless he is in fact dependent upon her for over one-half of his support....

Appellant Sharron Frontiero, a lieutenant in the United States Air Force, sought increased quarters allowances, and housing and medical benefits for her husband, appellant Joseph Frontiero, on the ground that he was her 'dependent.' Although such benefits would automatically have been granted with respect to the wife of a male member of the uniformed services, appellant's application was denied because she failed to demonstrate that her husband was dependent on her for more than one-half of his support. Appellants then commenced this suit, contending that, by making this distinction, the statutes unreasonably discriminate on the basis of sex....

Although the legislative history of these statutes sheds virtually no light on the purposes underlying the differential treatment accorded male and female members, a majority of the three-judge District Court surmised that Congress might reasonably have concluded that, since the husband in our society is generally the 'breadwinner' in the family—and the wife typically the 'dependent' partner—'it would be more economical to require married female members claiming husbands to prove actual dependency than to extend the presumption of dependency to such members.'... Indeed, given the fact that approximately 99% of all members of the uniformed services are male, the District Court speculated that such differential treatment might conceivably lead to a 'considerable saving of administrative expense and manpower.'...

At the outset, appellants contend that classifications based upon sex, like classifications based upon race, alienage, and national origin, are inherently suspect and must therefore be subjected to close judicial scrutiny. We agree and, indeed, find at least implicit support for such an approach in our unanimous decision only last Term in Reed v. Reed....

There can be no doubt that our Nation has had a long and unfortunate history of sex discrimination.... It is true, of course, that the position of women in America has improved markedly in recent decades. Nevertheless, it can hardly be doubted that, in part because of the high visibility of the sex characteristic, women still face pervasive, although at times more subtle, discrimination in our educational institutions, in the job market and, perhaps most conspicuously, in the political arena.... Moreover, since sex, like race and national origin, is an immutable characteristic determined solely by the accident of birth, the imposition of special disabilities upon the members of a particular sex because of their sex would seem to violate 'the basic concept of our system that legal burdens should bear some relationship to individual responsibility ...' ... And what differentiates sex from such non-suspect statuses as intelligence or physical disability, and aligns it with the recognized suspect criteria, is that the sex characteristic frequently bears no relation to ability to perform or contribute to society. As a result, statutory distinctions between the sexes often have the effect of invidiously relegating the entire class of females to inferior legal status without regard to the actual capabilities of its individual members....

With these considerations in mind, we can only conclude that classifications based upon sex, like classifications based upon race, alienage, or national origin, are inherently suspect, and must therefore be subjected to strict judicial scrutiny. Applying the analysis mandated by that stricter standard of review, it is clear that the statutory scheme now before us is constitutionally invalid....

The Government concedes that the differential treatment accorded men and women under these statutes serves no purpose other than mere 'administrative convenience.' In essence, the Government maintains that, as an empirical matter, wives in our society frequently are dependent upon their husbands, while husbands rarely are dependent upon their wives. Thus, the Government argues that Congress might reasonably have concluded that it would be both cheaper and easier simply conclusively to presume that wives of male members are financially dependent upon their husbands, while burdening female members with the task of establishing dependency in fact....

In any case, our prior decisions make clear that, although efficacious administration of governmental programs is not without some importance, 'the Constitution recognizes higher values than speed and efficiency.'... And when we enter the realm of 'strict judicial scrutiny,' there can be no doubt that 'administrative convenience' is not a shibboleth, the mere recitation of which dictates constitutionality.... On the contrary, any statutory scheme which draws a sharp line between the sexes, solely for the purpose of achieving administrative convenience, necessarily commands 'dissimilar treatment for men and women who are ... similarly situated,' and therefore involves the 'very kind of arbitrary legislative choice forbidden by the (Constitution)....' Reed v. Reed.

MR. JUSTICE POWELL, with whom THE CHIEF JUSTICE and MR. JUSTICE BLACK-MUN join, concurring in the judgment.

I agree that the challenged statutes constitute an unconstitutional discrimination against servicewomen in violation of the Due Process Clause of the Fifth Amendment, but I cannot join the opinion of Mr. Justice Brennan, which would hold that all classifications based upon sex, 'like classifications based upon race, alienage, and national origin,' are 'inherently suspect and must therefore be subjected to close judicial scrutiny.'... It is unnecessary for the Court in this case to characterize sex as a suspect classification, with all of the far-reaching implications of such a holding. Reed v. Reed, which abundantly supports our decision today, did not add sex to the narrowly limited group of classifications which are inherently suspect. In my view, we can and should decide this case on the authority of Reed and reserve for the future any expansion of its rationale.

There is another, and I find compelling, reason for deferring a general categorizing of sex classifications as invoking the strictest test of judicial scrutiny. The Equal Rights Amendment, which if adopted will resolve the substance of this precise question, has been approved by the Congress and submitted for ratification by the States. If this Amendment is duly adopted, it will represent the will of the people accomplished in the manner prescribed by the Constitution. By acting prematurely and unnecessarily, as I view it, the Court has assumed a decisional responsibility at the very time when state legislatures, functioning within the traditional democratic process, are debating the proposed Amendment. It seems to me that this reaching out to pre-empt by judicial action a major political decision which is currently in process of resolution does not reflect appropriate respect for duly prescribed legislative processes.

There are times when this Court, under our system, cannot avoid a constitutional decision on issues which normally should be resolved by the elected representatives of the people. But democratic institutions are weakened, and confidence in the restraint of the Court is impaired, when we appear unnecessarily to decide sensitive issues of broad social and political importance at the very time they are under consideration within the prescribed constitutional processes.

Review Questions and Explanations: *Frontiero*

1. Compare the justifications provided by the state in *Frontiero* to those presented in *Reed*. In what ways are they similar and different?

2. Justice Brennan, writing for a four justice plurality, applies strict scrutiny to the question presented. How does he justify this choice? Do you agree that strict scrutiny is appropriate here? Why or why not?

3. One reason Justice Brennan gives for applying strict scrutiny is that sex bears "no relation to [a woman's] ability to perform or contribute" to society. Compare this to Justice Bradley's opinion in *Bradwell.* Is either man doing anything other than asserting an opinion on this point? If so, why do we think (if we do) that Justice Brennan is obviously right and Justice Bradley obviously wrong?

4. Can you summarize Justice Powell's point?

Craig v. Boren

429 U.S. 190 (1976)

Majority: *Brennan,* White, Marshall, Powell, Stevens

Concurrences: *Blackmun; Stewart; Stevens; Powell* (all but Stevens omitted)

Dissents: *Burger* (CJ) (omitted); *Rehnquist*

MR. JUSTICE BRENNAN delivered the opinion of the Court.

The interaction of two sections of an Oklahoma statute, Okla.Stat., Tit. 37, §§ 241 and 245 (1958 and Supp.1976), prohibits the sale of "nonintoxicating" 3.2% beer to males under the age of 21 and to females under the age of 18. The question to be decided is whether such a gender-based differential constitutes a denial to males 18–20 years of age of the equal protection of the laws in violation of the Fourteenth Amendment....

Analysis may appropriately begin with the reminder that Reed emphasized that statutory classifications that distinguish between males and females are "subject to scrutiny under the Equal Protection Clause." ... To withstand constitutional challenge, previous cases establish that classifications by gender must serve important governmental objectives and must be substantially related to achievement of those objectives.... Reed v. Reed has also provided the underpinning for decisions that have invalidated statutes employing gender as an inaccurate proxy for other, more germane bases of classification. Hence, "archaic and overbroad" generalizations, ... concerning the financial position of servicewomen, Frontiero v. Richardson, and working women, Weinberger v. Wiesenfeld, could not justify use of a gender line in determining eligibility for certain governmental entitlements. Similarly, increasingly outdated misconceptions concerning the role of females in the home rather than in the "marketplace and world of ideas" were rejected as loose-fitting characterizations incapable of supporting state statutory schemes that were premised upon their accuracy.... In light of the weak congruence between gender and the characteristic or trait that gender purported to represent, it was necessary that the legislatures choose either to realign their substantive laws in a gender-neutral fashion, or to adopt procedures for identifying those instances where the sex-centered generalization actually comported with fact.... We turn then to the question whether, under Reed, the difference between males and females with respect to the purchase of 3.2% beer warrants the differential in age drawn by the Oklahoma statute. We conclude that it does not....

We accept for purposes of discussion the District Court's identification of the objective underlying §§ 241 and 245 as the enhancement of traffic safety. Clearly, the protection of public health and safety represents an important function of state and local governments. However, appellees' statistics in our view cannot support the conclusion that the gender-based distinction closely serves to achieve that objective and therefore the distinction cannot under Reed withstand equal protection challenge.... Even were this statistical evidence accepted as accurate, it nevertheless offers only a weak answer to the equal protection question presented here. The most focused and relevant of the statistical surveys, arrests of 18–20-year-olds for alcohol-related driving offenses, exemplifies the ultimate unpersuasiveness of this evidentiary record. Viewed in terms of the correlation between sex and the actual activity that Oklahoma seeks to regulate driving while under the influence of alcohol the statistics broadly establish that .18% of females and 2% of males in that age group were arrested for that offense. While such a disparity is not trivial in a statistical sense, it hardly can form the basis for employment of a gender line as a classifying device. Certainly if maleness is to serve as a proxy for drinking and driving, a correlation of 2% must be considered an unduly tenuous "fit." Indeed, prior cases have consistently rejected the use of sex as a decisionmaking factor even though the statutes in question certainly rested on far more predictive empirical relationships than this.

Moreover, the statistics exhibit a variety of other shortcomings that seriously impugn their value to equal protection analysis. Setting aside the obvious methodological problems, the surveys do not adequately justify the salient features of Oklahoma's gender-based traffic-safety law. None purports to measure the use and dangerousness of 3.2% beer as opposed to alcohol generally, a detail that is of particular importance since, in light of its low alcohol level, Oklahoma apparently considers the 3.2% beverage to be "nonintoxicating." ... Moreover, many of the studies, while graphically documenting the unfortunate increase in driving while under the influence of alcohol, make no effort to relate their findings to age-sex differentials as involved here. Indeed, the only survey that explicitly centered its attention upon young drivers and their use of beer albeit apparently not of the diluted 3.2% variety reached results that hardly can be viewed as impressive in justifying either a gender or age classification.

> FN14. The very social stereotypes that find reflection in age-differential laws, see Stanton v. Stanton (1975), are likely substantially to distort the accuracy of these comparative statistics. Hence "reckless" young men who drink and drive are transformed into arrest statistics, whereas their female counterparts are chivalrously escorted home.... Moreover, the Oklahoma surveys, gathered under a regime where the age-differential law in question has been in effect, are lacking in controls necessary for appraisal of the actual effectiveness of the male 3.2% beer prohibition. In this regard, the disproportionately high arrest statistics for young males and, indeed, the growing alcohol-related arrest figures for all ages and sexes simply may be taken to document the relative futility of controlling driving behavior by the 3.2% beer statute and like legislation, although we obviously have no means of estimating how many individuals, if any, actually were prevented from drinking by these laws.

There is no reason to belabor this line of analysis. It is unrealistic to expect either members of the judiciary or state officials to be well versed in the rigors of experimental or statistical technique. But this merely illustrates that proving broad sociological propositions by statistics is a dubious business, and one that inevitably is in tension with the normative philosophy that underlies the Equal Protection Clause. Suffice to say that the showing offered by the appellees does not satisfy us that sex represents a legitimate, accurate proxy for the regulation of drinking and driving. In fact, when it is further recognized that Oklahoma's statute prohibits only the selling of 3.2% beer to young males and not their drinking the beverage once acquired (even after purchase by their 18–20-year-old female companions), the relationship between gender and traffic safety becomes far too tenuous to satisfy Reed's requirement that the gender-based difference be substantially related to achievement of the statutory objective....

MR. JUSTICE STEVENS, concurring.

There is only one Equal Protection Clause. It requires every State to govern impartially. It does not direct the courts to apply one standard of review in some cases and a different standard in other cases. Whatever criticism may be leveled at a judicial opinion implying that there are at least three such standards applies with the same force to a double standard.

I am inclined to believe that what has become known as the two-tiered analysis of equal protection claims does not describe a completely logical method of deciding cases, but rather is a method the Court has employed to explain decisions that actually apply a single standard in a reasonably consistent fashion. I also suspect that a careful explanation of the reasons motivating particular decisions may contribute more to an identification of that standard than an attempt to articulate it in all-encompassing terms. It may therefore be appropriate for me to state the principal reasons which persuaded me to join the Court's opinion.

In this case, the classification is not as obnoxious as some the Court has condemned, nor as inoffensive as some the Court has accepted. It is objectionable because it is based on an accident of birth, because it is a mere remnant of the now almost universally rejected tradition of discriminating against males in this age bracket, and because, to the extent it reflects any physical difference between males and females, it is actually perverse. The question then is whether the traffic safety justification put forward by the State is sufficient to make an otherwise offensive classification acceptable.

> FN1. Men as a general class have not been the victims of the kind of historic, pervasive discrimination that has disadvantaged other groups.

The classification is not totally irrational. For the evidence does indicate that there are more males than females in this age bracket who drive and also more who drink. Nevertheless, there are several reasons why I regard the justification as unacceptable. It is difficult to believe that the statute was actually intended to cope with the problem of traffic safety, since it has only a minimal effect on access to a not very intoxicating beverage and does not prohibit its consumption. Moreover, the empirical data submitted by the State accentuate the unfairness of treating all 18–21-year-old males as inferior to their female counterparts. The legislation imposes a restraint on 100% of the males in the class allegedly because about 2% of them have probably violated one or more laws relating to the consumption of alcoholic beverages. It is unlikely that this law will have a significant deterrent effect either on that 2% or on the law-abiding 98%. But even assuming some such slight benefit, it does not seem to me that an insult to all of the young men of the State can be justified by visiting the sins of the 2% on the 98%.

MR. JUSTICE REHNQUIST, dissenting.

The Court's disposition of this case is objectionable on two grounds. First is its conclusion that men challenging a gender-based statute which treats them less favorably than women may invoke a more stringent standard of judicial review than pertains to most other types of classifications. Second is the Court's enunciation of this standard, without citation to any source, as being that "classifications by gender must serve important governmental objectives and must be substantially related to achievement of those objectives." ... The only redeeming feature of the Court's opinion, to my mind, is that it apparently signals a retreat by those who joined the plurality opinion in Frontiero v. Richardson, from their view that sex is a "suspect" classification for purposes of equal protection analysis. I think the Oklahoma statute challenged here need pass only the "rational basis" equal protection analysis expounded in cases such as McGowan v. Maryland (1961), and Williamson v. Lee Optical Co. (1955), and I believe that it is constitutional under that analysis.

In Frontiero v. Richardson, the opinion for the plurality sets forth the reasons of four Justices for concluding that sex should be regarded as a suspect classification for purposes of equal protection analysis. These reasons center on our Nation's "long and unfortunate history of sex discrimination," … which has been reflected in a whole range of restrictions on the legal rights of women, not the least of which have concerned the ownership of property and participation in the electoral process. Noting that the pervasive and persistent nature of the discrimination experienced by women is in part the result of their ready identifiability, the plurality rested its invocation of strict scrutiny largely upon the fact that "statutory distinctions between the sexes often have the effect of invidiously relegating the entire class of females to inferior legal status without regard to the actual capabilities of its individual members." …

Subsequent to Frontiero, the Court has declined to hold that sex is a suspect class, … and no such holding is imported by the Court's resolution of this case. However, the Court's application here of an elevated or "intermediate" level scrutiny, like that invoked in cases dealing with discrimination against females, raises the question of why the statute here should be treated any differently from countless legislative classifications unrelated to sex which have been upheld under a minimum rationality standard.…

Most obviously unavailable to support any kind of special scrutiny in this case, is a history or pattern of past discrimination, such as was relied on by the plurality in Frontiero to support its invocation of strict scrutiny. There is no suggestion in the Court's opinion that males in this age group are in any way peculiarly disadvantaged, subject to systematic discriminatory treatment, or otherwise in need of special solicitude from the courts.

The Court does not discuss the nature of the right involved, and there is no reason to believe that it sees the purchase of 3.2% beer as implicating any important interest, let alone one that is "fundamental" in the constitutional sense of invoking strict scrutiny. Indeed, the Court's accurate observation that the statute affects the selling but not the drinking of 3.2% beer … further emphasizes the limited effect that it has on even those persons in the age group involved. There is, in sum, nothing about the statutory classification involved here to suggest that it affects an interest, or works against a group, which can claim under the Equal Protection Clause that it is entitled to special judicial protection.

It is true that a number of our opinions contain broadly phrased dicta implying that the same test should be applied to all classifications based on sex, whether affecting females or males. E.g., Frontiero v. Richardson. However, before today, no decision of this Court has applied an elevated level of scrutiny to invalidate a statutory discrimination harmful to males, except where the statute impaired an important personal interest protected by the Constitution. There being no such interest here, and there being no plausible argument that this is a discrimination against females, the Court's reliance on our previous sex-discrimination cases is ill-founded. It treats gender classification as a talisman which without regard to the rights involved or the persons affected calls into effect a heavier burden of judicial review.

The Court's conclusion that a law which treats males less favorably than females "must serve important governmental objectives and must be substantially related to achievement of those objectives" apparently comes out of thin air. The Equal Protection Clause contains no such language, and none of our previous cases adopt that standard. I would think we have had enough difficulty with the two standards of review which our cases have recognized the norm of "rational basis," and the "compelling state interest" required where a "suspect classification" is involved so as to counsel weightily against the insertion of still another "standard" between those two. How is this Court to divine what objectives are important? How is it to determine whether a particular law is "substantially" related to the achievement of such objective, rather than related in some other way to its achievement? Both of the phrases used are so diaphanous and elastic as to invite subjective judicial preferences or prejudices relating to particular types of legislation, masquerading as judgments whether such legislation is directed at "important" objectives or, whether the relationship to those objectives is "substantial" enough.

I would have thought that if this Court were to leave anything to decision by the popularly elected branches of the Government, where no constitutional claim other than that of equal protection is invoked, it would be the decision as to what governmental objectives to be achieved by law are "important," and which are not. As for the second part of the Court's new test, the Judicial Branch is probably in no worse position than the Legislative or Executive Branches to determine if there is any rational relationship between a classification and the purpose which it might be thought to serve. But the introduction of the adverb "substantially" requires courts to make subjective judgments as to operational effects, for which neither their expertise nor their access to data fits them. And even if we manage to avoid both confusion and the mirroring of our own preferences in the development of this new doctrine, the thousands of judges in other courts who must interpret the Equal Protection Clause may not be so fortunate.

Review Questions and Explanations: *Craig*

1. The Court in *Craig* articulates for the first time what has come to be known as the "intermediate" standard of review. Identify the prongs of the test, and articulate how the majority justified creating and applying this new standard.

2. Justice Stevens and Chief Justice Rehnquist both object to the Court's creation of a new test, but do so for different reasons. Can you precisely articulate both justices' reasons for writing separately, as well as the differences between their two opinions?

3. After carefully articulating the tests preferred by Justice Stevens and Chief Justice Rehnquist, apply their respective tests to the facts presented in *Bradwell, Reed,* and *Frontiero.*

4. This would be a good point at which to consider the question posed at the beginning of this chapter: what work are the standards of review really doing in these cases? Do they guide the law, or are they legal-*sounding* standards that work as labels attached to conclusions reached for other reasons?

Professional Development Reflection Question

Justice Brennan, writing for a plurality of just four justices, adopts strict scrutiny in *Frontiero.* In *Craig,* he backs off of that, accepting intermediate scrutiny in order to security a majority opinion. Think for a moment about the ethics of this: if Justice Brennan believed that strict scrutiny was constitutionally compelled, should he have forfeited that position just to get five secure votes for a lesser but still heightened standard of review? How would you advise him if you were his law clerk?

Guided Reading Questions: *U.S. v. Virginia*

1. Pay close attention to how Justice Ginsburg describes and applies the intermediate standard of review. In particular, consider what role the "exceedingly

persuasive justification" language is playing. Is it part of the intermediate scrutiny test, a refinement of it, or something entirely new?

2. Note that the question actually presented in the case is whether Virginia's effort to remedy the problem created by VMI's exclusion of women was constitutionally adequate. Does this posture effect the outcome in any meaningful way?

United States v. Virginia

518 U.S. 515 (1996)

Majority: *Ginsburg*, Stevens, O'Connor, Kennedy, Souter, Breyer

Concurrence: *Rehnquist* (CJ) (omitted)

Dissent: *Scalia*

JUSTICE GINSBURG delivered the opinion of the Court.

Virginia's public institutions of higher learning include an incomparable military college, Virginia Military Institute (VMI). The United States maintains that the Constitution's equal protection guarantee precludes Virginia from reserving exclusively to men the unique educational opportunities VMI affords. We agree.

Founded in 1839, VMI is today the sole single-sex school among Virginia's 15 public institutions of higher learning. VMI's distinctive mission is to produce "citizen-soldiers," men prepared for leadership in civilian life and in military service. VMI pursues this mission through pervasive training of a kind not available anywhere else in Virginia. Assigning prime place to character development, VMI uses an "adversative method" modeled on English public schools and once characteristic of military instruction. VMI constantly endeavors to instill physical and mental discipline in its cadets and impart to them a strong moral code. The school's graduates leave VMI with heightened comprehension of their capacity to deal with duress and stress, and a large sense of accomplishment for completing the hazardous course.

VMI has notably succeeded in its mission to produce leaders; among its alumni are military generals, Members of Congress, and business executives. The school's alumni overwhelmingly perceive that their VMI training helped them to realize their personal goals. VMI's endowment reflects the loyalty of its graduates; VMI has the largest per-student endowment of all public undergraduate institutions in the Nation.

Neither the goal of producing citizen-soldiers nor VMI's implementing methodology is inherently unsuitable to women. And the school's impressive record in producing leaders has made admission desirable to some women. Nevertheless, Virginia has elected to preserve exclusively for men the advantages and opportunities a VMI education affords....

In contrast to the federal service academies, institutions maintained "to prepare cadets for career service in the armed forces," VMI's program "is directed at preparation for both military and civilian life"; "[o]nly about 15% of VMI cadets enter career military service....

VMI produces its "citizen-soldiers" through "an adversative, or doubting, model of education" which features "[p]hysical rigor, mental stress, absolute equality of treatment, absence of privacy, minute regulation of behavior, and indoctrination in desirable values." ... As one Commandant of Cadets described it, the adversative method " 'dissects the young student,'" and makes him aware of his " 'limits and capabilities,'" so that he knows " 'how far he can go with his anger, ... how much he can take under stress, ... exactly what he can do when he is physically exhausted.' " ...

VMI cadets live in spartan barracks where surveillance is constant and privacy nonexistent; they wear uniforms, eat together in the mess hall, and regularly participate in drills.... Entering students are incessantly exposed to the rat line, "an extreme form of the adversative model," comparable in intensity to Marine Corps boot camp.... Tormenting and punishing, the rat line bonds new cadets to their fellow sufferers and, when they have completed the 7-month experience, to their former tormentors....

VMI's "adversative model" is further characterized by a hierarchical "class system" of privileges and responsibilities, a "dyke system" for assigning a senior class mentor to each entering class "rat," and a stringently enforced "honor code," which prescribes that a cadet " 'does not lie, cheat, steal nor tolerate those who do.' " ... VMI attracts some applicants because of its reputation as an extraordinarily challenging military school, and "because its alumni are exceptionally close to the school." ... "[W]omen have no opportunity anywhere to gain the benefits of [the system of education at VMI]." ...

In 1990, prompted by a complaint filed with the Attorney General by a female high-school student seeking admission to VMI, the United States sued the Commonwealth of Virginia and VMI, alleging that VMI's exclusively male admission policy violated the Equal Protection Clause of the Fourteenth Amendment.... Trial of the action consumed six days and involved an array of expert witnesses on each side.... In the two years preceding the lawsuit, the District Court noted, VMI had received inquiries from 347 women, but had responded to none of them.... "[S]ome women, at least," the court said, "would want to attend the school if they had the opportunity." ... The court further recognized that, with recruitment, VMI could "achieve at least 10% female enrollment" — "a sufficient 'critical mass' to provide the female cadets with a positive educational experience." ... And it was also established that "some women are capable of all of the individual activities required of VMI cadets." ... In addition, experts agreed that if VMI admitted women, "the VMI ROTC experience would become a better training program from the perspective of the armed forces, because it would provide training in dealing with a mixed-gender army." ...

The District Court ruled in favor of VMI ... The Court of Appeals for the Fourth Circuit disagreed and vacated the District Court's judgment.... Remanding the case, the appeals court assigned to Virginia, in the first instance, responsibility for selecting a remedial course. The court suggested these options for the Commonwealth: Admit women to VMI; establish parallel institutions or programs; or abandon state support, leaving VMI free to pursue its policies as a private institution.... In response to the Fourth Circuit's ruling, Virginia proposed a parallel program for women: Virginia Women's Institute for Leadership (VWIL). The 4-year, state-sponsored undergraduate program would be located at Mary Baldwin College, a private liberal arts school for women, and would be open, initially, to about 25 to 30 students. Although VWIL would share VMI's mission — to produce "citizen-soldiers" — the VWIL program would differ, as does Mary Baldwin College, from VMI in academic offerings, methods of education, and financial resources....

The average combined SAT score of entrants at Mary Baldwin is about 100 points lower than the score for VMI freshmen.... Mary Baldwin's faculty holds "significantly fewer Ph.D.'s than the faculty at VMI," ... and receives significantly lower salaries.... While VMI offers degrees in liberal arts, the sciences, and engineering, Mary Baldwin, at the time of trial, offered only bachelor of arts degrees.... A VWIL student seeking to earn an engineering degree could gain one, without public support, by attending Washington University in St. Louis, Missouri, for two years, paying the required private tuition....

Experts in educating women at the college level composed the Task Force charged with designing the VWIL program; Task Force members were drawn from Mary Baldwin's own faculty and staff.... Training its attention on methods of instruction appropriate for "most women," the Task Force determined that a military model would be "wholly inappropriate" for VWIL....

VWIL students would participate in ROTC programs and a newly established, "largely ceremonial" Virginia Corps of Cadets but the VWIL House would not have a military format and VWIL would not require its students to eat meals together or to wear uniforms during the school day. In lieu of VMI's adversative method, the VWIL Task Force favored "a cooperative method which reinforces self-esteem." In addition to the standard bachelor of arts program offered at Mary Baldwin, VWIL students would take courses in leadership, complete an off-campus leadership externship, participate in community service projects, and assist in arranging a speaker series.

Virginia represented that it will provide equal financial support for in-state VWIL students and VMI cadets, ... and the VMI Foundation agreed to supply a $5.4625 million endowment for the VWIL program.... Mary Baldwin's own endowment is about $19 million; VMI's is $131 million.... Mary Baldwin will add $35 million to its endowment based on future commitments; VMI will add $220 million.... The VMI Alumni Association has developed a network of employers interested in hiring VMI graduates. The Association has agreed to open its network to VWIL graduates, ... but those graduates will not have the advantage afforded by a VMI degree....

The cross-petitions in this suit present two ultimate issues. First, does Virginia's exclusion of women from the educational opportunities provided by VMI-extraordinary opportunities for military training and civilian leadership development—deny to women "capable of all of the individual activities required of VMI cadets," ... the equal protection of the laws guaranteed by the Fourteenth Amendment? Second, if VMI's "unique" situation,—as Virginia's sole single-sex public institution of higher education—offends the Constitution's equal protection principle, what is the remedial requirement?

We note, once again, the core instruction of this Court's pathmarking decisions ... parties who seek to defend gender-based government action must demonstrate an "exceedingly persuasive justification" for that action.

Today's skeptical scrutiny of official action denying rights or opportunities based on sex responds to volumes of history. As a plurality of this Court acknowledged a generation ago, "our Nation has had a long and unfortunate history of sex discrimination." Frontiero. Through a century plus three decades and more of that history, women did not count among voters composing "We the People"; not until 1920 did women gain a constitutional right to the franchise.... And for a half century thereafter, it remained the prevailing doctrine that government, both federal and state, could withhold from women opportunities accorded men so long as any "basis in reason" could be conceived for the discrimination.

FN5: As Thomas Jefferson stated the view prevailing when the Constitution was new:

"Were our State a pure democracy ... there would yet be excluded from their deliberations ... [w]omen, who, to prevent depravation of morals and ambiguity of issue, could not mix promiscuously in the public meetings of men."

In 1971, for the first time in our Nation's history, this Court ruled in favor of a woman who complained that her State had denied her the equal protection of its laws. Reed v. Reed (holding unconstitutional Idaho Code prescription that, among "'several persons claiming and equally entitled to administer [a decedent's estate], males must be preferred to females'"). Since Reed, the Court has repeatedly recognized that neither federal nor state government acts compatibly with the equal protection principle when a law or official policy denies to women, simply because they are women, full citizenship stature—equal opportunity to aspire, achieve, participate in and contribute to society based on their individual talents and capacities....

Without equating gender classifications, for all purposes, to classifications based on race or national origin, the Court, in post-*Reed* decisions, has carefully inspected official action that closes a door or denies opportunity to women (or to men).... To summarize the Court's current directions for cases of official classification based on gender: Focusing on the differential treatment or denial of opportunity for which relief is sought, the reviewing court must determine whether the proffered justification is "exceedingly persuasive." The burden of justification is demanding and it rests entirely on the State.... The State must show "at least that the [challenged] classification serves 'important governmental objectives and that the discriminatory means employed' are 'substantially related to the achievement of those objectives.'" ... The justification must be genuine, not hypothesized or invented *post hoc* in response to litigation. And it must not rely on overbroad generalizations about the different talents, capacities, or preferences of males and females.

The heightened review standard our precedent establishes does not make sex a proscribed classification. Supposed "inherent differences" are no longer accepted as a ground for race or national origin classifications. See *Loving v. Virginia.* Physical differences between men and women, however, are enduring: "[T]he two sexes are not fungible; a community made up exclusively of one [sex] is different from a community composed of both." ...

"Inherent differences" between men and women, we have come to appreciate, remain cause for celebration, but not for denigration of the members of either sex or for artificial constraints on an individual's opportunity. Sex classifications may be used to compensate women "for particular economic disabilities [they have] suffered," ... to "promot[e] equal employment opportunity," ... to advance full development of the talent and capacities of our Nation's people. But such classifications may not be used, as they once were ... to create or perpetuate the legal, social, and economic inferiority of women.

Measuring the record in this case against the review standard just described, we conclude that Virginia has shown no "exceedingly persuasive justification" for excluding all women from the citizen-soldier training afforded by VMI. We therefore affirm the Fourth Circuit's initial judgment, which held that Virginia had violated the Fourteenth Amendment's Equal Protection Clause. Because the remedy proffered by Virginia—the Mary Baldwin VWIL program—does not cure the constitutional violation, *i.e.,* it does not provide equal opportunity, we reverse the Fourth Circuit's final judgment in this case.

The Fourth Circuit initially held that Virginia had advanced no state policy by which it could justify, under equal protection principles, its determination "to afford VMI's unique type of program to men and not to women." ... Virginia challenges that "liability" ruling and asserts two justifications in defense of VMI's exclusion of women. First, the Commonwealth contends, "single-sex education provides important educational benefits," ... and the option of single-sex education contributes to "diversity in educational approaches" ... Second, the Commonwealth argues, "the unique VMI method of character development and leadership training," the school's adversative approach, would have to be modified were VMI to admit women. We consider these two justifications in turn....

Single-sex education affords pedagogical benefits to at least some students, Virginia emphasizes, and that reality is uncontested in this litigation. Similarly, it is not disputed that diversity among public educational institutions can serve the public good. But Virginia has not shown that VMI was established, or has been maintained, with a view to diversifying, by its categorical exclusion of women, educational opportunities within the Commonwealth. In cases of this genre, our precedent instructs that "benign" justifications proffered in defense of categorical exclusions will not be accepted automatically; a tenable justification must describe actual state purposes, not rationalizations for actions in fact differently grounded....

> **FN8.** On this point, the dissent sees fire where there is no flame...."Both men and women can benefit from a single-sex education," the District Court recognized, although "the beneficial effects" of such education, the court added, apparently "are stronger among women than among men." ... The United States does not challenge that recognition ...:
>
>> The pluralistic argument for preserving all-male colleges is uncomfortably similar to the pluralistic argument for preserving all-white colleges.... The all-male college would be relatively easy to defend if it emerged from a world in which women were established as fully equal to men. But it does not. It is therefore likely to be a witting or unwitting device for preserving tacit assumptions of male superiority—assumptions for which women must eventually pay.

... In sum, we find no persuasive evidence in this record that VMI's male-only admission policy "is in furtherance of a state policy of 'diversity.'" ... No such policy, the Fourth Circuit observed, can be discerned from the movement of all other public colleges and universities in Virginia away from single-sex education.... That court also questioned "how one institution with autonomy, but with no authority over any other state institution, can give effect to a state policy of diversity among institutions." ... A purpose genuinely to advance an array of educational options, as the Court of Appeals recognized, is not served by VMI's historic and constant plan—a plan to "affor[d] a unique educational benefit only to males." ... However "liberally" this plan serves the Commonwealth's sons, it makes no provision whatever for her daughters. That is not *equal* protection.

Virginia next argues that VMI's adversative method of training provides educational benefits that cannot be made available, unmodified, to women. Alterations to accommodate women would necessarily be "radical," so "drastic," Virginia asserts, as to transform, indeed "destroy," VMI's program.... Neither sex would be favored by the transformation, Virginia maintains: Men would be deprived of the unique opportunity currently available to them; women would not gain that opportunity because their participation would "eliminat[e] the very aspects of [the] program that distinguish [VMI] from ... other institutions of higher education in Virginia." ...

The District Court forecast from expert witness testimony, and the Court of Appeals accepted, that coeducation would materially affect "at least these three aspects of VMI's program—physical training, the absence of privacy, and the adversative approach." ... And it is uncontested that women's admission would require accommodations, primarily in arranging housing assignments and physical training programs for female cadets.... It is also undisputed, however, that "the VMI methodology could be used to educate women." ... The District Court even allowed that some women may prefer it to the methodology a women's college might pursue.... "[S]ome women, at least, would want to attend [VMI] if they had the opportunity," the District Court recognized ... and "some women," the expert testimony established, "are capable of all of the individual activities required of VMI cadets...." The parties, furthermore, agree that "*some* women can meet the physical standards [VMI] now impose[s] on men." ... In sum, as the Court of Appeals stated, "neither the goal of producing citizen soldiers," VMI's *raison d'être,* "nor VMI's implementing methodology is inherently unsuitable to women." ...

It may be assumed, for purposes of this decision, that most women would not choose VMI's adversative method. As Fourth Circuit Judge Motz observed, however, in her dissent from the Court of Appeals' denial of rehearing en banc, it is also probable that "many men would not want to be educated in such an environment." ... (On that point, even our dissenting colleague might agree.) Education, to be sure, is not a "one size fits all" business. The issue, however, is not whether "women—or men—should be forced to attend VMI"; rather, the question is whether the Commonwealth can constitutionally deny to women who have the will and capacity, the training and attendant opportunities that VMI uniquely affords....

The notion that admission of women would downgrade VMI's stature, destroy the adversative system and, with it, even the school, is a judgment hardly proved, a prediction hardly different from other "self-fulfilling prophec[ies]," see Hogan, once routinely used to deny rights or opportunities. When women first sought admission to the bar and access to legal education, concerns of the same order were expressed.... Women's successful entry into the federal military academies, and their participation in the Nation's military forces, indicate that Virginia's fears for the future of VMI may not be solidly grounded. The Commonwealth's justification for excluding all women from "citizen-soldier" training for which some are qualified, in any event, cannot rank as "exceedingly persuasive," as we have explained and applied that standard.

> FN15. Inclusion of women in settings where, traditionally, they were not wanted inevitably entails a period of adjustment. As one West Point cadet squad leader recounted: "[T]he classes of '78 and '79 see the women as women, but the classes of '80 and '81 see them as classmates."

Virginia and VMI trained their argument on "means" rather than "end," and thus misperceived our precedent. Single-sex education at VMI serves an "important governmental objective," they maintained, and exclusion of women is not only "substantially related," it is essential to that objective. By this notably circular argument, the "straightforward" test [of Hogan] was bent and bowed.

The Commonwealth's misunderstanding and, in turn, the District Court's, is apparent from VMI's mission: to produce "citizen-soldiers," individuals imbued with love of learning, confident in the functions and attitudes of leadership, possessing a high sense of public service, advocates of the American democracy and free enterprise system, and ready ... to defend their country in time of national peril.

Surely that goal is great enough to accommodate women, who today count as citizens in our American democracy equal in stature to men. Just as surely, the Commonwealth's great goal is not substantially advanced by women's categorical exclusion, in total disregard of their individual merit, from the Commonwealth's premier "citizen-soldier" corps. Virginia, in sum, "has fallen far short of establishing the 'exceedingly persuasive justification,'" ... that must be the solid base for any gender-defined classification....

Virginia chose not to eliminate, but to leave untouched, VMI's exclusionary policy. For women only, however, Virginia proposed a separate program, different in kind from VMI and unequal in tangible and intangible facilities. Having violated the Constitution's equal protection requirement, Virginia was obliged to show that its remedial proposal "directly address[ed] and relate[d] to" the violation, ... the equal protection denied to women ready, willing, and able to benefit from educational opportunities of the kind VMI offers.... VWIL affords women no opportunity to experience the rigorous military training for which VMI is famed.... VWIL students participate in ROTC and a "largely ceremonial" Virginia Corps of Cadets, but Virginia deliberately did not make VWIL a military institute. The VWIL House is not a military-style residence and VWIL students need not live together throughout the 4-year program, eat meals together, or wear uniforms during the schoolday.... VWIL students thus do not experience the "barracks" life "crucial to the VMI experience," the spartan living arrangements designed to foster an "egalitarian ethic." ... "[T]he most important aspects of the VMI educational experience occur in the barracks," the District Court found, ... yet Virginia deemed that core experience nonessential, indeed inappropriate, for training its female citizen-soldiers.

VWIL students receive their "leadership training" in seminars, externships, and speaker series, ... episodes and encounters lacking the "[p]hysical rigor, mental stress, ... minute regulation of behavior, and indoctrination in desirable values" made hallmarks of VMI's citizen-soldier training.... Kept away from the pressures, hazards, and psychological bonding characteristic of VMI's adversative training, ... VWIL students will not know the "feeling of tremendous accomplishment" commonly experienced by VMI's successful cadets....

Virginia maintains that these methodological differences are "justified pedagogically," based on "important differences between men and women in learning and developmental needs," "psychological and sociological differences" Virginia describes as "real" and "not stereotypes." ... The Task Force charged with developing the leadership program for women, drawn from the staff and faculty at Mary Baldwin College, "determined that a military model and, especially VMI's adversative method, would be wholly inappropriate for educating and training *most women*." ... (noting Task Force conclusion that, while "some women would be suited to and interested in [a VMI-style experience]," VMI's adversative method "would not be effective for *women as a group*.") ...

As earlier stated, ... generalizations about "the way women are," estimates of what is appropriate for *most women*, no longer justify denying opportunity to women whose talent and capacity place them outside the average description. Notably, Virginia never asserted that VMI's method of education suits *most men*. It is also revealing that Virginia accounted for its failure to make the VWIL experience "the entirely militaristic experience of VMI" on the ground that VWIL "is planned for women who do not necessarily expect to pursue military careers." ... By that reasoning, VMI's "entirely militaristic" program would be inappropriate for men in general or *as a group*, for "[o]nly about 15% of VMI cadets enter career military service." ...

In contrast to the generalizations about women on which Virginia rests, we note again these dispositive realities: VMI's "implementing methodology" is not "inherently unsuitable to women," ... "some women ... do well under [the] adversative model," ... ; "some women, at least, would want to attend [VMI] if they had the opportunity," ... "some women are capable of all of the individual activities required of VMI cadets," ... and "can meet the physical standards [VMI] now impose[s] on men...." It is on behalf of these women that the United States has instituted this suit, and it is for them that a remedy must be crafted, a remedy that will end their exclusion from a state-supplied educational opportunity for which they are fit, a decree that will "bar like discrimination in the future."

In myriad respects other than military training, VWIL does not qualify as VMI's equal. VWIL's student body, faculty, course offerings, and facilities hardly match VMI's. Nor can the VWIL graduate anticipate the benefits associated with VMI's 157-year history, the school's prestige, and its influential alumni network.

Mary Baldwin College, whose degree VWIL students will gain, enrolls first-year women with an average combined SAT score about 100 points lower than the average score for

VMI freshmen.... The Mary Baldwin faculty holds "significantly fewer Ph.D.'s, ... and receives substantially lower salaries," ... than the faculty at VMI.

Mary Baldwin does not offer a VWIL student the range of curricular choices available to a VMI cadet. VMI awards baccalaureate degrees in liberal arts, biology, chemistry, civil engineering, electrical and computer engineering, and mechanical engineering.... VWIL students attend a school that "does not have a math and science focus," ... they cannot take at Mary Baldwin any courses in engineering or the advanced math and physics courses VMI offers....

For physical training, Mary Baldwin has "two multi-purpose fields" and "[o]ne gymnasium." ... VMI has "an NCAA competition level indoor track and field facility; a number of multi-purpose fields; baseball, soccer and lacrosse fields; an obstacle course; large boxing, wrestling and martial arts facilities; an 11-laps-to-the-mile indoor running course; an indoor pool; indoor and outdoor rifle ranges; and a football stadium that also contains a practice field and outdoor track." ...

Although Virginia has represented that it will provide equal financial support for in-state VWIL students and VMI cadets, ... and the VMI Foundation has agreed to endow VWIL with $5.4625 million, ... the difference between the two schools' financial reserves is pronounced. Mary Baldwin's endowment, currently about $19 million, will gain an additional $35 million based on future commitments; VMI's current endowment, $131 million—the largest public college per—student endowment in the Nation—will gain $220 million....

The VWIL student does not graduate with the advantage of a VMI degree. Her diploma does not unite her with the legions of VMI "graduates [who] have distinguished themselves" in military and civilian life ... and that closeness accounts, in part, for VMI's success in attracting applicants.... A VWIL graduate cannot assume that the "network of business owners, corporations, VMI graduates and non-graduate employers ... interested in hiring VMI graduates," ... will be equally responsive to her search for employment....

Virginia, in sum, while maintaining VMI for men only, has failed to provide any "comparable single-gender women's institution." ... Instead, the Commonwealth has created a VWIL program fairly appraised as a "pale shadow" of VMI in terms of the range of curricular choices and faculty stature, funding, prestige, alumni support and influence....

A prime part of the history of our Constitution, historian Richard Morris recounted, is the story of the extension of constitutional rights and protections to people once ignored or excluded. VMI's story continued as our comprehension of "We the People" expanded.... There is no reason to believe that the admission of women capable of all the activities required of VMI cadets would destroy the Institute rather than enhance its capacity to serve the "more perfect Union."

JUSTICE SCALIA, dissenting.

Today the Court shuts down an institution that has served the people of the Commonwealth of Virginia with pride and distinction for over a century and a half.... Much of the Court's opinion is devoted to deprecating the closed-mindedness of our forebears with regard to women's education, and even with regard to the treatment of women in areas that have nothing to do with education. Closed-minded they were—as every age is, including our own, with regard to matters it cannot guess, because it simply does not consider them debatable. The virtue of a democratic system with a First Amendment is that it readily enables the people, over time, to be persuaded that what they took for granted is not so, and to change their laws accordingly. That system is destroyed if the smug assurances of each age are removed from the democratic process and written into the Constitution. So to counterbalance the Court's criticism of our ancestors, let me say a word in their praise: They left us free to change. The same cannot be said of this most illiberal Court, which has embarked on a course of inscribing one after another of the current preferences of the society (and in some cases only the counter-majoritarian preferences of the society's law-trained elite) into our Basic Law. Today it enshrines the notion that no substantial educational value is to be served by an all-men's military academy—so that the decision by the people of Virginia to maintain such an institution denies equal protection to women who cannot attend that institution but can attend others. Since it is entirely clear that the Constitution of the United States—the old one—takes no sides in this educational debate, I dissent.

I shall devote most of my analysis to evaluating the Court's opinion on the basis of our current equal protection jurisprudence, which regards this Court as free to evaluate everything under the sun by applying one of three tests: "rational basis" scrutiny, intermediate scrutiny, or strict scrutiny. These tests are no more scientific than their names suggest, and a further element of randomness is added by the fact that it is largely up to us which test will be applied in each case. Strict scrutiny, we have said, is reserved for state "classifications based on race or national origin and classifications affecting fundamental rights."... It is my position that the term "fundamental rights" should be limited to "interest[s] traditionally protected by our society,"... but the Court has not accepted that view, so that strict scrutiny will be applied to the deprivation of whatever sort of right we consider "fundamental." We have no established criterion for "intermediate scrutiny" either, but essentially apply it when it seems like a good idea to load the dice. So far it has been applied to content-neutral restrictions that place an incidental burden on speech, to disabilities attendant to illegitimacy, and to discrimination on the basis of sex....

I have no problem with a system of abstract tests such as rational basis, intermediate, and strict scrutiny (though I think we can do better than applying strict scrutiny and intermediate scrutiny whenever we feel like it). Such formulas are essential to evaluating whether the new restrictions that a changing society constantly imposes upon private conduct comport with that "equal protection" our society has always accorded in the past. But in my view the function of this Court is to *preserve* our society's values regarding (among other things) equal protection, not to *revise* them; to prevent backsliding from the degree of restriction the Constitution imposed upon democratic government, not to prescribe, on our own authority, progressively higher degrees. For that reason it is my view that, whatever abstract tests we may choose to devise, they cannot supersede—and indeed ought to be crafted *so as to reflect*—those constant and unbroken national traditions that embody the people's understanding of ambiguous constitutional texts. More specifically, it is my view that "when a practice not expressly prohibited by the text of the Bill of Rights bears the endorsement of a long tradition of open, widespread, and unchallenged use that dates back to the beginning of the Republic, we have no proper basis for striking it down."...

The all-male constitution of VMI comes squarely within such a governing tradition. Founded by the Commonwealth of Virginia in 1839 and continuously maintained by it since, VMI has always admitted only men. And in that regard it has not been unusual. For almost all of VMI's more than a century and a half of existence, its single-sex status reflected the uniform practice for government-supported military colleges. Another famous Southern institution, The Citadel, has existed as a state-funded school of South Carolina since 1842. And all the federal military colleges—West Point, the Naval Academy at Annapolis, and even the Air Force Academy, which was not established until 1954—admitted only males for most of their history. Their admission of women in 1976 ... came not by court decree, but because the people, through their elected representatives, decreed a change.... In other words, the tradition of having government-funded military schools for men is as well rooted in the traditions of this country as the tradition of sending only men into military combat. The people may decide to change the one tradition, like the other, through democratic processes; but the assertion that either tradition has been unconstitutional through the centuries is not law, but politics-smuggled-into-law....

Today, however, change is forced upon Virginia, and reversion to single-sex education is prohibited nationwide, not by democratic processes but by order of this Court. Even while bemoaning the sorry, bygone days of "fixed notions" concerning women's education, ... the Court favors current notions so fixedly that it is willing to write them into the Constitution of the United States by application of custom-built "tests." This is not the interpretation of a Constitution, but the creation of one.

To reject the Court's disposition today, however, it is not necessary to accept my view that the Court's made-up tests cannot displace longstanding national traditions as the primary determinant of what the Constitution means. It is only necessary to apply honestly the test the Court has been applying to sex-based classifications for the past two decades. It is well settled, as Justice O'Connor stated some time ago for a unanimous Court, that we evaluate a statutory classification based on sex under a standard that lies "[b]etween th[e] extremes of rational basis review and strict scrutiny." ... Instead, however, the Court proceeds to interpret "exceedingly persuasive justification" in a fashion that contradicts the reasoning of Hogan and our other precedents.

That is essential to the Court's result, which can only be achieved by establishing that intermediate scrutiny is not survived if there are *some* women interested in attending VMI, capable of undertaking its activities, and able to meet its physical demands. Thus, the Court summarizes its holding as follows:

> In contrast to the generalizations about women on which Virginia rests, we note again these *dispositive* realities: VMI's implementing methodology is not *inherently* unsuitable to women; *some* women do well under the adversative model; *some* women, at least, would want to attend VMI if they had the opportunity; *some* women are capable of all of the individual activities required of VMI cadets and can meet the physical standards VMI now imposes on men.

Similarly, the Court states that "[t]he Commonwealth's justification for excluding all women from 'citizen-soldier' training for which some are qualified ... cannot rank as 'exceedingly persuasive'...." ...

Only the amorphous "exceedingly persuasive justification" phrase, and not the standard elaboration of intermediate scrutiny, can be made to yield this conclusion that VMI's single-sex composition is unconstitutional because there exist several women (or, one would have to conclude under the Court's reasoning, a single woman) willing and able to undertake VMI's program. Intermediate scrutiny has never required a least-restrictive-means analysis, but only a "substantial relation" between the classification and the state interests that it serves.... The reasoning in our other intermediate-scrutiny cases has similarly required only a substantial relation between end and means, not a perfect fit....

Not content to execute a *de facto* abandonment of the intermediate scrutiny that has been our standard for sex-based classifications for some two decades, the Court purports to reserve the question whether, even in principle, a higher standard (*i.e.*, strict scrutiny) should apply. "The Court has," it says, "*thus far* reserved most stringent judicial scrutiny for classifications based on race or national origin...," ... ; and it describes our earlier cases as having done no more than decline to "equat[e] gender classifications, *for all purposes,* to classifications based on race or national origin".... The wonderful thing about these statements is that they are not actually false—just as it would not be actually false to say that "our cases have thus far reserved the 'beyond a reasonable doubt' standard of proof for criminal cases," or that "we have not equated tort actions, for all purposes, to criminal prosecutions." But the statements are misleading, insofar as they suggest that we have not already categorically *held* strict scrutiny to be inapplicable to sex-based classifications....

The Court's intimations are particularly out of place because it is perfectly clear that, if the question of the applicable standard of review for sex-based classifications were to be regarded as an appropriate subject for reconsideration, the stronger argument would be not for elevating the standard to strict scrutiny, but for reducing it to rational-basis review. The latter certainly has a firmer foundation in our past jurisprudence: Whereas no majority of the Court has ever applied strict scrutiny in a case involving sex-based classifications, we routinely applied rational-basis review until the 1970s.... And of course normal, rational-basis review of sex-based classifications would be much more in accord with the genesis of heightened standards of judicial review, the famous footnote in United States v. Carolene Products Co., which said (intimatingly) that we did not have to inquire in the case at hand

> whether prejudice against discrete and insular minorities may be a special condition, which tends seriously to curtail the operation of those political processes ordinarily to be relied upon to protect minorities, and which may call for a correspondingly more searching judicial inquiry.

It is hard to consider women a "discrete and insular minorit[y]" unable to employ the "political processes ordinarily to be relied upon," when they constitute a majority of the electorate. And the suggestion that they are incapable of exerting that political power smacks of the same paternalism that the Court so roundly condemns....

With this explanation of how the Court has succeeded in making its analysis seem orthodox—and indeed, if intimations are to be believed, even overly generous to VMI-I now proceed to describe how the analysis should have been conducted. The question to be answered, I repeat, is whether the exclusion of women from VMI is "substantially related to an important governmental objective."

It is beyond question that Virginia has an important state interest in providing effective college education for its citizens. That single-sex instruction is an approach substantially related to that interest should be evident enough from the long and continuing history in this country of men's and women's colleges ... But besides its single-sex constitution, VMI is different from other colleges in another way. It employs a "distinctive educational method," sometimes referred to as the "adversative, or doubting, model of education." ... "Physical rigor, mental stress, absolute equality of treatment, absence of privacy, minute regulation of behavior, and indoctrination in desirable values are the salient attributes of the VMI educational experience." ... No one contends that this method is appropriate for all individuals; education is not a "one size fits all" business. Just as a State may wish to support junior colleges, vocational institutes, or a law school that emphasizes case practice instead of classroom study, so too a State's decision to maintain within its system one school that provides the adversative method is "substantially related" to its goal of good education. Moreover, it was uncontested that "if the state were to establish a women's VMI-type [*i.e.,* adversative] program, the program would attract an insufficient number of participants to make the program work," ... and it was found by the District Court that if Virginia were to include women in VMI, the school "would eventually find it necessary to drop the adversative system altogether...." Thus, Virginia's options were an adversative method that excludes women or no adversative method at all.

There can be no serious dispute that, as the District Court found, single-sex education and a distinctive educational method "represent legitimate contributions to diversity in the Virginia higher education system." ... As a theoretical matter, Virginia's educational interest would have been *best* served (insofar as the two factors we have mentioned are concerned) by six different types of public colleges—an all-men's, an all-women's, and a coeducational college run in the "adversative method," and an all-men's, an all-women's, and a coeducational college run in the "traditional method." But as a practical matter, of course, Virginia's financial resources, like any State's, are not limitless, and the Commonwealth must select among the available options. Virginia thus has decided to fund, in addition to some 14 coeducational 4-year colleges, one college that is run as an all-male school on the adversative model: the Virginia Military Institute....

Finally, the absence of a precise "all-women's analogue" to VMI is irrelevant.... Although there is no precise female-only analogue to VMI, Virginia has created during this litigation the Virginia Women's Institute for Leadership (VWIL), a state-funded all-women's program run by Mary Baldwin College. I have thus far said nothing about VWIL because it is, under our established test, irrelevant, so long as *VMI*'s all-male character is "substantially related" to an important state goal. But VWIL now exists, and the Court's treatment of it shows how far reaching today's decision is.

VWIL was carefully designed by professional educators who have long experience in educating young women. The program *rejects* the proposition that there is a "difference in the respective spheres and destinies of man and woman," ... and is designed to "provide an all-female program that will achieve substantially similar outcomes [to VMI's] in an all-female environment...." After holding a trial where voluminous evidence was submitted and making detailed findings of fact, the District Court concluded that "there is a legitimate pedagogical basis for the different means employed [by VMI and VWIL] to achieve the substantially similar ends." ... The Court of Appeals undertook a detailed review of the record and affirmed.... But it is Mary Baldwin College, which runs VWIL, that has made the point most succinctly:

> It would have been possible to develop the VWIL program to more closely resemble VMI, with adversative techniques associated with the rat line and barracks-like living quarters. Simply replicating an existing program would have required far less thought, research, and educational expertise. But such a facile approach would have produced a paper program with no real prospect of successful implementation....

... Under the constitutional principles announced and applied today, single-sex public education is unconstitutional. By going through the motions of applying a balancing test—asking whether the State has adduced an "exceedingly persuasive justification" for its sex-based classification—the Court creates the illusion that government officials in some future case will have a clear shot at justifying some sort of single-sex public education. Indeed, the Court seeks to create even a greater illusion than that: It purports to have said nothing of relevance to *other* public schools at all. "We address specifically and only an educational opportunity recognized ... as 'unique'" ...

The Supreme Court of the United States does not sit to announce "unique" dispositions. Its principal function is to establish *precedent*—that is, to set forth principles of law that every court in America must follow. As we said only this Term, we expect both ourselves and lower courts to adhere to the "*rationale* upon which the Court based the results of its earlier decisions." ... That is the principal reason we publish our opinions....

In an odd sort of way, it is precisely VMI's attachment to such old-fashioned concepts as manly "honor" that has made it, and the system it represents, the target of those who today succeed in abolishing public single-sex education. The record contains a booklet that all first-year VMI students (the so-called "rats") were required to keep in their possession at all times. Near the end there appears the following period piece, entitled "The Code of a Gentleman":

> Without a strict observance of the fundamental Code of Honor, no man, no matter how 'polished,' can be considered a gentleman. The honor of a gentleman demands the inviolability of his word, and the incorruptibility of his principles. He is the descendant of the knight, the crusader; he is the defender of the defenseless and the champion of justice ... or he is not a Gentleman.
>
> A Gentleman ...
>
> Does not discuss his family affairs in public or with acquaintances.
>
> Does not speak more than casually about his girl friend.
>
> Does not go to a lady's house if he is affected by alcohol. He is temperate in the use of alcohol.
>
> Does not lose his temper; nor exhibit anger, fear, hate, embarrassment, ardor or hilarity in public.
>
> Does not hail a lady from a club window.
>
> A gentleman never discusses the merits or demerits of a lady.
>
> Does not mention names exactly as he avoids the mention of what things cost.
>
> Does not borrow money from a friend, except in dire need. Money borrowed is a debt of honor, and must be repaid as promptly as possible. Debts incurred by a deceased parent, brother, sister or grown child are assumed by honorable men as a debt of honor.
>
> Does not display his wealth, money or possessions.
>
> Does not put his manners on and off, whether in the club or in a ballroom. He treats people with courtesy, no matter what their social position may be.
>
> Does not slap strangers on the back nor so much as lay a finger on a lady.
>
> Does not 'lick the boots of those above' nor 'kick the face of those below him on the social ladder.'
>
> Does not take advantage of another's helplessness or ignorance and assumes that no gentleman will take advantage of him.
>
> A Gentleman respects the reserves of others, but demands that others respect those which are his.
>
> A Gentleman can become what he wills to be.

I do not know whether the men of VMI lived by this code; perhaps not. But it is powerfully impressive that a public institution of higher education still in existence sought to have them do so. I do not think any of us, women included, will be better off for its destruction.

Review Questions and Explanations: *VMI*

1. Compare Justice Scalia's opinion in *VMI* to Justice Brennan's in *Reed* and Justice Bradley's in *Bradwell*. What vision of women's role in society does each justice have, and how does that vision influence his view of the constitutional question presented? Justice Scalia says that the majority is reading its view into the Constitution while he is not. In one sense, this certainly is correct, in that Justice Scalia is allowing decisions made by the elected branches of government to stand, while the majority is not. But consider the question at a deeper level. Given the doctrinal task in equal protection cases of determining what is and is not a sufficiently important state interest, how would *any* justice give substance to the clause without considering the appropriate role of woman in society?

2. Justice Ginsburg, writing for the majority in *VMI*, refuses to defer to the educational experts relied on by the state. Compare this to the deference to school authorities that Justice Breyer advocated for in his dissent in *Parents Involved*. Are these positions compatible?

E. Not-Quite-Suspect Classifications

As you will have realized when reading the above materials, when and if to designate something a "suspect" classification is a point of some contention on the Court. While giving heightened review to sex-based classifications no longer strikes many people as constitutionally extraordinary, the path to this point was not, as seen above, easy or straight.

But sex is not the only classification with which the Court has struggled. The next three cases explore the Court's efforts to decide how to review to classifications drawn on the basis of mental disability (*City of Cleburne*) and sexual orientation (*Romer* and *Lawrence*). When reading these cases, think about how the classifications drawn in these statutes are like and unlike classifications drawn on the basis of race and sex. Also consider the arguments for and against granting or denying heightened review in the below cases, and whether you find those arguments convincing. Finally, without spoiling any surprises, we can tell you that the Court purported to treat disability and sexual orientation as ordinary legislative classifications reviewed under the rational basis test. Yet they held that the challenged laws failed that test, striking them down as equal protection violations. Consider whether you agree with some commentators that these cases mark out a special category of rational basis analysis—sometimes referred to as "rational basis with bite."

Guided Reading Questions: *City of Cleburne* and *Romer v. Evans*

1. In *Cleburne* and *Romer*, the Court applies the rational basis test. Why doesn't the Court apply some form of heightened scrutiny? Is there an explanation given? If not, can you infer one?

2. Try to summarize the application of the rational basis test in each case. Why do the laws fail this test?

3. Do you think the Court applied some form of heightened scrutiny as a practical matter? Whether it did or not, should the Court have found either or both disability and sexual orientation to be suspect classes triggering heightened scrutiny?

City of Cleburne v. Cleburne Living Center

473 U.S. 432 (1985)

Majority: *White,* Powell, Rehnquist, O'Connor

Concurrence: *Stevens,* Burger (CJ)

Concurrence/Dissent: *Marshall,* Brennan, Blackmun

JUSTICE WHITE delivered the opinion of the Court.

A Texas city denied a special use permit for the operation of a group home for the mentally retarded, acting pursuant to a municipal zoning ordinance requiring permits for such homes. The Court of Appeals for the Fifth Circuit held that mental retardation is a "quasi-suspect" classification and that the ordinance violated the Equal Protection Clause because it did not substantially further an important governmental purpose. We hold that a lesser standard of scrutiny is appropriate, but conclude that under that standard the ordinance is invalid as applied in this case.

In July 1980, respondent Jan Hannah purchased a building at 201 Featherston Street in the city of Cleburne, Texas, with the intention of leasing it to Cleburne Living Center, Inc. (CLC), for the operation of a group home for the mentally retarded. It was anticipated that the home would house 13 retarded men and women, who would be under the constant supervision of CLC staff members. The house had four bedrooms and two baths, with a half bath to be added. CLC planned to comply with all applicable state and federal regulations.... The city informed CLC that a special use permit would be required for the operation of a group home at the site, and CLC accordingly submitted a permit application. In response to a subsequent inquiry from CLC, the city explained that under the zoning regulations applicable to the site, a special use permit, renewable annually, was required for the construction of "[h]ospitals for the insane or feeble-minded, or alcoholic [sic] or drug addicts, or penal or correctional institutions." ...

The city had determined that the proposed group home should be classified as a "hospital for the feebleminded." After holding a public hearing on CLC's application, the City Council voted 3 to 1 to deny a special use permit.... The District Court found that "[i]f the potential residents of the Featherston Street home were not mentally retarded, but the home was the same in all other respects, its use would be permitted under the city's zoning ordinance," and that the City Counsel's decision "was motivated primarily by the fact that the residents of the home would be persons who are mentally retarded." ... Even so, the District Court held the ordinance and its application constitutional. Concluding that no fundamental right was implicated and that mental retardation was neither a suspect nor a quasi-suspect classification, the court employed the minimum level of judicial scrutiny applicable to equal protection claims. The court deemed the ordinance, as written and applied, to be rationally related to the city's legitimate interests in "the legal responsibility of CLC and its residents, ... the safety and fears of residents in the adjoining neighborhood," and the number of people to be housed in the home....

The Equal Protection Clause of the Fourteenth Amendment commands that no State shall "deny to any person within its jurisdiction the equal protection of the laws," which is essentially a direction that all persons similarly situated should be treated alike.... Section 5 of the Amendment empowers Congress to enforce this mandate, but absent controlling congressional direction, the courts have themselves devised standards for determining the validity of state legislation or other official action that is challenged as denying equal protection. The general rule is that legislation is presumed to be valid and will be sustained if the classification drawn by the statute is rationally related to a legitimate state interest.... When social or economic legislation is at issue, the Equal Protection Clause allows the States wide latitude ... and the Constitution presumes that even improvident decisions will eventually be rectified by the democratic processes.

The general rule gives way, however, when a statute classifies by race, alienage, or national origin. These factors are so seldom relevant to the achievement of any legitimate state interest that laws grounded in such considerations are deemed to reflect prejudice and antipathy—a view that those in the burdened class are not as worthy or deserving as others. For these reasons and because such discrimination is unlikely to be soon rectified by legislative means, these laws are subjected to strict scrutiny and will be sustained only if they are suitably tailored to serve a compelling state interest.... Similar oversight by the courts is due when state laws impinge on personal rights protected by the Constitution....

Legislative classifications based on gender also call for a heightened standard of review. That factor generally provides no sensible ground for differential treatment. "[W]hat differentiates sex from such nonsuspect statuses as intelligence or physical disability ... is that the sex characteristic frequently bears no relation to ability to perform or contribute to society." Frontiero v. Richardson (1973). Rather than resting on meaningful considerations, statutes distributing benefits and burdens between the sexes in different ways very likely reflect outmoded notions of the relative capabilities of men and women. A gender classification fails unless it is substantially related to a sufficiently important governmental interest. Mississippi University for Women v. Hogan (1982); Craig v. Boren (1976). Because illegitimacy is beyond the individual's control and bears "no relation to the individual's ability to participate in and contribute to society," Mathews v. Lucas (1976), official discriminations resting on that characteristic are also subject to somewhat heightened review. Those restrictions "will survive equal protection scrutiny to the extent they are substantially related to a legitimate state interest." Mills v. Habluetzel (1982). We have declined, however, to extend heightened review to differential treatment based on age....

Against this background, we conclude for several reasons that the Court of Appeals erred in holding mental retardation a quasi-suspect classification calling for a more exacting standard of judicial review than is normally accorded economic and social legislation. First, it is undeniable, and it is not argued otherwise here, that those who are mentally retarded have a reduced ability to cope with and function in the everyday world. Nor are they all cut from the same pattern: as the testimony in this record indicates, they range from those whose disability is not immediately evident to those who must be constantly cared for. They are thus different, immutably so, in relevant respects, and the States' interest in dealing with and providing for them is plainly a legitimate one. How this large and diversified group is to be treated under the law is a difficult and often a technical matter, very much a task for legislators guided by qualified professionals and not by the perhaps ill-informed opinions of the judiciary. Heightened scrutiny inevitably involves substantive judgments about legislative decisions, and we doubt that the predicate for such judicial oversight is present where the classification deals with mental retardation.

Second, the distinctive legislative response, both national and state, to the plight of those who are mentally retarded demonstrates not only that they have unique problems, but also that the lawmakers have been addressing their difficulties in a manner that belies a continuing antipathy or prejudice and a corresponding need for more intrusive oversight by the judiciary....

Third, the legislative response, which could hardly have occurred and survived without public support, negates any claim that the mentally retarded are politically powerless in the sense that they have no ability to attract the attention of the lawmakers. Any minority can be said to be powerless to assert direct control over the legislature, but if that were a criterion for higher level scrutiny by the courts, much economic and social legislation would now be suspect.

Fourth, if the large and amorphous class of the mentally retarded were deemed quasi-suspect for the reasons given by the Court of Appeals, it would be difficult to find a principled way to distinguish a variety of other groups who have perhaps immutable disabilities setting them off from others, who cannot themselves mandate the desired legislative responses, and who can claim some degree of prejudice from at least part of the public at large. One need mention in this respect only the aging, the disabled, the mentally ill, and the infirm. We are reluctant to set out on that course, and we decline to do so.

Doubtless, there have been and there will continue to be instances of discrimination against the retarded that are in fact invidious, and that are properly subject to judicial correction under constitutional norms. But the appropriate method of reaching such instances is not to create a new quasi-suspect classification and subject all governmental action based on that classification to more searching evaluation. Rather, we should look to the likelihood that governmental action premised on a particular classification is valid as a general matter, not merely to the specifics of the case before us. Because mental retardation is a characteristic that the government may legitimately take into account in a wide range of decisions, and because both State and Federal Governments have recently committed themselves to assisting the retarded, we will not presume that any given legislative action, even one that disadvantages retarded individuals, is rooted in considerations that the Constitution will not tolerate.

Our refusal to recognize the retarded as a quasi-suspect class does not leave them entirely unprotected from invidious discrimination. To withstand equal protection review, legislation that distinguishes between the mentally retarded and others must be rationally related to a legitimate governmental purpose. This standard, we believe, affords government the latitude necessary both to pursue policies designed to assist the retarded in realizing their full potential, and to freely and efficiently engage in activities that burden the retarded in what is essentially an incidental manner. The State may not rely on a classification whose relationship to an asserted goal is so attenuated as to render the distinction arbitrary or irrational.... Furthermore, some objectives—such as "a bare ... desire to harm a politically unpopular group," ... are not legitimate state interests.... Beyond that, the mentally retarded, like others, have and retain their substantive constitutional rights in addition to the right to be treated equally by the law.

We turn to the issue of the validity of the zoning ordinance insofar as it requires a special use permit for homes for the mentally retarded. We inquire first whether requiring a special use permit for the Featherston home in the circumstances here deprives respondents of the equal protection of the laws. If it does, there will be no occasion to decide whether the special use permit provision is facially invalid where the mentally retarded are involved, or to put it another way, whether the city may never insist on a special use permit for a home for the mentally retarded in an R-3 zone. This is the preferred course of adjudication since it enables courts to avoid making unnecessarily broad constitutional judgments....

The constitutional issue is clearly posed. The city does not require a special use permit in an R-3 zone for apartment houses, multiple dwellings, boarding and lodging houses, fraternity or sorority houses, dormitories, apartment hotels, hospitals, sanitariums, nursing homes for convalescents or the aged (other than for the insane or feebleminded or alcoholics or drug addicts), private clubs or fraternal orders, and other specified uses. It does, however, insist on a special permit for the Featherston home, and it does so, as the District Court found, because it would be a facility for the mentally retarded. May the city require the permit for this facility when other care and multiple-dwelling facilities are freely permitted?

It is true, as already pointed out, that the mentally retarded as a group are indeed different from others not sharing their misfortune, and in this respect they may be different from those who would occupy other facilities that would be permitted in an R-3 zone without a special permit. But this difference is largely irrelevant unless the Featherston home and those who would occupy it would threaten legitimate interests of the city in a way that other permitted uses such as boarding houses and hospitals would not. Because in our view the record does not reveal any rational basis for believing that the Featherston home would pose any special threat to the city's legitimate interests, we affirm the judgment below insofar as it holds the ordinance invalid as applied in this case....

In the courts below the city also urged that the ordinance is aimed at avoiding concentration of population and at lessening congestion of the streets. These concerns obviously fail to explain why apartment houses, fraternity and sorority houses, hospitals and the like, may freely locate in the area without a permit. So, too, the expressed worry about fire hazards, the serenity of the neighborhood, and the avoidance of danger to other residents fail rationally to justify singling out a home such as 201 Featherston for the special use permit, yet imposing no such restrictions on the many other uses freely permitted in the neighborhood.

The short of it is that requiring the permit in this case appears to us to rest on an irrational prejudice against the mentally retarded, including those who would occupy the Featherston facility and who would live under the closely supervised and highly regulated conditions expressly provided for by state and federal law.

The judgment of the Court of Appeals is affirmed insofar as it invalidates the zoning ordinance as applied to the Featherston home. The judgment is otherwise vacated, and the case is remanded.

JUSTICE STEVENS, with whom THE CHIEF JUSTICE joins, concurring.

The Court of Appeals disposed of this case as if a critical question to be decided were which of three clearly defined standards of equal protection review should be applied to a legislative classification discriminating against the mentally retarded. In fact, our cases have not delineated three—or even one or two—such well-defined standards. Rather, our cases reflect a continuum of judgmental responses to differing classifications which have been explained in opinions by terms ranging from "strict scrutiny" at one extreme to "rational basis" at the other. I have never been persuaded that these so-called "standards" adequately explain the decisional process. Cases involving classifications based on alienage, illegal residency, illegitimacy, gender, age, or—as in this case—mental retardation, do not fit well into sharply defined classifications.

FN2. ... Commenting on the intermediate standard of review in his dissent in Craig v. Boren (1976), Justice REHNQUIST wrote:

I would think we have had enough difficulty with the two standards of review which our cases have recognized—the norm of 'rational basis,' and the 'compelling state interest' required where a 'suspect classification' is involved—so as to counsel weightily against the insertion of still another 'standard' between those two. How is this Court to divine what objectives are important? How is it to determine whether a particular law is 'substantially' related to the achievement of such objective, rather than related in some other way to its achievement? Both of the phrases used are so diaphanous and elastic as to invite subjective judicial preferences or prejudices relating to particular types of legislation, masquerading as judgments whether such legislation is directed at 'important' objectives or, whether the relationship to those objectives is 'substantial' enough.

"I am inclined to believe that what has become known as the [tiered] analysis of equal protection claims does not describe a completely logical method of deciding cases, but rather is a method the Court has employed to explain decisions that actually apply a single standard in a reasonably consistent fashion." Craig v. Boren (1976) (Stevens, J., concurring). In my own approach to these cases, I have always asked myself whether I could find a "rational basis" for the classification at issue. The term "rational," of course, includes a requirement that an impartial lawmaker could logically believe that the classification would serve a legitimate public purpose that transcends the harm to the members of the disadvantaged class. Thus, the word "rational" —for me at least—includes elements of legitimacy and neutrality that must always characterize the performance of the sovereign's duty to govern impartially.

The rational-basis test, properly understood, adequately explains why a law that deprives a person of the right to vote because his skin has a different pigmentation than that of other voters violates the Equal Protection Clause. It would be utterly irrational to limit the franchise on the basis of height or weight; it is equally invalid to limit it on the basis of skin color. None of these attributes has any bearing at all on the citizen's willingness or ability to exercise that civil right. We do not need to apply a special standard, or to apply "strict scrutiny," or even "heightened scrutiny," to decide such cases.

In every equal protection case, we have to ask certain basic questions. What class is harmed by the legislation, and has it been subjected to a "tradition of disfavor" by our laws? What is the public purpose that is being served by the law? What is the characteristic of the disadvantaged class that justifies the disparate treatment? In most cases the answer to these questions will tell us whether the statute has a "rational basis." The answers will result in the virtually automatic invalidation of racial classifications and in the validation of most economic classifications, but they will provide differing results in cases involving classifications based on alienage, gender, or illegitimacy. But that is not because we apply an "intermediate standard of review" in these cases; rather it is because the characteristics of these groups are sometimes relevant and sometimes irrelevant to a valid public purpose, or, more specifically, to the purpose that the challenged laws purportedly intended to serve.

JUSTICE MARSHALL, with whom JUSTICE BRENNAN and JUSTICE BLACKMUN join, concurring in the judgment in part and dissenting in part.

... The Court holds the ordinance invalid on rational-basis grounds and disclaims that anything special, in the form of heightened scrutiny, is taking place. Yet Cleburne's ordinance surely would be valid under the traditional rational-basis test applicable to economic and commercial regulation. In my view, it is important to articulate, as the Court does not, the facts and principles that justify subjecting this zoning ordinance to the searching review—the heightened scrutiny—that actually leads to its invalidation.... Because I dissent from this novel and truncated remedy, and because I cannot accept the Court's disclaimer that no "more exacting standard" than ordinary rational-basis review is being applied, ... I write separately....

The refusal to acknowledge that something more than minimum rationality review is at work here is, in my view, unfortunate in at least two respects. The suggestion that the traditional rational-basis test allows this sort of searching inquiry creates precedent for this Court and lower courts to subject economic and commercial classifications to similar and searching "ordinary" rational-basis review—a small and regrettable step back toward the days of Lochner v. New York (1905). Moreover, by failing to articulate the factors that justify today's "second order" rational-basis review, the Court provides no principled foundation for determining when more searching inquiry is to be invoked. Lower courts are thus left in the dark on this important question, and this Court remains unaccountable for its decisions employing, or refusing to employ, particularly searching scrutiny. Candor requires me to acknowledge the particular factors that justify invalidating Cleburne's zoning ordinance under the careful scrutiny it today receives.

I have long believed the level of scrutiny employed in an equal protection case should vary with "the constitutional and societal importance of the interest adversely affected and the recognized invidiousness of the basis upon which the particular classification is drawn." ... When a zoning ordinance works to exclude the retarded from all residential districts in a community, these two considerations require that the ordinance be convincingly justified as substantially furthering legitimate and important purposes....

First, the interest of the retarded in establishing group homes is substantial. The right to "establish a home" has long been cherished as one of the fundamental liberties embraced by the Due Process Clause. See Meyer v. Nebraska (1923). For retarded adults, this right means living together in group homes, for as deinstitutionalization has progressed, group homes have become the primary means by which retarded adults can enter life in the community.... Excluding group homes deprives the retarded of much of what makes for human freedom and fulfillment—the ability to form bonds and take part in the life of a community.

Second, the mentally retarded have been subject to a "lengthy and tragic history," University of California Regents v. Bakke (1978) (opinion of POWELL, J.), of segregation and discrimination that can only be called grotesque. During much of the 19th century, mental retardation was viewed as neither curable nor dangerous and the retarded were largely left to their own devices. By the latter part of the century and during the first decades of the new one, however, social views of the retarded underwent a radical trans-formation. Fueled by the rising tide of Social Darwinism, the "science" of eugenics, and the extreme xenophobia of those years, leading medical authorities and others began to portray the "feeble-minded" as a "menace to society and civilization ... responsible in a large degree for many, if not all, of our social problems." A regime of state-mandated seg-regation and degradation soon emerged that in its virulence and bigotry rivaled, and indeed paralleled, the worst excesses of Jim Crow. Massive custodial institutions were built to warehouse the retarded for life; the aim was to halt reproduction of the retarded and "nearly extinguish their race." Retarded children were categorically excluded from public schools, based on the false stereotype that all were ineducable and on the purported need to protect nonretarded children from them. State laws deemed the retarded "unfit for citizenship."

Romer v. Evans

517 U.S. 620 (1996)

Majority: *Kennedy*, Stevens, O'Connor, Souter, Ginsburg, Breyer

Dissent: *Scalia*, Rehnquist (CJ), Thomas

JUSTICE KENNEDY delivered the opinion of the Court.

One century ago, the first Justice Harlan admonished this Court that the Constitution "neither knows nor tolerates classes among citizens." Plessy v. Ferguson (1896) (dissenting opinion). Unheeded then, those words now are understood to state a commitment to the law's neutrality where the rights of persons are at stake. The Equal Protection Clause enforces this principle and today requires us to hold invalid a provision of Colorado's Constitution.

The enactment challenged in this case is an amendment to the Constitution of the State of Colorado, adopted in a 1992 statewide referendum. The parties and the state courts refer to it as "Amendment 2," its designation when submitted to the voters. The impetus for the amendment and the contentious campaign that preceded its adoption came in large part from ordinances that had been passed in various Colorado municipalities. For example, the cities of Aspen and Boulder and the city and County of Denver each had enacted ordinances which banned discrimination in many transactions and activities, including housing, employment, education, public accommodations, and health and welfare services.... What gave rise to the statewide controversy was the protection the ordinances afforded to persons discriminated against by reason of their sexual orientation. See Boulder Rev. Code § 12-1-1 (defining "sexual orientation" as "the choice of sexual partners, i. e., bisexual, homosexual or heterosexual"); Denver Rev. Municipal Code, Art. IV, § 28-92 (defining "sexual orientation" as "the status of an individual as to his or her hetero-sexuality, homosexuality or bisexuality"). Amendment 2 repeals these ordinances to the extent they prohibit discrimination on the basis of "homosexual, lesbian or bisexual orientation, conduct, practices or relationships."

Yet Amendment 2, in explicit terms, does more than repeal or rescind these provisions. It prohibits all legislative, executive or judicial action at any level of state or local government designed to protect the named class, a class we shall refer to as homosexual persons or gays and lesbians. The amendment reads:

> No Protected Status Based on Homosexual, Lesbian or Bisexual Orientation. Neither the State of Colorado, through any of its branches or departments, nor any of its agencies, political subdivisions, municipalities or school districts, shall enact, adopt or enforce any statute, regulation, ordinance or policy whereby homosexual, lesbian or bisexual orientation, conduct, practices or relationships shall constitute or otherwise be the basis of or entitle any person or class of persons to have or claim any minority status, quota preferences, protected status or claim of discrimination. This Section of the Constitution shall be in all respects self-executing.

... The trial court granted a preliminary injunction to stay enforcement of Amendment 2, and an appeal was taken to the Supreme Court of Colorado. Sustaining the interim injunction and remanding the case for further proceedings, the State Supreme Court held that Amendment 2 was subject to strict scrutiny under the Fourteenth Amendment because it infringed the fundamental right of gays and lesbians to participate in the political process.... To reach this conclusion, the state court relied on our voting rights cases ... and on our precedents involving discriminatory restructuring of governmental decisionmaking.... On remand, the State advanced various arguments in an effort to show that Amendment 2 was narrowly tailored to serve compelling interests, but the trial court found none sufficient. It enjoined enforcement of Amendment 2, and the Supreme Court of Colorado, in a second opinion, affirmed the ruling.... We granted certiorari, ... and now affirm the judgment, but on a rationale different from that adopted by the State Supreme Court.

The State's principal argument in defense of Amendment 2 is that it puts gays and lesbians in the same position as all other persons. So, the State says, the measure does no more than deny homosexuals special rights. This reading of the amendment's language is implausible....

Sweeping and comprehensive is the change in legal status effected by this law. So much is evident from the ordinances the Colorado Supreme Court declared would be void by operation of Amendment 2. Homosexuals, by state decree, are put in a solitary class with respect to transactions and relations in both the private and governmental spheres. The amendment withdraws from homosexuals, but no others, specific legal protection from the injuries caused by discrimination, and it forbids reinstatement of these laws and policies.

The change Amendment 2 works in the legal status of gays and lesbians in the private sphere is far reaching, both on its own terms and when considered in light of the structure and operation of modern antidiscrimination laws. That structure is well illustrated by contemporary statutes and ordinances prohibiting discrimination by providers of public accommodations. "At common law, innkeepers, smiths, and others who 'made profession of a public employment,' were prohibited from refusing, without good reason, to serve a customer." ... The duty was a general one and did not specify protection for particular groups. The common-law rules, however, proved insufficient in many instances, and it was settled early that the Fourteenth Amendment did not give Congress a general power to prohibit discrimination in public accommodations, Civil Rights Cases (1883). In consequence, most States have chosen to counter discrimination by enacting detailed statutory schemes.

Colorado's state and municipal laws typify this emerging tradition of statutory protection and follow a consistent pattern. The laws first enumerate the persons or entities subject to a duty not to discriminate. The list goes well beyond the entities covered by the common law. The Boulder ordinance, for example, has a comprehensive definition of entities deemed places of "public accommodation." They include "any place of business engaged in any sales to the general public and any place that offers services, facilities, privileges, or advantages to the general public or that receives financial support through solicitation of the general public or through governmental subsidy of any kind." ... The Denver ordinance is of similar breadth, applying, for example, to hotels, restaurants, hospitals, dental clinics, theaters, banks, common carriers, travel and insurance agencies, and "shops and stores dealing with goods or services of any kind...."

These statutes and ordinances also depart from the common law by enumerating the groups or persons within their ambit of protection. Enumeration is the essential device used to make the duty not to discriminate concrete and to provide guidance for those who must comply. In following this approach, Colorado's state and local governments have not limited antidiscrimination laws to groups that have so far been given the protection of heightened equal protection scrutiny under our cases.... Rather, they set forth an extensive catalog of traits which cannot be the basis for discrimination, including age, military status, marital status, pregnancy, parenthood, custody of a minor child, political affiliation, physical or mental disability of an individual or of his or her associates — and, in recent times, sexual orientation. . . .

Amendment 2 bars homosexuals from securing protection against the injuries that these public-accommodations laws address. That in itself is a severe consequence, but there is more. Amendment 2, in addition, nullifies specific legal protections for this targeted class in all transactions in housing, sale of real estate, insurance, health and welfare services, private education, and employment. . . .

Not confined to the private sphere, Amendment 2 also operates to repeal and forbid all laws or policies providing specific protection for gays or lesbians from discrimination by every level of Colorado government. The State Supreme Court cited two examples [a state executive order prohibiting employment discrimination against state on the basis of sexual orientation; and various provisions prohibiting discrimination based on sexual orientation at state colleges].

Amendment 2's reach may not be limited to specific laws passed for the benefit of gays and lesbians. It is a fair, if not necessary, inference from the broad language of the amendment that it deprives gays and lesbians even of the protection of general laws and policies that prohibit arbitrary discrimination in governmental and private settings. . . . At some point in the systematic administration of these laws, an official must determine whether homosexuality is an arbitrary and, thus, forbidden basis for decision. Yet a decision to that effect would itself amount to a policy prohibiting discrimination on the basis of homosexuality, and so would appear to be no more valid under Amendment 2 than the specific prohibitions against discrimination the state court held invalid.

If this consequence follows from Amendment 2, as its broad language suggests, it would compound the constitutional difficulties the law creates. . . . [W]e cannot accept the view that Amendment 2's prohibition on specific legal protections does no more than deprive homosexuals of special rights. To the contrary, the amendment imposes a special disability upon those persons alone. Homosexuals are forbidden the safeguards that others enjoy or may seek without constraint. They can obtain specific protection against discrimination only by enlisting the citizenry of Colorado to amend the State Constitution or perhaps, on the State's view, by trying to pass helpful laws of general applicability. This is so no matter how local or discrete the harm, no matter how public and widespread the injury. We find nothing special in the protections Amendment 2 withholds. These are protections taken for granted by most people either because they already have them or do not need them; these are protections against exclusion from an almost limitless number of transactions and endeavors that constitute ordinary civic life in a free society.

The Fourteenth Amendment's promise that no person shall be denied the equal protection of the laws must coexist with the practical necessity that most legislation classifies for one purpose or another, with resulting disadvantage to various groups or persons. . . . We have attempted to reconcile the principle with the reality by stating that, if a law neither burdens a fundamental right nor targets a suspect class, we will uphold the legislative classification so long as it bears a rational relation to some legitimate end. . . .

Amendment 2 fails, indeed defies, even this conventional inquiry. First, the amendment has the peculiar property of imposing a broad and undifferentiated disability on a single named group, an exceptional and, as we shall explain, invalid form of legislation. Second, its sheer breadth is so discontinuous with the reasons offered for it that the amendment seems inexplicable by anything but animus toward the class it affects; it lacks a rational relationship to legitimate state interests.

Taking the first point, even in the ordinary equal protection case calling for the most deferential of standards, we insist on knowing the relation between the classification adopted and the object to be attained. The search for the link between classification and objective gives substance to the Equal Protection Clause; it provides guidance and discipline for the legislature, which is entitled to know what sorts of laws it can pass; and it marks the limits of our own authority. In the ordinary case, a law will be sustained if it can be said to advance a legitimate government interest, even if the law seems unwise or works to the disadvantage of a particular group, or if the rationale for it seems tenuous.... The laws challenged in the cases just cited were narrow enough in scope and grounded in a sufficient factual context for us to ascertain some relation between the classification and the purpose it served. By requiring that the classification bear a rational relationship to an independent and legitimate legislative end, we ensure that classifications are not drawn for the purpose of disadvantaging the group burdened by the law....

Amendment 2 confounds this normal process of judicial review. It is at once too narrow and too broad. It identifies persons by a single trait and then denies them protection across the board. The resulting disqualification of a class of persons from the right to seek specific protection from the law is unprecedented in our jurisprudence. The absence of precedent for Amendment 2 is itself instructive; "discriminations of an unusual character especially suggest careful consideration to determine whether they are obnoxious to the constitutional provision."...

It is not within our constitutional tradition to enact laws of this sort. Central both to the idea of the rule of law and to our own Constitution's guarantee of equal protection is the principle that government and each of its parts remain open on impartial terms to all who seek its assistance. "'Equal protection of the laws is not achieved through indiscriminate imposition of inequalities.'"... Respect for this principle explains why laws singling out a certain class of citizens for disfavored legal status or general hardships are rare. A law declaring that in general it shall be more difficult for one group of citizens than for all others to seek aid from the government is itself a denial of equal protection of the laws in the most literal sense....

Laws of the kind now before us raise the inevitable inference that the disadvantage imposed is born of animosity toward the class of persons affected. "If the constitutional conception of 'equal protection of the laws' means anything, it must at the very least mean that a bare ... desire to harm a politically unpopular group cannot constitute a *legitimate* governmental interest."... Even laws enacted for broad and ambitious purposes often can be explained by reference to legitimate public policies which justify the incidental disadvantages they impose on certain persons. Amendment 2, however, in making a general announcement that gays and lesbians shall not have any particular protections from the law, inflicts on them immediate, continuing, and real injuries that outrun and belie any legitimate justifications that may be claimed for it. We conclude that, in addition to the far-reaching deficiencies of Amendment 2 that we have noted, the principles it offends, in another sense, are conventional and venerable; a law must bear a rational relationship to a legitimate governmental purpose ... and Amendment 2 does not.

The primary rationale the State offers for Amendment 2 is respect for other citizens' freedom of association, and in particular the liberties of landlords or employers who have personal or religious objections to homosexuality. Colorado also cites its interest in conserving resources to fight discrimination against other groups. The breadth of the Amendment is so far removed from these particular justifications that we find it impossible to credit them....

We must conclude that Amendment 2 classifies homosexuals not to further a proper legislative end but to make them unequal to everyone else. This Colorado cannot do. A State cannot so deem a class of persons a stranger to its laws. Amendment 2 violates the Equal Protection Clause, and the judgment of the Supreme Court of Colorado is affirmed.

JUSTICE SCALIA, with whom THE CHIEF JUSTICE and JUSTICE THOMAS join, dissenting.

The Court has mistaken a Kulturkampf for a fit of spite. The constitutional amendment before us here is not the manifestation of a "'bare ... desire to harm'" homosexuals, ... but is rather a modest attempt by seemingly tolerant Coloradans to preserve traditional sexual mores against the efforts of a politically powerful minority to revise those mores through use of the laws. That objective, and the means chosen to achieve it, are not only unimpeachable under any constitutional doctrine hitherto pronounced (hence the opinion's heavy reliance upon principles of righteousness rather than judicial holdings); they have been specifically approved by the Congress of the United States and by this Court.

In holding that homosexuality cannot be singled out for disfavorable treatment, the Court contradicts a decision, unchallenged here, pronounced only 10 years ago, see Bowers v. Hardwick (1986), and places the prestige of this institution behind the proposition that opposition to homosexuality is as reprehensible as racial or religious bias. Whether it is or not is *precisely* the cultural debate that gave rise to the Colorado constitutional amendment (and to the preferential laws against which the amendment was directed). Since the Constitution of the United States says nothing about this subject, it is left to be resolved by normal democratic means, including the democratic adoption of provisions in state constitutions. This Court has no business imposing upon all Americans the resolution favored by the elite class from which the Members of this institution are selected, pronouncing that "animosity" toward homosexuality ... is evil. I vigorously dissent.

The Colorado Supreme Court concluded] that "general laws and policies that prohibit arbitrary discrimination" would continue to prohibit discrimination on the basis of ho-mosexual conduct as well. This analysis, which is fully in accord with (indeed, follows inescapably from) the text of the constitutional provision, lays to rest such horribles, raised in the course of oral argument, as the prospect that assaults upon homosexuals could not be prosecuted. The amendment prohibits *special treatment* of homosexuals, and nothing more. It would not affect, for example, a requirement of state law that pensions be paid to all retiring state employees with a certain length of service; homosexual employees, as well as others, would be entitled to that benefit. But it would prevent the State or any municipality from making death-benefit payments to the "life partner" of a homosexual when it does not make such payments to the long-time roommate of a non-homosexual employee. Or again, it does not affect the requirement of the State's general insurance laws that customers be afforded coverage without discrimination unrelated to anticipated risk. Thus, homosexuals could not be denied coverage, or charged a greater premium, with respect to auto collision insurance; but neither the State nor any municipality could require that distinctive health insurance risks associated with homosexuality (if there are any) be ignored....

The only denial of equal treatment [the Court] contends homosexuals have suffered is this: They may not obtain *preferential* treatment without amending the state constitution. That is to say, the principle underlying the Court's opinion is that one who is accorded equal treatment under the laws, but cannot as readily as others obtain *preferential* treatment under the laws, has been denied equal protection of the laws. If merely stating this alleged "equal protection" violation does not suffice to refute it, our constitutional jurisprudence has achieved terminal silliness.

The central thesis of the Court's reasoning is that any group is denied equal protection when, to obtain advantage (or, presumably, to avoid disadvantage), it must have recourse to a more general and hence more difficult level of political decisionmaking than others. The world has never heard of such a principle, which is why the Court's opinion is so long on emotive utterance and so short on relevant legal citation. And it seems to me most unlikely that any multilevel democracy can function under such a principle. For *whenever* a disadvantage is imposed, or conferral of a benefit is prohibited, at one of the higher levels of democratic decisionmaking (*i. e.*, by the state legislature rather than local government, or by the people at large in the state constitution rather than the legislature), the affected group has (under this theory) been denied equal protection. To take the simplest of examples, consider a state law prohibiting the award of municipal contracts to relatives of mayors or city councilmen. Once such a law is passed, the group composed of such relatives must, in order to get the benefit of city contracts, persuade the state legislature—unlike all other citizens, who need only persuade the municipality. It is ridiculous to consider this a denial of equal protection, which is why the Court's theory is unheard of.

The Court might reply that the example I have given is *not* a denial of equal protection only because the same "rational basis" (avoidance of corruption) which renders constitutional the *substantive discrimination* against relatives (*i. e.*, the fact that they alone cannot obtain city contracts) also automatically suffices to sustain what might be called the *electoral-procedural discrimination* against them (*i. e.*, the fact that they must go to the state level to get this changed). This is of course a perfectly reasonable response, and would explain why "electoral-procedural discrimination" has not hitherto been heard of: A law that is valid in its substance is automatically valid in its level of enactment. But the Court cannot afford to make this argument, for as I shall discuss next, there is no doubt of a rational basis for the substance of the prohibition at issue here. The Court's entire novel theory rests upon the proposition that there is something *special*—something that cannot be justified by normal "rational basis" analysis—in making a disadvantaged group (or a nonpreferred group) resort to a higher decision-making level. That proposition finds no support in law or logic.

I turn next to whether there was a legitimate rational basis for the substance of the constitutional amendment—for the prohibition of special protection for homosexuals. 1 It is unsurprising that the Court avoids discussion of this question, since the answer is so obviously yes. The case most relevant to the issue before us today is not even mentioned in the Court's opinion: In Bowers v. Hardwick, we held that the Constitution does not prohibit what virtually all States had done from the founding of the Republic until very recent years—making homosexual conduct a crime. That holding is unassailable, except by those who think that the Constitution changes to suit current fashions. But in any event it is a given in the present case: Respondents' briefs did not urge overruling Bowers, and at oral argument respondents' counsel expressly disavowed any intent to seek such overruling.... If it is constitutionally permissible for a State to make homosexual conduct criminal, surely it is constitutionally permissible for a State to enact other laws merely *disfavoring* homosexual conduct....

[Even] assuming that, in Amendment 2, a person of homosexual "orientation" is someone who does not engage in homosexual conduct but merely has a tendency or desire to do so, Bowers still suffices to establish a rational basis for the provision. If it is rational to criminalize the conduct, surely it is rational to deny special favor and protection to those with a self-avowed tendency or desire to engage in the conduct. Indeed, where criminal sanctions are not involved, homosexual "orientation" is an acceptable stand-in for homosexual conduct. A State "does not violate the Equal Protection Clause merely because the classifications made by its laws are imperfect...." Just as a policy barring the hiring of methadone users as transit employees does not violate equal protection simply because *some* methadone users pose no threat to passenger safety, ... and just as a mandatory retirement age of 50 for police officers does not violate equal protection even though it prematurely ends the careers of many policemen over 50 who still have the capacity to do the job, ... Amendment 2 is not constitutionally invalid simply because it could have been drawn more precisely so as to withdraw special antidiscrimination protections only from those of homosexual "orientation" who actually engage in homosexual conduct. As Justice Kennedy wrote, when he was on the Court of Appeals, in a case involving discharge of homosexuals from the Navy: "Nearly any statute which classifies people may be irrational as applied in particular cases. Discharge of the particular plaintiffs before us would be rational, under minimal scrutiny, not because their particular cases present the dangers which justify Navy policy, but instead because the general policy of discharging all homosexuals is rational."...

Moreover, even if the provision regarding homosexual "orientation" *were* invalid, respondents' challenge to Amendment 2—which is a facial challenge—must fail.... It would not be enough for respondents to establish (if they could) that Amendment 2 is unconstitutional as applied to those of homosexual "orientation"; since, under Bowers, Amendment 2 is unquestionably constitutional as applied to those who engage in homosexual conduct, the facial challenge cannot succeed. Some individuals of homosexual "orientation" who do not engage in homosexual acts might successfully bring an as-applied challenge to Amendment 2, but so far as the record indicates, none of the respondents is such a person....

The Court's opinion contains grim, disapproving hints that Coloradans have been guilty of "animus" or "animosity" toward homosexuality, as though that has been established as un-American. Of course it is our moral heritage that one should not hate any human being or class of human beings. But I had thought that one could consider certain conduct reprehensible—murder, for example, or polygamy, or cruelty to animals—and could exhibit even "animus" toward such conduct. Surely that is the only sort of "animus" at issue here: moral disapproval of homosexual conduct, the same sort of moral disapproval that produced the centuries-old criminal laws that we held constitutional in Bowers. The Colorado amendment does not, to speak entirely precisely, prohibit giving favored status to people who are *homosexuals;* they can be favored for many reasons—for example, because they are senior citizens or members of racial minorities. But it prohibits giving them favored status *because of their homosexual conduct*—that is, it prohibits favored status *for homosexuality.*

But though Coloradans are, as I say, *entitled* to be hostile toward homosexual conduct, the fact is that the degree of hostility reflected by Amendment 2 is the smallest conceivable. The Court's portrayal of Coloradans as a society fallen victim to pointless, hate-filled "gay-bashing" is so false as to be comical. Colorado not only is one of the 25 States that have repealed their antisodomy laws, but was among the first to do so.... But the society that eliminates criminal punishment for homosexual acts does not necessarily abandon the view that homosexuality is morally wrong and socially harmful; often, abolition simply reflects the view that enforcement of such criminal laws involves unseemly intrusion into the intimate lives of citizens....

There is a problem, however, which arises when criminal sanction of homosexuality is eliminated but moral and social disapprobation of homosexuality is meant to be retained.

The Court cannot be unaware of that problem; it is evident in many cities of the country, and occasionally bubbles to the surface of the news, in heated political disputes over such matters as the introduction into local schools of books teaching that homosexuality is an optional and fully acceptable "alternative life style." The problem (a problem, that is, for those who wish to retain social disapprobation of homosexuality) is that, because those who engage in homosexual conduct tend to reside in disproportionate numbers in certain communities ... and, of course, care about homosexual-rights issues much more ardently than the public at large, they possess political power much greater than their numbers, both locally and statewide. Quite understandably, they devote this political power to achieving not merely a grudging social toleration, but full social acceptance, of homosexuality....

I do not mean to be critical of these legislative successes; homosexuals are as entitled to use the legal system for reinforcement of their moral sentiments as is the rest of society. But they are subject to being countered by lawful, democratic counter-measures as well.

That is where Amendment 2 came in. It sought to counter both the geographic concentration and the disproportionate political power of homosexuals by (1) resolving the controversy at the statewide level, and (2) making the election a single-issue contest for both sides. It put directly, to all the citizens of the State, the question: Should homosexuality be given special protection? They answered no. The Court today asserts that this most democratic of procedures is unconstitutional. Lacking any cases to establish that facially absurd proposition, it simply asserts that it *must* be unconstitutional, because it has never happened before....

The Court today ... employs a constitutional theory heretofore unknown to frustrate Colorado's reasonable effort to preserve traditional American moral values. The Court's stern disapproval of "animosity" towards homosexuality might be compared with what an earlier Court (including the revered Justices Harlan and Bradley) said in Murphy v. Ramsey (1885), rejecting a constitutional challenge to a United States statute that denied the franchise in federal territories to those who engaged in polygamous cohabitation:

> Certainly no legislation can be supposed more wholesome and necessary in the founding of a free, self-governing commonwealth, fit to take rank as one of the co-ordinate States of the Union, than that which seeks to establish it on the basis of the idea of the family, as consisting in and springing from the union for life of one man and one woman in the holy estate of matrimony; the sure foundation of all that is stable and noble in our civilization; the best guaranty of that reverent morality which is the source of all beneficent progress in social and political improvement.

I would not myself indulge in such official praise for heterosexual monogamy, because I think it no business of the courts (as opposed to the political branches) to take sides in this culture war.

But the Court today has done so, not only by inventing a novel and extravagant constitutional doctrine to take the victory away from traditional forces, but even by verbally disparaging as bigotry adherence to traditional attitudes.... When the Court takes sides in the culture wars, it tends to be with the knights rather than the villains—and more specifically with the Templars, reflecting the views and values of the lawyer class from which the Court's Members are drawn. How that class feels about homosexuality will be evident to anyone who wishes to interview job applicants at virtually any of the Nation's law schools. The interviewer may refuse to offer a job because the applicant is a Republican; because he is an adulterer; because he went to the wrong prep school or belongs to the wrong country club; because he eats snails; because he is a womanizer; because she wears real-animal fur; or even because he hates the Chicago Cubs. But if the interviewer should wish not to be an associate or partner of an applicant because he disapproves of the applicant's homosexuality, *then* he will have violated the pledge which the Association of American Law Schools requires all its member schools to exact from job interviewers: "assurance of the employer's willingness" to hire homosexuals.... This law-school view of what "prejudices" must be stamped out may be contrasted with the more plebeian attitudes that apparently still prevail in the United States Congress, which has been unresponsive to repeated attempts to extend to homosexuals the protections of federal civil rights laws.

Review Questions and Explanation: *Cleburne* and *Romer*

1. Are you convinced by the *Cleburne* majority opinion that disability should not be deemed a suspect class? Why or why not?

2. Is there a meaningful difference between (1) a law expressly imposing discriminatory treatment on gays and lesbians (e.g., a law banning gay or lesbian night clubs from a certain area of a city); (2) a law permitting private parties to engage in such discrimination (e.g., making it legal for a commercial landlord to deny a lease to a gay or lesbian night club); or (3) the law struck down in *Romer*?

3. What is Justice Scalia getting at in his *Romer* dissent? "Kulturkampf" is an unfortunate word choice, if Justice Scalia meant to suggest a legitimate subject of the kind of morals legislation that is classically within the police powers of the states and that does not trigger close judicial scrutiny. (It is German for "cultural struggle" and apparently derives from late-nineteenth century German laws discriminating against Catholics and the Catholic Church—laws that would be struck down using strict scrutiny under current American constitutional doctrine.) What view of gays and lesbians underlies the assertion that laws like that at issue in *Romer* can be enacted as routine morals legislation, like regulating gambling? Is there a counterpoint to this view in the majority opinion? If so, what is it?

4. Reconsider the following Guided Reading Question: Did the Court in fact apply heightened scrutiny in *Cleburne* or *Romer*? If no, should it have? If yes, should it have done so explicitly?

The next case, *Lawrence v. Texas*, also deals with gay rights. The majority opinion, written by Justice Kennedy, held that a Texas "sodomy" law violated the Due Process clause. Because of their focus on substantive due process, we presented the majority and dissenting opinions in *Lawrence* in Chapter 7. Here, we present Justice O'Connor's concurrence in the judgment, which argues that the case should have been decided on equal protection grounds. Turn back to that Chapter 7 to refresh your recollection of the facts of the case. Among its other significant aspects, *Lawrence* provides another illustration of how legislative classifications can be challenged under either due process or equal protection theories, or both.

Lawrence v. Texas

539 U.S. 558 (2003)

Majority: *Kennedy*, Stevens, Souter, Ginsburg, Breyer (omitted)

Concurrence in the judgment: *O'Connor*

Dissents: *Scalia*, Rehnquist (CJ), *Thomas* (both omitted)

JUSTICE O'CONNOR, concurring in the judgment.

The Court today overrules Bowers v. Hardwick, 478 U.S. 186 (1986). I joined Bowers, and do not join the Court in overruling it. Nevertheless, I agree with the Court that Texas' statute banning same-sex sodomy is unconstitutional. Rather than relying on the substantive component of the Fourteenth Amendment's Due Process Clause, as the Court does, I base my conclusion on the Fourteenth Amendment's Equal Protection Clause.

The Equal Protection Clause of the Fourteenth Amendment "is essentially a direction that all persons similarly situated should be treated alike." Cleburne v. Cleburne Living Center, Inc., 473 U.S. 432 (1985). Under our rational basis standard of review, "legislation is presumed to be valid and will be sustained if the classification drawn by the statute is rationally related to a legitimate state interest." Laws such as economic or tax legislation that are scrutinized under rational basis review normally pass constitutional muster, since "the Constitution presumes that even improvident decisions will eventually be rectified by the democratic processes." We have consistently held, however, that some objectives, such as "a bare ... desire to harm a politically unpopular group," are not legitimate state interests. When a law exhibits such a desire to harm a politically unpopular group, we have applied a more searching form of rational basis review to strike down such laws under the Equal Protection Clause.

We have been most likely to apply rational basis review to hold a law unconstitutional under the Equal Protection Clause where, as here, the challenged legislation inhibits personal relationships. In Department of Agriculture v. Moreno, for example, we held that a law preventing those households containing an individual unrelated to any other member of the household from receiving food stamps violated equal protection because the purpose of the law was to "'discriminate against hippies.'" The asserted governmental interest in preventing food stamp fraud was not deemed sufficient to satisfy rational basis review. In Eisenstadt v. Baird, we refused to sanction a law that discriminated between married and unmarried persons by prohibiting the distribution of contraceptives to single persons. Likewise, in Cleburne v. Cleburne Living Center, *supra*, we held that it was irrational for a State to require a home for the mentally disabled to obtain a special use permit when other residences—like fraternity houses and apartment buildings—did not have to obtain such a permit. And in Romer v. Evans, we disallowed a state statute that "impos[ed] a broad and undifferentiated disability on a single named group"—specifically, homosexuals.

The statute at issue here makes sodomy a crime only if a person "engages in deviate sexual intercourse with another individual of the same sex." Sodomy between opposite-sex partners, however, is not a crime in Texas. That is, Texas treats the same conduct differently based solely on the participants. Those harmed by this law are people who have a same-sex sexual orientation and thus are more likely to engage in behavior prohibited by § 21.06.

The Texas statute makes homosexuals unequal in the eyes of the law by making particular conduct—and only that conduct—subject to criminal sanction. It appears that prosecutions under Texas' sodomy law are rare. This case shows, however, that prosecutions under § 21.06 *do* occur. And while the penalty imposed on petitioners in this case was relatively minor, the consequences of conviction are not. It appears that petitioners' convictions, if upheld, would disqualify them from or restrict their ability to engage in a variety of professions, including medicine, athletic training, and interior design. Indeed, were petitioners to move to one of four States, their convictions would require them to register as sex offenders to local law enforcement.

And the effect of Texas' sodomy law is not just limited to the threat of prosecution or consequence of conviction. Texas' sodomy law brands all homosexuals as criminals, thereby making it more difficult for homosexuals to be treated in the same manner as everyone else.... Texas attempts to justify its law, and the effects of the law, by arguing that the statute satisfies rational basis review because it furthers the legitimate governmental interest of the promotion of morality. In Bowers, we held that a state law criminalizing sodomy as applied to homosexual couples did not violate substantive due process.... *Bowers* did not hold that moral disapproval of a group is a rational basis under the Equal Protection Clause to criminalize homosexual sodomy when heterosexual sodomy is not punished.

This case raises a different issue than *Bowers* whether, under the Equal Protection Clause, moral disapproval is a legitimate state interest to justify by itself a statute that bans homosexual sodomy, but not heterosexual sodomy. It is not. Moral disapproval of this group, like a bare desire to harm the group, is an interest that is insufficient to satisfy rational basis review under the Equal Protection Clause. See, *e.g.*, Department of Agriculture v. Moreno, 413 U.S., at 534, 93 S.Ct. 2821; Romer v. Evans, 517 U.S. Indeed, we have never held that moral disapproval, without any other asserted state interest, is a sufficient rationale under the Equal Protection Clause to justify a law that discriminates among groups of persons.

Moral disapproval of a group cannot be a legitimate governmental interest under the Equal Protection Clause because legal classifications must not be "drawn for the purpose of disadvantaging the group burdened by the law." Texas' invocation of moral disapproval as a legitimate state interest proves nothing more than Texas' desire to criminalize homosexual sodomy. But the Equal Protection Clause prevents a State from creating "a classification of persons undertaken for its own sake." And because Texas so rarely enforces its sodomy law as applied to private, consensual acts, the law serves more as a statement of dislike and disapproval against homosexuals than as a tool to stop criminal behavior. The Texas sodomy law "raise[s] the inevitable inference that the disadvantage imposed is born of animosity toward the class of persons affected."

Texas argues, however, that the sodomy law does not discriminate against homosexual persons. Instead, the State maintains that the law discriminates only against homosexual conduct. While it is true that the law applies only to conduct, the conduct targeted by this law is conduct that is closely correlated with being homosexual. Under such circumstances, Texas' sodomy law is targeted at more than conduct. It is instead directed toward gay persons as a class. "After all, there can hardly be more palpable discrimination against a class than making the conduct that defines the class criminal." When a State makes homosexual conduct criminal, and not "deviate sexual intercourse" committed by persons of different sexes, "that declaration in and of itself is an invitation to subject homosexual persons to discrimination both in the public and in the private spheres."

Indeed, Texas law confirms that the sodomy statute is directed toward homosexuals as a class. In Texas, calling a person a homosexual is slander *per se* because the word "homosexual" "impute[s] the commission of a crime." The State has admitted that because of the sodomy law, being homosexual carries the presumption of being a criminal. See State v. Morales, 826 S.W.2d, at 202–203 ("[T]he statute brands lesbians and gay men as criminals and thereby legally sanctions discrimination against them in a variety of ways unrelated to the criminal law"). Texas' sodomy law therefore results in discrimination against homosexuals as a class in an array of areas outside the criminal law. In Romer v. Evans, we refused to sanction a law that singled out homosexuals "for disfavored legal status." The same is true here. The Equal Protection Clause " 'neither knows nor tolerates classes among citizens.' " Id., at 623, 116 S.Ct. 1620 (quoting Plessy v. Ferguson, 163 U.S. 537 (1896) (Harlan, J., dissenting))....

"The framers of the Constitution knew, and we should not forget today, that there is no more effective practical guaranty against arbitrary and unreasonable government than to require that the principles of law which officials would impose upon a minority be imposed generally. Conversely, nothing opens the door to arbitrary action so effectively as to allow those officials to pick and choose only a few to whom they will apply legislation and thus to escape the political retribution that might be visited upon them if larger numbers were affected." Railway Express Agency, Inc., v. New York, 336 U.S. 106 (1949) (concurring opinion)....

A law branding one class of persons as criminal based solely on the State's moral disapproval of that class and the conduct associated with that class runs contrary to the values of the Constitution and the Equal Protection Clause, under any standard of review. I therefore concur in the Court's judgment that Texas' sodomy law banning "deviate sexual intercourse" between consenting adults of the same sex, but not between consenting adults of different sexes, is unconstitutional.

Review Questions and Explanations: *Lawrence* (O'Connor opinion)

1. Is there a practical difference between deciding *Lawrence* on equal protection grounds versus substantive due process grounds?

2. Write out the claim asserted in *Lawrence* in both equal protection and due process terms. Which claim seems stronger to you? Why?

Recap: Not-Quite-Suspect Classifications

1. As you have seen, the Court reviews classifications based on race and gender with heightened scrutiny, and does so regardless of whether the classification is meant to help or hurt the traditionally discriminated against group. You also have seen that the Court has declined to use heightened scrutiny to review classifications based on mental disability and—so far—sexual orientation. Are these decisions consistent? Can you create a list of criteria that explains the Court's decisions in each issue area?

2. Contrast the Court's consideration of sex-based classifications with its cases involving sexual orientation. Is the Court following the same path in the sexual orientation cases that it did in sex discrimination cases? In what ways are sex and sexual orientation alike and different? What is the legal relevance of the similarities and differences you have identified? Put them in the language of legal

doctrine, and then consider the strengths and weaknesses, for equal protection purposes, of the comparison.

3. Justice White, writing in *Cleburne,* explains that classifications based on mental disability do not warrant heightened judicial scrutiny because advocates for the mentally disabled have been able to obtain victories at the legislative level. He frames the issue like this: "[L]awmakers have been addressing their difficulties in a manner that belies a continuing antipathy or prejudice and a corresponding need for more intrusive oversight by the judiciary." This is not dissimilar from the point Justice Scalia makes, writing in dissent, in *Romer.* Justice Scalia, however, frames the issue in terms of a "politically powerful minority" that "possesses political power much greater than their numbers." Other than tone, is there any difference between the points being made by these two justices?

4. Do you agree with Justice O'Connor that *Lawrence* should have been decided under the Equal Protection clause rather than the Due Process clause?

Exercise: Equal Protection

In February 2004, the mayor of San Francisco instructed city and county officials to begin issuing marriage licenses to same sex couples. Thousands of such licenses were issued. The issuance of the licenses was challenged in the state courts. The California Supreme Court held that a state law prohibiting same sex couples from entering into state-recognized civil marriages violated the California Constitution. The California high Court found that the "equal respect and dignity" of marriage is a basic civil right that could not be withheld from same-sex couples. The court also held that, like race and sex, sexual orientation is a protected class and that any classification or discrimination on the basis of sexual orientation would be subject to strict scrutiny under the Equal Protection clause of the California constitution.

Reaction to the California court's decision was swift. Opponents of the decision immediately initiated a ballot drive. Under California law, the state constitution can be amended by referendum. The ballot initiative, which became known as Proposition 8, was descriptively titled *Eliminates Right of Same-Sex Couples to Marry Act.* The proposed constitutional amendment did just that: it inserted language into the state constitution limiting civil marriages to those between one man and one woman. The language did not affect civil unions conferring the legal benefits of marriage, which also were allowed under state law.

The proposed amendment appeared on the California general election ballot in November 2008. It passed with a 52% majority. The prohibition was then challenged in the federal courts. The challengers argued that the amendment to the state constitution violated both the Equal Protection clause and the Due Process clause of the U.S. Constitution.

Write a memo analyzing these claims. You have already studied the Due Process clause, so you can use this problem to refresh your recollection of what know about that doctrine. Reviewing your understanding of substantive due process will have the additional benefit of helping you understand how the Due Process clause and the Equal Protection clause embody distinct but related claims.

F. Equal Protection and Fundamental Rights

So far, our examination of the Equal Protection clause has focused on how that clause governs statutes drawing classifications between different groups, and which types of classifications are subject to more searching scrutiny. You will have noticed in the cases, however, that the justices frequently note that classifications drawn on suspect classes *or infringing fundamental rights* are subject to more exacting review. We now turn our attention to that issue.

As you learned in Chapter 7, many rights deemed "fundamental" for constitutional purposes are found in the Bill of Rights. Classifications that infringe on those rights are subject to strict scrutiny under the Equal Protection clause. Since such laws also directly infringe the specifically enumerated right in question, the equal protection analysis is often of secondary concern. Where strict scrutiny for classifications infringing fundamental rights has more punch is in classifications involving rights that are *not* explicitly enumerated in the Bill of Rights, but that nonetheless have been deemed fundamental by the Court. As you know from Chapter 7, infringements on such rights can be challenged under the Due Process clause; such challenges also sometimes can be brought under the Equal Protection clause. The main distinction between the two claims is that a due process challenge requires the state to justify the infringement itself, while an equal protection challenge requires the state to justify depriving one group of the right but not another group.

The next two cases examine the Court's work in this area. The first, *Harper v. Virginia,* shows the application of equal protection analysis to a classification affecting the right to vote. The second, *Rodriguez v. San Antonio School District,* involves whether or not the right to education should be deemed fundamental, thereby subjecting unequal deprivations of it to heightened review under the Equal Protection clause.

Guided Reading Questions: *Harper v. Virginia* and *San Antonio v. Rodriguez*

1. When reading *Harper* and *Rodriguez,* try to identify the key differences between the rights being asserted in each of these cases. Why does the Court deem voting fundamental and not education?

2. Both *Harper* and *Rodriguez* were decided before the Court fully articulated its multi-tiered system of review. In *Harper,* this means that the language of the Court does not map completely on to the tiered system laid out above. In *Rodriguez,* it gives us a chance to consider Justice Marshall's view on the then-evolving tiered system. Compare Justice Marshall's views to those expressed by Justice Stevens.

3. When reading *Harper* and *Rodriguez,* consider the differences between a due process claim that a state action infringes on a fundamental right and therefore warrants heightened review, and an equal protection claim asserting that a state action infringes a fundamental right and that the classification drawn within it must therefore satisfy heightened review.

Harper v. Virginia State Bd. of Elections

383 U.S. 663 (1966)

Majority: *Douglas*, Warren (CJ), Clark, Brennan, White, Fortas

Dissents: *Black*; *Harlan*, Stewart (both omitted)

JUSTICE DOUGLAS delivered the opinion of the Court.

These are suits by Virginia residents to have declared unconstitutional Virginia's poll tax. The three-judge District Court, feeling bound by our [earlier decisions] dismissed the complaint. The cases came here on appeal and we noted probable jurisdiction.

While the right to vote in federal elections is conferred by Art. I, s 2, of the Constitution, the right to vote in state elections is nowhere expressly mentioned. It is argued that the right to vote in state elections is implicit, particularly by reason of the First Amendment and that it may not constitutionally be conditioned upon the payment of a tax or fee. We do not stop to canvass the relation between voting and political expression. For it is enough to say that once the franchise is granted to the electorate, lines may not be drawn which are inconsistent with the Equal Protection Clause of the Fourteenth Amendment. That is to say, the right of suffrage 'is subject to the imposition of state standards which are not discriminatory and which do not contravene any restriction that Congress, acting pursuant to its constitutional powers, has imposed.' Lassiter v. Northampton County Board of Elections, 360 U.S. 45. We were speaking there of a state literacy test which we sustained, warning that the result would be different if a literacy test, fair on its face, were used to discriminate against a class. But the Lassiter case does not govern the result here, because, unlike a poll tax, the 'ability to read and write... has some relation to standards designed to promote intelligent use of the ballot.'

We conclude that a State violates the Equal Protection Clause of the Fourteenth Amendment whenever it makes the affluence of the voter or payment of any fee an electoral standard. Voter qualifications have no relation to wealth nor to paying or not paying this or any other tax. Our cases demonstrate that the Equal Protection Clause of the Fourteenth Amendment restrains the States from fixing voter qualifications which invidiously discriminate. Thus without questioning the power of a State to impose reasonable residence restrictions on the availability of the ballot we held that a State may not deny the opportunity to vote to a bona fide resident merely because he is a member of the armed services. 'By forbidding a soldier ever to controvert the presumption of non-residence, the Texas Constitution imposes an invidious discrimination in violation of the Fourteenth Amendment.' Previously we had said that neither homesite nor occupation 'affords a permissible basis for distinguishing between qualified voters within the State.' We think the same must be true of requirements of wealth or affluence or payment of a fee.

Long ago in Yick Wo v. Hopkins, the Court referred to 'the political franchise of voting' as a 'fundamental political right, because preservative of all rights.' Recently in Reynolds v. Sims, we said, 'Undoubtedly, the right of suffrage is a fundamental matter in a free and democratic society. Especially since the right to exercise the franchise in a free and unimpaired manner is preservative of other basic civil and political rights, any alleged infringement of the right of citizens to vote must be carefully and meticulously scrutinized.' There we were considering charges that voters in one part of the State had greater representation per person in the State Legislature than voters in another part of the State. We concluded:

A citizen, a qualified voter, is no more nor no less so because he lives in the city or on the farm. This is the clear and strong command of our Constitution's Equal Protection Clause. This is an essential part of the concept of a government of laws and not men. This is at the heart of Lincoln's vision of 'government of the people, by the people, (and) for the people.' The Equal Protection Clause demands no less than substantially equal state legislative representation for all citizens, of all places as well as of all races.

We say the same whether the citizen, otherwise qualified to vote, has $1.50 in his pocket or nothing at all, pays the fee or fails to pay it. The principle that denies the State the right to dilute a citizen's vote on account of his economic status or other such factors by analogy bars a system which excludes those unable to pay a fee to vote or who fail to pay.

It is argued that a State may exact fees from citizens for many different kinds of licenses; that if it can demand from all an equal fee for a driver's license, it can demand from all an equal poll tax for voting. But we must remember that the interest of the State, when it comes to voting, is limited to the power to fix qualifications. Wealth, like race, creed, or color, is not germane to one's ability to participate intelligently in the electoral process. Lines drawn on the basis of wealth or property, like those of race, are traditionally disfavored. To introduce wealth or payment of a fee as a measure of a voter's qualifications is to introduce a capricious or irrelevant factor. The degree of the discrimination is irrelevant. In this context—that is, as a condition of obtaining a ballot—the requirement of fee paying causes an 'invidious' discrimination that runs afoul of the Equal Protection Clause. Levy 'by the poll,' as stated in is an old familiar form of taxation; and we say nothing to impair its validity so long as it is not made a condition to the exercise of the franchise. Breedlove v. Suttles sanctioned its use as 'a prerequisite of voting.' To that extent the Breedlove case is overruled.

We agree, of course, with Mr. Justice Holmes that the Due Process Clause of the Fourteenth Amendment 'does not enact Mr. Herbert Spencer's Social Statics.' Likewise, the Equal Protection Clause is not shackled to the political theory of a particular era. In determining what lines are unconstitutionally discriminatory, we have never been confined to historic notions of equality, any more than we have restricted due process to a fixed catalogue of what was at a given time deemed to be the limits of fundamental rights. Notions of what constitutes equal treatment for purposes of the Equal Protection Clause do change. This Court in 1896 held that laws providing for separate public facilities for white and Negro citizens did not deprive the latter of the equal protection and treatment that the Fourteenth Amendment commands. Plessy v. Ferguson, 163 U.S. 537. Seven of the eight Justices then sitting subscribed to the Court's opinion, thus joining in expressions of what constituted unequal and discriminatory treatment that sound strange to a contemporary ear. When, in 1954—more than a half-century later—we repudiated the 'separate-but-equal' doctrine of Plessy as respects public education. We stated: 'In approaching this problem, we cannot turn the clock back to 1868 when the Amendment was adopted, or even to 1896 when Plessy v. Ferguson was written.'

We have long been mindful that where fundamental rights and liberties are asserted under the Equal Protection Clause, classifications which might invade or restrain them must be closely scrutinized and carefully confined. Those principles apply here. For to repeat, wealth or fee paying has, in our view, no relation to voting qualifications; the right to vote is too precious, too fundamental to be so burdened or conditioned.

Reversed.

JUSTICE BLACK, dissenting.

I think the interpretation that this Court gave the Equal Protection Clause in Breedlove was correct. The mere fact that a law results in treating some groups differently from others does not, of course, automatically amount to a violation of the Equal Protection Clause. To bar a State from drawing any distinctions in the application of its laws would practically paralyze the regulatory power of legislative bodies. Consequently 'The constitutional command for a state to afford "equal protection of the laws" sets a goal not attainable by the invention and application of a precise formula.' Voting laws are no exception to this principle. All voting laws treat some persons differently from others in some respects. Some bar a person from voting who is under 21 years of age; others bar those under 18. Some bar convicted felons or the insane, and some have attached a freehold or other property qualification for voting. The Breedlove case upheld a poll tax which was imposed on men but was not equally imposed on women and minors, and the Court today does not overrule that part of Breedlove which approved those discriminatory provisions. And in Lassiter v. Northampton Election Board, this Court held that state laws which disqualified the illiterate from voting did not violate the Equal Protection Clause. From these cases and all the others decided by this Court interpreting the Equal Protection Clause it is clear that some discriminatory voting qualifications can be imposed without violating the Equal Protection Clause.

A study of our cases shows that this Court has refused to use the general language of the Equal Protection Clause as though it provided a handily instrument to strike down state laws which the Court feels are based on bad governmental policy. The equal protection cases carefully analyzed boil down to the principle that distinctions drawn and even discriminations imposed by state laws do not violate the Equal Protection Clause so long as these distinctions and discriminations are not 'irrational,' 'irrelevant,' 'unreasonable,' 'arbitrary,' or 'invidious.' These vague and indefinite terms do not, of course, provide a precise formula or an automatic mechanism for deciding cases arising under the Equal Protection Clause. The restrictive connotations of these terms, however (which in other contexts have been used to expand the Court's power inordinately), are a plain recognition of the fact that under a proper interpretation of the Equal Protection Clause States are to have the broadest kind of leeway in areas where they have a general constitutional competence to act. In view of the purpose of the terms to restrain the courts from a wholesale invalidation of state laws under the Equal Protection Clause it would be difficult to say that the poll tax requirement is 'irrational' or 'arbitrary' or works 'invidious discriminations.' State poll tax legislation can 'reasonably,' 'rationally' and without an 'invidious' or evil purpose to injure anyone be found to rest on a number of state policies including (1) the State's desire to collect its revenue, and (2) its belief that voters who pay a poll tax will be interested in furthering the State's welfare when they vote. Certainly it is rational to believe that people may be more likely to pay taxes if payment is a prerequisite to voting. And if history can be a factor in determining the 'rationality' of discrimination in a state law ... then whatever may be our personal opinion, history is on the side of 'rationality' of the State's poll tax policy. Property qualifications existed in the Colonies and were continued by many States after the Constitution was adopted. Although I join the Court in disliking the policy of the poll tax, this is not in my judgment a justifiable reason for holding this poll tax law unconstitutional. Such a holding on my part would, in my judgment, be an exercise of power which the Constitution does not confer upon me....

I find no statement in the Court's opinion, however, which advances even a plausible argument as to why the alleged discriminations which might possibly be effected by Virginia's poll tax law are 'irrational,' 'unreasonable,' 'arbitrary,' or 'invidious' or have no relevance to a legitimate policy which the State wishes to adopt. The Court gives no reason at all to discredit the long-standing beliefs that making the payment of a tax a prerequisite to voting is an effective way of collecting revenue and that people who pay their taxes are likely to have a far greater interest in their government. The Court's failure to give any reasons to show that these purposes of the poll tax are 'irrational,' 'unreasonable,' 'arbitrary,' or 'invidious' is a pretty clear indication to me that none exist. I can only conclude that the primary, controlling, predominate, if not the exclusive reason for declaring the Virginia law unconstitutional is the Court's deep-seated hostility and antagonism, which I share, to making payment of a tax a prerequisite to voting.

San Antonio Independent School District v. Rodriguez
411 U.S. 1 (1973)

Majority: *Powell*, Burger (CJ), Rehnquist, Blackmun

Concurrence: *Stewart* (omitted)

Dissent: *Marshall*, Douglas; *Brennan* (omitted); *White* (omitted)

MR. JUSTICE POWELL delivered the opinion of the Court.

This suit attacking the Texas system of financing public education was initiated by Mexican-American parents whose children attend the elementary and secondary schools in the Edgewood Independent School District, an urban school district in San Antonio, Texas. They brought a class action on behalf of schoolchildren throughout the State who are members of minority groups or who are poor and reside in school districts having a low property tax base. Named as defendants were the State Board of Education, the Commissioner of Education, the State Attorney General, and the Bexar County (San Antonio) Board of Trustees. The complaint was filed in the summer of 1968 and a three-judge court was impaneled in January 1969. In December 1971 the panel rendered its judgment in a per curiam opinion holding the Texas school finance system unconstitutional under the Equal Protection Clause of the Fourteenth Amendment. The State appealed, and we noted probable jurisdiction to consider the far-reaching constitutional questions presented. For the reasons stated in this opinion, we reverse the decision of the District Court....

Until recent times, Texas was a predominantly rural State and its population and property wealth were spread relatively evenly across the State. Sizable differences in the value of assessable property between local school districts became increasingly evident as the State became more industrialized and as rural-to-urban population shifts became more pronounced. The location of commercial and industrial property began to play a significant role in determining the amount of tax resources available to each school district. These growing disparities in population and taxable property between districts were responsible in part for increasingly notable differences in levels of local expenditure for education....

The school district in which appellees reside, the Edgewood Independent School District, has been compared throughout this litigation with the Alamo Heights Independent School District. This comparison between the least and most affluent districts in the San Antonio area serves to illustrate the manner in which the dual system of finance operates and to indicate the extent to which substantial disparities exist despite the State's impressive progress in recent years....

Substantial interdistrict disparities in school expenditures found by the District Court to prevail in San Antonio and in varying degrees throughout the State still exist. And it was these disparities, largely attributable to differences in the amounts of money collected through local property taxation, that led the District Court to conclude that Texas' dual system of public school financing violated the Equal Protection Clause. The District Court held that the Texas system discriminates on the basis of wealth in the manner in which education is provided for its people. Finding that wealth is a 'suspect' classification and that education is a 'fundamental' interest, the District Court held that the Texas system could be sustained only if the State could show that it was premised upon some compelling state interest. On this issue the court concluded that '(n)ot only are defendants unable to demonstrate compelling state interests ... they fail even to establish a reasonable basis for these classifications.'...

Texas virtually concedes that its historically rooted dual system of financing education could not withstanding the strict judicial scrutiny that this Court has found appropriate in reviewing legislative judgments that interfere with fundamental constitutional rights or that involve suspect classifications.... The precedents of this Court provide the proper starting point. The individuals, or groups of individuals, who constituted the class discriminated against in our prior cases shared two distinguishing characteristics: because of their impecunity they were completely unable to pay for some desired benefit, and as a consequence, they sustained an absolute deprivation of a meaningful opportunity to enjoy that benefit....

[I]t is clear that appellees' suit asks this Court to extend its most exacting scrutiny to review a system that allegedly discriminates against a large, diverse, and amorphous class, unified only by the common factor of residence in districts that happen to have less taxable wealth than other districts. The system of alleged discrimination and the class it defines have none of the traditional indicia of suspectness: the class is not saddled with such disabilities, or subjected to such a history of purposeful unequal treatment, or relegated to such a position of political powerlessness as to command extraordinary protection from the majoritarian political process.

We thus conclude that the Texas system does not operate to the peculiar disadvantage of any suspect class. But in recognition of the fact that this Court has never heretofore held that wealth discrimination alone provides an adequate basis for invoking strict scrutiny, appellees have not relied solely on this contention. They also assert that the State's system impermissibly interferes with the exercise of a 'fundamental' right and that accordingly the prior decisions of this Court require the application of the strict standard of judicial review....

We agree with the court below that 'the grave significance of education both to the individual and to our society' cannot be doubted. But the importance of a service performed by the State does not determine whether it must be regarded as fundamental for purposes of examination under the Equal Protection Clause....

It is not the province of this Court to create substantive constitutional rights in the name of guaranteeing equal protection of the laws. Thus, the key to discovering whether education is 'fundamental' is not to be found in comparisons of the relative societal significance of education as opposed to subsistence or housing. Nor is it to be found by weighing whether education is as important as the right to travel. Rather, the answer lies in assessing whether there is a right to education explicitly or implicitly guaranteed by the Constitution....

Education, of course, is not among the rights afforded explicit protection under our Federal Constitution. Nor do we find any basis for saying it is implicitly so protected. As we have said, the undisputed importance of education will not alone cause this Court to depart from the usual standard for reviewing a State's social and economic legislation. It is appellees' contention, however, that education is distinguishable from other services and benefits provided by the State because it bears a peculiarly close relationship to other rights and liberties accorded protection under the Constitution. Specifically, they insist that education is itself a fundamental personal right because it is essential to the effective exercise of First Amendment freedoms and to intelligent utilization of the right to vote. In asserting a nexus between speech and education, appellees urge that the right to speak is meaningless unless the speaker is capable of articulating his thoughts intelligently and persuasively. The 'marketplace of ideas' is an empty forum for those lacking basic communicative tools. Likewise, they argue that the corollary right to receive information becomes little more than a hollow privilege when the recipient has not been taught to read, assimilate, and utilize available knowledge....

Even if it were conceded that some identifiable quantum of education is a constitutionally protected prerequisite to the meaningful exercise of either [First Amendment rights or the right to vote] we have no indication that the present levels of educational expenditures in Texas provide an education that falls short. Whatever merit appellees' argument might have if a State's financing system occasioned an absolute denial of educational opportunities to any of its children, that argument provides no basis for finding an interference with fundamental rights where only relative differences in spending levels are involved and where—as is true in the present case—no charge fairly could be made that the system fails to provide each child with an opportunity to acquire the basic minimal skills necessary for the enjoyment of the rights of speech and of full participation in the political process.

It should be clear, for the reasons stated above and in accord with the prior decisions of this Court, that this is not a case in which the challenged state action must be subjected to the searching judicial scrutiny reserved for laws that create suspect classifications or impinge upon constitutionally protected rights.... The foregoing considerations buttress our conclusion that Texas' system of public school finance is an inappropriate candidate for strict judicial scrutiny. These same considerations are relevant to the determination whether that system, with its conceded imperfections, nevertheless bears some rational relationship to a legitimate state purpose. It is to this question that we next turn our attention.

[T]o the extent that the Texas system of school financing results in unequal expenditures between children who happen to reside in different districts, we cannot say that such disparities are the product of a system that is so irrational as to be invidiously discriminatory.... The Texas plan is not the result of hurried, ill-conceived legislation. It certainly is not the product of purposeful discrimination against any group or class. On the contrary, it is rooted in decades of experience in Texas and elsewhere, and in major part is the product of responsible studies by qualified people.... The constitutional standard under the Equal Protection Clause is whether the challenged state action rationally furthers a legitimate state purpose or interest. We hold that the Texas plan abundantly satisfies this standard.

Mr. Justice MARSHALL, with whom Mr. Justice DOUGLAS concurs, dissenting.

The Court today decides, in effect, that a State may constitutionally vary the quality of education which it offers its children in accordance with the amount of taxable wealth located in the school districts within which they reside.

A number of theories of discrimination have, to be sure, been considered in the course of this litigation. Thus, the District Court found that in Texas the poor and minority group members tend to live in property-poor districts, suggesting discrimination on the basis of both personal wealth and race. The Court goes to great lengths to discredit the data upon which the District Court relied, and thereby its conclusion that poor people live in property-poor districts. Although I have serious doubts as to the correctness of the Court's analysis in rejecting the data submitted below, I have no need to join issue on these factual disputes. I believe it is sufficient that the overarching form of discrimination in this case is between the schoolchildren of Texas on the basis of the taxable property wealth of the districts in which they happen to live.

To understand both the precise nature of this discrimination and the parameters of the disadvantaged class it is sufficient to consider the constitutional principle which appellees contend is controlling in the context of educational financing. In their complaint appellees asserted that the Constitution does not permit local district wealth to be determinative of educational opportunity. This is simply another way of saying, as the District Court concluded, that consistent with the guarantee of equal protection of the laws, 'the quality of public education may not be a function of wealth, other than the wealth of the state as a whole.' Under such a principle, the children of a district are excessively advantaged if that district has more taxable property per pupil than the average amount of taxable property per pupil considering the State as a whole. By contrast, the children of a district are disadvantaged if that district has less taxable property per pupil than the state average....

To begin, I must once more voice my disagreement with the Court's rigidified approach to equal protection analysis. The Court apparently seeks to establish today that equal protection cases fall into one of two neat categories which dictate the appropriate standard of review-strict scrutiny or mere rationality. But this Court's decisions in the field of equal protection defy such easy categorization. A principled reading of what this Court has done reveals that it has applied a spectrum of standards in reviewing discrimination allegedly violative of the Equal Protection Clause. This spectrum clearly comprehends variations in the degree of care with which the Court will scrutinize particular classifications, depending, I believe, on the constitutional and societal importance of the interest adversely affected and the recognized invidiousness of the basis upon which the particular classification is drawn. I find in fact that many of the Court's recent decisions embody the very sort of reasoned approach to equal protection analysis for which I previously argued—that is, an approach in which 'concentration [is] placed upon the character of the classification in question, the relative importance to individuals in the class discriminated against of the governmental benefits that they do not receive, and the asserted state interests in support of the classification.'

I therefore cannot accept the majority's labored efforts to demonstrate that fundamental interests, which call for strict scrutiny of the challenged classification, encompass only established rights which we are somehow bound to recognize from the text of the Constitution itself. To be sure, some interests which the Court has deemed to be fundamental for purposes of equal protection analysis are themselves constitutionally protected rights. Thus, discrimination against the guaranteed right of freedom of speech has called for strict judicial scrutiny. Further, every citizen's right to travel interstate, although nowhere expressly mentioned in the Constitution, has long been recognized as implicit in the premises underlying that document: the right 'was conceived from the beginning to be a necessary concomitant of the stronger Union the Constitution created.' Consequently, the Court has required that a state classification affecting the constitutionally protected right to travel must be 'shown to be necessary to promote a compelling governmental interest.' But it will not do to suggest that the 'answer' to whether an interest is fundamental for purposes of equal protection analysis is always determined by whether that interest 'is a right ... explicitly or implicitly guaranteed by the Constitution.'

The majority is, of course, correct when it suggests that the process of determining which interests are fundamental is a difficult one. But I do not think the problem is insurmountable. And I certainly do not accept the view that the process need necessarily degenerate into an unprincipled, subjective 'picking-and-choosing' between various interests or that it must involve this Court in creating 'substantive constitutional rights in the name of guaranteeing equal protection of the laws.' Although not all fundamental interests are constitutionally guaranteed, the determination of which interests are fundamental should be firmly rooted in the text of the Constitution. The task in every case should be to determine the extent to which constitutionally guaranteed rights are dependent on interests not mentioned in the Constitution. As the nexus between the specific constitutional guarantee and the nonconstitutional interest draws closer, the non-constitutional interest becomes more fundamental and the degree of judicial scrutiny applied when the interest is infringed on a discriminatory basis must be adjusted accordingly....

The majority suggests, however, that a variable standard of review would give this Court the appearance of a 'super-legislature.' I cannot agree. Such an approach seems to me a part of the guarantees of our Constitution and of the historic experiences with oppression of and discrimination against discrete, powerless minorities which underlie that document. In truth, the Court itself will be open to the criticism raised by the majority so long as it continues on its present course of effectively selecting in private which cases will be afforded special consideration without acknowledging the true basis of its action....

Education directly affects the ability of a child to exercise his First Amendment rights, both as a source and as a receiver of information and ideas, whatever interests he may pursue in life.... Education [also] serves the essential function of instilling in our young an understanding of and appreciation for the principles and operation of our governmental processes. Education may instill the interest and provide the tools necessary for political discourse and debate. Indeed, it has frequently been suggested that education is the dominant factor affecting political consciousness and participation. A system of '(c)ompetition in ideas and governmental policies is at the core of our electoral process and of the First Amendment freedoms.'... But of most immediate and direct concern must be the demonstrated effect of education on the exercise of the franchise by the electorate. The right to vote in federal elections is conferred by Art. I, s 2, and the Seventeenth Amendment of the Constitution, and access to the state franchise has been afforded special protection because it is 'preservative of other basic civil and political rights.' Data from the Presidential Election of 1968 clearly demonstrate a direct relationship between participation in the electoral process and level of educational attainment; and, as this Court recognized, the quality of education offered may influence a child's decision to 'enter or remain in school.' It is this very sort of intimate relationship between a particular personal interest and specific constitutional guarantees that has heretofore caused the Court to attach special significance, for purposes of equal protection analysis, to individual interests such as procreation and the exercise of the state franchise.

When evaluated with these considerations in mind, it seems to me that discrimination on the basis of group wealth in this case likewise calls for careful judicial scrutiny.

Review Questions and Explanations: *Harper* and *Rodriguez*

1. Both *Harper* and *Rodriguez* flirt with deeming poverty a suspect class, but neither does. Should classifications that distinguish people on the basis of wealth be treated as suspect? Consider this question in light of *Carolene Products* footnote 4, as well as the cases studied above.

2. *Harper* nicely illustrates the way fundamental rights work within the equal protection clause: poverty (the asserted basis of the classification) is not treated

as suspect and thus does not trip strict scrutiny under equal protection or due process. But strict scrutiny is nonetheless applied because the thing one class but not the other is being deprived of—the right to vote—is deemed fundamental.

3. The Guided Reading Questions before *Harper* asked you consider the differences between a due process claim that a state action infringes on a fundamental right and therefore warrants heightened review, and an equal protection claim asserting that a state action infringes a fundamental right and that the classification drawn within it must therefore satisfy heightened review. Test yourself now: write out precisely how both the due process claim and the equal protection claim underlying both *Harper* and *Rodriguez* would be articulated if presented to a court today.

PART FIVE

THE FIRST AMENDMENT

The First Amendment provides for the protection of several rights:

> Congress shall make no law respecting an establishment of religion, or prohibiting the free exercise thereof; or abridging the freedom of speech, or of the press; or the right of the people peaceably to assemble, and to petition the government for a redress of grievances.

Traditionally, courts and commentators organize First Amendment doctrine into two parts, the "speech clauses" and the "religion clauses," and this Part follows that practice. The speech clauses—the cluster of rights related to "the freedom of speech," the press, assembly, and petition—are addressed first. The religion clauses—establishment and free exercise—are considered in the succeeding chapter.

The dominant topic in Chapter 9 is free speech. It is easy to conceive of how freedom of the press and the rights of assembly and petition all work together in support of the concept of freedom of speech. While it also is conceivable that press, assembly, and petition rights protect things distinct from speech, most doctrinal developments relating to freedom of the press, and the rights of petition and assembly, are subsumed under free speech analysis: the press is treated as just a particularly noteworthy speaker, whereas petition and assembly are seen as modes by which the people engage in "political speech" (which numerous Court decisions have recognized as lying at the "core" of the First Amendment). In addition to the enumerated rights, the Court also has read a right to "freedom of association" into the First Amendment, viewing it as a right with speech implications whose existence is inferred from the rights to speech and assembly.

Figure 9.1. Freedom of Speech Analytical Flow Chart

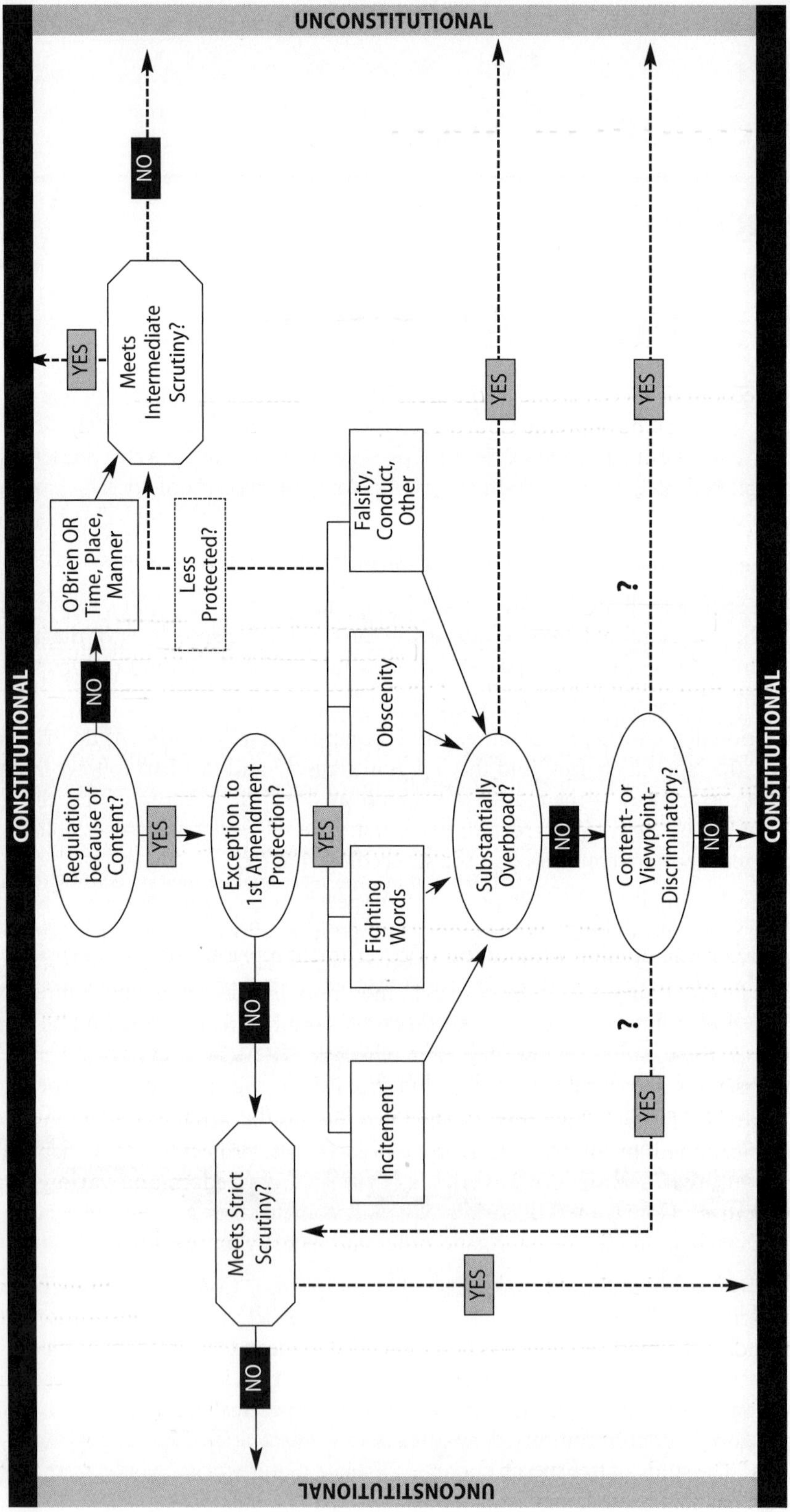

Chapter 9

Freedom of Speech

A. Overview

Freedom of speech is one of the areas of constitutional law that has received the most attention from the Supreme Court. Free speech doctrine is so extensively developed that many law school curricula devote an upper level survey course to the subject. There are several dedicated First Amendment casebooks, and freedom of speech chapters usually take up hundreds of pages even in general constitutional law books like this one.

By observing that free speech doctrine is extensively developed, we don't mean to suggest that the doctrines are clear. Regrettably, the opposite is often true. Free speech case law is exceedingly complex and confusing, not only because of the sheer number of cases, but also because of the range of strong opinions held by individual justices. The passion with which justices come to these cases has led to many highly charged (though often subtle) disagreements and doctrinal shifts over time.

Three additional factors contribute considerably to the volume and density of free speech case law. First is the sheer ubiquity of speech. So much of human activity is conducted through verbal expression or through acts intended to convey meaning. Rational government necessarily requires some direct regulation of these expressive activities; moreover, many regulations of societal affairs necessarily affect speech indirectly.

Second, free speech—understood as the ability to express one's views and convey information and opinion without fear of government reprisal—is (quite sensibly) deemed fundamental to democratic government. Moreover, it is one of the few substantive rights of the individual that is expressly identified in the Constitution. Perhaps for this reason, courts in general, and the Supreme Court in particular, have felt more justified in exercising non-deferential judicial review in this area.

The third factor follows from the first two. Because speech is so ubiquitous, and courts are so confident of what they see as their obligation to protect freedom of speech, judges are continually confronting conflicts between this freedom and various regulatory imperatives. Courts are thus continually challenged to strike the delicate balance between speech rights, on the one hand, and order and security on the other.

This last point should make clear that the phrase "Congress shall make no law ... abridging the freedom of speech" is not taken literally in our constitutional law. The Amendment almost certainly was never intended to mean that "freedom of speech" imposes an absolute prohibition on any regulatory action that infringes any speech interests. Instead, "freedom of speech," like all other constitutional rights, has been understood throughout our constitutional history to mean something like "freedom within reasonable limits." The study of free speech doctrine therefore requires delving into where the Supreme Court has said those limits are.

Figure 9.1, our Freedom of Speech Analytical Flow Chart, shows one way to approach free speech questions. We acknowledge that there are many ways into this doctrine; we have found this approach to be highly useful.

Free speech doctrine is implicated whenever two elements are present: (1) governmental action that (2) restricts communication or expression. The first element is the "state action" requirement—the requirement that the right being asserted was violated by a state, local, *or* federal governmental actor.[1] As in almost all constitutional rights claims, this requirement is fully applicable to First Amendment claims: conduct by private property owners or private employers does not trigger First Amendment scrutiny in the absence of some law or governmental involvement. Element two requires that the action being challenged restricts some type of communication or expression. "Speech"—the word actually used in the text—includes spoken or written expression, but is not limited to that: the Court has extended it to other conduct intended to convey ideas or information. Hence, the concept is sometimes referred to as "freedom of *expression*." (This latter term is used in the text of more recently enacted human rights documents, such as the European Convention on Human Rights.) In the flow chart, the presence of a claim that communication or expression has been limited by some governmental action is assumed. In other words, we assume (for purposes of the flow chart) the presence of a free speech issue, and pick up the analysis from there.

The first question to answer in addressing any free speech issue is whether the regulation being challenged is "content-based" or "content-neutral." A content-based law regulates speech *because* of what it says; a content-neutral law, in contrast, is a law aimed at something else that only incidentally captures and restricts speech. Content-neutral laws are reviewed less strictly than laws that attempt to regulate speech because of what is being said.

If the law is content-based (or, worse, discriminates against a particular viewpoint), it will be reviewed under strict scrutiny, *unless* it is deemed to fall into one of the unprotected categories of speech carved out by the Court. These include "fighting words," obscenity, defamation, words that incite "imminent lawless action" and a few others.

Even if the law is aimed at regulation of unprotected speech, however, there remain certain constitutional objections based on how the law is constructed. For example, a law regulating unprotected speech that is unduly "vague" or "overbroad," may still be unconstitutional. And regulation of unprotected speech that discriminates against particular points of view also may be unconstitutional.

Figure 9.1 does not exhaust all possible free speech issues. Creating a manageable chart requires simplifying matters somewhat. Some of these miscellaneous issues are covered at the end of this chapter. Section E deals with special rules for laws limiting speech in specific contexts (campaign finance, government employment, schools and commercial speech), while section F looks at the speech-related rights of association, press, petition, and assembly.

Finally, you should note that while the concept of heightened scrutiny applies in First Amendment cases, the terminology and the formulations of the tests will sometimes differ from analogous tests used in the Equal Protection/Substantive Due Process contexts. For example, content-neutral restrictions on speech are reviewed under an intermediate scrutiny-type test that asks whether the regulation burdens more speech than necessary and leaves open alternative avenues for the regulated speaker.

---

1. Note that despite its textual restriction to "Congress," the First Amendment, like most other specific provisions of the Bill of Rights, has been incorporated against the states through the Due Process clause of the Fourteenth Amendment (see Chapter 7).

B. Foundational Doctrine

1. Basic Principles

The following very short excerpts are intended to illustrate some basic free speech principles as well as the variety of ways in which regulations of speech raising First Amendment issues may arise. In famous separate opinions arising out of prosecutions of anti-war activists and leftists in the aftermath of World War I, Justices Holmes and Brandeis articulated ideas that have now become fundamental to free speech doctrine. In *Abrams v. United States*, 250 U.S. 616 (1919), Holmes dissented from a decision upholding the conviction of an anti-war leafletter, and set out his famous "marketplace of ideas" metaphor:

> [W]hen men have realized that time has upset many fighting faiths, they may come to believe even more than they believe the very foundations of their own conduct that the ultimate good desired is better reached by free trade in ideas — that the best test of truth is the power of the thought to get itself accepted in the competition of the market, and that truth is the only ground upon which their wishes safely can be carried out. That at any rate is the theory of our Constitution. Id., at 630 (Holmes, J., dissenting)

In *Whitney v. California*, 274 U.S. 357 (1925), the Court upheld a California criminal statute making it a crime to advocate using unlawful force to bring about political change. The holding is no longer good law, and the following excerpt from Justice Brandeis's separate opinion has been frequently quoted with approval over the years:

> Those who won our independence believed ... that public discussion is a political duty; and that this should be a fundamental principle of the American government. They recognized the risks to which all human institutions are subject. But they knew that order cannot be secured merely through fear of punishment for its infraction; that it is hazardous to discourage thought, hope and imagination; that fear breeds repression; that repression breeds hate; that hate menaces stable government; that the path of safety lies in the opportunity to discuss freely supposed grievances and proposed remedies; and that the fitting remedy for evil counsels is good ones. Believing in the power of reason as applied through public discussion, they eschewed silence coerced by law — the argument of force in its worst form. Recognizing the occasional tyrannies of governing majorities, they amended the Constitution so that free speech and assembly should be guaranteed. Id., at 375–376 (1925) (Brandeis, J., concurring).

In *New York Times v. Sullivan*, 376 U.S. 254 (1964), the Court applied the First Amendment to curtail a state's power to punish criticism of public officials under state libel laws:

> .... It is true that the First Amendment was originally addressed only to action by the Federal Government.... But this distinction was eliminated with the adoption of the Fourteenth Amendment and the application to the States of the First Amendment's restrictions.

> The fear of damage awards under a rule such as that invoked by the Alabama courts here may be markedly more inhibiting than the fear of prosecution under a criminal statute.... Plainly the Alabama law of civil libel is "a form of regulation that creates hazards to protected freedoms markedly greater than those that attend reliance upon the criminal law."

The state rule of law is not saved by its allowance of the defense of truth.... Allowance of the defense of truth, with the burden of proving it on the defendant, does not mean that only false speech will be deterred. Even courts accepting this defense as an adequate safeguard have recognized the difficulties of adducing legal proofs that the alleged libel was true in all its factual particulars. Under such a rule, would-be critics of official conduct may be deterred from voicing their criticism, even though it is believed to be true and even though it is in fact true, because of doubt whether it can be proved in court or fear of the expense of having to do so. They tend to make only statements which "steer far wider of the unlawful zone." The rule thus dampens the vigor and limits the variety of public debate. It is inconsistent with the First and Fourteenth Amendments.

And in *Paris Adult Theatre I v. Slaton*, 413 U.S. 49 (1973), Justice Brennan's dissent argued that even efforts to regulate obscenity could undermine important free speech values, particularly where the prohibitions of speech are vague or overbroad:

[N]o person, not even the most learned judge much less a layman, is capable of knowing in advance of an ultimate decision in his particular case by this Court whether certain material comes within the area of "obscenity".... In addition to problems that arise when any criminal statute fails to afford fair notice of what it forbids, a vague statute in the areas of speech and press creates a second level of difficulty.... [by] potentially inhibiting effect on speech; a man may the less be required to act at his peril here, because the free dissemination of ideas may be the loser....

If, as the Court today assumes, "a state legislature may ... act on the ... assumption that commerce in obscene books, or public exhibitions focused on obscene conduct, have a tendency to exert a corrupting and debasing impact leading to antisocial behavior," then it is hard to see how state-ordered regimentation of our minds can ever be forestalled. For if a State, in an effort to maintain or create a particular moral tone, may prescribe what its citizens cannot read or cannot see, then it would seem to follow that in pursuit of that same objective a State could decree that its citizens must read certain books or must view certain films....

In short, while I cannot say that the interests of the State—apart from the question of juveniles and unconsenting adults—are trivial or nonexistent, I am compelled to conclude that these interests cannot justify the substantial damage to constitutional rights and to this Nation's judicial machinery that inevitably results from state efforts to bar the distribution even of unprotected material to consenting adults. *Id.* at 87–88, 110, 112 (Brennan, J. dissenting).

2. Vagueness and Overbreadth

In the free speech context, you will encounter attacks on statutes as being vague or overbroad. These two terms often go together, and indeed they overlap, particularly in this area. But they also differ significantly. Vagueness and overbreadth are each a type of statutory drafting problem. They are therefore substantive in nature, but they also have certain procedural implications for legal challenges.

"Vagueness" is an argument that the law is so imprecise that a person of ordinary intelligence can't understand what conduct it prohibits or permits. "Overbreadth" is an argument that the law goes beyond permissible regulation of speech to include some speech regulation that violates free speech rights. A law can be either overbroad, or vague, or both. Both vagueness and overbreadth raise the same First Amendment problem: they can have a "chilling effect" on speech. A person unsure about whether his speech will provoke a criminal prosecution or other regulatory consequences (tort damages or civil enforcement penalties, for instance) may refrain from engaging in constitutionally protected expression rather than run the risk of being held liable under the law. Vague and overbroad laws can thus create wide gray areas of ambiguous application, areas that many people would naturally wish to give a wide berth.

a. Vagueness — Due Process violation of fair notice.

A law will be held unconstitutionally vague ("void for vagueness") if, in the words of the Court, it "fails to provide a person of ordinary intelligence fair notice of what is prohibited, or is so standardless that it authorizes or encourages seriously discriminatory enforcement." *E.g., United States v. Williams*, 553 U.S. 285, 304 (2008). Vagueness is thus not really a First Amendment issue as such, but a problem of due process, whose fundamental requirement is fair notice. It is unfair to punish a person without clear warning that conduct was prohibited. Moreover, vague laws allow excessive interpretive leeway to enforcement officers and thereby create a high risk of discriminatory enforcement. In *Papachristou v. City of Jacksonville*, 405 U.S. 156 (1972), the Court struck down a vagrancy statute that allowed misdemeanor arrests and convictions for "Rogues and vagabonds, or dissolute persons[.]" The Court held that the statute was unduly standardless and vague, and therefore subject to discriminatory enforcement.

A vagueness case dealing more directly with First Amendment issues is *Coates v. City of Cincinnati*, 402 U.S. 611 (1971), in which the appellants were convicted under a statute making it a misdemeanor for "three or more persons to assemble ... on any of the sidewalks ... and there conduct themselves in a manner annoying to persons passing by[.]" The Court struck down the statute as unconstitutionally vague under the Due Process clause, but went on to note that the statute also violated the First Amendment (presumably on overbreadth grounds, though the Court did not use the term):

> the vice of the ordinance lies not alone in its violation of the due process standard of vagueness. The ordinance also violates the constitutional right of free assembly and association. Our decisions establish that mere public intolerance or animosity cannot be the basis for abridgment of these constitutional freedoms. The First and Fourteenth Amendments do not permit a State to make criminal the exercise of the right of assembly simply because its exercise may be "annoying" to some people. If this were not the rule, the right of the people to gather in public places for social or political purposes would be continually subject to summary suspension through the good-faith enforcement of a prohibition against annoying conduct. And such a prohibition, in addition, contains an obvious invitation to discriminatory enforcement against those whose association together is "annoying" because their ideas, their lifestyle, or their physical appearance is resented by the majority of their fellow citizens.

Although vagueness is technically a due process problem, *Coates* and other cases suggest that vague laws which chill constitutionally protected speech will be reviewed more stringently than other types of vague laws.

Impermissibly vague laws may take one of two forms. A law may be entirely vague in all its applications such that it "simply has no core." *Smith v. Goguen*, 415 U.S. 566, 578

(1974). The vagrancy and anti-gathering laws in *Papachristou* and *Coates* illustrate this type. Or a law may have a core of permissible applications but be vague in the full extent of its reach or at the margins. For example, a law making it a crime to "provide assistance to a terrorist organization" would clearly prohibit making a weapons purchase on behalf of Al-Qaeda. But what about writing an op-ed piece advocating recognition of the Palestine Liberation Organization as the rightful government of a Palestinian state?

This category—permissible core, vague at the margins—is probably more common than laws with no core; indeed, given the inherent limitations and ambiguities of language, and the ingenuity of well-trained lawyers, it is all to easy to come up with examples of vagueness of statutes in marginal applications.

The "permissible core, vague at the margins" category also raises a significant procedural issue. "A plaintiff who engages in some conduct that is clearly proscribed cannot complain of the vagueness of the law as applied to the conduct of others." *Hoffman Estates v. Flipside, Hoffman Estates, Inc.*, 455 U.S. 489, 495 (1982). In other words, someone who violates the core prohibition of a statute can't successfully challenge the statute by arguing that it is vague in more marginal situations in other potential cases. In the example above, the arms dealer who supplied weapons to Al-Qaeda will not be heard to argue that the statute is void for vagueness because it could hypothetically be applied to the op-ed writer.

b. Overbreadth

A law is "overbroad" if it prohibits both conduct that may be constitutionally prohibited (or regulated) as well as conduct whose prohibition (or regulation) is deemed unconstitutional. Although the concept of overbreadth could apply, in theory, to many areas of constitutional law, it has been used only in the free speech context. So, more specifically, overbroad laws prohibit (or regulate) more speech than constitutionally allowed even though some aspects of the prohibition may be constitutional.

This general definition of overbreadth is qualified by three important aspects of the overbreadth doctrine. First, overbreadth doctrine provides a special, and wider avenue for raising facial challenges to laws restricting speech, in contrast to other kinds of laws. As explained in the introductory chapter to this book, a facial challenge to a law argues that the law is unconstitutional in all circumstances and cases: "A facial challenge to a legislative Act is, of course, the most difficult challenge to mount successfully, since the challenger must establish that no set of circumstances exists under which the Act would be valid." *United States v. Salerno*, 481 U.S. 739, 745 (1987). But overbreadth doctrine creates an exception to this rule in free speech cases: a law may be challenged as unconstitutional "on its face" on First Amendment grounds if it is shown to be "substantially overbroad," that is, if "a substantial number of its applications are unconstitutional, judged in relation to the statute's plainly legitimate sweep." *Washington State Grange v. Washington State Republican Party*, 552 U.S. 442, 449 (2008).

Second, as suggested by the just-quoted language, the overbreadth must be substantial in order for a facial overbreadth challenge to succeed. *Broadrick v. Oklahoma*, 413 U.S. 601 (1973). "We have never held that a statute should be held invalid on its face merely because it is possible to conceive of a single impermissible application[.]" *Houston v. Hill*, 482 U.S. 451, 458 (1987). That frequent quotation is a bit of an understatement, since substantial overbreadth undoubtedly may require showing more than a few unconstitutional applications infringing speech. Indeed, the Court has pointed out that striking down a statute on substantial overbreadth grounds is "strong medicine," *Broadrick, supra*, suggesting that it is to be avoided if the statute is "readily susceptible" to a narrowing construction.

Third, substantial overbreadth as a substantive concept gives rise to a special doctrine of standing in free speech cases. As explained in Chapter 6, the Court has created a judge-made prudential rule that generally precludes third party standing—parties are not generally allowed to assert the rights of third parties not before the court. However, this prohibition is relaxed when a law is challenged on First Amendment overbreadth grounds. Specifically, a party whose conduct is constitutionally prohibited by a law may nevertheless assert the rights of third parties not before the court, and argue that the speech rights of those third parties (even hypothetical third parties) would be unconstitutionally infringed by the law.

Here's an example, loosely based on *Reno v. ACLU* (a case we present below, in Section D.4). Suppose Congress enacts a law making it a crime to post any verbal or visual depiction of sexual acts or sex organs on an internet web site, except one that is password-protected and accessible to adults only (which is what the law challenged in *Reno* did). The terms of this law would apply to obscene matter; but also would apply to an online anatomy text or an article advocating safe-sex practices. And it would unduly restrict adults' access to the material on non-password-protected web sites. The law would not be unconstitutional as applied to obscene matter (because, as noted above, obscenity is one of the categories of speech deemed unprotected). But a person charged under this law for posting obscene matter could nevertheless challenge the statute as substantially overbroad, and therefore facially invalid, because it infringes the rights of others, such as those who might post the anatomy text. In such a case, the Court could strike down the law in its entirety, and the obscene poster would win his case even though the law would have been constitutional as applied to him.

Why allow this liberalization of third party standing for substantial overbreadth challenges? The answer lies in concerns about the chilling effect. The persons who want to post the anatomy text and the safe-sex article might refrain from doing so for fear of prosecution. Society then loses the benefit of their speech. While they might have standing to challenge the law and get a declaratory judgment, they might not have the time, resources, or interest in doing so. Meanwhile, the obscene poster has been criminally charged, so he has a huge incentive to raise the constitutional issues. Substantial overbreadth doctrine allows him to do so as a proxy for the others, because of the social benefit in promoting judicial resolution of the free speech rights of the non-litigants.

Can a challenger to a law show that it is unconstitutionally overbroad as applied to him even though it is not otherwise substantially overbroad? Well … yes and no, but really, no. It's not that such an argument is illogical, but just that the concept of overbreadth is not used that way. A law that is overbroad in certain applications, but generally constitutional, can be successfully subject to an "as-applied" challenge by a party whose speech is unconstitutionally prohibited by the statute. "As-applied" challenges, in contrast to facial challenges, attack the constitutionality of a law only as applied to the facts of the case at hand. In other words, "as-applied" challenges don't employ an overbreadth analysis.

c. Vagueness and Overbreadth Compared

Let's return to comparing and contrasting vagueness and overbreadth. To begin with, a key difference between the two doctrines should be apparent. A party whose First Amendment rights have not been infringed by a statute can nevertheless argue that it is substantially overbroad based on its unconstitutional application to others. But a party whose due process "notice" rights have not been infringed—whose conduct clearly falls within a statutory prohibition—cannot argue that the statute is void because it is unconstitutionally vague as to others. The relaxed third party standing concept in substantial overbreadth challenges thus does not carry over into vagueness challenges.

A statute can be overbroad but not vague. The above example, making it a crime to "post on an internet web site, except one that is password-protected and accessible to adults only, any verbal or visual depiction of sexual acts or sex organs," is reasonably specific—likely enough to withstand a vagueness challenge. But it is plainly overbroad, and substantially so, for reasons discussed above.

A statute also can be vague, but not overbroad. A law that prohibits the posting on the internet of "obscene material that shocks the conscience" seems vague—what does "shock the conscience" mean? But the law is not overbroad, since obscene material is not protected and the law, by its terms, prohibits only (a subset) of the publication of obscene material. In *FCC v. Fox Television Stations*, 567 U.S. ___, 132 S. Ct. 2307 (2012) the Court ruled that an inconsistently applied FCC policy that permitted some "fleeting expletives," while banning other foul language was "void for vagueness." The policy was too unclear and inconsistently applied to provide adequate notice to broadcasters. The policy was not "overbroad," however, because controlling precedent has allowed prohibition of "indecent" speech on broadcast television.

Finally, a statute can be both vague and overbroad. This is not uncommon, since the boundaries of a vague statute, because of its vagueness, can be extensive and reach a lot of constitutionally permissible conduct. Suppose the internet statute were written to prohibit "any patently offensive verbal or visual depiction of sexual acts or sex organs." The law is substantially overbroad, as discussed above. Now it is impermissibly vague as well. Perhaps the anatomy text and safe-sex article will be permitted under the law because they aren't "patently offensive." But, on the other hand, maybe they are. Offensive to whom? The phrase is highly subjective and ambiguous, raising significant vagueness problems. Another example is provided by *Coates v. City of Cincinnati*, above, in which the Court ultimately found the law in question to be both vague and overbroad.

C. Content-Based and Content-Neutral Regulation

In this section we consider the important distinction between speech-restricting laws that are content-based and those that are content-neutral. A law is deemed content-based (also sometimes referred to as content-discriminatory) if it regulates some subjects or categories of expression while leaving others unregulated. A law is content-neutral if, despite its tendency to restrict speech in some way, it is not designed to regulate particular subjects or categories of expression. A law prohibiting "the public burning of a cross to signify a message of white supremacy" is content-based. A law prohibiting "the setting of a fire in a public place, except in designated firepits or barbeques, without a permit" is content-neutral, even though it might limit the "speech" of a group that wanted to burn a cross as a white supremacist message.

Content-neutral laws may or may not specifically seek to regulate speech. In some cases, a law aimed at regulating conduct might incidentally extend to certain expressive conduct. The above example of a law against "setting a fire in a public place" is illustrative of this issue; so would be a law against littering, if applied to a person trying to distribute leaflets, or a law against sleeping overnight in a public park if applied to a group conducting a "sleep-in" to raise public awareness of homelessness. Again, these kinds of laws do not appear to target speech, and were probably not intended to do so, aiming instead at a range of non-expressive conduct; but they may nevertheless limit expressive conduct.

Another subset of content-neutral laws might indeed seek to regulate expressive activity, but in a way not based on the content of expression. Examples of this sort of regulation includes restrictions on the time or place of using sound amplification equipment, or on the size or placement of signs and billboards in a residential neighborhood. These kinds of laws are often referred to as "time, place, or manner" restrictions: that is, they are intended to regulate the time, place, or manner of communication. They are thus *direct* regulations of speech, but they are not targeted at the *content* of the speech.

One caveat is in order about content-neutral laws. Although time, place, or manner regulations are one *type* of content-neutral law, attempts to regulate time, place, or manner are not automatically, or always, content-neutral. A law that limits "political parades or demonstrations in a public street" to "the last Saturday of each month" certainly regulates "time" and "place," but also discriminates on the basis of content — if it does not similarly restrict all other parades or demonstrations, such as civic festivities, graduation celebrations, etc. By the same token, it might be argued that a law prohibiting the burning of the American flag is not intended to eliminate the underlying protest message, but only to regulate the particular mode or manner in which the message is conveyed. But such a law is properly deemed content-based, since the mode of expression is so highly correlated with certain types of message.

The content-based/content-neutral distinction is important because the courts will apply strict scrutiny to content-based regulations of speech but an intermediate level of scrutiny to content-neutral laws.

There is one further concept to be aware of: the Court has identified a special subcategory of content-based speech regulation, referred to as "viewpoint discrimination." A law prohibiting "the placement of signs endorsing a candidate for public office within 500 feet of a public building" discriminates on the basis of content: it regulates a particular topic or subject matter of speech. A law prohibiting "the placement of signs endorsing a Democratic candidate for public office within 500 feet of a public building" discriminates on the basis of viewpoint: it singles out a particular point of view within a particular subject matter. While viewpoint discrimination, like content discrimination, is reviewed under strict scrutiny, viewpoint discrimination rarely survives this review: few (if any) compelling state interests justify discriminating on the basis of viewpoint.

Review the First Amendment flow chart. We are now at the first node of that chart, determining whether the law is content-neutral. But that's only the first step of the inquiry, telling us which of two tests to apply: strict scrutiny or intermediate scrutiny.

Subsection 1 considers laws that do not seek to regulate speech, but nevertheless restrict speech indirectly when the regulated conduct is used for expressive purposes. Subsection 2 examines laws that do regulate speech but attempt to achieve content-neutrality by regulating its time, place, or manner.

1. Content-Neutral Regulation of Expressive Conduct

The problem of content-neutrality arises repeatedly in situations where a law regulates conduct and, on occasion, that conduct is used expressively, to communicate an idea or message.

When studying First Amendment cases, you will encounter two analytical points that are treated as important in *some* judicial opinions or academic commentary, but that we find misleading and unhelpful in figuring out free speech doctrine. First, you will occasionally see some debates about whether the person making the free speech challenge to the law has engaged in "speech" or "conduct." The point of that distinction (to those who draw it) is that the First Amendment protects speech but not conduct. While that notion is undoubtedly true in some sense, and despite occasional judicial handwringing over a "speech or conduct" question, the Court has rarely, if ever, decided a case by characterizing even arguably expressive conduct as conduct, not speech.

A better way to think about these issues is to recognize that speech may be verbal or non-verbal, that is, it may take the form of words or conduct. Rather than engaging in sterile debates about whether a specific example of expressive conduct should be treated as "speech" or "pure conduct," the Court has tended to give the "speech" characterization the benefit of the doubt. In none of the cases in this chapter was arguably expressive conduct — burning a draft card or a flag or a cross, sleeping in a park in protest, standing silently during the pledge of allegiance, to cite a few examples — treated as non-speech by the Court.

A related point is whether expressive conduct is somehow a distinct category of speech, subject to special rules. In short, it is not. Again, some courts occasionally imply that it is; casebook and study aid writers likewise imply that expressive conduct is a special type of speech by naming chapters after the concept. But the Court has consistently treated expressive conduct as the equivalent of verbal speech for First Amendment free speech purposes.

There is, of course, a reason why expressive conduct raises problems that may not be raised by verbal speech in First Amendment case law. That is the simple fact that many laws are intended to regulate conduct without giving consideration to how that conduct might, in particular circumstances, be used expressively. The law banning sleeping in the park, discussed in the *Clark* case below, is an example. A particular doctrine has emerged to answer *that* question, but the question answered by that doctrine is not whether expressive speech deserves full First Amendment protection (it does), but whether the law *really was* aimed at the conduct rather than at the expression embodied in it.

In sum, the significance of expressive conduct is not whether it can be placed in a mere conduct box and denied protection. Rather its significance arises when expressive conduct falls within a regulation genuinely aimed at the conduct, independent of its expressive intent. The following cases illustrate this problem.

Guided Reading Questions: *United States v. O'Brien*

1. Subsequent cases have referred to the "four-part O'Brien" test for permissible regulation of conduct that may sometimes be combined with speech. Identify that test.

2. How does the Court reach the conclusion that the law against draft card burning meets this test?

3. How do we know that the law, and its purported rationale, are not merely a pretext to punish draft card burnings for protest? Is the Court concerned about this? How would the analysis change if the Court believed this to be the case?

United States v. O'Brien

391 U.S. 367 (1968)

Majority: *Warren* (CJ), Black, Harlan, Brennan, Stewart, White, Fortas

Concurrence: *Harlan*

Dissent: *Douglas* (Marshall did not take part)

MR. CHIEF JUSTICE WARREN delivered the opinion of the Court.

On the morning of March 31, 1966, David Paul O'Brien and three companions burned their Selective Service registration certificates on the steps of the South Boston Courthouse. A sizable crowd, including several agents of the Federal Bureau of Investigation, witnessed the event. Immediately after the burning, members of the crowd began attacking O'Brien and his companions. An FBI agent ushered O'Brien to safety inside the courthouse. After he was advised of his right to counsel and to silence, O'Brien stated to FBI agents that he had burned his registration certificate because of his beliefs, knowing that he was violating federal law. He produced the charred remains of the certificate, which, with his consent, were photographed.

For this act, O'Brien was indicted, tried, convicted, and sentenced in the United States District Court for the District of Massachusetts. The District Court rejected [O'Brien's First Amendment challenge to the statute prohibiting the destruction of a draft certificate, and held] that the statute on its face did not abridge First Amendment rights.... The Court of Appeals for the First Circuit [reversed].... We hold that the 1965 Amendment is constitutional both as enacted and as applied. We therefore vacate the judgment of the Court of Appeals and reinstate the judgment and sentence of the District Court ...

By the 1965 Amendment [to § 12(b)(3) of the Universal Military Training and Service Act of 1951], Congress added ... the provision here at issue, subjecting to criminal liability not only one who "forges, alters, or in any manner changes" but also one who "knowingly destroys, [or] knowingly mutilates" a [draft] certificate. We note at the outset that the 1965 Amendment plainly does not abridge free speech on its face, and we do not understand O'Brien to argue otherwise.... The Amendment does not distinguish between public and private destruction, and it does not punish only destruction engaged in for the purpose of expressing views....

O'Brien first argues that the 1965 Amendment is unconstitutional as applied to him because his act of burning his registration certificate was protected "symbolic speech" within the First Amendment. His argument is that the freedom of expression which the First Amendment guarantees includes all modes of "communication of ideas by conduct," and that his conduct is within this definition because he did it in "demonstration against the war and against the draft." ...

We cannot accept the view that an apparently limitless variety of conduct can be labeled "speech" whenever the person engaging in the conduct intends thereby to express an idea.

However, even on the assumption that the alleged communicative element in O'Brien's conduct is sufficient to bring into play the First Amendment, it does not necessarily follow that the destruction of a registration certificate is constitutionally protected activity. This Court has held that when "speech" and "nonspeech" elements are combined in the same course of conduct, a sufficiently important governmental interest in regulating the nonspeech element can justify incidental limitations on First Amendment freedoms.... [W]e think it clear that a government regulation is sufficiently justified if it is within the constitutional power of the Government; if it furthers an important or substantial governmental interest; if the governmental interest is unrelated to the suppression of free expression; and if the incidental restriction on alleged First Amendment freedoms is no greater than is essential to the furtherance of that interest. We find that the 1965 Amendment to §12 (b)(3) of the Universal Military Training and Service Act meets all of these requirements, and consequently that O'Brien can be constitutionally convicted for violating it....

The constitutional power of Congress to raise and support armies and to make all laws necessary and proper to that end is broad and sweeping. Pursuant to this power, Congress may establish a system of registration for individuals liable for training and service, and may require such individuals within reason to cooperate in the registration system. The issuance of certificates indicating the registration and eligibility classification of individuals is a legitimate and substantial administrative aid in the functioning of this system. And legislation to insure the continuing availability of issued certificates serves a legitimate and substantial purpose in the system's administration.

.... [T]he registration certificate ... serves purposes in addition to initial notification. Many of these purposes would be defeated by the certificates' destruction or mutilation. Among these are:

1. The registration certificate serves as proof that the individual described thereon has registered for the draft.... 2. The information supplied on the certificates facilitates communication between registrants and local boards, simplifying the system and benefiting all concerned.... 3. Both certificates carry continual reminders that the registrant must notify his local board of any change of address, and other specified changes in his status. 4. The regulatory scheme involving Selective Service certificates includes clearly valid prohibitions against the alteration, forgery, or similar deceptive misuse of certificates. The destruction or mutilation of certificates obviously increases the difficulty of detecting and tracing abuses such as these. Further, a mutilated certificate might itself be used for deceptive purposes.

The many functions performed by Selective Service certificates establish beyond doubt that Congress has a legitimate and substantial interest in preventing their wanton and unrestrained destruction and assuring their continuing availability by punishing people who knowingly and wilfully destroy or mutilate them....

O'Brien finally argues that the 1965 Amendment is unconstitutional as enacted because what he calls the "purpose" of Congress was "to suppress freedom of speech." We reject this argument because under settled principles the purpose of Congress, as O'Brien uses that term, is not a basis for declaring this legislation unconstitutional.

It is a familiar principle of constitutional law that this Court will not strike down an otherwise constitutional statute on the basis of an alleged illicit legislative motive.... Inquiries into congressional motives or purposes are a hazardous matter. When the issue is simply the interpretation of legislation, the Court will look to statements by legislators for guidance as to the purpose of the legislature, because the benefit to sound decisionmaking in this circumstance is thought sufficient to risk the possibility of misreading Congress' purpose. It is entirely a different matter when we are asked to void a statute that is, under well-settled criteria, constitutional on its face, on the basis of what fewer than a handful of Congressmen said about it. What motivates one legislator to make a speech about a statute is not necessarily what motivates scores of others to enact it, and the stakes are sufficiently high for us to eschew guesswork.... There was little floor debate on this legislation in either House.... The portions of [the Senate and House Armed Services Committees'] reports explaining the purpose of the Amendment are reproduced in the Appendix ... While both reports make clear a concern with the "defiant" destruction of so-called "draft cards" and with "open" encouragement to others to destroy their cards, both reports also indicate that this concern stemmed from an apprehension that unrestrained destruction of cards would disrupt the smooth functioning of the Selective Service System.

.... [W]e vacate the judgment of the Court of Appeals, and reinstate the judgment and sentence of the District Court....

APPENDIX TO OPINION OF THE COURT.

Portions of the Reports of the Committees on Armed Services of the Senate and House Explaining the 1965 Amendment

The "Explanation of the Bill" in the Senate Report is as follows:

"Section 12 (b)(3) of the Universal Military Training and Service Act of 1951, as amended, provides, among other things, that a person who forges, alters, or changes a draft registration certificate is subject to a fine of not more than $ 10,000 or imprisonment of not more than 5 years, or both. There is no explicit prohibition in this section against the knowing destruction or mutilation of such cards.

"The committee has taken notice of the defiant destruction and mutilation of draft cards by dissident persons who disapprove of national policy. If allowed to continue unchecked this contumacious conduct represents a potential threat to the exercise of the power to raise and support armies.

"For a person to be subject to fine or imprisonment the destruction or mutilation of the draft card must be 'knowingly' done. This qualification is intended to protect persons who lose or mutilate draft cards accidentally." S. Rep. No. 589, 89th Cong., 1st Sess. (1965).

And the House Report explained:

"Section 12 (b)(3) of the Universal Military Training and Service Act of 1951, as amended, provides that a person who forges, alters, or in any manner changes his draft registration card, or any notation duly and validly inscribed thereon, will be subject to a fine of $ 10,000 or imprisonment of not more than 5 years. H. R. 10306 would amend this provision to make it apply also to those persons who knowingly destroy or knowingly mutilate a draft registration card.

"The House Committee on Armed Services is fully aware of, and shares in, the deep concern expressed throughout the Nation over the increasing incidences in which individuals and large groups of individuals openly defy and encourage others to defy the authority of their Government by destroying or mutilating their draft cards.

"While the present provisions of the Criminal Code with respect to the destruction of Government property may appear broad enough to cover all acts having to do with the mistreatment of draft cards in the possession of individuals, the committee feels that in the present critical situation of the country, the acts of destroying or mutilating these cards are offenses which pose such a grave threat to the security of the Nation that no question whatsoever should be left as to the intention of the Congress that such wanton and irresponsible acts should be punished.

"To this end, H. R. 10306 makes specific that knowingly mutilating or knowingly destroying a draft card constitutes a violation of the Universal Military Training and Service Act and is punishable thereunder; and that a person who does so destroy or mutilate a draft card will be subject to a fine of not more than $ 10,000 or imprisonment of not more than 5 years." H. R. Rep. No. 747, 89th Cong., 1st Sess. (1965).

MR. JUSTICE HARLAN, concurring.

.... I wish to make explicit my understanding that this passage does not foreclose consideration of First Amendment claims in those rare instances when an "incidental" restriction upon expression, imposed by a regulation which furthers an "important or substantial" governmental interest and satisfies the Court's other criteria, in practice has the effect of entirely preventing a "speaker" from reaching a significant audience with whom he could not otherwise lawfully communicate. This is not such a case, since O'Brien manifestly could have conveyed his message in many ways other than by burning his draft card.

MR. JUSTICE DOUGLAS, dissenting.

The Court states that the constitutional power of Congress to raise and support armies is "broad and sweeping" and that Congress' power "to classify and conscript manpower for military service is 'beyond question.'" This is undoubtedly true in times when, by declaration of Congress, the Nation is in a state of war. The underlying and basic problem in this case, however, is whether conscription is permissible in the absence of a declaration of war. That question has not been briefed nor was it presented in oral argument; but it is, I submit, a question upon which the litigants and the country are entitled to a ruling. ...

Review Questions and Explanations: *O'Brien*

1. Notice how the Court bemoans "the view that an apparently limitless variety of conduct can be labeled 'speech'" but then goes on to analyze the case on the assumption that burning a draft card in protest is speech.

2. Can you locate this decision on Figure 9.1? *O'Brien* does not use either the terms intermediate scrutiny or content-neutrality. However, both these concepts are reflected in the four part test. The first part of the test ("it is within the power of government") relates to enumerated powers rather than the First Amendment. The rest of the test has become a standard for content-neutral laws that limit speech: if indeed the "the governmental interest is unrelated to the suppression of free expression" (i.e., is a content-neutral regulation of conduct), the law will be upheld "if it furthers an important or substantial governmental interest ..."

and if the incidental restriction on alleged First Amendment freedoms is no greater than is essential to the furtherance of that interest."

3. Note the Court's comment in *O'Brien* that the Court "will not strike down an otherwise constitutional statute on the basis of an alleged illicit legislative motive." Compare this to the Court's discussions of discriminatory intent or purpose in the Equal Protection context.

Guided Reading Questions: *Clark v. Community for Creative Non-Violence*

1. Try to determine whether and how *Clark* applies the *O'Brien* test.

2. The Court says that it could apply either the *O'Brien* test or a time, place, or manner test, and reach the same result. How do these tests differ?

3. Is there an argument that the no-sleeping rule is content-based? If not, what argument is there that the restriction is unconstitutional?

4. How does the Court deal with the argument that the government's interest could have been served without banning the sleep-in? Is the argument persuasive?

Clark v. Community for Creative Non-Violence
468 U.S. 288 (1984)

Majority: *White*, Burger (CJ), Blackmun, Powell, Rehnquist, Stevens, O'Connor

Concurrence: *Burger* (CJ)

Dissent: *Marshall*, Brennan

JUSTICE WHITE delivered the opinion of the Court.

The issue in this case is whether a National Park Service regulation prohibiting camping in certain parks violates the First Amendment when applied to prohibit demonstrators from sleeping in Lafayette Park and the Mall in connection with a demonstration intended to call attention to the plight of the homeless. We hold that it does not and reverse the contrary judgment of the Court of Appeals.

The Interior Department, through the National Park Service, is charged with responsibility for the management and maintenance of the National Parks and is authorized to promulgate rules and regulations for the use of the parks in accordance with the purposes for which they were established.

The network of National Parks includes the National Memorial-core parks, Lafayette Park and the Mall, which are set in the heart of Washington, D. C., and which are unique resources that the Federal Government holds in trust for the American people. Lafayette Park is a roughly 7-acre square located across Pennsylvania Avenue from the White House. Although originally part of the White House grounds, President Jefferson set it aside as a park for the use of residents and visitors. It is a "garden park with a … formal landscaping of flowers and trees, with fountains, walks and benches." The Mall is a stretch of land running westward from the Capitol to the Lincoln Memorial some two miles away. It includes the Washington Monument, a series of reflecting pools, trees, lawns, and other greenery. It is bordered by, inter alia, the Smithsonian Institution and the National Gallery of Art. Both the Park and the Mall were included in Major Pierre L'Enfant's original plan for the Capital. Both are visited by vast numbers of visitors from around the country, as well as by large numbers of residents of the Washington metropolitan area.

Under the regulations involved in this case, camping in National Parks is permitted only in campgrounds designated for that purpose. 36 CFR § 50.27(a). No such campgrounds have ever been designated in Lafayette Park or the Mall. Camping is defined as

> the use of park land for living accommodation purposes such as sleeping activities, or making preparations to sleep (including the laying down of bedding for the purpose of sleeping), or storing personal belongings, or making any fire, or using any tents or ... other structure ... for sleeping or doing any digging or earth breaking or carrying on cooking activities.

These activities, the regulation provides,

> constitute camping when it reasonably appears, in light of all the circumstances, that the participants, in conducting these activities, are in fact using the area as a living accommodation regardless of the intent of the participants or the nature of any other activities in which they may also be engaging.

Demonstrations for the airing of views or grievances are permitted in the Memorial-core parks, but for the most part only by Park Service permits. 36 CFR § 50.19. Temporary structures may be erected for ["symbolizing a message or meeting logistical needs such as first aid facilities, lost children areas or the provision of shelter for electrical and other sensitive equipment or displays"] but may not be used for camping.

In 1982, the Park Service issued a renewable permit to respondent Community for Creative Non-Violence (CCNV) to conduct a wintertime demonstration in Lafayette Park and the Mall for the purpose of demonstrating the plight of the homeless. The permit authorized the erection of two symbolic tent cities: 20 tents in Lafayette Park that would accommodate 50 people and 40 tents in the Mall with a capacity of up to 100. The Park Service, however, relying on the above regulations, specifically denied CCNV's request that demonstrators be permitted to sleep in the symbolic tents.

CCNV and several individuals then filed an action to prevent the application of the no-camping regulations to the proposed demonstration, which, it was claimed, was not covered by the regulation. It was also submitted that the regulations were unconstitutionally vague, had been discriminatorily applied, and could not be applied to prevent sleeping in the tents without violating the First Amendment. The District Court granted summary judgment in favor of the Park Service. The Court of Appeals, sitting en banc, reversed. The 11 judges produced 6 opinions.... We granted the Government's petition for certiorari, and now reverse.

We need not differ with the view of the Court of Appeals that overnight sleeping in connection with the demonstration is expressive conduct protected to some extent by the First Amendment.... Expression, whether oral or written or symbolized by conduct, is subject to reasonable time, place, or manner restrictions. We have often noted that restrictions of this kind are valid provided that they are justified without reference to the content of the regulated speech, that they are narrowly tailored to serve a significant governmental interest, and that they leave open ample alternative channels for communication of the information.

It is also true that a message may be delivered by conduct that is intended to be communicative and that, in context, would reasonably be understood by the viewer to be communicative. Symbolic expression of this kind may be forbidden or regulated if the conduct itself may constitutionally be regulated, if the regulation is narrowly drawn to further a substantial governmental interest, and if the interest is unrelated to the suppression of free speech. United States v. O'Brien, supra.

… [T]he regulation forbidding sleeping is defensible either as a time, place, or manner restriction or as a regulation of symbolic conduct.… [The "no camping"] provisions, including the ban on sleeping, are clearly limitations on the manner in which the demonstration could be carried out. That sleeping, like the symbolic tents themselves, may be expressive and part of the message delivered by the demonstration does not make the ban any less a limitation on the manner of demonstrating, for reasonable time, place, or manner regulations normally have the purpose and direct effect of limiting expression but are nevertheless valid. Neither does the fact that sleeping, arguendo, may be expressive conduct, rather than oral or written expression, render the sleeping prohibition any less a time, place, or manner regulation. To the contrary, the Park Service neither attempts to ban sleeping generally nor to ban it everywhere in the parks. It has established areas for camping and forbids it elsewhere, including Lafayette Park and the Mall. Considered as such, we have very little trouble concluding that the Park Service may prohibit overnight sleeping in the parks involved here.

…. [T]he prohibition on camping, and on sleeping specifically, is content-neutral and is not being applied because of disagreement with the message presented. Neither was the regulation faulted, nor could it be, on the ground that without overnight sleeping the plight of the homeless could not be communicated in other ways. The regulation otherwise left the demonstration intact, with its symbolic city, signs, and the presence of those who were willing to take their turns in a day-and-night vigil. Respondents do not suggest that there was, or is, any barrier to delivering to the media, or to the public by other means, the intended message concerning the plight of the homeless.

It is also apparent to us that the regulation narrowly focuses on the Government's substantial interest in maintaining the parks in the heart of our Capital in an attractive and intact condition, readily available to the millions of people who wish to see and enjoy them by their presence. To permit camping—using these areas as living accommodations—would be totally inimical to these purposes, as would be readily understood by those who have frequented the National Parks across the country and observed the unfortunate consequences of the activities of those who refuse to confine their camping to designated areas.

It is urged by respondents, and the Court of Appeals was of this view, that if the symbolic city of tents was to be permitted and if the demonstrators did not intend to cook, dig, or engage in aspects of camping other than sleeping, the incremental benefit to the parks could not justify the ban on sleeping, which was here an expressive activity said to enhance the message concerning the plight of the poor and homeless. We cannot agree. In the first place, we seriously doubt that the First Amendment requires the Park Service to permit a demonstration in Lafayette Park and the Mall involving a 24-hour vigil and the erection of tents to accommodate 150 people. Furthermore, although we have assumed for present purposes that the sleeping banned in this case would have an expressive element, it is evident that its major value to this demonstration would be facilitative. Without a permit to sleep, it would be difficult to get the poor and homeless to participate or to be present at all. This much is apparent from the permit application filed by respondents: "Without the incentive of sleeping space or a hot meal, the homeless would not come to the site." The sleeping ban, if enforced, would thus effectively limit the nature, extent, and duration of the demonstration and to that extent ease the pressure on the parks.

Beyond this, however, it is evident from our cases that the validity of this regulation need not be judged solely by reference to the demonstration at hand. Absent the prohibition on sleeping, there would be other groups who would demand permission to deliver an asserted message by camping in Lafayette Park. Some of them would surely have as credible a claim in this regard as does CCNV, and the denial of permits to still others would present difficult problems for the Park Service. With the prohibition, however, as is evident in the case before us, at least some around-the-clock demonstrations lasting for days on end will not materialize, others will be limited in size and duration, and the purposes of the regulation will thus be materially served. Perhaps these purposes would be more effectively and not so clumsily achieved by preventing tents and 24-hour vigils entirely in the core areas. But the Park Service's decision to permit nonsleeping demonstrations does not, in our view, impugn the camping prohibition as a valuable, but perhaps imperfect, protection to the parks. If the Government has a legitimate interest in ensuring that the National Parks are adequately protected, which we think it has, and if the parks would be more exposed to harm without the sleeping prohibition than with it, the ban is safe from invalidation under the First Amendment as a reasonable regulation of the manner in which a demonstration may be carried out.... [T]he regulation "responds precisely to the substantive problems which legitimately concern the [Government]."

... [T]he foregoing analysis demonstrates that the Park Service regulation is sustainable under the four-factor standard of United States v. O'Brien, 391 U.S. 367 (1968), for validating a regulation of expressive conduct, which, in the last analysis is little, if any, different from the standard applied to time, place, or manner restrictions.

> FN8. Reasonable time, place, or manner restrictions are valid even though they directly limit oral or written expression. It would be odd to insist on a higher standard for limitations aimed at regulable conduct and having only an incidental impact on speech. Thus, if the time, place, or manner restriction on expressive sleeping, if that is what is involved in this case, sufficiently and narrowly serves a substantial enough governmental interest to escape First Amendment condemnation, it is untenable to invalidate it under O'Brien on the ground that the governmental interest is insufficient to warrant the intrusion on First Amendment concerns or that there is an inadequate nexus between the regulation and the interest sought to be served. We note that only recently, in a case dealing with the regulation of signs, the Court framed the issue under O'Brien and then based a crucial part of its analysis on the time, place, or manner cases. City Council of Los Angeles v. Taxpayers for Vincent, 466 U.S. 789 (1984).

No one contends that aside from its impact on speech a rule against camping or overnight sleeping in public parks is beyond the constitutional power of the Government to enforce. And for the reasons we have discussed above, there is a substantial Government interest in conserving park property, an interest that is plainly served by, and requires for its implementation, measures such as the proscription of sleeping that are designed to limit the wear and tear on park properties. That interest is unrelated to suppression of expression.

.... The Court of Appeals' suggestions that the Park Service minimize the possible injury by reducing the size, duration, or frequency of demonstrations would still curtail the total allowable expression in which demonstrators could engage, whether by sleeping or otherwise, and these suggestions represent no more than a disagreement with the Park Service over how much protection the core parks require or how an acceptable level of preservation is to be attained. We do not believe, however, that either United States v. O'Brien or the time, place, or manner decisions assign to the judiciary the authority to replace the Park Service as the manager of the Nation's parks or endow the judiciary with the competence to judge how much protection of park lands is wise and how that level of conservation is to be attained. Accordingly, the judgment of the Court of Appeals is reversed.

CHIEF JUSTICE BURGER, concurring.

.... Respondents' attempt at camping in the park is a form of "picketing"; it is conduct, not speech. Moreover, it is conduct that interferes with the rights of others to use Lafayette Park for the purposes for which it was created....

JUSTICE MARSHALL, with whom JUSTICE BRENNAN joins, dissenting.

.... Missing from the majority's description is any inkling that Lafayette Park and the Mall have served as the sites for some of the most rousing political demonstrations in the Nation's history....

The primary purpose for making *sleep* an integral part of the demonstration was "to re-enact the central reality of homelessness," and to impress upon public consciousness, in as dramatic a way as possible, that homelessness is a widespread problem, often ignored, that confronts its victims with life-threatening deprivations.... Here respondents clearly intended to protest the reality of homelessness by sleeping outdoors in the winter in the near vicinity of the magisterial residence of the President of the United States. In addition to accentuating the political character of their protest by their choice of location and mode of communication, respondents also intended to underline the meaning of their protest by giving their demonstration satirical names. Respondents planned to name the demonstration on the Mall "Congressional Village," and the demonstration in Lafayette Park, "Reaganville II."

Nor can there be any doubt that in the surrounding circumstances the likelihood was great that the political significance of sleeping in the parks would be understood by those who viewed it. Certainly the news media understood the significance of respondents' proposed activity; newspapers and magazines from around the Nation reported their previous sleep-in and their planned display. Ordinary citizens, too, would likely understand the political message intended by respondents. This likelihood stems from the remarkably apt fit between the activity in which respondents seek to engage and the social problem they seek to highlight....

Although sleep in the context of this case is symbolic speech protected by the First Amendment, it is nonetheless subject to reasonable time, place, and manner restrictions. I agree with the standard enunciated by the majority: "[Restrictions] of this kind are valid provided that they are justified without reference to the content of the regulated speech, that they are narrowly tailored to serve a significant governmental interest, and that they leave open ample alternative channels for communication of the information." I conclude, however, that the regulations at issue in this case, as applied to respondents, fail to satisfy this standard....

The issue posed by this case is not whether the Government is constitutionally compelled to permit the erection of tents and the staging of a continuous 24-hour vigil; rather, the issue is whether any substantial Government interest is served by banning sleep that is part of a political demonstration.... The First Amendment requires the Government to justify *every* instance of abridgment.... Moreover, the stringency of that requirement is not diminished simply because the activity the Government seeks to restrain is supplemental to other activity that the Government may have permitted out of grace but was not constitutionally compelled to allow. If the Government cannot adequately justify abridgment of protected expression, there is no reason why citizens should be prevented from exercising the first of the rights safeguarded by our Bill of Rights.

The majority's second argument is comprised of the suggestion that, although sleeping contains an element of expression, "its major value to [respondents'] demonstration would have been facilitative." While this observation does provide a hint of the weight the Court attached to respondents' First Amendment claims, it is utterly irrelevant to whether the Government's ban on sleeping advances a substantial Government interest.

FN7. The facilitative purpose of the sleep-in takes away nothing from its independent status as symbolic speech. Moreover, facilitative conduct that is closely related to expressive activity is itself protected by First Amendment considerations.

.... The Court's erroneous application of the standard for ascertaining a reasonable time, place, and manner restriction is also revealed by the majority's conclusion that a substantial governmental interest is served by the sleeping ban because it will discourage "around-the-clock demonstrations for days" and thus further the regulation's purpose "to limit wear and tear on park properties." The majority cites no evidence indicating that sleeping engaged in as symbolic speech will cause *substantial* wear and tear on park property. Furthermore, the Government's application of the sleeping ban in the circumstances of this case is strikingly underinclusive. The majority acknowledges that a proper time, place, and manner restriction must be "narrowly tailored." Here, however, the tailoring requirement is virtually forsaken inasmuch as the Government offers no justification for applying its absolute ban on sleeping yet is willing to allow respondents to engage in activities—such as feigned sleeping—that is no less burdensome.

In short, there are no substantial Government interests advanced by the Government's regulations as applied to respondents....

The Court's salutary skepticism of governmental decisionmaking in First Amendment matters suddenly dissipates once it determines that a restriction is not content-based. The Court evidently assumes that the balance struck by officials is deserving of deference so long as it does not appear to be tainted by content discrimination. What the Court fails to recognize is that public officials have strong incentives to overregulate even in the absence of an intent to censor particular views. This incentive stems from the fact that of the two groups whose interests officials must accommodate—on the one hand, the interests of the general public and, on the other, the interests of those who seek to use a particular forum for First Amendment activity—the political power of the former is likely to be far greater than that of the latter.

Review Questions and Explanations: *Clark*

1. *Clark* presents a classic example of a content-neutral law that comes into conflict with an instance of expressive conduct. A no-camping rule seems pretty standard for parks, or sections of parks; even if the intention in this inner-city park was to target homeless people, it doesn't seem to have been targeting their *speech*. And yet the question still arises whether, in application to this particular protest, the law nevertheless restricted more speech than necessary. Justice Marshall makes the case for why a sleep-in had particular significance to this particular protest. The majority seems to finesse that point by arguing that if this group is allowed to sleep-in, then every protest group will want to sleep-in. Is that plausible?

2. Does the choice of location for a protest itself become a form of expressive conduct, or part of the expressive conduct? Justice Marshall seems to think so. Should this have gotten any weight in the majority analysis?

3. *Clark* also illustrates a regrettable tendency of the Court to create confusion in its already exceedingly complex First Amendment doctrinal frameworks by misusing or changing its own terminology. The Court does this in at least two ways. First, it describes *O'Brien* as a test for "regulation of expressive conduct." But *O'Brien* deals with regulation of generally *non-expressive* conduct that may on occasion be used expressively. Second, it says that the law could be upheld as

a "time, place, or manner" regulation. To be sure, "time, place, or manner" regulations are another form of content-neutral law; but they are laws that regulate the "time, place, or manner" of *speech*. It is not the doctrinal category to use for laws regulating generally non-expressive conduct—like sleeping in a park.

4. An argument that expressive conduct is "conduct, not speech" continues to pop up in separate opinions, but not majority opinions. *See, e.g., Virginia v. Black* (below) (Thomas, J., dissenting). Here, Chief Justice Burger's assertion that picketing is conduct and not speech is his own view, not a correct statement of the case law. *See, e.g., Frisby v. Schultz* (below).

Guided Reading Questions: *Texas v. Johnson*

1. Read the Texas statute carefully (it is in the Court's footnote 1). Does it prohibit only flag burning? Does it prohibit only expressive conduct? Or can you think of conduct that would "intentionally or knowingly desecrate" a venerated object that is not expressive?

2. The opinion sets out the *O'Brien* framework, and then tries to organize its analysis around that. The first question is whether Johnson's conduct is expressive. How does the Court decide this?   *[handwritten: Question #1]*

3. The next step is to ask whether the state's justification for its law is "unrelated to the suppression of speech." The Court identifies two justifications. What are they, and are they speech-related? (This is fundamentally the same as asking whether the law is content-based.)   *[handwritten: Question #2]*

4. Note that a law may be speech-related or content-based *in part*, that is, with respect to some speech or expressive conduct, but not all. It is typical in such cases to consider an as-applied rather than a facial challenge to the law: that's an argument that the law can't be constitutionally applied to regulate the particular conduct in the case before the Court. A facial challenge says that all (or most) applications of the law are unconstitutional, so the entire law is struck down. Which approach does the Court take here?   *[handwritten: Laws that are partially speech-related or content-based. "As applied" challenge, not "facial challenge"]*

5. Because the Court determines that the law is content-based, it applies strict scrutiny. (See Figure 9.1.) The question now becomes whether the state interests justifying the law, albeit speech related, are compelling; and whether the law is narrowly tailored to achieve those interests. What does the Court say?

Texas v. Johnson
491 U.S. 397 (1989)

Majority: *Brennan*, Marshall, Blackmun, Scalia, Kennedy

Concurrence: *Kennedy*

Dissent: *Rehnquist* (CJ), White, O'Connor; *Stevens*

JUSTICE BRENNAN delivered the opinion of the Court.

After publicly burning an American flag as a means of political protest, Gregory Lee Johnson was convicted of desecrating a flag in violation of Texas law. This case presents the question whether his conviction is consistent with the First Amendment. We hold that it is not.

While the Republican National Convention was taking place in Dallas in 1984, respondent Johnson participated in a political demonstration dubbed the "Republican War Chest Tour." As explained in literature distributed by the demonstrators and in speeches made by them, the purpose of this event was to protest the policies of the Reagan administration and of certain Dallas-based corporations. The demonstrators marched through the Dallas streets, chanting political slogans and stopping at several corporate locations to stage "die-ins" intended to dramatize the consequences of nuclear war. On several occasions they spray-painted the walls of buildings and overturned potted plants, but Johnson himself took no part in such activities. He did, however, accept an American flag handed to him by a fellow protestor who had taken it from a flagpole outside one of the targeted buildings.

The demonstration ended in front of Dallas City Hall, where Johnson unfurled the American flag, doused it with kerosene, and set it on fire. While the flag burned, the protestors chanted: "America, the red, white, and blue, we spit on you." After the demonstrators dispersed, a witness to the flag burning collected the flag's remains and buried them in his backyard. No one was physically injured or threatened with injury, though several witnesses testified that they had been seriously offended by the flag burning.

Of the approximately 100 demonstrators, Johnson alone was charged with a crime. The only criminal offense with which he was charged was the desecration of a venerated object in violation of Tex. Penal Code Ann. § 42.09(a)(3). After a trial, he was convicted, sentenced to one year in prison, and fined $ 2,000. The Court of Appeals for the Fifth District of Texas at Dallas affirmed Johnson's conviction, but the Texas Court of Criminal Appeals reversed, (1988), holding that the State could not, consistent with the First Amendment, punish Johnson for burning the flag in these circumstances.

FN1. Texas Penal Code Ann. § 42.09 (1989) provides in full:

§ 42.09. Desecration of Venerated Object

(a) A person commits an offense if he intentionally or knowingly desecrates: (1) a public monument; (2) a place of worship or burial; or (3) a state or national flag.

(b) For purposes of this section, "desecrate" means deface, damage, or otherwise physically mistreat in a way that the actor knows will seriously offend one or more persons likely to observe or discover his action.

(c) An offense under this section is a Class A misdemeanor.

…. Because it reversed Johnson's conviction on the ground that § 42.09 was unconstitutional as applied to him, the state court did not address Johnson's argument that the statute was, on its face, unconstitutionally vague and overbroad. We granted certiorari, and now affirm.

Johnson was convicted of flag desecration for burning the flag rather than for uttering insulting words. This fact somewhat complicates our consideration of his conviction under the First Amendment. We must first determine whether Johnson's burning of the flag constituted expressive conduct, permitting him to invoke the First Amendment in challenging his conviction. See, e.g., Spence v. Washington, 418 U.S. 405, 409–411 (1974). If his conduct was expressive, we next decide whether the State's regulation is related to the suppression of free expression. See, e.g., United States v. O'Brien, 391 U.S. 367, 377 (1968). If the State's regulation is not related to expression, then the less stringent standard we announced in United States v. O'Brien for regulations of noncommunicative conduct controls. If it is, then we are outside of O'Brien's test, and we must ask whether this interest justifies Johnson's conviction under a more demanding standard.

FN3. Although Johnson has raised a facial challenge to Texas' flag-desecration statute, we choose to resolve this case on the basis of his claim that the statute as applied to him violates the First Amendment. Section 42.09 regulates only physical conduct with respect to the flag, not the written or spoken word, and although one violates the statute only if one "knows" that one's physical treatment of the flag "will seriously offend one or more persons likely to observe or discover his action," Tex. Penal Code Ann. § 42.09(b), this fact does not necessarily mean that the statute applies only to expressive conduct protected by the First Amendment. A tired person might, for example, drag a flag through the mud, knowing that this conduct is likely to offend others, and yet have no thought of expressing any idea; neither the language nor the Texas courts' interpretations of the statute precludes the possibility that such a person would be prosecuted for flag desecration. Because the prosecution of a person who had not engaged in expressive conduct would pose a different case, and because this case may be disposed of on narrower grounds, we address only Johnson's claim that § 42.09 as applied to political expression like his violates the First Amendment.

[handwritten margin note: Court narrows the grounds of its holding.]

A third possibility is that the State's asserted interest is simply not implicated on these facts, and in that event the interest drops out of the picture.

The First Amendment literally forbids the abridgment only of "speech," but we have long recognized that its protection does not end at the spoken or written word.... In deciding whether particular conduct possesses sufficient communicative elements to bring the First Amendment into play, we have asked whether "[a]n intent to convey a particularized message was present, and [whether] the likelihood was great that the message would be understood by those who viewed it." Hence, we have recognized the expressive nature of students' wearing of black armbands to protest American military involvement in Vietnam, Tinker v. Des Moines Independent Community School Dist., 393 U.S. 503, 505 (1969); of a sit-in by blacks in a "whites only" area to protest segregation, Brown v. Louisiana, 383 U.S. 131, 141–142 (1966); of the wearing of American military uniforms in a dramatic presentation criticizing American involvement in Vietnam, Schacht v. United States, 398 U.S. 58 (1970); and of picketing about a wide variety of causes.

Especially pertinent to this case are our decisions recognizing the communicative nature of conduct relating to flags. Attaching a peace sign to the flag, Spence, supra, at 409–410; refusing to salute the flag, Barnette, 319 U.S., at 632; and displaying a red flag, Stromberg v. California, 283 U.S. 359, 368–369 (1931), we have held, all may find shelter under the First Amendment.... The very purpose of a national flag is to serve as a symbol of our country; it is, one might say, "the one visible manifestation of two hundred years of nationhood." Id., at 603 (Rehnquist, J., dissenting). Thus, we have observed:

> [T]he flag salute is a form of utterance. Symbolism is a primitive but effective way of communicating ideas. The use of an emblem or flag to symbolize some system, idea, institution, or personality, is a short cut from mind to mind. Causes and nations, political parties, lodges and ecclesiastical groups seek to knit the loyalty of their followings to a flag or banner, a color or design. Barnette, supra, at 632.

Pregnant with expressive content, the flag as readily signifies this Nation as does the combination of letters found in "America."

.... The State of Texas conceded for purposes of its oral argument in this case that Johnson's conduct was expressive conduct, Tr. of Oral Arg. 4, and this concession seems to us as prudent as was Washington's in Spence. Johnson burned an American flag as part—indeed, as the culmination—of a political demonstration that coincided with the convening of the Republican Party and its renomination of Ronald Reagan for President.

The expressive, overtly political nature of this conduct was both intentional and overwhelmingly apparent....

The government generally has a freer hand in restricting expressive conduct than it has in restricting the written or spoken word. It may not, however, proscribe particular conduct *because* it has expressive elements. "[W]hat might be termed the more generalized guarantee of freedom of expression makes the communicative nature of conduct an inadequate *basis* for singling out that conduct for proscription. A law *directed at* the communicative nature of conduct must, like a law directed at speech itself, be justified by the substantial showing of need that the First Amendment requires." It is, in short, not simply the verbal or nonverbal nature of the expression, but the governmental interest at stake, that helps to determine whether a restriction on that expression is valid.

Thus, although we have recognized that where "'speech' and 'nonspeech' elements are combined in the same course of conduct, a sufficiently important governmental interest in regulating the nonspeech element can justify incidental limitations on First Amendment freedoms," O'Brien, supra, at 376, we have limited the applicability of O'Brien's relatively lenient standard to those cases in which "the governmental interest is unrelated to the suppression of free expression." In stating, moreover, that O'Brien's test "in the last analysis is little, if any, different from the standard applied to time, place, or manner restrictions," Clark v. Community for Creative Non-Violence, 468 U.S. 288, 298 (1984), we have highlighted the requirement that the governmental interest in question be unconnected to expression in order to come under O'Brien's less demanding rule....

Texas claims that its interest in preventing breaches of the peace justifies Johnson's conviction for flag desecration. However.... [t]he only evidence offered by the State at trial to show the reaction to Johnson's actions was the testimony of several persons who had been seriously offended by the flag burning.

The State's position, therefore, amounts to a claim that an audience that takes serious offense at particular expression is necessarily likely to disturb the peace and that the expression may be prohibited on this basis. Our precedents do not countenance such a presumption. On the contrary, they recognize that a principal "function of free speech under our system of government is to invite dispute. It may indeed best serve its high purpose when it induces a condition of unrest, creates dissatisfaction with conditions as they are, or even stirs people to anger." Terminiello v. Chicago, 337 U.S. 1, 4 (1949). It would be odd indeed to conclude both that "if it is the speaker's opinion that gives offense, that consequence is a reason for according it constitutional protection," FCC v. Pacifica Foundation, 438 U.S. 726, 745 (1978) (opinion of Stevens, J.), and that the government may ban the expression of certain disagreeable ideas on the unsupported presumption that their very disagreeableness will provoke violence.

Thus, we have not permitted the government to assume that every expression of a provocative idea will incite a riot, but have instead required careful consideration of the actual circumstances surrounding such expression, asking whether the expression "is directed to inciting or producing imminent lawless action and is likely to incite or produce such action." Brandenburg v. Ohio, 395 U.S. 444, 447 (1969) (reviewing circumstances surrounding rally and speeches by Ku Klux Klan). To accept Texas' arguments that it need only demonstrate "the potential for a breach of the peace," Brief for Petitioner 37, and that every flag burning necessarily possesses that potential, would be to eviscerate our holding in Brandenburg. This we decline to do.

Nor does Johnson's expressive conduct fall within that small class of "fighting words" that are "likely to provoke the average person to retaliation, and thereby cause a breach of the peace." Chaplinsky v. New Hampshire, 315 U.S. 568, 574 (1942). No reasonable onlooker would have regarded Johnson's generalized expression of dissatisfaction with the policies of the Federal Government as a direct personal insult or an invitation to exchange fisticuffs.

We thus conclude that the State's interest in maintaining order is not implicated on these facts....

The State also asserts an interest in preserving the flag as a symbol of nationhood and national unity. In Spence, we acknowledged that the government's interest in preserving the flag's special symbolic value "is directly related to expression in the context of activity" such as affixing a peace symbol to a flag. We are equally persuaded that this interest is related to expression in the case of Johnson's burning of the flag. The State, apparently, is concerned that such conduct will lead people to believe either that the flag does not stand for nationhood and national unity, but instead reflects other, less positive concepts, or that the concepts reflected in the flag do not in fact exist, that is, that we do not enjoy unity as a Nation. These concerns blossom only when a person's treatment of the flag communicates some message, and thus are related "to the suppression of free expression" within the meaning of O'Brien. We are thus outside of O'Brien's test altogether.

It remains to consider whether the State's interest in preserving the flag as a symbol of nationhood and national unity justifies Johnson's conviction.... Johnson was not, we add, prosecuted for the expression of just any idea; he was prosecuted for his expression of dissatisfaction with the policies of this country, expression situated at the core of our First Amendment values.

Moreover, Johnson was prosecuted because he knew that his politically charged expression would cause "serious offense." If he had burned the flag as a means of disposing of it because it was dirty or torn, he would not have been convicted of flag desecration under this Texas law: federal law designates burning as the preferred means of disposing of a flag "when it is in such condition that it is no longer a fitting emblem for display," 36 U.S.C. §176(k), and Texas has no quarrel with this means of disposal. Brief for Petitioner 45. The Texas law is thus not aimed at protecting the physical integrity of the flag in all circumstances, but is designed instead to protect it only against impairments that would cause serious offense to others. Texas concedes as much: "Section 42.09(b) reaches only those severe acts of physical abuse of the flag carried out in a way likely to be offensive. The statute mandates intentional or knowing abuse, that is, the kind of mistreatment that is not innocent, but rather is intentionally designed to seriously offend other individuals."

Whether Johnson's treatment of the flag violated Texas law thus depended on the likely communicative impact of his expressive conduct.... [T]his restriction on Johnson's expression is content-based.... We must therefore subject the State's asserted interest in preserving the special symbolic character of the flag to "the most exacting scrutiny."

Texas argues that its interest in preserving the flag as a symbol of nationhood and national unity survives this close analysis.... According to Texas, if one physically treats the flag in a way that would tend to cast doubt on either the idea that nationhood and national unity are the flag's referents or that national unity actually exists, the message conveyed thereby is a harmful one and therefore may be prohibited.

If there is a bedrock principle underlying the First Amendment, it is that the government may not prohibit the expression of an idea simply because society finds the idea itself offensive or disagreeable.... We have not recognized an exception to this principle even where our flag has been involved.... In short, nothing in our precedents suggests that a State may foster its own view of the flag by prohibiting expressive conduct relating to it.

To bring its argument outside our precedents, Texas attempts to convince us that even if its interest in preserving the flag's symbolic role does not allow it to prohibit words or some expressive conduct critical of the flag, it does permit it to forbid the outright destruction of the flag.... Texas' focus on the precise nature of Johnson's expression, moreover, misses the point of our prior decisions: their enduring lesson, that the government may not prohibit expression simply because it disagrees with its message, is not dependent on the particular mode in which one chooses to express an idea....

We never before have held that the Government may ensure that a symbol be used to express only one view of that symbol or its referents.... There is, moreover, no indication — either in the text of the Constitution or in our cases interpreting it — that a separate juridical category exists for the American flag alone.

.... It cannot be gainsaid that there is a special place reserved for the flag in this Nation, and thus we do not doubt that the government has a legitimate interest in making efforts to "preserv[e] the national flag as an unalloyed symbol of our country." Spence, 418 U.S., at 412.... To say that the government has an interest in encouraging proper treatment of the flag, however, is not to say that it may criminally punish a person for burning a flag as a means of political protest. "National unity as an end which officials may foster by persuasion and example is not in question. The problem is whether under our Constitution compulsion as here employed is a permissible means for its achievement." Barnette, 319 U.S., at 640....

We are tempted to say, in fact, that the flag's deservedly cherished place in our community will be strengthened, not weakened, by our holding today. Our decision is a reaffirmation of the principles of freedom and inclusiveness that the flag best reflects, and of the conviction that our toleration of criticism such as Johnson's is a sign and source of our strength. Indeed, one of the proudest images of our flag, the one immortalized in our own national anthem, is of the bombardment it survived at Fort McHenry. It is the Nation's resilience, not its rigidity, that Texas sees reflected in the flag — and it is that resilience that we reassert today.... The judgment of the Texas Court of Criminal Appeals is therefor affirmed.

JUSTICE KENNEDY, concurring.

I write not to qualify the words Justice Brennan chooses so well, for he says with power all that is necessary to explain our ruling. I join his opinion without reservation, but with a keen sense that this case, like others before us from time to time, exacts its personal toll.... It is poignant but fundamental that the flag protects those who hold it in contempt....

CHIEF JUSTICE REHNQUIST, with whom JUSTICE WHITE and JUSTICE O'CONNOR join, dissenting.

In holding this Texas statute unconstitutional, the Court ignores Justice Holmes' familiar aphorism that "a page of history is worth a volume of logic." New York Trust Co. v. Eisner, 256 U.S. 345, 349 (1921). For more than 200 years, the American flag has occupied a unique position as the symbol of our Nation, a uniqueness that justifies a governmental prohibition against flag burning in the way respondent Johnson did here....

Both Congress and the States have enacted numerous laws regulating misuse of the American flag. Until 1967, Congress left the regulation of misuse of the flag up to the States. Now, however, 18 U.S.C. § 700(a) provides that: "Whoever knowingly casts contempt upon any flag of the United States by publicly mutilating, defacing, defiling, burning, or trampling upon it shall be fined not more than $1,000 or imprisoned for not more than one year, or both." Congress has also prescribed, inter alia, detailed rules for the design of the flag, 4 U.S.C. § 1, the time and occasion of flag's display, 36 U.S.C. § 174, the position and manner of its display, § 175, respect for the flag, § 176, and conduct during hoisting, lowering, and passing of the flag, § 177....

The American flag, then, throughout more than 200 years of our history, has come to be the visible symbol embodying our Nation. It does not represent the views of any particular political party, and it does not represent any particular political philosophy. The flag is not simply another "idea" or "point of view" competing for recognition in the marketplace of ideas. Millions and millions of Americans regard it with an almost mystical reverence regardless of what sort of social, political, or philosophical beliefs they may have. I cannot agree that the First Amendment invalidates the Act of Congress, and the laws of 48 of the 50 States, which make criminal the public burning of the flag....

The Court concludes its opinion with a regrettably patronizing civics lecture, presumably addressed to the Members of both Houses of Congress, the members of the 48 state legislatures that enacted prohibitions against flag burning, and the troops fighting under that flag in Vietnam who objected to its being burned: "The way to preserve the flag's special role is not to punish those who feel differently about these matters. It is to persuade them that they are wrong." The Court's role as the final expositor of the Constitution is well established, but its role as a Platonic guardian admonishing those responsible to public opinion as if they were truant schoolchildren has no similar place in our system of government....

JUSTICE STEVENS, dissenting.

As the Court analyzes this case, it presents the question whether the State of Texas, or indeed the Federal Government, has the power to prohibit the public desecration of the American flag. The question is unique. In my judgment rules that apply to a host of other symbols, such as state flags, armbands, or various privately promoted emblems of political or commercial identity, are not necessarily controlling. Even if flag burning could be considered just another species of symbolic speech under the logical application of the rules that the Court has developed in its interpretation of the First Amendment in other contexts, this case has an intangible dimension that makes those rules inapplicable....

Review Questions and Explanations: *Johnson*

1. Apparently Texas tried, as its first line of argument, to defend the statute under *O'Brien*, on the theory that the statute regulated conduct to further a state interest "unrelated to the suppression of free expression." Do you think the Texas anti-desecration law is distinguishable from the law against destroying a draft card in *O'Brien*?

2. The Court spends a page analyzing whether intentional flag burning in this case is expressive conduct, only to conclude by saying that the lawyers for Texas had conceded the point, which was "overwhelmingly obvious" from the get go! The "expressive conduct" problem here is not whether Johnson's conduct was expressive, but whether the statute can be justified as regulating non-expressive conduct.

Can you imagine cases in which a flag is defaced or destroyed (1) intentionally and (2) with knowledge that it will cause serious offense, if indeed no expressive conduct is at issue? Indeed, the distinction between "desecration" and "damage" has to do with the ideas and symbolism attached to the former. The Court itself had a hard time thinking of examples: note the implausibility of the Court's example of the person who drags a flag through the mud because he's too tired to carry it. If such examples are hard to dream up, what does that suggest about how to analyze the statute?

3. Can a state ban highly provocative political expression on the strength of its interest to "keep the peace" or "prevent violence"? What does the Court say? Is it accurate that, as the Court concludes, "the State's interest in maintaining order is not implicated on these facts"? This issue also arises in the "fighting words" context, and some commentators analyze *Johnson* as a "fighting words" case. The problem of protected speech being shut down due to listeners' disruptive reactions is sometimes called "the heckler's veto." That is, a heckler can effectively induce law enforcement to stop a speaker by creating a disturbance in the audience.

4. The dissents seem to be arguing for some sort of special "flag burning exception" to the First Amendment. What is the basis for that? Is it that flag burning should be deemed unprotected speech, like fighting words? Note that a general "test" for unprotected speech is that it has no value for "any exposition of ideas." Doesn't the debate between the majority and dissenters undermine such a characterization of flag burning as protest? If flag burning is not valueless as expressive conduct, perhaps the constitutional argument for permitting its prohibition is that there is a compelling interest in banning ideological flag burning. Is there such a compelling interest?

2. Time, Place, or Manner Regulations

Laws that regulate the time, place, or manner of speech have been upheld in recognition of the principle that "even protected speech is not equally permissible in all places and at all times." *Cornelius v. NAACP Legal Def. & Ed. Fund*, 473 U.S. 788, 799 (1985). In contrast to laws regulating conduct that may sometimes happen to be expressive, "time, place, or manner" regulations *are* intended to regulate speech. But they are defensible if they do not distinguish speech on the basis of its content and do not unduly suppress speech (that is, restrict more speech than necessary to accomplish the substantial governmental interest underlying the law). Commonplace examples are ordinances banning parades or demonstrations in city streets or after certain hours in residential neighborhoods. A frequently cited illustration comes from *Kovacs v. Cooper*, 336 U.S. 77 (1949), in which the Court upheld a city ordinance banning the use of "sound trucks"—trucks mounted with sound amplification equipment. The problem with the trucks was not the content of the messages, but the noise. (Ironically, given the frequent citation to the case, there was no agreed majority rationale in *Kovacs*.)

Guided Reading Questions: *Frisby v. Schultz* and *City of Ladue v. Gilleo*

1. In *Frisby* and *Ladue*, identify the test used by the Court to assess the constitutionality of the law and the reasons for choosing the particular test.

2. Next, examine how the Court applies the test. First, this will involve identifying the government's interest (the purposes or justifications for the law).

Is the interest even legitimate? If so, how strong is it (compelling, significant, substantial, etc.)?

3. The Court will then look at legislative fit: Does the conduct prohibition match up with the purported goal? If so, how carefully does the law target the "evil" without collateral damage to other (speech-related) interests? These questions are analyzed as narrow tailoring, which is the doctrinal mechanism used to ensure that the law prohibits no more speech than necessary to accomplish the state's goals.

Frisby v. Schultz

487 U.S. 474 (1988)

Majority: *O'Connor*, Rehnquist (CJ), Blackmun, Scalia, Kennedy

Concurrence in the judgment: *White*

Dissent: *Brennan*, Marshall; *Stevens*

JUSTICE O'CONNOR delivered the opinion of the Court.

.... Brookfield, Wisconsin, is a residential suburb of Milwaukee with a population of approximately 4,300. The appellees, Sandra C. Schultz and Robert C. Braun, are individuals strongly opposed to abortion and wish to express their views on the subject by picketing on a public street outside the Brookfield residence of a doctor who apparently performs abortions at two clinics in neighboring towns. Appellees and others engaged in precisely that activity, assembling outside the doctor's home on at least six occasions between April 20, 1985, and May 20, 1985, for periods ranging from one to one and a half hours. The size of the group varied from 11 to more than 40. The picketing was generally orderly and peaceful; the town never had occasion to invoke any of its various ordinances prohibiting obstruction of the streets, loud and unnecessary noises, or disorderly conduct. Nonetheless, the picketing generated substantial controversy and numerous complaints.

[On May 15, 1985, the Town Board enacted a] flat ban on all residential picketing: "It *RULE* is unlawful for any person to engage in picketing before or about the residence or dwelling of any individual in the Town of Brookfield."

The ordinance itself recites the primary purpose of this ban: "the protection and preservation of the home" through assurance "that members of the community enjoy in their homes and dwellings a feeling of well-being, tranquility, and privacy." The Town Board believed that a ban was necessary because it determined that "the practice of picketing before or about residences and dwellings causes emotional disturbance and distress to the occupants ... [and] has as its object the harassing of such occupants." The ordinance also evinces a concern for public safety, noting that picketing obstructs and interferes with "the free use of public sidewalks and public ways of travel."

On May 18, 1985, appellees were informed by the town attorney that enforcement of the ... ordinance would begin on May 21, 1985. Faced with this threat of arrest and prosecution, appellees ceased picketing in Brookfield and filed this lawsuit in the United States District Court for the Eastern District of Wisconsin. The complaint was brought under 42 U.S.C. § 1983 and sought declaratory as well as preliminary and permanent injunctive relief on the grounds that the ordinance violated the First Amendment. Appellees named appellants—the three members of the Town Board, the Chief of Police, the town attorney, and the town itself—as defendants. The District Court granted appellees' motion for a preliminary injunction.... A divided panel of the United States Court of Appeals for the Seventh Circuit affirmed.

The antipicketing ordinance operates at the core of the First Amendment by prohibiting appellees from engaging in picketing on an issue of public concern. Because of the importance of "uninhibited, robust, and wide-open" debate on public issues, New York Times Co. v. Sullivan, 376 U.S. 254, 270 (1964), we have traditionally subjected restrictions on public issue picketing to careful scrutiny. Of course, "[e]ven protected speech is not equally permissible in all places and at all times."

To ascertain what limits, if any, may be placed on protected speech, we have often focused on the "place" of that speech, considering the nature of the forum the speaker seeks to employ. Our cases have recognized that the standards by which limitations on speech must be evaluated "differ depending on the character of the property at issue." Perry Education Assn. v. Perry Local Educators' Assn., 460 U.S. 37, 44 (1983). Specifically, we have identified three types of fora: "the traditional public forum, the public forum created by government designation, and the nonpublic forum."

.... [W]e have repeatedly referred to public streets as the archetype of a traditional public forum.... Our prior holdings make clear that a public street does not lose its status as a traditional public forum simply because it runs through a residential neighborhood.... No particularized inquiry into the precise nature of a specific street is necessary; all public streets are held in the public trust and are properly considered traditional public forā.... The residential character of those streets may well inform the application of the relevant test, but it does not lead to a different test; the antipicketing ordinance must be judged against the stringent standards we have established for restrictions on speech in traditional public fora:

> [the state] must show that its regulation is necessary to serve a compelling state interest and that it is narrowly drawn to achieve that end.... The State may also enforce regulations of the time, place, and manner of expression which are content-neutral, are narrowly tailored to serve a significant government interest, and leave open ample alternative channels of communication. Perry, supra, at 45 (citations omitted).

.... [T]he appropriate level of scrutiny is initially tied to whether the statute distinguishes between prohibited and permitted speech on the basis of content.... Following our normal practice, "we defer to the construction of a state statute given it by the lower federal courts ... to reflect our belief that district courts and courts of appeals are better schooled in and more able to interpret the laws of their respective States." Thus, we accept the lower courts' conclusion that the Brookfield ordinance is content-neutral. Accordingly, we turn to consider whether the ordinance is "narrowly tailored to serve a significant government interest" and whether it "leave[s] open ample alternative channels of communication."

.... [T]he ordinance is readily subject to a narrowing construction that avoids constitutional difficulties. Specifically, the use of the singular form of the words "residence" and "dwelling" suggests that the ordinance is intended to prohibit only picketing focused on, and taking place in front of, a particular residence.... This narrow reading is supported by the representations of counsel for the town at oral argument, which indicate that the town takes, and will enforce, a limited view of the "picketing" proscribed by the ordinance. Thus, generally speaking, "picketing would be having the picket proceed on a definite course or route in front of a home." Tr. of Oral Arg. 8. The picket need not be carrying a sign, but in order to fall within the scope of the ordinance the picketing must be directed at a single residence. General marching through residential neighborhoods, or even *ample alternative Channels of Communication* walking a route in front of an entire block of houses, is not prohibited by this ordinance. Id., at 15. Accordingly, we construe the ban to be a limited one; only focused picketing taking place solely in front of a particular residence is prohibited.

So narrowed, the ordinance permits the more general dissemination of a message. As appellants explain, the limited nature of the prohibition makes it virtually self-evident that ample alternatives remain:

> Protestors have not been barred from the residential neighborhoods. They may enter such neighborhoods, alone or in groups, even marching.... They may go door-to-door to proselytize their views. They may distribute literature in this manner ... or through the mails. They may contact residents by telephone, short of harassment." Brief for Appellants 41–42 (citations omitted).

We readily agree that the ordinance preserves ample alternative channels of communication and thus move on to inquire whether the ordinance serves a significant government interest....

"The State's interest in protecting the well-being, tranquility, and privacy of the home is certainly of the highest order in a free and civilized society." Carey v. Brown, 447 U.S., at 471. Our prior decisions have often remarked on the unique nature of the home, "the last citadel of the tired, the weary, and the sick," and have recognized that "[p]reserving the sanctity of the home, the one retreat to which men and women can repair to escape from the tribulations of their daily pursuits, is surely an important value."

One important aspect of residential privacy is protection of the unwilling listener. Although in many locations, we expect individuals simply to avoid speech they do not want to hear, the home is different.... [A] special benefit of the privacy all citizens enjoy within their own walls, which the State may legislate to protect, is an ability to avoid intrusions. Thus, we have repeatedly held that individuals are not required to welcome unwanted speech into their own homes and that the government may protect this freedom. See, e.g., FCC v. Pacifica Foundation, 438 U.S. 726, 748–749 (1978) (offensive radio broadcasts); Rowan, supra (offensive mailings); Kovacs v. Cooper, 336 U.S. 77, 86–87 (1949) (sound trucks).... There simply is no right to force speech into the home of an unwilling listener.

It remains to be considered, however, whether the Brookfield ordinance is narrowly tailored to protect only unwilling recipients of the communications. A statute is narrowly tailored if it targets and eliminates no more than the exact source of the "evil" it seeks to remedy. A complete ban can be narrowly tailored, but only if each activity within the proscription's scope is an appropriately targeted evil. For example, in Taxpayers for Vincent we upheld an ordinance that banned all signs on public property because...."the substantive evil—visual blight—[was] not merely a possible byproduct of the activity, but [was] created by the medium of expression itself."

The same is true here. The type of focused picketing prohibited by the Brookfield ordinance is fundamentally different from more generally directed means of communication that may not be completely banned in residential areas. In such cases "the flow of information [is not] into ... household[s], but to the public." Here, in contrast, the picketing is narrowly directed at the household, not the public. The type of picketers banned by the Brookfield ordinance generally do not seek to disseminate a message to the general public, but to intrude upon the targeted resident, and to do so in an especially offensive way. Moreover, even if some such picketers have a broader communicative purpose, their activity nonetheless inherently and offensively intrudes on residential privacy. The devastating effect of targeted picketing on the quiet enjoyment of the home is beyond doubt.... ("[There] are few of us that would feel comfortable knowing that a stranger lurks outside our home").... The resident is figuratively, and perhaps literally, trapped within the home, and because of the unique and subtle impact of such picketing is left with no ready means of avoiding the unwanted speech. Thus, the "evil" of targeted residential picketing, "the very presence of an unwelcome visitor at the home," is "created by the medium of expression itself." Accordingly, the Brookfield ordinance's complete ban of that particular medium of expression is narrowly tailored.

Of course, this case presents only a facial challenge to the ordinance. Particular hypothetical applications of the ordinance — to, for example, a particular resident's use of his or her home as a place of business or public meeting, or to picketers present at a particular home by invitation of the resident — may present somewhat different questions.... The contrary judgment of the Court of Appeals is reversed.

JUSTICE WHITE, concurring in the judgment.

I agree with the Court that an ordinance which only forbade picketing before a single residence would not be unconstitutional on its face....

The Court endorses a narrow construction of the ordinance by relying on the town counsel's representations, made at oral argument, that the ordinance forbids only single-residence picketing. In light of the view taken by the lower federal courts and the apparent failure of counsel below to press on those courts the narrowing construction that has been suggested here, I have reservations about relying on counsel's statements as an authoritative statement of the law....

There is nevertheless sufficient force in the town counsel's representations about the reach of the ordinance to avoid application of the overbreadth doctrine in this case, which as we have frequently emphasized is such "strong medicine" that it "has been employed by the Court sparingly and only as a last resort." ...

JUSTICE BRENNAN, with whom JUSTICE MARSHALL joins, dissenting.

The Court today sets out the appropriate legal tests and standards governing the question presented, and proceeds to apply most of them correctly. Regrettably, though, the Court errs in the final step of its analysis, and approves an ordinance banning significantly more speech than is necessary to achieve the government's substantial and legitimate goal. Accordingly, I must dissent.

.... The mere fact that speech takes place in a residential neighborhood does not automatically implicate a residential privacy interest.... [So] long as the speech remains outside the home and does not unduly coerce the occupant, the government's heightened interest in protecting residential privacy is not implicated.

The ... last prong of the time, place, and manner test [whether the ordinance is narrowly tailored to achieve the governmental interest] requires that the government demonstrate that the offending aspects of the prohibited manner of speech cannot be separately, and less intrusively, controlled....

Without question there are many aspects of residential picketing that, if unregulated, might easily become intrusive or unduly coercive. Indeed, some of these aspects are illustrated by this very case. As the District Court found, before the ordinance took effect up to 40 sign-carrying, slogan-shouting protesters regularly converged on Dr. Victoria's home and, in addition to protesting, warned young children not to go near the house because Dr. Victoria was a "baby killer." Further, the throng repeatedly trespassed onto the Victorias' property and at least once blocked the exits to their home. Surely it is within the government's power to enact regulations as necessary to prevent such intrusive and coercive abuses. Thus, for example, the government could constitutionally regulate the number of residential picketers, the hours during which a residential picket may take place, or the noise level of such a picket. In short, substantial regulation is permitted to neutralize the intrusive or unduly coercive aspects of picketing around the home. But to say that picketing may be substantially regulated is not to say that it may be prohibited in its entirety. Once size, time, volume, and the like have been controlled to ensure that the picket is no longer intrusive or coercive, only the speech itself remains, conveyed perhaps by a lone, silent individual, walking back and forth with a sign. Such speech, which no longer implicates the heightened governmental interest in residential privacy, is nevertheless banned by the Brookfield law. Therefore, the ordinance is not narrowly tailored.

A valid time, place, or manner law neutrally regulates speech only to the extent necessary to achieve a substantial governmental interest, and no further. Because the Court is unwilling to examine the Brookfield ordinance in light of the precise governmental interest at issue, it condones a law that suppresses substantially more speech than is necessary. I dissent.

JUSTICE STEVENS, dissenting.

.... The picketing that gave rise to the ordinance enacted in this case was obviously intended to do more than convey a message of opposition to the character of the doctor's practice; it was intended to cause him and his family substantial psychological distress.... As is often the function of picketing, during the periods of protest the doctor's home was held under a virtual siege. I do not believe that picketing for the sole purpose of imposing psychological harm on a family in the shelter of their home is constitutionally protected. I do believe, however, that the picketers have a right to communicate their strong opposition to abortion to the doctor, but after they have had a fair opportunity to communicate that message, I see little justification for allowing them to remain in front of his home and repeat it over and over again simply to harm the doctor and his family. Thus, I agree that the ordinance may be constitutionally applied to the kind of picketing that gave rise to its enactment.

On the other hand, the ordinance is unquestionably "overbroad" in that it prohibits some communication that is protected by the First Amendment.... My hunch is that the town will probably not enforce its ban against friendly, innocuous, or even brief unfriendly picketing, and that the Court may be right in concluding that its legitimate sweep makes its overbreadth insubstantial. But.... [the] scope of the ordinance gives the town officials far too much discretion in making enforcement decisions; while we sit by and await further developments, potential picketers must act at their peril.... [It] it is a simple matter for the town to amend its ordinance and to limit the ban to conduct that unreasonably interferes with the privacy of the home and does not serve a reasonable communicative purpose. Accordingly, I respectfully dissent.

Review Questions and Explanations: *Frisby*

1. The idea of imposing a limiting construction—interpreting a statute in a way that narrows its scope without unduly changing its fundamental meaning or intent—to avoid unconstitutional applications (or even constitutional close calls) is a recurring theme throughout constitutional adjudication, but particularly

in the First Amendment area. Note how the Court here comes up with a limiting construction through a sort of interactive process with the lawyers for Brookfield—relying on their briefs and statements at oral argument. To what extent is it appropriate for an attorney to "collude" in narrowing a legislative act in this way?

2. Justice Stevens prefers to see the limiting constructions formally written into a new ordinance, rather than waiting to see how the town counsel's enforcement intentions unfold. Do you agree that it is "a simple matter" to amend the ordinance to protect residential privacy without prohibiting protected speech?

3. What is the basis of disagreement between the majority and the Brennan dissent?

City of Ladue v. Gilleo
512 U.S. 43 (1994)

Unanimous decision: *Stevens*, Rehnquist (CJ), Blackmun, O'Connor, Scalia, Kennedy, Souter, Thomas, Ginsburg

Concurrence: *O'Connor* (omitted)

JUSTICE STEVENS delivered the opinion of the Court.

[Respondent Margaret P. Gilleo had placed an 8.5- by 11-inch sign in the second story window of her home stating, "For Peace in the Gulf." This sign appeared to be in violation of a City of Ladue ordinance that prohibited homeowners from displaying any signs on their property except "residence identification" signs, "for sale" signs, and signs warning of safety hazards. The ordinance also permitted commercial establishments, churches, and nonprofit organizations to erect certain signs that are not allowed at residences. The stated purpose of the ordinance was to control "ugliness, visual blight and clutter" in the area, to preserve the "special ambience of the community," and to prevent signs from causing "safety and traffic hazards to motorists, pedestrians, and children." Gilleo filed suit under 42 U.S.C. § 1983 challenging the ordinance. The District Court held the ordinance unconstitutional, and the Court of Appeals affirmed.]

While signs are a form of expression protected by the Free Speech Clause, they pose distinctive problems that are subject to municipalities' police powers. Unlike oral speech, signs take up space and may obstruct views, distract motorists, displace alternative uses for land, and pose other problems that legitimately call for regulation. It is common ground that governments may regulate the physical characteristics of signs—just as they can, within reasonable bounds and absent censorial purpose, regulate audible expression in its capacity as noise....

[Our] decisions identify two analytically distinct grounds for challenging the constitutionality of a municipal ordinance regulating the display of signs. One is that the measure in effect restricts too little speech because its exemptions discriminate on the basis of the signs' messages. Alternatively, such provisions are subject to attack on the ground that they simply prohibit too much protected speech.... [Even if the exemptions in the sign-prohibition ordinance do not constitute impermissible content or viewpoint discrimination, exemptions of this sort] may diminish the credibility of the government's rationale for restricting speech in the first place. In this case, at the very least, the exemptions from Ladue's ordinance demonstrate that Ladue has concluded that the interest in allowing certain messages to be conveyed by means of residential signs outweighs the City's esthetic interest in eliminating outdoor signs. Ladue has not imposed a flat ban on signs because it has determined that at least some of them are too vital to be banned.

... [T]he City might theoretically remove [this defect] in its ordinance by simply repealing all of the exemptions. If, however, the ordinance is also vulnerable because it prohibits too much speech, that solution would not save it.... Therefore, we first ask whether Ladue may properly *prohibit* Gilleo from displaying her sign, and then, only if necessary, consider the separate question whether it was improper for the City simultaneously to *permit* certain other signs....

Gilleo and other residents of Ladue are forbidden to display virtually any "sign" on their property.... Ladue has almost completely foreclosed a venerable means of communication that is both unique and important. It has totally foreclosed that medium to political, religious, or personal messages. Signs that react to a local happening or express a view on a controversial issue both reflect and animate change in the life of a community. Often placed on lawns or in windows, residential signs play an important part in political campaigns, during which they are displayed to signal the resident's support for particular candidates, parties, or causes. They may not afford the same opportunities for conveying complex ideas as do other media, but residential signs have long been an important and distinct medium of expression.

.... Although prohibitions foreclosing entire media may be completely free of content or viewpoint discrimination, the danger they pose to the freedom of speech is readily apparent—by eliminating a common means of speaking, such measures can suppress too much speech.

Ladue contends, however, that its ordinance is a mere regulation of the "time, place, or manner" of speech because residents remain free to convey their desired messages by other means, such as *hand-held* signs, "letters, handbills, flyers, telephone calls, newspaper advertisements, bumper stickers, speeches, and neighborhood or community meetings." However, even regulations that do not foreclose an entire medium of expression, but merely shift the time, place, or manner of its use, must "leave open ample alternative channels for communication." In this case, we are not persuaded that adequate substitutes exist for the important medium of speech that Ladue has closed off.

Displaying a sign from one's own residence often carries a message quite distinct from placing the same sign someplace else, or conveying the same text or picture by other means. Precisely because of their location, such signs provide information about the identity of the "speaker." As an early and eminent student of rhetoric observed, the identity of the speaker is an important component of many attempts to persuade. A sign advocating "Peace in the Gulf" in the front lawn of a retired general or decorated war veteran may provoke a different reaction than the same sign in a 10-year-old child's bedroom window or the same message on a bumper sticker of a passing automobile....

Residential signs are an unusually cheap and convenient form of communication. Especially for persons of modest means or limited mobility, a yard or window sign may have no practical substitute. Even for the affluent, the added costs in money or time of taking out a newspaper advertisement, handing out leaflets on the street, or standing in front of one's house with a hand-held sign may make the difference between participating and not participating in some public debate. Furthermore, a person who puts up a sign at her residence often intends to reach *neighbors*, an audience that could not be reached nearly as well by other means.

A special respect for individual liberty in the home has long been part of our culture and our law; that principle has special resonance when the government seeks to constrain a person's ability to *speak* there. Most Americans would be understandably dismayed, given that tradition, to learn that it was illegal to display from their window an 8- by 11-inch sign expressing their political views. Whereas the government's need to mediate among various competing uses, including expressive ones, for public streets and facilities is constant and unavoidable, its need to regulate temperate speech from the home is surely much less pressing....

... Ladue's ban on almost all residential signs violates the First Amendment.... It bears mentioning that individual residents themselves have strong incentives to keep their own property values up and to prevent "visual clutter" in their own yards and neighborhoods—incentives markedly different from those of persons who erect signs on others' land, in others' neighborhoods, or on public property. Residents' self-interest diminishes the danger of the "unlimited" proliferation of residential signs that concerns the City of Ladue. We are confident that more temperate measures could in large part satisfy Ladue's stated regulatory needs without harm to the First Amendment rights of its citizens. As currently framed, however, the ordinance abridges those rights. Accordingly, the judgment of the Court of Appeals is affirmed.

Review Questions and Explanations: *City of Ladue v. Gilleo*

1. *Ladue* discusses a recurring problem in legislative drafting, of "overinclusiveness" (prohibiting too much) and "underinclusiveness" (prohibiting too little). These problems arise in the First Amendment, equal protection and due process areas. "Overinclusiveness" means that a law prohibits at least some conduct that can't constitutionally be banned. "Underinclusiveness" means, not literally that the law regulates "too little conduct," but that it improperly plays favorites by permitting some conduct that should, under the law's stated rationale, be banned. Here, the law is about controlling visual clutter, yet it is hard to argue that "for sale" signs create less clutter than political signs. Underinclusive laws can raise equal protection problems. In the speech context, they can be criticized on two grounds: they discriminate based on content, and they raise doubts about whether the stated reason for the law is the real reason. Maybe Ladue was less concerned about visual clutter than political controversy in the neighborhood. But the town counsel would have to know that tamping down political controversy is not a legitimate state interest.

2. Although the Court flags the underinclusivess issue, it doesn't rely on that for its decision. Underinclusiveness can be cured by eliminating the favoritism—here, by eliminating the exemptions from the ban. But that would fail to cure the overinclusiveness problem. The Court decides that the law bans too much speech. What is its rationale?

Recap: Content-Based and Content-Neutral Laws

1. A key threshold question in analyzing First Amendment cases is whether the challenged law is content-based or content-neutral. Content-based laws identify certain subject matters of speech for regulation, and are reviewed under

strict scrutiny. Content-neutral laws do not have that characteristic, and are reviewed under various formulations of intermediate scrutiny.

2. Laws may be (or may try to be) content-neutral in either of two ways. First, a law that regulates conduct without reference to speech is likely to be content-neutral. The ban on sleeping in the park upheld in *Clark* is a paradigm example. The *O'Brien* Court also held that the prohibition on destroying a draft card was content-neutral. In both cases, the purpose of the law was to regulate non-expressive conduct; the fact that the regulated conduct could be employed expressively in particular circumstances was incidental to the purpose of the law.

3. Second, a law may be (or may try to be) content-neutral by regulating speech explicitly but in an impartial way, that is, without reference to particular content. A law banning all signs in a residential neighborhood is content-neutral; a law banning all *political* signs in a residential neighborhood is not. Supposedly content-neutral speech regulations are typically sought to be justified as time, place, or manner regulations, on the theory that protected speech is not equally permissible in all places and at all times and delivered in any manner whatsoever.

4. Both categories of content-neutral regulation are subject to something less than strict scrutiny. The standards are probably analogous to the intermediate scrutiny found in the equal protection context, but worded somewhat differently. Regulation of (non-expressive) conduct that incidentally restricts some expressive conduct will be upheld, under the *O'Brien* test, if, as the Court put it in that case, "it furthers an important or substantial governmental interest unrelated to the suppression of free expression" and restricts no more speech than necessary to achieve that interest.

5. Time, place, or manner regulations will be upheld under a test fundamentally analogous to the *O'Brien* test. (*See* the Court's footnote 8 in *Clark v. CCNV*.) Regrettably for lawyers and law students trying to master this area of doctrine, the Court has settled on a formulation for the time, place, or manner intermediate scrutiny test that not only differs from the *O'Brien* test, but also uses language that sounds something like strict scrutiny: the law must be "narrowly tailored to serve a significant government interest, and leave open ample alternative channels of communication." *Frisby, supra.* The elements of that test, as used by the Court in various cases, are as follows:

   (a) A "significant" government interest is something less demanding than a "compelling" one. Most governmental interests in public order, safety, and health will qualify, such as traffic and noise control, sanitation, and even aesthetic concerns like control of visual clutter.

   (b) The "ample alternative channels" formulation is similar to "restricts no more speech than necessary" from the *O'Brien* test. The Court will consider whether the alternatives are comparable in cost and ability to reach the intended audience.

   (c) More confusing, however, is the use of "narrowly tailored." The Court has made clear — if "clear" is the right word here — that this "narrow tailoring" is not as strict as "narrow tailoring" in the strict scrutiny test in substantive due process, equal protection ... or even other free speech analysis! "Narrow tailoring" of time, place, and manner laws does not require that the government use the least restrictive means to achieve the state's regulatory interest, but need only choose means that are "not substantially broader than necessary." Sorry—we don't write the doctrine, we just report it.

6. *Frisby* alludes to heighted scrutiny of time, place, or manner restrictions of speech in "traditional public fora." (Fora are "gathering places.") There is language in some earlier cases suggesting that speech restrictions in places that have traditionally been used "for public assembly and debate" (streets, sidewalks, parks, public squares) are reviewed under strict scrutiny. It is true that the Court distinguishes such traditional public fora from non-public fora (e.g., the mailroom of a government office) and fora created specially by the government (e.g., a municipal theater), and allows more scope for regulating speech in the two latter categories. However, it seems apparent from *Frisby* and other cases that content-neutral time, place, or manner regulations of traditional public fora are reviewed under the above intermediate scrutiny test.

7. Despite occasional statements suggesting otherwise, mostly in separate opinions, the Court does not set much stock in deciding cases by determining that a challenger's expressive conduct is non-expressive conduct and therefore not speech. The Court typically either agrees, or else assumes arguendo, that the challenger's conduct is expressive. And the Court treats expressive conduct as a form of speech, no less entitled to protection than verbal speech. Where the distinction matters is in analyzing a *statute*, not the challenger's actions. Statutes that regulate conduct without reference to expression are content-neutral. A statute like the Texas "anti-desecration" law becomes problematic because a great deal of what it tries to prohibit seems to be expressive conduct.

---

3. Viewpoint Discrimination

Content-based laws discriminate against particular subject matters of speech, and are generally reviewed under strict scrutiny. Laws that discriminate against a particular point of view within a subject area are especially disfavored. Thus, a law prohibiting the posting of political campaign signs within 50 feet of a government building is an example of content-discrimination, since it singles out a particular subject matter: political campaign messages. But a law prohibiting only such signs that advocate the defeat of an incumbent (or that advocate Republican candidates) would be an example of *viewpoint* discrimination.

There are instances where the distinction between content and viewpoint discrimination is debatable. In *Texas v. Johnson*, the majority flirts with the suggestion that the law discriminates on the basis of viewpoint, but the Court reaches no conclusion on the point. But think about it: does anyone who burns a flag expressively do so to signal *support* for U.S. government policies? The Court also toys with finding viewpoint discrimination in *R.A.V. v. St. Paul* (presented below), since the racist speech banned by the law tended to be reflective of a particular viewpoint.

What is the significance of *viewpoint* (as opposed to *content*) discrimination? Perhaps not a lot: despite frequent language to the effect that viewpoint discrimination is particularly disfavored, and almost never justifiable under strict scrutiny, it makes most sense to think of it as a particularly egregious category of content discrimination—rather than as a separate doctrinal avenue. (At least in regard to governmental *regulation*. Governmental spending on its *own* speech raises a host of distinct issues, but the Court has held that the government need not be viewpoint-neutral as a speaker: it can, for example, fund a "just say no to drugs" campaign without also funding a pro-drug message.) Viewpoint discrimination is in many cases most relevant as evidence that an asserted justification for content-based laws is unconvincing. In the example above, if the stated purpose of the political sign ban is to protect government employees from electioneering pressure, that supposed purpose seems to be undermined by permitting signs of incumbents while prohibiting only the signs of challengers. Finally, the distinction between content and viewpoint discrimination will not always be clear — or even necessary to decide the case. For example, in *Boos v. Barry*, 485 U.S. 312 (1988), the Court reviewed a Washington, D.C. ordinance that prohibited displaying signs critical of the policies of a foreign government within 500 feet of that government's embassy. The law did not prohibit signs *supporting* the foreign governments. Somewhat strangely, the Court concluded that the law did *not* discriminate on the basis of viewpoint, but nevertheless struck down the law as impermissible content regulation.

Exercise: Content-Based and Content-Neutral Laws

Lakeshore Bluffs is an incorporated town consisting predominantly of detached single family homes in the greater metropolitan area of New Berg, a large city. Lakeshore Bluffs residents have complained to the mayor about a recent surge in door-to-door solicitations of all kinds: sales, political campaigns, non-profit fundraising, and the like. Residents are particularly annoyed that many of these doorbell-ringing interruptions occur during family dinner times. The mayor has asked the Town Attorney to draft an ordinance restricting or banning such soliciting, but has specifically asked that the ordinance contain an exception for fundraising by students of Lakeshore Bluff schools for school-related activities.

"NewBeak" is the New Berg Environmental Information Committee, a non-profit group that conducts door-to-door canvassing to raise funds, solicit membership and distribute literature on environmental issues. NewBeak will want to challenge the ordinance in court.

With one or more fellow students, play the roles of Town Attorney and counsel for NewBeak.

(a) Draft the ordinance.

(b) Present a challenge to, and defense of, the ordinance. (Have a fellow student play the role of judge.)

D. Unprotected Speech

This section looks at categories of speech that may not be protected under First Amendment doctrine. The basic idea behind these categories is that certain speech can be regulated or even prohibited precisely because its content is seen as harmful, and its social value as negligible; these categories of speech are typically referred to as unprotected. As we will see, however, some of the categories below might have constitutional protection despite their resemblance to unprotected speech; and even where unprotected speech is involved, there may nonetheless be some constitutional restrictions on how it can be regulated.

The cases in this section involve content-based laws. To return to Figure 9.1, this means that the answer to the first question on the flow chart is "yes" and the analysis has proceeded to the next question. As you will see in the cases, speech that falls into one of the categorically unprotected areas can be flatly prohibited notwithstanding the First Amendment. Unprotected speech is thus an exception to the rule that content-based regulations are given strict scrutiny.

Yet the regulation of unprotected speech is far from simple. It can be very difficult to draft a law that prohibits unprotected speech without also restricting protected speech. The cases in each of the following subsections raise different versions of this problem. We will consider, in turn, the following categories of speech and the extent to which they are unprotected: "incitement" (the tendency of speech to cause recipients of the speech to commit unlawful acts); "fighting words" (speech that provokes violence against the speaker); "hate speech" (speech intended to abuse historically oppressed or victimized groups); and "obscenity" and "indecency." These categories are not all unprotected, nor do they exhaust the categories of unprotected speech. However, they provide good illustrations of the problems surrounding unprotected speech.

1. Incitement

The well-worn example of unprotected speech is falsely shouting "fire" in a crowded theater. Such speech maliciously causes harm (a panicked rush for the exit in a confined space, emotional upset, and potential physical injury), without communicating a message of any social value. But what about a speaker who says to a small crowd: "Theater owners are nothing but fat-cat capitalists who take money from the poor! Let's go into a bunch of theaters and shout 'fire!' That'll show them!" Perhaps that speech is unprotected too. Despite its political content, perhaps its overriding purpose is to encourage others to engage in a malicious act that has no social value. Or does it? What if the message is more overtly political and the recommended acts are not purely malicious, but have a political purpose—like violently overthrowing the government?

The Court struggled with this issue repeatedly throughout the first seven decades of the twentieth century as it ruled on criminal prosecutions under a variety of federal and state laws aimed at communists and "subversives." The Court had not always actively used its power to review speech-infringing laws under the First Amendment. The foundations of modern free speech doctrine arose relatively late, and grew out of federal prosecutions of speech-related activities by opponents of U.S. involvement in World War I. Soon thereafter, federal and state authorities began prosecuting political leftists under so-called "anti-syndicalism" laws, which made it a crime to advocate the violent overthrow of the United States government or the capitalist system of industrial organization.

While these cases planted the seeds of the Court's modern jurisprudence in this area, those seeds are found in dissenting or concurring, not majority opinions. In three sets of cases, none of which were the finest hours of the Supreme Court or its free speech doctrine, the Court virtually always upheld the prosecutions and convictions of individuals for their speech activities under speech-restrictive laws. In *Schenck v. United States*, 249 U.S. 47 (1919), *Frohwerk v. United States*, 249 U.S. 204 (1919), and *Debs v. United States*,

1st Set

249 U.S. 211 (1919), the Court unanimously upheld convictions of anti-war leafletters and speakers under the Espionage Act of 1917. That law, among other things, broadly prohibited speech intended to interfere with the war effort. The decisions, each written by Justice Holmes, purported to adopt a test under which advocacy speech could be punished if there is a "clear and present danger" that the words will bring about "substantive evils" that Congress has a right to prevent. "Clear and present danger" implies a likelihood of imminent and effective action, yet in none of the cases did the Court require any specific evidence that the speech was likely to incite the listeners or readers to act in ways that posed any danger to the war effort. Instead, the Court found it sufficient to assume that words were likely to have their intended persuasive effect and incite action; and that, in a wartime setting, the action would be assumed dangerous.

The second set of cases is distinguished by what appears to have been an evolution in the views of Justices Holmes and Brandeis. *Abrams v. United States*, 250 U.S. 616 (1919), was another prosecution of an anti-war leafletter under the Espionage Act. *Gitlow v. New York*, 268 U.S. 652 (1925) and *Whitney v. California*, 274 U.S. 357 (1927), both involved prosecutions of communists under state "anti-syndicalism" laws for publishing literature or engaging in political organizing. Holmes and Brandeis parted ways with the rest of the Court in these cases, arguing that the "clear and present danger test" required some evidence that advocacy would in fact incite unlawful action. But the majority of the justices continued to believe that the intent to persuade to unlawful action was sufficient in itself to make advocacy fall outside First Amendment protection.[2]

The third set of cases arose during the height of the Cold War, in the aftermath of World War II, when many Americans feared the spread of international communism through subversive activities directed by the Soviet Union. The Court continued to review prosecutions of communists and communist sympathizers under state criminal syndicalism laws and the federal Smith Act. By the post-war period, the views of Holmes and Brandeis had become ascendant in the courts and the legal academy. However, the Court continued to be plagued by the question of how close a connection between advocacy and illegal action was required for speech to lose its First Amendment protection. The leading case in this anti-communist era—and perhaps the nadir of free speech protection—is *Dennis v. United States*, 341 U.S. 494 (1951), in which the Court upheld the Smith Act conviction of several defendants for teaching books by Marx, Lenin, and Stalin. A plurality of the Court purported to apply a modified version of the "clear and present danger test," as articulated by court of appeals judge Learned Hand: "In each case [courts] must ask whether the gravity of the 'evil,' discounted by its improbability, justifies such invasion of free speech as is necessary to avoid the danger." *Id.* at 510. The plurality viewed the danger of communist subversion as extremely grave—indeed, unprecedented ("Justices Holmes and Brandeis.... were not confronted with any situation comparable to the instant one"). The "clear and present danger test," according to the plurality,

> cannot mean that before the Government may act, it must wait until the *putsch* is about to be executed, the plans have been laid and the signal is awaited. If Government is aware that a group aiming at its overthrow is attempting to indoctrinate its members and to commit them to a course whereby they will strike when the leaders feel the circumstances permit, action by the Government is required.

---

2. Holmes dissented in *Abrams* and (joined by Brandeis) in *Gitlow*; Brandeis, joined by Holmes, concurred in the judgment in *Whitney*.

Id., at 509. Accordingly, the plurality did not require much evidence at all of the "probability" that the defendants' teaching activities would lead to subversion or revolution.

In the 1960s, the Court haltingly moved toward greater protection of advocacy speech. The culmination of this doctrinal odyssey, beginning with *Schenck*, is the decision in *Brandenburg v. Ohio*, which follows.

Guided Reading Questions: *Brandenburg v. Ohio*

1. Identify as clearly as you can the elements of the crime for which Brandenburg has been charged.

2. Identify as clearly as you can the elements of the *Brandenburg* "test" for unprotected incitement.

3. How does the Ohio statute fail the test?

4. What does the Court mean by distinguishing "mere advocacy" from "incitement"?

Brandenburg v. Ohio
395 U.S. 444 (1969)

Unanimous: Warren (CJ), Black, Douglas, Harlan, Brennan, Stewart, White, Marshall

PER CURIAM.

The appellant, a leader of a Ku Klux Klan group, was convicted under the Ohio Criminal Syndicalism statute for "advocat[ing] ... the duty, necessity, or propriety of crime, sabotage, violence, or unlawful methods of terrorism as a means of accomplishing industrial or political reform" and for "voluntarily assembl[ing] with any society, group, or assemblage of persons formed to teach or advocate the doctrines of criminal syndicalism." Ohio Rev. Code Ann. § 2923.13. He was fined $ 1,000 and sentenced to one to 10 years' imprisonment. [The Ohio appellate and supreme courts affirmed without issuing opinions.]

The record shows that a man, identified at trial as the appellant, telephoned an announcer-reporter on the staff of a Cincinnati television station and invited him to come to a Ku Klux Klan "rally" to be held at a farm in Hamilton County. With the cooperation of the organizers, the reporter and a cameraman attended the meeting and filmed the events. Portions of the films were later broadcast on the local station and on a national network.

The prosecution's case rested on the films and on testimony identifying the appellant as the person who communicated with the reporter and who spoke at the rally. The State also introduced into evidence several articles appearing in the film, including a pistol, a rifle, a shotgun, ammunition, a Bible, and a red hood worn by the speaker in the films.

One film showed 12 hooded figures, some of whom carried firearms. They were gathered around a large wooden cross, which they burned. No one was present other than the participants and the newsmen who made the film. Most of the words uttered during the scene were incomprehensible when the film was projected, but scattered phrases could be understood that were derogatory of Negroes and, in one instance, of Jews.

FN1. The significant portions that could be understood were:

.... "This is what we are going to do to the niggers".... "A dirty nigger".... "Send the Jews back to Israel".... "Let's go back to constitutional betterment".... "Bury the niggers".... "We intend to do our part".... "Give us our state rights".... "Freedom for the whites"....

Another scene on the same film showed the appellant, in Klan regalia, making a speech. The speech, in full, was as follows:

> This is an organizers' meeting. We have had quite a few members here today which are—we have hundreds, hundreds of members throughout the State of Ohio. I can quote from a newspaper clipping from the Columbus, Ohio Dispatch, five weeks ago Sunday morning. The Klan has more members in the State of Ohio than does any other organization. We're not a revengent organization, but if our President, our Congress, our Supreme Court, continues to suppress the white, Caucasian race, it's possible that there might have to be some revengeance taken.
>
> We are marching on Congress July the Fourth, four hundred thousand strong. From there we are dividing into two groups, one group to march on St. Augustine, Florida, the other group to march into Mississippi. Thank you.

The second film showed six hooded figures one of whom, later identified as the appellant, repeated a speech very similar to that recorded on the first film. The reference to the possibility of "revengeance" was omitted, and one sentence was added: "Personally, I believe the nigger should be returned to Africa, the Jew returned to Israel." Though some of the figures in the films carried weapons, the speaker did not.

The Ohio Criminal Syndicalism Statute was enacted in 1919. From 1917 to 1920, identical or quite similar laws were adopted by 20 States and two territories. In 1927, this Court sustained the constitutionality of California's Criminal Syndicalism Act, the text of which is quite similar to that of the laws of Ohio. Whitney v. California, 274 U.S. 357 (1927). The Court upheld the statute on the ground that, without more, "advocating" violent means to effect political and economic change involves such danger to the security of the State that the State may outlaw it. But Whitney has been thoroughly discredited by later decisions. See Dennis v. United States, 341 U.S. 494, 507 (1951). These later decisions have fashioned the principle that the constitutional guarantees of free speech and free press do not permit a State to forbid or proscribe advocacy of the use of force or of law violation except where such advocacy is directed to inciting or producing imminent lawless action and is likely to incite or produce such action....

Measured by this test, Ohio's Criminal Syndicalism Act cannot be sustained. The Act punishes persons who "advocate or teach the duty, necessity, or propriety" of violence "as a means of accomplishing industrial or political reform"; or who publish or circulate or display any book or paper containing such advocacy; or who "justify" the commission of violent acts "with intent to exemplify, spread or advocate the propriety of the doctrines of criminal syndicalism"; or who "voluntarily assemble" with a group formed "to teach or advocate the doctrines of criminal syndicalism." Neither the indictment nor the trial judge's instructions to the jury in any way refined the statute's bald definition of the crime in terms of mere advocacy not distinguished from incitement to imminent lawless action.

Accordingly, we are here confronted with a statute which, by its own words and as applied, purports to punish mere advocacy and to forbid, on pain of criminal punishment, assembly with others merely to advocate the described type of action. 4Such a statute falls within the condemnation of the First and Fourteenth Amendments. The contrary teaching of Whitney v. California, supra, cannot be supported, and that decision is therefore overruled. Reversed.

MR. JUSTICE BLACK, concurring.

I agree with the views expressed by MR. JUSTICE DOUGLAS in his concurring opinion in this case that the "clear and present danger" doctrine should have no place in the interpretation of the First Amendment. I join the Court's opinion, which, as I understand it, simply cites Dennis v. United States, 341 U.S. 494 (1951), but does not indicate any agreement on the Court's part with the "clear and present danger" doctrine on which Dennis purported to rely.

MR. JUSTICE DOUGLAS, concurring.

While I join the opinion of the Court, I desire to enter a caveat.

The "clear and present danger" test was adumbrated by Mr. Justice Holmes in a case arising during World War I—a war "declared" by the Congress, not by the Chief Executive. The case was Schenck v. United States, 249 U.S. 47, 52, where the defendant was charged with attempts to cause insubordination in the military and obstruction of enlistment. The pamphlets that were distributed urged resistance to the draft, denounced conscription, and impugned the motives of those backing the war effort. The First Amendment was tendered as a defense. Mr. Justice Holmes in rejecting that defense said:

> The question in every case is whether the words used are used in such circumstances and are of such a nature as to create a clear and present danger that they will bring about the substantive evils that Congress has a right to prevent. It is a question of proximity and degree.

Frohwerk v. United States, 249 U.S. 204, also authored by Mr. Justice Holmes, involved prosecution and punishment for publication of articles very critical of the war effort in World War I. Schenck was referred to as a conviction for obstructing security "by words of persuasion." And the conviction in Frohwerk was sustained because "the circulation of the paper was in quarters where a little breath would be enough to kindle a flame."

Debs v. United States, 249 U.S. 211, was the third of the trilogy of the 1918 Term. Debs was convicted of speaking in opposition to the war where his "opposition was so expressed that its natural and intended effect would be to obstruct recruiting." "If that was intended and if, in all the circumstances, that would be its probable effect, it would not be protected by reason of its being part of a general program and expressions of a general and conscientious belief." Ibid.

In the 1919 Term, the Court applied the Schenck doctrine to affirm the convictions of other dissidents in World War I. Abrams v. United States, 250 U.S. 616, was one instance. Mr. Justice Holmes, with whom Mr. Justice Brandeis concurred, dissented. While adhering to Schenck, he did not think that on the facts a case for overriding the First Amendment had been made out: "It is only the present danger of immediate evil or an intent to bring it about that warrants Congress in setting a limit to the expression of opinion where private rights are not concerned. Congress certainly cannot forbid all effort to change the mind of the country." Id., at 628. [See also the Holmes and Brandeis dissents in Schafer and Pierce.]

.... Those, then, were the World War I cases that put the gloss of "clear and present danger" on the First Amendment. Whether the war power—the greatest leveler of them all—is adequate to sustain that doctrine is debatable. The dissents in Abrams, Schaefer, and Pierce show how easily "clear and present danger" is manipulated to crush what Brandeis called "the fundamental right of free men to strive for better conditions through new legislation and new institutions" by argument and discourse even in time of war. Though I doubt if the "clear and present danger" test is congenial to the First Amendment in time of a declared war, I am certain it is not reconcilable with the First Amendment in days of peace.

The Court quite properly overrules Whitney v. California, 274 U.S. 357, which involved advocacy of ideas which the majority of the Court deemed unsound and dangerous.

Mr. Justice Holmes, though never formally abandoning the "clear and present danger" test, moved closer to the First Amendment ideal when he said in dissent in Gitlow v. New York, 268 U.S. 652, 673:

> Every idea is an incitement. It offers itself for belief and if believed it is acted on unless some other belief outweighs it or some failure of energy stifles the movement at its birth. The only difference between the expression of an opinion and an incitement in the narrower sense is the speaker's enthusiasm for the result. Eloquence may set fire to reason. But whatever may be thought of the redundant discourse before us it had no chance of starting a present conflagration. If in the long run the beliefs expressed in proletarian dictatorship are destined to be accepted by the dominant forces of the community, the only meaning of free speech is that they should be given their chance and have their way.

We have never been faithful to the philosophy of that dissent.

.... Out of the "clear and present danger" test came other offspring. Advocacy and teaching of forcible overthrow of government as an abstract principle is immune from prosecution. Yates v. United States, 354 U.S. 298, 318. But an "active" member, who has a guilty knowledge and intent of the aim to overthrow the Government by violence, may be prosecuted. Scales v. United States, 367 U.S. 203, 228. And the power to investigate, backed by the powerful sanction of contempt, includes the power to determine which of the two categories fits the particular witness. Barenblatt v. United States, 360 U.S. 109, 130. And so the investigator roams at will through all of the beliefs of the witness, ransacking his conscience and his innermost thoughts.

.... I see no place in the regime of the First Amendment for any "clear and present danger" test, whether strict and tight as some would make it, or free-wheeling as the Court in Dennis rephrased it.

When one reads the opinions closely and sees when and how the "clear and present danger" test has been applied, great misgivings are aroused. First, the threats were often loud but always puny and made serious only by judges so wedded to the status quo that critical analysis made them nervous. Second, the test was so twisted and perverted in Dennis as to make the trial of those teachers of Marxism an all-out political trial which was part and parcel of the cold war that has eroded substantial parts of the First Amendment.

.... One's beliefs have long been thought to be sanctuaries which government could not invade. Barenblatt is one example of the ease with which that sanctuary can be violated. The lines drawn by the Court between the criminal act of being an "active" Communist and the innocent act of being a nominal or inactive Communist mark the difference only between deep and abiding belief and casual or uncertain belief. But I think that all matters of belief are beyond the reach of subpoenas or the probings of investigators. That is why the invasions of privacy made by investigating committees were notoriously unconstitutional. That is the deep-seated fault in the infamous loyalty-security hearings which, since 1947 when President Truman launched them, have processed 20,000,000 men and women. Those hearings were primarily concerned with one's thoughts, ideas, beliefs, and convictions. They were the most blatant violations of the First Amendment we have ever known.

The line between what is permissible and not subject to control and what may be made impermissible and subject to regulation is the line between ideas and overt acts.

The example usually given by those who would punish speech is the case of one who falsely shouts fire in a crowded theatre.

This is, however, a classic case where speech is brigaded with action. See Speiser v. Randall, 357 U.S. 513, 536–537 (DOUGLAS, J., concurring). They are indeed inseparable and a prosecution can be launched for the overt acts actually caused. Apart from rare instances of that kind, speech is, I think, immune from prosecution. Certainly there is no constitutional line between advocacy of abstract ideas as in Yates and advocacy of political action as in Scales. The quality of advocacy turns on the depth of the conviction; and government has no power to invade that sanctuary of belief and conscience.

Review Questions and Explanations: *Brandenburg v. Ohio*

1. Does *Brandenburg* significantly change the law on speech that is unprotected due to its tendency to threaten social order? If so, how?

2. The Court overrules *Whitney v. California*, a case that purported to apply Holmes's "clear and present danger" test. Why not overrule *Dennis* as well? Can *Dennis* and *Brandenburg* be harmonized?

Exercise: Incitement

A Montana statute prohibits "criminal syndicalism," defined as "the advocacy of crime, malicious damage or injury to property, violence, or other unlawful methods of terrorism as a means of accomplishing industrial or political ends." The statute further provides: "A person commits the offense of criminal syndicalism if he purposely or knowingly, orally or by means of writing, advocates or promotes the doctrine of criminal syndicalism[.]" An historian of the Irish Republican Army ("IRA") has written a book in which he claims that, "For better or worse, the bombings and other terrorist acts committed by the IRA have been effective in keeping 'the troubles' in Northern Ireland as a high priority item on the agenda of successive British governments and as a focus of concern on the world stage." The author, Sean O'Fallon, repeats this statement at a book signing at Barnes and Noble in Missoula, Montana, where he is arrested by the county sheriff for criminal syndicalism. According to charges filed against the author, the quoted statement "clearly promotes IRA terrorism as a means of advancing its political ends." The criminal complaint also alleges that O'Fallon's book has been "widely read by IRA members, who have made several terrorist attacks since the book's publication."

With one ore more fellow students, play the roles of state's attorney for Montana, defense counsel for O'Fallon, and judge. Outline and argue a motion to dismiss the indictment on First Amendment grounds.

---

2. Fighting Words and Offensive Speech

In the previous section, "inciting" speech was deemed to be unprotected because of its likelihood of causing imminent harm. The value (or lack of value) of the speech in contributing to political debate was not a factor in the analysis. In this section, dealing with "fighting words" and offensive speech, the doctrine looks not only at the impact of the speech, but also its "social value" in the "exposition of ideas." Fighting words are perhaps a paradigmatic example of such "low value" speech — or at least have sometimes been viewed as such.

Guided Reading Questions: *Chaplinksy v. New Hampshire; Cohen v. California*

1. Can you articulate a test for unprotected "fighting words" based your reading of the two cases?

2. Are *Chaplinksy* and *Cohen* consistent with each other?

3. Can wearing a jacket with a provocative message on it, as in *Cohen*, be analyzed as regulation of "conduct" rather than speech?

4. Does the Court in *Cohen* say that it would be unconstitutional to enact a statute prohibiting the use of profane language in a courthouse?

Chaplinsky v. New Hampshire
315 U.S. 568 (1942)

Unanimous decision: *Murphy*, Stone (CJ), Roberts, Black, Reed, Frankfurter, Douglas, Byrnes, Jackson

MR. JUSTICE MURPHY delivered the opinion of the Court.

Appellant, a member of the sect known as Jehovah's Witnesses, was convicted in the municipal court of Rochester, New Hampshire, for violation of Chapter 378, § 2, of the Public Laws of New Hampshire:

> No person shall address any offensive, derisive or annoying word to any other person who is lawfully in any street or other public place, nor call him by any offensive or derisive name, nor make any noise or exclamation in his presence and hearing with intent to deride, offend or annoy him, or to prevent him from pursuing his lawful business or occupation....

There is no substantial dispute over the facts. Chaplinsky was distributing the literature of his sect on the streets of Rochester on a busy Saturday afternoon. Members of the local citizenry complained to the City Marshal, Bowering, that Chaplinsky was denouncing all religion as a "racket." Bowering told them that Chaplinsky was lawfully engaged, and then warned Chaplinsky that the crowd was getting restless. Some time later, a disturbance occurred and the traffic officer on duty at the busy intersection started with Chaplinsky for the police station, but did not inform him that he was under arrest or that he was going to be arrested. On the way, they encountered Marshal Bowering, who had been advised that a riot was under way and was therefore hurrying to the scene. Bowering repeated his earlier warning to Chaplinsky, who then addressed to Bowering the words set forth in the complaint.

Chaplinsky's version of the affair was slightly different. He testified that, when he met Bowering, he asked him to arrest the ones responsible for the disturbance. In reply,

Bowering cursed him and told him to come along. Appellant admitted that he said the words charged in the complaint, with the exception of the name of the Deity.

Over appellant's objection the trial court excluded, as immaterial, testimony relating to appellant's mission "to preach the true facts of the Bible," his treatment at the hands of the crowd, and the alleged neglect of duty on the part of the police. [After his municipal court conviction, Chaplinsky was again found guilty in a trial de novo before the superior court. His conviction was affirmed by the state supreme court.]

.... There are certain well-defined and narrowly limited classes of speech, the prevention and punishment of which have never been thought to raise any Constitutional problem. These include the lewd and obscene, the profane, the libelous, and the insulting or "fighting" words—those which by their very utterance inflict injury or tend to incite an immediate breach of the peace. It has been well observed that such utterances are no essential part of any exposition of ideas, and are of such slight social value as a step to truth that any benefit that may be derived from them is clearly outweighed by the social interest in order and morality. "Resort to epithets or personal abuse is not in any proper sense communication of information or opinion safeguarded by the Constitution, and its punishment as a criminal act would raise no question under that instrument." Cantwell v. Connecticut, 310 U.S. 296, 309–310.

The state statute here challenged comes to us authoritatively construed by the highest court of New Hampshire. It has two provisions—the first relates to words or names addressed to another in a public place; the second refers to noises and exclamations. The court said: "The two provisions are distinct. One may stand separately from the other. Assuming, without holding, that the second were unconstitutional, the first could stand if constitutional." We accept that construction of severability and limit our consideration to the first provision of the statute.

> FN6. Since the complaint charged appellant only with violating the first provision of the statute, the problem of Stromberg v. California, 283 U.S. 359, is not present. [Editors' note: the reference is to expressive conduct.]

On the authority of its earlier decisions, the state court declared that the statute's purpose was to preserve the public peace, no words being "forbidden except such as have a direct tendency to cause acts of violence by the persons to whom, individually, the remark is addressed." It was further said:

> The word "offensive" is not to be defined in terms of what a particular addressee thinks.... The test is what men of common intelligence would understand would be words likely to cause an average addressee to fight.... The English language has a number of words and expressions which by general consent are "fighting words" when said without a disarming smile.... Such words, as ordinary men know, are likely to cause a fight. So are threatening, profane or obscene revilings. Derisive and annoying words can be taken as coming within the purview of the statute as heretofore interpreted only when they have this characteristic of plainly tending to excite the addressee to a breach of the peace.... The statute, as construed, does no more than prohibit the face-to-face words plainly likely to cause a breach of the peace by the addressee, words whose speaking constitutes a breach of the peace by the speaker—including "classical fighting words", words in current use less "classical" but equally likely to cause violence, and other disorderly words, including profanity, obscenity and threats.

We are unable to say that the limited scope of the statute as thus construed contravenes the Constitutional right of free expression. It is a statute narrowly drawn and limited to define and punish specific conduct lying within the domain of state power, the use in a public place of words likely to cause a breach of the peace. This conclusion necessarily disposes of appellant's contention that the statute is so vague and indefinite as to render a conviction thereunder a violation of due process. A statute punishing verbal acts, carefully drawn so as not unduly to impair liberty of expression, is not too vague for a criminal law.

Appellant need not therefore have been a prophet to understand what the statute condemned.

Nor can we say that the application of the statute to the facts disclosed by the record substantially or unreasonably impinges upon the privilege of free speech. Argument is unnecessary to demonstrate that the appellations "damned racketeer" and "damned Fascist" are epithets likely to provoke the average person to retaliation, and thereby cause a breach of the peace.... Affirmed.

Cohen v. California
403 U.S. 15 (1971)

Majority: *Harlan*, Douglas, Brennan, Stewart, Marshall

Dissent: *Blackmun*, Burger (CJ), Black, White (in part)

MR. JUSTICE HARLAN delivered the opinion of the Court.

This case may seem at first blush too inconsequential to find its way into our books, but the issue it presents is of no small constitutional significance.

Appellant Paul Robert Cohen was convicted in the Los Angeles Municipal Court of violating that part of California Penal Code § 415 which prohibits "maliciously and willfully disturb[ing] the peace or quiet of any neighborhood or person ... by ... offensive conduct...." He was given 30 days' imprisonment. The facts upon which his conviction rests are detailed in the opinion of the Court of Appeal of California, ... as follows:

> On April 26, 1968, the defendant was observed in the Los Angeles County Court-house in the corridor outside of division 20 of the municipal court wearing a jacket bearing the words 'Fuck the Draft' which were plainly visible. There were women and children present in the corridor. The defendant was arrested. The defendant testified that he wore the jacket knowing that the words were on the jacket as a means of informing the public of the depth of his feelings against the Vietnam War and the draft.

> The defendant did not engage in, nor threaten to engage in, nor did anyone as the result of his conduct in fact commit or threaten to commit any act of violence. The defendant did not make any loud or unusual noise, nor was there any evidence that he uttered any sound prior to his arrest.

In affirming the conviction the Court of Appeal held that "offensive conduct" means "behavior which has a tendency to provoke others to acts of violence or to in turn disturb the peace," and that the State had proved this element because, on the facts of this case, "it was certainly reasonably foreseeable that such conduct might cause others to rise up to commit a violent act against the person of the defendant or attempt to forceably remove his jacket." The California Supreme Court declined review.... We now reverse.

The conviction quite clearly rests upon the asserted offensiveness of the words Cohen used to convey his message to the public. The only "conduct" which the State sought to punish is the fact of communication. Thus, we deal here with a conviction resting solely upon "speech," cf. Stromberg v. California, 283 U.S. 359 (1931), not upon any separately identifiable conduct which allegedly was intended by Cohen to be perceived by others as expressive of particular views but which, on its face, does not necessarily convey any message and hence arguably could be regulated without effectively repressing Cohen's ability to express himself. Cf. United States v. O'Brien, 391 U.S. 367 (1968). Further, the State certainly lacks power to punish Cohen for the underlying content of the message the inscription conveyed. At least so long as there is no showing of an intent to incite disobedience to or disruption of the draft, Cohen could not, consistently with the First and Fourteenth Amendments, be punished for asserting the evident position on the inutility or immorality of the draft his jacket reflected. Yates v. United States, 354 U.S. 298 (1957).

Appellant's conviction, then, rests squarely upon his exercise of the "freedom of speech" protected from arbitrary governmental interference by the Constitution and can be justified, if at all, only as a valid regulation of the manner in which he exercised that freedom, not as a permissible prohibition on the substantive message it conveys. This does not end the inquiry, of course, for the First and Fourteenth Amendments have never been thought to give absolute protection to every individual to speak whenever or wherever he pleases, or to use any form of address in any circumstances that he chooses. In this vein, too, however, we think it important to note that several issues typically associated with such problems are not presented here.

.... Any attempt to support this conviction on the ground that the statute seeks to preserve an appropriately decorous atmosphere in the courthouse where Cohen was arrested must fail in the absence of any language in the statute that would have put appellant on notice that certain kinds of otherwise permissible speech or conduct would nevertheless, under California law, not be tolerated in certain places.

This Court has also held that the States are free to ban the simple use, without a demonstration of additional justifying circumstances, of so-called "fighting words," those personally abusive epithets which, when addressed to the ordinary citizen, are, as a matter of common knowledge, inherently likely to provoke violent reaction. Chaplinsky v. New Hampshire, 315 U.S. 568 (1942). While the four-letter word displayed by Cohen in relation to the draft is not uncommonly employed in a personally provocative fashion, in this instance it was clearly not "directed to the person of the hearer." Cantwell v. Connecticut, 310 U.S. 296, 309 (1940). No individual actually or likely to be present could reasonably have regarded the words on appellant's jacket as a direct personal insult. Nor do we have here an instance of the exercise of the State's police power to prevent a speaker from intentionally provoking a given group to hostile reaction. There is, as noted above, no showing that anyone who saw Cohen was in fact violently aroused or that appellant intended such a result.

.... [Nor is this] an obscenity case. Whatever else may be necessary to give rise to the States' broader power to prohibit obscene expression, such expression must be, in some significant way, erotic.

Finally, in arguments before this Court much has been made of the claim that Cohen's distasteful mode of expression was thrust upon unwilling or unsuspecting viewers, and that the State might therefore legitimately act as it did in order to protect the sensitive from otherwise unavoidable exposure to appellant's crude form of protest. Of course, the mere presumed presence of unwitting listeners or viewers does not serve automatically to justify curtailing all speech capable of giving offense. See, e.g., Organization for a Better Austin v. Keefe, 402 U.S. 415 (1971). While this Court has recognized that government may properly act in many situations to prohibit intrusion into the privacy of the home of unwelcome views and ideas which cannot be totally banned from the public dialogue, we have at the same time consistently stressed that "we are often 'captives' outside the sanctuary of the home and subject to objectionable speech." The ability of government, consonant with the Constitution, to shut off discourse solely to protect others from hearing it is, in other words, dependent upon a showing that substantial privacy interests are being invaded in an essentially intolerable manner. Any broader view of this authority would effectively empower a majority to silence dissidents simply as a matter of personal predilections.

.... Given the subtlety and complexity of the factors involved, if Cohen's "speech" was otherwise entitled to constitutional protection, we do not think the fact that some unwilling "listeners" in a public building may have been briefly exposed to it can serve to justify this breach of the peace conviction where, as here, there was no evidence that persons powerless to avoid appellant's conduct did in fact object to it, and where that portion of the statute upon which Cohen's conviction rests evinces no concern, either on its face or as construed by the California courts, with the special plight of the captive auditor, but, instead, indiscriminately sweeps within its prohibitions all "offensive conduct" that disturbs "any neighborhood or person."

Against this background, the issue flushed by this case stands out in bold relief. It is whether California can excise, as "offensive conduct," one particular scurrilous epithet from the public discourse, either upon the theory of the court below that its use is inherently likely to cause violent reaction or upon a more general assertion that the States, acting as guardians of public morality, may properly remove this offensive word from the public vocabulary.

The rationale of the California court is plainly untenable. At most it reflects an "undifferentiated fear or apprehension of disturbance [which] is not enough to overcome the right to freedom of expression." Tinker v. Des Moines Indep. Community School Dist., 393 U.S. 503, 508 (1969). We have been shown no evidence that substantial numbers of citizens are standing ready to strike out physically at whoever may assault their sensibilities with execrations like that uttered by Cohen. There may be some persons about with such lawless and violent proclivities, but that is an insufficient base upon which to erect, consistently with constitutional values, a governmental power to force persons who wish to ventilate their dissident views into avoiding particular forms of expression. The argument amounts to little more than the self-defeating proposition that to avoid physical censorship of one who has not sought to provoke such a response by a hypothetical coterie of the violent and lawless, the States may more appropriately effectuate that censorship themselves....

.... The constitutional right of free expression is powerful medicine in a society as diverse and populous as ours. It is designed and intended to remove governmental restraints from the arena of public discussion, putting the decision as to what views shall be voiced largely into the hands of each of us, in the hope that use of such freedom will ultimately produce a more capable citizenry and more perfect polity and in the belief that no other approach would comport with the premise of individual dignity and choice upon which our political system rests. See Whitney v. California, 274 U.S. 357, 375–377 (1927) (Brandeis, J., concurring).

To many, the immediate consequence of this freedom may often appear to be only verbal tumult, discord, and even offensive utterance. These are, however, within established limits, in truth necessary side effects of the broader enduring values which the process of open debate permits us to achieve. That the air may at times seem filled with verbal cacophony is, in this sense not a sign of weakness but of strength. We cannot lose sight of the fact that, in what otherwise might seem a trifling and annoying instance of individual distasteful abuse of a privilege, these fundamental societal values are truly implicated. That is why "wholly neutral futilities ... come under the protection of free speech as fully as do Keats' poems or Donne's sermons," Winters v. New York, 333 U.S. 507, 528 (1948) (Frankfurter, J., dissenting), and why "so long as the means are peaceful, the communication need not meet standards of acceptability," Organization for a Better Austin v. Keefe, 402 U.S. 415, 419 (1971).

.... Surely the State has no right to cleanse public debate to the point where it is grammatically palatable to the most squeamish among us. Yet no readily ascertainable general principle exists for stopping short of that result were we to affirm the judgment below. For, while the particular four-letter word being litigated here is perhaps more distasteful than most others of its genre, it is nevertheless often true that one man's vulgarity is another's lyric. Indeed, we think it is largely because governmental officials cannot make principled distinctions in this area that the Constitution leaves matters of taste and style so largely to the individual.

... [M]uch linguistic expression serves a dual communicative function: it conveys not only ideas capable of relatively precise, detached explication, but otherwise inexpressible emotions as well. In fact, words are often chosen as much for their emotive as their cognitive force. We cannot sanction the view that the Constitution, while solicitous of the cognitive content of individual speech, has little or no regard for that emotive function which, practically speaking, may often be the more important element of the overall message sought to be communicated. Indeed, as Mr. Justice Frankfurter has said, "one of the prerogatives of American citizenship is the right to criticize public men and measures—and that means not only informed and responsible criticism but the freedom to speak foolishly and without moderation." Baumgartner v. United States, 322 U.S. 665, 673–674 (1944).

Finally, and in the same vein, we cannot indulge the facile assumption that one can forbid particular words without also running a substantial risk of suppressing ideas in the process. Indeed, governments might soon seize upon the censorship of particular words as a convenient guise for banning the expression of unpopular views....

It is, in sum, our judgment that, absent a more particularized and compelling reason for its actions, the State may not, consistently with the First and Fourteenth Amendments, make the simple public display here involved of this single four-letter expletive a criminal offense. Because that is the only arguably sustainable rationale for the conviction here at issue, the judgment below must be reversed.

MR. JUSTICE BLACKMUN, with whom THE CHIEF JUSTICE and MR. JUSTICE BLACK join. MR. JUSTICE WHITE concurs in Paragraph 2....

.... Cohen's absurd and immature antic, in my view, was mainly conduct and little speech.... As a consequence, this Court's agonizing over First Amendment values seems misplaced and unnecessary.

[Paragraph 2:] I am not at all certain that the California Court of Appeal's construction of § 415 is now the authoritative California construction.... Inasmuch as this Court does not dismiss this case, it ought to be remanded to the California Court of Appeal for reconsideration in the light of the subsequently rendered decision by the State's highest tribunal [interpreting § 415].

CASE NOTE: Offensive Speech—*Boos v. Barry* and *Hustler Magazine v. Falwell*. In *Boos v. Barry*, 485 U.S. 312, 321 (1988), the Court struck down a Washington, D.C.

ordinance that prohibited displaying messages critical of the policies of a foreign government within 500 feet of that government's embassy. The law was justified, in part, by international treaty obligations to protect the "dignity" of foreign emissaries to the U.S. The Court said:

> As a general matter, we have indicated that in public debate our own citizens must tolerate insulting, and even outrageous, speech in order to provide "adequate 'breathing space' to the freedoms protected by the First Amendment." Hustler Magazine, Inc. v. Falwell, 485 U.S. 46, 56 (1988). See also, e.g., New York Times Co. v. Sullivan, 376 U.S., at 270. A "dignity" standard, like the "outrageousness" standard that we rejected in Hustler, is so inherently subjective that it would be inconsistent with "our longstanding refusal to [punish speech] because the speech in question may have an adverse emotional impact on the audience." Hustler Magazine, 485 U.S., at 55.

In *Hustler Magazine*, the pornographic magazine Hustler had published a lewd and offensive satire, in the form of a parody advertisement, of a nationally known and politically outspoken evangelical minister, Jerry Falwell. Falwell sued the magazine and its publisher for defamation and intentional infliction of emotional distress. A jury found against Falwell on his libel claim on the ground that the parody could not "reasonably be understood as describing actual facts about [Falwell] or actual events in which [he] participated." However, the jury awarded him damages on the emotional distress claim. The Supreme Court reversed the emotional distress verdict. With no dissenters, the Court held that the "outrageousness" of the satire could not make otherwise protected speech actionable; and since the speech was not defamatory, it fell into no other exceptions to First Amendment protection. The Court cited *Chaplinsky*, but did not even consider applying a "fighting words" exception to the satire.

Review Questions and Explanations: *Chaplinsky* and *Cohen*

1. In both cases, involving appeals from state law convictions, the Court makes a point of reciting the state court's interpretation of the statute. In general, the U.S. Supreme Court will refrain from making an independent interpretation of state statutes if a state appellate court has construed the statute; instead, the Supreme Court will treat the state court explanation of statutory meaning as authoritative.

The New Hampshire Supreme Court in *Chaplinsky* interpreted the "offensive words" prohibition as including "only" words that "ordinary men know, are likely to cause a fight." The U.S. Supreme Court seems to say that this "objective" or "reasonable person" test resolves any constitutional objection to the statute. Do you agree?

2. *Chaplinsky* has never been overruled, and remains the classic citation for the proposition that "fighting words" are not protected by the First Amendment. Even assuming that some sort of "fighting words exception" to speech protection still exists, do you think *Chaplinsky* would be decided the same way today? Why or why not?

3. Is there a constitutional distinction between fighting words directed personally to an individual and fighting words directed indiscriminately at no particular person? Note the language derived from *Cantwell v. Connecticut*, quoted in *Cohen*, that fighting words must be "directed to the person of the hearer."

4. The *Cohen* court makes a big deal out of the fact that no one present was actually provoked to fight. Why is that relevant? The statutes reviewed in *Chaplinsky* and *Cohen* both required only a showing that the words had a "tendency" to provoke a fight. Is the Court in *Cohen* adding an element to the constitutional test for fighting words that they must not only tend to, but actually provoke violence?

5. Does *Cohen* state or imply that edgy or provocative speech must be used in service of a political message in order to be protected?

Recap: Fighting Words

1. *Boos* and *Hustler* state that "adverse emotional impact on the audience" does not make speech unprotected. If that is a correct doctrinal statement, what if anything remains of the idea that "fighting words" are unprotected speech?

2. *Chaplinsky* defines fighting words in terms of whether an "ordinary person" would be provoked to fight. This is very much like a "reasonable person" standard: its intent, clearly, is to factor out of the constitutional equation the reactions of hypersensitive or exceptionally quick-tempered people. But is it ever "reasonable" to be provoked to violence by mere words?

Exercise: Fighting Words

Try drafting a statute that prohibits fighting words that would stand up to First Amendment scrutiny. Be sure to consider potential problems of vagueness and overbreadth.

3. Hate Speech

"Hate speech" is not particularly new, but laws regulating or prohibiting it in this country are a relatively recent phenomena. A common-sense definition of "hate speech" is speech that has the purpose and effect of abusing or intimidating members of historically victimized or oppressed groups. Clearly, hate speech overlaps with fighting words, to some degree, but there are also significant differences. Fighting words can be any highly provocative language, and may be targeted to individuals' sensitivities without respect to their membership in a group, their race, ethnicity, or other group identification. Hate speech may provoke "fighting" reactions, but may also intimidate the hearer; its force typically arises out of an historical context in which the hearer's identity group has been the victim of past oppression or invidious discrimination. But because oppression is often the result of political regimes and movements, the very context that makes hate speech offensive can carry political overtones and thus raise possible First Amendment concerns.

At the end of the day, it is not clear that hate speech as a category is in fact unprotected speech. If identity-based discrimination and oppression are political acts, then prohibiting speech promoting or advocating such discrimination or oppression can be seen as taking sides in a political controversy. Does the First Amendment permit the government to take sides in that way, even if the goal is to promote a just society? The following case delves into some of these issues.

Guided Reading Questions: *R.A.V. v. St. Paul*

1. Try to articulate the majority's first key point in section I, regarding impermissible content-based distinctions within an unprotected or "proscribable" category of speech.

2. Try to articulate the majority's second key point in section I of the opinion, regarding when it is *permissible* to make content-based distinctions within an unprotected or "proscribable" category of speech.

3. Summarize in a few sentences how these two key doctrinal points are applied to the St. Paul ordinance in section II.

4. Content discrimination, as you know from the flow chart and prior cases, can be upheld if it meets strict scrutiny: if the prohibition is "narrowly tailored" or "necessary" [both formulations appear in various First Amendment cases] "to achieve a compelling state interest." Where does the majority apply this test, and what does it conclude?

5. Try to articulate the main differences of opinion between the majority and the White and Stevens concurrences in the judgment.

R.A.V. v. St. Paul
505 U.S. 377 (1992)

Majority: *Scalia,* Rehnquist (CJ), Kennedy, Souter, Thomas

Concurrences in the judgment: *White, Blackmun* (omitted), *Stevens,* O'Connor

JUSTICE SCALIA delivered the opinion of the Court.

In the predawn hours of June 21, 1990, petitioner and several other teenagers allegedly assembled a crudely made cross by taping together broken chair legs. They then allegedly burned the cross inside the fenced yard of a black family that lived across the street from the house where petitioner was staying. Although this conduct could have been punished under any of a number of laws, one of the two provisions under which respondent city of St. Paul chose to charge petitioner (then a juvenile) was the St. Paul Bias-Motivated Crime Ordinance, St. Paul, Minn., Legis. Code § 292.02 (1990), which provides:

> Whoever places on public or private property a symbol, object, appellation, characterization or graffiti, including, but not limited to, a burning cross or Nazi swastika, which one knows or has reasonable grounds to know arouses anger, alarm or resentment in others on the basis of race, color, creed, religion or gender commits disorderly conduct and shall be guilty of a misdemeanor.

Petitioner moved to dismiss this count on the ground that the St. Paul ordinance was substantially overbroad and impermissibly content-based and therefore facially invalid under the First Amendment. The trial court granted this motion, but the Minnesota Supreme Court reversed.... We granted certiorari.

I

In construing the St. Paul ordinance, we are bound by the construction given to it by the Minnesota court. Accordingly, we accept the Minnesota Supreme Court's authoritative statement that the ordinance reaches only those expressions that constitute "fighting words" within the meaning of Chaplinsky v. New Hampshire, 315 U.S. 568, 672 (1942).... Assuming, arguendo, that all of the expression reached by the ordinance is proscribable under the "fighting words" doctrine, we nonetheless conclude that the ordinance is facially unconstitutional in that it prohibits otherwise permitted speech solely on the basis of the subjects the speech addresses.

The First Amendment generally prevents government from proscribing speech, or even expressive conduct, because of disapproval of the ideas expressed. Content-based regulations are presumptively invalid. From 1791 to the present, however, our society, like other free but civilized societies, has permitted restrictions upon the content of speech in a few limited areas, which are "of such slight social value as a step to truth that any benefit that may be derived from them is clearly outweighed by the social interest in order and morality." Chaplinsky, 315 U.S. at 572....

We have sometimes said that these categories of expression are "not within the area of constitutionally protected speech".... What [we] mean is that these areas of speech can, consistently with the First Amendment, be regulated *because of their constitutionally proscribable content* (obscenity, defamation, etc.)—not that they are categories of speech entirely invisible to the Constitution, so that they may be made the vehicles for content discrimination unrelated to their distinctively proscribable content. Thus, the government may proscribe libel; but it may not make the further content discrimination of proscribing *only* libel critical of the government....

The proposition that a particular instance of speech can be proscribable on the basis of one feature (*e.g.*, obscenity) but not on the basis of another (*e.g.*, opposition to the city government) is commonplace and has found application in many contexts.... [J]ust as the power to proscribe particular speech on the basis of a noncontent element (*e.g.*, noise) does not entail the power to proscribe the same speech on the basis of a content element; so also, the power to proscribe it on the basis of *one* content element (*e.g.*, obscenity) does not entail the power to proscribe it on the basis of *other* content elements.

In other words, the exclusion of "fighting words" from the scope of the First Amendment simply means that, for purposes of that Amendment, the unprotected features of the words are, despite their verbal character, essentially a "nonspeech" element of communication. Fighting words are thus analogous to a noisy sound truck: Each is, as Justice Frankfurter recognized, a "mode of speech"; both can be used to convey an idea; but neither has, in and of itself, a claim upon the First Amendment. As with the sound truck, however, so also with fighting words: The government may not regulate use based on hostility—or favoritism—towards the underlying message expressed.

The concurrences describe us as setting forth a new First Amendment principle that prohibition of constitutionally proscribable speech cannot be "underinclusive,"—a First Amendment "absolutism" whereby "within a particular 'proscribable' category of expression, ... a government must either proscribe *all* speech or no speech at all," (STEVENS, J., concurring in judgment). That easy target is of the concurrences' own invention. In our view, the First Amendment imposes not an "underinclusiveness" limitation but a "content discrimination" limitation upon a State's prohibition of proscribable speech. There is no problem whatever, for example, with a State's prohibiting obscenity (and other forms of proscribable expression) only in certain media or markets, for although that prohibition would be "underinclusive," it would not discriminate on the basis of content.

Even the prohibition against content discrimination that we assert the First Amendment requires is not absolute. It applies differently in the context of proscribable speech than in the area of fully protected speech. The rationale of the general prohibition, after all, is that content discrimination "raises the specter that the Government may effectively drive certain ideas or viewpoints from the marketplace." But content discrimination among various instances of a class of proscribable speech often does not pose this threat.

When the basis for the content discrimination consists entirely of the very reason the entire class of speech at issue is proscribable, no significant danger of idea or viewpoint discrimination exists. Such a reason, having been adjudged neutral enough to support exclusion of the entire class of speech from First Amendment protection, is also neutral enough to form the basis of distinction within the class. To illustrate: A State might choose to prohibit only that obscenity which is the most patently offensive *in its prurience* — *i.e.*, that which involves the most lascivious displays of sexual activity. But it may not prohibit, for example, only that obscenity which includes offensive *political* messages. And the Federal Government can criminalize only those threats of violence that are directed against the President, see 18 U.S.C. § 871 — since the reasons why threats of violence are outside the First Amendment (protecting individuals from the fear of violence, from the disruption that fear engenders, and from the possibility that the threatened violence will occur) have special force when applied to the person of the President. See Watts v. United States, 394 U.S. 705, (1969) (upholding the facial validity of § 871 because of the "overwhelming interest in protecting the safety of [the] Chief Executive and in allowing him to perform his duties without interference from threats of physical violence"). But the Federal Government may not criminalize only those threats against the President that mention his policy on aid to inner cities. And to take a final example (one mentioned by JUSTICE STEVENS), a State may choose to regulate price advertising in one industry but not in others, because the risk of fraud (one of the characteristics of commercial speech that justifies depriving it of full First Amendment protection, see Virginia State Bd. of Pharmacy v. Virginia Citizens Consumer Council, Inc., 425 U.S. 748, 771–772 (1976)) is in its view greater there. But a State may not prohibit only that commercial advertising that depicts men in a demeaning fashion.

Another valid basis for according differential treatment to even a content-defined subclass of proscribable speech is that the subclass happens to be associated with particular "secondary effects" of the speech, so that the regulation is *"justified* without reference to the content of the … speech," Renton v. Playtime Theatres, Inc., 475 U.S. 41, 48, (1986). A State could, for example, permit all obscene live performances except those involving minors. Moreover, since words can in some circumstances violate laws directed not against speech but against conduct (a law against treason, for example, is violated by telling the enemy the Nation's defense secrets), a particular content-based subcategory of a proscribable class of speech can be swept up incidentally within the reach of a statute directed at conduct rather than speech. Thus, for example, sexually derogatory "fighting words," among other words, may produce a violation of Title VII's general prohibition against sexual discrimination in employment practices. Where the government does not target conduct on the basis of its expressive content, acts are not shielded from regulation merely because they express a discriminatory idea or philosophy.

These bases for distinction refute the proposition that the selectivity of the restriction is "even arguably conditioned upon the sovereign's agreement with what a speaker may intend to say." There may be other such bases as well. Indeed, to validate such selectivity (where totally proscribable speech is at issue) it may not even be necessary to identify any particular "neutral" basis, so long as the nature of the content discrimination is such that there is no realistic possibility that official suppression of ideas is afoot. (We cannot think of any First Amendment interest that would stand in the way of a State's prohibiting only those obscene motion pictures with blue-eyed actresses.) Save for that limitation, the regulation of "fighting words," like the regulation of noisy speech, may address some offensive instances and leave other, equally offensive, instances alone.

II

Applying these principles to the St. Paul ordinance, we conclude that, even as narrowly construed by the Minnesota Supreme Court, the ordinance is facially unconstitutional.... [T]he ordinance applies only to "fighting words" that insult, or provoke violence, "on the basis of race, color, creed, religion or gender." Displays containing abusive invective, no matter how vicious or severe, are permissible unless they are addressed to one of the specified disfavored topics. Those who wish to use "fighting words" in connection with other ideas— to express hostility, for example, on the basis of political affiliation, union membership, or homosexuality—are not covered. The First Amendment does not permit St. Paul to impose special prohibitions on those speakers who express views on disfavored subjects.

In its practical operation, moreover, the ordinance goes even beyond mere content discrimination, to actual viewpoint discrimination. Displays containing some words— odious racial epithets, for example—would be prohibited to proponents of all views. But "fighting words" that do not themselves invoke race, color, creed, religion, or gender— aspersions upon a person's mother, for example—would seemingly be usable ad libitum in the placards of those arguing *in favor* of racial, color, etc., tolerance and equality, but could not be used by those speakers' opponents. One could hold up a sign saying, for example, that all "anti-Catholic bigots" are misbegotten; but not that all "papists" are, for that would insult and provoke violence "on the basis of religion." St. Paul has no such authority to license one side of a debate to fight freestyle, while requiring the other to follow Marquis of Queensberry rules.

What we have here, it must be emphasized, is not a prohibition of fighting words that are directed at certain persons or groups (which would be *facially* valid if it met the requirements of the Equal Protection Clause); but rather, a prohibition of fighting words that contain (as the Minnesota Supreme Court repeatedly emphasized) messages of "bias motivated" hatred and in particular, as applied to this case, messages "based on virulent notions of racial supremacy." One must wholeheartedly agree with the Minnesota Supreme Court that "it is the responsibility, even the obligation, of diverse communities to confront such notions in whatever form they appear," but the manner of that confrontation cannot consist of selective limitations upon speech. St. Paul's brief asserts that a general "fighting words" law would not meet the city's needs because only a content-specific measure can communicate to minority groups that the "group hatred" aspect of such speech "is not condoned by the majority." The point of the First Amendment is that majority preferences must be expressed in some fashion other than silencing speech on the basis of its content....

The content-based discrimination reflected in the St. Paul ordinance comes within neither any of the specific exceptions to the First Amendment prohibition we discussed earlier nor a more general exception for content discrimination that does not threaten censorship of ideas. It assuredly does not fall within the exception for content discrimination based on the very reasons why the particular class of speech at issue (here, fighting words) is proscribable. As explained earlier, the reason why fighting words are categorically excluded from the protection of the First Amendment is not that their content communicates any particular idea, but that their content embodies a particularly intolerable (and socially unnecessary) *mode* of expressing *whatever* idea the speaker wishes to convey. St. Paul has not singled out an especially offensive mode of expression—it has not, for example, selected for prohibition only those fighting words that communicate ideas in a threatening (as opposed to a merely obnoxious) manner. Rather, it has proscribed fighting words of whatever manner that communicate messages of racial, gender, or religious intolerance. Selectivity of this sort creates the possibility that the city is seeking to handicap the expression of particular ideas. That possibility would alone be enough to render the ordinance presumptively invalid, but St. Paul's comments and concessions in this case elevate the possibility to a certainty.

St. Paul argues that the ordinance comes within another of the specific exceptions we mentioned, the one that allows content discrimination aimed only at the "secondary effects" of the speech, see Renton v. Playtime Theatres, Inc., 475 U.S. 41 (1986). According to St. Paul, the ordinance is intended, "not to impact on [sic] the right of free expression of the accused," but rather to "protect against the victimization of a person or persons who are particularly vulnerable because of their membership in a group that historically has been discriminated against." Even assuming that an ordinance that completely proscribes, rather than merely regulates, a specified category of speech can ever be considered to be directed only to the secondary effects of such speech, it is clear that the St. Paul ordinance is not directed to secondary effects within the meaning of *Renton.* As we said in *Boos v. Barry,* 485 U.S. 312 (1988), "Listeners' reactions to speech are not the type of 'secondary effects' we referred to in *Renton.*" "The emotive impact of speech on its audience is not a 'secondary effect.'" . . .

Finally, St. Paul and its *amici* defend the conclusion of the Minnesota Supreme Court that, even if the ordinance regulates expression based on hostility towards its protected ideological content, this discrimination is nonetheless justified because it is narrowly tailored to serve compelling state interests. Specifically, they assert that the ordinance helps to ensure the basic human rights of members of groups that have historically been subjected to discrimination, including the right of such group members to live in peace where they wish. We do not doubt that these interests are compelling, and that the ordinance can be said to promote them. But the "danger of censorship" presented by a facially content-based statute requires that that weapon be employed only where it is "*necessary* to serve the asserted [compelling] interest." The existence of adequate content-neutral alternatives thus "undercuts significantly" any defense of such a statute, casting considerable doubt on the government's protestations that "the asserted justification is in fact an accurate description of the purpose and effect of the law." The dispositive question in this case, therefore, is whether content discrimination is reasonably necessary to achieve St. Paul's compelling interests; it plainly is not. An ordinance not limited to the favored topics, for example, would have precisely the same beneficial effect. In fact the only interest distinctively served by the content limitation is that of displaying the city council's special hostility towards the particular biases thus singled out. That is precisely what the First Amendment forbids. The politicians of St. Paul are entitled to express that hostility—but not through the means of imposing unique limitations upon speakers who (however benightedly) disagree.

Let there be no mistake about our belief that burning a cross in someone's front yard is reprehensible. But St. Paul has sufficient means at its disposal to prevent such behavior without adding the First Amendment to the fire.

The judgment of the Minnesota Supreme Court is reversed, and the case is remanded for proceedings not inconsistent with this opinion.

JUSTICE WHITE, with whom JUSTICE BLACKMUN and JUSTICE O'CONNOR join, and with whom JUSTICE STEVENS joins except as to Part I-A, concurring in the judgment.

I agree with the majority that the judgment of the Minnesota Supreme Court should be reversed. However, our agreement ends there.

[Today] the Court announces that earlier Courts did not mean their repeated statements that certain categories of expression are "not within the area of constitutionally protected speech."...

To the contrary, those statements meant precisely what they said: The categorical approach is a firmly entrenched part of our First Amendment jurisprudence....

The majority's observation that fighting words are "quite expressive indeed," is no answer. Fighting words are not a means of exchanging views, rallying supporters, or registering a protest; they are directed against individuals to provoke violence or to inflict injury. Chaplinsky, 315 U.S. at 572. Therefore, a ban on all fighting words or on a subset of the fighting words category would restrict only the social evil of hate speech, without creating the danger of driving viewpoints from the marketplace.

Therefore, the Court's insistence on inventing its brand of First Amendment under-inclusiveness puzzles me. The overbreadth doctrine has the redeeming virtue of attempting to avoid the chilling of protected expression, but the Court's new "underbreadth" creation serves no desirable function. Instead, it permits, indeed invites, the continuation of expressive conduct that in this case is evil and worthless in First Amendment terms, until the city of St. Paul cures the underbreadth by adding to its ordinance a catchall phrase such as "and all other fighting words that may constitutionally be subject to this ordinance."

Any contribution of this holding to First Amendment jurisprudence is surely a negative one, since it necessarily signals that expressions of violence, such as the message of intimidation and racial hatred conveyed by burning a cross on someone's lawn, are of sufficient value to outweigh the social interest in order and morality that has traditionally placed such fighting words outside the First Amendment. Indeed, by characterizing fighting words as a form of "debate," the majority legitimates hate speech as a form of public discussion.

Furthermore, the Court obscures the line between speech that could be regulated freely on the basis of content (*i.e.*, the narrow categories of expression falling outside the First Amendment) and that which could be regulated on the basis of content only upon a showing of a compelling state interest (*i.e.*, all remaining expression). By placing fighting words, which the Court has long held to be valueless, on at least equal constitutional footing with political discourse and other forms of speech that we have deemed to have the greatest social value, the majority devalues the latter category.

.... Assuming, arguendo, that the St. Paul ordinance is a content-based regulation of protected expression, it nevertheless would pass First Amendment review under settled law upon a showing that the regulation "is necessary to serve a compelling state interest and is narrowly drawn to achieve that end." .... The Court expressly concedes that [the anti-discrimination] interest is compelling.... [However, under] the majority's view, a narrowly drawn, content-based ordinance could never pass constitutional muster if the object of that legislation could be accomplished by banning a wider category of speech....

Although the First Amendment does not apply to categories of unprotected speech, such as fighting words, the Equal Protection Clause requires that the regulation of unprotected speech be rationally related to a legitimate government interest. A defamation statute that drew distinctions on the basis of political affiliation or "an ordinance prohibiting only those legally obscene works that contain criticism of the city government," would unquestionably fail rational-basis review....

Although I disagree with the Court's analysis, I do agree with its conclusion: The St. Paul ordinance is unconstitutional. However, I would decide the case on overbreadth grounds....

In construing the St. Paul ordinance, the Minnesota Supreme Court.... ruled that St. Paul may constitutionally prohibit expression that "by its very utterance" causes "anger, alarm or resentment."

Our fighting words cases have made clear, however, that such generalized reactions are not sufficient to strip expression of its constitutional protection. The mere fact that expressive activity causes hurt feelings, offense, or resentment does not render the expression unprotected.

.... Although the ordinance reaches conduct that is unprotected, it also makes criminal expressive conduct that causes only hurt feelings, offense, or resentment, and is protected by the First Amendment. The ordinance is therefore fatally overbroad and invalid on its face.

JUSTICE STEVENS, with whom JUSTICE WHITE and JUSTICE BLACKMUN join as to Part I, concurring in the judgment.

Conduct that creates special risks or causes special harms may be prohibited by special rules. Lighting a fire near an ammunition dump or a gasoline storage tank is especially dangerous; such behavior may be punished more severely than burning trash in a vacant lot. Threatening someone because of her race or religious beliefs may cause particularly severe trauma or touch off a riot, and threatening a high public official may cause substantial social disruption; such threats may be punished more severely than threats against someone based on, say, his support of a particular athletic team. There are legitimate, reasonable, and neutral justifications for such special rules.

.... [M]y colleagues today wrestle with two broad principles: first, that certain "categories of expression [including 'fighting words'] are 'not within the area of constitutionally protected speech'"; and second, that "content-based regulations [of expression] are presumptively invalid." Although in past opinions the Court has repeated both of these maxims, it has—quite rightly—adhered to neither with the absolutism suggested by my colleagues....

I

Fifty years ago, the Court articulated a categorical approach to First Amendment jurisprudence.

> There are certain well-defined and narrowly limited classes of speech, the prevention and punishment of which have never been thought to raise any Constitutional problem.... It has been well observed that such utterances are no essential part of any exposition of ideas, and are of such slight social value as a step to truth that any benefit that may be derived from them is clearly outweighed by the social interest in order and morality. Chaplinsky v. New Hampshire, 315 U.S. 568, 571–572 (1942).

The Court today revises this categorical approach. It is not, the Court rules, that certain "categories" of expression are "unprotected," but rather that certain "elements" of expression are wholly "proscribable." To the Court, an expressive act, like a chemical compound, consists of more than one element. Although the act may be regulated because it contains a proscribable element, it may not be regulated on the basis of another (nonproscribable) element it also contains. Thus, obscene antigovernment speech may be regulated because it is obscene, but not because it is antigovernment. It is this revision of the categorical approach that allows the Court to assume that the St. Paul ordinance proscribes *only* fighting words, while at the same time concluding that the ordinance is invalid because it imposes a content-based regulation on expressive activity.

As an initial matter, the Court's revision of the categorical approach seems to me something of an adventure in a doctrinal wonderland, for the concept of "obscene antigovernment" speech is fantastical. The category of the obscene is very narrow; to be obscene, expression must be found by the trier of fact to "appeal to the prurient interest, ... depict or describe, in a patently offensive way, sexual conduct, [and], taken as a whole, *lack serious literary, artistic, political, or scientific value.*" Miller v. California, 413 U.S. 15 (1973) (emphasis added). "Obscene antigovernment" speech, then, is a contradiction in terms: If expression is anti-government, it does not "lack serious ... political ... value" and cannot be obscene.

The Court attempts to bolster its argument by likening its novel analysis to that applied to restrictions on the time, place, or manner of expression or on expressive conduct. It is true that loud speech in favor of the Republican Party can be regulated because it is loud, but not because it is pro-Republican; and it is true that the public burning of the American flag can be regulated because it involves public burning and not because it involves the flag. But these analogies are inapposite. In each of these examples, the two elements (*e.g.*, loudness and pro-Republican orientation) can coexist; in the case of "obscene antigovernment" speech, however, the presence of one element ("obscenity") by definition means the absence of the other. To my mind, it is unwise and unsound to craft a new doctrine based on such highly speculative hypotheticals.

I am, however, even more troubled by the second step of the Court's analysis—namely, its conclusion that the St. Paul ordinance is an unconstitutional content-based regulation of speech. Drawing on broadly worded dicta, the Court establishes a near-absolute ban on content-based regulations of expression and holds that the First Amendment prohibits the regulation of fighting words by subject matter. Thus, while the Court rejects the "all-or-nothing-at-all" nature of the categorical approach, it promptly embraces an absolutism of its own: Within a particular "proscribable" category of expression, the Court holds, a government must either proscribe *all* speech or no speech at all....

Although the Court has, on occasion, declared that content-based regulations of speech are "never permitted," Police Dept. of Chicago v. Mosley, 408 U.S. 92, 99 (1972).... our decisions demonstrate that content-based distinctions, far from being presumptively invalid, are an inevitable and indispensable aspect of a coherent understanding of the First Amendment.

.... [O]ur entire First Amendment jurisprudence creates a regime based on the content of speech. The scope of the First Amendment is determined by the content of expressive activity: [Categories of unprotected speech are necessarily determined by their content.].... Even within categories of protected expression, the First Amendment status of speech is fixed by its content. New York Times Co. v. Sullivan, 376 U.S. 254 (1964), ... establish[es] that the level of protection given to speech depends upon its subject matter: Speech about public officials or matters of public concern receives greater protection than speech about other topics. It can, therefore, scarcely be said that the regulation of expressive activity cannot be predicated on its content: Much of our First Amendment jurisprudence is premised on the assumption that content makes a difference.

Consistent with this general premise, we have frequently upheld content-based regulations of speech....

Our First Amendment decisions have created a rough hierarchy in the constitutional protection of speech. Core political speech occupies the highest, most protected position; commercial speech and nonobscene, sexually explicit speech are regarded as a sort of second-class expression; obscenity and fighting words receive the least protection of all. Assuming that the Court is correct that this last class of speech is not wholly "unprotected," it certainly does not follow that fighting words and obscenity receive the *same* sort of protection afforded core political speech. Yet in ruling that proscribable speech cannot be regulated based on subject matter, the Court does just that. Perversely, this gives fighting words *greater* protection than is afforded commercial speech. If Congress can prohibit false advertising directed at airline passengers without also prohibiting false advertising directed at bus passengers and if a city can prohibit political advertisements in its buses while allowing other advertisements, it is ironic to hold that a city cannot regulate fighting words based on "race, color, creed, religion or gender" while leaving un-regulated fighting words based on "union membership ... or homosexuality." The Court today turns First Amendment law on its head: Communication that was once entirely unprotected (and that still can be wholly proscribed) is now entitled to greater protection than commercial speech—and possibly greater protection than core political speech.

Perhaps because the Court recognizes these perversities, it quickly offers some ad hoc limitations on its newly extended prohibition on content-based regulations. First, the Court states that a content-based regulation is valid "when the basis for the content discrimination consists entirely of the very reason the entire class of speech ... is proscribable." ...

As I understand this opaque passage, Congress may choose from the set of unprotected speech (all threats) to proscribe only a subset (threats against the President) because those threats are particularly likely to cause "fear of violence," "disruption," and actual "violence."

Precisely this same reasoning, however, compels the conclusion that St. Paul's ordinance is constitutional. Just as Congress may determine that threats against the President entail more severe consequences than other threats, so St. Paul's City Council may determine that threats based on the target's race, religion, or gender cause more severe harm to both the target and to society than other threats. This latter judgment—that harms caused by racial, religious, and gender-based invective are qualitatively different from that caused by other fighting words—seems to me eminently reasonable and realistic. *[handwritten: Stevens' view]*

Next, the Court recognizes that a State may regulate advertising in one industry but not another because "the risk of fraud (one of the characteristics ... that justifies depriving [commercial speech] of full First Amendment protection ...)" in the regulated industry is "greater" than in other industries. Again, the same reasoning demonstrates the constitutionality of St. Paul's ordinance. "One of the characteristics that justifies" the constitutional status of fighting words is that such words "by their very utterance inflict injury or tend to incite an immediate breach of the peace." Chaplinsky, 315 U.S. at 572. Certainly a legislature that may determine that the risk of fraud is greater in the legal trade than in the medical trade may determine that the risk of injury or breach of peace created by race-based threats is greater than that created by other threats. *[handwritten: if Cts can proscribe speech, can't it prohibit speech? why can't it be threatening speech?]*

[handwritten at bottom: Reminds me of Plessy: "Black folks ~~do~~ choose to be offended by the law, it's not actually offensive though.]

Similarly, it is impossible to reconcile the Court's analysis of the St. Paul ordinance with its recognition that "a prohibition of fighting words that are directed at certain persons or groups ... would be facially valid." A selective proscription of unprotected expression designed to protect "certain persons or groups" (for example, a law proscribing threats directed at the elderly) would be constitutional if it were based on a legitimate determination that the harm created by the regulated expression differs from that created by the unregulated expression (that is, if the elderly are more severely injured by threats than are the nonelderly). Such selective protection is no different from a law prohibiting minors (and only minors) from obtaining obscene publications. St. Paul has determined—reasonably in my judgment—that fighting-word injuries "based on race, color, creed, religion or gender" are qualitatively different and more severe than fighting-word injuries based on other characteristics. Whether the selective proscription of proscribable speech is defined by the protected target ("certain persons or groups") or the basis of the harm (injuries "based on race, color, creed, religion or gender") makes no constitutional difference: What matters is whether the legislature's selection is based on a legitimate, neutral, and reasonable distinction....

III

As the foregoing suggests, I disagree with both the Court's and part of JUSTICE WHITE's analysis of the constitutionality of the St. Paul ordinance. Unlike the Court, I do not believe that all content-based regulations are equally infirm and presumptively invalid; unlike JUSTICE WHITE, I do not believe that fighting words are wholly unprotected by the First Amendment....

Not all content-based regulations are alike; our decisions clearly recognize that some content-based restrictions raise more constitutional questions than others....

First, as suggested above, the scope of protection provided expressive activity depends in part upon its content and character. We have long recognized that when government regulates political speech or "the expression of editorial opinion on matters of public importance," "First Amendment protection is 'at its zenith.'" In comparison, we have recognized that "commercial speech receives a limited form of First Amendment protection," and that "society's interest in protecting [sexually explicit films] is of a wholly different, and lesser, magnitude than [its] interest in untrammeled political debate." The character of expressive activity also weighs in our consideration of its constitutional status. As we have frequently noted, "the government generally has a freer hand in restricting expressive conduct than it has in restricting the written or spoken word."

The protection afforded expression turns as well on the context of the regulated speech. [Varying First Amendment analyses apply in employment, school, university, and "captive audience" contexts.] Perhaps the most familiar embodiment of the relevance of context is our "fora" jurisprudence, differentiating the levels of protection afforded speech in different locations.

.... More particularly to the matter of content-based regulations, we have implicitly distinguished between restrictions on expression based on *subject matter* and restrictions based on *viewpoint,* indicating that the latter are particularly pernicious....

Finally, in considering the validity of content-based regulations we have also looked more broadly at [whether speech was prohibited entirely or subject only to certain time, place, or manner restriction]....

All of these factors play some role in our evaluation of content-based regulations on expression. Such a multifaceted analysis cannot be conflated into two dimensions. Whatever the allure of absolute doctrines, it is just too simple to declare expression "protected" or "unprotected" or to proclaim a regulation "content-based" or "content-neutral."

In applying this analysis to the St. Paul ordinance, I assume, *arguendo*—as the Court does—that the ordinance regulates *only* fighting words and therefore is *not* overbroad. Looking to the content and character of the regulated activity, two things are clear. First, by hypothesis the ordinance bars only low-value speech, namely, fighting words. By definition such expression constitutes "no essential part of any exposition of ideas, and [is] of such slight social value as a step to truth that any benefit that may be derived from [it] is clearly outweighed by the social interest in order and morality." Chaplinsky, 315 U.S. at 572. Second, the ordinance regulates "expressive conduct [rather] than ... the written or spoken word." Texas v. Johnson, 491 U.S. at 406.

.... Whether words are fighting words is determined in part by their context. Fighting words are not words that merely cause offense; fighting words must be directed at individuals so as to "by their very utterance inflict injury." By hypothesis, then, the St. Paul ordinance restricts speech in confrontational and potentially violent situations. The case at hand is illustrative. The cross burning in this case—directed as it was to a single African-American family trapped in their home—was nothing more than a crude form of physical intimidation. That this cross burning sends a message of racial hostility does not automatically endow it with complete constitutional protection.

Significantly, the St. Paul ordinance regulates speech not on the basis of its subject matter or the viewpoint expressed, but rather on the basis of the *harm* the speech causes. In this regard, the Court fundamentally misreads the St. Paul ordinance.... as regulating expression "addressed to one of [several] specified disfavored *topics*[.]" ... [But] the ordinance regulates only a subcategory of expression that causes *injuries based on* "race, color, creed, religion or gender," not a subcategory that involves *discussions* that concern those characteristics. The ordinance, as construed by the Court, criminalizes expression that "one knows ... [by its very utterance inflicts injury on] others on the basis of race, color, creed, religion or gender." ...

Contrary to the suggestion of the majority, the St. Paul ordinance does *not* regulate expression based on viewpoint. The Court contends that the ordinance requires proponents of racial intolerance to "follow the Marquis of Queensberry rules" while allowing advocates of racial tolerance to "fight freestyle." The law does no such thing.

.... The response to a sign saying that "all [religious] bigots are misbegotten" is a sign saying that "all advocates of religious tolerance are misbegotten." Assuming such signs could be fighting words (which seems to me extremely unlikely), neither sign would be banned by the ordinance for the attacks were not "based on ... religion" but rather on one's beliefs about tolerance. Conversely (and again assuming such signs are fighting words), just as the ordinance would prohibit a Muslim from hoisting a sign claiming that all Catholics were misbegotten, so the ordinance would bar a Catholic from hoisting a similar sign attacking Muslims.

The St. Paul ordinance is evenhanded. In a battle between advocates of tolerance and advocates of intolerance, the ordinance does not prevent either side from hurling fighting words at the other on the basis of their conflicting ideas, but it does bar *both* sides from hurling such words on the basis of the target's "race, color, creed, religion or gender." To extend the Court's pugilistic metaphor, the St. Paul ordinance simply bans punches "below the belt" — *by either party*. It does not, therefore, favor one side of any debate.

Finally, it is noteworthy that the St. Paul ordinance is, as construed by the Court today, quite narrow. The St. Paul ordinance does not ban all "hate speech," nor does it ban, say, all cross burnings or all swastika displays. Rather it only bans a subcategory of the already narrow category of fighting words. Such a limited ordinance leaves open and protected a vast range of expression on the subjects of racial, religious, and gender equality. As construed by the Court today, the ordinance certainly does not "raise the specter that the Government may effectively drive certain ideas or viewpoints from the marketplace." Petitioner is free to burn a cross to announce a rally or to express his views about racial supremacy, he may do so on private property or public land, at day or at night, so long as the burning is not so threatening and so directed at an individual as to "by its very [execution] inflict injury." Such a limited proscription scarcely offends the First Amendment.

In sum, the St. Paul ordinance (as construed by the Court) regulates expressive activity that is wholly proscribable and does so not on the basis of viewpoint, but rather in recognition of the different harms caused by such activity. Taken together, these several considerations persuade me that the St. Paul ordinance is not an unconstitutional content-based regulation of speech. Thus, were the ordinance not overbroad, I would vote to uphold it.

Review Questions and Explanations: *R.A.V.*

1. The majority's rule suggests that content discrimination is generally prohibited within a regulation of "proscribable" or "unprotected" speech, with a significant exception (or set of exceptions). What are these exceptions? Why doesn't hate speech fit into the exception? Both the White and Stevens opinions take issue with this.

2. Viewpoint discrimination is deemed even worse than content discrimination. While content discrimination regulates subject matter, viewpoint discrimination regulates some but not all opinions within that subject matter. Admittedly, the distinction between content and viewpoint discrimination can be fuzzy.

The majority ventures to suggest that this law might well entail viewpoint discrimination, but does not insist on that view, falling back on its argument that the law impermissibly discriminates on content. The viewpoint discrimination argument centers around the paragraph concluding that the law forces one side of the debate "to follow Marquis of Queensberry rules." Review that paragraph and the response in Justice Stevens' dissent. Is it correct that the law would permit racial or religious slurs to be used in support of tolerance?

3. The majority indicates that interest in tolerance for social diversity is compelling, but holds that the St. Paul ordinance is not necessary to achieve that interest, because there are content-neutral alternatives. What are those alternatives?

4. Both the White and Stevens concurrences disagree sharply with the majority's analysis about impermissible content discrimination within a regulation of fighting words. But they (and thus all nine justices) apparently agree that the St. Paul ordinance was unconstitutionally overbroad on its face.

5. This note refers you back to Figure 9.1. As suggested by the White and Stevens opinions, the *R.A.V.* decision seems to engage in some doctrinal innovation that makes it difficult locate in the First Amendment scheme. We suggest that you can locate *R.A.V.* on our flow chart in the very bottom node, which asks — for the second time in the analytical flow — whether the law is content-discriminatory. In essence, the case proceeds down the flow from top to bottom in a more-or-less straight line: the law is content-based because it focuses on a

category of speech; that category, according to the Minnesota Supreme Court's interpretation was fighting words, one of the unprotected types of speech; the White and Stevens opinions both find the law overbroad, and thereby take a sharp right turn at the second-to-last node ("substantially overbroad?"); but the majority goes to the last question ("content or viewpoint discriminatory?"). This reiteration of the content-discrimination question should be understood to refer to *R.A.V.*'s analysis: is there content-discrimination within a category of unprotected speech? *R.A.V.* answers that question yes, and then proceeds to a brief analysis of whether the law meets strict scrutiny (following the arrow to the left and up). The reason there is an arrow off to the right, directly to a finding of unconstitutionality—with question marks in each direction—reflects an ambiguity in *R.A.V.* It is arguable that viewpoint-discriminatory laws never meet strict scrutiny, and *R.A.V.* hinted that this law may have been viewpoint-discriminatory.

Exercise: *R.A.V.*

You are an assistant city attorney and have been assigned the responsibility to draft a section of a municipal "human rights" ordinance that prohibits (1) hate speech based on race, sex, ethnicity, national origin, or religion; and (2) cross-burning. Your instructions are to avoid constitutional problems laid out in the fighting words cases and *R.A.V.* while, at the same time, not banning conduct so broadly that you obscure the statute's purpose:

> To ensure the basic human rights of members of groups that have historically been subjected to discrimination, including the right of such group members to live in peace where they wish.

Try drafting this part of the ordinance. Consider whether you should put the hate speech and cross-burning bans in separate, severable subsections. Note that the city charter authorizes the city to define and punish misdemeanors, but not felonies.

---

4. Obscenity and Indecency

Obscenity and indecency are related, in that both types of speech tend to trigger a similar "censorship" regulatory motivation. But they are treated as distinct concepts in free speech doctrine. Obscenity is specifically defined, involves depictions of sexual conduct, and is unprotected speech that may, under the First Amendment, be banned outright. Indecency is not specifically defined, and is not limited to sexual depictions; it refers to expression that is protected under the First Amendment but that may nevertheless be subject to time, place, or manner regulations because its offensive character may make it inappropriate to certain circumstances. As Justice Stevens once colorfully described it, indecent speech "may be merely a right thing in the wrong place,—like a pig in the parlor instead of the barnyard." *Federal Communications Commission v. Pacifica Foundation*, 438 U.S. 726 (1978).

Obscenity is another category of speech that is viewed as having little or no value to the exposition of ideas while creating harmful effects. The definition of obscenity, though specific, is arguably vague. In a pair of 1973 decisions, *Miller v. California*, 413 U.S. 15 (1973), and *Paris Adult Theatre I v. Slaton*, 413 U.S. 49 (1973), the Court set out the test for obscenity that remains applicable under current law. Expression is obscene if (1) the average person, applying contemporary community standards, would find that the work, taken as a whole, appeals to the prurient interest; (2) the work depicts or describes, in a patently offensive way, sexual conduct specifically defined by the applicable state law; and (3) the work, taken as a whole, lacks serious literary, artistic, political, or scientific value. The *Miller/Paris Adult Theatre* test was the culmination of a 20-year struggle by the Supreme Court to find a workable definition of obscenity. This doctrinal struggle produced such highlights as Justice Stewart's famous acknowledgment of futility ("I know it when I see it," *Jacobellis v. Ohio*, 378 U.S. 184, 197 (1964) (Stewart, J., concurring)), and the infamous "Redrup" procedure of case-by-case adjudication, *see Redrup v. New York*, 386 U.S. 767 (1967), requiring the justices themselves to repeatedly undertake the "absurd business of perusing and viewing the miserable [pornographic] stuff" to determine whether it met the varying judicial tests for obscenity. *See Paris Adult Theatre I*, 413 U.S. at 92 (Brennan, J., dissenting). The *Miller/Paris Adult Theatre* approach changed the legal question of obscenity to a fact-intensive inquiry into "community standards" that has made jury and lower court resolutions more predominant.

Indecency is different. Whether there is a formal category of "indecent" speech is doctrinally unclear. Justice Stevens did not win colleagues over to his theory that it is less protected than other speech. However, in *Federal Communications Commission v. Pacifica Foundation*, 438 U.S. 726 (1978), the Court upheld the FCC's statutory authority to regulate and penalize "indecent" broadcasts over the radio. The case involved a public radio station's airing of a recording of comedian George Carlin's satiric monologue called "Filthy Words," in which Carlin repeatedly uttered and commented on "the words you couldn't say on the public airwaves." Five justices (*Stevens*, Burger (CJ), Rehnquist, Blackmun, Powell) agreed that the broadcast was subject to the FCC's indecency restrictions because the broadcast medium and time of day (the afternoon) made it likely that children could hear the broadcast. A three-justice plurality (*Stevens*, Burger, and Rehnquist) argued that the "patently offensive" nature of the language alone made the speech less "valuable" than other protected speech and thus subject to indecency regulations. In dissent, Justice Brennan pointed out the irony of that plurality view that Carlin's monologue had no "valuable" content: "Carlin is not mouthing obscenities, [but] is merely using words to satirize as harmless and essentially silly our attitudes towards those words." Significantly, for present purposes, neither the FCC nor the plurality contended that the Carlin monologue was "obscene" or otherwise entirely without First Amendment protection. (On the First Amendment Flow Chart, "indecency" is represented by the dotted line on the right side of the "unprotected speech" categories heading back up to intermediate scrutiny.)

The indecency issue returned to the Supreme Court in *FCC v. Fox Television Stations*, 567 U.S. ___, 132 S. Ct. 2307 (2012). There, Fox Television and ABC challenged the constitutionality of penalties imposed on them for momentary foul language and nudity in live broadcasts despite an FCC policy that permitted "fleeting expletives" and some nudity. A unanimous Court vacated the penalties. A seven-justice majority opinion authored by Justice Kennedy held that the "fleeting expletive" policy—banning some instances of expletive use and nudity but not others—was "void for vagueness." The Court did not decide whether, as argued by the broadcasters, the continued ban on broadcast "indecency" upheld in *Pacifica* violated the First Amendment. Justice Ginsburg, concurring in the judgment, argued that *Pacifica* should be overruled.

The next case is the first major Supreme Court decision to consider First Amendment issues in the context of internet-based speech. The lengthy factual description may be familiar to you, but recall this opinion was issued 15 years ago, when the internet was still unfamiliar to many people. You should read the facts carefully, since they bear significantly on the First Amendment analysis. In reading this case, a key point to bear in mind is the obscenity/indecency distinction, set out above.

Guided Reading Questions: *Reno v. American Civil Liberties Union*

1. The discussion of the statute in section II starts by pointing out that the challenged provisions were contained in an amendment slipped into a larger bill on related but different subject matter. Why point this out?

2. Read the statutes carefully. Since the statute creates a criminal offense, try identifying, in a few bullet points, the "elements" of the crime.

3. Sections IV and V of the opinion distinguish prior cases in which regulation was upheld and note significant technological features of the internet. What is the point of these sections? What do they tell us about the appropriate level of scrutiny and the strength of the governmental interest?

4. Sections VI and VII of the opinion ultimately deal with narrow tailoring. How does the vagueness argument fit in? Summarize in a few sentences how the Court reaches the conclusion that the law is not narrowly tailored.

5. Sections VIII and IX consider and reject arguments that limiting language defining the crimes, as well as affirmative defenses, save the statute's constitutionality. Why do these arguments fail?

6. Section X deals with the government's argument that the Court should interpret the statute to save it from unconstitutionality and, if necessary, sever unconstitutional portions and uphold the rest. What does the Court do with this?

Reno v. American Civil Liberties Union
521 U.S. 844 (1997)

Majority: *Stevens*, Scalia, Kennedy, Souter, Thomas, Ginsburg, Breyer

Partial dissent: *O'Connor*, Rehnquist (CJ)

JUSTICE STEVENS delivered the opinion of the Court.

At issue is the constitutionality of two statutory provisions enacted to protect minors from "indecent" and "patently offensive" communications on the Internet. Notwithstanding the legitimacy and importance of the congressional goal of protecting children from harmful materials, we agree with the three-judge District Court that the statute abridges "the freedom of speech" protected by the First Amendment.

I

.... Anyone with access to the Internet may take advantage of a wide variety of communication and information retrieval methods. These methods are constantly evolving and difficult to categorize precisely.... Any person or organization with a computer connected to the Internet can "publish" information.... Publishers may either make their material available to the entire pool of Internet users, or confine access to a selected group, such as those willing to pay for the privilege. "No single organization controls any membership in the Web, nor is there any centralized point from which individual Web sites or services can be blocked from the Web."

Sexually explicit material on the Internet includes text, pictures, and chat and "extends from the modestly titillating to the hardest-core." These files are created, named, and posted in the same manner as material that is not sexually explicit, and may be accessed either deliberately or unintentionally during the course of an imprecise search. "Once a provider posts its content on the Internet, it cannot prevent that content from entering any community." ...

Though such material is widely available, users seldom encounter such content accidentally. "A document's title or a description of the document will usually appear before the document itself ... and in many cases the user will receive detailed information about a site's content before he or she need take the step to access the document. Almost all sexually explicit images are preceded by warnings as to the content." For that reason, the "odds are slim" that a user would enter a sexually explicit site by accident. Unlike communications received by radio or television, "the receipt of information on the Internet requires a series of affirmative steps more deliberate and directed than merely turning a dial. A child requires some sophistication and some ability to read to retrieve material and thereby to use the Internet unattended."

Systems have been developed to help parents control the material that may be available on a home computer with Internet access. A system may either limit a computer's access to an approved list of sources that have been identified as containing no adult material, it may block designated inappropriate sites, or it may attempt to block messages containing identifiable objectionable features. "Although parental control software currently can screen for certain suggestive words or for known sexually explicit sites, it cannot now screen for sexually explicit images." Nevertheless, the evidence indicates that "a reasonably effective method by which parents can prevent their children from accessing sexually explicit and other material which parents may believe is inappropriate for their children will soon be available."

The problem of age verification differs for different uses of the Internet. The District Court categorically determined that there "is no effective way to determine the identity or the age of a user who is accessing material through e-mail, mail exploders, newsgroups or chat rooms." ... Moreover, even if it were technologically feasible to block minors' access to newsgroups and chat rooms containing discussions of art, politics or other subjects that potentially elicit "indecent" or "patently offensive" contributions, it would not be possible to block their access to that material and "still allow them access to the remaining content, even if the overwhelming majority of that content was not indecent."

Technology exists by which an operator of a Web site may condition access on the verification of requested information such as a credit card number or an adult password. Credit card verification is only feasible, however, either in connection with a commercial transaction in which the card is used, or by payment to a verification agency. Using credit card possession as a surrogate for proof of age would impose costs on non-commercial Web sites that would require many of them to shut down.... Moreover, the imposition of such a requirement "would completely bar adults who do not have a credit card and lack the resources to obtain one from accessing any blocked material."

Commercial pornographic sites that charge their users for access have assigned them passwords as a method of age verification. The record does not contain any evidence concerning the reliability of these technologies. Even if passwords are effective for commercial purveyors of indecent material, the District Court found that an adult password requirement would impose significant burdens on noncommercial sites, both because they would discourage users from accessing their sites and because the cost of creating and maintaining such screening systems would be "beyond their reach."

II

The Telecommunications Act of 1996 was an unusually important legislative enactment. As stated on the first of its 103 pages, its primary purpose was to reduce regulation and encourage "the rapid deployment of new telecommunications technologies." The major components of the statute have nothing to do with the Internet; they were designed to promote competition in the local telephone service market, the multichannel video market, and the market for over-the-air broadcasting. The Act includes seven Titles, six of which are the product of extensive committee hearings and the subject of discussion in Reports prepared by Committees of the Senate and the House of Representatives. By contrast, Title V—known as the "Communications Decency Act of 1996" (CDA)—contains provisions that were either added in executive committee after the hearings were concluded or as amendments offered during floor debate on the legislation. An amendment offered in the Senate was the source of the two statutory provisions challenged in this case. They are informally described as the "indecent transmission" provision and the "patently offensive display" provision.

The first, 47 U.S.C. A. § 223(a), prohibits the knowing transmission of obscene or indecent messages to any recipient under 18 years of age. It provides in pertinent part:

(a) Whoever—(1) in interstate or foreign communications—.... (B) by means of a telecommunications device knowingly—(i) makes, creates, or solicits, and (ii) initiates the transmission of,

any comment, request, suggestion, proposal, image, or other communication which is obscene or indecent, knowing that the recipient of the communication is under 18 years of age, regardless of whether the maker of such communication placed the call or initiated the communication; [or]

(2) knowingly permits any telecommunications facility under his control to be used for any activity prohibited by paragraph (1) with the intent that it be used for such activity,

shall be fined under Title 18, or imprisoned not more than two years, or both.

The second provision, § 223(d), prohibits the knowing sending or displaying of patently offensive messages in a manner that is available to a person under 18 years of age. It provides:

(d) Whoever—(1) in interstate or foreign communications knowingly—(A) uses an interactive computer service to send to a specific person or persons under 18 years of age, or (B) uses any interactive computer service to display in a manner available to a person under 18 years of age,

any comment, request, suggestion, proposal, image, or other communication that, in context, depicts or describes, in terms patently offensive as measured by contemporary community standards, sexual or excretory activities or organs, regardless of whether the user of such service placed the call or initiated the communication; or

(2) knowingly permits any telecommunications facility under such person's control to be used for an activity prohibited by paragraph (1) with the intent that it be used for such activity,

shall be fined under Title 18, or imprisoned not more than two years, or both.

The breadth of these prohibitions is qualified by two affirmative defenses. See § 223(e)(5). One covers those who take "good faith, reasonable, effective, and appropriate actions" to restrict access by minors to the prohibited communications. § 223(e)(5)(A). The other covers those who restrict access to covered material by requiring certain designated forms of age proof, such as a verified credit card or an adult identification number or code. § 223(e)(5)(B).

III

On February 8, 1996, immediately after the President signed the statute, 20 plaintiffs filed suit against the Attorney General of the United States and the Department of Justice challenging the constitutionality of §§ 223(a)(1) and 223(d). A week later, based on his conclusion that the term "indecent" was too vague to provide the basis for a criminal prosecution, District Judge Buckwalter entered a temporary restraining order against enforcement of § 223(a)(1)(B)(ii) insofar as it applies to indecent communications. A second suit was then filed by 27 additional plaintiffs, the two cases were consolidated, and a three-judge District Court was convened pursuant to § 561 of the Act. After an evidentiary hearing, that Court entered a preliminary injunction against enforcement of both of the challenged provisions. Each of the three judges wrote a separate opinion, but their judgment was unanimous....

The judgment of the District Court enjoins the Government from enforcing the prohibitions in § 223(a)(1)(B) insofar as they relate to "indecent" communications, but expressly preserves the Government's right to investigate and prosecute the obscenity or child pornography activities prohibited therein. The injunction against enforcement of §§ 223(d)(1) and (2) is unqualified because those provisions contain no separate reference to obscenity or child pornography.

The Government appealed under the Act's special review provisions, § 561, and we noted probable jurisdiction. In its appeal, the Government argues that the District Court erred in holding that the CDA violated both the First Amendment because it is overbroad and the Fifth Amendment because it is vague. While we discuss the vagueness of the CDA because of its relevance to the First Amendment overbreadth inquiry, we conclude that the judgment should be affirmed without reaching the Fifth Amendment issue. We begin our analysis by reviewing the principal authorities on which the Government relies. Then, after describing the overbreadth of the CDA, we consider the Government's specific contentions, including its submission that we save portions of the statute either by severance or by fashioning judicial limitations on the scope of its coverage.

IV

In arguing for reversal, the Government contends that the CDA is plainly constitutional under three of our prior decisions: (1) Ginsberg v. New York, 390 U.S. 629 (1968); (2) FCC v. Pacifica Foundation, 438 U.S. 726 (1978); and (3) Renton v. Playtime Theatres, Inc., 475 U.S. 41 (1986). A close look at these cases, however, raises — rather than relieves — doubts concerning the constitutionality of the CDA.

In Ginsberg, we upheld the constitutionality of a New York statute that prohibited selling to minors under 17 years of age material that was considered obscene as to them even if not obscene as to adults. We rejected the defendant's broad submission that "the scope of the constitutional freedom of expression secured to a citizen to read or see material concerned with sex cannot be made to depend on whether the citizen is an adult or a minor." In rejecting that contention, we relied not only on the State's independent interest in the well-being of its youth, but also on our consistent recognition of the principle that "the parents' claim to authority in their own household to direct the rearing of their children is basic in the structure of our society." In four important respects, the statute upheld in Ginsberg was narrower than the CDA. First, we noted in Ginsberg that "the prohibition against sales to minors does not bar parents who so desire from purchasing the magazines for their children." Under the CDA, by contrast, neither the parents' consent—nor even their participation—in the communication would avoid the application of the statute. Second, the New York statute applied only to commercial transactions, whereas the CDA contains no such limitation. Third, the New York statute cabined its definition of material that is harmful to minors with the requirement that it be "utterly without redeeming social importance for minors." The CDA fails to provide us with any definition of the term "indecent" as used in §223(a)(1) and, importantly, omits any requirement that the "patently offensive" material covered by §223(d) lack serious literary, artistic, political, or scientific value. Fourth, the New York statute defined a minor as a person under the age of 17, whereas the CDA, in applying to all those under 18 years, includes an additional year of those nearest majority.

In Pacifica, we upheld a declaratory order of the Federal Communications Commission, holding that the broadcast of a recording of a 12-minute monologue entitled "Filthy Words" that had previously been delivered to a live audience "could have been the subject of administrative sanctions." The Commission had found that the repetitive use of certain words referring to excretory or sexual activities or organs "in an afternoon broadcast when children are in the audience was patently offensive" and concluded that the monologue was indecent "as broadcast." ... Relying on the premise that "of all forms of communication" broadcasting had received the most limited First Amendment protection, the Court concluded that the ease with which children may obtain access to broadcasts, "coupled with the concerns recognized in Ginsberg," justified special treatment of indecent broadcasting.

... [T]here are significant differences between the order upheld in Pacifica and the CDA. First, the order in Pacifica, issued by an agency that had been regulating radio stations for decades, targeted a specific broadcast that represented a rather dramatic departure from traditional program content in order to designate when—rather than whether—it would be permissible to air such a program in that particular medium. The CDA's broad categorical prohibitions are not limited to particular times and are not dependent on any evaluation by an agency familiar with the unique characteristics of the Internet. Second, unlike the CDA, the Commission's declaratory order was not punitive; we expressly refused to decide whether the indecent broadcast "would justify a criminal prosecution." Finally, the Commission's order applied to a medium which as a matter of history had "received the most limited First Amendment protection," in large part because warnings could not adequately protect the listener from unexpected program content. The Internet, however, has no comparable history. Moreover, the District Court found that the risk of encountering indecent material by accident is remote because a series of affirmative steps is required to access specific material.

In Renton, we upheld a zoning ordinance that kept adult movie theatres out of residential neighborhoods. The ordinance was aimed, not at the content of the films shown in the theaters, but rather at the "secondary effects"—such as crime and deteriorating property values—that these theaters fostered. According to the Government, the CDA is constitutional because it constitutes a sort of "cyberzoning" on the Internet. But the CDA applies broadly to the entire universe of cyberspace. And the purpose of the CDA is to protect children from the primary effects of "indecent" and "patently offensive" speech, rather than any "secondary" effect of such speech. Thus, the CDA is a content-based blanket restriction on speech, and, as such, cannot be "properly analyzed as a form of time, place, and manner regulation." ...

[Our] precedents, then, surely do not require us to uphold the CDA and are fully consistent with the application of the most stringent review of its provisions.

V

... "[E]ach medium of expression ... may present its own problems." Thus, some of our cases have recognized special justifications for regulation of the broadcast media that are not applicable to other speakers.

Those factors are not present in cyberspace. Neither before nor after the enactment of the CDA have the vast democratic fora of the Internet been subject to the type of government supervision and regulation that has attended the broadcast industry. Moreover, the Internet is not as "invasive" as radio or television. The District Court specifically found that "communications over the Internet do not 'invade' an individual's home or appear on one's computer screen unbidden. Users seldom encounter content 'by accident.'" It also found that "almost all sexually explicit images are preceded by warnings as to the content," and cited testimony that "'odds are slim' that a user would come across a sexually explicit sight by accident." ...

Finally, unlike the conditions that prevailed when Congress first authorized regulation of the broadcast spectrum, the Internet can hardly be considered a "scarce" expressive commodity. It provides relatively unlimited, low-cost capacity for communication of all kinds. The Government estimates that "as many as 40 million people use the Internet today, and that figure is expected to grow to 200 million by 1999." ... Through the use of chat rooms, any person with a phone line can become a town crier with a voice that resonates farther than it could from any soapbox. Through the use of Web pages, mail exploders, and newsgroups, the same individual can become a pamphleteer. As the District Court found, "the content on the Internet is as diverse as human thought." We agree with its conclusion that our cases provide no basis for qualifying the level of First Amendment scrutiny that should be applied to this medium.

VI

Regardless of whether the CDA is so vague that it violates the Fifth Amendment, the many ambiguities concerning the scope of its coverage render it problematic for purposes of the First Amendment. For instance, each of the two parts of the CDA uses a different linguistic form. The first uses the word "indecent," 47 U.S.C. A. § 223(a), while the second speaks of material that "in context, depicts or describes, in terms patently offensive as measured by contemporary community standards, sexual or excretory activities or organs," § 223(d). Given the absence of a definition of either term, this difference in language will provoke uncertainty among speakers about how the two standards relate to each other and just what they mean. Could a speaker confidently assume that a serious discussion about birth control practices, homosexuality, the First Amendment issues raised by the Appendix to our Pacifica opinion, or the consequences of prison rape would not violate the CDA? This uncertainty undermines the likelihood that the CDA has been carefully tailored to the congressional goal of protecting minors from potentially harmful materials.

The vagueness of the CDA is a matter of special concern for two reasons. First, the CDA is a content-based regulation of speech. The vagueness of such a regulation raises special First Amendment concerns because of its obvious chilling effect on free speech. Second, the CDA is a criminal statute. In addition to the opprobrium and stigma of a criminal conviction, the CDA threatens violators with penalties including up to two years in prison for each act of violation. The severity of criminal sanctions may well cause speakers to remain silent rather than communicate even arguably unlawful words, ideas, and images. As a practical matter, this increased deterrent effect, coupled with the "risk of discriminatory enforcement" of vague regulations, poses greater First Amendment concerns than those implicated by ... civil regulation.

The Government argues that the statute is no more vague than the obscenity standard this Court established in Miller v. California, 413 U.S. 15 (1973). But that is not so.... Having struggled for some time to establish a definition of obscenity, we set forth in Miller the test for obscenity that controls to this day:

> (a) whether the average person, applying contemporary community standards would find that the work, taken as a whole, appeals to the prurient interest; (b) whether the work depicts or describes, in a patently offensive way, sexual conduct specifically defined by the applicable state law; and (c) whether the work, taken as a whole, lacks serious literary, artistic, political, or scientific value.

.... The Government's assertion is incorrect as a matter of fact. The second prong of the Miller test—the purportedly analogous standard—contains a critical requirement that is omitted from the CDA: that the proscribed material be "specifically defined by the applicable state law." This requirement reduces the vagueness inherent in the open-ended term "patently offensive" as used in the CDA. Moreover, the Miller definition is limited to "sexual conduct," whereas the CDA extends also to include (1) "excretory activities" as well as (2) "organs" of both a sexual and excretory nature.

The Government's reasoning is also flawed. Just because a definition including three limitations is not vague, it does not follow that one of those limitations, standing by itself, is not vague.

> FN38. Even though the word "trunk," standing alone, might refer to luggage, a swimming suit, the base of a tree, or the long nose of an animal, its meaning is clear when it is one prong of a three-part description of a species of gray animals.

Each of Miller's additional two prongs—(1) that, taken as a whole, the material appeals to the "prurient" interest, and (2) that it "lack serious literary, artistic, political, or scientific value"—critically limits the uncertain sweep of the obscenity definition. The second requirement is particularly important because, unlike the "patently offensive" and "prurient interest" criteria, it is not judged by contemporary community standards. This "societal value" requirement, absent in the CDA, allows appellate courts to impose some limitations and regularity on the definition by setting, as a matter of law, a national floor for socially redeeming value. The Government's contention that courts will be able to give such legal limitations to the CDA's standards is belied by Miller's own rationale for having juries determine whether material is "patently offensive" according to community standards: that such questions are essentially ones of *fact*.

VII

.... We are persuaded that the CDA lacks the precision that the First Amendment requires when a statute regulates the content of speech. In order to deny minors access to potentially harmful speech, the CDA effectively suppresses a large amount of speech that adults have a constitutional right to receive and to address to one another. That burden on adult speech is unacceptable if less restrictive alternatives would be at least as effective in achieving the legitimate purpose that the statute was enacted to serve.

In evaluating the free speech rights of adults, we have made it perfectly clear that "sexual expression which is indecent but not obscene is protected by the First Amendment.".... [The] governmental interest in protecting children from harmful materials.... does not justify an unnecessarily broad suppression of speech addressed to adults....

In arguing that the CDA does not so diminish adult communication, the Government relies on the incorrect factual premise that prohibiting a transmission whenever it is known that one of its recipients is a minor would not interfere with adult-to-adult communication. The findings of the District Court make clear that this premise is untenable. Given the size of the potential audience for most messages, in the absence of a viable age verification process, the sender must be charged with knowing that one or more minors will likely view it. Knowledge that, for instance, one or more members of a 100-person chat group will be minor—and therefore that it would be a crime to send the group an indecent message—would surely burden communication among adults.

The District Court found that at the time of trial existing technology did not include any effective method for a sender to prevent minors from obtaining access to its communications on the Internet without also denying access to adults.... By contrast, the District Court found that "despite its limitations, currently available *user-based* software suggests that a reasonably effective method by which *parents* can prevent their children from accessing sexually explicit and other material which *parents* may believe is inappropriate for their children will soon be widely available."

The breadth of the CDA's coverage is wholly unprecedented. Unlike the regulations upheld in Ginsberg and Pacifica, the scope of the CDA is not limited to commercial speech or commercial entities. Its open-ended prohibitions embrace all nonprofit entities and individuals posting indecent messages or displaying them on their own computers in the presence of minors. The general, undefined terms "indecent" and "patently offensive" cover large amounts of nonpornographic material with serious educational or other value.

> FN44. Transmitting obscenity and child pornography, whether via the Internet or other means, is already illegal under federal law for both adults and juveniles. See 18 U.S.C. §§ 1464–1465 (criminalizing obscenity); § 2251 (criminalizing child pornography). In fact, when Congress was considering the CDA, the Government expressed its view that the law was unnecessary because existing laws already authorized its ongoing efforts to prosecute obscenity, child pornography, and child solicitation. See 141 Cong. Rec. S8342 (June 14, 1995) (letter from Kent Markus, Acting Assistant Attorney General, U.S. Department of Justice, to Sen. Leahy).

Moreover, the "community standards" criterion as applied to the Internet means that any communication available to a nation-wide audience will be judged by the standards of the community most likely to be offended by the message. The regulated subject matter includes any of the seven "dirty words" used in the Pacifica monologue, the use of which the Government's expert acknowledged could constitute a felony. It may also extend to discussions about prison rape or safe sexual practices, artistic images that include nude subjects, and arguably the card catalogue of the Carnegie Library.

For the purposes of our decision, we need neither accept nor reject the Government's submission that the First Amendment does not forbid a blanket prohibition on all "indecent" and "patently offensive" messages communicated to a 17-year old—no matter how much value the message may contain and regardless of parental approval. It is at least clear that the strength of the Government's interest in protecting minors is not equally strong throughout the coverage of this broad statute. Under the CDA, a parent allowing her 17-year-old to use the family computer to obtain information on the Internet that she, in her parental judgment, deems appropriate could face a lengthy prison term. See 47 U.S.C. A. § 223(a)(2). Similarly, a parent who sent his 17-year-old college freshman information on birth control via e-mail could be incarcerated even though neither he, his child, nor anyone in their home community, found the material "indecent" or "patently offensive," if the college town's community thought otherwise.

The breadth of this content-based restriction of speech imposes an especially heavy burden on the Government to explain why a less restrictive provision would not be as effective as the CDA. It has not done so. The arguments in this Court have referred to possible alternatives such as requiring that indecent material be "tagged" in a way that facilitates parental control of material coming into their homes, making exceptions for messages with artistic or educational value, providing some tolerance for parental choice, and regulating some portions of the Internet—such as commercial web sites—differently than others, such as chat rooms. Particularly in the light of the absence of any detailed findings by the Congress, or even hearings addressing the special problems of the CDA, we are persuaded that the CDA is not narrowly tailored if that requirement has any meaning at all.

VIII

In an attempt to curtail the CDA's facial overbreadth, the Government advances three additional arguments for sustaining the Act's affirmative prohibitions....

The Government first contends that, even though the CDA effectively censors discourse on many of the Internet's modalities—such as chat groups, newsgroups, and mail exploders—it is nonetheless constitutional because it provides a "reasonable opportunity" for speakers to engage in the restricted speech on the World Wide Web. This argument is unpersuasive because the CDA regulates speech on the basis of its content. A "time, place, and manner" analysis is therefore inapplicable. It is thus immaterial whether such speech would be feasible on the Web (which, as the Government's own expert acknowledged, would cost up to $ 10,000 if the speaker's interests were not accommodated by an existing Web site, not including costs for database management and age verification). The Government's position is equivalent to arguing that a statute could ban leaflets on certain subjects as long as individuals are free to publish books. In invalidating a number of laws that banned leafletting on the streets *regardless of* their content—we explained that "one is not to have the exercise of his liberty of expression in appropriate places abridged on the plea that it may be exercised in some other place." Schneider v. State (Town of Irvington), 308 U.S. 147, 163 (1939).

The Government also asserts that the "knowledge" requirement of both §§ 223(a) and (d), especially when coupled with the "specific child" element found in § 223(d), saves the CDA from overbreadth. Because both sections prohibit the dissemination of indecent messages only to persons known to be under 18, the Government argues, it does not require transmitters to "refrain from communicating indecent material to adults; they need only refrain from disseminating such materials to persons they know to be under 18." This argument ignores the fact that most Internet fora—including chat rooms, newsgroups, mail exploders, and the Web—are open to all comers. The Government's assertion that the knowledge requirement somehow protects the communications of adults is therefore untenable. Even the strongest reading of the "specific person" requirement of § 223(d) cannot save the statute. It would confer broad powers of censorship, in the form of a "heckler's veto," upon any opponent of indecent speech who might simply log on and inform the would-be discoursers that his 17-year-old child—a "specific person ... under 18 years of age," 47 U.S.C. A. § 223(d)(1)(A)—would be present.

Finally, we find no textual support for the Government's submission that material having scientific, educational, or other redeeming social value will necessarily fall outside the CDA's "patently offensive" and "indecent" prohibitions.

IX

The Government's three remaining arguments focus on the defenses provided in § 223(e)(5). First, relying on the "good faith, reasonable, effective, and appropriate actions" provision, the Government suggests that "tagging" provides a defense that saves the constitutionality of the Act. The suggestion assumes that transmitters may encode their indecent communications in a way that would indicate their contents, thus permitting recipients to block their reception with appropriate software. It is the requirement that the good faith action must be "effective" that makes this defense illusory. The Government recognizes that its proposed screening software does not currently exist. Even if it did, there is no way to know whether a potential recipient will actually block the encoded material. Without the impossible knowledge that every guardian in America is screening for the "tag," the transmitter could not reasonably rely on its action to be "effective."

For its second and third arguments concerning defenses—which we can consider together—the Government relies on the latter half of § 223(e)(5), which applies when the transmitter has restricted access by requiring use of a verified credit card or adult identification.... Under the findings of the District Court, however, it is not economically feasible for most noncommercial speakers to employ such verification. Accordingly, this defense would not significantly narrow the statute's burden on noncommercial speech. Even with respect to the commercial pornographers that would be protected by the defense, the Government failed to adduce any evidence that these verification techniques actually preclude minors from posing as adults. Given that the risk of criminal sanctions "hovers over each content provider, like the proverbial sword of Damocles," the District Court correctly refused to rely on unproven future technology to save the statute. The Government thus failed to prove that the proffered defense would significantly reduce the heavy burden on adult speech produced by the prohibition on offensive displays.

We agree with the District Court's conclusion that the CDA places an unacceptably heavy burden on protected speech, and that the defenses do not constitute the sort of "narrow tailoring" that will save an otherwise patently invalid unconstitutional provision. [In an analogous case,] we remarked that the speech restriction at issue there amounted to "burning the house to roast the pig." The CDA, casting a far darker shadow over free speech, threatens to torch a large segment of the Internet community.

X

At oral argument, the Government relied heavily on its ultimate fall-back position: If this Court should conclude that the CDA is insufficiently tailored, it urged, we should save the statute's constitutionality by honoring the severability clause, and construing nonseverable terms narrowly. In only one respect is this argument acceptable.

A severability clause requires textual provisions that can be severed.... The "indecency" provision, 47 U.S.C. A. § 223(a), applies to "any comment, request, suggestion, proposal, image, or other communication which is *obscene or indecent*" (emphasis added). Appellees do not challenge the application of the statute to obscene speech, which, they acknowledge, can be banned totally because it enjoys no First Amendment protection. Therefore, we will sever the term "or indecent" from the statute, leaving the rest of §223(a) standing. In no other respect, however, can §223(a) or §223(d) be saved by such a textual surgery.

... [T]he statute that grants our jurisdiction for this expedited review, 47 U.S.C. A. §561, limits that jurisdictional grant to actions challenging the CDA "on its face." Consistent with §561, the plaintiffs who brought this suit and the three-judge panel that decided it treated it as a facial challenge. We have no authority, in this particular posture, to convert this litigation into an "as-applied" challenge. Nor, given the vast array of plaintiffs, the range of their expressive activities, and the vagueness of the statute, would it be practicable to limit our holding to a judicially defined set of specific applications.

.... In considering a facial challenge, this Court may impose a limiting construction on a statute only if it is "readily susceptible" to such a construction. The open-ended character of the CDA provides no guidance whatever for limiting its coverage.

This case is therefore unlike those in which we have construed a statute narrowly because the text or other source of congressional intent identified a clear line that this Court could draw.... [We] decline[] to "draw one or more lines between categories of speech covered by an overly broad statute, when Congress has sent inconsistent signals as to where the new line or lines should be drawn" because doing so "involves a far more serious invasion of the legislative domain." ...

For the foregoing reasons, the judgment of the district court is affirmed.

JUSTICE O'CONNOR, with whom THE CHIEF JUSTICE joins, concurring in the judgment in part and dissenting in part.

... I view the Communications Decency Act of 1996 (CDA) as little more than an attempt by Congress to create "adult zones" on the Internet. Our precedent indicates that the creation of such zones can be constitutionally sound. Despite the soundness of its purpose, however, portions of the CDA are unconstitutional because they stray from the blueprint our prior cases have developed for constructing a "zoning law" that passes constitutional muster....

Our cases make clear that a "zoning" law is valid only if adults are still able to obtain the regulated speech. If they cannot, the law does more than simply keep children away from speech they have no right to obtain — it interferes with the rights of adults to obtain constitutionally protected speech and effectively "reduces the adult population ... to reading only what is fit for children." ...

The Court in Ginsberg concluded that the New York law created a constitutionally adequate adult zone simply because, on its face, it denied access only to minors. The Court did not question — and therefore necessarily assumed — that an adult zone, once created, would succeed in preserving adults' access while denying minors' access to the regulated speech. Before today, there was no reason to question this assumption, for the Court has previously only considered laws that operated in the physical world....

The electronic world is fundamentally different. Because it is no more than the interconnection of electronic pathways, cyberspace allows speakers and listeners to mask their identities.... [At the same time,] it is possible to construct barriers in cyberspace and use them to screen for identity, making cyberspace more like the physical world and, consequently, more amenable to zoning laws. This transformation of cyberspace is already underway....

Although the prospects for the eventual zoning of the Internet appear promising, I agree with the Court that we must evaluate the constitutionality of the CDA as it applies to the Internet as it exists today. Given the present state of cyberspace, I agree with the Court that the "display" provision cannot pass muster....

The "indecency transmission" and "specific person" provisions present a closer issue, for they are not unconstitutional in all of their applications. As discussed above, the "indecency transmission" provision makes it a crime to transmit knowingly an indecent message to a person the sender knows is under 18 years of age....

So construed, both provisions are constitutional as applied to a conversation involving only an adult and one or more minors—e.g., when an adult speaker sends an e-mail knowing the addressee is a minor, or when an adult and minor converse by themselves or with other minors in a chat room. In this context, these provisions are no different from the law we sustained in Ginsberg....

The analogy to Ginsberg breaks down, however, when more than one adult is a party to the conversation. If a minor enters a chat room otherwise occupied by adults, the CDA effectively requires the adults in the room to stop using indecent speech....

But these two provisions do not infringe on adults' speech in *all* situations.... I do not find that the provisions are overbroad in the sense that they restrict minors' access to a substantial amount of speech that minors have the right to read and view....

.... Where, as here, "the parties challenging the statute are those who desire to engage in protected speech that the overbroad statute purports to punish ... the statute may forthwith be declared invalid to the extent that it reaches too far, but otherwise left intact." There is no question that Congress intended to prohibit certain communications between one adult and one or more minors. There is also no question that Congress would have enacted a narrower version of these provisions had it known a broader version would be declared unconstitutional. I would therefore sustain the "indecency transmission" and "specific person" provisions to the extent they apply to the transmission of Internet communications where the party initiating the communication knows that all of the recipients are minors.

Review Questions and Explanations: *Reno v. ACLU*

1. First Amendment doctrine often has very practical underpinnings in terms of the expressive activities at stake. Review the two statutory provisions at the beginning of the opinion; then try making a list of all the kinds of speech and expression that could be posted to or received via the internet that would potentially be restricted by this criminal law—but that, in your view, the First Amendment should protect. Skim through the opinion again, and compare your list to the examples the Court gives of protected speech implicated by the statute.

2. After all the dust has settled, what is prohibited and what is permitted under the remaining constitutionally valid provisions, if any, of the CDA? What would Justice O'Connor have permitted?

3. Why does the Court speak, in sections VI through VIII, both in terms of lack of narrow tailoring *and* substantial overbreadth? Are those two concepts redundant, or are they different?

4. This case pulls together precedents dealing with the related, but different, concepts of obscenity and indecency. You should be able to articulate the difference

between these two concepts in First Amendment doctrine. Is the Court's handling of them consistent within the *Reno* case itself and consistent with the precedents?

E. Free Speech Doctrine in Special Contexts

As suggested in Justice Stevens' opinion concurring in the judgment in *R.A.V.*, free speech doctrine can be context-specific: the general rules may (at least arguably) be modified in particular settings. In this section we consider four such contexts: campaign finance, government employment, schools, and commercial speech.

1. Campaign Finance

The Federal Election Campaign Act of 1971 made comprehensive reforms of federal election campaign finance law, established the framework of campaign finance regulation that still governs federal elections, and created the Federal Election Commission as an independent agency to oversee the law's ongoing regulatory functions. Several constitutional challenges were soon made both to the regulatory impact of the law and to the Commission, on both separation-of-powers and First Amendment grounds. The separation-of-powers part of the case was excerpted in Chapter 3. Here we present the First Amendment part of the case.

Guided Reading Questions: *Buckley v. Valeo*

1. The majority begins by considering an argument that campaign expenditures and contributions should be treated as only incidentally affecting speech rights. This argument is based in part on *United States v. O'Brien,* where the speech interest harmed by the prohibition on burning draft cards was seen as only incidental to the non-speech need of the selective service to operate the draft effectively. Under this argument, the target of the campaign finance regulation is not the content of the speech, but the distorting effects the need to raise and spend money has on representative government. As you will see, the Court rejected this argument. The Court also considered an argument that campaign finance regulations should be treated as time, place, and manner regulations and thereby subjected to less rigorous review. The Court rejected this position as well. The idea that "money is speech" in the campaign finance context now seems beyond debate. Should it be? Money certainly facilities speech, but so do lots of other things, many of which we regulate without regard to the First Amendment.

2. The Court treats campaign contributions (money given to candidates) differently than it treats campaign expenditures (money spent by candidates or individuals to purchase campaign speech). The Court sees these two acts—giving money and spending money—as carrying different constitutional weight. Pay attention to the Court's argument on this point: it is complicated but important.

3. What compelling interest(s) does the government put forward as supporting the need to regulate contributions and expenditures? Which interest(s) does the Court recognize as constitutionally sufficient? Is it sufficient to justify restrictions on contributions *and* expenditures?

Buckley v. Valeo
424 U.S. 1 (1976)

[The Court decided these challenges in a lengthy and complicated set of opinions that ran to over 90,000 words and well over 150 pages in the U.S. Reports. Although issued as a "per curiam" opinion (see introductory chapter for a definition), there was not unanimity on all of the large number of substantive points in the case. However, each conclusion in the per curiam opinion received at least five votes. It was eventually revealed that Justice Brennan was the author of the per curiam opinion. It was joined in its entirety by Justices Stewart and Powell. The other five justices, Burger, White, Marshall, Blackmun and Rehnquist, each wrote a separate opinion concurring in part and dissenting in part. (Justice Stevens did not take part in the case, because he did not take his seat on the Court until December 19, 1975, shortly after the case was argued.) The positions of the other justices and the final voting alignment is as follows:]

Holdings (votes):

I-B-1: The $ 1,000 Limitation on Contributions by Individuals and Groups to Candidates and Authorized Campaign Committees—**constitutional** (6–2, Burger (CJ) and Blackmun dissenting)

I-B-2 (omitted): The $ 5,000 Limitation on Contributions by Political Committees—**constitutional** (6–2, Burger and Blackmun dissenting)

I-C-1: The $ 1,000 Limitation on Expenditures "Relative to a Clearly Identified Candidate"—*un*constitutional (7–1, White dissenting)

I-C-2: Limitation on Expenditures by Candidates from Personal or Family Resources—*un*constitutional (6–2, White and Marshall dissenting)

I-C-3: Limitations on Campaign Expenditures—*un*constitutional (7–1, White dissenting)

II—Disclosure Requirements—**constitutional** (7–1, Burger dissenting)

III—Public financing of presidential election campaigns—**constitutional** (6–2, Burger and Rehnquist dissenting)

[Burger (CJ), White, Marshall, Blackmun and Rehnquist all wrote separate opinions. These are omitted except for Justice White's.]

PER CURIAM.

These appeals present constitutional challenges to the key provisions of the Federal Election Campaign Act of 1971, (Act) and related provisions of the Internal Revenue Code of 1954, all as amended in 1974.

The Court of Appeals, in sustaining the legislation in large part against various constitutional challenges, viewed it as "by far the most comprehensive reform legislation [ever] passed by Congress concerning the election of the President, Vice-President, and members of Congress." The statutes at issue summarized in broad terms, contain the following provisions: individual political contributions are limited to $1,000 to any single candidate per election, with an overall annual limitation of $25,000 by any contributor; independent expenditures by individuals and groups "relative to a clearly identified candidate" are limited to $1,000 a year; campaign spending by candidates for various federal offices and spending for national conventions by political parties are subject to prescribed limits; (b) contributions and expenditures above certain threshold levels must be reported and publicly disclosed; (c) a system for public funding of Presidential campaign activities is established by Subtitle H of the Internal Revenue Code; and (d) a Federal Election Commission is established to administer and enforce the legislation....

The complaint sought both a declaratory judgment that the major provisions of the Act were unconstitutional and an injunction against enforcement of those provisions.... [A] majority of the Court of Appeals rejected, for the most part, appellants' constitutional attacks....

I. Contribution And Expenditure Limitations

The intricate statutory scheme adopted by Congress to regulate federal election campaigns includes restrictions on political contributions and expenditures that apply broadly to all phases of and all participants in the election process. The major contribution and expenditure limitations in the Act prohibit individuals from contributing more than $25,000 in a single year or more than $1,000 to any single candidate for an election campaign and from spending more than $1,000 a year "relative to a clearly identified candidate." Other provisions restrict a candidate's use of personal and family resources in his campaign and limit the overall amount that can be spent by a candidate in campaigning for federal office....

A. General Principles

The Act's contribution and expenditure limitations operate in an area of the most fundamental First Amendment activities.... The First Amendment affords the broadest protection to such political expression in order "to assure [the] unfettered interchange of ideas for the bringing about of political and social changes desired by the people." ... The First Amendment protects political association as well as political expression.... "[E]ffective advocacy of both public and private points of view, particularly controversial ones, is undeniably enhanced by group association." ...

.... Appellees contend that what the Act regulates is conduct, and that its effect on speech and association is incidental at most.... [T]his Court has never suggested that the dependence of a communication on the expenditure of money operates itself to introduce a nonspeech element or to reduce the exacting scrutiny required by the First Amendment.... The interests served by the Act include restricting the voices of people and interest groups who have money to spend and reducing the overall scope of federal election campaigns. Although the Act does not focus on the ideas expressed by persons or groups subjected to its regulations, it is aimed in part at equalizing the relative ability of all voters to affect electoral outcomes by placing a ceiling on expenditures for political expression by citizens and groups. Unlike [United States v. O'Brien, 391 U.S. 367 (1968)], where the Selective Service System's administrative interest in the preservation of draft cards was wholly unrelated to their use as a means of communication, it is beyond dispute that the interest in regulating the alleged "conduct" of giving or spending money "arises in some measure because the communication allegedly integral to the conduct is itself thought to be harmful." 391 U.S. at 382.

Nor can the Act's contribution and expenditure limitations be sustained, as.... reasonable time, place, and manner regulations, which do not discriminate among speakers or ideas, in order to further an important governmental interest unrelated to the restriction of communication.... The critical difference between this case and those time, place and manner cases is that the present Act's.... restriction on the amount of money a person or group can spend on political communication during a campaign necessarily reduces the quantity of expression by restricting the number of issues discussed, the depth of their exploration, and the size of the audience reached....

A restriction on the amount of money a person or group can spend on political communication during a campaign necessarily reduces the quantity of expression by restricting the number of issues discussed, the depth of their exploration, and the size of the audience reached. This is because virtually every means of communicating ideas in today's mass society requires the expenditure of money. The distribution of the humblest handbill or leaflet entails printing, paper, and circulation costs. Speeches and rallies generally necessitate hiring a hall and publicizing the event. The electorate's increasing dependence on television, radio, and other mass media for news and information has made these expensive modes of communication indispensable instruments of effective political speech.

The expenditure limitations contained in the Act represent substantial rather than merely theoretical restraints on the quantity and diversity of political speech. The $1,000 ceiling on spending "relative to a clearly identified candidate would appear to exclude all citizens and groups except candidates, political parties, and the institutional press from any significant use of the most effective modes of communication. Although the Act's limitations on expenditures by campaign organizations and political parties provide substantially greater room for discussion and debate, they would have required restrictions in the scope of a number of past congressional and Presidential campaigns and would operate to constrain campaigning by candidates who raise sums in excess of the spending ceiling.

By contrast with a limitation upon expenditures for political expression, a limitation upon the amount that any one person or group may contribute to a candidate or political committee entails only a marginal restriction upon the contributor's ability to engage in free communication. A contribution serves as a general expression of support for the candidate and his views, but does not communicate the underlying basis for the support. The quantity of communication by the contributor does not increase perceptibly with the size of his contribution, since the expression rests solely on the undifferentiated, symbolic act of contributing. At most, the size of the contribution provides a very rough index of the intensity of the contributor's support for the candidate. A limitation on the amount of money a person may give to a candidate or campaign organization thus involves little direct restraint on his political communication, for it permits the symbolic expression of support evidenced by a contribution but does not in any way infringe the contributor's freedom to discuss candidates and issues. While contributions may result in political expression if spent by a candidate or an association to present views to the voters, the transformation of contributions into political debate involves speech by someone other than the contributor.

Given the important role of contributions in financing political campaigns, contribution restrictions could have a severe impact on political dialogue if the limitations prevented candidates and political committees from amassing the resources necessary for effective advocacy. There is no indication, however, that the contribution limitations imposed by the Act would have any dramatic adverse effect on the funding of campaigns and political associations. The overall effect of the Act's contribution ceilings is merely to require candidates and political committees to raise funds from a greater number of persons and to compel people who would otherwise contribute amounts greater than the statutory limits to expend such funds on direct political expression, rather than to reduce the total amount of money potentially available to promote political expression.

The Act's contribution and expenditure limitations also impinge on protected associational freedoms. Making a contribution, like joining a political party, serves to affiliate a person with a candidate. In addition, it enables like-minded persons to pool their resources in furtherance of common political goals. The Act's contribution ceilings thus limit one important means of associating with a candidate or committee, but leave the contributor free to become a member of any political association and to assist personally in the association's efforts on behalf of candidates. And the Act's contribution limitations permit associations and candidates to aggregate large sums of money to promote effective advocacy. By contrast, the Act's $ 1,000 limitation on independent expenditures "relative to a clearly identified candidate" precludes most associations from effectively amplifying the voice of their adherents, the original basis for the recognition of First Amendment protection of the freedom of association. See NAACP v. Alabama, 357 U.S. at 460....

In sum, although the Act's contribution and expenditure limitations both implicate fundamental First Amendment interests, its expenditure ceilings impose significantly more severe restrictions on protected freedoms of political expression and association than do its limitations on financial contributions.

B. Contribution Limitations

1. The $1,000 Limitation on Contributions by Individuals and Groups to Candidates and Authorized Campaign Committees

Section 608 (b) provides, with certain limited exceptions, that "no person shall make contributions to any candidate with respect to any election for Federal office which, in the aggregate, exceed $1,000." ...

.... According to the parties and amici, the primary interest served by the limitations and, indeed, by the Act as a whole, is the prevention of corruption and the appearance of corruption spawned by the real or imagined coercive influence of large financial contributions on candidates' positions and on their actions if elected to office. Two "ancillary" interests underlying the Act are also allegedly furthered by the $ 1,000 limits on contributions. First, the limits serve to mute the voices of affluent persons and groups in the election process and thereby to equalize the relative ability of all citizens to affect the outcome of elections. Second, it is argued, the ceilings may to some extent act as a brake on the skyrocketing cost of political campaigns and thereby serve to open the political system more widely to candidates without access to sources of large amounts of money.

It is unnecessary to look beyond the Act's primary purpose — to limit the actuality and appearance of corruption resulting from large individual financial contributions — in order to find a constitutionally sufficient justification for the $ 1,000 contribution limitation. Under a system of private financing of elections, a candidate lacking immense personal or family wealth must depend on financial contributions from others to provide the resources necessary to conduct a successful campaign. The increasing importance of the communications media and sophisticated mass-mailing and polling operations to effective campaigning make the raising of large sums of money an ever more essential ingredient of an effective candidacy. To the extent that large contributions are given to secure political quid pro quo's from current and potential office holders, the integrity of our system of representative democracy is undermined. Although the scope of such pernicious practices can never be reliably ascertained, the deeply disturbing examples surfacing after the 1972 election demonstrate that the problem is not an illusory one.

Of almost equal concern as the danger of actual quid pro quo arrangements is the impact of the appearance of corruption stemming from public awareness of the opportunities for abuse inherent in a regime of large individual financial contributions.... Congress could legitimately conclude that the avoidance of the appearance of improper influence "is also critical ... if confidence in the system of representative Government is not to be eroded to a disastrous extent."

Appellants contend that the contribution limitations must be invalidated because bribery laws and narrowly drawn disclosure requirements constitute a less restrictive means of dealing with "proven and suspected quid pro quo arrangements." But laws making criminal the giving and taking of bribes deal with only the most blatant and specific attempts of those with money to influence governmental action. And while disclosure requirements serve the many salutary purposes discussed elsewhere in this opinion, Congress was surely entitled to conclude that disclosure was only a partial measure....

The Act's $1,000 contribution limitation focuses precisely on the problem of large campaign contributions—the narrow aspect of political association where the actuality and potential for corruption have been identified—while leaving persons free to engage in independent political expression, to associate actively through volunteering their services, and to assist to a limited but nonetheless substantial extent in supporting candidates and committees with financial resources.

.... We find that, under the rigorous standard of review established by our prior decisions, the weighty interests served by restricting the size of financial contributions to political candidates are sufficient to justify the limited effect upon First Amendment freedoms caused by the $1,000 contribution ceiling....

C. Expenditure Limitations

1. The $1,000 Limitation on Expenditures "Relative to a Clearly Identified Candidate"

.... Although "expenditure," "clearly identified," and "candidate" are defined in the Act, there is no definition clarifying what expenditures are "relative to" a candidate. The use of so indefinite a phrase as "relative to" a candidate fails to clearly mark the boundary between permissible and impermissible speech.... Candidates, especially incumbents, are intimately tied to public issues involving legislative proposals and governmental actions. Not only do candidates campaign on the basis of their positions on various public issues, but campaigns themselves generate issues of public interest.... [In] order to preserve the provision against invalidation on vagueness grounds, § 608 (e)(1) must be construed to apply only to expenditures for communications that in express terms advocate the election or defeat of a clearly identified candidate for federal office.

> FN52. This construction would restrict the application of s 608 (e)(1) to communications containing express words of advocacy of election or defeat, such as "vote for," "elect," "support," "cast your ballot for," "Smith for Congress," "vote against," "defeat," "reject."

We turn then to the basic First Amendment question—whether § 608 (e)(1) even as thus narrowly and explicitly construed, impermissibly burdens the constitutional right of free expression.... The discussion in Part I-A, supra, explains why the Act's expenditure limitations impose far greater restraints on the freedom of speech and association than do its contribution limitations....

We find that the governmental interest in preventing corruption and the appearance of corruption is inadequate to justify § 608 (e)(1)'s ceiling on independent expenditures.... So long as persons and groups eschew expenditures that in express terms advocate the election or defeat of a clearly identified candidate, they are free to spend as much as they want to promote the candidate and his views. The exacting interpretation of the statutory language necessary to avoid unconstitutional vagueness thus undermines the limitation's effectiveness as a loophole-closing provision by facilitating circumvention by those seeking to exert improper influence upon a candidate or officeholder....

.... The parties defending § 608 (e)(1) contend that it is necessary to prevent would-be contributors from avoiding the contribution limitations by the simple expedient of [making] expenditures controlled by or coordinated with the candidate and his campaign.... Yet such controlled or coordinated expenditures are treated as contributions [subject to] Section 608 (b)'s contribution ceilings.... By contrast, § 608(e)(1) limits expenditures for express advocacy of candidates made totally independently of the candidate and his campaign.... The absence of prearrangement and coordination of an expenditure with the candidate or his agent not only undermines the value of the expenditure to the candidate, but also alleviates the danger that expenditures will be given as a quid pro quo for improper commitments from the candidate....

It is argued [further] that the ancillary governmental interest in equalizing the relative ability of individuals and groups to influence the outcome of elections serves to justify the limitation on express advocacy of the election or defeat of candidates imposed by § 608 (e)(1)'s expenditure ceiling. But the concept that government may restrict the speech of some elements of our society in order to enhance the relative voice of others is wholly foreign to the First Amendment, [whose] protection against governmental abridgment of free expression cannot properly be made to depend on a person's financial ability to engage in public discussion.

.... [W]e conclude that § 608 (e)(1)'s independent expenditure limitation is unconstitutional under the First Amendment.

2. Limitation on Expenditures by Candidates from Personal or Family Resources

The Act also sets limits on expenditures by a candidate "from his personal funds, or the personal funds of his immediate family, in connection with his campaigns during any calendar year." § 608 (a)(1). These ceilings vary from $50,000 for Presidential or Vice Presidential candidates to $35,000 for senatorial candidates, and $25,000 for most candidates for the House of Representatives.

The ceiling on personal expenditures by candidates on their own behalf, ... imposes a substantial restraint on the ability of persons to engage in protected First Amendment expression. The candidate, no less than any other person, has a First Amendment right to engage in the discussion of public issues and vigorously and tirelessly to advocate his own election and the election of other candidates. Indeed, it is of particular importance that candidates have the unfettered opportunity to make their views known so that the electorate may intelligently evaluate the candidates' personal qualities and their positions on vital public issues before choosing among them on election day....

The primary governmental interest served by the Act—the prevention of actual and apparent corruption of the political process—does not support the limitation on the candidate's expenditure of his own personal funds.... Indeed, the use of personal funds reduces the candidate's dependence on outside contributions and thereby counteracts the coercive pressures and attendant risks of abuse to which the Act's contribution limitations are directed.

The ancillary interest in equalizing the relative financial resources of candidates competing for elective office,.... is clearly not sufficient to justify the provision's infringement of fundamental First Amendment rights.... [T]he First Amendment simply cannot tolerate § 608 (a)'s restriction upon the freedom of a candidate to speak without legislative limit on behalf of his own candidacy. We therefore hold that § 608 (a)'s restriction on a candidate's personal expenditures is unconstitutional.

3. Limitations on Campaign Expenditures

Section 608 (c) places limitations on overall campaign expenditures by candidates seeking nomination for election and election to federal office. Presidential candidates may spend $ 10,000,000 in seeking nomination for office and an additional $ 20,000,000 in the general election campaign. §§ 608 (c)(1)(A), (B). The ceiling on Senatorial campaigns is pegged to the size of the voting-age population of the State....

No governmental interest that has been suggested is sufficient to justify the restriction on the quantity of political expression imposed by § 608 (c)'s campaign expenditure limitations. The major evil associated with rapidly increasing campaign expenditures is the danger of candidate dependence on large contributions. The interest in alleviating the corrupting influence of large contributions is served by the Act's contribution limitations and disclosure provisions rather than by § 608 (c)'s campaign expenditure ceilings.... Extensive reporting, auditing, and disclosure requirements applicable to both contributions and expenditures by political campaigns are designed to facilitate the detection of illegal contributions....

The interest in equalizing the financial resources of candidates competing for federal office is no more convincing a justification for restricting the scope of federal election campaigns. Given the limitation on the size of outside contributions, the financial resources available to a candidate's campaign, like the number of volunteers recruited, will normally vary with the size and intensity of the candidate's support. There is nothing invidious, improper, or unhealthy in permitting such funds to be spent to carry the candidate's message to the electorate. Moreover, the equalization of permissible campaign expenditures might serve not to equalize the opportunities of all candidates but to handicap a candidate who lacked substantial name recognition or exposure of his views before the start of the campaign.

The campaign expenditure ceilings appear to be designed primarily to serve the governmental interests in reducing the allegedly skyrocketing costs of political campaigns. Appellees and the Court of Appeals stressed statistics indicating that spending for federal election campaigns increased almost 300% between 1952 and 1972 in comparison with a 57.6% rise in the consumer price index during the same period.... The First Amendment denies government the power to determine that spending to promote one's political views is wasteful, excessive, or unwise. In the free society ordained by our Constitution it is not the government but the people—individually as citizens and candidates and collectively as associations and political committees—who must retain control over the quantity and range of debate on public issues in a political campaign.

For these reasons we hold that § 608 (c) is constitutionally invalid.

II. Reporting and Disclosure Requirements

.... [The Act's] disclosure provisions impose reporting obligations on "political committees" and candidates. "Political committee" is defined in § 431 (d) as a group of persons that receives "contributions" or makes "expenditures" of over $1,000 in a calendar year....

Each political committee is required to register with the Commission, §433, and to keep detailed records of both contributions and expenditures, §§432 (c), (d). These records must include the name and address of everyone making a contribution in excess of $ 10, along with the date and amount of the contribution. If a person's contributions aggregate more than $ 100, his occupation and principal place of business are also to be included. These files are subject to periodic audits and field investigations by the Commission. §438 (a)(8).

Each committee and each candidate also is required to file quarterly reports. §434 (a). The reports are to contain detailed financial information, including the full name, mailing address, occupation, and principal place of business of each person who has contributed over $ 100 in a calendar year, as well as the amount and date of the contributions. §434 (b). They are to be made available by the Commission "for public inspection and copying." §438 (a)(4). Every candidate for federal office is required to designate a "principal campaign committee," which is to receive reports of contributions and expenditures made on the candidate's behalf from other political committees and to compile and file these reports, together with its own statements, with the Commission. §432 (f).

Every individual or group, other than a political committee or candidate, who makes "contributions" or "expenditures" of over $ 100 in a calendar year "other than by contribution to a political committee or candidate" is required to file a statement with the Commission. §434 (e). Any violation of these recordkeeping and reporting provisions is punishable by a fine of not more than $1,000 or a prison term of not more than a year, or both. §441 (a).

A. General Principles

.... [We] have repeatedly found that compelled disclosure, in itself, can seriously infringe on privacy of association and belief guaranteed by the First Amendment.... Since NAACP v. Alabama we have required that the subordinating interests of the State must survive exacting scrutiny.... [Group] association is protected because it enhances "[e]ffective advocacy." NAACP v. Alabama, supra, at 460. The right to join together "for the advancement of beliefs and ideas," is diluted if it does not include the right to pool money through contributions, for funds are often essential if "advocacy" is to be truly or optimally "effective." Moreover, the invasion of privacy of belief may be as great when the information sought concerns the giving and spending of money as when it concerns the joining of organizations, for "[f]inancial transactions can reveal much about a person's activities, associations, and beliefs." Our past decisions have not drawn fine lines between contributors and members but have treated them interchangeably....

The governmental interests sought to be vindicated by the disclosure requirements.... fall into three categories. First, disclosure provides the electorate with information "as to where political campaign money comes from and how it is spent by the candidate" in order to aid the voters in evaluating those who seek federal office. It allows voters to place each candidate in the political spectrum more precisely than is often possible solely on the basis of party labels and campaign speeches.... Second, disclosure requirements deter actual corruption and avoid the appearance of corruption by exposing large contributions and expenditures to the light of publicity.... Third, and not least significant, recordkeeping, reporting, and disclosure requirements are an essential means of gathering the data necessary to detect violations of the contribution limitations described above.

The disclosure requirements, as a general matter, directly serve substantial governmental interests. In determining whether these interests are sufficient to justify the requirements we must look to the extent of the burden that they place on individual rights.

It is undoubtedly true that public disclosure of contributions to candidates and political parties will deter some individuals who otherwise might contribute. In some instances, disclosure may even expose contributors to harassment or retaliation. [However,] we note and agree with appellants' concession that disclosure requirements—certainly in most applications—appear to be the least restrictive means of curbing the evils of campaign ignorance and corruption that Congress found to exist....

B. Application to Minor Parties and Independents

Appellants contend that the Act's requirements are overbroad insofar as they apply to contributions to minor parties and independent candidates because the governmental interest in this information is minimal and the danger of significant infringement on First Amendment rights is greatly increased.... [But no] record of harassment on a [scale similar to NAACP v. Alabama] was found in this case.... NAACP vs. Alabama is inapposite where, as here, any serious infringement on First Amendment rights brought about by the compelled disclosure of contributors is highly speculative.

.... Minor parties [could make an as-applied challenge to disclosure requirements by showing] a reasonable probability that the compelled disclosure of a party's contributors' names will subject them to threats, harassment, or reprisals from either Government officials or private parties. The proof may include, for example, specific evidence of past or present harassment of members due to their associational ties.... New parties that have no history upon which to draw may be able to offer evidence of reprisals and threats directed against individuals or organizations holding similar views.

Where it exists the type of chill and harassment identified in NAACP vs. Alabama can be shown.... in future cases. We therefore conclude that a blanket exemption is not required.

C. Section 434 (e)

Section 434 (e) requires "[e]very person (other than a political committee or candidate) who makes contributions or expenditures" aggregating over $100 in a calendar year "other than by contribution to a political committee or candidate" to file a statement with the Commission. Unlike the other disclosure provisions, this section does not seek the contribution list of any association. Instead, it requires direct disclosure of what an individual or group contributes or spends.

.... The provision is responsive to the legitimate fear that efforts would be made, as they had been in the past, to avoid the disclosure requirements by routing financial support of candidates through avenues not explicitly covered by the general provisions of the Act. In its effort to be all-inclusive, however, the provision raises serious problems of vagueness....

Due process requires that a criminal statute provide adequate notice to a person of ordinary intelligence that his contemplated conduct is illegal, for "no man shall be held criminally responsible for conduct which he could not reasonably understand to be proscribed.".... §434(e) as construed [by us], imposes independent reporting requirements on individuals and groups that are not candidates or political committees only in the following circumstances: (1) when they make contributions earmarked for political purposes or authorized or requested by a candidate or his agent, to some person other than a candidate or political committee, and (2) when they make expenditures for communications that expressly advocate the election or defeat of a clearly identified candidate.... §434 (e), as construed, bears a sufficient relationship to a substantial governmental interest. As narrowed, § 434 (e), like § 608 (e)(1), does not reach all partisan discussion for it only requires disclosure of those expenditures that expressly advocate a particular election result....

In summary, we find no constitutional infirmities in the recordkeeping, reporting, and disclosure provisions of the Act.

III. Public Financing of Presidential Election Campaigns

[The Court upheld the constitutionality of the Presidential Election Campaign Fund, financed from general revenues, which offers major political parties $2,000,000 (adjusted for inflation, using 1974 as the base year) to defray the cost of their nominating conventions, provided the parties do not spend more than that amount on their conventions. It also upheld the Presidential Primary Matching Payment Account to aid campaigns by candidates seeking Presidential nomination "by a political party," in "primary elections." Once a candidate raises at least $5,000 in each of 20 States, the candidate is entitled to a sum equal to the total private contributions received (counting only the first $250 from each person contributing to the candidate). The candidate must abide by a set expenditure ceiling, and payments from the Account may not exceed 50% of the overall expenditure ceiling accepted by the candidate.]

It cannot be gainsaid that public financing as a means of eliminating the improper influence of large private contributions furthers a significant governmental interest. In addition, the limits on contributions necessarily increase the burden of fund-raising, and Congress properly regarded public financing as an appropriate means of relieving major-party Presidential candidates from the rigors of soliciting private contributions....

We also reject as without merit appellants' argument that the matching formula favors wealthy voters and candidates. The thrust of the legislation is to reduce financial barriers and to enhance the importance of smaller contributions. Some candidates undoubtedly could raise large sums of money and thus have little need for public funds, but candidates with lesser fundraising capabilities will gain substantial benefits from matching funds. In addition, one eligibility requirement for matching funds is acceptance of an expenditure ceiling, and candidates with little fundraising ability will be able to increase their spending relative to candidates capable of raising large amounts in private funds.

C. Severability

.... [W]e have no difficulty in concluding that Subtitle H is severable. "Unless it is evident that the Legislature would not have enacted those provisions which are within its power, independently of that which is not, the invalid part may be dropped if what is left is fully operative as a law." Our discussion of "what is left" leaves no doubt that the value of public financing is not dependent on the existence of a generally applicable expenditure limit. We therefore hold Subtitle H severable from those portions of the legislation today held constitutionally infirm....

MR. JUSTICE WHITE, concurring in part and dissenting in part.

.... [In] Burroughs v. United States, 290 U.S. 534, 546–548 (1934) ... the Court sustained the Federal Corrupt Practices Act of 1925, which, among other things, required political committees to keep records and file reports concerning all contributions and expenditures received and made by political committees for the purposes of influencing the election of candidates for federal office. The Court [stated]:

> The power of Congress to protect the election of President and Vice President from corruption being clear, the choice of means to that end presents a questions

primarily addressed to the judgment of Congress. If it can be seen that the means adopted are really calculated to attain the end, the degree of their necessity, the extent to which they conduce to the end, the closeness of the relationship between the means adopted and the end to be attained, are matters for congressional determination alone.

Pursuant to this undoubted power of Congress to vindicate the strong public interest in controlling corruption and other undesirable uses of money in connection with election campaigns, the Federal Election Campaign Act substantially broadened the reporting and disclosure requirements that so long have been a part of the federal law. Congress also concluded that limitations on contributions and expenditures were essential if the aims of the Act were to be achieved fully. In another major innovation, aimed at insulating candidates from the time-consuming and entangling task of raising huge sums of money, provision was made for public financing of political campaigns for federal office. A Federal Election Commission (FEC) was also created to administer the law.

.... [Neither] the limitations on contributions nor those on expenditures directly or indirectly purport to control the content of political speech by candidates or by their supporters or detractors. What the Act regulates is giving and spending money, acts that have First Amendment significance not because they are themselves communicative with respect to their qualifications of the candidate, but because money may be used to defray the expenses of speaking or otherwise communicating about the merits or demerits of federal candidates for election. The act of giving money to political candidates, however, may have illegal or other undesirable consequences: it may be used to secure the express or tacit understanding that the giver will enjoy political favor if the candidate is elected. Both Congress and this Court's cases have recognized this as a mortal danger against which effective preventive and curative steps must be taken.

Since the contribution and expenditure limitations are neutral as to the content of speech and are not motivated by fear of the consequences of the political speech of particular candidates or of political speech in general, this case depends on whether the nonspeech interests of the Federal Government in regulating the use of money in political campaigns are sufficiently urgent to justify the incidental effects that the limitations visit upon the First Amendment interests of candidates and their supporters....

It would make little sense to me and apparently made none to Congress, to limit the amounts an individual may give to a candidate or spend with his approval but fail to limit the amounts that could be spent on his behalf. Yet the Court permits the former while striking down the latter limitation.... For constitutional purposes it is difficult to see the difference between the two situations. I would take the word of those who know—that limiting independent expenditures is essential to prevent transparent and widespread evasion of the contribution limits.

.... [T]he argument that money is speech and that limiting the flow of money to the speaker violates the First Amendment proves entirely too much. Compulsory bargaining and the right to strike, both provided for or protected by federal law, inevitably have increased the labor costs of those who publish newspapers, which are in turn an important factor in the recent disappearance of many daily papers. Federal and state taxation directly removes from company coffers large amounts of money that might be spent on larger and better newspapers. The antitrust laws are aimed at preventing monopoly profits and price fixing, which gouge the consumer. It is also true that general price controls have from time to time existed and have been applied to the newspapers or other media. But it has not been suggested, nor could it be successfully, that these laws, and many others, are invalid because they siphon off or prevent the accumulation of large sums that would otherwise be available for communicative activities.

In any event, as it should be unnecessary to point out, money is not always equivalent to or used for speech, even in the context of political campaigns. I accept the reality that communicating with potential voters is the heart of an election campaign and that widespread communication has become very expensive. There are, however, many expensive campaign activities that are not themselves communicative or remotely related to speech. Furthermore, campaigns differ among themselves. Some seem to spend much less money than others and yet communicate as much as or more than those supported by enormous bureaucracies with unlimited financing. The record before us no more supports the conclusion that the communicative efforts of congressional and Presidential candidates will be crippled by the expenditure limitations that it supports the contrary....

.... [E]xpenditure ceilings reinforce the contribution limits and help eradicate the hazard of corruption. The.... expenditure limit imposed on candidates plays its own role in lessening the chance that the contribution ceiling will be violated. Without limits on total expenditures, campaign costs will inevitably and endlessly escalate. Pressure to raise funds will constantly build and with it the temptation to resort in "emergencies" to those sources of large sums, who, history shows, are sufficiently confident of not being caught to risk flouting contribution limits. Congress would save the candidate from the predicament by establishing a reasonable ceiling on all candidates. This is a major consideration in favor of the limitation. It should be added that many successful candidates will also be saved from large, over-hanging campaign debts which must be paid off with money raised while holding public office and at a time when they are already preparing or thinking about the next campaign. The danger to the public interest in such situations is self-evident....

I have little doubt in addition that limiting the total that can be spent will ease the candidate's understandable obsession with fundraising, and so free him and his staff to communicate in more places and ways unconnected with the fundraising function. There is nothing objectionable — indeed it seems to me a weighty interest in favor of the provision — in the attempt to insulate the political expression of federal candidates from the influence inevitably exerted by the endless job of raising increasingly large sums of money. I regret that the Court has returned them all to the treadmill.

It is also important to restore and maintain public confidence in federal elections. It is critical to obviate or dispel the impression that federal elections are purely and simply a function of money, that federal offices are bought and sold or that political races are reserved for those who have the facility — and the stomach — for doing whatever it takes to bring together those interests, groups, and individuals that can raise or contribute large fortunes in order to prevail at the polls.

The ceiling on candidate expenditures represents the considered judgment of Congress that elections are to be decided among candidates none of whom has overpowering advantage by reason of a huge campaign war chest. At least so long as the ceiling placed upon the candidates is not plainly too low, elections are not to turn on the difference in the amounts of money that candidates have to spend. This seems an acceptable purpose and the means chosen a commonsense way to achieve it. The Court nevertheless holds that a candidate has a constitutional right to spend unlimited amounts of money, mostly that of other people, in order to be elected. The holding perhaps is not that federal candidates have the constitutional right to purchase their election, but many will so interpret the Court's conclusion in this case. I cannot join the Court in this respect.

I will also disagree with the Court's judgment that § 608(a), which limits the amount of money that a candidate or his family may spend on his campaign, violates the Constitution. Although it is true that this provision does not promote any interest in preventing the corruption of candidates, the provision does, nevertheless, serve salutary purposes related to the integrity of federal campaigns. By limiting the importance of personal wealth, § 608(a) helps assure that only individuals with a modicum of support from others will be viable candidates. This in turn would tend to discourage any notion that the outcome of elections is primarily a function of money. Similarly, § 608 (a) tends to equalize access to the political arena, encouraging the less wealthy, unable to bankroll their own campaigns, to run for political office.

As with the campaign expenditure limits, Congress was entitled to determine that personal wealth ought to play a less important role in political campaigns than it has in the past. Nothing in the First Amendment stands in the way of that determination.

Review Questions and Explanations: *Buckley v. Valeo*

1. Now that you've read Justice White's dissent, let's return to the idea that "money is speech" in the campaign finance context. Is that proposition fairly debatable? How persuaded are you by Justice White's argument that unlimited campaign spending *restricts* speech in certain ways?

2. The majority suggests that even reducing somewhat, let alone fully equalizing, candidate's electoral opportunities is completely impermissible as a governmental objective under the First Amendment. How does the Court justify this distinction? Do you agree?

3. What are the doctrinal consequences of adopting the "money is speech" position or, instead, Justice White's position that it is not? What level of scrutiny did the Court use to evaluate the regulation of contributions? Of expenditures?

4. Pay attention to the section on severability. In refusing to strike down the entire Act and instead upholding limitations on contributions while striking down limitations on expenditures, the Court created a campaign finance regime in which the ability to raise money is tightly controlled but the need for it is not. Not surprisingly, this drove a lot of political money out of the hands of candidates (who can only raise money in relatively small chunks) and into independent expenditures made by individuals or groups that are — at least officially — not coordinated with the candidates. Is this a good result? It certainly is not one that anyone in Congress ever voted for.

5. Are there governmental interests supporting campaign finance regulation that did not get due consideration from the majority? What about the idea that unequal financial resources can distort the flow of information and ideas in an election campaign?

The Court has issued numerous campaign finance decisions since *Buckley* was decided in 1974. All of these, however, have followed the basic dichotomies set out in *Buckley*: contributions and expenditures are treated as distinct, and the prevention of corruption or the appearance of corruption is a constitutionally acceptable justification for limiting contributions (but not expenditures) while the promotion of equality is not. A third dichotomy, not addressed in *Buckley* but arising frequently in this area, involves the distinction between corporate general revenue funds and other sources of money. State and federal laws have long prohibited corporations from making contributions to candidates out of general revenue funds. The Bipartisan Campaign Reform Act of 2002 (the McCain-Feingold Act) also prohibited corporations from using corporate general revenue to purchase certain types of political advertising that clearly identified a candidate for federal office. The Supreme Court struck down this provision of the law in 2010 in *Citizens United v. Federal Election Commission*, 558 U.S. 50 (2010). *Citizens United* thus prohibits treating corporate general revenue funds differently from other sources of money for purposes of political expenditures. The case did not address whether corporations could be prohibited from making political contributions out of general revenue funds, nor did it challenge the constitutional distinction, drawn in *Buckley*, between contributions and expenditures.

Between the complex statutory scheme regulating federal election law, which has been amended more than once since 1971, and the numerous Supreme Court decisions on campaign finance (mostly decided under the First Amendment), campaign finance law has grown into a subspeciality in itself. Some practicing lawyers specialize in that area, and some law school courses are devoted entirely to it. If you find these materials engaging, we highly recommend you take an advanced Election Law course if available at your school.

2. Government Employment

You can imagine numerous situations in which an employer might discipline or fire an employee based on the employee's speech. Where the employer is a governmental entity, such actions constitute state action and thus raise First Amendment issues. Moreover, because government employees are involved in implementation of policies that are almost by definition matters of public concern, there may often be a public interest in hearing critical comments from government employees that may be in tension with the government's interest in efficiently implementing those policies. These concerns underlie the following case.

Guided Reading Questions: *Garcetti v. Ceballos*

1. What is the test for whether a public employee's speech will be afforded First Amendment protection, derived from the *Pickering* case, discussed in *Garcetti*?

2. If the employee's speech is protected, is the government employer's power to restrict that speech the same as if the speaker were not an employee?

3. In applying the doctrine to the facts of the case in section III, does the Court qualify *Pickering*? What, in a sentence or two, is the holding of *Garcetti*?

4. What test would the dissenters have applied?

Garcetti v. Ceballos

547 U.S. 410 (2006)

Majority: *Kennedy,* Roberts (CJ), Scalia, Thomas, Alito

Dissents: *Stevens, Souter,* Ginsburg, *Breyer* (omitted)

JUSTICE KENNEDY delivered the opinion of the Court.

.... The question presented by the instant case is whether the First Amendment protects a government employee from discipline based on speech made pursuant to the employee's official duties.

Respondent Richard Ceballos has been employed since 1989 as a deputy district attorney for the Los Angeles County District Attorney's Office. [In February 2000, Ceballos had a discussion with a defense attorney in a pending case about alleged factual inaccuracies in a search warrant. Ceballos investigated and determined that the search warrant's supporting affidavit contained serious misrepresentations. After receiving unsatisfactory explanations from the warrant affiant, a deputy sheriff from the Los Angeles County Sheriff's Department, Ceballos recommended in a March 2, 2000 memo to his supervisors, Carol Najera and Frank Sundstedt, that the case be dismissed. A meeting was held with Ceballos, his supervisors, and members of the Sheriff's Department to discuss the matter, at which heated words were exchanged.]

Despite Ceballos' concerns, Sundstedt decided to proceed with the prosecution, pending disposition of the defense motion to traverse. The trial court held a hearing on the motion. Ceballos was called by the defense and recounted his observations about the affidavit, but the trial court rejected the challenge to the warrant.

Ceballos claims that in the aftermath of these events he was subjected to a series of retaliatory employment actions. The actions included reassignment from his calendar deputy position to a trial deputy position, transfer to another courthouse, and denial of a promotion. Ceballos initiated an employment grievance, but the grievance was denied based on a finding that he had not suffered any retaliation. Unsatisfied, Ceballos sued [Sunstedt, Najara and LA District Attorney Gil Garcetti] in the United States District Court for the Central District of California, asserting, as relevant here, a claim under 42 U.S.C. § 1983. He alleged petitioners violated the First and Fourteenth Amendments by retaliating against him based on his memo of March 2.

[The District Court granted summary judgment for the defendants.] The Court of Appeals for the Ninth Circuit reversed, holding that "Ceballos's allegations of wrongdoing in the memorandum constitute protected speech under the First Amendment." ... We granted certiorari, and we now reverse.

.... Public employees do not surrender all their First Amendment rights by reason of their employment. Rather, the First Amendment protects a public employee's right, in certain circumstances, to speak as a citizen addressing matters of public concern. See, e.g., Pickering v. Bd. of Educ., 391 U.S. 563, 568 (1968); Connick v. Myers, 461 U.S. 138, 147 (1983).

Pickering provides a useful starting point in explaining the Court's doctrine. There the relevant speech was a teacher's letter to a local newspaper addressing issues including the funding policies of his school board. "The problem in any case," the Court stated, "is to arrive at a balance between the interests of the teacher, as a citizen, in commenting upon matters of public concern and the interest of the State, as an employer, in promoting the efficiency of the public services it performs through its employees." The Court found the teacher's speech "neither [was] shown nor can be presumed to have in any way either impeded the teacher's proper performance of his daily duties in the classroom or to have interfered with the regular operation of the schools generally." Thus, the Court concluded that "the interest of the school administration in limiting teachers' opportunities to contribute to public debate is not significantly greater than its interest in limiting a similar contribution by any member of the general public."

Pickering and the cases decided in its wake identify two inquiries to guide interpretation of the constitutional protections accorded to public employee speech. The first requires determining whether the employee spoke as a citizen on a matter of public concern. If the answer is no, the employee has no First Amendment cause of action based on his or her employer's reaction to the speech. If the answer is yes, then the.... question becomes whether the relevant government entity had an adequate justification for treating the employee differently from any other member of the general public.... A government entity has broader discretion to restrict speech when it acts in its role as employer, but the restrictions it imposes must be directed at speech that has some potential to affect the entity's operations.

When a citizen enters government service, the citizen by necessity must accept certain limitations on his or her freedom. Government employers, like private employers, need a significant degree of control over their employees' words and actions; without it, there would be little chance for the efficient provision of public services. Public employees, moreover, often occupy trusted positions in society. When they speak out, they can express views that contravene governmental policies or impair the proper performance of governmental functions.

At the same time, the Court has recognized that a citizen who works for the government is nonetheless a citizen. The First Amendment limits the ability of a public employer to leverage the employment relationship to restrict, incidentally or intentionally, the liberties employees enjoy in their capacities as private citizens. So long as employees are speaking as citizens about matters of public concern, they must face only those speech restrictions that are necessary for their employers to operate efficiently and effectively.

.... The First Amendment interests at stake extend beyond the individual speaker. The Court has acknowledged the importance of promoting the public's interest in receiving the well-informed views of government employees engaging in civic discussion. Pickering.... noted that teachers are "the members of a community most likely to have informed and definite opinions" about school expenditures.... The Court's more recent cases have expressed similar concerns.... [But while] the First Amendment invests public employees with certain rights, it does not empower them to "constitutionalize the employee grievance." Connick, 461 U.S., at 154.

III

With these principles in mind we turn to the instant case.... That Ceballos expressed his views inside his office, rather than publicly, is not dispositive. Employees in some cases may receive First Amendment protection for expressions made at work. Many citizens do much of their talking inside their respective workplaces, and it would not serve the goal of treating public employees like "any member of the general public," Pickering, 391 U.S., at 573, to hold that all speech within the office is automatically exposed to restriction.

The memo concerned the subject matter of Ceballos' employment, but this, too, is nondispositive. The First Amendment protects some expressions related to the speaker's job. As the Court noted in Pickering: "Teachers are, as a class, the members of a community most likely to have informed and definite opinions as to how funds allotted to the operation of the schools should be spent. Accordingly, it is essential that they be able to speak out freely on such questions without fear of retaliatory dismissal." The same is true of many other categories of public employees.

The controlling factor in Ceballos' case is that his expressions were made pursuant to his duties as a calendar deputy. See Brief for Respondent 4 ("Ceballos does not dispute that he prepared the memorandum 'pursuant to his duties as a prosecutor'"). That consideration—the fact that Ceballos spoke as a prosecutor fulfilling a responsibility to advise his supervisor about how best to proceed with a pending case—distinguishes Ceballos' case from those in which the First Amendment provides protection against discipline. We hold that when public employees make statements pursuant to their official duties, the employees are not speaking as citizens for First Amendment purposes, and the Constitution does not insulate their communications from employer discipline.

.... Restricting speech that owes its existence to a public employee's professional responsibilities does not infringe any liberties the employee might have enjoyed as a private citizen. It simply reflects the exercise of employer control over what the employer itself has commissioned or created. Contrast, for example, the expressions made by the speaker in Pickering, whose letter to the newspaper had no official significance and bore similarities to letters submitted by numerous citizens every day.

.... Refusing to recognize First Amendment claims based on government employees' work product does not prevent them from participating in public debate. The employees retain the prospect of constitutional protection for their contributions to the civic discourse. This prospect of protection, however, does not invest them with a right to perform their jobs however they see fit.

.... Employers have heightened interests in controlling speech made by an employee in his or her professional capacity. Official communications have official consequences, creating a need for substantive consistency and clarity. Supervisors must ensure that their employees' official communications are accurate, demonstrate sound judgment, and promote the employer's mission. Ceballos' memo is illustrative. It demanded the attention of his supervisors and led to a heated meeting with employees from the sheriff's department. If Ceballos' superiors thought his memo was inflammatory or misguided, they had the authority to take proper corrective action.

Ceballos' proposed contrary rule, adopted by the Court of Appeals, would commit state and federal courts to a new, permanent, and intrusive role, mandating judicial oversight of communications between and among government employees and their superiors in the course of official business. This displacement of managerial discretion by judicial supervision finds no support in our precedents. When an employee speaks as a citizen addressing a matter of public concern, the First Amendment requires a delicate balancing of the competing interests surrounding the speech and its consequences. When, however, the employee is simply performing his or her job duties, there is no warrant for a similar degree of scrutiny. To hold otherwise would be to demand permanent judicial intervention in the conduct of governmental operations to a degree inconsistent with sound principles of federalism and the separation of powers.

The Court of Appeals.... suggested it would be inconsistent to compel public employers to tolerate certain employee speech made publicly but not speech made pursuant to an employee's assigned duties. This objection misconceives the theoretical underpinnings of our decisions. Employees who make public statements outside the course of performing their official duties retain some possibility of First Amendment protection because that is the kind of activity engaged in by citizens who do not work for the government. The same goes for writing a letter to a local newspaper, or discussing politics with a co-worker. When a public employee speaks pursuant to employment responsibilities, however, there is no relevant analogue to speech by citizens who are not government employees.

.... A public employer that wishes to encourage its employees to voice concerns privately retains the option of instituting internal policies and procedures that are receptive to employee criticism. Giving employees an internal forum for their speech will discourage them from concluding that the safest avenue of expression is to state their views in public....

Two final points warrant mentioning. First, as indicated above, the parties in this case do not dispute that Ceballos wrote his disposition memo pursuant to his employment duties. We thus have no occasion to articulate a comprehensive framework for defining the scope of an employee's duties in cases where there is room for serious debate. We reject, however, the suggestion that employers can restrict employees' rights by creating excessively broad job descriptions....

Second, Justice Souter suggests today's decision may have important ramifications for academic freedom, at least as a constitutional value.... We need not, and for that reason do not, decide whether the analysis we conduct today would apply in the same manner to a case involving speech related to scholarship or teaching.

IV

Exposing governmental inefficiency and misconduct is a matter of considerable significance. As the Court noted in Connick, public employers should, "as a matter of good judgment," be "receptive to constructive criticism offered by their employees." The dictates of sound judgment are reinforced by the powerful network of legislative enactments — such as whistle-blower protection laws and labor codes — available to those who seek to expose wrongdoing. Cases involving government attorneys implicate additional safeguards in the form of, for example, rules of conduct and constitutional obligations apart from the First Amendment. See, e.g., Cal. Rule Prof. Conduct 5-110 (2005) ("A member in government service shall not institute or cause to be instituted criminal charges when the member knows or should know that the charges are not supported by probable cause"); Brady v. Maryland, 373 U.S. 83, (1963). These imperatives, as well as obligations arising from any other applicable constitutional provisions and mandates of the criminal and civil laws, protect employees and provide checks on supervisors who would order unlawful or otherwise inappropriate actions.

We reject, however, the notion that the First Amendment shields from discipline the expressions employees make pursuant to their professional duties.... The judgment of the Court of Appeals is reversed, and the case is remanded for proceedings consistent with this opinion.

JUSTICE STEVENS, dissenting.

The proper answer to the question "whether the First Amendment protects a government employee from discipline based on speech made pursuant to the employee's official duties," is "Sometimes," not "Never." Of course a supervisor may take corrective action when such speech is "inflammatory or misguided." But what if it is just unwelcome speech because it reveals facts that the supervisor would rather not have anyone else discover?

.... Over a quarter of a century has passed since then-Justice Rehnquist, writing for a unanimous Court, rejected "the conclusion that a public employee forfeits his protection against governmental abridgment of freedom of speech if he decides to express his views privately rather than publicly." Givhan v. Western Line Consol. School Dist., 439 U.S. 410, 414 (1979). We had no difficulty recognizing that the First Amendment applied when Bessie Givhan, an English teacher, raised concerns about the school's racist employment practices to the principal. Our silence as to whether or not her speech was made pursuant to her job duties demonstrates that the point was immaterial. That is equally true today, for it is senseless to let constitutional protection for exactly the same words hinge on whether they fall within a job description. Moreover, it seems perverse to fashion a new rule that provides employees with an incentive to voice their concerns publicly before talking frankly to their superiors.

JUSTICE SOUTER, with whom JUSTICE STEVENS and JUSTICE GINSBURG join, dissenting.

.... [The] significant, albeit qualified, protection of public employees who irritate the government is understood to flow from the First Amendment, in part, because a government paycheck does nothing to eliminate the value to an individual of speaking on public matters, and there is no good reason for categorically discounting a speaker's interest in commenting on a matter of public concern just because the government employs him. Still, the First Amendment safeguard rests on something more, being the value to the public of receiving the opinions and information that a public employee may disclose. "Government employees are often in the best position to know what ails the agencies for which they work."

The reason that protection of employee speech is qualified is that it can distract co-workers and supervisors from their tasks at hand and thwart the implementation of legitimate policy, the risks of which grow greater the closer the employee's speech gets to commenting on his own workplace and responsibilities. It is one thing for an office clerk to say there is waste in government and quite another to charge that his own department pays full-time salaries to part-time workers. Even so, we have regarded eligibility for protection by Pickering balancing as the proper approach when an employee speaks critically about the administration of his own government employer....

The difference between a case like Givhan and this one is that the subject of Ceballos's speech fell within the scope of his job responsibilities, whereas choosing personnel was not what the teacher was hired to do. The effect of the majority's constitutional line between these two cases, then, is that a Givhan schoolteacher is protected when complaining to the principal about hiring policy, but a school personnel officer would not be if he protested that the principal disapproved of hiring minority job applicants. This is an odd place to draw a distinction....

.... The majority is rightly concerned that the employee who speaks out on matters subject to comment in doing his own work has the greater leverage to create office uproars and fracture the government's authority to set policy to be carried out coherently through the ranks.... Up to a point, then, the majority makes good points: government needs civility in the workplace, consistency in policy, and honesty and competence in public service.

But why do the majority's concerns, which we all share, require categorical exclusion of First Amendment protection against any official retaliation for things said on the job?.... [An] adjustment using the basic Pickering balancing scheme is perfectly feasible here.... [An] employee commenting on subjects in the course of duties should not prevail on balance unless he speaks on a matter of unusual importance and satisfies high standards of responsibility in the way he does it.

.... First Amendment protection less circumscribed than what I would recognize has been available in the Ninth Circuit for over 17 years, and neither there nor in other Circuits that accept claims like this one has there been a debilitating flood of litigation....

For that matter, the majority's position comes with no guarantee against factbound litigation over whether a public employee's statements were made "pursuant to ... official duties." In fact, the majority invites such litigation by describing the enquiry as a "practical one," apparently based on the totality of employment circumstances. Are prosecutors' discretionary statements about cases addressed to the press on the courthouse steps made "pursuant to their official duties"? Are government nuclear scientists' complaints to their supervisors about a colleague's improper handling of radioactive materials made "pursuant" to duties? ...

Ceballos's action against petitioners under 42 U.S.C. § 1983 claims that the individuals retaliated against him for exercising his First Amendment rights in submitting the memorandum, discussing the matter with Najera and Sundstedt, testifying truthfully at the hearing, and speaking at the bar meeting.... [The] Court of Appeals saw no need to address the protection afforded to Ceballos's statements other than the disposition memorandum, which it thought was protected under the Pickering test. Upon remand, it will be open to the Court of Appeals to consider the application of Pickering to any retaliation shown for other statements; not all of those statements would have been made pursuant to official duties in any obvious sense, and the claim relating to truthful testimony in court must surely be analyzed independently to protect the integrity of the judicial process.

Review Questions and Explanations: *Garcetti*

1. Why don't public employees "surrender their First Amendment rights"? Why shouldn't a government employer have a right to demand that employees be team players?

2. Does the majority's rule create an incentive for complaining public employees to go public with problems and complaints rather than to their supervisors? Or does the majority's rule protecting statements outside of job responsibilities create an incentive for government *employers* to create internal policies encouraging non-retaliatory in-house handling of complaints?

3. Is there anything wrong with Justice Souter's recommended case-by-case approach of weighing the government's interest in efficiency and internal discipline against the public's interest in the government employee's speech? Consider the majority's worry about embroiling courts in government employment disputes, and contrast that with Justice Souter's response, that the majority's rule will not result in less litigation.

---

3. Public Schools

As in the government employment context, there are situations in which the First Amendment rights of students are robustly protected, but also other situations in which the Court has upheld limitations on students' speech that are more restrictive than elsewhere in society.

Two famous First Amendment cases upheld speech rights for grade school/high school students. In *West Virginia State Bd. of Ed. v. Barnette*, 319 U.S. 624 (1943), several Jehovah's

Witness parents of public school children challenged a school district policy requiring participation in a "flag salute" ceremony each morning in school. The flag salute involved reciting the Pledge of Allegiance while raising a stiff right arm toward the flag (a gesture many parents felt too closely resembled the Nazi-Fascist salute of that era). Refusal to participate was "regarded as an act of insubordination, and shall be dealt with accordingly." The students in question were expelled for insisting on remaining silent and not raising their arms in salute, and their parents were threatened with prosecution for failure to comply with compulsory school attendance laws.

A six-justice majority (*Jackson*, Stone, Black, Douglas, Murphy, Rutledge) held that the compulsory flag salute violated the First Amendment. (Roberts, Reed and *Frankfurter* dissented.) Noting that "the refusal of these persons to participate in the ceremony" was "peaceable and orderly" and "does not interfere with or deny rights of others to do so," the Court framed the issue as whether "a Bill of Rights which guards the individual's right to speak his own mind, left it open to public authorities to compel him to utter what is not in his mind." The Court concluded: "compelling the flag salute and pledge transcends constitutional limitations on their power and invades the sphere of intellect and spirit which it is the purpose of the First Amendment to our Constitution to reserve from all official control." Given the wartime context, which undoubtedly heightened the tensions of this case, the Court felt compelled to state:

> To enforce those rights today is not to choose weak government over strong government. It is only to adhere as a means of strength to individual freedom of mind in preference to officially disciplined uniformity for which history indicates a disappointing and disastrous end.... To believe that patriotism will not flourish if patriotic ceremonies are voluntary and spontaneous instead of a compulsory routine is to make an unflattering estimate of the appeal of our institutions to free minds. 319 U.S. at 636–37, 641.

In *Tinker v. Des Moines Independent Community School Dist.*, 393 U.S. 503 (1969), a small group of high- and middle-school students and their parents, met in December 1965 and decided that the students would wear black armbands to school for the last two weeks of December, to protest United States military involvement in Vietnam. The school district learned of this meeting and hastily enacted a policy that any student wearing the black armband would be suspended unless and until he or she complied with an instruction to remove it. On December 16, the students showed up at school wearing the armbands; they refused orders to remove them and were suspended and sent home. They did not return to school until after the two weeks of their planned protest. The parents sued in district court, seeking an injunction against any further disciplinary consequences and nominal damages. The district court ruled for the school district and the Court of Appeals affirmed.

The Supreme Court reversed. Eight justices (*Fortas*, Warren, Black, Douglas, Brennan, Stewart, White, Marshall) over one dissent (*Harlan*) agreed that the school district's actions violated the First Amendment. The Court began its discussion by observing that, notwithstanding "special characteristics of the school environment.... [it] can hardly be argued that either students or teachers shed their constitutional rights to freedom of speech or expression at the schoolhouse gate." The Court noted that there was no evidence that the armband-wearing created any disturbance or interfered with other students' rights or ability to do their schoolwork. The Court also found it "relevant that the school authorities did not purport to prohibit the wearing of all symbols of political or controversial significance. The record shows that students in some of the schools wore buttons relating to national political campaigns[.]" Finally, the Court reasoned that communicative interaction among students outside the classroom was an important part of the educational process. The school could not restrict student speech without "a showing that the students' activities would materially and substantially disrupt the work and discipline of the school."

Review Questions and Explanations: *Hazelwood School District v. Kuhlmeier*

1. Does this case differ in a factually significant way from *Barnette* and *Tinker*? If so, how?

2. Why does the Court examine evidence regarding the latitude actually given the students by the school in putting together Spectrum? What does that have to do with First Amendment principles for student speech?

3. Why does the Court go on so much about school authority over the curriculum as a limit on student speech rights? What would be the alternative?

4. The dissent begins with an extract from the course description for Journalism II and the board policy. Do the dissenters agree that these define the contours of the students' speech rights, or do they propose a broader rule for student speech?

Hazelwood School District v. Kuhlmeier
484 U.S. 260 (1988)

Majority: *White*, Rehnquist (CJ), Stevens, O'Connor, Scalia

Dissent: *Brennan*, Marshall, Blackmun (Kennedy did not take part)

JUSTICE WHITE delivered the opinion of the Court.

.... Petitioners are the Hazelwood School District in St. Louis County, Missouri; various school officials; Robert Eugene Reynolds, the principal of Hazelwood East High School; and Howard Emerson, a teacher in the school district. Respondents are three former Hazelwood East students who were staff members of Spectrum, the school newspaper. They contend that school officials violated their First Amendment rights by deleting two pages of articles from the May 13, 1983, issue of Spectrum.

Spectrum was written and edited by the Journalism II class at Hazelwood East. The newspaper was published every three weeks or so during the 1982–1983 school year. More than 4,500 copies of the newspaper were distributed during that year to students, school personnel, and members of the community.

[Most of the costs associated with the newspaper—such as supplies, textbooks, and a portion of the journalism teacher's salary—were borne by the Board, offset slightly by revenue from sales of the paper.]

The practice at Hazelwood East during the spring 1983 semester was for the journalism teacher to submit page proofs of each Spectrum issue to Principal Reynolds for his review prior to publication. On May 10, Emerson delivered the proofs of the May 13 edition to Reynolds, who objected to two of the articles scheduled to appear in that edition. One of the stories described three Hazelwood East students' experiences with pregnancy; the other discussed the impact of divorce on students at the school.

Reynolds was concerned that, although the pregnancy story used false names "to keep the identity of these girls a secret," the pregnant students still might be identifiable from the text. He also believed that the article's references to sexual activity and birth control were inappropriate for some of the younger students at the school. In addition, Reynolds was concerned that a student identified by name in the divorce story had complained that her father "wasn't spending enough time with my mom, my sister and I" prior to the divorce, "was always out of town on business or out late playing cards with the guys," and "always argued about everything" with her mother. Reynolds believed that the students' parents should have been given an opportunity to respond to these remarks or to consent to their publication. He was unaware that Emerson had deleted the student's name from the final version of the article.

Reynolds believed that there was no time to make the necessary changes in the stories before the scheduled press run and that the newspaper would not appear before the end of the school year if printing were delayed to any significant extent. He concluded that his only options under the circumstances were to publish a four-page newspaper instead of the planned six-page newspaper, eliminating the two pages on which the offending stories appeared, or to publish no newspaper at all. Accordingly, he directed Emerson to withhold from publication the two pages containing the stories on pregnancy and divorce. He informed his superiors of the decision, and they concurred.

Respondents subsequently commenced this action in the United States District Court for the Eastern District of Missouri seeking a declaration that their First Amendment rights had been violated, injunctive relief, and monetary damages. After a bench trial, the District Court denied an injunction, holding that no First Amendment violation had occurred....

The Court of Appeals for the Eighth Circuit reversed.... [The] Court of Appeals found "no evidence in the record that the principal could have reasonably forecast that the censored articles or any materials in the censored articles would have materially disrupted classwork or given rise to substantial disorder in the school." School officials were entitled to censor the articles on the ground that they invaded the rights of others, according to the court, only if publication of the articles could have resulted in tort liability to the school. The court concluded that no tort action for libel or invasion of privacy could have been maintained against the school by the subjects of the two articles or by their families. Accordingly, the court held that school officials had violated respondents' First Amendment rights by deleting the two pages of the newspaper. We granted certiorari, and we now reverse.

Students in the public schools do not "shed their constitutional rights to freedom of speech or expression at the schoolhouse gate." They cannot be punished merely for expressing their personal views on the school premises—whether "in the cafeteria, or on the playing field, or on the campus during the authorized hours," unless school authorities have reason to believe that such expression will "substantially interfere with the work of the school or impinge upon the rights of other students."

We have nonetheless recognized that the First Amendment rights of students in the public schools "are not automatically coextensive with the rights of adults in other settings," and must be "applied in light of the special characteristics of the school environment." A school need not tolerate student speech that is inconsistent with its "basic educational mission," even though the government could not censor similar speech outside the school. Accordingly, we [have] held ... that a student could be disciplined for having delivered a speech that was "sexually explicit" but not legally obscene at an official school assembly, because the school was entitled to "disassociate itself" from the speech in a manner that would demonstrate to others that such vulgarity is "wholly inconsistent with the 'fundamental values' of public school education." We thus recognized that "[t]he determination of what manner of speech in the classroom or in school assembly is inappropriate properly rests with the school board," rather than with the federal courts....

.... The public schools do not possess all of the attributes of streets, parks, and other traditional public forums that "time out of mind, have been used for purposes of assembly, communicating thoughts between citizens, and discussing public questions." Hence, school facilities may be deemed to be public forums only if school authorities have "by policy or by practice" opened those facilities "for indiscriminate use by the general public," or by some segment of the public, such as student organizations. If the facilities have instead been reserved for other intended purposes, "communicative or otherwise," then no public forum has been created, and school officials may impose reasonable restrictions on the speech of students, teachers, and other members of the school community. "The government does not create a public forum by inaction or by permitting limited discourse, but only by intentionally opening a nontraditional forum for public discourse."

.... Hazelwood School Board Policy 348.51.... provided that "[s]chool sponsored publications are developed within the adopted curriculum and its educational implications in regular classroom activities." The Hazelwood East Curriculum Guide described the Journalism II course as a "laboratory situation in which the students publish the school newspaper applying skills they have learned in Journalism I."... [The district court found that school officials] did not evince either "by policy or by practice," any intent to open the pages of Spectrum to "indiscriminate use," by its student reporters and editors, or by the student body generally. Instead, they "reserve[d] the forum for its intended purpos[e]," as a supervised learning experience for journalism students. Accordingly, school officials were entitled to regulate the contents of Spectrum in any reasonable manner.

The question whether the First Amendment requires a school to tolerate particular student speech—the question that we addressed in Tinker v. Des Moines Independent Community School Dist., 393 U.S. 503 (1969)—is different from the question whether the First Amendment requires a school affirmatively to promote particular student speech. The former question addresses educators' ability to silence a student's personal expression that happens to occur on the school premises. The latter question concerns educators' authority over school-sponsored publications, theatrical productions, and other expressive activities that students, parents, and members of the public might reasonably perceive to bear the imprimatur of the school. These activities may fairly be characterized as part of the school curriculum, whether or not they occur in a traditional classroom setting, so long as they are supervised by faculty members and designed to impart particular knowledge or skills to student participants and audiences.

Educators are entitled to exercise greater control over this second form of student expression to assure that participants learn whatever lessons the activity is designed to teach, that readers or listeners are not exposed to material that may be inappropriate for their level of maturity, and that the views of the individual speaker are not erroneously attributed to the school. Hence, a school may in its capacity as publisher of a school newspaper or producer of a school play "disassociate itself," not only from speech that would "substantially interfere with [its] work ... or impinge upon the rights of other students," Tinker, 393 U.S., at 509, but also from speech that is, for example, ungrammatical, poorly written, inadequately researched, biased or prejudiced, vulgar or profane, or unsuitable for immature audiences. A school must be able to set high standards for the student speech that is disseminated under its auspices—standards that may be higher than those demanded by some newspaper publishers or theatrical producers in the "real" world—and may refuse to disseminate student speech that does not meet those standards. In addition, a school must be able to take into account the emotional maturity of the intended audience in determining whether to disseminate student speech on potentially sensitive topics, which might range from the existence of Santa Claus in an elementary school setting to the particulars of teenage sexual activity in a high school setting. A school must also retain the authority to refuse to sponsor student speech that might reasonably be perceived to advocate drug or alcohol use, irresponsible sex, or conduct otherwise inconsistent with "the shared values of a civilized social order," or to associate the school with any position other than neutrality on matters of political controversy. Otherwise, the schools would be unduly constrained from fulfilling their role as "a principal instrument in awakening the child to cultural values, in preparing him for later professional training, and in helping him to adjust normally to his environment." ...

This standard is consistent with our oft-expressed view that the education of the Nation's youth is primarily the responsibility of parents, teachers, and state and local school officials, and not of federal judges. It is only when the decision to censor a school-sponsored publication, theatrical production, or other vehicle of student expression has no valid educational purpose that the First Amendment is so "directly and sharply implicate[d]," as to require judicial intervention to protect students' constitutional rights....

We conclude that Principal Reynolds acted reasonably in requiring the deletion from the May 13 issue of Spectrum of the pregnancy article, the divorce article, and the remaining articles that were to appear on the same pages of the newspaper.... [Reynolds] could reasonably have concluded that the students who had written and edited these articles had not sufficiently mastered those portions of the Journalism II curriculum that pertained to the treatment of controversial issues and personal attacks, the need to protect the privacy of individuals whose most intimate concerns are to be revealed in the newspaper, and "the legal, moral, and ethical restrictions imposed upon journalists within [a] school community" that includes adolescent subjects and readers. Finally, we conclude that the principal's decision to delete two pages of Spectrum, rather than to delete only the offending articles or to require that they be modified, was reasonable under the circumstances as he understood them. Accordingly, no violation of First Amendment rights occurred. The judgment of the Court of Appeals for the Eighth Circuit is therefore reversed.

JUSTICE BRENNAN, with whom JUSTICE MARSHALL and JUSTICE BLACKMUN join, dissenting.

When the young men and women of Hazelwood East High School registered for Journalism II, they expected a civics lesson. Spectrum, the newspaper they were to publish, "was not just a class exercise in which students learned to prepare papers and hone writing skills, it was a ... forum established to give students an opportunity to express their views while gaining an appreciation of their rights and responsibilities under the *First Amendment to the United States Constitution....*" "[A]t the beginning of each school year," the student journalists published a Statement of Policy—tacitly approved each year by school authorities—announcing their expectation that "*Spectrum*, as a student-press publication, accepts all rights implied by the First Amendment.... Only speech that 'materially and substantially interferes with the requirements of appropriate discipline' can be found unacceptable and therefore prohibited." The school board itself affirmatively guaranteed the students of Journalism II an atmosphere conducive to fostering such an appreciation and exercising the full panoply of rights associated with a free student press. "School sponsored student publications," it vowed, "will not restrict free expression or diverse viewpoints within the rules of responsible journalism." (Board Policy 348.51)....

In my view the principal broke more than just a promise. He violated the First Amendment's prohibitions against censorship of any student expression that neither disrupts classwork nor invades the rights of others, and against any censorship that is not narrowly tailored to serve its purpose....

Free student expression undoubtedly sometimes interferes with the effectiveness of the school's pedagogical functions. Some brands of student expression do so by directly preventing the school from pursuing its pedagogical mission: The young polemic who stands on a soapbox during calculus class to deliver an eloquent political diatribe interferes with the legitimate teaching of calculus. And the student who delivers a lewd endorsement of a student-government candidate might so extremely distract an impressionable high school audience as to interfere with the orderly operation of the school. Other student speech, however, frustrates the school's legitimate pedagogical purposes merely by expressing a message that conflicts with the school's, without directly interfering with the school's expression of its message: A student who responds to a political science teacher's question with the retort, "socialism is good," subverts the school's inculcation of the message that capitalism is better. Even the maverick who sits in class passively sporting a symbol of protest against a government policy, cf. Tinker v. Des Moines Independent Community School Dist., 393 U.S. 503 (1969), or the gossip who sits in the student commons swapping stories of sexual escapade could readily muddle a clear official message condoning the government policy or condemning teenage sex. Likewise, the student newspaper that, like Spectrum, conveys a moral position at odds with the school's official stance might subvert the administration's legitimate inculcation of its own perception of community values.

If mere incompatibility with the school's pedagogical message were a constitutionally sufficient justification for the suppression of student speech, school officials could censor each of the students or student organizations in the foregoing hypotheticals, converting our public schools into "enclaves of totalitarianism," that "strangle the free mind at its source," West Virginia Board of Education v. Barnette. The First Amendment permits no such blanket censorship authority....

In Tinker, this Court struck the balance. We held that official censorship of student expression — there the suspension of several students until they removed their armbands protesting the Vietnam war — is unconstitutional unless the speech "materially disrupts classwork or involves substantial disorder or invasion of the rights of others...." School officials may not suppress "silent, passive expression of opinion, unaccompanied by any disorder or disturbance on the part of" the speaker. The "mere desire to avoid the discomfort and unpleasantness that always accompany an unpopular viewpoint," or an unsavory subject, does not justify official suppression of student speech in the high school....

Tinker teaches us that the state educator's undeniable, and undeniably vital, mandate to inculcate moral and political values is not a general warrant to act as "thought police" stifling discussion of all but state-approved topics and advocacy of all but the official position.... Thus, the State cannot constitutionally prohibit its high school students from recounting in the locker room "the particulars of [their] teen-age sexual activity," nor even from advocating "irresponsible se[x]" or other presumed abominations of "the shared values of a civilized social order." Even in its capacity as educator the State may not assume an Orwellian "guardianship of the public mind." ...

The case before us aptly illustrates how readily school officials (and courts) can camouflage viewpoint discrimination as the "mere" protection of students from sensitive topics. Among the grounds that the Court advances to uphold the principal's censorship of one of the articles was the potential sensitivity of "teenage sexual activity." Yet the District Court specifically found that the principal "did not, as a matter of principle, oppose discussion of said topi[c] in Spectrum." That much is also clear from the same principal's approval of the "squeal law" article on the same page, dealing forthrightly with "teenage sexuality," "the use of contraceptives by teenagers," and "teenage pregnancy." If topic sensitivity were the true basis of the principal's decision, the two articles should have been equally objectionable. It is much more likely that the objectionable article was objectionable because of the viewpoint it expressed: It might have been read (as the majority apparently does) to advocate "irresponsible sex."

The sole concomitant of school sponsorship that might conceivably justify the distinction that the Court draws between sponsored and nonsponsored student expression is the risk "that the views of the individual speaker [might be] erroneously attributed to the school." ...

Dissociative means short of censorship are available to the school. It could, for example, require the student activity to publish a disclaimer, such as the "Statement of Policy" that Spectrum published each school year announcing that "[a]ll ... editorials appearing in this newspaper reflect the opinions of the Spectrum staff, which are not necessarily shared by the administrators or faculty of Hazelwood East," or it could simply issue its own response clarifying the official position on the matter and explaining why the student position is wrong. Yet, without so much as acknowledging the less oppressive alternatives, the Court approves of brutal censorship.

Since the censorship served no legitimate pedagogical purpose, it cannot by any stretch of the imagination have been designed to prevent "materia[l] disrup[tion of] classwork," Tinker, 393 U.S., at 513. Nor did the censorship fall within the category that Tinker described as necessary to prevent student expression from "inva[ding] the rights of others." If that term is to have any content, it must be limited to rights that are protected by law. "Any yardstick less exacting than [that] could result in school officials curtailing speech at the slightest fear of disturbance," a prospect that would be completely at odds with this Court's pronouncement that the "undifferentiated fear or apprehension of disturbance is not enough [even in the public school context] to overcome the right to freedom of expression." Tinker, supra, at 508. And, as the Court of Appeals correctly reasoned, whatever journalistic impropriety these articles may have contained, they could not conceivably be tortious, much less criminal.

Review Questions and Explanations: *Hazelwood School District*

1. Which position, majority or dissent, do you find more persuasive, and why?

2. Do you think there was viewpoint discrimination going on here? (Recall the hint of viewpoint discrimination alluded to, but apparently not made the basis of decision in *Tinker*—that the school allowed the wearing of political campaign buttons, but not the armbands.) The dissent's argument illustrates how the presence of viewpoint discrimination can undercut the rationale for a content-based regulation of speech.

3. Is the K–12 (grade and high school) environment a "special context" where First Amendment rules apply differently, or does the school environment simply present a particular set of state interests that can and should be evaluated under standard First Amendment doctrine?

4. What if anything do the majority and dissenting opinions imply in answer to the previous question? The dissent can be read to suggest that (a) the *Tinker* test is a "compelling interest" formulation for school speech: that is, the state has a compelling interest in preventing "material and substantial disruption of the work and discipline of the school"; and (b) that "dissociation" of the school from student speech is not a compelling interest (or that censorship in this case is not narrowly tailored to achieve it).

What about the majority: Does that opinion suggest that barring the student speech here was narrowly tailored to meet some compelling state interest in curricular goals? The language suggesting that Courts must adopt a deferential, "hands off" attitude toward schools implies that strict scrutiny is not being applied.

4. Commercial Speech

Even commercial, non-political advertising is "speech." What sort of protection, if any, does it get from the First Amendment?

Guided Reading Questions: *Virginia State Bd. of Pharmacy*

1. What are the arguments for and against according First Amendment protection to commercial speech? What is at stake in doing so?

2. As you read the case, try to distinguish between advertising generally and the specific context of advertising in this case: price and product information that is being withheld from consumers in order to protect the anticompetitive economic interests of pharmacists.

3. Compare the Court's treatment of commercial speech cases with its approach to campaign finance regulations. What arguments can you make for treating these two areas the same? What arguments support treating them differently? Which approach has the Court taken? Review *Buckley* carefully before answering that question.

Virginia State Board of Pharmacy v. Virginia Citizens Consumer Counsel

425 U.S. 748 (1976)

Majority: *Blackmun*, Burger (CJ), Brennan, Stewart, White, Marshall, Powell

Concurrences: *Burger* (CJ) (omitted), *Stewart*

Dissent: *Rehnquist* (Stevens took no part)

MR. JUSTICE BLACKMUN delivered the opinion of the Court.

The plaintiff-appellees in this case attack ... that portion of § 54-524.35 of Va. Code Ann. (1974), which provides that a pharmacist licensed in Virginia is guilty of unprofessional conduct if he "(3) publishes, advertises or promotes, directly or indirectly, in any manner whatsoever, any amount, price, fee, premium, discount, rebate or credit terms ... for any drugs which may be dispensed only by prescription." The three-judge District Court declared the quoted portion of the statute "void and of no effect," and enjoined the defendant-appellants, the Virginia State Board of Pharmacy and the individual members of that Board, from enforcing it. We noted probable jurisdiction of the appeal....

The "practice of pharmacy" is statutorily declared to be "a professional practice affecting the public health, safety and welfare," and to be "subject to regulation and control in the public interest." Va. Code Ann. §54-524.2 (a) (1974). Indeed, the practice is subject to extensive regulation aimed at preserving high professional standards. [The] appellant Virginia State Board of Pharmacy.... is broadly charged by statute with various responsibilities, including the "[m]aintenance of the quality, quantity, integrity, safety and efficacy of drugs or devices distributed, dispensed or administered." §54-524.16 (a). It also is to concern itself with "[ma]intaining the integrity of, and public confidence in, the profession and improving the delivery of quality pharmaceutical services to the citizens of Virginia." §54-524.16 (d)....

The Board is also the licensing authority. It may issue a license, necessary for the practice of pharmacy in the State, only upon evidence that the applicant is "of good moral character," is a graduate in pharmacy of a school approved by the Board, and has had "a suitable period of experience [the period required not to exceed 12 months] acceptable to the Board." §54-524.21. The applicant must pass the examination prescribed by the Board....

Once licensed, a pharmacist is subject to a civil monetary penalty, or to revocation or suspension of his license, if the Board finds that he "is not of good moral character," or has violated any of a number of stated professional standards (among them that he not be "negligent in the practice of pharmacy" or have engaged in "fraud or deceit upon the consumer ... in connection with the practice of pharmacy"), or is guilty of "unprofessional conduct." §54-524.22:1. "Unprofessional conduct" is specifically defined in §54-524.35, the third numbered phrase of which relates to advertising of the price for any prescription drug, and is the subject of this litigation.

Inasmuch as only a licensed pharmacist may dispense prescription drugs in Virginia, §54-524.48, advertising or other affirmative dissemination of prescription drug price information is effectively forbidden in the State. Some pharmacies refuse even to quote prescription drug prices over the telephone....

The present ... attack on the statute is one made not by one directly subject to its prohibition, that is, a pharmacist, but by prescription drug consumers who claim that they would greatly benefit if the prohibition were lifted and advertising freely allowed....

Certainly that information may be of value. Drug prices in Virginia, for both prescription and nonprescription items, strikingly vary from outlet to outlet even within the same locality. It is stipulated, for example, that in Richmond "the cost of 40 Achromycin tablets ranges from $2.59 to $6.00, a difference of 140% [sic]," and that in the Newport News-Hampton area the cost of tetracycline ranges from $1.20 to $9.00, a difference of 650%....

The question first arises whether, even assuming that First Amendment protection attaches to the flow of drug price information, it is a protection enjoyed by the appellees as recipients of the information, and not solely, if at all, by the advertisers themselves who seek to disseminate that information.

Freedom of speech presupposes a willing speaker. But where a speaker exists, as is the case here, the protection afforded is to the communication, to its source and to its recipients both.... [This] Court has referred to a First Amendment right to "receive information and ideas," and that freedom of speech "necessarily protects the right to receive." ... If there is a right to advertise, there is a reciprocal right to receive the advertising, and it may be asserted by these appellees....

The appellants contend that the advertisement of prescription drug prices is outside the protection of the First Amendment because it is "commercial speech." There can be no question that in past decisions the Court has given some indication that commercial speech is unprotected.

Here ... the question whether there is a First Amendment exception for "commercial speech" is squarely before us. Our pharmacist does not wish to editorialize on any subject, cultural, philosophical, or political. He does not wish to report any particularly newsworthy fact, or to make generalized observations even about commercial matters. The "idea" he wishes to communicate is simply this: "I will sell you the X prescription drug at the Y price." ...

.... [Clearly,] speech does not lose its First Amendment protection because money is spent to project it, as in a paid advertisement of one form or another. Speech likewise is protected even though it is carried in a form that is "sold" for profit [such as books, motion pictures, religious literature], and even though it may involve a solicitation to purchase or otherwise pay or contribute money. [E.g.,] New York Times Co. v. Sullivan....

If there is a kind of commercial speech that lacks all First Amendment protection, therefore, it must be distinguished by its content. Yet the speech whose content deprives it of protection cannot simply be speech on a commercial subject. No one would contend that our pharmacist may be prevented from being heard on the subject of whether, in general, pharmaceutical prices should be regulated, or their advertisement forbidden. Nor can it be dispositive that a commercial advertisement is noneditorial, and merely reports a fact. Purely factual matter of public interest may claim protection.

.... [W]e may assume that the advertiser's interest is a purely economic one.... As to the particular consumer's interest in the free flow of commercial information, that interest may be as keen, if not keener by far, than his interest in the day's most urgent political debate. Appellees' case in this respect is a convincing one. Those whom the suppression of prescription drug price information hits the hardest are the poor, the sick, and particularly the aged. A disproportionate amount of their income tends to be spent on prescription drugs; yet they are the least able to learn, by shopping from pharmacist to pharmacist, where their scarce dollars are best spent. When drug prices vary as strikingly as they do, information as to who is charging what becomes more than a convenience. It could mean the alleviation of physical pain or the enjoyment of basic necessities.

Generalizing, society also may have a strong interest in the free flow of commercial information. Even an individual advertisement, though entirely "commercial," may be of general public interest. The facts of decided cases furnish illustrations: advertisements stating that referral services for legal abortions are available, that a manufacturer of artificial furs promotes his product as an alternative to the extinction by his competitors of fur-bearing mammals, and that a domestic producer advertises his product as an alternative to imports that tend to deprive American residents of their jobs. Obviously, not all commercial messages contain the same or even a very great public interest element. There are few to which such an element, however, could not be added. Our pharmacist, for example, could cast himself as a commentator on store-to-store disparities in drug prices, giving his own and those of a competitor as proof. We see little point in requiring him to do so, and little difference if he does not.

Moreover, there is another consideration that suggests that no line between publicly "interesting" or "important" commercial advertising and the opposite kind could ever be drawn. Advertising, however tasteless and excessive it sometimes may seem, is nonetheless dissemination of information as to who is producing and selling what product, for what reason, and at what price. So long as we preserve a predominantly free enterprise economy, the allocation of our resources in large measure will be made through numerous private economic decisions. It is a matter of public interest that those decisions, in the aggregate, be intelligent and well informed. To this end, the free flow of commercial information is indispensable.... [It] is also indispensable to the formation of intelligent opinions as to how that system ought to be regulated or altered....

Arrayed against these substantial individual and societal interests are a number of justifications for the advertising ban. These have to do principally with maintaining a high degree of professionalism on the part of licensed pharmacists. Indisputably, the State has a strong interest in maintaining that professionalism. It is exercised in a number of ways for the consumer's benefit....

Price advertising, it is argued, will place in jeopardy the pharmacist's expertise and, with it, the customer's health. It is claimed that the aggressive price competition that will result from unlimited advertising will make it impossible for the pharmacist to supply professional services in the compounding, handling, and dispensing of prescription drugs. Such services are time consuming and expensive; if competitors who economize by eliminating them are permitted to advertise their resulting lower prices, the more painstaking and conscientious pharmacist will be forced either to follow suit or to go out of business. It is also claimed that prices might not necessarily fall as a result of advertising. If one pharmacist advertises, others must, and the resulting expense will inflate the cost of drugs. It is further claimed that advertising will lead people to shop for their prescription drugs among the various pharmacists who offer the lowest prices, and the loss of stable pharmacist-customer relationships will make individual attention—and certainly the practice of monitoring—impossible. Finally, it is argued that damage will be done to the professional image of the pharmacist. This image, that of a skilled and specialized craftsman, attracts talent to the profession and reinforces the better habits of those who are in it. Price advertising, it is said, will reduce the pharmacist's status to that of a mere retailer.

The strength of these proffered justifications is greatly undermined by the fact that high professional standards, to a substantial extent, are guaranteed by the close regulation to which pharmacists in Virginia are subject. And this case concerns the retail sale by the pharmacist more than it does his professional standards. Surely, any pharmacist guilty of professional dereliction that actually endangers his customer will promptly lose his license. At the same time, we cannot discount the Board's justifications entirely. The Court regarded justifications of this type sufficient to sustain the advertising bans challenged on due process and equal protection grounds. [See, e.g.,] Williamson v. Lee Optical Co.

The challenge now made, however, is based on the First Amendment. This casts the Board's justifications in a different light, for on close inspection it is seen that the State's protectiveness of its citizens rests in large measure on the advantages of their being kept in ignorance. The advertising ban does not directly affect professional standards one way or the other. It affects them only through the reactions it is assumed people will have to the free flow of drug price information. There is no claim that the advertising ban in any way prevents the cutting of corners by the pharmacist who is so inclined. That pharmacist is likely to cut corners in any event. The only effect the advertising ban has on him is to insulate him from price competition and to open the way for him to make a substantial, and perhaps even excessive, profit in addition to providing an inferior service. The more painstaking pharmacist is also protected but, again, it is a protection based in large part on public ignorance....

There is, of course, an alternative to this highly paternalistic approach. That alternative is to assume that this information is not in itself harmful, that people will perceive their own best interests if only they are well enough informed, and that the best means to that end is to open the channels of communication rather than to close them. If they are truly open, nothing prevents the "professional" pharmacist from marketing his own assertedly superior product, and contrasting it with that of the low-cost, high-volume prescription drug retailer. But the choice among these alternative approaches is not ours to make or the Virginia General Assembly's. It is precisely this kind of choice, between the dangers of suppressing information, and the dangers of its misuse if it is freely available, that the First Amendment makes for us. Virginia is free to require whatever professional standards it wishes of its pharmacists; it may subsidize them or protect them from competition in other ways. But it may not do so by keeping the public in ignorance of the entirely lawful terms that competing pharmacists are offering....

In concluding that commercial speech, like other varieties, is protected, we of course do not hold that it can never be regulated in any way. Some forms of commercial speech regulation are surely permissible. We mention a few only to make clear that they are not before us and therefore are not foreclosed by this case.

There is no claim, for example, that the prohibition on prescription drug price advertising is a mere time, place, and manner restriction. We have often approved restrictions of that kind provided that they are justified without reference to the content of the regulated speech, that they serve a significant governmental interest, and that in so doing they leave open ample alternative channels for communication of the information....

Nor is there any claim that prescription drug price advertisements are forbidden because they are false or misleading in any way. Untruthful speech, commercial or otherwise, has never been protected for its own sake. Obviously, much commercial speech is not provably false, or even wholly false, but only deceptive or misleading. We foresee no obstacle to a State's dealing effectively with this problem. The First Amendment, as we construe it today, does not prohibit the State from insuring that the stream of commercial information flow cleanly as well as freely.

Also, there is no claim that the transactions proposed in the forbidden advertisements are themselves illegal in any way. Finally, the special problems of the electronic broadcast media are likewise not in this case.

What is at issue is whether a State may completely suppress the dissemination of concededly truthful information about entirely lawful activity, fearful of that information's effect upon its disseminators and its recipients. Reserving other questions, we conclude that the answer to this one is in the negative. The judgment of the District Court is affirmed.

MR. JUSTICE STEWART.

.... I write separately to explain why I think today's decision does not preclude ... governmental regulation [of false advertising].

.... [T]he Constitution does not provide absolute protection for false factual statements that cause private injury. In Gertz v. Robert Welch, Inc., 418 U.S. 323, 340, the Court concluded that "there is no constitutional value in false statements of fact." As the Court had previously recognized in New York Times Co. v. Sullivan, 376 U.S. 254, however, factual errors are inevitable in free debate, and the imposition of liability for erroneous factual assertions can "dampe[n] the vigor and limi[t] the variety of public debate" by inducing "self-censorship." In order to provide ample "breathing space" for free expression, the Constitution places substantial limitations on the discretion of government to permit recovery for libelous communications.

The principles recognized in the libel decisions suggest that government may take broader action to protect the public from injury produced by false or deceptive price or product advertising than from harm caused by defamation. In contrast to the press, which must often attempt to assemble the true facts from sketchy and sometimes conflicting sources under the pressure of publication deadlines, the commercial advertiser generally knows the product or service he seeks to sell and is in a position to verify the accuracy of his factual representations before he disseminates them. The advertiser's access to the truth about his product and its price substantially eliminates any danger that governmental regulation of false or misleading price or product advertising will chill accurate and non-deceptive commercial expression. There is, therefore, little need to sanction "some falsehood in order to protect speech that matters."...

Commercial price and product advertising differs markedly from ideological expression because it is confined to the promotion of specific goods or services. The First Amendment protects the advertisement because of the "information of potential interest and value" conveyed, rather than because of any direct contribution to the interchange of ideas. Since the factual claims contained in commercial price or product advertisements relate to tangible goods or services, they may be tested empirically and corrected to reflect the truth without in any manner jeopardizing the free dissemination of thought. Indeed, the elimination of false and deceptive claims serves to promote the one facet of commercial price and product advertising that warrants First Amendment protection—its contribution to the flow of accurate and reliable information relevant to public and private decisionmaking.

MR. JUSTICE REHNQUIST, dissenting.

The logical consequences of the Court's decision in this case, a decision which elevates commercial intercourse between a seller hawking his wares and a buyer seeking to strike a bargain to the same plane as has been previously reserved for the free marketplace of ideas, are far reaching indeed....

The Court speaks of the importance in a "predominantly free enterprise economy" of intelligent and well-informed decisions as to allocation of resources. While there is again much to be said for the Court's observation as a matter of desirable public policy, there is certainly nothing in the United States Constitution which requires the Virginia Legislature to hew to the teachings of Adam Smith in its legislative decisions regulating the pharmacy profession....

Both Congress and state legislatures have by law sharply limited the permissible dissemination of information about some commodities because of the potential harm resulting from those commodities, even though they were not thought to be sufficiently demonstrably harmful to warrant outright prohibition of their sale. Current prohibitions on television advertising of liquor and cigarettes are prominent in this category, but apparently under the Court's holding so long as the advertisements are not deceptive they may no longer be prohibited.

Review Questions and Explanations: *Virginia Pharmacy*

1. *Virginia State Board of Pharmacy* is the leading case establishing some degree of First Amendment protection for commercial speech. The Court has—

at least so far—made clear that commercial speech is entitled to lesser protection than non-commercial speech. What justifications can you think of for such a distinction?

2. The advertising ban in this case seems to have been part of a broader system designed, in part, to maintain a professional "guild." This concept, which goes back many centuries, centers on a category of specialized work in which group norms are imposed on both the quality of work and the ethical behavior of group members; entry into the guild is restricted by requiring special training, experience, apprenticeships and/or examinations, with the benefit to group members that the ensuing limitation on membership allows guild members to command higher prices for their services. The legal profession, of course, is an example of such a professional guild.

Guilds are somewhat anti-competitive in a free market sense, as is the restriction of price information at issue in this case. Is the *Virginia Pharmacy* decision driven by an underlying belief in the virtue of the free market? Free speech has often been analogized as promoting a "free market in ideas"; in *Virginia Pharmacy*, the connection between free speech and the free market is made more literal. To what extent do you think the First Amendment should protect a free economic market?

3. Might Justice Rehnquist's dissent be right? The Court applies some sort of heightened scrutiny to regulation of commercial speech as a result of the *Virginia Pharmacy* decision. The objection to the advertising ban ultimately seems to be its anti-competitive impact. Why not leave regulation of the economy to the state legislature? Arguably, the reason the law exists is that pharmacists were sufficiently powerful as an interest group to win special interest legislation. But so was the dairy industry in *Carolene Products* and the optometrist industry in *Williamson v. Lee Optical*, both cases in which the Court decided it needed to adopt a deferential, "rational basis" review of even protectionist economic laws in order to eschew the *Lochner* approach to judicial review. Does *Virginia Pharmacy* raise the specter of a return to heightened judicial scrutiny of economic legislation, with the First Amendment standing in for substantive due process?

F. Speech-Related Rights

As mentioned at the outset of this chapter, the Court has treated the freedom of the press, and the right to peaceably assemble and to petition the government for a redress of grievances, both found in the text of the First Amendment, as specific examples of free speech rather than as additions to it. The Court has found one additional, non-textual right within the First Amendment: the right to freedom of association.

1. Freedom of Association

Though not expressly mentioned in the First Amendment, the Court has held that a right of free association can be inferred from the freedom of speech and assembly, and even to an extent from the free exercise of religion. An early case discussing association rights, *NAACP v. Alabama*, is presented below.

Guided Reading Questions: *NAACP v. Alabama*

1. Why would freedom of association entail a right to keep organizational membership confidential?

2. Is the right to resist compelled disclosure of a group's membership list unconditional? What sort of a showing does the Court seem to look for?

3. How does the Court address the argument that any infringement on the NAACP's speech and association would come from private parties, so that state action is lacking?

4. What are the state's interests in disclosure? How strong do you think they are? Do you think stronger state interests would have generated a different result?

National Association for the Advancement of Colored People v. Alabama ex rel. Patterson
357 U.S. 449 (1958)

Unanimous decision: *Harlan*, Warren (CJ), Black, Frankfurter, Douglas, Burton, Clark, Brennan, Whittaker

MR. JUSTICE HARLAN delivered the opinion of the Court.

We review from the standpoint of its validity under the Federal Constitution a judgment of civil contempt entered against petitioner, the National Association for the Advancement of Colored People, in the courts of Alabama. The question presented is whether Alabama, consistently with the Due Process Clause of the Fourteenth Amendment, can compel petitioner to reveal to the State's Attorney General the names and addresses of all its Alabama members and agents, without regard to their positions or functions in the Association. The judgment of contempt was based upon petitioner's refusal to comply fully with a court order requiring in part the production of membership lists. Petitioner's claim is that the order, in the circumstances shown by this record, violated rights assured to petitioner and its members under the Constitution.

[In 1956, Alabama Attorney General Patterson brought suit in Alabama state court to enjoin the NAACP from conducting further activities within, and to oust it from, the State. The complaint alleged that the NAACP had opened a regional offices in Alabama, and conducted civil rights activities, without obtaining a corporate charter from the state, as required by Alabama law. The state court issued a temporary restraining order, without prior notice to the NAACP, prohibiting it from conducting further activities in the state. The NAACP moved to dismiss the suit, contending that its activities did not subject it to the corporate qualification requirements of the statute. Before the date for that hearing, the State moved for the production of a large number of the Association's records and papers, including bank statements, leases, deeds, and records containing the names and addresses of all Alabama "members" and "agents" of the Association. It alleged that all such documents were necessary for adequate preparation for the hearing, in view of petitioner's denial of the conduct of intrastate business within the meaning of the qualification statute. Over petitioner's objections, the court ordered the production of a substantial part of the requested records, including the membership lists. The NAACP refused to produce its membership lists, and the court held the NAACP in civil contempt, imposing a $100,000 fine (equal to approximately $800,000 in 2012). Under Alabama law the contempt adjudication also foreclosed the NAACP from obtaining a hearing on the merits of the underlying case until the contempt was purged by compliance with the order. The State Supreme Court denied review of the final contempt judgment, and the U.S. Supreme Court granted certiorari.]

The Association both urges that it is constitutionally entitled to resist official inquiry into its membership lists, and that it may assert, on behalf of its members, a right personal to them to be protected from compelled disclosure by the State of their affiliation with the Association as revealed by the membership lists. We think that petitioner argues more appropriately the rights of its members, and that its nexus with them is sufficient to permit that it act as their representative before this Court. In so concluding, we reject respondent's argument that the Association lacks standing to assert here constitutional rights pertaining to the members, who are not of course parties to the litigation.... If petitioner's rank-and-file members are constitutionally entitled to withhold their connection with the Association despite the production order, it is manifest that this right is properly assertable by the Association. To require that it be claimed by the members themselves would result in nullification of the right at the very moment of its assertion.

.... Petitioner argues that in view of the facts and circumstances shown in the record, the effect of compelled disclosure of the membership lists will be to abridge the rights of its rank-and-file members to engage in lawful association in support of their common beliefs. It contends that governmental action which, although not directly suppressing association, nevertheless carries this consequence, can be justified only upon some overriding valid interest of the State.

Effective advocacy of both public and private points of view, particularly controversial ones, is undeniably enhanced by group association, as this Court has more than once recognized by remarking upon the close nexus between the freedoms of speech and assembly. It is beyond debate that freedom to engage in association for the advancement of beliefs and ideas is an inseparable aspect of the "liberty" assured by the Due Process Clause of the Fourteenth Amendment, which embraces freedom of speech. Of course, it is immaterial whether the beliefs sought to be advanced by association pertain to political, economic, religious or cultural matters, and state action which may have the effect of curtailing the freedom to associate is subject to the closest scrutiny.

The fact that Alabama, so far as is relevant to the validity of the contempt judgment presently under review, has taken no direct action to restrict the right of petitioner's members to associate freely, does not end inquiry into the effect of the production order. In the domain of these indispensable liberties, whether of speech, press, or association, the decisions of this Court recognize that abridgment of such rights, even though unintended, may inevitably follow from varied forms of governmental action.... The governmental action challenged may appear to be totally unrelated to protected liberties. Statutes imposing taxes upon rather than prohibiting particular activity have been struck down when perceived to have the consequence of unduly curtailing the liberty of freedom of press assured under the Fourteenth Amendment.

It is hardly a novel perception that compelled disclosure of affiliation with groups engaged in advocacy may constitute as effective a restraint on freedom of association as the forms of governmental action in the cases above were thought likely to produce upon the particular constitutional rights there involved. This Court has recognized the vital relationship between freedom to associate and privacy in one's associations.... Inviolability of privacy in group association may in many circumstances be indispensable to preservation of freedom of association, particularly where a group espouses dissident beliefs.

We think that the production order, in the respects here drawn in question, must be regarded as entailing the likelihood of a substantial restraint upon the exercise by petitioner's members of their right to freedom of association. Petitioner has made an uncontroverted showing that on past occasions revelation of the identity of its rank-and-file members has exposed these members to economic reprisal, loss of employment, threat of physical coercion, and other manifestations of public hostility. Under these circumstances, we think it apparent that compelled disclosure of petitioner's Alabama membership is likely to affect adversely the ability of petitioner and its members to pursue their collective effort to foster beliefs which they admittedly have the right to advocate, in that it may induce members to withdraw from the Association and dissuade others from joining it because of fear of exposure of their beliefs shown through their associations and of the consequences of this exposure.

It is not sufficient to answer, as the State does here, that whatever repressive effect compulsory disclosure of names of petitioner's members may have upon participation by Alabama citizens in petitioner's activities follows not from *state* action but from *private* community pressures. The crucial factor is the interplay of governmental and private action, for it is only after the initial exertion of state power represented by the production order that private action takes hold.

We turn to the final question whether Alabama has demonstrated an interest in obtaining the disclosures it seeks from petitioner which is sufficient to justify the deterrent effect which we have concluded these disclosures may well have on the free exercise by petitioner's members of their constitutionally protected right of association. Such a " ... subordinating interest of the State must be compelling."

It is important to bear in mind that petitioner asserts no right to absolute immunity from state investigation, and no right to disregard Alabama's laws. As shown by its substantial compliance with the production order, petitioner does not deny Alabama's right to obtain from it such information as the State desires concerning the purposes of the Association and its activities within the State. Petitioner has not objected to divulging the identity of its members who are employed by or hold official positions with it. It has urged the rights solely of its ordinary rank-and-file members. This is therefore not analogous to a case involving the interest of a State in protecting its citizens in their dealings with paid solicitors or agents of foreign corporations by requiring identification.

.... The issues in the litigation commenced by Alabama by its bill in equity were whether the character of petitioner and its activities in Alabama had been such as to make petitioner subject to the registration statute, and whether the extent of petitioner's activities without qualifying suggested its permanent ouster from the State. Without intimating the slightest view upon the merits of these issues, we are unable to perceive that the disclosure of the names of petitioner's rank-and-file members has a substantial bearing on either of them. As matters stand in the state court, petitioner (1) has admitted its presence and conduct of activities in Alabama since 1918; (2) has offered to comply in all respects with the state qualification statute, although preserving its contention that the statute does not apply to it; and (3) has apparently complied satisfactorily with the production order, except for the membership lists, by furnishing the Attorney General with varied business records, its charter and statement of purposes, the names of all of its directors and officers, and with the total number of its Alabama members and the amount of their dues.

We hold that the immunity from state scrutiny of membership lists which the Association claims on behalf of its members is here so related to the right of the members to pursue their lawful private interests privately and to associate freely with others in so doing as to come within the protection of the Fourteenth Amendment. And we conclude that Alabama has fallen short of showing a controlling justification for the deterrent effect on the free enjoyment of the right to associate which disclosure of membership lists is likely to have. Accordingly, the judgment of civil contempt and the $100,000 fine which resulted from petitioner's refusal to comply with the production order in this respect must fall....

For the reasons stated, the judgment of the Supreme Court of Alabama must be reversed and the case remanded for proceedings not inconsistent with this opinion.

Review Questions and Explanations: *NAACP v. Alabama*

1. Does the state's investigation, and the state court's extremely high contempt fine, suggest a concerted state effort to undermine the civil rights organization? Do you think this influenced the Supreme Court's ruling?

2. The end of the opinion refers to a "showing" expected of Alabama. What triggers that obligation?

The next two cases considered associational rights to exclude persons from an organization — specifically, in these cases, gays and lesbians.

Guided Reading Questions: *Hurley v. Irish-Am. Gay, Lesbian & Bisexual Group*

1. Pay close attention to how the concept of "public accommodation" is defined in Massachusetts law. How does it relate to the case?

2. Does the Court hold that a state public accommodations law prohibiting discrimination in privately owned places of public accommodation violates the First Amendment right to freedom of association?

3. How does the Court characterize the parade? Is it like "a boardwalk or other public highway [or] ... a place of public amusement, recreation, sport, exercise or entertainment" or is it something different? What is the legal significance of the characterization?

4. Why isn't enforcement of state antidiscrimination law a compelling interest that would justify an abridgement of speech in this case? Does the Court even go through that analysis?

Hurley v. Irish-American Gay, Lesbian and Bisexual Group of Boston

515 U.S. 557 (1995)

Unanimous decision: *Souter*, Rehnquist (CJ), Stevens, O'Connor, Scalia, Kennedy, Thomas, Ginsburg, Breyer

JUSTICE SOUTER delivered the opinion of the Court.

The issue in this case is whether Massachusetts may require private citizens who organize a parade to include among the marchers a group imparting a message the organizers do not wish to convey. We hold that such a mandate violates the First Amendment.

[The petitioner South Boston Allied War Veterans Council, an unincorporated association of individuals elected from various South Boston veterans groups, had applied for and received a permit for a St. Patrick's Day parade every year since 1947, when the city of Boston ceased formal sponsorship of the parade. The parade has included as many as 20,000 marchers and drawn up to 1 million watchers.] No other applicant has ever applied for that permit. Through 1992, the city allowed the Council to use the city's official seal, and provided printing services as well as direct funding.

In 1992, a number of gay, lesbian, and bisexual descendants of the Irish immigrants joined together with other supporters to form the respondent organization, GLIB, to march in the parade as a way to express pride in their Irish heritage as openly gay, lesbian, and bisexual individuals, to demonstrate that there are such men and women among those so descended, and to express their solidarity with like individuals who sought to march in New York's St. Patrick's Day Parade. Although the Council denied GLIB's application to take part in the 1992 parade, GLIB obtained a state-court order to include its contingent, which marched "uneventfully" among that year's 10,000 participants and 750,000 spectators.

In 1993, after the Council had again refused to admit GLIB to the upcoming parade, the organization and some of its members filed this suit against the Council, the individual petitioner John J. "Wacko" Hurley, and the city of Boston, alleging violations of the State and Federal Constitutions and of the state public accommodations law, which prohibits "any distinction, discrimination or restriction on account of ... sexual orientation ... relative to the admission of any person to, or treatment in any place of public accommodation, resort or amusement." Mass. Gen. Laws § 272:98 (1992). After finding that "for at least the past 47 years, the Parade has traveled the same basic route along the public streets of South Boston, providing entertainment, amusement, and recreation to participants and spectators alike," the state trial court ruled that the parade fell within the statutory definition of a public accommodation, which includes "any place ... which is open to and accepts or solicits the patronage of the general public and, without limiting the generality of this definition, whether or not it be ... (6) a boardwalk or other public highway [or] ... (8) a place of public amusement, recreation, sport, exercise or entertainment," Mass. Gen. Laws § 272:92A (1992). The court found that the Council had no written criteria and employed no particular procedures for admission, voted on new applications in batches, had occasionally admitted groups who simply showed up at the parade without having submitted an application, and did "not generally inquire into the specific messages or views of each applicant." The court consequently rejected the Council's contention that the parade was "private" (in the sense of being exclusive), holding instead that "the lack of genuine selectivity in choosing participants and sponsors demonstrates that the Parade is a public event." It found the parade to be "eclectic," containing a wide variety of "patriotic, commercial, political, moral, artistic, religious, athletic, public service, trade union, and eleemosynary themes," as well as conflicting messages. While noting that the Council had indeed excluded the Ku Klux Klan and ROAR (an antibusing group), it attributed little significance to these facts, concluding ultimately that "the only common theme among the participants and sponsors is their public involvement in the Parade."

The court rejected the Council's assertion that the exclusion of "groups with sexual themes merely formalized [the fact] that the Parade expresses traditional religious and social values," and found the Council's "final position [to be] that GLIB would be excluded because of its values and its message, i.e., its members' sexual orientation." This position, in the court's view, was not only violative of the public accommodations law but "paradoxical" as well, since "a proper celebration of St. Patrick's and Evacuation Day[3] requires diversity and inclusiveness." .... The Supreme Judicial Court of Massachusetts affirmed....

[Despite winning the issue in the courts below, respondents dropped their equal protection claim under the Fourteenth Amendment, grounded in part on the City of Boston's continued involvement in the parade.] In this Court, then, their claim for inclusion in the parade rests solely on the Massachusetts public accommodations law.

If there were no reason for a group of people to march from here to there except to reach a destination, they could make the trip without expressing any message beyond the fact of the march itself. Some people might call such a procession a parade, but it would not be much of one. Real "parades are public dramas of social relations, and in them performers define who can be a social actor and what subjects and ideas are available for communication and consideration." S. Davis, Parades and Power: Street Theatre in Nineteenth-Century Philadelphia 6 (1986). Hence, we use the word "parade" to indicate marchers who are making some sort of collective point, not just to each other but to bystanders along the way. Indeed, a parade's dependence on watchers is so extreme that nowadays, as with Bishop Berkeley's celebrated tree, "if a parade or demonstration receives no media coverage, it may as well not have happened."[4] Parades are thus a form of expression, not just motion, and the inherent expressiveness of marching to make a point explains our cases involving protest marches....

The protected expression that inheres in a parade is not limited to its banners and songs, however, for the Constitution looks beyond written or spoken words as mediums of expression. Noting that "symbolism is a primitive but effective way of communicating ideas," West Virginia Bd. of Ed. v. Barnette, 319 U.S. 624, 632 (1943), our cases have recognized that the First Amendment shields such acts as saluting a flag (and refusing to do so), wearing an armband to protest a war, Tinker v. Des Moines Independent Community School Dist., 393 U.S. 503, 505–506 (1969), displaying a red flag, Stromberg v. California, 283 U.S. 359, 369 (1931), and even "marching, walking or parading" in uniforms displaying the swastika, National Socialist Party of America v. Skokie, 432 U.S. 43 (1977). As some of these examples show, a narrow, succinctly articulable message is not a condition of constitutional protection, which if confined to expressions conveying a "particularized message," would never reach the unquestionably shielded painting of Jackson Pollock, music of Arnold Schoenberg, or Jabberwocky verse of Lewis Carroll.

---

3. Editors' note: March 17 is also celebrated as the anniversary of the evacuation of Boston by British troops in 1776.

4. Editors' note: Justice Souter apparently refers to the conundrum: "if a tree falls in the forest and there is no one to hear it, does it make a sound?"

Not many marches, then, are beyond the realm of expressive parades, and the South Boston celebration is not one of them. Spectators line the streets; people march in costumes and uniforms, carrying flags and banners with all sorts of messages (*e.g.,* "England get out of Ireland," "Say no to drugs"); marching bands and pipers play; floats are pulled along; and the whole show is broadcast over Boston television. To be sure, we agree with the state courts that in spite of excluding some applicants, the Council is rather lenient in admitting participants. But a private speaker does not forfeit constitutional protection simply by combining multifarious voices, or by failing to edit their themes to isolate an exact message as the exclusive subject matter of the speech. Nor, under our precedent, does First Amendment protection require a speaker to generate, as an original matter, each item featured in the communication. Cable operators, for example, are engaged in protected speech activities even when they only select programming originally produced by others. For that matter, the presentation of an edited compilation of speech generated by other persons is a staple of most newspapers' opinion pages, which, of course, fall squarely within the core of First Amendment security, Miami Herald Publishing Co. v. Tornillo, 418 U.S. 241, 258 (1974), as does even the simple selection of a paid noncommercial advertisement for inclusion in a daily paper, see New York Times, 376 U.S. at 265–266. The selection of contingents to make a parade is entitled to similar protection.

Respondents' participation as a unit in the parade was equally expressive. GLIB was formed for the very purpose of marching in it, as the trial court found, in order to celebrate its members' identity as openly gay, lesbian, and bisexual descendants of the Irish immigrants, to show that there are such individuals in the community, and to support the like men and women who sought to march in the New York parade. The organization distributed a fact sheet describing the members' intentions, and the record otherwise corroborates the expressive nature of GLIB's participation. In 1993, members of GLIB marched behind a shamrock-strewn banner with the simple inscription "Irish American Gay, Lesbian and Bisexual Group of Boston." GLIB understandably seeks to communicate its ideas as part of the existing parade, rather than staging one of its own.

The Massachusetts public accommodations law under which respondents brought suit has a venerable history. At common law, innkeepers, smiths, and others who "made profession of a public employment," were prohibited from refusing, without good reason, to serve a customer. As one of the 19th-century English judges put it, the rule was that "the innkeeper is not to select his guests[;] he has no right to say to one, you shall come into my inn, and to another you shall not, as every one coming and conducting himself in a proper manner has a right to be received; and for this purpose innkeepers are a sort of public servants." Rex v. Ivens, 7 Car. & P. 213, 219, 173 Eng. Rep. 94, 96 (N. P. 1835).

After the Civil War, the Commonwealth of Massachusetts was the first State to codify this principle to ensure access to public accommodations regardless of race.... As with many public accommodations statutes across the Nation, the legislature continued to broaden the scope of legislation, to the point that the law today prohibits discrimination on the basis of "race, color, religious creed, national origin, sex, sexual orientation...., deafness, blindness or any physical or mental disability or ancestry" in "the admission of any person to, or treatment in any place of public accommodation, resort or amusement." Mass. Gen. Laws § 272:98 (1992). Provisions like these are well within the State's usual power to enact when a legislature has reason to believe that a given group is the target of discrimination, and they do not, as a general matter, violate the First or Fourteenth Amendments. Nor is this statute unusual in any obvious way, since it does not, on its face, target speech or discriminate on the basis of its content, the focal point of its prohibition being rather on the act of discriminating against individuals in the provision of publicly available goods, privileges, and services on the proscribed grounds.

In the case before us, however, the Massachusetts law has been applied in a peculiar way.... Although the state courts spoke of the parade as a place of public accommodation, once the expressive character of both the parade and the marching GLIB contingent is understood, it becomes apparent that the state courts' application of the statute had the effect of declaring the sponsors' speech itself to be the public accommodation. Under this approach any contingent of protected individuals with a message would have the right to participate in petitioners' speech, so that the communication produced by the private organizers would be shaped by all those protected by the law who wished to join in with some expressive demonstration of their own. But this use of the State's power violates the fundamental rule of protection under the First Amendment, that a speaker has the autonomy to choose the content of his own message.

.... Indeed this general rule, that the speaker has the right to tailor the speech, applies not only to expressions of value, opinion, or endorsement, but equally to statements of fact the speaker would rather avoid ... Nor is the rule's benefit restricted to the press, being enjoyed by business corporations generally and by ordinary people engaged in unsophisticated expression as well as by professional publishers. Its point is simply the point of all speech protection, which is to shield just those choices of content that in someone's eyes are misguided, or even hurtful.

.... [T]he Council clearly decided to exclude a message it did not like from the communication it chose to make, and that is enough to invoke its right as a private speaker to shape its expression by speaking on one subject while remaining silent on another. The message it disfavored is not difficult to identify. Although GLIB's point (like the Council's) is not wholly articulate, a contingent marching behind the organization's banner would at least bear witness to the fact that some Irish are gay, lesbian, or bisexual, and the presence of the organized marchers would suggest their view that people of their sexual orientations have as much claim to unqualified social acceptance as heterosexuals and indeed as members of parade units organized around other identifying characteristics. The parade's organizers may not believe these facts about Irish sexuality to be so, or they may object to unqualified social acceptance of gays and lesbians or have some other reason for wishing to keep GLIB's message out of the parade. But whatever the reason, it boils down to the choice of a speaker not to propound a particular point of view, and that choice is presumed to lie beyond the government's power to control.

.... Unlike the programming offered on various channels by a cable network, the parade does not consist of individual, unrelated segments that happen to be transmitted together for individual selection by members of the audience. Although each parade unit generally identifies itself, each is understood to contribute something to a common theme, and accordingly there is no customary practice whereby private sponsors disavow "any identity of viewpoint" between themselves and the selected participants. Practice follows practicability here, for such disclaimers would be quite curious in a moving parade.... In this case, of course, there is no assertion ... that some speakers will be destroyed in the absence of the challenged law. True, the size and success of petitioners' parade makes it an enviable vehicle for the dissemination of GLIB's views, but that fact, without more, would fall far short of supporting a claim that petitioners enjoy an abiding monopoly of access to spectators. Considering that GLIB presumably would have had a fair shot (under neutral criteria developed by the city) at obtaining a parade permit of its own, respondents have not shown that petitioners enjoy the capacity to "silence the voice of competing speakers".... Nor has any other legitimate interest been identified in support of applying the Massachusetts statute in this way to expressive activity like the parade.

The statute, Mass. Gen. Laws § 272:98 (1992), is a piece of protective legislation that announces no purpose beyond the object both expressed and apparent in its provisions, which is to prevent any denial of access to (or discriminatory treatment in) public accommodations on proscribed grounds, including sexual orientation. On its face, the object of the law is to ensure by statute for gays and lesbians desiring to make use of public accommodations what the old common law promised to any member of the public wanting a meal at the inn, that accepting the usual terms of service, they will not be turned away merely on the proprietor's exercise of personal preference. When the law is applied to expressive activity in the way it was done here, its apparent object is simply to require speakers to modify the content of their expression to whatever extent beneficiaries of the law choose to alter it with messages of their own. But in the absence of some further, legitimate end, this object is merely to allow exactly what the general rule of speaker's autonomy forbids.

.... Disapproval of a private speaker's statement does not legitimize use of the Commonwealth's power to compel the speaker to alter the message by including one more acceptable to others. Accordingly, the judgment of the Supreme Judicial Court is reversed and the case remanded for proceedings not inconsistent with this opinion.

Review Questions and Explanations: *Hurley*

1. As explained at some length in the opinion, a place of public accommodation is generally understood as a privately owned establishment that is open to the public for business. Some state laws may define this concept more expansively. The basic idea is that such establishments are subject to certain amounts of regulation restricting their right to pick and choose their customers, since members of the public may justifiably rely on their own right to do business with such establishments. Imagine the hardship imposed on a family traveling on an interstate road trip late at night being turned away from one motel after another due to race discrimination.

2. The key analytical move the Court makes is to define the parade as speech or expressive conduct rather than as a public accommodation. Do you agree with that characterization?

3. The doctrinal implication of defining the parade as speech is that it puts the state law in the position of government compulsion of speech — somewhat like the compulsory flag salute in *Barnette*. The Court treats compelled speech as an infringement of freedom of speech to the same extent as a prohibition on speech, for reasons summarized in *Barnette*.

4. On what basis, if any, could the St. Patrick's Day Parade in Boston, consistently with the First Amendment, be permitted to exclude the Klan and the anti-busing group ROAR from marching, but be required to include GLIB? Here's a related question: if the parade were organized by the City of Boston, rather than private groups, could the Klan or GLIB be excluded?

5. If there is there a flaw in the Court's analysis, is it that (a) the parade simply can't reasonably be defined as a private event; or (b) however expressive the parade might be, its message is so amorphous that its First Amendment interest

in excluding GLIB is weak; or (c) something else? Should the Court distinguish this parade from a more ideologically focused march or demonstration?

Guided Reading Questions: *Boy Scouts of America v. Dale*

1. Try to define as precisely as you can the right of expressive association that emerges from *Dale*. Does any association have a First Amendment right to exclude unwanted persons or are there limitations to such a right?

2. The Court seems critical of an expansive state-law definition of public accommodation. Does the Court suggest that it is unconstitutional to apply an antidiscrimination law to public accommodations that are not a "place" of business?

3. What level of scrutiny does the Court apply to the state accommodations law, and how does the Court apply it?

4. Is the outcome of this case mandated by *Hurley*, or is *Hurley* distinguishable?

5. How does the Court determine whether or not the Boy Scouts as an organization espouse disapproval of homosexuality? Consider the majority opinion's handling of the evidence on this point carefully.

Boy Scouts of America v. Dale

530 U.S. 640 (2000)

Majority: *Rehnquist* (CJ), O'Connor, Scalia, Kennedy, Thomas

Dissents: *Stevens, Souter*, Ginsburg, Breyer

CHIEF JUSTICE REHNQUIST delivered the opinion of the Court.

Petitioners are the Boy Scouts of America and the Monmouth Council, a division of the Boy Scouts of America (collectively, Boy Scouts). The Boy Scouts is a private, not-for-profit organization engaged in instilling its system of values in young people. The Boy Scouts asserts that homosexual conduct is inconsistent with the values it seeks to instill. Respondent is James Dale, a former Eagle Scout whose adult membership in the Boy Scouts was revoked when the Boy Scouts learned that he is an avowed homosexual and gay rights activist. The New Jersey Supreme Court held that New Jersey's public accommodations law requires that the Boy Scouts admit Dale. This case presents the question whether applying New Jersey's public accommodations law in this way violates the Boy Scouts' First Amendment right of expressive association. We hold that it does.

I

James Dale entered scouting in 1978 at the age of eight by joining Monmouth Council's Cub Scout Pack 142. Dale became a Boy Scout in 1981 and remained a Scout until he turned 18. By all accounts, Dale was an exemplary Scout. In 1988, he achieved the rank of Eagle Scout, one of Scouting's highest honors.

Dale applied for adult membership in the Boy Scouts in 1989. The Boy Scouts approved his application for the position of assistant scoutmaster of Troop 73. Around the same time, Dale left home to attend Rutgers University. After arriving at Rutgers, Dale first acknowledged to himself and others that he is gay. He quickly became involved with, and eventually became the copresident of, the Rutgers University Lesbian/Gay Alliance. In 1990, Dale attended a seminar addressing the psychological and health needs of lesbian and gay teenagers. A newspaper covering the event interviewed Dale about his advocacy of homosexual teenagers' need for gay role models. In early July 1990, the newspaper published the interview and Dale's photograph over a caption identifying him as the copresident of the Lesbian/Gay Alliance.

Later that month, Dale received a letter from Monmouth Council Executive James Kay revoking his adult membership. Dale wrote to Kay requesting the reason for Monmouth Council's decision. Kay responded by letter that the Boy Scouts "specifically forbid membership to homosexuals."

In 1992, Dale filed a complaint against the Boy Scouts in the New Jersey Superior Court. The complaint alleged that the Boy Scouts had violated New Jersey's public accommodations statute and its common law by revoking Dale's membership based solely on his sexual orientation. New Jersey's public accommodations statute prohibits, among other things, discrimination on the basis of sexual orientation in places of public accommodation. N. J. Stat. Ann. §§ 10:5-4 and 10:5-5.

The New Jersey Superior Court's Chancery Division granted summary judgment in favor of the Boy Scouts.... The New Jersey Superior Court's Appellate Division affirmed the dismissal of Dale's common-law claim, but otherwise reversed and remanded for further proceedings.... The New Jersey Supreme Court affirmed the judgment of the Appellate Division. It held that the Boy Scouts was a place of public accommodation subject to the public accommodations law, that the organization was not exempt from the law under any of its express exceptions, and that the Boy Scouts violated the law by revoking Dale's membership based on his avowed homosexuality....

We granted the Boy Scouts' petition for certiorari to determine whether the application of New Jersey's public accommodations law violated the First Amendment.

II

In Roberts v. United States Jaycees, 468 U.S. 609 (1984), we observed that "implicit in the right to engage in activities protected by the First Amendment" is "a corresponding right to associate with others in pursuit of a wide variety of political, social, economic, educational, religious, and cultural ends." This right is crucial in preventing the majority from imposing its views on groups that would rather express other, perhaps unpopular, ideas. Government actions that may unconstitutionally burden this freedom may take many forms, one of which is "intrusion into the internal structure or affairs of an association" like a "regulation that forces the group to accept members it does not desire." 468 U.S. at 623. Forcing a group to accept certain members may impair the ability of the group to express those views, and only those views, that it intends to express. Thus, "[f]reedom of association ... plainly presupposes a freedom not to associate."

The forced inclusion of an unwanted person in a group infringes the group's freedom of expressive association if the presence of that person affects in a significant way the group's ability to advocate public or private viewpoints. But the freedom of expressive association, like many freedoms, is not absolute. We have held that the freedom could be overridden "by regulations adopted to serve compelling state interests, unrelated to the suppression of ideas, that cannot be achieved through means significantly less restrictive of associational freedoms." Roberts, supra, at 623.

To determine whether a group is protected by the First Amendment's expressive associational right, we must determine whether the group engages in "expressive association." The First Amendment's protection of expressive association is not reserved for advocacy groups. But to come within its ambit, a group must engage in some form of expression, whether it be public or private.

Because this is a First Amendment case where the ultimate conclusions of law are virtually inseparable from findings of fact, we are obligated to independently review the factual record to ensure that the state court's judgment does not unlawfully intrude on free expression. The record reveals the following. The Boy Scouts is a private, nonprofit organization. According to its mission statement:

> It is the mission of the Boy Scouts of America to serve others by helping to instill values in young people and, in other ways, to prepare them to make ethical choices over their lifetime in achieving their full potential.

> The values we strive to instill are based on those found in the Scout Oath and Law:

> Scout Oath: "On my honor I will do my best—To do my duty to God and my country—and to obey the Scout Law;—To help other people at all times;—To keep myself physically strong,—mentally awake, and morally straight.

> Scout Law: "A Scout is:—Trustworthy Obedient—Loyal Cheerful—Helpful Thrifty—Friendly Brave—Courteous Clean—Kind Reverent."

Thus, the general mission of the Boy Scouts is clear: "To instill values in young people." The Boy Scouts seeks to instill these values by having its adult leaders spend time with the youth members, instructing and engaging them in activities like camping, archery, and fishing. During the time spent with the youth members, the scoutmasters and assistant scoutmasters inculcate them with the Boy Scouts' values—both expressly and by example. It seems indisputable that an association that seeks to transmit such a system of values engages in expressive activity....

The values the Boy Scouts seeks to instill are "based on" those listed in the Scout Oath and Law. The Boy Scouts explains that the Scout Oath and Law provide "a positive moral code for living; they are a list of 'do's' rather than 'don'ts.'" Brief for Petitioners 3. The Boy Scouts asserts that homosexual conduct is inconsistent with the values embodied in the Scout Oath and Law, particularly with the values represented by the terms "morally straight" and "clean."

Obviously, the Scout Oath and Law do not expressly mention sexuality or sexual orientation. And the terms "morally straight" and "clean" are by no means self-defining. Different people would attribute to those terms very different meanings. For example, some people may believe that engaging in homosexual conduct is not at odds with being "morally straight" and "clean." And others may believe that engaging in homosexual conduct is contrary to being "morally straight" and "clean." The Boy Scouts says it falls within the latter category.

The New Jersey Supreme Court analyzed the Boy Scouts' beliefs and found that the "exclusion of members solely on the basis of their sexual orientation is inconsistent with Boy Scouts' commitment to a diverse and 'representative' membership ... [and] contradicts Boy Scouts' overarching objective to reach 'all eligible youth.'" The court concluded that the exclusion of members like Dale "appears antithetical to the organization's goals and philosophy." But our cases reject this sort of inquiry; it is not the role of the courts to reject a group's expressed values because they disagree with those values or find them internally inconsistent.

The Boy Scouts asserts that it "teaches that homosexual conduct is not morally straight," Brief for Petitioners 39, and that it does "not want to promote homosexual conduct as a legitimate form of behavior," Reply Brief for Petitioners 5. We accept the Boy Scouts' assertion. We need not inquire further to determine the nature of the Boy Scouts' expression with respect to homosexuality. But because the record before us contains written evidence of the Boy Scouts' viewpoint, we look to it as instructive, if only on the question of the sincerity of the professed beliefs.

[The opinion goes on to summarize various "position statements" of the Boy Scouts' Executive Committee, expressing disapproval of homosexuality.] We cannot doubt that the Boy Scouts sincerely holds this view.

We must then determine whether Dale's presence as an assistant scoutmaster would significantly burden the Boy Scouts' desire to not "promote homosexual conduct as a legitimate form of behavior." Reply Brief for Petitioners 5. As we give deference to an association's assertions regarding the nature of its expression, we must also give deference to an association's view of what would impair its expression. That is not to say that an expressive association can erect a shield against antidiscrimination laws simply by asserting that mere acceptance of a member from a particular group would impair its message. But here Dale, by his own admission, is one of a group of gay Scouts who have "become leaders in their community and are open and honest about their sexual orientation." Dale was the copresident of a gay and lesbian organization at college and remains a gay rights activist. Dale's presence in the Boy Scouts would, at the very least, force the organization to send a message, both to the youth members and the world, that the Boy Scouts accepts homosexual conduct as a legitimate form of behavior.

Hurley is illustrative on this point. . . . As the presence of GLIB in Boston's St. Patrick's Day parade would have interfered with the parade organizers' choice not to propound a particular point of view, the presence of Dale as an assistant scoutmaster would just as surely interfere with the Boy Scout's choice not to propound a point of view contrary to its beliefs.

. . . . [A]ssociations do not have to associate for the "purpose" of disseminating a certain message in order to be entitled to the protections of the First Amendment. An association must merely engage in expressive activity that could be impaired in order to be entitled to protection. For example, the purpose of the St. Patrick's Day parade in Hurley was not to espouse any views about sexual orientation, but we held that the parade organizers had a right to exclude certain participants nonetheless. . . .

Having determined that the Boy Scouts is an expressive association and that the forced inclusion of Dale would significantly affect its expression, we inquire whether the application of New Jersey's public accommodations law to require that the Boy Scouts accept Dale as an assistant scoutmaster runs afoul of the Scouts' freedom of expressive association. We conclude that it does.

State public accommodations laws were originally enacted to prevent discrimination in traditional places of public accommodation—like inns and trains. Over time, the public accommodations laws have expanded to cover more places. New Jersey's statutory definition of "'[a] place of public accommodation'" is extremely broad. The term is said to "include, but not be limited to," a list of over 50 types of places. Many on the list are what one would expect to be places where the public is invited. For example, the statute includes as places of public accommodation taverns, restaurants, retail shops, and public libraries. But the statute also includes places that often may not carry with them open invitations to the public, like summer camps and roof gardens. In this case, the New

Jersey Supreme Court went a step further and applied its public accommodations law to a private entity without even attempting to tie the term "place" to a physical location. As the definition of "public accommodation" has expanded from clearly commercial entities, such as restaurants, bars, and hotels, to membership organizations such as the Boy Scouts, the potential for conflict between state public accommodations laws and the First Amendment rights of organizations has increased.

We recognized in cases such as Roberts ... that States have a compelling interest in eliminating discrimination against women in public accommodations. But in each of these cases we went on to conclude that the enforcement of these statutes would not materially interfere with the ideas that the organization sought to express.... [A]fter finding a compelling state interest, the Court went on to examine whether or not the application of the state law would impose any "serious burden" on the organization's rights of expressive association. So in these cases, the associational interest in freedom of expression has been set on one side of the scale, and the State's interest on the other.

Dale contends that we should apply the intermediate standard of review enunciated in United States v. O'Brien, 391 U.S. 367 (1968), to evaluate the competing interests. There the Court enunciated a four-part test for review of a governmental regulation that has only an incidental effect on protected speech — in that case the symbolic burning of a draft card. A law prohibiting the destruction of draft cards only incidentally affects the free speech rights of those who happen to use a violation of that law as a symbol of protest. But New Jersey's public accommodations law directly and immediately affects associational rights, in this case associational rights that enjoy First Amendment protection. Thus, O'Brien is inapplicable.

In Hurley, we applied traditional First Amendment analysis to hold that the application of the Massachusetts public accommodations law to a parade violated the First Amendment rights of the parade organizers. Although we did not explicitly deem the parade in Hurley an expressive association, the analysis we applied there is similar to the analysis we apply here. We have already concluded that a state requirement that the Boy Scouts retain Dale as an assistant scoutmaster would significantly burden the organization's right to oppose or disfavor homosexual conduct. The state interests embodied in New Jersey's public accommodations law do not justify such a severe intrusion on the Boy Scouts' rights to freedom of expressive association. That being the case, we hold that the First Amendment prohibits the State from imposing such a requirement through the application of its public accommodations law.

.... "While the law is free to promote all sorts of conduct in place of harmful behavior, it is not free to interfere with speech for no better reason than promoting an approved message or discouraging a disfavored one, however enlightened either purpose may strike the government." Hurley, 515 U.S. at 579.

The judgment of the New Jersey Supreme Court is reversed, and the cause remanded for further proceedings not inconsistent with this opinion.

JUSTICE STEVENS, with whom JUSTICE SOUTER, JUSTICE GINSBURG and JUSTICE BREYER join, dissenting.

New Jersey "prides itself on judging each individual by his or her merits" and on being "in the vanguard in the fight to eradicate the cancer of unlawful discrimination of all types from our society." Peper v. Princeton Univ. Bd. of Trustees, 77 N.J. 55, 80, 389 A.2d 465, 478 (1978). Since 1945, it has had a law against discrimination. The law broadly protects the opportunity of all persons to obtain the advantages and privileges "of any place of public accommodation." N. J. Stat. Ann. §10:5-4. The New Jersey Supreme

Court's construction of the statutory definition of a "place of public accommodation" has given its statute a more expansive coverage than most similar state statutes. And as amended in 1991, the law prohibits discrimination on the basis of nine different traits including an individual's "sexual orientation." The question in this case is whether that expansive construction trenches on the federal constitutional rights of the Boy Scouts of America (BSA).

Because every state law prohibiting discrimination is designed to replace prejudice with principle, Justice Brandeis' comment on the States' right to experiment with "things social" is directly applicable to this case.

> To stay experimentation in things social and economic is a grave responsibility. Denial of the right to experiment may be fraught with serious consequences to the Nation. It is one of the happy incidents of the federal system that a single courageous State may, if its citizens choose, serve as a laboratory; and try novel social and economic experiments without risk to the rest of the country. This Court has the power to prevent an experiment. We may strike down the statute which embodies it on the ground that, in our opinion, the measure is arbitrary, capricious or unreasonable. We have power to do this, because the due process clause has been held by the Court applicable to matters of substantive law as well as to matters of procedure. But in the exercise of this high power, we must be ever on our guard, lest we erect our prejudices into legal principles. If we would guide by the light of reason, we must let our minds be bold. New State Ice Co. v. Liebmann, 285 U.S. 262 (1932) (dissenting opinion).

In its "exercise of this high power" today, the Court does not accord this "courageous State" the respect that is its due.

... New Jersey's law.... does not "impose any serious burdens" on BSA's "collective effort on behalf of [its] shared goals," Roberts v. United States Jaycees, 468 U.S. 609, 622 (1984), nor does it force BSA to communicate any message that it does not wish to endorse. New Jersey's law, therefore, abridges no constitutional right of the Boy Scouts.

James Dale joined BSA as a Cub Scout in 1978, when he was eight years old. Three years later he became a Boy Scout, and he remained a member until his 18th birthday. Along the way, he earned 25 merit badges, was admitted into the prestigious Order of the Arrow, and was awarded the rank of Eagle Scout—an honor given to only three percent of all Scouts. In 1989, BSA approved his application to be an Assistant Scoutmaster.

On July 19, 1990, after more than 12 years of active and honored participation, the Boys Scouts sent Dale a letter advising him of the revocation of his membership. The letter stated that membership in BSA "is a privilege" that may be denied "whenever there is a concern that an individual may not meet the high standards of membership which the BSA seeks to provide for American youth." Expressing surprise at his sudden expulsion, Dale sent a letter requesting an explanation of the decision. In response, BSA sent him a second letter stating that the grounds for the decision "are the standards for leadership established by the Boy Scouts of America, which specifically forbid membership to homosexuals." At that time, no such standard had been publicly expressed by BSA.

In this case, Boy Scouts of America contends that it teaches the young boys who are Scouts that homosexuality is immoral. Consequently, it argues, it would violate its right to associate to force it to admit homosexuals as members, as doing so would be at odds with its own shared goals and values. This contention, quite plainly, requires us to look at what, exactly, are the values that BSA actually teaches.

BSA's mission statement reads as follows: "It is the mission of the Boy Scouts of America to serve others by helping to instill values in young people and, in other ways, to prepare them to make ethical choices over their lifetime in achieving their full potential." Its federal charter declares its purpose is "to promote, through organization, and cooperation with other agencies, the ability of boys to do things for themselves and others, to train them in scoutcraft, and to teach them patriotism, courage, self-reliance, and kindred values, using the methods which were in common use by Boy Scouts on June 15, 1916." 36 U.S.C. § 23. BSA describes itself as having a "representative membership," which it defines as "boy membership [that] reflects proportionately the characteristics of the boy population of its service area." In particular, the group emphasizes that "neither the charter nor the bylaws of the Boy Scouts of America permits the exclusion of any boy.... To meet these responsibilities we have made a commitment that our membership shall be representative of *all* the population in every community, district, and council" (emphasis in original)....

It is plain as the light of day that neither one of these principles—"morally straight" and "clean"—says the slightest thing about homosexuality. Indeed, neither term in the Boy Scouts' Law and Oath expresses any position whatsoever on sexual matters.

BSA's published guidance on that topic underscores this point. Scouts, for example, are directed to receive their sex education at home or in school, but not from the organization: "Your parents or guardian or a sex education teacher should give you the facts about sex that you must know." Boy Scout Handbook (1992) (reprinted in App. 211). To be sure, Scouts are not forbidden from asking their Scoutmaster about issues of a sexual nature, but Scoutmasters are, literally, the last person Scouts are encouraged to ask: "If you have questions about growing up, about relationships, sex, or making good decisions, ask. Talk with your parents, religious leaders, teachers, or Scoutmaster." Moreover, Scoutmasters are specifically directed to steer curious adolescents to other sources of information[.]

[The dissent reviewed the factual record, including the BSA policy statements relied on by the majority.] It is clear, then, that nothing in these policy statements supports BSA's claim. The only policy written before the revocation of Dale's membership was an equivocal, undisclosed statement that evidences no connection between the group's discriminatory intentions and its expressive interests. The later policies demonstrate a brief—though ultimately abandoned—attempt to tie BSA's exclusion to its expression, but other than a single sentence, BSA fails to show that it ever taught Scouts that homosexuality is not "morally straight" or "clean," or that such a view was part of the group's collective efforts to foster a belief. Furthermore, BSA's policy statements fail to establish any clear, consistent, and unequivocal position on homosexuality. Nor did BSA have any reason to think Dale's sexual *conduct*, as opposed to his orientation, was contrary to the group's values....

BSA's claim finds no support in our cases. We have recognized "a right to associate for the purpose of engaging in those activities protected by the First Amendment—speech, assembly, petition for the redress of grievances, and the exercise of religion." Roberts, 468 U.S. at 618. And we have acknowledged that "when the State interferes with individuals' selection of those with whom they wish to join in a common endeavor, freedom of association ... may be implicated." But "the right to associate for expressive purposes is not ... absolute"; rather, "the nature and degree of constitutional protection afforded freedom of association may vary depending on the extent to which ... the constitutionally protected liberty is at stake in a given case." 468 U.S. at 623, 618. Indeed, the right to associate does not mean "that in every setting in which individuals exercise some discrimination in choosing associates, their selective process of inclusion and exclusion is protected by the

Constitution." For example, we have routinely and easily rejected assertions of this right by expressive organizations with discriminatory membership policies, such as private schools, law firms, and labor organizations. In fact, until today, we have never once found a claimed right to associate in the selection of members to prevail in the face of a State's antidiscrimination law. To the contrary, we have squarely held that a State's antidiscrimination law does not violate a group's right to associate simply because the law conflicts with that group's exclusionary membership policy....

Several principles are made perfectly clear by Jaycees and Rotary Club. First, to prevail on a claim of expressive association in the face of a State's antidiscrimination law, it is not enough simply to engage in *some kind* of expressive activity. Both the Jaycees and the Rotary Club engaged in expressive activity protected by the First Amendment, yet that fact was not dispositive. Second, it is not enough to adopt an openly avowed exclusionary membership policy. Both the Jaycees and the Rotary Club did that as well. Third, it is not sufficient merely to articulate *some* connection between the group's expressive activities and its exclusionary policy. The Rotary Club, for example, justified its male-only membership policy by pointing to the "aspect of fellowship ... that is enjoyed by the [exclusively] male membership" and by claiming that only with an exclusively male membership could it "operate effectively" in foreign countries. Rotary Club, 481 U.S. at 541.

Rather, in Jaycees, we asked whether Minnesota's Human Rights Law requiring the admission of women "imposed any serious burdens" on the group's "collective effort on behalf of [its] shared goals."... The relevant question is whether the mere inclusion of the person at issue would "impose any serious burden," "affect in any significant way," or be "a substantial restraint upon" the organization's "shared goals," "basic goals," or "collective effort to foster beliefs." Accordingly, it is necessary to examine what, exactly, are BSA's shared goals and the degree to which its expressive activities would be burdened, affected, or restrained by including homosexuals.

The evidence before this Court makes it exceptionally clear that BSA has, at most, simply adopted an exclusionary membership policy and has no shared goal of disapproving of homosexuality. BSA's mission statement and federal charter say nothing on the matter; its official membership policy is silent; its Scout Oath and Law—and accompanying definitions—are devoid of any view on the topic; its guidance for Scouts and Scoutmasters on sexuality declare that such matters are "not construed to be Scouting's proper area," but are the province of a Scout's parents and pastor; and BSA's posture respecting religion tolerates a wide variety of views on the issue of homosexuality. Moreover, there is simply no evidence that BSA otherwise teaches anything in this area, or that it instructs Scouts on matters involving homosexuality in ways not conveyed in the Boy Scout or Scoutmaster Handbooks. In short, Boy Scouts of America is simply silent on homosexuality. There is no shared goal or collective effort to foster a belief about homosexuality at all—let alone one that is significantly burdened by admitting homosexuals.... [T]here is no evidence here that BSA's policy was necessary to—or even a part of—BSA's expressive activities or was ever taught to Scouts.

Equally important is BSA's failure to adopt any clear position on homosexuality. BSA's temporary, though ultimately abandoned, view that homosexuality is incompatible with being "morally straight" and "clean" is a far cry from the clear, unequivocal statement necessary to prevail on its claim. Despite the solitary sentences in the 1991 and 1992 policies, the group continued to disclaim any single religious or moral position as a general matter and actively eschewed teaching any lesson on sexuality.... As noted earlier, nothing in our cases suggests that a group can prevail on a right to expressive association if it, effectively, speaks out of both sides of its mouth. A State's antidiscrimination law does not impose a "serious burden" or a "substantial restraint" upon the group's "shared goals" if the group itself is unable to identify its own stance with any clarity.

The majority pretermits this entire analysis. It finds that BSA in fact "teaches that homosexual conduct is not morally straight." This conclusion, remarkably, rests entirely on statements in BSA's briefs. Moreover, the majority insists that we must "give deference to an association's assertions regarding the nature of its expression" and "we must also give deference to an association's view of what would impair its expression." So long as the record "contains written evidence" to support a group's bare assertion, "we need not inquire further." Once the organization "asserts" that it engages in particular expression, "we cannot doubt" the truth of that assertion.

This is an astounding view of the law. I am unaware of any previous instance in which our analysis of the scope of a constitutional right was determined by looking at what a litigant asserts in his or her brief and inquiring no further. It is even more astonishing in the First Amendment area, because, as the majority itself acknowledges, "we are obligated to independently review the factual record." It is an odd form of independent review that consists of deferring entirely to whatever a litigant claims....

Even if BSA's right to associate argument fails, it nonetheless might have a First Amendment right to refrain from including debate and dialogue about homosexuality as part of its mission to instill values in Scouts.... "One important manifestation of the principle of free speech is that one who chooses to speak may also decide 'what not to say.'" Hurley, 515 U.S. at 573....

BSA has not contended, nor does the record support, that Dale had ever advocated a view on homosexuality to his troop before his membership was revoked.... Dale's inclusion in the Boy Scouts is nothing like the case in Hurley. His participation sends no cognizable message to the Scouts or to the world. Unlike GLIB, Dale did not carry a banner or a sign; he did not distribute any fact sheet; and he expressed no intent to send any message.... [I]t is not likely that BSA would be understood to send any message, either to Scouts or to the world, simply by admitting someone as a member. Over the years, BSA has generously welcomed over 87 million young Americans into its ranks. In 1992 over one million adults were active BSA members. The notion that an organization of that size and enormous prestige implicitly endorses the views that each of those adults may express in a non-Scouting context is simply mind boggling. Indeed, in this case there is no evidence that the young Scouts in Dale's troop, or members of their families, were even aware of his sexual orientation, either before or after his public statements at Rutgers University. It is equally farfetched to assert that Dale's open declaration of his homosexuality, reported in a local newspaper, will effectively force BSA to send a message to anyone simply because it allows Dale to be an Assistant Scoutmaster. For an Olympic gold medal winner or a Wimbledon tennis champion, being "openly gay" perhaps communicates a message— for example, that openness about one's sexual orientation is more virtuous than concealment; that a homosexual person can be a capable and virtuous person who should be judged like anyone else; and that homosexuality is not immoral—but it certainly does not follow that they necessarily send a message on behalf of the organizations that sponsor the activities in which they excel.... Surely the organizations are not forced by antidiscrimination laws to take any position on the legitimacy of any individual's private beliefs or private conduct.

.... [Anti-homosexual] prejudices are still prevalent and that they have caused serious and tangible harm to countless members of the class New Jersey seeks to protect are established matters of fact that neither the Boy Scouts nor the Court disputes. That harm can only be aggravated by the creation of a constitutional shield for a policy that is itself the product of a habitual way of thinking about strangers. As Justice Brandeis so wisely advised, "we must be ever on our guard, lest we erect our prejudices into legal principles."

If we would guide by the light of reason, we must let our minds be bold. I respectfully dissent.

___

Review Questions and Explanations: *Boy Scouts of America v. Dale*

1. The majority and dissent disagree over how closely to scrutinize BSA's claim that its organization espouses an anti-homosexual message. Is the disagreement over how to interpret particular ambiguous facts, or about how to approach factfinding more broadly? What does the dissent mean when it says: "It is an odd form of independent review that consists of deferring entirely to whatever a litigant claims"?

2. The majority says that in expressive association cases, "the associational interest in freedom of expression has been set on one side of the scale, and the State's interest on the other." Doesn't that require a careful look at how important it is to BSA in fact to express a message against homosexuality?

3. How relevant is it that, as the dissent argues, Dale himself was not using his position as a scoutmaster to make statements about homosexuality—in contrast to GLIB, which wanted to join the parade in order to engage in expressive activity?

___

Recap: *Hurley* and *Dale*

1. Try to articulate in a few sentences the prevailing doctrine of expressive association, based on *Hurley* and *Dale*.

2. *Hurley* was a unanimous decision, joined by all four of the *Dale* dissenters. Do you think this is explained by a evolution of opinions of those four justices in the five intervening years, by some factual and doctrinal grounds to distinguish the two cases, or by what might be seen as the compelling human side of Dale's case?

3. Assuming that a neo-Nazi party or the Klan would enforce a policy to exclude, for instance Black or Jewish members, such an exclusionary policy may strike one as far less troublesome than the exclusion of GLIB from the St. Patrick's Day parade in *Hurley* or the exclusion of Dale from the BSA in *Dale*. If that characterizes your view of things, can you explain why you hold that view? Is it that some organizations are more amorphous in their expressive premises than others? Or (a related idea) that once an organization holds itself out as broadly inclusive, it somehow waives its right (at least to a degree) to be selectively exclusive—or, more pointedly, to practice invidious discrimination?

___

Exercise: Freedom of Association

You are a law clerk to a federal district judge who is considering the case of *Rollins v. American Revolutionary Heritage Society*. Gerilyn Rollins is President of the Queens, New York chapter of the American Revolutionary Heritage Society ("ARHS"). The record presented on cross-motions for summary judgment establishes the following facts.

ARHS is a national organization with over 100,000 members nationwide, organized into 250 local chapters. It is "dedicated to promoting patriotism and preserving American history and values." The organization engages in public education and charitable activities. Membership in the organization is open to anyone "who is able to prove himself or herself an authentic American Patriot," which the organization's pre-2011 bylaws defined as "having lineal descent from a member of the Continental Army or state militia who fought for American independence in the American Revolution."

Until 2008, all members of ARHS were white. That year, six African Americans were admitted into the Queens, New York chapter of ARHS after furnishing proof that they were directly descended from among the 5,000 black soldiers who fought on the American side in the Revolutionary War. One of these members, Gerilyn Rollins, was elected chapter president in 2010.

In 2011, the ARHS banned representatives from the Queens chapter from marching in the ARHS contingent of the Fourth of July parade down New York City's Fifth Avenue. Although the parade is sponsored by the City, the City takes no responsibility for participation decisions of groups that take part in the march. In 2011, the national ARHS adopted new bylaws amending the definition of "authentic American patriot" to mean "any white person who can prove lineal descent … [etc.]" Based on this, the ARHS "decertified" the Queens chapter and no longer recognizes any of its members as members of the national ARHS organization. ARHS, which has long been associated with conservative political positions, says in its briefs to the court that "ARHS has always maintained that the success of America is due to the talents and efforts of white people who first settled North America and who fought the Revolution, as well as their descendents."

Rollins and the 18 black and white members of the Queens chapter have sued ARHS seeking injunctive relief restoring them to ARHS membership and directing that they be allowed to march in the ARHS contingent in future July 4th parades.

Draft or outline a "bench memo" proposing how the judge should resolve this case, in light of *Hurley* and *Dale*.

---

2. Press and Petition

Freedom of the press is integral to the First Amendment, but has not generated a significant body of doctrine separate from free speech case law more generally. A handful of cases deal with special problems relating to the press. For example, "the press" is the usual beneficiary of the doctrine that a prior restraint on speech (blocking the publication of allegedly harmful speech) is presumptively invalid. *See Near v. Minnesota*, 283 U.S. 697 (1931); *New York Times Co v. United States*, 403 U.S. 713 (1971). Case authority supporting a "journalist's privilege" to decline to reveal a news source may also derive, at least in part, from freedom of the press. *See Branzburg v. Hayes*, 408 U.S. 665 (1972) (rejecting a general constitutional journalist's privilege, but leaving open possibility that such a privilege could be found in particular cases). We have also seen cases raising "special concern" about abridgment of press freedom coming from regulations not necessarily aimed at the press. *See, e.g., Citizens United* (expressing concern about *Austin*'s affect on "media corporations"). Generally speaking, however, the press is not given any particular privileged position in First Amendment doctrine.[5]

The right to "petition the government for a redress of grievances" undoubtedly folds into freedom of speech in most situations. Indeed, the Court has stated that "Petitions are a form of expression, and [plaintiffs] who invoke the Petition Clause in most cases could invoke as well the Speech Clause of the First Amendment." *Borough of Duryea, Pennsylvania v. Guarnieri*, 131 S. Ct. 2488 (2011). Some cases have stated that "the right of access to courts for redress of wrongs is an aspect of the First Amendment right to petition the government." *Sure-Tan, Inc. v. NLRB*, 467 U.S. 883, 896–897 (1984). Justice Scalia has argued that it only applies to petitions to the executive and legislative branches. *See Guarnieri*, 131 S. Ct. at 2503 (Scalia, J., dissenting in part).

---

5. Not all scholars agree that Press Clause should simply be subsumed into the free speech clause, however. Sonja West, for example, has argued that while the Speech Clause protects rights of expression, publication, and dissemination, the Press Clause could function separately to safeguard journalists in the act of newsgathering. Such constitutional protections could include rights of access to government property, information on meetings, or legal protections from government subpoenas or search warrants. Sonja R. West, *Awakening the Press Clause*, 58 U.C.L.A. L. Rev. 1025 (2011).

Chapter 10

Religious Freedom

A. Overview

We now move from freedom of speech to the First Amendment's guarantee of freedom of religion. The religion clauses of the First Amendment read as follows:

"Congress shall make no law respecting an establishment of religion, or prohibiting the free exercise thereof."

These clauses operate to protect religious freedom in two ways. The Establishment Clause prohibits the official establishment of religion by government. The Free Exercise clause bars laws that unduly burden religious practice. As with "the freedom of speech," however, these elegant phrases help frame the constitutional questions in particular cases, but can do little on their own to resolve them. The Court, as in other areas of constitutional law, has thus necessarily built up doctrine in this area, using precedent, history, principle and policy considerations to evaluate the disputes that arise under the religion clauses.

B. Establishment Clause

The concern with government establishing religion was intended, in the broadest sense, to depart from the practice of European monarchs practice of sanctioning one "true" religion and permitting various degrees of persecution for the rest. Some of the ideas embodied in the Establishment Clause are developed in James Madison's famous "Memorial and Remonstrance Against Religious Assessments" presented to the Virginia state assembly. (That document is discussed in *Everson v. Board of Education* and is reprinted below as an appendix to the Court's opinion in that case.) In modern First Amendment doctrine, the Establishment Clause has been applied to more incremental instances of official government involvement with religion. In doing so, the Court has relied on array of arguments—including Madison's Memorial and Remonstrance, and the ideas contained within it. As you will see in the following cases, determining just what constitutes an unconstitutional establishment of religion has been difficult for the Court. It is an question that, at least at the margins, has eluded clear answers.

1. Foundational Doctrine: State Support for Religious Institutions

---

Guided Reading Questions: *Everson v. Board of Education*

1. Identify precisely the nature of the government involvement with religion in this case.

2. What is the basis of the ruling upholding the New Jersey law?

Everson v. Board of Education

330 U.S. 1 (1947)

Majority: *Black*, Vinson (CJ), Reed, Douglas, Murphy

Dissents: *Jackson*, Frankfurter, *Rutledge*, Burton

MR. JUSTICE BLACK delivered the opinion of the Court.

A New Jersey statute authorizes its local school districts to make rules and contracts for the transportation of children to and from schools. The appellee, a township board of education, acting pursuant to this statute, authorized reimbursement to parents of money expended by them for the bus transportation of their children on regular busses operated by the public transportation system. Part of this money was for the payment of transportation of some children in the community to Catholic parochial schools. These church schools give their students, in addition to secular education, regular religious instruction conforming to the religious tenets and modes of worship of the Catholic Faith. The superintendent of these schools is a Catholic priest.

The appellant, in his capacity as a district taxpayer, filed suit in a state court challenging the right of the Board to reimburse parents of parochial school students. He contended that the statute and the resolution passed pursuant to it violated both the State and the Federal Constitutions. That court held that the legislature was without power to authorize such payment under the state constitution. 132 N. J. L. 98, 39 A. 2d 75. The New Jersey Court of Errors and Appeals reversed....

The New Jersey statute is challenged as a "law respecting an establishment of religion." The First Amendment, as made applicable to the states by the Fourteenth, Murdock v. Pennsylvania, 319 U.S. 105, commands that a state "shall make no law respecting an establishment of religion, or prohibiting the free exercise thereof...." These words of the First Amendment reflected in the minds of early Americans a vivid mental picture of conditions and practices which they fervently wished to stamp out in order to preserve liberty for themselves and for their posterity. Doubtless their goal has not been entirely reached; but so far has the Nation moved toward it that the expression "law respecting an establishment of religion," probably does not so vividly remind present-day Americans of the evils, fears, and political problems that caused that expression to be written into our Bill of Rights. Whether this New Jersey law is one respecting an "establishment of religion" requires an understanding of the meaning of that language, particularly with respect to the imposition of taxes....

The "establishment of religion" clause of the First Amendment means at least this: Neither a state nor the Federal Government can set up a church. Neither can pass laws which aid one religion, aid all religions, or prefer one religion over another. Neither can force nor influence a person to go to or to remain away from church against his will or force him to profess a belief or disbelief in any religion. No person can be punished for entertaining or professing religious beliefs or disbeliefs, for church attendance or non-attendance. No tax in any amount, large or small, can be levied to support any religious activities or institutions, whatever they may be called, or whatever form they may adopt to teach or practice religion. Neither a state nor the Federal Government can, openly or secretly, participate in the affairs of any religious organizations or groups and vice versa. In the words of Jefferson, the clause against establishment of religion by law was intended to erect "a wall of separation between church and State." Reynolds v. United States, supra at 164.

We must consider the New Jersey statute in accordance with the foregoing limitations imposed by the First Amendment. But we must not strike that state statute down if it is within the State's constitutional power even though it approaches the verge of that power. New Jersey cannot consistently with the "establishment of religion" clause of the First Amendment contribute tax-raised funds to the support of an institution which teaches the tenets and faith of any church. On the other hand, other language of the amendment commands that New Jersey cannot hamper its citizens in the free exercise of their own religion.... While we do not mean to intimate that a state could not provide transportation only to children attending public schools, we must be careful, in protecting the citizens of New Jersey against state-established churches, to be sure that we do not inadvertently prohibit New Jersey from extending its general state law benefits to all its citizens without regard to their religious belief.

Measured by these standards, we cannot say that the First Amendment prohibits New Jersey from spending tax-raised funds to pay the bus fares of parochial school pupils as a part of a general program under which it pays the fares of pupils attending public and other schools. It is undoubtedly true that children are helped to get to church schools. There is even a possibility that some of the children might not be sent to the church schools if the parents were compelled to pay their children's bus fares out of their own pockets when transportation to a public school would have been paid for by the State. The same possibility exists where the state requires a local transit company to provide reduced fares to school children including those attending parochial schools, or where a municipally owned transportation system undertakes to carry all school children free of charge. Moreover, state-paid policemen, detailed to protect children going to and from church schools from the very real hazards of traffic, would serve much the same purpose and accomplish much the same result as state provisions intended to guarantee free transportation of a kind which the state deems to be best for the school children's welfare. And parents might refuse to risk their children to the serious danger of traffic accidents going to and from parochial schools, the approaches to which were not protected by policemen. Similarly, parents might be reluctant to permit their children to attend schools which the state had cut off from such general government services as ordinary police and fire protection, connections for sewage disposal, public highways and sidewalks. Of course, cutting off church schools from these services, so separate and so indisputably marked off from the religious function, would make it far more difficult for the schools to operate. But such is obviously not the purpose of the First Amendment. That Amendment requires the state to be a neutral in its relations with groups of religious believers and non-believers; it does not require the state to be their adversary. State power is no more to be used so as to handicap religions than it is to favor them....

The First Amendment has erected a wall between church and state. That wall must be kept high and impregnable. We could not approve the slightest breach. New Jersey has not breached it here. Affirmed.

MR. JUSTICE JACKSON, dissenting.

.... The Township of Ewing is not furnishing transportation to the children in any form; it is not operating school busses itself or contracting for their operation; and it is not performing any public service of any kind with this taxpayer's money. All school children are left to ride as ordinary paying passengers on the regular busses operated by the public transportation system. What the Township does, and what the taxpayer complains of, is at stated intervals to reimburse parents for the fares paid, provided the children attend either public schools or Catholic Church schools. This expenditure of tax funds has no possible effect on the child's safety or expedition in transit. As passengers on the public busses they travel as fast and no faster, and are as safe and no safer, since their parents are reimbursed as before.

In addition to thus assuming a type of service that does not exist, the Court also insists that we must close our eyes to a discrimination which does exist. The resolution which authorizes disbursement of this taxpayer's money limits reimbursement to those who attend public schools and Catholic schools. That is the way the Act is applied to this taxpayer.

The New Jersey Act in question makes the character of the school, not the needs of the children, determine the eligibility of parents to reimbursement. The Act permits payment for transportation to parochial schools or public schools but prohibits it to private schools operated in whole or in part for profit. Children often are sent to private schools because their parents feel that they require more individual instruction than public schools can provide, or because they are backward or defective and need special attention. If all children of the state were objects of impartial solicitude, no reason is obvious for denying transportation reimbursement to students of this class, for these often are as needy and as worthy as those who go to public or parochial schools. Refusal to reimburse those who attend such schools is understandable only in the light of a purpose to aid the schools, because the state might well abstain from aiding a profit-making private enterprise. Thus, under the Act and resolution brought to us by this case, children are classified according to the schools they attend and are to be aided if they attend the public schools or private Catholic schools, and they are not allowed to be aided if they attend private secular schools or private religious schools of other faiths.

If we are to decide this case on the facts before us, our question is simply this: Is it constitutional to tax this complainant to pay the cost of carrying pupils to Church schools of one specified denomination?

.... [W]e cannot have it both ways. Religious teaching cannot be a private affair when the state seeks to impose regulations which infringe on it indirectly, and a public affair when it comes to taxing citizens of one faith to aid another, or those of no faith to aid all. If these principles seem harsh in prohibiting aid to Catholic education, it must not be forgotten that it is the same Constitution that alone assures Catholics the right to maintain these schools at all when predominant local sentiment would forbid them. Pierce v. Society of Sisters, 268 U.S. 510. Nor should I think that those who have done so well without this aid would want to see this separation between Church and State broken down. If the state may aid these religious schools, it may therefore regulate them....

MR. JUSTICE FRANKFURTER joins in this opinion.

MR. JUSTICE RUTLEDGE, with whom MR. JUSTICE FRANKFURTER, MR. JUSTICE JACKSON and MR. JUSTICE BURTON agree, dissenting.

.... The [First] Amendment's purpose was.... broader than separating church and state in this narrow sense. It was to create a complete and permanent separation of the spheres of religious activity and civil authority by comprehensively forbidding every form of public aid or support for religion. In proof the Amendment's wording and history unite with this Court's consistent utterances whenever attention has been fixed directly upon the question.

"Religion" appears only once in the Amendment. But the word governs two prohibitions and governs them alike. It does not have two meanings, one narrow to forbid "an establishment" and another, much broader, for securing "the free exercise thereof." ... "Religion" and "establishment" were not used in any formal or technical sense. The prohibition broadly forbids state support, financial or other, of religion in any guise, form or degree. It outlaws all use of public funds for religious purposes.

.... No provision of the Constitution is more closely tied to or given content by its generating history than the religious clause of the First Amendment. It is at once the refined product and the terse summation of that history. The history includes not only Madison's authorship and the proceedings before the First Congress, but also the long and intensive struggle for religious freedom in America, more especially in Virginia, of which the Amendment was the direct culmination. In the documents of the times, particularly of Madison, who was leader in the Virginia struggle before he became the Amendment's sponsor, but also in the writings of Jefferson and others and in the issues which engendered them is to be found irrefutable confirmation of the Amendment's sweeping content.

.... As a member of the [Virginia] General Assembly in 1779 [Madison] threw his full weight behind Jefferson's historic Bill for Establishing Religious Freedom. That bill was a prime phase of Jefferson's broad program of democratic reform undertaken on his return from the Continental Congress in 1776 and submitted for the General Assembly's consideration in 1779 as his proposed revised Virginia code. With Jefferson's departure for Europe in 1784, Madison became the Bill's prime sponsor. Enactment failed in successive legislatures from its introduction in June, 1779, until its adoption in January, 1786. But during all this time the fight for religious freedom moved forward in Virginia on various fronts with growing intensity....

The climax came in the legislative struggle of 1784–1785 over the Assessment Bill. See Supplemental Appendix hereto. This was nothing more nor less than a taxing measure for the support of religion, designed to revive the payment of tithes suspended since 1777. So long as it singled out a particular sect for preference it incurred the active and general hostility of dissentient groups. It was broadened to include them, with the result that some subsided temporarily in their opposition. As altered, the bill gave to each taxpayer the privilege of designating which church should receive his share of the tax. In default of designation the legislature applied it to pious uses. But what is of the utmost significance here, "in its final form the bill left the taxpayer the option of giving his tax to education."

Madison was unyielding at all times, opposing with all his vigor the general and nondiscriminatory as he had the earlier particular and discriminatory assessments proposed. The modified Assessment Bill passed second reading in December, 1784, and was all but enacted. Madison and his followers, however, maneuvered deferment of final consideration until November, 1785. And before the Assembly reconvened in the fall he issued his historic Memorial and Remonstrance.

This is Madison's complete, though not his only, interpretation of religious liberty. It is a broadside attack upon all forms of "establishment" of religion, both general and particular, nondiscriminatory or selective. Reflecting not only the many legislative conflicts over the Assessment Bill and the Bill for Establishing Religious Freedom but also, for example, the struggles for religious incorporations and the continued maintenance of the glebes, the Remonstrance is at once the most concise and the most accurate statement of the views of the First Amendment's author concerning what is "an establishment of religion." Because it behooves us in the dimming distance of time not to lose sight of what he and his coworkers had in mind when, by a single sweeping stroke of the pen, they forbade an establishment of religion and secured its free exercise, the text of the Remonstrance is appended at the end of this opinion for its wider current reference, together with a copy of the bill against which it was directed.

The Remonstrance, stirring up a storm of popular protest, killed the Assessment Bill. It collapsed in committee shortly before Christmas, 1785. With this, the way was cleared at last for enactment of Jefferson's Bill for Establishing Religious Freedom. Madison promptly drove it through in January of 1786, seven years from the time it was first introduced. This dual victory substantially ended the fight over establishments [in Virginia], settling the issue against them....

APPENDIX.

Memorial and Remonstrance Against Religious Assessments.
To the Honorable the General Assembly of the Commonwealth of Virginia.

We, the subscribers, citizens of the said Commonwealth, having taken into serious consideration, a Bill printed by order of the last Session of General Assembly, entitled "A Bill establishing a provision for Teachers of the Christian Religion," and conceiving that the same, if finally armed with the sanctions of a law, will be a dangerous abuse of power, are bound as faithful members of a free State, to remonstrate against it, and to declare the reasons by which we are determined. We remonstrate against the said Bill,

1. Because we hold it for a fundamental and undeniable truth, "that Religion or the duty which we owe to our Creator and the Manner of discharging it, can be directed only by reason and conviction, not by force or violence."....

2. Because if religion be exempt from the authority of the Society at large, still less can it be subject to that of the Legislative Body....

3. Because, it is proper to take alarm at the first experiment on our liberties....

4. ... If "all men are by nature equally free and independent," all men are to be considered as entering into Society on equal conditions; as relinquishing no more, and therefore retaining no less, one than another, of their natural rights. Above all are they to be considered as retaining an "equal title to the free exercise of Religion according to the dictates of conscience." Whilst we assert for ourselves a freedom to embrace, to profess and to observe the Religion which we believe to be of divine origin, we cannot deny an equal freedom to those whose minds have not yet yielded to the evidence which has convinced us. If this freedom be abused, it is an offence against God, not against man: To God, therefore, not to men, must an account of it be rendered. As the Bill violates equality by subjecting some to peculiar burdens; so it violates the same principle, by granting to others peculiar exemptions.

5. Because the bill implies either that the Civil Magistrate is a competent Judge of Religious truth; or that he may employ Religion as an engine of Civil policy....

6. Because the establishment proposed by the Bill is not requisite for the support of the Christian Religion....

7. Because experience witnesseth that ecclesiastical establishments, instead of maintaining the purity and efficacy of Religion, have had a contrary operation....

8. Because the establishment in question is not necessary for the support of Civil Government....

9. Because the proposed establishment is a departure from that generous policy, which, offering an asylum to the persecuted and oppressed of every Nation and Religion, promised a lustre to our country, and an accession to the number of its citizens. What a melancholy mark is the Bill of sudden degeneracy? Instead of holding forth an asylum to the persecuted, it is itself a signal of persecution. It degrades from the equal rank of Citizens all those whose opinions in Religion do not bend to those of the Legislative authority....

10. Because, it will have a like tendency to banish our Citizens....

11. Because, it will destroy that moderation and harmony which the forbearance of our laws to intermeddle with Religion, has produced amongst its several sects. Torrents of blood have been spilt in the old world, by vain attempts of the secular arm to extinguish Religious discord, by proscribing all difference in Religious opinions. Time has at length revealed the true remedy. Every relaxation of narrow and rigorous policy, wherever it has been tried, has been found to assuage the disease....

15. Because, finally, "the equal right of every citizen to the free exercise of his Religion according to the dictates of conscience" is held by the same tenure with all our other rights....

Review Questions and Explanations: *Everson*

1. Carefully identify the position taken by Justice Black's majority, Justice Jackson's dissent, and Justice Rutledge's dissent. Do the justices disagree about the facts, the law, or both? What does each justice see as the most significant constitutional problem presented in the case?

2. Read the last paragraph of Justice Jackson's opinion carefully. He is making a point about the relationship between the Establishment Clause and the Free Exercise clause. The second paragraph of Justice Rutledge's opinion is doing something similar. You have not yet studied the Free Exercise clause, but try to understand what the justices are concerned about in these paragraphs.

3. Is it necessary to prohibit incremental government aid to religious institutions to maintain a "wall of separation" between church and state? If so, why? Does the word "respecting" in the Establishment Clause invite scrutiny of such incremental steps?

4. Is there a distinction between extending police and fire protection to religious schools and paying transportation costs of students attending such schools? What if, instead, school buses were supplied to all public and parochial schools at taxpayer expense—would that be legally distinguishable from the facts presented in *Everson*? What about reimbursing parents for the costs of school books

(assuming school books were provided free of charge to public school students)? What about reimbursing tuition?

5. What relevance, if any, does Madison's "Remonstrance" have on the question before the Court?

Guided Reading Questions: *Lemon v. Kurtzman*

1. Identify as precisely as you can how the state law operated to support religious schools.

2. What are the elements of the "*Lemon* test"?

3. The "entanglement" prong of the *Lemon* test is itself described in subsequent cases as having three components. Try when reading the case to anticipate what they are.

4. Whether or not you agree with the *Lemon* test as an appropriate standard in Establishment Clause cases, was the test applied correctly to the facts of *Lemon*?

Lemon v. Kurtzman
403 U.S. 602 (1971)

Majority: *Burger* (CJ), Black, Douglas, Harlan, Stewart, Marshall, Blackmun

Concurrence: *Douglas*, Black, Marshall

Partial concurrences, partial dissents: *Brennan*, *White*

MR. CHIEF JUSTICE BURGER delivered the opinion of the Court.

[The case consolidated citizen/taxpayer suits filed in Rhode Island and Pennsylvania claiming that state support for private religious schools violated the religion clauses of the First Amendment. The Rhode Island statute offered payment of up to 15-percent of the annual salary of private elementary school teachers, so long as they taught only secular subjects and were paid less than public school teachers. The statute further required that the average per-pupil expenditure on secular education at the private school receiving funds had to be less than the public school average, that the private school would have to allow its financial records to be audited by the state, and that the subsidized teacher would teach only those subjects offered in the public schools, using teaching materials used in the public schools. Teachers receiving supplements were required to first agree in writing not to teach a course in religion while receiving the supplements. The district court, finding that virtually all the subsidies under this statute went to teachers at Roman Catholic schools, and that the teaching of secular subjects at these schools was an integral part of their religious mission, held the law unconstitutional under the Establishment Clause of the First Amendment.

[The Pennsylvania statute provided for state reimbursement of private elementary and secondary schools for the costs of teachers' salaries, textbooks, and instructional materials in specified secular subjects, but prohibited reimbursement for any course containing religious subject matter. Under the Pennsylvania statute, the participating schools were required to maintain prescribed accounting procedures to identify the cost of secular educational service. Such accounts were subject to state audit, reimbursement was limited to courses presented in the public schools' curricula, and textbooks and instructional materials were subject to approval by the state. The Pennsylvania suit alleged that religious schools were the primary beneficiaries of this law, which therefore violated the Establishment Clause, but the District Court dismissed the suit for failure to state a claim. The Supreme Court heard the cases as a direct appeal from the district court.]

In Everson v. Board of Education, 330 U.S. 1 (1947), this Court upheld a state statute that reimbursed the parents of parochial school children for bus transportation expenses. There MR. JUSTICE BLACK, writing for the majority, suggested that the decision carried to "the verge" of forbidden territory under the Religion Clauses. Candor compels acknowledgment, moreover, that we can only dimly perceive the lines of demarcation in this extraordinarily sensitive area of constitutional law.

The language of the Religion Clauses of the First Amendment is at best opaque, particularly when compared with other portions of the Amendment. Its authors did not simply prohibit the establishment of a state church or a state religion, an area history shows they regarded as very important and fraught with great dangers. Instead they commanded that there should be "no law respecting an establishment of religion." A law may be one "respecting" the forbidden objective while falling short of its total realization. A law "respecting" the proscribed result, that is, the establishment of religion, is not always easily identifiable as one violative of the Clause. A given law might not establish a state religion but nevertheless be one "respecting" that end in the sense of being a step that could lead to such establishment and hence offend the First Amendment.

In the absence of precisely stated constitutional prohibitions, we must draw lines with reference to the three main evils against which the Establishment Clause was intended to afford protection: "sponsorship, financial support, and active involvement of the sovereign in religious activity." Walz v. Tax Commission, 397 U.S. 664, 668 (1970).

Every analysis in this area must begin with consideration of the cumulative criteria developed by the Court over many years. Three such tests may be gleaned from our cases. First, the statute must have a secular legislative purpose; second, its principal or primary effect must be one that neither advances nor inhibits religion; finally, the statute must not foster "an excessive government entanglement with religion." Walz, supra, at 674.

Inquiry into the legislative purposes of the Pennsylvania and Rhode Island statutes affords no basis for a conclusion that the legislative intent was to advance religion. On the contrary, the statutes themselves clearly state that they are intended to enhance the quality of the secular education in all schools covered by the compulsory attendance laws.... A State always has a legitimate concern for maintaining minimum standards in all schools it allows to operate....

The two legislatures, however, have also recognized that church-related elementary and secondary schools have a significant religious mission and that a substantial portion of their activities is religiously oriented. They have therefore sought to create statutory restrictions designed to guarantee the separation between secular and religious educational functions and to ensure that State financial aid supports only the former. All these provisions are precautions taken in candid recognition that these programs approached, even if they did not intrude upon, the forbidden areas under the Religion Clauses. We need not decide whether these legislative precautions restrict the principal or primary effect of the programs to the point where they do not offend the Religion Clauses, for we conclude that the cumulative impact of the entire relationship arising under the statutes in each State involves excessive entanglement between government and religion.

In Walz v. Tax Commission, supra, the Court upheld state tax exemptions for real property owned by religious organizations and used for religious worship. That holding, however, tended to confine rather than enlarge the area of permissible state involvement with religious institutions by calling for close scrutiny of the degree of entanglement involved in the relationship. The objective is to prevent, as far as possible, the intrusion of either into the precincts of the other.

Our prior holdings do not call for total separation between church and state; total separation is not possible in an absolute sense. Some relationship between government and religious organizations is inevitable. Fire inspections, building and zoning regulations, and state requirements under compulsory school-attendance laws are examples of necessary and permissible contacts. Indeed, under the statutory exemption before us in Walz, the State had a continuing burden to ascertain that the exempt property was in fact being used for religious worship....

In order to determine whether the government entanglement with religion is excessive, we must examine the character and purposes of the institutions that are benefited, the nature of the aid that the State provides, and the resulting relationship between the government and the religious authority. MR. JUSTICE HARLAN, in a separate opinion in Walz, supra, echoed the classic warning as to "programs, whose very nature is apt to entangle the state in details of administration...." Id., at 695. Here we find that both statutes foster an impermissible degree of entanglement.

(a) Rhode Island program

.... On the basis of [extensive factual] findings the District Court concluded that the parochial schools constituted "an integral part of the religious mission of the Catholic Church" [and thus].... involve substantial religious activity and purpose.

The substantial religious character of these church-related schools gives rise to entangling church-state relationships of the kind the Religion Clauses sought to avoid. Although the District Court found that concern for religious values did not inevitably or necessarily intrude into the content of secular subjects, the considerable religious activities of these schools led the legislature to provide for careful governmental controls and surveillance by state authorities in order to ensure that state aid supports only secular education.

The dangers and corresponding entanglements are enhanced by the particular form of aid that the Rhode Island Act provides. Our decisions from Everson to Allen have permitted the States to provide church-related schools with secular, neutral, or nonideological services, facilities, or materials. Bus transportation, school lunches, public health services, and secular textbooks supplied in common to all students were not thought to offend the Establishment Clause. We note that the dissenters in Allen seemed chiefly concerned with the pragmatic difficulties involved in ensuring the truly secular content of the textbooks provided at state expense.

In Allen the Court refused to make assumptions, on a meager record, about the religious content of the textbooks that the State would be asked to provide. We cannot, however, refuse here to recognize that teachers have a substantially different ideological character from books. In terms of potential for involving some aspect of faith or morals in secular subjects, a textbook's content is ascertainable, but a teacher's handling of a subject is not. We cannot ignore the danger that a teacher under religious control and discipline poses to the separation of the religious from the purely secular aspects of pre-college education. The conflict of functions inheres in the situation.

In our view the record shows these dangers are present to a substantial degree. The Rhode Island Roman Catholic elementary schools are under the general supervision of the Bishop of Providence and his appointed representative, the Diocesan Superintendent of Schools. In most cases, each individual parish, however, assumes the ultimate financial responsibility for the school, with the parish priest authorizing the allocation of parish funds. With only two exceptions, school principals are nuns appointed either by the Superintendent or the Mother Provincial of the order whose members staff the school. By 1969 lay teachers constituted more than a third of all teachers in the parochial elementary schools, and their number is growing. They are first interviewed by the superintendent's office and then by the school principal. The contracts are signed by the parish priest, and he retains some discretion in negotiating salary levels. Religious authority necessarily pervades the school system.

The schools are governed by the standards set forth in a "Handbook of School Regulations," which has the force of synodal law in the diocese. It emphasizes the role and importance of the teacher in parochial schools: "The prime factor for the success or the failure of the school is the spirit and personality, as well as the professional competency, of the teacher...." The Handbook also states that: "Religious formation is not confined to formal courses; nor is it restricted to a single subject area." Finally, the Handbook advises teachers to stimulate interest in religious vocations and missionary work. Given the mission of the church school, these instructions are consistent and logical.

.... [T]he District Court found that religious values did not necessarily affect the content of the secular instruction. But what has been recounted suggests the potential if not actual hazards of this form of state aid. The teacher is employed by a religious organization, subject to the direction and discipline of religious authorities, and works in a system dedicated to rearing children in a particular faith. These controls are not lessened by the fact that most of the lay teachers are of the Catholic faith. Inevitably some of a teacher's responsibilities hover on the border between secular and religious orientation.

We need not and do not assume that teachers in parochial schools will be guilty of bad faith or any conscious design to evade the limitations imposed by the statute and the First Amendment. We simply recognize that a dedicated religious person, teaching in a school affiliated with his or her faith and operated to inculcate its tenets, will inevitably experience great difficulty in remaining religiously neutral. Doctrines and faith are not inculcated or advanced by neutrals. With the best of intentions such a teacher would find it hard to make a total separation between secular teaching and religious doctrine. What would appear to some to be essential to good citizenship might well for others border on or constitute instruction in religion. Further difficulties are inherent in the combination of religious discipline and the possibility of disagreement between teacher and religious authorities over the meaning of the statutory restrictions.

.... The State must be certain, given the Religion Clauses, that subsidized teachers do not inculcate religion—indeed the State here has undertaken to do so. To ensure that no trespass occurs, the State has therefore carefully conditioned its aid with pervasive restrictions. An eligible recipient must teach only those courses that are offered in the public schools and use only those texts and materials that are found in the public schools. In addition the teacher must not engage in teaching any course in religion.

A comprehensive, discriminating, and continuing state surveillance will inevitably be required to ensure that these restrictions are obeyed and the First Amendment otherwise respected. Unlike a book, a teacher cannot be inspected once so as to determine the extent and intent of his or her personal beliefs and subjective acceptance of the limitations imposed by the First Amendment. These prophylactic contacts will involve excessive and enduring entanglement between state and church.

There is another area of entanglement in the Rhode Island program that gives concern. The statute excludes teachers employed by nonpublic schools whose average per-pupil expenditures on secular education equal or exceed the comparable figures for public schools. In the event that the total expenditures of an otherwise eligible school exceed this norm, the program requires the government to examine the school's records in order to determine how much of the total expenditures is attributable to secular education and how much to religious activity. This kind of state inspection and evaluation of the religious content of a religious organization is fraught with the sort of entanglement that the Constitution forbids. It is a relationship pregnant with dangers of excessive government direction of church schools and hence of churches....

(b) Pennsylvania program

.... [The Pennsylvania statute and the structure of the parochial schools are very similar to those in the Rhode Island case.] The Pennsylvania statute, moreover, has the further defect of providing state financial aid directly to the church-related school. This factor distinguishes both Everson and Allen, for in both those cases the Court was careful to point out that state aid was provided to the student and his parents — not to the church-related school. In Walz v. Tax Commission, supra, at 675, the Court warned ... [that] "a direct money subsidy ... could encompass sustained and detailed administrative relationships for enforcement of statutory or administrative standards[.]" ... [G]overnment grants of a continuing cash subsidy ... have almost always been accompanied by varying measures of control and surveillance....

A broader base of entanglement of yet a different character is presented by the divisive political potential of these state programs. In a community where such a large number of pupils are served by church-related schools, it can be assumed that state assistance will entail considerable political activity. Partisans of parochial schools, understandably concerned with rising costs and sincerely dedicated to both the religious and secular educational missions of their schools, will inevitably champion this cause and promote political action to achieve their goals. Those who oppose state aid, whether for constitutional, religious, or fiscal reasons, will inevitably respond and employ all of the usual political campaign techniques to prevail. Candidates will be forced to declare and voters to choose. It would be unrealistic to ignore the fact that many people confronted with issues of this kind will find their votes aligned with their faith.

Ordinarily political debate and division, however vigorous or even partisan, are normal and healthy manifestations of our democratic system of government, but political division along religious lines was one of the principal evils against which the First Amendment was intended to protect. The potential divisiveness of such conflict is a threat to the normal political process. To have States or communities divide on the issues presented by state aid to parochial schools would tend to confuse and obscure other issues of great urgency.... The history of many countries attests to the hazards of religion's intruding into the political arena or of political power intruding into the legitimate and free exercise of religious belief.

Of course, as the Court noted in Walz, "adherents of particular faiths and individual churches frequently take strong positions on public issues." Walz v. Tax Commission, supra, at 670. We could not expect otherwise, for religious values pervade the fabric of our national life. But in Walz we dealt with a status under state tax laws for the benefit of all religious groups. Here we are confronted with successive and very likely permanent annual appropriations that benefit relatively few religious groups. Political fragmentation and divisiveness on religious lines are thus likely to be intensified.

The potential for political divisiveness related to religious belief and practice is aggravated in these two statutory programs by the need for continuing annual appropriations and the likelihood of larger and larger demands as costs and populations grow....

In Walz it was argued that a tax exemption for places of religious worship would prove to be the first step in an inevitable progression leading to the establishment of state churches and state religion. That claim could not stand up against more than 200 years of virtually universal practice imbedded in our colonial experience and continuing into the present.

The progression argument, however, is more persuasive here. We have no long history of state aid to church-related educational institutions comparable to 200 years of tax exemption for churches. Indeed, the state programs before us today represent something of an innovation.... Nor can we fail to see that in constitutional adjudication some steps, which when taken were thought to approach "the verge," have become the platform for yet further steps. A certain momentum develops in constitutional theory and it can be a "downhill thrust" easily set in motion but difficult to retard or stop. Development by momentum is not invariably bad; indeed, it is the way the common law has grown, but it is a force to be recognized and reckoned with. The dangers are increased by the difficulty of perceiving in advance exactly where the "verge" of the precipice lies. As well as constituting an independent evil against which the Religion Clauses were intended to protect, involvement or entanglement between government and religion serves as a warning signal.

Finally, nothing we have said can be construed to disparage the role of church-related elementary and secondary schools in our national life. Their contribution has been and is enormous....

The merit and benefits of these schools, however, are not the issue before us in these cases.... Under our system the choice has been made that government is to be entirely excluded from the area of religious instruction and churches excluded from the affairs of government. The Constitution decrees that religion must be a private matter for the individual, the family, and the institutions of private choice, and that while some involvement and entanglement are inevitable, lines must be drawn.

The judgment of the Rhode Island District Court in No. 569 and No. 570 is affirmed. The judgment of the Pennsylvania District Court in No. 89 is reversed, and the case is remanded for further proceedings consistent with this opinion.

MR. JUSTICE DOUGLAS, whom MR. JUSTICE BLACK joins, concurring.

.... In Walz v. Tax Commission, 397 U.S. 664, 674, the Court in approving a tax exemption for church property said:

> Determining that the legislative purpose of tax exemption is not aimed at establishing, sponsoring, or supporting religion does not end the inquiry, however. We must also be sure that the end result — the effect — is not an excessive government entanglement with religion.

There is in my view such an entanglement here. The surveillance or supervision of the States needed to police grants involved in these three cases, if performed, puts a public investigator into every classroom and entails a pervasive monitoring of these church agencies by the secular authorities. Yet if that surveillance or supervision does not occur the zeal of religious proselytizers promises to carry the day and make a shambles of the Establishment Clause. Moreover, when taxpayers of many faiths are required to contribute money for the propagation of one faith, the Free Exercise Clause is infringed.

The analysis of the constitutional objections to these two state systems of grants to parochial or sectarian schools must start with the admitted and obvious fact that the raison d'etre of parochial schools is the propagation of a religious faith. They also teach secular subjects; but they came into existence in this country because Protestant groups were perverting the public schools by using them to propagate their faith. The Catholics naturally rebelled. If schools were to be used to propagate a particular creed or religion, then Catholic ideals should also be served. Hence the advent of parochial schools....

Public financial support of parochial schools puts those schools under disabilities with which they were not previously burdened.... [O]nce one of the States finances a private school, it is duty-bound to make certain that the school stays within secular bounds and does not use the public funds to promote sectarian causes....

When Madison in his Remonstrance attacked a taxing measure to support religious activities, he advanced a series of reasons for opposing it. One that is extremely relevant here was phrased as follows: "It will destroy that moderation and harmony which the forbearance of our laws to intermeddle with Religion, has produced amongst its several sects." Intermeddling, to use Madison's word, or "entanglement," to use what was said in Walz, has two aspects. The intrusion of government into religious schools through grants, supervision, or surveillance may result in establishment of religion in the constitutional sense when what the State does enthrones a particular sect for overt or subtle propagation of its faith. Those activities of the State may also intrude on the Free Exercise Clause by depriving a teacher, under threats of reprisals, of the right to give sectarian construction or interpretation of, say, history and literature, or to use the teaching of such subjects to inculcate a religious creed or dogma.

Under these laws there will be vast governmental suppression, surveillance, or meddling in church affairs.... If the government closed its eyes to the manner in which these grants are actually used it would be allowing public funds to promote sectarian education. If it did not close its eyes but undertook the surveillance needed, it would, I fear, intermeddle in parochial affairs in a way that would breed only rancor and dissension....

MR. JUSTICE MARSHALL, who took no part in the consideration or decision of [the Pennsylvania case], concurs in MR. JUSTICE DOUGLAS' opinion covering [the Rhode Island case].

MR. JUSTICE BRENNAN.

I agree that the judgments in [the Rhode Island case] must be affirmed. In my view the judgment in [the Pennsylvania case] must be reversed outright....

The common feature of [the] statutes before us is the provision of a direct subsidy from public funds for activities carried on by sectarian educational institutions. We have sustained the reimbursement of parents for bus fares of students under a scheme applicable to both public and nonpublic schools, Everson v. Board of Education, 330 U.S. 1 (1947). We have also sustained the loan of textbooks in secular subjects to students of both public and nonpublic schools, Board of Education v. Allen, 392 U.S. 236 (1968).... In sharp contrast to the "undeviating acceptance given religious tax exemptions from our earliest days as a Nation," subsidy of sectarian educational institutions became embroiled in bitter controversies very soon after the Nation was formed....

... [F]or more than a century, the consensus, enforced by legislatures and courts with substantial consistency, has been that public subsidy of sectarian schools constitutes an impermissible involvement of secular with religious institutions.... These are involvements that threaten "dangers—as much to church as to state—which the Framers feared would subvert religious liberty and the strength of a system of secular government." Schempp, 374 U.S., at 295 (BRENNAN, J., concurring). "Government and religion have discrete interests which are mutually best served when each avoids too close a proximity to the other. It is not only the nonbeliever who fears the injection of sectarian doctrines and controversies into the civil polity, but in as high degree it is the devout believer who fears the secularization of a creed which becomes too deeply involved with and dependent upon the government." Id., at 259 (BRENNAN, J., concurring). [The Rhode Island and Pennsylvania] statutes require "too close a proximity" of government to the subsidized sectarian institutions and in my view create real dangers of "the secularization of a creed."... The picture of state inspectors prowling the halls of parochial schools and auditing classroom instruction surely raises more than an imagined specter of governmental "secularization of a creed."...

Moreover, when a sectarian institution accepts state financial aid it becomes obligated under the Equal Protection Clause of the Fourteenth Amendment not to discriminate in admissions policies and faculty selection. The District Court in the Rhode Island case pinpointed the dilemma: .... "At some point the school becomes 'public' for more purposes than the Church could wish. At that point, the Church may justifiably feel that its victory on the Establishment Clause has meant abandonment of the Free Exercise Clause."

In any event, I do not believe that elimination of these aspects of "too close a proximity" would save these three statutes. I expressed the view in Walz that.... :

.... "in the case of direct subsidy, the state forcibly diverts the income of both believers and nonbelievers to churches, while in the case of an exemption, the state merely refrains from diverting to its own uses income independently generated by the churches through voluntary contributions." Thus, "the symbolism of tax exemption is significant as a manifestation that organized religion is not expected to support the state; by the same token the state is not expected to support the church."

.... The common ingredient of the three prongs of the test set forth at the outset of this opinion is whether the statutes involve government in the "essentially religious activities" of religious institutions. My analysis of the operation, purposes, and effects of these statutes leads me inescapably to the conclusion that they do impermissibly involve the States ... with the "essentially religious activities" of sectarian educational institutions. More specifically, for the reasons stated, I think each government uses "essentially religious means to serve governmental ends, where secular means would suffice." This Nation long ago committed itself to primary reliance upon publicly supported public education to serve its important goals in secular education. Our religious diversity gave strong impetus to that commitment.

MR. JUSTICE WHITE, concurring in the judgment [in the Pennsylvania case] and dissenting in [the Rhode Island case].

.... It is enough for me that the States ... are financing a separable secular function of overriding importance in order to sustain the legislation here challenged. That religion and private interests other than education may substantially benefit does not convert these laws into impermissible establishments of religion.... I would sustain both the ... Rhode Island program[] at issue in these cases.... Although I would also reject the facial challenge to the Pennsylvania statute,.... I do agree, however, that the complaint should not have been dismissed for failure to state a cause of action. Although it did not specifically allege that the schools involved mixed religious teaching with secular subjects, the complaint did allege that the schools were operated to fulfill religious purposes and one of the legal theories stated in the complaint was that the Pennsylvania Act "finances and participates in the blending of sectarian and secular instruction." At trial under this complaint, evidence showing such a blend in a course supported by state funds would appear to be admissible and, if credited, would establish financing of religious instruction by the State. Hence, I would reverse the judgment of the District Court and remand the case for trial, thereby holding the Pennsylvania legislation valid on its face but leaving open the question of its validity as applied to the particular facts of this case.

Review Questions and Explanations: *Lemon*

1. The *Lemon* test has been criticized by Supreme Court justices and commentators, but it remains good law if only because of the absence of agreement on a better approach. The *Lemon* opinion opens with the disclaimer that "we can only dimly perceive the lines of demarcation in this extraordinarily sensitive area of constitutional law." The candor is refreshing, perhaps, but how accurate is the point? Is the Court more challenged to draw clear lines here than in any other First Amendment area? (Or in Commerce Clause cases, for that matter?) Moreover, if the Court's perception is dim, should that warrant more institutional modesty, in the form of greater deference to (less strict judicial review of) the decisions of other governmental institutions?

2. What aspects of the three part test does the Court rely on for its decision, and why? Do the Douglas and Brennan concurrences make any new or different arguments, or do they just repeat what the majority says?

3. Should direct subsidies to schools be allowed on the ground that religious schools are taking on some of society's burden of providing K–12 education? Could the "surveillance" or "audit" problem be resolved simply by doing away with restrictions on how the money is used? Would this alleviate or aggravate the Establishment Clause problem?

4. What do you make of the argument in section IV of the majority opinion: that "excessive entanglement" is made worse by creating a highly contentious subject of political debate that will divide voters along religious lines. Is that a legitimate basis to strike down a law under the Establishment Clause?

5. Section V makes the slippery slope argument about religious establishment. Do you find it persuasive?

---

2. School Prayer

The issue of prayer in public schools has arisen only intermittently before the Court, but offers a window into the limits of Establishment Clause jurisprudence more generally. The Court's decisions in this area remain controversial. When reading the cases, try to disaggregate the arguments the different justices are making, and to ascertain the underlying concerns driving the justices in these cases. What is it that the justices voting against the constitutionality of organized school prayers fear? What is that their judicial opponents fear? Is either position self-evidently required by the text of the First Amendment?

Guided Reading Questions: *Engel v. Vitale* and *Lee v. Weisman*

1. Identify carefully the facts surrounding the prayers in the two cases. For example, were the prayers affiliated with a particular religion? Was participation compulsory? Was attendance?

2. What doctrine about school prayer can you discern from the two cases?

3. Do you agree that the prayers at issue violated the Establishment Clause?

Engel v. Vitale
370 U.S. 421 (1962)

Majority: *Black*, Warren (CJ), Clark, Harlan, Brennan,

Concurrence in the judgment: *Douglas*

Dissent: *Stewart* (Frankfurter and White took no part)

MR. JUSTICE BLACK delivered the opinion of the Court.

The respondent Board of Education of Union Free School District No. 9, New Hyde Park, New York, acting in its official capacity under state law, directed the School District's principal to cause the following prayer to be said aloud by each class in the presence of a teacher at the beginning of each school day: "Almighty God, we acknowledge our dependence upon Thee, and we beg Thy blessings upon us, our parents, our teachers and our Country."

This daily procedure was adopted on the recommendation of the State Board of Regents, a governmental agency created by the State Constitution to which the New York Legislature has granted broad supervisory, executive, and legislative powers over the State's public school system....

[The parents of ten pupils brought this action in a New York State Court challenging the use of this official prayer as a violation of the Establishment Clause of the First Amendment, made applicable to the State of New York by the Fourteenth Amendment. The New York courts upheld the prayer.]

We think that by using its public school system to encourage recitation of the Regents' prayer, the State of New York has adopted a practice wholly inconsistent with the Establishment Clause. There can, of course, be no doubt that New York's program of daily classroom invocation of God's blessings as prescribed in the Regents' prayer is a religious activity.... [T]he constitutional prohibition against laws respecting an establishment of religion must at least mean that in this country it is no part of the business of government to compose official prayers for any group of the American people to recite as a part of a religious program carried on by government.

It is a matter of history that this very practice of establishing governmentally composed prayers for religious services was one of the reasons which caused many of our early colonists to leave England and seek religious freedom in America.... It is an unfortunate fact of history that when some of the very groups which had most strenuously opposed the established Church of England found themselves sufficiently in control of colonial governments in this country to write their own prayers into law....

By the time of the adoption of the Constitution, our history shows that there was a widespread awareness among many Americans of the dangers of a union of Church and State. These people knew, some of them from bitter personal experience, that one of the greatest dangers to the freedom of the individual to worship in his own way lay in the Government's placing its official stamp of approval upon one particular kind of prayer or one particular form of religious services....

It has been argued that to apply the Constitution in such a way as to prohibit state laws respecting an establishment of religious services in public schools is to indicate a hostility toward religion or toward prayer. Nothing, of course, could be more wrong.... There were men of ... faith in the power of prayer who led the fight for adoption of our Constitution and also for our Bill of Rights with the very guarantees of religious freedom that forbid the sort of governmental activity which New York has attempted here. These men knew that the First Amendment, which tried to put an end to governmental control of religion and of prayer, was not written to destroy either. They knew rather that it was written to quiet well-justified fears which nearly all of them felt arising out of an awareness that governments of the past had shackled men's tongues to make them speak only the religious thoughts that government wanted them to speak and to pray only to the God that government wanted them to pray to. It is neither sacrilegious nor antireligious to say that each separate government in this country should stay out of the business of writing or sanctioning official prayers and leave that purely religious function to the people themselves and to those the people choose to look to for religious guidance.

The judgment of the Court of Appeals of New York is reversed and the cause remanded for further proceedings not inconsistent with this opinion. Reversed and remanded.

MR. JUSTICE DOUGLAS, concurring.

.... Plainly, our Bill of Rights would not permit a State or the Federal Government to adopt an official prayer and penalize anyone who would not utter it. This, however, is not that case, for there is no element of compulsion or coercion in New York's regulation requiring that public schools be opened each day with [a] prayer.... [T]he only one who need utter the prayer is the teacher; and no teacher is complaining of it. Students can stand mute or even leave the classroom, if they desire....

.... I cannot say that to authorize this prayer is to establish a religion in the strictly historic meaning of those words. A religion is not established in the usual sense merely by letting those who choose to do so say the prayer that the public school teacher leads. Yet once government finances a religious exercise it inserts a divisive influence into our communities.... I therefore join the Court in reversing the judgment below.

MR. JUSTICE STEWART, dissenting.

.... I cannot see how an "official religion" is established by letting those who want to say a prayer say it. On the contrary, I think that to deny the wish of these school children to join in reciting this prayer is to deny them the opportunity of sharing in the spiritual heritage of our Nation.

.... The Court today says that the state and federal governments are without constitutional power to prescribe any particular form of words to be recited by any group of the American people on any subject touching religion. One of the stanzas of "The Star-

Spangled Banner," made our National Anthem by Act of Congress in 1931, contains these verses:

> Blest with victory and peace, may the heav'n rescued land
>
> Praise the Pow'r that hath made and preserved us a nation!
>
> Then conquer we must, when our cause it is just,
>
> And this be our motto "In God is our Trust."

In 1954 Congress added a phrase to the Pledge of Allegiance to the Flag so that it now contains the words "one Nation under God, indivisible, with liberty and justice for all." In 1952 Congress enacted legislation calling upon the President each year to proclaim a National Day of Prayer. Since 1865 the words "IN GOD WE TRUST" have been impressed on our coins.

.... I do not believe that this Court, or the Congress, or the President has by the actions and practices I have mentioned established an "official religion" in violation of the Constitution. And I do not believe the State of New York has done so in this case. What each has done has been to recognize and to follow the deeply entrenched and highly cherished spiritual traditions of our Nation—traditions which come down to us from those who almost two hundred years ago avowed their "firm Reliance on the Protection of divine Providence" when they proclaimed the freedom and independence of this brave new world. I dissent.

Lee v. Weisman

505 U.S. 577 (1992)

Majority: *Kennedy*, Blackmun, Stevens, O'Connor, Souter

Concurrences: *Blackmun*, *Souter*, Stevens, O'Connor

Dissent: *Scalia*, Rehnquist (CJ), White, Thomas

JUSTICE KENNEDY delivered the opinion of the Court.

> [The Providence, Rhode Island school board permitted public school principals to invite members of the clergy to offer invocation and benediction prayers as part of the formal graduation ceremonies for middle schools and for high schools. One school principal, petitioner Robert E. Lee, invited Rabbi Leslie Gutterman, of the Temple Beth El in Providence, to deliver prayers at the graduation exercises for Nathan Bishop Middle School, a public school in Providence, at a formal ceremony in June 1989. It had been the custom of Providence school officials to provide invited clergy with a pamphlet entitled "Guidelines for Civic Occasions," prepared by the National Conference of Christians and Jews. The Guidelines recommend that public prayers at nonsectarian civic ceremonies be composed with "inclusiveness and sensitivity," though they acknowledge that "prayer of any kind may be inappropriate on some civic occasions." Pursuant to these guidelines, and on advice from Principal Lee, Rabbi Gutterman gave non-sectarian prayers for an invocation and a benediction. Daniel Weisman, father of 14 year-old Deborah Weisman, had sought a temporary restraining order in the district court to prohibit school officials from including an invocation or benediction in the graduation ceremony. The court denied the motion for lack of adequate time to consider it. Deborah and her family attended the graduation, where the prayers were recited. In July 1989, Daniel Weisman filed an amended complaint seeking

a permanent injunction barring petitioners, various officials of the Providence public schools, from inviting the clergy to deliver invocations and benedictions at future graduations. The district court held that the practice of including invocations and benedictions in public school graduations violated the Establishment Clause of the First Amendment, and it enjoined petitioners from continuing the practice. The First Circuit affirmed. The Supreme Court granted certiorari. It found that Deborah Weisman had standing because she was now enrolled as a student at Classical High School in Providence "and from the record it appears likely, if not certain, that an invocation and benediction will be conducted at her high school graduation." The Court proceeded to the merits.]

These dominant facts mark and control the confines of our decision: State officials direct the performance of a formal religious exercise at promotional and graduation ceremonies for secondary schools. Even for those students who object to the religious exercise, their attendance and participation in the state-sponsored religious activity are in a fair and real sense obligatory, though the school district does not require attendance as a condition for receipt of the diploma.

.... We can decide the case without reconsidering the general constitutional framework by which public schools' efforts to accommodate religion are measured. Thus we do not accept the invitation of petitioners and amicus the United States to reconsider our decision in Lemon v. Kurtzman. The government involvement with religious activity in this case is pervasive, to the point of creating a state-sponsored and state-directed religious exercise in a public school. Conducting this formal religious observance conflicts with settled rules pertaining to prayer exercises for students, and that suffices to determine the question before us.

The principle that government may accommodate the free exercise of religion does not supersede the fundamental limitations imposed by the Establishment Clause. It is beyond dispute that, at a minimum, the Constitution guarantees that government may not coerce anyone to support or participate in religion or its exercise, or otherwise act in a way which "establishes a [state] religion or religious faith, or tends to do so." Lynch v. Donelly. The State's involvement in the school prayers challenged today violates these central principles....

The State's role did not end with the decision to include a prayer and with the choice of a clergyman. Principal Lee provided Rabbi Gutterman with a copy of the "Guidelines for Civic Occasions," and advised him that his prayers should be nonsectarian. Through these means the principal directed and controlled the content of the prayers. Even if the only sanction for ignoring the instructions were that the rabbi would not be invited back, we think no religious representative who valued his or her continued reputation and effectiveness in the community would incur the State's displeasure in this regard. It is a cornerstone principle of our Establishment Clause jurisprudence that "it is no part of the business of government to compose official prayers for any group of the American people to recite as a part of a religious program carried on by government," Engel v. Vitale, 370 U.S. 421 (1962), and that is what the school officials attempted to do....

We are asked to recognize the existence of a practice of nonsectarian prayer, prayer within the embrace of what is known as the Judeo-Christian tradition, prayer which is more acceptable than one which, for example, makes explicit references to the God of Israel, or to Jesus Christ, or to a patron saint. There may be some support, as an empirical observation, ... that there has emerged in this country a civic religion, one which is tolerated when sectarian exercises are not. If common ground can be defined which permits once conflicting faiths to express the shared conviction that there is an ethic and a morality which transcend human invention, the sense of community and purpose sought by all decent societies might be advanced. But though the First Amendment does not allow the government to stifle prayers which aspire to these ends, neither does it permit the government to undertake that task for itself.

The First Amendment's Religion Clauses mean that religious beliefs and religious expression are too precious to be either proscribed or prescribed by the State.... [W]hile concern must be given to define the protection granted to an objector or a dissenting nonbeliever, these same Clauses exist to protect religion from government interference. James Madison, the principal author of the Bill of Rights, did not rest his opposition to a religious establishment on the sole ground of its effect on the minority. A principal ground for his view was: "Experience witnesseth that ecclesiastical establishments, instead of maintaining the purity and efficacy of Religion, have had a contrary operation."

.... By the time they are seniors, high school students no doubt have been required to attend classes and assemblies and to complete assignments exposing them to ideas they find distasteful or immoral or absurd or all of these. Against this background, students may consider it an odd measure of justice to be subjected during the course of their educations to ideas deemed offensive and irreligious, but to be denied a brief, formal prayer ceremony that the school offers in return. This argument cannot prevail, however....

The First Amendment protects speech and religion by quite different mechanisms. Speech is protected by ensuring its full expression even when the government participates, for the very object of some of our most important speech is to persuade the government to adopt an idea as its own. The method for protecting freedom of worship and freedom of conscience in religious matters is quite the reverse. In religious debate or expression the government is not a prime participant, for the Framers deemed religious establishment antithetical to the freedom of all. The Free Exercise Clause embraces a freedom of conscience and worship that has close parallels in the speech provisions of the First Amendment, but the Establishment Clause is a specific prohibition on forms of state intervention in religious affairs with no precise counterpart in the speech provisions.... A state-created orthodoxy puts at grave risk that freedom of belief and conscience which are the sole assurance that religious faith is real, not imposed....

As we have observed before, there are heightened concerns with protecting freedom of conscience from subtle coercive pressure in the elementary and secondary public schools. Our decisions ... recognize, among other things, that prayer exercises in public schools carry a particular risk of indirect coercion. The concern may not be limited to the context of schools, but it is most pronounced there....

The injury caused by the government's action, and the reason why Daniel and Deborah Weisman object to it, is that the State, in a school setting, in effect required participation in a religious exercise. It is, we concede, a brief exercise during which the individual can concentrate on joining its message, meditate on her own religion, or let her mind wander. But the embarrassment and the intrusion of the religious exercise cannot be refuted by arguing that these prayers, and similar ones to be said in the future, are of a de minimis character....

Inherent differences between the public school system and a session of a state legislature distinguish this case from Marsh v. Chambers, 463 U.S. 783 (1983). The considerations we have raised in objection to the invocation and benediction are in many respects similar to the arguments we considered in Marsh. But there are also obvious differences. The at-mosphere at the opening of a session of a state legislature where adults are free to enter and leave with little comment and for any number of reasons cannot compare with the constraining potential of the one school event most important for the student to attend.... Our Establishment Clause jurisprudence remains a delicate and fact-sensitive one, and we cannot accept the parallel relied upon by petitioners and the United States between the facts of Marsh and the case now before us. Our decisions in Engel v. Vitale, and School Dist. of Abington v. Schempp, supra, require us to distinguish the public school context.

We do not hold that every state action implicating religion is invalid if one or a few citizens find it offensive. People may take offense at all manner of religious as well as non-religious messages, but offense alone does not in every case show a violation. We know too that sometimes to endure social isolation or even anger may be the price of conscience or nonconformity....

.... We recognize that, at graduation time and throughout the course of the educational process, there will be instances when religious values, religious practices, and religious persons will have some interaction with the public schools and their students. But these matters, often questions of accommodation of religion, are not before us. The sole question presented is whether a religious exercise may be conducted at a graduation ceremony in circumstances where, as we have found, young graduates who object are induced to conform. No holding by this Court suggests that a school can persuade or compel a student to participate in a religious exercise. That is being done here, and it is forbidden by the Establishment Clause of the First Amendment.

For the reasons we have stated, the judgment of the Court of Appeals is affirmed.

JUSTICE BLACKMUN, with whom JUSTICE STEVENS and JUSTICE O'CONNOR join, concurring.

Nearly half a century of review and refinement of Establishment Clause jurisprudence has distilled one clear understanding: Government may neither promote nor affiliate itself with any religious doctrine or organization, nor may it obtrude itself in the internal affairs of any religious institution. The application of these principles to the present case mandates the decision reached today by the Court....

In 1971, Chief Justice Burger reviewed the Court's past decisions and found: "Three ... tests may be gleaned from our cases." Lemon v. Kurtzman, 403 U.S. 602. In order for a statute to survive an Establishment Clause challenge, "first, the statute must have a secular legislative purpose; second, its principal or primary effect must be one that neither advances nor inhibits religion; finally the statute must not foster an excessive government entanglement with religion." After Lemon, the Court continued to rely on these basic principles in resolving Establishment Clause disputes.

Application of these principles to the facts of this case is straightforward. There can be "no doubt" that the "invocation of God's blessings" delivered at Nathan Bishop Middle School "is a religious activity." Engel, 370 U.S. at 424. In the words of Engel, the rabbi's prayer "is a solemn avowal of divine faith and supplication for the blessings of the Almighty. The nature of such a prayer has always been religious." The question then is whether the government has "placed its official stamp of approval" on the prayer. As the Court ably demonstrates, when the government "composes official prayers," selects the member of the clergy to deliver the prayer, has the prayer delivered at a public school event that is planned, supervised, and given by school officials, and pressures students to attend and participate in the prayer, there can be no doubt that the government is advancing and pro-moting religion. As our prior decisions teach us, it is this that the Constitution prohibits.

I join the Court's opinion today because I find nothing in it inconsistent with the essential precepts of the Establishment Clause developed in our precedents. The Court holds that the graduation prayer is unconstitutional because the State "in effect required participation in a religious exercise." Although our precedents make clear that proof of government coercion is not necessary to prove an Establishment Clause violation, it is sufficient. Government pressure to participate in a religious activity is an obvious indication that the government is endorsing or promoting religion.

But it is not enough that the government restrain from compelling religious practices: It must not engage in them either. See Schempp, 374 U.S. at 305 (Goldberg, J., concurring). The Court repeatedly has recognized that a violation of the Establishment Clause is not predicated on coercion. . . .

The mixing of government and religion can be a threat to free government, even if no one is forced to participate. When the government puts its *imprimatur* on a particular religion, it conveys a message of exclusion to all those who do not adhere to the favored beliefs. A government cannot be premised on the belief that all persons are created equal when it asserts that God prefers some. . . .

JUSTICE SOUTER, with whom JUSTICE STEVENS and JUSTICE O'CONNOR join, concurring.

I join the whole of the Court's opinion, and fully agree that prayers at public school graduation ceremonies indirectly coerce religious observance. I write separately nonetheless on two issues of Establishment Clause analysis that underlie my independent resolution of this case. . . .

Since Everson, we have consistently held the Clause applicable no less to governmental acts favoring religion generally than to acts favoring one religion over others. . . . Such is the settled law. Here, as elsewhere, we should stick to it absent some compelling reason to discard it.

Some have challenged this precedent by reading the Establishment Clause to permit "nonpreferential" state promotion of religion. The challengers argue that, as originally understood by the Framers, "the Establishment Clause did not require government neutrality between religion and irreligion nor did it prohibit the Federal Government from providing nondiscriminatory aid to religion." While a case has been made for this position, it is not so convincing as to warrant reconsideration of our settled law; indeed, I find in the history of the Clause's textual development a more powerful argument supporting the Court's jurisprudence following Everson.

. . . . [O]ne further concern animates my judgment. In many contexts, including this one, non-preferentialism requires some distinction between "sectarian" religious practices and those that would be, by some measure, ecumenical enough to pass Establishment Clause muster. Simply by requiring the enquiry, nonpreferentialists invite the courts to engage in comparative theology. I can hardly imagine a subject less amenable to the competence of the federal judiciary, or more deliberately to be avoided where possible. . . .

Nor does it solve the problem to say that the State should promote a "diversity" of religious views; that position would necessarily compel the government and, inevitably, the courts to make wholly inappropriate judgments about the number of religions the State should sponsor and the relative frequency with which it should sponsor each. In fact, the prospect would be even worse than that. As Madison observed in criticizing religious Presidential proclamations, the practice of sponsoring religious messages tends, over time, "to narrow the recommendation to the standard of the predominant sect." . . .

Petitioners rest most of their argument on a theory that, whether or not the Establishment Clause permits extensive nonsectarian support for religion, it does not forbid the state to sponsor affirmations of religious belief that coerce neither support for religion nor participation in religious observance. I appreciate the force of some of the arguments supporting a "coercion" analysis of the Clause. But we could not adopt that reading without abandoning our settled law, a course that, in my view, the text of the Clause would not readily permit. Nor does the extratextual evidence of original meaning stand so unequivocally at odds with the textual premise inherent in existing precedent that we should fundamentally reconsider our course....

JUSTICE SCALIA, with whom THE CHIEF JUSTICE, JUSTICE WHITE, and JUSTICE THOMAS join, dissenting.

.... In holding that the Establishment Clause prohibits invocations and benedictions at public school graduation ceremonies, the Court—with nary a mention that it is doing so—lays waste a tradition that is as old as public school graduation ceremonies themselves, and that is a component of an even more longstanding American tradition of nonsectarian prayer to God at public celebrations generally....

Our national celebration of Thanksgiving likewise dates back to President Washington.... This tradition of Thanksgiving Proclamations—with their religious theme of prayerful gratitude to God—has been adhered to by almost every President.

The other two branches of the Federal Government also have a long-established practice of prayer at public events. As we detailed in Marsh, congressional sessions have opened with a chaplain's prayer ever since the First Congress.

In addition to this general tradition of prayer at public ceremonies, there exists a more specific tradition of invocations and benedictions at public school graduation exercises....

The Court presumably would separate graduation invocations and benedictions from other instances of public "preservation and transmission of religious beliefs" on the ground that they involve "psychological coercion.".... The Court's argument that state officials have "coerced" students to take part in the invocation and benediction at graduation ceremonies is, not to put too fine a point on it, incoherent.

.... The Court's notion that a student who simply sits in "respectful silence" during the invocation and benediction (when all others are standing) has somehow joined—or would somehow be perceived as having joined—in the prayers is nothing short of ludicrous. We indeed live in a vulgar age. But surely "our social conventions," have not coarsened to the point that anyone who does not stand on his chair and shout obscenities can reasonably be deemed to have assented to everything said in his presence. Since the Court does not dispute that students exposed to prayer at graduation ceremonies retain (despite "subtle coercive pressures") the free will to sit, there is absolutely no basis for the Court's decision. It is fanciful enough to say that "a reasonable dissenter," standing head erect in a class of bowed heads, "could believe that the group exercise signified her own participation or approval of it." It is beyond the absurd to say that she could entertain such a belief while pointedly declining to rise.

But let us assume the very worst, that the nonparticipating graduate is "subtly coerced" ... to stand! Even that half of the disjunctive does not remotely establish a "participation" (or an "appearance of participation") in a religious exercise....

I also find it odd that the Court concludes that high school graduates may not be subjected to this supposed psychological coercion, yet refrains from addressing whether "mature adults" may. I had thought that the reason graduation from high school is regarded as so significant an event is that it is generally associated with transition from adolescence to young adulthood. Many graduating seniors, of course, are old enough to vote. Why, then, does the Court treat them as though they were first-graders? Will we soon have a jurisprudence that distinguishes between mature and immature adults?

The other "dominant fact" identified by the Court is that "state officials direct the performance of a formal religious exercise" at school graduation ceremonies.... [But] the Court identifies nothing in the record remotely suggesting that school officials have ever drafted, edited, screened, or censored graduation prayers, or that Rabbi Gutterman was a mouthpiece of the school officials....

The deeper flaw in the Court's opinion does not lie in its wrong answer to the question whether there was state-induced "peer-pressure" coercion; it lies, rather, in the Court's making violation of the Establishment Clause hinge on such a precious question. The coercion that was a hallmark of historical establishments of religion was coercion of religious orthodoxy and of financial support by force of law and threat of penalty....

Thus, while I have no quarrel with the Court's general proposition that the Establishment Clause "guarantees that government may not coerce anyone to support or participate in religion or its exercise," I see no warrant for expanding the concept of coercion beyond acts backed by threat of penalty—a brand of coercion that, happily, is readily discernible to those of us who have made a career of reading the disciples of Blackstone rather than of Freud....

Our Religion Clause jurisprudence has become bedeviled (so to speak) by reliance on formulaic abstractions that are not derived from, but positively conflict with, our long-accepted constitutional traditions. Foremost among these has been the so-called Lemon test, see Lemon v. Kurtzman, 403 U.S. 602, 612–613 (1971), which has received well-earned criticism from many Members of this Court. The Court today demonstrates the irrelevance of Lemon by essentially ignoring it, and the interment of that case may be the one happy byproduct of the Court's otherwise lamentable decision....

Review Questions and Explanations: *Engel* and *Lee*

1. *Engel* is a pre-*Lemon* case, but *Lee* was decided post-*Lemon*. Was the *Lemon* test necessary or helpful to the decision in *Lee*? Or could *Lee* have been decided merely by applying *Engel*?

2. Why the two concurring opinions in *Lee*? Did they clarify or distinguish any points made in the majority opinion?

3. Can *Lee* be distinguished from *Engel* on the ground that, as pointed out in the dissent, the prayer was an instance of "a longstanding American tradition of nonsectarian prayer to God at public celebrations generally"—that is, at graduation rather than as a daily exercise to start the school day?

4. The dissent ridicules the notion that sitting through the prayer is in any sense psychologically coercive, and further disagrees that such coercion should be part of an Establishment Clause analysis regardless. Maybe the dissenters have a point. But couldn't their concerns also be addressed by a flat ban on prayers at public school functions of any kind—thereby eliminating the need for all the fine-grained factual analysis relied on by the majority?

5. Put yourself in the position of a high school student sitting at your graduation ceremony and hearing a prayer with which you deeply disagree. Do any of the opinions in *Engel* or *Lee* capture how you think you would react to this situation?

What is the link between the justices' perceptions of how students would react and the constitutional rule they adopt?

3. Ten Commandments Displays

Like the school prayer cases, the Court's cases involving the display of the Ten Commandments in public buildings have been controversial. When reading the next case, think about the ways in which these displays are and are not like organized prayer in schools. Would you tend to find the displays more or less "coercive" than the middle school graduation ceremony prayers? Why?

Guided Reading Questions: *McCreary County v. ACLU*

1. Recall James Madison's Memorial and Remonstrance. Madison talked about equality of citizenship as one reason for avoiding governmental engagement with religion. Justice Souter's concern with religious neutrality echoes these concerns. Do you think Souter's reasoning is consistent with, an extension of, or distinct from, Madison's?

2. Justice Scalia, writing in dissent, also claims adherence to the founders' intentions. Is his position consistent with, an extension of, or distinct from, Madison's?

McCreary County, Kentucky v. American Civil Liberties Union of Kentucky
545 U.S. 844 (2005)

Majority: *Souter,* Stevens, O'Connor, Ginsburg, Breyer

Concurrence: *O'Connor*

Dissent: *Scalia,* Rehnquist (CJ), Thomas, Kennedy (concurring in Part and dissenting in Part)

JUSTICE SOUTER delivered the opinion of the Court.

In the summer of 1999, petitioners McCreary County and Pulaski County, Kentucky (hereinafter Counties), put up in their respective courthouses large, gold-framed copies of an abridged text of the King James version of the Ten Commandments, including a citation to the Book of Exodus. In McCreary County, the placement of the Commandments responded to an order of the county legislative body requiring "the display [to] be posted in 'a very high traffic area' of the courthouse." In Pulaski County, amidst reported controversy over the propriety of the display, the Commandments were hung in a ceremony presided over by the county Judge-Executive, who called them "good rules to live by" and who recounted the story of an astronaut who became convinced "there must be a divine God" after viewing the Earth from the moon. The Judge-Executive was accompanied by the pastor of his church, who called the Commandments "a creed of ethics" and told the press after the ceremony that displaying the Commandments was "one of the greatest things the judge could have done to close out the millennium."

In November 1999, respondents American Civil Liberties Union of Kentucky sued the Counties in Federal District Court ... and sought a preliminary injunction against maintaining the displays, which the ACLU charged were violations of the prohibition of religious establishment included in the First Amendment of the Constitution. Within a month, and before the District Court had responded to the request for injunction, the legislative body of each County authorized a second, expanded display, by nearly identical resolutions reciting that the Ten Commandments are "the precedent legal code upon which the civil and criminal codes of ... Kentucky are founded," and stating several grounds for taking that position: that "the Ten Commandments are codified in Kentucky's civil and criminal laws"; that the Kentucky House of Representatives had in 1993 "voted unanimously ... to adjourn ... 'in remembrance and honor of Jesus Christ, the Prince of Ethics'"; that the "County Judge and ... magistrates agree with the arguments set out by Judge [Roy] Moore" in defense of his "display [of] the Ten Commandments in his courtroom"; and that the "Founding Father[s] [had an] explicit understanding of the duty of elected officials to publicly acknowledge God as the source of America's strength and direction."

As directed by the resolutions, the Counties expanded the displays of the Ten Commandments in their locations, presumably along with copies of the resolution, which instructed that it, too, be posted. In addition to the first display's large framed copy of the edited King James version of the Commandments, the second included eight other documents in smaller frames, each either having a religious theme or excerpted to highlight a religious element. The documents were the "endowed by their Creator" passage from the Declaration of Independence; the Preamble to the Constitution of Kentucky; the national motto, "In God We Trust"; a page from the Congressional Record of February 2, 1983, proclaiming the Year of the Bible and including a statement of the Ten Commandments; a proclamation by President Abraham Lincoln designating April 30, 1863, a National Day of Prayer and Humiliation; an excerpt from President Lincoln's "Reply to Loyal Colored People of Baltimore upon Presentation of a Bible," reading that "[t]he Bible is the best gift God has ever given to man"; a proclamation by President Reagan marking 1983 the Year of the Bible; and the Mayflower Compact.

After argument, the District Court entered a preliminary injunction on May 5, 2000, ordering that the "display ... be removed from [each] County Courthouse."... The Counties filed a notice of appeal from the preliminary injunction but voluntarily dismissed it after hiring new lawyers. They then installed another display in each courthouse, the third within a year. No new resolution authorized this one, nor did the Counties repeal the resolutions that preceded the second. The posting consists of nine framed documents of equal size, one of them setting out the Ten Commandments explicitly identified as the "King James Version" at Exodus 20:3–17, and quoted at greater length than before.... Assembled with the Commandments are framed copies of the Magna Carta, the Declaration of Independence, the Bill of Rights, the lyrics of the Star Spangled Banner, the Mayflower Compact, the National Motto, the Preamble to the Kentucky Constitution, and a picture of Lady Justice. The collection is entitled "The Foundations of American Law and Government Display" and each document comes with a statement about its historical and legal significance. The comment on the Ten Commandments reads:

> The Ten Commandments have profoundly influenced the formation of Western legal thought and the formation of our country. That influence is clearly seen in the Declaration of Independence, which declared that 'We hold these truths to be self-evident, that all men are created equal, that they are endowed by their

Creator with certain unalienable Rights, that among these are Life, Liberty, and the pursuit of Happiness.' The Ten Commandments provide the moral background of the Declaration of Independence and the foundation of our legal tradition.

Ever since Lemon v. Kurtzman summarized the three familiar considerations for evaluating Establishment Clause claims, looking to whether government action has "a secular legislative purpose" has been a common, albeit seldom dispositive, element of our cases. Though we have found government action motivated by an illegitimate purpose only four times since Lemon, and "the secular purpose requirement alone may rarely be determinative...", it nevertheless serves an important function." ... The touchstone for our analysis is the principle that the "First Amendment mandates governmental neutrality between religion and religion, and between religion and nonreligion." When the government acts with the ostensible and predominant purpose of advancing religion, it violates that central Establishment Clause value of official religious neutrality, there being no neutrality when the government's ostensible object is to take sides. Manifesting a purpose to favor one faith over another, or adherence to religion generally, clashes with the "understanding, reached ... after decades of religious war, that liberty and social stability demand a religious tolerance that respects the religious views of all citizens...." By showing a purpose to favor religion, the government "sends the ... message to ... nonadherents 'that they are outsiders, not full members of the political community, and an accompanying message to adherents that they are insiders, favored members....'"

Indeed, the purpose apparent from government action can have an impact more significant than the result expressly decreed: when the government maintains Sunday closing laws, it advances religion only minimally because many working people would take the day as one of rest regardless, but if the government justified its decision with a stated desire for all Americans to honor Christ, the divisive thrust of the official action would be inescapable. This is the teaching of McGowan v. Maryland (1961), which upheld Sunday closing statutes on practical, secular grounds after finding that the government had forsaken the religious purposes behind centuries-old predecessor laws.

Despite the intuitive importance of official purpose to the realization of Establishment Clause values, the Counties ask us to abandon Lemon's purpose test, or at least to truncate any enquiry into purpose here. Their first argument is that the very consideration of purpose is deceptive: according to them, true "purpose" is unknowable, and its search merely an excuse for courts to act selectively and unpredictably in picking out evidence of subjective intent. The assertions are as seismic as they are unconvincing. Examination of purpose is a staple of statutory interpretation that makes up the daily fare of every appellate court in the country, and governmental purpose is a key element of a good deal of constitutional doctrine, e.g., Washington v. Davis (1976) (discriminatory purpose required for Equal Protection violation); Hunt v. Washington State Apple Advertising Comm'n (1977) (discriminatory purpose relevant to dormant Commerce Clause claim); Churck of Lukumi Babalu Aye, Inc. v. Hialeah (1993) (discriminatory purpose raises level of scrutiny required by free exercise claim). With enquiries into purpose this common, if they were nothing but hunts for mares' nests deflecting attention from bare judicial will, the whole notion of purpose in law would have dropped into disrepute long ago....

After declining the invitation to abandon concern with purpose wholesale, we also have to avoid the Counties' alternative tack of trivializing the enquiry into it. The Counties would read the cases as if the purpose enquiry were so naive that any transparent claim to secularity would satisfy it, and they would cut context out of the enquiry, to the point of ignoring history, no matter what bearing it actually had on the significance of current circumstances. There is no precedent for the Counties' arguments, or reason supporting them.

Lemon said that government action must have "a secular ... purpose," and after a host of cases it is fair to add that although a legislature's stated reasons will generally get deference, the secular purpose required has to be genuine, not a sham, and not merely secondary to a religious objective.... As we said, the Court often does accept governmental statements of purpose, in keeping with the respect owed in the first instance to such official claims. But in those unusual cases where the claim was an apparent sham, or the secular purpose secondary, the unsurprising results have been findings of no adequate secular object, as against a predominantly religious one.

The Counties' second proffered limitation can be dispatched quickly. They argue that purpose in a case like this one should be inferred, if at all, only from the latest news about the last in a series of governmental actions, however close they may all be in time and subject. But the world is not made brand new every morning, and the Counties are simply asking us to ignore perfectly probative evidence; they want an absentminded objective observer, not one presumed to be familiar with the history of the government's actions and competent to learn what history has to show.... The Counties' position just bucks common sense: reasonable observers have reasonable memories, and our precedents sensibly forbid an observer "to turn a blind eye to the context in which [the] policy arose."

... Once the Counties were sued, they modified the exhibits and invited additional insight into their purpose in a display that hung for about six months.... [T]he second version was required to include the statement of the government's purpose expressly set out in the county resolutions, and underscored it by juxtaposing the Commandments to other documents with highlighted references to God as their sole common element. The display's unstinting focus was on religious passages, showing that the Counties were posting the Commandments precisely because of their sectarian content. That demonstration of the government's objective was enhanced by serial religious references and the accompanying resolution's claim about the embodiment of ethics in Christ. Together, the display and resolution presented an indisputable, and undisputed, showing of an impermissible purpose. Today, the Counties make no attempt to defend their undeniable objective, but instead hopefully describe version two as "dead and buried." Their refusal to defend the second display is understandable, but the reasonable observer could not forget it.

After the Counties changed lawyers, they mounted a third display, without a new resolution or repeal of the old one. The result was the "Foundations of American Law and Government" exhibit, which placed the Commandments in the company of other documents the Counties thought especially significant in the historical foundation of American government. In trying to persuade the District Court to lift the preliminary injunction, the Counties cited several new purposes for the third version, including a desire "to educate the citizens of the county regarding some of the documents that played a significant role in the foundation of our system of law and government." The Counties' claims did not, however, persuade the court, intimately familiar with the details of this litigation, or the Court of Appeals, neither of which found a legitimizing secular purpose in this third version of the display. "'When both courts [that have already passed on the case] are unable to discern an arguably valid secular purpose, this Court normally should hesitate to find one.'" The conclusions of the two courts preceding us in this case are well warranted.

These new statements of purpose were presented only as a litigating position, there being no further authorizing action by the Counties' governing boards. And although repeal of the earlier county authorizations would not have erased them from the record of evidence bearing on current purpose, the extraordinary resolutions for the second display passed just months earlier were not repealed or otherwise repudiated.... No reasonable observer could swallow the claim that the Counties had cast off the objective so unmistakable in the earlier displays.

Nor did the selection of posted material suggest a clear theme that might prevail over evidence of the continuing religious object. In a collection of documents said to be "foundational" to American government, it is at least odd to include a patriotic anthem, but to omit the Fourteenth Amendment, the most significant structural provision adopted since the original Framing. And it is no less baffling to leave out the original Constitution of 1787 while quoting the 1215 Magna Carta even to the point of its declaration that "fish-weirs shall be removed from the Thames." If an observer found these choices and omissions perplexing in isolation, he would be puzzled for a different reason when he read the Declaration of Independence seeking confirmation for the Counties' posted explanation that the Ten Commandments' "influence is clearly seen in the Declaration"; in fact the observer would find that the Commandments are sanctioned as divine imperatives, while the Declaration of Independence holds that the authority of government to enforce the law derives "from the consent of the governed." If the observer had not thrown up his hands, he would probably suspect that the Counties were simply reaching for any way to keep a religious document on the walls of courthouses constitutionally required to embody religious neutrality.

In holding the preliminary injunction adequately supported by evidence that the Counties' purpose had not changed at the third stage, we do not decide that the Counties' past actions forever taint any effort on their part to deal with the subject matter. We hold only that purpose needs to be taken seriously under the Establishment Clause and needs to be understood in light of context; an implausible claim that governmental purpose has changed should not carry the day in a court of law any more than in a head with common sense.... Nor do we have occasion here to hold that a sacred text can never be integrated constitutionally into a governmental display on the subject of law, or American history. We do not forget, and in this litigation have frequently been reminded, that our own courtroom frieze was deliberately designed in the exercise of governmental authority so as to include the figure of Moses holding tablets exhibiting a portion of the Hebrew text of the later, secularly phrased Commandments; in the company of 17 other lawgivers, most of them secular figures, there is no risk that Moses would strike an observer as evidence that the National Government was violating neutrality in religion....

The importance of neutrality as an interpretive guide is no less true now than it was when the Court broached the principle in Everson v. Board of Ed. of Ewing (1947), and a word needs to be said about the different view taken in today's dissent. We all agree, of course, on the need for some interpretative help. The First Amendment contains no textual definition of "establishment," and the term is certainly not self-defining. No one contends that the prohibition of establishment stops at a designation of a national (or with Fourteenth Amendment incorporation, a state) church, but nothing in the text says just how much more it covers. There is no simple answer, for more than one reason.

The prohibition on establishment covers a variety of issues from prayer in widely varying government settings, to financial aid for religious individuals and institutions, to comment on religious questions. In these varied settings, issues of interpreting inexact Establishment Clause language, like difficult interpretative issues generally, arise from the tension of competing values, each constitutionally respectable, but none open to realization to the logical limit.

The First Amendment has not one but two clauses tied to "religion," the second forbidding any prohibition on "the free exercise thereof," and sometimes, the two clauses compete: spending government money on the clergy looks like establishing religion, but if the government cannot pay for military chaplains a good many soldiers and sailors would be kept from the opportunity to exercise their chosen religions. At other times, limits on governmental action that might make sense as a way to avoid establishment could arguably limit freedom of speech when the speaking is done under government auspices. The dissent, then, is wrong to read [some prior cases] as a rejection of neutrality on its own terms, for tradeoffs are inevitable, and an elegant interpretative rule to draw the line in all the multifarious situations is not to be had. Given the variety of interpretative problems, the principle of neutrality has provided a good sense of direction: the government may not favor one religion over another, or religion over irreligion, religious choice being the prerogative of individuals under the Free Exercise Clause. The principle has been helpful simply because it responds to one of the major concerns that prompted adoption of the Religion Clauses. The Framers and the citizens of their time intended not only to protect the integrity of individual conscience in religious matters, but to guard against the civic divisiveness that follows when the government weighs in on one side of religious debate; nothing does a better job of roiling society, a point that needed no explanation to the descendants of English Puritans and Cavaliers (or Massachusetts Puritans and Baptists). A sense of the past thus points to governmental neutrality as an objective of the Establishment Clause, and a sensible standard for applying it. To be sure, given its generality as a principle, an appeal to neutrality alone cannot possibly lay every issue to rest, or tell us what issues on the margins are substantial enough for constitutional significance, a point that has been clear from the founding era to modern times. *E.g.,* Letter from J. Madison to R. Adams (1832), in 5 The Founders' Constitution 107 (P. Kurland & R. Lerner eds. 1987) ("[In calling for separation] I must admit moreover that it may not be easy, in every possible case, to trace the line of separation between the rights of religion and the Civil authority with such distinctness as to avoid collisions & doubts on unessential points"). But invoking neutrality is a prudent way of keeping sight of something the Framers of the First Amendment thought important.

The dissent, however, puts forward a limitation on the application of the neutrality principle, with citations to historical evidence said to show that the Framers understood the ban on establishment of religion as sufficiently narrow to allow the government to espouse submission to the divine will. The dissent identifies God as the God of monotheism, all of whose three principal strains (Jewish, Christian, and Muslim) acknowledge the religious importance of the Ten Commandments. On the dissent's view, it apparently follows that even rigorous espousal of a common element of this common monotheism is consistent with the establishment ban. But the dissent's argument for the original understanding is flawed from the outset by its failure to consider the full range of evidence showing what the Framers believed. The dissent is certainly correct in putting forward evidence that some of the Framers thought some endorsement of religion was compatible with the establishment ban; the dissent quotes the first President as stating that "[n]ational morality [cannot] prevail in exclusion of religious principle," and it cites his first Thanksgiving proclamation giving thanks to God. Surely if expressions like these from Washington and his contemporaries were all we had to go on, there would be a good case that the neutrality principle has the effect of broadening the ban on establishment beyond the Framers' understanding of it (although there would, of course, still be the question of whether the historical case could overcome some 60 years of precedent taking neutrality as its guiding principle).

But the fact is that we do have more to go on, for there is also evidence supporting the proposition that the Framers intended the Establishment Clause to require governmental neutrality in matters of religion, including neutrality in statements acknowledging religion. The very language of the Establishment Clause represented a significant departure from early drafts that merely prohibited a single national religion, and the final language instead "extended [the] prohibition to state support for 'religion' in general." The historical record, moreover, is complicated beyond the dissent's account by the writings and practices of figures no less influential than Thomas Jefferson and James Madison. Jefferson, for example, refused to issue Thanksgiving Proclamations because he believed that they violated the Constitution. See Letter to S. Miller (Jan. 23, 1808), in 5 The Founders' Constitution, supra, at 98. And Madison, whom the dissent claims as supporting its thesis, post, at 2749–2750, criticized Virginia's general assessment tax not just because it required people to donate "three pence" to religion, but because "it is itself a signal of persecution. It degrades from the equal rank of Citizens all those whose opinions in Religion do not bend to those of the Legislative authority." [Citations omitted.]

The fair inference is that there was no common understanding about the limits of the establishment prohibition, and the dissent's conclusion that its narrower view was the original understanding, stretches the evidence beyond tensile capacity. What the evidence does show is a group of statesmen, like others before and after them, who proposed a guarantee with contours not wholly worked out, leaving the Establishment Clause with edges still to be determined. And none the worse for that. Indeterminate edges are the kind to have in a constitution meant to endure, and to meet "exigencies which, if foreseen at all, must have been seen dimly, and which can be best provided for as they occur." McCulloch v. Maryland, 4 Wheat. 316, 415, 4 L.Ed. 579 (1819).

While the dissent fails to show a consistent original understanding from which to argue that the neutrality principle should be rejected, it does manage to deliver a surprise. As mentioned, the dissent says that the deity the Framers had in mind was the God of monotheism, with the consequence that government may espouse a tenet of traditional monotheism. This is truly a remarkable view. Other Members of the Court have dissented on the ground that the Establishment Clause bars nothing more than governmental preference for one religion over another, but at least religion has previously been treated inclusively. Today's dissent, however, apparently means that government should be free to approve the core beliefs of a favored religion over the tenets of others, a view that should trouble anyone who prizes religious liberty. Certainly history cannot justify it; on the contrary, history shows that the religion of concern to the Framers was not that of the monotheistic faiths generally, but Christianity in particular, a fact that no Member of this Court takes as a premise for construing the Religion Clauses. Justice Story probably reflected the thinking of the framing generation when he wrote in his Commentaries that the purpose of the Clause was "not to countenance, much less to advance, Mahometanism, or Judaism, or infidelity, by prostrating Christianity; but to exclude all rivalry among Christian sects." The Framers would, therefore, almost certainly object to the dissent's unstated reasoning that because Christianity was a monotheistic "religion," monotheism with Mosaic antecedents should be a touchstone of establishment interpretation. Even on originalist critiques of existing precedent there is, it seems, no escape from interpretative consequences that would surprise the Framers. Thus, it appears to be common ground in the interpretation of a Constitution "intended to endure for ages to come," McCulloch v. Maryland, that applications unanticipated by the Framers are inevitable....

Given the ample support for the District Court's finding of a predominantly religious purpose behind the Counties' third display, we affirm the Sixth Circuit in upholding the preliminary injunction.

JUSTICE SCALIA, with whom THE CHIEF JUSTICE and JUSTICE THOMAS join, and with whom JUSTICE KENNEDY joins as to Parts II and III, dissenting.

… Besides appealing to the demonstrably false principle that the government cannot favor religion over irreligion, today's opinion suggests that the posting of the Ten Commandments violates the principle that the government cannot favor one religion over another. That is indeed a valid principle where public aid or assistance to religion is concerned, or where the free exercise of religion is at issue, but it necessarily applies in a more limited sense to public acknowledgment of the Creator. If religion in the public forum had to be entirely nondenominational, there could be no religion in the public forum at all. One cannot say the word "God," or "the Almighty," one cannot offer public supplication or thanksgiving, without contradicting the beliefs of some people that there are many gods, or that God or the gods pay no attention to human affairs. With respect to public acknowledgment of religious belief, it is entirely clear from our Nation's historical practices that the Establishment Clause permits this disregard of polytheists and believers in unconcerned deities, just as it permits the disregard of devout atheists. The Thanksgiving Proclamation issued by George Washington at the instance of the First Congress was scrupulously nondenominational—but it was monotheistic. In Marsh v. Chambers, supra, we said that the fact the particular prayers offered in the Nebraska Legislature were "in the Judeo-Christian tradition," posed no additional problem, because "there is no indication that the prayer opportunity has been exploited to proselytize or advance any one, or to disparage any other, faith or belief."

Historical practices thus demonstrate that there is a distance between the acknowledgment of a single Creator and the establishment of a religion. The former is, as Marsh v. Chambers put it, "a tolerable acknowledgment of beliefs widely held among the people of this country." The three most popular religions in the United States, Christianity, Judaism, and Islam—which combined account for 97.7% of all believers— are monotheistic. All of them, moreover (Islam included), believe that the Ten Commandments were given by God to Moses, and are divine prescriptions for a virtuous life. Publicly honoring the Ten Commandments is thus indistinguishable, insofar as discriminating against other religions is concerned, from publicly honoring God. Both practices are recognized across such a broad and diverse range of the population—from Christians to Muslims—that they cannot be reasonably understood as a government endorsement of a particular religious viewpoint.…

Review Questions and Explanations: *McCreary County*

1. Does Justice Souter's majority opinion follow *Lemon* or change it?

2. The attorneys for McCreary County made a point, as Justice Souter notes, of reminding the Court that the Supreme Court building, like the McCreary County courthouse, contains depictions of Moses as a law giver. Justice Souter distinguishes the two displays. Are you convinced by his reasoning?

3. The Supreme Court has declined to hear cases addressing the constitutionality of things like the stamping of "In God We Trust" on U.S. money and the addition of "Under God" to the Pledge of Allegiance. Under the test set out in *McCreary County,* what are the best arguments for and against the constitutionality of these things?

Exercise: Establishment Clause

Work through the following review question. Be prepared to discuss your work in class.

The Young Christian Club (YCC) at Joseph Story Memorial High School, a Massachusetts public school, obtained Principal Dan Murphy's assent to be listed as an "official" school club, which permits the club to reserve classroom space for meetings after normal instructional hours. Recognized school clubs are also generally permitted to use the school photocopier and office supplies up to a value of $50 per month, and to post club announcement in designated posting areas.

Concerned about Establishment Clause issues, Murphy has forbidden the YCC to receive the $50 copy/supplies allowance, but has allowed the organization to post material created at its own expense.

The YCC also has requested permission to lead a "non-sectarian" prayer at the beginning of Story High's Friday afternoon pep rally, an event regularly scheduled to celebrate that evening's varsity football game. The pep rally is held right after instructional hours, and attendance is optional. The school has for several years allowed the Dance Club and a small contingent of the marching band to perform at pep rallies. No other student organizations have expressed an interest in doing so. Principal Murphy granted permission to the YCC to lead this prayer.

Two potential lawsuits are now under consideration.

Jason Tolliver, YCC's leader, and his parents want to know whether YCC can sue the school to obtain the $50 copy/supplies allowance.

Priya Singh and her parents want to know whether they can sue the school to block the prayers at the pep rallies, and to force the school to withdraw its official recognition of the YCC as a student club.

With one or more fellow students, assume the roles of attorney and client, discuss how you would advise your clients.

C. The Free Exercise Clause

The First Amendment states that "Congress shall make no law respecting an establishment of religion, *or prohibiting the free exercise thereof.*" As in the Establishment Clause cases, the Supreme Court has struggled to develop workable doctrines from these sparse words. We focus here on a basic question: to what extent does the Free Exercise clause require the government to exempt religious practices from the reach of generally applicable laws? Consider, for example, a statute requiring all employers who provide health care plans to their employees to include within their plan insurance coverage for contraception. Does the Free Exercise clause prohibit the state from applying that law against an employer who also is a church with moral objections to birth control? Do churches have a right to be exempt from statutes prohibiting discrimination, in non-pastoral employment positions, on the basis of race or sex? What about families holding sincere religious beliefs about things like educating girls and forcing children into arranged marriages? Are they entitled to exemptions from generally applicable laws regulating these things? If your answer is "it depends," what does it depend on—what test, in other words, should courts use to decide such questions?

The first two cases below, *Sherbert v. Verner* and *Employment Division v. Smith*, give different answers to this basic question. Each position, as you will see, has distinct strengths and weaknesses. The final case, *Church of the Lukumi Babalu Aye v. City of Hialeah*, illustrates the Supreme Court's most recent thoughts on this issue.

Guided Reading Questions: *Sherbert v. Verner*

1. What is the religious exercise or observance at issue in *Sherbert* and how does the government place a burden on it?

2. How does the Court resolve the case? Can you distill a doctrinal principal from the decision?

3. The Court applies strict scrutiny in this case. What triggers that level of scrutiny? Why? How does the Court apply it?

Sherbert v. Verner

374 U.S. 398 (1963)

Majority: *Brennan*, Warren (CJ), Black, Douglas, Clark, Goldberg

Concurrence: *Douglas* (omitted)

Concurrence in the result: *Stewart*

Dissent: *Harlan*, White

MR. JUSTICE BRENNAN delivered the opinion of the Court.

Appellant, a member of the Seventh-day Adventist Church, was discharged by her South Carolina employer because she would not work on Saturday, the Sabbath Day of her faith. When she was unable to obtain other employment because from conscientious scruples she would not take Saturday work, she filed a claim for unemployment compensation benefits under the South Carolina Unemployment Compensation Act. That law provides that, to be eligible for benefits, a claimant must be "able to work and … available for work"; and, further, that a claimant is ineligible for benefits "if … he has failed, without good cause … to accept available suitable work when offered him by the employment office or the employer.…" The appellee Employment Security Commission, in administrative proceedings under the statute, found that appellant's restriction upon her availability for Saturday work brought her within the provision disqualifying for benefits insured workers who fail, without good cause, to accept "suitable work when offered … by the employment office or the employer.…" The Commission's finding was sustained by the Court of Common Pleas for Spartanburg County. That court's judgment was in turn affirmed by the South Carolina Supreme Court, which rejected appellant's [Free Exercise Clause challenge]. We reverse the judgment of the South Carolina Supreme Court …

The door of the Free Exercise Clause stands tightly closed against any governmental regulation of religious *beliefs* as such. Government may neither compel affirmation of a repugnant belief, nor penalize or discriminate against individuals or groups because they hold religious views abhorrent to the authorities, nor employ the taxing power to inhibit the dissemination of particular religious views. On the other hand, the Court has rejected challenges under the Free Exercise Clause to governmental regulation of certain overt acts prompted by religious beliefs or principles, for "even when the action is in accord with one's religious convictions, [it] is not totally free from legislative restrictions." The conduct or actions so regulated have invariably posed some substantial threat to public safety, peace or order.

Plainly enough, appellant's conscientious objection to Saturday work constitutes no conduct prompted by religious principles of a kind within the reach of state legislation. If, therefore, the decision of the South Carolina Supreme Court is to withstand appellant's constitutional challenge, it must be either because her disqualification as a beneficiary represents no infringement by the State of her constitutional rights of free exercise, or because any incidental burden on the free exercise of appellant's religion may be justified by a "compelling state interest in the regulation of a subject within the State's constitutional power to regulate...." NAACP v. Button, 371 U.S. 415, 438.

We turn first to the question whether the disqualification for benefits imposes any burden on the free exercise of appellant's religion. We think it is clear that it does.... For "if the purpose or effect of a law is to impede the observance of one or all religions or is to discriminate invidiously between religions, that law is constitutionally invalid even though the burden may be characterized as being only indirect." Here.... [t]he ruling forces her to choose between following the precepts of her religion and forfeiting benefits, on the one hand, and abandoning one of the precepts of her religion in order to accept work, on the other hand. Governmental imposition of such a choice puts the same kind of burden upon the free exercise of religion as would a fine imposed against appellant for her Saturday worship.

Nor may the South Carolina court's construction of the statute be saved from constitutional infirmity on the ground that unemployment compensation benefits are not appellant's "right" but merely a "privilege." It is too late in the day to doubt that the liberties of religion and expression may be infringed by the denial of or placing of conditions upon a benefit or privilege.... In Speiser v. Randall, 357 U.S. 513, we emphasized that conditions upon public benefits cannot be sustained if they so operate, whatever their purpose, as to inhibit or deter the exercise of First Amendment freedoms. We there struck down a condition which limited the availability of a tax exemption to those members of the exempted class who affirmed their loyalty to the state government granting the exemption. While the State was surely under no obligation to afford such an exemption, we held that the imposition of such a condition upon even a gratuitous benefit inevitably deterred or discouraged the exercise of First Amendment rights of expression and thereby threatened to "produce a result which the State could not command directly." 357 U.S., at 526.... Likewise, to condition the availability of benefits upon this appellant's willingness to violate a cardinal principle of her religious faith effectively penalizes the free exercise of her constitutional liberties.

Significantly South Carolina expressly saves the Sunday worshipper from having to make the kind of choice which we here hold infringes the Sabbatarian's religious liberty. When in times of "national emergency" the textile plants are authorized by the State Commissioner of Labor to operate on Sunday, "no employee shall be required to work on Sunday ... who is conscientiously opposed to Sunday work; and if any employee should refuse to work on Sunday on account of conscientious … objections he or she shall not jeopardize his or her seniority by such refusal or be discriminated against in any other manner." S. C. Code, § 64-4. No question of the disqualification of a Sunday worshipper for benefits is likely to arise, since we cannot suppose that an employer will discharge him in violation of this statute. The unconstitutionality of the disqualification of the Sabbatarian is thus compounded by the religious discrimination which South Carolina's general statutory scheme necessarily effects.

We must next consider whether some compelling state interest enforced in the eligibility provisions of the South Carolina statute justifies the substantial infringement of appellant's First Amendment right. It is basic that no showing merely of a rational relationship to some colorable state interest would suffice; in this highly sensitive constitutional area, "only the gravest abuses, endangering paramount interests, give occasion for permissible limitation," Thomas v. Collins, 323 U.S. 516, 530. No such abuse or danger has been advanced in the present case. The appellees suggest no more than a possibility that the filing of fraudulent claims by unscrupulous claimants feigning religious objections to Saturday work might not only dilute the unemployment compensation fund but also hinder the scheduling by employers of necessary Saturday work. But…. there is no proof whatever to warrant such fears of malingering or deceit as those which the respondents now advance. Even if…. the possibility of spurious claims did threaten to dilute the fund and disrupt the scheduling of work, it would plainly be incumbent upon the appellees to demonstrate that no alternative forms of regulation would combat such abuses without infringing First Amendment rights.

In these respects, then, the state interest asserted in the present case is wholly dissimilar to the interests which were found to justify the less direct burden upon religious practices in Braunfeld v. Brown, supra. The Court recognized that the Sunday closing law which that decision sustained undoubtedly served "to make the practice of [the Orthodox Jewish merchants'] … religious beliefs more expensive," 366 U.S., at 605. But the statute was nevertheless saved by a countervailing factor which finds no equivalent in the instant case—a strong state interest in providing one uniform day of rest for all workers. That secular objective could be achieved, the Court found, only by declaring Sunday to be that day of rest. Requiring exemptions for Sabbatarians, while theoretically possible, appeared to present an administrative problem of such magnitude, or to afford the exempted class so great a competitive advantage, that such a requirement would have rendered the entire statutory scheme unworkable. In the present case no such justifications underlie the determination of the state court that appellant's religion makes her ineligible to receive benefits.

In holding as we do, plainly we are not fostering…. that involvement of religious with secular institutions which it is the object of the Establishment Clause to forestall. Nor does the recognition of the appellant's right to unemployment benefits under the state statute serve to abridge any other person's religious liberties. Nor do we, by our decision today, declare the existence of a constitutional right to unemployment benefits on the part of all persons whose religious convictions are the cause of their unemployment. This is not a case in which an employee's religious convictions serve to make him a nonproductive member of society….

The judgment of the South Carolina Supreme Court is reversed and the case is remanded for further proceedings not inconsistent with this opinion.

MR. JUSTICE STEWART, concurring in the result.

Although fully agreeing with the result which the Court reaches in this case, I cannot join the Court's opinion…. I think that the Court's approach to the Establishment Clause has on occasion, and specifically in Engel, Schempp and Murray, been not only insensitive, but positively wooden, and that the Court has accorded to the Establishment Clause a meaning which neither the words, the history, nor the intention of the authors of that specific constitutional provision even remotely suggests.... [T]he result is that there are many situations where legitimate claims under the Free Exercise Clause will run into head-on collision with the Court's insensitive and sterile construction of the Establishment Clause. The controversy now before us is clearly such a case....

To require South Carolina to so administer its laws as to pay public money to the appellant under the circumstances of this case is ... to require the State to violate the Establishment Clause as construed by this Court. This poses no problem for me, because I think the Court's mechanistic concept of the Establishment Clause is historically unsound and constitutionally wrong. I think the process of constitutional decision in the area of the relationships between government and religion demands considerably more than the invocation of broad-brushed rhetoric of the kind I have quoted. And I think that the guarantee of religious liberty embodied in the Free Exercise Clause affirmatively requires government to create an atmosphere of hospitality and accommodation to individual belief or disbelief. In short, I think our Constitution commands the positive protection by government of religious freedom—not only for a minority, however small—not only for the majority, however large—but for each of us....

My second difference with the Court's opinion is that I cannot agree that today's decision can stand consistently with Braunfeld v. Brown, supra.... I think the Braunfeld case was wrongly decided and should be overruled....

MR. JUSTICE HARLAN, whom MR. JUSTICE WHITE joins, dissenting.

.... South Carolina's Unemployment Compensation Law was enacted.... to tide people over, and to avoid social and economic chaos, during periods when *work was unavailable.* But at the same time there was clearly no intent to provide relief for those who for purely personal reasons were or became *unavailable for work.* In accordance with this design, the legislature provided, in § 68-113, that "an unemployed insured worker shall be eligible to receive benefits with respect to any week *only* if the Commission finds that ... he is able to work and is available for work...." (emphasis added).

The South Carolina Supreme Court has uniformly applied this law in conformity with its clearly expressed purpose. It has consistently held that one is not "available for work" if his unemployment has resulted not from the inability of industry to provide a job but rather from personal circumstances, no matter how compelling. The reference to "involuntary unemployment" in the legislative statement of policy, whatever a sociologist, philosopher, or theologian might say, has been interpreted not to embrace such personal circumstances. In the present case all that the state court has done is to apply these accepted principles. Since virtually all of the mills in the Spartanburg area were operating on a six-day week, the appellant was "unavailable for work," and thus ineligible for benefits, when personal considerations prevented her from accepting employment on a full-time basis in the industry and locality in which she had worked. The fact that these personal considerations sprang from her religious convictions was wholly without relevance to the state court's application of the law. Thus in no proper sense can it be said that the State discriminated against the appellant on the basis of her religious beliefs or that she was denied benefits *because* she was a Seventh-day Adventist. She was denied benefits just as any other claimant would be denied benefits who was not "available for work" for personal reasons.

.... [T]he implications of the present decision are far more troublesome than its apparently narrow dimensions would indicate at first glance. The meaning of today's holding, as already noted, is that the State must furnish unemployment benefits to one who is unavailable for work if the unavailability stems from the exercise of religious convictions. The State, in other words, must *single out* for financial assistance those whose behavior is religiously motivated, even though it denies such assistance to others whose identical behavior (in this case, inability to work on Saturdays) is not religiously motivated.

.... I cannot subscribe to the conclusion that the State is constitutionally *compelled* to carve out an exception to its general rule of eligibility in the present case. Those situations in which the Constitution may require special treatment on account of religion are, in my view, few and far between, and this view is amply supported by the course of constitutional litigation in this area. See, e.g., Braunfeld v. Brown, supra. Such compulsion in the present case is particularly inappropriate in light of the indirect, remote, and insubstantial effect of the decision below on the exercise of appellant's religion and in light of the direct financial assistance to religion that today's decision requires.

For these reasons I respectfully dissent from the opinion and judgment of the Court.

Review Questions and Explanations: *Sherbert v. Verner*

1. Does *Sherbert*'s holding depend on the fact that the law accommodated Sunday Sabbath observance? In other words, does the First Amendment allow government to burden religious exercises that have no analogue in mainstream religious observances accommodated by the government?

2. The First Amendment speaks in terms of laws "*prohibiting* the free exercise" of religion. Is it appropriate, then, for the Court to focus on whether the law imposes a "burden" on free exercise?

3. Are you persuaded by the majority's effort to distinguish *Braunfield v. Braun*, which upheld Sunday closing laws (a/k/a "blue laws") prohibiting businesses from being open on Sunday in order to further a compelling state interest in a "uniform day of rest"?

4. The dissent in *Sherbert* seems troubled by the notion that religious reasons for declining Saturday work receive preferential treatment over other personal reasons. Does the dissent have a good point here—that free exercise doesn't require the state to bend over backwards to make religious exercise cost free? Is the opposite notion attributable to the Court's substitution of the word "burden" for "prohibition" in considering free exercise claims?

Guided Reading Questions: *Employment Division v. Smith*

1. Review the facts of *Smith* carefully. What happened to Smith and what are his claims? How close are these facts to the facts of *Sherbert*?

2. What does the Court say about the *Sherbert* test? After *Smith*, what is the doctrinal status of that test?

3. What test does the Court apply instead of the *Sherbert* test?

4. What tests are proposed in the concurring and dissenting opinions?

Employment Division, Department of Human Resources of Oregon v. Smith

494 U.S. 872 (1990)

Majority: *Scalia*, Rehnquist (CJ), White, Stevens, Kennedy

Concurrence in the judgment: *O'Connor*, Brennan, Marshall, Blackmun (joining in parts I and II only, without concurring in the judgment)

Dissent: *Blackmun*, Brennan, Marshall

JUSTICE SCALIA delivered the opinion of the Court.

This case requires us to decide whether the Free Exercise Clause of the First Amendment permits the State of Oregon to include religiously inspired peyote use within the reach of its general criminal prohibition on use of that drug, and thus permits the State to deny unemployment benefits to persons dismissed from their jobs because of such religiously inspired use.

Oregon law prohibits the knowing or intentional possession of a "controlled substance" unless the substance has been prescribed by a medical practitioner. The law defines "controlled substance" as a drug classified in Schedules I through V of the Federal Controlled Substances Act, 21 U. S. C. §§ 811–812, as modified by the State Board of Pharmacy. Ore. Rev. Stat. § 475.005(6). Persons who violate this provision by possessing a controlled substance listed on Schedule I are "guilty of a Class B felony." § 475.992(4)(a). As compiled by the State Board of Pharmacy under its statutory authority, see § 475.035, Schedule I contains the drug peyote, a hallucinogen. . . .

Respondents Alfred Smith and Galen Black (hereinafter respondents) were fired from their jobs with a private drug rehabilitation organization because they ingested peyote for sacramental purposes at a ceremony of the Native American Church, of which both are members. When respondents applied to petitioner Employment Division (hereinafter petitioner) for unemployment compensation, they were determined to be ineligible for benefits because they had been discharged for work-related "misconduct." The Oregon Court of Appeals reversed that determination, holding that the denial of benefits violated respondents' free exercise rights under the First Amendment. . . . The Oregon Supreme Court [affirmed, on the grounds] that the criminality of respondents' peyote use was irrelevant to resolution of their constitutional claim—since the purpose of the "misconduct" provision under which respondents had been disqualified was not to enforce the State's criminal laws but to preserve the financial integrity of the compensation fund, and since that purpose was inadequate to justify the burden that disqualification imposed on respondents' religious practice. Citing our decisions in Sherbert v. Verner, 374 U.S. 398 (1963), and Thomas v. Review Bd. of Indiana Employment Security Div., 450 U.S. 707 (1981), the court concluded that respondents were entitled to payment of unemployment benefits. We granted certiorari.

Before this Court in 1987, petitioner continued to maintain that the illegality of respondents' peyote consumption was relevant to their constitutional claim. We agreed, concluding that "if a State has prohibited through its criminal laws certain kinds of religiously motivated conduct without violating the First Amendment, it certainly follows that it may impose the lesser burden of denying unemployment compensation benefits to persons who engage in that conduct." Employment Div., Dept. of Human Resources of Oregon v. Smith, 485 U.S. 660, 670 (1988) (Smith I). We noted, however, that the Oregon Supreme Court had not decided whether respondents' sacramental use of peyote was in fact proscribed by Oregon's controlled substance law, and that this issue was a matter of dispute between the parties. Being "uncertain about the legality of the religious use of peyote in Oregon," we determined that it would not be "appropriate for us to decide whether the practice is protected by the Federal Constitution." Accordingly, we vacated the judgment of the Oregon Supreme Court and remanded for further proceedings.

On remand, the Oregon Supreme Court held that respondents' religiously inspired use of peyote fell within the prohibition of the Oregon statute, which "makes no exception for the sacramental use" of the drug. It then considered whether that prohibition was valid under the Free Exercise Clause, and concluded that it was not. The court therefore reaffirmed its previous ruling that the State could not deny unemployment benefits to respondents for having engaged in that practice. We again granted certiorari.

II

Respondents' claim for relief rests on our decisions in Sherbert v. Verner, supra, Thomas v. Review Bd. of Indiana Employment Security Div., supra, and Hobbie v. Unemployment Appeals Comm'n of Florida, 480 U.S. 136 (1987), in which we held that a State could not condition the availability of unemployment insurance on an individual's willingness to forgo conduct required by his religion. As we observed in Smith I, however, the conduct at issue in those cases was not prohibited by law. We held that distinction to be critical. . . . Now that the Oregon Supreme Court has confirmed that Oregon does prohibit the religious use of peyote, we proceed to consider whether that prohibition is permissible under the Free Exercise Clause.

A

The Free Exercise Clause of the First Amendment, which has been made applicable to the States by incorporation into the Fourteenth Amendment, see Cantwell v. Connecticut, 310 U.S. 296, 303 (1940), provides that "Congress shall make no law respecting an establishment of religion, or prohibiting the free exercise thereof. . . ." The free exercise of religion means, first and foremost, the right to believe and profess whatever religious doctrine one desires. Thus, the First Amendment obviously excludes all "governmental regulation of religious beliefs as such." Sherbert v. Verner, supra, at 402. The government may not compel affirmation of religious belief, punish the expression of religious doctrines it believes to be false, impose special disabilities on the basis of religious views or religious status, or lend its power to one or the other side in controversies over religious authority or dogma.

But the "exercise of religion" often involves not only belief and profession but the performance of (or abstention from) physical acts: assembling with others for a worship service, participating in sacramental use of bread and wine, proselytizing, abstaining from certain foods or certain modes of transportation. It would be true, we think (though no case of ours has involved the point), that a State would be "prohibiting the free exercise [of religion]" if it sought to ban such acts or abstentions only when they are engaged in for religious reasons, or only because of the religious belief that they display. It would doubtless be unconstitutional, for example, to ban the casting of "statues that are to be used for worship purposes," or to prohibit bowing down before a golden calf.

Respondents in the present case, however, seek to carry the meaning of "prohibiting the free exercise [of religion]" one large step further. They contend that their religious motivation for using peyote places them beyond the reach of a criminal law that is not specifically directed at their religious practice, and that is concededly constitutional as applied to those who use the drug for other reasons. They assert, in other words, that "prohibiting the free exercise [of religion]" includes requiring any individual to observe a generally applicable law that requires (or forbids) the performance of an act that his religious belief forbids (or requires). As a textual matter, we do not think the words must be given that meaning. It is no more necessary to regard the collection of a general tax, for example, as "prohibiting the free exercise [of religion]" by those citizens who believe support of organized government to be sinful, than it is to regard the same tax as "abridging the freedom ... of the press" of those publishing companies that must pay the tax as a condition of staying in business. It is a permissible reading of the text, in the one case as in the other, to say that if prohibiting the exercise of religion (or burdening the activity of printing) is not the object of the tax but merely the incidental effect of a generally applicable and otherwise valid provision, the First Amendment has not been offended.

Our decisions reveal that the latter reading is the correct one. We have never held that an individual's religious beliefs excuse him from compliance with an otherwise valid law prohibiting conduct that the State is free to regulate. On the contrary, the record of more than a century of our free exercise jurisprudence contradicts that proposition. As described succinctly by Justice Frankfurter in Minersville School Dist. Bd. of Ed. v. Gobitis, 310 U.S. 586, 594–595 (1940): "Conscientious scruples have not, in the course of the long struggle for religious toleration, relieved the individual from obedience to a general law not aimed at the promotion or restriction of religious beliefs. The mere possession of religious convictions which contradict the relevant concerns of a political society does not relieve the citizen from the discharge of political responsibilities." ...

Our most recent decision involving a neutral, generally applicable regulatory law that compelled activity forbidden by an individual's religion was United States v. Lee, 455 U.S., at 258–261. There, an Amish employer, on behalf of himself and his employees, sought exemption from collection and payment of Social Security taxes on the ground that the Amish faith prohibited participation in governmental support programs. We rejected the claim that an exemption was constitutionally required. There would be no way, we observed, to distinguish the Amish believer's objection to Social Security taxes from the religious objections that others might have to the collection or use of other taxes....

The only decisions in which we have held that the First Amendment bars application of a neutral, generally applicable law to religiously motivated action have involved not the Free Exercise Clause alone, but the Free Exercise Clause in conjunction with other constitutional protections, such as freedom of speech and of the press, or the right of parents, acknowledged in Pierce v. Society of Sisters, 268 U.S. 510 (1925), to direct the education of their children, see Wisconsin v. Yoder, 406 U.S. 205 (1972). Some of our cases prohibiting compelled expression, decided exclusively upon free speech grounds, have also involved freedom of religion, cf. Wooley v. Maynard, 430 U.S. 705 (1977) (invalidating compelled display of a license plate slogan that offended individual religious beliefs); West Virginia Bd. of Education v. Barnette, 319 U.S. 624 (1943) (invalidating compulsory flag salute statute challenged by religious objectors). And it is easy to envision a case in which a challenge on freedom of association grounds would likewise be reinforced by Free Exercise Clause concerns.

The present case does not present such a hybrid situation, but a free exercise claim unconnected with any communicative activity or parental right. Respondents urge us to hold, quite simply, that when otherwise prohibitable conduct is accompanied by religious convictions, not only the convictions but the conduct itself must be free from governmental regulation. We have never held that, and decline to do so now. There [is] no contention that Oregon's drug law represents an attempt to regulate religious beliefs, the communication of religious beliefs, or the raising of one's children in those beliefs....

B

Respondents argue that even though exemption from generally applicable criminal laws need not automatically be extended to religiously motivated actors, at least the claim for a religious exemption must be evaluated under the balancing test set forth in Sherbert v. Verner, 374 U.S. 398 (1963). Under the Sherbert test, governmental actions that substantially burden a religious practice must be justified by a compelling governmental interest.... We have never invalidated any governmental action on the basis of the Sherbert test except the denial of unemployment compensation. Although we have sometimes purported to apply the Sherbert test in contexts other than that, we have always found the test satisfied. In recent years we have abstained from applying the Sherbert test (outside the unemployment compensation field) at all....

Even if we were inclined to breathe into Sherbert some life beyond the unemployment compensation field, we would not apply it to require exemptions from a generally applicable criminal law. The Sherbert test, it must be recalled, was developed in a context that lent itself to individualized governmental assessment of the reasons for the relevant conduct. [A] distinctive feature of unemployment compensation programs is that their eligibility criteria invite consideration of the particular circumstances behind an applicant's unemployment: "The statutory conditions [in Sherbert and Thomas] provided that a person was not eligible for unemployment compensation benefits if, 'without good cause,' he had quit work or refused available work. The 'good cause' standard created a mechanism for individualized exemptions.".... [O]ur decisions in the unemployment cases stand for the proposition that where the State has in place a system of individual exemptions, it may not refuse to extend that system to cases of "religious hardship" without compelling reason.

Whether or not the decisions are that limited, they at least have nothing to do with an across-the-board criminal prohibition on a particular form of conduct.... We conclude today that the sounder approach, and the approach in accord with the vast majority of our precedents, is to hold the test inapplicable to such challenges. The government's ability to enforce generally applicable prohibitions of socially harmful conduct, like its ability to carry out other aspects of public policy, "cannot depend on measuring the effects of a governmental action on a religious objector's spiritual development." To make an individual's obligation to obey such a law contingent upon the law's coincidence with his religious beliefs, except where the State's interest is "compelling"—permitting him, by virtue of his beliefs, "to become a law unto himself," contradicts both constitutional tradition and common sense.

Nor is it possible to limit the impact of respondents' proposal by requiring a "compelling state interest" only when the conduct prohibited is "central" to the individual's religion. It is no more appropriate for judges to determine the "centrality" of religious beliefs before applying a "compelling interest" test in the free exercise field, than it would be for them to determine the "importance" of ideas before applying the "compelling interest" test in the free speech field.... Repeatedly and in many different contexts, we have warned that courts must not presume to determine the place of a particular belief in a religion or the plausibility of a religious claim.

If the "compelling interest" test is to be applied at all, then, it must be applied across the board, to all actions thought to be religiously commanded. Moreover, if "compelling interest" really means what it says (and watering it down here would subvert its rigor in the other fields where it is applied), many laws will not meet the test. Any society adopting such a system would be courting anarchy, but that danger increases in direct proportion to the society's diversity of religious beliefs, and its determination to coerce or suppress none of them. Precisely because "we are a cosmopolitan nation made up of people of almost every conceivable religious preference," Braunfeld v. Brown, 366 U.S., at 606, and precisely because we value and protect that religious divergence, we cannot afford the luxury of deeming presumptively invalid, as applied to the religious objector, every regulation of conduct that does not protect an interest of the highest order. The rule respondents favor would open the prospect of constitutionally required religious exemptions from civic obligations of almost every conceivable kind—ranging from compulsory military service, see, e.g., Gillette v. United States, 401 U.S. 437 (1971), to the payment of taxes, see, e.g., United States v. Lee, supra; to health and safety regulation such as manslaughter and child neglect laws, see, e.g., Funkhouser v. State, 763 P. 2d 695 (Okla. Crim. App. 1988), compulsory vaccination laws, see, e.g., Cude v. State, 237 Ark. 927, 377 S. W. 2d 816 (1964), drug laws, see, e.g., Olsen v. Drug Enforcement Administration, 279 U. S. App. D. C. 1, 878 F. 2d 1458 (1989), and traffic laws, see Cox v. New Hampshire, 312 U.S. 569 (1941); to social welfare legislation such as minimum wage laws, see Tony and Susan Alamo Foundation v. Secretary of Labor, 471 U.S. 290 (1985), child labor laws, see Prince v. Massachusetts, 321 U.S. 158 (1944), animal cruelty laws, see, e.g., Church of the Lukumi Babalu Aye Inc. v. City of Hialeah, 723 F. Supp. 1467 (SD Fla. 1989), cf. State v. Massey, 229 N. C. 734, 51 S. E. 2d 179, appeal dism'd, 336 U.S. 942 (1949), environmental protection laws, see United States v. Little, 638 F. Supp. 337 (Mont. 1986), and laws providing for equality of opportunity for the races, see, e.g., Bob Jones University v. United States, 461 U.S. 574, 603–604 (1983). The First Amendment's protection of religious liberty does not require this.

Values that are protected against government interference through enshrinement in the Bill of Rights are not thereby banished from the political process. Just as a society that believes in the negative protection accorded to the press by the First Amendment is likely to enact laws that affirmatively foster the dissemination of the printed word, so also a society that believes in the negative protection accorded to religious belief can be expected to be solicitous of that value in its legislation as well. It is therefore not surprising that a number of States have made an exception to their drug laws for sacramental peyote use. But to say that a nondiscriminatory religious-practice exemption is permitted, or even that it is desirable, is not to say that it is constitutionally required, and that the appropriate occasions for its creation can be discerned by the courts. It may fairly be said that leaving accommodation to the political process will place at a relative disadvantage those religious practices that are not widely engaged in; but that unavoidable consequence of democratic government must be preferred to a system in which each conscience is a law unto itself or in which judges weigh the social importance of all laws against the centrality of all religious beliefs.

Because respondents' ingestion of peyote was prohibited under Oregon law, and because that prohibition is constitutional, Oregon may, consistent with the Free Exercise Clause, deny respondents unemployment compensation when their dismissal results from use of the drug. The decision of the Oregon Supreme Court is accordingly reversed.

JUSTICE O'CONNOR, with whom JUSTICE BRENNAN, JUSTICE MARSHALL, and JUSTICE BLACKMUN join as to Parts I and II, concurring in the judgment.*

* Although Justice Brennan, Justice Marshall, and Justice Blackmun join Parts I and II of this opinion, they do not concur in the judgment.

I

.... The Court today ... interprets the [free exercise] Clause to permit the government to prohibit, without justification, conduct mandated by an individual's religious beliefs, so long as that prohibition is generally applicable. But a law that prohibits certain con-duct — conduct that happens to be an act of worship for someone — manifestly does prohibit that person's free exercise of his religion.... [E]ven if the law is generally applicable, [it] does ... at least implicate First Amendment concerns.

.... The First Amendment, however, does not distinguish between laws that are generally applicable and laws that target particular religious practices. Indeed, few States would be so naive as to enact a law directly prohibiting or burdening a religious practice as such. Our free exercise cases have all concerned generally applicable laws that had the effect of significantly burdening a religious practice. If the First Amendment is to have any vitality, it ought not be construed to cover only the extreme and hypothetical situation in which a State directly targets a religious practice....

In my view, however, the essence of a free exercise claim is relief from a burden imposed by government on religious practices or beliefs, whether the burden is imposed directly through laws that prohibit or compel specific religious practices, or indirectly through laws that, in effect, make abandonment of one's own religion or conformity to the religious beliefs of others the price of an equal place in the civil community.... The Sherbert compelling interest test applies in both kinds of cases.... I would reaffirm that principle today: A neutral criminal law prohibiting conduct that a State may legitimately regulate is, if anything, more burdensome than a neutral civil statute placing legitimate conditions on the award of a state benefit....

III

.... There is no dispute that Oregon's criminal prohibition of peyote places a severe burden on the ability of respondents to freely exercise their religion. Peyote is a sacrament of the Native American Church and is regarded as vital to respondents' ability to practice their religion....

Thus, the critical question in this case is whether exempting respondents from the State's general criminal prohibition "will unduly interfere with fulfillment of the governmental interest." Although the question is close, I would conclude that uniform application of Oregon's criminal prohibition is "essential to accomplish," its overriding interest in preventing the physical harm caused by the use of a Schedule I controlled sub-stance....

I would therefore adhere to our established free exercise jurisprudence and hold that the State in this case has a compelling interest in regulating peyote use by its citizens and that accommodating respondents' religiously motivated conduct "will unduly interfere with fulfillment of the governmental interest." Lee, supra, at 259. Accordingly, I concur in the judgment of the Court.

JUSTICE BLACKMUN, with whom JUSTICE BRENNAN and JUSTICE MARSHALL join, dissenting.

This Court over the years painstakingly has developed a consistent and exacting standard to test the constitutionality of a state statute that burdens the free exercise of religion. Such a statute may stand only if the law in general, and the State's refusal to allow a religious exemption in particular, are justified by a compelling interest that cannot be served by less restrictive means.

.... It is not the State's broad interest in fighting the critical "war on drugs" that must be weighed against respondents' claim, but the State's narrow interest in refusing to make an exception for the religious, ceremonial use of peyote. Failure to reduce the competing interests to the same plane of generality tends to distort the weighing process in the State's favor.

The State's interest in enforcing its prohibition, in order to be sufficiently compelling to outweigh a free exercise claim, cannot be merely abstract or symbolic. The State cannot plausibly assert that unbending application of a criminal prohibition is essential to fulfill any compelling interest, if it does not, in fact, attempt to enforce that prohibition. In this case, the State actually has not evinced any concrete interest in enforcing its drug laws against religious users of peyote. Oregon has never sought to prosecute respondents, and does not claim that it has made significant enforcement efforts against other religious users of peyote. The State's asserted interest thus amounts only to the symbolic preservation of an unenforced prohibition. But a government interest in "symbolism, even symbolism for so worthy a cause as the abolition of unlawful drugs," cannot suffice to abrogate the constitutional rights of individuals.

Similarly, this Court's prior decisions have not allowed a government to rely on mere speculation about potential harms, but have demanded evidentiary support for a refusal to allow a religious exception. In this case, the State's justification for refusing to recognize an exception to its criminal laws for religious peyote use is entirely speculative.

The State proclaims an interest in protecting the health and safety of its citizens from the dangers of unlawful drugs. It offers, however, no evidence that the religious use of peyote has ever harmed anyone....

> FN4. This dearth of evidence is not surprising, since the State never asserted this health and safety interest before the Oregon courts; thus, there was no opportunity for factfinding concerning the alleged dangers of peyote use. What has now become the State's principal argument for its view that the criminal prohibition is enforceable against religious use of peyote rests on no evidentiary foundation at all.

The fact that peyote is classified as a Schedule I controlled substance does not, by itself, show that any and all uses of peyote, in any circumstance, are inherently harmful and dangerous. The Federal Government, which created the classifications of unlawful drugs from which Oregon's drug laws are derived, apparently does not find peyote so dangerous as to preclude an exemption for religious use. [See 21 CFR § 1307.31 (1989) ("The listing of peyote as a controlled substance in Schedule I does not apply to the nondrug use of peyote in bona fide religious ceremonies of the Native American Church, and members of the Native American Church so using peyote are exempt from registration.")].... The State also seeks to support its refusal to make an exception for religious use of peyote by invoking its interest in abolishing drug trafficking. There is, however, practically no illegal traffic in peyote....

Finally, the State argues that granting an exception for religious peyote use would erode its interest in the uniform, fair, and certain enforcement of its drug laws.... [But the] State's apprehension of a flood of other religious claims is purely speculative. Almost half the States, and the Federal Government, have maintained an exemption for religious peyote use for many years, and apparently have not found themselves overwhelmed by claims to other religious exemptions. Allowing an exemption for religious peyote use would not necessarily oblige the State to grant a similar exemption to other religious groups. The unusual circumstances that make the religious use of peyote compatible with the State's interests in health and safety and in preventing drug trafficking would not apply to other religious claims. Some religions, for example, might not restrict drug use to a limited ceremonial context, as does the Native American Church. Some religious claims, involve drugs such as marijuana and heroin, in which there is significant illegal traffic, with its attendant greed and violence, so that it would be difficult to grant a religious exemption without seriously compromising law enforcement efforts.... Though the State must treat all religions equally, and not favor one over another, this obligation is fulfilled by the uniform application of the "compelling interest" test to all free exercise claims, not by reaching uniform results as to all claims....

Finally, although I agree with Justice O'Connor that courts should refrain from delving into questions whether, as a matter of religious doctrine, a particular practice is "central" to the religion, I do not think this means that the courts must turn a blind eye to the severe impact of a State's restrictions on the adherents of a minority religion.

Respondents believe, and their sincerity has *never* been at issue, that the peyote plant embodies their deity, and eating it is an act of worship and communion. Without peyote, they could not enact the essential ritual of their religion. See Brief for Association on American Indian Affairs et al. as Amici Curiae 5–6.... This potentially devastating impact must be viewed in light of the federal policy—reached in reaction to many years of religious persecution and intolerance—of protecting the religious freedom of Native Americans....

The American Indian Religious Freedom Act, in itself, may not create rights enforceable against government action restricting religious freedom, but this Court must scrupulously apply its free exercise analysis to the religious claims of Native Americans, however unorthodox they may be. Otherwise, both the First Amendment and the stated policy of Congress will offer to Native Americans merely an unfulfilled and hollow promise.... I dissent.

Review Questions and Explanations: *Smith*

1. Does *Smith's* reasoning remind you at all of the *O'Brien* test from the speech context? A law that regulates conduct without reference to religious practices is challenged by someone who employs that conduct as part of a religious practice. The burden on religion, like the burden on speech, is incidental to the purpose the law; and the law is reviewed under something less than strict scrutiny. Under *O'Brien*, the Court applies intermediate scrutiny. What level of scrutiny does the Court apply in *Smith*?

2. What danger is there, if any, in allowing an exemption from general criminal laws to accommodate religious beliefs? Would such a rule put courts in the position of having to distinguish between sincere, as opposed to opportunistic, professions of religious belief? Why is the majority concerned with getting courts involved in this type of inquiry?

3. Do you agree or disagree with the argument in the majority's second-to-last paragraph, that allowing democratic processes to look after religious accommodation is preferable to "a system in which each conscience is a law unto itself or in which judges weigh the social importance of all laws against the centrality of all religious beliefs"?

4. Do you find the dissent persuasive? The dissent implies that opportunistic claims for exemptions from other drug (or criminal) laws can be handled by

states, and reviewed by courts, case by case, by examining the state's interest in enforcement of its general laws, rather than by scrutinizing the sincerity of the claimed religious belief. Between that point, and the suggestion that, empirically speaking, states have not been flooded with such requests for exemptions, has the dissent addressed the majority's concern about opening a floodgate of religious exemptions?

Guided Reading Questions: *Church of the Lukumi Babalu Aye, Inc. v. City of Hialeah*

1. Consider both the express provisions of the Hialeah ordinance and its circumstances. Is this a "religion-neutral, generally applicable" law like the one in *Smith*? (Note that no one dissents from the decision to strike down the ordinance, suggesting that *Smith* must be distinguishable.)

2. What is the rationale the majority uses to strike down the ordinance?

3. What level of scrutiny does the Court apply to the law, and why?

Church of the Lukumi Babalu Aye, Inc. v. City of Hialeah

508 U.S. 520 (1993)

Majority (all but part II-A-2): *Kennedy,* Rehnquist (CJ), White (except part II-A), Stevens, Scalia, Souter (except part II), Thomas

Opinion (part II-A-2): *Kennedy,* Stevens

Concurrences in part and in the judgment: *Scalia*, Rehnquist (CJ); *Souter*

Concurrence in the judgment: *Blackmun*, O'Connor

JUSTICE KENNEDY delivered the opinion of the Court, except as to Part II-A-2.

.... This case involves practices of the Santeria religion, which originated in the 19th century. When hundreds of thousands of members of the Yoruba people were brought as slaves from western Africa to Cuba, their traditional African religion absorbed significant elements of Roman Catholicism. The resulting syncretion, or fusion, is Santeria, "the way of the saints." The Cuban Yoruba express their devotion to spirits, called orishas, through the iconography of Catholic saints, Catholic symbols are often present at Santeria rites, and Santeria devotees attend the Catholic sacraments.

The Santeria faith teaches that every individual has a destiny from God, a destiny fulfilled with the aid and energy of the orishas. The basis of the Santeria religion is the nurture of a personal relation with the orishas, and one of the principal forms of devotion is an animal sacrifice. 13 Encyclopedia of Religion, supra, at 66. The sacrifice of animals as part of religious rituals has ancient roots....

According to Santeria teaching, the orishas are powerful but not immortal. They depend for survival on the sacrifice. Sacrifices are performed at birth, marriage, and death rites, for the cure of the sick, for the initiation of new members and priests, and during an annual celebration. Animals sacrificed in Santeria rituals include chickens, pigeons, doves, ducks, guinea pigs, goats, sheep, and turtles. The animals are killed by the cutting of the carotid arteries in the neck. The sacrificed animal is cooked and eaten, except after healing and death rituals.

Santeria adherents faced widespread persecution in Cuba, so the religion and its rituals were practiced in secret. The open practice of Santeria and its rites remains infrequent. The religion was brought to this Nation most often by exiles from the Cuban revolution. The District Court estimated that there are at least 50,000 practitioners in South Florida today. See 723 F. Supp. at 1470.

Petitioner Church of the Lukumi Babalu Aye, Inc. (Church), is a not-for-profit corporation organized under Florida law in 1973. The Church and its congregants practice the Santeria religion. The president of the Church is petitioner Ernesto Pichardo, who is also the Church's priest and holds the religious title of Italero, the second highest in the Santeria faith. In April 1987, the Church leased land in the city of Hialeah, Florida, and announced plans to establish a house of worship as well as a school, cultural center, and museum. Pichardo indicated that the Church's goal was to bring the practice of the Santeria faith, including its ritual of animal sacrifice, into the open. The Church began the process of obtaining utility service and receiving the necessary licensing, inspection, and zoning approvals. Although the Church's efforts at obtaining the necessary licenses and permits were far from smooth, see it appears that it received all needed approvals by early August 1987.

The prospect of a Santeria church in their midst was distressing to many members of the Hialeah community, and the announcement of the plans to open a Santeria church in Hialeah prompted the city council to hold an emergency public session on June 9, 1987 [at which several resolutions were passed]....

First, the city council adopted Resolution 87-66, which noted the "concern" expressed by residents of the city "that certain religions may propose to engage in practices which are inconsistent with public morals, peace or safety," and declared that "the City reiterates its commitment to a prohibition against any and all acts of any and all religious groups which are inconsistent with public morals, peace or safety." Next, the council approved an emergency ordinance, Ordinance 87-40, which incorporated in full, except as to penalty, Florida's animal cruelty laws. Fla. Stat. ch. 828 (1987). Among other things, the incorporated state law subjected to criminal punishment "whoever ... unnecessarily or cruelly ... kills any animal." § 828.12....

In September 1987, the city council adopted three substantive ordinances addressing the issue of religious animal sacrifice.... All ordinances and resolutions passed the city council by unanimous vote. Violations of each of the four ordinances were punishable by fines not exceeding $500 or imprisonment not exceeding 60 days, or both.

Following enactment of these ordinances, the Church and Pichardo filed this action pursuant to 42 U.S.C. § 1983 in the United States District Court for the Southern District of Florida. [The district court ruled in favor of the defendants, and the Court of Appeals for the Eleventh Circuit affirmed.]

II

The Free Exercise Clause of the First Amendment, which has been applied to the States through the Fourteenth Amendment, provides that "Congress shall make no law respecting an establishment of religion, or *prohibiting the free exercise thereof....*" (emphasis added). The city does not argue that Santeria is not a "religion" within the meaning of the First Amendment.... Given the historical association between animal sacrifice and religious worship, petitioners' assertion that animal sacrifice is an integral part of their religion "cannot be deemed bizarre or incredible." Frazee v. Illinois Dept. of Employment Security, 489 U.S. 829, 834, n.2 (1989). Neither the city nor the courts below, moreover, have questioned the sincerity of petitioners' professed desire to conduct animal sacrifices for religious reasons....

In addressing the constitutional protection for free exercise of religion, our cases establish the general proposition that a law that is neutral and of general applicability need not be justified by a compelling governmental interest even if the law has the incidental effect of burdening a particular religious practice. Employment Div., Dept. of Human Resources of Ore. v. Smith, supra. Neutrality and general applicability are interrelated, and, as becomes apparent in this case, failure to satisfy one requirement is a likely indication that the other has not been satisfied. A law failing to satisfy these requirements must be justified by a compelling governmental interest and must be narrowly tailored to advance that interest. These ordinances fail to satisfy the Smith requirements. We begin by discussing neutrality.

A

In our Establishment Clause cases we have often stated the principle that the First Amendment forbids an official purpose to disapprove of a particular religion or of religion in general....

At a minimum, the protections of the Free Exercise Clause pertain if the law at issue discriminates against some or all religious beliefs or regulates or prohibits conduct because it is undertaken for religious reasons.... In McDaniel v. Paty, 435 U.S. 618, 55 L. Ed. 2d 593, 98 S. Ct. 1322 (1978), for example, we invalidated a state law that disqualified members of the clergy from holding certain public offices, because it "impose[d] special disabilities on the basis of ... religious status[.]" On the same principle, in Fowler v. Rhode Island, supra, we found that a municipal ordinance was applied in an unconstitutional manner when interpreted to prohibit preaching in a public park by a Jehovah's Witness but to permit preaching during the course of a Catholic mass or Protestant church service.

1

Although a law targeting religious beliefs as such is never permissible, if the object of a law is to infringe upon or restrict practices because of their religious motivation, the law is not neutral, see Employment Div., Dept. of Human Resources of Ore. v. Smith, supra, at 878–879; and it is invalid unless it is justified by a compelling interest and is narrowly tailored to advance that interest.... A law lacks facial neutrality if it refers to a religious practice without a secular meaning discernible from the language or context.... [But] facial neutrality is not determinative.... The Free Exercise Clause protects against governmental hostility which is masked as well as overt....

.... The subject at hand does implicate, of course, multiple concerns unrelated to religious animosity, for example, the suffering or mistreatment visited upon the sacrificed animals and health hazards from improper disposal. But the ordinances when considered together disclose an object remote from these legitimate concerns. The design of these laws accomplishes instead ... an impermissible attempt to target petitioners and their religious practices.

... [A]lmost the only conduct subject to Ordinances 87-40, 87-52, and 87-71 is the religious exercise of Santeria church members. The texts show that they were drafted in tandem to achieve this result.... Thus, religious practice is being singled out for discriminatory treatment.

We also find significant evidence of the ordinances' improper targeting of Santeria sacrifice in the fact that they proscribe more religious conduct than is necessary to achieve their stated ends. It is not unreasonable to infer, at least when there are no persuasive indications to the contrary, that a law which visits "gratuitous restrictions" on religious conduct, seeks not to effectuate the stated governmental interests, but to suppress the conduct because of its religious motivation.

The legitimate governmental interests in protecting the public health and preventing cruelty to animals could be addressed by restrictions stopping far short of a flat prohibition of all Santeria sacrificial practice. If improper disposal, not the sacrifice itself, is the harm to be prevented, the city could have imposed a general regulation on the disposal of organic garbage. It did not do so. Indeed, counsel for the city conceded at oral argument that, under the ordinances, Santeria sacrifices would be illegal even if they occurred in licensed, inspected, and zoned slaughterhouses....

.... With regard to the city's interest in ensuring the adequate care of animals, regulation of conditions and treatment, regardless of why an animal is kept, is the logical response to the city's concern, not a prohibition on possession for the purpose of sacrifice. The same is true for the city's interest in prohibiting cruel methods of killing. Under federal and Florida law and Ordinance 87-40, which incorporates Florida law in this regard, killing an animal by the "simultaneous and instantaneous severance of the carotid arteries with a sharp instrument"—the method used in kosher slaughter—is approved as humane. See 7 U.S.C. § 1902(b); Fla. Stat. § 828.23(7)(b) (1991); Ordinance 87-40, § 1. The District Court found that, though Santeria sacrifice also results in severance of the carotid arteries, the method used during sacrifice is less reliable and therefore not humane. If the city has a real concern that other methods are less humane, however, the subject of the regulation should be the method of slaughter itself, not a religious classification that is said to bear some general relation to it.

Ordinance 87-72—unlike the three other ordinances—does appear to apply to substantial nonreligious conduct and not to be overbroad.... We need not decide whether Ordinance 87-72 could survive constitutional scrutiny if it existed separately; it must be invalidated because it functions, with the rest of the enactments in question, to suppress Santeria religious worship.

2

In determining if the object of a law is a neutral one under the Free Exercise Clause, we can also find guidance in our equal protection cases.... Here, as in equal protection cases, we may determine the city council's object from both direct and circumstantial evidence. Arlington Heights v. Metropolitan Housing Development Corp., 429 U.S. 252, 266 (1977). Relevant evidence includes, among other things, the historical background of the decision under challenge, the specific series of events leading to the enactment or official policy in question, and the legislative or administrative history, including contemporaneous statements made by members of the decisionmaking body. These objective factors bear on the question of discriminatory object.

That the ordinances were enacted "'because of,' not merely 'in spite of,'" their suppression of Santeria religious practice, is revealed by the events preceding their enactment. Although respondent claimed at oral argument that it had experienced significant problems resulting from the sacrifice of animals within the city before the announced opening of the Church, Tr. of Oral Arg. 27, 46, the city council made no attempt to address the supposed problem before its meeting in June 1987, just weeks after the Church announced plans to open.

The minutes and taped excerpts of the June 9 session, both of which are in the record, evidence significant hostility exhibited by residents, members of the city council, and other city officials toward the Santeria religion and its practice of animal sacrifice. The public crowd that attended the June 9 meetings interrupted statements by council members critical of Santeria with cheers and the brief comments of Pichardo with taunts. When Councilman Martinez, a supporter of the ordinances, stated that in prerevolution Cuba "people were put in jail for practicing this religion," the audience applauded. Taped excerpts of Hialeah City Council Meeting, June 9, 1987. [Other council members and city officials] made comparable comments.... This history discloses the object of the ordinances to target animal sacrifice by Santeria worshippers because of its religious motivation.

In sum, the neutrality inquiry leads to one conclusion: The ordinances had as their object the suppression of religion. The pattern we have recited discloses animosity to Santeria adherents and their religious practices; the ordinances by their own terms target this religious exercise; the texts of the ordinances were gerrymandered with care to proscribe religious killings of animals but to exclude almost all secular killings; and the ordinances suppress much more religious conduct than is necessary in order to achieve the legitimate ends asserted in their defense. These ordinances are not neutral, and the court below committed clear error in failing to reach this conclusion.

B

We turn next to a second requirement of the Free Exercise Clause, the rule that laws burdening religious practice must be of general applicability. Employment Div., Dept. of Human Resources of Ore. v. Smith, 494 U.S. at 879–881. All laws are selective to some extent, but categories of selection are of paramount concern when a law has the incidental effect of burdening religious practice. The Free Exercise Clause "protect[s] religious observers against unequal treatment," and inequality results when a legislature decides that the governmental interests it seeks to advance are worthy of being pursued only against conduct with a religious motivation....

Respondent claims that Ordinances 87-40, 87-52, and 87-71 advance two interests: protecting the public health and preventing cruelty to animals. The ordinances are underinclusive for those ends. They fail to prohibit nonreligious conduct that endangers these interests in a similar or greater degree than Santeria sacrifice does. The underinclusion is substantial, not inconsequential. Despite the city's proffered interest in preventing cruelty to animals, the ordinances are drafted with care to forbid few killings but those occasioned by religious sacrifice. Many types of animal deaths or kills for nonreligious reasons are either not prohibited or approved by express provision....

The ordinances are underinclusive as well with regard to the health risk posed by consumption of uninspected meat. Under the city's ordinances, hunters may eat their kill and fishermen may eat their catch without undergoing governmental inspection. Likewise, state law requires inspection of meat that is sold but exempts meat from animals raised for the use of the owner and "members of his household and nonpaying guests and employees." Fla. Stat. § 585.88(1)(a) (1991). The asserted interest in inspected meat is not pursued in contexts similar to that of religious animal sacrifice.

Ordinance 87-72, which prohibits the slaughter of animals outside of areas zoned for slaughterhouses, is underinclusive on its face. The ordinance includes an exemption for "any person, group, or organization" that "slaughters or processes for sale, small numbers of hogs and/or cattle per week in accordance with an exemption provided by state law." See Fla. Stat. § 828.24(3) (1991)....

We conclude, in sum, that each of Hialeah's ordinances pursues the city's governmental interests only against conduct motivated by religious belief....

III

A law burdening religious practice that is not neutral or not of general application must undergo the most rigorous of scrutiny. To satisfy the commands of the First Amendment, a law restrictive of religious practice must advance "interests of the highest order" and must be narrowly tailored in pursuit of those interests.... A law that targets religious conduct for distinctive treatment or advances legitimate governmental interests only against conduct with a religious motivation will survive strict scrutiny only in rare cases. It follows from what we have already said that these ordinances cannot withstand this scrutiny.

First, even were the governmental interests compelling, the ordinances are not drawn in narrow terms to accomplish those interests. As we have discussed, all four ordinances are overbroad or underinclusive in substantial respects....

Respondent has not demonstrated, moreover, that, in the context of these ordinances, its governmental interests are compelling. Where government restricts only conduct protected by the First Amendment and fails to enact feasible measures to restrict other conduct producing substantial harm or alleged harm of the same sort, the interest given in justification of the restriction is not compelling. It is established in our strict scrutiny jurisprudence that "a law cannot be regarded as protecting an interest 'of the highest order'... when it leaves appreciable damage to that supposedly vital interest unprohibited."....

The Free Exercise Clause commits government itself to religious tolerance, and upon even slight suspicion that proposals for state intervention stem from animosity to religion or distrust of its practices, all officials must pause to remember their own high duty to the Constitution and to the rights it secures.... Legislators may not devise mechanisms, overt or disguised, designed to persecute or oppress a religion or its practices. The laws here in question were enacted contrary to these constitutional principles, and they are void. Reversed.

JUSTICE SCALIA, with whom THE CHIEF JUSTICE joins, concurring in part and concurring in the judgment.

.... I join the judgment of the Court and all of its opinion except section 2 of Part II-A[,] because it departs from the opinion's general focus on the object of the laws at issue to consider the subjective motivation of the lawmakers, i.e., whether the Hialeah City Council actually intended to disfavor the religion of Santeria. As I have noted elsewhere, it is virtually impossible to determine the singular "motive" of a collective legislative body, and this Court has a long tradition of refraining from such inquiries.

.... The First Amendment does not refer to the purposes for which legislators enact laws, but to the effects of the laws enacted: "Congress shall make no law ... prohibiting the free exercise [of religion]...." This does not put us in the business of invalidating laws by reason of the evil motives of their authors.... Had the ordinances here been passed with no motive on the part of any councilman except the ardent desire to prevent cruelty to animals (as might in fact have been the case), they would nonetheless be invalid.

JUSTICE SOUTER, concurring in part and concurring in the judgment.

This case turns on a principle about which there is no disagreement, that the Free Exercise Clause bars government action aimed at suppressing religious belief or practice.

The Court holds that Hialeah's animal-sacrifice laws violate that principle, and I concur in that holding without reservation.

Because prohibiting religious exercise is the object of the laws at hand, this case does not present the more difficult issue addressed in our last free-exercise case, Employment Div., Dept. of Human Resources of Ore. v. Smith, 494 U.S. 872, 108 L. Ed. 2d 876, 110 S. Ct. 1595 (1990), which announced the rule that a "neutral, generally applicable" law does not run afoul of the Free Exercise Clause even when it prohibits religious exercise in effect. The Court today refers to that rule in dicta, and despite my general agreement with the Court's opinion I do not join Part II, where the dicta appear, for I have doubts about whether the Smith rule merits adherence....

JUSTICE BLACKMUN, with whom JUSTICE O'CONNOR joins, concurring in the judgment.

The Court holds today that the city of Hialeah violated the First and Fourteenth Amendments when it passed a set of restrictive ordinances explicitly directed at petitioners' religious practice. With this holding I agree. I write separately to emphasize that the First Amendment's protection of religion extends beyond those rare occasions on which the government explicitly targets religion (or a particular religion) for disfavored treatment, as is done in this case. In my view, a statute that burdens the free exercise of religion "may stand only if the law in general, and the State's refusal to allow a religious exemption in particular, are justified by a compelling interest that cannot be served by less restrictive means." Employment Div., Dept. of Human Resources of Ore. v. Smith, 494 U.S. 872, 907, 108 L. Ed. 2d 876, 110 S. Ct. 1595 (1990) (dissenting opinion).... I continue to believe that Smith was wrongly decided, because it ignored the value of religious freedom as an affirmative individual liberty and treated the Free Exercise Clause as no more than an antidiscrimination principle. See 494 U.S. at 908–909....

.... This case does not present, and I therefore decline to reach, the question whether the Free Exercise Clause would require a religious exemption from a law that sincerely pursued the goal of protecting animals from cruel treatment. The number of organizations that have filed amicus briefs on behalf of this interest, however, demonstrates that it is not a concern to be treated lightly.

Review Questions and Explanations:
Church of the Lukumi Babalu Aye

1. Perhaps the analogy to free speech and *O'Brien* can be extended here to include *Texas v. Johnson*. There, the problem with the Texas statute was the difficulty in viewing it as primarily a regulation of non-expressive conduct. Here, the difficulty is in viewing the Hialeah ordinance as a general law against animal sacrifice: the circumstances virtually compel the conclusion that the law was expressly aimed at the Church's religious observance. The case also invites comparison to the Court's treatment of legislative purpose and discriminatory intent in the equal protection context.

2. Justices Blackmun, O'Connor, and Souter took the opportunity to express the view that *Smith* was wrongly decided. Was there any occasion to overrule *Smith* in this case? If so, how could such a decision have been written?

Appendix

The Constitution of the United States

We the People of the United States, in Order to form a more perfect Union, establish Justice, insure domestic Tranquility, provide for the common defence, promote the general Welfare, and secure the Blessings of Liberty to ourselves and our Posterity, do ordain and establish this Constitution for the United States of America.

ARTICLE 1

Section 1.   All legislative Powers herein granted shall be vested in a Congress of the United States, which shall consist of a Senate and House of Representatives.

Section 2.   The House of Representatives shall be composed of Members chosen every second Year by the People of the several States, and the Electors in each State shall have the Qualifications requisite for Electors of the most numerous Branch of the State Legislature.

No Person shall be a Representative who shall not have attained to the Age of twenty five Years, and been seven Years a Citizen of the United States, and who shall not, when elected, be an Inhabitant of that State in which he shall be chosen.

[Representatives and direct Taxes shall be apportioned among the several States which may be included within this Union, according to their respective Numbers, which shall be determined by adding to the whole Number of free Persons, including those bound to Service for a Term of Years, and excluding Indians not taxed, three fifths of all other Persons.] The actual Enumeration shall be made within three Years after the first Meeting of the Congress of the United States, and within every subsequent Term of ten Years, in such Manner as they shall by Law direct. The Number of Representatives shall not exceed one for every thirty Thousand, but each State shall have at Least one Representative; and until such enumerations shall be made, the State of New Hampshire shall be entitled to chuse three, Massachusetts eight, Rhode-Island and Providence Plantations one, Connecticut five, New-York six, New Jersey four, Pennsylvania eight, Delaware one, Maryland six, Virginia ten, North Carolina five, South Carolina five, and Georgia three.

When vacancies happen in the Representation from any State, the Executive Authority thereof shall issue Writs of Election to fill such Vacancies.

The House of Representatives shall chuse their speaker and other Officers; and shall have the sole Power of Impeachment.

Section 3.   The Senate of the United States shall be composed of two Senators from each State, [chosen by the Legislature thereof,] for six Years; and each Senator shall have one Vote.

Immediately after they shall be assembled in Consequence of the first Election, they shall be divided as equally as may be into three Classes. The Seats of the Senators of the first Class shall be vacated at the Expiration of the second Year, of the second Class at the Expiration of the fourth Year, and of the third Class at the Expiration of the sixth Year, so that one third may be chosen every second Year; [and if Vacancies happen by Resignation, or otherwise, during the Recess of the Legislature of any State, the Executive thereof may make temporary Appointments until the next Meeting of the Legislature, which shall then fill such Vacancies.]

No Person shall be a Senator who shall not have attained to the Age of thirty Years, and been nine Years a Citizen of the United States, and who shall not, when elected, be an Inhabitant of that State for which he shall be chosen.

The Vice President of the United States shall be President of the Senate, but shall have no Vote, unless they be equally divided.

The Senate shall chuse their other Officers, and also a President pro tempore, in the Absence of the Vice President, or when he shall exercise the Office of President of the United States.

The Senate shall have the sole Power to try all Impeachments. When sitting for that Purpose, they shall be on Oath or Affirmation. When the President of the United States is tried, the Chief Justice shall preside: And no Person shall be convicted without the concurrence of two thirds of the Members present. Judgment in Cases of Impeachment shall not extend further than to removal from Office, and disqualification to hold and enjoy any Office of honor, Trust or Profit under the United States: but the Party convicted shall nevertheless be liable and subject to Indictment, Trial, Judgment and Punishment, according to law.

Section 4. The Times, Places and Manner of holding Elections for Senators and Representatives, shall be prescribed in each State by the Legislature thereof; but the Congress may at any time by Law make or alter such Regulations, except as to the Places of chusing Senators.

The Congress shall assemble at least once in every Year, and such Meeting shall be [on the first Monday in December,] unless they shall by Law appoint a different Day.

Section 5. Each House shall be the Judge of the Elections, Returns and Qualifications of its own Members, and a Majority of each shall constitute a Quorum to do business; but a smaller Number may adjourn from day to day, and may be authorized to compel the Attendance of absent Members, in such Manner, and under such Penalties as each House may provide.

Each House may determine the Rules of its Proceedings, punish its Members for disorderly Behaviour, and, with the Concurrence of two thirds, expel a Member.

Each House shall keep a Journal of its Proceedings, and from time to time publish the same, excepting such Parts as may in their Judgment require Secrecy; and the yeas and Nays of the Members of either House on any question shall, at the Desire of one fifth of those Present, be entered on the Journal.

Neither House, during the Session of Congress, shall, without the Consent of the other, adjourn for more than three days, nor to any other place than that in which the two Houses shall be sitting.

Section 6. The Senators and Representatives shall receive a Compensation for their Services, to be ascertained by Law, and paid out of the Treasury of the United States. They shall in all Cases, except Treason, Felony and Breach of the Peace, be privileged from Arrest during their Attendance at the Session of their respective Houses, and in going to and returning from the same; and for any Speech or Debate in either House, they shall not be questioned in any other Place.

No Senator or Representative shall, during the Time for which he was elected, be appointed to any civil Office under the Authority of the United States, which shall have been created, or the Emoluments whereof shall have been increased during such time; and no Person holding any Office under the United States, shall be a Member of either House during his Continuance in Office.

Section 7. All Bills for raising Revenue shall originate in the House of Representatives; but the Senate may propose or concur with Amendments as on other Bills.

Every Bill which shall have passed the House of Representatives and the Senate, shall, before it become a Law, be presented to the President of the United States; If he approve he shall sign it, but if not he shall return it, with his Objections to that House in which it shall have originated, who shall enter the Objections at large on their Journal, and proceed to reconsider it. If after such Reconsideration two thirds of that House shall agree to pass the Bill, it shall be sent, together with the Objections, to the other House, by which it shall likewise be reconsidered, and if approved by two thirds of that House, it shall become a Law. But in all such Cases the Votes of both Houses shall be determined by yeas and Nays, and the Names of the Persons voting for and against the Bill shall be entered on the Journal of each House respectively. If any Bill shall not be returned by the President within ten Days (Sundays excepted) after it shall have been presented to him, the Same shall be a Law, in like Manner as if he had signed it, unless the Congress by their Adjournment prevent its Return, in which Case it shall not be a Law.

Every Order, Resolution, or Vote to which the Concurrence of the Senate and House of Representatives may be necessary (except on a question of Adjournment) shall be presented to the President of the United States; and before the Same shall take Effect, shall be approved by him, or being disapproved by him, shall be repassed by two thirds of the Senate and House of Representatives, according to the Rules and Limitations prescribed in the Case of a Bill.

Section 8. The Congress shall have Power To lay and collect Taxes, Duties, Imposts and Excises, to pay the Debts and provide for the common Defence and general Welfare of the United States; but all duties, Imposts and Excises shall be uniform throughout the United States;

To borrow Money on the Credit of the United States;

To regulate Commerce with foreign Nations, and among the several States, and with the Indian Tribes;

To establish an uniform Rule of Naturalization, and uniform Laws on the subject of Bankruptcies throughout the United States;

To coin Money, regulate the Value thereof, and of foreign Coin, and fix the Standard of Weights and Measures;

To provide for the Punishment of counterfeiting the Securities and current Coin of the United States;

To establish Post Offices and post Roads;

To promote the Progress of Science and useful Arts, by securing for limited Times to Authors and Inventors exclusive Right to their respective Writings and Discoveries;

To constitute Tribunals inferior to the supreme Court;

To define and punish Piracies and Felonies committed on the high Seas, and Offences against the Law of Nations;

To declare War, grant Letters of Marque and Reprisal, and make rules concerning Captures on Land and Water;

To raise and support Armies, but no Appropriation of Money to that Use shall be for a longer Term than two Years;

To provide and maintain a Navy;

To make rules for the Government and Regulation of the land and naval Forces;

To provide for calling forth the Militia to execute the Laws of the Union, suppress Insurrections and repel Invasions;

To provide for organizing, arming, and disciplining, the Militia, and for governing such Part of them as may be employed in the Service of the United States, reserving to the States respectively, the Appointment of the Officers, and the Authority of training the Militia according to the discipline prescribed by Congress;

To exercise exclusive Legislation in all Cases whatsoever, over such District (not exceeding ten Miles square), as may, by Cession of particular States, and the Acceptance of Congress, become the Seat of the Government of the United States, and to exercise like Authority over all Places purchased by the Consent of the Legislature of the State in which the Same shall be for the Erection of Forts, Magazines, Arsenals, dock-Yards, and other needful Buildings; — And

To make all Laws which shall be necessary and proper for carrying into Execution the foregoing Powers, and all other Powers vested by this Constitution in the Government of the United States, or in any Department or Officer thereof.

Section 9.   The Migration or Importation of such Persons as any of the States now existing shall think proper to admit, shall not be prohibited by the Congress prior to the Year one thousand eight hundred and eight, but a Tax or duty may be imposed on such Importation, not exceeding ten dollars for each Person.

The Privilege of the Writ of Habeas Corpus shall not be suspended, unless when in Cases of Rebellion or Invasion the public Safety may require it.

No Bill of Attainder or ex post facto Law shall be passed.

[No Capitation, or other direct, Tax shall be laid, unless in Proportion to the Census or Enumeration herein before directed to be taken.]

No Tax or Duty shall be laid on Articles exported from any State.

No Preference shall be given by any Regulation of Commerce or Revenue to the Ports of one State over those of another: nor shall Vessels bound to, or from, one State, be obliged to enter, clear, or pay Duties in another.

No money shall be drawn from the Treasury, but in Consequence of Appropriations made by Law; and a regular Statement and Account of the Receipts and Expenditures of all public Money shall be published from time to time.

No Title of Nobility shall be granted by the United States: And no Person holding any Office of Profit or Trust under them, shall, without the Consent of the Congress, accept of any present, Emolument, Office, or Title, of any kind whatever, from any King, Prince, or foreign State.

Section 10.   No State shall enter into any Treaty, Alliance, or Confederation; grant Letters of Marque and Reprisal; coin Money; emit Bills of Credit; make any Thing but gold and silver Coin a Tender in Payment of Debts; pass any Bill of Attainder, ex post facto Law, or Law impairing the Obligation of Contracts, or grant any Title of Nobility.

No State shall, without the Consent of the Congress, lay any Imposts or Duties on Imports or Exports, except what may be absolutely necessary for executing it's inspection Laws: and the net Produce of all Duties and Imposts, laid by any State on Imports or Exports, shall be for the Use of the Treasury of the United States; and all such Laws shall be subject to the Revision and Controul of the Congress.

No State shall, without the Consent of Congress, lay any Duty of Tonnage, keep Troops, or Ships of War in time of Peace, enter into any Agreement or Compact with another State, or with a foreign Power, or engage in War, unless actually invaded, or in such imminent Danger as will not admit of delay.

ARTICLE II

Section 1.   The executive Power shall be vested in a President of the United States of America. He shall hold his Office during the Term of four Years, and, together with the Vice President, chosen for the same term, be elected, as follows

Each State shall appoint, in such Manner as the Legislature thereof may direct, a Number of Electors, equal to the whole Number of Senators and Representatives to which the State may be entitled in the Congress: but no Senator or Representative, or Person holding an Office of Trust or Profit under the United States, shall be appointed an Elector.

[The Electors shall meet in their respective States, and vote by Ballot for two Persons, of whom one at least shall not be an Inhabitant of the same State with themselves. And they shall make a List of all the Persons voted for, and of the Number of Votes for each; which List they shall sign and certify, and transmit sealed to the Seat of the Government of the United States, directed to the President of the Senate. The President of the Senate shall, in the Presence of the Senate and House of Representatives, open all the Certificates, and the Votes shall then be counted. The Person having the greatest Number of Votes shall be the President, if such Number be a Majority of the whole Number of Electors appointed; and if there be more than one who have such Majority, and have an equal Number of Votes, then the House of Representatives shall immediately chuse by Ballot one of them for President: and if no Person have a Majority, then from the five highest on the List the said House shall in like Manner chuse the President. But in chusing the President, the Votes shall be taken by States, the Representation from each State having one Vote; A quorum for this Purpose shall consist of a Member or Members from two thirds of the States, and a Majority of all the States shall be necessary to a Choice. In every Case, after the Choice of the President, the Person having the greatest Number of Votes of the Electors shall be the Vice President. But if there should remain two or more who have equal Votes, the Senate shall chuse from them by Ballot the Vice President.]

The Congress may determine the Time of chusing the Electors, and the Day on which they shall give their Votes; which Day shall be the same throughout the United States.

No Person except a natural born Citizen, or a Citizen of the United States, at the time of the Adoption of this Constitution, shall be eligible to the Office of President; neither shall any Person be eligible to that Office who shall not have attained to the Age of thirty five Years, and been fourteen Years a Resident within the United States.

[In Case of the Removal of the President from Office, or of his Death, Resignation, or Inability to discharge the Powers and Duties of the said Office, the Same shall devolve on the Vice President, and the Congress may by Law provide for the Case of Removal, Death, Resignation or Inability, both of the President and Vice President, declaring what Officer shall then act as President, and such Officer shall act accordingly, until the Disability be removed, or a President shall be elected.]

The President shall, at stated Times, receive for his Services, a Compensation, which shall neither be encreased nor diminished during the Period for which he shall have been elected, and he shall not receive within that Period any other Emolument from the United States, or any of them.

Before he enter on the Execution of his Office, he shall take the following Oath or Affirmation: — "I do solemnly swear (or affirm) that I will faithfully execute the Office of President of the United States, and will to the best of my Ability, preserve, protect and defend the Constitution of the United States."

Section 2.   The President shall be Commander in Chief of the Army and Navy of the United States, and of the Militia of the several States, when called into the actual Service of the United States; he may require the Opinion, in writing, of the principal Officer in each of the executive Departments, upon any Subject relating to the Duties of their respective Offices, and he shall have Power to grant Reprieves and Pardons for Offences against the United States, except in Cases of Impeachment.

He shall have Power, by and with the Advice and Consent of the Senate, to make Treaties, provided two thirds of the Senators present concur; and he shall nominate, and by and with the Advice and Consent of the Senate, shall appoint Ambassadors, other public Ministers and Consuls, Judges of the supreme Court, and all other Officers of the United States, whose Appointments are not herein otherwise provided for, and which shall be established by Law; but the Congress may by Law vest the Appointment of such inferior Officers, as they think proper, in the President alone, in the Courts of Law, or in the Heads of Departments.

The President shall have Power to fill up all Vacancies that may happen during the Recess of the Senate, by granting Commissions which shall expire at the End of their next Session.

Section 3. He shall from time to time give to the Congress Information of the State of the Union, and recommend to their Consideration such Measures as he shall judge necessary and expedient; he may, on extraordinary Occasions, convene both Houses, or either of them, and in Case of Disagreement between them, with Respect to the Time of Adjournment, he may adjourn them to such Time as he shall think proper; he shall receive Ambassadors and other public Ministers; he shall take Care that the Laws be faithfully executed, and shall Commission all the Officers of the United States.

Section 4. The President, Vice President and all civil Officers of the United States, shall be removed from Office on Impeachment for, and Conviction of, Treason, Bribery, or other High Crimes and Misdemeanors.

ARTICLE III

Section 1. The judicial Power of the United States, shall be vested in one supreme Court, and in such inferior Courts as the Congress may from time to time ordain and establish. The Judges, both of the supreme and inferior Courts, shall hold their Offices during good Behaviour, and shall, at stated Times, receive for their Services, a Compensation, which shall not be diminished during their Continuance in Office.

Section 2. The judicial Power shall extend to all Cases, in Law and Equity, arising under this Constitution, the Laws of the United States, and Treaties made, or which shall be made, under their Authority;—to all Cases affecting Ambassadors, other public Ministers and Consuls;—to all Cases of admiralty and maritime Jurisdiction;—to Controversies to which the United States shall be a Party;—to Controversies between two or more States; [between a State and Citizens of another State;]—between Citizens of different States;—between Citizens of the same State claiming Lands under Grants of different States, [and between a State, or the Citizens thereof, and foreign States, Citizens or Subjects.]

In all Cases affecting Ambassadors, other public Ministers and Consuls, and those in which a State shall be Party, the supreme Court shall have original Jurisdiction. In all the other Cases before mentioned, the supreme Court shall have appellate Jurisdiction, both as to Law and Fact, with such Exceptions, and under such Regulations as the Congress shall make.

The Trial of all Crimes, except in Cases of Impeachment, shall be by Jury; and such Trial shall be held in the State where the said Crimes shall have been committed; but when not committed within any State, the Trial shall be at such Place or Places as the Congress may by Law have directed.

Section 3. Treason against the United States, shall consist only in levying War against them, or in adhering to their Enemies, giving them Aid and Comfort. No Person shall be convicted of Treason unless on the Testimony of two Witnesses to the same overt Act, or on Confession in open Court.

The Congress shall have Power to declare the Punishment of Treason, but no Attainder of Treason shall work Corruption of Blood, or Forfeiture except during the Life of the Person attainted.

ARTICLE IV

Section 1.   Full Faith and Credit shall be given in each State to the public Acts, Records, and judicial Proceedings of every other State. And the Congress may by general Laws prescribe the Manner in which such Acts, Records and Proceedings shall be proved, and the Effect thereof.

Section 2.   The Citizens of each State shall be entitled to all Privileges and Immunities of Citizens in the several States.

A Person charged in any State with Treason, Felony, or other Crime, who shall flee from Justice, and be found in another State, shall on Demand of the executive Authority of the State from which he fled, be delivered up, to be removed to the State having Jurisdiction of the Crime.

[No person held to Service or Labour in one State, under the Laws thereof, escaping into another, shall, in Consequence of any Law or Regulation therein, be discharged from such Service or Labour, but shall be delivered up on Claim of the Party to whom such Service or Labour may be due.]

Section 3.   New States may be admitted by the Congress into this Union; but no new State shall be formed or erected within the Jurisdiction of any other State; nor any State be formed by the Junction of two or more States, or Parts of States, without the Consent of the Legislatures of the States concerned as well as of the Congress.

The Congress shall have Power to dispose of and make all needful Rules and Regulations respecting the Territory or other Property belonging to the United States; and nothing in this Constitution shall be so construed as to Prejudice any Claims of the United States, or of any particular State.

Section 4.   The United States shall guarantee to every State in this Union a Republican Form of Government, and shall protect each of them against Invasion; and on Application of the Legislature, or of the Executive (when the Legislature cannot be convened) against domestic Violence.

ARTICLE V

The Congress, whenever two thirds of both Houses shall deem it necessary, shall propose Amendments to this Constitution, or, on the Application of the Legislatures of two thirds of the several States, shall call a Convention for proposing Amendments, which, in either Case, shall be valid to all Intents and Purposes, as Part of this Constitution, when ratified by the Legislatures of three fourths of the several States, or by Conventions in three fourths thereof, as the one or the other Mode of Ratification may be proposed by the Congress; Provided that no Amendment which may be made prior to the Year One thousand eight hundred and eight shall in any Manner affect the first and fourth Clauses in the Ninth Section of the first Article; and that no State, without its Consent, shall be deprived of its equal Suffrage in the Senate.

ARTICLE VI

All Debts contracted and Engagements entered into, before the Adoption of this Constitution, shall be as valid against the United States under this Constitution, as under the Confederation.

This Constitution, and the Laws of the United States which shall be made in Pursuance thereof; and all Treaties made, or which shall be made, under the Authority of the United States, shall be the supreme Law of the Land; and the Judges in every State shall be bound thereby, any Thing in the Constitution or Laws of any State to the Contrary notwithstanding.

The Senators and Representatives before mentioned, and the Members of the several State Legislatures, and all executive and judicial Officers, both of the United States and of the several States, shall be bound by Oath or Affirmation, to support this Constitution; but no religious Test shall ever be required as a Qualification to any Office or public Trust under the United States.

ARTICLE VII

The Ratification of the Conventions of nine States, shall be sufficient for the Establishment of this Constitution between the States so ratifying the Same.

AMENDMENTS

(The first 10 Amendments were ratified December 15, 1791, and form what is known as the "Bill of Rights")

AMENDMENT 1

Congress shall make no law respecting an establishment of religion, or prohibiting the free exercise thereof; or abridging the freedom of speech, or of the press; or the right of the people peaceably to assemble, and to petition the Government for a redress of grievances.

AMENDMENT 2

A well regulated Militia, being necessary to the security of a free State, the right of the people to keep and bear Arms, shall not be infringed.

AMENDMENT 3

No Soldier shall, in time of peace be quartered in any house, without the consent of the Owner, nor in time of war, but in a manner to be prescribed by law.

AMENDMENT 4

The right of the people to be secure in their persons, houses, papers, and effects, against un-reasonable searches and seizures, shall not be violated, and no Warrants shall issue, but upon probable cause, supported by Oath or affirmation, and particularly describing the place to be searched, and the persons or things to be seized.

AMENDMENT 5

No person shall be held to answer for a capital, or otherwise infamous crime, unless on a presentment or indictment of a Grand Jury, except in cases arising in the land or naval forces, or in the Militia, when in actual service in time of War or public danger; nor shall any person be subject for the same offence to be twice put in jeopardy of life or limb; nor shall be com-pelled in any criminal case to be a witness against himself, nor be deprived of life, liberty, or property, without due process of law; nor shall private property be taken for public use, without just compensation.

AMENDMENT 6

In all criminal prosecutions, the accused shall enjoy the right to a speedy and public trial, by an impartial jury of the State and district wherein the crime shall have been committed, which district shall have been previously ascertained by law, and to be informed of the nature and cause of the accusation; to be confronted with the witnesses against him; to have com-pulsory process for obtaining witnesses in his favor, and to have the Assistance of Counsel for his defence.

AMENDMENT 7

In Suits at common law, where the value in controversy shall exceed twenty dollars, the right of trial by jury shall be preserved, and no fact tried by a jury, shall be otherwise re-examined in any Court of the United States, than according to the rules of the common law.

AMENDMENT 8

Excessive bail shall not be required, nor excessive fines imposed, nor cruel and unusual pun-ishments inflicted.

AMENDMENT 9

The enumeration in the Constitution, of certain rights, shall not be construed to deny or disparage others retained by the people.

AMENDMENT 10

The powers not delegated to the United States by the Constitution, nor prohibited by it to the States, are reserved to the States respectively, or to the people.

AMENDMENT 11
(Ratified February 7, 1795)

The Judicial power of the United States shall not be construed to extend to any suit in law or equity, commenced or prosecuted against one of the United States by Citizens of another State, or by Citizens or Subjects of any Foreign State.

AMENDMENT 12
(Ratified July 27, 1804)

The Electors shall meet in their respective states and vote by ballot for President and Vice-President, one of whom, at least, shall not be an inhabitant of the same state with themselves; they shall name in their ballots the person voted for as President, and in distinct ballots the person voted for as Vice-President, and they shall make distinct lists of all persons voted for as President, and of all persons voted for as Vice-President, and of the number of votes for each, which lists they shall sign and certify, and transmit sealed to the seat of the government of the United States, directed to the President of the Senate; — The President of the Senate shall, in the presence of the Senate and House of Representatives, open all the certificates and the votes shall then be counted; — The person having the greatest number of votes for President, shall be the President, if such number be a majority of the whole number of Electors appointed; and if no person have such majority, then from the persons having the highest numbers not exceeding three on the list of those voted for as President, the House of Representatives shall choose immediately, by ballot, the President. But in choosing the President, the votes shall be taken by states, the representation from each state having one vote; a quorum for this purpose shall consist of a member or members from two-thirds of the states, and a majority of all the states shall be necessary to a choice. [And if the House of Representatives shall not choose a President whenever the right of choice shall devolve upon them, before the fourth day of March next following, then the Vice-President shall act as President, as in the case of the death or other constitutional disability of the President. —] The person having the greatest number of votes as Vice-President, shall be the Vice-President, if such number be a majority of the whole number of Electors appointed, and if no person have a majority, then from the two highest numbers on the list, the Senate shall choose the Vice-President; a quorum for the purpose shall consist of two-thirds of the whole number of Senators, and a majority of the whole number shall be necessary to a choice. But no person constitutionally ineligible to the office of President shall be eligible to that of Vice-President of the United States.

AMENDMENT 13
(Ratified December 6, 1865)

Section 1.   Neither slavery nor involuntary servitude, except as a punishment for crime whereof the party shall have been duly convicted, shall exist within the United States, or any place subject to their jurisdiction.

Section 2.   Congress shall have power to enforce this article by appropriate legislation.

AMENDMENT 14
(Ratified July 9, 1868)

Section 1.   All persons born or naturalized in the United States, and subject to the jurisdiction thereof, are citizens of the United States and of the State wherein they reside. No State shall make or enforce any law which shall abridge the privileges or immunities of citizens of the United States; nor shall any State deprive any person of life, liberty, or property, without due process of law; nor deny to any person within its jurisdiction the equal protection of the laws.

Section 2.   Representatives shall be apportioned among the several States according to their respective numbers, counting the whole number of persons in each State, excluding Indians not taxed. But when the right to vote at any election for the choice of electors for President and Vice President of the United States, Representatives in Congress, the Executive and Judicial officers of a State, or the members of the Legislature thereof, is denied to any of the male inhabitants of such State, being twenty-one years of age, and citizens of the United States, or in any way abridged, except for participation in rebellion, or other crime, the basis of representation therein shall be reduced in the proportion which the number of such male citizens shall bear to the whole number of male citizens twenty-one years of age in such State.

Section 3.   No person shall be a Senator or Representative in Congress, or elector of President and Vice President, or hold any office, civil or military, under the United States, or under any State, who, having previously taken an oath, as a member of Congress, or as an officer of the United States, or as a member of any State legislature, or as an executive or judicial officer of any State, to support the Constitution of the United States, shall have engaged in insurrection or rebellion against the same, or given aid or comfort to the enemies thereof. But Congress may by a vote of two-thirds of each House, remove such disability.

Section 4.   The validity of the public debt of the United States, authorized by law, including debts incurred for payment of pensions and bounties for services in suppressing insurrection or rebellion, shall not be questioned. But neither the United States nor any State shall assume or pay any debt or obligation incurred in aid of insurrection or rebellion against the United States, or any claim for the loss or emancipation of any slave; but all such debts, obligations and claims shall be held illegal and void.

Section 5.   The Congress shall have power to enforce, by appropriate legislation, the provisions of this article.

AMENDMENT 15
(Ratified February 3, 1870)

Section 1.   The right of citizens of the United States to vote shall not be denied or abridged by the United States or by any State on account of race, color, or previous condition of servitude.

Section 2.   The Congress shall have power to enforce this article by appropriate legislation.

AMENDMENT 16
(Ratified February 3, 1913)

The Congress shall have power to lay and collect taxes on incomes, from whatever source derived, without apportionment among the several States, and without regard to any census or enumeration.

AMENDMENT 17
(Ratified April 8, 1913)

The Senate of the United States shall be composed of two Senators from each State, elected by the people thereof for six years; and each Senator shall have one vote. The electors in each State shall have the qualifications requisite for electors of the most numerous branch of the State legislatures.

When vacancies happen in the representation of any State in the Senate, the executive authority of such State shall issue writs of election to fill such vacancies: *Provided,* That the legislature of any State may empower the executive thereof to make temporary appointments until the people fill the vacancies by election as the legislature may direct.

This amendment shall not be so construed as to affect the election or term of any Senator chosen before it becomes valid as part of the Constitution.

AMENDMENT 18
(Ratified January 16, 1919. Repealed December 5, 1933 by Amendment 21)

Section 1.   After one year from the ratification of this article the manufacture, sale, or transportation of intoxicating liquors within, the importation thereof into, or the exportation thereof from the United States and all territory subject to the jurisdiction thereof for beverage purposes is hereby prohibited.

Section 2.   The Congress and the several States shall have concurrent power to enforce this article by appropriate legislation.

Section 3.   This article shall be inoperative unless it shall have been ratified as an amendment to the Constitution by the legislatures of the several States as provided in the Constitution, within seven years from the date of the submission hereof to the States by the Congress.

AMENDMENT 19
(Ratified August 18, 1920)

The right of citizens of the United States to vote shall not be denied or abridged by the United States or by any State on account of sex.

Congress shall have power to enforce this article by appropriate legislation.

AMENDMENT 20
(Ratified January 23, 1933)

Section 1.   The terms of the President and Vice President shall end at noon on the 20th day of January, and the terms of Senators and Representatives at noon on the 3d day of January, of the years in which such terms would have ended if this article had not been ratified; and the terms of their successors shall then begin.

Section 2.   The Congress shall assemble at least once in every year, and such meeting shall begin at noon on the 3d day of January, unless they shall by law appoint a different day.

Section 3.   If, at the time fixed for the beginning of the term of the President, the President elect shall have died, the Vice President elect shall become President. If a President shall not have been chosen before the time fixed for the beginning of his term, or if the President elect shall have failed to qualify, then the Vice President elect shall act as President until a President shall have qualified; and the Congress may by law provide for the case wherein neither a President elect nor a Vice President elect shall have qualified, declaring who shall then act as President, or the manner in which one who is to act shall be selected, and such person shall act accordingly until a President or Vice President shall have qualified.

Section 4.   The Congress may by law provide for the case of the death of any of the persons from whom the House of Representatives may choose a President whenever the right of choice shall have devolved upon them, and for the case of the death of any of the persons from whom the Senate may choose a Vice President whenever the right of choice shall have devolved upon them.

Section 5.   Sections 1 and 2 shall take effect on the 15th day of October following the ratification of this article.

Section 6.   This article shall be inoperative unless it shall have been ratified as an amendment to the Constitution by the legislatures of three-fourths of the several States within seven years from the date of its submission.

AMENDMENT 21
(Ratified December 5, 1933)

Section 1.   The eighteenth article of amendment to the Constitution of the United States is hereby repealed.

Section 2.   The transportation or importation into any State, Territory, or possession of the United States for delivery or use therein of intoxicating liquors, in violation of the laws thereof, is hereby prohibited.

Section 3.   This article shall be inoperative unless it shall have been ratified as an amendment to the Constitution by conventions in the several States, as provided in the Constitution, within seven years from the date of the submission hereof to the States by the Congress.

AMENDMENT 22
(Ratified February 27, 1951)

Section 1.   No person shall be elected to the office of the President more than twice, and no person who has held the office of President, or acted as President, for more than two years of a term to which some other person was elected President shall be elected to the office of the President more than once. But this Article shall not apply to any person holding the office of President when this Article was proposed by the Congress, and shall not prevent any person who may be holding the office of President, or acting as President, during the term within which this Article becomes operative from holding the office of President or acting as President during the remainder of such term.

Section 2. This article shall be inoperative unless it shall have been ratified as an amendment to the Constitution by the legislatures of three-fourths of the several States within seven years from the date of its submission to the States by the Congress.

AMENDMENT 23
(Ratified March 29, 1961)

Section 1. The District constituting the seat of Government of the United States shall appoint in such manner as the Congress may direct:

A number of electors of President and Vice President equal to the whole number of Senators and Representatives in Congress to which the District would be entitled if it were a State, but in no event more than the least populous State; they shall be in addition to those appointed by the States, but they shall be considered, for the purposes of the election of President and Vice President, to be electors appointed by a State; and they shall meet in the District and perform such duties as provided by the twelfth article of amendment.

Section 2. The Congress shall have power to enforce this article by appropriate legislation.

AMENDMENT 24
(Ratified January 23, 1964)

Section 1. The right of citizens of the United States to vote in any primary or other election for President or Vice President, for electors for President or Vice President, or for Senator or Representative in Congress, shall not be denied or abridged by the United States or any State by reason of failure to pay any poll tax or other tax.

Section 2. The Congress shall have power to enforce this article by appropriate legislation.

AMENDMENT 25
(Ratified February 10, 1967)

Section 1. In case of the removal of the President from office or of his death or resignation, the Vice President shall become President.

Section 2. Whenever there is a vacancy in the office of the Vice President, the President shall nominate a Vice President who shall take office upon confirmation by a majority vote of both Houses of Congress.

Section 3. Whenever the President transmits to the President pro tempore of the Senate and the Speaker of the House of Representatives his written declaration that he is unable to discharge the powers and duties of his office, and until he transmits to them a written declaration to the contrary, such powers and duties shall be discharged by the Vice President as Acting President.

Section 4. Whenever the Vice President and a majority of either the principal officers of the executive departments or of such other body as Congress may by law provide, transmit to the President pro tempore of the Senate and the Speaker of the House of Representatives their written declaration that the President is unable to discharge the powers and duties of his office, the Vice President shall immediately assume the powers and duties of the office as Acting President.

Thereafter, when the President transmits to the President pro tempore of the Senate and the Speaker of the House of Representatives his written declaration that no inability exists, he shall resume the powers and duties of his office unless the Vice President and a majority of either the principal officers of the executive department or of such other body as Congress may by law provide, transmit within four days to the President pro tempore of the Senate and the Speaker of the House of Representatives their written declaration that the President is unable to discharge the powers and duties of his office. Thereupon Congress shall decide the issue, assembling within forty-eight hours for that purpose if not in session. If the Congress, within twenty-one days after receipt of the latter written declaration, or, if Congress is not in session, within twenty-one days after Congress is required to assemble, determines by two-thirds vote of both Houses that the President is unable to discharge the powers and duties of his office, the Vice President shall continue to discharge the same as Acting President; otherwise, the President shall resume the powers and duties of his office.

AMENDMENT 26
(Ratified July 1, 1971)

Section 1.   The right of citizens of the United States, who are eighteen years of age or older, to vote shall not be denied or abridged by the United States or by any State on account of age.

Section 2.   The Congress shall have the power to enforce this article by appropriate legislation.

AMENDMENT 27
(Ratified May 7, 1992)

No law, varying the compensation for the services of the Senators and Representatives, shall take effect, until an election of Representatives shall have intervened.

Index

Note: *f* denotes figure; *n*, note